American Sports

American Sports

A HISTORY OF ICONS, IDOLS, AND IDEAS

Volume 4: S–Z

MURRY R. NELSON

Editor

GREENWOOD

AN IMPRINT OF ABC-CLIO, LLC
Santa Barbara, California • Denver, Colorado • Oxford, England

Library of Congress Cataloging-in-Publication Data

American sports : a history of icons, idols, and ideas / Murry R. Nelson, editor.
    4 v.   p. cm.
  Includes bibliographical references and index.
   ISBN 978-0-313-39752-3 (hardcover : alk. paper) — ISBN 978-0-313-39753-0 (ebook)
  1. Sports—United States—History—Encyclopedias.   2. Athletes—United States—History—
Encyclopedias.   I. Nelson, Murry R.
   GV583.A637   2013
   796.0973—dc23   2012039243

ISBN: 978-0-313-39752-3
EISBN: 978-0-313-39753-0

17 16 15 14 13   1 2 3 4 5

This book is also available on the World Wide Web as an eBook.
Visit www.abc-clio.com for details.

Greenwood
An Imprint of ABC-CLIO, LLC

ABC-CLIO, LLC
130 Cremona Drive, P.O. Box 1911
Santa Barbara, California 93116-1911

This book is printed on acid-free paper ∞

Manufactured in the United States of America

Contents

VOLUME 3

Preface

The four volumes that constitute *American Sports: A History of Icons, Idols, and Ideas* represent more than three years of planning, writing, editing, and proofing. The volume provides a current reference on important topics in modern American sports for high school and college students and for interested nonspecialists. *American Sports* contains over 480 entries on a mixture of contemporary topics that stretch in time from the present to the early 20th century, with the earliest topics still holding relevance today. The entries were selected for inclusion by a knowledgeable editorial advisory board. Each of the board members made suggestions that were then shared with the rest of the board for comments and advice on inclusion of those entries. In the course of this process, it became apparent that the greatest factor for inclusion was the sustainability of the entry, that is, does that entry seem to have applicability to today's culture and is it likely to retain that applicability in the near future? The editorial board also suggested authors for entries, contributors who had strong knowledge and insight into today's society and its view of sport. The limiting factor was the culture of the United States, thus providing historic and geographic parameters that were only violated a few times and for obvious reasons.

Most of the more than 140 individuals who contributed to these volumes are in higher education, but a number of highly respected independent scholars and other professionals in various fields are represented in these volumes. Many are historians, but there are also anthropologists, educators, artists, musicians, literary experts, and communication arts scholars. The contributors used a variety of books, archives, websites, and articles, as well as their own expertise, to shape a coherent, informative, and readable set of entries.

The entries, which cover people, events, organizations, ideas, movements, books, films, and other topics, are listed alphabetically across the volumes. Each entry concludes with a listing of further information resources, including books, articles, and websites. Most entries also contain a list of "See also" cross references that lead the reader to related entries in the volumes as well as a sidebar, which offers more in-depth insight into an interesting related topic or idea. A Guide to Related Topics helps readers quickly trace broad ideas of themes by organizing entries into general categories and relevant subcategories, such as Individuals/Tennis Players or Places/Racing Venues. A selected bibliography, found in the last volume, also lists important general information resources.

Such a massive undertaking could not have been successfully completed without the assistance of many people. At ABC-CLIO, my editor Christian Green provided great and continual feedback. After he left near the end of the project, John Wagner came on board and saw this work through to completion. Barbara Patterson coordinated the project, assisting with contracts, contributor credits, and overall troubleshooting. The editorial advisory board of Ron Briley, Sarah Fields, Keith Harrison, Daniel Nathan, and Jaime Schultz provided insight, encouragement, and suggestions on authors and entries. A number of folks did yeoman work in completing many more entries than initially expected, including Ron Briley, Sarah Fields, Jaime Schultz, David Skinner, and Maureen Smith. The willingness of some authors to take on entries at short notice, after these had been returned by initial writers who were unable to complete the tasks in a timely manner, was really appreciated. Thus, I am deeply indebted to Matthew De-Fraga, Kevin Hagopian, Keith Harrison, Jarrod Jonsrud, Ric Jensen, Rich Macales, Fred Mason, David Skinner, Maureen Smith, Elizabeth Tobey, and Theresa Walton for their willingness to take on tasks at a late date and do them well.

Murry R. Nelson, Editor

Introduction

Sport has a long history in the United States; in fact, it predates the formation of the nation, for sports and games were a part of American colonial experiences. Rather than recapitulate that history, four volumes of *American Sports: A History of Icons, Idols, and Ideas* seek to highlight those people, places, events, ideas, books, films, and phenomena in sports that endure, that have become an accepted part of American culture. Many of the more than 480 entries in these volumes do look at the history of sports in this country, but many are also reflective of a contemporary snapshot of the place sport has in today's culture. In 50 years, most of the subjects of these entries will endure and will be part of another such work, but, certainly, there will also be some that would not be, that have much shorter half-lives, but burn so intensely in this period that they cannot help but be noticed and acknowledged.

Thus, *American Sports* tries to convey to students and general readers how sports and popular culture intersect in the United States today. The editor and contributors did not assume a deep knowledge of sports on the part of the reader, although that would not be a detriment; rather, they assumed that the reader is aware of his or her surroundings and is interested in how those compare with the general ideas of sport and culture in the public space.

A unique emphasis in these volumes is on various arts and sport. In terms of music, the entries include a number of songs, traditional ones like "Take Me Out to the Ballgame" and more recent ones like "Talkin' Baseball." Artists like Norman Rockwell and LeRoy Neiman, who have gained additional fans because of their iconic sports paintings, are profiled. And famous plays that have sport as a major or minor theme are also included, such as *That Championship Season* by Jason Miller, *Fences* by August Wilson, *Golden Boy* by Clifford Odets, and the recent revival on Broadway of *Death of a Salesman* by Arthur Miller. Also covered are a number of novels with sport themes, including *The Natural* by Bernard Malamud, *Bang the Drum Slowly* by Mark Harris, and *North Dallas Forty* by Peter Gent. Some fine nonfiction pieces are also included, such as *Paper Lion* by George Plimpton and *Friday Night Lights* by Buzz Bissinger, as well as a number of sports memoirs like *Ball Four* by Jim Bouton.

Another aspect of *American Sports* concerns entries on well-known products that have become identified with sport or sports figures, such as "Hot Dogs," "Gatorade," "Wheaties—The Breakfast of Champions," and "Sports Food" and "Sports Drinks." This theme is extended by a general entry on "Sports Clothing" and specific entries on companies that have become part of the overall culture, like Nike, Adidas, and Puma.

In compiling *American Sports*, difficult decisions had to be addressed regarding which topics to include and which to exclude. Reflective of the notion of "sustainability" described above, it seems useful to provide some examples to illustrate the rationale used in choosing entry topics. Since there are so many topics, a few examples will have to suffice. Individuals, especially historical ones, often left the editor and editorial board with dilemmas. Thus, a baseball player like Babe Ruth or Joe DiMaggio would be included because they were "bigger than baseball." Ruth's visage and references to his name still are easily recognizable to even a casual sports fan. DiMaggio's life and his likely unbreakable 56-game hitting streak make him a continued and recognizable part of American culture, not just of baseball or sport. So, too, with more modern players like Willie Mays or Mickey Mantle, but not so, unfortunately, for their great contemporary Duke Snider or Mantle's Yankee teammate Whitey Ford.

Some players needed to be included both because of their talent and because of their social importance. These included the first African Americans in various aspects of sport, such as Jackie Robinson playing Major League Baseball, Frank Robinson as the first African American manager, Hank Greenberg and Sandy Koufax as Hall of Fame players and practicing Jews, Dana Torres as a medal-winning and over-40 Olympian, and Tiger Woods as a Grand Slam champion and mixed-race groundbreaker. There are a very few non-Americans, but their inclusion comes as a result of their athletic success and their common appearances in advertising or social circles in this country. Two of the best examples would be Roger Federer, the all-time Grand Slam champion, who has appeared in a number of advertisements in American magazines for, among other products, Rolex watches and Nike gear, and Wayne Gretzky, who not only made the Los Angeles Kings "fashionable" when he was traded there, but who also has been a hockey executive and coach with the Phoenix Coyotes and is married to an American film actress, making him a fixture in glitterati L.A. He has also appeared in numerous films and television shows, including a stint as a judge on *Dance Fever*.

Specific plays that have become famous are also included, such as "The Catch" of Dwight Clark on a pass from Joe Montana to win the NFC championship in 1982 and the "Immaculate Reception" of Franco Harris of the Pittsburgh Steelers in December 1972 to win the AFC crown. Plays and games that have become seared into Americans' consciousness are included, although some people might include other plays, some of which might be found as sidebars or highlights in a player's entry.

The sidebars that over 300 entries include are either relevant and logical extensions of the entry itself or some engaging, tangential topic inspired by or alluded to by the main entry. Examples of the former include the Arthur Ashe entry sidebar, which discusses his pioneering inspiration for other African Americans in tennis, the Yogi Berra entry sidebar, which highlights the Yogi Berra Museum and Stadium, and the Wilt Chamberlain sidebar, which focuses on his 100-point game. Examples of the latter, more esoteric sidebars include the Roger Maris sidebar, which is devoted to the Billy Crystal–produced movie *61**, the James Naismith sidebar, which describes the results of a 2010 auction of the original 13 Rules of basketball, and the George Plimpton sidebar, which talks about the mythical Sidd Finch.

The volumes of *American Sports* are meant to convey the importance and ubiquitous nature of sport in American culture. Whereas the entire field of sports as an academic endeavor was once seen rather skeptically, there is no question that the various aspects of sport in culture now constitute a legitimate and vital part of social science and literary research and study. The economics of professional sports franchises and the impact that they and big-time college sports have on a region's economy are readily acknowledged today, and many books, journals, and reports are devoted to analyzing and using these topics. Legal journals such as the *Harvard Journal of Sport and Law*, the *Journal of Sports Law and Contemporary Problems*, and the *Marquette Sports Law Review* are illustrative of this trend, and the Sports Lawyers Association produces three different publications on the topic of sport and law.

Certainly, sports have affected social mobility in this country, and that is an area of dynamic research in sociology, history, and geography, among the social sciences. Books and journals focused on sport and its impact on social growth and ethnic advancement have become commonplace.

Over the past two decades larger compendia have presented aspects of sport in American history or American society. Many have had an academic focus with the intended audience being students of sport history in higher education. More recently, there have been efforts to provide these same topics in a format readily available and understandable to high school and undergraduate students and to the general reader. Thus, works like *Encyclopedia of Sports in America: A History from Foot Races to Extreme Sports* (Murry Nelson, ed., Greenwood Press, 2009) have set a new standard for popular interest in the broader notion of sport in this nation. However, works that are much more historical in scope do not offer the same contemporary, popular attention that *American Sports* provides.

Guide to Related Topics

EVENTS

Baseball Events
All-Star Game (Baseball)
Black Sox Scandal
Disco Demolition Night
Earthquake World Series
Little League World Series
Mazeroski Homer, Game Seven, 1960 World Series
McGwire, Mark and Sosa, Sammy
Pine Tar Incident
Presidents and Opening Day in Baseball
Shot Heard 'Round the World
Spring Training
World Series

Basketball Events
CCNY 1950 Double Championships
College Basketball Scandals
Final Four
March Madness
Point Shaving and 1950s College Basketball
Slam Dunk Contest
Texas Western Wins the 1966 NCAA Basketball Title

Boxing Events
The Long Count
Thrilla in Manila

Football Events
Bowl Games
Bud Bowl
"The Catch"
Immaculate Reception
Lingerie Bowl

Monday Night Football
NBA Draft
1972 Miami Dolphins
Nipplegate
Super Bowl
"Super Bowl Shuffle"

Horse Racing Events
Kentucky Derby
Triple Crown

International Events
America's Cup
Boston Marathon
Gay Games
Iditarod
Indianapolis 500
1994 FIFA World Cup
1999 FIFA Women's World Cup
1958 NFL Championship Game
1932 Olympic Games, Lake Placid
1932 Olympic Games, Los Angeles
1960 Olympic Games, Squaw Valley
1968 Olympic Games, Mexico City
1984 Olympic Games, Los Angeles
1996 Olympic Games, Atlanta
1975 World Series Sixth Game
Paralympic Games
Ryder Cup Matches
2002 Olympic Games, Salt Lake City

Other Events
ESPY Awards
The Masters
Spelling Bees

Strikes and Lockouts
Westminster Kennel Club/Westminster Dog Show
X Games

GROUPS AND ORGANIZATIONS

Amateur/College Organizations/Teams
AAU Basketball
Bowl Championship Series (BCS)
Dream Team
Fab Five
Four Horsemen
Magnificent Seven
NCAA (National Collegiate Athletic Association)
Notre Dame Fighting Irish Football
2008 Redeem Team
UCLA Basketball

Media Organizations
Chicago Defender
ESPN Channels
Fox Sports
The Sporting News
Sports Illustrated
Turner Broadcasting System (TBS)
WGN Television

Professional Organizations
All-American Girls Professional Baseball League (AAGPBL)
American Basketball Association (ABA)
American Football League (AFL)
Arena Football
The A's (Athletics)
Big Red Machine
Boston Celtics
Boston Red Sox
Brooklyn Dodgers
Chicago Bears
Chicago Bulls
Chicago Cubs
Cleveland Indians
Dallas Cowboys
Dream Team
The Greatest Show on Turf, 1999–2001 St. Louis Rams

Green Bay Packers
Harlem Globetrotters
Homestead Grays
Indianapolis Clowns
Los Angeles Dodgers
Los Angeles Lakers
Murderers' Row
NASCAR (National Association for Stock Car Auto Racing)
National Basketball Association (NBA)
National Football League (NFL)
Negro Leagues
New Orleans Saints
New York Mets
New York Rens (Renaissance)
New York Yankees
Philadelphia Phillies
Pittsburgh Crawfords
Rodeo
Roller Derby
St. Louis Cardinals
Ultimate Fighting Championship (UFC) and Mixed Martial Arts (MMA)
Women's National Basketball Association (WNBA)
Women's Professional Basketball League (WBL)
Women's Tennis Association (WTA)
Women's United Soccer Association (WUSA)
World Wrestling Entertainment (WWE)
XFL

IDEAS AND MOVEMENTS

Physical/Sporting Actions
Chest Bump
Concussion
High Five
Miniature Golf
Skateboarding
Tailgating
Three-Point Shot
Violence, Guns, and Sport

Sociopolitical Movements and Ideas
Black Power Salute (1968 Olympics)
Fantasy Leagues
Ladies' Day

Legal Decisions
Mitchell Report
Rooney Rule
Soccer Moms
Title IX

Substances
Dipping and Baseball
Sports and Drugs/Doping
Steroids
Substance Abuse

INDIVIDUALS

Activists
Scott, Jack

**Baseball Players, Managers, Owners,
 Commissioners**
Aaron, Hank
Autry, Gene
Banks, Ernest "Ernie"
Berra, Yogi
Blue, Vida
Bonds, Barry
Brosnan, Jim
Clemens, Roger
Clemente, Roberto
Dean, Dizzy
DiMaggio, Joe
Feller, Bob
Finch, Jennie
Finley, Charlie
Flood, Curt
Gehrig, Lou
Gibson, Bob
Gibson, Josh
Greenberg, Hank
Griffey, Ken, Jr.
Gwynn, Tony
Hunter, Jim "Catfish"
Jackson, Bo
Jackson, Reggie
Jeter, Derek
Koufax, Sandy
Landis, Kenesaw Mountain
Mantle, Mickey

Marichal, Juan
Maris, Roger
Mays, Willie
Musial, Stan "The Man"
Paige, Satchel
Pujols, Albert
Ramirez, Manny
Ripken, Cal, Jr.
Robinson, Frank
Robinson, Jackie
Rodriguez, Alex
Rose, Pete
Ruth, Babe
Ryan, Nolan
Seaver, Tom
Selig, Bud
Steinbrenner, George
Stengel, Casey
Turner, Ted
Uecker, Bob
Valenzuela, Fernando
Veeck, Bill
Williams, Ted

Basketball Players, Coaches, Owners
Abdul-Jabbar, Kareem
Auerbach, Arnold "Red"
Auriemma, Geno
Barkley, Charles
Barry, Rick
Bird, Larry
Blazejowski, Carol
Bryant, Kobe
Chamberlain, Wilt
Cooper, Cynthia
Cousy, Bob
Cuban, Mark
Durant, Kevin
Erving, Julius
Hawkins, Connie
Iverson, Allen
Jackson, Phil
James, LeBron
Johnson, Earvin "Magic"
Jordan, Michael
Knight, Bobby

Krzyzewski, Mike
Leslie, Lisa
Lieberman, Nancy
Maravich, Peter "Pete"
Mikan, George
Miller, Cheryl
Naismith, James
Olajuwon, Hakeem
O'Neal, Shaquille
Robertson, Oscar
Russell, Bill
Saperstein, Abe
Stern, David
Stringer, C. Vivian
Summitt, Pat
Swoopes, Sheryl
Taurasi, Diana
VanDerveer, Tara
Walton, Bill
West, Jerry
Wooden, John
Yao Ming

Boxers and Boxing Promoters
Ali, Laila
Ali, Muhammad
Johnson, Jack
Louis, Joe
Tyson, Mike

Broadcasters and Journalists
Allen, Mel
Caray, Harry
Cosell, Howard
Costas, Bob
Deford, Frank
Enberg, Dick
Facenda, John
Madden, John
Rice, Grantland
Scully, Vin
Smith, Red
Vitale, Richard J. (Dick)

Entertainers, Writers, Artists
Burns, Ken

Fogerty, John
Harris, Mark
Imus, Don
James, Bill
Lardner, Ring
Lee, Spike
Neiman, LeRoy
Plimpton, George
Rockwell, Norman
Schulz, Charles and *Peanuts*
Shelton, Ron

Football Players, Coaches
Belichick, Bill
Bradshaw, Terry
Brown, Jim
Bryant, Paul "Bear"
Butkus, Dick
Davis, Al
Davis, Ernie
Ditka, Mike
Dungy, Tony
Favre, Brett
Flutie, Doug
Four Horsemen
Grange, Red
Halas, George
Hayes, Bob
Hayes, Woody
Jackson, Bo
Lombardi, Vincent T.
Madden, John
Manning, Peyton
Montana, Joe
Namath, Joe
Owens, Terrell "T. O." and Ochocinco, Chad
Paterno, Joe
Payton, Walter
Rice, Jerry
Robinson, Eddie G.
Rockne, Knute
Roethlisberger, Ben
Sanders, Barry
Sayers, Gale
Simpson, O. J.
Smith, Emmitt

Steel Curtain
Strode, Woody
Thorpe, Jim
Tillman, Pat
Unitas, John
Vick, Michael
Walker, Herschel
Williams, Doug

Golfers
Jones, Bobby
Lopez, Nancy
Nicklaus, Jack
Palmer, Arnold
Rodriguez, Chi Chi
Trevino, Lee
Woods, Tiger

Hockey Players
Gretzky, Wayne Douglas

Horse Racing: Horses and Jockeys
Citation
Krone, Julie
Man O' War
Seabiscuit
Secretariat

Olympians
Armstrong, Lance
Benoit Samuelson, Joan
Blair, Bonnie
Chastain, Brandi
Coachman, Alice
Crabbe, Buster
Didrikson, Babe
Ederle, Gertrude
Fleming, Peggy
Griffith Joyner, Florence
Hamill, Dorothy
Hamm, Mia
Hayes, Bob
Heiden, Eric
Hyman, Flo
Jansen, Dan
Jenner, Bruce

Johnson, Michael
Johnson, Rafer
Jones, Marion
Joyner-Kersee, Jackie
Kahanamoku, Duke
Lewis, Carl
Louganis, Greg
Ohno, Apolo
Owens, Jesse
Phelps, Michael
Retton, Mary Lou
Rudolph, Wilma Glodean
Spitz, Mark
Street, Picabo
Thorpe, Jim
Tonya Harding–Nancy Kerrigan Scandal
Torres, Dara
Weissmuller, Johnny
White, Shaun
White, Willye Bertha

Race Car Drivers
Earnhardt, Ralph Dale, Sr. and Earnhardt, Ralph
    Dale, Jr.
Gordon, Jeff
Johnson, Jimmie
Patrick, Danica
Petty, Richard

Tennis Players
Agassi, Andre
Ashe, Arthur
Connors, Jimmy
Evert, Chris
Federer, Roger
Gibson, Althea
King, Billie Jean
McEnroe, John
Navratilova, Martina
Sampras, Pete
Williams, Serena
Williams, Venus

X-treme Sports Stars
Hawk, Tony
White, Shaun

OBJECTS AND ARTIFACTS

Awards
Heisman Trophy
Parade Magazine All-Americans
Stanley Cup

Companies, Products, and Advertising
Adidas
Advertising and Sport
Baseball Cards
Chuck Taylor All Stars
EA Sports
Gatorade
Hot Dogs
Jumbotron
Madden NFL
Nike, Inc.
Puma
Sports Bars
Sports Clothing
Sports Drinks
Sports Food
Sports Memorabilia, Vintage and Autographed
Wheaties—The Breakfast of Champions

Films and Television
Angels in the Outfield
The Babe Ruth Story
The Bad News Bears
The Blind Side
Breaking Away
Brian's Song
Bull Durham
Caddyshack
Champion
Cinderella Man
Coach
Cobb
Cool Runnings
Cornbread, Earl and Me
ESPN *College Game Day*
Fear Strikes Out
Field of Dreams
The Fighter
Finding Forrester

Friday Night Lights
Golden Boy
Happy Gilmore
Hoop Dreams
Hoosiers
The Hustler
I Spy
Jerry Maguire
A League of Their Own
Love & Basketball
Million Dollar Baby
Miracle on Ice
Monday Night Football
Moneyball
Murderball
The Natural
North Dallas Forty
Paper Lion
The Pride of the Yankees
Raging Bull
Remember the Titans
Rocky
Rudy
Slap Shot
Space Jam
The White Shadow

Human Condition
Cheerleading
Collective Bargaining Agreement (CBA)
Dunk
Marching Band
Sports Agents
Tommy John Surgery

Literature/Books, Short Stories, Poems
"Alibi Ike"
Ball Four
Bang the Drum Slowly
"Baseball's Sad Lexicon"
"Casey at the Bat"
Moneyball
North Dallas Forty
Paper Lion
"Spahn and Sain and Pray for Rain"
Sports Metaphors

Literature/Plays, Musicals, Songs, Routines
Damn Yankees
Death of a Salesman
Fences
The Great White Hope
Take Me Out
"Take Me Out to the Ballgame"
"Talkin' Baseball"
That Championship Season
White Men Can't Jump
The White Shadow
"Who's on First?"
The Winning Team

Oddities
Cheeseheads
Honus Wagner Card
Schilling, Curt, Bloody Sock of

PLACES

College Stadia and Arenas
The Big House (Michigan Stadium)
Death Valley, LSU Football
Happy Valley, Penn State Football
Ohio Stadium
The Pit

Rose Bowl
The Swamp

Halls of Fame
Baseball Hall of Fame
Naismith Memorial Basketball Hall of Fame
Pro Football Hall of Fame and Museum

Other Legendary Sites
Lake Placid
Las Vegas and Sports Betting
Rucker Park

Pro Stadia and Arenas
Astrodome
Cowboys Stadium
Fenway Park
Madison Square Garden
Superdome
Wrigley Field
Yankee Stadium

Racing Venues
Bonneville Salt Flats
Daytona International Speedway
Saratoga Springs, New York

S

Sampras, Pete (1971–)

Pete Sampras is seen as one of the best tennis players of all time. He was a professional tennis player for 15 years before retiring in 2003. In his professional career, spanning from 1988 to 2002, Sampras won 14 Grand Slam singles tournaments.

Sampras was born in Maryland in 1971 to parents who were both of Greek heritage. His Greek heritage and upbringing in the Greek Orthodox Church were important aspects of Sampras's life. He began playing tennis at the age of three after discovering a tennis racquet in his parents' basement. From an early age, Sampras would spend hours hitting the tennis ball against the wall to improve his abilities. His parents saw such an immense talent and athletic ability in Sampras that in 1978, they moved their family to California for Pete to have more opportunities to play tennis and improve his skills. Sampras's tennis idol was Rod Laver; at the age of 11, he had the opportunity to meet and play against Laver, fulfilling his childhood dream.

In 1988, Sampras made his professional debut on the men's tournament circuit at the age of 16 at the rank of 893 in the world. Through various wins and losses throughout the year, he was able to move up the ranks to close out the year at 97.

The year 1990 was the breakout year for Pete Sampras. At the beginning of the competitive season, he ranked at number 61 in the world, but by the end of the year, he had moved up considerably to number five. He did this by advancing well in a number of major tournaments that year, beating higher-ranked players like fellow American Tim Mayotte (then ranked number eight in the world) at the Australian Open and defeating John McEnroe in the Canadian Open. Sampras also won his first professional tour title in 1990, earning the top spot at the Ebel U.S. Pro Indoor Championship in Philadelphia. At this tournament, he beat Andre Agassi and Mayotte, and faced Andres Gomez of Ecuador in the final. Winning that tournament propelled him into the top 20 category in world rankings for the first time in his career.

That same year, Sampras earned his first-ever Grand Slam title at the U.S. Open. At that tournament, Sampras beat Ivan Lendl and John McEnroe before facing Andre Agassi in the final. Agassi ranked number four in the world at the time. When Sampras won, he was the youngest singles male to ever win the title—he was 19 years old. While Sampras was in the top field of male players from 1990 through 1992, it was not until 1993 that he earned the honor of number one ranked in the world.

Pete Sampras earned a spot to represent the United States at the 1992 Olympic Games in Barcelona, Spain. He played in both the men's singles and doubles tournament, where he partnered with Jim Courier. He lost in the third round of the men's singles tournament and the second round of the doubles.

Interestingly, Sampras earned top ranking in April 1993 even after losing in the semifinals of the Australian Open and quarterfinals of the French Open. This achievement was met with a great deal of controversy by many in the tennis world because in the past, top-ranked players were those who had won the most recent Grand Slam title, which Sampras had not done in that tournament year. Despite this, Sampras's wins at smaller tournaments gave him the credibility needed for the ranking. And a mere three months later, Sampras proved his worthiness of the number one ranking by winning his first Wimbledon title, beating fellow

Pete Sampras returns the ball during the semifinals of the U.S. Open in New York, September 9, 1995. (AP Photo/ Ron Frehm.)

American and former number one–ranked Jim Courier in the final. Just two months later, he followed that win with another victory at the U.S. Open. At the end of the 1993 season he had proved to all that he deserved the number one spot, as well as becoming the first player on the men's circuit to serve more than 1,000 aces in a season.

Pete Sampras was a powerhouse at Wimbledon, winning at the tournament every year he appeared after 1993 until 2003, with the only exception being in 1996 when he lost to Dutch player Richard Krajicek. Sampras holds the record for the most wins at Wimbledon by a single male tennis player with seven.

His wins at Wimbledon and the U.S. Open left the Australian and French Opens for him to win. In 1994, he achieved the first of two Australian championships, beating American Todd Martin. Sampras reached the 1995 final in Australia as well, but lost to Andre Agassi. During the 1995 tournament, Sampras's longtime coach, Tom Gullikson, collapsed shortly before

his quarterfinal match with American Jim Courier. Sampras was so emotionally affected by the event that during his match with Courier, he openly wept while he played. Gullikson was later diagnosed with brain cancer, dying a year later. His death had a profound impact on Pete Sampras.

Sampras was a powerhouse on grass courts, as evidenced by his seven Wimbledon titles. An overall well-rounded player who had a fierce competitive side, Sampras's weakness on clay courts may have been his only drawback as a player. The farthest he ever went in the tournament at the French Open occurred in 1996 when he reached the semifinals before losing to Yevgeny Kafelnikov of Russia. He won smaller tournaments played on clay surfaces, but was never victorious at the famous Roland Garros stadium.

Sampras won his second and last Australian title in 1997, beating Spanish player Carlos Moya. After winning both Wimbledon and a number of other titles including the ATP Tour World Championship, Sampras ended the year with over $6 million in prize money and a win/loss record of 10–1 against the top-ranked players of the men's circuit. He was the number one–ranked player for the entirety of 1997. This distinction earned him honors with Jimmy Connors as the only men to be number one at the end of a tournament season for five consecutive years.

While Pete Sampras played increasingly well in almost all the tournaments he entered, his 1999 Wimbledon final against fellow American Andre Agassi is seen by tennis enthusiasts as one of his greatest competitions in the history of his career. The rivalry between Agassi and Sampras was at a pinnacle—the game was an excellent show of their athleticism and superior tennis skills. For Sampras the match was even more impressive because he was experiencing back pain, which was later diagnosed as a herniated disc, an injury that forced him to withdraw from the U.S. Open tournament that year. That withdrawal, as well as Sampras's not competing in that season's Australian Open, dropped him out of the world top rating, a position Andre Agassi gained from him.

In 2000, Sampras's rivalry with Agassi would continue to play out, losing to him in the semifinals of the Australian Open. Pete Sampras would win Grand Slam title number 13 at the Wimbledon tournament that summer, an amazing feat not only for the new re-cords he set, but also because he was battling multiple injuries at the time. His 2000 win at Wimbledon be-came a new record for number of consecutive wins in a Grand Slam final, which as of this writing, Sampras still holds at eight. His losses in the 2000 and 2001 U.S. Open, combined with injuries, led many in the tennis world to believe that Sampras might have been on the back side of his amazing athletic career. In 2001, Sampras lost at Wimbledon in the fourth round to Swiss player Roger Federer, whose records and wins in tennis rivals and in some cases surpasses the records held by Sampras.

Sampras continued to play the men's circuit in 2001 and 2002 despite setbacks in tournaments. His final Grand Slam appearance was at the 2002 U.S. Open where Sampras was up against longtime rival Agassi. The irony of the matching was not lost on the world of tennis—Agassi had been Sampras's oppo-nent for his first-ever Grand Slam appearance 12 years earlier. The match was captivating and had the atten-tion of the nation, tennis fans or not. Sampras's victory marked the last Grand Slam win of his career, as well as another new marker in tennis history. His 2002 U.S. Open win gave him his 14th Grand Slam career title and he tied the U.S. Open record for wins by a single male player at five; he shares the record with Jimmy Connors. Roger Federer would also join this club for U.S. Open wins.

Of the great rivalries within the world of sports, one of the longest may be between Sampras and Andre Agassi. They met each other 34 times on the men's tournament during Sampras's professional career. Of those 34 matches, Sampras won 20 of them. They faced each other at almost every level of play at vari-ous tournaments, the most notable being in semifinals and finals of the Grand Slam tournaments. Their 2001 U.S. Open quarterfinal match is one of the most often replayed series of tennis. During this meeting, there were no breaks of serve during the entire match. Both Sampras and Agassi were superior tennis players.

After his setbacks in 2000 through 2002, it seemed to all that Sampras would most likely announce his re-tirement after the U.S. Open win, leaving the game on top. It was not until the following year that Sampras announced his retirement. At the U.S. Open in 2003,

---

Sampras versus Agassi

The rivalry between Pete Sampras and Andre Agassi is one of the most storied within the field of sports his-tory and most definitely one of the top in tennis history. Their rivalry spans almost the entire length of both of their professional careers on the men's circuit, beginning with Sampras's first Grand Slam win in 1994 at the U.S. Open when he beat the higher-ranking Agassi. For both men, career successes and losses are frequently linked together, the most memorable being the 2002 quarter-final match at the U.S. Open. These giants of the tennis world showed the public not only the ultimate in tennis skill and athleticism, but pure rivalry and competition at work. This struggle against each other continues into their retirements as well, because they frequently play each other in charity tennis tournaments.

Sampras was honored for his illustrious career in ten-nis, declared by many as the best tennis player of all time. Sampras also won two doubles titles and ranked number one a total of 286 weeks—the most for any player, setting a high record for excellence in the field of men's tennis. Roger Federer has since surpassed Sampras's record of 14 Grand Slam titles. The record was broken in 2009 when Federer won the U.S. Open against Andy Roddick; Pete Sampras was present at the match. His record had stood for seven years.

Pete Sampras holds a number of records for the modern open era of tennis. For six consecutive years from 1993 to 1998, Sampras held the number one ranking at the end of each year. Sampras also holds the record for most men's singles titles at Wimbledon, a distinction he shares with 19th-century British player William Renshaw. In addition, Sampras also holds five ATP World Tour championship titles, tied with Ivan Lendl of Czechoslovakia and Federer.

Much has been written about Sampras's prowess on the tennis court. His competitive spirit and desire to always improve himself and his game had a big impact on his tennis wins. Sampras played his entire career using the same type of racquet, a Wilson Pro Staff Original with a custom-built handle. Sampras played the court well, often putting his opponents on the defensive and earning points by moving to the net to score. His serve was powerful and effective, earning numerous aces throughout his career. In addition, his forehand while running to the net was powerful and effective. Sampras popularized the "jump smash" technique, where he would jump high to hit the ball and slam it to the opponent's court.

In his retirement, Sampras has played in a number of exhibition games, both as part of the ATP tour and for charitable fundraisers. Some of these matches include games against longtime rival Agassi, Roger Federer, Rafael Nadal, Patrick Rafter, and John McEnroe.

Sampras married actress Bridgette Wilson in 2000. The couple has two sons, Christian and Ryan, born in 2002 and 2005, respectively. In November 2010, Pete Sampras suffered a personal setback when a number of his trophies and awards from his tennis career were stolen from a storage facility in Los Angeles. They included the trophy from his first Australian Open win, a ring from the Olympics, and other items. Almost all of the items were found and returned to Sampras.

As of this writing, Pete Sampras is the last American male to win the men's singles championship at Wimbledon. He is also the last American male singles player to reach the ATP World Cup finals. He was inducted into the International Tennis Hall of Fame in 2007.

Kristen Costa

See also Agassi, Andre; Connors, Jimmy; Federer, Roger; McEnroe, John

Suggested Resources
Boughn, Michael. *Pete Sampras*. Lynchburg, VA: Warwick House, 1999.
Branham, H. A. *Sampras: A Legend in the Works*. Los Angeles: Bonus Books, 1996.
"Pete Sampras." International Tennis Hall of Fame and Museum. http://www.tennisfame.com/hall-of-famers/pete-sampras. Accessed November 12, 2011.
Pete Sampras Website. http://www.petesampras.com/. Accessed November 12, 2011.
Sampras, Pete. *A Champion's Mind: Lessons from a Life in Tennis*. London: Aurum Press, 2009.

Sanders, Barry (1968–)

Barry Sanders is a former NFL running back who spent his entire 10-year career with the Detroit Lions and retired at age 30, just short of the all-time rushing record. He is currently the third-leading rusher all-time in NFL history.

Sanders was born and grew up in Wichita, Kansas, on July 16, 1968. He attended North High School, but was not a starting running back until his senior year, when he gained over 1,300 yards in just seven games. Despite making the all-state team, Sanders was not heavily recruited because of his height; he was just 5'8" and weighed less than 200 pounds.

He received a football scholarship to Oklahoma State, where he played behind all-American running back Thurman Thomas, but became a starter in his junior year. In his junior year Sanders gained over 2,600 yards, averaged 7.6 yards per carry, over 200 yards per game, and had 344 carries. He rushed for over 300 yards in four games, won the Heisman Trophy, then scored five touchdowns and ran for over 200 yards in the 62–14 Holiday Bowl romp over Wyoming in December 1988. Following that season, Sanders declared himself eligible for the NFL draft and was taken in the first round (third overall) of the 1989 NFL draft.

Sanders continued his elusive running in the NFL, finishing second in the league in rushing (1,470 yards), second in rushing touchdowns (14), and won the Offensive Rookie of the Year award. The Lions improved from 4–12 in 1988 to 7–9. The next year Sanders led the league in rushing and rushing touchdowns.

Over the next eight years, Sanders continued to dominate on the field, finishing in the top five in rushing every year and leading the league three more times. In 1997 he was voted Most Valuable Player in the NFL after leading the league with 2,023 yards rushing, 128 yards per game rushing, and 2,358 yards from scrimmage. At the end of the 1988 season, he had gained 15,269 yards and averaged 5.0 yards per carry, while scoring 109 rushing touchdowns. The yardage record was held by the recently retired Walter Payton, with 16,726 (subsequently broken by Emmitt Smith in 2004).

Sanders had always let his work on the field speak for him; his biggest off-the-field controversy was his early retirement. Many felt that he should continue and break the record and try to get the Lions into the Super Bowl. Sanders did lead the team to the playoffs five

Oklahoma State running back Barry Sanders poses with his Heisman Trophy on December 8, 1988. (AP Photo/Susan Ragan.)

times in his 10 years; after his retirement the Lions failed to make the playoffs again until 2011.

Sanders's announcement of retirement shocked the football world, but he felt that he would rather retire without significant injury while his children were still young, than play until he was either too hurt or incapable of doing well. There was also speculation that he wanted to play for a contender, which Detroit seemed to be failing at being. Sanders was elected to the Pro Football Hall of Fame in 2004. He was rated the most elusive runner of all time by NFL.com. Sanders holds a number of NFL records, the most significant of which include most seasons rushing for over 1,000 yards (10, tied with Walter Payton).

Sanders has always been quiet and modest, avoiding the spotlight. He has four children, three with his wife, Lauren Campbell, a television personality in Detroit. Sanders's son was a freshman at Stanford in 2012–2013 and has been an all-state running back in Oklahoma. In February 2012, Sanders and his wife announced that they were divorcing. Sanders has recently worked as an endorser for Comcast and did the opening for the Lions-Bears game in October 2011.

Murry R. Nelson

See also Heisman Trophy; Payton, Walter; Pro Football Hall of Fame and Museum; Smith, Emmitt

Suggested Resources
"Barry Sanders." Pro Football Hall of Fame. http://www .profootballhof.com/hof/member.aspx?PLAYER_ ID=187. Accessed February 28, 2012.
"Barry Sanders." Pro-Football-Reference.com. http://www .pro-football-reference.com/players/S/SandBa00.htm. Accessed February 28, 2012.
"Barry Sanders." SR/College Football. http://www.sports -reference.com/cfb/players/barry-sanders-1.html. Accessed February 28, 2012.
Crompton, Samuel W. *Barry Sanders (Football Superstars)*. New York: Chelsea House, 2009.
Sanders, Barry, with Mark McCormick, contributor. *Barry Sanders Now You See Him: His Story in His Own Words*. Cincinnati: Clerisy Press, 2005.

Saperstein, Abe (1902–1966)

Abe Saperstein was a basketball and show business entrepreneur who gained his greatest fame by taking over a team that he renamed the Harlem Globetrotters and making them a worldwide brand.

Saperstein was born in London in 1902, the son of immigrant Jews who had fled Poland. In 1906 his father, Louis, came to the United States and found work as an apprentice tailor in Chicago, after spending time working in the garment district of New York City. He sent for the rest of the family, who arrived the next year, by which time Louis had become the owner of a tailor shop. Besides his mother, Abe had three younger siblings and five more followed over the next few years, a total of nine children.

Saperstein and his family moved a lot during his childhood, but remained within the environs of Ravenswood on the near north side of Chicago. He attended Ravenswood Elementary School and Lake View High School, one of the oldest in the city, where he played intramural sports until his senior year. He made the varsity basketball and baseball team. Saperstein only

grew to 5'3", but was able to coax lots of walks because of his shortness. In basketball he excelled as a guard on the bantamweight squad. At that time basketball was more of a floor game with little jumping. High school teams were divided into heavyweight, lightweight, and bantamweight with the latter having a 115-pound limit. Saperstein was a good ball handler and ran well; shooting was minimal in the games with scores usually in the teens and 20s. His team finished second in the city championships and he graduated from high school in 1920.

For the next six years Saperstein worked a variety of jobs and played or coached amateur basketball teams on the side. In 1926 he landed a job at a city park, Welles Park, with duties of organizing and managing recreational programs, as well as coaching the local park amateur team, the Chicago Reds. Through this job he met a lot of sportsmen in Chicago, both white and black, and one of them was Walter Ball. He hired Saperstein to do bookings in the Midwest for his Negro baseball team, figuring a white man would be more convincing to white representatives in the midwestern towns than a black man. Saperstein was great at this and maintained a contact with Negro League baseball for nearly 30 years in the capacity of booking agent/promoter.

In late 1926 Saperstein, upon Ball's recommendation, began doing some bookings for an all-black basketball team from the Giles Post American Legion team that had been playing around Chicago. Their manager, Dick Hudson, thought that they could succeed as barnstormers, at least within the region, playing local white teams. The players were largely from the south side of Chicago and most had attended Wendell Phillips High School, so they had played together for a number of years. The first tour of Wisconsin was preceded by a barrage of hyperbole regarding the players and their backgrounds, as well as the team and its national success, all of which was likely the product of Saperstein's promotional excess, though it was never proved.

In the fall of 1927, the Savoy Ballroom opened on Chicago's south side and the owner booked Hudson's team to play games there in January 1928 against Howard University. Hudson now called the team the Savoy Bear Cats, but soon changed that name to the

Wilt "the Stilt" Chamberlain, former University of Kansas star, holds two basketballs over the head of the diminutive owner of the Harlem Globetrotters, Abe Saperstein, after accepting a one-year contract to tour with the Globetrotters, June 18, 1958. (AP Photo/Anthony Camerano.)

Savoy Big Five. The team was successful, both financially and in winning, its first games. But during the season players were added, some quit over losing their starting positions, and later greater dissension arose over payments to some of the new players. The team broke up at the end of the season and that might have been the end of them as a team in April 1928.

Saperstein, meanwhile, had lost most of his booking jobs and had managed to wrangle a patronage job from his local ward boss, working as a forester in Chicago's Lincoln Park. Basically he coordinated and managed the jobs that tree surgeons did throughout the park.

In fall of 1928 when the Savoy Big Five came together, there was a new manager and a number of new players. Six or seven of the previous Big Five squad had started their own team called the Globetrotters, but they seemed to disappear for months. Meanwhile the new Savoy Big Five had a great year, winning 33

of 37 games. The Globetrotters had changed their name to the Tommy Brookins' Globetrotters (one of the original Wendell Phillips players who later became a singer, entertainer, and nightclub owner and the husband of Ethel Waters, the famous jazz singer). Then they changed their name again to the Original Chicago Globe Trotters and beat most of the teams they played.

Now Brookins and the team manager, Dick Hudson, formerly with the Savoy Big Five, wanted to do a tour of Wisconsin and Michigan and turned to Saperstein to do their bookings. He was hired for a 10 percent booking fee. Saperstein also took a number of players, started his own team, and booked them on a similar tour, calling them the Globe Trotters, too. Brookins was initially angry with Saperstein, but ended up accepting Abe's dealings since Brookins was ready to abandon the road and concentrate on the singing gigs that he had been offered. Saperstein agreed to take the other Globe Trotters as part of his squad and

Tommy Brookins's involvement with the Globe Trotters ended.

Saperstein's involvement was just beginning and it would become much more pronounced and have greater longevity than anyone could have imagined at the time. The Harlem name came about in an effort to try to add some "worldliness" to the team, since Harlem was almost foreign to many midwesterners, and a bit exotic. Initially the name that Saperstein used was "New York Harlem Globe Trotters," but "New York" eventually was dropped because of the obvious redundancy and the readily identifiable team itself (as well as the cost of two more words in telegrams). Saperstein devoted himself to the team as manager, booking agent, chauffeur, publicist, and, at times, substitute player. The touring squad usually carried only five players. Starting in the early 1930s the team began playing about 150 games per year. Saperstein spent most of his time on the road with the team, although he did find the time to get married in May 1934 to Sylvia Franklin of Kenosha, Wisconsin. Saperstein maintained his business office in his parents' home, also his residence until his marriage. He and his wife had two children, a son and a daughter.

The Globetrotters began adding entertainment "shticks" to their play and the pregame during this period, although they still played the game straight. In 1939, they were third in the World Professional Basketball Tournament, and in 1940, they won the tournament title. Saperstein was also busy in the basketball off-season by continuing to promote Negro League baseball, which was enormously popular until the integration of the major leagues in 1947, after which league attendance began to fall as the talent drained into the major leagues.

The integration of basketball concerned Saperstein because he would lose a large talent pool and he used his leverage to encourage the NBA not to integrate. In the earliest years of the NBA (1946–1950), the Globetrotters often appeared as part of a doubleheader with the NBA game following. These were by far the biggest paydays for NBA teams and the owners were loath to cross Saperstein and give up this financial boon. Nevertheless the NBA finally did integrate in 1950 and lost the Saperstein/Globetrotter connection, although not entirely.

Earlier, in the 1940s the Globetrotters had begun adding clowning to their game repertoire, and eventually Saperstein was supporting a team that traveled with the Globetrotters as their foil, the designated loser. By 1947 Saperstein owned a number of "opposition" teams—the House of David, the Kansas City Stars, the San Francisco All-Nations, and the Hawaii All-Stars. Still, the Trotters were loaded with real talent, and in February 1948, they topped the Minnesota Lakers, the top team in the NBL and the best team in basketball, with George Mikan as their star. Saperstein had combined his East and West Globetrotters squads to make a powerhouse team and the tactic worked that night.

Saperstein created and promoted a tour in the 1940s with the Trotters playing a team of college all-stars, but it was dropped after a year. The tour was resurrected in 1950 and continued until 1962, but it was killed by an AAU ruling that jeopardized the scholarships of the college seniors. Abe was always promoting something. In the late 1940s he began sending the Globetrotters to tours in Mexico, Cuba, and Hawaii. In the 1950s Saperstein booked them on tours of Europe and beyond. Their first "round the world" tour was in 1952.

In 1959, at the behest of the Department of State, the Globetrotters toured in the Soviet Union, where Saperstein met Soviet premier Nikita Khrushchev. Saperstein and the Globetrotters also entertained U.S. servicemen overseas, resulting in commendations from the U.S. government.

Saperstein recognized that he and his team were seen more as entertainers than basketball players and he thought that when the NBA expanded, he would have the inside track on a franchise in the league, specifically on the West Coast. This was seen as kind of a payoff for continuing to schedule NBA doubleheaders with the Globetrotters, following the integration of the NBA. In the spring of 1960, new Lakers owner Bob Short was allowed to move his franchise from Minneapolis to Los Angeles and Saperstein felt aggrieved. He had already been contemplating a new professional basketball league, but this sealed the deal. He lined up a number of franchise owners and in August the American Basketball League was announced as a new entity, one that would begin play in the fall of 1961 with Saperstein as the league commissioner. He also

Abe's Tall Tales?

Abe Saperstein was a great showman and entrepreneur who told great stories of his accomplishments, most of which were either untrue or greatly exaggerated. Many sources have repeated his claims, almost verbatim. According to Abe, he was a great baseball, track, and basketball star in high school. Records indicate he didn't run track, got two hits on the baseball team in his senior year, and was a starter on the bantamweight basketball team. He claimed to have played or been cut from the University of Illinois basketball team, but university records indicate he was never enrolled there. Even Abe's height was hard to "measure" as various sources claim that he was 5', 5'3", and 5'5". Saperstein also spun stories about his early Globetrotter players, claiming most had college degrees, when none had. Saperstein learned early that in promotion, stretching the truth made for good copy.

would own, at least initially, the Chicago franchise in the eight-team league.

Over the next two years he divided his energies between the Globetrotters and the off-season touring, usually overseas, and his new league and franchise. The ABL had a number of innovative concepts. First was the three-point shot, which would be awarded from shots beyond 25 feet. Second was a trapezoidal center lane, one seen now in international basketball. Another was a 30-second, rather than 24-second clock to allow for more plays to be set up. The league had a franchise in Hawaii and Saperstein devised a schedule that had visiting teams making three-game road trips to the Islands for games. He also used his Globetrotters for ABL doubleheaders and drew huge crowds, as he had for the NBA.

Nevertheless, the league lost far more than anticipated (more than $1.5 million) and midway through its second year, the ABL folded. Saperstein took Connie Hawkins, whom the NBA had blacklisted and was the ABL's Most Valuable Player, onto the Globetrotters, the second big star (after Wilt Chamberlain) to come to the team, but Hawkins left the team in 1966 when his contract was not renewed for negotiating an attempted entrance to the NBA.

By 1965, Saperstein was pushing himself way too hard and, on a four-month world tour to meet with promoters, had a mild heart attack in Australia. He was in and out of the hospital for the next few months until he was told he needed prostate surgery, which was scheduled for March 11, 1966. While being prepped for the operation, he suffered a heart attack and died in the hospital on March 15, 1966.

In 1970, Saperstein was elected to the Naismith Memorial Basketball Hall of Fame as a contributor and in 1979 he was inducted into the International Jewish Sports Hall of Fame. Despite his death nearly 50 years ago, Saperstein's name is still indelibly tied to the Harlem Globetrotters, who have continued to thrive as the greatest showmen in basketball.

Murry R. Nelson

See also Chamberlain, Wilt; Harlem Globetrotters; Los Angeles Lakers; Naismith Memorial Basketball Hall of Fame; National Basketball Association; New York Rens

Suggested Resources

"Abe Saperstein." Hoopedia. http://hoopedia.nba.com/index.php?title=Abe_Saperstein. Accessed March 25, 2011.

"Abe Saperstein." International Jewish Sports Hall of Fame. http://www.jewishsports.net/BioPages/AbeSaperstein.htm. Accessed March 25, 2011.

Green, Ben. *Spinning the Globe: The Rise, Fall and Return to Greatness of the Harlem Globetrotters*. New York: Amistad, 2005.

"Saperstein, Abe." Hickoksports.com. http://www.hickoksports.com/biograph/sapersteinabe.shtml. Accessed March 25, 2011.

Siegman, Joseph. *Jewish Sports Legends: The International Jewish Hall of Fame*. Washington, DC: Potomac Books, 2005.

Saratoga Springs, New York

A popular resort town with a rich history and 26,000 year-round residents, Saratoga Springs, New York, is located 30 miles north of Albany and close to the Hudson River and the southern Adirondacks. During the summer, the town almost trebles in size, as tourists come to enjoy themselves, especially during the six-week-long thoroughbred horse racing season. A street sign on the outskirts of town welcoming visitors reads

The Saratoga clubhouse at the racetrack in Saratoga Springs, New York, is the alleged birthplace of the club sandwich in the late 1800s. (Library of Congress.)

"Health, History, Horses." This encapsulates what makes Saratoga Springs distinctive. These subjects are intertwined.

According to local historians and archeologists, long before 18th-century white settlers arrived in the area, Native Americans used it for hunting and fishing. Eventually, the Mohawk called the area Sarach-togue, which meant "hillside of a great river" or "place of the swift water." In the summer, a variety of indigenous peoples gathered in the area because of the natural springs, which were believed to have healing powers.

Even before the pivotal Battle of Saratoga in 1777 during the Revolutionary War, in which the Americans unexpectedly defeated British general John Burgoyne's army (near what is now Schuylerville, New York), a few white settlers had made Saratoga their home. In general, New Englanders and people from southern New York settled Saratoga Springs. Among them was Gideon Putnam, a young miller and entrepreneur from Massachusetts, who settled in 1789. He purchased and cleared land, and built and operated a tavern and a boardinghouse. Later, he built a hotel,

helped plan a broad avenue, and donated "land for a church, school and cemetery," explains historian Timothy Holmes.

Because of Putnam and others who grew the village, and because the burgeoning leisure class was looking for places and opportunities for "relaxation, recreation and entertainment" outside of increasingly industrializing urban centers, Saratoga Springs became a more and more popular destination. People from all over the country came to take the waters (that is, to bathe in and drink them), to socialize (which included gambling and drinking), to conduct business, and to be entertained by traveling musicians and performers. An expanding railroad system reached Saratoga in 1832 and hastened the town's growth.

"During the 19th century," writes antiquarian Robert Joki, "the village flourished, attracting ever-increasing numbers of travelers, climaxing in the post–Civil War Victorian era." At the time, Joki adds, visitors "stayed in magnificent hotels and boarding houses, enjoying sumptuous feasts in fine dining rooms." In addition to attending festive balls and parties and promenading up and down the town's piazzas and covered porches, tourists spent time in gaming houses. Former pugilist John Morrissey, an Irish immigrant who became a Tammany Hall politician and businessman, established perhaps the most famous of them: Morrissey's Club House Casino in what is now Congress Park. "The casino drew in all sorts of gamblers," reports gaming expert Ed Hertel. "Those who were reported to have visited the club include American presidents Chester A. Arthur and Rutherford B. Hayes, as well as Civil War generals Grant, Sherman and Sheridan. Tycoons with the names Vanderbilt and Rockefeller were enthusiastically welcomed frequent patrons. The Club House quickly became the meeting place for the social and economic elite." After Morrissey's death in 1878, his establishment eventually became the lavish Canfield Casino, until the city outlawed gambling in the early 20th century. As a result, Richard Canfield sold the building to the city. (Today, it houses the Saratoga Springs History Museum and is used for social events.)

Adding to the town's popularity, the Saratoga Race Course opened in 1863—thanks to New York businessman William R. Travers, horseman John R. Hunter, and other likeminded men who appreciated the "Sport of Kings" and thought it would appeal to summer visitors. A year later, the track moved to its current location on the eastside of town, on the still fashionable Union Avenue. Often proclaimed "the oldest race track in America," the Saratoga Race Course has been renovated several times, most famously in 1902, when it took on much of its current Victorian appearance. Local historians assert that "with the exception of 1911 and 1912, when the track closed in response to gambling reforms, and 1943–45, when meets were canceled due to World War II," the track has been in continuous operation. During those years, it has featured numerous successful horses (e.g., War Admiral, Seabiscuit, Secretariat, and local favorite Funny Cide) and famous races, most notably the Travers Stakes, which some consider to be the fourth jewel in the Triple Crown. Since the 1950s, the New York Racing Association (NYRA), a not-for-profit private corporation, has administered the track, sometimes ineptly.

The Saratoga Race Course is the community's primary economic engine. However, Saratoga Springs has numerous other important cultural institutions. In 1900, for instance, the financier Spencer Trask and his wife Katrina founded Yaddo, an artists' community on a bucolic 400-acre estate. Yaddo promotes many art forms (literature, musical composition, painting, etc.) by awarding residencies that allow artists "to work without interruption in a supportive environment." In 1903, Lucy Skidmore Scribner, the widow of one of Charles Scribner's sons, founded the Young Women's Industrial Club to provide young women with vocational and professional training. After growing and evolving, the institution became an accredited four-year women's college (Skidmore) in 1922. Today, it is a respected coeducational liberal arts college with 2,500 students and a $280 million endowment. Additionally, just south of downtown is the Saratoga Spa State Park, which is listed as a National Historic Landmark. It includes the Saratoga Performing Arts Center (which hosts the New York City Ballet, the Philadelphia Orchestra, and music festivals and concerts in the summer), the Spa Little Theater, the National Museum of Dance, the Gideon Putnam Resort, the Roosevelt Baths and Spa, and a golf course, as well as traditional recreation opportunities like hiking and fishing.

Since the Gilded Age, arguably the pinnacle of its popularity and prestige, Saratoga Springs has changed significantly—architecturally, demographically, economically, and culturally. Still, this upstate New York town remains a popular summer tourist destination. As recently as 2012, *Travel and Leisure* magazine cited its historic Broadway as one of "America's Greatest Main Streets."

Daniel A. Nathan

See also Seabiscuit; Secretariat; Triple Crown

Suggested Resources

Chambers, Thomas A. *Drinking the Waters: Creating an American Leisure Class at Nineteenth-Century Mineral Springs*. Washington, DC: Smithsonian Institution Press, 2002.

City of Saratoga Springs. http://www.saratoga-springs.org/. Accessed May 15, 2012.

Corbett, Theodore. *The Making of American Resorts: Saratoga Springs, Ballston Spa, Lake George*. New Brunswick, NJ: Rutgers University Press, 2001.

Holmes, Timothy. *Saratoga Springs, New York: A Brief History*. Charleston, SC: The History Press, 2008.

Horne, Field. *The Saratoga Reader: Writing about an American Village, 1749–1900.* Saratoga Springs, NY: Kiskatom, 2004.

Hotaling, Edward. *They're Off!: Horse Racing at Saratoga.* Syracuse, NY: Syracuse University Press, 1995.

Joki, Robert. *Saratoga Lost: Images of Victorian America.* Hensonville, NY: Black Dome Press, 1998.

Saratoga Racetrack. http://www.saratogaracetrack.com/. Accessed May 15, 2012.

Swanner, Grace Maguire. *Saratoga, Queen of Spas: A History of the Saratoga Spa and the Mineral Springs of the Saratoga and Ballston Areas.* Utica, NY: North Country Books, 1988.

Sayers, Gale (1943–)

Gale Sayers in his Chicago Bears uniform. (AP Photo.)

Gale Sayers was a running back for the University of Kansas who became one of the greatest runners in the National Football League for the Chicago Bears, before injuries ended his career prematurely. He later became an athletic administrator and businessman and lives in Chicago.

Gale Eugene Sayers was born in 1943 in Wichita, Kansas, but was raised in rural Speed, Kansas, before his family moved to Omaha when he was about 10. He attended Omaha Central High School where he played football and ran track, setting a state record in the long jump, his senior year.

After Sayers's all-state selection, he decided to attend the University of Kansas because he liked the Jayhawks' coach, Jack Mitchell. At that time athletes could not play varsity ball until sophomore year, but Sayers burst on the Kansas scene by gaining over 1,100 yards as a sophomore in just 10 games, including 283 yards in one game against Oklahoma State. Sayers was an All-American running back in both his junior and senior seasons. He ended his career at KU with nearly 2,700 yards rushing and over 3,900 all-purpose yards gained. He was the fourth selection of the first round in the National Football League draft, taken by the Chicago Bears, who had been scouting him since high school.

Sayers became a starter in the third game of the season and proceeded to improve every week in his running and throwing of the option pass. The Bears lost their first three games, but with Sayers in the lineup and his rookie counterpart, Dick Butkus, settling into the middle linebacker position, the Bears won 9 of their final 11 games to finish 9–5 in the Western Conference, two games behind Green Bay and Baltimore. Sayers, however, was the Rookie of the Year in the league after gaining 867 yards rushing, 507 yards receiving, and 898 return yards in the 14-game season. He also scored 22 touchdowns, including 6 in one game against the San Francisco 49ers. Sayers was also voted First-Team All-Pro.

Also a rookie that year, but on the taxi squad (players signed by the team, but not on the roster) was Brian Piccolo, another running back, who had gone undrafted out of Wake Forest and signed as a free agent. Sayers first encountered him at an all-star game in Buffalo after the 1964 collegiate season had ended. Since they were both signed by the Bears, they said hello, but not much more. In 1966, Piccolo became Sayers's backup at running back.

Following his great rookie year, Sayers responded with an even better sophomore year. He led the league in rushing with 1,231 yards, had 447 yards receiving on 34 catches, and had 718 yards on kickoff returns. He scored 11 touchdowns and was again First-Team All-Pro. The Bears, however, went only five and seven with two ties. The team was aging on both sides of the ball and opposing teams keyed on Sayers, so his rushing title was that much more impressive.

In 1967 the Bears had a new young quarterback, Jack Concannon, and he provided a better passing game, which took some pressure off Sayers. Sayers still rushed for 880 yards from scrimmage (third in the league) and was First-Team All-Pro once again. The Bears finished at 7–6–1, good for second in the new six-division organization that came about after the NFL and AFL merged that year.

During that year, the Bears' regular fullback was injured and Brian Piccolo became the fullback, playing in the backfield with Sayers. In training camp the two had become roommates (the NFL's first interracial roommates), and this allowed them to become close friends.

In 1968, Sayers was leading the league in rushing, when he injured his knee in the ninth game of the season. He missed the rest of the year, but his 856 yards rushing were still fifth in the league and his average yards rushed per game (95.1) were first in the league. Sayers was again named First-Team All-Pro, but his injury threatened his career.

The surgery by Dr. Ted Fox, Bear team physician, was successful and Sayers rehabbed diligently. He came back in 1969, but didn't have the ability to cut as sharply as before; he became more of a power runner on a very weak team. The Bears went 1–13 in 1969, but Sayers led the league in rushing with 1,032 yards and was First-Team All-Pro.

Midway through the season, Brian Piccolo began coughing quite a bit and couldn't shake the cough. Finally, in November he went to a doctor who found a large tumor on his lung. Piccolo had never smoked and the assumption was that the tumor had been there since birth and, for some reason, had become active and malignant. Surgery was performed to remove the tumor and the hope was that the cancer would not return, but it did. Twice more surgery was done and Piccolo grew progressively weaker with his surgery.

The Greatest Performance Ever?

On December 12, 1965, Sayers and the Bears took the field against the San Francisco 49ers at Wrigley Field. There had been rain and the field was muddy, sloppy, and slippery. Players dropped passes, fell making cuts, and missed easy tackles. Sayers, however, seemed unaffected as he ran and tacklers literally fell over trying to grasp him. In three quarters he scored five touchdowns from scrimmages and the Bears had a commanding lead. Coach George Halas pulled Sayers, but reinserted him to return a punt because of the fans' chanting to put him back in. Sayers returned the punt 85 yards for a sixth touchdown, a record that still stands. The NFL calls it the greatest game by any player ever.

At the end of the season Sayers received an award for being the most courageous player in the NFL, having come back to lead the league in rushing after the devastating knee injury of the year before. At the ceremony where Sayers received the award, he said that he was giving the award to Piccolo, truly the most courageous man in the NFL. In June 1970 Piccolo died. Sayers himself was hospitalized in Omaha at the time, but after being discharged, he went to New York and gave the trophy he won to Piccolo's widow. The Sayers-Piccolo relationship became the subject of a television film, *Brian's Song*, which was broadcast in 1971 (and won three Emmy awards), and later remade and broadcast in 2001.

In the second game of the 1970 season, Sayers reinjured his knee and underwent surgery once again. He attempted a comeback in 1971, but, after two games, it was clear that he would never recover his elusiveness and was essentially running on one leg. He tried another comeback in 1972, but quit before the end of the exhibition season. Sayers retired and became a stockbroker (he had been taking classes in the offseason).

In 1977, Sayers became the youngest former player (34) ever elected to the Professional Football Hall of Fame. Despite his short career, Sayers had made an indelible impact on the game. He set a number of records including most touchdowns in a season (22), most in a game (6, tied with Ernie Nevers and Dub Jones), highest career kickoff return average (30.56), and most return touchdowns in a game (2, tied with multiple players). He led the league in rushing twice and finished in the top five all five years that he played at least nine games, and he was First-Team All-Pro every year.

After football, Sayers finished his undergraduate degree at Kansas and also received a master's degree and accepted a job as director of athletics at Southern Illinois University in 1976. He remained in that position until 1981. Sayers then returned to Chicago and worked in private business before returning to Lawrence as the University of Kansas assistant athletics director. He also spent a year as director of athletics at Tennessee State University in Nashville. He is chairman of a technology company, Sayers 40, and active in many philanthropic causes in Chicago.

Because of the many sports channels and the NFL's own film series, Sayers's amazing runs have been seen by new generations of football fans, and he is recognized as the most elusive runner ever to play professional football.

See also *Brian's Song*; Butkus, Dick; Chicago Bears; Green Bay Packers; Halas, George; Pro Football Hall of Fame and Museum

Murry R. Nelson

Suggested Resources

Davis, Jeff. *Chicago Bears: Yesterday and Today.* Lincolnwood, IL: Publications International, 2009.

"Gale Sayers." Pro Football Hall of Fame. http://www.profootballhof.com/hof/member.aspx?PLAYER_ID=188. Accessed February 10, 2011.

"Gale Sayers." Pro-Football-Reference.com. http://www.pro-football-reference.com/players/S/SayeGa00.htm. Accessed February 10, 2011.

Sayers, Gale, with Al Silverman. *I Am Third.* New York: Bantam Books, 1974.

Sayers, Gale, with Fred Mitchell. *Sayers, My Life and Times.* Chicago: Triumph Books, 2007.

"Sayers' Greatest Performance." NFL.com. http://www.nfl.com/videos/nfl-game-highlights/09000d5d801b36bb/Sayers-Greatest-Performance. Accessed February 14, 2011.

Schilling, Curt, Bloody Sock of (2004)

During the second game of the 2004 World Series, Curt Schilling, pitching for the Boston Red Sox, had his sock slowly darken with blood in the middle innings of the game, yet he stayed in the game and he and the Red Sox won the contest.

Curt Schilling (1966–) was a veteran pitcher in 2004, who was originally drafted by the Red Sox, but traded before reaching the major leagues. He made his debut with the Baltimore Orioles in 1988, but pitched only in relief for the Orioles and Houston Astros, who acquired him in 1991. Before the 1992 season, he was traded to the Philadelphia Phillies, who made him a starter, and he won 101 games for the Phillies over the next nine years. In mid-season of 2000, he was traded to the Arizona Diamondbacks, where he won 58 games in four years, including two 20-win seasons and a World Series victory in 2001. In 2003, he was traded by the Diamondbacks to the Boston Red Sox, a team that had not won a World Series since 1918.

The Red Sox were in the World Series only in 1946, 1967, 1975, and 1986, but lost in seven games in each instance. Their lack of success was called the "Curse of the Bambino" and linked to the trade of Babe Ruth from the Red Sox to the Yankees in 1920. With Ruth they appeared in and won three World Series titles in five years. After his trade their demise began, or so the curse seemed to be.

In 2004, the Red Sox finished second in the Eastern Division to the New York Yankees, their traditional rival and nemesis, but made the American League playoffs as the wild card team. They also had the second-best record in the league. Curt Schilling won 22 games for the Red Sox and finished second in the league in Cy Young Award voting. He pitched 6.2 innings in game one against the Anaheim Angels and won, 9–3. He aggravated an ankle injury, however, and it was questionable whether he would be able to pitch again in the postseason. The Red Sox swept the series in three games, so Schilling had a little more time to rest the ankle.

The opponents in the American League Championship Series would be the New York Yankees, who had topped the Minnesota Twins in four games. Schilling started game one, but was pounded by the Yankees for six runs in three innings as the New Yorkers won, 10–7. They then won the next two games and the Red Sox curse seemed to be working once again. But something amazing happened. Down 4–3 in the bottom of the ninth inning, the Red Sox tied the game,

The Schilling Tendon Procedure

Schilling's tendon procedure was unique at the time, but it has now become a recognized medical procedure, named after Schilling and initiated by Dr. William Morgan, the Red Sox team physician. It involves placing three sutures through the skin anterior to the path of the peroneus brevis tendon and into the underlining deep connective tissue. This provides a temporary barrier, preventing the tendon from moving anteriorly over the malleolus (the bone on each side of the ankle). Stitches must be removed immediately after play.

then won in 12 innings, 6–4. Game five was similar with the Red Sox tying the game in the bottom of the 8th inning, then adding a run in the bottom of the 14th to win, 5–4.

In game six, the Red Sox went back to Schilling, who pitched seven innings and gave up only one run on four hits, and the Red Sox won, 4–2. More impressive, however, was the fact that Schilling was pitching with a torn tendon sheath in his right ankle, which had been sutured by the doctors, connecting the skin with ligament and deep connective tissue. By the fifth inning, his sock was soaked with blood seeping through the sutures, yet he stayed in and pitched. The next game the Red Sox completed the improbable sweep, winning 10–3 and advancing to the World Series. Was the curse broken?

The World Series was played against the St. Louis Cardinals and the Red Sox won game one, 11–9. Curt Schilling started game two. His ankle had been sutured the day before and he was in discomfort. When one stitch was removed, he was treated with antibiotics, felt better, and then pitched six innings, allowing only one unearned run. Blood stained his sock almost immediately, but he continued to pitch and win the game, and the Red Sox won the Series in four straight games. Doctors said that the procedure might be too dangerous to attempt a third time, but they did not have to with the Series ending.

In 2005, Schilling donated the sock to the Baseball Hall of Fame in Cooperstown, New York, where it was displayed as part of a Red Sox exhibition celebrating the four-game sweep of the Cardinals. In 2007, Baltimore Orioles' broadcaster Gary Thorne claimed

that the blood on the sock was actually red paint, but retracted his statement after strong denials by Schilling, his teammates, and the doctors involved. Schilling offered $1 million if someone could prove it was not blood. The sock had become a mythical baseball icon.

Murry R. Nelson

See also Baseball Hall of Fame; Boston Red Sox; St. Louis Cardinals; World Series

Suggested Resources

Boston Red Sox, 2004 Championship. http://mlb.mlb.com/bos/history/championship04.jsp. Accessed January 28, 2011.

Golenbock, Peter. *Red Sox Nation: An Unexpurgated History of the Red Sox.* Chicago: Triumph Books, 2005.

"Hall Enshrines Schilling's Bloody Sock." nbcsports.com. February 11, 2005. http://nbcsports.msnbc.com/id/6948862/ Accessed January 28, 2011.

O'Nan, Stewart, and Stephen King. *Faithful: Two Diehard Boston Red Sox Fans Chronicle the Historic 2004 Season.* New York: Scribner, 2005.

Shaughnessy, Dan. *Reversing the Curse: Inside the 2004 Boston Red Sox.* Boston: Mariner Books, 2006.

"2004 World Series." Baseball Almanac. http://www.baseball-almanac.com/ws/yr2004ws.shtml. Accessed January 28, 2011.

Schulz, Charles (1922–2000) and *Peanuts*

Charles Schulz was an American cartoonist who created the popular and lasting comic strip *Peanuts*. On October 2, 1950, at the age of 27, Schulz's first *Peanuts* strip appeared in eight newspapers nationwide. At its peak, the comic was syndicated to over 2,600 newspapers in 75 countries, translated into more than 20 languages, and attracted an estimated readership of 355 million. Schulz wrote and illustrated one of the 17,897 *Peanuts* strips every week for nearly 50 years until December 14, 1999, when at the age of 77, his struggle with colon cancer forced him to retire. The last original panel was published on February 13, 2000—the day following his death. Throughout the strip, he demonstrated his passion for sports as a fan and participant. *Peanuts* is generally recognized as one of the most influential comic strips in history and is still reprinted daily in newspapers across the world.

Charles Schulz, seated at drawing table with drawing of Charlie Brown. (Library of Congress.)

Born in Minneapolis, Minnesota, and raised in Saint Paul, Schulz's early childhood and adolescent years were very significant for his future work. Like Charlie Brown, his father was a barber, while his mother raised him at home. His dog Spike provided the influence for Snoopy. He began drawing in kindergarten and played sports informally throughout his youth, including baseball, ice skating, and ice hockey. As a teenager, he fell in love with golf and dreamed of becoming a successful amateur golfer, as well as a cartoonist.

While a senior in high school, Schulz enrolled in a correspondence course with an emphasis on cartooning at Art Instruction Schools in Minneapolis. Shortly after graduation, he submitted cartoons to many major magazines, but without success. In 1943, he was drafted into the U.S. Army and served as a sergeant with the 20th Armored Division in Europe during World War II. Following the war, he earned a position

lettering comics for *Timeless Topix*, the publisher of a series of Catholic comic magazines. Shortly thereafter, he joined the staff at Art Instruction Schools. He continued producing his own cartoons and sold 15 strips to the *Saturday Evening Post* between 1948 and 1950.

Schulz also developed and sold a weekly feature to the *St. Paul Pioneer Press* called *Li'l Folks.* He persisted in mailing his work to major syndicates and in the spring of 1950, United Feature Syndicate in New York City decided to publish the strip. *Peanuts* emerged after he signed with United Media in 1950. The characters, except for Snoopy and his sidekick Woodstock, are children who cope with adult-themed issues and relationships. The comic revolved around the experiences of small children because his own children were very young at the time. Initially, readers observed the characters from an adult perspective. Gradually, he adopted the characters' point of view as the children developed their own adult sophistication.

The *Peanuts* gang frequently refer to topics ranging from religion and destiny to psychiatry and identity, and from love and loneliness to music and sports. Sports, in particular, continued to hold a prominent role in Schulz's adult life. He operated an ice rink and played hockey, golf, and tennis well into his 70s, and he felt that the challenges confronted while playing sports worked well in his comic strip to depict the more serious tests encountered in life. Games and athletics became an essential part of *Peanuts*, as he used sport as a metaphor to represent life as a challenge, filled with hope and possibility.

United Feature Syndicate estimates that nearly 10 percent of the strips dealt with baseball, Schulz's favorite sport to utilize for the characters' musings. The *Peanuts* gang, however, can also be seen bowling, figure skating, and flying kites, not to mention playing basketball, checkers, croquet, football, golf, hockey, marbles, soccer, and tennis. Usually, the sports-themed segments detail the dismal failures of Charlie Brown. One of the most well-known and often repeated strips throughout *Peanuts*'s 50 years shows a determined Charlie Brown ready to kick a football held in place by Lucy. Once every year from 1952 to 1999, she maliciously removes the ball at the exact moment before his foot would boot it, sending him head over heels in yet another tumbling catastrophe. Most frequently, however, the lovable loser's endless suffering and tragic defeats occur from his position on the pitcher's mound of a baseball diamond. The only time he won a baseball game was when the other team forfeited.

While his friends and not-so-loyal dog often lose sight of the game in daydreams and reflections, Charlie Brown urgently presses them on toward victory. Despite his efforts, his baseball clubs lose by scores of 40–0, 123–0, and even 200–0. In one contest he is called in to pitch the ninth inning with a 50–0 lead. He, of course, blows the game and the team falls 51–50. Yet amid the endless heartache and disappointment, he never quits. His character illustrates the notion that through sport, everyone is familiar with losing, while his peers' lack of concern for the outcome demonstrates that sport is not the most important thing in the world.

If Charlie Brown is the realistic portrayal of the plucky, noble athlete in defeat, his dog Snoopy represents the elusive fantasy of triumph and glory. He frequently dives into the depths of his imagination to reemerge as a variety of alter-personae, including a fighter pilot. In his athletic pursuits, he escapes the sandlot in his owner's neighborhood and envisions himself competing in some of professional sport's ultimate competitions, including Wimbledon, the North American Figure Skating Championships, the Masters, and Summer Olympic Games. He dances, surfs, skateboards, swims, and shoots hoops, but also plays alongside legends such as Peggy Fleming and Billie Jean King. Once, he even broke Babe Ruth's home run record (before Hank Aaron and Barry Bonds passed him). Snoopy represents the eternal optimism many Americans find in sport, while another character personifies a never-say-die attitude.

Portrayed as a fearless tomboy, Peppermint Patty is the most accomplished athlete of the group. She excels in baseball, football, golf, and skating, and reads sport literature on fishing, motorcycles, mountain climbing, and wrestling. She is never shy about offering to protect "Chuck" from others, as only she can call him, with threats of "knuckle sandwiches" and good old-fashioned poundings. The pair also carry on many conversations about baseball.

Other characters are woven in and out of the *Peanuts*'s sporting adventures. The egotistical Lucy Van Pelt is a harsh and unforgiving opponent. She finds no redeeming qualities in sport, yet consistently belittles Charlie Brown for his miscues. Her brother and Charlie Brown's faithful friend, Linus, often takes the field only to stumble with life's biggest questions and over his blanket. The tiny bird Woodstock is typically knocked around and confused, like the youngster on the block too little to play with older children. Schroeder, the young piano prodigy, is willing to join the rest as long as it does not interfere with his passion for Beethoven.

Schulz received global acclaim for his work. He also made significant contributions to the world of sport, particularly through his service to hockey. He formed the world's largest senior hockey tournament, which features an over-70 league. Among the several awards received throughout his lifetime, he was inducted into the Cartoonist Hall of Fame and the U.S. Hockey Hall of Fame in 1986 and 1993, respectively, and earned a star on Hollywood's Walk of Fame in 1996. Five years later he posthumously received the Congressional Gold Medal, the highest civilian honor awarded by the U.S. Congress. That same year, in 2001, the City of Saint Paul renamed its Highland Arena the Charles Schulz Arena in honor of his work developing ice hockey for senior athletes. He was inducted into the U.S. Figure Skating Hall of Fame in 2007 for his lifelong contribution to the sport, including building the Redwood Empire Ice Arena (Santa Rosa, California), which opened in 1969.

Schulz also left an enduring legacy in American culture. In 2002, the Charles M. Schulz Museum and Research Center opened, housing almost 6,000 of his drawings. Additionally, the amusement park theme at the Mall of America in Bloomington, Minnesota, featured the *Peanuts* characters from 1992 to 2006. Between 2000 and 2004, representatives of his hometown paid tribute to their native cartoonist through "Peanuts on Parade" by placing over 100 statues of Snoopy, Charlie Brown, Linus, and Lucy around the city.

Peanuts continues to resonate with audiences old and new. The success of the comic strip spawned several successful television specials, some of which won Emmy awards and are broadcast to this day. The brand made its way into theater with the musical *You're a Good Man, Charlie Brown* and into mainstream culture through a line of merchandise. At least part of this success can be attributed to Schulz's eloquence in revealing that for every winner, there is a loser, and for every serious moment, there is absurdity. Perhaps most importantly for fans and athletes at any level, he demonstrated that in failure or success, sport offers a place where people, big and little, can dream.

Dain TePoel

Suggested Resources

Charles M. Schulz Museum and Research Center. http://www.schulzmuseum.org. Accessed September 26, 2011.

Michaelis, David. *Schulz and Peanuts: A Biography.* New York: HarperCollins, 2007.

Peanuts Website. http://www.peanuts.com/. Accessed September 26, 2011.

Schulz, Charles. *Celebrating Peanuts: 60 Years.* Kansas City: Andrews McMeel, 2009.

Schulz, Charles. *My Life with Charlie Brown.* Jackson: University Press of Mississippi, 2010.

Scott, Jack (1943–2008)

When Jack Scott died of cancer in February 2008, many obituaries focused upon his connections with the Symbionese Liberation Army (SLA) and Patty Hearst during the mid-1970s, rather than the educator's challenge to the sport establishment during the late 1960s and early 1970s. As the author of *The Athletic Revolution* (1971), athletic director at Oberlin College from 1972 to 1974, and director of the Institute for the Study of Sport and Society, Scott argued that collegiate athletic programs and coaches often exploited athletes. While Scott's critics complained that he was opposed to competition, Scott insisted that he envisioned a more democratic sporting culture that would provide athletes a greater voice in the managing of collegiate sport programs. Embracing pure athletic competition, Scott asserted that he wanted to alter the sexism, racism, and commercialism that all too often dominated the world of sport.

Born in 1943, Scott grew up in Scranton, Pennsylvania, where as a quarterback he led his high school to a city championship. A strong student, Scott attended Villanova and Stanford University, where he ran track until becoming disillusioned with the Stanford program. Returning to the Northeast, he enrolled at Syracuse University and participated in track as a member of the sprint relay team. After graduation from Syracuse in 1966, Scott continued to work with three of his former track teammates as an informal coach, accusing the Syracuse coaching staff of racism. However, the three black athletes were dismissed from the team for their association with Scott. A disillusioned Scott denounced the Syracuse administration and praised the athletes whose times improved under his direction. The runners, nevertheless, were not reinstated.

Scott and his wife, Micki, moved to Berkeley where he pursued a doctorate in sport sociology from the University of California. While engaged in his studies, Scott supported his family by serving as an editor for the radical magazine *Ramparts*. In 1968, he covered the Mexico City Olympics for *Ramparts*, expressing support for the Black Power salutes of sprinters John Carlos and Tommie Smith, who were expelled from the U.S. Olympic team. He also worked closely with University of California, Berkeley professor

Harry Edwards, who advocated the boycott of track-and-field events by black athletes to protest racial conditions in the United States and apartheid regimes in Rhodesia and South Africa.

After earning his doctorate in 1970, Scott and his wife formed the Institute for the Study of Sport and Society in Oakland. They invited athletes such as former St. Louis Cardinals linebacker Dave Meggyesy to use the institute's facilities in writing memoirs and reports challenging the nation's sporting establishment. In addition, Scott privately published *Athletics for Athletes* after the *Track & Field News* reneged on an agreement to distribute the book. *Athletics for Athletes* would become the basis for *The Athletic Revolution*, published by The Free Press in 1971. In *The Athletic Revolution*, Scott exposed the excessive commercialization of sport, which led to violence, drug use, and recruiting violations; the employment of sport as a male rite of passage; the myth of sport in providing social mobility for blacks; and the growing gap between professional and recreational sports with most Americans becoming passive spectators.

In the fall of 1970, Scott taught a course at the University of California, Berkeley campus entitled Intercollegiate Athletics and Higher Education. The university expected an enrollment of between 50 and 100 students. Instead, approximately 400 students, including many varsity athletes, enrolled for the popular course. Accordingly, in 1971 the University of Washington offered Scott a position in the physical education department. After considerable internal pressure and protest by the athletic department and football coach Jim Owens, the offer was rescinded. Scott, in turn, sued the University of Washington, and he was awarded the amount of his one-year contract, $10,500.

But in 1972 Scott was destined to make a much larger splash on the national scene when young, reform-minded Oberlin College president Robert Fuller hired Scott as athletic director and chairman of the physical education department with a four-year contract. With its liberal reputation as an institution that prided itself on being the first white college to admit blacks (1835) and graduate women (1837), the Ohio college seemed to be a perfect fit for Scott. Oberlin's liberal image was suffering, and 35-year-old President

Dave Meggyesy

Among the first clients of Jack Scott's Oakland-based Institute for the Study of Sport and Society was former St. Louis Cardinals linebacker Dave Meggyesy, whose bestselling 1970 memoir *Out of Their League*, echoed Scott's critique of professional football. In *Out of Their League*, Meggyesy denounced the sexism, racism, violence, and exploitation of athletes in the National Football League (NFL).

Meggyesy was born November 1, 1941, in Cleveland, Ohio. His father was a working-class immigrant from Hungary. Meggyesy's high school performance on the football field earned him an athletic scholarship at 1959 national champion Syracuse University under Coach Ben Schwartzwalder. In his memoir, Meggyesy described how the Syracuse coaching staff discouraged academic pursuits while making cash payments to players and condoning sexual exploitation of women by the athletes.

Meggyesy was selected by the St. Louis Cardinals in the 1963 NFL draft. Meggyesy played for the Cardinals from 1963 to 1969. In *Out of Their League*, Meggyesy describes his discontent with the hypocrisy of professional football. He denounces the racial segregation practiced by Cardinals management as well as the promotion of homophobia and militarism within the culture of professional football. Meggyesy quit after the 1969 season and accepted Scott's invitation to work on *Out of Their League* at the Institute for the Study of Sport and Society. After living briefly in Colorado, Meggyesy accepted a position teaching the sociology of sport at Stanford University. In the 1980s, he began a career with the National Football Players Association, working with the labor organization until his retirement in 2007. With the life expectancy of former professional football players averaging 55 years of age, many of the issues raised by Meggyesy in his memoir remain of major concern.

Fuller was upset by the dismissal of a star baseball player for failure to shave his beard.

Scott quickly made his presence felt, launching what would become known as the "Oberlin experiment." In his first major hiring decision, Scott named Tommie Smith, the winner of the 200-meter gold medal at the 1968 Mexico City Olympics and perhaps best known for his Black Power salute at the games, as assistant athletic director and track coach. In response to the appointments of Scott and Smith, four members of the athletic department, including the head basketball and football coaches, departed Oberlin.

Seeking to empower athletes, Scott decided to enlist the football squad in the recruitment of a new coach. After consulting with the players, former professional player Cass Jackson was selected to lead the team, becoming the first black to assume the head coaching duties at a predominantly white institution. Jackson immediately turned the Oberlin football program around after a winless season before Scott's arrival. He also increased spending on women's athletics from $1,000 to $7,000 and expanded participation in the school's physical education program, offering new classes such as Sports and Racism, Sports and Politics, and Sports and the News Media. To erase the distinction between revenue and nonrevenue sports, Scott introduced the concept of not charging for admission to Oberlin athletic contests. Even mainstream media outlets such as *Time* praised Scott's quest for "excellence without dehumanizing the athlete."

The Oberlin faculty, however, was not supportive of Scott, claiming that he was often abusive in his interaction with colleagues. After 16 turbulent months, Fuller decided to dismiss Scott. While President Fuller officially praised Scott for his contributions to the Oberlin athletic program, the conflict between Scott and Fuller may be perceived as reflective of the New Left, which sought to work outside the system, while Fuller was a liberal who sought reform within the system. Tommie Smith asserted that white liberals at Oberlin were simply uncomfortable with the number of black coaches, students, and athletes Scott was attracting to Oberlin.

After leaving Oberlin, Scott returned to the Bay Area and began to pursue a book manuscript on the revolutionary Symbionese Liberation Army (SLA). His interest in the SLA brought Scott into contact with Patty Hearst, the kidnapped heiress who was then a fugitive wanted for bank robbery. In 1974, Scott reportedly helped Hearst escape a FBI dragnet by driving her across the country to a safe house in Pennsylvania. Although questioned by authorities, Scott was never indicted for conspiring with Hearst and other members of the SLA.

After the controversy surrounding the Hearst case, Scott maintained a low profile. In 1975, he moved to Oregon where he employed the use of microcurrent theory to increase circulation and promote healing. Among his clients were such prominent track-and-field performers as Carl Lewis, Ben Johnson, and Mary Decker Slaney. When he died from throat cancer on February 6, 2000, Scott was, unfortunately, perhaps best remembered for his association with the Hearst case and the SLA rather than his radical challenge to the collegiate sporting establishment, which he attempted to implement at Oberlin from 1972 to 1974. And Scott's critique of major college sports continues to contain a great deal of validity.

Ron Briley

See also Black Power Salute; Lewis, Carl; 1968 Olympic Games, Mexico City

Suggested Resources

Brown, Gwilym S. "Jeepers! Peepers Is in Charge Now." October 23, 1972. http://sportsillustrated.cnn.com/vault/article/magazine/MAG1086676/index.htm. 10 June 2011.

Meggyesy, Dave. *Out of Their League*. San Francisco: Ramparts Press, 1970.

Scott, Jack. *The Athletic Revolution*. New York: The Free Press, 1971.

Scully, Vin (1927–)

Vin Scully has been a staple of Major League Baseball for over 50 years as a broadcaster for the Dodgers organization. Born in the Bronx, New York, on November 29, 1927, Vincent Edward Scully was the son of a silk salesman and a homemaker. An Irish Catholic, Scully first attended school at Fordham Preparatory School. After moving to the Washington Heights neighborhood of Manhattan, Scully knew from a young age that he wanted to be a sports announcer. During World War II, he worked as a delivery boy to make money after asking his father not to accept a more lucrative job in a combat zone.

While attending college at Fordham University (1944–1949), Scully helped found WFUV, an FM radio station for the college. Scully was also assistant sports editor of *The Fordham Ram* during his senior year. In addition to playing center field for the varsity teams in high school and college, Scully called games on the radio for baseball, football, and basketball. He graduated in June 1949, having served for a year in the navy.

The summer after graduation, Scully worked as an intern at WTOP, a 50,000-watt CBS affiliate, in Washington, D.C. During the fall, the illness of the regular broadcaster for a Boston University–Maryland football game played at Fenway Park gave Scully an opportunity to demonstrate his talents for a national audience. The broadcast caught the attention of Red Barber, the CBS sports director. Shortly thereafter, Barber recommended Scully to Brooklyn Dodgers president Branch Rickey to replace Ernie Harwell, who had left for the New York Giants. The 22-year-old took his position as the third member of the broadcast team behind Red Barber and Connie Desmond.

Scully began his tenure as a Dodger broadcaster during spring training in 1950. He would usually call the third and seventh innings and developed a style that Barber and Desmond mentored. In 1951, Scully was in the booth for the heartbreaking Dodger loss to the New York Giants in the final game of a three-game playoff for the pennant with a home run by Bobby Thomson. Just two years later, Scully became the youngest person to call a World Series. At 25, Scully replaced Barber in announcing the Dodgers-Yankees World Series with Mel Allen for television in 1953. Barber then took a job with the New York Yankees, and Scully took the first position on the team for the 1954 season.

Vin Scully called games in such a descriptive, melodic way that sometimes simplicity fit the moment more than numerous words. In 1955, when the Brooklyn Dodgers defeated the New York Yankees to win the World Series, Scully simply said, "Ladies and gentlemen, the Brooklyn Dodgers are the champions of the world." The Dodgers and Yankees had played one another five times in 14 years, and this was the first Dodger victory and the only championship they would take in Brooklyn.

In 1957, Dodger owner Walter O'Malley decided to move the Dodgers west to Los Angeles, breaking the hearts of millions of fans in Brooklyn. The move, along with the New York Giants' relocation to San Francisco, marked the first time Major League Baseball had moved west of St. Louis. Vin Scully moved west with the team. Maintaining the same style of broadcasting, Scully quickly found fans in the Southern California audience. Jerry Doggett joined Scully in the broadcast booth in 1956. O'Malley considering hiring a local personality to connect with the fans in Los Angeles, but Scully argued to keep him. They would work together, alternating innings, for another 30 years.

When the Dodgers moved to Los Angeles, they played at the Los Angeles Coliseum while a new stadium was constructed in Chavez Ravine. The size of the Coliseum and the newness of the major league game in Southern California led fans to bring transistor radios to the game to hear Scully's play-by-play. In a culture dominated by cars and with most Dodger away games, except those against the San Francisco Giants, starting at 5 p.m. (8 p.m. Eastern), West Coast fans could listen to the game while driving home from work.

In their first two seasons on the West Coast, the Los Angeles Dodgers went from seventh to first place, winning the 1959 world championship. Three years later, the new ballpark at Chavez Ravine opened. Over the years, Scully called many historic baseball moments including Sandy Koufax's perfect game against the Cubs on September 9, 1965, at Dodger Stadium. On April 8, 1974, he announced the game as Henry Aaron surpassed Babe Ruth's all-time home run record in the fourth inning with a home run off Dodger pitcher Al Downing. After 30 seconds of silence, Scully said, "What a marvelous moment for baseball; what a marvelous moment for Atlanta and the state of Georgia; what a marvelous moment for the country and the world. A black man is getting a standing ovation in the Deep South for breaking a record of an all-time baseball idol. And it is a great moment for all of us, and particularly for Henry Aaron." On October 15, 1988, Scully made the call as the Dodgers played in game one of the 1988 World Series. With a man on base, an injured Kirk Gibson hobbled to the plate to hit a home run that would win the game and provide enough momentum for the Dodgers to win the Series.

Scully was also present for the growth of Fernando-mania, the support for and excitement about Fernando Valenzuela, a 20-year-old left-handed pitcher from Mexico who was the dominant pitcher for the Dodgers starting in 1981. In addition to building support from the Latino community, Fernando pitched great games throughout the 1980s including a no-hitter on June 29, 1990. Scully was in the broadcast booth for all six of the Dodger world championships (1955, 1959, 1963, 1965, 1981, 1988) and 12 All-Star Games.

In addition to calling play-by-play for the Dodgers, Scully called national games for radio and television. From 1975 to 1982, Scully worked as the weekend sportscaster for CBS broadcasting for tennis, golf, and professional football. From 1983 to 1989, he called games for the weekly national program *NBC Saturday Game*. In 1997, he retired from all other broadcast duties to focus wholly on the Dodgers. Over time, Scully reduced his travel to games in the West Division of the National League, but his announcing continues in part on radio and in part on television.

Vin Scully's illustrious broadcasting career has included tragedy in his personal life. In 1958, Scully married Joan Crawford, who was not related to the famous actress. Together they had three children. In 1972, Joan died of an accidental medical overdose at the age of 35. In late 1973, Scully married Sandra Hunt, a woman who had two children of her own. Together they had one child. In 1994, his eldest son Michael died in a helicopter crash at the age of 33.

During his career, Vin Scully has been recognized in every possible way. In 1982, he won the Ford C. Frick Award from the Baseball Hall of Fame. He was inducted into the National Radio Hall of Fame in 1995. He won a Lifetime Achievement Emmy in 1996. The National Sportscasters and Sportswriters named him Sportscaster of the Year three times. He was a winner

of the Peabody Award for broadcast excellence. In 2008, Fordham University's WFUV Radio gave Scully a Lifetime Achievement Award in Sports Broadcasting. He was given a star on the Hollywood Walk of Fame. In 2011, the Dodgers paid to have it patched, due to cracks. Scully, or his voice, has "appeared" on numerous television shows, movies, and video games, including the 1999 Kevin Costner film *For Love of the Game* and documentary filmmaker Ken Burns's series *Baseball* in 1994. Scully's tenure at the Dodgers is the longest of any broadcaster with one team. In 2012, the Dodgers signed Vin Scully to broadcast for another season, his 63rd with the Dodgers.

Amy Essington

See also Aaron, Hank; Baseball Hall of Fame; Brooklyn Dodgers; Koufax, Sandy; Los Angeles Dodgers; Shot Heard 'Round the World; Valenzuela, Fernando

Suggested Resources
Kattan, Larry. *The Voice of the Dodgers*. Bloomington, IN: Trafford, 2011.
Los Angeles Dodgers Website. http://losangeles.dodgers.mlb.com/team/broadcasters.jsp?c_id=la. Accessed October 25, 2011.
Smith, Curt. *Pull Up a Chair: The Vin Scully Story*. Washington, DC: Potomac Books, 2009.
Smith, Curt. *Voice of the Game: The Acclaimed Chronicle of Baseball Radio and Television Broadcasting from 1921 to the Present*. New York: A Fireside Book, 1987.
"Vin Scully." Radio Hall of Fame. http://www.radiohof.org/sportscasters/vinscully.html. Accessed October 25, 2011.
Wolfe, Rich. *Vin Scully: I Saw It on the Radio*. Archbald, PA: A Tribute Book, n.d.

Seabiscuit

Seabiscuit was the quintessential American racehorse. Born in 1933, a descendant of the great Man O' War through his sire Hard Tack, he came to embody the struggle, grit, and spirit of the Great Depression. Despite his pedigree, Seabiscuit's charm stemmed not from the storied history of his ancestors, but rather from the way in which he continually overcame adversity to take on and beat the best horses around the country. Born to a body ill-suited for racing, Seabiscuit spent the early years of his career being overraced and

Jockey Red Pollard rides Seabiscuit to victory in the 28th Yonkers Handicap in 1937. (Library of Congress.)

poorly treated. In 1936, midway through his second racing season, the horse came into the capable hands of owner Charles Howard, trainer Tom Smith, and jockey Johnny "Red" Pollard, the men who would lead Seabiscuit to countless racing victories over the next four years. By overcoming serious injuries and continually defeating bigger, more physically impressive horses, Seabiscuit became the favorite of millions of struggling Americans who flocked to tracks to watch him run or huddled around radios to hear the call. It is this "little horse that could" aspect of the story, captured in Laura Hillenbrand's 2001 bestseller, *Seabiscuit: An American Legend*, and in the 2003 movie that followed, that gives Seabiscuit his legendary status and permanent place in American popular culture.

As a young colt, Seabiscuit's prospects as a race horse seemed dim. First, he inherited nothing of Hard Tack's clean lines and physical prowess. Small by thoroughbred standards, he was built too low to the ground and had crooked front legs and an awkward gait. Second, Seabiscuit, unlike his fast but unruly sire, quickly earned a reputation for being quiet and content to the point of laziness. He preferred sleeping to any other activity and showed little interest in training or competing. James Fitzsimmons, the colt's first trainer, did his best to coax Seabiscuit's latent talent out of him by advising his jockeys to use the whip liberally and by putting the young colt through a grueling training and racing schedule. Despite a handful of wins and glimmers of promise, Seabiscuit mostly turned sour as a result of this approach.

By the time Seabiscuit's first owners, Gladys Phipps and her brother Ogden Mills, sold their unpromising colt to Charles Howard for $8,000 in August 1936, he had raced an astonishing 47 times. In his first season alone, as a young two-year-old, he raced 35 times and traveled more than 6,000 miles. For Seabiscuit, the move to the Howard barn and into the steady hands of unconventional trainer Tom Smith and hard-luck jockey Red Pollard marked a new beginning.

The men who surrounded Seabiscuit during his rise from obscurity to legendary status are a study in contrasts. The intersection of their remarkable lives with Seabiscuit's is part of what makes his story compelling and enduring in popular culture. Charles Howard, a powerful man who had made his fortune in the nascent automobile industry in San Francisco in the first decades of the 20th century, had, by the time he bought Seabiscuit in 1936, endured the accidental death of a teenaged son, had divorced his first wife, and had married his second wife and fellow horse enthusiast, Marcela Zabala. Generous and kind by nature, he was a bold, ambitious risk-taker who loved nothing more than to talk and to promote his horse.

By contrast, Tom Smith was a notoriously quiet and experienced horseman who had spent his youth and young adulthood taming mustangs and working on cattle ranches. When Howard hired him, he had been living, most recently, in a horse stall at a track in Mexico. By all accounts, Smith had a special way with horses and knew how to make them thrive. He preferred their company to people's and tolerated but did not embrace the steady stream of reporters and friends that Howard invited into their circle.

Red Pollard was 26 when he met Howard and Smith and had already spent a dozen years trying to eke out a living as a jockey. An avid reader and willing fighter—Pollard used prizefighting to supplement his income—he brought to the partnership a rare combination of intellect, nerve, and patience with troubled horses. Like Smith, Pollard came to understand Seabiscuit perfectly.

Although different by disposition and experience, Howard, Smith, and Pollard shared an unwavering belief in Seabiscuit's potential and spent the late summer and early fall of 1936 earning the horse's trust and rebuilding his confidence. Within several weeks Seabiscuit responded to his new training regime and started to win races at a variety of distances and locations. Smith knew that he was training a once-in-a-lifetime kind of horse. The Howards, giddy with excitement over their horse's early success, decided that Seabiscuit would be ready for the big-time Santa Anita Handicap, also known as the hundred-grander for its staggering $100,000 purse, scheduled for February 1937 on a recently built track just outside of Los Angeles, California. Seabiscuit ran an excellent race, but placed second by a nose when Pollard failed to urge him in the final stretch. Sportswriters blamed Pollard for the loss and praised Seabiscuit's talent and heart. The Howards' horse would never again go unnoticed.

Following the race, Charles Howard decided to take his horse to the East Coast and challenge "all comers." He wanted to prove that Seabiscuit could compete with top horses around the country and, as he boldly predicted, Seabiscuit won race after race in 1937. Along the way, he amassed a huge base of fan support and, before long, folks began to clamor for a match race between Seabiscuit and War Admiral, the impressive 1937 Triple Crown winner. After difficult negotiations, the race was scheduled for November 1, 1938, at Pimlico Race Track in Maryland.

Americans, nine years into the Great Depression, were nothing less than captivated by this one-on-one race. The 40 million people who listened to the call on their radios expected War Admiral to win, but rooted for the underdog, Seabiscuit. They were not disappointed. Ridden that day by George Woolf, a highly successful and well-respected jockey filling in for an injured Red Pollard, Seabiscuit bolted quickly at the start of the race and led the whole way, except for a brief moment before the last turn when Woolf, on Pollard's advice, slowed his horse long enough for War Admiral to make eye contact. Pollard knew that seeing the look of challenge in an opponent's eye was all his horse needed to run with a vengeance.

Rather than retire after the match race, as expected, Seabiscuit continued to train. Six weeks later, however, the horse sustained a potentially career-ending suspensory ligament injury and was forced to return to the Howard barn in California to recuperate. There, he and the injured Pollard recovered together, slowly, over many months. By late 1939, the Howards decided that Seabiscuit, who was then sound but approaching the advanced age of seven, would make one more attempt at the Santa Anita Handicap scheduled for March 1940. Perhaps even more surprisingly, Red Pollard planned to ride him. They were a "couple of old cripples," as Pollard liked to say.

Seabiscuit won the 1940 Santa Anita Handicap in his signature fashion with Pollard guiding the way. Boxed in on the final turn, Pollard threaded the needle

Johnny "Red" Pollard

Red Pollard, born in 1909 in Edmonton, Alberta, spent his young adulthood in the grip of the Great Depression. Born into a loving but financially strapped family, Red left home to become a jockey at 15. He spent the first dozen years of his career moving from track to track looking for mounts and supplementing his meager income by boxing. When Red met Tom Smith in 1936, he had several things working against him as a jockey. He was taller (5'7") than most jockeys and fought a constant and grueling battle to keep his weight down. He had no real record of success as a jockey, having routinely been given the least talented and most difficult horses to ride. Perhaps most importantly, Pollard had no vision in his right eye as the result of an accident early in his career. For a jockey, this loss of vision made racing not only difficult, but incredibly dangerous. Knowing that he would never be allowed to ride if people knew, Pollard kept his condition a secret from the racing world and allowed people to think that he made "mistakes" for other reasons. In addition, Pollard's career before, during, and after his years with Seabiscuit was plagued with serious, sometimes life-threatening injuries. Although sustained by his love for horses, good literature, and by the affection of friends and love of his wife and children, Red Pollard had a hard life. His most joyous and successful years were those he spent riding Seabiscuit.

and found running room for his mount down the final stretch. For a moment it appeared that Kayak, a horse known for his strong finishing speed, might surpass Seabiscuit, but it did not happen. Seabiscuit caught Kayak's eye and, as he had done so many times before, surged to victory one last time, thrilling millions of fans along the way.

Horse racing was popular in the United States throughout the 20th century and many great thoroughbreds made their mark on the sport, but few had Seabiscuit's claim on the hearts of so many Americans. Fans followed his career passionately through radio and newspapers and could not get enough of their rags-to-riches champion. In fact, Hillenbrand points out that Seabiscuit was the single biggest newsmaker of 1938, beating both Franklin Delano Roosevelt and Adolf Hitler in press coverage. Charles Howard played his part in making his beloved horse

a cultural icon by encouraging the press coverage, responding on demand to reporters from around the country and sending them Seabiscuit Christmas cards and other mementos.

Seabiscuit and the men who guided his remarkable career personified traits that Americans, especially those living through the grim years of the Great Depression, hoped to see in themselves. With courage, will, and endurance, Seabiscuit surveyed the landscape with its many obstacles and rose to meet it. He gamely took on all challengers. For Howard, it was better to rise to the challenge and lose than never to rise at all. He continued to believe in his horse and jockey in their darkest hours, knowing that they would come back stronger, and they did. For all those people who were suffering and down on their luck, the ungainly Seabiscuit provided inspiration and hope. This will always be true for those who read his story.

Sarah D. Bair

See also Man O' War

Suggested Resources

Bowen, Edward L. *The Jockey Club's Illustrated History of Thoroughbred Racing in America.* Boston: Bulfinch Press, 1994.

Hillenbrand, Laura. *Seabiscuit: An American Legend.* New York: Ballentine. 2001.

Hotaling, Edward. *They're Off! Horse Racing at Saratoga.* Syracuse, NY: Syracuse University Press, 1995.

"Seabiscuit." American Experience. PBS.org. http://www.pbs.org/wgbh/americanexperience/films/seabiscuit/player/. Accessed November 1, 2011.

Simon, Mary, and Mark Simon. *Racing Through the Century: The Story of Thoroughbred Racing in America.* Mission Viejo, CA: Bowtie Press, 2003.

Seaver, Tom (1944–)

One of the signature major league pitchers of the second half of the 20th century, Tom Seaver almost singlehandedly brought respect to the lackluster New York Mets team. The collected right-hander led the team to its first World Series in the astonishing 1969 season and won three Cy Young Awards during his 11½ years in New York. For good reason Mets fans called him "The Franchise."

George Thomas Seaver was born on November 17, 1944, in Fresno, California. His father, Charlie, was a top-ranked amateur golfer who played on the 1932 American Walker Cup team. Tom was small for his age but developed ability as a high school pitcher. Following a year in the U.S. Marine Reserves he attended Fresno City College and spent a summer pitching for the Alaska Goldpanners of Fairbanks collegiate baseball team before transferring to the University of Southern California. At USC he was coached by the legendary Ron Dedeaux. During Seaver's junior year he signed a contract with the Atlanta Braves, but his contract was nullified by Major League Baseball over a question of his collegiate eligibility. Other teams were invited to offer him contracts, including the Cleveland Indians, New York Mets, and Philadelphia Phillies. The Mets won the rights in a special lottery drawing.

The Mets had been a national punch line since their inaugural 1962 season when they lost a record 120 games; from 1962 through 1966 they finished a collective 287 games under the .500 mark. Seaver had no patience for the "lovable losers" stereotype: "I didn't laugh. I hadn't been raised on the Mets legend; I wasn't part of that losing history. I never did find defeat particularly funny." After a 12–12 season with the Mets' farm club in Jacksonville in 1966, Seaver joined the big league rotation for the 1967 season. He debuted on April 13, 1967, at Shea Stadium against the visiting Pittsburgh Pirates, earning a no-decision while allowing two earned runs in five-and-one-third innings. Seaver finished 1967 with a 16–13 record, the first Mets starter ever with a winning record, and received the National League's Rookie of the Year award. Through a strong farm system and a series of savvy trades, the Mets were slowly building the pieces of a contender. Seaver was joined in the Mets rotation by Jerry Koosman and a young fireballer named Nolan Ryan. Seaver exuded confidence in the doldrums of the Mets universe. "There are only two places in this league," he said, "first place and no place."

The story of the 1969 Mets remains one of the greatest in major league history. Improbably playing over .500 baseball in midseason, they won 38 of their final 49 regular-season games to topple the Chicago Cubs and win the National League Eastern Division title. Seaver went 25–7 with a 2.21 ERA; that July 8 he even took a perfect game against the Cubs into the ninth inning before Jimmy Qualls singled with one out. After beating Atlanta in the National League Championship Series, the Mets faced the dominant Baltimore Orioles in the World Series, who were cocky. In the first inning of game one leadoff batter Don Buford homered off Seaver, who left after five innings with a defeat. The Mets won the next two games, however, and Seaver bounced back in game four, throwing all 10 innings of a 2–1 win. The Mets clinched the Series the following afternoon.

In the wake of the Mets championship Seaver became a superstar. Madison Avenue sought him out for TV commercials due to his collegiate background, good looks, and pretty wife, Nancy. He was also appreciated by most of New York's tough-minded sportswriters for his perceptive commentary. Mets general manager Bing Devine said of Seaver, "He was a very bright guy. He could have done anything else," but Seaver once said, "The owners think if I wasn't in baseball, I'd be out digging ditches or something. . . . How can they be in baseball and not see what it's all about? Pitching is a beautiful thing. It's an art."

A series of injuries and the presence of the Pittsburgh Pirates in the National League East prevented the Mets from establishing a dynasty, but Seaver continued to be one of the game's top pitchers. On April 22, 1970, Seaver struck out 19 San Diego Padres, fanning the last 10 batters in a row (still a record as of 2011). He enjoyed arguably his top season in 1971 with a 20–10 record and a 1.76 ERA, though he lost the NL Cy Young Award to Ferguson Jenkins. In 1973 Seaver won the Cy Young with a 19–11 record as the Mets rallied in the season's final weeks to clinch the Eastern Division and upset Cincinnati in the playoffs. The Mets lost the World Series to Oakland in seven games, but the A's respected Seaver. Slugger Reggie Jackson said of Seaver, "Blind people come to the park just to listen to him pitch."

Seaver unexpectedly slumped in 1974 to an 11–11 record, but rebounded with his third Cy Young Award in 1975 with a 22–9 record as he relied less on his fastball and more on his curve. As baseball salaries started rising in the early days of the free agent era, Seaver sought a new, more expensive contract from Mets management.

In mid-June 1977, following an evening when Seaver and the Mets verbally agreed on a new deal, New York *Daily News* sports columnist Dick Young (whose son-in-law was a Mets executive) reported that Nancy Seaver demanded a new salary for Tom because she was jealous of Nolan Ryan's contract with the California Angels. Seaver, angered that his wife was gratuitously brought into the conflict, immediately told the Mets front office, "Everything I said last night is forgotten. I want out. The attack on my family is something that I just can't take." The Mets then engineered a last-minute deal at the June 15 trade deadline, sending Seaver to the Cincinnati Reds for several prospects. He gave an emotional press conference thanking the New York fans. Mets fans young and old alike wept upon learning of Seaver's departure. In *The New Yorker*, Roger Angell called the trade "a shocking and mystifying affair." With the Reds, declining from their "Big Red Machine" heyday of 1975–1976, Seaver won 14 of 17 decisions to finish 21–6, but the Reds still finished second to the Los Angeles Dodgers. And the Mets would not return to contention until the mid-1980s.

On June 16, 1978, almost one year to the day of his trade to the Reds, Seaver threw the one no-hitter of his major league career, beating St. Louis 4–0. Though Seaver remained sharp over the next three seasons and helped Cincinnati to the 1979 NL West Division title, he would play in no more World Series. Following a shocking 5–13 record in 1982, the 38-year-old Seaver found himself trade bait. Improbably, a deal was made that December sending him back to the Mets. An overflow crowd returned to Shea Stadium on Opening Day 1983 as Seaver defeated Steve Carlton and the Phillies 2–0. Seaver finished the year with a subpar 9–13 record, but most of that was due to the mediocrity of his teammates; his 3.55 ERA was actually slightly better than the league average. Shockingly, the Mets management accidentally left Seaver off its list of players protected from free agent compensation, and in January 1984 the Chicago White Sox claimed him. In Chicago he had his last stellar years, with a 16–11 record in 1985 at the age of 40. That August 4, he won his 300th career game against the Yankees in Yankee Stadium, where 54,032 fans cheered the opposing team's pitcher in a complete-game 4–1 win. He was traded to

The 1969 World Series

"The last miracle I did was the 1969 Mets," George Burns as the Almighty confides to John Denver in the 1977 movie comedy *Oh, God!* "Before that, I think you have to go back to the Red Sea." The Mets had stunned the baseball world merely by winning the National League Eastern Division and then the National League. However, they were decided underdogs in the 66th World Series against the mighty Baltimore Orioles, who had won 109 games in the regular season. The club featured future Hall of Famers Jim Palmer, Frank Robinson, and Brooks Robinson, who declared before the Series began, "We're here to prove there is no Santa Claus." And when they easily defeated Tom Seaver 4–1 in the opening game, many predicted a Baltimore sweep. Yet the Mets took charge over the next four games with a combination of great starting pitching, clutch hitting from Al Weis (hitting just .215 in the regular season, he hit .455 in the five-game Series) and Series MVP Donn Clendenon (who homered three times), and remarkable outfield catches by Tommie Agee and Ron Swoboda. At 3:17 on October 16, Davey Johnson's fly ball landed in left fielder Cleon Jones's glove for the final out of the Series. Fans stormed the Shea Stadium field and tore up much of the sod in celebration.

the Boston Red Sox in the summer of 1986; ineligible for the postseason, he watched the Sox lose the World Series to the Mets. He unsuccessfully attempted a comeback in the Mets minor league system before retiring in 1987. In July 1988, the Mets officially retired his uniform number 41.

Four years later, Seaver was elected to the Baseball Hall of Fame on the first ballot, receiving a record 98.84 percent of the votes from the Baseball Writers of America Association (Seaver needed merely 75 percent for induction). In retirement, Seaver has been a broadcaster for the Mets and Yankees and began his own vineyard in northern California in 2002.

Andrew Milner

See also Baseball Hall of Fame; Jackson, Reggie; New York Mets; Ryan, Nolan

Suggested Resources
Angell, Roger. *Late Innings: A Baseball Companion.* New York: Ballantine, 1983.

Golenbock, Peter. *Amazin': The Miraculous History of New York's Most Beloved Baseball Team.* New York: St. Martin's Press, 2002.

James, Bill, and Rob Neyer. *The Neyer/James Guide to Pitchers.* New York: Fireside, 2002.

"Tom Seaver." Baseball-Reference.com. http://www.baseball-reference.com/players/s/seaveto01.shtml. Accessed October 30, 2011.

"Tom Seaver's MLB Game." YouTube.com. http://www.youtube.com/watch?v=3GB_kkbFVhk. Accessed October 30, 2011.

Secretariat

Secretariat is considered by racing historians as one of the greatest racehorses of the American turf. In 1973, he became the first horse since Citation (1948) to sweep racing's Triple Crown series, and his 31-length triumph in the Belmont Stakes is perhaps the single most impressive performance by an American racehorse in history. Secretariat's winning time for the Belmont (2:24) remains a North American record on dirt. Although the champion was euthanized in 1989, several books and a movie, *Secretariat* (2010), have kept his memory alive.

Secretariat, a strapping chestnut colt with a blaze and three white stockings, was foaled on March 29, 1970, at Christopher T. Chenery's Meadow Stud in Doswell, Virginia. Secretariat's sire, Bold Ruler, won the 1957 Preakness Stakes and was named Horse of the Year for that year. Bold Ruler had led the sire list in progeny earnings seven years in a row, but his offspring seemed to lack the necessary stamina for the longer classic races of the Triple Crown. Somethingroyal, Secretariat's dam, was a daughter of Princequillo, who excelled at longer distances. Somethingroyal had already produced two very good racehorses in Sir Gaylord and Syrian Sea. Christopher Chenery's daughter, Helen "Penny" Chenery Tweedy, decided to name the chestnut colt Secretariat in honor of Meadow Stud's secretary, Elizabeth Ham.

Secretariat received his early breaking and training as a yearling at Meadow Stud. Sent to Florida in January 1972 for training, Secretariat was placed in the hands of veteran French-Canadian trainer Lucien Laurin, who also trained the Chenerys' Triple Crown

contender, Riva Ridge. Riva Ridge would proceed later that spring to win the 1972 Kentucky Derby and Belmont Stakes. Ron Turcotte, who was to ride Secretariat in 18 of his 21 races, rode the chestnut colt during some of his early workouts. Initially, Secretariat showed few signs of his blistering speed but improved as the year progressed and made his initial start at Belmont Park in Elmont, New York, on July 4, 1972, in a 5½-furlong maiden race ("maiden" indicates the horses have never won a race). Ridden by Paul Feliciano, Secretariat was jostled and blocked throughout the race and finished fourth after making a late charge at the end. He made his next start in a six-furlong contest at Aqueduct Racetrack and this time galloped to a six-length victory.

Secretariat remained unbeaten for the remaining seven races of his two-year-old season. He captured the Sanford and Hopeful Stakes at Saratoga Race Course in Saratoga Springs, New York, in August 1972. Moving on to Belmont Park in Elmont, New York, on Long Island, Secretariat defeated Stop the Music in the 6½-furlong Futurity Stakes and then again in the one-mile Champagne Stakes, but was disqualified to second place after bumping the bay colt in the stretch. Both moved on to Laurel Park in Maryland for the 1¹/₁₆-mile Laurel Futurity, in which Secretariat defeated Stop the Music by eight lengths. His winning time of 1:42⁴/₅ was a stakes record and just ¹/₅ second shy of the track record. In his final start of 1972, Secretariat won the Garden State Stakes at Garden State Park in New Jersey, triumphing over Angle Light by 3½ lengths in the 1¹/₁₆-mile race. In addition to receiving the award as Champion Two-Year-Old colt, Secretariat became the first two-year-old to win the Horse of the Year title since the National Turf Writers Association, the Thoroughbred Racing Association, and the Daily Racing Form combined their polls beginning in 1972.

On January 3, 1973, Christopher Chenery, owner of Meadow Stud, passed away at age 87 following a chronic debilitating illness. Penny Tweedy and her siblings recognized that they would need to raise a considerable amount of money to pay the death taxes on their father's estate or risk losing Meadow Farm. Since Secretariat was the estate's most valuable asset, Tweedy engaged Seth Hancock of Claiborne Farm to syndicate the horse for future breeding purposes.

Thirty-two breeders purchased shares in the horse at $190,000 a share for a total record value of $6.08 million. The contract stipulated that Secretariat would continue to race in the Meadow Stable colors through November 15, 1973, at which time he would be retired to stud at Claiborne Farm in Kentucky.

Lucien Laurin chose the seven-furlong Bay Shore Stakes at Aqueduct on March 17 for Secretariat's first start as a three-year-old. The big chestnut colt triumphed by four-and-a-half lengths over a sloppy track. The Gotham Mile, also at Aqueduct, on April 7 came next, and Secretariat did not disappoint, winning by three lengths over Champagne Charlie and equaling the track record in 1:33²/₅.

Laurin pointed Secretariat toward the 1¹/₈-mile Wood Memorial at Aqueduct on April 27 as the final prep race for the Kentucky Derby. The morning of the Wood, veterinarian Dr. Manuel Gilman noticed a small abscess on the horse's upper lip, but Laurin decided to start him anyway. Secretariat's groom, Edward "Eddie" Sweat, noticed while saddling the colt that he showed an uncharacteristic reluctance to accept the bit in his mouth. The colt performed dully in the Wood, finishing third to Angle Light and Sham in front of a stunned crowd. Although many attributed Secretariat's loss to the lip abscess, others speculated that he was lame or, like his sire, Bold Ruler, lacked the stamina for the 1¼-mile Derby.

A then-record crowd of 137,476 fans flocked to Churchill Downs in Louisville, Kentucky, on May 5, 1973, to witness the 99th edition of the "Run for the Roses." Secretariat surged past Sham and Our Native in the final furlong of the Derby, winning by 2½ lengths in 1:59²/₅, the fastest Derby ever, eclipsing Northern Dancer's record of 2:00 flat. Secretariat's opponents may have looked slow in comparison, but were great athletes in their own right. Runner-up Sham also finished the race in less than two minutes. The bay gelding Forego finished fourth and, as an older horse, won Horse of the Year titles for three consecutive years from 1974 to 1976. No victor in the Kentucky Derby has ever surpassed Secretariat's winning time, although Monarchos came the closest, winning the 2001 running in 1:59.97.

Two weeks later, Secretariat started in the 1³/₁₆-mile Preakness Stakes, the second leg of the Triple

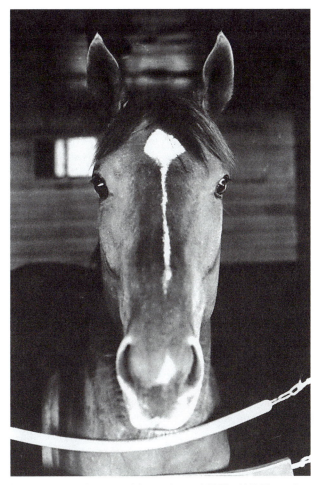

Secretariat is shown in November of 1973. (AP Photo.)

Crown, at Pimlico Race Course in Baltimore, Maryland. Secretariat easily triumphed by 2½ lengths over Sham and Our Native. Pimlico's electronic timer stopped the clock at 1:55, but others recorded a stakes-record 1:53²/₅. Track stewards later revised the official time to 1:54²/₅. In 2012, the record was officially lowered to 1:53 after a film review.

Anticipation built during the three weeks leading to the June 9 Belmont Stakes and Secretariat's photo graced the covers of *Time*, *Newsweek*, and *Sports Illustrated* during the same week, but some naysayers doubted the colt had the stamina to endure the 1½-mile Belmont. During the first five furlongs of the Belmont, Secretariat and Sham battled for the lead at a torrid pace, but then the chestnut powerhouse began pulling away from Sham. Around the final turn of Belmont Park's gigantic 1½-mile track, Secretariat pulled far ahead of his struggling rivals and finished 31 lengths in front in a then–world record time of 2:24. He had run each

Secretariat's Record as a Sire

When Secretariat began his first year at stud in 1974, breeders hoped that he would prove as great a sire as he was a racehorse. Although Secretariat never met these inflated expectations, most breeding experts agree that he had a good record as a stallion, if not spectacular. His first major stakes winner, General Assembly, won the 1979 Travers Stakes at Saratoga. His greatest runner was the gray filly Lady's Secret, who earned Horse of the Year honors in 1986. She earned over $3 million in purse money, beat males in the 1986 Whitney Handicap at Saratoga, and triumphed in the 1986 Breeder's Cup Distaff for fillies and mares. Secretariat's best colt was Risen Star, who won the latter two-thirds of the Triple Crown in 1988. Other distinguished offspring of Secretariat include Pancho Villa, Tinners Way, Terlingua, and Kingston Rule.

Secretariat's greatest legacy as a stallion is as a sire of broodmares. Stallions that are sons of distinguished broodmares (Somethingroyal produced multiple talented racehorses) often excel at siring exceptional fillies and mares. Not only were Secretariat's fillies generally superior to his colts, but they also produced important racehorses and sires. Secretariat still exerts great influence over the Thoroughbred breed through three of his daughters, who produced leading sires. Terlingua foaled Storm Cat (by Storm Bird) in 1983; Weekend Surprise produced Horse of the Year and 1992 Belmont Stakes winner A.P. Indy (by Seattle Slew) in 1989 and 1990 Preakness winner Summer Squall (by Storm Bird) in 1987; and Secrettame foaled leading sire Gone West in 1984 (by Mr. Prospector). These three stallions were all top sires and their descendants include top racehorses Giant's Causeway, Smarty Jones, Mineshaft, Bernardini, and Charismatic.

successive quarter mile faster than the previous one, an unbelievable accomplishment in a 1½-mile race.

Secretariat raced six more times in 1973. On June 30, he captured the 1⅛-mile Arlington Invitational at Arlington Park in Chicago. He suffered two losses during the remainder of 1973, finishing second to Onion in the Whitney Handicap at Saratoga and second to Prove Out in the Woodward Stakes at Belmont. The big chestnut colt redeemed himself by crushing a field of top older horses in the 1⅛-mile Marlboro Cup at Belmont on September 15, 1973, defeating his stablemate Riva Ridge, as well as Onion and Key to the Mint. On October 8, Secretariat tried running on a turf (grass) track surface for the first time, easily winning the 1½-mile Man O' War Stakes at Belmont in the course-winning time of 2:24⁴/₅. Secretariat headed to Ontario, Canada, for the final start of his career at Woodbine Park on October 28 in the 1⅝-mile Canadian International Championship. Piloted in his final race by jockey Eddie Maple, Secretariat galloped to a 6½-length victory. Secretariat retired to Claiborne Farm after his final victory with 16 wins, 3 seconds, and one third-place finish in 21starts and earnings of $1,316,808. He received a second consecutive Horse of the Year title, as well as awards as Champion Three-Year-Old Colt and Champion Grass Horse. Turf journalist Charles Hatton, who had witnessed the career of the great Man O' War in 1919–1920, proclaimed Secretariat the Horse of the Century.

Secretariat sired 56 stakes winners during his stud career and attracted thousands of visitors to Claiborne Farm during his retirement years. Sadly, he developed laminitis in September 1989, an incurable and very painful disease of the equine foot. On October 4, 1989, Secretariat was euthanized at age 19 and buried in the Claiborne Farm stallion cemetery.

Elizabeth M. Tobey

See also Citation; Kentucky Derby; Man O' War; *Sports Illustrated*; Triple Crown

Suggested Resources

Capps, Timothy T. *Secretariat.* Thoroughbred Legends 19. Lexington, KY: Blood-Horse, 2003.

Drager, Marvin. *The Most Glorious Crown: The Story of America's Triple Crown Thoroughbreds from Sir Barton to Secretariat.* New York: Winchester Press, 1975.

Nack, William. *Secretariat: The Making of a Champion.* New York: Da Capo Press, 1975.

Secretariat. IMDb. http://www.imdb.com/title/tt1028576/. Accessed January 30, 2012.

Secretariat Website. http://www.secretariat.com/. Accessed January 30, 2012.

Selig, Bud (1934–)

Bud Selig is the commissioner of Major League Baseball (MLB)—the ninth person in baseball history to hold that title—and the former owner of the Milwaukee Brewers. As commissioner, Selig guided MLB through numerous changes, including a players' strike, two rounds of team expansions, the implementation of interleague regular-season play, the founding of the World Baseball Classic, and the reformatting of the MLB playoffs and the All-Star Game. Although Selig has provided a calm, steady presence and increased MLB's revenue, his tenure has been decried by fan and media critics for pro-ownership decisions that weren't necessarily in the best interests of baseball and its fans. He has also been criticized frequently for his alleged tendency to avoid making tough decisions and for his handling of MLB's steroids scandal during the 2000s. Selig has the unqualified support of MLB's owners, however, as many of his decisions as commissioner have directly benefited the finances of MLB teams. Selig is one of the richest executives in professional sports, earning a yearly salary of over $14 million.

Allan Huber "Bud" Selig was born on July 30, 1934, in Milwaukee, Wisconsin, to parents from European Jewish immigrant families. After graduating from the University of Wisconsin–Milwaukee and serving a stint in the U.S. Army, he went to work for his father, Ben, who owned a car-leasing business. As the business flourished, Selig bought a considerable amount of public stock in the Milwaukee Braves.

After the Braves moved to Atlanta in 1965, Selig founded a local group in Milwaukee that worked toward bringing MLB back to the city. He persuaded the Chicago White Sox to play some of their home games in Milwaukee County Stadium, and the high attendance at these games marked Milwaukee as a promising site for a future MLB club.

After a failed attempt to buy the White Sox, Selig bought the bankrupt Seattle Pilots in 1970 and moved the franchise to Milwaukee. He renamed the team the Brewers after the minor league team he had watched as a kid. Though the Brewers initially struggled to compete in the American League, they made the World Series in 1982, led by stars such as Paul Molitor, Cecil Cooper, and Robin Yount.

Under Selig, the Brewers were generally recognized as a successful organization, despite their lack of on-field success. By the 1980s, Selig had emerged as a leader among MLB owners. This was not always

seen as a positive, however, and he was implicated in collusion (whereby MLB owners agreed to artificially hold down MLB players' salaries) during the middle of the decade.

After owner disaffection, led by Selig, forced MLB commissioner Fay Vincent to leave his post in 1992, Selig took over as interim commissioner. Although he quickly transferred ownership of the Brewers to his daughter, Wendy Selig-Prieb, to maintain a semblance of neutrality, it was widely speculated that he continued to run the franchise behind the scenes, and the MLB Players' Association (MLBPA), among others, charged him with bias in favor of MLB owners. Selig was the first MLB owner to take over the position of commissioner, which had previously been bestowed upon executives from outside the game.

Upon assuming his duties as commissioner, Selig immediately moved to boost the prosperity of MLB ownership by expanding the National and American League playoffs to two rounds and adding a wild card playoff team. Moving the total number of playoff teams from four to eight added another week of postseason media coverage and increased ticket proceeds, much to the delight of the owners. The postseason was expanded even further in 2012, despite objections from some baseball insiders, who protested the extension of the season into November.

At the same time, MLB's labor situation was growing contentious. The owners' collective bargaining agreement with the MLBPA expired after the 1993 season, and negotiations on a new contract bogged down over attempts by the owners to impose a salary cap and gain greater control over players' futures with their teams. When the two sides couldn't reach an agreement, the players went on strike, canceling the 1994 postseason. The strike, which was finally resolved the following spring, is widely considered the most disastrous work stoppage in professional sports history.

Despite his initial inability to calm the waters of baseball's labor situation, the owners voted in Selig as permanent commissioner in 1998, and many of his early accomplishments rewarded the owners' faith. He did a masterful job of bringing disaffected fans back to games after the 1994–1995 strike, instituting interleague play (which was immediately popular) in 1997 and tirelessly working with the mass media to promote the sport. After the 1998 season, which witnessed the exciting race by sluggers Mark McGwire and Sammy Sosa to break Roger Maris's single-season home run record, baseball (and Selig) was at a high in popularity.

In 2000, Selig eliminated the posts of American and National League presidents by merging the administrative functions of both leagues into the commissioner's office, which increased the efficiency of baseball operations. Two years later, Selig prevented another players' strike by hammering out a collective bargaining agreement that benefited both the MLBPA and the MLB owners. He also presided over two rounds of MLB expansion—in 1993 (the Florida Marlins and Colorado Rockies) and 1998 (the Arizona Diamondbacks and Tampa Bay Devil Rays). All four franchises have enjoyed success, each having reached the World Series at least once since its founding.

Though Selig was popular with the owners and did much to ensure the smooth running of MLB operations, he came increasingly under fire from the media during the 2000s, and many of his public actions and statements have been controversial. In late 2001, Selig and Montreal Expos owner Jeffrey Loria were forced into an expensive out-of-court settlement; the two men were sued for racketeering by the Expos' minority shareholders after they allegedly worked in secret to try to merge the Expos with the Minnesota Twins.

At the 2002 All-Star Game, baseball reporters and fans reacted angrily when Selig declared the contest a 7–7 tie, purportedly because his supporters among the owners didn't want to risk their pitchers in extra innings. Selig's apologetic response to the outcry did little to soothe public criticism, and his attempt, soon after, to make All-Star Games more important (by declaring that the winner of future games would decide home-field advantage during each season's World Series) was derided as arbitrary and self-serving.

In 2005, Selig faced a crisis that was, perhaps, bigger than the 1994–1995 players' strike. Revelations of MLB players' widespread use of steroids and other performance-enhancing drugs (PEDs) during the 1990s and 2000s were made public, and the commissioner was called to testify on the issue before Congress. Selig denied knowledge of PED use among players, which, in the eyes of media and fans, made him appear to be either a liar or clueless. When the full extent of PED use became clear, he drew even more criticism by refusing to level any blame on either the owners or the commissioner's office, despite substantial evidence indicating that many owners were happy to turn a blind eye to PED use when it was clear that home runs would bring fans back after the 1994–1995 strike.

The following year, Selig commissioned an independent panel, led by former Maine senator George Mitchell, to look into PED allegations. The resulting Mitchell Report (released in 2007) named 89 players as PED users. However, Mitchell's status as a Boston Red Sox executive cast the neutrality of the report in doubt, and no prominent current Red Sox or Brewers players were listed; the latter was claimed to be proof that Selig hired Mitchell knowing that he would temper the report's results. The Mitchell Report did recommend a program of drug testing (and affiliated punishments for transgressors), and Selig reached an agreement with the MLBPA soon after to begin limited testing. Though Selig garnered some praise for finally implementing a comprehensive drug-testing policy, his critics claimed that he only did so after most of the damage to baseball's reputation had been done.

Although Selig continues to create controversy (for example, over his recent handling of organization problems with the New York Mets and Los Angeles Dodgers and his introduction of instant replay into baseball), his status as commissioner remains safe. In early 2012, MLB ownership granted him an extension as commissioner through 2014, despite promises that he would retire after 2012.

Matt DeFraga

See also Landis, Kenesaw Mountain; McGwire, Mark and Sosa, Sammy; Sports and Drugs/Doping; Strikes and Lockouts; World Series

Suggested Resources

Bud Selig Website. www.budselig.com. Accessed February 12, 2012.

Costas, Bob. *Fair Ball: A Fan's Case for Baseball.* New York: Broadway, 2001.

Gould, William B. *Bargaining with Baseball: Labor Relations in an Age of Prosperous Turmoil.* Jefferson, NC: McFarland, 2011.

Major League Baseball Website. www.mlb.com. Accessed February 12, 2012.

Moffi, Larry. *The Conscience of the Game: Baseball's Commissioners from Landis to Selig.* Lincoln, NE: Bison Books, 2006.

Okrent, Daniel. *Nine Innings.* New York: Mariner Books, 2000.

Zimbalist, Andrew. *In the Best Interests of Baseball?: The Revolutionary Reign of Bud Selig.* Hoboken, NJ: Wiley, 2007.

Shelton, Ron (1945–)

Ron Shelton, a former minor league baseball player, is an acclaimed filmmaker best known for his films dealing with American sport, especially baseball. *Bull Durham* (1988), which incorporates elements of realism and comedy in its depiction of minor league baseball, was selected by *Sports Illustrated* as the Greatest Sports Movie of All Time.

Shelton was born September 15, 1945, in Whittier, California, after his father relocated from Texas to seek work in the California oil fields. The oldest of four brothers, Shelton was drawn to sports, playing baseball for Santa Barbara High School and Westmont College, where he gained a degree in English literature. From 1967 to 1971, Shelton pursued a career in professional baseball. As a second baseman in the Baltimore Orioles' minor league system, Shelton reached the Triple A level with the Rochester Red Wings. Frustration regarding the baseball labor stoppage of 1972 and the difficulty of advancing in the talent-laden Orioles system convinced Shelton to leave the game. Shelton studied sculpture at the University of Arizona where he earned an MFA degree. Following his graduation, he returned to his native California and worked at various blue-collar jobs in addition to trying his hand at writing.

After publishing several short stories, Shelton's first produced screenplay was the war correspondent drama *Under Fire* (1983), starring Nick Nolte and focusing on the contemporary civil conflicts in Central America. Continuing to work with director Roger Spottiswoode, Shelton in 1986 wrote his first screenplay dealing with sports, *The Best of Times*. Featuring Robin Williams and Kurt Russell, *The Best of Times* tells the story of two former high school football players who attempt to stage a replay of the big game they lost 15 years earlier.

> ### Blue Chips
>
> In 1994, Shelton explored the sport of basketball with his screenplay for *Blue Chips*, directed by William Friedkin, starring Nick Nolte, and featuring appearances by well-known basketball coaches and players. Nolte plays Pete Bell, a coach for the Western University Dolphins, whose basketball program is in decline. To attract top "blue chip" recruits, Bell works with booster Happy (J. T. Walsh) who is able to attract star players such as Neon Boudeaux (Shaquille O'Neal) and Butch McRae (Penny Hardaway) by engaging in illegal payments to the athletes.
>
> His estranged wife, Jenny (Mary McDonnell), and a local reporter (Ed O'Neill) attempt to resurrect Bell's conscience, to no avail. However, after he learns that one of his former players was engaged in point shaving, Bell has had enough. When his team defeats the number one–ranked University of Indiana, Bell exposes the corruption of his team during a press conference. The team faces a suspension from the NCAA, and Bell is out of college coaching before he finds a job in the high school ranks. The film included cameo appearances by college basketball coaches Bob Knight, Jim Boeheim, Nolan Richardson, and Rick Pitino; and the picture was filmed in French Lick, Indiana, the home of basketball legend Larry Bird. Despite these appeals to basketball fans, this sport morality tale failed to find an audience and was generally panned by critics.

Following this experience, Shelton was ready to write and direct his own film. Drawing on his own baseball background, Shelton's *Bull Durham* depicts a legendary minor league catcher, Crash Davis (Kevin Costner), who never makes it to the big leagues but wins the heart of Annie Savoy (Susan Sarandon) while establishing a minor league home run mark. Audiences loved the film, and Shelton received an Academy Award nomination for his screenplay.

Seeking to avoid being typecast as a sports film director, Shelton followed *Bull Durham* with the less successful political film *Blaze* starring Paul Newman and Lolita Davidovich, whom Shelton wed after the collapse of his first marriage. Shelton found greater commercial viability when he returned to sport subjects for his filmmaking. In *White Men Can't Jump* (1992), Woody Harrelson and Wesley Snipes explore issues of racial stereotyping as basketball hustlers. A more serious effort was Shelton's 1994 biographical picture, *Cobb*. Basing his screenplay on the Ty Cobb biography by sportswriter Al Stump (Robert Wuhl), Shelton depicts an aging and angry Cobb portrayed by Tommy Lee Jones. Despite the strong performances, viewers found the film overly pessimistic and dark, while many baseball fans were disappointed by the lack of playing field action in the picture. A more pleasing film for audiences was the athletic and handsome Kevin Costner as golfer Ron McAvoy in *Tin Cup* (1996) attempting to qualify for the U.S. Open and gain the affections of Rene Russo. The Costner and Shelton pairing again produced box office dividends.

However, Shelton's films following *Tin Cup* have failed to find an audience. *Play It to the Bone* (1999), *Dark Blue* (2002), *Hollywood Homicide* (2003), and *Bad Boys II* (2003) were commercial and critical failures. Striving to regain some of that magic he displayed with *Bull Durham*, Shelton returned in 2011 to the topics of baseball and the minor leagues. For the acclaimed ESPN documentary series *30 for 30*, Shelton produced *Jordan Rides the Bus*, focusing on Michael Jordan's 1994 season with the Double A Birmingham Barons as the athlete pursued a career in baseball after winning three basketball championships with the Chicago Bulls. In addition, Shelton wrote and produced a comedy series, *Hound Dogs*, for television (TBS), chronicling the travails of a minor league team. Shelton is also at work on a screenplay dealing with American baseball players in the Mexican League. With these new projects, Shelton is reconnecting with the sport and the baseball arenas where he enjoyed his early popular success as a screenwriter and director.

Ron Briley

See also *Bull Durham*; Chicago Bulls; *Cobb*; ESPN Channels; Jordan, Michael; *Sports Illustrated*; *White Men Can't Jump*

Suggested Resources

Erickson, Hal. *The Baseball Filmography, 1915 through 2001*. Jefferson, NC: McFarland, 2002.

"Ron Shelton." IMDb. http://www.imbd.com/name/nn005421/. Accessed June 6, 2011.

"Ron Shelton." http://thehollywoodinterview.blogspot.com/2009/06/ron-shelton-hollywood-interview.html. Accessed June 14, 2011.

Wood, Stephen C., and J. David Pincus, eds. *Reel Baseball: Essays and Interviews on the National Pastime, Hollywood and American Culture*. Jefferson, NC: McFarland, 2002.

Shot Heard 'Round the World

The shot heard 'round the world refers to the pennant-winning home run of Bobby Thomson to win the 1951 National League pennant for the New York Giants against their rivals, the Brooklyn Dodgers. The name borrows from Ralph Waldo Emerson's 1837 poem and referred to the shot fired at Lexington Green on April 19, 1775, that initiated the American Revolutionary War.

In 1951, the Brooklyn Dodgers were the favorites to win the National League pennant. They had also been favored in 1950, when the Philadelphia Phillies defeated the Dodgers in a playoff to capture the pennant and stop the Dodgers from winning their third pennant in four years. The postwar Dodgers were the first team in baseball to integrate, beginning with Jackie Robinson in 1947, then adding Roy Campanella and Don Newcombe in 1948 and 1949. They joined a powerful squad headed by Duke Snider, Pee Wee Reese, Gil Hodges, Carl Furillo, Ralph Branca, Preacher Roe, and Carl Erskine.

The Giants, on the other hand, had fallen on hard times since their last pennant in 1937. Once the best teams in the league from the early 1900s until the late 1930s, the Giants struggled to reach the first division in the 1940s. Both the Giants and the Dodgers were charter members of the National League and their rivalry was seen as the most heated in baseball, if not all of sport.

The 1951 Giants were managed by Leo Durocher, former manager of the Dodgers (1938–1948), who loved beating the Giants when he managed the Dodgers, but now lived, it seemed, to defeat the Dodgers as manager of the Giants. The Giants had finished third in 1950, their highest finish since 1942. Their roster was composed of veteran starting pitchers (Sal Maglie, Larry Jansen, Jim Hearn) and younger hitters. Except for Monte Irvin, one of the first African Americans in the league, who was 32, most of the

New York Giants Bobby Thomson hits his famous home run off Ralph Branca of the Brooklyn Dodgers at the Polo Grounds in New York, October 3, 1951. (AP Photo.)

everyday players were in their 20s. These included Wes Westrum, Whitey Lockman, Alvin Dark, Don Mueller, Bobby Thomson, and the new superstar, Willie Mays, who was just 20.

The Giants had high hopes for the season, but the Dodgers broke out fast in the spring and kept winning, even when the Giants were playing better and better. By August, the Dodgers had a 13½ game lead and the pennant was all but conceded to the Brooklyn squad. But then the Giants caught fire, winning 50 of their last 62 games to catch the Dodgers on the last day of the season and force a three-game playoff for the pennant and a trip to the World Series to meet the New York Yankees, the American League champion.

In the history of the National League there had been just one other playoff, in 1946, when the Dodgers and the St. Louis Cardinals had tied for the pennant and the Cards triumphed in two straight games to advance to the World Series. Now, just five years later, the Dodgers were involved in a playoff once again.

Game one, played October 1, 1951, had both the Giants and the Dodgers sending their number three starters out to the mound. Both teams had had to use their top pitchers to get into the playoff, so it was anticipated that the game might be a slugfest, especially in the Dodgers' Ebbets Field, a small park tucked into the Flatbush section of Brooklyn on Sullivan Place. Instead it was a pitcher's duel with Jim Hearn throwing a five-hitter, stifling the Dodgers' bats, and winning 3–1 behind home runs by Monte Irvin and Bobby Thomson. Ralph Branca took the loss, pitching eight innings.

For games two and three, the teams moved to the Giants' home field, the Polo Grounds, located at 155th Street and Eighth Avenue in Harlem, just across the river from Yankee Stadium in the Bronx. The Polo Grounds were unusually shaped with short right and left field lines and an impossibly deep center field of 483 feet. The game two starters were Sheldon Jones, a journeyman who had won just six games that year, and Clem Labine, a promising rookie who had pitched in just 13 games, five as a starter. He was 4–1 with an earned run average of 2.20.

Labine pitched magnificently, allowing just six hits and no runs in a complete game victory. Jones gave up two runs and was pulled in the third inning in favor of George Spencer, who was followed by Al Corwin. The Dodgers pounded the relievers in the 10–0 victory, getting home runs from Jackie Robinson, Gil Hodges, Andy Pafko, and Rube Walker. The series was now tied at one game each.

The next day, October 3, both teams sent their aces to the mound. Sal Maglie, nicknamed "the Barber" because of his willingness to pitch inside, very close to batters, had gone 23–6 for the Giants with four saves. Maglie was 34 and had returned to the Giants in 1950 after jumping to the Mexican League in 1946, then had been banned from the major leagues until 1949. The Dodgers gave the ball to Don Newcombe, a big 25-year-old right-hander who had won 20 games for the Dodgers with 18 complete games. He was also one of the best-hitting pitchers in baseball.

In the top of the first Robinson singled in a run and that was the scoring until the seventh inning. In the bottom of the inning, Irvin doubled, advanced on a sacrifice, and scored on a sacrifice fly to tie the score. In the top of the eighth, the Dodgers came back to score three runs on four singles and a wild pitch, to lead 4–1. The Giants failed to score in the bottom of the inning and the Dodgers also went down scoreless in the ninth against reliever Larry Jansen.

The Giants rallied in the bottom of the ninth. Alvin Dark led off with a single and Don Mueller also singled. Irvin popped out, but Whitey Lockman doubled, scoring Dark and sending Mueller to third. Muller had done a half-slide at third and torn tendons in his ankle. He was carted off the field on a stretcher and a pinch runner, Clint Hartung, entered.

Newcombe was exhausted after going 8⅓ innings and Manager Charlie Dressen, after consulting with his pitching coach, called for Ralph Branca from the bullpen. Branca had pitched eight innings two days before, but there was no tomorrow. He said that he was ready. He would face Bobby Thomson, who had homered off him in game one and had hit two other homers off Branca that year.

The Friendship of Branca and Thomson

Ralph Branca won 68 games between 1947 and 1951, but after the 1951 season, he won only 12 more games and retired in 1954 at the age of 28 (he did appear in one game in 1956). The 1951 playoffs seemed to have sapped his vitality. Thomson played 10 more years and ended his career at 36 with over 1,700 hits and almost 250 home runs. Their careers seemed to have taken opposite directions, but in the 1990s the two began to appear at sports memorabilia shows together and became good friends. They continued this "partnership" until about 2008. Thomson died in 2010. Regarding the revelation of the "spy in the clubhouse," Branca showed no resentment, saying, "Bobby still had to hit the ball."

What none of the Dodgers knew, as Thomson stepped into the box, was that the Giants had a spy deep in center field in the Giants' clubhouse, who was picking up the catcher's signals using a telescope and then relaying what the pitch was via a buzzer system that had been installed in the dugout. So Thomson was able to know what pitch was coming and could adjust for that.

Branca threw a fastball for a strike, then another. On the second, Thomson swung and hit a low line shot to left field that cleared the left field wall and dropped into the second row of seats to give the Giants a 5–4 victory and the National League pennant. At this point, announcer Russ Hodges began what has become a staple of archival baseball footage, screaming, "The Giants win the pennant! The Giants win the pennant! The Giants win the pennant! The Giants win the pennant! The Giants win the pennant!" Hodges was broadcasting on radio, although the game was telecast on WPIX and nationally shown on NBC with Ernie Harwell doing the play-by-play. The number of televisions in American homes at that time was extremely small.

Video footage shows Thomson taking about five strides, then running, then leaping into the air and sailing around the bases, where he again leaps onto the plate and is met by his entire team. The field was then swamped by Giants' fans.

The Giants went on to lose the World Series to the Yankees in six games, but the glow of the impossible victory remained for years afterward. The Giants abandoned the Polo Grounds and New York after the 1957 season and moved to San Francisco, but the glow of the 1951 playoffs continues each time it is broadcast on television during a baseball season.

ESPN ranked this game number 2 of the 10 greatest games of the 20th century. References to the game abound in fiction and film, including *The Godfather*, the television series *M*A*S*H*, and an episode of *The Wonder Years*. The novel *The Underworld* by Don DeLillo opens as a young man sneaks into this game. There is probably no baseball event more well known or replayed than the Thomson homer to end this contest; the game seems to transcend time.

Murry R. Nelson

Suggested Resources

"Dodgers-Giants Box Score." Baseball-Reference.com. http://www.baseball-reference.com/boxes/NY1/NY1195110030.shtml. Accessed February 23, 2011.

Prager, Joshua. *The Echoing Green: The Untold Story of Bobby Thomson, Ralph Branca and the Shot Heard 'Round the World*. New York: Pantheon Books, 2006.

Robinson, Ray. *The Home Run Heard 'Round the World*. New York. HarperCollins, 1991.

"The Shot Heard 'Round the World." YouTube.com. http://www.youtube.com/watch?v=lrI7dVj90zs&feature=related. Accessed February 23, 2011.

Simpson, O. J. (1947–)

The story of football great Orenthal James "O. J." Simpson is an American tragedy of almost epic proportions. Simpson came from humble beginnings and a somewhat troubled youth but went on to achieve a level of athletic greatness and pan-cultural popularity enjoyed by only a select few, which led to immense commercial success. Through the decades of the 1970s, 1980s, and into the 1990s Simpson was one of the most well-liked and wildly popular sports celebrities in the United States. But all of that changed in June 1994 when Simpson was arrested and charged with the murder of his ex-wife, Nicole Brown-Simpson, and her friend Ronald Goldman. The ensuing O. J. Simpson murder trial was televised live. Dubbed "The Trial of the Century," it played out as a spectacular

media event that both featured and created any number of popular culture "celebrities." The trial concluded on October 3, 1995, with a verdict of not guilty, but Simpson was found liable in a 1997 wrongful death civil trial and ordered to pay some $33 million in damages, almost none of which has been collected. In the fall of 2007 Simpson was arrested in Las Vegas, Nevada, for a number of felonies, including robbery and kidnapping. In October 2008, Simpson was found guilty of all charges and sentenced in December 2008 to 33 years in prison. Simpson is eligible for parole in 2017, when he will be 70 years of age. Simpson's life and times mirror several themes in American popular culture, especially the rags-to-riches myth often associated with athletic excellence, the almost universal admiration and consequent celebrity bestowed upon great athletes, and, during the Simpson murder trial, racial prejudice by the Los Angeles Police Department that can be traced from the Watts riots of 1965 through the South Central (Rodney King) riots of 1992.

Simpson was born in San Francisco, California. His mother, Eunice Durden, was a hospital administrator and his father, James "Jimmie" Lee Simpson, was a cook and bank custodian. Simpson's parents divorced in 1952, and he and his three siblings (brother Melvin and sisters Shirley and Carmelita) were raised by Eunice in the Potrero Hill section of San Francisco. Simpson, to treat a case of rickets, wore braces on his legs until he was five years old. As a result, Simpson is slightly bow-legged, a characteristic many believe contributed to his relatively injury-free football career. While growing up in Potrero Hill, Simpson was a member of a gang called the Persian Kings (aka the Persian Warriors) and following an altercation in 1962 was sent for a short time to the local juvenile detention center. Simpson attended Galileo High School where he was a star football player. From Galileo he went on to play football in 1965 and 1966 for City College of San Francisco, where he was named to the Junior College All-American Team as a running back. So impressive was Simpson as a running back that he earned a scholarship to the University of Southern California (USC), and it is at USC that Simpson would burst onto the national scene as one of the best collegiate running backs of all time and begin to emerge as a popular culture icon.

O. J. Simpson (32), running back of the Buffalo Bills, strides over some teammates as he latches on to Joe DeLamielleurs (68) at Rich Stadium, Buffalo, New York, September 3, 1977. (AP Photo.)

Simpson's football career at USC was remarkable. Simpson possessed the combination of size, 6'2" and 210 pounds, and world-class speed (Simpson ran the third leg of USC's world record–setting 440-yard sprint relay team in the 1967 NCAA track championships) that made him virtually unstoppable as the USC tailback during the 1967 and 1968 NCAA football seasons. Simpson led the nation in rushing in each of those seasons, tallying 1,451 yards as a junior and 1,709 yards as a senior. On November 18, 1967, Simpson led his number four ranked Trojans into Los Angeles Memorial Coliseum to meet the undefeated archrival and number one ranked UCLA Bruins with a trip to the Rose Bowl and possible national championship on the line. With USC trailing 20–14 in the fourth quarter, Simpson exploded for a 64-yard touchdown run that, with the PAT, ultimately secured the 21–20 victory, a berth in the Rose Bowl versus Indiana, which USC won 14–7, and the 1967 AP national championship. During the 1968 season Simpson was

equally spectacular. He ended the season in a losing effort by rushing for 171 yards in the Rose Bowl versus Ohio State, the 1968 AP national champions. Simpson concluded his USC football career as a two-time consensus All-American, the 1968 Heisman Trophy winner, the 1968 Maxwell Award winner, and a two-time winner of the Walter Camp Award. Simpson was selected on January 28, 1969, as the number one overall pick in the NFL draft by the Buffalo Bills.

Simpson's career in the National Football League with the Bills was every bit as spectacular as his college career at USC, despite the slow start. During Simpson's first three seasons in Buffalo he rushed for 697, 488, and 742 yards for the lowly Bills. Then Buffalo brought back as head coach Lou Saban, who had coached them to consecutive AFL Championships in 1964 and 1965. Saban pledged to rely heavily on Simpson and the potential rushing attack he represented. In 1972, Saban's first year as Simpson's coach, O. J. ran for 1,251 yards on 21 attempts per game. The following season, 1973, was magical for Simpson and his Bills teammates. In the first game of that season, at New England versus the Patriots, Simpson rushed for a NFL single-game record 250 yards. As Simpson, nicknamed "The Juice," continued to pile up the yardage, he and his offensive line, nicknamed "the Electric Company," anchored by All-Pro pulling guards Reggie McKenzie and Joe DeLamielleure, became the top story of the NFL. Simpson and the Electric Company were regularly featured on the Howard Cosell narrated "Halftime Highlights" segment of *Monday Night Football*. The entire sporting nation was mesmerized by the possibility of a running back breaking the great Jim Brown's 1963 single-season rushing record of 1,863 yards and of breaking the once thought unbreakable 2,000-yard barrier. Simpson entered the 14th and final game of the season on a cold and snowy day at Shea Stadium versus the New York Jets with 1,803 yards, needing only 61 to break Brown's record. Simpson responded with 200 yards on 34 carriers, breaking both Brown's record and becoming the first and only player to rush for over 2,000 yards in 14 games. In all, Simpson played 11 NFL seasons—the first nine with Buffalo and the final two with the San Francisco 49ers in the city of his birth. Simpson rushed for a total of 11,236 yards on 2,404 carries, was the 1973 NFL Player of the Year, played in the Pro Bowl on six occasions, was First-Team All-Pro five times, rushed for over 200 yards in a game on six different occasions—a record that stands to this day—and in 1985 was a first-ballot inductee into the Pro Football Hall of Fame.

Simpson played prominently in American pop culture off the field even more than he did on the gridiron. Simpson had a warm and likable public persona, complete with a charming smile and childlike innocence that allowed him to relate equally well to black and white, male and female, young and old. The *Los Angeles Times* credited Simpson in 1994 with pioneering endorsement deals with team sport stars before anyone had even coined the term "sports marketing." Simpson's most popular endorsement deal was with Hertz Rental Car, and in these television ads he could be seen running (and even flying) through airports, while an elderly white woman—or some other "every person"—might shout "Go, O. J., go!" In addition to helping Hertz maintain its hold as the number one rental car company in the United States, Simpson also endorsed a variety of other products, including Royal Crown Cola, Schick, Foster Grant, and Dingo Cowboy Boots. Simpson also has appeared in over 30 television programs and motion pictures, including *Dragnet*, *In the Heat of the Night*, *The Towering Inferno*, *Capricorn One*, *Roots*, *Saturday Night Live* (as host), *Monday Night Football* and *The NFL on NBC* (as expert commentator), and perhaps most famously as Detective Nordberg in the *Naked Gun* trilogy. He even won a Golden Raspberry Award for worst supporting actor in *Naked Gun 33⅓: The Final Insult* in March 1995, while on trial for murder.

Given the enormous celebrity and near universal appeal of Simpson, his trial for murder—*People of the State of California v. Orenthal James Simpson*—was arguably the single largest American popular culture "media event" of the 20th century. On June 12, 1994, the bodies of Simpson's ex-wife, Nicole Brown-Simpson, and her friend Ronald Goldman were found dead outside Brown's condominium in Brentwood, California. Brown had been stabbed multiple times in the head and her throat was cut with such ferocity that her larynx was visible. Physical evidence gathered at the scene led investigators to suspect Simpson, who in 1989 had pleaded no contest to a domestic violence charge against Brown. Simpson was charged with these murders. After failing to turn himself in to authorities, Simpson on June 17, 1994, with friend A. C. Cowlings driving, led police on a slow-speed chase in the now infamous "White Bronco Scene." In one of the more surreal scenes in media history, the 20-car police pursuit of the white Bronco was picked up live by ABC, NBC, CBS, CNN, and numerous local news channels, with an approximate viewing audience of 100 million. NBC even used a split-screen format to broadcast the chase live during game five of the NBA Finals between the Houston Rockets and New York Knicks from Madison Square Garden. Simpson was arrested later that evening and arraigned on June 20, where he pleaded "Absolutely, 100 percent, not guilty."

The ensuing trial, which played out from January to October 1995, reads like a who's who of popular culture. Simpson's first attorney and personal friend, the late Robert Kardashian, is the father of "The Kardashians"—Kim, Khloe, and Kourtney—who were some of the first, in the reality TV generation, to be "famous for being famous." The mother of the Kardashian children was Kris Kardashian, one of Brown's closest friends, who later married Olympic decathlon champion turned celebrity Bruce Jenner. Simpson's primary defense team consisted of F. Lee Bailey, who tried the Sam Sheppard murder case, the "Boston Strangler" case, and the Patty Hearst case; Johnnie Cochran, who also has represented Michael Jackson, Tupac Shakur, Todd Bridges, NFL great Jim Brown, and rapper/actor Snoop Dogg; and Robert Shapiro, who has represented baseball players Darryl Strawberry, Jose Canseco, and Vince Coleman along with celebrities Johnny Carson, Christian Brando, and—who else—the Kardashians. During the trial Simpson was visited by Rosey Grier, a Christian minister, former member of the Los Angeles Rams "Fearsome Foursome," and bodyguard to friend Robert Kennedy when Kennedy was assassinated by Sirhan Sirhan. After that visit Grier is reported to have taken Simpson's words as an admission of guilt.

The issue of race figured prominently in the media coverage of the trial and in the trial itself. In terms of media coverage, *Time Magazine*, on its June 27, 1994, cover, featured a mug shot of Simpson and *Newsweek* featured on its June 27 cover the same mug shot. The *Time* mug shot had been "darkened" via digital enhancement, and it fomented a public outcry of racism. *Time* managing editor James Gaines issued a formal explanation, stating that there was no racial implication, but apologized to all who were offended. In the trial itself, race played a prominent role in the presence of Los Angeles police detective Mark Fuhrman. Fuhrman testified in March that he had gone to Simpson's house on the night of the murder and found that no one was home, at which time he jumped a wall to gain entrance to the property. Once on the property, according to Fuhrman, he found blood marks in the drive and a leather glove, which had on it the blood of Brown, Goldman, and Simpson. During his testimony, Fuhrman denied that he was a racist and swore under oath that had not used the word "nigger" in the past 10 years. Then in September Fuhrman was recalled and the defense team produced a tape recording made in 1986 in which Fuhrman used the word "nigger" some 41 times. Under further questioning, Fuhrman pleaded

Simpson's Record-Setting 1973 NFL Season—Yards Rushing by Game	
Week 1 at New England Patriots	250 yards
Week 2 at San Diego Chargers	103 yards
Week 3 vs. New York Jets	123 yards
Week 4 vs. Philadelphia Eagles	171 yards
Week 5 vs. Baltimore Colts	166 yards
Week 6 at Miami Dolphins	55 yards
Week 7 vs. Kansas City Chiefs	157 yards
Week 8 at New Orleans Saints	79 yards
Week 9 vs. Cincinnati Bengals	99 yards
Week 10 vs. Miami Dolphins	120 yards
Week 11 at Baltimore Colts	124 yards
Week 12 at Atlanta Falcons	137 yards
Week 13 vs. New England Patriots	219 yards
Week 14 at New York Jets	200 yards

TOTAL: 2,003 yards on 332 carries averaging 6.0 yards per carry

the Fifth Amendment, and later pleaded no contest to one count of perjury.

Simpson was, in the end, found not guilty, and Los Angeles avoided the race riot for which it was prepared. Americans were sharply divided along racial lines in their opinion of the outcome. In any number of public opinion polls, most African Americans thought justice had been served, while most white Americans thought Simpson had, quite literally, gotten away with murder. Whether or not Simpson actually committed these heinous murders, one can be certain that O. J. Simpson, who once had it all, will occupy a space of infamy in American popular culture for decades to come.

Chris B. Geyerman

See also Advertising and Sport; Brown, Jim; Cosell, Howard; Heisman Trophy; *Monday Night Football*; National Football League; Pro Football Hall of Fame and Museum

Suggested Resources

Gilbert, Mike. *How I Helped O.J. Get Away with Murder*. Washington, DC: Regency, 2008.
"O.J. Simpson." NFL.com. http://www.nfl.com/player/o.j.simpson/2525705/careerstats. Accessed January 17, 2012.
"O.J. Simpson." Pro-Football-Reference.com. http://www.pro-football-reference.com/players/S/SimpO.00.htm. Accessed January 17, 2012.

Simpson, O. J. *If I Did It: Confessions of a Killer.* New York: Beaufort Books, 2007.

Simpson Trial Transcripts. http://simpson.walraven.org/. Accessed January 17, 2012.

Skateboarding

Skateboarding has been touted as an alternative to mainstream sport. Unlike basketball or baseball, skateboarding does not have formal rules or a standardized venue. It can be performed in a variety of ways and virtually in any space that has pavement. Although there are some formal competitions such as the X Games, skateboarding is regularly practiced as a more individualistic, creative, and process-oriented activity. Because of this orientation, skill and innovation are more valued than winning. It is not referees who judge skill, but other participants. Fundamentally, skateboarding is participant-run; it thrives on a do-it-yourself (DIY) ethos.

The everyday practice of skateboarding may be different from more traditional sports, but skateboarding is clearly in the mainstream. Skateboarding is growing faster than any other sport in the United States. In 1998, 5.8 million people were skating and in 2007 there were 10.1 million participants, a 74 percent growth rate with the 12–17-year-olds generating most of this increase. Current estimates range from 9 to 12 million participants in the United States. To meet and encourage this demand skate parks have been built in municipalities using both public and private funds. In the early 1990s there were fewer than 200 skate parks in the United States; today there are over 2,000. The popularity of skateboarding is also evident in young adults' role models. In 2008, Tony Hawk, the public face of skateboarding, was rated the top overall athlete, surpassing more traditional sport athletes such as baseball player Derek Jeter and basketball player LeBron James. Skateboarding's popularity can also be identified by its fiscal value. In the late 2000s, the global skateboarding industry has an estimated worth between $4.9 and $5.5 billion. Additionally, top athletes are attractive to mainstream corporate sponsorship. Tony Hawk earned $12 million in 2008, all through sponsorships, his traveling road shows, and his top-rated video games, as he retired from professional skateboarding in 1999.

The youth market has always been the target audience for skateboarding, but it was not until the 1980s that the industry intentionally distinguished itself from surfing, creating an identity that highlighted skateboarders as rebellious, cool, and street savvy. To maximize appeal for a youthful market, the industry promoted a whole lifestyle including music, art, and fashion around skateboarding. In the 1990s the millennial generation (people born between 1978 and 1995) was the most highly sought after market due to its numbers and wealth, and skateboarding's "packaged" lifestyle was a perfect avenue for mainstream commercial interests to reach this audience. The wealth and scope of such corporations as ESPN and the X Games, Mountain Dew, Nike, NBC, Adidas, and McDonald's engages with alternative sports. Skateboarding and other "action" or "extreme" sports became the marker of the cool, independent teen. By the early 2000s there were 1,141 registered trademarked products with "extreme" in their name. Additionally, skateboarding's DIY ethos and emphasis on creativity and innovation is currently striking a chord with an audience that doesn't necessarily skate, but that does support the tenets of entrepreneurialism. Skateboarding's broader appeal is due, in part, because it resonates with the American ideals of rugged individualism, creativity, and entrepreneurialism.

Development of Skateboarding's Cultural Meanings

The promotional messages and strategies around skateboarding provide an avenue to understand how particular meanings and values have become commonly associated with the activity. Although skateboarding has many different meanings for those who participate, the industry is in a more powerful position to promote their ideals through advertising and promotions.

Since its mass-marketed inception in the early 1960s, promotional strategies have remained very similar: Companies create and sponsor teams to advertise their wares in contests and in magazines, which also happened to be produced by people in the skateboarding business. Media coverage is crucial as it creates images and narratives of legitimacy and authenticity by highlighting cutting-edge styles and personalities. What has changed is the image of a skateboarder. Initially, skateboarding was being promoted as a dry land equivalent to surfing, referred to as "sidewalk surfing." Not surprisingly, skateboarding was promoted by a few California surfers and the surfing industry was also behind the first skateboard magazine, the *Quarterly Skateboarder*. The images of skateboarders were primarily white teenaged males, but occasionally white females. Most of the tricks consisted of gymnastic-like moves or slalom style. The industry included female divisions of contests, and female images were picked up by mass media such as *Life Magazine*, which used a picture on their cover of Patti McGee, the national girls' champion, doing a handstand while riding her board.

In 1975 the magazine *Quarterly Skateboarder* was revived as *Skateboarder*. This magazine set the standard for the format that most others would follow: action shots, technical coverage of skills, coverage of interesting places to skate, profiles of skateboarders, and related commentary on the skateboarding social scene. *Skateboarder*, and more specifically writer and photographer Craig Stecyk, played a critical role in shifting the image of a skateboarder from a regular suburban teenager to a rebellious urban youth. Stecyk was an artist and friend of two surfers, Jeff Ho and Skip Engblom, who ran a shop and sponsored both a surf and skate team called the Z-boys. Stecyk chronicled the Z-Boys in *Skateboarder*, and in one article wrote, "Skaters by their very nature are urban guerillas," helping to promote a different vision of skateboarding than what had dominated before. Instead of white suburban youth doing freestyle and gymnastic-like tricks, Z-Boys represented a more ethnically diverse and economically disadvantaged group. One of the top Z-Boy skaters was Stacy Peralta, who would later work in the industry in promotions and media and who has heavily influenced the culture. The visual and story line that Stecyk created was of marginalized kids who were challenging conventions, being aggressive, and being innovative. However, while the Z-Boys were featured regularly in magazines during the

mid-1970s, most skaters and contests were still made up of freestyle, slalom, and downhill skateboarding.

The reliance on surfing images and businesses was soon tempered as skateboarding took on an urban punk style and former skateboarders began their own successful companies. The 1980s also witnessed a merging of surf and punk styles as the freestyle and ramp skating of the 1970s was modified to work in urban spaces, ultimately morphing into the "street style" that has become the signature of skateboarding.

Fausto Vitello was a key stakeholder who owned a skateboard parts company, Independent Trucks, and started a niche magazine, *Thrasher*, in the early 1980s that emphasized a more punk, DIY orientation to skateboarding. *Thrasher* claimed to be for "core" skaters and not big business, and its motto was "Skate and Destroy." Fausto collaborated with Stacy Peralta and Craig Stecyk to develop ways to reinvigorate the market when skateboarding slumped in the early 1980s. Their strategy was to make skateboarding more widely accessible while creating an antiestablishment activity that was simultaneously "cool." To do this, they promoted very local types of contests, such as ramp jams staged in participants' backyards, giving the appearance of local as opposed to corporate control. They also worked at promoting street-style skating to increase their consumer base; because it doesn't require special apparatus (in fact, one simply uses everyday elements of the street), more people could potentially participate. *Thrasher* started promoting street contests in 1983 and purposely made them gritty by creating a harsh urban atmosphere by staging old cars and painted graffiti on ramps. The ideas of DIY and a form of streetwise masculinity were promoted by many stakeholders early in the 1980s.

Larry Balma and other skateboarding advocates such as Neil Blender and Grant Brittain were part of the organization United Skate Front, and in 1983 they started publishing *Transworld Skateboarding*. Their intention was to make skateboarding accessible to a wide audience including more mainstream companies and parents who often oversaw what their children purchased. To differentiate their audience from *Thrasher*, they downplayed the antiestablishment ethos and took up the motto, "Skate and Create."

The niche media including magazines and videos played a crucial role in promoting particular forms of authenticity as they highlighted different lifestyles of a skateboarder. The contention was primarily in the degree of rebelliousness that should be embraced. The industry had to play a balancing act between appealing to a broad audience for financial reasons and simultaneously appealing to hard-core skaters to "keep it real." Nonetheless, the 1980s saw the establishment of DIY as a standard of legitimacy that most stakeholders upheld. The urban environment and style along with this outlaw and streetwise image generated appeal, as the late 1980s saw the highest number of participants ever for skateboarding, not surpassed until the early 2000s.

The ultimate boost to the sport's global popularity has been the widespread appeal of the X Games to a youthful audience. In 1995, ESPN, a subsidiary of the Disney Corporation, capitalized on the appeal that the cultural meanings of alternative sport had for young people. They created the X Games, which are meant to be the Olympics of alternative sport. Currently the X Games have contests globally in the winter and summer. Another media form that has been credited with engaging a mainstream audience with skateboarding is video games. In particular, Tony Hawk's series of video games have been perennial top sellers since they came on the market in 1999. His games have generated over a billion dollars. These games represent well-known skate spots and have avatars of other famous skateboarders.

Current Status within Popular Culture

Skateboarding has established a strong presence in our culture beyond the actual practice of skateboarding. Its influence can be seen in various forms of media including art, film, literature, and television. Skateboarding's emphasis on creativity has been parlayed into artistic credibility. In the past two decades there have been numerous local and regional art exhibitions featuring skateboarders' work or the use of skateboards as art. *Beautiful Losers* is one particular exhibition that has gained mainstream recognition. It opened in 2004 and was billed as a multimedia art exhibit that featured art from street culture. The exhibit included installations, sculpture, drawings, graffiti, paintings, toys, graphics

for magazines and album covers, film, photography, skateboards, and an actual skateboarding apparatus, a ramp-like bowl, which was used as part of the exhibit. Works of skaters Ed Templeton and Mark Gonzales were also displayed. The industry is quite aware of the cultural appeal of skateboarding and art. One apparel company, RVCA, actually supports an artist network program with a quarterly publication called *ANP*. Additionally, Nike was one sponsor of *Beautiful Losers*, and more recently supported the creation of a "skateable" art installation at the Museum of Contemporary Art, Los Angeles, called "Art in the Street." And Oakley has sponsored the annual "love and guts" skate/art show since 2005. Mainstream settings have also included shows on skateboarding. In 2010 *Ramp It Up: Skateboard Culture in Native America* was exhibited in Washington, D.C., at the Smithsonian National Museum of the American Indian. Also in 2010 an exhibit featuring the history of African Americans in the sport, *How We Roll*, was shown at the California African American Museum.

Films and books have been other artistic forums for skateboarding. In the 2000s there were several films that focused on the culture of skateboarding. Most significant was the award-winning documentary *Dogtown and Z-Boys*, which told the story of the rise of aggressive street skateboarding. This 2001 film was directed by Stacy Peralta and partially funded by Vans. Another award-winning film was Gus Van Sant's 2007 adaptation of the novel *Paranoid Park*, which addresses the life of teenagers in Portland, Oregon. Another film highlighting urban teenagers' relationship with skateboarding was Larry Clark's 2005 film *Wassup Rockers*. Mainstream authors also used skateboarding as the means to convey teenage culture in the 2000s. Nick Hornby, the author of *About a Boy* and *Fever Pitch*, wrote the 2007 novel *Slam*, in which a teenage boy partly relies on the image of Tony Hawk as counsel for his own transition into adulthood.

Television is a major contributor to facilitating skateboarding's place in young-adult lives. MTV has used the antiauthoritarian and DIY lifestyle of skaters to create the series *Jackass*, which has been developed into two successful feature-length films. MTV played off the success of that program and worked with professional skateboarder Rob Dyrdek to create the series

Rob and Big, which focused on the friendship of Rob and his bodyguard, "Big." After that series ended, MTV featured another Dyrdek program called *Fantasy Factor*, which displayed the creative and entrepreneurial workings of his corporation and how they developed different products including the world's largest skateboard. MTV also worked with Ryan Scheckler in creating the reality show called *The Life of Ryan*, and another reality program called *Skater Girls*. MTV's investment in action sports was also established in a new company in 2008, Alli Sports, created through the partnership with NBC Sports.

Skateboarding has also been used for mainstream educational and humanitarian purposes. For example, "Skate Pass" is a popular curriculum that incorporates skateboarding with traditional physical education classes and "Drop into Skateboarding" promotes strategies to incorporate skateboarding into public recreation and school facilities. In 2007 two skaters from Australia started a skateboarding school in Kabul, Afghanistan, called Skateistan. The informal education has turned to a permanent skate park and school where participation for young boys and girls is blossoming and has captured the attention of skaters across the globe who volunteer their time and supplies. Plans are being made to build a similar school in Phnom Penh, Cambodia. Similar efforts to use skateboarding as an outreach to disenfranchised youth are happening in Durban, South Africa.

The popularity of the sport is based, in part, on the control the participants have, which has translated into a subcultural identity that focuses on creativity, independence, and antiauthoritarianism. That avantgarde image has been widely used by popular cultural industries to reach a youth audience. This synergistic relationship of skateboarding and cultural industries has promoted the significance of the skateboarding values and meanings within popular culture.

Becky Beal

See also Adidas; ESPN Channels; Hawk, Tony; James, LeBron; Jeter, Derek; Nike, Inc.; X Games

Suggested Resources

Beal, Becky. *Skateboarding: The Ultimate Guide*. Santa Barbara, CA: ABC-CLIO, 2013.

Borden, Iain. *Skateboarding, Space, and the City: Architecture and the Body*. Oxford: Berg, 2001.

Browne, David. *Amped: How Big Air, Big Dollars, and a New Generation Took Sports to the Extreme*. New York: Bloomsbury, 2004.

Chivers Yochim, Emily. *Skate Life: Re-Imaging White Masculinity*. Ann Arbor: University of Michigan Press, 2010.

I Skate Therefore I Am. http://blog.istia.tv/. Accessed January 5, 2012.

Skateboarding. http://skateboard.about.com/. Accessed January 5, 2012.

Wheaton, Belinda. *Lifestyle Sport: The Cultural Politics of Alternative Sports*. London: Routledge Press, 2012.

Willard, Michael. "Séance, Tricknowlogy, Skateboarding, and the Space of Youth." In Joe Austin and Michael N. Willard, eds. *Generations of Youth: Youth Cultures and History in Twentieth-Century America*. New York: New York University Press, 1998, pp. 327–346.

Slam Dunk Contest

The Slam Dunk Contest, originally created as a spectacle for the American Basketball Association (ABA), has become one of America's favorite annual sport contests, showcasing supreme athleticism. The contest is held annually during the NBA All-Star Weekend, falling on a mid-February Saturday evening. Once coveted by the who's who of the NBA for participation, recent years have seen perennial All-Stars such as LeBron James, Dwyane Wade, and others scoff at the contest due to the risk of potential injury. This trend may be changing, however, with the augment of the use of props during dunks. Players such as Dwight Howard and Blake Griffin have come out of phone booths à la Superman and jumped over a car, respectively. This increased flare has brought the fanfare back to the contest that was one of the greatest spectacles in all of professional sports in the 1980s.

The first contest was held in 1976 in Denver, Colorado. The mile-high city saw one of the most memorable dunks in history as Julius "Dr. J" Erving soared through the air, taking off from the foul line, confidently throwing the ball through the hoop. After the 1976 ABA All-Star Game, there was an eight-year hiatus from the contest due to the ABA and NBA merger.

In 1984, the Slam Dunk Contest returned to Denver. The mile-high city highlighted Dr. J's return to the competition with a free throw line dunk similar to the one with which he wowed basketball fans eight years prior. Erving lost to a lanky young Larry Nance who stood 6'10" and effortlessly dunked the ball while looking down into the basket. The Atlanta Hawk's Dominique Wilkins also shone that year, one of the most powerful dunkers in basketball history.

After a successful renaissance, the Slam Dunk Contest came to Indianapolis, Indiana, in 1985. Most notably billed as Dr. J's last contest, it was a passing of the torch from one great high-flyer to another. The show was taken over by a rookie named Michael Jordan and an already seasoned Dominique Wilkins. It was a show of power versus soaring grace and was ultimately won by "the human highlight film," Wilkins. After 1985, it was clear the contest had returned with style as it created one of the great dunk rivalries in history.

The anticipated contest in 1986 was headlined by an injured Michael Jordan. The contest did not lose any excitement, however, as an unknown 5'7" Anthony "Spud" Webb stole the spotlight. He and his Atlanta teammate, Wilkins, went back and forth as fans marveled at the unbelievable leaping ability of Webb. Wilkins was not able to defend his title, as Webb won the fans and the judges' approval, taking home the trophy.

The year 1987 brought the return of Michael "Air" Jordan to Seattle and a reign of unforgettable moments in Slam Dunk Contest history as Wilkins and Webb were sidelined with injuries. Jordan ran away with the contest with his famous double-pump "free throw line dunk." The following year, the contest was held in Chicago in front of Jordan's home crowd. Wilkins was healthy again, which made for perhaps the most memorable year in Slam Dunk Contest history. Jordan once again leaped from the free throw line and edged out Wilkins by two points for a final score of 147–145.

Houston, Texas, welcomed the 1989 contest when the hometown favorite Clyde "The Glide" Drexler returned to the city of his alma mater. Drexler was unable to defeat Kenny "Sky" Walker, as Walker contorted his body and effortlessly threw the ball into the hoop. Walker, relatively unknown except for his leaping abilities, won the contest only once.

In 1990, the event in Miami brought what would be the final contest for Wilkins and the end of spectacular contests in the late 1980s. Wilkins won the contest with

Washington Wizards JaVale McGee dunks during the Slam Dunk Contest at the NBA All-Star Weekend, Saturday, February 19, 2011, in Los Angeles. (AP Photo/Mark J. Terrill.)

his vintage-style showcase of power dunks, outlasting three-point sharpshooter Kenny "The Jet" Smith.

Wilkins's final contest passed the torch to a new era of dunk contests. The new decade ushered in the gradual decline in the popularity of the contest. Wilkins and Jordan were no longer competing and the years of superstar player participants began to subside. The year 1991, however, began the era of more creative dunks, when showmanship outshone athletic dunking ability. Dee Brown was the contest's winner in 1991 with the famous "no look dunk." It is disputed today whether or not Brown could actually see through his arm as it covered his eyes during the left-handed slam.

The 1992 contest returned to Florida, highlighting the three-year-old arena in Orlando, which hosted the expansion team Orlando Magic. Once again the trickery returned as Cedric Ceballos of the Phoenix Suns won the contest with the "blindfolded dunk." Larry Johnson, nicknamed "Grandmama," was runner-up that year. His purely power dunks were no match for the creativity of Ceballos.

The following year, the contest went west to Salt Lake City where Harold "Baby Jordan" Miner started a trend of increasingly athletic dunks. Minor preferred the double-pump reverse dunk, which won him the title. In 1994, the most famous dunk since the foul line dunk was born. Isaiah Rider won the contest with a between-the-legs dunk, which has since been duplicated and modified many times.

The 1995 contest came to Phoenix to see the past two champions duel on the court; however, the performances were mostly unexciting. Due to missed opportunities on Rider's part, Minor easily defeated the participants and walked away with his second title.

A year later, Brent Barry, son of Hall of Famer Rick Barry, brought back the free throw line dunk made famous 20 years prior by Julius Erving. Barry effortlessly glided through the air with a warm-up jacket on and immediately ignited the crowd. When asked about his victory during the broadcast of the 2011 dunk contest, Barry noted that he currently uses his trophy as a dip bowl.

The final contest in the 1990s took place in Cleveland where the 50 greatest players in NBA history were honored. The dunk contest was overshadowed in 1997 by the spectacular collection of basketball talent that came together that year. In what proved to be an underwhelming contest, a young 17-year-old Kobe Bryant went on to win what would be his only dunk title in a career of many achievements. After the pageantry at the All-Star Game in 1997, the NBA faced a dark age in the late 1990s that involved a lockout, overall apathy after Michael Jordan's departure in 1998, and the lack of a superstar to take Jordan's place.

The dunk contest did not return until 2000 as the millennium welcomed perhaps the best dunker of all time in Vince Carter. The former University of North Carolina Tar Heel won the contest with a between-the-legs dunk off an alley-oop. As teammates and cousins, Carter and Tracy McGrady put on arguably the best

show in dunk contest history. Some critics say this was the final great contest for many years as the event declined in popularity in the following years.

In 2001, a relatively unknown Desmond Mason held off a cocky DeShawn Stevenson to take the title in the nation's capital, Washington, D.C. The years 2002 and 2003 saw the contest's first back-to-back winner since Michael Jordan in 1987 and 1988. Jason Richardson brought superb athleticism to the contest, but the television ratings remained low. In 2004, Richardson sought to become the contest's first three-peat champion, but was beaten by Fred Jones. The dunk contest was no longer filled with superstars as lucrative contracts left the league's best players wary of injury.

With discussions of canceling the contest due to the lack of star power, the 2005 contest was a pivotal competition for the future as casual basketball fans had lost interest. The Atlanta Hawks' young star Josh Smith ran away with the competition, leaping over the Denver Nuggets' Kenyon Martin. Perhaps the best dunk of the competition was the assist from Steve Nash to Amar'e Stoudemire off Nash's head.

The flare of the contest returned in 2006 with the arrival of 5'9" Nate Robinson. Robinson brought the 1986 champion Spud Webb to aid in his dunk as he jumped over Webb to clinch the 2006 title. Robinson went on to win the title two more times in 2009 and 2010 to become the only person in dunk contest history to win three times.

Robinson's attempt to repeat in 2007 made him the fan favorite. The year 2007, however, began the era of props and creativity in the contest. Dwight Howard affixed a sticker to the top of the backboard. Gerald Green paid homage to fellow Celtic Dee Brown by completing the "no look dunk," giving him the title.

The year 2008 continued the trend of trickery and dunking props. Dwight Howard brought a new element both creatively and athletically to the contest. The game had never seen a man at 6'11" with the athleticism that Howard possessed. Howard beat Green despite Green blowing out a candle on a cupcake placed delicately on the rim. Howard won by dressing like Superman in a cape. He flew through the air, violently throwing the ball through the rim in a dunk unlike any seen in history.

Phi Slama Jama

Phi Slama Jama was a nickname given to the University of Houston Cougar basketball team in the early 1980s. The two most recognizable players on the team were Clyde Drexler and Hakeem Olajuwon. Coach Guy Lewis was infamous for letting his players play basketball with a free, up-tempo, pickup basketball type of mentality. With the supreme athleticism the team possessed, they were collectively known as "Texas's Tallest Fraternity." Phi Slama Jama is a play off the three Greek letters in the names of traditional fraternities. The nickname was first given to the team by writer Thomas Bonk in a 1983 article in the *Houston Post*. Phi Slama Jama set a precedent for collegiate basketball with its athletic, up-tempo, above-the-rim, fast-paced style of play.

The following year, Robinson regained his crown by jumping effortlessly over his adversary, Dwight Howard, who made his appearance at the contest exiting a phone booth. Robinson dressed all in green and used a green ball simulating Kryptonite, which symbolically was the demise of Superman.

The year 2010 brought a much-anticipated contest to Dallas; however, the contest had little excitement and was largely a disappointment. Robinson once again ran away with the contest as the creativity suffered from the previous year.

The 2011 contest took place in Los Angeles, where the creativity returned. Serge Ibaka snagged a stuffed animal at the rim with his teeth and JaVale McGee dunked three balls simultaneously. Rookie Blake Griffin stole the show, jumping over a Kia brand car. Griffin showed an incredible display of athleticism and power.

The 2011 contest brought the dunk contest to an all-time high of creativity. The 1980s were fraught with star power in Jordan and Wilkins. The 1990s brought increasing athleticism and the 2000s brought props and creativity. The contest had never seen the use of a car as part of the show until 2011. In 2012 the fans were given complete voting power with the use of text messaging after each dunk. Reggie Evans of Utah won, the first winner for a Jazz player. The future of the contest is sure to be entertaining, as the creativity and spectacle of the contest becomes increasingly popular.

Dean Bring

See also American Basketball Association; Bryant, Kobe; Erving, Julius: Jordan, Michael

Suggested Resources
Graham, Brad. "A Slam Dunk Contest Never Hurt Anyone." February 9, 2010. http://www.slamonline.com/online/blogs/isolation-play/2010/02/high-definition/. Accessed October 4, 2011.
Mallozzi, Vincent. *Doc: The Rise and Rise of Julius Erving*. New York: Wiley, 2009.
"NBA Slam Dunk Contest." Insidehoops.com. February 25, 2012. http://www.insidehoops.com/slam-dunk-contest.shtml. Accessed October 4, 2011.
Schuman, Jeff. "History of the NBA Dunk Contest." April 4, 2007. http://www.associatedcontent.com/article/192650/history_of_the_nba_dunk_contest.html. Accessed October 4, 2011.
"Slam Dunk Contest." ESPN.com. http://espn.go.com/nba/topics/_/page/sprite-slam-dunk-contest. Accessed October 4, 2011.

Slap Shot (1977)

Early in George Roy Hill's gritty hockey classic, *Slap Shot*, Reggie Dunlop (Paul Newman) reads the *Hockey News* as his Charlestown Chiefs board a charter bus. On the magazine's cover is Bobby Clarke of the Philadelphia Flyers, an image that places the film within its historical context.

The years 1976–1977 were an era of transition for the NHL; the Flyers, led by the likes of Andre "Moose" Dupont, Dave "the Hammer" Schultz, and Bob "Hound Dog" Kelly, played a brand of goon hockey and were affectionately labeled "The Broad Street Bullies." Clarke, the team captain, was infamous for deliberately breaking the ankle of Soviet star Valeri Kharlamov in the 1972 Summit Series.

Moreover, the Flyers themselves were part of an international controversy. On January 11, 1976, in a "friendly" exhibition match between them and the Red Army at the Spectrum, Flyer defenseman Ed Van Impe wiped out Kharlamov (once again) with a clean but crushing check. Kharlamov lay on the ice for over a minute, and the Soviets, protesting that no penalty was called, left the ice, threatening not to return.

By the end of the decade, goon hockey was slowly replaced with the faster, more up-tempo style of the Montreal Canadiens (who won four Stanley Cups from 1976 to 1979). During the 1980s the game had evolved into a free-wheeling style epitomized by Wayne Gretzky and the Edmonton Oilers. Today, with the opening of the red line (no more offside calls for two-line passes) and the removal of the clutch-and-grab defense (courtesy of more tightly officiated games and the enforcement of holding and hooking penalties), the game is faster than ever.

Slap Shot writer Nancy Dowd based her screenplay on the experiences of her brother Ned. The pregame brawl between the Chiefs and the Patriots and the Chiefs climbing over the glass to attack fans who threw a set of keys at Jeff Hanson really happened. And the flavorful depiction of Olgie Oglethorpe, a goon mentioned throughout the film as someone to be wary of, is loosely modeled on Bill "Goldie" Goldthorpe, who once accrued a whopping 25 major penalties before Christmas. Unfortunately the 1970s was an era when violence sold tickets.

Nancy Dowd captures this flavor and the authentic feel of minor league hockey. The players constantly drop "F-bombs," are homophobic, play poker during long bus rides, and obsess over sex; and their wives are unhappy, living in a desolate community and turning to drink.

But all of these authentic facts aside, it is the Philadelphia Flyers of the 1970s and their notorious antics that most audience members in 1977 would have seen as the contextual intersection between the film world (the Charlestown Chiefs of the Federal League) and the real world watched by hockey fans across North America (the Flyers and the National Hockey League).

Shot on location in Johnstown, Pennsylvania, Pittsburgh, and upstate New York, the film is set in a dying rustbelt community. The mill is closing and 10,000 workers will be without jobs. The hockey team represents the distilled dreams and hopes and sense of worth of the town. In a way, the film predates the slow death of cities like Detroit and Cleveland, and the support of these cities' zealous fans who love their teams. Anonymous people constantly approach player-coach Dunlop—on the streets, in bars—and offer advice on improving the Chiefs, such as bolstering the power play.

The team is going to be sold and Dunlop, struggling to maintain morale, concocts a false story about interest in the club by a retirement community in Florida. This gives the players hope and, in a drive to increase support, advertising, and exposure for his club, Dunlop decides to "goon it up."

Paul Newman plays Dunlop with a mix of con man and rebel cool. Tapping into his legendary persona by restructuring elements of his Lew Harper from *Harper* and Henry Gondorff from *The Sting*, Newman's Dunlop is a slightly underhanded figure who gets everyone believing in a rough-and-tumble style of hockey, courtesy of the Hanson brothers, three bespectacled thugs who arrive on a 4:15 bus.

At first, Dunlop doesn't play the three arrested adolescents (after all, he thinks they're "retards" because they play with slot cars and enjoy sipping on orange and grape sodas), but in a hilarious three-minute montage, Dunlop lets them loose on the ice and they commit a series of belligerent infractions: crosschecking, high-sticking, boarding, and low-bridging other players. Steve Hanson even cruises by the opponent's bench and whacks several players with the blade of his stick.

Players buy into the concept, including Dave Carlson, who gives himself the nickname "Killer" and sports a Dracula cape as part of his pregame ritual, and Denis Lemieux, the team's French Canadian goalie, who replaces his blank fiberglass mask with one plastered with a menacing skull and crossbones.

Ned Braden (Michael Ontkean), an American (which was a rarity back then; now up to 17 percent of all pro players are U.S. born) and a Princeton graduate, refuses to goon it up and is disgusted by Dunlop's manipulations and newfound tough-guy posturing.

Dunlop eventually comes clean, drops his conman persona, and tells the truth. After meeting with the mysterious team owner and discovering that she cares nothing about hockey, the guilt-ridden coach tells the fellas that he wants to return to old-time hockey, no more goon stuff.

In the championship game, their opponent loads up with goons, including the aforementioned Oglethorpe. The unsuspecting Chiefs get hammered in the first period. The second begins with a huge line brawl and that's when Ned Braden, the film's moral center, swings into action. Disgusted with the on-ice violence, he removes all of his equipment to a bump-and-grind beat. The crowd raucously cheers, the line brawl

Jacques Plante: The Innovator

On November 1, 1959, a rising slap shot from the Rangers' Andy Bathgate broke Habs goalie Jacques Plante's nose. Goalies didn't wear masks back then, and Plante had to leave the ice to get stitched up. Since there were no backups, the Madison Square Garden crowd had to wait for his return. After being stitched up, Plante told Coach Toe Blake he would not return to the nets unless he could wear a mask he had been trying out in practice since 1956. Blake, with no options, agreed. In the dim light of the Garden, Plante, sporting a crude mask, now looked like a post-Halloween ghoul.

After that night, Plante never played a game without a mask, and the goalie fraternity was forever changed. Plante's first mask eventually gave way to a pretzel design before he invented the form-fitting fiberglass model that would be worn by many goaltenders in the 1970s. It is that model that Denis Lemieux in *Slap Shot* also sports. Lemieux, played by Yvon Barrette, is a comical character. In the opening set piece to the film, he explains the finer nuances of the game, and how if you commit an infraction you go to the box and "feel shame." His character is French Canadian, and, as such, writer Nancy Dowd gives a shout-out to Plante and all the French Canadian goalies who have populated the game (including then-Flyers goalie Bernie Parent, who was mentored by Plante for two years in the early 1970s).

In 2000, the Canadian government recognized Plante's innovations in the sport of hockey, as a 46-cent stamp bearing his likeness was commissioned.

breaks apart, and Chiefs play-by-play announcer Jim Carr labels the striptease "disgusting."

But is it disgusting? Isn't all of the blood on the ice and the freak show fighting a bigger disgrace? Through a burlesque act, Braden burlesques the fighting in the game of hockey. His perverse genius deconstructs the tough-guy antics.

And perhaps Braden's philosophy has won the day. Most NHL teams no longer carry an "enforcer" (they can't keep up with the game's fast pace and skill); international hockey doesn't allow fighting; and the junior leagues are thinking of following suit. The goon game is gone and soon fighting might be as passé as well.

Underappreciated upon its initial release, *Slap Shot* has gained in cult status. *Hockey News* declared it the greatest hockey film ever made. In 1998, *Maxim* called it the "best guy film of all time." *Entertainment Weekly* voted it number 31 of its top 50 cult films. *Slap Shot* is screened on team charter buses across the United States and Canada. The fictional Hanson brothers (Jeff Carlson, Steve Carlson, and Dave Hanson) still make appearances in their Chiefs jerseys at hockey venues everywhere, and McFarlane Toys captured their likenesses in a series of action figures.

Grant Tracey

See also Gretzky, Wayne

Suggested Resources
Denault, Todd. *Jacques Plante: The Man Who Changed the Face of Hockey.* Toronto: McLelland & Stewart, 2009.
Jackson, Jim. *Walking Together Forever: The Broad Street Bullies, Then and Now.* Champaign, IL: Sport Publishing, 2005.
Jackson, Jonathon. *The Making of* Slap Shot: *Behind the Scenes of the Greatest Hockey Movie Ever Made.* Mississauga, Ontario: John Wiley and Sons, 2011.
Slap Shot. IMDb. http://www.imdb.com/title/tt0076723/. Accessed March 11, 2012.

Smith, Emmitt (1969–)

On October 27, 2002, Emmitt Smith accomplished a singular achievement, one for which he'd been preparing ever since he was a young man growing up in Pensacola, Florida. Midway through his 13th National Football League season, in the fourth quarter versus the Seattle Seahawks at Dallas's Texas Stadium, he took a handoff, ran left off-tackle, and gained 11 yards. With that carry, Smith amassed 16,728 career yards and became the NFL's all-time leading rusher, eclipsing Hall of Famer Walter Payton's career mark of 16,726.

The run had not been easy. As Smith cut through the hole, he was hit hard by a defender, stumbled, and almost lost his balance; yet instinctively, he placed his hand on the ground to regain his footing and then lurched forward several more yards before he was finally tackled. In many ways, the run personified Smith's career. Not blessed with great size, blazing speed, or tremendous explosiveness, he succeeded through hard work, commitment, and determination. Indeed, it was

Emmitt Smith of the Dallas Cowboys eludes a Buffalo Bills defender during Super Bowl XXVIII in Atlanta, Georgia, on January 30, 1994. (AP Photo/Bob Galbraith.)

those qualities that over his 15-year career made Smith one of the most durable and prolific running backs in the history of the National Football League.

At just 5'9" tall and 200 pounds, Smith was smaller than the prototypical NFL running back. By the time he arrived in the professional ranks, though, he had proven time and again that regardless of his size, he was a natural runner. He ran on instinct, sensing almost instantaneously where holes developed in the offensive line. Once he found the hole, whatever he lacked in speed was more than offset by his intensity and desire to make yardage. Smith's powerful legs never stopped moving, and invariably it took more than one defender to bring him down.

It had been that way at every level of competition. No matter the strength or skill of the opponent, whenever Smith was handed the ball, the result was usually one rushing record after another. In four years at Escambia High School in Pensacola, his numbers were staggering. On the way to a career total of 8,804 yards rushing, he tallied 45 100-yard games and scored 106 touchdowns. Twice he led his team to state championships.

Soon, college scouts from all over the country descended on Pensacola, attempting to recruit Smith. Ultimately, however, he chose to stay in his home state and attend the University of Florida. Again, records fell. In just his second collegiate game, Smith ran for over 100 yards; the next week, versus Southeastern Conference rival Alabama, he set a school record by rushing for 224 yards. In that freshman season, his 1,341 rushing yards set a school record and also led the conference.

But that was just a prelude to his junior year. After missing the 1,000-yard mark by two yards as a sophomore due to an injury, the next year Smith came back with a vengeance. On October 21, 1989, he ran for 316 yards against the University of New Mexico in a 27–21 Florida victory, and he finished the season with a school record and conference-leading total of 1,599 yards rushing; he also tied the single-season school mark of 14 touchdowns. By the end of that season, Smith had rushed for a three-year collegiate total of 3,938 yards, including 23 100-yard games; scored 37 touchdowns; and set 58 school records. Moreover, on the basis of his tremendous junior season, he was named both SEC Player of the Year as well as a first-team All-American.

Smith was now one of the best collegiate running backs in the nation. Yet there was little left for him to prove at that level. So in 1990 he decided it was time to become a professional, and he declared himself a junior-eligible for the NFL's annual draft. Assured of his talent, prior to the draft Smith wrote down his professional goals: lead the NFL in rushing; win the NFL Rookie of the Year; become the NFL's all-time leading rusher; make the Professional Football Hall of Fame; and become the greatest running back in history. By the time his career was ended, three of his four measurable goals would be accomplished.

As the draft approached, Smith felt confident he was ready for the next level. To help ensure his chances of being an early first-round pick, his agent held an open workout to allow NFL scouts to assess Smith's skills. While the running back excelled at blocking, pass catching, and strength, however, his time in the 40-yard run was a somewhat pedestrian 4.59 seconds, not the sort of speed NFL teams preferred at the position. So, despite his collegiate heroics, 16 teams bypassed Smith in the first round. Finally, with the 17th pick, the Dallas Cowboys selected him as the second running back taken. (Penn State's Blair Thomas, the second overall pick, was the first running back selected.)

Understandably, Smith was disappointed in his low selection. From that point forward, he always felt he had something to prove. Luckily, in the Cowboys, he had joined a team that was on the verge of greatness. Following an abysmal 1988 season during which the team finished with a 3–13 record, new owner Jerry Jones had fired the only coach the Cowboys had ever known, legendary future Hall of Famer Tom Landry, and replaced him with Jimmy Johnson, a highly successful college coach. Johnson immediately went about transforming an old, slow team into one built on youth, strength, and speed. Together with quarterback Troy Aikman and wide receiver Michael Irvin, both of whom, like Smith, would later be enshrined in the Pro Football Hall of Fame, the trio powered an offense that eventually led the Cowboys to three Super Bowl victories in the next five years.

Smith's rushing was the catalyst of the potent offensive attack. In his rookie season of 1990, when the Cowboys improved their record from 1–15 in their first year under Johnson to 7–9, Smith gained 937 yards and was named the NFL's Rookie of the Year; for the first of eight seasons, he was also named to the Pro Bowl. Yet he was just getting started. The following season he won the first of four NFL rushing titles, while also leading the league for the first of three times in carries. (He was also named First-Team All-Pro for the first of four consecutive seasons.) That performance put Smith, in just his third season, among the elite running backs in the league. More importantly, however, after an absence of 15 years, it helped return the Cowboys to championship status.

By 1992, Johnson's rebuilding project was complete. In the preseason, *Sports Illustrated* magazine predicted that the Cowboys would win the Super Bowl, and after a 13–3 regular season, that prediction proved accurate: On January 31, 1993, Dallas demolished the Buffalo Bills, 52–17, to win the third Super Bowl in team history. Afterward, Smith, who had carried 22 times for 108 yards, was naturally elated, and he cried tears of joy in the locker room.

The next season may have been his finest. Once again, Smith led the league in rushing yards, and for the only time in his career, he also led the league in yards per carry, with a single-season career-best 5.3. (He would finish his career with an average of 4.2 yards per carry.) So dominant was Smith in the Cowboys backfield in 1993 that he was named both the NFL's regular-season Player of the Year and Most Valuable Player. And to top off his stellar season, Smith was also named MVP of Super Bowl XXVIII, as for the second year in a row the Cowboys defeated the Buffalo Bills, 30–13.

That season, Smith also gave what was undoubtedly the most courageous performance of his career. As the 11–4 Cowboys traveled to take on their divisional rival, the New York Giants, in the final game of the regular season, Dallas was once again playing for a top seed in the playoffs. With Dallas leading 13–0 late in the second quarter, Smith broke off a 46-yard run, but as he was tackled he landed hard on his left shoulder; halftime X-rays later confirmed it had been separated. After the tackle, Smith left the game for two plays, but then returned and stayed in the game. Teammates later told reporters they could hear Smith screaming in pain at the bottom of piles each time he was tackled. Nonetheless, he finished the regulation game with 168 rushing yards.

By the fourth quarter, the Giants had tied the score, and the game went into overtime. Despite his injury, however, Smith remained in the game—and was instrumental in the outcome. During the extra session he carried five times and caught three passes, helping to set up the game-winning field goal, as Dallas defeated New York, 16–13. After the game, Smith spent 15 hours in the hospital receiving an IV filled with pain medication. He had proven his commitment to the team's success.

There would be one final championship for Smith and the Cowboys: On January 28, 1996, in Super Bowl XXX, Dallas defeated the Pittsburgh Steelers, 27–17. The 1995 regular season, however, turned out to be Smith's final stellar performance. With a single-season-best 1,773 rushing yards, Smith earned his fourth and final rushing title; moreover, he also set a then–league record by scoring 25 rushing touchdowns. Yet even though he exceeded 1,000 rushing yards for the next six seasons, none of those performances equaled what he had accomplished in the championship years,

---

The NFL Career Rushing Leaders

Since 1932, when the NFL began keeping statistics, only six players have held the record for career rushing yardage. Each of them was inducted into the Professional Football Hall of Fame. They are listed below in chronological order:

Cliff Battles, 3,511 yards—Washington Redskins, Boston Braves, 1932, Boston Redskins, 1932–1936, Washington Redskins, 1937. Elected to the Hall of Fame in 1968.

Clarke Hinkle, 3,860 yards—Green Bay Packers, 1932–1941. At 5'11" tall, 202 pounds, Hinkle played during an era of two-way football, when players played both offense and defense. Elected to the Hall of Fame in 1964.

Steve Van Buren, 5,860 yards—Philadelphia Eagles, 1944–1951. The Eagles' number one draft pick in 1944, he won the NFL single-season rushing title four times. Elected to the Hall of Fame in 1965.

Joe Perry, 8,378 yards—San Francisco 49ers, 1948–1960, 1963; Baltimore Colts, 1961–1962. Nicknamed "The Jet," Perry was the first player to exceed 1,000 yards rushing in two consecutive seasons. Elected to the Hall of Fame in 1969.

Jim Brown, 12,312 yards—Cleveland Browns, 1957–1965. The 6'2", 232-pound fullback led the NFL in rushing a record eight times. He was Rookie of the Year in 1957 and a three-time Most Valuable Player. Elected to the Hall of Fame in 1971.

Walter Payton, 16,726 yards—Chicago Bears, 1975–1987. Nicknamed "Sweetness," the 5'10", 200-pound Payton had 77 games of over 100 rushing yards. He was named an All-Pro seven times and played in nine Pro Bowls. For many years he held the single-game rushing record of 275 yards. Tragically, Payton died of kidney disease at the age of 45 on November 1, 1999. Elected to the Hall of Fame in 1993.

Emmitt Smith, 18,355 yards

---

nor did the Cowboys ever return to their previous level of excellence. Although he broke Payton's record in 2002, that season, for the first time since his rookie year, Smith failed to reach 1,000 yards. When the season was ended, he and the Cowboys parted ways, and he spent two final frustrating seasons with the lowly Arizona Cardinals before finally ending his career following the 2004 season. By then, he had also set the record for most career carries, 4,409, and rushing touchdowns, 164. But most amazing, he had pushed the career rushing total to an unfathomable 18,355 yards. That record will be hard to beat.

As expected, over the years Smith has received many football accolades. In 2001, he was named the All-Time Offensive Player on *USA Today*'s 20th Anniversary All-USA team; he has also been named a member of the College Football Hall of Fame, as well as both the Texas and Florida Sports Halls of Fame. Further, in 1995, Smith was inducted, along with Michael Irvin and Troy Aikman, into the Dallas Cowboys Ring of Honor; and finally, the ultimate honor, in 2010, the first year of his eligibility, Smith was elected to the Professional Football Hall of Fame.

In retirement, he has kept right on running. Keeping a promise to his mother, in 1996 he returned to the University of Florida and earned his college degree. That has undoubtedly enhanced his postfootball career. Today, Smith is the majority partner and cochairman of ESmith Legacy, Inc., a Dallas-based commercial real estate and investment company; he and his wife, Pat, still live in Dallas with their four children. And in 2010, Smith realized one more accomplishment when he won the reality-based TV show, ABC's *Dancing with the Stars*. With Smith's perseverance and hard work, there are assuredly many more accomplishments to come.

Chip Greene

See also Brown, Jim; Dallas Cowboys; Payton, Walter; Pro Football Hall of Fame and Museum; Super Bowl

Suggested Resources

"Emmitt Smith." Pensapedia. http://www.pensapedia.com/wiki/Emmitt_Smith. Accessed October 9, 2011.

"Emmitt Smith." Pro Football Hall of Fame. http://www.profootballhof.com/hof/member.aspx?PlayerId=97. Accessed October 9, 2011.

"Emmitt Smith." Pro-Football-Reference.com. http://www
.pro-football-reference.com/players/S/SmitEm00.htm.
Accessed October 9, 2011.

Emmitt Smith Website. http://www.emmittsmith.com. Accessed October 9, 2011.

Pearlman, Jeff. *Boys Will Be Boys: The Glory Days and
Party Nights of the Dallas Cowboys Dynasty*. New
York: Harper, 2008.

Smith, Emmitt, with Steve Delsohn. *The Emmitt Zone*. New
York: Crown, 1994.

Smith, Red (1905–1982)

Red Smith was a Pulitzer Prize–winning journalist who wrote commentaries and columns on sport for such newspapers as the *Philadelphia Record*, *New York Herald Tribune*, and the *New York Times* from the 1930s until his death in 1982. Smith initially wanted to be a writer and journalist, but settled into the sports role. Reflective of his earlier ambitions, Smith's columns were noted for their literary qualities and absence of sport clichés, often reading more like short stories. In awarding Smith the Pulitzer, the selection committee praised Smith's sport commentary as "unique in the erudition, the literary quality, the vitality and freshness of viewpoint." Smith labored over his writing and took pride in his work, quipping, "Writing is easy, I just open a vein and bleed." As a writer, Smith's prose transcended the world of sport.

Smith was born Walter Wellesly Smith on September 25, 1905, in Green Bay, Wisconsin. His father operated a small grocery store, and the family was of modest means. As a young man, Smith enjoyed the outdoors, engaging in hiking, camping, and fishing. Many of his later columns would comment upon his passion for fishing, but often in a self-deprecating manner. Although Smith would later gain fame commenting on such team sports as baseball and football, he was not particularly drawn to athletics in his youth. Smith was a fine student with a passion for books, and he enjoyed reading the classical works of literature available in a credenza in the family living room. In 1922, Smith earned his high school degree from East High School in Green Bay.

After a brief stint as a filing clerk for a hardware company, Smith entered the University of Notre Dame in South Bend, Indiana, in the fall of 1923. Smith was a journalism major at Notre Dame, and by his junior year served as editor for the school yearbook, *The Dome*. He praised his journalism professors for fostering the habits of factual accuracy in reporting, a straightforward writing style, and a willingness to move beyond one's comfort level.

Following his graduation from Notre Dame in 1927, Smith pursued a career in journalism, accepting a position as a general assignment reporter for the *Milwaukee Sentinel* after he received little response from the more than 100 newspapers to which he sent letters of inquiry. Covering events from the social calendar to the crime beat, Smith lasted a year with the *Sentinel*. In 1928, he accepted a raise from $25 to $40 a week to work as a copy editor with the *St. Louis Star*. Serving as a copy editor, Smith learned a great deal about writing from some of the incoherent prose that came across his desk. While at the *Star-Times* (after a St. Louis newspaper consolidation), Smith was assigned to the sports page after most of the paper's sports staff was fired by the managing editor. His first assignment was a night football game, and Smith wrote the piece from the perspective of a glowworm that was attracted to the lights of the game.

After eight years in St. Louis, Smith was lured east by the *Philadelphia Record* to serve as a sportswriter and columnist. Smith accepted the position in Philadelphia because he received an increase in salary and the move brought him closer to New York City, which he considered to be the focal point for American writing. Although he still harbored literary ambitions beyond the sports page, Smith's output was increasingly focused upon sport. He wrote about baseball, football, boxing, and horse racing, while displaying little interest in basketball or hockey, which he termed "back and forth" sports. He would, however, occasionally enjoy the opportunity to venture beyond the world of sport. For example, in 1937 when the Philadelphia Athletics were training in Mexico City, Smith secured an interview with exiled Bolshevik Leon Trotsky, although the conservative Smith's portrayal of the revolutionary was hardly flattering.

With the *Philadelphia Record*, Smith began to write a full-time column and employed the byline of

Red Smith at the Belmont Park race track on opening day in 1951. (Library of Congress.)

Red Smith, reflecting both his red hair and disdain for his given name of Walter Wellesly. Beyond draft age in World War II, Smith continued to write his column, asserting that sport, and in some small ways his own writing, contributed to wartime national morale. And still seeking to expand his writing beyond the sports page, Smith was delighted when the *Saturday Evening Post* published one of his stories in 1944.

Smith's ambitions as a newspaperman, however, were realized in 1945 when sports editor Stanley Woodward of the *New York Herald* summoned the writer to the center of the American publishing world. Smith wrote his column for the *Herald Tribune* from 1945 until the folding of the paper in 1966. Although he would later receive his Pulitzer Prize while writing for the *New York Times*, Smith's 21 years with the *Herald Tribune* are usually considered to be his best work. He was syndicated in over 90 newspapers, and with the death of Grantland Rice in 1954, Smith's columns

were syndicated in more papers that any other sportswriter in the nation.

Although known for his direct style, Smith could engage in a little hyperbole. When describing the New York Giants' Bobby Thomson's "Shot Heard 'Round the World" home run in the 1951 National League playoffs, capping the greatest comeback in baseball history, Smith wrote, "Now the story ends. And there is no way to tell it. The art of fiction is dead. Reality has strangled invention. Only the utterly impossible, the inexpressibly fantastic, can ever be plausible again." But the Giants could work no magic against the New York Yankees in the 1951 World Series. Smith lamented, "But you don't beat the Yankees with a witch's broomstick. Not the Yankees, when there's money to be won." In fact, Smith had little use for the Yankees, asserting that rooting for them on the ball field was similar to rooting for U.S. Steel in labor negotiations.

As a journalist, Smith did not actively campaign for baseball integration, and his biographer, Ira Berkow, suggests that he was a little late on the Jackie Robinson story. Nevertheless, Smith became a great admirer of Robinson, and his description "the unconquerable doing the impossible" perhaps best captures the combative spirit of the racial pioneer. While able to grow in his appreciation of Robinson, Smith never forgave Dodger owner Walter O'Malley for moving the Dodgers from Brooklyn to Los Angeles. Smith described O'Malley's actions as "an unrelieved calamity, a grievous loss to the city and to baseball."

Confronted with a financial crisis, the *Herald Tribune* became part of the *World Journal Tribune* in 1966, but the paper folded within a year. Seeking an outlet for his columns, Smith wrote for the *Long Island Press* and *Women's Wear Daily*. In 1971, however, Smith believed that he had reached the pinnacle of his journalistic career when the 66-year-old writer joined the *New York Times*. Smith's columns for the *Times* were syndicated to 175 newspapers in the United States and over 200 papers in 30 nations. Smith continued to work hard at his craft, asserting that he was attempting to be "simpler, straighter, and purer in my language." Smith was awarded a Pulitzer Prize in 1976 for his *New York Times* columns, but many of his readers considered the award a quarter-century overdue.

Smith was also perceived as becoming more liberal in his old age, incorporating more political commentary into his columns. For example, while covering the 1968 Democratic National Convention in a nonsporting assignment, Smith condemned Mayor Richard Daley for the police state tactics employed in the streets of Chicago against demonstrators. He was also critical of the hypocrisy demonstrated by Olympic officials such as Avery Brundage, labeling the decision to continue the 1972 Munich Olympic Games after terrorist attacks on Israeli athletes as stupid. Smith also criticized the International Olympic Committee for attempting to impose 19th-century standards on 20th-century athletics.

On the other hand, Smith was not impressed with Muhammad Ali, and he considered Ali's rival Joe Frazier to be the better fighter. He condemned Ali's draft resistance during the Vietnam War, describing the boxer as a "slacker" and a "draft dodger." Smith displayed little patience for Ali's antics and politics as the writer considered himself a patriot and an anti-communist. Thus, following the 1979 invasion of Afghanistan by the Soviet Union, Smith proposed a boycott of the 1980 Moscow Olympic Games. Several weeks after Smith's column, President Jimmy Carter endorsed the boycott proposal.

Although he continued to write his columns, Smith's health was fading in the 1970s as he was suffering from cancer. In January 1982, Smith announced to his readers that he was going to cut back on his writing from four to three columns per week. However, this proved to be Smith's final column as on January 8, 1982, Smith died from a heart attack.

For nearly five decades Smith's writing graced the sport pages of America's newspapers. He set a high standard in which a literary approach was applied to the writing of sport in a humorous and direct fashion. Although Smith initially aspired to be a writer whose work would transcend sport, he never wrote a complete book. Numerous collections of his work, however, were published. Smith's self-deprecating style was perhaps best evident in his introduction to the 1974 collection *Strawberries in the Wintertime* when he wrote, "Finding a title for such a mixed bag can be a problem. I considered using a catchier title like *War and Peace*, *Wuthering Heights*, or *The Holy Bible*, but they struck me as dated." Smith's legacy continues to be recognized and honored by the University of Notre Dame with the Red Smith Lecture initiated in 1983. The Red Smith Lecture discusses journalism and the craft of writing. Among the distinguished recipients of the Red Smith Lectureship are James Reston, Art Buchwald, David Remnick, Ted Koppel, Jim Lehrer, Judy Woodruff, Tim Russert, and Frank Deford. Red Smith's passion for the written word remains alive and well.

See also Ali, Muhammad; New York Yankees; Rice, Grantland; Shot Heard 'Round the World

Ron Briley

Suggested Resources

Berkow, Ira. *Red: A Biography of Red Smith*. Lincoln, NE: Bison Books, 2007.

Berkow, Ira. "Red Smith, Sports Columnist Who Won Pulitzer, Dies at 76." January 16, 1982. http://www

.nytimes.com/1982/01/16/obituaries/red-smith-sports-columnist-who-won-pulitzer-dies-at-76.html. Accessed July 9, 2011.

Holtzman, Jerome. *No Cheering in the Press Box*. New York: Henry Holt, 1995.

Smith, Red. *Red Smith on Baseball: The Game's Greatest Writer on the Game's Greatest Years*. New York: Ivan R. Dee, 2001.

Smith, Red. *Red Smith Reader*. New York: Vantage, 1982.

Smith, Red. *Strawberries in the Wintertime*. New York: Quadrangle, 1974.

Smith, Red. *To Absent Friends*. New York: Atheneum, 1982.

Soccer Moms

The term "soccer moms" is as much, if not more, a political, rather than sports term. It refers mostly to the greater recognition of women between the ages of 30 and 45, approximately, as a potent political bloc that can have a significant influence on the outcome of elections, local, state, and national.

The term may have first appeared in the 1970s, but its use then was quite literal, that is, moms who transport, raise money for, and watch their kids play soccer. The rise in sports parity access as a result of Title IX was partly responsible for the rise in young girls playing soccer, but the sport has grown in interest among both genders in the past 20 years because of more exposure on television as well as the perceived limiting factors of size and strength that may shut many youngsters out of playing highly competitive football and basketball.

In the 1990s "soccer mom" was used by some political candidates to try to empower a voting base that had not received much attention before. A candidate for Denver City Council, Susan Casey, used the slogan, "A Soccer Mom for City Council" to show how much she was like the average member of the electorate. Casey was elected to the council.

The voting bloc became a real source of attention in the 1996 presidential election that pitted President Bill Clinton against the challenge of Republican senator Bob Dole. The challenger's campaign staff claimed that Clinton was appealing to a voting demographic that was referred to as soccer moms, that is,

A Soccer Mom Film

In 2008, a film was released directly to video entitled *Soccer Mom* and starring Emily Osment and Kristin Wilson. It had no political messages or aspirations; rather, it was a comedy about a teenage girls' soccer team and a mom who takes over as their coach, masquerading as a well-known European mentor when efforts at hiring the European collapse. Reviews found it humorous and possessed of nice messages about young girls and competition.

overburdened, middle-income working mothers who ferry their kids to various sports practices. The media picked up on the demographic and it was isolated in polls as suburban women, who overwhelmingly cast their ballots for Clinton.

The group has been described as college-educated, often not working or working from home, Caucasian, and antagonistic toward mothers who work outside the home. Nevertheless, there are still groups that are appealing to soccer moms on the basis of the interest in soccer, not just politics.

Since then, the term has sometimes been seen as a negative, as mothers who are overly involved in their kids' activities and overly protective of their children. Terms like "Tiger moms" have been associated with the same demographic.

Today, the demographic is not clearly either Democratic (as it was in 1996) or Republican, as President Bush hoped when his reelection team coined the term "security moms" and hoped to shift the "soccer moms" into that category. Women of that demographic still lean more Democratic in elections because of the appeal to their greater empowerment, rather than an appeal to them as conservative traditionalists.

Murry R. Nelson

Suggested Resources

Araton, Harvey. *Alive and Kicking: When Soccer Moms Take the Field and Change Their Lives Forever*. New York: Simon & Schuster, 2001.

Hong, Fan, and J. A. Mangan. *Soccer, Women, Sexual Liberation: Kicking off a New Era*. London: Frank Cass, 2004.

"Soccer Moms—We're Not a New Species But a Powerful Political Force." January 11, 1997. http://community

Lauren Sveen, right, of Westport Connecticut, kicks a soccer ball to her daughter Emma, 5, on the sidelines during a soccer game in Westport, October 14, 2000. (AP Photo/Douglas Healey.)

.seattletimes.nwsource.com/archive/?date=19970111 &slug=2518157. Accessed March 28, 2012.
"What Is a Soccer Mom?" wisegeek.com. http://www .wisegeek.com/what-is-a-soccer-mom.htm. Accessed March 28, 2012.

Sosa, Sammy

See McGwire, Mark and Sosa, Sammy

Space Jam (1996)

Space Jam is a Warner Bros. Entertainment, Inc. live action/animated film starring Michael Jordan, Wayne Knight, Bill Murray, and the entire Looney Tunes cast. Looney Tunes—also produced by Warner Bros.— is an animated cartoon series that famously features Bugs Bunny and Daffy Duck. Directed by Joe Pytka and released in 1996, *Space Jam* presents an alternate reason for Jordan's return to professional basketball after his retirement from the National Basketball Association (NBA) in 1994, during which time he competed in minor league baseball. The film showcases Jordan's unhappiness in baseball and simultaneously demonstrates the persistent extent of his basketball fame. Despite mixed reception, *Space Jam* opened as the number one movie the first weekend after its release in the United States and grossed over $230 million worldwide.

The movie begins with a press conference in which Jordan announces his decision to retire from the NBA. Solemnly, he expresses his desire to fulfill a childhood goal of playing professional baseball, an ambition connected to the recent and untimely death of his father. The former three-time NBA champion and two-time Most Valuable Player then commences a rather unsuccessful career in the minor leagues with the Birmingham Barons. Despite Jordan's basketball reprieve and baseball inconsequentiality, people nevertheless continue to fanatically worship "His Royal Airness." During one game, for example, following his fourth strikeout the fans award him with an exuberant standing ovation and a teammate comments that Jordan's failed attempt was a "good-looking strikeout."

At the same time, the film's greedy animated villain, Swackhammer, owner of the decrepit amusement park planet Moron Mountain, lusts for new attractions to increase his income. After discovering the comedic talents of the Looney Tunes, he decides that these characters would be a welcomed feature to counteract the sinister ambiance of the park. To obtain his newly desired possessions, Swackhammer sends the Nerdlucks—his enslaved, bow-tie-wearing minions—to bring the Tunes back to Moron Mountain. Opposed to a future of imprisonment, Bugs Bunny tricks the Nerdlucks into agreeing to compete for the Looney Tunes' fate. If the Tunes win, they remain free. If not, they become Moron Mountain's newest exhibit. Due to the Nerdlucks' small stature, Bugs Bunny picks basketball as the destiny-deciding contest.

Aware of their physical disadvantages and determined to abduct the Looney Tunes, the Nerdlucks travel to Earth to poach skills from the best players in the NBA. After scouting the options, the minions burglarize Charles Barkley, Muggsy Bogues, Shawn Bradley, Patrick Ewing, and Larry Johnson of talent, leaving the five professional athletes devoid of all ability and coordination, unable to even catch or throw a basketball. With these stolen goods—encased in a golden basketball—the previously miniature, un-athletic Nerdlucks transform into the powerful and terrifying Monstars.

Because he was not in the NBA at the time of the Nerdlucks' hijacking, Jordan's basketball aptitude remains intact. Therefore, fearful of a future that involves tedious nightly stand-up routines for humorless aliens, Bugs Bunny forcibly seeks his assistance. While Jordan is golfing with friends Larry Bird, Bill Murray, and publicist Stan Podolak (Wayne Knight), Yosemite Sam, the irate animated gunslinging cowboy, lassos Jordan's arm and pulls him through a hole, forcing him into the underground world of the Looney Tunes.

As soon as Jordan arrives, the Tunes surround him in excited awe—his iconic status even transcends spatial dimensions. Porky Pig, the affable animated pig most recognized for his stutter, immediately asks for Jordan's autograph. Also recognizing "His Airness," Tweety Bird, the animated yellow canary, alters his familiar slogan that describes a cat sighting ("I thought I taw a puddy tat. I did, I did see a puddy tat!") to "I did, I did see Michael Jordan!" After the hype dwindles, the Tunes explain the severity of the stakes. Jordan is initially reluctant to help the characters, stating that he now competes in baseball, not basketball. Only when Bugs Bunny suggests that Jordan's hesitance is due to a loss of talent does he agree to play.

To prepare for the Monstars, Jordan holds a practice for the Looney Tunes. There he meets his new animated teammates: Bugs Bunny, Daffy Duck, Pepe Le Pew, Porky Pig, Sylvester, the Tazmanian Devil, Tweety Bird, and Yosemite Sam. Within minutes, Jordan realizes the hopelessness of the situation. While very adept at comedy, the Tune Squad is quite inept at basketball. Yosemite Sam, for example, prefers shooting the ball with his gun rather than dribbling it with his hand.

The situation improves when the previously unknown Lola Bunny enters the gym. Created specifically for *Space Jam*, Lola Bunny combines athletic prowess with seductive charm. When she asks to try out for the team, a clearly infatuated Bugs Bunny challenges her to a game of "one on one," mistakenly

Chicago Bulls Michael Jordan poses with a cutout of Bugs Bunny at a news conference, Tuesday, June 20, 1995, in New York. (AP Photo/Marty Lederhandler.)

calling her "doll" in the process. Enraged, Lola Bunny defeats him, literally running circles around him before ending the contest with a slam dunk.

With the team formed, only one problem remains, a lack of proper footwear. Jordan, famously known for wearing Nikes while competing, was abducted during a golf outing and consequently only has golf shoes. To resolve the issue, Bugs Bunny and Daffy Duck travel to "3-D land" and successfully locate both the sneakers and Jordan's University of North Carolina shorts, which he wore under his Chicago Bulls uniform for every game. With the appropriate shoes and shorts, "Air Jordan" makes his reappearance in basketball.

Unfortunately, the Monstars finish the first half of the game ahead, 66–18, and a life of comedic bondage seems likely for the Tune Squad. In the locker room, the mangled and beaten Looney Tunes are ready to embrace defeat when Bugs Bunny passes around a water bottle filled with "Michael's Secret Stuff," a liquid form of Jordan's talents.

Unbeknown to the animated protagonists, however, the libation is not a magical ability-generating concoction but merely tap water. Nonetheless, bolstered by the placebo, the Looney Tunes resurge in the second half and strategically utilize their wackiness. Wile E. Coyote lights dynamite to steal the ball, Yosemite Sam shoots the opponents with his gun, and Pepe Le Pew deploys his skunk-stench to clear the lane. Through these eccentric techniques, the Tune Squad pulls to within one point of the Monstars. With little time remaining, the Tune Squad steals the ball and gives it to Jordan. As the final seconds tick down, Jordan literally flies from half-court for the game-winning dunk. The Looney Tunes remain free, the Nerdlucks rebel against Swackhammer, and the five dejected NBA players are reinvigorated with basketball talent. Most importantly, Jordan returns to professional basketball.

Grossing over $90 million domestically, *Space Jam* is the highest-earning basketball movie to date. Popular with children, the film finished fourth out of all the PG-rated movies released the same year. The inspirational song featured in the film, "I Believe I Can Fly," performed by R. Kelley, won a Grammy for "Best Song Written Specifically for a Motion Picture or Television" and was also nominated for the MTV Movie Award, "Best Movie Song."

Despite the popular reception, reviewers critiqued *Space Jam* for its overt commercialism. The movie itself was inspired by Nike television advertisements that featured Jordan and Bugs Bunny competing against alien cartoon characters. Realizing the campaign's success, Warner Bros. conceptualized the film. Furthermore, several occurrences in the movie suggest a commercial intent. For example, Jordan insists upon playing in his Nikes, a demand that not only produces a miniature quest for Bugs Bunny and Daffy Duck but also allows for favorable recognition from the Monstars. Warner Bros. also engaged in self-promotion; when explaining the composition of the Looney Tunes to Jordan, Daffy Duck shows him the WB logo taped to his backside, then proceeds to kiss it. Finally, along with overcommercialization, *Space Jam* was critiqued for poor integration of live action and animation. Several critics compared it negatively to Touchstone's 1988 film *Who Framed Roger Rabbit*, the only live action/animated movie to date that has won three Academy Awards.

Although many perceived the commercialization negatively, certain sequences suggest the writers were purposefully mocking Jordan's long-lasting fame and fandom. For example, when Jordan strikes out in the beginning of the movie, the coach tells the assistant that Jordan "looks good in that uniform" and that "you can't teach that." Similarly, Jordan's publicist later exclaims, "C'mon, Michael, it's game time. Get your Hanes on, lace up your Nikes, grab your Wheaties and your Gatorade, and we'll pick up a Big Mac on the way to the ballpark." The film clearly plays upon Jordan's celebrity and endorsements. Thus, despite his leave from basketball, unsuccessful attempt in baseball, and mediocre venture into acting, *Space Jam* demonstrates that Jordan's reputation is everlasting.

Lindsay Parks Pieper

See also Advertising and Sport; Barkley, Charles; Bird, Larry; Gatorade; Jordan, Michael; National Basketball Association; Nike, Inc.; Wheaties

Suggested Resources
Carney, Charles, and Gina Misiroglu. *Space Jammin': Michael and Bugs Hit the Big Screen*. Nashville, TN: Rutledge Hill Press, 1996.
Space Jam. IMDb. http://www.imdb.com/title/tt0117705/fullcredits#cast. Accessed October 10, 2011.
Space Jam. Roger Ebert Reviews. http://rogerebert.suntimes.com/apps/pbcs.dll/article?AID=/19961115/REVIEWS/611150. Accessed October 10, 2011.
Space Jam. Rottentomatoes.com. http://www.rottentomatoes.com/m/space_jam/. Accessed October 10, 2011.

"Spahn and Sain and Pray for Rain"

Warren Spahn (1921–2003) and Johnny Sain (1917–2006) were the two mainstay pitchers for the Boston Braves during their 1948 pennant race. Their significance to the team was memorialized in a poem in the September 14, 1948, *Boston Post* by the sports editor, Gerry Hern. Hern hoped that the left-handed Spahn and the right-handed Sain would be healthy enough to pitch on one-day rest and rainouts and thus carry the pitching staff and the team to victory. The full poem is given below, though the Boston faithful shortened the poem to "Spahn and Sain and Pray for Rain."

First we'll use Spahn
then we'll use Sain
Then an off day
followed by rain
Back will come Spahn
followed by Sain
And followed
we hope
by two days of rain.

The poem was inspired by an amazing 12-day stretch in early September when the two combined to win eight games. No other pitcher started for Boston because the only days Spahn or Sain did not start were scheduled off days or rain days. Thanks in large part to their performances, Boston won the 1948 National League pennant, the team's last pennant in that city. They lost, however, to the Cleveland Indians in six games in the World Series. Sain won the opening game and lost game four. Spahn started and lost game

Warren Spahn, left, and Johnny Sain, the pitching mainstays of the Boston Braves, pose during a workout in preparation for the upcoming World Series against the Cleveland Indians, on October 5, 1948. (AP Photo.)

two and won game five after entering the game in relief in the fourth inning. In game six, Spahn entered in relief in the eighth inning with the Braves losing by two; although Spahn held the Indians to one more run, the Braves still lost.

Together Spahn and Sain had a good season in 1948, and Sain had a remarkable one. Sain was the runner-up for the National League Most Valuable Player award that year after leading the league in wins, complete games, and innings pitched. He won 24 games and lost 15. Spahn won 15 games and lost 12. This is not to diminish the skills of the other two pitchers, Bill Voiselle, who won and lost 13 games, and Vern Bickford, who won 11 and lost 5. Thanks to the hot streak at the end of the regular season, however, Spahn and Sain got the poem and a certain degree of immortality.

Although Sain had a much better 1948 season, Spahn had an amazing career as a pitcher. Born and raised in Buffalo, New York, after he married his home

became Oklahoma where he and his family had a ranch outside of Tulsa. He entered the major leagues in 1942 but was sent to the minors after just a few games. At the end of that season, he entered the military and served three years in the European theater during World War II as a combat engineer. When he returned to the major leagues in 1946, he began what would become a Hall of Fame career that lasted through 1965. During that time he won more games than any other left-handed pitcher in baseball history (363) with an ERA of 3.09. He was named to 17 All-Star teams, won four National League Pitcher of the Year awards (1952, 1957, 1958, and 1961), and won the Cy Young Award in 1957. That same year of 1957 he helped the (now) Milwaukee Braves win the World Series.

As a player, Spahn was noted for his lanky build and his amazingly high leg-kick. He attributed his success as a pitcher to his year-round conditioning and his concentration on the game. Although he started

Modern Couplets

The lyric catchiness of "Spahn and Sain and Pray for Rain" has endured for over 60 years, and baseball writers revive the line for a variety of reasons.

Some use it to criticize the modern pitching techniques of only pitching a few innings and having multiple days of rest. Sain in 1948 had at one point pitched nine complete games in 29 days. In 1986, pitchers averaged four days of rest and *Chicago Tribune* columnist Jerome Holtzman bemoaned the modern weakness.

Sometimes when a team has two dominant pitchers, the writers try to use similar poetry. In 1977 *New York Times* columnist Deane McGowen suggested "Reuschel and Sutter and stay out of the clutter." Rick Reuschel finished third in the Cy Young voting that year and won 20 games, and Bruce Sutter had 31 saves that year. In 2006 Sutter was elected to the Hall of Fame, but in 1977 the Cubs failed to win the pennant and the rhyme disappeared.

In 2004, when Pedro Martinez and Curt Schilling won a combined 37 games (16 for Martinez and 21 for Schilling), *New York Times* columnist Richard Goldstein suggested during the American League playoffs that Boston fans adopt the phrase "It's Martinez and Schilling if the weather is willing." Although Boston swept the St. Louis Cardinals to win the Red Sox's first World Series since 1918, the phrase did not catch on.

his career as a fastball pitcher, as he aged he added a range of additional pitches and he focused on the batters. He kept track of their strengths and weaknesses and pitched to them accordingly.

Spahn's consistency and his years of success made it difficult for him to retire from the game. At the age of 43, the Braves traded him to the Mets, but he continued to try to pitch the next season. In 1966, he was a pitching coach in Mexico, and he pitched in a game there at the age of 45. He was elected to the Hall of Fame in 1973, his first year of eligibility.

Johnny Sain, born in Arkansas, had a solid career in baseball. He pitched in the major leagues from 1942 through 1955 (less three years in the navy during World War II) and won 139 games while losing 116. His career ERA was 3.49. Toward the end of his career, he became a relief pitcher and in 1954 had a league-leading 22 saves for the New York Yankees. He played on three World Series–winning Yankee teams (1951, 1952, and 1953).

After retiring as a player, Sain became a successful if somewhat controversial pitching coach. His success was reflected in part when he coached on three World Series champions (the 1961 and 1962 Yankees and the 1968 Detroit Tigers). He was noted for emphasizing to his pitchers the power of positive thinking and the power of deviousness. He taught his pitchers to use the best mechanics for their style and taught them to believe in themselves. In 1969 *New York Times* columnist Bill Surface argued he was the best in the business.

Sain's confidence in his pitchers sometimes resulted in conflict with his managers. Sain firmly believed that any pitch that got a batter out was a good pitch even if the pitch resulted in a line drive and a leaping catch by a fielder to make that out. His manager felt differently and Sain refused to apologize. Sain was fired, only to be hired by another team at one of the highest salaries a pitching coach had ever been paid.

See also Boston Red Sox; St. Louis Cardinals; World Series

Sarah K. Fields

Suggested Resources
Caruso, Gary. *The Braves Encyclopedia*. Philadelphia: Temple University Press, 1995.
Kaese, Harold. *The Boston Braves, 1871–1953*. Boston: Northeastern University Press, 2004.
"Spahn and Sain and Pray for Rain." Baseball Almanac. www.baseball-almanac.com. Accessed December 21, 2010.
"Spahn and Sain and Pray for Rain." Baseball-Reference .com. www.baseball-reference.com. Accessed December 21, 2010.
Surface, Bill. "Johnny Sain Teaches the Power of Positive Thinking." April 20, 1969. http://selct.nytimes.com/gst/abstract.html?res=F10B1FFD3A5913748DDDA90A94DC405B898AF1D3&scp=1&sq=johnny+sain+teaches&st=p. Accessed September 18, 2011.

Spelling Bees

In the 2000s, the spelling bee, an American pastime since cold winter nights in 18th-century Puritan New England, cropped up in a range of popular media. Most prominently, the documentary *Spellbound* (2002) was nominated for the Academy Award for best documentary, edged out by Michael Moore's *Bowling for Columbine*. In 2007, the International Documentary Association named it the fourth-best documentary of all time (right behind *Bowling for Columbine*). Spelling bees were also critical to the plots of the feature film *Akeelah and the Bee* (2006); the Broadway musical comedy *The 25th Annual Putnam County Spelling Bee* (2005); the novel *Bee Season* (2000), which was made into a movie of the same name in 2005; and the young adult novel *Spelldown* (2007).

Millions of children—about two million in 1925, the year of the first national bee, and about 10 million today—participate in local bees every year. The winners proceed to regional bees, which are sponsored by English-language newspapers, and then to the national bee, currently known as the Scripps National Spelling Bee and sponsored by the E. W. Scripps Company since 1941. Into the 1970s, the national bee had 40 to 50 competitors; since then the number of sponsors, and hence the number of spellers, has climbed to 288.

Since 1994, the later rounds of the bee have been broadcast on ESPN, increasing the bee's exposure in popular culture. Writer/director Doug Atchison says he first got the idea for *Akeelah and the Bee* after watching the 1994 broadcast. Since 2006—likely reflecting the increasing popularity of the bee after *Spellbound*—the finals have been broadcast on ABC during prime time. Many spellers set the goal of making it to the televised rounds.

The broadcasts produce unlikely media darlings: brilliant, often awkward middle-schoolers who spell words few English speakers have ever encountered. Akshay Buddiga made many a blooper reel in 2004 when he fainted, then popped up to quickly spell his word correctly, eventually coming in second. So did 1997 winner Rebecca Sealfon, the first home-schooler to win the bee, when she had the chance to spell the championship word. She was so sure she knew "euonym" that she screamed each letter into the microphone while triumphantly pumping her fists in the air with each letter.

All words are drawn from the *Webster's Unabridged Dictionary*, and some competitors, like 2004 champion David Tidmarsh, report they have studied the whole thing. Spellers rely less on memorization, though, than on extensive knowledge of word roots and the spelling patterns of languages such as German, Spanish, French, Italian, Latin, and Greek.

Any serious national competitor is quick to point out that there are no guarantees at the national bee. The luck of the draw fells many top contenders, while many winners admit they would have missed some words given to others. No one knows this better than Samir Patel. In 2003, the audience fell in love with the pint-sized nine-year-old. Given the word "onychophagy," he did not ask for the definition. Instead he asked, "Does it mean the biting of fingernails?" To the audience's delight, it did. The oldest competitors are 14, and they towered over Samir, who was still a child but who had already stunned followers of the bee circuit by winning the North South Foundation's bee, an event that helps Indian American students train for the national bee, when he was only seven. But Samir, who finished third in 2003, never won the National Spelling Bee. He competed four more times and placed 27th, 2nd, 14th, and, in his last year of eligibility, 34th.

Spellbound follows competitors in the 1999 National Spelling Bee who represent the diversity among bee-goers. Though the documentary is structured with profiles first and the suspenseful bee second, some of the students profiled seem to have been interviewed after the bee, including the film's most eccentric character, the rubber-faced Harry Altman, and the champion, Nupur Lala.

The film begins with Angela Arenivar of Perryton, Texas, winning her regional bee. Angela is the daughter of Mexican immigrants who speak little English. As they stand around at the ranch where her father, Ubaldo, has worked for 20 years, her brother, Jorge, interprets. His father came to the United States to give his children a better life, Jorge explains. The opportunity to see his daughter on stage at the National Spelling Bee, Jorge remarks, shows that he achieved his goal.

The bee is characterized by a large number of children of immigrants, including two of the other students profiled, the winner, Nupur, and Neil Kadakia. Neil exemplifies three other characteristics of many top spellers: he is the younger sibling of a previous top speller, he is returning to the national bee, and he has

Rebecca Sealfon, 13, of Brooklyn, New York, reacts after winning the 70th annual National Spelling Bee in Washington, D.C., May 29, 1997. (AP Photo/Ron Edmonds.)

a parent who is heavily invested in preparing his son for the contest. Indeed, Neil's father overshadows his son in *Spellbound* as he expounds on the value of hard work and the ability of anyone with the right work ethic to make it in America. In a slyly humorous moment, Neil's father mispronounces "epitome" while speed drilling his son.

April DeGideo of Ambler, Pennsylvania, represents middle America. Her always-smiling mother has decorated the house with a bee motif in honor of April's pursuit. Her father, a bar owner who shrugs and says he does not consider himself a success story, shines with pride as his daughter finishes among the top spellers at nationals. Ted Brigham of Rolla, Missouri, who grew up in a double-wide trailer and has had trouble fitting in at a new school, looks forward

to being around his intellectual peers at the national bee. In many ways he is the socioeconomic opposite of Emily Stagg of New Haven, Connecticut, whose au pair once traveled with her family to the national bee and who is returning for the third time.

Ashley White, an African American girl being raised by a single mother in Washington, D.C., rounds out the portrait of the bee as a ticket to using one's brain power to rise above one's circumstances. Her mother reveals much about their context in poverty-stricken D.C. when she expresses her hope to see Ashley graduate from high school, a goal that for many bee parents is only a hoop to be jumped through on the way to advanced postgraduate degrees.

The film tenderly and humorously presents these children as a cross-section of America, lingering on shots of the enormous American flag that hangs in the center of the Grand Hyatt in Washington, D.C., the long-time site of the bee. This does not take into account that, despite its official name, the bee does include non-Americans because several English-language newspapers around the world sponsor spellers. In 1998, the champion was Jody-Anne Maxwell of Kingston, Jamaica, and spellers from Canada have often placed well.

The documentary's tagline, "Everyone wants the last word," is a reminder that only one person can win a spelling bee. (The exception is if the last two spellers at nationals exhaust all 25 championship words. There were co-champions in 1950, 1957, and 1962.) Champion Rebecca Sealfon told a reporter she thought the spelling bee should be abolished—after all, every competitor but her was suffering at that moment from having lost.

Akeelah and the Bee is a fictional rendering of the National Spelling Bee. Producer Sid Ganis attributes the fact that *Akeelah and the Bee* was funded due to the success of *Spellbound*. The film follows 11-year-old Akeelah Anderson (KeKe Palmer), an African American girl growing up in a poor area of Los Angeles and being raised by her single mother (Angela Bassett) after her father's death from random street violence. After Akeelah shows promise as a speller and wins her disadvantaged school's first-ever bee, her principal hopes Akeelah's spelling career can bring positive publicity and even funding to the school. But Akeelah feels uncomfortable with her talent and fears she will not be able to fit in if she follows an intellectual pursuit.

The principal persuades his old college friend, Dr. Joshua Larabee (Laurence Fishburne), an English professor who competed in the National Bee as a child, to coach Akeelah. The relationship between Akeelah, who has lost her father, and Dr. Larabee, who has lost a daughter, reveals over the course of the film that competitive spelling encompasses issues of character development, work ethic, confidence in oneself, and poise. The film also stresses the way individual spelling success can affect a community and make learning attractive. When Akeelah prevails in the district bee she becomes a local celebrity. She finds she has "50,000 coaches"—everyone from an elderly man at a coffee shop to her brother's gang leader wants to drill her on spelling words. The scenes at the National Spelling Bee are imbued with a sense of authenticity by Dr. Jacques Bailly, the National Spelling Bee pronouncer and 1980 national champion. Bailly also served as the film's technical adviser.

The musical comedy *The 25th Annual Putnam County Spelling Bee* features six middle-schoolers competing for a trip to the National Spelling Bee. In each performance, four audience members also compete. Often, a local celebrity such as a politician or television newscaster is invited to compete. Some versions of the show are labeled "Parent-Teacher Conferences," with the humor geared toward adults.

The Putnam County spellers represent a range of personalities, such as the former champion favored to win again who in his arrogance misspeaks and is disqualified; a lonely girl whose parents do not bother to attend the bee; an overstressed, overachieving student who misspells a word to escape the bee; and William Barfée (whose name is constantly mispronounced "barfy"), who taps the letters with one foot while spelling. An ex-convict named Mitch is performing his community service by comforting the students with juice boxes after their misspellings, perhaps a nod to the "comfort room" at the National Spelling Bee that students enter directly after misspelling.

The novel *Bee Season* by Myla Goldberg is about the younger daughter of a rabbi who feels like the only unsuccessful person in her family until she discovers her talent for spelling. It treats darker situations than most spelling bee tales. Eliza's father, interested in Jewish mysticism, sees her talent for letters as a sign of her greater propensity for mysticism than his and pays attention to her for the first time. The novel proceeds from the innocence of Eliza winning her first class bee to the collapse of her family as her mother is admitted to a psychiatric hospital and her brother leaves home to join the International Society for Krishna Consciousness. The 2005 movie stars Richard Gere and Juliette Binoche as the troubled parents. The young adult novel *Spelldown* by Karon Luddy is set in 1968 South Carolina. It traces a young girl's budding love for language and the influence that her Latin teacher has on her despite her chaotic life.

Brooke Sherrard

Suggested Resources

Maguire, James. *American Bee: The National Spelling Bee and the Culture of Word Nerds.* Emmaus, PA: Rodale, 2006.
National Spelling Bee Website. http://www.spellingbee.com/. Accessed October 4, 2011.
Spellbound. IMDb. http://www.imdb.com/title/tt0334405/. Accessed October 4, 2011.

Spitz, Mark (1950–)

Mark Andrew Spitz has made an important contribution to sports and American popular culture as the first athlete to win seven gold medals in an Olympics. He earned these medals at the 1972 Munich Olympics, setting world records for his swimming times. In addition to these seven gold medals, he also earned four medals (two gold, one silver, and one bronze) at the 1968 Olympics. He was named World Swimmer of the Year in 1969, 1971, and 1972. Within two years of retiring from swimming in 1974, Spitz had monetized his athletic success into corporate sponsorships that made him a millionaire. In 1999, his 33 world records were still such an outstanding example of athletic success that he was the only swimmer to make ESPN's *Sports Century 50 Greatest Athletes* list, coming in at number 33 on the list. His record number of seven gold medals earned at one Olympics was not broken until 2008 when Michael Phelps, another world record–setting swimmer, won eight gold medals. Spitz is one of only

Teammates Jerry Heidenreich, left, and Tom Bruce carry U.S. superswimmer Mark Spitz on their shoulders after they won the gold medal in the Olympic 4 ×100-meter medley relay in Munich, Germany, June 2, 1972. (AP Photo/fls.)

five Olympians to win nine or more career gold medals (the others are Larisa Latynina, Paavo Nurmi, Carl Lewis, and Michael Phelps).

Spitz is a Jewish American who grew up in Hawaii and California. He was born on February 10, 1950, in Modesto, California. He is the oldest of three children. Between ages two and six, his family lived in Honolulu, Hawaii, and he learned to swim at Waikiki Beach. When his family returned to the mainland, they moved to Sacramento. Between ages 6 and 14 (1956–1963), Spitz swam and competed for the private Arden Hills Swim and Tennis Club. His coach was Sherm Chavoor, who trained and developed a host of other Olympic swimming champions including Mike Burton (1968 Mexico Olympics—two gold medals and 1972 Munich Olympics—1 gold medal); Ellie Daniel (1968 Mexico

Olympics—one gold medal, one silver medal, and one bronze medal); Jeff Float (1984 Los Angeles Olympics—one gold medal); Debbie Meyer (1968 Mexico Olympics—three gold medals); Sue Pederson (1968 Mexico Olympics—two gold medals and two silver medals); and John Nelson (1964 Tokyo Olympics—one silver medal and 1968 Mexico Olympics—one gold medal and one bronze medal). Under Chavoor's guidance, Spitz earned 17 national records and had one world record by the time he was 10 years old.

Between 1964 and 1968, while he was in high school, Mark Spitz trained with swimming coach George F. Haines at the Santa Clara Swim Club. While Mark Spitz was training at the Santa Clara Swim Club with Coach Haines, he attended Santa Clara High School. In 1965, he qualified for his first international competition. He was selected to become a member of the U.S. delegation attending the seventh Maccabiah Games in Tel Aviv. The Maccabiah Games are an international athletic competition held every four years in Israel and they are similar to the Olympics. In August 1965, 1,200 athletes from 25 different countries participated in the games. It was the largest event since World War II and brought an estimated 10,000 tourists to Israel. Team USA had 200 athletes and a strong swim team that included 15-year-old Mark Spitz. He won four gold medals, broke three Maccabiah records, and was named the most outstanding athlete.

Throughout high school, Spitz continued to break records. In 1966, at age 16, he won his first National U.S. Amateur Athletic Union (AAU) title in the 100-meter butterfly. This was the first out of a total 31 National U.S. AAU titles that he would acquire during his swimming career. In 1967, he broke his first world record with a time of 4:10.60 in the 400-meter freestyle. That summer, he went to the Pan American Games in Winnipeg, Canada, and won five gold medals. By 1968, he held 10 world records.

At the 1968 Mexico City Olympics, Mark Spitz expected to be a standout. He won two team gold medals in the 4×100-meter freestyle relay and the 4×200-meter freestyle relay. However, he was disappointed in his quest to earn gold medals in individual events. Although he held the world record in the 100-meter butterfly, he was unable to meet his own time and came in second to fellow American Doug Russell to win a silver medal. In the 100-meter freestyle he came in third for a bronze medal.

In the fall of 1968, he enrolled as a predental student at Indiana University and later became a member of Phi Kappa Psi fraternity. He chose Indiana University so that he could train with swimming coach James Edward "Doc" Counsilman, who had been the coach of Team USA swimming at the 1968 Mexico City Olympics. Coach Counsilman also coached at the 1964 and 1976 Olympics. Throughout his career, he would coach over 60 Olympic swimmers. As head swimming coach at Indiana University (1957–1990), his teams won numerous titles and championships. A pioneer and innovator in the sport, he was known for watching his swimmers underwater and using film to study their training practice sessions and meets. Never one to miss an opportunity, in 1979 he became the then-oldest person to swim the English Channel. While swimming at Indiana University with Doc Counsilman between 1968 and 1972, Spitz was known by his fellow swimming teammates as "The Shark." As a college student, he earned eight individual NCAA titles. In 1969, he attended the eighth Maccabiah Games, won six gold medals, and for the second time was named outstanding athlete of the Maccabiah Games. In 1971, he was awarded the James E. Sullivan Award as the top amateur athlete in the United States based on merit including qualities of leadership, character, and sportsmanship.

Spitz earned his triumph and fame as a top Olympian with seven gold medals at the 1972 Munich Olympic Games. He not only earned the gold medals, in each event he set new world records. These included: (1) 100-meter freestyle, 00:51:22; (2) 200-meter freestyle, 01:52:78; (3) 100-meter butterfly, 00:54:27; (4) 200-meter butterfly, 02:00:70; (5) 4×100-meter freestyle relay, 03:26:42; (6) 4x200-meter freestyle relay, 07:35:78; and (7) 4×100-meter medley relay, 03:48:16. It was at the 1972 Olympics that Mark Spitz became known for his classic mustached swimmer image that would help him win major corporate endorsements and become known in American popular culture as a sports celebrity. At the time, many swimmers believed that shaving body hair helped increased their times. In a complete reversal of this mindset, Spitz swam with a mustache. He has said that he grew it in response to a college challenge that he couldn't grow one and had

planned to shave it off. However, because it became the subject of so much discussion, he decided to keep it.

Spitz made another impression at the 1972 Munich Olympics when he arrived barefoot carrying his shoes to receive his gold medal for the 200-meter freestyle race. After the playing of the American national anthem, he waved with his shoes in his hands. He was later questioned by the International Olympic Committee about whether he was promoting the manufacturer of his shoes. He explained that this had been accidental, that he had in fact been rushed to get to the podium and had not had time to put his shoes on. He was cleared of any product placement charges.

A third image came out of the 1972 Munich Olympics. On September 5, early in the morning and only hours after Spitz had won his final medal, Palestinian terrorists attacked the Olympic Village. They killed two Israeli athletes and took another nine athletes hostage. Spitz was unharmed, although he had been sleeping near where the attacks took place. Attending a press conference the next day he expressed his concern for the hostages. He then left for London before the closing ceremonies. He would be criticized by some in the media for moving on and discussing his future plans and potential endorsements before the hostage crisis was over. Unfortunately, all nine hostages were killed during the rescue attempt.

Following the Munich Olympics, at the age of 22, Spitz retired from swimming. Immediately, he signed with the William Morris Agency, a world-renowned talent agency, to promote his good-looking, athletic, Olympic-gold, mustache image. He was soon doing commercials for Schick razors, the California Milk Advisory Board, Adidas, Speedo, and other products. He was featured in a famous and very popular "pin-up" poster that showed him in a swimsuit with his seven gold medals. Within the next two years (1972–1974), he made an estimated $7 million. This immediate success with endorsements, however, did not translate into commercials or an acting career in Hollywood. He did make numerous guest appearances on TV shows between 1973 and 1974 but received a lukewarm reception. These included *The Tonight Show with Johnny Carson*, *Bob Hope Special*, *The Sonny and Cher Comedy Hour*, and *The Dean Martin Celebrity Roast*.

Santa Clara Swim Club

Over the years, swimmers from this club (including Mark Spitz) have earned 71 Olympic medals: 42 gold, 18 silver, and 11 bronze. In 1960, Coach Haines was selected as head coach for the U.S. swim team headed to the Rome Olympics. Seven of his swimmers from the Santa Clara Swim Club qualified to make the trip with him. During the 1960, 1964, and 1968 Olympics, his swimmers from the Santa Clara Swim Club on the medal podium included Lynn Burke (1960 Rome Olympics—two gold medals); Steve Clark (1964 Tokyo Olympics—three gold medals); Donna de Varona (1964 Tokyo Olympics—two gold medals); George Harrison (1960 Rome Olympics—one gold medal); Paul Hait (1960 Rome Olympics—one gold medal); Claudio Kolb (1964 Tokyo Olympics—one silver medal and 1968 Mexico City Olympics—two gold medals); Don Schollander (1964 Tokyo Olympics—four gold medals and one silver medal, the most medals of anyone at that Olympics); and Chris von Saltza (1960 Rome Olympics—three gold medals and one silver medal). Haines left the Santa Clara Swim Club in 1974 to become an NCAA coach at UCLA and later Stanford University.

Spitz became a family man and sports commentator. In May 1973, he married Suzy Weiner in a traditional Jewish service at the Beverly Hills Hotel. She was a graduate of UCLA and a daughter of one of his father's business acquaintances. They had two sons, Matthew, born in 1981, and Justin, born in 1991. Spitz was a TV sports commentator at the 1976 Montreal Olympics and 1984 Los Angeles Olympics. He continued to be honored for his outstanding swimming accomplishments including inductions into the International Hall of Fame in 1977, International Jewish Sports Hall of Fame in 1979, and United States Olympic Hall of Fame in 1983. In 1985, he returned to the Maccabiah games to light the opening torch. Aside from sports, he ran a successful real estate company in Beverly Hills, became an entrepreneur, and took up blue water ocean racing (sailing). In 1981, he competed in his third Trans-Pac Yacht Race from Los Angeles to Hawaii, finishing third.

In the 1990s, Spitz returned to swimming without his mustache. According to a *Sports Illustrated* article from February 1988, after thinking about shaving off his mustache for a year, he finally did. The next year,

at age 39, he started training for a comeback with his eye on the 1992 Barcelona Olympic tryouts. He failed to qualify for the Olympics in the 50-meter butterfly by 2.44 seconds.

After his attempted Olympic comeback, Spitz returned to his private business investments. He also makes motivational speeches and the occasional commercial endorsement. These include a 1998 TV commercial for PlayStation that featured him with Evel Knievel; a 2004 TV commercial for Sprint PCS; spokesperson work for Medco Pharmacy; a 2007 Go-Daddy TV commercial with Amanda Beard; and a 2007 Orbitrek Elite fitness workout. In 2005, he made several appearances for the 17th Maccabiah Games including participating as a member of the U.S. delegation and as a speaker at the JCC Maccabiah Opening Ceremonies in Richmond, Virginia. In 2006, he narrated *Freedom Fury*, a documentary produced by Quentin Tarantino and Lucy Liu that debuted at the Tribeca Film Festival. The movie was about one of the most famous matches in water polo history known as "Blood in the Water," held during the 1956 Melbourne Olympics between Hungary and Russia at the same time that these two countries were involved in the Hungarian Revolution of 1956.

In 2008, Spitz received a great deal of media attention before and after Michael Phelps broke Spitz's gold medal–winning record at the 2008 Beijing Olympics. Rumors abound that Spitz did not attend the Olympics because he did not want to witness Phelps's success in person. On August 14, 2008, Spitz appeared on NBC's *Today Show* and Los Angeles KNBC-4's *Today in L.A.* to set the record straight. He let the world know that he had not been invited to attend the 2008 Olympics in any type of official capacity, which is why he was not there in person. He praised Michael Phelps and called his 100-meter butterfly race "epic."

Margaret Carroll Boardman

See also Advertising and Sport; ESPN Channels; Lewis, Carl; 1968 Olympic Games, Mexico City; Phelps, Michael; *Sports Illustrated*

Suggested Resources
Brody, Seymour. "Mark Spitz." Jewish Virtual Library. http://www.jewishvirtuallibrary.org/jsource/biography/Spitz.html. Accessed February 20, 2012.

Bruns, Bill. "The Shark Gets Soft." July 8, 1974. http://www.people.com/people/archive/article/0,,20064247,00.html. Accessed February 12, 2012.

Foster, Richard J. *Mark Spitz: The Extraordinary Life of an Olympic Champion*. Santa Monica, CA: Santa Monica Press, 2008.

Goodman, Dean. "Mark Spitz Makes Splash about Beijing Invite." August 2, 2008. http://www.reuters.com/article/sportsNews/idUSN1935785920080802?feedType=RSS&feedName=sportsNews. Accessed January 30, 2012.

"Mark Spitz: It's Time Somebody Else Takes the Throne." 2008. http://www.msnbc.msn.com/id/26194898/. Accessed January 30, 2012.

Mark Spitz Website. www.markspitzusa.com/. Accessed February 15, 2012.

Spitz, Mark, and Mickey Herskowitz. *Seven Golds: Mark Spitz' Own Story: The Growing Up of a Gold Medal Swimmer*. Garden City, NY: Doubleday, 1984.

The Sporting News

The Sporting News was founded as a weekly newspaper in St. Louis, Missouri, on St. Patrick's Day in March 1886 by Alfred H. Spink. Spink had a lifelong association with baseball's beginnings as America's national pastime and his national sports newspaper emerged right after World War I. For many years, *The Sporting News* was considered the top chronicler in the field of professional baseball. Prior to founding *The Sporting News*, Spink had been the sports editor of the *Missouri Chronicle* and *St. Louis Chronicle*. He had also been the founding editor of the *St. Louis World*, focusing on sports, especially baseball, horse racing, and other popular forms of entertainment, including theater. He also wrote for the *St. Louis Dispatch*. He liked to say that he was attracted to the drama and the excitement of real life, and especially sports. For a short time he ran a racetrack and at one point, this founder of what would become one of the nation's most celebrated sports publications invested heavily in a theatrical production, a play about the Kentucky Derby entitled *The Derby Winner*. But the play flopped very badly.

Spink emerged from an extended family tradition of writing, with an emphasis on sportswriting. His brother William C. "Billy" Spink once served as the sports editor of the *St. Louis Globe-Democrat*. As early as four years prior to founding *The Sporting News*, Spink became instrumental in the creation of the American Association. Alfred Spink was also one of the organizers of the St. Louis Brown Stockings, a team that resigned from the National League due to a gambling scandal and an enormous amount of accumulated debt, and then later was reborn in another form as the St. Louis Browns.

Spink recruited Christian von der Ahe to serve as that team's owner, a means of helping form a club association to compete with teams in comparable locations. He aggressively promoted the sport when the original Browns first went out of business. The Browns joined with five other baseball clubs. They invested in improvements in the physical plant of the St. Louis stadium, Sportsman's Park, a move repeated in other cities. Construction led to further interest in the game and *The Sporting News* eventually began to cover minor league teams. The publication was eventually taken over by Spink's brother Charles.

Priced initially at just five cents per issue or $2.50 per year, the paper's size was eight pages in length, 17 by 22 inches in layout, and often sported a cover drawing by a leading artist. While early issues of *The Sporting News* made a point to cover the entire sports scene, baseball was considered its primary focus and the publication was often referred to as "The Bible of Baseball," a title it warmly embraced. Charles Spink is credited with having increased circulation and advertising rates to make the paper more competitive nationally. As a result, the size of *The Sporting News* grew to 12 pages and circulation increased by nearly 20,000, growing from 40,000 to almost 60,000 in just one year, highlighting the growing popularity of baseball.

Charles Spink's son, John George Taylor Spink, or Taylor Spink as he came to be known, was born just two years after his uncle founded the newspaper. He started working there while he was still in elementary school when his father gave him an initial sales quota to attract four sales a week, a goal he quickly accomplished in very short order. Immersed in news and sports, he just barely completed grade school and then begged his parents to permit him to drop out of high school to pursue his first loves, sports, sportswriting, and sports reporting, and they acquiesced to all his wishes. His father helped him to gain a beginning job at the Rawlings Sporting Goods Company and then again as a copyboy for the *St. Louis Post-Dispatch*.

Once he proved his total devotion to the field, at least enough to impress his father, he was then invited to join the family publishing business. He worked very hard and at the age of 21, sought an appointment to also work as the American League's official scorer for the World Series, a position sought by many of the more senior, more seasoned sportswriters. His mastery of sports statistics and information about baseball people as well as his commitment to the work of publishing the nation's top baseball journal became legendary. He took over as the sole publisher of *The Sporting News* in 1914 while also overseeing publication of the trade monthly *Sporting Goods Dealer*. When his father passed away, Taylor took over all of the company publications on a full-time basis. He gained attention nationally when he took part in an extended editorial campaign to support the American and National Leagues in opposition to the addition of a brand-new league, the Federal League. Spink said that two leagues were enough and the fortunes of the emerging third league lost out and were more or less buried in less than two years.

When a major scandal involving the Chicago White Sox hit baseball over an attempt to throw the 1919 World Series to gambling interests, Spink endorsed the position of American League president Byron Bancroft Johnson, a close friend of his father's, in trying to clean up the mess that ensued. In what became known as the Black Sox scandal, Spink contributed a number of investigative stories and provided story leads involving some of the gamblers, a few of whom had close connections to crime in St. Louis. His interest in this story and the manner in which it unfolded held him in good stead later on, when his newspaper, with a very solid track record as well as strong commercial ties, was willing to fulfill an advocacy role in keeping the sport above many of the competing interests.

Spink became legendary in the newspaper business for his stern independence on all issues affecting the game of baseball and also for making tremendous demands on his employees, often in some rather

extreme and salty language, symbolized by many follow-up questions and queries involving stories that they had reported or edited involving important national sources. Arthur Daley of the *New York Times* said that Spink would have made a great city editor because "he could smell a story at 1,000 paces," adding: "When he couldn't find one, he sought out others. He was a great idea man."

There are many stories about Spink continually firing his writers, editors, and news managers because of some news-gathering transgression, a decision involving a source, or just some poorly researched or badly written story and using some direct language, for effect, in carrying out the dismissal. He often then repeated the same behavior involving the exact same people—firing them again and for the same (or at least a similar) mistake on some another occasion, which led to a number of jokes about the level of seriousness involved, in spite of many apparent fits of rage. Those who defended Spink's methods and his rugged demeanor tended to point out that he was merely expecting the same level of total commitment to his trade that he had established for himself, reading every piece of copy written for the paper, consulting at length with those involved, and then attributing the information to the most important, highly credible sources. Spink spared no cost and was said to have spent over $6,500 on long-distance phone calls annually as a means of following up with his writers, reporters, and editors and also $10,000 on added telegraph toll-lines to keep up or gain exclusive stories on developing stories. This was at a time when an average salary in the United States was about $1,200.

The upshot of all of this personal involvement and emerging national profile was some degree of emerging jealousy and vitriol. This activity started to produce a national image of someone totally committed to the game of baseball but also someone above the petty politics that a business bureaucracy in the sport might produce. Of course, this placed Spink on a collision course with some of those controlling the fortunes of the game, including another very strong figure in baseball at that time, the game's commissioner, also an extremely colorful figure in his own right, Kenesaw Mountain Landis. Landis, always very forceful and outspoken concerning the interests of the game, was someone who regarded the moniker of "Mr. Baseball" as his sole domain. This perception extended to the recognition players received for their efforts on the field, including designation for outstanding performance such as Most Valuable Player, recognition that the major leagues once dropped, but Spinks continued to maintain as part of *The Sporting News*. He regularly identified such awards and recognition in his publication simply because he decided that they were much too important to be eliminated. This placed him at odds with those who ran the teams and the leagues, including Commissioner Landis, but won him praise among many baseball fans and some sportswriters who were in total agreement.

Faced with periodic challenges, not the least of which were economic pressures tied to the Great Depression, Spinks took strong editorial stands to support innovations of his day at a time when they were considered somewhat controversial. These included enhanced regular radio broadcasts, station affiliations with teams, broadcast of baseball play-by-play, and also the development and broadcast of night games. Spink supported all of these innovations as a means of getting American sports society to adapt to a changing environment. Baseball purists argued that expansion would dilute the game, but Spink editorialized how they would add to the national interest level and help baseball to reach a newer, younger generation, extended to an even wider and broader public appeal.

When World War II emerged, baseball, just like the rest of the country, was faced with severe material shortages, and for newspapers such as *The Sporting News*, this included a shortage of newsprint, the material used in production of the paper. Additional challenges included maintaining commercial advertising from companies hit with a variety of new limitations. During World War II, Spink had 400,000 copies of the newspaper distributed to servicemen overseas. This appealed to the public as a very positive service gesture but also helped to keep the publication and the sport of baseball in the public eye and let the soldiers know what was happening in the sport back home. To achieve this, Spink produced a tabloid format of just five columns with shorter, more tightly edited stories. This added to circulation at war's end and the World Series spiked the readership to a million.

During the war, Spink asked President Franklin D. Roosevelt to issue draft exemptions from military service for baseball players. This was opposed by baseball commissioner Landis for fear that such a policy might be interpreted by some people as offering a special privilege. Roosevelt commented on the importance of the game as a morale booster and diversion from grim war news and the level of details on reporting was further enhanced. In the early 1940s, Spink took over and publicized the publication of baseball statistical publications when the organization that had the long-term franchise, Spalding and Brothers Company, decided to give up the endeavor. Spink sought permission from baseball commissioner Landis to publish the official guides in 1942. It seemed as if any rift between the commissioner and Spink was over. But a few months later a national article about Spink appeared in the *Saturday Evening Post*, which formally dubbed him "Mr. Baseball," a title Landis held dear and regarded as his description. It was said in some circles that as a direct result of the use of the term, the publication of an "official" baseball guide would need to come directly from the baseball commissioner's office, a development Spink simply chose to ignore. The commissioner's guide was published but it came out late, well after the baseball season had begun, and the effort was subsequently abandoned by that office when Landis died in 1944, ironically in favor of it being published once again by Spink and his prize, *The Sporting News*.

The home of *The Sporting News*, St. Louis, Missouri, was also home base for one of the two most successful teams during the developing era of both the game and this premier sports publication. St. Louis was also home to one of the most colorful baseball owners, and his "stunts" also created an occasional stir. Bill Veeck used an undersized player and also employed the use of a one-armed outfielder, Pete Gray, who fielded fly balls by catching them, throwing them into the air, then switching his glove and throwing the ball home. Gray batted .218 for the St. Louis Browns in 1945. Radio descriptions of such exploits by an otherwise disabled person created additional interest and admiration, even if conditions of the war years and a shortage of players due to military service actually made this possible. Later on, one of the Negro Leagues' star players, James "Cool Papa" Bell, known as "the black Ty Cobb," was offered a chance to play for the St. Louis Browns, but he opted instead for the opportunity to function as a professional baseball scout as a means of helping up and coming African American players. He was in his mid-40s by this time and did not want to play when he was no longer at his peak as a ballplayer.

During the decade of the 1940s, another St. Louis franchise formed one of two National League teams that dominated baseball: the St. Louis Cardinals and the Brooklyn Dodgers. Those teams won seven National League pennants during the decade, and in both 1941 and 1942, the championship was determined on the last day of play between the two. By the middle of that decade, the same two teams tied for first place and a playoff was required to determine league champion. At different times, the teams had the same general manager, Branch Rickey, who helped the Cardinals win nine National League pennants by developing an effective farm system, before departing for Brooklyn, and the Dodgers, whom he would also assist. Until baseball expansion occurred later, prompting moves by such teams as the Dodgers, the Cardinals were the team geographically located farthest west and south. This resulted in a following for that franchise in southern and western states, especially due to coverage by *The Sporting News* and the "clear channel" broadcast status of KMOX Radio with Dizzy Dean, Harry Caray, and Jack Buck at the microphone. These developments assisted the growth of the game but also provided additional interest in its key contributors in the press.

The commitment Spink brought to his publication during this era of growth of baseball set a most demanding tone, which was easy to understand but hard to duplicate. He worked seven days a week, always arriving at the publication well before anyone else and leaving after everyone else on the staff had departed. He had expanded the staff to over 250 correspondents and he communicated with them regularly. He regularly bellowed orders to his staff about whatever he wanted, and whatever it was, he got it—and very quickly. He was demanding and impatient. When he was asked by the members of his family to refrain from working on Sundays, he would merely work from home. He conducted long-distance interviews

with some of the best-known figures in baseball. He was a good friend to many baseball legends such as Ty Cobb, who, like Spink, was regarded as a very tough character to know and like. But Spink was regarded by those in his hometown of St. Louis to be a generous person who helped a lot of people privately and who often extended quiet support for important local causes. He knew all of the employees of *The Sporting News* by first name and they relied on him for assistance when times were tough. He valued loyalty above all else. But these efforts were overshadowed by his symbolic gruff manner and demanding temperament.

In terms of his unique approach to the business of reporting baseball, Taylor Spink initiated a strategy of having contributing correspondents situated in all of the cities with a major league team. The colorful details accompanying box scores increased reader and fan interest, and made the paper more attractive and more readable. For a short time, the paper was edited by Ring Lardner, who attracted attention with a series about sports figures, another strategy duplicated at the *Saturday Evening Post*. Taylor Spink became legendary in sports publishing because of his attention to detail and the massive amount of colorful correspondence he conducted with contributors and some readers, as well as an expansive business model earning revenue from the minor league teams, accomplished by publishing their box scores. He would often comment on the importance of covering the up-and-coming players to the game, at least as important, he would say, as covering stars like Mickey Mantle or Stan Musial, because of their potential future impact on the game.

Spink later coauthored a book with sportswriter Fred Lieb about his presumed baseball nemesis, entitled *Judge Landis and 25 Years of Baseball*, and publication of the book was regarded as something of a classy move, coming from someone with whom he had had so many public disputes. Six years before his death, two branches of the United States military service, the U.S. Army and Air Force, honored Spink for having recognized the importance of serving the leisure-time needs of those who served the nation. The contributions of Taylor Spink were also recognized nationally when he passed away in 1962. The Baseball Hall of Fame, located in Cooperstown, New York, named its prize for meritorious service to baseball and journalism in his honor, while also designating him as the award's first recipient.

His son Charles Spink II, known as Johnson Spink, is remembered for ushering in the modern era of color photography and offset presses, eliminating traditional column rules, and further improving and increasing the paper's visual attractiveness. Johnson Spink arrived at the paper for his first day of work in a coat and tie and was told by his father to immediately remove himself to the stockroom and get to work. His exposure to the production end of the business was said to have left an indelible impression on him and the next generation of the publication, with the enhanced work of well-known artists, cartoonists, and photographers on display on the front covers with story boards for visual storytelling. He expanded on the growth and recognition of his publication's role as a sounding board for baseball.

This publisher also expanded the parameters of the publication to include investigative reporting, which often trended toward advocacy, once the background on a situation had been fully explored—telling the whole story, often offering the reader an "insider's" perspective on people and events. He also took a special interest in kids and the younger generations of enthusiastic Americans when it came to baseball. As a result, he offered a special supplement for many years about American Legion baseball, where many of the major leaguers had gotten their start in the game. He was asked to oversee an executive program on youth fitness and editorialized on the importance of that subject. He initially wrote against the signing of the first African American player, Jackie Robinson, by the Brooklyn Dodgers, but once Robinson demonstrated his skill, Spink pleaded for fairness and tolerance. He also extended interest in the sport on an international basis and promoted semiprofessional baseball tournaments abroad with a great deal of attention in *The Sporting News* to a special trip to Japan in 1950.

Under Johnson Spink's leadership, *The Sporting News* dropped the "*The*" and became known as *Sporting News*. It increased its offerings of statistical compilations and books devoted to a variety of sporting endeavors. It eventually made the transition to going totally online and like many legacy companies, relinquished most of its print holdings in favor of the Internet and a new generation of American sports enthusiasts. Online auctions of photos later offered rare originals from the company's archive, which highlighted the important role it had played in America and the spread of American sports culture, especially the game of baseball. The paper eventually stopped publishing minor league box scores and a competing publication, *Baseball Weekly*, took over that arena. Another competitor with roots in broadcasting, *ESPN the Magazine*, provided feature material.

Johnson Spink sold the publication to the Times-Mirror Company for $18 million in 1977. When he took over, it had a circulation of less than 200,000. When he sold it, circulation was slightly less than one-half million. He continued as editor-in-chief for five years as part of an agreement with Times-Mirror. The publication eventually reached a circulation of over 500,000, and by the time it was sold again, this time to Vulcan Ventures in 2000, it went for $100 million. As online opportunities proliferated, by comparison, *ESPN the Magazine* had an 850,000 circulation with its online edition, within just two years of its launch. In 2006, *Sporting News* was sold again, this time to American City Business Journals. The first free online daily edition of *Sporting News Today* appeared July 23, 2008.

Before his death 80 years before his publication went online, founder Alfred Spink wrote one of the first authoritative histories of baseball, *The National Game*. It was replete with information on teams and sportswriters. Spink and his family's premier baseball publication had for years helped to create a level of interest and enthusiasm for that one game, the one that would become so highly regarded, and also so uniquely engrained in American culture and the national consciousness.

Michael D. Murray

See also Baseball Hall of Fame; Black Sox Scandal; Brooklyn Dodgers; Caray, Harry; Dean, Dizzy; Landis, Kenesaw Mountain; Lardner, Ring; Mantle, Mickey; Musial, Stan "The Man"; Negro Leagues; Robinson, Jackie; St. Louis Cardinals; Veeck, Bill

Suggested Resources

"J. G. Taylor Spink." National Baseball Hall of Fame. http://baseballhall.org/museum/awards/j-g-taylor-spink. Accessed July 28, 2011.

Rygelski, Jim. "Baseball's 'Boss President': Chris Von Der Ahe and the Nineteenth Century St. Louis Browns." *Gateway Heritage* 13 (Summer 1992).

Spink, Al. *The National Game.* 2nd ed. Carbondale: Southern Illinois University Press, 2000.

Sporting News Website. http://aol.sportingnews.com/. Accessed July 28, 2011.

Sports Agents

Sports agents are business professionals who assist professional athletes and coaches in contract negotiations. Athletes and coaches often do not have a financial or legal background, which creates the need for agents to negotiate contracts and advise the players and coaches. In some cases, agents have become comparable to lifestyle managers and deal with their clients' schedules, appearances, finances, and other aspects of day-to-day life. These relationships have become an integral part of professional sports.

When athletes decide to enter a professional sports league, they usually enter through the league's draft system. Once athletes declare they are entering the draft, they are free to choose an agent to negotiate their initial professional contract and endorsement contracts. Contact with athletes before their draft declaration is strictly forbidden. High-profile athletes will receive pamphlets, letters, phone calls, and other promotional materials from the various agents. These marketing materials attempt to demonstrate the value of having that agent represent them. The athlete then has to research which clients the agent represents and the lucrative contracts he or she has negotiated. Once signed, the athlete hands the negotiations over to the agent to handle. Negotiations are not always salary focused, as agents will often construct their endorsement deals with other companies as well. Today, massive contracts are being negotiated by sports agents, which make the negotiations more contentious.

The man credited as the first sports agent was Charles C. "Cash and Carry" Pyle. Pyle represented Harold "Red" Grange, who played halfback for the Chicago Bears. Through negotiations between Pyle and the Bears, Grange received a $3,000 per game contract and more than $300,000 for movie rights, which included several miscellaneous items such as a Grange doll. This was a significant deal with Grange receiving far more money than the traditional athlete. Other Pyle clients included Suzanne Lenglen, who after signing a $50,000 deal with Pyle became the first professional tennis player. Other original sports agents included Hollywood movie producer J. William Hayes (represented pitchers Sandy Koufax and Don Drysdale) and cartoonist Christy Walsh (represented Babe Ruth). These agents and others paved the way for the industry to take shape.

Agent compensation usually follows one of four methods. The first is a percentage fee of whatever the athlete earns on the negotiated deal. Different leagues have different policies on how much an agent can earn. For example, the NFL caps its agent compensation at 3 percent, while the National Basketball Association does not allow over 4 percent. If an NFL quarterback signs a one-year $15,000,000 deal, the agent can make up to $450,000 under this model. The second model is an hourly rate, which usually ranges from $200 to $1,000 per hour. Lon Babby, current president of basketball operations for the Phoenix Suns, is credited with introducing the hourly fee to athlete representation. In addition, the agent could charge a flat fee based on completion of the contract. Finally, the agent could choose a combination method of the above financing methods. Each method aims to ensure that successful agents will have lucrative careers. Team sport athletes paid their agents approximately $500 million in 2010.

Currently, there are very low barriers to entry in the sports agent business. To start, there are generally no formal educational requirements to become an agent, although some agents pursue a law degree to better understand contracts and legal concepts. Prospective agents have to pass a certification test with the league that they hope to work with as well as pay a one-time fee for the test. If the agent fails the test, he or she must wait one year to reapply. The number of agents in the industry has made for an extremely competitive atmosphere. Currently, only a few agents and companies represent the majority of athletes in the professional leagues. For example, approximately 70 to 75 percent

Philadelphia Flyers head coach Fred Shero, center, signs a sample contract for photographers during a news conference in Philadelphia on Monday, July 23, 1974. Shero's agent, Mark Stewart, left, and Flyers general manager Keith Allen also are shown. (AP Photo/Brian Horton.)

of all NFL players are represented by a small number of agents and agencies; only one-third of the registered agents have active clients in the NBA; and only about half of baseball's agents are considered active. This has created "superagents" and powerful agencies.

With large contracts being negotiated by agents for players, there needs to be some restrictions placed upon the agents. An example of this is the Uniform Athlete Agents Act (UAAA). The UAAA requires that the contract have certain elements between the athlete and agent such as a stated amount of and method for compensation, a description of any expenses the agent will reimburse for the athlete, a description of the services to be provided to the athlete, and the duration of the contract. Restrictions put on these contracts include the inability to give the athlete anything of value before the contract is signed and approved, the prohibition of false information, and the illegality of not informing the athlete of provisions that may result in

the athlete becoming illegible. Currently, the UAAA has been passed in 40 states as well as the District of Columbia and the U.S. Virgin Islands.

Additionally, there is the Sports Agent Responsibility and Trust Act (SPARTA). Passed in 2004 by the United States Congress, the act further defined the role of sports agents. The act's classification of an athlete agent is "an individual who enters into an agency contract with a student athlete, or directly or indirectly recruits or solicits a student athlete to enter into an agency contract, and does not include a spouse, parent, sibling, grandparent, or guardian of such student athlete." The act also defines the role of the athletic director and explains how their role differs from that of an agent. These regulations provide a clearer framework for sports agents and their roles.

A perceived lack of regulations, an excess of unethical behavior, and strong personalities of superagents have created a population that does not consider sports agents as positive figures or role models. Minnesota Vikings cornerback Antoine Winfield described his agent Dunyasha Yetts and the amount of money Yetts spent on him before he was drafted into the NFL. Yetts apparently paid Winfield and several others money for apartment rent, trips to Las Vegas, and luxurious suits. In 2007, Yetts was convicted for his involvement in an investment scheme and marijuana trafficking. Additionally, former agent Donald Lukens, who represented several players including NBA player Kurt Thomas, filed for bankruptcy in 2002 claiming he was $47 million in debt because of the high-risk investments he made on behalf of his clients. Yetts and Lukens represent a select group of agents who, due to the large publicity their issues receive, have in part created the perception that agents are not ethical people.

Additional issues in the sports agent field include agents leaving their current companies to join other agencies and bringing their clients with them. In July 2011, Tiger Woods and agent Mark Steinberg left International Management Group (IMG) for Excel Sports Management, which left a large hole for IMG to fill. Also, multirepresentation has become an increasingly apparent topic. When an agent decides to represent multiple athletes in the same sports, there is the chance that the agent will have to negotiate on behalf of both athletes' best interests in the same deal. This can become extremely difficult for all parties involved and sometimes creates a conflict of interest for the agent.

In conclusion, sports agents, whether viewed positively or negatively, must be dealt with in negotiations with the athletes and coaches in professional sports. Teams can create positive relationships with the agents, which will allow for more productive negotiations in the future. Sports agents, when following the legal and ethical guidelines imposed on them, can assure that their clients will receive compensation and avoid being taken advantage of by teams and endorsers. Due to their clients' lack of crucial education, the need for agents will continue and portrayals of the business from movies such as *Jerry Maguire* will continue to motivate individuals to attempt to enter the business. It is clear from the current industry that the agent business will continue to be competitive and only the best agents and agencies will survive.

Stephen D. Thiel

See also Grange, Red; *Jerry Maguire*; Koufax, Sandy; Ruth, Babe; Woods, Tiger

Suggested Resources
Davis, Timothy, and Kenneth L. Shropshire. *The Business of Sports Agents.* 2nd ed. Philadelphia: University of Pennsylvania Press, 2008.
Ruxin, Robert H. *An Athlete's Guide to Agents: Fifth Edition.* Sudbury, MA: Jones and Bartlett, 2010.
Shropshire, Kenneth L. *Agents of Opportunity: Sports Agents and Corruption in College Sports.* Philadelphia: University of Pennsylvania Press, 1990.
Sports Agent Directory. http://www.sports-agent-directory .com/. Accessed November 1, 2011.
Stein, Mel. *How to Be a Sports Agent.* London: High Stakes, 2008.

Sports and Drugs/Doping

The history of performance-enhancing drug use in sport dates back to ancient times. Scholars in classical studies suggest that athletes in ancient Greece competing at the festivals in Olympia consumed herbal teas, mushrooms, and dried figs in an attempt to maximize their athletic performance. Similarly, ancient Egyptians are thought to have consumed a drink made from oil, roses, and donkey hooves to enhance their physical abilities, and ancient Roman gladiators are believed to have consumed stimulants to restore and enhance their energy levels.

The term "doping" is thought to stem from the word "dop," which refers to the grapeskin extract consumed by Zulu warriors in South Africa for the purpose of enhancing endurance and strength. The resulting alcoholic beverage was referred to as "dop" by the Afrikaans population in South Africa and as "doop" in Dutch, which translated to "sauce." Dutch canal swimmers who consumed stimulants in the 1860s are generally thought to be the first modern athletes to have engaged in doping practices. The term "doping" entered the English language as "dope" at the end of the 19th century. Popular extreme endurance events at the time, such as pedestrianism (competitive race-walking), encouraged stimulant use to maximize competitors' performance by allowing them to compete longer. Stimulants were thus viewed in a positive light and performance-enhancing drug use in sport was not yet viewed negatively.

Research in the late 19th century contributed to the use of ergogenic substances in sport. Early insight into exercise physiology and the possibility of using nutrition and drugs to enhance athletic performance came from the French physiologist Philippe Tissié. Experimenting on cyclists to better understand human functioning, not athletic performance specifically, Tissié tested a wide array of substances, including rum, champagne, and milk, to determine which substances functioned as stimulants. Coca leaves from South America and kola nuts from Africa were also studied in the late 19th century to gain insight into the ability of various substances to relieve fatigue. These food products were the original performance-enhancing substances used in sport to enhance athletic performance.

It was not until the 20th century that the meaning of the word "drug" expanded to include not only medicinal products intended to restore health, but also street drugs, particularly narcotics and cocaine, which were taken for pleasure and were associated with moral decline. While some people embraced the use of drugs to help workers labor more efficiently, temperance campaigners opposed the use of drugs and established a negative association between drug use and addiction, crime, prostitution, and social degeneracy. Drug users were often portrayed as deceitful, corrupt, and immoral. Societal disapproval of recreational drug use is thought to have contributed to the opposition to drug use in sport.

Endurance sports have a history of athletes using drugs, beverages, and other concoctions to fuel their performances. Thomas Hicks, winner of the marathon at the 1904 Olympic Games, held in St. Louis, was open about his consumption of small amounts of sulphate of strychnine and brandy to help him finish the grueling race. At the next Olympic Games, the Italian runner Dorando Pietri was disqualified for receiving assistance in crossing the marathon finish line. Throughout the race, doctors had given him the stimulants strychnine and atropine. The crowd was outraged at Pietri's disqualification despite knowing he was using drugs to fuel his performance. At the time, drugs were not prohibited in sport, and there was little to no opposition to Olympic athletes consuming performance-enhancing substances. The idea of creating drug bans that would punish athletes by rendering them ineligible to compete was far from the forefront of most people's concerns, and drug use in sport was not considered a violation of fair play or sportsmanship.

The first drug bans applied in the sporting context prohibited the use of drugs to enhance one's own or sabotage a competitor's racehorse. In 1903 the English Jockey Club banned doping of horses, and by 1910 tests were developed to detect cocaine and heroin in horse saliva. Early leaders in banning doping among human competitors included the International Amateur Athletics Federation (IAAF) in 1928. However, because the IAAF lacked tests to detect the use of banned drugs by athletes, competitors were expected to simply accept the rules and adhere to the antidoping restrictions voluntarily. Very little attention was given to the issue of drug use in sport until allegations of athletes dying from drug use surfaced. Welsh cyclist Arthur Linton reportedly died from an overdose of the drug trimethyl or strychnine in a cycling race in France in 1879 or 1886. However, contradictory evidence shows that Linton did not die from doping but succumbed to typhoid fever in 1896. Linton's case demonstrates the extent to which many early examples of doping were based on unsubstantiated rumors.

During the interwar years between the First and Second World Wars, sports became increasingly modernized with more emphasis placed on coaching, training, and sport science. The international significance and prestige of winning Olympic medals increased and athletes began gaining national and international recognition. Sport historians have demonstrated that after the end of World War II, when international sport was gaining momentum, drug use in sport became increasingly prevalent. Amphetamines and other pep pills that were used frequently by many people for many reasons after the war were also used in sport. Throughout the 1940s, 1950s, and 1960s, amphetamines, cocaine, caffeine, and steroids were consumed by some athletes to fuel their performances. Doping was considered an open secret in many sports, and it was thought to be a necessary part of keeping up with the demands of being a high-performance athlete.

Despite the prevalence of drugs available to athletes, drug use in sport, particularly steroid use, eventually gained a negative image and came to be met with disdain by sports fans. Several factors contributed to the shift from neutral tolerance to fierce opposition to drug use in sport. An association between steroid use and Nazi soldiers in WWII contributed to the negative stigma forming around steroid users. Sports fans in the West attributed the success of athletes from Communist countries in the East to steroid use and a win-at-all-costs mentality, which further solidified the growing dislike of performance-enhancing drug use. In addition, the resulting androgenization of female athletes consuming steroids sparked fears of what steroids could do to women's bodies. Steroid use by women posed a challenge to the natural gender order and was viewed with suspicion and contempt. Thus, in the West, steroid use gained a negative reputation through associations with German atrocities and aggression during the Second World War, perceived Soviet aspirations to create machine-like athletes, and the masculinization of female athletes. Together these factors functioned to attach a negative label to steroid users and steroid use. Sports fans began fearing what "unnatural" drugs could do to athletes' bodies.

The death of 23-year-old Danish cyclist Knud E. Jensen at the 1960 Olympic Games in Rome, Italy, midway through the course contributed to the demand for antidoping policies in sport. Jensen was not the first athlete to die from using performance-enhancing drugs (and it is debatable whether or not performance drugs even contributed to his death), but his death, having occurred at the Olympic Games, was the first to cause the International Olympic Committee (IOC) distress. Seven years later, British cyclist Tommy Simpson met the same fate as Jensen when he died in July 1967 during a stage of the Tour de France. Simpson's death, however, occurred during a live television broadcast of the race and gathered much greater media attention. When reports from Simpson's autopsy revealed amphetamines, methylamphetamines, and cognac in his bloodstream, many people attributed his death to doping, and a very negative association began to form between high-performance sport and doping. Opposition to doping in sport was also influenced by amateur ideals as well as religious and political values.

Because of the negative public reaction to the possible drug-induced deaths of high-performance athletes, the IOC began discussing what it could do to prevent similar situations in the future. At the 57th session of the IOC in San Francisco, California, in 1960, not long after Jensen's death, the IOC Executive Board appointed a Doping Committee, which consisted of Sir Arthur Porritt of New Zealand, Dr. Josef Gruss of the former Czechoslovakia, Ryotaro Azuma of Japan, and Agustin Sosa of Panama. Amid increasing public concern about steroids and the masculinization of female competitors, in 1967 the IOC created a Medical Commission to address doping and sex testing in sport, and to create a list of drugs that the members of the commission felt should be banned in sport. In 1968, the Medical Commission decided to perform dope tests on the top six competitors at the Olympic Games, two athletes drawn at random from the rest of the field, and two athletes from each team participating in a team sport. This decision set the stage for drug testing in the Olympic Games, which officially started at the 1968 Summer Games in Mexico City. Athletes at the 1964 Olympic Games in Tokyo and in Grenoble at the Winter Games in 1968 were subjected to unofficial drug tests prior to the first official testing protocols at the Mexico City Games. Four years prior to the IOC's decision to create a Medical Commission, the government of France attempted to pass antidoping legislation, and the Council of Europe's Committee on Drugs began discussing drug use in sport. Moreover, in 1966 the International Sports Federations for football and cycling instigated drug testing at major competitions. While the IOC Medical Commission was the first organization to create a list of banned substances in sport applicable to all athletes competing at the Olympics, it was not the leader in instigating drug tests in sport.

Despite bans on steroids and other performance-enhancing drugs, the tests used by the IOC Medical Commission at the Olympic Games to detect metabolites of banned drugs in athletes' urine samples were not foolproof. After the fall of the Berlin Wall on November 9, 1989, files emerged that confirmed the fears of many in the sporting community who suspected the former East Germany of running state-sponsored, systemic doping. Professor Werner Franke and Brigitte Berendonk's translations of State Plan 14:25 provide further evidence. According to these files, most, if not all, athletes competing for East Germany in the strength and speed events were given anabolic steroids. Moreover, the Stasi files reveal that several hundred of East Germany's finest physicians and researchers administered and researched unapproved experimental drugs given to thousands of athletes, including athletes who were 14 years of age and younger, without gaining consent from the athletes or the parents of underage athletes. Additional files published in *Swimming World* magazine in December 1994 show that every top East German athlete was doped. German historian Giselher Spitzer reports that the Stasi files reveal over 10,000 East German athletes were given performance-enhancing drugs.

Drug testing at the Olympic Games did not catch the athletes who competed drug-free at the Olympics but used drugs in their training regiments. The tests also failed to identify athletes who were using effective and undetectable masking agents to avoid failing a doping test. In 1996, newspaper headlines across the globe reported that East Germany's knowledge of how to avoid detection of drugs during doping tests was so great that they set up a medical facility on the fringe of the Olympic Village at the 1976 Olympics in Montreal and administered steroids and other performance-enhancing drugs throughout the Games. Following the closing ceremonies, the director of state security, Peter Busse, allegedly dumped 10 suitcases filled with used syringes and drugs into the St. Lawrence River. Although less evidence exists, the former Soviet Union and other Soviet bloc countries are also believed to have participated in systemic doping. In contrast, in the West, doping use was facilitated by individual trainers, coaches, and physicians without centralized government influence.

At the 1980 Olympic Games in Moscow, zero athletes tested positive for banned drugs. However, scientists retroactively examining the samples and testing procedures estimate that 20 percent of the athletes tested had traces of banned substances in their systems.

Similar controversies and coverups are attached to the 1984 Olympic Games in Los Angeles. While 12 athletes tested positive in L.A., another nine positive tests went missing and the names attached to the tests were shredded. The 1988 Olympic Games in Seoul thrust doping back into the public spotlight when Canadian sprinter Ben Johnson had his gold medal in the 100-meter sprint revoked after testing positive for the steroid stanozolol. At the Atlanta Olympics in 1996, 16 samples raised doping suspicions; however, only two athletes were punished. Of the remaining 14 positive samples, the IOC Medical Commission dismissed 7 of them because the drug in question, Bromantan, had only recently been added to the banned substance list, 5 because of technical doubt, and 2 without giving a reason. Over time, the public and "clean" athletes became very mistrustful of the IOC Medical Commission's ability to detect and punish "drug cheats" when the frequency of scandals involving drug-related incidents continued to build steadily.

The IOC Medical Commission attempted to stay ahead of the drug cheats and develop tests to detect the performance-enhancing substances that athletes were using. Some newly invented drugs could be used for several years before a detection method was developed. While amphetamines reigned as the performance-enhancing drug of choice in the 1960s and early 1970s, anabolic steroids replaced them in the 1970s and 1980s, followed by the use of human growth hormones (hGH) and erythropoietin (EPO). The testing procedures implemented by the IOC Medical Commission caught some drug cheats, but even members of the commission were well aware that many other doped athletes were slipping through their fingers. In 1994, in an attempt to unify anti-doping rules, procedures, and sanctions, the IOC Medical Commission developed a standardized set of doping agreements that international sports federations had to agree to accept if they wished to participate in the 1996 Olympics. The acceptance that the IOC Medical Commission was looking for did not transpire immediately. The international soccer federation, FIFA, declared it was unwilling to adhere to the IOC Medical Commission's rules. However, in response, the IOC ratified the Medical Commission's standards and made them binding by adding them to the Olympic Charter as an annex. This move forced FIFA to comply, or risk having soccer removed from the Olympic program. Rule 29A of the Olympic Charter was amended to read, "Doping is forbidden. The IOC Medical Commission shall prepare a list of prohibited classes of drugs and of banned procedures." With this addition, the first international antidoping policy was put into effect.

Despite its efforts to add a doping clause to the Olympic Charter, the IOC Medical Commission seemed to ignore the prevalence of performance-enhancing substances used by many cyclists and the blatant doping that went on at the Tour de France. However, the French authorities did not do the same. During raids of participants, coaches, and officials' living quarters during the 1998 Tour de France, police found large quantities of EPO and other performance-enhancing drugs. The Tour de France doping scandal served as the last straw for many people when the French police took the initiative to try to free cycling from doping while the IOC Medical Commission merely observed their efforts. On July 27, 1998, amid the peak of the Tour de France scandal when teams were dropping out in protest of the treatment they received from the police, riders were sabotaging the races, and the French police were detaining individual riders, the IOC issued a press release informing the world of its plan to host an International Conference on Doping. Also scheduled was an emergency meeting of the IOC Executive Board to discuss doping in sport. IOC Executive Board member Kevan Gospar of Australia voiced his strong support for the meeting and put forth the idea of a "full-time IOC watchdog" that would have direct supervision of athletes year round, not just during the two weeks of the Olympic Games every four years. A proposal was put forth to create an agency to coordinate the worldwide fight against doping in sport. This agency was to eventually perform random, unannounced, year-round testing and receive funding from the IOC via its TV revenue funds as well as from national governments.

The IOC invited a diverse assortment of individuals and organizations associated with sport, drug legislation, and human welfare to the World Conference in Sport, which was held in Lausanne, Switzerland, in February 1999. At this gathering, the groundwork to create an independent, transparent, and accountable antidoping agency that would govern high-performance sport emerged, and the Lausanne Declaration on Doping in Sport was created. This document set out the parameters for the creation of what would eventually become known as the World Anti-Doping Agency (WADA). Initial financial contributions to support the international collaborative agency were shared between the IOC and national governments of the countries that compete at the Olympic Games, and dues ranged from just $200 to over $1 million based on how much each country could afford to pay. The resulting agency, known as WADA, was to be housed in Montreal, Canada, under the leadership of IOC member and lawyer Richard (Dick) W. Pound.

The World Anti-Doping Code came into effect on January 1, 2004, and is updated annually. International sports federations competing at the Olympic Games are required to adopt the World Anti-Doping Code and follow all of the antidoping rules and restrictions contained within it. The Olympic Charter stipulates that athletes participating at the Olympic Games must respect the spirit of fair play and comply with all aspects of the World Anti-Doping Code if they wish to take part. The main categories of banned substances included in the World Anti-Doping Code are anabolic agents, peptide hormones and growth factors, beta-2-agonists, hormone antagonists, diuretics and masking agents, narcotics, cannabinoids, and glucocorticosteroids. Alcohol and beta-blockers are banned in competition for some sports but not all. Methods prohibited under the World Anti-Doping Code include enhancing oxygen transfer using blood doping or related techniques, chemically and physically manipulating urine and blood samples, and gene doping.

Therapeutic use exemptions (TUEs) are approved if an athlete would experience impaired health as a result of restricting a medication that he or she requires to treat an acute or chronic health condition. TUEs are granted only if equally effective, alternative, and approved methods of treating the condition do not exist. Banned substances for which athletes can gain a TUE to use must merely restore the athlete to normal health, rather than produce performance advantages. Examples of TUEs include insulin for athletes with diabetes mellitus and methylpenidate for athletes diagnosed with attention deficit hyperactivity disorder (ADHD).

WADA maintains that all of the substances and methods banned under the provisions set out in the World Anti-Doping Code meet two of three following criteria: (1) the substance or method causes harm; (2) the substance or method enhances athletic performance; and (3) use of the substance or method violates the spirit of sport. Drugs meeting only one of the three criteria theoretically would not be banned in sport. The fairness of antidoping rules in sport has been challenged by some competitors, researchers, and sports administrators. These critics maintain that the inclusion or exclusion of substances on the banned list is arbitrary and based on social or political motivations. For example, marijuana use was not banned in sport until Canadian snowboarder Ross Rebagliati's urine sample at the 1998 Winter Olympics in Nagano, Japan, was found to contain traces of tetrahydrocannabinol (THC) from passively inhaling secondhand marijuana smoke. Rebagliati was disqualified but eventually had his gold medal returned after arguing successfully that THC was not included on the banned substance list at the time. Not long after, WADA added THC to the banned substance list despite a lack of consensus among scientists regarding whether the drug constitutes a health risk or provides performance-enhancing benefits, and thereby meets the required two or three criteria for banning substances and methods.

The bans on erythropoietin (EPO) and blood doping also challenge some people's perceptions of the accuracy and fairness of the banned substance list. EPO is a glycohormone produced in the kidneys, and in smaller amounts in the liver and brain, which is produced in response to hypoxia in the tissues. Sport scientists agree that one of the most effective ways to improve athletic performance is to enhance the delivery of oxygen to the working muscles. Increasing the amount of red blood cells in the body increases the body's capacity to carry oxygen. Athletes seeking to maximize their oxygen kinetics and increase their red blood cell concentrations can do so in four ways: (1) through training at high altitude, (2) through mimicking the conditions of training at high altitude by sleeping in a hypobaric chamber, (3) through blood doping, which involves transfusing either one's own or another person's blood to provide additional red blood cells, or (4) through the use of EPO or similar drugs. The first

and second methods of increasing the concentration of red blood cells in the body are permitted, while the latter two options are prohibited and, if caught, will lead to a doping violation and corresponding period of ineligibility from participating in sport. Blood doping in sport has been banned since the early 1980s due to the health risks associated with a high haematocrit and the deaths of several cyclists and skiers allegedly linked to blood doping. The IOC Medical Commission banned EPO use in sport in 1990, but several variants of the drugs were subsequently created to avoid detection in the tests used by accredited doping laboratories.

The banned substance list is a fluid document that is evaluated and updated regularly. For example, in recent years, antiasthma medications, such as Salbutamol, have been banned, permitted with therapeutic use exemptions for athletes with medical diagnoses of asthma or exercise-induced asthma, and permitted for all athletes in small doses. The statuses of caffeine, pseudoephedrine, ephedrine, and phenylpropanolamine on the banned list have also changed several times in the last decade.

In addition to establishing and maintaining the list of banned substances and methods in sport, the primary responsibilities of WADA are to coordinate the protocols for collecting and analyzing urine and blood samples, and to determine the criteria for allowing TUEs for athletes who require the use of a banned substance or method for a legitimate health purpose as prescribed by a medical doctor. Other functions of WADA include advocating unified doping sanctions by courts around the world and funding research in both antidoping tests and antidoping education programs. In doing so, WADA seeks to protect athletes' rights to compete in doping-free competitions.

The creation of the World Anti-Doping Agency has not eradicated the use of banned substances and methods in sport. Since its creation, WADA has had to deal with the creation of second, third, and fourth generations of EPO, "The Clear" (THG), and derivatives of these drugs, for which designing reliable tests has been difficult. Popular athletes such as sprinters Marion Jones and Dwain Chambers, cyclists Floyd Landis and Tyler Hamilton, and baseball players Alex Rodriguez and Manny Ramirez are among the many Olympic and professional athletes who have failed doping tests

Gene Doping

There are numerous gene transfer procedures under development by medical researchers to treat genetic diseases and disorders. The use of these techniques in healthy athletes with the intention of enhancing performance has worried WADA officials since the late 1990s. Scientists have identified many genes that contribute to strength, endurance, oxygen kinetics, inflammation and repair, pain, and flexibility. If athletes could use gene therapies nontherapeutically to manipulate their bodies' production of desirable genes, it is speculated that the performance-enhancing benefits that result would be extremely hard to detect using conventional testing methods. The use of gene therapies for enhancement purposes in sport evokes many ethical issues. One of the most pronounced of these issues is the uncertainty involved in distinguishing elective enhancements from medically necessary therapies for athletes, particularly injured athletes who could heal at a faster rate with the assistance of banned procedures and drugs. The therapy/enhancement distinction is complicated for banned drugs, but is even less clear in the context of athletes' potential use of genetic therapies.

or admitted they had intentionally broken antidoping rules. New developments in the "fight" against doping in sport include storing samples and retesting them up to eight years after the competition, and imposing penalties based on indirect evidence as opposed to a positive analytical finding. WADA's efforts to coordinate the drug testing at recent Olympic Games have shown many athletes are still using performance-enhancing drugs. At the Beijing Olympic Games in 2008, nine athletes and six horses were disqualified for committing doping violations. Six more positive tests for the drug CERA were detected after the Games when 948 samples were retested using a more accurate testing method recently developed. Prior to the 2010 Olympic Games in Vancouver, more than 30 athletes committed doping violations and were thus ineligible to compete.

Opponents of drug bans in sport claim that unless doping harms people other than the athletes taking the drugs or using the banned methods, prohibiting athletes from making informed decisions about whether or not to use legal drugs is a paternalistic act that fails to respect athletes' autonomy. Other rationales for easing up or removing doping rules include the lack of success in eradicating doping from sport and the idea that medically approved doping would be safer for the athletes involved. Concerns about athletes' privacy in the drug-testing process also provide impetus to people looking to relax the doping restrictions. In addition to physical violations of privacy that come from providing a urine sample, high-performance athletes are also required to provide their whereabouts to WADA so that drug testers can locate them to conduct random unannounced tests. Athletes failing to file their whereabouts for a one-hour period each day, or failing to be present at the location they had previously indicated, are charged with a missed test and whereabouts strike. An antidoping rule violation can be applied for missing tests, often if an athlete receives three whereabouts strikes in an 18-month period. People who reject these arguments against relaxing doping restrictions contend that without doping bans high-performance sport would be a competition between scientists and pharmacists, not athletes.

See also Jones, Marion; 1984 Olympic Games, Los Angeles; 1996 Olympic Games, Atlanta; Ramirez, Manny; Rodriguez, Alex; Steroids

Sarah J. Teetzel

Suggested Resources
Beamish, Rob, and Ian Ritchie. *Fastest, Highest, Strongest: A Critique of High-Performance Sport.* New York: Routledge, 2006.
Olympic Charter. http://www.olympic.org/Documents/olympic_charter_en.pdf. Accessed October 17, 2011.
Olympic Medical Commission. http://www.olympic.org/medical-commission. Accessed October 17, 2011.
Ungerleider, Steven. *Faust's Gold: Inside the East German Doping Machine.* New York: St. Martin's Press, 2001.
Waddington, Ivan, and Andy Smith. *An Introduction to Drugs in Sport: Addicted to Winning?* 2nd ed. London: Routledge, 2009.
World Anti-doping Agency. http://www.wada-ama.org. Accessed October 17, 2011.

Sports Bars

Bars are commonly categorized by either the kind of patrons who frequent them (e.g., college bars, cop bars, biker bars) or the kind of entertainment that they offer (e.g., sports bars, live music bars, blues bars). Sports bars, in particular, are specialized in offering sports fans the possibility of watching games on large-screen televisions. Along with a good beer selection and other drinks, generally all sports bars propose a menu that consists of at least burgers, sandwiches, pizza, and appetizers.

Televisions are aligned in such a way that all customers can watch the game, and they are typically tuned to different channels to show an assortment of games and sports. In the case of sports bars, owners spend a larger-than-average portion of their revenues to purchase the newest releases in the audio and video market. Sports bars are not just fun environments where people can relax after work, like any other bars. Their main attraction is sporting events. One of the key defining factors of a sports bar's success or failure is, indeed, its entertainment. The sports bar concept relies on providing a setting in which customers can enjoy themselves while watching their favorite sporting event. Providing as many televisions as necessary with state-of-the-art equipment in highly visible areas of the restaurant is therefore essential.

The furniture and other furnishing equipment of sports bars must be particularly comfortable, for guests tend to spend long hours in the bar to follow the game. Sports bars are also typically decorated so as to celebrate the hometown teams, with photos, jerseys, and other memorabilia hanging behind the counter. Dart boards, pool tables, and videogames are also there to complete the entertainment offer in most bars.

As far as the establishment's capacity is concerned, there are no fixed or average requirements. Sports bars can be a themed version of the small neighborhood tavern or they can be as big as multistory nightclubs.

While nothing compares to the excitement of being at a game in the stadium, sports bars nevertheless grant sports fans a series of benefits. Stadium tickets are often hard to find, and some people cannot afford the price anyway, whereas going to the local sports bar allows all categories of fans to spend according to their means. Going to the sports bar is also particularly popular among businesspeople, whose hectic lifestyle makes it difficult for them to devote but a limited amount of time to leisure and who often find themselves away from home the night of the big game.

In that sense, we may say that sports bars reflect one of the main social merits of sport, in that they democratically attract all categories of fans regardless of their social, cultural, or professional background.

The sports bars concept has considerably evolved over time. People have always talked about the game in bars. When sports highlights were only made available *ex post facto*, by word of mouth or in the next morning's newspaper, this all happened after the game. Fans gathered in the bar to discuss the latest exploits of their favorite champions over a drink. The advent of radio allowed people to listen to the game, but that did not fundamentally alter the fans' habits in sports bars or the nature of these environments. Things started to evolve more significantly in the 1930s with the opening of Jack Dempsey's (former world heavyweight boxing champion) Restaurant across from Madison Square Garden, and in the 1940s with the opening of the legendary Toots Shor's in the middle of Manhattan at 51 West 1st Street. Bernard (Toots) Shor, the founder and owner of the establishment, had the idea, like Dempsey, of inviting sports champions to the bar along with sportswriters and sports executives. One could meet there Joe DiMaggio and the other players of the city's teams, but also Broadway entertainers, politicians, beat writers. A new concept was launched. Traditional and new bars across the United States started to assume a sports-centered identity and to bring in sports players, typically after the game. As the demand for the new concept grew, the number of bars with a sport-driven personality continued to expand.

The advent of TV sets, as from the 1950s, provided sports bars with a new, pivotal device to attract customers. Then, the following turning point and booster to the spreading of sports bars occurred in the 1980s with the rise of sport as a highly professionalized and mercantile phenomenon, and the interest of sponsors naturally converging toward all that could be commercially exploited around sports, including sports bars.

The mass-mediazation of sports and the explosion in the market of TV rights for sport events toward the end of the 20th century has further accentuated the trend toward sport as a TV phenomenon. For sports bars, the key word is no longer, or not only, entertainment but technology. The modernity of equipment becomes the *conditio sine qua non* for sports bars to stay in the market. Making large TV screens available is no longer enough: It is about displaying the latest plasma model, tableside monitors, digital scoreboards for betting purposes, wi-fi Internet access from everywhere on the premises.

The race to the latest state-of-the-art equipment has also extended to all that contributes to create a place where people can not only watch sports but also play them. Some sports bars, especially the biggest ones, provide on-site boxing rings, shuffleboards, and playgrounds of all sorts. Online videogames, in particular, have grown extremely popular in the first decade of the 21st century. In addition to giving customers the possibility to play, in an increasing number of sports bars one or more TV sets are switched to Internet broadcasts of professional videogame matches happening hundreds or thousands of miles away. For sports bars, the fans of online games represent a new and growing source of revenue coming especially, although not exclusively, from the youngest patrons.

New-generation bars, with their need for continuously upgraded technology and larger surfaces, clearly demand much higher investments than their predecessors. Similar to family-owned businesses, which have found it increasingly hard to survive in the face of big retailers, so have little bars often found it difficult to compete with high-tech megabars. Yet, big and costly establishments are riskier businesses, requiring strong and sustained earning streams. This is why they are normally implanted in touristic or densely populated areas, not always with long-lasting results. Size and technology do not guarantee success. Small bars are places where patrons, owners, and bartenders know one another and develop personal relationships, while megabars are comparatively more impersonal and cannot focus on clients' loyalty. Small bars therefore maintain a certain competitive edge thanks to their hardly irreplaceable "human touch."

Sports bars are recurrently evoked in the discussions on the link between alcohol and sports, a subject that becomes particularly critical in the case of college sports bars, where it concerns young students and athletes. Drinking in sports bars reflects, in fact, a link that exists at a more general level between socializing, not necessarily around sports, and alcohol consumption, especially in the cultures where drinking is not regarded as a simple complement to food but as the quintessential or most common social activity, and the ability to drink large quantities of alcoholic beverages even becomes a sign of adulthood and strength. Indeed, the problem arises with overdrinking and the health and social consequences of that habit. The sport-alcohol nexus, and notably the excesses in the consumption of alcoholic beverages that may surround sports certainly emerge as an especially paradoxical phenomenon, in view of what is supposed to be one of the main social values of sport, that is, teaching a correct, disciplined, and salubrious lifestyle.

Regarding the population that frequents sports bars, these have long been a favorite destination and an almost exclusive territory for men. They operated on the traditionally gender-based combination of alcohol, sports, and hegemonic masculinity. With the mass diffusion and "spectacularization" of sports, in the final decades of the 20th century, the public of sports has expanded, and so has the community of sports bars. Women are nowadays regular guests of sports bars, too, and the concept has generally evolved to include finer dining and family fun. In the collective imagery, the sport-and-beer mixture continues to be naturally identified with men's lifestyle. It is still mostly men who go to sports bars for the sport-centered camaraderie they can find there, and overdrinking while watching the game is still a typically masculine behavior, socially acceptable for men and certainly not for women in the vast majority of cultures. Nevertheless, the changing trend in the composition of sports bars communities mirrors broader changes in social relations, notably the increased flexibility of gender roles and the progressive diminution of hegemonic masculinity.

If on the one hand the mass diffusion of sports has brought in new sets of clients, such as women and families, the other side of the coin has been the wholesale multiplication of competitors to sports bars. The quantity of nonthemed bars and restaurants that show the game on large flat-screen TVs has never stopped growing. One does not need to go to a sports bar to watch a match with friends. Sports bars are therefore more than ever obliged to offer additional services to distinguish themselves from nonthemed establishments, such as featured events around special games, exclusive agreements with the local broadcasters, or personalized parties for clients, as a way to reinforce the loyalty bond with their clients.

Sports bars can be fruitfully observed beneath the surface to explore how society, sports, and gender relations have evolved in the United States over the last decades. They are one of the most recognizable symbols of the way Americans live and enjoy sports.

Rosarita Cuccoli

Suggested Resources

Ballard, Chris. "Finding the Perfect Sports Bar." February 7, 2005. http://sportsillustrated.cnn.com/vault/article/magazine/MAG1108512/index.htm. Accessed November 1, 2011.

Efrati, Amir. "Geeks Beat Jocks as Bar Fight Breaks Out over Control of the TV." August 23, 2011. http://online.wsj.com/article/SB10001424053111904070604576516462736084234.html Accessed November 1, 2011.

Klink, William R. "Sports Bar." In Dennis Hall and Susan G. Susan, eds. *American Icons: An Encyclopedia of the People, Places, and Things That Have Shaped Our Culture*. Vol. 3. Westport, CT: Greenwood Press, 2006, pp. 641–647.

Wenner, Lawrence A. "In Search of the Sports Bars: Masculinity, Alcohol, Sports, and the Mediation of Public Space." In Geneviève Rail, ed. *Sport and Postmodern Times*. Albany: State University of New York Press, 1998, pp. 301–332.

Wenner, Lawrence A., and Jackson, Steven J., eds. *Sport, Beer, and Gender: Promotional Culture and Contemporary Social Life*. New York: Peter Lang, 2009.

Sports Clothing

Sports clothing is what individuals wear when they engage in physical activity; for competitive athletes, the clothing is intended to maximize the wearer's performance. Athletes must be able to move their bodies freely and to protect themselves from the elements to perform effectively. Sports clothing illustrates technological advancements in form and function of fabric. Thus, clothing selection is relevant to one's athletic success. Sports clothing is also socially relevant beyond the elite playing fields. Recreational athletes or even sport fans wear sport-specific attire. In addition, the clothing is specific to historical periods and highlights the values of the era. Sports clothing demonstrates society's athletic expectations of those wearing it and athletes' responses to these expectations.

Technology and Clothing

Changes in technology influence sports clothing. Advancements in production and the materials used have impacted athletic performances and participation. The industrial revolution of the mid-18th to mid-19th centuries and the sewing machine, utilized in manufacturing by the 1850s, enabled the mass production of fabric, which increased the production and lowered the cost of clothing. The demand for activewear also increased with the amount of leisure time afforded to the populace. The growth of women's participation in physical activity further generated an increased demand for activewear.

Prominent materials in sports clothing include wool, jersey, cotton, Lycra, nylon, and polyester. The natural fibers wool and cotton are good for weather conditions; wool serves as protection from cold temperatures, whereas cotton is absorbent and adequate for summer weather. Jersey, a wool-based fabric, appeared in the late 1800s as a fabric that permitted the wearer flexibility in movement; it offered give but would still retain its shape. Synthetics, such as Lycra, polyester, and nylon, are sometimes seen as superior for athletic participation because they can be constructed to answer specific needs. Polyester, first used for sports clothing in the 1950s, is resistant to stretching and color-fading in chlorine. It also, along with polyamide (nylon), blends with other fabrics to create microfibers, which are utilized in many current forms of sport clothing. In addition to more traditional fabrics, both natural and synthetic, sports clothing consists of other materials, such as silicone, glass, metals, and carbon.

Activewear responds to several demands, but focuses on protecting the wearer from outdoor conditions, maximizing the wearer's comfort, and improving performance. To answer these demands, clothing designers utilized developments from military and space-program research. For sports that take place in the elements, athletes need to be protected from cold, wind, rain, and heat conditions. Designers must plan for extreme conditions to sustain the wearer, for instance, if a surfer must stay in the water for extended periods of time. The wetsuit protects the wearer partially due to its neoprene, or synthetic rubber, construction; the wetsuit is waterproof and stretches without losing density, so that the body remains dry and warm. The advancement of Gore-Tex in the 1970s was critical in protecting outdoor athletes from the wet and cold temperatures. The outer membrane of Gore-Tex consists of small holes that allow water vapor from sweat to escape, but the holes are too small to allow outside water from rain to penetrate the fabric. The microfibers popular in the 21st century are dense and act as a water repellent. Protection is also needed against the sun's rays. Metal combined with textiles can create protection from the ultraviolet rays that cause skin damage. Athletes who engage in outdoor activities for extended periods of time, such as golfing and sailing, benefit from this technology. Microscopic spheres of glass can also be mixed with ink and applied to fabric to create reflective clothing; this reflection protects the night-time cyclist or runner in conditions with poor visibility.

To maximize comfort, activewear strives to maintain the wearer's body temperature and to allow freedom of movement. Currently tech fibers serve to wick sweat away from the body with the goal of maintaining body temperature whether in cold or hot weather. The material draws the perspiration off the body and transports the sweat to the outer layer so that it may evaporate. A wetsuit also allows for maximum movement; the addition of layers for protection does not encumber activity. That is a primary concern for sports in cold conditions; a cross-country skier needs to stay warm and move effectively. Stretchy fabrics, such as Lycra, are also important for maximizing the body's ability to move.

Performance is critical to competitive athletes, and clothing is constructed with the intent of aiding athletes in improving their times. For instance, clothing with silicone strips can reduce drag. Competitive-swimsuit designers are constantly working to develop new technology to limit drag in the water and to create the fastest suit. Full-body swimsuits free of stitching and comprised of polyurethane and neoprene to increase buoyancy were prominent features at the 2008 Beijing Olympic Games. These technological features have also been quite contentious and led to the international governing body of swimming, Federation Internationale de Natation (FINA), to review some swimsuits to determine whether they give swimmers an unfair advantage. Effective in 2010, FINA banned full-body swimsuits, as well as suits made from polyurethane and neoprene, and announced that swimsuits may only be produced from textile fibers.

Technology has also made substantial gains in balancing the relation of fashion, performance, and waste. Companies that began to meet the specific needs of those in outdoor activities, such as hiking, endurance races, and kayaking, are leading the way in creating sustainable clothing materials. A goal of such companies as North Face, REI, and Patagonia is to limit the negative impact of clothing production on the environment. As a result, recyclable materials and postconsumer waste, such as plastic bottles, limited chemicals, and organic and biodegradable fibers are used in the construction of their products.

Clothing, Gender, and Society

Attire is a means through which the wearer's body responds to power dynamics, whether there are cultural expectations of how one should dress for a particular sport or activity or actual formal restrictions on dress. Together with the type of sport, relevant identity categories that impact the role of a participant's clothing selections include race, class, gender, and sexuality. For instance, women and men have dressed differently for different activities.

Historically, women's athletic participation has been marked by the presence of a skirt. It was not until after World War II that women regularly wore pants in everyday life, and into the 21st century many women continue to wear skirts while being physically active. Female athletes were frequently accused of being mannish or lesbian, both considered negative in a society that promotes defined gender roles and heterosexual relationships. Since athleticism has been viewed as counter to expectations of the female body and societal roles of women, women's athletic attire and general appearance in sports has been framed around the need to maintain femininity and counter such claims. Often women's clothing perpetuated social expectations so that they would be considered normal; skirts served to suggest social normalcy.

Dresses and skirts have changed over time in regard to length, layers, and even circumference. To participate in athletics, women wore long skirts that enabled movement but also maintained ideals of femininity in public. In the early to mid-1800s, women wore wide skirts with a hooped petticoat. This expansive form had a tendency to flip inside out while walking or skating in wind, so women began to wear fashionable undergarments. They also began using a skirt elevator, a device to heighten the skirt, so that women would not trip over their long skirts while skating and walking.

In 1851, Amelia Bloomer broke from the skirt when she adjusted it to create a baggy pair of pants, commonly referred to as "bloomers." This scandalous modification became a symbol of the women's movement of the era, as bloomers enabled greater freedom in mobility when riding the bicycle. But even bloomers worn while cycling were covered by long skirts so that passersby would not see the bloomers. The bicycle also brought challenges to the corset, worn by women in public whether participating in physical activity or not. Along with bloomers many women wore an undergarment with a bounded waist that enabled more comfort than the corset while moving on the bicycle.

There were fewer social restrictions on women's attire when men were not present. In private or in same-sex company, women had greater flexibility in their clothing choices. While participating in physical education classes, women wore a gym suit with bloomers, which resembled a loose, shorter skirt. The divided skirt still did not visually resemble pants. The schools developed uniform gym suits once the women began participating in team sports, such as basketball, in the late 19th century.

Women's athletic participation followed Victorian ideals of modesty well into the 20th century. Even though bloomers were first worn in the 1850s, women continued to wear skirts when engaging in physical activity. Changes to these skirts have generated at times scandalous reactions. Suzanne Lenglen wore a knee-length skirt at Wimbledon in 1919; at first it was shocking, then it started a trend and tennis skirts became shorter. The shorter skirts allowed for greater freedom of movement. Tennis, a sport that has represented white middle-class ideals, has a custom of white clothing; the color is indicative of the free time

and labor needed to sustain itself. Wimbledon still requires its male and female participants to dress predominantly in white.

Throughout the 20th century, skirts became shorter and at times used to promote (hetero)sex appeal in addition to femininity. Made famous by the film *A League of Their Own* (1992), the All-American Girls Professional Baseball League required its participants to wear a belted pastel tunic that fell above the knee, despite the reality that men's baseball players at the time, and still today, wear pants to play the sport.

Although women in most sports now wear shorts or pants, some sports still require, or it is the culture in that sport, to wear a skirt/kilt, for instance, field hockey, lacrosse, and tennis. In lacrosse in particular, some prominent collegiate teams have moved toward wearing shorts, and that has been met with much resistance within the sport's community. Within competitive and recreational running groups, there has been a resurgence of the skirt in the form of the running skirt. Running skirts are marketed as skirts that allow a runner to be feminine and active. They also may be less revealing than tight running attire; the freedom of the skirt allows for more bodily coverage.

Similar to skirts, advancements in swimwear for women have been rooted in concerns of modesty. The water generated unique dilemmas for clothing designers; when wet, bathing and swimming clothing became heavier, form fitting, and translucent. Thus, in the 19th century, women had more freedom in their swimwear choices when in private. The different styles of swimwear have been directly related to the public nature of outdoor swimming. For bathing, women in the 19th century wore clothing that resembled their attire on land, namely trousers under a skirt, but the skirts were knee length or longer. Women wore a corset as well. Once women began to actually swim as opposed to bathe, the costumes became a bit more practical. To prevent drag, swimsuit sleeves were less baggy and then later were eliminated. Swimsuits were one piece with legs extended to the knee and later cut in brief style to enable more movement. Fabric remained a concern until World War II and the resultant advancements in nylon and synthetics with elasticity. In the latter half of the 20th century, elite swimmers wore tight, trim swimsuits that functioned as a second skin;

some competitive teams even advocated competing nude to glide through the water with less resistance. Now, partially due to the advancements in technology, swimsuits cover more parts of the body again. According to the 2010 FINA regulations noted above, women's suits may not extend above the shoulders or below the knees.

In other sports, however, swimsuits have become more revealing. Women participants in beach volleyball, a sport for which players wear swimwear but no one enters the water, conventionally wear bikinis for contests. Those marketing women's athletics sometimes use bikinis as a means to advertise women's sports through the promotion of sex appeal. In summer 2011, the Russian women's soccer team grabbed international headlines when they held matches with players in bikinis to attract a greater following and specifically male soccer fans.

Modesty was also a concern for men in their swimsuits. Only in the 1930s did society's views on exposing the male chest start to change. Earlier men's tank suits covered the body at least up to the armpits. Swim trunks became popular in the 1930s, and men's swimwear since has primarily maintained a one-piece, exposed-chest standard. Spandex greatly impacted swimming competitions, as the form-fitting material created less drag. Elite competitive swimmers wore briefs until the early 21st century, when they were largely replaced by the more technology-driven suits addressed above. According to the 2010 FINA regulations, men's suits may not extend above the navel or below the knee. Recreational swimsuits and surf wear for men at the beginning of the 21st century consist primarily of baggy shorts, some extending to the knee and fitting low on the hips.

Male participants in physical activity have also had changes in their attire in the past century. Dress reformers in the late 19th century claimed trousers trapped air in the legs and led to unbalanced heating for the body. Thus, men wore knee-length pants with wool stockings. The trend did not catch on for everyday attire but did for those engaging in outdoor activities such as golf. "Plus fours," or knickerbockers that extended four inches below the knee, became popular in the 1920s when baggy pants were in style for gentlemen. Some male golf competitors still wear knickerbockers and

argyle socks, but primarily they wear long trousers during competition. Short trousers took years to become popular for public sporting events. In 1932, Bunny Austin wore "ventilated pants" at the U.S. men's tennis championships and was mocked by the press; by the 1940s it was common to wear shorts for athletic competition. In contrast, many women currently wear shorts for golf competitions but not tennis.

The polo shirt has been a staple for men's sporting activities since the beginning of the 1900s. As the name suggests, the garment was originally designed for polo, and the shirt allowed the athlete freedom of movement during competition. By the 1920s the polo shirt became a part of everyday fashion and was the first article of sport clothing to cross over into mainstream attire. Tennis champion René Lacoste, nicknamed the Crocodile, marketed a version of the polo shirt that he wore when playing in the 1920s. The shirt's collar allowed for a slightly formal look while remaining casual, and the longer back enabled the shirt to remain tucked in during competition. Lacoste, among many other manufacturers, continues to make polo shirts for athletic and everyday wear.

Aesthetics and Self-Expression

Sport clothing may also be a means of personal expression for the athletes. Figure skating outfits balance function and aesthetics. Both men's and women's outfits on the ice need to be tight to allow movement but also to prevent injury; if an article of clothing were to hit the ice or become caught in the skates, injury could easily occur. Even as the garments demonstrate artistic expression, they also focus on the body's safety. Women primarily wear short skirts with tight pants that protect them from cold and injury. Sheer mesh fabric gives the appearance of bare skin when in fact the body is quite covered. Men wear tight pants when they compete. Both men and women wear tight, flashy costumes in this sport, and men's outfits are becoming increasingly ornate as gender roles change in the broader society.

Clothing design serves as a creative means of expression for some prominent athletes. The Williams sisters, Venus and Serena, demonstrate their artistic talents on and off the tennis court. Both sisters have worn their own designs while competing in major tournaments. Serena assisted in designing a media-dubbed "catsuit" at the 2002 U.S. Open; her outfit proved to be controversial partially due to its black, fake-leather fabric and body-clinging shape. Similarly, Venus received attention in 2011 not for her performance at Wimbledon but for her self-designed jumper. In addition, Serena has started her own nonsports-related clothing line, Aneres Designs.

Regulations and Reactions

Although some developments and policies in sports clothing have offered the wearer greater freedom and an opportunity to excel athletically, others have limited participants' opportunities. Athletes as individuals and as groups have responded. For instance, after Muslim American Kulsoom Abdullah's appeals, the International Weightlifting Federation ruled in 2011 that women could wear a unitard under the lifting singlet. As part of their faith and efforts to maintain modesty, many Muslim women cover their legs, arms, and hair when in public or mixed company. Since it is expected and sometimes required in many sports to wear clothing that would violate a Muslim woman's faith to participate, the rules and demonstration of religion are in conflict with each other. This compromise meets the athletes' modesty requirements as well as the officials' need to view the body to check for legal lifts. Increasingly, sports organizations are making exceptions to their dress codes and allowing Muslim women to dress in accordance with their faith while competing.

Athletes in other sports have used clothing as an opportunity to rebel against the norms of dominant society. Baggy shorts in basketball, for instance, fit these criteria. Michael Jordan first wore baggy shorts as part of his uniform in the late 1980s, and this trend has continued to the present day. Such baggy shorts are emblematic of black hip-hop culture; clothing functions as a means through which wearers express themselves in relation to their position in society. Hip-hop fashions challenge and subvert authority, while playing with ideas of consumption and power. The National Basketball Association (NBA) has responded to these fashions and has adopted a formal dress code

Fab Five and Fashion

The "Fab Five," five first-year students at the University of Michigan who led the men's basketball team to NCAA Division I finals in 1992 and 1993, faced criticism for their style of play. Dominant white expectations concerning how college basketball players should look and act did not align with the black athletes' approach to the game. Although their clothing was only part of their controversial appeal, their baggy shorts and black shoes and socks continue to be identified as critical components of their challenges to the sport. Now, the fashions they inspired are commonplace in basketball at all levels.

Juwan Howard, Ray Jackson, Jimmy King, Jalen Rose, and Chris Webber represented a new generation of style in the college game. Partially for comfort, they chose the biggest shorts from the uniform selection; the Fab Five's uniforms were loose fitting and extended to and even below the knee, similar to Michael Jordan's at the professional level. Only three years prior, the Michigan championship-winning team wore substantially shorter shorts that fell just below the end of the buttocks and revealed most of the thigh. In addition, the Fab Five's donning of black socks with their black shoes was coordinated. What could have been a fashion faux pas—white socks were the norm—became a marketable trend.

Following the Fab Five's success, Michigan apparel sales soared. After their first season, the school's athletic royalties jumped from $2.4 to $4.4 million. Although unable to financially benefit from these sales, the athletes were aware of the profits their fashions generated. In response, they utilized some of the same articles that caused them controversy to protest the commodification of their style. During the starting lineup announcements at a game, they wore plain navy T-shirts—a look that would not be marketed as unique.

for its athletes both on and off the court. According to the 2005 code, after sporting events when players appeared on television or in a professional setting, they needed to be dressed in business casual, which included the removal of large medallions and oversized clothing. League officials also began to enforce a rule that required uniform shorts to not extend below 0.1 inch above the knee, a rule that had been on the books for years but had not been enforced. Reactions to these rules have been mixed; some athletes have refused to follow them and face fines for each violation. Scholars and journalists have argued that the NBA dress code was an example of white authority attempting to rein in the actions of black athletes.

Notably, baggy basketball jerseys and sport attire are worn by individuals and groups off the court as well. In the early 2000s, hip-hop generated a new retro jersey market. Retro jerseys serve as homage to those who made social advancements prior to the acceptance of the black athlete. Rapper and music producer P-Diddy (Sean Combs) helped launch the retro craze when he wore a series of jerseys at the American Music Awards in 2001. Celebrities pay hundreds of dollars for exact replicas of vintage uniforms, and they wear these uniforms at the games as spectators and in everyday public life. Those who have no affiliation with the team may wear them as a representation of black success in the athletic arena. What began as a political expression has become a mass market. Increasingly fans of all races enjoy replica jerseys representing athletes of all races as a form of nostalgia.

Skateboarding communities have also used clothing as a means to rebel against the dominant culture. These activities embody an alternative culture; alternative activities were developed as a means of expression and anticompetition in contrast to mainstream sport and society. Skateboarders reject the notion of wearing athletic or sport-specific attire to skate. Having a set style would go against their ideals; what they wear to skate is what they already have been wearing that day. They typically wear T-shirts and denim jeans, either baggy or skinny jeans to allow movement while performing tricks. The focus is on comfort and self-expression as opposed to conformity. Although there is no set uniform, there is a skateboarding clothing market, which is popular among skaters and nonskaters. As the above examples demonstrate, sports clothing serves many purposes, including resisting athletic norms and assisting in developing an arena for alternative interpretations of mainstream sports.

Melissa C. Wiser

See also Fab Five; Jordan, Michael; National Basketball Association; Williams, Serena; Williams, Venus

Suggested Resources
Costantino, Maria. *Men's Fashion in the Twentieth Century: From Frock Coats to Intelligent Fibres.* London: BT Batsford, 1997.
FINA Requirements for Swimwear Approval. http://www.fina.org/H2O/docs/rules/SWIMWEAR_APPROVAL_from_01012010.pdf. Accessed October 1, 2011.
NBA Player Dress Code. http://www.nba.com/news/player_dress_code_051017.html. Accessed October 1, 2011.
O'Mahony, Marie, and Sarah E. Braddock. *Sportstech: Revolutionary Fabrics, Fashion, and Design.* New York: Thames & Hudson, 2002.
Warner, P. C. *When the Girls Came Out to Play: The Birth of American Sportswear.* Amherst: University of Massachusetts Press, 2006.

Sports Drinks

Sports drinks are meant to rehydrate athletes before, during, and after their athletic performances. Historical discussions on how to do this go back to ancient Greek texts discussing whether Olympians should consume wine or refrain from it during their competitions. In the modern era, the first commercialized sports drink was Gatorade, invented at the University of Florida in 1965. Through the early 1990s there were a host of competitors including Powerade, 10K-Thirst, All Sport, Nautilus, Powerburst, Enduro, BodyAid, Dragonade, Starter Fluids, and Quenchade. Through the present day, Gatorade has continued to dominate the sports drink market with approximately 75 percent market share. One of the reasons for this has been the "science" contained in more than 100 studies conducted by the Gatorade Sports Science Institute, which support Gatorade's health claims. A second reason has been successful sports marketing centered on key sports endorsements. Until recently, the only two other sports drink to survive and compete against Gatorade's success have been Coca-Cola's Powerade and, on a smaller scale, Monarch Beverage's (formerly PepsiCo's) All Sport. However, since 2004, new competitors have emerged including Vitaminwater (owned by Coca-Cola) and ZICO Pure Premium Coconut Water.

Some might consider Red Bull Energy drink an "ergogenic" sports drink. In fact, since the 1970s there

Pittsburgh Penguins goalie Marc-Andre Fleury consumes a sports drink during the NHL hockey team's practice in Pittsburgh, April 17, 2012. (AP Photo/Gene J. Puskar.)

have been nutritional studies demonstrating that caffeine enhances athletic performance, especially when consumed before exercise. Red Bull was first introduced in 1987 in Austria. It is not covered in any further detail in this article because in the United States, the National Federation of State High School Associations has recommended that athletes not consume Red Bull to enhance or recover from sports performance. They have categorized it as an energy drink, not a sports drink.

Gatorade, the first sports drink, was discovered in 1965 at the University of Florida, Gainesville. Gator football players attributed their first-time victory at the Orange Bowl in 1966 to Gatorade's success in reviving them by adequately replacing fluids and electrolytes. Gatorade soon developed a following among college and professional football players. As a Stokely-Van Camp product, it reached its high point in 1983 when it was named the official sports drink of the National Football League (NFL), a title that it still holds today.

As a market, the sports drink beverage sector changed rapidly in the 1980s and 1990s. In 1983, QuakerOats purchased Stokely-Van Camp for $220 million. At the time, Gatorade had an estimated $100 million in sales. Under QuakerOats's sports marketing campaign, Michael Jordan was signed to endorse Gatorade. Sales skyrocketed and by 2001 Gatorade had $2.2 billion in sales. During this same period, other sports drinks such as 10-K Thirst Quencher were eliminated or relegated to a small market share. 10-K Thirst Quencher had been Florida State University football's sports drink of preference. In 1987, it was subject of a New Orleans television commercial featuring football and basketball coaches from the New Orleans Saints, Louisiana State University, and Tulane University. By 2002, it had disappeared from the U.S. market. In contrast, Powerade, launched by the Coca-Cola Company in 1988, has been successful in carving out its own identity in the sports drink market. It debuted in 1988 and alongside Japanese sports drinks Aquarius, it has shared the title of official sports drink at the Olympics Games under a key sponsorship agreement with the International Olympic Committee (IOC).

A third Gatorade competitor still in business today is All Sport. This sports drink product line was launched by PepsiCo in 1993. In 2001, PepsiCo wanted to acquire Gatorade. It purchased the QuakerOats Company for $13 billion. This created a shakeup in the sports drinks market. As part of the merger, in compliance with antitrust regulations, All Sport was sold. It was acquired by Monarch Beverage Company who later sold it in 2007 to All Sport, Inc., based in Austin, Texas. All Sport's product line of sports drinks is currently distributed by the Dr. Pepper Snapple Group.

Since 2001, in an attempt to gain greater market share over PepsiCo's Gatorade, the Coca-Cola Company has made various changes to its Powerade product line. First, it reformulated Powerade to include vitamins B_3, B_6, and B_{12}. Second, it created a low-calorie sports drink, Powerade Option, to compete with Gatorade Propel. Third, it began acquiring additional sports drink brands that may compete with Gatorade directly in the future. This includes the 2005 purchase of Aquarius, a mineral sports drink that since 1988 has shared the title of official sports drink at the Olympic Games with Powerade. The Coca-Cola Company has not marketed Aquarius sports drinks in the United States to date. However, it has used the Aquarius brand to rename its Dannon spring water line. Another related acquisition in the sports drink sector was Coca-Cola's 2007 purchase of Glaceau for $4.1 billion. Glaceau's VitaminWater product line has been placed under Powerade's management. A fourth change made in the Powerade line was the creation since 2008 of two new products: Powerade Zero, a zero-calorie sports drink, and Powerade ION4, a formula that contains four specific electrolytes.

In 2008, the sports drink market in the United States had an estimated $7.6 billion in retail sales. In 2010, Gatorade dominated this market with 77.2 percent of the market share, followed by Powerade with 21.7 percent of the market. One of the new companies interested in creating a new niche in the growing and lucrative sports drink market is ZICO Pure Premium Coconut Water. According to the company's advertising materials, coconut water is a healthy alternative that has traditionally been used in tropical cultures to rehydrate and replenish electrolytes, as well as vitamins and amino acids. It also has potassium, magnesium, and cytokinins (plant hormones). ZICO is committed to harvesting its products in the developing world through sustainable practices. Outside of the traditional sports market, it is creating a new following that includes runners, cyclists, tri-athletes, yogis, and surfers. In 2009, the Coca-Cola Company took notice and acquired a small investment (less than 20 percent) in the company.

In 2009, following a 2 percent decline in sales, Gatorade rebranded a major portion of its product line around the G Series. This classified different Gatorade products into Prime 01 (before), Perform 02 (during), and Recover 03 (after) sports categories. A new G Series Pro line was created for professional athletes, as was a G Natural line that was marketed in Whole Foods grocery stores. Last, a line of G Series FIT fruit-and-nut bites and postworkout protein smoothies was created.

The growth in the sports drinks market and the growing concern about childhood obesity has sparked questions about the marketing of high-calorie drinks at schools. This has sparked questions about soda, as well as sports drinks. As part of this debate, in 2010, California governor Arnold Schwarzenegger sponsored a bill (SB 1295) to ban the sale of sports drinks in California schools. The bill did not pass but it raised the issue about the role of sugar, calories, and general nutrition in sports drinks, and their prevalence in school-sponsored sporting events.

Sports drinks are part of American popular culture and they represent a growing sector of the beverage and sports marketing industries. One of the best examples of this is in the movie *The Waterboy* when Adam Sandler is told that Gatorade is better than water. Gatorade sponsors many professional athletes and has been endorsed by superstar athletes such as Michael Jordan and Tiger Woods. Powerade has its own line of endorsements. It is the official sports drink of the U.S. Olympic Team (excluding U.S.A. Basketball and U.S. Soccer, which have deals with Gatorade). Through its parent Coca-Cola, it has many national and international contracts. All Sport's sport marketing is more limited but it does include PGA and NASCAR celebrities.

See also Advertising and Sport; Gatorade; Jordan, Michael; New Orleans Saints; Woods, Tiger

Margaret Carroll Boardman

Suggested Resources

Fredrix, Emily. "Pepsi Suing Coca-Cola over Powerade Ads." April 13, 2009. http://www.huffington post.com/2009/04/14/pepsi-suing-cocacola-over_n_ 186709.html. Accessed February 26, 2012.

McWilliams, Jeremiah. "PepsiCo Revamps 'Formable' Gatorade Franchise after Rocky 2009." March 23, 2010. http://www.ajc.com/business/pepsico-revamps-formi dable-gatorade-397505.html. Accessed February 23, 2012.

Picchi, Aimee. "Gatorade's Rebranding: So Confusing It Requires an Ad to Explain It." May 6. 2010. http:// www.dailyfinance.com/story/company-news/gato rades-rebranding-so-confusing-it-requires-a-new-ad -to-expl/19467659/?icid=sphere_copyright. Accessed February 24, 2012.

"Position Statement and Recommendations for the Use of Energy Drinks by Young Athletes." National Federation of State High School Associations. http://www .ahsaa.com/Portals/0/pdf/other/energy%20drinks.pdf. Accessed February 29, 2012.

Rovell, Darren. *First in Thirst: How Gatorade Turned the Science of Sweat into a Cultural Phenomenon.* New York: American Management Association, 2006.

Spector, Bennett. "Gatorade Conquers Hydration." February 1, 2010. http://bleacherreport.com/articles/337710 -gatorade-concurs-hydration-debuting-g-series-technol ogy-at-super-bowl-xliv, Accessed February 23, 2012.

"ZICO Beverages, LLC Announces $15 Million Investment from Key Strategic Partners." Press Release. http:// www.reuters.com/article/2009/09/01/idUS151359+01 -Sep-2009+PRN20090901. Accessed March 1, 2012.

Sports Food

Americans have been picking up sports food to eat while watching and participating in athletic events since the colonial period. Since the 19th century, baseball parks and football stadiums initially had vendors walking through the spectator stands with baskets of food. This would have been similar to the food available at state and local fairs. With time, sports parks installed permanent concession areas and common spectator fare included popcorn, roasted nuts, ice cream, pretzels, sodas, hot dogs, and nachos. Since the 1990s, sports food has evolved to also include a new category of high-energy endurance bars targeted at athletes, which have increasingly become popular snacks for spectators.

Harry M. Stevens was one of the first modern concessionaires to build a business empire by selling sports food. Beginning in 1894, he acquired the concession rights to sell food at New York's Polo Grounds (home of the New York Giants), Madison Square Garden, Ebbets Field, Yankee Stadium, and several major New York racetracks including Saratoga and Belmont. He and his sons continued to expand until they were providing concessions across the United States. Stevens is credited for introducing the hot dog to baseball sports fans.

Cracker Jack is another sports food whose popularity and success is closely associated with baseball. It is made from a mixture of peanuts and popcorn coated with molasses syrup. It was created by German immigrants Fritz and Louis Rueckheim who made it to sell at the 1893 World's Fair. In 1908, sales received a boost from publicity created by Jack Norworth and Albert Von Tilzer who composed the song "Take Me Out to the Ballgame" with its one line, "buy me some peanuts and Cracker Jack!" The Cracker Jack Company was purchased by Borden in 1964 and later acquired in 1997 by Frito-Lay, a wholly owned subsidiary of PepsiCo. In 2004, when Frito-Lay replaced the traditional cardboard box packaging with a seven-ounce bag, Yankee Stadium concessions canceled sales and began selling as a substitute Crunch 'n Munch. Protests from the fans were so great that the Yankees' chief operating officer rescinded the decision and made Cracker Jack available to fans at Yankee Stadium.

Nachos are a sports food closely associated with professional football. According to a story told in the *San Antonio Express-News* in 2002 by Ignacio Anaya Jr., nachos were first created and named by his father Ignacio (nicknamed "Nacho") Araya in 1943 at the Victory Club in Piedras Negras, Mexico. He put the dish together quickly when a group of U.S. military wives came across the Rio Grande from Fort Duncan in Eagle Pass, Texas, and stopped in his Victory Club restaurant. Nachos gained national fame in the late

Cracker Jack and peanuts are seen during a spring training baseball game in March of 2010 in Peoria, Arizona. (AP Photo/Charlie Neibergall.)

1970s. Starting in 1977, Frank Liberto began selling nachos in the concession stand at Arlington Stadium near Dallas, Texas. Their popularity grew after Howard Cosell talked glowingly about how much he enjoyed eating them before his television broadcasts on *Monday Night Football*. "Nacho cheese" is a generic term frequently used in American popular culture to describe the melted cheese sauce poured over the corn chips. Frito-Lays sells a cheese dip with this name and Taco Bell uses it in their fast-food menu.

Between 1999 and 2011, eight major football and baseball stadiums underwent new construction or renovation. In the process, they upgraded their food and beverage concessions. Recognition was given to the importance of sports food as each stadium made an effort to introduce more upscale or gourmet food, while still maintaining traditional sports food options. Beginning in July 1999, Safeco Field in Seattle, home to the Seattle Mariners, became known as the stadium with the healthiest sports food including sushi rolls, organic smoothies, veggie hot dogs, and peel-and-eat shrimp cocktail. In August 2008, $720 million Lucas Oil Stadium, home to the Indianapolis Colts and Super Bowl XLVI in 2012, centered its sports food on a pork theme—fried pork tenderloin sandwiches, pork-shank lollipops with a sweet chile glaze, and pork poppers.

Four stadiums changed their sports food menus in 2009. The newly renovated Kauffman Stadium, home to the Kansas City Royals, made barbeque the main food theme—Royals All-Star Barbeque BBW ribs, smoked prime rib, beef brisket and pork-shoulder sandwiches, barbecue baked potatoes, the All-Star BBQ hot dog, and barbeque pulled-pork sandwiches. At the new $1.5 billion Yankee Stadium, sports food now includes Brother Jimmy's barbecue, Johnny Rockets sandwiches, 33 different beers from Beers of the World, garlic fries with cheese, and Lobel's dry-aged prime rib. The new $800 million Mets Stadium at Citi Field, New York, provides more food options than its predecessor at Shea Stadium. This includes lobster rolls, crab cake sandwiches, clam chowder, soft tacos, and Mexican-style corn on the cob. At the renovated Dallas Cowboys Stadium in Arlington, Texas, prime beef and Tex-Mex are the food themes. This includes cheesesteaks, chopped beef barbecue sandwiches, Black Angus cheeseburgers, lots of nachos, the "Cowboyritas" cocktails (similar to margaritas), and green-chile Kobe burgers topped with jalapeño jack cheese.

In 2010, two more stadiums upgraded their sports food. The $517 million Minnesota Twins stadium at Target Field in Minneapolis provides favorites from local restaurants including steak sandwiches, pork chops on a stick, chili, wild rice soup, and a root beer float made with Killebrew root beer (a brand from former Twins star Harmon Killebrew). Last, the new $1.7 billion New Meadowlands Stadium, home to the Giants and Jets, focuses on Italian American cuisine items such as peppers and eggs, roast pork with provolone and hot peppers, Italian hot dogs, Taylor pork rolls, and meatball hoagies.

Switching from spectator sports food to high-energy sports food for endurance athletes, two American companies stand out as innovators in this new sector worth approximately $1.9 billion in worldwide sales in 2005. The first is PowerBar, founded in 1986 by Canadian entrepreneur and athlete Brian Maxwell in Berkeley, California. PowerBar's original formula was created in 1983 by Jennifer Biddulph, a nutritionist who later married Maxwell. Its first target market was marathon runners and cyclists. This expanded to surfers, mountain bikers, soccer players, and triathlon athletes who run, cycle, and swim. By the early 1990s, the company was doing between $6 and $7 million in sales. In 1992, it was ranked as the 22nd fastest growing company in the United States by *Inc. 500* magazine. By 1999, sales reached $150 million. Then Nestlé, the world's largest food company, purchased PowerBar for $375 million. PowerBar was a sponsor of the U.S. Olympics team in 2000. The following year, it launched its line of Pria bars especially formulated for the nutritional needs of female athletes. Between 2005 and 2008, PowerBar was the exclusive global sponsor of all U.S. and international Ironman triathlon championships.

PowerBar's main competitor, ClifBar, was created in 1992 by Gary Erickson. His goal was to take away 20 percent of PowerBar's market share. As the part owner of a bakery in the San Francisco Bay Area, he formulated various recipes, then made an initial 30,000 shipment of ClifBars to his distributors. Sales were $700,000 the first year, $1.2 million the second year. By 1994, sales surpassed $2 million. In 2000, Erickson turned down an offer to sell ClifBar to QuakerOats for $120 million. He continued building his company so successfully that between 2006 and 2009, Forbes ranked the company as the number one "breakway brand" in the United States.

ClifBar's target market includes athletes and fans of winter sports, cycling, cyclo-cross, mountain biking, triathlons, climbing, surfing, and running. The company sponsors 1,000 sports and charity events annually. A percentage of all its profits go to the Breast Cancer Fund in San Francisco. This includes profits from its product line of Luna Bars, created in 1999 as the first energy bars formulated especially for women. (PowerBar's Pria line was created in 2001 to compete with Luna Bars.) In 2000, Luna Bars established Lunafest, a philanthropic traveling film festival with films written and directed by women. This has raised over $456,000 for the Breast Cancer Fund and $785,000 for other women's organizations. In 2001, both the ClifBar and Luna product lines began sponsoring the LUNA Pro Team, a women's professional mountain biking team. In 2002, this expanded into Team LUNA Chix, a group of mountain biking, running, triathlon, and cycling teams that fundraises for the Breast Cancer Fund, as well as promotes women's sports. Luna Bars have received unpaid celebrity endorsements in *Self* and *U.S. Weekly* from Carrie Underwood and Cameron Diaz.

Margaret Carroll Boardman

See also Cosell, Howard; Cowboys Stadium: Hot Dogs; *Monday Night Football*; New York Yankees; Super Bowl; "Take Me Out to the Ballgame"; Yankee Stadium

Suggested Resources

America's Best Sports Stadium Food. http://www.departures.com/slideshows/americas-best-sports-stadium-food/1. Accessed March 6, 2012.

Byrd, Veronica. "Hungry for Power." October 22, 2001. http://www.people.com/people/archive/article/0,20135536,00.html Accessed February 29, 2012.

"Crunch 'n Munch Waived by Yankees." http://www.washingtonpost.com/wp-dyn/articles/A14400-2004Jun3.html. Accessed March 2, 2012.

"Food Consumption to Set New Mark." http://query.nytimes.com/gst/abstract.html?res=F60C12FC3C551A738DDDA90B94DE405B818EF1D3 Accessed March 10, 2012.

Heintz, Nadine, Bo Burlingham, and Ryan McCarthy. "Starting Up in a Down Economy." May 1, 2008. http://www.inc.com/magazine/20080501/starting-up-in-a-down-economy_pagen_4.html. Accessed March 6, 2012.

Powerbar and Ironman Announce Global Sponsorship Agreement. Press Release. http://ironman.com/mediacenter/pressreleases/powerbar-and-ironman-announce-global-sponsorship-agreement#ixzz1oZKVN7fp. http://ironman.com/mediacenter/pressreleases/powerbar-and-ironman-announceglobal-sponsorship-agreement#ixzz1oZJiP3Rp. Accessed March 5, 2012.

Sports Illustrated

Sports Illustrated is a weekly magazine, begun in 1954, that has been the leading sports magazine in the United States since that time. Its specialty swimsuit issue, published each February, may be the biggest publication, in terms of issues printed and sold, of any national magazine.

In 1954, Henry Luce, the publisher of *Time* and many other journals, decided that the company needed to add another magazine to his empire. He wanted another weekly like *Time* or *Life*, but the topic was open, until it was narrowed down to sports after a number of months of secret meetings by a development team. At that time there was no weekly sports magazine and there was a belief that a desire for one did not exist among the readership of mostly young males. The most popular regular sports magazines were monthlies like *Sport*, *True*, and *Field and Stream* with seasonal publications for baseball, football, and basketball seeming to fill in the remainder of demand. There was a belief that sports readers were too highly specialized to make a weekly general sports magazine successful.

After months of meetings, planning, and establishment of a editorial team, *Sports Illustrated* debuted in August 1954 and, from the beginning, there was uncertainty about who the readership was that the magazine sought. Compounding this was the writing staff who represented a few very distinct backgrounds. First, there were the large number of former Ivy Leaguers who had an interest in traditional sports like baseball and college football, but also were taken with yachting, horse racing, and mountain climbing, sports that were limited, generally, to those with more financial means.

A second group of writers were more "good old boys" in being from the more southern states like Texas and Georgia. Equally well educated, their interests extended more into college and professional football, hunting, fishing, and auto racing (just in its infancy). Many of the writers had strong literary backgrounds, while some had more journalistic credentials. It would take a number of years to establish an identity for the magazine as the readership slowly climbed.

The first two issues of the magazine contained insert baseball card reproductions based on the 1954 Topps baseball cards. Some were exact reproductions and others were facsimiles created for the magazine and not existent in the 1954 Topps card set. Few adults would have been excited by these inserts, but 10–12-year-old boys would have been. The appeal, then, would have been to their dads to buy the magazine and give the cards (made of paper, not cardboard) to their grateful kids.

In the late 1950s into the 1960s the magazine continued to cover sports in a larger, more cultural sense, which included sports clothing, hunting, hiking in other countries, and bridge. Charles Goren had a regular bridge column. Red Smith had pieces in *SI* and Grantland Rice's last piece (most likely) was in the first issue (he had died a month prior).

Subscription sales reached 1,000,000 in 1960 and continued to climb, but seven years into the magazine, it still lost money. That would finally turn around in the mid-1960s and eventually make *SI* the leading money-maker in the *Time-Life* empire.

From its inception *Sports Illustrated* was a writer's magazine with editors doing the minimum necessary to publish a piece. Readers looked forward to the work of Dan Jenkins, George Plimpton, Robert Creamer, Tex Maule, Roy Blount Jr., Frank Deford, and Rick Reilly, among others. Most of them published novels or longer works of nonfiction, inspired by or developed from their work on *Sports Illustrated* pieces.

As managing editors changed, the magazine began to shift its contents and developed a broader demographic, even as it narrowed its foci to the so-called big six—college football, pro football, college basketball, pro basketball, hockey, and baseball. The magazine also continued to provide more and greater photographs, first by introducing more color, before subsequently switching to all color photographs in the late 1960s/early 1970s.

The Swimsuit Issue

In 1964, Jule Campbell was asked by managing editor Andre Laguerre to go "some place beautiful and put a pretty girl on the cover" of the magazine. *SI* had had a couple small fashion shoots with swimwear in the previous year or two, but this would be a dedicated focus that would grab the attention of men interested in pretty girls as well as travel. The shoot was in Baja Mexico (Cabo San Lucas) and the result was a series of letters that indicated how provocative the issue was. It was repeated in 1965 and the tradition was born. It only grew with the only constant for more than 30 years being Jule Campbell, who spent much of the year planning where to shoot and which models to use, often introducing new models who then became superstars in that field, often because their names were used, unlike in fashion magazines where there was relative anonymity.

The great *SI* photographers, including Tony Triolo, Walter Iooss, and Neil Leifer, made these editions as special as they were. The swimsuit photos were accompanied by a travel piece, reflecting the location of the shoot. In the 1970s, Cheryl Tiegs was one of the first of the new supermodels and her photo in 1978, taken by Walter Iooss in Brazil for that year's issue, became a sensation, leading to enormous newsstand sales of *SI*. Campbell discovered Christie Brinkley as well as Elle Macpherson (for whom Campbell became a sort of surrogate mother/sister), Kathy Ireland, Paula Porzikova, and Carol Alt. Newsstand sales on the "sunshine issue" reached 451,000 in 1984 and by 1987 were just under 1.5 million. The 25th anniversary swimsuit issue in 1989 generated sales of nearly $10 million and video sales were over $5 million.

Campbell handled her last issue in 1996, her 32nd, with Tyra Banks on the cover. By that time, the issue had generated a lot of controversy both from feminists and conservatives. In addition, *SI* was having a hard time finding innovative ways to produce and photograph the models. Since 1997, the swimsuit issue has become a separate issue that subscribers can opt out of if they wish. Over these last few years a few innovations have emerged: the use of athletes, both male and female, as well as the absence of swimsuits, totally, replaced by creative use of body paint.

Special Issues

One of the first special issues was a five-part series in 1968 on the plight of the black athlete, "The Black Athlete, a Shameful Story." It was critically acclaimed, but also aroused the initial ire of the bosses at Time-Life. After the articles elicited thousands of letters,

Henry R. Luce (1898–1967), founder of *Sports Illustrated*. (Library of Congress.)

almost all positive, and the series won awards for the magazine, a new threshold had been crossed in *SI*'s efforts at covering civil rights.

Most of the other special issues were less controversial with annual editions devoted to the big six sports, as well as Olympic previews and summaries, among others. A series on women in sports garnered less controversy, but still made an impact on the magazine and its readership.

Sports Illustrated for Kids

In January 1989, *SI* brought out a new monthly magazine, *Sports Illustrated for Kids*, with top writers and photographers producing a magazine for children, ages 8–13. Michael Jordan was on the first cover and has appeared on it three other times, second only to Shaquille O'Neal's five covers. By its second year, it had 500,000 subscribers and the magazine broke even in its third year, two years ahead of schedule. Circulation now runs close to a million per month. This magazine has won the Parents' Choice Magazine Award seven

Sports Illustrated Covers

Despite the so-called *Sports Illustrated* jinx, wherein those appearing on the cover of the magazine soon have unexpected losses or injuries, it is a singular honor to appear on those covers. Over the nearly 60 years of the magazine, the most portrayed individual has been Michael Jordan with 58 covers, distantly followed by Muhammad Ali with 38 and Tiger Woods with 24 (as of early 2012). The top five list as of that time:

Michael Jordan	58
Muhammad Ali	38
Tiger Woods	24
Magic Johnson	23
Kareem Abdul-Jabbar	22

times and the Distinguished Achievement for Excellence in Educational Publishing 11 times. Building on the success of this magazine, *SI* produced *Sports Illustrated for Women*, a bimonthly, starting in 2000. During the course of the production, the magazine name was changed to simply *Sports Illustrated Women*, but it failed to find a real niche and *SI* ceased producing it with the December 2002 edition.

Over the past 20 years, *Sports Illustrated* has focused more and more on the major sports, but there has been growing coverage of soccer and extreme sports. Critics have cited the dearth of great writers, which early editions had, with more emphasis and control by the editors, whose bottom line is always the bottom line. *SI* has become the biggest moneymaker in the Time-Warner stable of magazines, with profits topping $100 million in many years.

Television and Sports Illustrated

In 1984, a few years after its inception in 1979, ESPN was put on the market and *Sports Illustrated* seriously considered purchasing it. Instead, they took a bye and ABC (subsequently purchased by Disney in 1996) stepped in and purchased the channel, infusing it with money and creating the biggest challenge to *SI* ever, a daily account of sports that *SI* could only match on a weekly basis with more in-depth writing. *SI* was not sure how to address the new total sports programming, particularly ESPN's *SportsCenter*, and

considered their own cable channel, increased advertising of the magazine and its videos on ESPN, as well as a joint partnership with CNN, CNN/SI. The latter debuted in 1996 as a 24-hour channel, but it was unable to make an impact, either in viewership or profit. It folded in 2002, but the website survives. Of even greater concern to *SI* was the creation and continued publication of a rival print magazine, *ESPN, the Magazine*, which debuted in 1998 as a biweekly. *SI* is seen as more serious and provides more depth than *ESPN, the Magazine*, but there has certainly been an effect on *SI*'s readership numbers. As of the end of 2011, *Sports Illustrated* had a circulation figure of 3.3 million; *ESPN, the Magazine*'s was 2.1 million.

As of 2012, *Sports Illustrated* continues to be the most circulated and most respected sports magazine in the United States. Its various videos and special editions of games or series sell well and its various awards for sportspersons of the year and other honors are well respected in and out of the sports world. The magazine has become a solid part of American sports culture and continues to thrive on excellent writing, photography, and editing.

Murry R. Nelson

See also Deford, Frank; ESPN Channels; Jordan, Michael; O'Neal, Shaquille; Plimpton, George; Rice, Grantland

Suggested Resources

Fleder, Rob. *Sports Illustrated 50: The Anniversary Book.* New York: Time, 2005.

Kelly, Greg, and the Editors of *Sports Illustrated. Sports Illustrated, the Covers.* New York: Sports Illustrated, 2010.

MacCambridge, Michael. *The Franchise: A History of* Sports Illustrated *Magazine.* New York: Hyperion, 1997.

Sports Illustrated for Kids. http://www.sikids.com/. Accessed March 13, 2012.

Sports Memorabilia, Vintage and Autographed

Cecil "Tex" Hughson, a Boston Red Sox pitcher in the 1940s, once expressed amazement that wiry kids would take the most mangled scraps of paper, even remnants of boxes of popcorn, and thrust it in front

Mark Friedland from Aspen, Colorado, proudly shows off a 1938 Lou Gehrig bat and jersey he bought at an auction for $52,000 and $220,000, respectively, in San Francisco on September 4, 1991. (AP Photo/Brad Mangin.)

of his face in quest of his autograph. When he recognized the source of such adoration was the same youngster, he asked, "What could you possibly want with my autograph on these beat-up slivers of paper?" The young man answered innocently, "'Cause we can trade five of yours for one Ted Williams." Such is the fun and spirit of collecting autographed sports memorabilia. The hobby is clearly more sophisticated than that Rockwell-esque snapshot.

Collectors of vintage and autographed sports memorabilia commonly started their habits with trading cards. As they grew to appreciate and witness moments in sports—a World Series, a Super Bowl, an All-Star Game, a decisive series final, a milestone moment, or the history of a player, a team, or a sport—their desire to take away something beside sheer joy or grave disappointment blossomed as well. Tickets, programs,

and other keepsakes documented these memories; mementos acquired over time documented history.

Fans collect mementos and inherit others. The orb stuffed in a sock and stored in the blackness of a safety deposit box was one of countless baseballs autographed by the Bambino, Babe Ruth, who relished public appearances and signing for young admirers. Still others acquired items purely by chance and captured signatures on anything from menus to programs at fundraising events. Maybe they invested time in a flattering, well-crafted missive and received a response or simply an autographed index card. Or they endeared themselves to ballplayers who remembered their childhood trips to the ballpark and rewarded a youngster for his devotion with a well-worn jersey. Or maybe someone with a team contact had access to jerseys stored in a stadium, warehouse, or filing cabinet. Such was the genesis of collecting vintage and autographed sports memorabilia. The desire continues as an obsession in round-the-clock media attention as collectors seek a more physical connection with heroes.

American sports began to tell their stories formally and in a collective manner in 1939, when baseball's Hall of Fame and Museum opened in Cooperstown, New York. (Its first inductees actually were elected in 1936.) Twenty years after the Hall opened in upstate New York, the Naismith Memorial Basketball Hall of Fame opened; and the Pro Football Hall of Fame followed in 1963. These shrines were depositories of artifacts, and they became managed by curators. Many artifacts came from sports legends or patriarchal families of the sports teams. Over time, other individuals would come forward with items that gained the approval of Hall of Fame accessions committees. Like any museum, the Halls of Fame's supply of artifacts and memorabilia would far outstrip display space. Their roles as caretakers of history would come into play. Sports museums wowed visitors and stimulated urges to dig through closets, attics, basements, garage sales, and junk shops for old stuff.

Early collectors of artifacts, like card collectors, possessed moxie for requesting and receiving items from retired and active players and managers. Scoring one item was enough to set in motion a passion for widening tactics that would beget further collecting. None of these characters was as successful or cunning in gathering items as Barry Halper, a New Jersey kid who began his passion at age nine, played college baseball for Jimmie Foxx, and became a businessman, which led him to become a minority owner of the New York Yankees. The relationships he built during his lifetime allowed him to amass an immense collection, so abundant and expansive that the relatively few who saw it swore it exceeded the overall quality of the museum in Cooperstown.

In 1999, Hall of Fame officials admittedly filled in many of the museum's gaps by arranging through Major League Baseball to purchase a significant portion of Halper's collection for $25 million and a space that bears his name. He converted rooms in his Livingston, New Jersey, home and covered virtually every square inch of the space with vintage collectibles. He owned more than 200 vintage jerseys and stored them

in a closet equipped with a revolving rack common to all dry cleaning shops. Other individuals had a similar passion and embarked on missions to scour the countryside seeking visits with old ballplayers and other athletes to talk sports and ask for something from their playing days. Old gear and keepsakes had relatively little value to many athletes or their widows. Offspring, if there were any, showed little interest in keeping the stuff. More savvy individuals would unveil dreams, most of them pipe dreams, of building museums to exhibit items. They'd leave with an armful or a trunk full of items. Worse yet, as Negro Leaguers gained some attention for their contributions to the history of baseball, eager, often unscrupulous collectors would virtually prey on such legendary players as James "Cool Papa" Bell and gather what little that might have survived the time for a couple of hundred dollars.

Another milestone in baseball history that stirred passions for heroes and their legacies were the East Coast departures of the Brooklyn Dodgers and New York Giants as they moved to Los Angeles and San Francisco, respectively. Generations of Dodgers and Giants fans remain scarred from the cross-country move and, even worse, the destruction of the historic Polo Grounds and Ebbets Field. Seats, turnstiles, bricks, signage, and other items were casualties of the moves, but reclamation efforts preceded the wrecking ball, and some of these items were salvaged. Crosley Field and so many other stadia would follow. In 1973, the House that Ruth Built was overhauled with new seats. Many of the old seats were sold for $10 apiece. The rush to collecting vintage autographs was off to a fast start.

Hunting season opened for remnants of sports history. Sports fans also found ways to correspond with old timers, like "Goose" Goslin, "Gabby" Hartnett, "Smokey" Joe Wood, Ernie Lombardi, Roy Campanella, Jackie Robinson, Joe DiMaggio, and so many more survivors from earlier decades. Letter writers would regularly correspond with enclosures of index cards and self-addressed envelopes, then race home daily to check the mailbox to check the day's bounty. All of these transactions took place for the cost of envelopes and postage. With all of the searching high and low for all kinds of memorabilia and letter writing, a market emerged.

Swap meet promoters with tables of hobbyists added method to the collecting madness. Heroes were paid fees to sign as show guests. The costs were recouped by charging adoring fans, who never dreamed that getting an autograph would be so easy, despite the cost. Early in this process, Mickey Mantle signed for $10 apiece; Bob Feller for $3. The idea of athletes signing for fees transformed the hobby into an industry. Dealers from coast to coast soon would conceive a national convention for collectors in 1980, and the inaugural National Sports Collectors Convention would be held in Los Angeles. Meanwhile, Sotheby's and Christie's, auction houses known for selling paintings by Renaissance and modern masters for tens of millions of dollars, were attracted by this new collecting niche and brought vintage and autographed sports memorabilia to a broader audience.

Prices soared with the increase in demand. The hobby became increasingly popular and weekend warriors who would sell memorabilia, quit real jobs to build a livelihood through the sports memorabilia business. The Internet and other digital media outlets contributed to explosive sales and a burgeoning hobby evolved into a billion-dollar business. The high-stakes business, however, also revealed a fraudulent side of activity, including forgeries. In the 1990s, the Federal Bureau of Investigation conducted a sting operation called Operation Bullpen that would bust a ring of forgers and distributors that stretched from coast to coast. Because they tend to fetch the most money in the marketplace, forgers tend to focus on the priciest signatures (Babe Ruth, Lou Gehrig, Jimmie Foxx, Roberto Clemente, Mickey Mantle, Roger Maris, Ted Williams, Joe DiMaggio) and those with few, if any, exemplars (19th-century Hall of Famers and other vintage players, managers and owners; most Negro Leaguers).

As a result, professional sports leagues got into the sports memorabilia game by validating memorabilia associated with famous firsts or other milestones. Of course, they also recognized memorabilia as a potential revenue stream. Accounting firms validated such items and affixed holograms to memorabilia before placing them on their own website auctions. Milestone baseballs kept by lucky fans meant instant fortunes at auction. Comic book creator and music producer Todd McFarlane paid $3 million for Mark McGwire's 70th

Collecting Wisdom That Lasts Forever

Sports memorabilia collectors are passionate about their favorite teams and players. They often say that owning a signed piece of memorabilia or an artifact draws them closer to that hero, a team, a stadium, a point in time. People who seek this feeling surround themselves with favorite, interesting, and artful objects and should follow the advice of an assortment of wise and experienced hobbyists. Consider the following:

- For beginners, don't be impulsive. Build your collection slowly, thoughtfully, and cautiously.
- When acquiring autographs, get them in person, at least initially. Build an autograph collection gradually, not overnight.
- Educate yourself. Ask questions of dealers be a scrutinizing consumer. Research your hobby the way you would any product or service.
- Graduate to buying items from dealers who can document that they acquired items from shows or private signings.
- Make sure the history of the signed object squares with the time frame of the signer. Babe Ruth, for example, didn't sign any baseballs dated 1949 and beyond. He died on August 16, 1948. Ballpoint pens became popular in the United States after his death.
- If you have *any* thoughts that the item you're considering for purchase is bogus, then pass on it.
- Pay more attention to provenance than a certificate of authenticity. Certificates of authenticity do not necessarily guarantee authenticity; what is guaranteed is that they do make people *feel* that what they're buying is authentic.
- You may have to live without autographs from some Hall of Famers, particularly where exemplars are few, unverifiable, or nonexistent.
- Major collectors who purchase or trade vintage items urge others to buy the best quality or condition you can find.

home run ball slugged in 1999. Four years later, Barry Bonds hit 73 home runs and McFarlane stepped up to the plate again, this time to purchase this ball for $450,000. Alleged steroid use would cause a reassessment of the historic value of the ball in many ways. A seven-figure benchmark was created in basketball in December 2010, when David Booth, a mutual fund CEO, purchased the two typed pieces of paper on which Dr. James Naismith laid out the rules of basket ball in 1891. He paid $4.3 million for the document at Sotheby's. He plans to have it displayed at his alma mater, the University of Kansas, where Naismith coached and college basketball remains a premier sport.

Eye-popping sums of money equal the passion and hero-worship of sports celebrities so long as prices advance and sports economics bulge. Concurrently, consumer advocacy and authenticity will forever be part of the vintage and sports memorabilia collection landscape. Law enforcement, legendary representatives, authenticators, and forensic experts are increasingly involved to police an aspect of society that parallels the fun and hazards of American sport.

Charles Kaufman

See also Baseball Cards; Baseball Hall of Fame; Honus Wagner Card; McGwire, Mark and Sosa, Sammy; Naismith, James; Negro Leagues; Rockwell, Norman; Ruth, Babe

Suggested Resources

Collectors Universe Message Boards. http://forums.collectors.com/categories.cfm?catid=11. Accessed June 13, 2011.

Keating, Kevin, and Mike Kolleth. *The Negro Leagues Autograph Guide*. Norfolk, VA: Tuff Stuff Publications, December 1998.

Mortenson, Tom. *The Standard Catalog of Sports Autographs*. Iola, WI: Krause Publications, 2000.

Nelson, Kevin. *Operation Bullpen: The Inside Story of the Biggest Forgery Scam in American History*. Benicia, CA: Southampton Books, 2006.

O'Keeffe, Michael, and Teri Thompson. *The Card: Collectors, Con Men and the True Story of History's Most Desired Baseball Card*. New York: William Morrow, 2007.

Sweet Spot Online. www.sweetspotnews.com. Accessed June 13, 2011.

Sports Metaphors

A metaphor is a figure of speech. It is an expression in which words are used in a creative, inventive, or imaginative way rather than in a literal way, to clarify, describe, explain, or express meaning. When used correctly, a metaphor simplifies a difficult concept in terms of a common, recognizable idea. Consider the following example: "If Marcus misses school again he will be skating on thin ice." The metaphor "skating on thin ice" does not mean that Marcus is actually skating on ice that may be too fragile to support his weight; instead it implies that Marcus is taking unnecessary risks. By comparing Marcus's unstable situation at school with the danger of treading on thin ice, readers come to understand that Marcus is in a perilous position. The metaphor connects the urgency of his situation in school to an understandable experience.

While a metaphor explains one thing in terms of another, a sports metaphor, such as "skating on thin ice," draws on the experience of sport to make a connection to something else. Even though metaphors can be created using common ideas other than sport, such as weather ("you are my sunshine" or "my memory is a little foggy"), Americans' passion for competition makes sporting experiences particularly accessible and, therefore, a logical tool for creating recognizable associations. In simple terms, a sports metaphor enables people to understand an abstract idea by linking a *less* familiar concept to a *more* familiar, sport-based concept. By creating this practical connection to the unfamiliar through the familiar, sports metaphors put unknown ideas into human perspective.

This language of shared meanings between sport and other subjects, sometimes referred to as "sport-speak," is widespread in American life and originates from many different forms of competition. To be average is to be "par for the course" (golf), to remind someone of something is to "ring a bell" (boxing), and to concentrate is to "keep your eye on the ball" (tennis, golf, football, baseball). Many commonly used sports metaphors derived from sports that are now illegal or not practiced in the United States such as "crestfallen" (cockfighting) and "take the bull by the horns" (bullfighting); nevertheless they remain effective expressions. On the other hand, some sports metaphors are so commonplace they are considered cliché or no longer metaphorically impactful. They are so familiar that we fail to notice the original sporting experience that once connected them to everyday life. For example, if speakers approach a topic indirectly rather than addressing it straightforwardly, they are "beating around the bush." While many audiences may recognize this stalling tactic, they may not realize that its source is mid-19th-century hunting, when men called "beaters" would scare game out of hiding so that it could be shot by the hunters. Another frequently used metaphor rooted in sport is employed in situations that become out of control or "get out of hand." Though "get out of hand" is used today in reference to a heated argument or a fight, it originated in equestrian sports. To "get out of hand" meant the rider lost the reins to the horse, thus losing control of the animal's power.

Even though some sports metaphors may have lost their obvious relationship to sport, many continue to thrive in the English language. In 1989, two lexicographers (persons who compile, edit, and write dictionaries) listed over 1,700 metaphors commonly used in the English language that stem from terminology related to sport, games, and recreation. Research shows that some of these metaphors originated as early as the 16th century. For instance, the expression "to hoodwink," meaning to trick someone, comes from the Renaissance sport of falconry and refers to the practice of blindfolding a falcon with a hood prior to releasing it for flight. In the 18th and 19th centuries, the use of sport metaphors expanded. As Americans recognized the importance of physical health in an increasingly industrialized society, sport, games, and recreation flourished. With this rise of physical activity, speaking with sports metaphors became so customary that the expressions extended beyond the boundaries of the playing field. For example, sports metaphors are often heard in politics, business, advertising, news, and science. While studies may not exist that identify the number of sports metaphors in our daily discourse, James Geary, a best-selling author who studies language, notes that, on average, Americans use one metaphor for every 10 to 25 words of spoken English. Considering the depth to which sport is embedded in American culture, "sportspeak" expressions are likely to be included in that count.

The dialogue of American politics, in particular, counts the language of sport as an essential ingredient. Like sport, American politics is a contest built on a belief in competition that is guided by rules and fair play. This similarity enables politicians to readily borrow from the language of sport. One of the most commonly used metaphorical expressions for fair play is to "level the playing field" or to situate the field of play so neither team has to start the competition by running uphill. Indeed, just as all sporting competitions begin with a 0–0 score, all U.S. elections include laws that try to ensure each candidate begins with an equal chance to win.

Applying sporting metaphor to political ideas is a well-documented practice. Theodore Roosevelt, U.S. president from 1901 to 1909 and an avid sportsman, made the use of boxing metaphors popular. He famously proclaimed his run for the presidency with the phrase, "My hat's in the ring." Today, boxing expressions are almost expected to be woven into political conversation. Political remarks might include metaphors such as those noted in the following sentences: The candidates are "evenly matched" and will likely go "head-to-head" in a "free-for-all." They are each "hard-nosed" "contenders" who will "spar" until one of them is "knocked out" of the campaign. Without metaphor, the same sentence might read as follows: "The candidates are of equal ability and will likely directly confront each other in a competition that is open to all spectators. They are each tough and insensitive candidates for office who will engage in impromptu debate until one of them suffers a defeat in the campaign." Needless to say, the metaphorical version is more vivid and engaging, providing a colorful picture of the pending contest.

Politicians and political news reporters also use metaphors related to running. Candidates enter a "race" and sometimes "make great strides" in a "come-from-behind," "runaway" victory. Voting constituents too, can join in on the sports metaphor chorus by voicing horse-racing phrases such as "backing the wrong horse" (voting for the wrong candidate) or anticipating the winner of a campaign that is "neck and neck" (tied for the lead). Boxing, running, and horse racing are but a small sampling of the sports that have been metaphorically referenced in political debate; however, in today's win-at-all-costs culture, two sports stand out as politics' metaphorical jackpots—baseball and football.

Though baseball is often called "America's sport," fanaticism around Friday-night high school football contests, Saturday college games, and Sunday professional games makes football arguably the most popular sport in the United States. Regardless of which sport's popularity is greater, the obvious attractiveness of each provides politicians with a plethora of sporting metaphors. From baseball: Political challengers who do not win an election "strike out." Though they may be "in the ballpark" with a large percentage of the vote, they might not be "in the same league with" their opponent. Former Speaker of the House Tip O'Neill welcomed newly elected president Ronald Reagan to office with the phrase, "you're in 'the big leagues' now." Even U.S. Supreme Court Chief Justice John Roberts used a sports metaphor to illustrate the difficulty in making judicial decisions. In his confirmation hearing he stated that judges are like umpires, "they make sure everybody plays by the rules." Associate Justice Elena Kagan added that judicial decisions are tough: "They are not easy calls."

In reference to football, candidates "kick off" a campaign and create a "game plan" of political strategy. They also support policy by "carrying the ball." They sometimes make unfair remarks about their opponents by "taking cheap shots," and many political reporters second-guess candidates' strategies with their "Monday-morning quarterback" commentary. There are many examples of presidential football metaphors: John F. Kennedy often referenced his beloved sport of football when describing how similar politics is to the gridiron, "if you see daylight, go through the hole"; Gerald Ford, a star center and lineman on the University of Michigan's 1932 and 1933 national championship football teams, promised to "hold the line" on inflation during his 1973–1977 term; and not surprisingly, sports-loving Teddy Roosevelt once said that the principle of life was "to hit the line hard."

Football not only provides plenty of colorful metaphors to illuminate political dialogue, but it also uses metaphors to intensify its own narrative. Metaphors derived from warfare are often used in football to promote its image as a violent and brutal game. The similarities between the two, such as victory through aggression, strength, and courage, make their vocabulary seemingly interchangeable. Hostile war metaphors such as "blitz," "bomb," "battlefield," "combat," "field attack," "air assault" populate football television and radio commentary. Descriptions of stoic "field

generals" (the coaches), strong "arsenals" (the team members), and promising "recruits" (young players) waiting in "the trenches" (on the sidelines) pepper sporting periodicals. It is important to note, however, that although these metaphors are commonly assumed to be sporting metaphors, instead they are military metaphors that originated in warfare. This conflation, or fusion, of football and war terms is an example of how frequent use of metaphors can lessen or erase their historical sources.

Using the language of war to promote football may seem to some audiences an excessive and inappropriate use of metaphor, but can a line of appropriate use be drawn? Advertisers regularly create links between sporting ideas and consumer goods in an effort to increase sales. Subaru's advertising slogan, "Driven by what's inside," accompanied by an image of Lance Armstrong on his bike, encouraged consumers to imagine themselves as winners whose lives resembles that of the Tour de France champion. (Amusingly, Subaru explained Armstrong's physicality by using another sporting metaphor, auto racing: "He is engineered like no other to perform like no other.") Gatorade's successful 1991 advertising campaign, "Be like Mike," promised consumers that drinking the popular thirst-quencher could bring them athletic success similar to that of NBA star Michael Jordan. Jordan's NBA championship run with the Chicago Bulls made the phrase omnipresent in American households. But it wasn't recited only by hopeful hoopsters, rather it extended beyond the boundary of sport. The concept of greatness inspired by "Be like Mike" applied to principles of success in business, fashion, and education. Using these analogies of sporting success, advertisers create a virtual bridge to success in other fields. The idea of winning and the image of a winning athlete permeate American culture and persuade, according to sports-smitten advertisers, as no other idea can. And as long as the athlete and the sporting idea are respected by the public, the use of their accomplishments as metaphor is accepted.

The business of advertising may be an obvious example of the popularity of sports metaphor, but from a broader perspective, the "business" of business depends on sports metaphor for its success. As 19th-century industrialist Andrew Carnegie once said,

Mixed Sports Metaphors: Amateur Attempts at Using Figurative Language

Sports metaphors are so popular that they are sometimes remembered and reused incorrectly. Inaccurate metaphor-users often combine two unrelated metaphors, creating what is known as a "mixed metaphor." For example, "take it in stride" implies that even though a team didn't win the game, it should be pleased with the way it played. A similar sport metaphor is "take the ball and run with it," implying that a team should make the most of any opportunity. However, jumbling these two familiar metaphors, "take the ball in stride," has no meaning at all. Should the players be content with their performance or should they be angry that they lost?

Amateurs aren't the only ones to use mixed metaphors. In fact, there are several mixed sporting metaphors that passed an editor's eye and producer's ear. A large city newspaper once printed the following headline of a baseball story, "Step Up to the Plate and Fish or Cut Bait." In a regional radio broadcast of a soccer match, the commentator mixed racing and fighting metaphors, "In a two-horse race, always back the underdog." And another soccer sports reporter described a midfielder under attack with the phrase, "He took to . . . the midfield like a duck to the slaughter." Huh?

Though they are often amusing, mixed metaphors block understanding rather than support it. When in doubt about whether a sports metaphor is accurate, take a "mulligan" and try another expression.

Sports metaphors are applicable to nearly any situation that involves competition. Endeavors that involve planning, foresight, and management provide an obvious place for "sportspeak." Still, there are times where sports metaphors apply to subjects completely outside of the competitive sphere. Fashion, for example, has inherited sports metaphors. Men's loose-fitting undershorts, "boxer shorts," are called such because they resemble the shorts worn by prize-fighters. The name "boxer shorts" became popular in the early 1940s, most likely supported by the emergence of television broadcasts of boxing matches. Previously, newspaper and radio supplied the public with reports of boxing bouts, but television gave fans their first look at a real match and with it the masculine fashion of the sportswear shorts. Other examples of noncompetitive applications of sports metaphor include fleeing the scene of an accident or "hit and run" (baseball), falling in love or falling "head over heels" (football or soccer), being a "southpaw" or left-hander (baseball), and even appearing attractive or as "a knockout" (boxing).

Whether they continue to be associated with sport or have taken on adapted meaning, sports metaphors will continue to be relied upon as valuable tools for successful communication. After all, sport works "across the board" to give everyone the chance "to play ball" on a "level playing field" of understanding.

Beth Emery

"Business is the greatest game in the world." Not only is business a game of risk and strategy, but it uses sports metaphors to motivate employees, to lift the spirits or "rally the troops" toward achievement or "victory." Sports metaphors are used to excite, to stir, to arouse interest in competition, such as: "We're in the bottom of the ninth; it's time to show the competition what we're made of," "It's crunch time," and "Let's bat a thousand." Sports metaphors are used to inspire a collective work force: "Let's bat an idea around," "cover all the bases," and "get the ball rolling." Sports metaphors are used to imply a challenge: "We're working against all odds," "all bets are off," and "we're behind the eight ball." And sports metaphors are used to praise good performances: "good hustle," "way to knock 'em dead," and "you made a killing."

See also Advertising and Sports; Chicago Bulls; Gatorade; Jordan, Michael

Suggested Resources
Ammer, Christine. *Southpaws and Sunday Punches.* New York: Penguin Books, 1993.
"Bush Runs White House with Sports Metaphors." MSNBC. July 15, 2007. http://www.msnbc.msn.com/id/19774480/ns/politics. Accessed April 18, 2011.
Grothe, Mardy. *I Never Metaphor I Didn't Like.* New York: HarperCollins, 2008.
Herman, Gail. *Snowboarding Similes and Metaphors.* Pleasantville, NY: Gareth Stevens Publishing, 2010.
Lakoff, G., and M. Johnson. *Metaphors We Live By.* Chicago: University of Chicago Press, 1980.
McCallum, Jack. "Fighting Words." October 1, 2001. http://sportsillustrated.cnn.com/vault/article/magazine/MAG1023778/index.htm. Accessed August 5, 2011.

Palmatier, Robert A., and Harold L. Ray. *Sports Talk: A Dictionary of Sports Metaphors.* Westport, CT: Greenwood Press, 1989.

Spring Training

Spring training is Major League Baseball's preseason, typically running from mid-February, when pitchers and catchers report to camp, until the first game of the regular season in early April. Spring training is unlike the preseason for the other major American sports. While the preseasons for the National Hockey League and the National Basketball Association can come and go with little fanfare, baseball fans often start counting down the days until pitchers and catchers report for spring training as soon as the World Series ends. The spring training atmosphere is often described by players, coaches and managers as laid-back, in contrast to the National Football League, where players are regularly subjected to grueling preseason workouts in full uniform in the late-summer heat.

For baseball fans, part of the allure of spring training is the intimacy of the spring training ballparks and the access to the players that is unequaled during the regular season. Spring training games are played in smaller ballparks in Arizona and Florida, which not only allows fans close-up views of their favorite players and ample autograph opportunities, but also a respite from the winter weather that still grips the home cities of the teams from the North and Midwest. It is not unusual for the public address announcer's report of weather conditions in cities such as Chicago or Kansas City to elicit cheers from crowds basking in the sunshine in Phoenix.

Spring training was not always a tourist attraction. In fact, in baseball's earliest years, few teams could afford to travel to the South. Even if they could afford it, many players did not want to go. The majority of teams were from the North and players still harbored bitterness about the South from the Civil War. The first reported instance of a team going to the South for spring training was in 1869. The New York Mutuals was an amateur team of New York City employees with financial backing from notorious politician William "Boss" Tweed. The team was a moneymaking venture for

Tweed and he sent the players to the warmer climate of New Orleans, Louisiana, to prepare for the season. Other teams combined training camps with barnstorming trips through Arkansas, Georgia, and Mississippi.

The first report of a professional team holding spring training in the South was in 1870, when the Cincinnati Red Stockings, baseball's first professional franchise, went to New Orleans. In 1885, Cap Anson, player and manager for the Chicago White Stockings, took his team and a reporter to Hot Spring, Arkansas, for training camp. The White Stockings went on to win the pennant that year and the following season. In 1888, Florida hosted spring baseball for the first time when the Washington Senators went to Jacksonville, although several hotels, already familiar with the reputation of the Senators for raucous behavior, turned the team away. Baltimore Orioles manager Ned Hanlon is credited with bringing more structure to training camp by implementing scheduled drills eight hours a day for eight weeks when his team trained in Macon, Georgia, in 1894. The Orioles went on to win three consecutive pennants.

Organized spring training officially began in Florida in 1913 when Tampa's mayor, D. B. McKay, agreed to pay the Chicago Cubs up to $100 per player if they would prepare for the season at Plant Field, named for the owner of the nearby Tampa Bay Hotel, Henry B. Plant. The Cubs attracted some attention from curious tourists, including William Jennings Bryan, who was about to be sworn in as secretary of state for the Woodrow Wilson administration. Fans could buy a bleacher ticket for 25 cents to watch the Cubs take on a team from Havana, Cuba, which featured several American college players. Meanwhile, the Cleveland Indians began training in Pensacola that same year.

Florida's Grapefruit League began to take shape after the opening of Sunshine Park in St. Petersburg in 1914, which hosted the St. Louis Browns in its first year, then the Philadelphia Phillies from 1916 to 1918. Sunshine Park was the first multipurpose baseball training facility, complete with sliding pits, batting cages, and a 5,000-seat grandstand. It was the project of former Pittsburgh businessman Al Lang. As mayor of St. Petersburg, he was one of spring training baseball's strongest advocates. He developed friendships and business relationships with many of baseball's

Atlanta Braves teammates Felipe Alou (29), Joe Torre (15), and Hank Aaron (44) perform conditioning exercises during spring training in West Palm Beach, Florida, March 1, 1968. (AP Photo.)

most influential owners and sportswriters, promoting Florida as an ideal spring training location at a time when Florida was still considered by northerners to be little more than swampland. It was Lang who orchestrated a 99-year lease on a piece of waterfront property for the city of St. Petersburg in 1921, which hosted spring training for 85 years.

It was also Lang who, in 1925, convinced New York Yankees owner Jake Ruppert to move his team's spring training camp from New Orleans to St. Petersburg. It was a move that removed the temptations of Bourbon Street from his star player, Babe Ruth, and brought contingents of reporters to Florida. There were few stars like Ruth in the 1920s and reporters followed his every move. For six weeks out of the year, any news on Ruth came from St. Petersburg. This, combined with the great land boom in Florida, put the Grapefruit League on the map. New tourists, prospective business owners, and residents streamed into the state and lobbying for a spring training team became an essential element of the economic development plan for nearly every city in Florida.

Residents and business owners looked forward to the time when all Major League Baseball teams would hold spring training in Florida. The closest the Grapefruit League came to being the exclusive home of spring training was in the early 1950s, when 14 of the 16 major league franchises trained in Florida. Another warm weather state entered the spring training picture in 1946—Arizona. Fifteen of the 30 Major League Baseball teams now train in Arizona and all have home ballparks in the Phoenix metropolitan area. Previously, Yuma, in far western Arizona near the California border, was the spring training home of the Baltimore Orioles in 1954 and the San Diego Padres from 1969 until 1993. Tucson was the site of the first game between Bill Veeck's Indians and Horace Stoneham's Giants in 1946 and hosted spring training baseball every year after that through 2010. At various times, the Los Angeles Angels have played all or some of their games in Palm Springs, California, before settling full-time at Tempe Diablo Stadium in Tempe in 1992, and Las Vegas, Nevada, often hosts various teams for a brief series.

In 1946, Cleveland Indians owner Bill Veeck convinced Horace Stoneham, owner of the New York Giants, to move his team's spring training to Phoenix, Arizona. Veeck, who owned a ranch in Tucson, also began scouting African American slugger Larry Doby, unbeknown to Doby. One issue that Veeck knew he would encounter by signing Doby was that Jim Crow laws of the time did not permit Doby to stay in the same hotel as the rest of his teammates in spring training in Florida. Veeck believed that the racial climate in Arizona would be more welcoming to Doby, who made his major league debut three months after Jackie Robinson's debut with the Dodgers in 1947. In 1951, the Giants and the Yankees swapped spring training sites and the Yankees spent their only season training in Arizona so their owner, Del Webb, could keep close tabs on his team, as well as his new real estate ventures in the Valley of the Sun. The Yankees played two games against the Chicago Cubs that spring, who were officially training on Catalina Island off the coast of southern California, but had trouble finding other teams to play.

The following year, thanks to a deal brokered by Mesa rancher Dwight Patterson, the Cubs moved their spring training camp to Mesa, east of the Phoenix metropolitan area. The Cubs moved their training camp to California in 1966, but moved to Scottsdale, Arizona, the following year after discovering their training facility was nothing more than a Little League field. The Cubs returned to Mesa in 1979, where they have had spring training every year since. The Cubs are perennially one of the biggest attractions in the Cactus League, as well as a major contributor to the city of Mesa's economy. When the Cubs threatened to leave Mesa in 2010, voters approved a $99 million bond to construct new facilities for the team, while the Cubs promised to finance a nearby shopping and entertainment district.

The first official year of the Cactus League was 1954, when the Baltimore Orioles opened spring training camp in Yuma, near the California-Arizona border. The Indians and the Giants met in the "Cactus League World Series" that year, which the Giants won in four games. The two teams met again in the regular-season World Series, with similar results as the Giants swept the Indians for the championship. After much shifting back and forth between spring training sites over the next several years, the Cactus League hosted eight teams in the same eight venues for nearly 10 years in the late 1970s through the late 1980s. Along with the Cubs, Arizona hosted the Indians, the San Francisco Giants, the Milwaukee Brewers, the California Angels, the San Diego Padres, the Oakland A's, and the Seattle Mariners.

In 1991, Florida launched its strongest challenge to lure spring training teams from Arizona. In the mid-1980s, Florida instituted a tax on hotel rooms and the millions of dollars that were generated went toward the construction of new spring training facilities. In 1991, the original Cactus League team, the Cleveland Indians, announced that it was leaving Tucson for Homestead, Florida, where plans were underway to build the Homestead Sports Complex. Other Cactus League teams threatened to follow suit, presenting the real possibility that the Cactus League would lose all of its teams. The loss of the Cactus League would have been a serious financial blow to Maricopa County, where most of the Arizona teams trained. The $220 million generated each spring by the Cactus League was the equivalent of hosting the Super Bowl each year.

In response to the threat waged by the State of Florida, Arizona enacted legislation that permitted the creation of stadium districts in any county that hosted spring training or planned to do so. A car rental surcharge, similar to Florida's hotel tax, funneled millions of dollars to the stadium districts, which in turn provided funding for the construction of new spring training facilities. No other teams left the Cactus League, but in 2000, it was Florida's Grapefruit League that faced a threat. Just as the spring training contracts for the Reds, the Orioles, the Dodgers, the Toronto Blue Jays, the Houston Astros, the Kansas City Royals, and the Texas Rangers were set to expire, Las Vegas, Nevada, proposed the Oasis League. All of the teams in the league would play and practice in a single mega-complex, with teams rotating in and out of a larger stadium near the Las Vegas Strip. The idea went as far as a summit between all of the proposed teams, which made spring training officials in both Florida and Arizona concerned about the prospect of losing teams at some point. However, the concept never developed and eventually the Reds, the Royals, the Rangers, and the Dodgers moved to the Cactus League.

As baseball training and conditioning has become more sophisticated, so have the needs of players. Until the advent of multimillion-dollar contracts that accompanied free agency in the 1970s, spring training was literally a time for players to get their bodies into baseball condition. Many players worked at jobs in the off-season because they did not make enough money during the baseball season to sustain them financially through the fall and winter. It was rare for players to spend winters working out in a gym. Even players who did not have jobs were less likely to stay physically fit in the off-season, expecting to run themselves into shape in spring training.

However, the vast majority of modern players do not need off-season jobs. Pressure to live up to their contracts and changing expectations for players drives many ballplayers to arrive at spring training already in shape. Many players even participate in pre–spring training drills, particularly to work on their hitting or pitching fundamentals. When spring training begins, even more time is spent working on fundamentals or going through drills that simulate game scenarios. Modern spring training facilities, particularly in the Cactus League, have multiple full practice fields, half fields, batting cages, plush clubhouses, and state-of-the-art miniature stadiums that typically seat between 10,000 and 11,000 fans. Salt River Fields at Talking Stick, the spring training home of the Arizona Diamondbacks and the Colorado Rockies, features weight rooms, classrooms, meeting rooms, a theater, 12 practice fields, and an array of audiovisual equipment as part of its "video coaching" system.

Spring training has also grown into a vacation destination for fans. Approximately three million fans attend spring training games in Arizona and Florida every year. However, the rise in popularity of spring training has not been entirely positive for fans. Increased interest means that tickets are harder to come by. Tickets to see some of the most popular teams, such as the Giants and the Cubs in Arizona or the Yankees and the Red Sox in Florida, often sell out before spring training begins. This eliminates the ability for some fans to spontaneously decide to drop in to see a ball game. Increased interest also equates to higher ticket prices and some teams charge more for so-called premium games against the more popular draws. In Arizona, some spring training tickets for a Saturday afternoon game between the Giants and the Diamondbacks cost more than a regular season Giants versus Diamondbacks game.

The competition between cities to attract teams has, in turn, created a void in some communities that used to be known as spring training mainstays. Vero Beach, Florida, was the spring training home for the Dodgers for six decades, dating back to when the team was based in Brooklyn. A former U.S. naval base was transformed into a spring training facility that served the team's needs well after the signing of Jackie Robinson. Florida's segregation laws, which led to the Indians moving their spring training camp to Arizona, prevented Robinson from staying in the same hotel as the rest of the Dodgers. The navy barracks were converted into sleeping quarters for the team and eventually Dodgertown was built. All of the players' needs were met, including a post office, canteen, and barbershop just for players and coaches. Dodgertown was such a novelty it was the subject of a *Life* magazine cover story in 1948. Soon, Vero Beach and the Dodgers were synonymous. The Vero Beach community considered the Dodgers their own team for six weeks a year. Nearby streets are named for Dodger Hall of Famers. Then the relationship between the team's management and county officials soured. The Dodgers moved to a new facility in Glendale, Arizona, in 2008, leaving Vero Beach without spring training for the first time since 1947.

A similar fate befell Tucson, where spring training baseball in Arizona began. In 2010, both of Tucson's spring training facilities, Tucson Electric Park and Hi Corbett Field, hosted their final spring training games. Tucson Electric Park opened in 1998 and was the home of the Chicago White Sox and the National League's new entry, the Arizona Diamondbacks. The owner of the Diamondbacks, Jerry Colangelo, wanted the team to train away from Phoenix and he wanted to share the team with the state's second-largest city. However, after Colangelo's departure, new ownership struck a deal with the Salt River Pima Maricopa Indian Community and the first spring training facility on Indian land was built. The White Sox left Tucson in 2008 to join the Dodgers at Camelback Ranch in Glendale.

Spring Training on Catalina Island

In 1916, William Wrigley Jr., who made his fortune selling chewing gum, purchased a share of the Chicago Cubs. Three years later, he bought Catalina Island, an undeveloped piece of land 25 miles off the coast of Los Angeles. By 1921, Wrigley was the principal owner of the Cubs and decided that the team would hold spring training on his island. Wrigley spent millions developing Avalon, the island's only town, including building hotels, installing streetlights, and opening the largest dance hall in the world, the Avalon Grand Casino. For his players, Wrigley built a baseball diamond with the exact same dimensions as its home park in Chicago, Wrigley Field. The field was just below Wrigley's country club, which housed the players' locker rooms. The majority of the games were intrasquad games, but occasionally other teams would visit the island to provide new competition before the Cubs headed to the mainland of California to complete the spring training season. While the Cub players loved the beauty of the island, the fact that few other teams traveled to Catalina, combined with several springs of inclement weather—including snow in 1951—led to the Cubs leaving Catalina Island for Mesa, Arizona, in 1952.

The Colorado Rockies had been training at Hi Corbett Field and left to share Salt River Fields with the Diamondbacks. With Colangelo out of the picture, Tucson no longer had an advocate for spring training and after 63 years spring training left town.

Despite the infusion of business and politics into spring training, the culture of baseball's preseason remains largely intact. Scores are still irrelevant and fans still cluster in the stands near the dugout, calling out to their favorite players for autographs. The elements that attracted baseball fans to spring training decades ago still exist, from the warm spring weather in Arizona and Florida to the chances to glimpse baseball stars of the past, present, and future. Attendance briefly dipped throughout spring training in 2008, when the economy forced many fans to forgo spring training vacation plans. Within two years, attendance was on the rise again, with several teams setting attendance records. By 2011, total spring training attendance was over 3.5 million fans, the third-highest total ever recorded.

See also Brooklyn Dodgers; Chicago Cubs; Cleveland Indians; Los Angeles Dodgers; New York Yankees; Robinson, Jackie; Ruth, Babe; Veeck, Bill; Wrigley Field; World Series

Amy Lively

Suggested Resources

Cactus League Website. http://www.cactusleague.com/. Accessed November 28, 2011.

Fountain, Charles. *Under the March Sun: The Story of Spring Training.* New York: Oxford University Press, 2009.

Grapefruit League Website. http://www.floridagrapefruitleague.com/. Accessed November 28, 2011.

Rich, Wilbur C., ed. *The Economics and Politics of Sports Facilities.* Westport, CT: Quorum Books, 2000.

"Timeline: A History of Spring Training." NPR.org. http://www.npr.org/templates/story/story.php?storyId=125308274. Accessed November 28, 2011.

St. Louis Cardinals

The first iteration of the St. Louis Cardinals took the field in 1882. Called the St. Louis Brown Stockings, they were members of the American Association Baseball League. As the "Stockings" they won four Association pennants in a row (1885–1888) and played in a championship series that predated the World Series. Two of the series competitions were against the forerunners of the Chicago Cubs, the Chicago White Stockings, with Chicago and St. Louis each winning one. The rivalry developed in those games set the tone for the annual Cardinal/Cub meetings that still exists today.

In 1893 the Brown Stockings moved to the National League after the American Association went bankrupt. Here, in 1899, they became the St. Louis Perfectos. In 1900 the team was again renamed to its present title, the St. Louis Cardinals. Unfortunately, despite the name changes the Brown Stockings, Perfectos, or Cardinals did not win a pennant for over 30 years as a member of the National League.

Initial Success

In 1920, Sam Breadon bought the team and hired Branch Rickey. Under Rickey's on- and off-field leadership the Cardinals began to sign young players and

St. Louis Cardinals pitcher Blake Hawksworth delivers a pitch July 26, 2009, against the Phillies in Philadelphia. (Aspen Photo/Shutterstock.com.)

build an extensive minor league system that would produce many future major league stars and become a model that other baseball organizations would emulate over the next two decades. At the same time future Hall of Famers such as Rogers Hornsby, winner of the Triple Crown (highest batting average, most runs batted in, and most home runs in a season) in 1922 and 1925, and Grover Cleveland "Pete" Alexander were added to Cardinal lineups. As a result, the Cardinals won their first pennant and World Series in 1926, with Pete Alexander winning two games and saving the seventh Series game by striking out Tony Lazzeri of the Yankees with the bases loaded in the seventh inning and pitching two scoreless eighth and ninth innings.

National Recognition

The Cardinals' winning tradition, begun in the late 1920s, continued into the 1930s with back-to-back pennants in 1930 and 1931 and a World Series victory over the Philadelphia Athletics in 1931. Although

highly popular throughout the Midwest and South, mainly due to radio broadcasts of all Cardinal games on St. Louis station KMOX, the team did not receive any real national recognition until the "Gashouse Gang" appeared in 1934.

Named after the plants that produced town gas for lighting and cooking from coal that emitted awful odors, the team was tough, quick, and a fan favorite. It was led by Leo Durocher, Rip Collins, Joe Medwick, and "the Wild Horse of the Osage"—Pepper Martin. The pitching staff included brothers Paul and Dizzy Dean. "Diz" won 30 games that year, the last National League pitcher to accomplish this feat, and quickly became a national celebrity through his radio and movie appearances. The Dean brothers won all four games for the Cardinals in the 1934 Series victory over the Detroit Tigers. The Cardinals were led at the plate by Medwick hitting .379 and driving in five runs.

Although his batting statistics were most impressive during the 1934 series, "Ducky" Medwick is probably best known for being the only player ever to be pulled from a World Series game by a commissioner, Kenesaw Mountain Landis, after being hit by garbage thrown by Detroit Tiger fans when he returned to his outfield position after a hard slide into third base. Medwick would go on to become the National League's Most Valuable Player in 1937 after winning the Triple Crown, the last National Leaguer to do so.

Faster and Quicker

After the team failed to win any pennants from 1934 through the 1941 season, Cardinal fans' hopes for a new winning era began to take shape with the arrival of Stan "The Man" Musial in 1941. Other youngsters from the Cardinal farm system, including shortstop Marty Marion and outfielder Enos "Country" Slaughter, joined Musial, who was to become a superstar spending 22 years in a Redbird uniform. These young, quick newcomers were called the "St. Louis Swifties," winning three straight pennants from 1942 through 1944 and two World Series titles in 1942 and 1944. In doing so they won a franchise-record 105 games in 1942, 1943, and 1944.

The 1944 pennant and Series wins were particularly sweet as the Cardinals played the team that they shared Sportsman's Park with, the St. Louis Browns, for the series title. In the only St. Louis "streetcar" series the Cardinals easily beat the Brownies.

The last pennant win for the Cardinals in the 1940s came in 1946. After finishing the regular season in a tie with the Brooklyn Dodgers they went on to beat the "Bums" in a three-game playoff series, allowing them to face a star-laden Boston Red Sox team in the first postwar World Series.

The Sox, led by Ted Williams and Johnny Pesky, were heavy favorites to win the title. With the series tied three games apiece Enos Slaughter made history in game seven with his "Mad Dash" to home from first base on a double in the bottom of the eighth, by Harry "The Hat" Walker, to seal a Cardinal championship, their last for the next 18 years.

Going Nowhere

The 1950s were a "dead era" for most Cardinal fans. No pennants, no World Series, with the club finishing mostly in the middle of the National League races. There were, however, significant changes during this era beginning in 1953 when the Anheuser-Busch brewery, chaired by its owner August "Gussie" Busch, bought the team and Sportsman's Park, the home field of the Cardinals.

After renovating and renaming the park Busch Stadium, "Gussie" also made history in 1954 by signing and playing the first African American in Cardinal history, Tom Alston.

Back on Top

Through trades and making the most of the players developed in their minor league system, the Cardinals began to slowly regain their championship aura during the early 1960s. Players such as Bill White, Julian Javier, Curt Flood, who would later challenge baseball's reserve clause, and Tim McCarver made the team into a strong offensive power. Added to this was the pitching of Bob Gibson, a hard-throwing, no-nonsense right-hander. However it wasn't until June 15, 1964, when Lou Brock was obtained by the Cardinals as part of a six-player trade from the Chicago Cubs, that the final piece of this era's champions fell into place.

The Brock for Broglio steal/deal, as it came to be known, brought a new meaning to lopsided baseball trades. After joining the Cardinals in June 1964, Brock went on to hit .384 for the rest of the season, leading the Cardinals to their first World Series title, over the New York Yankees, since 1946. This set the tone for his Hall of Fame career where he collected numerous base-stealing records and over 3,000 hits. Broglio would win four games for the Cubs in 1964 after the trade while never reaching stardom throughout the rest of his career.

The Cardinals repeated their pennant success in 1967 and 1968. In both seasons the pitching of Bob Gibson set a tone for the team. In 1967 Gibson pitched three complete game wins in the World Series as the Cardinals beat the Boston Red Sox. Named pitcher of the year for 1968, his earned run average was 1.12. He also pitched another three games in the 1968 Series, but lost to the Detroit Tigers, striking out a record 17 batters in the first game.

Although the Cardinals did achieve individual success, with Bob Gibson receiving his second Cy Young Award in 1970 and Joe Torre named Most Valuable Player for the 1971 season, following their back-to-back pennants in 1967 and 1968 they did not win a pennant during the 1970s.

"Whitey Ball"

Hired in 1980, "Whitey" Herzog brought back the emphasis on speed and defense that the Cardinals had been noted for throughout their history. Fleet outfielders such as Willie McGee and base stealer Vince Coleman epitomized Herzog's baseball philosophy. But just as in 1964 a trade would be the catalyst for winning seasons for the rest of the decade.

In 1982, the Cardinals sent shortstop Gary Templeton to the San Diego Padres for shortstop Ozzie Smith. Smith was regarded as a good-fielding, light-hitting player. Despite this reputation, Herzog saw in Smith an ability to lead a team to a championship. The payoff was immediate as the Cardinals won the 1982 pennant and a World Series title over the Milwaukee Brewers (then in the American League). They repeated as league champions in 1985 and 1987 but failed to win either World Series.

Winning and Records

Whitey Ball lasted through 1990 when former MVP Joe Torre took over as the Cardinal manager. Despite winning seasons the Cardinals continually failed to make the playoffs until Tony La Russa took over the Cardinal dugout in 1996. The team responded by winning the National League Central Division and the division series over the Padres before losing to Atlanta in the National League Championship Series.

Per La Russa's suggestion the Cardinals added slugger Mark McGwire to their roster. McGwire had played for La Russa when he managed the Oakland Athletics and added a power-hitting dimension to a team that had relied on pitching and defense.

"Big Mac" greeted fans in his new home by breaking the single-season major league home record in 1998, in a race with Chicago Cub outfielder Sammy Sosa, by hitting 70 round-trippers. For many fans this

---

St. Louis Cardinals Statistics, Ballparks, and Hall of Fame Players

Statistics

Through the 2010 season the St. Louis Cardinals had won 10 World Series titles, 17 National League pennants, 4 American Association pennants, 8 National League Central Division titles, 3 National League East Division titles, and 1 National League wild card berth. In addition, 16 Cardinal players had been awarded the Most Valuable Player award—a National League record.

Ballparks

Since their inception the Cardinals have played in six named stadiums but in only four distinct parks. These are:

1. Sportsman's Park, 1882–1892
2. Robison Field or New Sportsman's Park, 1893–1920
3. Original Sportsman's Park,* 1920–1953
4. Busch Stadium I,** 1954–1966
5. Busch Stadium II, 1966–2005
6. Busch Stadium III, 2006–present

* Same field as 1882 Sportsman's Park
** Same field as Sportsman's Park but renamed after Cardinals were purchased by the Busch family

Hall of Fame Players

Forty-two members of the National Baseball Hall of Fame played for the Cardinals. Ten who were elected have the Cardinal logo on their plaque. Another seven list the Cardinals as their primary team. Those wearing the Cardinal insignia include Lou Brock, Dizzy Dean, Bob Gibson, Whitey Herzog, Stan Musial, Albert "Red" Schoendienst, Enos Slaughter, Ozzie Smith, Billy Southworth, and Bruce Sutter.

Four former Cardinal broadcasters have been given the Ford C. Frick Broadcasting Award and are enshrined in the Hall of Fame: Jack Buck, Harry Carry, Joe Garagiola, and Milo Hamilton. A former Cardinal player, Bob Uecker, has also been honored with this award.

---

mark is tainted as McGwire later revealed that he was taking steroids while chasing the record.

The Cardinals continued to win as a new century began by capturing the National League Central Division in 2000, 2001, 2002, 2004, 2005, 2006, and 2009 and winning the World Series for the 11th time in 2011. In 2004 the team won a major league high of

105 games and in 2009, when they defeated the San Diego Padres in the playoffs, they became only the fourth team to win 10,000 games.

New stars such as slugger Albert Pujols and defensive stalwart catcher Yadier Molina joined pitchers Chris Carpenter and Adam Wainwright in maintaining the Cardinal tradition of baseball excellence. After Pujols left in 2012, the Cardinals looked to Carlos Beltran and Lance Berkman to maintain their power.

Cardinal fans supported their team in record numbers and, as announcer Jack Buck said, continued to "Go Crazy" as the "Red Out" tradition of Redbird baseball begun in 1882 rolled on.

Richard Diem

See also Boston Red Sox; Brooklyn Dodgers; Dean, Dizzy; Gibson, Bob; Landis, Kenesaw Mountain; McGwire, Mark and Sosa, Sammy; Musial, Stan "The Man"; Pujols, Albert

Suggested Resources

Broeg, Bob, and Vickery, Jerry. *The St. Louis Cardinals Encyclopedia.* New York: Masters Press, 1998.

Feldman, Doug. *St. Louis Cardinals Past and Present.* Minneapolis: MVP Books, 2009.

Golenback, Peter. *The Spirit of St. Louis: A History of the St. Louis Cardinals and Browns.* New York: HarperCollins, 2000.

Herman, Bruce, and Smith, Ozzie. *Yesterday and Today: St. Louis Cardinals.* New York: Publications International, 2009.

"St. Louis Cardinals." Baseball Almanac. http://www.baseball-almanac.com/teams/cards.shtml. Accessed September 18, 2011.

St. Louis Cardinals Website. http://stlouis.cardinals.mlb.com/index.jsp?c_id=stl. Accessed September 18, 2011.

Stanley Cup

The Stanley Cup is the oldest trophy in sport and is annually awarded to the winner of the National Hockey League (NHL) playoffs. Each team plays an eighty-two game regular season and the top eight teams from both the Eastern and Western Conferences compete in the conference quarterfinals. Following this round is the conference semifinals and then the conference finals. The Stanley Cup series is between the winners of the Eastern and Western Conference finals. Each round of the playoffs is a best-of-seven series and to win the championship, a team needs to win a total of sixteen games.

History

The Stanley Cup is the oldest trophy in professional athletics; however, it was first given because Lord Stanley of Preston wanted to do something to honor the champion of Canada's amateur hockey teams. At a time when goals were only portable poles with no nets, Lord Stanley ordered a silver bowl from England that was lined with gold. It was 35¼ inches tall and weighed 34½ pounds. It cost $48.67 and was originally known as the Dominion Hockey Challenge Cup. A pair of trustees was hired to take care of the trophy. Lord Stanley returned to England before he ever saw a championship game. The Montreal Amateur Athletic Association (AAA) first won the Cup in 1893.

In the early years, only amateurs competed for the Cup, but as the years went on, some athletes moved from club to club for pay. Within 20 years of the introduction of Lord Stanley's Cup, only professionals competed for it. The National Hockey League was formed in 1917 and for the next decade the trophy was awarded to the winner of a playoff between the NHL and its rival, the Pacific Coast Hockey League (PCHL). Then, when the PCHL dissolved in 1927, the Cup became the de facto championship trophy of the NHL.

Only two times since the inception of the Stanley Cup has it not been awarded. In 1919, it was not awarded because of a Spanish flu pandemic. During the 2004–2005 season, there was a labor dispute between the NHL's owners and the NHL Players Association that resulted in the cancellation of the season.

Currently there are three Stanley Cups. The original bowl was purchased and donated by Lord Stanley. It is currently displayed in the Hockey Hall of Fame in Toronto, Ontario. It was awarded to each champion for the first 71 years of competition until the presentation cup was created in 1963. Carl Petersen, a Montreal silversmith, crafted it. This is the cup that is now given to the players on the ice each year at the conclusion of the championship playoff series. The Stanley Cup travels more than 320 days a year to various charitable and official NHL functions. The replica cup was created in

1993 by Louise St. Jacques, another Montreal silversmith, and cost $75,000. This cup is on display at the Hockey Hall of Fame and is used as a stand-in whenever the presentation cup is unavailable.

The first team to have the players' names engraved on it was the 1907 Montreal Wanderers and, from then on, players could pay to have their names put on the Cup. In 1924, the Montreal Canadiens won the championship, and ever since then, all champions' names have been engraved on the Cup.

The criteria for a player to have his name inscribed on the Cup include either playing in at least 40 regular-season games for the championship team or playing in a least one game of the finals. Key front office personnel also have their names etched on the Cup. There are more than 2,500 names chiseled onto the Cup, although not all are on it at the same time. There is a five-band barrel and each band displays a total of 13 winning teams. When all five bands are full, the top and oldest band is removed from the Cup and put on exhibition in the Hockey Hall of Fame. Because the oldest band is replaced by a blank one every 13 years, the Cup never gets any taller. Also, players can expect to have their names on the Cup for about 65 years before their band is retired.

Stanley Cup Winners
Anaheim Ducks—2007
Boston Bruins—1929, 1939, 1941, 1970, 1972, 2011
Calgary Flames—1989
Carolina Hurricanes—2006
Chicago Blackhawks—1934, 1938, 1961, 2010
Colorado Avalanche—1996, 2001
Dallas Stars—1999
Detroit Red Wings—1936, 1937, 1943, 1950, 1952, 1954, 1955, 1997, 1998, 2002, 2008
Edmonton Oilers—1984, 1985, 1987, 1988, 1990
Kenora Thistles—1907*
Los Angeles Kings—2012
Montreal AAA—1893*, 1894*, 1902*, 1903*
Montreal Canadiens—1916*, 1924#, 1930, 1931, 1944, 1946, 1953, 1956, 1957, 1958, 1959, 1960, 1965, 1966, 1968, 1969, 1971, 1973, 1976, 1977, 1978, 1979, 1986, 1993
Montreal Maroons—1926#, 1935

Montreal Shamrocks—1899*, 1900* (2)
Montreal Victorias—1895*, 1897*, 1898*
Montreal Wanderers—1906*, 1907*, 1908*, 1910*
New Jersey Devils—1995, 2000, 2003
New York Islanders—1980, 1981, 1982, 1983
New York Rangers—1928, 1933, 1940, 1994
Ottawa Senators—1903* (2), 1904*, 1905*, 1906*, 1909*, 1911*, 1920#, 1921#, 1923#, 1927
Ottawa Silver Seven—1905*
Philadelphia Flyers—1974, 1975
Pittsburgh Penguins—1991, 1992, 2009
Quebec Bulldogs—1912*, 1913*
Seattle Metropolitans—1917#
Tampa Bay Lightning—2004
Toronto Maple Leafs—1932, 1942, 1945, 1947, 1948, 1949, 1951, 1962, 1963, 1964, 1967
Toronto Arenas—1918#
Toronto Blueshirts—1914*
Toronto St. Patricks—1922#
Vancouver Millionaires—1915*
Victoria Cougars—1925#
Winnipeg Victoria—1896*, 1901*, 1902*
1919—No decision (Spanish flu pandemic)
2005—Lockout

*Amateur champion (some years, there was more than one champion)

#Champion of the National Hockey League (NHL) and Pacific Coast Hockey League (PCHL)

Day with Stanley

All players of the winning team get to have the Stanley Cup for a day during the summer. Players enjoy taking it around town to celebrate and sharing it with their family, friends, and fans. Some players have had some crazy adventures on their "Day with Stanley."

The winning team drinks champagne out of the Cup, which has been a tradition since 1896. Since then, other things have been consumed from it including raw clams and oysters, popcorn, and chicken wings. Players of the New Jersey Devils made a gigantic margarita in it while celebrating in a nightclub. Edmonton's Doug Weight made an ice cream sundae, and Carolina's Cam Ward ate fruit loops out of it.

Ted Lindsay of the Detroit Red Wings kisses the Stanley Cup after the Wings beat the New York Rangers, April 23, 1950, in Detroit, Michigan. (AP Photo/AE.)

People have not been the only beings to consume from the Cup. In 1980, New York Islander Clark Gillies allowed his dog, Hombre, to eat from the Stanley Cup. Horses have also had their meals out of the Cup on several occasions. In 1994 Ed Olczyk of the New York Rangers let Kentucky Derby winner Go for Gin eat oats from the Cup at the Belmont racetrack. In 1995, Neal Broten, a New Jersey player, let one of his wife's favorite horses have some oats out of the Cup.

The Cup has had other uses as well. In 1907, the Cup served as a flowerpot because members of the Montreal Wanderers forgot the Cup at the home of a local photographer. The photographer's mother decided to use the Cup as a flowerpot in her garden. Several weeks later, the players remembered where they left it and then retrieved it.

The Cup has also been used as a baptismal font for newborn children. In 1996, Sylvain Lefebvre of the Colorado Avalanche had his daughter Alexzandra baptized in it. In 2008 Tomas Holmstrom of the Detroit Red Wings brought the Stanley Cup home to Pitea, Sweden, where he encouraged his cousin Robert to baptize his daughter, little Alva Felicia Holmstrom, in the Stanley Cup, and she was.

Players have cleaned the Stanley Cup for various reasons. Red Wing player Steve Yzerman took a shower with the Cup in 1997. In 2008, Detroit Red Wing Kris Draper's newborn daughter, Kamryn, pooped in the Cup. However, Draper reassured everyone that he thoroughly cleaned the Cup after his daughter's "accident" and even drank out of it later that same night.

Players love to take Lord Stanley's Cup to memorable places for photographs. Stanley has been brought to Red Square in Moscow, the Hollywood sign in Los Angeles, the Parliament building in Canada, the White House in Washington, D.C., and Niagara Falls. It has also been tubing on Island Lake, wearing a life vest, as well as visiting Finland for a traditional sauna. Perhaps the most thrilling experience the Stanley Cup has had so far is when it was under attack from an incoming missile in Afghanistan in 2007. It was brought there by the NHL and its Players Association and was photographed with soldiers from Canada and the United States. Luckily, it emerged unscratched despite being in the middle of an active war zone.

However, there have been restrictions to players' freedom in how they celebrate with the Cup. In 1991, as the Pittsburgh Penguins were celebrating their win, Stanley hit the bottom of Mario Lemieux's swimming pool. The Cup sustained damage since chlorine damages silver and nickel alloy. Due to this incident and others, like bringing the Cup to casinos and strip clubs, the NHL and the Hockey Hall of Fame decided that there had to be some rules regarding how to treat the Cup. Some of the celebrations with the Cup caused bad public relations and showed disrespect to the history and tradition of the Cup. Therefore they decided that Stanley should have a bodyguard, a "Cup-keeper" who is with it at all times. The Cup-keeper travels with the Cup, delivers it to each player, and stays with it for the entire 24-hour period as a passive observer to make sure that Stanley does not get damaged in any way and that its tradition and history are respected. One rule that is enforced by the Cup-keeper is that fans are not allowed to raise the Cup themselves and drink from it anymore. Only the players who have won the championship and therefore earned it are allowed to do this.

Superstition

Like any other professional sport, hockey is no stranger to its own unique superstitions. Some even go so far as to say that hockey is the most superstitious sport around, from the growth of the playoff beard until the fleeting moment of hoisting Lord Stanley way above the head or when a team takes its long and disappointing journey home with no Stanley Cup in tow. Needless to say, superstitions that start in this sport are carried on for decades.

From the taping of one's stick to the order of putting pads on, no superstition in hockey is greater or more revered than the touching or the nontouching of trophies during the Stanley Cup playoffs. During each conference title game, the winning team is presented with the Prince of Wales Trophy in the Eastern Conference or the Clarence S. Campbell Bowl in the Western Conference. Superstition states that no one on the winning conference team should touch their conference trophy or Lord Stanley's Cup will not make it to his hands. NHL players believe that the Stanley Cup is the true championship trophy and only it should be lifted up. However, exceptions have occurred and resulted in the team ultimately winning the Stanley Cup despite touching their conference trophy. Sidney Crosby touched the Price of Wales Trophy in 2008 and ultimately won the Cup that year. The year prior, it was not touched and the Pittsburgh Penguins lost to the Detroit Red Wings. According to ESPN.com, since 2001, teams that have left the trophy alone have won the Cup four times and those who have touched it have lost four times. Superstition or not, tradition is a core value in the NHL.

When a team wins the Stanley Cup, it is proudly lifted up in the arms of the captain for the fans to see. This tradition began in 1950 when Detroit Red Wing captain Ted Lindsay was the first captain to hoist the trophy in the air and skate around the rink. The captain

The Tradition of the Playoff Beard

The tradition of the playoff beard is one of the greatest traditions in sports. The players do not shave for the duration of their playoff run. This ritual was started in the early 1980s by the New York Islanders, who had a string of successes at the time, winning four consecutive Stanley Cups by defeating opponents for 19 playoff series in a row. The beard can be explained as an act of team unity.

Even if a player does not like a thick beard, he is doing it as part of the team. It is a constant reminder of team unity and a shared mission since each player starts to think about the playoffs from the very first glimpse in the mirror each morning.

The playoff beard is a superstition, and even if the origin of the tradition is not purely superstitious, it is well known that athletes do not talk about the beard in public since this would jinx the team. For example, the Detroit Red Wings had the slogan "The beard is back" for the final series in 2009 and ended up losing to the Pittsburgh Penguins in the Stanley Cup finals. If a team suffers a tough loss during the playoffs, modifications to the facial hair such as trimming, primping, and grooming might be made to try to change the team's luck.

The tradition has spread to other hockey leagues in North America and Europe; it is even practiced by many hockey fans who do not shave their beard until their team either loses a playoff series or is crowned champion.

then always hands the Cup off to a player on the team or a coach. This is a time-honored tradition and often a superstition in that whoever is handed the Cup from the captain is extremely important to the captain and team. The fans are most excited about this, due to no one knowing to whom the captain will hand Lord Stanley until the moment it happens. Each and every player on the winning team is handed the Cup and skates around the rink hoisting it as high as possible.

There have been three notable exceptions to this tradition. In 1993, Montreal Canadien Guy Carbonneau handed the Cup to Denis Savard because many fans had wanted the team to draft him in 1980. In 1998, before hoisting the Cup, Detroit Red Wing Steve Yzerman handed it to Vladimir Konstantinov who was in a wheelchair because he had suffered severe injuries from an automobile accident in 1997. Joe Sakic handed the Cup directly to his Colorado Avalanche teammate Ray Bourque in 2001. Bourque had spent his first 21 years as a Boston Bruin and had never won the Cup. In his 22nd and final year in the NHL, he finally won the coveted championship.

It is also again an extreme superstition that NHL players will never, ever touch the Stanley Cup until their team has rightfully won it. That means in photos, advertisements, or in passing, the Cup will never be touched. It is said that he who touches the Stanley Cup without rightfully earning it will be denied the chance to touch it again. Or so they say.

Ulrika Billme, Susannah Kaye Knust,
and Katelyn Rockenbach

Suggested Resources

Bernstein, Ross. *Raising Stanley: What It Takes to Claim Hockey's Ultimate Prize.* Chicago: Triumph Books, 2010.

Diamond, Dan, James Duplacey, and Eric Zweig. *The Ultimate Prize: The Stanley Cup.* Kansas City, MO: Andrews McMeel, 2003.

"Kris Draper's Daughter Makes Mess in Stanley Cup." June 12, 2008. http://sportsbybrooks.com/kris-drapers -daughter-makes-mess-in-stanley-cup-18771. Accessed September 29, 2011.

Podnieks, Andrew. *Lord Stanley's Cup.* Bolton, Ontario: Fenn, 2004.

Stanley Cup Winners—The Complete List. http://proice hockey.about.com/od/stanleycupbunker/a/stanley_ cuplist.htm. Accessed November 4, 2011.

Wyshyski, Greg. "The 10 Oddest Places the Stanley Cup Has Ever Visited." May 31, 2010. http://sports.yahoo .com/nhl/blog/puck_daddy/post/The-10-oddest-places -the-Stanley-Cup-has-ever-vi?urn=nhl-wp6036. Accessed October 15, 2011.

Steel Curtain

The "Steel Curtain" is a nickname given to the heralded defense of the 1970s Pittsburgh Steelers football team. High school student Gregory Kronz entered the name in a contest sponsored by Pittsburgh area radio station WTAE in 1971. The Steel Curtain is a neologism, or play on words, reflecting a famous Cold War–era speech given by British prime minister Winston Churchill. In that speech, Churchill

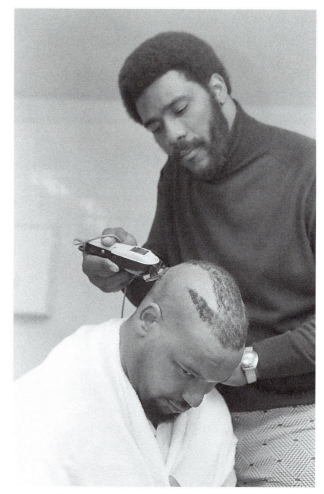

Pittsburgh Steelers defensive tackle Joe Greene shaves the arrow off the head of teammate Ernie Holmes, also a defensive tackle, in the Steelers dressing room in Pittsburgh following a Super Bowl IX victory parade through downtown Pittsburgh in 1975. (AP Photo.)

referred to the spread of communism—particularly the influence of the Soviet Union—as an Iron Curtain descending across Eastern Europe. While the term has been used to describe the Pittsburgh defense of the 1970s in general, and continues to be used to describe Steeler defenses, the "Steel Curtain" generally refers to the 1976 squad—specifically the four defensive linemen, arguably the best defensive unit in the history of the NFL. The 1976 Steelers defense had eight selections to the Pro Bowl that year, and four players would eventually be selected for the NFL Hall of Fame. In the 1976 season, the Steeler defense ranked first overall, giving up only 138 points, accumulating 22 interceptions, 24 fumble recoveries, and five shutouts.

Mean Joe Greene and Coca-Cola

Mean Joe Greene is famous for a Coca-Cola commercial that aired during Super Bowl XIV in which he gives a young fan his game jersey. The commercial begins with Greene limping off through the stadium tunnel, apparently leaving the game. A young boy says hello and tells Greene that he is the greatest, to which Greene scoffs. The boy then offers him his bottle of Coca-Cola, which Greene drinks in one long gulp. The boy looks on sheepishly as Greene drinks the soda, then begins to walk away. Greene finishes the soda and says, "Hey kid ... catch," and tosses the young fan his jersey. The boy exclaims, "Wow, thanks, Mean Joe!" The commercial was immensely popular even in countries where Joe Greene was not well known. The commercial won a Clio Award, which recognizes creativity in advertising and communication, and has been parodied many times.

The defensive line—the Steel Curtain—included Hall of Famer "Mean" Joe Greene, L. C. Greenwood, Dwight White, and Ernie Holmes. Greene and Greenwood were drafted by the Steelers in 1969—NFL Hall of Fame Chuck Noll's first draft as head coach. Greene, who attended North Texas State, was selected NFL Rookie of the Year and selected as the NFL's Defensive Player of the Year in 1972 and 1974. Greene's selection is recognized as the beginning of what would become the Pittsburgh dynasty team of the 1970s. While Pittsburgh-area newspapers printed the headline "Joe Who?" following the draft, Greene went on to be a leader on and off the field. Greenwood, from Arkansas AM&N (now University of Arkansas at Pine Bluff), led the Steelers in sacks six times and was selected to the Pro Bowl six times. Dwight White and Ernie Holmes were drafted in 1971—White from East Texas State and Holmes from Texas Southern University.

The four would go on to accumulate a combined total of 238 quarterback sacks in their careers. This is an unofficial statistic since the NFL did not keep sack totals as a statistic until 1982. The four were known to be good friends off the field as they all shared similar humble backgrounds. Greene played for 13 seasons and was inducted into the Pro Football Hall of Fame in 1987; White and Greenwood played for 10, and Holmes played for 8. The four helped cement the Pittsburgh Steelers' reputation as the "team of the 1970s." During their tenure, the Steel Curtain contributed to the Steelers winning six consecutive AFC titles (1974–1979) and Super Bowls IX, X, XIII, and XIV.

Vincent W. Youngbauer

See also Advertising and Sport; "Immaculate Reception"; Pro Football Hall of Fame and Museum; Super Bowl

Suggested Resources
"Coca-Cola Classic Ad: Mean Joe Green." YouTube.com. http://www.youtube.com/watch?v=xffOCZYX6F8. Accessed December 2, 2011.
Fulks, Matt. *The Good, the Bad, and the Ugly: Heart-pounding, Jaw-dropping, and Gut-wrenching Moments from Pittsburgh Steelers History.* Chicago: Triumph Books, 2008.
"The Immaculate Reception." Pro Football Hall of Fame. http://www.profootballhof.com/history/release.aspx?release_id=762. Accessed October 21, 2011.
Loed, Matt. *100 Things Steelers Fans Should Know and Do before They Die.* Chicago: Triumph Books, 2010.
Mendelson, Abby. *The Pittsburgh Steelers: The Official Team History.* 3rd ed. Lanham, MD: Taylor, 2011.
Steel Curtain Website. http://www.steelergridiron.com/history/curtain.html. Accessed November 12, 2011.

Steinbrenner, George (1930–2010)

George Steinbrenner, principal owner and managing general partner of the New York Yankees from 1973 until his death in 2010, was a controversial figure, reviled more than respected and hated more than loved. Yankee fans in two eras tended to forgive and forget, as he twice brought the team out of the doldrums, using his considerable resources to produce a string of American League and World Series champions. In between the glory years, however, the Yankees were again mired in the depths of mediocrity. Steinbrenner's autocratic style and abusive personality led to a longer skein of futility than the team had endured in the lean years before he purchased the club. He had inherited the family Great Lakes shipping business and eventually expanded it successfully, and had a brief spell as the owner of a professional basketball franchise, but it was in baseball that the Steinbrenner name was best known, as he became the most recognized owner in American sports. A convicted felon who was twice

George Steinbrenner, left, principal owner of the New York Yankees, chatting with Reggie Jackson at Royals Stadium in Kansas City, October 1976. (AP Photo/File.)

banned from baseball for his illegal activities, Steinbrenner's meddlesome tactics, tendency to arbitrarily hire and fire managers, and disparaging remarks about his players always rankled even when his team enjoyed success on the field. Yet his love for the game of baseball was undeniable, outstripping his knowledge and outweighing his judgment, and during his long reign, "King George" Steinbrenner was always the Yankees' biggest fan every bit as much as he was "the Boss," his well-deserved nickname.

George Michael Steinbrenner III, born on July 4, 1930, in Rocky River, Ohio, the only son of Henry George Steinbrenner II and the former Rita Haley, was named after his paternal grandfather. Henry had been a world-class hurdler while attending the Massachusetts Institute of Technology, from which he graduated with a degree in engineering. The elder Steinbrenner then went on to take over the Kinsman Marine Transit Company

from his father and himself became a wealthy shipping magnate as owner of the company that young George's grandfather had purchased from a relative in 1901, managing freighters that transported ore and grain on the Great Lakes. George grew up in Lakewood, Ohio, a western suburb of Cleveland, and attended Culver Military Academy in Indiana, graduating in 1948. He was awarded a BA degree from Williams College in Massachusetts in 1952, where he was an average student, who was a hurdler like his father on the track-and-field team, halfback on the football team, and sports editor of the student newspaper.

Following graduation, George Steinbrenner was commissioned as a second lieutenant in the U.S. Air Force, heading the sports program at Lockbourne Air Base in Columbus, Ohio, before his honorable discharge in 1954, with a coffee stand business as a sideline that grew to six pickup trucks. Steinbrenner remained in Columbus where he attended Ohio State University, earning his master's degree in physical education in 1955. While there he served as graduate assistant to legendary football coach Woody Hayes, as the undefeated Buckeyes won the 1954 national championship and the Rose Bowl. George also was an assistant football coach at Northwestern in 1955 and Purdue in 1956–1957. In Columbus he met Elizabeth Joan Zieg, and the two were married on May 12, 1956. The couple would have two sons, Hank and Hal, and two daughters, Jessica and Jennifer.

George went to work for the family business in 1957 and, breaking away from his father's domination, bought the Cleveland Pipers of the National Industrial Basketball League for $125,000 in 1960, much to the dismay of the elder Steinbrenner. The team would go on to win both the 1960–1961 NIBL and national AAU championships. The Pipers were led by the legendary black college coach John McClendon, who would become the first African American to coach a professional basketball team when the Pipers joined the fledgling American Basketball League for its 1961–1962 debut. The ABL under founder Abe Saperstein attempted to break the monopoly held by the National Basketball Association. Steinbrenner displayed outrageous behavior in his drive to win, and he bought players regardless of his coach's wishes, insisting that they play when and where he chose. His greatest coup, though, was signing away Dick Barnett from the NBA Syracuse Nationals. The flamboyant Barnett, a future star with the New York Knicks, had played for McClendon at Tennessee A&I. When the Pipers lost the first half playoff of the ABL split season, Steinbrenner refused to pay his players. McClendon, supporting his players, quit as financial problems beset the team and the league. Owner Steinbrenner displayed the contempt for his coach that later became a hallmark in his treatment of Yankee managers. He readily replaced the dignified but reserved McClendon with former NBA star Bill Sharman, the coach of the ABL's Los Angeles Jets, who had folded in December, and the Pipers went on to win the ABL's only championship in 1962. The league dissolved early in its second season, and Steinbrenner lost a great deal of money, though George reportedly paid off all of his creditors and partners within the next few years.

Working hard to restore Kinsman to financial stability, Steinbrenner would focus on grain rather than ore shipments, and bought out his father when Henry retired in 1963. He was the majority shareholder among a group that in 1967 purchased the American Shipbuilding Company, one of the country's largest shipbuilders, and he became its chairman and chief executive officer. The company flourished, eventually merging with Kinsman. George began to dabble in Broadway theatrical production beginning in 1967, investing in half a dozen plays from then until 1988, including *Seesaw*, nominated for a Tony Award as Best Musical of 1974. From the early 1970s he was also involved in Thoroughbred horse racing, operating a stable and stud farm in Ocala, Florida.

Steinbrenner became actively involved in the political arena as well, lobbying in favor of the Merchant Marine Act of 1970 on behalf of the Great Lakes shipping industry. In this context he supported the campaign of liberal Democrat Jack Gilligan for governor of Ohio, and curried favor with both Democratic senator Ted Kennedy of Massachusetts and Republican president Richard Nixon, who would fulfill a 1968 campaign promise by signing the bill in question into law. Steinbrenner did his bit by tendering illegal contributions to the campaigns of a group of politicians. George had chaired a committee to raise funds for Democratic U.S. senatorial candidates, and in 1972 donated $100,000 to CREEP, the notorious Committee to Re-elect the President. For this he faked employee bonuses and used corporate funds from American Shipbuilding Company. It was this gift to the Nixon campaign and his subsequent lying about it to federal investigators that led to his 1974 guilty plea for the illegal contribution and a felony charge of obstruction of justice. He admitted to making a "false and misleading" explanation regarding $25,000 of his donation to CREEP and trying to intimidate employees to give false information to a grand jury. He was fined a mere $15,000 and his company an additional $20,000, and Republican president Ronald Reagan pardoned him for his crimes as he was leaving office in 1989.

Under the ownership of CBS since 1965, the New York Yankees had experienced a period of futility unprecedented since the arrival of Babe Ruth in 1920. Between 1921 and 1964, they had won 29 American

League pennants and 20 World Series. In the CBS years they had won none of either. In 1972, Yankee president Michael Burke had been told the club had to be sold, and he was given the opportunity to purchase the franchise if he could get the necessary financial backing. George Steinbrenner, who had recently failed in a bid to buy the Cleveland Indians, was introduced to Burke by former Indians executive Gabe Paul. On January 3, 1973, with Burke as minority partner, Steinbrenner led a group of investors who purchased the New York Yankees from CBS. The net cost to the consortium was later determined to have been $8.8 million. Burke continued as club president, but quit when he felt his authority had been undermined by Paul, who succeeded him in the position in April 1973. Steinbrenner was now effectively in full control of the team, and after the 1973 season Manager Ralph Houk and General Manager Lee MacPhail departed as well. After attempts to hire recently resigned Oakland Athletics manager Dick Williams were foiled because he was still under contract, the Yankees hired former Pittsburgh Pirates field boss Bill Virdon as their manager for the 1974 season.

George Steinbrenner would become as well known for his megalomaniacal personality as he would for producing championship baseball teams. Biographer Peter Golenbock identified traits of both obsessive-compulsive and narcissistic personality disorders as consistent with the Yankee owner's actions over the years. These were manifested by his meddling in team affairs, attempted total control of the lives of players, and constant turnover of management. In 23 seasons, Steinbrenner changed field managers 20 times, including the five times he fired and rehired Billy Martin. Until the position was finally stabilized in later years under Brian Cashman, general managers were also an endangered species on the Steinbrenner Yankees, with 11 men holding that position over the first 30 years of King George's reign. He was famous for his military-style dress and grooming codes. No facial hair other than mustaches was allowed for players, managers, coaches, and male executives, and head hair could not be grown below the collar. As a new owner, before he even learned the names of his players, the Boss identified several by number and ordered Manager Houk

to have them cut their hair. These policies were never rescinded, with Yankee captain Don Mattingly falling afoul of them more than once, the last time in 1995. Pitcher David Wells was later able to flaunt the facial hair ban, however, defiantly sporting a goatee on occasion. Uniform employees were always required to wear jackets and ties while traveling with the team. A soft touch in some unexpected ways, Steinbrenner was always ready to give players a second or even third chance, particularly those with drug problems. Dwight Gooden, Darryl Strawberry, and Steve Howe were all signed to Yankee contracts and made positive contributions on the field after well-publicized struggles with cocaine abuse had led to their suspensions by MLB while playing for other clubs.

In November 1974, baseball commissioner Bowie Kuhn suspended George Steinbrenner as the result of his felony conviction, banning him from any involvement with baseball and his team's affairs for two years, though the suspension was later reduced to 15 months after the Yankees supported Kuhn's bid for reelection. Shortly after Steinbrenner gained control of the Yankees in 1973, he had told a college friend that he wanted to sign slugger Reggie Jackson and hire former Yankee sparkplug Billy Martin as manager. King George was back on his throne by the end of spring training in 1976, but even before that Virdon had been let go by the Yankees and Martin, recently fired by the Texas Rangers, took over as Yankee manager for the final two months of the 1975 season. The club flourished under Billy's tutelage, winning the 1976 pennant before being swept by the Cincinnati Reds in the World Series. Jackson provided the final component that would return New York to the top of the baseball world, after George wooed and won him in time for the 1977 AL campaign. Martin never liked the charismatic Jackson, and though the Yanks would defeat the Los Angeles Dodgers in the Series in 1977 and 1978, the fiery skipper would famously feud with his star and his boss, missing the latter Fall Classic after resigning under pressure, to be replaced by former Cleveland Indians Hall of Fame pitcher Bob Lemon. The incident that led to Martin's first departure was a statement he made to reporters after suspending Jackson for bunting against his orders, telling the press regarding Jackson and Steinbrenner, "They deserve each other. One's a born liar, and the other's convicted." The reference about Steinbrenner being convicted of course referred to the Yankee owner's guilty plea for obstruction of justice after lying about his illegal contribution to the Nixon campaign.

Martin returned briefly in 1979, but was then fired after an off-season fight in a Minneapolis hotel. Billy would come back to manage the Yanks in 1983, 1985, and 1988, but he never lasted for more than a season. Managers came and went on a regular basis, but another title eluded the Boss's grasp. Most notable among the fired managers was Yankee great Yogi Berra, whom Steinbrenner hired in 1984 and fired early in 1985 shortly after giving his skipper a vote of confidence, leading to a long-term rupture in relations between Berra and the club. The team under Dick Howser lost the American League Championship Series to the Kansas City Royals in 1980. Steinbrenner went back to the free agent market, signing Dave Winfield of the San Diego Padres to a 10-year, $23 million contract, which made him the highest paid player in baseball. Lemon was again brought in as manager after Gene Michael had led the team to the first-half title in the strike-shortened 1981 season, but the Yanks lost the Series to the Dodgers, Jackson was allowed to leave for the California Angels, and the team went into a tailspin, failing to make the postseason again during Winfield's time with the ball club. Steinbrenner put the blame for the team's failures on his expensive star, and after Winfield failed to deliver in an important series late in the 1985 season, the Boss was quoted by the *New York Times* asking, "Where is Reggie Jackson? We need a Mr. October [Jackson's nickname, for his postseason heroics] or a Mr. September. Winfield is Mr. May." Steinbrenner characteristically heaped criticism on his other stars as well, but it was always Winfield who seemed to receive the brunt of it. Then in July 1990 his mistreatment of the dignified outfielder led to Steinbrenner being suspended from the day-to-day operation of the club, this time permanently, by baseball commissioner Fay Vincent. The Boss had paid a gambler named Howie Spera $40,000 to dig up dirt on Winfield, who was suing his employers for breach of contract for failing

The Bad Side of Steinbrenner

In life, New York Yankees principal owner George Steinbrenner was a newsmaker, frequently stealing headlines from his players even while insulting them. After his death, the Boss proved to be literally a larger-than-life figure, as he continued to make news.

In December 2010, five months after his demise, the FBI released documents detailing how in 1973 Steinbrenner tried to dodge the Feds, who wanted to question him regarding an illegal contribution made to President Richard Nixon's 1972 reelection campaign. Steinbrenner pleaded guilty in 1974 to making the illegal contribution and to a felony obstruction of justice charge. More documents released by the FBI in May 2011 stated that the Yankee owner assisted the agency in two investigations, one of them a terrorism probe, before he was pardoned for his crimes by President Ronald Reagan.

Steinbrenner's name again appeared in the news in July 2011 following the discovery of the body of former Yankee pitcher Hideki Irabu. After an impressive debut in 1997, the pitcher billed as "the Japanese Nolan Ryan" failed to live up to such lofty expectations. As virtually every news story about Irabu's death pointed out, George Steinbrenner helped destroy his self-confidence by branding his expensive acquisition a "fat … toad" when the overweight hurler failed to cover first base during an exhibition game in April 1999. Traded after the 1999 season, Irabu remained in MLB for three more seasons without achieving any notable success. He began to drink heavily and was arrested for assault on a bartender in Japan in August 2008 and for driving under the influence in Gardena, California, in May 2010, before apparently committing suicide at age 42 by hanging himself in his Rancho Palos Verdes, California, home.

to contribute a mandated $300,000 to the Dave Winfield Foundation, the player's charitable organization.

Steinbrenner was reinstated in 1993, and after General Manager Gene Michael and farm director Bill Livesay had put the Yankee house in order during his absence, the team had begun to win, and Steinbrenner, despite occasional outbursts to the media and abusive comments about players, began to leave the operation of his team in the hands of his baseball people. He had moved his business and personal interests to Tampa,

Florida, and while he never became a hands-off owner, he allowed wiser heads to prevail. General managers Bob Watson and Brian Cashman were given more or less free rein to do as they saw fit, and the results were spectacular. The 1994 strike deprived the Yankees of a pennant, but they won the AL East in 1995 under Buck Showalter, and after unsuccessful NL manager Joe Torre took over as field boss in 1996, the Yanks would dominate Major League Baseball for the remainder of the century. After 14 years without a playoff appearance and 18 years without a World Series victory, more than the 12 and 15 years under CBS and the early Steinbrenner era, the Yankees regained their standing as baseball's greatest team. Eschewing expensive sluggers for small ball, the Torre-led Yanks featured solid hitting, fielding, and pitching to great effect, making the playoffs every season through 2007, winning the AL pennant in 1996, 1998–2001, and 2003, and the World Series in 1996 and 1998–2000. As Steinbrenner's health began to decline in 2006, he handed over operation of the team to sons Hank and Hal, under whose stewardship a new Yankee Stadium was built in the Bronx, and another pennant and World Series were won under manager Joe Girardi when the facility opened in 2009. In his last years the Boss was seldom seen or heard from, mostly remaining in his Tampa home. George Steinbrenner died in Tampa of a heart attack on July 13, 2010.

As a baseball entrepreneur, George Steinbrenner's legacy is unblemished. He revolutionized the game by being the first owner to sell cable TV rights, and later created the Yankees' own YES network. The franchise, which was valued at $10 million when he acquired it in 1993, was estimated to be worth $1.2 billion by 2005. Despite, or because of, his authoritarian ownership style, he became a cultural icon regardless of whether he was loved or hated. He hosted *Saturday Night Live*, did commercials for Miller Lite beer (with Yankee manager Billy Martin) and Visa credit cards (with Yankee captain Derek Jeter), was satirized on *The Simpsons*, and featured as a character on *Seinfeld*. He was generous in his contributions to charitable causes, especially in the Tampa Bay area, where a new high school was named for him in Lutz, Florida, in 2009. Legends Field in Tampa, the Yankees' spring training facility and home field for their farm club in the Class A Florida State League, was renamed George M. Steinbrenner

Field in March 2008, and a life-size bronze statue of the Boss was placed in front of the ballpark in January 2011. After his death, the Yankees wore a commemorative patch on the left breast of their uniforms, and in September 2010 the Steinbrenner family had a monument to his memory added to those in Monument Park behind the center field fence of Yankee Stadium. Despite all the honors, his abrasive manner and disregard for the feelings of his employees tarnished the Steinbrenner legacy. Though he was always popular with the media for his willingness to talk to them, his potential enshrinement as an executive in the Baseball Hall of Fame is far from assured. Placed on the 2011 ballot by the Historical Overview Committee, consisting of veteran baseball writers, his fate lies in the hands of players, as well as writers and executives, on the Veterans Committee. His rejection by more than 50 percent of the voters in his first appearance on the ballot indicates that it will be an uphill climb to convince them that the good that George Steinbrenner did for baseball outweighed the bad.

David C. Skinner

See also Berra, Yogi; Big Red Machine; Cleveland Indians; Hayes, Woody; Jackson, Reggie; Jeter, Derek; Los Angeles Dodgers; New York Yankees; Saperstein, Abe; World Series

Suggested Resources

"George Steinbrenner." Baseball Almanac. http://www .baseball-almanac.com/articles/george_steinbrenner_ biography.shtml. Accessed December 2010.

"George Steinbrenner." Biography.com. http://www.biog raphy.com/articles/George-Steinbrenner-583100. Accessed December 2010.

Golenbock, Peter. *George: The Poor Little Rich Boy Who Built the Yankee Empire.* Hoboken, NJ: John Wiley & Sons, 2009.

Madden, Bill. *Steinbrenner: The Last Lion of Baseball.* New York: HarperCollins, 2010.

Mahler, Jonathan. *Ladies and Gentlemen, the Bronx Is Burning: 1977, Baseball, Politics, and the Battle for the Soul of the City.* New York: Farrar, Straus and Giroux, 2005.

Merron, Jeff. "The List: Steinbrenner's Worst." ESPN.com. http://espn.go.com/page2/s/list/steinbrenner.html Accessed December 2010.

Schaap, Dick. *Steinbrenner!* New York: G. P. Putnam's Sons, 1982.

Stengel, Casey (1890–1975)

Charles Dillon Stengel, a major league outfielder from 1912 to 1925, achieved Hall of Fame status as manager of the New York Yankees from 1949 to 1960, though success eluded him while piloting poor National League teams before and after his fabulous run with the "Bronx Bombers." Always a colorful character in victory and defeat, he became well known for his zany antics as a player and his double-talk, so-called Stengelese, as a manager. Born in Kansas City, Missouri, on July 30, 1890, his original baseball nickname was Dutch, commonly applied to those of German ancestry at the time, but he became better known as Casey, a variant of K. C., for his hometown. To his family he was always Charley. As a manager, his strategic maneuvering, including the platooning of position players with left-handed hitters in the lineup against right-handed pitchers and righty hitters facing lefty pitchers, won him the sobriquet of "The Ole Perfesser."

Casey's father, Louis, was an insurance agent of German ancestry, and his mother, the former Jennie Jordan, was of Irish stock. Both parents were first-generation Americans, their families having emigrated to the United States around 1850. Young Charles attended Woodland Grade School and Central High School in his native city, starring in baseball, football, and basketball at the latter institution before attending Western Dental College for three years. In 1910 he signed a $135 a month contract as a left-handed outfielder for his hometown AAA Kansas City Blues, who optioned him to the Kankakee (Illinois) Kays of the Class D Northern Association. (Minor leagues were arranged hierarchically with AA being the highest and D the lowest level of the minors.)

When his league disbanded in July 1910, Stengel moved on to the Shelbyville (Kentucky) Millers of the similarly classified Blue Grass League. Casey was on the move again the following month as his team became the Maysville Rivermen, and he finished the season hitting .223 for the last-place club. The following season he led the Class C Wisconsin-Illinois League with a .352 average and 148 hits for the Aurora (Illinois) Blues, who finished seventh in the eight-team circuit. His .290 average in 1912 for the Montgomery (Alabama) Rebels of the Class A Southern League, another second-division team, was good enough for him to be called up to the Brooklyn Superbas (formerly known as the Dodgers) of the National League, whose owner, Charles Ebbets, had previously purchased his contract for $500. Casey would never again play in the minors until his big league career had concluded.

Stengel proved to be a solid player as a major league outfielder, a decent hitter with an above-average throwing arm. He was good, but by no means a superstar. He had four hits in four at-bats with a walk in his first big league contest and went on to hit .284 in 1,277 games over 14 seasons in the National League with Brooklyn (1912–1917), Pittsburgh Pirates (1918–1919), Philadelphia Phillies (1920–1921), New York Giants (1921–1923), and Boston Braves (1924–1925). He hit .316 for the 1914 Brooklyn Robins with a league-leading .404 on-base percentage and batted .368 and .339 in fewer games for John McGraw's 1922–1923 Giants. His home run against the Phillies allowed Brooklyn to clinch the 1916 NL pennant. He achieved career highs in games (150), at-bats (549), runs (69), hits (141), and RBIs (73) with the 1917 Robins. Raising his game in the World Series, he hit .393 in three Fall Classics, batting .364 in 1916, .400 in 1922, and .417 in 1923, the latter two with the New York Giants. Though the Giants lost in 1923, Casey won two games with home runs at the ripe old age of 33, including a ninth-inning, inside-the-park blast, the first home run in the first postseason game in Yankee Stadium, prompting lavish praise from the local press and this inspired bit of doggerel from Damon Runyon in the *New York American*:

> This is the way old "Casey" Stengel ran yesterday afternoon, running his home run home.
> This is the way old "Casey" Stengel ran running his home run home in a Giant victory by a score of 5 to 4 in the first game of the world's series of 1923.
> This is the way old "Casey" Stengel ran, running his home run home, when two were out in the ninth inning and the score was tied and the ball was still bounding inside the Yankee yard.
> This is the way—
> His mouth wide open.

His warped old legs bending beneath him at
  every stride.
His arms flying back and forth like those of a
  man swimming with a crawl stroke.
His flanks heaving, his breath whistling, his head
  far back.

Playing in Ebbets Field, his old home ballpark,
with the Pirates in 1919, Stengel literally gave the
crowd the bird. Having a bad day at the plate and in
right field, on his way to the dugout after the sixth inning Casey stopped by the Brooklyn bullpen in foul
territory along the right field wall. Pitcher Leon Cadore was holding a confused sparrow that had wan-
dered there. Casey took the bird from Cadore, and
before he batted, stuck it under his cap. As he stepped
to the plate, the fans mockingly cheered and good-
naturedly booed him. Casey bowed toward the stands
and doffed his cap, and as he did so the bird flew off,
to the laughter of all those present.

Casey Stengel met Edna Lawson of Glendale,
California, in the summer of 1923 through his Giants'
teammate Emil "Irish" Meusel. Casey was immediately smitten with Edna, a good friend of Meusel's
wife, Van, and quickly asked her to marry him. It took
about a year for her to consent, and the two were wed
the following August. Like many players of his era,
Stengel returned to the minor leagues after his big
league career had run its course. Released by Boston
in May 1925, he accepted the offer of Boston Braves
owner Judge Emil Fuchs to be player-manager and
president of the Worcester Panthers, a team the judge
owned in the Class A Eastern League. He hit .320
and was a success at his first managing job, lifting the
cellar-dwelling club to a third-place finish.

After the season Stengel moved up to AAA, signing on as player-manager for the American Association Toledo Mud Hens at the suggestion of John
McGraw, who had an interest in the club, which was
partly owned by the Giants. Casey thought he had the
freedom to do this, releasing himself as a player, firing himself as manager, and resigning as president, but
Fuchs balked, and baseball's all-powerful commissioner Judge Kenesaw Mountain Landis upheld the
Braves' claim to his services. Fuchs then agreed to let
him leave, and Casey took the reins of a club that had

finished seventh and never won a pennant. He stayed
there for six years, and as his on-field skills diminished
he gradually reduced his playing time from 88 games
in 1926 to none in 1930 and 2 in 1931. He had mixed
success as the Toledo manager, winning the league
title in 1927 but finishing last twice, including his last
year there. He was dropped after the season from the
club, which suffered severe Depression-related financial problems and entered receivership, causing Casey
to lose his and Edna's money, which he had invested
in the team.

As the 1932 season began, Stengel found himself back in Ebbets Field. Wilbert Robinson had been
dropped as Brooklyn president and manager over the
winter, and for the first time in 18 years the team nickname reverted to the Dodgers. Casey's former Pirate
teammate Max Carey was the club's new skipper, and
when Casey asked him for a job, management agreed,
reasoning that he might supply some of the color lost
with the dismissal of Uncle Robbie. After two years
as a coach, he replaced Carey as Dodgers field boss
and became a major league manager for the first time.
Casey supplied the necessary laughs and tried to do
well at his job, always teaching, though not always
understood, and often frustrated by his charges' inability to carry out his strategies. He was always a father figure to his young ballplayers, never having any
children of his own, but he could be mean as well. The
talent was thin in Brooklyn, and frustration was more
common than gratification, just as failure won over
success. The team finished sixth, fifth, and seventh,
and Casey was let go after the 1936 season.

Stengel stayed out of baseball for the first time
in his adult life in 1937, but his time was well spent.
The Stengels had invested the then-princely sum of
$10,000 from Edna's family money in the oil com-
pany owned by the family of Randy Moore, a Texan
who played briefly for Casey in 1936. He and Edna
spent the year in east Texas, where Casey learned the
oil business, and he was able to live on the money he
made from it for the rest of his life, freeing him from
dependency on his wife's inheritance. Casey missed
baseball, however, and the opportunity arose for him
to return to Boston, where Judge Fuchs was out of the
picture and the team was run by Bob Quinn, his old
boss in Brooklyn. Quinn changed the team nickname

from the Braves to the Bees and gave Casey the opportunity for him and Edna to buy part of the club, which Casey would also manage.

Casey managed Boston for six years, but he had another bad ball club and would never finish higher than fifth. As always he tried to teach, but there was little young talent, and the has-beens and never-would-bes weren't about to learn any new tricks. He liked the city, but the feeling wasn't mutual. He was entertaining, but the team wasn't, and the fans stayed away in droves. Before the start of the 1943 season, Casey was hit by a car and broke his leg. He missed two months, and the best he could do on his return was bring the team in sixth after a string of seventh-place finishes. *Boston Record* columnist Dave Egan recognized the driver who hit Stengel and kept him away from his job as the man who did the most for Boston baseball in 1943.

It was back to the minors for Stengel in 1944. The season had opened to find him at home in Glendale, but in May he was hired by co-owner Charlie Grimm to manage the Milwaukee Brewers of the American Association when Charlie moved from Milwaukee to Chicago to manage the Cubs. Grimm's partner, Bill Veeck, serving with the marines in the Pacific, couldn't be reached, but was furious when he got the news. Casey won the pennant with the Brewers and the hearts of their fans, but after he read the scathing letter Veeck had written about his hiring, declined to return for 1945 despite the returned Veeck's urging him to stay on. He moved on to the helm of the Kansas City Blues, the Yankee farm club in the same league, but with the New York system depleted by the war, the Blues finished seventh despite Casey's efforts.

Still longing for a return to the majors, Casey faced the reality that no managerial positions were available, and instead took a job piloting the Oakland Oaks of the AAA Pacific Coast League. He loved it there, being closer to Edna and enjoying life in the Bay Area, beloved by the Oakland fans and the sportswriters as well. The Oaks finished second and fourth in 1946 and 1947, but made it to the finals of the league playoffs each season before succumbing. Then in 1948 they won it all, finishing first and taking the playoffs, beating Seattle four games to one in the final round, as Casey was named minor league manager of

Casey Stengel as a young manager with the Brooklyn Dodgers in the 1930s. (Library of Congress.)

the year. The team had many veteran ballplayers, but more significantly, a local kid from Berkeley High School named Alfred Manuel Martin. The manager took to the young Billy, whose pugnacious attitude and willingness to learn from the old master, coupled with an ability to play several positions, made him the perfect Stengel player. The feeling was mutual, and Martin would some day follow in Casey's footsteps.

Yankees general manager George Weiss and Casey Stengel had a longstanding relationship from the time Casey was in Worcester and Weiss at New Haven in the Eastern League. Weiss did not like Manager Bucky Harris and had long wanted to bring Stengel to New York. The Yanks finished third in 1948, and Weiss fired Harris after the season. He convinced the owners to let him hire Stengel, and Casey was overjoyed to be back in the big leagues. Skepticism about his

Stengel and the Negro Leagues

Casey Stengel has been credited by numerous writers with recommending the players that formed the nucleus of the Negro Leagues' first dynasty, the Kansas City Monarchs of the early 1920s, including Hall of Fame pitching and hitting star Bullet Rogan, to owner J. L. Wilkinson. But did he?

In the fall of 1919, Casey was temporarily unemployed after refusing to report to the Phillies following a trade from the Pirates. He returned home to Kansas City where he put together a group of semipros and former minor leaguers to barnstorm through the plains and Southwest. One stop on the tour was Nogales, Arizona, where his KC All Stars played a series against the black army team stationed there, the 25th Infantry Wreckers. Rogan was the team captain, and other future Monarchs on the roster included Dobie Moore, Bob Fagan, Hurley McNair, Lemuel Hawkins, Heavy Johnson, and Andy Cooper, another future Hall of Fame pitcher.

Although Stengel never claimed any role in his signing, he would later reminisce about playing near the Mexican border against Rogan, who in his autobiography he called Grogan, and said next to Satchel Paige he was the best black pitcher he had ever seen. The upcoming games were front-page news in the *Nogales Daily Herald*, which stated that Rogan and his best hitters would not play for the army team. Coverage of the games themselves was spotty and lacked box scores, but, as far as can be determined, only Moore, whom Casey recalled in his memoir, Fagan, and possibly Johnson played against Stengel's squad.

Stengel may have seen Rogan play earlier when they were both in Kansas City, or Rogan may have played against him in Nogales after all. But there is no evidence that Casey had anything to do with the Monarchs signing him.

chances of success abounded. The public liked Harris, who had won the World Series in 1947, and the press doubted Casey's abilities. He had been a losing manager in the National League, and his reputation was as a hothead and a clown. It didn't take long for Casey to sway the opinion of most, but not all Yankees players despite immediate success on the field. Joe DiMaggio, the team's biggest star and most valuable asset, never warmed to Stengel. Weiss hired a new coaching staff, one that Stengel would keep together for most of his tenure, and in spring training they divided up the team and began instructing the players. Casey was still devoted to teaching, and though the veterans resented it, youngsters like infielder Jerry Coleman and catcher Yogi Berra appreciated the tutelage and thrived under the system.

When the team was beset by injuries, Stengel began to platoon his players, and this and other strategic moves raised his stature from clown to genius. The Yankees began winning and never stopped as long as Casey was at the helm. They won a never-equaled five consecutive World Series from 1949 through 1953 and took the American League pennant again from 1955 through 1958 and in 1960, copping two more Series crowns in 1956 and 1958. DiMaggio retired after the 1951 season, but new superstar Mickey Mantle was already there to take his place atop the Yankee pantheon. Whitey Ford came along around the same time, and the little lefty would anchor the Yankee pitching staff for years to come. Not on the same skill level, but another valuable addition was Billy Martin, who as "Casey's boy" provided the kind of versatility and hardnosed attitude that the manager counted on, and like his skipper had risen to greater heights on the field in the Fall Classic, while learning at Stengel's side the strategies that would make him a great manager a couple of decades later.

Despite having won his 10th AL title in 12 seasons at the Yankee helm, Stengel was fired after losing the 1960 World Series to the Pirates. He was perceived to be too old and was no longer garnering respect from the younger players. He retired to California as a wealthy man with a position as director of a bank, but retirement lasted only one season. In 1962 at age 71 he returned to the NL as manager of the expansion New York Mets, completing the cycle of having played for or managed all four 20th-century New York teams. The Mets were terrible, worse than the Brooklyn and Boston teams he had failed with previously. They set a record for futility in their first season and finished 10th in each of Casey's four years with the club. Still, the team was loved, and so was Casey, who dubbed them "amazin'." By the end of his tenure he was falling asleep on the bench, drinking too much, and was more sarcastic and caustic than ever with his players. He broke his hip in a fall in late July and retired before the end of the 1965 season, finishing his managerial career with a record of 1,905 wins and 1,842 losses. He was elected to the Hall of Fame in 1966 and had his uniform number 37 retired by both the Yankees and the Mets. Casey Stengel died of cancer in Glendale, California, on September 29, 1975.

Always entertaining as a player and manager, Casey Stengel made baseball fun for the fans and writers if not always for his players. Few who participated in the national pastime were held in higher affection by the public than the Ole Perfesser. On the road from clown to genius and back again, he presided over the greatest dynasty the game has known. He never stopped teaching and was always driven to win, no matter how unlikely the prospect. His perfection of the platoon system changed the nature of the game, and his wit and wisdom left their mark on several generations during his 55 years in professional baseball.

David C. Skinner

See also Baseball Hall of Fame; Berra, Yogi; Brooklyn Dodgers; DiMaggio, Joe; Mantle, Mickey; New York Mets, New York Yankees; Veeck, Bill; Yankee Stadium

Suggested Resources

"Casey Stengel." Baseball Almanac. http://www.baseball-almanac.com/quotes/casey_stengel_senate_testimony.shtml. Accessed August 29, 2011.

"Casey Stengel." National Baseball Hall of Fame. http://baseballhall.org/hof/stengel-casey. Accessed August 29, 2011.

Casey Stengel Website. http://www.caseystengel.com. Accessed August 29, 2011.

Creamer, Robert W. *Stengel: His Life and Times*. New York: Simon & Schuster, 1984.

Goldman, Steven. *Forging Genius: The Making of Casey Stengel*. Washington, DC: Potomac Books, 2005.

Stengel, Casey, as told to Harry T. Paxton. *Casey at the Bat: The Story of My Life in Baseball*. New York: Random House, 1962.

Stern, David (1942–)

David Stern was born on September 22, 1942, in Teaneck, New Jersey, just outside of New York City, and began his business career at his family's Jewish delicatessen in New York City. Living in New York City, Stern developed a love for the New York Knicks. He

never had formal basketball training, nor did he play organized basketball; however, Stern is arguably the most successful NBA commissioner in the history of the league.

He matriculated from Rutgers University, the largest state school in New Jersey, in 1963 with degrees in political science and history. He was also a member of the Sigma Alpha Mu fraternity at Rutgers. After his undergraduate education, Stern entered law school at the prestigious Columbia Law School where he graduated in 1966. Stern is still actively involved at both Rutgers and Columbia, serving on the board of trustees at Columbia currently. After law school, Stern entered the law firm of Proskauer Rose LLP in New York City. Proskauer Rose was founded in 1875 and is one of the nation's oldest and largest law firms. Stern began handling the NBA's legal work at Proskauer Rose as outside counsel at age 24. He proved to be highly capable as a young lawyer handling the legal business of the NBA.

Based on his impressive performance with Proskauer Rose, Stern was hired as the NBA's legal counsel in 1978. Six years later, Stern became the NBA's fourth commissioner in 1984, a pivotal year for the league. The NBA was declining in popularity and revenue for the league left much to be desired. In February 1984, the dunk contest returned to professional basketball, a spectacle that had been created in the ABA and last seen in 1976. More importantly, the third pick of the NBA draft in the summer of 1984 was Michael Jordan. The combination of Stern and Jordan completely changed the way the league was run and revolutionized the way a professional sports league made money.

When Stern entered as the NBA's fourth commissioner, the league was in financial trouble and had an embarrassing reputation. The league was tainted with drug use and unrest between the players and owners, and it was financially failing. During his time with the NBA, Stern helped implement a drug-testing program that cleaned up what was a drug-abusing league.

Many argue that Stern was the benefactor of good timing as the fourth NBA commissioner. When he began as the commissioner in 1984, the Houston Rockets drafted Akeem Olajuwon (now Hakeem) with the first pick and the Chicago Bulls drafted Michael

NBA commissioner David Stern speaks during a basketball news conference following a Board of Governors meeting in New York, October 25, 2012. (AP Photo/ Kathy Willens.)

The NBA commissioner deals with much more than just basketball. Stern is, first and foremost, an attorney, addressing the legal issues of one of the largest businesses in the world. In addition to legal issues, Stern must be a global ambassador. Since his tenure began in 1984, international players have entered the NBA at an astonishing rate. There are currently players from Iran, Israel, and Italy, just to name a few of many. As a result, Stern has helped make basketball arguably the most popular world sport, only behind soccer. Stern also has to be a business-savvy CEO. He helps negotiate television contracts, team acquisitions, and overall business dealings daily. He also has to deal with work stoppages (also known as a "lockout") when players and owners cannot come to an agreement for salaries and benefits. As a result, the league will not continue with the season until a mutual agreement exists. Stern is also the face behind the league. He is the person that addresses the media on all things NBA, and any time there is a controversial issue with a player or team, on or off the court, Stern is the person that ultimately decides the fate of that team or player.

Stern is also a boss. He oversees the conduct of each player, owner, administrator, and organization. Any boss must make difficult decisions and Stern is not exempt. One of Stern's more controversial decisions was to implement a mandatory dress code for the entire league. The new policy stated that players must dress in business casual clothing when arriving and leaving the arena. The players may not wear "throwback" jerseys, do-rags, jeans, flat-brimmed hats, and gaudy jewelry. The pointed criticism stems from an attempt to suppress hip-hop culture in the NBA. For many years, hip-hop culture and the NBA have been one and the same. Stern's argument for the new dress code was to bring more class and professionalism to the game. Many players thought the new code was racist, targeting a stereotypical audience and trying to unnecessarily suppress a style purely based on race. The policy was implemented in 2005, largely created due to players like Allen Iverson and Ron Artest, who were notoriously outspoken and critical about the league. After six years, the dress code is still a part of the game. Many players use the new policy to showcase different fashions of business attire, which has largely been accepted by the majority of the players.

Jordan with the third pick. Other notables from that draft include Charles Barkley, who was drafted by the Philadelphia 76ers with the fifth pick, and John Stockton, selected by the Utah Jazz with the 16th pick. The combination of an incredible influx of talent and Stern's intelligence and savvy allowed the league to rebound into an international powerhouse.

The NBA commissioner position had only been occupied by three men previous to David Stern. Maurice Podoloff, Walter Kennedy, and Larry O'Brien were Stern's predecessors, with the current NBA Finals trophy named after O'Brien. After Stern entered the league in 1978, he had already been exposed to the legal and business aspects of the league, making the transition to commissioner a relatively smooth one.

The following year, Stern instituted a new basketball, which was not well received. The old Spalding brand basketball, made of real leather and part of the NBA for 35 seasons, eventually returned. The new ball only lasted a couple months, as the old leather ball returned January 1, 2007. Stern, notorious for his steadfast decision making and stubborn personality, acquiesced after much player ridicule. Future NBA Hall of Famer Shaquille O'Neal, one of the best centers in NBA history, said of the ball, "It feels like one of those cheap balls that you buy at the toy store." Many of the players at that time agreed. In fact, the new ball was so unpopular among the players that the players' union filed a formal complaint to the National Labor Relations Board asking to go back to the original ball. This remains one of the few major decisions Stern was forced to revisit and change in his remarkably long tenure as NBA commissioner.

During the same time period, from 2005 to 2007, the NBA had perhaps the worst scandal a sport league would have to address in game fixing and gambling. Former referee Tim Donaghy was a longtime official in the NBA. During the 2007 season, Donaghy was accused of gambling during games he was officiating. Donaghy was sentenced to 15 months in prison, but more importantly the scandal brought scrutiny and uncertainty to professional basketball. Stern was quick to act, however, and revised the rules for officials regarding gambling. He also began programs to analyze the statistical relationship between officials, gambling, and game outcomes. Many officials had admitted to gambling on sports in general. Stern took the problem very seriously and acted swiftly to curb the problem that threatened the integrity of not only the NBA, but also sports everywhere. To date, Donaghy's scandal has been the only significant scandal with referees' gambling in the NBA. Stern was able to identify and correct the problem quickly. He restored credibility to NBA officiating, which seems to be untainted since the scandal. Stern controlled the problem and changed the rules, fixing the problem. Another successful change Stern instituted was the creation of the NBA Development League. This is the NBA's minor league basketball affiliation, which has been largely popular since its inception in 2001. Stern created the league with the idea of developing an intense game. He uses Major League Baseball's concept of farming players until they are ready for the game's highest level of play.

Until 2001, the NBA had never had a true developmental league that was part of the NBA. Smaller leagues, like the Continental Basketball Association (CBA), acted as leagues where players could perfect their skills before entering the more prestigious NBA. The NBDL has been very successful over its 10-year period, now containing 16 teams all across the country. The final four teams were added in 2006 from the CBA, including the Dakota Wizards, Sioux Falls Skyforce, Idaho Stampede, and the Colorado 14ers.

The NBDL allows teams to draft players on potential who may not be ready to play in the NBA right away. Stern recognized the possibility of developing players in smaller-market cities, where basketball may be popular, but not popular enough for a large NBA franchise. Stern has introduced professional basketball to 16 smaller cities where professional sports are often absent. In the 10 years the NBDL has been in existence, the league has been highly successful and has given previously unknown players an opportunity to develop and eventually become successful in the NBA.

Along with Stern's successful expansion of basketball domestically with new NBA franchises and the new NBDL, Stern has also expanded the game globally. Stern is considered by many to be a pioneer with his ability to expand an American game worldwide. Stern encouraged the recruitment of international talent, beginning with the 7'7" Manute Bol from Sudan in 1983, to Vlade Divac from Serbia in 1989. The 1990s experienced an influx of NBA players from Eastern Europe and Africa. As the game began to expand, Yao Ming was drafted to the Houston Rockets in 2002 from China. Since then, the game has seen players from Italy, Iran, Israel, Argentina, Brazil, Puerto Rico, Germany, Lithuania, and many other countries. Over the past 20 years, basketball has become arguably the second most popular sport, globally, behind soccer. This expansion of the game can be largely attributed to Stern's ability to promote the NBA worldwide.

Not only has Stern made the game a successful global enterprise financially, but also philanthropically as well. During the 1990s, numerous international players joined the NBA as the game became a global enterprise. During the international expansion, many international players, such as Dikembe Mutombo, spearheaded the movement to international charity in the NBA. In 1994, Mutombo, as well as Commissioner Stern and other NBA players, made a trip to South Africa to visit a country torn apart by apartheid. It was this on trip that Stern recognized the impact NBA charity could have on an entire continent. Stern was introduced to African leaders and recognized an opportunity within Africa for global expansion of the game. Now, the NBA has offices in South Africa.

After this trip in 1994, Stern and his NBA team began developing ideas for programs that could utilize the NBA name and develop charities abroad. Starting with Basketball Without Borders in 2003, then expanding to NBA Cares in 2005. Stern observed the success international players were having with their international charities and recognized both a moral opportunity and a business opportunity.

Stern started Basketball Without Borders in 2003 in an effort to spread the game of basketball outside of the United States. It also was an attempt to bring stability and charity to war-torn nations. Many of the countries the NBA helps have native players that return to their home country after playing in the NBA with resources and human capital to improve the nation's quality of life. Since its inception, Basketball Without Borders has been a successful program. Many NBA players, both American and international, travel annually abroad to help construct buildings, build schools, and practice other forms of charity.

Stern saw the success of Basketball Without Borders and decided to form another charitable organization named NBA Cares in 2005. NBA Cares is mainly a domestic program that Stern started where NBA players perform charity in local communities. The players often help build playgrounds, read to local schoolchildren, and perform other similar community services. Like Basketball Without Borders, NBA Cares has also been incredibly successful.

No other professional American sport has an international following like the NBA. This is largely attributed to Stern's efforts to globalize the game. Stern has grown the NBA into a professional sports league that is arguably the most popular international league. In his 27-year tenure as commissioner, Stern revived a crumbling league and added philanthropic programs

NBA Lockout

The NBA lockout is the term for a work stoppage in professional basketball. The lockout occurs when players and owners are unable to reach an agreement on many issues, including the amount the players are compensated by the owners. There have been four lockouts in the history of the NBA, most recently in 2011 and previously in 1998. The lockout in 1998 shortened the season to 50 games. The 2011 lockout resulted in a shortened season of 66 games. Unlike previous lockouts, there is now an alternative to playing domestically in the NBA. International basketball has become popular and competitive for professional basketball leagues worldwide. Not only are the international leagues competitive, they are able to offer financial incentives for the NBA's superstars to travel abroad to play. Many NBA players opted to sign contracts to play in China, Italy, France, Turkey, and other countries due to the work stoppage in the NBA. Even though international basketball is not a true threat to the NBA, it offers an alternative that many players involved in the lockout are evaluating.

that few other professional leagues around the world enjoy. Even though Stern has enjoyed success over the years, his next challenge will be solving the current lack of parity in the league. With the exception of a select few teams that thrive, many small-market NBA teams are losing money. The recent trend of NBA superstars "teaming up" to win a championship also creates a challenge for Stern.

During the summer of 2010, the entire basketball community tuned into ESPN to watch "The Decision" when LeBron James announced to the world which team he would play with for the upcoming NBA season. James chose the Miami Heat, joining superstars Dwyane Wade and Chris Bosh. This could be a common and potentially detrimental trend in the NBA. Since Michael Jordan won six NBA championships, NBA superstars will not receive the respect and admiration they desire without a championship ring. Because of this desire, everything, including money, becomes secondary to being a champion. If the trend continues, the parity in the league will diminish. Stern will have to address this challenge as smaller-market teams that do not employ a big-name superstar struggle to compete financially and on the basketball court. Another challenge Stern is currently facing is the NBA lockout. Also known as a work stoppage, the NBA lockout is occurring because players and owners cannot agree on many issues, most of which deal with money. The last work stoppage occurred in 1998, when the league shortened its season to 50 games. Stern managed to overcome this lockout, coupled with the decline of the league's popularity after Michael Jordan retired from the Chicago Bulls.

Stern has managed to address and solve many problems during his tenure as commissioner. From the officiating scandals, to the change to a new basketball, Stern has usually managed to be successful. As the league continues to grow, Stern may face his largest challenge yet. Even though he has faced a lockout before, Stern has not faced the increasing disparity in the league. Franchises such as Cleveland, Sacramento, and Minnesota struggle annually, with no signs of improvement. As superstar players continue to join the same team to win championships, the problems will only become worse. The salary cap and NBA lottery draft system is meant to make sure the league maintains competitive and financial parity, but it is clear that this system is no longer working. Stern must find a way to dissuade players from "teaming up," otherwise many of the league's teams may crumble. Given Stern's successful ability to problem solve over his tenure of commissioner, his NBA team will likely find a solution to keep the NBA a profitable, popular, and viable league for years to come.

Dean Bring

See also Barkley, Charles; Iverson, Allen; James, LeBron; Jordan, Michael; National Basketball Association; Olajuwon, Hakeem; O'Neal, Shaquille; Strikes and Lockouts; Yao Ming

Suggested Resources

Biography on David Stern. http://www.associatedcontent .com/article/1589090/a_biography_on_david_stern .html?cat=14. Accessed October 31, 2011.

"David J. Stern." PBS.org. http://www.pbs.org/wttw/ceo exchange/episodes/ceo_dstern.html. Accessed October 31, 2011.

Keteyian, Armen. *Inside the New NBA: Money Players.* New York: Pocket Books, 1998.

Robbins, Liz. "A Whole New Ballgame: NBA Admits Its Mistake." December 6, 2006. http://www.nytimes .com/2006/12/06/sports/basketball/06ball.html?hp& ex=1165467600&en=08728757c39f319b&ei=5094& partner=homepage. Accessed October 31, 2011.

Thomsen, Ian. "The Commissioner's Lasting Legacy." January 29, 2009.http://sportsillustrated.cnn.com/2009/ writers/ian_thomsen/01/29/stern.international/. Accessed October 31, 2011.

Steroids

Anabolic androgenic steroids, commonly known simply as steroids, are derivatives of the hormone testosterone. The term "steroids," however, is inclusive of not only androgens (testosterone), but also estrogens (estradiol), progestagens, and cortisol. The term "androgens" refers to all of the compounds in the human body with male hormone–like activity. Testosterone, specifically, is the androgen in the body responsible for androgenic (virilizing) and anabolic (cell growth) effects witnessed in males once puberty has occurred. The adrenal glands, ovaries in females, and testes in males all secrete testosterone.

In 1927, two researchers at the University of Chicago isolated testosterone from bull testicles for the first time. Synthetic forms of testosterone date back to 1935, when scientists in the former Yugoslavia discovered how to isolate and synthesize the hormone in the lab. This research breakthrough led to several pharmaceutical companies being able to develop and supply both oral and injectable forms of testosterone to the medical community. By the 1940s, testosterone was heavily marketed by several pharmaceutical companies in many areas of the world to older and middle-aged men. These preparations promised to reinvigorate tired bodies, restore manhood, and counter the effects of aging. Moreover, testosterone was thought to alleviate depression and melancholia. At the same time, estrogen replacement therapies were heavily marketed to women for similar reasons.

Over the next 20 years, scientists and medical researchers refined and developed many variations of steroids. The original medical function of testosterone supplementation in the form of anabolic androgenic steroids was to restore and reinvigorate aging male bodies. Once inside the body and across the membrane of the cell, the anabolic steroid binds to androgen receptors. The hormone and receptor then together enter the nucleus of the cell via diffusion to alter the gene transcription and messenger RNA synthesis. The result is a increase in proteins forming muscle cells and a decrease in cortisol production. Among the medical uses of testosterone are its anabolic effects in stimulating changes in the somatic and nonreproductive tissues that result in muscle growth, bone development, and increased appetite in patients battling cancer, AIDS, and other diseases that cause muscle atrophy. Testosterone is also known for its androgenic effects and role in stimulating the development of the male sex characteristics associated with puberty in boys. However, taken in sufficiently high doses, testosterone creates androgenic effects in both women and men, including acne and increased body hair growth. Therapeutic doses of testosterone are prescribed for males with hypogonadism to stimulate and maintain secondary sex characteristics, for transgender men transitioning from female to male, and sometimes for boys who have not started puberty by their mid-teens. Testosterone supplementation in boys is discouraged because it affects the epiphyseal center of bone and can impact growth.

Testosterone influences most tissues in the body. While the hormone has a direct impact on the sex organs and sex-linked muscles, it also exerts indirect influence on the kidneys, liver, heart, bone, bone marrow, bladder, and skin, among others. Testosterone supplementation exerts a reverse influence on other areas of the body by decreasing the size of the thymus, spleen, lymph glands, and adrenal glands, in addition to contributing to baldness. Long-term use of steroids at above-therapeutic doses is associated with high blood pressure, changed cholesterol profile, liver damage, and thickening of the left ventricle of the heart. Psychiatric symptoms, including addiction, mood disorders, depression, and "'roid rage" are associated with steroid use, but have not been confirmed in reputable studies. Male users can experience gynecomastia, enlarged prostates, atrophied testes, and temporary infertility when consuming large doses of steroids. Female users taking high doses of steroids tend to experience increased body hair, enlargement of the clitoris, amenorrhea, and enlargement of the

larynx and thickening of the vocal cords resulting in the deepening of the voice. Steroid use in both men and women is thought to contribute to arrhythmias, heart attacks, and congestive heart failure, but compelling evidence is not available due to the difficulty in obtaining research ethics approval to study the effects of high doses of steroid consumption. Following the cessation of a steroid program, former users report experiencing gradual decreases in body weight and muscle size as well as a period of hypogonadism in men before normal testicular function resumes.

There is ample empirical evidence from controlled, double-blind studies that anabolic androgenic steroids produce increased weight gain and scores on the 1-RM bench press test. When taken by healthy men and women, anabolic androgenic steroids assist in building muscle and decreasing body fat; hence, steroid use is associated with cosmetic modification of the body's shape and size. Taken in large doses, steroids can lead to extreme changes in users' physiques. Studies from many countries indicate that steroid use is highest among recreational male users intending to sculpt a muscular physique. Other user groups include people in the entertainment industry and people participating in the bodybuilding culture. However, steroids in media reports are often associated with high-performance athletes seeking to enhance their athletic performance.

Several of the first known uses of steroids to enhance athletic performance occurred not in male athletes but in horses used in the sport of horse racing. Sport historians acknowledge that steroids were used by athletes competing at the Olympics since at least 1952 in Helsinki, Finland, when athletes competing for the Soviet Union dominated the weightlifting events. Anecdotal evidence suggests that John Zeigler, the American sports doctor who developed steroids for American athletes in the mid-1950s, engaged in discussions with a physician from the former USSR in Vienna, Austria, at the 1954 World Weightlifting Championships, who confirmed that athletes competing in the heavy sports in the 1952 Olympic Games had been taking steroids. Zeigler's story served to suggest that American athletes were unaware of the performance-enhancing benefits of steroids in the early 1950s; however, this assertion is unlikely to be true given the extent to which testosterone was marketed and sold in the United States during the previous two decades. Zeigler, with the assistance of a U.S. pharmaceutical company, developed and marketed the steroid Dianabol, which promised fewer unwanted androgenic effects compared to earlier anabolic androgenic steroids. Steroids now come in many forms. Oral tablets that are swallowed are rapidly absorbed, but are quickly converted to inactive metabolites and are more damaging to the liver. Intramuscular oil-based and water-based forms of steroids are injected directly into a muscle using a needle and are longer acting than oral versions. Steroids can also be taken into the body using transdermal patches, nasal sprays, and gels rubbed into the skin.

Throughout the 1960s, many other steroids were created, including Stanozolol (Winstrol), Halotestin, Durabolin, and Adroyd. Many historians now believe that steroid use was widespread in sport and body-building during the 1950s and 1960s. However, at that time, there were few rules against steroid use and it was not widely considered cheating to use many of the drugs now prohibited in the World Anti-Doping Code. When the International Olympic Committee (IOC)'s Medical Commission formed in 1967, the main task of its members was to address the growing issue of steroid use in sport. The IOC Medical Commission began this task by creating a list of substances to ban. By the 1968 Summer Olympic Games in Mexico City, the IOC had a drug-testing program in place. However, tests to detect steroid use in athletes were still under-developed, and the IOC Medical Commission lacked a reliable test to detect the use of steroids in athletes' urine. By 1973 scientists had created tests to identify exogenous steroid use in urine; yet these rudimentary tests were not infallible, and athletes from many countries, but most notably from East Germany, continued to pass doping detection tests throughout the 1970s and 1980s, despite widespread acknowledgment that many athletes' performances were fueled by steroids.

Evidence released after the collapse of the communist German state revealed that East German athletes, in addition to athletes from the former Soviet Union, Eastern bloc countries, and other areas of the world, consumed large doses of steroids, despite very few of the athletes producing positive drug tests

BALCO founder Victor Conte holds a photo of San Francisco Giants Barry Bonds with the letters ZMA, a drug that Conte makes, on his hat, in his office in Burlingame, California, October 21, 2003. (AP Photo/Paul Sakuma.)

in competitions. When researchers were permitted to view and analyze previously classified files that documented East Germany's systematic program of state-sponsored doping, they were able to confirm that sport scientists could accurately and consistently mask the use of steroids in athletes' urine. Sport scientists working with high-performance athletes had developed masking agents and tests to detect steroids that were more advanced and accurate than the tests used by scientists working with the IOC Medical Commission. Testing athletes before competitions allowed countries to withdraw athletes from competing, rather than risk detection by the official testers, if an athlete tested positive for steroids.

The long-term effects and health risks of steroid use remain unknown. Medical studies examining low, therapeutic doses do not correlate steroid consumption with markedly enhanced performance or serious health risks; however, the doses used by athletes seeking performance-enhancing benefits are much higher than the doses used therapeutically and approved for study by research ethics boards. Consequently, credible information about steroid use coming from medical professionals is hard to find. A popular source for bodybuilders seeking information on using large doses of steroids was Dan Duchaine's *Underground Steroid Users' Handbook*, which contained information on types of steroids, suggested combinations, and tips for avoiding failing a urinalysis test. Sources of this nature explained the concept of taking cycles of steroids over 6- to 12-week periods and using more than one steroid at a time, known as stacking, to gain synergistic effects by activating more receptor sites. Staggering and overlapping the consumption of different steroids allowed the user to avoid plateauing or developing a tolerance for a particular steroid. To help negate the side effects of injecting or consuming multiple steroids, users were recommended to also consume diuretics and aromatase inhibitors as well as antiestrogens and antiacne and anti-inflammatory medications.

While steroid use is often associated with the extremely muscular physique associated with some male athletes and bodybuilders, women have also been implicated in many steroid scandals in sport. The program of systemic, state-sponsored doping in East Germany, in effect between 1972 and 1989, facilitated athletic success in many women's sports and led to many East German women winning international medals. Officials and coaches of the German Democratic Republic's sports schools required children as young as 10 years old to consume "vitamins," which were in fact the steroid oral-Turinabol. Through careful observation and distribution of these pills to many young women, optimal doses to enhance training and avoid detection in international competitions with drug testing were established. The performing-enhancing effects were more noticeable in the girls and young women compared to the performance benefits gained by boys and young men.

A second case of widespread steroid use associated with female athletes occurred in the 1990s when swimmers and track-and-field athletes from China starting consistently winning medals at international events. Despite the women's extremely muscular builds, Chinese coaches claimed their athletes' success was due to rigorous training and the use of traditional Chinese herbs. However, the steroid dehydrotestosterone (DHT) was soon detected in many athletes' urine samples and pointed to an extensive network of doping with ties to coaches' and clubs' desire to win prize money and endorsement contracts for their teams.

The use of steroids by several professional athletes played a prominent role in the trial of Victor Conte, the founder of the Bay Area Laboratory Co-operative (BALCO). Through a raid of Conte's records, allegations of rampant steroid use by several professional athletes were made public. Similar allegations of widespread steroid use in Major League Baseball were made by retired baseball player Ken Caminiti in *Sports Illustrated* in 2002, when he claimed that steroid use in Major League Baseball was rampant and half of all players used steroids. Similar allegations followed from former player Jose Canseco, who suggested in his book *Juiced: Wild Times, Rampant 'Roids, Smash Hits and How Baseball Got Big* (2005) that approximately 85 percent of MLB players were using steroids. Canseco's allegations were dismissed as an attempt to gain revenge on a league that would no longer employ him, but subsequent attention to a culture of using or condoning the use of steroids in MLB followed a year later with the publication of *San Francisco Chronicle* investigative reporters Lance Williams and Mark Fainaru-Wada's book *Game of Shadows* (2006). Allegations of this nature led the MLB commissioner, Allan H. (Bud) Selig, to request a study of drug use in professional baseball by former U.S. senator George J. Mitchell. The resulting report, *The Report to the Commissioner of Baseball of an Independent Investigation into the Illegal Use of Steroids and Other Performance Enhancing Substances by Players in Major League Baseball*, published in December 2007, identified more than 80 current and former players who used steroids and established that steroid use was tolerated by not only the players, but also by owners and the Major League Baseball Players Association. In addition to baseball players, other athletes named in Conte's records received considerable media attention for their use of banned steroids

Charles-Édouard Brown-Séquard

Neurologist and physiologist Charles-Édouard Brown-Séquard undertook groundbreaking research when he removed dog and guinea pig testicles, added the mixture to a salt solution, and injected the resulting concoction into his body. After injecting various combinations of the mixture over a three-week period, he reported radical changes in his physical and mental energies, culminating in feelings of rejuvenation. Brown-Séquard reported his discovery at a meeting of the Société de Biologie in Paris in 1889 and published an article entitled "The effects produced in man by subcutaneous injections of a liquid obtained from the testicles of animals," in the *Lancet*. Brown-Séquard's anecdotal evidence was discredited by his peers. Yet despite the scientific community's initial rejection of his ideas, the field of organotherapy soon developed based on similar principles of injecting extracts from animal and human testicles to restore energy and vigor in men.

to fuel athletic performance. For example, American sprinter Marion Jones, who won five medals at the 2000 Olympic Games in Sydney and denied using steroids throughout her career, was found guilty of perjury and sent to jail when evidence obtained in the BALCO investigations linked Jones to steroids. She eventually acknowledged her steroid use and, at the IOC's request, returned her Olympic medals.

Because steroids are banned by the World Anti-Doping Agency and illegal to use in many areas of the world without a doctor's prescription, obtaining accurate data on steroid use can be difficult. Much of what is known about athletes' steroid use comes from investigative journalists who have infiltrated organized doping rings. Based on testimonials from and interviews with former and current athletes and informants, reporters have confirmed that steroid use is common in many populations. However, the accuracy of the information provided by the informants is hard to determine. Athletes admitting to steroid use can face disqualification and bans, have their endorsements and contracts canceled, and have past records and honors revoked. Other sources of information on steroid use in sport come from government investigations and university-based research projects. However, the resulting reports often include nonrandom

samples and are thwarted by athletes' unwillingness to disclose information that could be potentially damaging to their careers. Information from drug-testing organizations is similarly problematic. Not all athletes are tested, and attempts can be made to sabotage the accuracy of the test using masking agents. Complicating the issue is the black market steroid trade, which is thought to supply many recreational users with steroids. Consequently, the extent of steroid use in sport is very difficult to determine.

Sarah J. Teetzel

See also Jones, Marion; Selig, Bud; Sports and Drugs/Doping; *Sports Illustrated*

Suggested Resources
Fainaru-Wada, Mark, and Lance Williams. *Game of Shadows*. New York: Gotham, 2006.
Steroid.com. http://www.steroid.com. Accessed October 7, 2011.
"Steroids in Baseball." SI.com. http://sportsillustrated.cnn.com/vault/cover/featured/9855/index.htm. Accessed October 7, 2011.
Yesalis, Charles. *Anabolic Steroids in Sport and Exercise*. Champaign, IL: Human Kinetics, 2000.

Street, Picabo (1971–)

Picabo Street was a three-time Olympic skier and winner of nine World Cup alpine ski events during nearly 15 years of international competitive skiing. Her two World Cup championships in women's downhill skiing in 1995 and 1996, along with a silver medal at the 1994 Winter Olympic Games and a gold medal at the 1998 Olympics, made Street the most successful American downhill skier in history at that time. Her success as an American in a sport dominated by Europeans, coupled with her ferocity on the slopes, engaging personality, and high-profile sponsorships, catapulted her to international fame during the 1990s.

Born in the tiny town of Triumph, Idaho (pop. 50), Picabo Street was the second child and only daughter of counterculture parents Stubby and Dee Street. Although she was called "Baby Girl" during the first years of her life, at age three she was given the name "Picabo" in honor of an Idaho town close to Triumph. The name means either "shining waters" or "silver

Picabo Street displays her gold medal, right, won in the womens downhill at the World Alpine Ski Championships in Sierra Nevada, Spain, on February 18, 1996, and her silver medal won earlier in the women's Super-G. (AP Photo/Stefano Rellandini.)

creek" in the language spoken by Idaho's Shoshone and Bannock Native American tribes. As the only girl in her male-dominated peer group, Street participated and excelled in sports traditionally associated with males, including tackle football and BMX racing. A self-described tomboy and fierce competitor with her older brother, Roland, she began skiing at age six on the nearby slopes of Sun Valley, Idaho, a mecca for alpine skiing. Less than a decade later, at age 15, Street joined the U.S. junior ski team. In 1988 she became the national junior champion in the downhill and super giant (Super G) events.

Street's status as a junior national champion earned her a spot on the U.S. national ski team, with whom she began training in 1989 at age 17. This did not immediately lead to success, however, as Street's defiance of her coaches and inability to adhere to the team's training regimen resulted in her dismissal from the team in 1990. Seeing this as a wake-up call, she moved to Hawaii to train, completed her high school studies, and was eventually reinstated to the team in 1990. Although she had curbed her hard-partying ways, her forthright personality continued to polarize some coaches and teammates, and she was always more popular with both the American and European publics than she was with most of her training partners and fellow competitors.

Two years after rejoining the U.S. national team, Street's finishes in international downhill and Super G competitions had earned her a world ranking of eighth among female alpine skiers in 1992. She built on this success the following year by winning a silver medal at the world championships in Morioka, Japan, in the combined alpine event; she also placed 10th in the downhill at the same competition. But it was her silver medal in the downhill competition, with a time of 1:36.59, at the 1994 Winter Olympic Games in Lillehammer, Norway, which secured her international reputation and brought her to the attention of the mainstream American media. During those same games she also competed in the women's combined alpine event—in which scores from downhill and slalom runs are tabulated together—earning a respectable 10th place. At a Winter Olympics dominated by the bizarre Nancy Kerrigan–Tonya Harding figure skating drama, Street's bold and brash personality, along with her fearless and powerful command of the slopes, made her an instant hit with the American public. She was featured in publications such as *Sports Illustrated* and *Vogue*, and she increased her profile after the Games by appearing on popular television shows like *American Gladiators* and *Sesame Street*. Her all-American good looks, fanciful moniker, and willingness to engage with her legions of fans made her an instant role model for children, especially for young girls.

Following the 1994 Winter Olympics, Street built on her burgeoning success and fame by becoming the first American skier, male or female, to win a World Cup season title in downhill skiing in 1995. She accomplished this by clinching six out of the nine individual World Cup title events that year. In 1996 she repeated this feat, and that same year she won a gold medal in downhill and a bronze in the Super G event at the world championships in Spain. With this domination of the sport came corporate sponsorships, and in December 1995 Nike signed Street to a marketing contract requiring her to continue to wear Nike apparel during competition and appear in company advertisements. Picabo Street thus became the first woman to represent Nike, as well as the first winter Olympian to have a signature shoe designed for her. Her groundbreaking deal with Nike led to additional sponsorships and advertising opportunities with other leading companies, including Rolex, PepsiCo, ChapStick, and United Airlines. She also promoted a Picabo Street–inspired ski gear line with outdoor sports equipment company Rossignol.

Just as her career seemed to crest, however, Street suffered a major setback by tearing her left anterior cruciate ligament (ACL) for the second time during a practice downhill run in Vail, Colorado. She had reconstructive surgery on her ACL and then endured a punishing training regimen that included cross-training workouts on land and in water, along with intensive strength-building and conditioning workouts on exercise bikes and treadmills. Though she regained her strength, this brutal rehabilitation schedule took its toll: In a September 2000 interview with *The New York Times*, Street revealed that she had suffered depression during the first months of her injury. Her discipline and fierce desire to compete helped her overcome both her physical and mental scars and return to competition nearly a year earlier than expected, with her sights focused on capturing gold at the 1998 Winter Olympics. These hopes were nearly dashed, however, when Street suffered a sickening crash in Are, Switzerland, during her final competition prior to the Olympic Games. Traveling at nearly 80 miles per hour, she collided with a fence and was knocked unconscious. Although she suffered a concussion, she was able to walk away from the crash under her own power. She later said that the ordeal galvanized her resolve to deliver a commanding performance at the upcoming Olympics.

In 1998, at the Winter Olympic Games in Nagano, Japan, Street's herculean training efforts reaped the most coveted award in international sports: a gold medal. Posting a time of 1:18.02, Street bested her fellow skiers by only .01 of a second to secure the top spot in the women's Super G event, a surprise win given her domination of downhill rather than Super G events in World Cup competitions. In addition, she finished sixth in the downhill event that year with a time of 1:29.54. Street described her winning of an Olympic gold medal as the magical fulfillment of a lifelong dream. Yet her Olympic success was cut short only a few months later when she suffered a horrific crash at a World Cup race in Switzerland in March 1998. Traveling at nearly 70 miles per hour, she lost control on the downhill course, breaking her left femur in nine places and tearing her right ACL. Although most commentators and experts at the time believed this spelled the end of her career, the 27-year-old Street vowed to return to international competition and win a spot on the 2002 U.S. Olympic team bound for Salt Lake City, Utah. She accomplished her goal by representing the United States once again at the Olympics after enduring nearly two years of painful rehabilitation. Following her somewhat disappointing 16th-place finish in the downhill event with a time of 1:41.17, Street retired permanently from international competition at the age of 30, having cemented her reputation as the most powerful and successful female alpine skier in American sport history.

Despite retiring in 2002, Picabo Street maintained a public presence by devoting herself to sports and philanthropic organizations and by appearing on television shows like *Hollywood Squares* and *America's Funniest Home Videos* as a celebrity judge and contestant. She also served as a commentator and analyst for CBS Sports and NBC Sports. Immediately following her retirement in 2002, she founded Picabo's Street of Dreams Foundation to help children achieve their sports goals, but in subsequent years devoted herself to fighting child abuse. In this capacity she became a spokesperson and advocate for the National Children's Alliance (NCA). Her Picabo Ski Challenge, an annual fundraiser for the NCA started in 2005 to coincide with the Sundance Film Festival in Park City, Utah, has raised hundreds of thousands of dollars for victims of child abuse. In addition to earning numerous honors and awards for her philanthropic endeavors, in 2005 Street was inducted into the U.S. Ski and Snowboard Hall of Fame. She also wrote an autobiography entitled *Picabo: Nothing to Hide*, which was published by McGraw-Hill in 2002.

Natalie Deibel

See also Nike, Inc.; *Sports Illustrated*; Tonya Harding–Nancy Kerrigan Scandal; 2002 Olympic Games, Salt Lake City

Suggested Resources

Anderson, Kelli. "Picabo Street." June 27, 2007. http://sportsillustrated.cnn.com/2007/more/06/25/watn.picabo/. Accessed November 15, 2011.

Clarke, John, Jr. "Skiing: Street Looking Forward to a Life Off the Slopes." November 24, 2002. http://www.nytimes.com/2002/11/24/sports/skiing-street-looking-forward-to-a-life-off-the-slopes.html. Accessed November 19, 2011.

Dippold, Joel. *Picabo Street: Downhill Dynamo*. Minneapolis: Lerner, 1998.

Street, Picabo, and Dana White. *Picabo: Nothing to Hide*. New York: McGraw-Hill, 2002.

Strikes and Lockouts

Many fans view professional sports as a hobby, pastime, or passion. It is easy to forget that the sports entertainment industry is not immune to the financial and legal issues that plague the business world.

Players in the big four sports (football, baseball, basketball, and hockey) are unionized. The players unions we know today began in the mid-1950s with the first being the Players Association of the National Basketball Association (NBA). The last to unionize were the players of Major League Baseball (MLB) in the late 1960s; however, they lay claim to be the first players' union to negotiate a collective bargaining agreement, more commonly known as a CBA. As in other industries, a sports CBA is an agreement between the employers and employees that outlines categories, including work conditions, wages, grievance processes, and the like. Typically, CBAs are negotiated between individual employers and their specific set of employees, but sometimes, as in the case of professional sports, CBAs can be negotiated nationwide within an industry affecting multiple employers and their employees.

Strikes and lockouts in the sports entertainment industry occur when there are unresolved disagreements between the players and the owners over matters like free agency and player salaries. Strikes are a strategy utilized by the players where they refuse to take the field and perform the functions of their job. Often, owners are forced to evaluate the money lost during these periods versus the demands of the players. Lockouts occur when the owners literally lock the players out of the workplace and refuse to allow the players to work. Like player strikes, owner lockouts are a strategic move that force the players to consider the amount of money they are losing each day in salary.

One counterstrategy owners have against strikes is the ability to use replacement players. These players act like scabs, crossing the picket line and taking over the position of the players who are involved in the strike. This scenario was depicted in the 2000 movie *The Replacements* starring Gene Hackman and Keanu Reeves, which followed a team of replacement players during a professional football strike.

Players in Major League Baseball struck in 1981 over a proposed stipulation in free agency that would cost the players leverage when seeking contracts in the free agent market, and in 1994 players struck again (for 232 days), forcing the league to cancel parts of two seasons, totaling over 900 games, including the 1994 postseason and World Series. Owners and players disagreed over salary cap issues and revenue sharing. Even after settlement, the strikes caused great animosity between fans and baseball and it took a

---

The Economics of a Strike

If the 2011 NFL lockout had prevented the season from taking place, Adam Shefter of ESPN projected the league would lose $9 billion in revenue from ticket, merchandise, and food and beverage sales, and advertisement, television, and sponsor contracts. However, this does not cover total monies lost. When you factor in money lost in Fantasy Football (a $1 billion industry) and monies lost by sports bars, businesses surrounding stadiums, and sports news outlets that specialize or focus on football talk, that number would have easily surpassed $12 billion.

Basketball fanatic and radio station employee Marty Anderson gives a jubilant double thumbs-up to passing, honking traffic in Portland, Oregon, January 6, 1999, after hearing that the NBA owners and players union had come to an agreement. (AP Photo/Don Ryan.)

number of years for Major League Baseball to draw many of these fans back to the game.

Most recently, the NFL owners locked out the NFL players for the 2011 off-season. The CBA was set to expire after the conclusion of the 2010 playoffs. Mediation was attempted; however, the owners could not come to terms on a new agreement during this process. Thus, the leaguewide lockout began. After the lockout, the players' union decertified and individual players including superstar quarterbacks Peyton Manning (Indianapolis Colts), Drew Brees (New Orleans Saints), and Tom Brady (New England Patriots) filed antitrust lawsuits against the owners of their teams. The grounds for this lawsuit were that since the players were no longer unionized, the owners were violating their rights by locking them out. Eventually, the dispute was resolved. A new CBA was laid out by the

owners, ratified, and sent to the players. The players voted to ratify the new CBA in July 2011.

Also in 2011, a lockout affected the NBA as the league lockout forced league commissioner David Stern to cancel the season in part. The dispute between the players and owners lay mainly in revenue sharing and the structure of the salary cap. In the case of this particular lockout many players like Tony Parker (San Antonio Spurs) chose to play for professional or national teams overseas until an agreement was reached. Most had clauses in their international contracts allowing them to return to the United States as soon as a strike was settled, but a few players failed to insert "escape clauses" in their contracts and were unable to return to the NBA for the 2011–2012 season.

The season itself lost 16 of each team's scheduled 82 games. A new schedule of 66 games per team, beginning on Christmas Day 2011, was very uneven with some teams not meeting others at all. The delay in the season and a contract also forced players and owners to scramble to make roster adjustments such as trades and waivers in a very compressed period of time, and the entire league appeared in flux in early December.

Historically, strikes and lockouts come to an end after a period of time that can range from just a few weeks or result in a cancellation of an entire season as was the case for the 2004–2005 NHL season. As of this writing the 2012–2013 NHL season is in jeopardy as a result of a lockout. While it seems that the players and owners always come to an agreement, it is the faithful fans who are forced to bear the burden.

Alexandra Schierer

See also ESPN Channel; Fantasy Leagues; Manning, Peyton; National Basketball Association; National Football League; Sports Bars

Suggested Resources

"Impact of the Pro Football Strike: A Lost Sunday and Lost Dollars." http://www.nytimes.com/1982/09/27/sports/impact-of-the-pro-football-strike-a-lost-sunday-and-lost-dollars.html. Accessed December 16, 2011.

Latzko, David A. "Who Won the Major League Baseball Strikes?"http://www.personal.psu.edu/~dxl31/research/presentations/strikes.pdf. Accessed December 16, 2011.

McKelvey, G. Richard. *For It's One, Two, Three Strikes You're Out at the Owner's Ball Game*. Jefferson, NC: McFarland, 2001.

Riesgo, Nicko, and Russ Cohen. *"Strike Three!"—A Player's Journey through the Infamous Baseball Strike of 1994*. Kindle edition. Lulu.com, 2010.

10 Game-Changing Pro Sports Lockouts and Strikes. http://www.cnbc.com/id/41968930/10_Game_Changing_Pro_Sports_Lockouts_and_Strikes. Accessed December 16, 2011.

Stringer, C. Vivian (1948–)

Born March 16, 1948, in Edenborn, Pennsylvania, Charlaine Vivian Stringer boasts one of the most storied coaching careers in the history of college basketball. Only Tennessee's Pat Summitt and the University of Texas's Jody Conradt rank higher in the number

---

The "Don Imus Incident"

Radio shock-jock Don Imus snared the Rutgers women's basketball team within an unwelcomed controversy with a series of racist and sexist comments made during the 2007 finals of the NCAA Tournament. Among a host of despicable remarks he referred to the Rutgers women as "rough girls" and compared them to the NBA's Toronto Raptors. Perhaps his most incendiary statement was when he called the Scarlet Knights "nappy-headed hos." Amid strong and immediate protest, Imus issued a public apology.

Rutgers coach Vivian Stringer parlayed the controversy into an opportunity for Americans to engage in important discussions about prejudices toward female athletes and women of color. At a press conference, she articulated the hurt and anger his comments caused her team and women's sports in general. "Let me put a human face on this," she told those in attendance at a special press conference. "These young ladies are valedictorians of their class, future doctors, musical prodigies, and, yes, even Girl Scouts. They are all young ladies of class. They are distinctive, articulate."

She continued to personalize the incident, allowing players to identify themselves and to speak openly about the damage Imus's comments had done as well as their pride in what they had accomplished that season. He had "stolen a moment of pure grace from us," assessed captain Essence Carson.

As pundits and well-known personalities debated whether Imus should be allowed to continue his program, a number of sponsors pulled their ads from his show. CBS and NBC eventually fired Imus. He has since returned to the airwaves.

---

of wins in the women's division. Just seven coaches, male or female, before her have reached the distinguished 800-win mark. Stringer holds a special place of prominence all to herself, however, for she is the first coach—man or woman—in NCAA history to take teams from three different schools to the Final Four of the national championship (Cheyney State, 1982; Iowa, 1993; Rutgers, 2000 and 2007). Named the Naismith College Coach of the Year in 1993, she is a member of the Basketball Hall of Fame and the Women's Basketball Hall of Fame.

Stringer was a trailblazer from the start. She grew up in an era with few athletic opportunities for girls.

Rutgers coach Vivian Stringer encouraging her team in an NCAA Tournament basketball game, March 17, 2012, in Spokane, Washington. (AP Photo/Elaine Thompson.)

She found her opportunities further restricted by race when she entered high school. Denied a spot on the cheerleading squad, she sued the school for racial bias. The courts found in her favor and she joined her fellow classmates on the sidelines in 1964. A graduate of Slippery Rock University of Pennsylvania, Stringer began coaching and teaching in the early 1970s at Cheyney State College (now Cheyney University of Pennsylvania), a historically black school. She led her Cinderella team to the first NCAA-sanctioned women's basketball championship in 1982 where they advanced to the illustrious Final Four.

The following year she took her talents to the University of Iowa where she developed the women's basketball program into a national powerhouse. In 1993 she took the Hawkeyes to the Final Four. In 1995 Stringer began her career at Rutgers University.

A mere three years later the Scarlet Knights won the Big East title and advanced to the Sweet Sixteen of the NCAA Tournament. In 2000 and again in 2007, Rutgers reached the Final Four in postseason play.

Throughout her storied career she has been forced to deal with a number of challenges, including the untimely deaths of her father and her husband, her daughter's life-altering illness, and her own bout with cancer. In 2007 Stringer showed her characteristic dignity and strength when forced to address radio shock-jock Don Imus's derogatory comments about her Rutgers team.

In addition to her Hall of Fame inductions, Stringer has received a plethora of well-deserved accolades. Among them are a number of national coach of the year awards, an assistant coaching position with the 2004 gold medal–winning Olympic women's basketball team, and initiator of the Women's Basketball Coaches Association. In 1993 she garnered the Carol Eckman Award, granted to the coach in women's basketball who best exemplifies the character of its groundbreaking namesake. In 2008, Nike dedicated the C. Vivian Stringer Child Development Center on its World Campus Headquarters in Beaverton, Oregon. She is the third woman, second coach, and first African American woman to receive such a tribute on Nike's campus. Yet for all her success, Stringer has never won a national championship. It is a goal she calls her "heart's desire." Even if the title remains elusive, by any measure, she is a true and unparalleled champion.

Jaime Schultz

See also Imus, Don; Naismith Memorial Basketball Hall of Fame; Summitt, Pat

Suggested Resources

Rhoden, William C. "Stringer's Long, Rewarding Trip to the Hall of Fame." September 9, 2009. http://www.nytimes.com/2009/09/10/sports/basketball/10rhoden.html?ref=cvivianstringer. Accessed October 31, 2011.

Stringer, C. Vivian. *Standing Tall: A Memoir of Tragedy and Triumph.* New York: Crown Archetype, 2008.

Strode, Woody (1914–1994)

In 1946, Kenny Washington and Woody Strode integrated the National Football League. They were part of integration in sport after World War II. Born in Los Angeles, California, on July 25, 1914, in a three-bedroom house, Woodrow Wilson Woolwine "Woody" Strode's father named him after a president and a local district attorney. Woody was the second son of a black-Creek-Blackfoot father and a black-Cherokee mother. His older brother was Baylous Strode Junior.

The great-grandson of a slave who married a Creek Indian, Strode's grandfather married a Blackfoot Indian. In 1900, his grandfather moved from Washington, Louisiana, to Los Angeles, California, for a better life. Strode's father, a bricklayer from the age of 14, helped build downtown Los Angeles. Strode's mother, the daughter of a slave in New Orleans and a Cherokee descendant, graduated from college.

Woody Strode attended Holmes Avenue Grammar School. Growing up, Strode watched Western movies. He traveled around Los Angeles by Red Car (a trolley of the time) and played in the Los Angeles River. He grew up playing sports in the city parks and playgrounds. Strode attended McKinley Junior High School. During the Depression, he worked for the WPA in Griffith Park. Strode then moved to the vibrant African American community surrounding Central Avenue. At Jefferson High School, Strode first went out for football. Former USC footballer Harry Edelson was the coach. Strode played football and ran track. His senior year he played for and was captain of the All-City Football Team.

Woody Strode attended the University of California, Los Angeles, beginning in 1936, after two-and-a-half years of extension school to qualify him academically for college. The 21-year-old freshman soon met Kenny Washington. Washington and Strode became close friends and would integrate the Los Angeles Rams together 10 years later. A local reporter nicknamed them the "Goal Dust Twins" after a popular advertisement for Gold Dust soap, which featured two black boys. While at UCLA, Strode received a scholarship of $100 a month, an $11 meal ticket, and $20 under the table in exchange for maintenance work around the campus. Tuition was $25 a quarter. At the time Bill Ackerman was the graduate manager. In addition to helping them as athletes, Ackerman helped with their cultural education and made sure the black players were not segregated when traveling. The football coach was Bill Spaulding and his assistant was Cliff Simpson. The team members dressed up to travel by train to their away games. Strode and other black players were accepted by their teammates with the exception of one teammate from Oklahoma. Strode caught the attention of German filmmaker Leni Riefenstahl. In 1936, Riefenstahl hired an artist to paint a full body portrait of Strode, who she said had the greatest physique of any athlete she had seen.

During the summer of 1939 Strode began working in the service department of Warner Brothers Studio. He worked as an assistant to movie stars and directors during movie filmings. In his senior year, Jackie Robinson joined the team from Pasadena City College. UCLA fielded four African Americans, Strode,

Actor Kirk Douglas, left, in the title role as a Roman slave and gladiator, battles Woody Strode in the role of gladiator Draba in a scene from *Spartacus* filmed in Hollywood, California, April 1959. (AP Photo.)

Washington, Robinson, and Ray Bartlett. Strode and the football team traveled to play in Hawaii at the end of the season. They sailed from Long Beach on the *SS Masonia*. While there, Strode met his future wife, Princess Luukialuana Kalaeloa, also called Luana, a descendant of the last queen of Hawaii. In 1940, after the cancellation of the Winter Olympics, which Strode had planned to compete in, he left UCLA six months before graduation.

Soon after Strode ended his college career, Larry Sunbrock hired Woody and Kenny Washington to play in two special exhibition football games on a college all-star team and then to play for the Hollywood Bears. Sunbrock promoted a league that Paul Schissler had established. The Pacific Coast League for semi-pro football had five teams including the Los Angeles Bulldogs and the Hollywood Bears. During this time, Woody also worked for the district attorney in Los Angeles. After reuniting in Los Angeles in 1940, he and Luana eloped to Las Vegas and soon lived within

the Hawaiian community in Southern California. They would have two children, a son, Woodrow Wilson Kalaeloa, called Kalai, born in 1946, and a daughter, Junelehua Kalaeloa, called June, in 1948. Luana worked as a hula dancer and in the movies, including as a stand-in for Dorothy Lamour. Beginning in 1941, Strode trained as a wrestler with Baron Gindberg. He continued to play for the Hollywood Bears and wrestled in the off-season.

After Pearl Harbor, Paul Schissler, an army reservist, organized the March Field Fliers, an army football team, at March Field in Riverside, California. Strode was soon a member of the team and the Army Air Corps. He first experienced segregation in the military, living in a segregated area of the base called Dusty Acres, until Schissler arranged for the football team to live together in the gym. Strode played for the army team for three years. He traveled to Hawaii and Tinian (in the Northern Mariana Islands) and then served on Guam until August 1945.

The National Football League did not allow blacks to play from 1933 to 1946. Teams released African Americans in 1933 when the league restructured. In 1946, the Cleveland Rams moved to Los Angeles. Part of the agreement to play in the publicly owned Los Angeles Coliseum included signing a black player. Pressured by members of the local black press, the Rams agreed to include a black player on the roster. They signed Kenny Washington on March 21, 1946. The Rams asked Washington whom he would like as a roommate and Washington chose Woody Strode. Strode signed a contract on May 7, 1946. Strode's marriage to a Hawaiian woman created controversy and he spent more time on the bench than playing, but he still earned $350 a week. Strode recalled not having much trouble with other players, but noted that not all of the hotels welcomed him and Washington. The Rams cut him from the team that same year.

In 1947, Strode played for the Calgary Stampeders of the Western Interprovincial Football Union in Canada. His contract for the season included $5,000 in salary, $100 a week for expenses, and hotel and transportation costs. In 1948, Strode broke his ankle and separated his shoulder. His Canadian career ended the next season with two broken ribs.

In 1948, the Strode family moved from Hollywood to Montebello. Woody purchased a ranch on which they raised chickens and rabbits. After his football career, Strode became a full-time wrestler for a few years. To be closer to his family, Strode worked for Chrysler on the brake assembly line and then at a gas station. Woody then began working in television, first on the show *Ramar of the Jungle* and then *Jungle Jim*. Strode then began acting in films, first small parts in films in the 1940s, but then larger roles such as the Egyptian king in Cecile B. DeMille's *The Ten Commandments* (1956) and Private Franklin in *Pork Chop Hill* (1959). He was in *Sergeant Rutledge* (1960), a picture in which he played the starring role and during which he developed a close relationship with director John Ford. He also worked with Stanley Kubrick on *Spartacus* (1960) (in a role initially offered to Rafer Johnson) and starred in *The Professionals* (1966). Strode also acted in Europe for several years. His film career lasted until 1995 (with the release of Sam Raimi's *The Quick and the Dead*) and included more than 100 movies.

Luana died September 17, 1980, after a four-year struggle with Parkinson's disease. On May 10, 1982, Woody married Tina, who would be his wife until his death. Woody Strode died on December 31, 1994, in Glendale, California, of lung cancer. He is buried at the Riverside National Cemetery in Riverside, California.

Amy Essington

See also Johnson, Rafer; Robinson, Jackie

Suggested Resources
Strode, Woody, and Sam Young. *Gold Dust: An Autobiography*. Lanham, MD: Madison Books, 1990.
"Woody Strode." IMDb. http://www.imdb.com/name/nm0834754/. Accessed October 25, 2011.
"Woody Strode." Movie Maker. http://www.moviemaker.com/directing/article/woody_strode_3134/. Accessed October 25, 2011.

Substance Abuse

Substance abuse is the excessive use of drugs or other chemicals for their effect on the mind and the body. In sports, substance abuse is specifically aimed at enhancing athletic performance and endurance. The use of a drug or blood product to improve athletic performance is also commonly referred to as "doping," a word that more broadly designates the practice of adding impurities to something, for example, in chemistry and electronics.

Drugs may be very useful tools in sports medicine, for some medications are needed to treat serious infections, heal from pain in the wake of injuries or surgery, and in several other cases. Drugs per se are not the problem as long as they are used in a prescribed, legal manner and under the supervision of medical professionals. Problems arise because some athletes will do almost anything to win, and that often includes inappropriate medication usage and banned substances, in spite of the negative physical and psychological effects and the risk of being caught and disqualified.

Substance abuse may have grown as a major and public issue in sports over the last decades, with the professionalization of sports, on the one hand, and the progressive emergence of dedicated legislation, at both the national and international level, on the other. The phenomenon, however, dates from antiquity.

Men have always tried to find ways to increase their physical power to be able to work harder, or at least suffer less as they were doing so, with the methods and substances that matched the scientific and pharmacologic knowledge of their times. In the ancient Olympic Games (776 to 393 BCE), athletes used extracts of mushrooms and plant seeds, or feasted on goat and lamb testicles to boost stamina and athletic performance. The use of drugs in Roman history has been recorded, too. Gladiators are described as using hallucinogens and stimulants, including caffeine and strychnine, to combat fatigue and to mask pain.

In the 19th century, strychnine, caffeine, cocaine, and alcohol were often used by cyclists and other endurance athletes. The first case of death allegedly attributed to doping occurred in the second half of that century. In 1886, 24-year-old Welsh cyclist Arthur Linton died a few weeks after participating in the Bordeaux-Paris race. Official sources mentioned exhaustion and typhoid fever as the cause of death, but allegations were made that he had taken a stimulant. Linton was managed by the notorious James Edward "Choppy" Warburton, an English record-breaking runner and then a cycling coach who was frequently questioned about claims that he was an instigator of drug taking. The facts of the case in Linton's death were never fully ascertained: The symptoms that brought Linton to death were consistent with typhoid fever and there was no evidence to state categorically that drugs had played a part in it. Warburton, however, was also involved in another dubious case. Another of Warburton's protégés, Welsh cyclist Jimmy Michael, was said, according to the *New York Times*, to have accused Warburton of poisoning him, although the facts in that case were never fully ascertained either.

Until then, drug use in sport was not cheating. It was only in the 1920s that the need for restrictions regarding drug use in sports became evident. The International Association of Athletics Federation (IAAF) was the first international sporting federation to prohibit doping by athletes, in 1928.

The Olympic Games in Berlin in 1936, under the Nazi regime, were replete with rumors of stimulants used by German athletes. Germans won more Olympic medals than any other country.

In the Second World War, amphetamines were widely used by soldiers of different nationalities to counteract fatigue and heighten endurance. The use of such substances crossed over into sports in the early 1950s. In Italy, these drugs were famously nicknamed by Italian cyclists as "*la bomba.*"

In the mid-1950s, John Ziegler, physician for the U.S. weightlifting team, developed methandrostenolone, commonly regarded as one of the world's first anabolic steroids. Such substances mimic the effects of testosterone and dihydrotestosterone—male sex hormones—in the body. They increase protein synthesis within cells, which results in the growth of cellular tissue (anabolism), especially in muscles. They also have virilizing properties, including the development of masculine characteristics. Methandrostenolone was unleashed in the United States in 1958 and found its way across the country, mostly into weightlifter training programs. It would later be banned by the Food and Drug Administration (FDA) under the Controlled Substances Act, in 1970. Ziegler himself, later in life, would publicly condemn the abuse of steroids in sports.

In 1960, Danish cyclist Knut Jensen died during the Summer Olympics in Rome. He collapsed near the end of a 62-mile road race, fractured his skull, and was pronounced dead shortly thereafter at a hospital in Rome. His autopsy revealed that he had taken a combination of drugs. It was a tragic fact within a lot of rumors concerning the use of drugs in sports, allegations that the world of sport angrily denied. In November of the same year, *Sports Illustrated* published "Our Drug-Happy Athletes" by George Walsh, reporting the dangers in the use of amphetamines ("pep pills"), tranquilizers, stimulants, and other substances in elite sports.

In 1967 Tommy Simpson, the most successful English road-racing cyclist of the postwar years, died on the slopes of Mont Ventoux during the 13th stage of the Tour de France. Simpson had been named Sports Personality of the Year by the BBC in 1965. Postmortem analyses found that he had taken amphetamines and alcohol, a combination that, added to the difficulties of the race and the heat of that day, had proved fatal. Simpson's death at the peak of his career created widespread pressure to take action against doping. In the wake of Simpson's death, in the same year the International Olympic Committee

(IOC) established the Medical Commission to fight against doping in sports, and the International Union of Cycling (UCI) banned the use of any performance-enhancing drugs in the sport.

In 1968, the IOC instituted its first compulsory doping controls at the Winter Olympics in Grenoble, France, and again at the Summer Olympics in Mexico City in the same year.

In 1975, after the development of a test that was considered to be reliable by British professor Raymond Brooks, anabolic steroids were added to IOC's Banned Substances List.

In 1988, Canadian sprinter Ben Johnson was stripped of his gold medal at the Olympic Games in Seoul, Korea, after testing positive for an anabolic steroid. Johnson's world record time in the 100 meters (9.79 seconds) was deleted from record books. The event had an enormous echo in the world's media. Johnson was also the main challenger to legendary U.S. athlete Carl Lewis.

In 1991, the *New York Times* reported that a group of 20 former East German coaches had admitted to two decades of doping by East German swimmers. The stunning domination of international swimming by East German women for nearly two decades, from the late 1960s to the late 1980s, was built upon an organized system of anabolic-steroid use. In spite of allegations by rival coaches and athletes, no East German swimmer was ever caught or penalized for drug use at the time.

In 1992, NFL star Lyle Alzado died of brain cancer at the age of 43. *Sports Illustrated* highlighted him on the cover of the July 8, 1991, issue. In the magazine, Alzado admitted to massive use of steroids and human growth hormone during his career and affirmed that he believed these substances had caused his inoperable brain cancer.

In 1998, a major scandal erupted at the Tour de France when the Festina team was ejected from competition following the discovery of supplies of performance-enhancing drugs, including erythropoietin (EPO)—a substance that increases the oxygen-carrying capacity of blood—in the team masseur's car. Another six teams voluntarily dropped out of the Tour, citing police raids and mistreatment of participants. The initial field of 189 cyclists was reduced to fewer than 100.

In 1999, the World Anti-Doping Agency (WADA), an independent agency, was formed through a collective initiative led by the International Olympic Committee to promote, coordinate, and monitor the fight against drugs in sport. The IOC would later transfer the management of the prohibited list to WADA in 2004.

In 2000, the U.S. Anti-Doping Agency (USADA) was born. USADA is the independent antidoping agency for Olympic sports in the United States, with full authority on research, education, in-competition and out-of-competition testing, and adjudications for Olympic, Paralympic, and Pan Am athletes. USADA was created upon recommendation by the U.S. Olympic Committee (USOC) Select Task Force on Externalization, which advocated that an independent body manage the antidoping program on the USOC's behalf.

In 2005, UNESCO adopted the International Convention against Doping in Sport, which entered into force in 2007, to help governments act in concert with one another in the fight against doping in sport. More than 140 countries have aligned their legislation and policies with the Convention ever since.

With growing knowledge and legislation on doping, coming out about past drug abuse to enhance performance has become an increasingly common phenomenon in the world of sport. In 2002, retired baseball player Ken Caminiti admitted, in the June 3 issue of *Sports Illustrated*, that he was using steroids when he won the 1996 National League Most Valuable Player (MVP) award. A few years later, in 2005, retired baseball player Jose Canseco spoke of his use of steroids and of alleged use by home run kings Mark McGwire and Sammy Sosa in his massively publicized book *Juiced: Wild Times, Rampant 'Roids, Smash Hits, and How Baseball Got Big*. In 2010, American cyclist Floyd Landis, who was stripped of his victory at the Tour de France for doping in 2006, admitted to continual doping during his career, after years of denial.

Other allegations on the use of doping substances have surrounded other athletes and other sports over the years. The mediatization of sports has certainly contributed to raised awareness on doping by informing the public about practices that would otherwise remain largely covert. In spite of that, doping is not going away, in a time when the use of pills and substances of all sorts to enhance performance and endurance is widespread across society. It is difficult, although it is indispensable, to isolate sport from the rest in a society where high performance and economic financial gain are the ultimate parameters by which individuals are measured, regardless of the means that are used to get there. Doping substances in sport are becoming, in fact, more sophisticated to defeat detection tests, which are increasingly advanced. Performance-enhancing drugs are also more easily available to younger and younger athletes through the Internet and through local gyms.

Substance abuse in sports has major ethical, educational, and health implications, which affect professional athletes as well as amateurs. From an ethical point of view, doping is a fundamental hindrance to sports ethics. The very idea that an athlete takes substances to enhance performance, whether licit or illicit, evokes an instinctively negative reaction. However, on a closer look the question appears much more complex to judge than it seems. The life of a sportsman involves a variety of actors: the coach, the physician, the masseur, the nutritionist, the parents, and so on. And this is only the closer environment. There is a wider environment that includes the sports club, the sport federation, the organizers of sports events, sports brands and sponsors, pharmaceutical industry, the media, and so forth. The variety of actors and interests involved in the life of an athlete makes it difficult to interpret which instance is ultimately responsible for the decision-making process.

Health and medical implications are also more controversial to evaluate than it may seem. The lines between the medicating of an athlete to preserve his or her health and the inappropriate use of performance-enhancing drugs are blurred. Not every substance is unhealthy, and the level of risk depends on the dosage and on the interaction with other products, in most cases. Furthermore, even though substance abuse is generally acknowledged as a serious and risky business for health, things get more complicated when it is necessary to reach conclusive evidence on the specific risks associated with each substance, due to inconsistencies in the reporting of drug use among athletes, with the consequent difficulty in carrying out reliable studies and the widespread practice of taking mixed substances.

And what if an athlete takes drugs in training but is "clean" in competition? Where does cheating begin? In view of all these aspects, it is evident that the fight against doping, which is crucial to preserve the ultimate nature of sport, is a particularly challenging and controversial activity.

Beyond its medical and legal implications, the key issue in dealing with substance abuse in sport is first and foremost education. Sport is an educational tool for children, young people, and adults. Besides the physical aspects and the benefits for health, sport embodies a series of positive values that represent its very essence and that can be transposed to any other aspect of life: respect for others, fair competition, discipline, team playing, respect for the rules, and many others. Accepting the principle of fairness, in particular, is the core of sport. Without fair play, sport does not mean much. It is therefore essential that athletes be educated from a young age to the real and founding values of sport. When athletes cheat by doping, they harm their fellow athletes who are not cheating, they harm their sport, and they may seriously harm themselves, both in the short and the long run. Substance abuse becomes part of the picture whenever sport is reduced to the mere result of the game. Sport is much more than that.

Rosarita Cuccoli

See also Lewis, Carl; McGwire, Mark and Sosa, Sammy; 1968 Olympic Games, Mexico City; Sports and Drugs/Doping; *Sports Illustrated*; Steroids

Suggested Resources
"How We Got Here: A Timeline of Performance-Enhancing Drugs in Sports." March 11, 2008. http://sportsillustrated.cnn.com/2008/magazine/03/11/steroid.timeline/index.html. Accessed September 24, 2011.

Marriott-Lloyd, Paul. *Understanding the International Convention against Doping in Sport*. Paris: UNESCO, 2010.

Murray, Thomas H., Karen J. Maschke, and Angela A. Wasunna, eds. *Performance-Enhancing Technologies in Sports: Ethical, Conceptual, and Scientific Issues*. Baltimore: Johns Hopkins University Press, 2009.

The Prohibited List. Montreal: World Anti-Doping Agency, updated annually.

Rosen, Daniel M. *Dope: A History of Performance Enhancement in Sports from the Nineteenth Century to Today*. Westport, CT: Praeger, 2008.

Waddington, Ivan, and Andy Smith. *An Introduction to Drugs in Sport: Addicted to Winning?* Oxford: Routledge, 2009.

Summitt, Pat (1952–)

With nearly 40 seasons under her belt at the University of Tennessee, Pat Summitt is the most decorated coach in the history of college basketball. She is the all-time winningest coach in NCAA history. She is the only coach in NCAA history, man or woman, to record 1,000 wins. Her eight national championships with the Lady Volunteers ranks second only to UCLA's John Wooden (who has 10 titles). She has added a combined 31 Southeastern Conference (SEC) titles and, in the process, has been named the SEC Coach of the Year eight times and the NCAA Coach of the Year seven times. Inducted into the Women's Basketball Hall of Fame in 1999 and the Basketball Hall of Fame in 2000, Pat Summitt is the Naismith Coach of the 20th Century.

A native of Clarksville, Tennessee, Patricia Sue was the fourth of five children born to tobacco and dairy farmers Richard and Hazel Head. In between schoolwork and family chores, "Trish," as she was called, showed great tenacity and athletic talent. At a time when girls had few athletic opportunities and little social support to pursue them, the Heads were an exception. They even moved to the nearby town of Henrietta to give their daughter the chance to play basketball. At Cheatham County High School she started on the varsity team all four years and was named to the all-district team in 1970.

While her older two brothers were able to secure athletic scholarships to college, none were available for women at that time. Still, Summitt enrolled at the University of Tennessee–Martin, where she became a four-year starter. From 1970 to 1974, she led the Lady Pacers to a 64–29 record and two national tournament berths. With 1,045 points, she became their all-time leading scorer and graduated with a degree in physical education.

Her playing career extended beyond her time at Martin. In 1973 she made the U.S. World University Games team that won a silver medal. Two years later, Summitt was a member of the world championship

President Barack Obama awards the Medal of Freedom to Pat Summitt during a ceremony in the East Room of the White House in Washington, D.C., on May 29, 2012. (AP Photo/Charles Dharapak.)

team, the U.S. National Team, and the Pan American Games team that took home the gold medal. The year 1976 marked the first time that the Olympic Games sponsored women's basketball; Summitt co-captained the U.S. team that won the silver medal, finishing behind the Soviet Union.

Her international experience extended into coaching. In 1977 she guided the U.S. Junior National Team to two gold medals and, two years later, took the helm of the U.S. National Team. She coached the 1983 world championship team to a silver medal and earned great notoriety when the United States earned the gold medal at the 1984 Olympic Games in Los Angeles. But it has been with the Tennessee Vols where Summitt truly secured her legacy.

In 1974, at age 22, Summitt enrolled in the master's of physical education program at the University of Tennessee. She also accepted a graduate teaching assistantship and planned to assist head coach Margaret Hutson with the women's basketball team. But Huston took a sabbatical that year and Summitt stepped in. She earned a 16–11 record in her inaugural season—all the while training for the 1976 Olympic team. Since then, Summitt has never had a losing season at UT, making the NCAA Tournament every year since 1982—the first year that the event included women. Only once, in 2009, did the Vols fail to advance past the first round.

In 1987, Tennessee won its first national title, beating Louisiana Tech, 67–44. Throughout the 1990s, the Vols dominated the hardwood, earning them the 2000 ESPY award for Team of the Decade (an honor they shared with Florida State University's football team). To date, her teams have won 31 conference titles, 27 Sweet Sixteen, 18 NCAA Final Four appearances (and an additional 4 in the AIAW era), and 8 national championships.

As of 2011, the program boasts 12 Olympians, 20 Kodak All-Americans, and 75 All-SEC performers. Some of the top players in the game have donned the Vols' orange and white, including Dena Head, Kara Lawson, Candace Parker, Tamika Catchings, Daedra Charles, Holly Warlick, Nikki McCray, Semeka Randal, Bridgette Gordon, and Chamique Holdsclaw, the Naismith Player of the Century. Known for "the stare," a steely-eyed gaze that epitomizes her intensity, Summitt demands excellence on the court and in the classroom; of those players who have completed their eligibility at UT, an inconceivable 100 percent graduate with their college diplomas.

A number of honors bespeak Summitt's place of prominence. The basketball court at Cheatham County High School now bears her name, as does the hardwood at University of Tennessee–Martin's Skyhawk Arena, along with a campus street renamed Pat Head Summitt Avenue. The Knoxville campus has also designated a road in her honor and the court at the Thompson-Boling Arena is now "The Summitt," dedicated following her 880th victory. She is also the first coach in the women's game to make more than $1 million. Twice asked to coach the Tennessee men's squad,

> ## The Tennessee-UConn Rivalry
>
> Since their first meeting in 1995, the relationship between the University of Tennessee Volunteers and the University of Connecticut Huskies has been called "the meanest rivalry in sport" and "the greatest rivalry in women's team sports." It began when the number one-ranked, undefeated Vols accepted an invitation to play the number two–rated Huskies, who were also without a loss that season. The Huskies stunned the odds-on favorite by winning, 77–66. Just over two months later, the teams met again in the final of the NCAA Tournament. UConn came out on top once more, besting Tennessee by a score of 70–64 and becoming only the second women's team in history to go undefeated en route to the national title.
>
> Since then, the two teams have generated unprecedented interest in the game. Their contest for the 2004 NCAA national championship earned the highest television ratings on ESPN for any basketball game—men's or women's. As of the end of the 2007–2008 season, the teams had met 22 times in 13 years, each game airing on national television. Fifteen of those encounters took place during the regular season, while the other seven occurred in the context of the NCAA Tournament. This includes a regional final, two Final Four match-ups, and four national championship games. In each NCAA final event, the Huskies have bested the Lady Vols and in total UConn leads the rivalry by a score of 13–9.
>
> In 2007, Pat Summitt did not sign the contract that would continue Tennessee's regular-season contests with the University of Connecticut. She has declined to answer why she put an end to the highly anticipated contest, though many speculate it had something to do with her increasingly adversarial relationship with UConn's coach, Geno Auriemma.

she has declined and focused her attention on creating one of the preeminent programs in the country.

In August 2011, Summitt revealed that, at age 59, doctors had diagnosed her with early onset dementia, Alzheimer's type, an irreversible brain disease that, over time, destroys cognitive abilities and recall. She announced that she would continue at the helm of the Lady Vols program for the 2011–2012 season, giving greater responsibilities to her assistant coaches. She has since received enormous support from her university, her players, and the intercollegiate athletics community. The Southeastern Conference dedicated a week of all men and women's basketball games to its "We Back Pat" campaign to raise awareness about Alzheimer's and funds, which it will donate to the Pat Summitt Foundation.

In addition to her own foundation, Summitt has been the official spokesperson for a number of programs: Verizon Wireless's HopeLine, the United Way, The Race for the Cure, and Juvenile Diabetes. A former member of Big Brothers/Big Sisters, Summitt was the honorary chair for the Tennessee Easter Seal Society and the Tennessee chair of the American Heart Association. She has earned recognition for her efforts from the Boy Scouts of America, the Lupus Foundation, and the Tennessee Lung Association. She also fulfills engagements as a motivational speaker and was hired as a WNBA consultant, assisting the Washington Mystics with player personnel and the draft. Though her future as a coach remains uncertain, her past and continued successes ensure her legacy as one of the most venerated and lasting in all of sport.

Jaime Schultz and Sara Roser-Jones

See also Auriemma, Geno; ESPY Awards; 1984 Olympic Games, Los Angeles; Women's National Basketball Association

Suggested Resources
Grundy, Pamela, and Susan Shackelford. *Shattering the Glass: The Remarkable History of Women's Basketball*. New York: The New Press, 2005.
Pat Summitt Website. http://www.coachsummitt.com/. Accessed March 1, 2012.
Summitt, Pat, with Sally Jenkins. *Raise the Roof*. New York: Broadway Books, 1998.
Summitt, Pat, with Sally Jenkins. *Reach for the Summit*. New York: Broadway Books, 1998.
Tennesse Women's Basketball Website. http://www.utladyvols.com/sports/w-baskbl/tennw-w-baskbl-body.html. Accessed March 2, 2012.

Super Bowl

The Super Bowl came about due to the 1966 merger between the established National Football League (NFL) and the upstart American Football League (AFL). Part of the merger agreement included the decision to pit the winners of the two leagues in the NFL-AFL Championship Game. The term "Super Bowl" was coined by Lamar Hunt, owner of the AFL's Kansas City Chiefs, after watching his young daughter playing with her toy "Super Ball." After the two leagues officially combined, the NFL was reorganized into conferences (NFC and AFC) and the Super Bowl has since been contested between the winners of these conferences.

While the first Super Bowl failed to sell out the stadium, the game has since become a major part of the American entertainment calendar. Super Bowl Sunday has become an unofficial American holiday with Americans' food consumption during this weekend coming second only to Thanksgiving weekend. Super Bowl games make up nearly half of the top 45 highest rated television broadcasts in history. Beyond the game, the Super Bowl also includes dynamic halftime shows, having featured high profile performers such as Michael Jackson, U2, and the Rolling Stones. Additionally, due to its high ratings, the Super Bowl attracts marketers who often unveil new products and creative advertisements during the broadcast. In fact, the commercials are often as highly anticipated as the game itself.

Super Bowl I (January 15, 1967, Los Angeles, California): The first NFL-AFL Championship Game pitted the NFL's Green Bay Packers against the AFL's Kansas City Chiefs. Quarterback and Most Valuable Player Bart Starr and an unlikely hero, receiver Max McGee (subbing for the injured Boyd Dowler), led the Packers and their coach Vince Lombardi to a 35–10 victory, further solidifying the belief that the NFL played a superior brand of football.

Super Bowl II (January 14, 1968, Miami, Florida): The Packers again represented the NFL in this second championship game, easily defeating the AFL's Oakland Raiders, 33–14. This marked Green Bay's third consecutive NFL title and its second Super Bowl victory, marking a decade of dominance for the Packers, who won five titles in the 1960s under Hall of Fame coach Vince Lombardi. This game was Lombardi's last with the Packers and his last championship.

Super Bowl III (January 12, 1969, Miami, Florida): In one of the biggest upsets in sports history, the New York Jets won the first championship for the AFL, defeating the heavily favored Baltimore Colts, 16–7.

The Thunderbirds of the U.S. Air Force perform a flyover during the playing of the national anthem to start Super Bowl XLIII, February 1, 2009, in Tampa, Florida. (Courtesy of US Military/Staff Sgt. Bradley Lail, USAF.)

Prior to the game, brash Jets quarterback Joe Namath guaranteed a Jet victory. Namath backed up his boasting by earning MVP honors for guiding the Jets to a convincing win over the Colts, who were favored by 17.5 points. This showed that AFL teams could compete with the NFL.

Super Bowl IV (January 12, 1970, New Orleans, Louisiana): In the last Super Bowl played prior to the AFL-NFL merger, the AFL representative (Kansas City Chiefs) pulled yet another upset over the favored NFL team (Minnesota Vikings). Chief quarterback Len Dawson led the Chiefs to a 23–7 victory and took home MVP honors for his efficient passing day, completing 12 of 17 passes. The Chief defense also held the Vikings to only 67 yards rushing and forced five turnovers.

Super Bowl V (January 17, 1971, Miami, Florida): In the closest played game thus far, the Baltimore Colts won 16–13 over the Dallas Cowboys on a last-second field goal by Jim O'Brien. This was the first and still the only time that a player from the losing team was named Most Valuable Player, as Dallas linebacker Chuck Howley received the honor. The first championship played after the merger (AFC vs. NFC format) was played between two teams that had been members of the original NFL. This was also the first time the champion was awarded the Vince Lombardi Trophy, named after the legendary Packer coach who had died on September 3, 1970.

Super Bowl VI (January 16, 1972, New Orleans, Louisiana): The Cowboys reached the Super Bowl for the second consecutive year and soundly defeated the Miami Dolphins, 24–3. The Cowboys rode their running attack to victory, rushing for a record 252 yards. Their defense also helped win the game as they held the Dolphins to a season-low 185 total yards and kept them from scoring a touchdown. Dallas quarterback Roger Staubach won the MVP honors. The telecast of this game was the top-rated television broadcast at the time.

Super Bowl VII (January 14, 1973, Los Angeles, California): After losing the previous year, the Miami

Dolphins won their first title, defeating the Washington Redskins, 14–7. This victory marked the culmination of Miami's undefeated season: still the only time in the Super Bowl era that a team has finished undefeated. The 2007 New England Patriots had no losses going into the Super Bowl, but were upset by the New York Giants. Each year, surviving members of this Dolphins celebrate their accomplishment after the last undefeated team loses.

Super Bowl VIII (January 14, 1974, Houston, Texas): The Dolphins under Coach Don Shula won their second consecutive championship (after reaching their third Super Bowl in a row), defeating the Minnesota Vikings, 24–7. The Dolphins beat Minnesota behind a record 145 rushing yards earned by MVP Larry Csonka.

Super Bowl IX (January 12, 1975, New Orleans, Louisiana): The Minnesota Vikings represented the NFC for the second consecutive year, but came up short again, losing to the Pittsburgh Steelers, 16–6. For the second year in a row, the Vikings gave up a record rushing performance, this time by the Steelers' Franco Harris, whose 158 yards earned him MVP honors. This game featured two dominant defenses: the Vikings' "Purple People Eaters" and the Steelers' "Steel Curtain."

Super Bowl X (January 18, 1976, Miami, Florida): The Steelers won their second consecutive title, this time defeating the Dallas Cowboys (making their third trip to the Super Bowl). Quarterback Terry Bradshaw and MVP receiver Lynn Swann, whose 161 receiving yards (on four catches with one touchdown) were a Super Bowl record, led the Steelers to a 21–17 victory, marking one of the closest games in Super Bowl history.

Super Bowl XI (January 9, 1977, Pasadena, California): The Minnesota Vikings reached the Super Bowl for the fourth time in the decade, but were again soundly defeated, this time by the Oakland Raiders, 32–14. The Raiders rode a strong rushing attack and the receiving work of MVP Fred Belitnikoff to beat the Vikings. Minnesota's Hall of Fame coach Bud Grant remains the most successful coach in Vikings' history, but he was never able to win a Super Bowl. Only the Buffalo Bills, who lost four consecutive Super Bowls in the early 1990s, matched Minnesota's four Super Bowl appearances without a victory.

Super Bowl XII (January 15, 1978, New Orleans, Louisiana): Tom Landry's Dallas Cowboys won their second Super Bowl behind a dominating defense that forced eight turnovers by the Denver Broncos (four fumbles and four interceptions). Defensive linemen Randy White and Harvey Martin were named co-MVPs in recognition of their contribution to the Cowboys' defensive effort. The television audience was the largest to ever witness a sporting event.

Super Bowl XIII (January 21, 1979, Miami, Florida): The Cowboys made it to the Super Bowl for the second year in a row, but lost to the Pittsburgh Steelers. The Steelers, behind 318 passing yards from MVP Terry Bradshaw, became the first team to win three Super Bowls as they beat the Cowboys, 35–31. Near the end of the game, the Steelers scored two touchdowns in the span of 19 seconds to extend their lead to 35–17.

Super Bowl XIV (January 20, 1980, Pasadena, California): The Steelers won their second straight title and fourth overall by defeating the Los Angeles Rams, 31–19. Terry Bradshaw was again named the MVP behind another 300-yard passing day. With his success in this game, Bradshaw set Super Bowl career records for most passing yards (932) and most touchdown passes (9). The Steelers established their dominance as the "Team of the 1970s" by winning their fourth Super Bowl before any other team had won three.

Super Bowl XV (January 25, 1981, New Orleans, Louisiana): The Oakland Raiders won their second Super Bowl, defeating the Philadelphia Eagles, 27–10. MVP Jim Plunkett led the Raiders to victory despite not becoming the starting quarterback until the sixth game of the season. The Raiders also turned in a strong defensive performance, including a record three interceptions by Rod Martin. The Raiders became the first wild card team to win a Super Bowl after the playoffs were expanded.

Super Bowl XVI (January 24, 1982, Pontiac, Michigan): In his first Super Bowl, future Hall of Fame quarterback Joe Montana earned MVP honors by guiding the San Francisco 49ers to a 26–21 victory over the Cincinnati Bengals. The 49ers built up a 20–0 halftime lead and were leading 26–14 throughout most of the fourth quarter, before a late Bengals touchdown. This was the first time that the winning team was outgained as the Bengals racked up 356 yards to the 49ers' 275.

Super Bowl XVII (January 30, 1983, Pasadena, California): Washington Redskins fullback John Riggins (aka "The Diesel") bulled his way to a Super Bowl record 166 yards in a come-from-behind 27–17 victory for the Washington Redskins over the Miami Dolphins. The signature play came with 10:01 remaining in the game when Riggins took the hand-off on fourth down and 1 yard to go and rumbled over the left side for a 43-yard touchdown run. The Redskins held the Dolphins to 176 total yards and only 34 in the second half.

Super Bowl XVIII (January 22, 1984, Tampa, Florida): The Redskins were once again the NFC representative in the Super Bowl, but the results this year were quite different as they were blown out by the Los Angeles Raiders, 38–9, the most lopsided victory since the Packers' 35–10 win over the Chiefs in Super Bowl I. John Riggins's record rushing performance from the previous year was eclipsed by the Raiders' Marcus Allen, who earned MVP honors by running for 191 total yards, including a dynamic 74-yard touchdown run.

Super Bowl XIX (January 20, 1985, Palo Alto, California): Joe Montana won his second Super Bowl and took home his second MVP honors as the San Francisco 49ers dominated the Miami Dolphins and their outstanding quarterback, Dan Marino, winning 38–16. Montana became only the third player (Bart Starr of the Packers and Terry Bradshaw of the Steelers were the other two) to win two Super Bowl MVP awards. San Francisco set a new game record with 537 total yards and held a nearly 2–1 edge in time of possession.

Super Bowl XX (January 26, 1986, New Orleans, Louisiana): The NFC champion Chicago Bears' defense stymied the New England Patriots while their offense tallied a new Super Bowl record number of points as they won easily, 46–10. The defense totaled seven sacks, led by MVP Richard Dent's 1.5, and held the Patriots to only seven rushing yards in the entire game. The Bears also held an astounding 236-to-19 yardage edge at halftime. The Bears only had one loss on the season and are often mentioned alongside the Dolphins' undefeated team of 1972 as one of the best teams in NFL history.

Super Bowl XXI (January 25, 1987, Pasadena, California): The New York Giants won their first title since 1956 by defeating the Denver Broncos, 39–20, behind quarterback (and MVP) Phil Simms's record-setting passing day. Simms was the most efficient quarterback in Super Bowl history, completing 22 out of 25 passes. The game was close at halftime with the Broncos holding a slim 10–9 edge. But the Giants held Denver to only 10 yards in the third quarter. This was the first of five Super Bowl appearances for John Elway and the Broncos.

Super Bowl XXII (January 31, 1988, San Diego, California): For the second year, the Denver Broncos represented the AFC in the Super Bowl and were once again beaten soundly. Washington's quarterback and MVP Doug Williams, the first African American to start at quarterback in the Super Bowl, guided the Redskins to 35 points in the second quarter and a 42–10 victory. The Redskins' Timmy Smith (204 yards rushing and Ricky Sanders (193 receiving yards) had record-setting performances.

Super Bowl XXIII (January 22, 1989, Miami, Florida): The San Francisco 49ers won their third title of the decade with a dramatic 20–16 victory over the Cincinnati Bengals. Quarterback Joe Montana set a new Super Bowl record with 357 yards passing, while future Hall of Famer Jerry Rice took home MVP honors by setting a new receiving standard with 215 yards on 11 catches. After the Bengals took a 16–13 lead with 3:20 left in the game, Joe Montana led San Francisco on a dramatic 92-yard-game-winning touchdown drive.

Super Bowl XXIV (January 28, 1990, New Orleans, Louisiana): The 49ers won their fourth title with a 55–10 defeat of the Denver Broncos, tying the Pittsburgh Steelers for most Super Bowl victories. Joe Montana won his third game MVP award by throwing for a record five touchdown passes in the win. The Broncos and John Elway lost their third Super Bowl in four years and were thoroughly dominated in the game, being outgained by nearly 300 yards.

Super Bowl XXV (January 27, 1991, Tampa, Florida): The game was played in the aftermath of the first Iraq war, leading to a display of patriotic sentiment at the game. The New York Giants beat the Buffalo Bills, 20–19, in dramatic fashion after Bills kicker Scott Norwood's field goal attempt sailed wide right as time expired. While Bills running back Thurman Thomas gained 190 yards from scrimmage, the Giants and MVP running back Otis Anderson set a record for time of possession in holding the Bills' powerful offense at bay.

Super Bowl XXVI (January 26, 1992, Minneapolis, Minnesota): The Bills lost their second consecutive Super Bowl, this time to the Washington Redskins, by a 37–24 score. MVP quarterback Mark Rypien led the Redskins in a dominating performance as they had leads of 24–0 and 37–10 prior to the Bills adding two late touchdowns. The Redskins' defense also turned in a strong performance, limiting the AFC's leading rusher, Thurman Thomas, to only 13 yards rushing.

Super Bowl XXVII (January 31, 1993, Pasadena, California): The Dallas Cowboys won their third title in their record six Super Bowl appearances with a dominating 52–17 victory against the Buffalo Bills. Cowboys quarterback Troy Aikman was named the game's MVP, but the defense forced nine turnovers (four interceptions and five fumbles) that led to 35 Cowboy points. The Cowboy win was the ninth straight for the NFC over the AFC.

Super Bowl XXVIII (January 30, 1994, Atlanta, Georgia): In a rematch, the Dallas Cowboys again defeated the Buffalo Bills, this time by a 30–13 score. Running back Emmitt Smith was named the game's MVP after rushing for 132 yards and two touchdowns. The Cowboys became the fifth team to win back-to-back Super Bowl titles (including Green Bay, Miami, Pittsburgh, and San Francisco). The Bills' fourth straight Super Bowl defeat put them in the company of the Minnesota Vikings and Denver Broncos, who also lost four Super Bowls.

Super Bowl XXIX (January 29, 1995, Miami, Florida): In the highest-scoring Super Bowl in history, the San Francisco 49ers defeated the San Diego Chargers, 49–26. Game MVP Steve Young passed for a record six touchdowns, breaking the previous mark held by former 49ers quarterback Joe Montana. Wide receiver Jerry Rice set career Super Bowl marks for receptions, yards, and receiving touchdowns.

Super Bowl XXX (January 28, 1996, Tempe, Arizona): The Dallas Cowboys won their third title (and record tying fifth overall) in four years, beating the Pittsburgh Steelers, 27–17. Dallas cornerback Larry Brown was named the game's MVP for his two interceptions.

Both of his interceptions set up Dallas touchdowns, including the game clinger for the Cowboys.

Super Bowl XXXI (January 26, 1997, New Orleans, Louisiana): The NFL championship returned to "Titletown" as the Green Bay Packers won their first Super Bowl in 29 years. The Packers defeated the New England Patriots, 35–21, behind MVP Desmond Howard's 244 return yards (including a 99-yard kickoff return for a touchdown), quarterback Brett Favre's two touchdown passes, and Reggie White's record three sacks.

Super Bowl XXXII (January 25, 1998, San Diego, California): This game marked a turning point for the Denver Broncos as well as the AFC. The Broncos won their first title after four previous Super Bowl losses and their 31–24 victory over the Green Bay Packers also ended the NFC's streak of 13 consecutive Super Bowl victories. Denver running back Terrell Davis rushed for 157 yards and three touchdowns on the way to earning MVP honors.

Super Bowl XXXIII (January 31, 1999, Miami, Florida): In the last game of his Hall of Fame career, quarterback John Elway earned the game MVP while leading the Denver Broncos to a 34–19 victory over the Atlanta Falcons. Elway threw for 336 yards and one touchdown and also ran for a touchdown in leading the Broncos to the title. After losing three Super Bowls in the 1980s, Elway ended his career on a high note with his second consecutive championship.

Super Bowl XXXIV (January 30, 2000, Atlanta, Georgia): In one of the more dramatic Super Bowl finishes, St. Louis Ram linebacker Mike Jones tacked Tennessee Titan receiver Kevin Dyson on the one-yard line as time expired to preserve the Rams' 23–16 victory. The Rams' powerful offense, dubbed "The Greatest Show on Turf," was led by game MVP Kurt Warner's record 414 passing yards and two touchdowns.

Super Bowl XXXV (January 28, 2001, Tampa, Florida): The Baltimore Ravens turned in a dominant defensive performance, holding the New York Giants to merely 152 total yards and not allowing an offensive touchdown en route to a 34–7 win. Raven middle linebacker Ray Lewis was named MVP for his leadership of the Raven defense that forced five turnovers and sacked Giant quarterback Kerry Collins four times.

Super Bowl XXXVI (February 3, 2002, New Orleans, Louisiana): In the first Super Bowl played after the 9/11 terrorist attacks, the game ended dramatically as the New England Patriots' Adam Vinatieri kicked a last-second field goal to beat the St. Louis Rams, 20–17. The Patriots' MVP Tom Brady led his team to an upset of the Rams by leading the last-minute field goal drive after the Rams had tied the game with 1:30 remaining.

Super Bowl XXXVII (January 26, 2003, San Diego, California): The Tampa Bay Buccaneers defeated the Oakland Raiders, 48–21, in one of the most dominating defensive showings in Super Bowl history. The Bucs had five sacks and five interceptions, three of which were returned for touchdowns. MVP Dexter Jackson had two interceptions including one that led to a go-ahead field goal midway through the second quarter.

Super Bowl XXXVIII (February 1, 2004, Houston, Texas): The New England Patriots won their second title in three years with a dramatic 32–29 victory over the Carolina Panthers. While both teams struggled to score early, the fourth quarter featured a Super Bowl record 37 combined points. Once again, MVP Tom Brady led the Patriots to the Panthers' 23-yard line and Adam Vinatieri kicked a 41-yard field goal with four seconds remaining to give the Patriots the victory.

Super Bowl XXXIX (February 6, 2005, Jacksonville, Florida): In their third Super Bowl in four years and second consecutive appearance in the big game, the Patriots completed their dynasty with their third title. New England receiver Deion Branch earned MVP accolades with a record-tying 11 catches to go with 133 yards. The Patriots defeated the Philadelphia Eagles, 24–21, becoming the second team (after the Dallas Cowboys) to win three championships in four years.

Super Bowl XL (February 5, 2006, Detroit, Michigan): The Pittsburgh Steelers won their record-tying fifth Super Bowl title (tied with the Dallas Cowboys and San Francisco 49ers) with a 21–10 victory over the Seattle Seahawks. Pittsburgh wide receiver Hines Ward earned MVP honors for gaining 123 yards on five catches. The game was marred by several controversial calls by the officials that went against the Seahawks.

Super Bowl XLI (February 4, 2007, Miami, Florida): The Indianapolis Colts led by game MVP Peyton Manning defeated the Chicago Bears, 29–17, in a wet and rainy Miami night. The game began well for the Bears as rookie Devin Hester returned the game's opening kickoff 92 yards for a touchdown. The first half featured sloppy play with each team turning the ball over three times. The game featured the first Super Bowl matchup of African American coaches, as the Bears' Lovie Smith lost to Colts' coach Tony Dungy.

Super Bowl XLII (February 3, 2008, Glendale, Arizona): The New England Patriots entered the Super Bowl at 18–0, looking to become the first championship team to go undefeated since the 1972–1973 Miami Dolphins. However, the New York Giants pulled off a dramatic upset, winning 17–14 on a go-ahead touchdown pass from MVP Eli Manning to Plaxico Burress with 35 seconds left in the game. Manning's MVP performance came on the heels of his older brother Peyton's MVP in the previous year's Super Bowl.

Super Bowl XLIII (February 1, 2009, Tampa, Florida): The Pittsburgh Steelers' 27–23 victory over the Arizona Cardinals marked their record-setting sixth Super Bowl victory. The Cardinals' Kurt Warner failed in his bid to win a Super Bowl with his second team after having won Super Bowl XXXIV as a member of the St. Louis Rams. Pittsburgh receiver

Super Bowl Records

Individual Records:

Passing Yards: 414—Kurt Warner, St. Louis Rams, XXXIV
Touchdown Passes: 6—Steve Young, San Francisco 49ers, XXIX
Interceptions: 5—Rich Gannon, Oakland Raiders, XXXVII
Receiving Yards Gained: 215—Jerry Rice, San Francisco 49ers, XXIII
Receiving Touchdowns: 3—Jerry Rice, San Francisco 49ers, XXIX
Rushing Yards Gained: 204—Timmy Smith, Washington Redskins, XXII
Rushing Touchdowns: 3—Terrell Davis, Denver Broncos, XXXII
Interceptions By: 3—Rod Martin, Oakland Raiders, XV
Sacks By: 3—Reggie White, Green Bay Packers, XXXI, and Darnell Dockett, Arizona Cardinals, XLIII

Team Records:

Most Points: 55—San Francisco 49ers, XXIV
Fewest Points: 3—Miami Dolphins, VI
Most Yards Gained: 602—Washington Redskins, XXII
Fewest Yards Gained: 119—Minnesota Vikings, IX

Santonio Holmes was named the MVP after his game-winning reception with 35 seconds left in the game.

Super Bowl XLIV (February 7, 2010, Miami, Florida): The New Orleans Saints won their first title by defeating the favored Indianapolis Colts, 31–17. Saints quarterback Drew Brees was named MVP and set a record with 32 pass completions. In addition to Brees's efficient performance, the Saints' success was partially based on bold coaching decisions as they successfully executed an onside kick to start the second half, leading to a New Orleans touchdown.

Super Bowl XLV (February 6, 2011, Dallas, Texas): The Green Bay Packers behind MVP quarterback Aaron Rodgers won their fourth Super Bowl title and their record 13th NFL title. The Packers struggled with injuries during the regular season and had to win on the last day of the regular season to make the playoffs as the NFC's sixth seed. They won three road games to reach the Super Bowl, where they defeated the Pittsburgh Steelers, 31–25.

Super Bowl XLVI (February 5, 2012, Indianapolis, Indiana): The New York Giants, with a record of just 9–7, had battled their way into the playoffs and the Super Bowl, where they defeated the favored New England Patriots, 21–17. It was the Giants' fourth Super Bowl victory and the second under MVP quarterback Eli Manning, who had also won that award in the Giants' victory in 2008 against the same Patriots.

Super Bowl XLVII (February 3, 2013, New Orleans, Louisiana): In what became the longest Super Bowl ever (4 hours, 14 minutes), the Baltimore Ravens defeated the San Francisco 49ers, 34–31 at the Mercedes-Benz Superdome in New Orleans. The Ravens, led by quarterback Joe Flacco, were ahead 28–6 early in the third quarter but a 34-minute partial power outage slowed Baltimore's surge. After play resumed, San Francisco scored 17 unanswered points in the third quarter. But despite the 49ers' frenzied comeback, the Ravens would be victorious. Joe Flacco, named Super Bowl MVP, completed 22 of 33 passes for 287 yards, three touchdowns, and no interceptions.

Jeffrey T. Ramsey

See also American Football League; Bradshaw, Terry; Dallas Cowboys; Dungy, Tony; Favre, Brett; The Greatest Show on Turf; Green Bay Packers; Lombardi, Vincent T.; Manning, Peyton; 1972 Miami Dolphins; Montana, Joe; Namath, Joe; National Football League; New Orleans Saints; Rice, Jerry; Steel Curtain; Williams, Doug

Suggested Resources

McGinn, Bob. *The Ultimate Super Bowl Book: A Complete Reference to the Stats, Stars, and Stories Behind Football's Biggest Game—Why the Best Team Won*. Minneapolis, MN: MVP Books, 2009.

St. John, Allen. *The Billion Dollar Game: Behind the Scenes of the Greatest Day in American Sport—Super Bowl Sunday*. New York: Anchor Books, 2009.

Super Bowl. NFL.com. http://www.nfl.com/superbowl/. Accessed November 28, 2011.

Super Bowl History. http://www.superbowlhistory.net/. Accessed November 28, 2011.

"Super Bowl Shuffle"

"The Super Bowl Shuffle" is a rap song made famous by the Chicago Bears football team in 1985, prior to their appearance and subsequent 46–10 victory over the New England Patriots in Super Bowl XX. The song became an overnight sensation, selling more than a half-million copies and reaching number 41 on the U.S. *Billboard* Hot 100. The song was nominated for a Grammy Award in 1985.

Bears fan Richard Meyer co-wrote (with Melvin Owens), produced, and choreographed "The Super Bowl Shuffle" as a tribute to his favorite team's 15 wins (with only one loss) during the 1985–1986 National Football League season. The music was written by Bobby Daniels and Lloyd Barry, and the record was released by Red Label Records in 1985. Meyer and Owens's lyrics highlighted several Bears, many of whom sang their own parts. The Bears who performed the song and later appeared in the video were known as the Chicago Bears Shufflin' Crew, and they included running back Walter Payton, quarterback Jim McMahon, defensive star Mike Singletary, receiver Willie Gault, backup quarterback Steve Fuller, cornerback Mike Richardson, defensive end Richard Dent, free safety Gary Fencik, linebacker Otis Wilson, and fan favorite, defensive lineman William "Refrigerator" Perry.

Chicago mayor Harold Washington, center, laughs on December 16, 1985, at City Hall as Chicago Bears Richard Dent, left, and Otis Wilson, right, teach him a "Super Bowl Shuffle." (AP Photo/Charlie Bennett.)

Additional players appeared in the video as the Shufflin' Crew band. Band members included punter Maury Buford on the cowbell, backup quarterback Mike Tomczak on guitar, running back Calvin Thomas on saxophone, offensive lineman Stefan Humphries on drums, and defensive lineman Tyrone Keys on keyboard. Nine additional players sang as part of the Shufflin Crew Chorus: cornerback/safety Leslie Frazier, cornerback/safety Shaun Gayle, running back Dennis Gentry, linebacker Jim Morrisey, wide receiver Keith Ortego, defensive back Reggie Phillips, linebacker Dan Rains, running back Thomas Sanders, and defensive back Ken Taylor. Dan Hampton, defensive end, was asked to participate, but declined, explaining that the video might be perceived as arrogant.

Other sport teams have recorded songs together, but the Chicago Bears and their "Super Bowl Shuffle" was the first account of a team creating their own rap video. A year earlier, the San Francisco 49ers recorded "We Are the 49ers" and later released a second song, "49ers Rap." The popularity and success of the rap video led other teams to imitate the Bears and their musical efforts. In the fall of 1985, the Kansas Wesleyan football team won their conference title and recorded the "KCAC Shuffle," which aired locally. The New England Patriots, as a response to the Bears, recorded "New England, the Patriots and We" in 1986, which wrongly predicted their victory over the Bears in Super Bowl XX. The New York Giants released "Walk Like a Giant" following their victory in Super

Bowl XXI. The Minnesota Twins, after winning the 1987 World Series, released a video, "The Berengeur Boogie," named for their relief pitcher, Juan Berenguer. Perhaps the most notable imitation was the "Ickey Shuffle," named for Cincinnati Bengals rookie fullback Ickey Woods prior to their appearance in Super Bowl XXIII, which they lost.

A 20th-anniversary DVD was released in 2004, which included the music video as well as outtakes and the making of the video. Proceeds from the original video were donated to the Chicago Community Trust, benefiting families in need with food, clothing, and shelter. In 2010, some of the 1985 Chicago Bears reunited to film an updated version, which aired as a commercial for Boost Mobile during Super Bowl XLIV.

See also Chicago Bears; Payton, Walter; Super Bowl

Maureen Smith

Suggested Resources

Mullin, John. *The Rise and Self-Destruction of the Greatest Team in History: The Chicago Bears and Super Bowl XX.* Chicago: Triumph Books, 2005.

"Super Bowl Shuffle" Video. http://video.google.com/video play?docid=765019771919333912. Accessed March 8, 2012.

Superdome

The Louisiana Superdome was conceived in the mid-1960s as an economic development effort to attract major events whose universal appeal would ultimately play a part in any progress the city of New Orleans would make in rendering segregation an irrelevant historical artifact. But just weeks after its 30th anniversary, the roof and interior of the Superdome were virtually destroyed by Hurricane Katrina, leaving a searing image of more than 40,000 evacuees—mostly African Americans—crowded inside and outside of the facility, then serving as a "refuge of last resort."

By 2011, a multiphase total makeover was completed at twice the original construction cost of the Superdome, and in stark contrast to the images of those 40,000, the stadium struck a naming-rights deal by which it became branded with images renaming it the Mercedes-Benz Superdome.

The stadium was the brainchild of New Orleans art and antiques dealer Dave Dixon. Having visited the Houston Astrodome shortly after it opened in 1965, Dixon was convinced that a similar domed stadium could be built in New Orleans, but bigger and more useful. He envisioned a facility that would accommodate all kinds of events, including major sports, as well as concerts, conventions, and trade shows. While his efforts indicated more of an interest in economic boosterism, they would also serve to bridge racial and cultural divides.

While that vision was taking form, New Orleans, like much of the nation, was struggling with fractious race relations. Sports and entertainment often served as a rallying and almost unifying force, but not always.

The American Football League All-Star Game was scheduled for Tulane Stadium in New Orleans in 1965, years before Superdome plans crystallized. Local hotels and taxicab operators denied access to black players, who voted to boycott the game. The contest was moved to Houston and played in front of an integrated crowd of fans with no reports of any racial incidents.

Dixon and others working to attract a professional football franchise to New Orleans were bluntly told that things would have to change if the city wanted to pursue a team in earnest. Planners of the Superdome hoped it would play a part in any such change.

Dixon pitched the domed stadium idea to local and state politicians, primarily Governor John McKeithen. Both knew the project could not be realized by the city acting on its own. Statewide support would be critical. McKeithen was from the rural town of Columbia in the north-central parish (county) of Caldwell, a world away from New Orleans. Contrasting cultural imperatives then separated the mostly rural north and central parts of Louisiana from the largely tourist-driven economy in New Orleans. Planners anticipated strong opposition to the project, which might not readily be seen as beneficial beyond the metropolitan area.

Dixon suggested that the concept could best be promoted outside the city (and to local skeptics) as generating thousands of jobs in construction and ongoing operations. The project, Dixon said, would reinvigorate an economy sputtering from a decline in status of the Port of New Orleans and the loss of manufacturing

As Hurricane Katrina approaches, residents of New Orleans bring supplies and line up to enter the Superdome, which was opened as a hurricane shelter on August 28, 2005, for those unable to evacuate the city. (FEMA.)

jobs in the state. Furthermore, Dixon predicted, the plan would resurrect the moribund Poydras Street corridor in the city's central business district.

Planners were convinced the project could be built for $35 million, none of which would need to be financed or guaranteed by the State of Louisiana. Instead, the stadium would be built exclusively with funds generated from a 4 percent sales tax on hotel and motel rooms in the New Orleans area. A state-promoted bond issue would serve under the plan as a funding fallback.

McKeithen secured approval of the plan from the state legislature and campaigned hard for it as a proposed state constitutional amendment put to Louisiana voters in 1966. One week before the election, the National Football League announced it had awarded an expansion franchise to New Orleans. The amendment passed with 74 percent of the vote.

As cost and design details became known, opposition began to include local critics. In 1971, a gubernatorial election year, the opposition to the stadium was led by John Schwegmann Jr., a millionaire New Orleans grocer running for governor. He complained that construction costs had increased to several times the $35 million initially budgeted, and he was concerned about traffic flow.

Concerns about financing were not misplaced. Completion costs were underestimated by more than 250 percent. A single bond issue begat two more. Important national banks such as Chase Manhattan, lobbied hard by McKeithen and Dixon to underwrite the bond issues and by Schwegmann not to do so, declined to get involved. A consortium of local bankers, at the apparent urging of McKeithen, then took on the underwriting, conditioned on the state's guarantee of the principal and interest for 35 years.

Construction then quickly began in 1971 and proceeded apace, slowing only when backhoes began turning up bodies, which homicide investigators quickly determined were not those of anyone recently deceased. Part of the construction site had once been the Girod Street Cemetery. By 1957, the property was so neglected the city condemned it and its former owner, the Episcopal Church, deconsecrated the cemetery. As it reclaimed the property, the city sought to have relatives of those buried there reinter their ancestors elsewhere, and it announced that unclaimed remains would be moved to other cemeteries (whites to one, blacks to another—segregated in death as in life).

As builders of the Superdome found out in 1971, some souls were overlooked. While there is debate about how much of the Superdome building site is actually atop the old Girod Street Cemetery, there is general agreement that at least some of the stadium's parking garage is indeed so situated. This fact later gave rise to several rituals to remove a supposed curse on the facility.

The Louisiana Superdome officially opened on August 3, 1975, the four years of construction being completed only hours before the ceremony. The first major event there was an NFL exhibition game between the Superdome-occupying Saints and the Houston Oilers, occupants of the Astrodome. The Oilers won, 13–7. True to the planners' ambition, the Astrodome could fit inside the Superdome with room to spare. The Superdome stands 27 stories high at its peak and was the largest "room" in the world constructed with steel, unobstructed by posts. The roof comprises nearly 10 acres and, utilizing revolutionary technology, actually holds the stadium together as the walls hang from it.

Movable grandstands accommodate multiple configurations so the Superdome can host an array of different events, including major sports such as football, basketball, and baseball, as well as concerts, trade shows, and conventions. Its parking facility can accommodate some 5,000 vehicles, its largest setup can seat 90,000 people, and its "superscreen" television was the largest in existence on which fans could watch instant replays and commercials just as they might do at home.

Early tenants included the Saints, whose presence in town solidified the lucrative possibilities of hosting Super Bowl games. Super Bowl IX was scheduled to be held in the Dome on January 12, 1975, but the facility was not ready in time. The game was played instead at Tulane Stadium, also the site of Saints home games pending completion of the Dome. More Super Bowls have been played in the Louisiana Superdome than in any other stadium. Although he never was so undiplomatic as to publicly emphasize the point, it no doubt registered with the late Dave Dixon, the art dealer and Superdome visionary, that none was ever played in the Astrodome (although two were played elsewhere in Houston).

What was for a time the largest crowd to attend a regular-season NCAA basketball game showed up at the Superdome on January 20, 1990, as 68,112 saw LSU defeat Notre Dame, 87–64. The record stood for more than 10 years, broken by a crowd of 78,129 in Michigan watching Michigan State host Kentucky on December 13, 2003 (Kentucky won, 79–74).

Still standing is the record set in the Superdome for hosting the largest indoor crowd at a regular-season NCAA baseball game on April 20, 2002 (27,673 watched LSU defeat Tulane, 9–5).

Muhammad Ali regained the heavyweight boxing title from Leon Spinks in a 1978 battle in the Superdome, becoming the first three-time champion in that weight class, with a crowd of 64,000 on hand.

The Rolling Stones set a record in the Superdome for indoor concert attendance with a 1981 performance drawing 87,500, a record that still stands.

Pope John Paul II addressed more than 80,000 children in the Superdome on September 12, 1987. Many still wonder about the coincidence of that papal visit and the Saints' first winning season that year (12–3), which started a streak of winning seasons (they went 7–9 in the 1994 season).

George H. W. Bush was nominated for president of the United States at the Republican Convention held in the Dome in 1988.

Several Mardi Gras organizations hold massive annual balls in the Superdome. As their traditional parades through the city conclude by taking a lap around the inside of the stadium, "krewe" members change in the Dome locker rooms before joining their tuxedoed and ball-gowned families and friends for a usually massive musical blowout.

In September 2010, a local baker spent three days producing a special-edition Mardi Gras "King Cake," which encircled the Superdome twice for a Guinness Book world record. Festooned with black and gold frosting and glitter in honor of the Saints' championship, the cake was sold by the slice and raised $50,000 for charity.

Superdome dominance in the New Orleans skyline became a reflexively accepted sight, a part of the city's personality, defining the city as a big-league sports and entertainment destination and highlighting all that it was doing right politically and socially. Recollection faded that any objection to its construction had ever been lodged.

Then came Katrina, a hurricane of unprecedented fury, which, in tandem with a failed system of federally designed and built levees, practically wiped out the city on August 29, 2005. On the day before, people who had not evacuated began to flow in to the Superdome. Mayor Ray Nagin had, on that Sunday morning, after much vacillation, finally declared the building a "refuge of last resort" despite earlier public announcements that it would not be available.

Previous experience with using the Dome as a shelter had not gone well. In 1998, some of the 14,000 evacuees of Hurricane Georges walked out with furniture from luxury suites, and property damage was estimated at $40,000. Better order prevailed for Hurricanes Ivan in 2004 and Dennis in the early summer of 2005. There was some optimism that the lessons of Georges had been learned.

For Katrina, the elite Special Reaction Team of the National Guard began showing up on Sunday, as thousands—mostly African Americans—began lining up for the thorough and time-consuming security procedures required of anyone headed for the uncertainties inside.

The rain started before everyone could get in. Thinking the storm had arrived early, some of those still outside panicked and surged toward the gates. Also persuaded that the "shelter of last resort" was their best option were tourists from foreign countries unable to get a timely flight out and New Orleans Police Department personnel.

By 10:30 p.m. on Sunday, all those who wanted to get in to the Dome apparently did. Supplies of

---

The Curse of the Superdome

When construction of the Superdome began in 1971, backhoes began turning up bodies. Turns out part of the construction site had once been the Girod Street Cemetery, established by the Episcopal Congregation of Christ church in 1822 as a final resting place for non-Catholics.

In the following years, the Girod Street Cemetery became neglected and overgrown, and some reports refer to rumors that it had served as a site and source of supply for voodoo rituals. In 1955 the city seized the property, and in 1957 the Episcopal Church deconsecrated the cemetery. Descendants who could be identified and located were notified to transfer the remains of their relatives. In the cases of unclaimed remains, assurances were given that those of whites were moved by the city to one facility, while those of blacks were moved to another.

Apparently, some remains were overlooked. Those souls resented the disturbance of their rest, the "doomed stadium" theory went.

Several efforts were made to reverse the perceived curse. A radio station hired voodoo priestess Miriam Chamani to perform a "purification ritual" outside the Superdome before a game with the Cleveland Browns on October 31, 1999. Despite the live python, burning incense, and pumpkin, the Saints lost 21–16 on a last-second 56-yard touchdown pass from Tim Couch to Kevin Johnson.

The Saints hired Priestess Ava Kay Jones to perform a similar ritual inside the Dome before a playoff game against the St. Louis Rams on December 30, 2000. The crowd joined in the chanting, and Jones continued the ritual at her church during the game. The Saints preserved their first-ever playoff victory when Brian Milne recovered a Ram-fumbled punt in the last seconds.

But it didn't work twice. The team hired Jones for another pregame performance. Result: Rams 34, Saints 21.

---

bottled water and MREs (military-issue "Meals Ready to Eat") were running low and replenishment would not be possible if trucks were unable to get through quickly after the storm passed. Predictions on that score were not optimistic. And no way would there be enough portable toilets.

Later that night, the winds and rain from Katrina's outer bands started slapping the glass doors to the Superdome as evacuees tried to get comfortable in stadium seats. The eye of the storm was expected Monday morning, August 29.

By 6 a.m., it was there. Those who had been able to sleep were awakened by the noise of winds starting to shake and tear apart the roof of the Dome. The lights went out, the air conditioning shut off, and generators kicked in to turn on emergency lights.

Other lights—far less reassuring—also arrived as the noise got louder. Huge storm vent dampers, each said in news reports to be as large as a compact car, were being torn away from the very peak of the roof, bolt by bolt. The underlayer of the roof was exposed to the wind and rain, which tore gaping holes in it. Water cascaded to the floor 27 stories below, and the huddled evacuees scattered for cover. Dome officials who knew about the unique "walls hanging from the roof" design of the stadium were terrified about what would happen if huge pieces of the roof kept peeling off. That cascading water was going everywhere inside the stadium— destroying the luxury suites, hallways, and lighting as it went and jeopardizing the integrity of the generators.

As the broken levees caused waters to rise outside by millions of gallons per minute, the generators were gasping. So were the people inside, whose sanitary options became impossibly overburdened. Food and water supplies were diminishing and the story kept getting worse. Criminal incidents, apparently scattered, were causing panic inside and outside of the Dome. Talk began of sending everyone elsewhere, perhaps to the New Orleans Convention Center.

News images of thousands of desperate evacuees were telling a story of mostly black people who either could not or, by some accounts, deliberately would not be rescued.

On Thursday, September 1, four days after the Superdome refuge was opened, some semblance of a rescue actually happened. Buses that had been promised since Monday finally came. An estimate of how many people had actually been inside was finally available, made by multiplying the number of buses by 50 passengers: a total of 41,100.

Ten people were dead at the Superdome, six of apparent natural causes, one a reported suicide or accident, and three—apparent drowning victims from nearby floodwaters—were swept to the stadium.

Water and wind damage to the Superdome was compounded by mountains of human waste, trash, and clothing. Repairs and restoration took more than a year. The Saints played "home" games in New York, San Antonio, and Baton Rouge during the 2005 season.

But, in a moment of nationally cathartic proportions, the Superdome reopened on September 25, 2006, as the Saints defeated the Atlanta Falcons, 23–3. When Saints journeyman Steve Gleason blocked a punt early in the game and Curtis DeLoach fell on the ball for the Saints' first score, noise levels by some accounts exceeded those experienced when Saints kicker Garrett Hartley booted the team to victory in the Dome over the Vikings and into Super Bowl XLIV in 2010.

Rebuilding of the stadium came in phases, was completed in 2011, and cost more than $336 million, nearly twice as much as the original construction. Saints owner Tom Benson had lobbied the State of Louisiana for a new stadium to keep pace with other NFL cities, and rumors had it the team would be moved out of New Orleans without such a concession. But the rebuild cost less than half of what it cost to build new stadiums elsewhere (Indianapolis's Lucas Oil Stadium—$720 million—and Cowboys Stadium in Dallas—$1.8 billion) and produced what some describe as a nearly new facility.

The Superdome likewise apparently became the economic engine it was envisioned to be. A study by the University of New Orleans estimates that, since the facility's reopening in 2006, it has had an economic impact of more than $4.1 billion on the state's economy. So with that, and after Katrina in 2005, the Monday night return in 2006 and the Super Bowl in 2010, talk of a new stadium or a move for the Saints no longer registers. Nor does any memory of the 1965 AFL All-Star Game boycott.

See also Ali, Muhammad; American Football League; Astrodome; New Orleans Saints; Super Bowl

James Hashek

Suggested Resources
Dixon, Dave. *Saints, the Superdome and the Scandal.* Gretna, LA: Pelican, 2008.
Duncan, Jeff. "Superdome, Refuge of Last Resort." August 27, 2006. http://www.nola.com/katrina/index.ssf/2006/08/superdomerefuge.html. Accessed August 30, 2011.

Mule, Marty. *Superdome: Thirteen Acres That Changed New Orleans.* Mandeville, LA: Gulf South Books, 1996.

The Swamp

Despite its numerous traditions, certain places have come to symbolize college football and all of its folklore: the Coliseum in Los Angeles, the Cotton Bowl in Texas, and the Sugar Bowl in New Orleans. However, a discussion of college football in tradition-rich Florida begins and ends with Ben Hill Griffin Stadium at the University of Florida. Famously known as the Swamp, this orange and blue–clad stadium is the largest in the state of Florida and legends such as Steve Spurrier, Jack Youngblood, Emmitt Smith, Danny Wuerffel, and Tim Tebow have all graced Florida Field.

Originally named Florida Field, the Swamp was built in 1930 with a maximum capacity of 21,769 persons. Several additions were made to the stadium in December 1949 and December 1965 bringing its capacity to 62,800. One of its most significant facelifts was completed in August 1982 in which a training center, modern press box, skybox tower, and seating in the south end zone were added. Seven years later, the stadium was named after Ben Hill Griffin Jr., an avid Gator supporter who had contributed to various sectors throughout the University of Florida. Modern renovations were made to the stadium in 2003 and 2004, which included an expanded press box and luxury suites for the university president as well as Gator boosters.

Despite its sheer size and numerous renovations, the legend of the Ben Hill Griffin stadium did not grow until the 1990s when former Heisman-winning quarterback Steve Spurrier took over as head coach of the Florida Gators. Even with strong alumni support and a burgeoning list of resources, the University of Florida football program had long underachieved well into the late 1980s. Spurrier changed Florida football into the dominant program it is today, and much of that domination was attributed to the home field advantage the Gators enjoyed. In 1991, Spurrier coined the term "the Swamp" when describing this home advantage: "A swamp is where Gators live. We feel comfortable there, but we hope our opponents feel tentative. A swamp is hot and sticky and can be dangerous. Only gators get out alive."

Big Crowd

The Swamp was home to the largest crowd in the history of Florida with the November 2009 contest versus the Gators' rivals Florida State Seminoles producing a record of 90,907 in attendance.

Florida Field is a swamp indeed. Due to the numerous additions, Florida Field is enclosed on all sides, and the walls are built steep, placing fans just a few feet away from the teams' benches. Its architecture also creates a humid, intimidating, noisy atmosphere that is known to rattle opposing teams. Thousands of fans yell and do the "Gator chomp" in unison, adding to the intimidation factor. Through 2010, the Swamp has sold out 137 consecutive games and boasts the nation's best record of 117–16 from Spurrier's arrival in 1990 through 2010. The Swamp consistently ranks in the top 10 in college football for average attendance and is considered by many experts to be one of the toughest stadiums to play in college football.

Christopher Busey

Suggested Resources

Ben Hill Griffin Stadium. http://www.gatorzone.com/facilities/?venue=swamp&sport=footb. Accessed November 25, 2011.

Carlson, Norm. *University of Florida Football Vault.* Florence, AL: Whitman, 2007.

Dooley, Pat. *Game of My life: Memorable Stories of Gator Football.* Champaign, IL: Sports Publishing, 2007.

Florida Gators Football. http://www.coachwillmuschamp.com/pages/swamp. Accessed November 25, 2011.

Parkhurst, Jason. *Into the Swamp: Four Years of Photographs inside the Florida Gators Football Program.* Self-published, 2010.

Swoopes, Sheryl (1971–)

Sheryl Swoopes is affectionately known as the "female [Michael] Jordan" in light of her ability to single-handedly change the course of a basketball game and the Nike Air Swoopes basketball shoes that were created and sold in her honor. As a U.S. female basketball player who competed at the collegiate level in the early 1990s, Swoopes's sustained involvement in the sport reveals much about U.S. female athletes'

Houston Comets forward Sheryl Swoopes (22) drives down court under pressure from Minnesota Lynx's Tonya Edwards (13), July 6, 1999. (AP Photo/Pat Sullivan.)

increased access to opportunities and the professionalization of women's basketball.

She was born in Brownfield, Texas, in 1971 and after a storied high school career, Swoopes moved to Austin, Texas, to play for the University of Texas (UT). However, after only a few days at the university, Swoopes realized her heart was still in Brownfield and decided to drop out of UT and return home. While some felt this was a dangerous career move, Swoopes rebounded and enrolled at a local junior college, South Plains College (SPC). She played two years at SPC (1989–1991) and still holds a number of individual scoring records.

After completing two years at SPC, Swoopes transferred to Texas Tech University to utilize the remaining two years of her NCAA eligibility. At Texas Tech, Swoopes made an immediate impact and led her team to the 1993 NCAA Final Four during her senior season. In the nationally televised championship game and in front of a sellout crowd in Atlanta, Swoopes scored a remarkable 47 points to lead her

team to an 84–82 victory over Ohio State. This victory earned Texas Tech its first NCAA Division I championship. Her 47 points in the championship game remains an NCAA record, and her Texas Tech jersey (number 22) was retired in 1994. Further, her performance in that game reflected her season-long performance and earned her a variety of awards, including the 1993 Women's Basketball Coaches Association (WBCA) Player of the Year, the Naismith College Player of the Year, and a place on the Division I All-American team.

Since the majority of women's basketball games were not televised at this time, Swoopes's performance in a nationally televised game provided her with a vehicle through which she could become the face of U.S. women's basketball. However, after completing her eligibility at Texas Tech, Swoopes was in a difficult situation: She was a talented and marketable basketball player with no U.S.-based league to support her endeavors. So, like many other talented female athletes before her, Swoopes opted to play professionally outside of the United States and signed with a club team (Bari) in Italy. However, similar to her initial foray into university life, Swoopes found that basketball and life outside the United States did not suit her, so she returned to the United States as an athlete without a U.S. league of her own. Discouraged but not defeated, she continued to play in pickup games, coached intermittently, and then represented the United States formally in 1994 at both the Goodwill Games and FIBA World Championships.

Shortly thereafter, Swoopes's luck began to change. With a U.S.-based Olympics on the horizon (the 1996 Atlanta Summer Games), Swoopes was offered a chance to try out, and she subsequently earned a spot on the U.S. women's national team. On this team, Swoopes joined forces with veterans Teresa Edwards and Ruth Bolton to lead the team to a 5–0 record and a gold medal in the Games. Even more, the 1996 Games—frequently dubbed the "Year of U.S. Women in Sport" in light of the accomplishments of U.S. female athletes during these particular Olympic Games—helped to create a welcoming climate for not one, but two U.S. professional women's basketball leagues to emerge: the American Basketball League

(ABL) and the Women's National Basketball Association (WNBA). The ABL began in 1996, and the league signed a number of players who represented the United States on the 1996 gold medal team. Swoopes, however, was not one of them as she opted to sign with the WNBA in January 1997. She began her professional career in the United States as a member of the Houston Comets, and though she started the season late due to the birth of her first child, Swoopes combined with teammates Cynthia Cooper and Tina Thompson to lead the team to the championship during the inaugural season of the WNBA. Swoopes would remain a member of the Houston Comets for the next 11 years, and she spent her final year in the WNBA as a member of the Seattle Storm. During her 12 years in the league, she helped lead Houston to four titles (1997, 1998, 1999, and 2000) and would amass a number of individual awards. She was named the MVP of the WNBA three times (2000, 2002, and 2005) and was also named the league's Defensive Player of the Year three times as well (2000, 2002, and 2003). Swoopes's consistent contribution to the league as both a player and a key public figure were recognized when she was named to the WNBA's All-Decade Team in 2006.

During her stint with the Comets, Swoopes also represented the United States as a veteran member of the women's national teams. To her list of WNBA accomplishments, she added gold medals at the 2000 and 2004 Olympic Games and a bronze medal at the 2006 FIBA World Championships. And, like many of her WNBA counterparts, Swoopes took advantage of opportunities to play in Europe to hone her skills in the WNBA's off-season. She played for clubs in Russia in 2004–2005 and in Italy in 2005–2006.

Around this same time (October 2005) Swoopes garnered significant media attention in light of her decision to publicly come out as a gay athlete. Her coming out article in *ESPN: The Magazine* marked one of the few instances when a high-profile gay or lesbian athlete decided to publicly discuss his or her sexuality, and therefore proves to be an important moment for the history of gay and lesbian athletes in U.S. sport. Her status as one of the only African American female athletes to publicly discuss her gay identity put her in the spotlight. So, too, did her endorsement by Olivia

---

Professional Basketball Leagues for Women: The ABL and the WNBA

The American Basketball League (ABL) and the Women's National Basketball Association (WNBA) were not the first U.S. professional leagues for women, but they did appear at a pivotal moment for U.S. female basketball players. The U.S. women's basketball team won the gold medal at the 1996 Olympics on its home soil (Atlanta) and had a cadre of experienced and media-savvy players eager to display their talents in their home country. However, members of the 1996 team were soon faced with a difficult choice as the two leagues competed for their allegiances.

In the end, it seemed inevitable that only one league would survive, especially with the dispersal of talent and personalities into two distinct leagues. The ABL lasted only 2½ seasons; it suspended operations and filed for bankruptcy in December 1998. The WNBA, on the other hand, is still in existence and began its 16th season in the summer of 2012.

The ABL was an independent league with teams based in cities known for supporting women's basketball: Atlanta, Chicago, Columbus (Ohio), Hartford (Connecticut), Long Beach, Nashville, Portland (Oregon), Richmond (Virginia), San Jose (California), and Seattle. The ABL played their season during the winter months and offered higher salaries than the WNBA offered. The WNBA, however, had the backing and support of the NBA. Though they offered lower salaries, their players would compete during a shorter season and would perform in the summer months. In this way, they would not compete directly with NBA or NCAA basketball games, and players could still play for teams outside the United States during the winter months. In fact, many current WNBA players do this not only to stay in top form but to supplement the salaries paid by the WNBA.

Cruises and Resorts (a lesbian travel company), which occurred in concert with her coming out announcement. Swoopes's declaration garnered considerable media attention both within and outside of the sporting realm, and news of her announcement appeared in media outlets such as *The Nation*, *People Magazine*, *Newsweek*, and *The Advocate*.

Megan Chawansky

See also Jordan, Michael; 1996 Olympic Games, Atlanta; Women's National Basketball Association

Suggested Resources

Corbett, S. *Venus to the Hoop: A Gold Medal Year in Women's Basketball.* New York: Doubleday, 1997.

Grundy, P., and S. Shackleford. *Shattering the Glass: The Remarkable History of Women's Basketball.* New York: New Press, 2005.

Porter, K. *Mad Seasons: The Story of the First Women's Professional Basketball League, 1978–1981.* Lincoln: University of Nebraska Press, 2006.

"Sheryl Swoopes." Women's Basketball Hall of Fame. http://www.wbhof.com/about.html. Accessed March 20, 2011.

Terzieff, J. *Women of the Court: Inside the WNBA.* New York: Alyson, 2008.

WNBA Website. www.wnba.com. Accessed March 20, 2011.

T

Tailgating

Tailgating is an almost exclusively American activity, when fans gather together before games, and sometimes after, to drink, grill food, play games, and socialize. Tailgate parties generally occur in parking lots outside stadiums, with the name "tailgating" coming from serving from the open trunks of vehicles. Tailgating is primarily associated with college football, although it occurs at many NFL stadiums as well and has expanded into other sports and special events.

Tailgating has roots dating back as long as football itself. Exactly when and where it began is difficult to determine accurately, but alumni and supporters of a number of Ivy League football teams in the 1870s used to bring picnic lunches with them to consume before and at the game. This fits into middle- and upper-class traditions at the time of garden parties and picnics at special events. For example, there is evidence to suggest that a group of spectators brought a picnic lunch and watched the Battle of Bull Run from a hillside in 1861. Some writers also suggest that chuck wagons of the West served as an inspiration for later developments.

The term "tailgating" came into use in the 1960s and early 1970s, when station wagons became popular family vehicles. The tailgate could be opened and used as a serving platform. Tailgating really took off as a widespread activity at football games in this time frame, at the same time that college football grew in popularity.

Tailgate parties occur at every home game of many colleges and universities throughout the football season, involving hundreds, even thousands of fans. While some tailgaters (up to 30 percent) do not attend games and come just for the party, the majority are among the most loyal of fans, attending every home game and often a few away games every year. Research on tailgaters suggest that many have been involved in the activity for years, tailgating every week and structuring their social lives for that part of the year around the activity. The average tailgaters are male, college-educated, in their mid-30s to 40s, and reasonably well-off financially. Alumni naturally make up a fair proportion of tailgaters at different institutions, but people from the wider community are also heavily involved.

Food and drink are a central focus of tailgate parties, with massive consumption of calories a regular occurrence. Typical tailgating foods include things that can be easily grilled, such as hot dogs, bratwurst, hamburgers, and chicken, with all kinds of chilies, salads, and fried foods to accompany them. Former chef Joe Cahn, the self-professed "commissioner of tailgating" who has traveled around the country to attend hundreds of tailgates, notes that there is regional variety in tailgating foods with local specialties taking an important place. In Texas, for instance, one is likely to find varieties of beef brisket, while chowder and lobster are not unusual in New England. Most tailgaters show up several hours before kickoff or even the night before, so the day moves through breakfast foods to heartier fare, often with copious quantities of alcoholic beverages.

Because of concerns over drinking, fan behavior, and associated liabilities, several colleges and NFL teams have put restrictions on tailgating activities or even banned them outright. The most famous ban occurred in 2007, when the NFL banned tailgating activities for a one-mile radius around Dolphin Stadium

Tom Paoletta, left, and his brother David Paoletta cook food outside Ralph Wilson Stadium while tailgating before an NFL football game between the Buffalo Bills and the Tennessee Titans on Sunday, October 21, 2012, in Orchard Park, New York. (AP Photo/Bill Wippert.)

on Super Bowl Sunday. The league cited "security reasons," but many journalists and fans argued that it was an attempt to increase ticket sales at corporate-sponsored events. Drinking by underaged students is a particular worry for a number of colleges. While there is no denying the amount of alcohol consumed at tailgating events, tailgate parties are usually community events involving a diverse group of people, including families with children, and drinking is only one part of the experience for most participants.

When asked, regular tailgaters give a variety of reasons for their activities. Food and drink, of course, rank highly on the list. Fun and sociability also come up quite high in research conducted on tailgating

motivations. Most tailgaters bring sports equipment like Frisbees and footballs, and they set up lawn games to play over the day. Many fans indicate that they see tailgating as a necessary part of game day and the game atmosphere, with attendance at a game implying attendance at the tailgate before and after.

Tailgating is frequently a family affair, with generations of extended families getting together at tailgate parties. Regular tailgaters develop a strong sense of community with each other. Socializing by visiting the sites of other tailgaters is considered an important part of the activity, and with many participants returning for every home game, year after year, long-term acquaintances develop. Many tailgaters even occupy the same parking spot regularly, so that if one is new or visiting at an away game, it is an informal norm to ask if a spot is customarily occupied before taking it.

Tailgating also enables the creation of strong ties to the local college and team. Identification and display of being a fan of a particular club or institution becomes important in terms of self-identity and recognition from other fans. This necessitates wearing team clothing and finding creative ways to display team logos and colors on the tailgating site. Some college sports marketers have been picking up on this recently, with suggestions that colleges should find ways to encourage more tailgating and get more people involved, to tap into and build on this loyal fan base.

At the most basic level, tailgating only requires a vehicle, some food and drink, and a means of serving. However, regular tailgating often requires significant planning, organization, and financial investment. Beyond planning menus and cooking techniques, requiring grills, coolers, and all associated equipment, most regular tailgaters set up tents, flags, lawn chairs, and other types of furniture. Some bring stereos and speakers, and televisions to watch pre- and postgame shows, requiring generators for power. The most elaborate set-ups turn the parking lot into miniature living rooms, bars, or dance clubs, complete with tables, carpets, or dance floors. Some fans purchase RVs specifically for tailgating, or convert vans or buses into the tailgating vehicles, replete with team colors and all kinds of gadgetry. Some tailgaters take it seriously enough to practice packing their vehicles at the beginning of the season to ensure they can get in all they want to bring.

Most dedicated tailgaters would argue that their parties are the best. Meanwhile, the tailgating atmosphere at some places has become legendary. At the University of Mississippi, the tailgate occurs in "the Grove," a shaded, treed quad at the front of the campus. Because of the area, rules have been established that prohibit cars, fires, and generators, but fans set up elaborate rows of tents and shelters, and it is traditional to dress as if heading out for the evening. Louisiana State fans turn the area outside of what they call "Death Valley Stadium" into a carnival of Cajun cooking, big-screen televisions, and monster speakers. In Jacksonville, the annual Florida-Georgia game draws fans from both universities into a tailgate party that goes from Wednesday before the game to the Sunday after. It used to be known as the "World's Largest Outdoor Cocktail Party" until the connotations of drinking became frowned upon in recent years.

Tailgating has become big business, with a number of companies producing and marketing equipment specifically for tailgating, such as grills that attach to the back of a pickup truck like a bike rack. Beer companies and several corporations that produce foods frequently consumed at tailgate parties have included tailgating in advertising and marketing campaigns, sponsored special events at the tailgate for important games, and designed vehicles to travel the country with the purpose of appearing at tailgate parties. Industry research estimates that some 30 million Americans tailgate at least once for some sport in a year, and that the average football tailgater spends over $500 per year on the activity, so the commercial focus is understandable.

Tailgating has become so associated with football that since the early 1990s, many media outlets have broadcast their pregame shows for important contests from the tailgate party, or set up their stage to have a tailgate theme. Iconic broadcaster John Madden was known to frequently bring cameras into the tailgate area and even wrote a book about tailgating in 1998. There are magazines such as *Tailgater Monthly* devoted to tailgating and numerous websites that offer tailgating tips, recipes, and product reviews.

While associated primarily with football, tailgating has expanded in the last two decades into other sports and events. Fans regularly tailgate at college baseball games, although in much smaller numbers than for football. Tailgating at NASCAR races has become extremely popular, rivaling football in recent years in terms of size and spectacle. Given that many NASCAR fans travel to races and stay over the weekend, tailgating-type activities are a natural fit. Tailgating has also begun to appear at concerts and festivals, with fans of singer Jimmy Buffett being known for good tailgate parties. Tailgating has also trickled down to local, community-level sports, where families of teams set up tailgates as a means of support and feeding the athletes, and as a fundraising activity through selling food and drink.

Fred Mason

See also Death Valley, LSU Football; Madden, John; NASCAR

Suggested Resources

Drozda, Joe. *The Tailgater's Handbook.* Indianapolis: Masters Press, 1996.

Linn, Stephen. *The Ultimate Tailgater's Handbook.* Nashville: Rutledge Hill Press, 2005.

Madden, John, with Peter Kaminsky. *John Madden's Ultimate Tailgating.* New York: Viking, 1998.

Tailgating.com Website. www.tailgating.com. Accessed May 16, 2012.

"25 Facts You Never Knew About Tailgating." November 30, 2011. http://www.onlinecolleges.net/2011/11/30/25-facts-you-never-knew-about-tailgating/. Accessed May 16, 2012.

Take Me Out (2002)

Take Me Out is a play written by Richard Greenberg about an openly homosexual player on a Major League Baseball team. Along with the Richard Adler/Jerry Ross musical comedy *Damn Yankees* (1955) and the August Wilson play *Fences* (1985), it is one of the few successful works in the American theater about America's national pastime.

In the first of the play's three acts, Darren Lemming (Daniel Sunjata), the son of a white father and black mother and a superstar player on the defending world champion New York Empires baseball team, publicly announces he is gay. He is shown to have arrived at this decision shortly after chatting with his best friend Davey Battle (Kevin Carroll), a star player on a rival ball club, who encourages Lemming to let his "whole self [be] known" to the world. At first, there is little tension; his best friend on the Empires, Kippy Sunderstrom (Neal Huff), appears supportive. His new financial advisor, Mason Morzac (Denis O'Hare), also homosexual, congratulates him for coming out. The Empires then embark on a long losing streak, which only ends upon the arrival of a shy minor league pitcher named Shane Mungitt (Frederick Weller). The shy Mungitt eventually tells his teammates of his southern childhood, raised by relatives after his parents die in a murder-suicide. As the first act closes reporters ask Mungitt how he likes the major leagues. Mungitt innocently replies, "I don't mind the colored people—the gooks an' the spics an' the coons an' like that. But every night t'have'ta take a shower with a faggot? Do you know what I'm sayin'?"

In the second act, Mungitt is suspended for his remarks, but is quickly reinstated after he issues a contrite public apology. Lemming responds to Mungitt's return by considering retiring from baseball himself in the middle of his career, but is discouraged by Mason, who to his surprise has developed a fascination both with baseball and with Darren. Shane quietly returns before a ball game with Davey Battle's team. Sensing that Shane is a closeted homosexual, Darren propositions Shane in the Empires' locker room shower. Shane, enraged by the suggestion, comes in to relieve the following game, and fatally beans Davey Battle.

The third act begins after Davey's funeral. It is reported that Shane had been overheard making threats before the previous ball game. There is a flashback scene between Darren and Davey after Darren's coming out; Davey, a wholesome family man with a wife and three kids, is repulsed by Darren's homosexuality: "You will welter in profanity and vulgarity and every kind of ugliness." Shane is detained by the police for questioning. Darren and Kippy visit Shane in jail. Shane naively talks about returning to the Empires to help them in the pennant drive. When told that he's been permanently expelled from Major League Baseball, Shane screams about Darren's proposition and insists that Darren had wished for Davey to die: "He's the one who wisht it! He gave the order, I just executed." Shane also declares that Kippy actually wrote Shane's public apology. Shane is not charged in Davey's death, but winds up imprisoned after a string of vandalisms in the South. The denouement of the play occurs after the Empires win the World Series again. Darren and Kippy congratulate each other, though their friendship is obviously strained. A drunken Mason shows up in the clubhouse and Darren invites him to the team victory party. Thinking back on the traumatic past season, Mason plaintively asks in the play's closing line, "What will we do till spring?"

Several characters and situations in the play had precedents in baseball history. Darin's mixed-race background and tabloid celebrity as a New York baseball superstar at the turn of the 21st century was strongly reminiscent of New York Yankees shortstop Derek

Jeter. Shane Mungitt's character seemed loosely based upon Atlanta Braves reliever John Rocker, whose slurs against gays, foreigners, and the conduct of New York Mets fans in a 2000 *Sports Illustrated* story earned him a brief suspension from Major League Baseball. And Mungitt's fatal beaning of Davey Battle called to mind the only fatal on-field incident in major league history, when New York Yankee pitcher Carl Mays killed Cleveland Indian shortstop Ray Chapman with a pitch in August 1920 (Mays, unlike Mungitt, held no animosity toward the batter; unlike Mungitt, he was not thrown out of baseball and remained in the majors for another nine seasons).

Take Me Out originally opened at the off-Broadway Public Theater in September 2002 to mixed reviews from the critics. In February 2003 it opened on Broadway at the Walter Kerr Theatre. Ben Brantley of the *New York Times* declared of the off-Broadway production, "[A]t its best—which is when it's wallowing in ecstatic contemplation of data found on the back of bubble gum trading cards—'Take Me Out' is a happy, manically animated sheaf of a newborn fan's notes." However, he concluded that "what emerges is less three-dimensional characters than constructs who say just what has to be said to further the play's intellectual debates." Critics hailed Greenberg's philosophical dialogue, in particular Mason's digression about what he loves most about baseball: "[B]aseball is better than democracy—or at least than democracy as it's practiced in this country—because unlike democracy, baseball acknowledges loss. While conservatives will tell you, leave things alone and no one will lose, and liberals will tell you, interfere a lot and nobody will lose, baseball says: Someone will lose. Not only *says* it—insists upon it! So that baseball achieves the tragic vision that democracy evades. Evades and embodies."

The play's set design drew much attention, as it included a functioning shower, which actors used during the performance while completely naked. *Take Me Out* received the Tony Award as the best Broadway play of 2003 and closed on January 4, 2004, after a successful run of 355 performances.

Andrew Milner

See also *Damn Yankees*; *Fences*; Jeter, Derek; *Sports Illustrated*

Baseball and Homosexuality in Popular Culture

As of 2011, only two men who played Major League Baseball—Glenn Burke (1952–1995) and Billy Bean (1964–)—and former major league umpire David Pallone have ever acknowledged being homosexual. The subject has appeared in fictional works beyond *Take Me Out*. Peter Lefcourt's 1993 novel, *The Dreyfus Affair*, focused on the homosexual relationship of a double-play combination on a major league club. Bernie Bookbinder's *Out at the Old Ball Game* (1995) is about a major league team comprised entirely of homosexuals, and Chad Harbach's acclaimed debut novel, *The Art of Fielding* (2011), featured an openly gay player on a championship Division III baseball team at a fictional midwestern college. And a 1983 episode of the sitcom classic *Cheers*, titled "The Boys in the Bar," featured a former teammate of Sam Malone's announcing he's gay.

Suggested Resources
Greenberg, Richard. *Take Me Out*. New York: Dramatists Play Service, 2004.
Take Me Out. IMDb. http://ibdb.com/production.php?id=13460. Accessed October 15, 2011.

"Take Me Out to the Ballgame" (1908)

There are three things that are widely known when anyone hears the word "baseball": the poem "Casey at the Bat," Abbot and Costello's "Who's on First," and the song "Take Me Out to the Ballgame," written by Jack Norworth. For most people, this song is considered baseball's anthem and is considered an American tradition. To keep with tradition, it is supposed to be sung during the seventh-inning stretch. People recognize the song and can sing the chorus with ease. Very few people know the first and second verses. Throughout the years, it is the chorus that helps to create a sense of magic that makes this song so invigorating. Before Jack Norworth penned this sensational song, there were numerous songs attempting to capture the passion and excitement of the game. The first baseball song that was published was "The Base Ball Polka" by J. R. Blodgett in 1858. "Slide, Kelly, Slide!" (1889) was the first recorded hit and the first pop hit record.

Dedicated to the new woman was the song "Who Would Doubt That I'm a Man" (1895). Despite the other songs that were dedicated to fans ("The Baseball Song," 1888), players ("They All Know Cobb," 1913), or teams ("Red Stocking Schottisch," 1869), it was not until 1908 that Jack Norworth (January 5, 1879–September 1, 1959) and Albert Von Tilzer (March 29, 1871–October 1, 1956) presented to the American public the song that is not only timeless, but truly identifies Americana.

The origin of the song begins with Norworth traveling on a New York subway. As he looked up to a sign advertising a ball game, "Baseball Today at the Polo Grounds," he wrote lyrics to "Take Me Out to the Ballgame," and in less than 15 minutes, he wrote the lyrics (32 lines) on a piece of scrap paper. The premise of the song involves a woman named Katie Casey, who was asked by her beau to go "see a show," but she responded that she wanted to go to a ball game instead. The original lyrics from 1908 were: "Katie Casey was base ball mad. Had the fever and had it bad; Just to root for the home town crew. Every sou Katie blew. On a Saturday, her young beau Called to see if she'd like to go, To see a show, but Miss Katie said, 'No, I'll tell you what you can do. Take me out to the ball game, Take me out with the crowd, Buy me some peanuts and Cracker Jack, I don't care if I never get back, Let me root, root, root for the home team, If they don't win it's a shame, For it's one, two, three strikes you're out, At the old ball game.'" To prove how much of a baseball fan she is, the second verse begins, "Katie Casey saw all the games, Knew the players by their first names, Told the umpire he was wrong, All along good and strong. When the score was just two to two, Katie Casey knew what to do, Just to cheer up the boys she knew, She made the gang sing this song" followed by the chorus.

What makes this song quite curious is that the song is told from a woman's point of view. Traditionally, baseball has always been considered a man's game, and now Norworth writes about a woman who wants to go to a game, and is knowledgeable about the game. Most men would scoff at the idea of a woman knowing anything that had to do with sports. The first time the song was performed in front of an audience was at the Brooklyn Grand Opera House in 1908 by Jack Norworth and his actress wife, Nora Bayes. They were able to perform a skit of Katie Casey and her beau with lantern slides that encouraged the audience to sing the chorus, following the lines of the song at the bottom of the screen accompanied by the house pianist. The reception of the song was positive and the song became a hit. However, some of the critics felt differently about the song. According to one article, some critics have described the lyrics as crude, but singable and do not understand why the song was a success. Despite the criticism the fans, on the other hand, embraced the song. It energized them, and eventually ended up being used in stadiums all over the country. The first and third verses were not easily remembered, so the focus remained on the chorus. One of the components that led to the song's popularity was the fact that people were able to purchase the sheet music and recordings of the song. In the meantime, Norworth and Tilzer decided to promote the song at various vaudeville shows, and they discovered that entertainers from all walks of life began including the song in their acts. The first time it was performed at a ballpark was not until the 1934 World Series by the St. Louis Cardinals band.

Jack Norworth had already captured the music world and the theater as an entertainer and composer. Before "Take Me Out to the Ballgame," he was known for "Shine On Harvest Moon." He ended up composing over 2,500 songs. After Norworth completed the lyrics, he asked Tilzer to add music to his lyrics and after an hour, the song was finally finished. It was Tilzer who added the finishing touches on the song with "The Sensational Base Ball Song." Tilzer collaborated on numerous songs with Norworth, for example, "Put Your Arms Around Me Honey" and "I'll Be With You in Apple Blossom Time." Tilzer also owned York Publishing Company. He moved to California in 1930. Both men were successful during this time, referred to as the Tin Pan Era. Despite the success of "Take Me Out to the Ballgame," neither one of them had attended a game until decades later. When someone asked Norworth why he wrote the song, he replied that he thought it was also time for a baseball song. He continued that once he had the idea for the song, he realized that the song was good. With all the success and accolades from the song, they never collaborated

Actor Vince Vaughn sings "Take Me Out to the Ballgame" during the seventh inning stretch of a baseball game between the Chicago Cubs and the Cincinnati Reds on May 29, 2006, at Wrigley Field in Chicago. (AP Photo/Jeff Roberson.)

on another song, which created a sense of mystery as to why.

Another mystery regarding the song is who is J. A. Sternad and why was the song dedicated to him? According to some historians, Sternad did exist and some identified him as a sportsman, a lover of theater, and a lover of baseball. He is referred to in 1907 in the *Tribune*, when he participated in a benefit. His name was also listed with the South Chicago Amusement Company. Strasberg explains that Sternad also participated in the sport of pedestrianism, which involves walking long distances at top speed. The last time he was mentioned was in the *Tribune* in 1911 as having the J. A. Sternad Vaudeville Agency. Unfortunately, no one really knows why the song was dedicated to him.

In 1927, Norworth made some revisions to the song. The name of Katie Casey was changed to Nelly

Kelly and Katie's beau is now Nelly's boyfriend. The beau of Katie wants to take her to a show, while Nelly's boyfriend wants to go to Coney Isle. Despite the changes, the excitement, the thrill of the game, and the chorus remains the same.

"Nelly Kelly loved baseball games, Knew the players, knew all their names, You could see her there ev'ry day, Shout 'Hooray,' when they'd play. Her boy friend by the name of Joe said, 'To Coney Isle, dear, let's go.' Then Nelly started to fret and pout, And to him I heard her shout." The second verse is "Nelly Kelly was sure some fan, She would root just like any man, Told the umpire he was wrong, All along, good and strong. When the score was just two to two, Nelly Kelly knew what to do, Just to cheer up the boys she knew, She made the gang sing this song." The song has proved its timeliness by updating its heroine to meet with the new freedoms for women in the 1920s.

In the 1930s, the Tin Pan Alley era ended and fans replaced sheet music with radios and records. Ballparks in 1931 played "The Star Spangled Banner" before major games. Strasberg notes that it was not until 1945 that the song was associated with the seventh-inning stretch. Stadiums hired organists to entertain the fans and the players. For some players, hearing one of their favorite songs enables the player more leverage.

Even with the changes, one thing is certain; there will always be a seventh-inning stretch. There are many ideas and legends about when it originated. One of the stories involved Joseph Brennan, Manhattan College's prefect of discipline in the 1880s. He managed games and noticed that by the seventh inning, some of the fans were uncomfortable in their seats and needed to stretch. This became a ritual at every game. President Taft stood up to stretch his legs. When the fans observed President Taft stand up, people thought he was leaving, so they stood up out of respect. There are other stories about the seventh-inning stretch. Most of the teams have their own songs, but one thing that is certain, when the seventh-inning stretch takes place, "Take Me Out to the Ballgame" is sung. It wasn't until 1971 that Harry Caray reintroduced the song to the fans at Chicago Cubs games. "ALL RIGHT, let me hear ya. Ah one, ah two, ah three . . . Take me out to the ball game, take me out with the crowd . . ." and for anyone who has heard him, he would always end the song with, "Let's get some runs!" In a *Time* article, "Take Me Out to the Ball Game," Frances Romero writes about the time when Bill Veeck decided to set Caray up. Romero writes that Veeck "outfitted Caray's booth with a secret microphone, and a tradition was born." When Harry Caray passed away in 1998, the tradition still lived on with singers conducting the crowd. One thing is certain; there will always be a seventh-inning stretch.

Even though the song was written in 1908, it still has survived the numerous attempts to write a "better" one. In 1986, the major leagues tried to introduce a new baseball song, "Baseball Is More than a Game." The hope was that people would find it more up-to-date and it would replace the "old one," and the leagues would receive royalties. It was a marketing strategy that failed. In the 1950s, the public began to be interested in memorabilia with the title of the song. The fans were finding movies, books, parodies, plays, and memorabilia based on the song. In 1989, the movie *Field of Dreams* emerged on the screen and baseball captivated fans once again. The movie was sentimental and brought about a return to innocence. In 1999, the Post Office released a stamp commemorating Roger Maris beating Babe Ruth's score.

On May 2, 1908, Jack Norworth and Albert Von Tilzer had the song copyrighted. Although the first version of the song was copyrighted, it is now in the public domain. The second version is under new copyright laws, which will be in place until 2022.

One of the interesting tales regarding the song is that neither Jack Norworth nor Albert Von Tilzer ever attended a ball game until decades later. On June 27, 1940, Major League Baseball presented Norworth with a gold lifetime pass. After both men relocated to California, Norworth remained active establishing a Little League Baseball team in Laguna. In the end, they knew they had a hit, but no one would ever realize that this would be the definitive song for the great American pastime. One baseball executive applauded Jack Norworth for his contribution to the American people and the baseball world. In a bequest from the estate of Jack Norworth, he wanted to set up a program with ASCAP that provides young composers with royalties from "Take Me Out to the Ballgame."

Baseball is America's quintessential pastime. Every spring, people get ready to celebrate Opening Day at the ballpark. The game is heightened by the ubiquitous song "Take Me Out to the Ballgame," which is recognized as one of the three most popular songs in America, with "Happy Birthday" and "The Star Spangled Banner" as the top songs in the 20th century. Journalist Walter Winchell indicated in 1951 that he felt the song represented innocence and delight in the midst of a despairing world.

Today, the song is played 365 days a year and still energizes the fans. But there is still one question left to ask: Why do we sing "Take Me Out to the Ballgame" when we're already there?

Karen E. Holleran

See also Caray, Harry; "Casey at the Bat"; Chicago Cubs; Ladies' Day; Presidents and Opening Day in Baeball; Veeck, Bill; "Who's on First?"; World Series

Suggested Resources

Baseball Almanac. http://www.baseball-almanac.com. Accessed November 1, 2011.

Katz, Harry. *Baseball Americana: Treasures from the Library of Congress.* New York: HarperCollins, 2009.

McGuiggan, Amy Whorf. *Take Me Out to the Ball Game: The Story of the Sensational Baseball Song.* Lincoln: University of Nebraska Press, 2009.

National Baseball Hall of Fame. http://baseballhall.org/. Accessed November 1, 2011.

Romero, Frances. "Take Me Out to the Ball Game." http://www.time.com. Accessed April 8, 2010.

Strasberg, Andy, Bob Thompson, and Tim Wiles. *Baseball's Greatest Hit: The Story of Take Me Out to the Ballgame.* New York: Hal Leonard, 2008.

Ward, Geoffrey C., and Ken Burns. *Baseball: An Illustrated History.* New York: Alfred A. Knopf, 2005.

"Talkin' Baseball" (1981)

"Talkin' Baseball" was a song recorded by Terry Cashman in 1981, which has remained popular because of its lyrics, recalling the golden age of baseball in New York in the 1950s.

Terry Cashman (born Dennis Minogue) was born in New York in 1941 and was talented enough as a pitcher to be signed to a minor league contract by the Detroit Tigers in 1960, right out of high school. He played in low-level minor league teams in the South before recognizing that his talents would not take him to the major leagues.

After his brief time in professional baseball, Minogue went into the music business, first as a promoter, then as a songwriter and singer. His first big hit was in 1967 and was recorded by Spanky and Our Gang. "Sunday Will Never Be the Same" reached number nine in *Billboard* listings in the summer of 1967. Meanwhile, Minogue, now using the stage name of Cashman, was singing and recording as part of Cashman, Pistilli and West. The group had modest success through the 1970s.

In 1981, Cashman wrote "Talkin' Baseball," a paean to 1950s baseball in New York, when there were three major league teams and they had three of the best players in baseball, each of whom played center field—Mickey Mantle of the New York Yankees, Willie Mays of the New York Giants, and Edwin

"Duke" Snider of the Brooklyn Dodgers. The song was released when many fans of Major League Baseball were disheartened by the baseball strike that went from June 12 to July 31 of 1981. Waxing nostalgic for better times, fans made the song an enormous hit.

Cashman made a number of versions for various teams, including the Detroit Tigers, Minnesota Twins, New York Yankees, St. Louis Cardinals, New York Mets, Boston Red Sox, and California Angels. The lyrics in each of these highlight the greats and mention highlights of each of the teams in question. Still, the fame of the song comes from the initial famous refrain, "Willie, Mickey and the Duke."

In 2011, the Baseball Hall of Fame in Cooperstown, New York, honored Cashman and his song at the Hall of Fame induction ceremonies in July when Roberto Alomar, Bert Blyleven, and Pat Gillick were inducted into the Hall. The original sheet music for the song is part of the collection in Cooperstown.

The seven verses refer to a number of baseball events and people of the 1950s and, later, the 1980s. In verse one the "Whiz kids" refers to the 1950 Phillies who won the pennant in a playoff with the Brooklyn Dodgers. The Phillies had not won a pennant since 1915 and would not do so again until 1980. The Whiz kids were led by Richie Ashburn, Del Ennis, Grady Hamner, Stan Lopata, Robin Roberts, Curt Simmons, and Jim Konstanty. Later in the verse is a reference to Bobby Thomson having "done it," which refers to his home run in the 1951 playoff that gave the pennant to the New York Giants.

"Yogi read the comics" refers to Yogi Berra's penchant for "light reading," while the "national pastime went on trial" refers to attempts to break the monopoly that baseball had on player contracts by using antitrust legislation.

The next verse refers to Kluzewski (Ted, a power-hitting first baseman for the Cincinnati Reds), Campanella (Roy, a Hall of Fame catcher for the Brooklyn Dodgers), The Man (Stan Musial, Hall of Fame outfielder and first baseman for the St. Louis Cardinals), Bobby Feller (finishing a Hall of Fame pitching career for the Cleveland Indians that went from 1936 to 1956), the Scooter (Phil Rizzuto, Hall of Fame shortstop for the Yankees who had a long career as their television and radio announcer), the Barber (Sal Maglie, who shaved

Terry Cashman performs "Talkin' Baseball" during an awards ceremony at Doubleday Field in Cooperstown, New York, on July 23, 2011. (AP Photo/Mike Groll.)

the corners of the plate as a pitcher), and the Newk (Don Newcombe, Dodger pitcher who won the Cy Young Award in 1956). "Ike" was President Eisenhower, "the only one winning down in Washington" as the Senators were at the bottom of the American League, while Eisenhower won elections in 1952 and 1956.

Verse three says, "Casey was winning, Hank Aaron was beginning," referring to Casey Stengel, manager of the Yankees who led them to pennants from 1949 to 1953, then from 1955 to 1958, and finally in 1960. Aaron began with the Milwaukee Braves in 1954. The two Robbies then referred to were Jackie Robinson, the first African American in modern Major League Baseball, who retired after the 1956 season, and Frank Robinson, the Hall of Famer

who debuted with the Cincinnati Reds in that same year. Kiner refers to Ralph Kiner, Pittsburgh Pirate Hall of Famer, who led the league in home runs for seven straight years; and Midget Gaedel is Eddie Gaedel, a 3'6" player who batted once for Bill Veeck's St. Louis Browns in 1951. The Thumper was Boston Red Sox great Ted Williams, also better known as the "Splendid Splinter." Mel Parnell was a great lefty pitcher on that same team.

The next verse repeats players, but the following verse has two childhood friend references of Cashman's, Cookie and the Bachelor, the latter trying to imitate the Oklahoma Kid, another nickname for Mickey Mantle, also known as the "Commerce Comet." There are additional references to Mays and Snider.

The Simpsons Are Talkin' Baseball

Cashman wrote and sang a version of his song especially for a 1992 episode of *The Simpsons* entitled "Homer at the Bat." Internal references were to Mr. Burns, the power plant, and Homer Simpson.

The last two verses have players from the 1980s—Pete Rose (Reds, Phillies), George Brett (Kansas City Royals), Bobby Bonds (Giants, Angels, and father of Barry), Rusty Staub (Mets, Astros), Reggie Jackson (A's, Angels, and Yankees), Dan Quisenberry (Kansas City Royals), Rod Carew (Twins and Angels), Gaylord Perry (many teams in his Hall of Fame career), Tom Seaver (Mets, Reds, White Sox), Steve Garvey (Dodgers and San Diego Padres), Mike Schmidt (Phillies), and Vida Blue (A's and Giants). The last reference to the great Alexander refers to Grover Cleveland Alexander, a Hall of Fame pitcher for the Cardinals and Cubs in the 1920s and 1930s, who was portrayed by Ronald Reagan, elected president in 1980, in the 1952 film *The Winning Team*. The song is still played regularly at ballparks throughout the country.

Murry R. Nelson

See also Aaron, Hank; Baseball Hall of Fame; Berra, Yogi; Brooklyn Dodgers; Feller, Bob; Mantle, Mickey; Mays, Willie; Musial, Stan "The Man"; Stengel, Casey; New York Mets; New York Yankees; Robinson, Jackie; Rose, Pete; Seaver, Tom; St. Louis Cardinals; Veeck, Bill

Suggested Resources
"Hall of Fame to Honor Terry Cashman." ESPN.com. March 18, 2011. http://sports.espn.go.com/mlb/news/story?id=6232352. Accessed June 15, 2011.

"Talkin' Baseball." Baseball Almanac. http://www.baseball-almanac.com/poetry/po_stb.shtml. Accessed June 15, 2011.

Terry Cashman Biography. http://www.americanoriginalscds.com/terrycashmansbio.htm. Accessed June 15, 2011.

Taurasi, Diana (1982–)

Diana Taurasi was one of the most successful women's basketball players in the history of the sport. Considered by many to be the best women's collegiate player of all time, she led the University of Connecticut to three consecutive national titles between 2002 and 2004. As a member of the U.S. Women's National Basketball team, she won gold medals at the 2004 and 2008 Summer Olympic Games. In 2005 she joined the Phoenix Mercury of the Women's National Basketball Association (WNBA) as the number one overall draft pick. Taurasi earned many WNBA honors, including Rookie of the Year, multiple First-Team All-WNBA recognitions, and multiple league and finals MVP awards. During her storied college career she was a recipient of All-America First-Team honors, the Wade Trophy for the best player in women's college basketball, and the Naismith College Player of the Year Award. In 2009, *Sports Illustrated* magazine named her the College Player of the Decade in recognition of her complete dominance of the sport.

Diana Taurasi was born in 1982 and raised in Chino, California, the daughter of immigrant parents Mario and Liliano Taurasi. Her father, Mario, played professional soccer in Argentina before emigrating to the United States, and for a time Taurasi considered following in her father's footsteps. By middle school, however, she had decided to focus permanently on basketball. Taurasi's older sister, Jessika, served as her opponent in one-on-one competitions on the family's front porch. The late-night practice sessions paid off: By the time she stepped onto a varsity basketball court as a freshman at Don Antonio Lugo High School, Taurasi was already an extraordinary player. She was named MVP of her high school athletic league her freshman year, and by the end of her senior year she had amassed 3,047 career points and earned every conceivable award for a high school athlete. In 2000 she received the Cheryl Miller Award, given by the *Los Angeles Times* to the best girls' basketball player in Southern California. *Parade* magazine named her the National High School Player of the Year, and she also received the coveted Naismith Trophy for the Girl's High School Player of the Year. Chosen to play in the Women's Basketball Coaches Association (WBCA) High School All-America Game, Taurasi wowed spectators with her performance, for which she was named the game's MVP.

Arguably the most heavily recruited player in women's collegiate basketball history, in 2000 Taurasi

Diana Taurasi of the USA cuts between China's Hu Xiao-tao, left, and Miaop Lijie at the Helliniko Indoor Arena in Athens during the 2004 Olympic Games, August 22, 2004. (AP Photo/Michael Conroy.)

decided to play for the University of Connecticut Huskies under head coach Geno Auriemma. Despite being surrounded by numerous All-Americans on a squad that had just clinched a National Collegiate Athletic Association (NCAA) championship the previous year, Taurasi made an instant impact playing for the Big East Conference powerhouse. As a power and shooting forward, the 6'0", 160-pound Taurasi helped her team achieve unprecedented success over the course of her university career. During her sophomore season the Huskies went undefeated and clinched the NCAA championship against the University of Oklahoma. Taurasi was named to the Kodak/State Farm All-America Team that year, the first of three such honors. Taurasi's junior year saw UConn extend their winning streak to an NCAA record-breaking 70-straight games and recapture their national title in a matchup against their rival, the University of Tennessee Lady Volunteers. Taurasi capped off her phenomenal season by earning the Most Outstanding Player of the

NCAA Final Four prize. She was also awarded the Naismith National Player of the Year trophy and named the Player of the Year by the Associated Press and the United States Basketball Writers Association (USBWA). In addition, she took home the Wade Trophy and NCAA Honda Award, both of which are given to the nation's top women's college basketball player. Following that season the national profile of both UConn women's basketball and Diana Taurasi soared, and the team traveled to the White House to meet President George W. Bush. Taurasi personally graced the cover of *Sports Illustrated* magazine twice that year: An April 2003 issue showed her dribbling down the court in the NCAA finals, while a November issue featured her alongside UConn men's standout center Emeka Okafor.

During her final season with the Huskies, Taurasi led her team to its 69th consecutive home court victory, tying the NCAA record. These stellar performances at home helped lift the Huskies to a third consecutive NCAA championship over the University of Tennessee, making UConn only the second college squad in NCAA history to achieve this feat. Taurasi was again named the NCAA Tournament's Most Outstanding Player, and she gained national accolades when she received the Naismith and Honda awards for the second year running. Taurasi was further honored with the Nancy Lieberman Award from the Rotary Club of Detroit, given annually to the best point guard in Women's Division I basketball. Over the course of her four years at the University of Connecticut, Taurasi averaged 15 points per game while leading her team to an impressive 139–8 record. By the time she left UConn, Taurasi had become a national star, as evidenced by her 2003 and 2004 ESPY awards. To punctuate her total dominance of the sport, in 2009 *Sports Illustrated* named her its Player of the Decade in recognition of her distinguished college career.

After graduating in 2004, Taurasi joined the U.S. Women's National Basketball team to train for the upcoming Summer Olympics. At the XXVIII Olympiad in Athens, Greece, Taurasi helped lead the U.S. team to a gold medal over Australia, despite being the youngest member on the squad. Two years later Taurasi's scoring and playmaking ability propelled the U.S. team to a bronze medal at the 2006 International Basketball Federation (FIBA) World Championships in Brazil. Although this finish disappointed the women's team, Taurasi and her teammates fought back two years later to reclaim their gold medal at the 2008 Summer Olympics in Beijing, China. Already a two-time Olympian, Taurasi looked forward to a third Olympiad when she was chosen to represent the United States at the 2012 Summer Olympics in London. Her latest venture into international competition reunited Taurasi with her UConn head coach, Geno Auriemma, who was selected in 2009 to pilot the U.S. Women's National team.

Taurasi built upon her college and international experience by signing with the Phoenix Mercury of the WNBA as the number one overall draft pick in 2005. She immediately made an impact by capturing WNBA Rookie of the Year honors and earning a trip to the WNBA All-Star Game. During her next six seasons with the Mercury, Taurasi dominated the WNBA. She won the WNBA's Peak Performer Award for scoring five times, collecting the league records for most points scored in a season (741) and most points scored in a game (47) along the way. In 2007 Taurasi led the Mercury to their first WNBA playoff championship, a feat she repeated in 2009. That year she was also named the MVP of the WNBA Finals. With her 2009 WNBA title, she became one of only two WNBA players to win a scoring title, league championship, season MVP honors, and the MVP finals award in the same season. She was voted one of the top 15 WNBA players of all time by players, coaches, writers, and fans in 2011.

While still playing professionally in the United States, Taurasi moved to Moscow, Russia, in 2007 to play for Spartak Moscow, a EuroLeague Women franchise, during the WNBA off-season. While earning nearly 10 times more money with Spartak Moscow than with the Phoenix Mercury, Taurasi and fellow American star Sue Bird lifted Spartak to four consecutive EuroLeague titles. In 2010 Taurasi signed with the Turkish basketball club Fenerbahçe and played one season for them. Her contract was terminated by the club in January 2011 when she tested positive for the banned substance modafinil, a stimulant usually prescribed to treat narcolepsy and sleep apnea. Taurasi maintained her innocence on doping charges while she underwent additional testing, and she was vindicated in February 2011 when subsequent analysis prompted the Turkish Federation to lift Taurasi's provisional ban. Although cleared and reinstated by the Turkish basketball league, Taurasi expressed no interest in returning to play for her former team. Instead, she remained focused on training for the upcoming WNBA season with the Phoenix Mercury.

Taurasi's extraordinary playing ability netted her commercial as well as athletic success. As a pro she signed endorsement deals with Gatorade, Eight O'Clock Coffee, and the Nike corporation. She has appeared in commercials for Nike and has her own signature shoes with the company, including the Nike Air Taurasi and DT Shox. Although she was convicted of a drunken driving charge in 2009 and served one day in jail on a suspended sentence, this has not diminished her commercial or fan appeal. Off the court Taurasi pursued charity projects, including working with her own Diana Taurasi Foundation, and made public speaking appearances. As of 2011, she played for the Phoenix Mercury and was a member of the U.S. Women's National Basketball team, which had qualified for the 2012 Summer Olympics.

Natalie Deibel

See also Auriemma, Geno; Gatorade; Lieberman, Nancy; Miller, Cheryl; Nike, Inc.; *Parade Magazine* All-Americans; *Sports Illustrated*; Summit, Pat; Women's National Basketball Association

Suggested Resources

Anderson, Kelli. "The Trials of Diana Taurasi." September 12, 2011. http://sportsillustrated.cnn.com/vault/article/magazine/MAG1190262/index.htm. Accessed November 20, 2011.

Diana Taurasi Website. http://www.dianataurasi.com/home/. Accessed November 20, 2011.

Feinberg, Doug. "Former UConn Basketball Player Diana Taurasi, Cleared of Using Peformance-Enhancing Drug, Says 'The Truth Came Out.'" February 16, 2011. http://www.masslive.com/sports/index.ssf/2011/02/former_uconn_basketball_player.html. Accessed November 20, 2011.

Grundy, Pamela, and Susan Shackelford. *Shattering the Glass: The Remarkable History of Women's Basketball*. Chapel Hill: University of North Carolina Press, 2007.

Texas Western Wins the 1966 NCAA Basketball Title

In 1966, Texas Western University (now the University of Texas at El Paso or UTEP) won the 1966 NCAA basketball tournament with a starting five of all African American players, the first time this was the case. It was the culmination of decades of segregation in college sports that had continued into the 1960s in many southern universities.

Up to and through World War II, many university sports conferences or specific universities remained segregated and would not allow their athletic teams to play teams with African Americans on their rosters. Most of these schools were in the South, but not exclusively so. In the South, education was segregated from elementary school through higher education. The *Brown v. Board of Education* decision of 1954 (augmented by *Brown II* in 1955) mandated integration to eliminate the unequal schooling opportunities and facilities of African Americans. Many southern states had established systems of segregated colleges and universities for black citizens. Even many northern athletic conferences had maintained de facto, if not de jure segregation on sports teams. The Big Ten, for example, had no African American basketball players until 1947 when Bill Garrett took the floor for Indiana University. Other major universities also maintained all-white teams into the postwar period.

The integration of southern universities and sports facilities and teams for all major universities was a major thrust of the civil rights movement of the 1950s and early 1960s, which arose to facilitate the intransigence of states and institutions to fully implement integrate in a reasonably swift manner. (The Supreme Court mandated this to occur with "deliberate speed.")

In the early 1960s many Deep South states still prohibited integration on the basketball court. This was seen vividly when the Mississippi State basketball team secretly slipped out of Starkville, Mississippi, on a March night to avoid the serving of an injunction that a local judge had issued that would prevent them from playing in the NCAA basketball tournament against teams with African American players.

In 1956, the University of San Francisco won the NCAA basketball tournament with, for the first time, three African American starters. Then, in 1963, Loyola University of Chicago started four African American players. That team played Mississippi State when the Bulldogs secretly flew to Nashville, then on to Michigan State to open the NCAA tourney in a second-round game. Loyola won, 61–51, with both the participation of Mississippi State and the four African American starters making news. Even then, however, there were those who saw blacks as having deficiencies in their play that the Loyola team composition seemed to enforce. The one white starter, Johnny Egan, was a point guard and the folk belief was that blacks weren't disciplined enough to lead a team from that position successfully.

The next two tournaments, in 1964 and 1965, were both won by the University of California at Los Angeles, coached by John Wooden, but in 1966 UCLA had a brief down year before going on to win NCAA titles over the next seven years. Thus, the 1966 title was a tossup, with the University of Kentucky, coached by Adolph Rupp, the favorite. Rupp and his Wildcats had won four previous NCAA titles in 1948, 1949, 1951, and 1958. Rupp, in contrast to many of his regional neighboring institutions, had continued to recruit and sign only whites for his basketball team at Kentucky. Rupp finally recruited his first African American player, Tom Payne, in 1969.

Texas Western College was founded in 1914 as Texas State School of Mines and Metallurgy and became Texas Western in 1949. Being located in the farthest reaches of the South made the college much less concerned with integration and they were the first southern school (in 1956) to integrate their sports teams. Shortly after that George McCarty, the basketball coach, began recruiting a few black players. Not that many noticed until the 1961–1962 season when the school hired Don Haskins, who led them to a record of 18–6 in his first year as coach. The next two years the Miners had records of 19–7 and 25–3, both good enough to get them invited to the NCAA Tournament. In the latter year, they defeated Texas A&M, then lost to Kansas State in the regional semifinals, before beating Creighton to take third in the Midwest. The next

Thad Jaracz, 55, of Kentucky, and David Latin, 42, of Texas Western, vie for a rebound in the NCAA championship game in College Park, Maryland, on March 19, 1966. Kentucky players at rear are Tommy Kron, 30, and Larry Conley, 40. (AP Photo.)

year their record was only 16–8 and they lost in the first round of the National Invitational Tournament.

For the 1965–1966 season just over 50 percent of the top 235 NCAA teams had a black player and there were none in the Southeastern Conference where Kentucky was the top team. Texas Western, on the other hand, had seven African Americans on their roster and a starting five of black players. Haskins had recruited three students who had been having academic difficulties and dropped out of their initial universities—Nevil Shedd, Bobby Joe Hill, and David Lattin. Willie Cager had left high school without graduating and earned a high school diploma in El Paso before he could enroll at Texas Western. Cager, Shedd, and Willie Worsley

were from New York City. Hill was from Detroit, Orstin Artis from Gary, as was Henry Flournoy. Only Lattin was from Texas (Houston). These seven players would be the only Texas Western players to appear in the championship game.

Playing as an independent, Texas Western breezed through their first nine games against mostly regional and weaker opponents, with only a home game against Fresno State close (75–73). Then on December 30, 1965, they played the number four–ranked Iowa Hawkeyes in Memorial Gym in El Paso and destroyed them by a score of 88–68. After easily defeating Tulsa and Seattle, the Miners first appeared in the top 10, ranked number nine, with a record of 12–0. They then

And Then They Became ...

Much of the criticism against the Texas Western team was focused on the academic deficiencies of their players compared to Kentucky's. Of the seven players who took the floor for Texas Western, four graduated in four years and the other three later held meaningful jobs as a public relations executive, a police officer, and a senior buyer with a gas company. Until the mid-1970s, four of Kentucky's starting five, including Riley and Dampier, had not yet earned their college degrees. Both Riley and Dampier became starters in pro basketball, Dampier in the ABA and Riley in the NBA, and Riley gained his greatest fame as the coach of NBA championships in Los Angeles and Miami; he was inducted into the Hall of Fame in 2008 as a coach.

won their next 11 games in a row, defeating teams such as Arizona, Arizona State, Colorado State, New Mexico, and New Mexico State before losing their final scheduled game in Seattle to Seattle University on March 5 by a score of 74–72. Despite the loss, the team retained a national ranking of number two in the Associated Press poll and had been invited to play in the NCAA tournament.

Playing in the Midwest Regional in Wichita, Texas Western defeated Oklahoma City, 89–74, and faced Cincinnati in the regional semifinal. The Bearcats had won national titles in 1961 and 1962 and were a difficult but unranked opponent. The Miners barely eked out a win, 78–76. Now ranked number three, they squared off against the number four–ranked Kansas Jayhawks in the regional finals in Lubbock on March 12, 1966. In another tense game, the Miners edged Kansas, 81–80, to advance to the Final Four in College Park, Maryland, the next week.

Despite having lost only one game, the Miners were expected to exit quickly. Instead they topped Utah, 85–78, to set up a championship match against Kentucky, who had defeated Duke, 83–79. Both teams had one loss, but Kentucky with its All-Americans, Louie Dampier and Pat Riley, was the prohibitive favorite.

Texas Western, however, pulled into the lead at 16–11 and never was behind again, following two steals by the Miners that shook the confidence of the Wildcats. At the half, the Miners led by 34–31. In the second half, Kentucky closed to within a point, twice, but could never tie or take the lead. With just under nine minutes to play, Dampier and Riley made baskets to bring the Wildcats to within three at 52–49. Then Texas Western had a run and led 60–51 with just under seven minutes to play. Down the stretch, Kentucky was forced to foul to try to stop the clock, but the Miners hit their free throws, going 28 for 34. Bobby Joe Hill led all scorers with 20, while Riley and Dampier had 19 each for Kentucky.

Following the game, integration came swiftly to many Southeastern Conference teams and other southern schools. They now felt that they needed to recruit African Americans to remain competitive. The result has been a total alteration of the landscape of college basketball in the past 45 years, both in players and in the rise of African American coaches at predominantly white major universities.

The 1966 game was reintroduced to another generation when the movie *Glory Road*, based on the Texas Western title run, was released in 2008. Rupp's career was near an end (he was forced to retire in March 1972 at age 70 and died in 1977) and Haskins's was just developing in 1966. He went on to win over 700 games, but never another NCAA title. He was enshrined in the Naismith Memorial Basketball Hall of Fame in 1997 and died in 2008. Rupp was elected to the Hall in 1969 after winning 869 games.

Murry R. Nelson

See also Final Four; March Madness; Naismith Memorial Basketball Hall of Fame; Wooden, John

Suggested Resources
Fitzpatrick, Frank. *And the Walls Came Tumbling Down: The Basketball Game That Changed American Sports.* New York: Simon & Schuster, 1999.
Fitzpatrick, Frank. "Texas Western's 1966 Title Left Lasting Legacy." November 19, 2003. http://espn.go.com/classic/s/013101_texas_western_fitzpatrick.html. Accessed September 8, 2011.
Haskins, Don, as told to Ray Sanchez. *Haskins: The Bear Facts.* El Paso, TX: Mangan Books, 1987.
Martin, Charles. *Benching Jim Crow: The Rise and Fall of the Color Line in Southern College Sports, 1890–1980.* Urbana: University of Illinois Press, 2010.
The 1966 Men's NCAA Basketball Champion Texas Western Miners. http://www.squidoo.com/twcminers. Accessed September 8, 2011.

That Championship Season (1972)

That Championship Season is a play written by Jason Miller and first performed off Broadway in 1972. It received the Pulitzer Prize for Drama that year, then played on Broadway for 844 performances from fall of 1972 to spring of 1974. The play was awarded a Critic's Circle Award for 1973 as well as the Tony Award for Best Play of 1973. The play was later adapted for film as well as a made-for-television movie, then was revived off Broadway in 1999 and on Broadway for a limited run from March to May 2011.

The play is set in the Lackawanna Valley, south of Scranton, Pennsylvania, in the early 1970s. Four members of the 1952 state championship–winning basketball team return to their old coach's home for what has been an annual evening of reminiscing, although these four haven't all been there with the coach for the past three years. One member of the starting five does not appear, as usual, because of a long-standing feud with the coach, the substance of which is not revealed until the end of the play.

The coach is an old-school conservative whose heroes were Joseph McCarthy and Father Charles Coughlin, both right-wing bigots. Each of the players has had a life of disappointment in some way. One (George) has become the mayor, but is likely to lose a reelection bid and, what is most galling to the coach, to a Jewish candidate. The Daley brothers (Tom and James) are two of the others and Phil, a wealthy local car dealer and strip mine owner, is the last of the four former players.

The play is less about basketball than it is about hopes, dreams, disappointment, and betrayal. It deals with the terror of being middle-aged and a "loser." In that sense the play is universal for many men who grew up in the post–World War II era, but that universality extends beyond that period. The playwright, Miller, is represented by Tom Daley, who moved to California to pursue his dreams of success. He remains the outsider in the drama that plays out, making wry comments and, seemingly, glad not to be involved.

In the course of the play it is revealed that Phil, who has been the biggest financial supporter of George's campaigns for mayor, has also been having an affair with George's wife. James, George's campaign manager and a junior high school principal, indicates that he has political ambitions that would include him being named superintendent of schools in the town. He also pushes to have himself supported for mayor when it appears that support for George is flagging. Tom, who has become an alcoholic or nearly so, angers the coach with his lack of what he considers seriousness of purpose.

The coach preaches winning by any means necessary because the others (whoever they might be) will be merciless in their efforts to win. This attitude of "us versus them at all costs" finally is too much for Tom, who says that their years as champions has been a lie since they "stole the trophy." It is this that has kept Martin away, the fact that the coach told him to get that big black center (the coach uses much more vile language) out of the game, resulting in Martin giving the other player a shot to the ribs. That broke two of the young man's ribs and the team then managed to win by one point on a shot by Martin with two seconds left.

For many young men this kind of high school glory or near glory often has seemed like the highlight of a disappointing life. The nostalgia, burnished over time, has made the men seem greater than they ever were. Still, their friendship has much less depth than it initially seemed and this raises another universal question by Miller. Does a great team create friendships or does friendship create a great team? Many people see their old teammates as their best, most endearing friends, but this play puts the lie to much of that. It is a powerful, searing indictment of small-town prejudices and disappointments, covered over by the façade of teamwork, orchestrated by a vile coach who taught them real life lessons.

The coach's long soliloquy at the end shows his prejudicial views against not just Jews and blacks, but politicians and outsiders. He says that he will hold them together and his rant ends with a recorded radio broadcast of the last 30 seconds of their championship game. Then they revert to their initial facades of loving and supporting each other. The revival of the play indicated that the play was now more dated in tone and content than it had appeared before. It seems unlikely to be revived again on a national scale, but will certainly remain a challenging, but popular choice for regional and local theater companies.

Miller was both an actor and a playwright, but this play was the highlight of his career. As an actor, he appeared in the film *The Exorcist* and was nominated for an Academy Award, but he preferred acting in regional theater and television to filmmaking and chose to live in New York City, not Hollywood. He was married three times and his son from his first marriage to Linda Gleason, Jason Patric, is a noted actor. Patric appeared in the role of Tom (his father's alter ego) in the 2011 revival of the play on Broadway. Miller died of a sudden heart attack while at a Scranton bar in 2001, at the age of 62.

Murry R. Nelson

Suggested Resources

Brown, Dennis. "*That Championship Season* Catapulted Jason Miller to Overnight Success." August 4, 2010. http://www.riverfronttimes.com/2010-08-04/culture/that-championship-season-catapulted-jason-miller-overnight-success/. Accessed July 14, 2011.

Miller, Jason. *That Championship Season*. New York: Atheneum, 1972.

That Championship Season. IMDb. http://www.imdb.com/title/tt0084784/. Accessed July 14, 2011.

Thorpe, Jim (1888–1953)

Jim Thorpe, the greatest star in the early years of professional football, was one of the most versatile athletes that the United States has ever produced. He was born and grew up in Indian Territory of racially mixed ancestry, raised as a Sac and Fox. An All-American football player on the college level in 1911 and 1912 at Carlisle (Pennsylvania) Indian School, he also starred in track and field, winning Olympic gold medals for the United States in pentathlon and decathlon in the 1912 Summer Games. He was stripped of his medals for having earlier played minor league professional baseball, though he was reinstated as an amateur by the International Olympic Committee in 1982, and commemorative medals (the originals had been stolen) were presented to his family in 1983, 30 years after his death.

In 1920 Thorpe was one of the founders of what is now the National Football League, having played and coached, beginning in 1915, in the pioneering days of pro football, most notably for the Canton (Ohio) Bulldogs. The 6'1", 202 pound. Thorpe was a running back, defensive back, punter, and placekicker. He also was an outfielder in Major League Baseball for six seasons between 1913 and 1919, mostly with the New York Giants, and barnstormed with a touring semipro basketball team in 1927–1928. He preferred football, and that was the sport for which he was best known. Thorpe was one of 17 players inducted in 1963 as the initial group selected for membership in the Pro Football Hall of Fame in Canton, and he is honored there by a larger-than-life statue in the rotunda, as befitting the game's first big star. He was named "the Legend" on the all-time NFL team.

In 1950, in an Associated Press poll of nearly 400 sports journalists, Jim Thorpe was named both the greatest male athlete and the greatest American football player of the 20th century. In a 1999 AP poll, Thorpe was still ranked third among top athletes of the 20th century, behind Babe Ruth and Michael Jordan. The same year he was ranked seventh by ESPN on their list of the best North American athletes of the century. Both houses of the U.S. Congress in 1999 proclaimed Jim Thorpe "Athlete of the Century," and in 2000 he was named ABC's *Wide World of Sports* Athlete of the Century in an Internet poll prior to Super Bowl XXXIV. Jim Thorpe was plagued by alcoholism, and late in life he suffered from ill health and poverty. He is buried in Jim Thorpe, Pennsylvania, a town named for him, though his son brought suit in 2010 to have his remains reinterred among family members near his birthplace in Oklahoma, the state that refused to erect a memorial to him at the time of his death.

Born into obscurity though destined for greatness, Jim Thorpe's origins have provided a challenge to his biographers. Even his name is the subject of dispute. According to his estate, he was born on May 28, 1887, in a one-room cabin near Prague, Oklahoma, in what was then Indian Territory. Jim, however, gave his birth date as May 28, 1888, based on papers from the Indian Nations, and the place as Old Shawnee Trading Post. There is little controversy regarding his Indian name of *Wa-Tho-Huk* (or *Huck*), meaning Bright Path, or his birthplace in the loosely delineated Sac and Fox Nation. The cabin was built by his father from cottonwood and hickory on the North Canadian River shortly before the breakup of the reservations. Jim's heirs admit that there is much confusion about his birth date, which is putting it mildly. This is inevitable, as no birth certificate is known to exist. The Pro Football Hall of Fame gives Thorpe's birth date as May 28, 1888, as does ESPN's football encyclopedia, although their baseball encyclopedia shows May 28, 1887. Wheeler (1979) and Newcombe (1975) use the dates May 28, 1888, and May 27, 1887, respectively. While Cook (2011) sticks with Thorpe's preferred May 28, 1888, Crawford (2005) and Buford (2010) agree on a May 22, 1887, date. Crawford's source is baptismal records at Sacred Heart Church near Konawa, Oklahoma. Buford adds that the birthplace is registered as Bellemont. His name is usually given as James Francis Thorpe, but his confirmation name was Jacobus Franciscus Thorpe, and that is the name used in certain biographical material. To complicate matters further, spelling of the last name varies, usually written as Thorp or sometimes Tharp until the final "e" was standardized at Carlisle.

Jim was a fraternal twin; his brother Charles, called Charlie, died of pneumonia when they were nine. Their parents were Hiram Phillip Thorp and Charlotte Vieux (sometimes Vieau or View), "civilized Indians" in the parlance of the time (meaning Native Americans who dressed like Caucasian Americans and lived in houses), who met around 1880, probably at the Sac and Fox Agency, where that tribe and several others did business near the current Stroud, Oklahoma. Hiram was Sac and Fox, and Charlotte was Potawatomi. Hiram P.'s father, Hiram G., was an Irish immigrant, who was wedded to No-ten-o-quah, a member of the Thunder Clan of Black Hawk, the most famous Sac and Fox chief, noted for his athletic prowess, as Jim Thorpe would be in the next century. The younger Hiram was a bootlegger who sold whiskey to his fellow tribe members, awaiting them at the agency when they received their government payments. Charlotte also had Kickapoo, Menominee, and French in her ancestry. She was a devout Roman Catholic and all the children were raised in the church, though no marriage certificate has been found for her and Hiram. Together, Hiram and Charlotte had 11 children, of whom only Jim, his older brother George, younger sisters Mary and Adaline, and younger brother Edward survived to adulthood. When he died at age 52, Hiram had fathered

Jim Thorpe greeted by New York City mayor William Jay Gaynor, third from left, and other dignitaries in Olympic ceremony at City Hall in 1912. (Library of Congress.)

at least 11 surviving children with at least five different women. Charlie and Jim attended the Sac and Fox Indian Agency School in Stroud, but after his twin brother died, Jim repeatedly ran away. His father sent him to the Haskell Institute, an Indian boarding school in Lawrence, Kansas. When his mother died after childbirth complications, Jim became depressed, argued with his father, and ran away to work on a ranch. In 1904, Jim returned home, and then decided to attend Carlisle Indian Industrial School. That same year Hiram died from gangrene following a hunting accident. After the school year ended in June, Jim was sent to do farm labor while living with a white family as part of Carlisle's Indian outing system, used to acculturate the Native American "students" into the dominant society. He would not return to the school until 1907.

Prior to enrolling at Carlisle, Thorpe had competed successfully in the Indian games of medicine ball and lacrosse, as well as attracting attention on the baseball diamond with his pitching and base running for the Prague town team. At Carlisle he would compete in track, football, baseball, and lacrosse. After his return to the school, he faced punishment for running away from his last two outing assignments, but he was released from it in time to join the baseball team. One day on his way to practice, he passed a group of track-and-field athletes high jumping. After asking if he could try, he did so in street clothes and jumped 5 feet 9 inches to break the school record. A watching student told legendary coach Glenn "Pop" Warner what he had done, and Warner sent for Thorpe, putting him on the track team. This began what would be Jim's most important adult relationship, and until his death Thorpe would praise Warner as a coach. The coach quickly saw his potential and assigned track and football star Albert Exendine to be Jim's mentor. Thorpe had his initial dominating track-and-field performances that spring, and soon began to compete in intramural football for the tailoring team (his vocational program), having seldom touched a football before. One of his coaches recommended that Warner let him try out for the varsity. Pop was reluctant to risk injury to the skinny Thorpe, his most promising track star, but Jim wanted to play and finally he relented. Though Thorpe was initially assigned to the scrubs, his ability to run the ball against the regulars won him the position of backup left halfback. Carlisle cruised through the college opponents on their schedule, a loss to Princeton the only blemish on their 10–1 record. Thorpe sat for the first three games and played sparingly thereafter. Then at Penn in the seventh game of the 1907 season, starter Albert Payne hurt his knee in the first quarter. Thorpe subbed for him, and after a loss on his first carry, scored a touchdown on a 75-yard end around. From this point on, Jim Thorpe was starting left half for the Carlisle Indians.

Though Jim was the star of the Carlisle track team, competing with distinction in high and low hurdles, high and broad jumps, shot put, and hammer throw, he failed to qualify for the 1908 U.S. Olympic team. Disappointed but undeterred, his broken field and power running and his kicking for the 10–2–1 Indians began to receive national attention, as Thorpe was selected by Walter Camp to be a Third-Team All-American for 1908. Though he was the ace of the Carlisle pitching staff, he had to gradually phase out baseball since Warner gave preference to track as a spring sport. Thorpe competed in as many as nine events in a given track meet, winning consistently and drawing national attention to his skills in that sport. After the end of the 1909 spring season, Thorpe and three Carlisle teammates headed to North Carolina, hoping to catch on with a minor league team in the Class D Eastern Carolina League to play baseball for money. This decision to turn pro would cost Thorpe his 1912 Olympic medals. Signed by Rocky Mount for $15 a week, Jim pitched and played first base, going 9–10 and hitting .254 in 1909. In Raleigh, Thorpe spent his pay on alcohol and experienced his first arrest for disorderly conduct. After the season, rather than return to Carlisle, he went back to Oklahoma to do farm work. He played for Rocky Mount and Fayetteville in the ECL in 1910, going a cumulative 10–10 on the mound and hitting .242. Off the field, he was embroiled in more drunk and disorderly conduct. Again Thorpe went home rather than back to school, and after a mediocre season by the football team, Warner wrote to Jim encouraging him to return to Carlisle, where he had two years of football eligibility remaining. Thorpe, his weight up to 176 pounds, stepped back into his starting spot at left half without missing a beat, and the 1911 Indians would go 11–1, with Thorpe leading the way, rushing and kicking field goals. In 1912, Carlisle won the national championship, going 12–1–1, as Thorpe scored 25 touchdowns and 198 points with several runs of 90 or more yards. In Jim Thorpe's four seasons playing football for Carlisle, 1907–1908 and 1911–1912, the Indians were 43–5–2.

Thorpe qualified for and won the decathlon and pentathlon at the 1912 Summer Olympics in Stockholm, the new multievent titles consisting of running and field competitions, winning 8 of 15 total events. He also participated in the individual broad jump and high jump competitions, finishing seventh and fourth, respectively. In addition to the gold medals, he was awarded challenge prizes donated by King Gustav V of Sweden for the decathlon and Czar Nicholas II of Russia for the pentathlon. On presenting the prize to

Thorpe, King Gustav reportedly told him, "You, sir, are the greatest athlete in the world." He returned to a ticker-tape parade in his honor on Broadway, remembering later his pleasure and astonishment at the public acclaim, but his euphoria would be short-lived. In January 1913, several American newspapers published stories detailing Thorpe's summer sojourns playing baseball in North Carolina, which violated the strict rules forcing Olympic athletes to adhere to amateurism. Unlike most collegians who played pro ball during summer vacation, Thorpe had used his own name rather than a pseudonym. Later that year, the International Olympic Committee voted to strip Jim Thorpe of his titles, medals, and awards, and declared him a professional. This tragic circumstance was nevertheless a boon to Thorpe's career. Since he was now a declared pro and his last minor league baseball club in 1910 had disbanded, he was a rare reserve clause–era free agent sought after by major league teams, and he could choose to sign with whomever he wished. His choice was the reigning National League champion New York Giants, with whom he signed a three-year contract in February 1913 at $5,000 per year, making him the best-paid untried player to ever have been hired by a major league team.

Playing baseball for John McGraw's Giants, Thorpe barely made a splash in the big leagues. His playing time varied, as did his relationship with the fiery field boss, but the two seldom got along, and Jim would play only infrequently. The biggest knock against him was that he lacked patience at the plate and couldn't hit the curveball. McGraw's motives for signing Thorpe appear to be pure. The Giants always seemed to need outfielders, and Thorpe's speed and strong right arm sold the manager on the player's potential. McGraw didn't like him, however, questioned his training habits, and warned him about the dangers of drinking and playing cards. Unlike his other charges, Thorpe challenged the Little Napoleon. McGraw could not stand any questioning of his authority and, although Jim made the club out of spring training, had little use for him. Jim Thorpe made his MLB debut in the second game of the National League season on April 14, 1913, an unsuccessful pinch-hitting appearance. Thorpe sat on the bench near McGraw, being educated in the game, which his mentor was

always teaching. He learned well and became an adept outfielder, but McGraw's faith in him as a hitter was never rewarded. McGraw confronted Thorpe about his drinking, and Thorpe shot back with ethnic slurs about Indians and Irish (as Thorpe pointed out, he was part Irish himself) freely exchanged. After this, Thorpe would always be in the manager's doghouse. Pop Warner claimed that Thorpe's game would have improved had McGraw just played him more, but that wasn't about to happen. He did take part in the famous world tour of the Giants and Chicago White Sox following the 1913 season, which was successful in spreading the game around the globe. Thorpe had married after the World Series, in which he did not play. Both Jim and his bride, Iva, proved to be popular wherever the tourists ventured.

From 1913 through 1915, Thorpe played in 19, 30, and 17 games for the Giants, while batting .143, .194, and .231. McGraw decided to start him in the outfield for 1915, finally agreeing that more work might improve his play. His hitting never really came around, and before the end of April he had cleared waivers and been shipped across the Hudson to the Jersey City Skeeters of the AA (then the highest level of minor league ball) International League. In the third year of his $5,000 a year contract, Thorpe was the highest paid player in the minors. His off-field antics and high jinks with roommate Al Schacht got him in trouble in Jersey City, and he was sent off to Harrisburg in the same league, where he was said to have a disturbing influence on the team. He hit .303 in a combined 96 IL games, then spent all of 1916 with the Milwaukee Brewers of the AA American Association, batting .274, and led the league with 48 stolen bases. In April 1917, Jim Thorpe was ostensibly sold to the Cincinnati Reds for the waiver price of $1,500. In reality, the other NL owners agreed that McGraw could loan him to his disciple Christy Mathewson, then managing the Reds and in need of outfielders, with the right to recall him if Matty decided to release him. Thorpe fared better with Cinci, although unable to hit the curve or do much versus righties; he played more and raised his average to .247 in 77 games. But McGraw recalled him on August 1 and again he played little, batting .193 in 26 contests. He started for New York against the White Sox in game five of the 1917 World Series, his only appearance in the Fall Classic, but suffered the humiliation of being removed for a pinch hitter when the Chicago left-handed starter was replaced by a righty in the bottom of the first, never to appear at-bat in a Series game. Thorpe made it into 58 games for the Giants in 1918, batting .248. His flaunting his celebrity and his defiant attitude toward McGraw boiled over in early 1919, and either because he missed a sign from the manager and then chased him around the ballpark when Mac called him a "dumb Indian" (according to former roommate Schacht) or because he was a disturbing influence on the team (in McGraw's words), in May Thorpe was traded to the Boston Braves. He finished his big league career with his best season in 1919, batting a cumulative .327 in 62 games, all but two with Boston. He hit better over three more seasons in the minors, mostly at the AA level, to finish his seven-year career in 1922 with a .319 average in 2,737 at-bats. Jim Thorpe's major league average was .252 in 698 at-bats.

Though baseball was the well-established sport, providing a more substantial paycheck and more renown, Jim still preferred football and began to focus on it more in the fall of 1915. In September, Indiana University hired Thorpe as the first assistant football coach in charge of the backfield. The professional game had been limping along for over 20 years, based in western Pennsylvania and to a lesser degree upstate New York, but it began to spread westward and found fertile ground in the Midwest. In November Thorpe played for the Pine Village, Indiana, pro team, paid $250 for a game. Big-time pro football had its beginnings that year, with Canton fielding a team, long known as the Bulldogs, to face off against their ready-made nearby rival, the Massillon Tigers. The two northern Ohio cities had played each other early in the century, but stories of game fixing had caused the teams to revert to sandlot status. A gas company employee named Jack Cusack quit his job to work full time to bring the Bulldogs to fully professional status. Cusack offered Thorpe the same $250 to play in each of the two scheduled 1915 games versus the Tigers. Jim Thorpe became the first big name to play as a pro, and his presence sent Bulldogs attendance soaring from an average of about 1,200 per game to 8,000 for the Massillon contest, and the Tigers also

experienced a boost when he played there. Thorpe was an immediate success in every phase of the game, punting and kicking (he could dropkick or placekick), running with speed and power, blocking with authority, and tackling with ferocity. He was soon named team "captain," in actuality serving as coach, while the Bulldogs rose to the top of the pro gridiron world. In 1916, 1917, and 1919, led by Thorpe, Canton won unofficial championships. But pro football's future was in jeopardy, with nearly 250 teams scattered about the East and Midwest with little organization. Canton was losing money, and Massillon announced that they would not field a team for 1920. The answer seemed obvious. A nationwide league was needed.

Car dealer Ralph Hay had succeeded Cusack as manager of the Canton Bulldogs. Players, owners, and managers representing 11 pro football clubs met at Hay's Hupmobile showroom in the Odd Fellows Hall in Canton, Ohio, on September 17, 1920. The result was the formation of the American Professional Football Association, which would be renamed the National Football League in 1922, with Jim Thorpe elected as its first president. Thorpe's role was largely ceremonial, his fame lending immediate stature to the fledgling league, and when it was realized the APFA needed a more experienced leader, he was replaced, in 1921, by veteran Ohio sports executive Joe Carr. The aging Thorpe continued to play well on the field, moving from Canton in 1920 to the Cleveland Indians in 1921; and in 1922–1923 he formed and coached the Oorang Indians, an all–Native American aggregation representing Marion, Ohio, in the NFL, which played mainly on the road. When that club folded in 1923, Thorpe participated in exhibition games for the Toledo (Ohio) Maroons, and with his great skills finally beginning to erode in his late 30s, he signed with the Rock Island (Illinois) Independents for the 1924 NFL season. In 1925 he was with the newly formed New York Football Giants, reporting out of shape and performing poorly, before he was released and returned to play for Rock Island. He had a last bow with the Canton Bulldogs in 1926, then coached the World Famous Indians, an all-Indian basketball team, barnstorming around the East and Midwest over the winter of 1927–1928. Thorpe gave the NFL one more shot, playing a game for the Chicago Cardinals against the Chicago

Bears in December 1928, but he played badly, and he retired after being removed from the game.

After leaving professional sports, Thorpe struggled to support his family. He had four children with his first wife, Iva Miller, whom he met at Carlisle and married in 1913: Jim Jr., who died at age two, Gale, Charlotte, and Grace. The couple separated in 1923 and Iva divorced Jim in 1924 on grounds of desertion. In 1925, Jim Thorpe married Freeda Kirkpatrick, who bore him four sons: Carl Phillip, William, Richard, and John. Upon divorcing Jim in 1943, Freeda charged him with excessive drinking, but author William Cook claims that Jim's "wanderlust" helped bring about the divorce. Thorpe was a bouncer and security guard, worked construction and dug ditches, but never held a job for long, as his chronic alcoholism took its toll. He was in several Hollywood movies as a bit player, frequently in the role of an Indian chief. In 1945 in Tijuana he married Patricia Gladys Askew, a woman he knew only slightly, after a drinking binge, which left Thorpe unable to remember the events, which had led to a quick trip to Mexico to circumvent California's three-day waiting period. Patsy was an alcoholic with two adult daughters. She was a chronic liar, hated by Thorpe's children, who nevertheless would remain with Jim for the duration of his life. Turned down in his attempts to enlist in the military after Pearl Harbor due to his age, Thorpe eventually joined the U.S. merchant marine, shipping out 11 days after marrying Patricia, as carpenter on the SS *Southwestern Victory* in the late stages of the Pacific campaign. World War II ended before the cargo ship could complete its mission delivering fuel and bombs for the Allied war effort, and the vessel was ordered to return home.

Jim used the money he'd earned working at sea to buy a waterfront bar called the Bank Café in the San Pedro neighborhood of Los Angeles harbor, with himself as the seedy dive's main attraction, along with the prostitutes hired by the bartender to encourage customers to buy more drinks. Jim sold out, but after poor health rendered him unable to drink, he briefly operated another L.A. bar called The Champ. He and Patsy lived in a travel trailer, out of economic need, but well suited to Jim's wandering lifestyle. They were able to buy a hotel in Charleston, South Carolina, which they quickly sold, and lived briefly in New York with Jim's

Jim Thorpe, Pennsylvania

Jim Thorpe's story doesn't end with his death. Thorpe's body initially lay in state in California. From there, it was transported to Shawnee, Oklahoma. While his clan relatives and children were holding a traditional tribal ritual prior to burial, Thorpe's third wife, Patricia, came in a hearse and removed Jim's body to another cemetery, Garden Grove, where Jim Thorpe was laid to rest in a mausoleum in a Catholic ceremony. But since his widow was unable to pay for the crypt, he was moved again, this time to Tulsa. The children wanted to build a memorial for their father, but lacked the funds. Patricia Thorpe asked the State of Oklahoma to pay for his burial, but the governor, William H. Murray, refused to sign the spending bill authorizing the funds to build a monument.

When Patricia heard that the small Pennsylvania coal-mining towns of Mauch Chunk and East Mauch Chunk were desperate to attract business, in 1954 she was able to sell them on the idea of buying and burying her late husband's remains. The towns merged, built a tasteful monument for Jim Thorpe's tomb, dedicated in 1957, erected historical markers and two statues of him in athletic poses, and renamed themselves the Borough of Jim Thorpe.

All was well until 2010, when Thorpe's son filed a lawsuit against the borough, seeking to have his father's remains reinterred in his Oklahoma homeland under the Native American Graves Protection and Repatriation Act, so he could be buried on Native American land near his father, brother, and sisters. As of mid-2012, the suit had not yet been settled, and the borough had been rebuffed in its request for dismissal.

son Dick. Jim earned money traveling around the country to any event that would pay him to speak, but he and Patsy always spent it quickly. He played an assistant football coach in the 1949 movie *Yes Sir, That's My Baby*, did some radio, and attended sports dinners. He started a girls' softball team in L.A., Jim Thorpe's All-America Thunderbirds, but the public was not attracted by girls in shorts or Jim Thorpe coaching third. Jim quit to become assistant sales manager of a Hudson car dealership for a while, then worked as a greeter in a downtown Los Angeles restaurant and bar. He sporadically had small roles in major films, but he was apparently destitute in 1950, when he was hospitalized for lip cancer as a charity case. A movie was made about his life in 1951, for which Jim received $15,000 from Warner Brothers. *Jim Thorpe— All-American* starred Burt Lancaster in the title role with Billy Gray as the young Jim. He had two heart attacks as his health began to deteriorate further. Jim Thorpe suffered his third heart attack at home in his trailer in Lomita, California, and died shortly afterward on March 28, 1953.

David C. Skinner

See also ESPN Channels; Jordan, Michael; National Football League; Pro Football Hall of Fame and Museum; Ruth, Babe; Super Bowl

Suggested Resources

Buford, Kate. *Native American Son: The Life and Sporting Legend of Jim Thorpe.* New York: Alfred A. Knopf, 2010.

Cook, William A. *Jim Thorpe: A Biography.* Jefferson, NC: McFarland, 2011.

Crawford, Bill. *All American: The Rise and Fall of Jim Thorpe.* Hoboken, NJ: John Wiley and Sons, 2005.

"Jim Thorpe." Pro Football Hall of Fame. http://www.pro footballhof.com/hof/member.aspx?player_id=213. Accessed December 2011.

Jim Thorpe Rest in Peace. http://www.jimthorperestin peace.com. Accessed July 2012.

Jim Thorpe Website. http://www.cmgww.com/sports/ thorpe/index.html. Accessed December 2011.

Newcombe, Jack. *The Best of the Athletic Boys: The White Man's Impact on Jim Thorpe.* Garden City, NY: Doubleday, 1975.

Wheeler, Robert W. *Jim Thorpe: World's Greatest Athlete.* Rev. ed. Norman: University of Oklahoma Press, 1979.

Three-Point Shot

The three-point shot is basketball's version of the home run, whereby a player is credited with three points on any shot made beyond the arc, which varies in length in high school, college, and pro basketball.

The three-point shot was discussed as early as the 1930s and even experimented in some exhibition games (Fordham vs. Columbia in February 1945 was one), but there was little interest in actually implementing it on a regular basis until 1961. At that point, two factors had changed since the 1930s. First, players had gotten stronger and taller and there was much more pushing and shoving in the lane, especially in professional games. Second was the fact that players had become better shooters from the outside and the likelihood of taking and making a deep outside shot had risen dramatically from earlier eras when a shooting percentage of 30 percent was considered average to good.

With that in mind and seeking something that would set the league apart, the American Basketball League announced that it would use a three-point shot in its games when the league began in the fall of 1961. Measured from the backboard, the three-point shot would be 25 feet or beyond. The league was derided by its more established rival, the National Basketball Association (NBA), for a variety of reasons, with the three-point basket one of them. The fans, however, found the new scoring rule exciting, even if they failed to warm to the league as a whole. At season's end in the spring of 1962, Tony Jackson of the Chicago Majors had the most three-pointers in the league, 141 in 72 games with an astounding 12 in one game. He shot 37 percent from long range, which, in terms of scoring would be like shooting 56 percent from two-point range. Only one other player, Bucky Bolyard, made more than 100 three-pointers that season. The league maintained the shot the next season, but the league folded at the end of December 1962 and the three-pointer died with the league.

In 1967, a new professional league began, the American Basketball Association, and they adopted the three-point shot as part of their basic rules, again seeking to differentiate themselves and their league from the NBA in some manner. The shot was a popular aspect of the league as were the spirited dunks that the young ABA players seemed to specialize in executing. Steve Jones of the Oakland Oaks had the best percentage for the year, but took only 54 three-pointers, making 26 for a .426 percentage. Les Selvage, however, led the league in three-pointers made and attempted with 147 for 461, a .320 percentage. Teams often didn't use the shot except in desperate situations, usually with the clock running down or if they were down by a large number of points late in a game. The shot was not really a planned part of most teams' arsenals.

Derek Fisher shoots a three-point shot for the L.A. Lakers during a Christmas day NBA game versus the Miami Heat at the Staples Center in Los Angeles in 2010. (Joel Shawn/Shutterstock.com.)

Over the next two years, Louie Dampier of the Kentucky Colonels made nearly 200 three-pointers each season (191 and 199, respectively) as teams began to plan how to use the shot more. In 1970–1971 George Lehman of the Carolina Cougars had a three-point percentage of .403, while leading the league in three-pointers made with 154. After that no player made more than 100 in the rest of the life of the ABA, which was taken over by the NBA in 1976.

The three-point shot was again dropped after the ABA sent four teams to the NBA and the ABA ceased to exist, but in 1979 the NBA reintroduced the shot in the league at a distance of 23'9". No player made more than 90 for the year and three players shot better than 40 percent, led by "Downtown" Freddy Brown, who shot 44.3 percent.

The next year (1980) the NCAA instituted a three-point shot for college games at varying distances, ranging from 17'9" to 22'. The decision was up to

individual conferences. This made for confusion when teams from different conferences played as well as in the end-of-the-year tournaments. Thus, in 1986 the NCAA standardized the distance at 19'9". It was used in the NCAA Tournament for the first time in 1987, and the top three-point shooting team in the nation, Indiana, hitting over 50 percent of their attempts, won the national title. The relatively short distance altered many college offenses as coaches worked the three-pointer into their offensive schemes. The distance for college remained 19'9" until 2008 when the distance increased a foot to 20'9" for men and remained at 19'9" for women.

The NBA moved their three-point line in a bit beginning in 1994, shortening the distance to 22 feet. The result was an enormous increase in the number of three-point shots being taken and made; two players (Steve Kerr and Detlef Schrempf) actually shot over 50 percent from beyond the arc. This pattern continued the next year and in 1996–1997 at least three players made over 200 three-pointers and the NBA decided to revert to the prior distance of 23'9" for the 1997–1998 season. That has remained the distance since then. Despite that reversion to the greater distance, Ray Allen broke the three-point mark in 2005–2006 with 269 made three-point shots. Allen is also the career three-point leader as of 2012 with over 2,700.

Meanwhile, FIBA (the International Federation of Basketball Associations) began using a three-point line of 6.25 meters (20'5") for all of their federation games beginning in 1984. This would have little impact on American teams, except in international tournaments like the Olympics and the Pan American Games. College players who made these American teams would be at a slight disadvantage, but professionals would not, having gotten used to an even longer distance. In 1988, the United States took only a bronze medal at the Olympics in Seoul, South Korea, and the different, longer three-point distance was one of a number of factors cited in that disappointing result.

In 1986 the NBA began a three-point shooting contest as part of the NBA All-Star Game festivities. The initial winner was Larry Bird, who then won two more titles before Dale Ellis won in 1989. Starting in 1990, Craig Hodges of the Chicago Bulls won three straight three-point shooting titles. Other multiple winners were Mark Price of Cleveland (1992 and 1993), Jeff Hornacek of the Utah Jazz (1998 and 2000, with no contest in 1999), Peja Stojakovic of Scaramento (2002 and 2003), and Jason Kapono of Miami and Toronto in 2007 and 2008).

Starting in 1992, FIBA altered its rules to allow professionals to play in international tournaments and the different distance became less of an issue for American squads. The 1992 "Dream Team" dominated the Olympic tournament and the differing three-point distances were forgotten as a source of concern for American teams.

Through all of these years, various state high school associations have adopted the three-point shot for game use. By 1986, eight states had adopted use of the shot with the 19'9" distance, measured from the center of the basket, whereas colleges measured from the front of the rim. By 1990 all state high school associations had adopted the use of the shot.

Three-Point Shooting to Victory

In the first NCAA championship game that had the three-point shot, Indiana faced Syracuse, with the Hoosiers winning, 74–73, on a last-minute shot by Keith Smart. What is often overlooked is the fact that Steve Alford made seven three-pointers in the game, all of Indiana's three-point scores.

Today there are six three-point distances. The NBA has the 23'9" distance, the WNBA uses a 20' distance, the NCAA men's distance is 20'9", the women's college distance is 19'9", and high schools also 19'9", but measured from a different spot. FIBA has lengthened its distance to 6.75 meters (22.1'). The adjustment seems less difficult than it once was since players start shooting for distance in high school or practicing such a shot even earlier.

Because of the three-point shot the inside game has opened up more. A good-shooting three-point team requires defenders to come out farther to guard the shooters, thus leaving more room in the inside for bigger players to maneuver and score. Fans, as predicted by Abe Saperstein, who began the ABL in 1961, love the shot. The arc of the ball, the hang time of the shot, the excitement as the referee puts up two hands to signal the three-point conversion, all serve to excite the fans and motivate the players.

Murry R. Nelson

See also American Basketball Association; Bird, Larry; Dream Team; National Basketball Association; Saperstein, Abe; Women's National Basketball Association

Suggested Resources
Brennan, Eamonn. "Top 3-Point Shots in NCAA History." November 3, 2011. http://espn.go.com/mens-college-basketball/story/_/id/7181471/top-3-point-shots-ncaa-history-college-basketball. Accessed November 10, 2011.

Nelson, Murry. *Abe Saperstein and the American Basketball League, 1960–1963: The Upstarts Who Shot for Three and Lost to the NBA.* Jefferson, NC: McFarland, 2013.

"2012 NBA Three-Point Shootout." Inside Hoops.com. February 25, 2012. http://www.insidehoops.com/nba_history_3point_shootout.shtml. Accessed November 10, 2011.

Thrilla in Manila (1975)

The "Thrilla in Manila" was the third of three fights between Muhammad Ali and Joe Frazier over a five-year period, two of which were for the heavyweight championship of the world. Frazier won the first fight in 1971 and Ali the final two.

Muhammad Ali won the world heavyweight championship in 1964 at the age of 22. He was stripped of that championship in 1967, then failed to regain the heavyweight title in 1971 with his first fight against the new heavyweight champion, Joe Frazier. Frazier was the 12th child of a poor family in Beaufort, South Carolina, and had worked his way to New York, where he began a fighting career. In 1964 he replaced the injured Buster Mathis on the 1964 Olympic boxing team in Tokyo and then won the heavyweight gold medal, the only U.S. boxing victory in those Olympics. He then started his pro career.

After Ali was stripped of his title there were a number of bouts held to determine the new heavyweight champion, and eventually Jimmy Ellis, a former sparring partner for Ali, defeated Jerry Quarry in the World Boxing Association elimination tournament to become the new champion. Frazier had chosen not to participate as a protest because of the fact that he recognized Ali as the legitimate champion. In February 1970, Frazier defeated Ellis on a TKO in the fifth round to become the undisputed champion since Ali had announced his retirement before the bout.

Frazier went on to defend his title in 1970 against Bob Foster. Meanwhile, Ali's case went to the U.S. Supreme Court, which found that his arrest and incarceration for avoiding the draft was unconstitutional, and he decided to return to the ring once his boxing license was returned. Ali fought and defeated Jerry Quarry and Oscar Bonavena, then challenged Frazier and a heavyweight title fight was set for March

World heavyweight champion Muhammad Ali, left, points at challenger Joe Frazier at a news conference in New York City, Thursday, July 17, 1975, promoting the "Thrilla in Manila," promoted by Don King, between the fighters. (AP Photo.)

8, 1971, in Madison Square Garden. In a unanimous decision, Frazier, who had knocked down Ali with two mammoth punches in the fight, was declared the winner and retained his championship. Don King promoted all of these fights between Ali and Frazier.

Following the loss, Ali worked himself even harder in training, then defeated Jimmy Ellis before having his jaw broken by Ken Norton in the next fight. Ali won a rematch and another fight with Joe Frazier was slated for January 28, 1974. This was a nontitle fight, however.

Frazier had defended his title against Terry Daniels and Ron Stander to remain undefeated in his pro career, but then, in January 1973, he lost his heavyweight title to George Foreman in Kingston, Jamaica. Frazier then fought and defeated Joe Bugner in London to set up the fight with Ali. The winner would face Foreman, it was assumed, for the championship. Ali defeated Frazier in a unanimous decision in the fight, held again in Madison Square Garden.

Frazier went on to win bouts against Jerry Quarry and Jimmy Ellis to set up another fight with Ali. Ali had fought Foreman in Kinshasa, Zaire, in October 1974 and knocked out the champion in the eighth round to reclaim the title.

This led to the third of the Frazier-Ali bouts, held October 1, 1975, in Quezon City, a district of Manila, the Philippines. The belief was that Frazier was washed up so Ali didn't train as hard for this fight as he could and should have. Frazier, by contrast, worked enormously hard, trying to win back his championship and retire. The dictator of the Philippines, Ferdinand Marcos, offered to have the fight staged in Manila so that he could show that his country was open, free, and a good place for Western investment. All of that was not so, but Don King extracted a guarantee from both Marcos and various networks that made the bout an attractive moneymaker.

The fight began at 10:45 in the morning to accommodate a worldwide television audience, mostly in Europe and North America. For the first four rounds, it was mostly Ali, punching, dodging, and hoping to end Frazier's fight quickly with a knockout. Frazier did not fall and the strategy seemed to backfire when Ali began to tire in round five. For the next six rounds, Frazier was the dominating force, rocking Ali with

"Rumble in the Jungle"

The fight that started Don King's boxing promoter career was a heavyweight boxing contest in 1974 between world heavyweight champion George Foreman against the challenger Muhammad Ali. Both Ali and Foreman spent much of the summer in 1974 training in Zaire for the contest to get used to the climate conditions of tropical Africa.

Ali and Foreman fought on October 30, 1974. Ali began the fight by attacking Foreman with unconventional "right-hand leads." Ali was famed for his speed and technical skills, while Foreman's raw power was his greatest strength. Ali made use of the right-hand lead punch without setting up with a left-handed punch in a further effort to disorient Foreman. In the second round, Ali frequently leaned on the ropes and covered up, letting Foreman punch him on the arms and body. As a result Foreman spent his energy throwing punches that either did not hit Ali or were deflected in a way that made it difficult for Foreman to hit Ali's head. Ali dubbed this strategy the "rope-a-dope." This sapped Foreman's strength and was key to the rope-a-dope technique.

After several rounds of this, Foreman began to show signs of fatigue and his face was badly damaged from the hard and fast jabs that Ali threw. By the eighth round, Foreman's efforts became ineffective as the fatigue of throwing wild shots took its toll. Ali pounced as Foreman tried to pin him on the ropes, landing several right hooks over Foreman's jab followed by a five-punch combination culminating in a left hook that brought Foreman's head up into position and a hard right straight to the face that caused Foreman to fall. Foreman did not get up, and Ali regained the heavyweight championship.

monstrous blows and staggering him but never sending him to the canvas.

Frazier seemed to begin to tire from all of his punching in the 10th and 11th rounds. Ali became more animated in rounds 12 and 13 and caught Frazier with a number of powerful punches to the head, closing his left eye. Ali continued to batter Frazier's head, opening cuts in his mouth and closing his eyes greatly. In the 14th both fighters were laboring heavily, but Ali managed to bring Frazier's right eye nearly to full closure with the swelling caused by the blows.

At the end of the 14th round, Frazier's trainer, Eddie Futch, fearing that Frazier might be severely injured or even killed because of his near blindness, told his fighter that the bout was over. Frazier pleaded to continue, but Futch threw in the towel. Interestingly, Ali had ended the round, completely exhausted, and had instructed his cornermen to cut off his gloves; he was through. But then Frazier's corner conceded and Ali remained the champion.

Afterwards, the antipathy that had marked the runup to the fight was gone. Ali declared Frazier "the greatest fighter ever, after me." The two would still have a shaky relationship over the next 35 years, but at Frazier's death in November 2011, Ali said in a statement, "The world has lost a great champion. I will always remember Joe with respect and admiration."

The "Thrilla in Manila" was the subject of an HBO documentary and the bout was called the fifth greatest sports event ever by ESPN. YouTube has footage of most of the fight. This fight also started Ali on a downward slide physically from which he never recovered, and it was certainly a significant factor in his onset of Parkinson's disease. Despite fighting until 1981 with a number of comebacks, Ali was never the fighter that he was before the "Thrilla in Manila."

Murry R. Nelson and Dylan Williams

See also Ali, Muhammad; ESPN Channels; Madison Square Garden

Suggested Resources
Boxing Classics—the Muhammad Ali vs. Joe Frazier Trilogy—1971–1975. http://www.saddoboxing.com/boxing-article/Muhammad-Ali-v-Joe-Frazier.html. Accessed February 29, 2012.

Frazier, Joe, and Phil Berger. *Smokin' Joe: The Autobiography of a Heavyweight Champion of the World, Smokin' Joe Frazier*. New York: Macmillan, 1996.

Kram, Mark. *Ghosts of Manila*. New York: HarperCollins, 2001.

Tillman, Pat (1976–2004)

At 5'11" and barely 200 pounds, Pat Tillman was a long-haired, undersized linebacker, a true student-athlete who excelled in both football and academics at Arizona State University from 1994 through 1998. For his efforts on the field, he was posthumously inducted into the College Football Hall of Fame in 2010. He went on to a stellar career at safety with the Arizona Cardinals of the National Football League, named to the All-Pro team for 2000. Following the events of September 11, 2001, Tillman completed the NFL season, and then along with his brother Kevin, volunteered for military service, both joining the elite U.S. Army Rangers for tours of combat duty in Iraq and Afghanistan. Beloved by supporters of those wars for sacrificing his successful career as a professional athlete to serve his country, Pat Tillman was lauded as an American hero after he was killed in 2004 in the mountains of Afghanistan. After originally attributing his death to enemy action, the government later admitted to his family and the American public that Tillman died as the result of "friendly fire." His being shot by his own men, along with his family's attempts to cut through the official cover-up and understand the circumstances under which he lost his life, began to erode Pat's place as an icon of the pro-war right. When stories emerged about his belief that the war in Iraq was "f***ing illegal," Pat Tillman, after his tragic passing, made the transition from idol of the right to symbol of the horrors of the "war on terror," and in the process became to the antiwar left an example of the futility of the American combat mission in Afghanistan.

Patrick Daniel Tillman was born on November 6, 1976, in Fremont, California. Ironically, that Bay Area community contains the highest concentration of Afghans in the United States, anchored by a neighborhood called Little Kabul after the Afghani capital, with some 10,000 residing in the city of just over 200,000. Pat's mother, the former Mary Lydanne Spalding, known to all by her nickname Dannie, teaches seventh and eighth grade at Bret Harte Middle School in the Almaden Valley neighborhood of San Jose, California. His father, Patrick Kevin Tillman, is a lawyer based in San Jose. Before amicably divorcing, the couple had three sons; Pat was the eldest, followed by Kevin and Richard. Pat starred in football at Leland High School in Almaden Valley, near where the family had settled in the unincorporated Santa Clara County community of New Almaden, California. Dannie retained their small home in a wooded canyon in that former quicksilver mining district following her split with Patrick. Pat led his team to the Central Coast Division I football championship in 1993, the school's first title since winning the initial CCS crown 21 years earlier. In the

Arizona Cardinals safety Pat Tillman pulls in an interception with one hand during mini-camp in Tempe, Arizona, in May of 2001. (AP Photo/Paul Connors.)

playoff final, a 35–0 rout of Milpitas, he played a key offensive role, rushing for 79 yards on five carries, two of them for touchdowns. Kevin, who later played minor league baseball, was the placekicker.

Pat Tillman attended ASU on an athletic scholarship, reportedly the final one available. In Pat's junior year, the Sun Devils were undefeated in the regular season, losing the 1996 national championship to Florida after a loss to Ohio State in the 1997 Rose Bowl. Pat was voted Pac 10 Defensive Player of the Year for his 1997 senior season and received a number of other athletic and academic honors, as the Devils won the Sun Bowl for their first bowl victory in a decade. He earned his degree in marketing in 3½ years, graduating with a nearly perfect 3.85 grade point average. The Arizona Cardinals, who at the time played their home games at ASU's Sun Devil Stadium in Tempe, selected Pat Tillman in the seventh round with the 226th pick in the 1998 NFL draft. During his rookie season of 1998, Tillman started 10 of the 16 games for the Cardinals. Soon earning a regular starting position, he set a team record with 155 tackles during his All-Pro year of 2000. He showed loyalty to his club when in 2001 he turned down a five-year, $9 million offer from the St. Louis Rams, remaining with the Cardinals at a salary of $512,000 per year. After September 11, and following much research and thought, Pat decided to enlist in the armed forces, and Kevin agreed to join with him. Despite an offer from Arizona in April 2002, which would have rewarded him for his efforts to the tune of $3.6 million for three years, Pat Tillman walked away from his pro football career at the age of 25 to join the army on May 31, 2002. His four-year career record in the NFL shows 238 tackles in 60 games.

Before entering the service, Pat took time to marry his high school sweetheart, Marie Ugenti, and they were able to honeymoon on Bora-Bora before Pat and Kevin left for army duty. Marie played an active role in the brothers' decision to enlist and accepted Pat's choice, although her family and Pat's unsuccessfully attempted an intervention to keep him and Kevin from signing up. Pat's biographer, the noted author Jon Krakauer, writes that Marie never asked Pat why he decided to join, since she knew it was because, in her words, "If it was the right thing for people to go off and fight a war, he believed he should be part of it." In late 2002, the Tillmans completed the Ranger Indoctrination Program and were assigned to the second battalion of the 75th Ranger Regiment at Ft. Lewis, Washington. Pat and Marie were able to live off the post in nearby University Place before he was deployed to Iraq. Both Pat and Kevin were open in their criticism of the Iraq war, courageously speaking freely to their colleagues. Pat's journal entries clearly reflect his horror at the events of what the Pentagon dubbed Operation Iraqi Freedom, and his frustration at actions that he saw as damaging to U.S. interests. After participating in the initial stages of the invasion, Pat returned stateside and entered Ranger School at Ft. Benning, Georgia, in September 2003, graduating in November of that year, after which he was redeployed, this time to Afghanistan.

Pat Tillman was killed on April 22, 2004, outside Sperah, near the Pakistan border, 25 miles southwest of Khost, along with a soldier from the allied Afghan Militia Forces. The Army Special Operations Command initially claimed that Tillman and his unit were ambushed on a road outside the village. Well before the completion of an investigation by the Criminal Investigation Command, the army changed its story, stating that the two men were killed by friendly fire when they were mistakenly believed to be enemy combatants. According to the soldier who was with him when he died, Pat tried to get his fraternal assailants to cease their firing, yelling "I'm Pat F***ing Tillman" before he was cut down in a hail of bullets. Kevin, riding in a nearby vehicle, was kept from the truth, as the Rangers were quickly ordered to avoid giving out accurate information to the family. Although he knew within 24 hours of his death that Pat Tillman had been a victim

of "fratricide," Lt. Gen. Stanley McChrystal nevertheless approved the award of a Silver Star along with his Purple Heart and posthumous promotion to the rank of corporal, and the fallen hero was honored with a nationally televised memorial service on May 3. Richard Tillman responded angrily to speakers like Sen. John McCain and Maria Shriver, representing her husband, California governor Arnold Schwarzenegger, who had spoken of Pat as being "with God." Richard denied this, saying only that he was "f***ing dead." Noting that his brother wasn't religious, he uttered the phrase a second time.

The Tillman family's hurt and anger only escalated after it was disclosed to them and the media soon afterward that Pat Tillman had been the victim of friendly fire, shot and killed by his own men in what was now apparently assumed to have been a ghastly mistake. The family members were outraged that the incident had initially been subject to such a thorough and complete cover-up, and they have since sought unsuccessfully to understand the details of Pat's death. Investigations by Congress, the Pentagon, and one funded by the family confirmed only that Pat Tillman was indeed a victim of friendly fire, and that the Defense Department did act in a callous manner toward the Tillman family, withholding the information they had until after the memorial. It also came out that field commanders and their superiors in Washington went to the extent of having Tillman's clothing, notebooks, and even parts of his body destroyed. Dannie Tillman has speculated that Pat was murdered, based on the destruction of evidence, and retired Gen. Wesley Clark agreed that it was "very possible." In July 2007, Chris Matthews reported on MSNBC's *Hardball* that Pat Tillman might have been deliberately murdered. Martha Mendoza of the Associated Press, citing portions of a review conducted by the Department of Defense inspector general's office released under the Freedom of Information Act, reported that Tillman's wounds indicated murder to the chief of the armed forces medical examiners, who performed Pat's autopsy and told investigators that the medical evidence, which indicated the fatal bullets had been fired from 10 yards away, was inconsistent with the scenario that was presented. This contradicted the opinion of expert forensic pathologists, who had earlier concluded that Tillman

Pat Tillman and Noam Chomsky

When speculation that Pat Tillman had been deliberately murdered began to appear in the mainstream media in the summer of 2007, accusations that he had been targeted due to his antiwar views began to surface in the blogosphere. Pat had read books by Noam Chomsky, perhaps the most prominent academic critic of the Bush administration's global war on terror, as had his brother Kevin and other family members. According to Réka Cseresnyés, who had been Pat's college study partner, he agreed with many of the Massachusetts Institute of Technology linguistics professor's views on the subject, which Krakauer states were "perfectly aligned with Tillman's own sense of outrage over what he'd witnessed in Iraq." Pat prevailed upon Réka, whose husband had begun graduate studies at MIT in 2003, to set up a meeting for him with Chomsky when he returned to the States. To her surprise, Chomsky quickly indicated that he was open to the idea, and Tillman planned to contact him when he came back from Afghanistan.

Although the rumors that Pat intended to come home and lead the antiwar movement have not gone away, nothing has been offered as proof other than his stated opposition to the war, both before and during his military service, and his widely reported planned meeting with Chomsky. The video *Soldier Suicide, Afghanistan and Heroin*, uploaded to YouTube in May 2010, claims that Pat Tillman was assassinated because he discovered that the United States was in Afghanistan to control the heroin trade. Although that claimed discovery squares with information provided by respected scholars like Alfred W. McCoy of the University of Wisconsin, no evidence has surfaced to show that Pat Tillman knew anything new or shocking that would expose the CIA's complicity in the global drug trade.

was killed by a single burst from a squad automatic weapon (SAW). Krakauer contends that Mendoza and the examining pathologist did not know of that report, mistakenly assumed that the fatal wounds had been fired from an M16 or M4, both of which use the same ammunition as an SAW, and therefore concluded that the weapon responsible for Tillman's death had been fired at close range.

Honors have been lavished upon Pat Tillman in the years following his death. Arizona State has retired his number 42, as have the Arizona Cardinals his number 40. A memorial to his memory was erected in New Almaden, California, near where Pat grew up. Leland High School renamed its football field for its most famous alumnus, and the Pac 10 Conference (now the Pac 12) renamed its defensive player of the year award for Pat. The Sun Devils made a "PT-42" patch a permanent part of their football uniform and named the tunnel by which they enter Sun Devil Stadium in his honor. The Cardinals designated the area surrounding their new University of Phoenix Stadium in Glendale as Pat Tillman Freedom Plaza, and in 2006 they unveiled a bronze statue of their former defensive backfield ace. Bridges, streets, and scholarships now bear Pat Tillman's name, as does an NFL-financed USO center in Afghanistan, and less formally, various geographical features around the site where he lost his life. Following Tillman's death, the linebackers on the Ohio State football team as well as Buckeye center Nick Mangold, a future All-Pro for the New York Jets, grew out their hair. Pat's former ASU teammate Jake Plummer, then quarterback of the Denver Broncos, began to wear his hair long and sported a beard. These grooming alterations recalled Pat's appearance as his fellow athletes chose to remember him, before he cut his hair and shaved to conform to military regulations. A film about his life, death, and the ensuing cover-up, *The Tillman Story*, opened in theaters in 2010 after premiering at the Sundance Film Festival, where it was nominated for the Grand Jury Prize. Also nominated by numerous Film Critics Circles as Best Documentary, it won the prize in Florida and San Francisco, as well as an NBR Award as one of the year's top five documentaries as selected by the National Board of Review.

As of mid-2012, more than eight years after Pat Tillman was killed, his family was still angered at the way they were used and abused by the Pentagon, and they remained uncertain as to the cause of his death and what lay behind it. Dannie, whose book about Pat was published in 2008, continues, along with Patrick, to speak out about the injustice. Her anger was channeled into political action, as she campaigned to have Gen. McChrystal fired from his post as co-chair of a White House commission in support of military families, citing the lies that she and others were told, saying his appointment made President Barack Obama "look foolish." Kevin, like his elder brother, left his job as a professional athlete to join the army, abandoning his career as a second baseman in the Cleveland Indians organization after the 2001 season. More outspoken than ever in his condemnation of the Iraq war and U.S. foreign policy, Kevin passionately made his views known in a widely read 2006 online posting, as hopeful as it was bitter, and in 2008 he published a book that simply explains the war in step-by-step fashion easily understandable to young readers. As the American presence in Iraq wound down and similar troop reductions were promised for Afghanistan, with both countries now less stable than they had been before the United States invaded, Pat Tillman was remembered as a hero who patriotically sacrificed his athletic career and finally his life for what he had believed was the good of his country. In the minds of his family and many of his fellow citizens who shared his views about the illegality of the U.S. war in Iraq and its deleterious effects upon the people of both nations, that sacrifice appeared to have been in vain.

David C. Skinner

See also Rose Bowl

Suggested Resources

Krakauer, Jon. *Where Men Win Glory: The Odyssey of Pat Tillman*. New York: Doubleday, 2009.

"Pat Tillman." Biography.com. http://www.biography.com/people/pat-tillman-197041. Accessed February 2012.

Pat Tillman Foundation Website. http://www.pattillmanfoundation.org. Accessed February 2012.

Tillman, Kevin. "After Pat's Birthday." October 19, 2006. http://www.truthdig.com/report/item/200601019_after_pats_birthday. Accessed February 2012.

Tillman, Kevin. *The Transparent Pillage*. Charleston, SC: BookSurge, 2008.

Tillman, Mary, with Narda Zacchino. *Boots on the Ground by Dusk: My Tribute to Pat Tillman*. New York: Modern Times, 2008.

Title IX

Title IX of the Education Amendments of 1972 was signed into law by President Richard M. Nixon. A deceptively simply phrased law, it changed the gender of American education and American sport. Just 37 words long, it read: "No person in the United States shall, on the basis of sex, be excluded from participation in, be denied the benefits of, or be subjected to discrimination under any education program or activity receiving Federal financial assistance." Although the law was patterned after Title VI of the Civil Rights Act of 1964, which prohibits discrimination on the grounds of race, color, or national origin in any program or activity receiving federal financial assistance, Title IX was limited to educational programs.

Prior to the enactment of Title IX, public schools and universities were free to discriminate on the basis of gender. For example, high schools could refuse to allow girls to enroll in classes like chemistry and refuse to allow boys to enroll in home economics. Universities were able to deny financial aid to female students and to save it for the male students. They could also limit admission to just a few women or even exclude them altogether. For example, before Title IX, the University of Virginia, a state school, did not enroll women in the law school.

Just as they were excluded from classes, colleges, and financial aid, women and girls were also systematically excluded from sport. Sport in America was largely considered a masculine preserve, a place to teach boys how to be men. Although girls and women had participated in sports throughout history, they had done so in much smaller numbers than boys and men. In the 1971–1972 school year fewer than 300,000 girls participated in organized high school sports, which meant that girls comprised about 5 percent of all high school athletes. The National Collegiate Athletics Association (NCAA) only sponsored sports for men; any colleges offering sports for women in 1971 had to compete under the supervision of the Association for Interscholastic Athletics for Women (AIAW). Significant differences between the two systems existed. The NCAA had been founded in 1906 and allowed athletic scholarships, and the AIAW was founded in 1971 (although it evolved from organizations founded about five years earlier) and allowed no athletic scholarships. An estimated 35,000 women competed in college sport in the 1971–1972 school year, about 22 percent of all athletes. Funding at all levels of female sport was minimal compared to male sport. The AIAW disbanded in about 1982, roughly when the NCAA began to sponsor women's sport.

Fellow witnesses applaud Olympic gymnast Dominique Dawes, center, as she is introduced at a hearing on Title IX, at the Capitol, April 7, 2003 in Washington, D.C.. Left to right are Nancy Hogshead-Makar, Olympic swimmer and professor at the Florida Coastal School of Law, Marnie Shaul, a Government Accounting Office official, Dawes, and World Cup soccer champion Mia Hamm. (AP Photo/Gerald Herbert.)

Title IX was one of the last laws enacted during the women's liberation movement. Earlier federal laws mandating equal pay and banning gender discrimination in the workplace had been passed. A constitutional amendment banning gender discrimination entirely had been passed by Congress and signed by the president and was wending its way through the states in an unsuccessful attempt at ratification. Thus Title IX was not unusual for the era: It was the result of years of struggle for gender equity in America.

Title IX had a profound impact on the gender of higher education. In 1971 prior to the law's enactment, women had received 1 percent of dental, 7 percent of law, 9 percent of medical, and 14 percent of doctoral degrees. Large numbers of universities had previously denied or limited the enrollment of women in a variety of programs, and after the law's enactment, any school

that received any federal funding (which the vast majority of all colleges and universities did) had to open its doors equally to women. In 2008–2009, women received about 46 percent of dental and law degrees, about 49 percent of medical degrees, and over 57 percent of doctoral degrees. In 2010, more women than men in the United States had undergraduate degrees and more women than men had master's degrees.

When Congress enacted Title IX, they intended the law to have an impact on the gender of higher education, but they did not expect that the law would have an impact on sports. Soon after passage of the law, however, Congress realized that it could change sports and some legislators were concerned. In 1974 Senator John Tower (R-TX) introduced a bill to exempt revenue-producing sport from Title IX. His bill failed to define revenue producing and would have allowed a school or conference to determine what sports fit the definition; the assumption was that men's college football and basketball would be exempt. The amendment was not passed. Instead Congress passed the Javits Amendment, which said that because different sports cost different amounts, nothing in the law should be read as requiring equal spending for different collegiate sports.

As with all laws, after passage, the Department of Housing, Education, and Welfare, the administrative branch charged with enforcing the law, promulgated enforcement regulations. After extensive public debate, Congress approved these regulations, giving them the force of law. The enforcement regulations greatly limited the intrusion of Title IX into sport by exempting contact sport. The regulations stated that if a school offered a team for boys but not girls, girls had to be allowed to try out for that team "unless the sport involved is a contact sport." Contact sport was defined as "boxing, wrestling, rugby, ice hockey, football, basketball and other sports the purpose or major activity of which involved bodily contact." For all legal purposes, girls could not use Title IX to gain access to contact sports; they could only use the law to gain access to noncontact sports. Schools were given until 1978 to comply with the law.

A number of lawsuits, however, were filed that affected, both positively and negatively, the impact of Title IX on sport. In *Cannon v. University of Chicago* (1979) the U.S. Supreme Court decided that the law included a private right of action, meaning that anyone who had suffered discrimination under the law could file a lawsuit without going through a governmental agency first. In 1984, though, the Supreme Court essentially exempted all college sport from the law. *Grove City v. Bell* concluded that only the division of an institution that directly received federal funding needed to comply with the law. For example, if a faculty member of the medical school had a grant from the National Institutes of Health, then the medical school could not discriminate on the basis of gender. Athletic programs, however, almost never received direct federal funding, making them free from Title IX. In 1988, though, Congress enacted the Civil Rights Restoration Act, which nullified *Grove City* and stated that if any part of an institution received federal funding, then the entire institution needed to comply with Title IX. Thus Title IX did not clearly and unequivocally apply to sport programs until 1988.

Even after the application of Title IX to sport, girls and women could still only use the law to gain access to noncontact sports. If they wanted the legal right to try out for a contact sport, they needed to use the Equal Protection Clause of the Fourteenth Amendment of the U.S. Constitution. Over the years in a series of lawsuits about different sports, the courts ruled that if a school offered a contact sport team for males and not females, they had just three choices: They could drop the sport, they could create a comparable team for females, or they could allow females to try out for the male team. In essence, the Equal Protection Clause closed the contact sport exemption and held schools to the same standard for both contact and noncontact sports.

Thus the first major component of Title IX (with help from the Equal Protection Clause) was to give girls and women access to sport programs through their schools and communities, which received federal funding. The second major component was about making those experiences and opportunities for females comparable to males' experiences. The enforcement regulations had three areas of concentration to help programs make that happen: financial assistance; benefits, opportunities, and treatment; and effective accommodation of interests.

The first area, financial assistance, applied only to schools that awarded athletic scholarships. The law was simple: If you offered athletic scholarships to men, you had to offer them to women. Although at first the rule that the scholarships should be "substantially proportionate" was understood to mean that they did not need to be equal, in 1998, the Office of Civil Rights (OCR), which enforced the law, clarified it. Scholarship dollars needed to be divided proportionately. If 55 percent of the schools' athletes were female, then 55 percent (plus or minus 1 percent) of the schools' scholarship dollars needed to go to females. Similarly, private donations needed to be matched either with other donations or by the school. For example, if a donor gave $1 million for scholarships to men's programs, then the school needed to increase funding of women's scholarships by $1 million. In 2003–2004, about 44 percent of Division I athletes were female, and women received about 45 percent of scholarship dollars, thus putting most NCAA programs in compliance with this prong of the law, although that year about 54 percent of all undergraduates were women.

The second area of concentration was benefits, opportunities, and treatment. Over the years, 13 areas were highlighted as points to examine whether or not women's sporting experiences were comparable to men's.

1. Whether the selection of sports and the level of competition effectively accommodates the interests and abilities of the students
2. Provision of equipment and supplies
3. Scheduling of games and practice times
4. Travel and per diem allowance
5. Opportunity to receive coaching and academic tutoring
6. Assignment and compensation of coaches and tutors
7. Provision of locker rooms, practice, and competitive facilities
8. Provision of medical and training facilities and services
9. Provision of housing and dining facilities and services
10. Publicity
11. Recruitment
12. Support services
13. Financial assistance

Except for financial assistance, these areas have been evaluated based on whether or not the experience was comparable and not necessarily equal. For example, the equipment for football is very expensive, but the equipment for women's soccer is not; therefore a school is permitted to spend more on football equipment than it spends on equipment for the women's soccer team. What the school is not permitted to do is to buy new uniforms for the men's baseball team annually and then give the women's softball team the men's old uniforms. Compliance for this area is based on an overall evaluation of the male and female sports programs. Therefore, spending for boys' lacrosse might exceed that of the spending for girls' lacrosse at the same institution provided the overall spending in the total athletic budget was roughly equivalent.

Likewise the law only requires that if the coach of the men's basketball team is paid a living wage, the coach of the women's team must also be paid a living wage but those wages need not be equal.

The dollar amount actually spent on these areas, however, varies dramatically by gender, especially at the elite college level. For example, in 2003–2004 at the NCAA Division I level, schools spent 30 percent of their recruiting budget on women's sport. Similarly, schools at that level spent about 38 percent of their travel budget on women's sport. On average, Division I schools spent more money on men's programs in every single area except fundraising and marketing. The average total expenses for men's teams were $7,285,500 compared to $4,194,800 for women's teams, meaning that women's teams received on average just under 37 percent of the athletic budget at Division I schools.

The third area of concentration, effective accommodation of interest, has been the most divisive and complicated of the three. A 1979 Policy Interpretation from the OCR gave schools three different ways (called the three-prong test) to measure whether or not they were in compliance with this area. First, they could provide participation opportunities that are roughly proportional to undergraduate enrollment, thus if women are 45 percent of an undergraduate population, 45 percent of the athletes should be female. Second, a school could show that it had a history of expanding athletic opportunities for women. Third, a school could demonstrate that they had effectively accommodated the interests and abilities of their students. A school could use any single method to prove compliance; it did not have to prove all three.

The First Circuit Court of Appeals in *Cohen v. Brown* (1996), though, emphasized that the courts preferred the proportionality prong for determining compliance. Brown University had cut a number of women's varsity sports and some men's programs for budget reasons and the women of the gymnastics team sued, claiming the school violated Title IX. Brown argued that the proportionality prong was an illegal quota and that they were meeting the interests and abilities of their undergraduates. After a long legal battle, the courts concluded that Title IX and the associated regulations and policies were not quotas and that the three-prong test was an appropriate way to evaluate interests and abilities. The court rejected Brown's claim that women were inherently less interested in sport. The court noted that "interests and abilities rarely develop in a vacuum; they evolve as a function of opportunity and experience" and concluded that Brown University needed to fully meet the interests and abilities of its female students. The court was skeptical of a survey approach to satisfy the third prong of the test but noted that a survey approach was irrelevant in this case because Brown University was demoting women's teams that were filled with eligible, qualified, and clearly interested athletes. As Brown was cutting women's sport, the institution was unable to argue that they had a history of expanding women's sporting opportunities.

The proportionality prong, while favored by courts, has been the most challenging. Some schools in the past have counted athletes multiple times. For example, schools have said that a three-sport female athlete counts three times even if she only receives one scholarship. Other schools have counted roster spots rather than actual athletes. For instance, a school might say they have 100 slots for female cross-country runners even though only 15 women are on the team. Neither of these is permissible.

What is permissible under the law but that is problematic morally is something called addition by subtraction. The proportionality rule is just that—proportions. A school can change the proportion of female athletes not by increasing the number of female athletes (which is the real goal of Title IX activists) but by decreasing the number of male athletes. For example, a school might have an undergraduate population that is 50 percent female but of their 100 athletes, only 25 are female. The spirit of Title IX would suggest that the school add 50 female athletes so that of the new 150 athletes, 50 percent (75) are female. The law, however, allows the school to instead cut 50 athletes so that of the 50 athletes remaining, 50 percent (25) are female. Some schools have chosen to scapegoat Title IX to justify cutting men's athletic programs, leading some people inaccurately to blame Title IX for any loss to men's programs. Although male athletes have challenged the cuts to their programs, the courts have refused to dictate to schools what sports should be

---

What Has Changed?

Although Title IX and the social movement that spawned gender equity in America deserve a great deal of credit for increasing the number of female athletes in America, Title IX had an unintended consequence. Prior to the law's enactment, an estimated 90 percent of college and high school sports for females were coached and run by females. Often these female coaches and administrators had very little financial support from their institutions and men apparently had little interest in getting involved. All that changed with Title IX. The NCAA recognized the future in college sport, began offering women's championships in 1980–1981, and that marked the end of the AIAW. With the increased interest and revenue came male coaches and administrators of women's sport. Immediately after the law was passed many colleges and high schools merged any existing women's programs with the men's and a male athletic director usually ran the department. If a woman had run the women's program, she became the senior women's administrator, reporting to the male AD. Although a few colleges kept separate men's and women's athletic departments, most have merged.

In 2008, about 20.6 percent of all teams (male and female) at the college level were coached by women and less than 43 percent of women's teams were coached by women. Just over 21 percent of athletic directors were female and just over 27 percent of head athletic trainers were female. Nothing in Title IX applies to the gender of coaches and administrators. Despite the greater participation of females in sport, sport remains predominantly male.

---

offered and how their funding should be determined, provided that Title IX is not violated.

Men's sport, though, has not been substantially harmed by the law. In 2009–2010 over three million girls played high school sport, comprising about 42 percent of all athletes, but a record 4.45 million boys played as well. Similarly in 2006–2007, 172,534 women participated in NCAA sport, comprising about 43 percent of all athletes, but a record 230,259 men also played. Just as Title IX opened the classroom doors to women and girls, the law also opened the doors to the fields and the gymnasiums.

Sarah K. Fields

See also Legal Decisions; NCAA

Suggested Resources

Anderson, Kelli. "The Power of Play." May 7, 2012. http://sportsillustrated.cnn.com/vault/article/magazine/MAG1197977/2/index.htm. Accessed May 31, 2012.

Brake, Deborah L. *Getting in the Game: Title IX and the Women's Sports Revolution*. New York: New York University Press, 2010.

Carpenter, Linda Jean, and R. Vivian Acosta. *Title IX*. Champaign, IL: Human Kinetics, 2005.

"Education and Title IX." National Organization for Women Website. http://www.now.org/issues/title_ix/index.html. Accessed June 24, 2011.

Hogshead-Maker, Nancy, and Andrew Zimbalist, eds. *Equal Play: Title IX and Social Change*. Philadelphia: Temple University Press, 2007.

Waecher, Marv. "Sports Illustrated Title IX Anniversary Edition." May 11, 2012. http://stream.goodwin.drexel.edu/womenincoaching/2012/05/11/sports-illustratred-title-ix-anniversary-edition/. Accessed May 31, 2012.

Tommy John Surgery

Tommy John surgery refers to the replacement of a damaged ulnar collateral ligament (UCL) in a baseball player's (usually a pitcher's) arm with a tendon from another part of his body, usually the other arm, to allow the player to return to his former level of skill. It is named after Tommy John, a pitcher upon whom the surgery was first successfully performed.

In 1974, Tommy John was a 31-year-old left-handed pitcher for the Los Angeles Dodgers. He had been initially signed by the Cleveland Indians after high school in Terre Haute, Indiana, and made his first major league appearance in 1963 at the age of 20. John went 0–2, but he had an ERA of 2.21 and struck out nine, while walking only one. He made the Indians in 1964, but went only 2–9 and was traded at the end of the season to the Chicago White Sox in a three-team deal involving the Kansas City A's.

Decathlete Trey Hardee flexes his muscle as he shows the scar from his Tommy John surgery at the Texas Relays track meet, March 28, 2012, in Austin, Texas. (AP Photo/Eric Gay.)

John blossomed with the White Sox and in seven seasons with them won 82 games and lost 80. In three of those years he was one of the top pitchers in the league in ERA and he was selected for the 1968 All-Star team. In December 1971 he was traded to the Dodgers for Dick Allen. In just under three years with the Dodgers, he had won 40 games and lost just 15, when in late August 1974, he felt a tear in his arm and could no longer pitch. After rest and efforts at rehabilitation, he was faced with retirement at age 31 or a revolutionary surgical procedure that had never been done before. Dozens of great pitchers, among them Sandy Koufax, had had their careers ended prematurely as a result of such an injury.

Dr. Frank Jobe had done research and some similar surgery, but never something so radical on a person whose entire livelihood was based on his demanding use of his arm. Jobe estimated that the chances of a full recovery were 1 in 100, but he was really only guessing, since he had no real data to back up such an estimate.

The surgery was performed on September 25, 1974, then John spent the entire 1975 season in rehabilitation, not knowing if he would ever pitch again. During that time he worked with teammate Mike Marshall, a relief pitcher, who had been a kinesiology major at Michigan State, in altering his pitching motion so as to put less strain on his arm and knee. John returned to the Dodgers in 1976 and went 10–10, then pitched until 1989, when he was 46 years old, winning a total of 288 games, 164 after having had the surgery.

The success that Jobe had with this surgical procedure put him in high demand both to perform it for other pitchers who had "blown out their pitching arms" as well as to teach it to other orthopedic surgeons. Jobe and those who learned his technique, such as Dr. Robert Kerlan and Dr. James Andrews, saved the careers of dozens of major leaguers who, in previous years, would have had their careers ended as a result of the injury. These include major leaguers Orel Hershiser, Tom Candiotti, John Smoltz, Chris Carpenter, Paul Molitor, Joe Nathan, Brian Wilson, and, most recently, Stephen Strasburg. This is in addition to the thousands of players at other levels, including high school, who have successfully undergone such surgery. In 2004 one report stated that in 2002 and 2003, 75 of nearly 700 pitchers in the major leagues

---

A Trademark Surgery

Dr. Jobe, upon the success of his radical procedure, trademarked the name "Tommy John surgery." Technically it is an ulnar collateral ligament replacement procedure, but the name of the Dodger pitcher is forever identified with the procedure.

---

had successfully undergone the procedure and were "Tommy John survivors." In addition, football players, usually quarterbacks, have also been beneficiaries of such surgery. These include Jake Delhomme, Craig Erickson, Rob Johnson, and Deion Sanders.

Today the surgery is relatively common and is performed by a host of excellent orthopedic surgeons. The humerus, in the upper arm, connects to the two bones in the forearm (the radius and the ulna) by means of various connective tissues, the most important of which is the ulnar collateral ligament (UCL). The UCL provides the elbow stability necessary to withstand the torque and stress put on the elbow when a baseball is thrown with great force. Holes are drilled in the ulna and humerus bones, which are part of the elbow joint. The arm is opened up, the muscles separated, and the ulnar nerve lifted out and moved to provide greater access to the joint. The damaged tissue is removed. The tendon, which has been harvested from the player's body or a cadaver, is then woven in a figure-eight pattern through the tunnels that have been drilled in the bones. Over time the tendon "ligamentizes" itself, that is, it somehow takes on the ligamental structure and function. There is a risk of injury to the ulnar nerve, and Tommy John's was slightly damaged by the surgery, causing his recovery to be longer than after most such surgeries today. The estimated recovery time is one year for a pitcher and six months for a nonpitcher, but these vary, depending on the individual. The success rate is about 85 percent.

The procedure has been adapted to accommodate other joints, where viable, such as the shoulder. In short, the Tommy John procedure has revolutionized sport surgery and become a part of American, if not global, culture. In recent years a movement has grown to have Dr. Jobe voted into the Baseball Hall of Fame as a contributor to the game.

Murry R. Nelson

See also Baseball Hall of Fame; Koufax, Sandy; Los Angeles Dodgers

Suggested Resources

Dr. Frank Jobe. http://mlb.mlb.com/news/press_releases/ press_release.jsp?ymd=20080221&content_id= 2382458&vkey=pr_la&fext=.jsp&c_id=la. Accessed July 26, 2011.

"Interview with Dr. Frank Jobe." http://assets.espn.go.com/ mlb/columns/bp/1431308.html. Accessed July 26, 2011.

John, Tommy. *T.J.: My 26 Years in Baseball.* New York: Bantam, 1992.

John, Tommy, with Sally John and Joe Musser. *The Tommy John Story.* Old Tappan, NY: F. H. Revell, 1978.

Tonya Harding–Nancy Kerrigan Scandal (1994)

Perhaps it is unfair to constantly link Tonya Harding and Nancy Kerrigan together, but their legacies are forever intertwined. The women, initially rivals in the world of figure skating, form two sides of one of the most sensational scandals ever to rock the history of sports. It began in 1994, just before the U.S. National Figure Skating Championships, when an assailant used a metal baton to strike Kerrigan in the leg. The public soon learned that Kerrigan's attacker had ties to Harding, who was eventually convicted for her role in the attack. The incident incited a media frenzy that the international ice-skating community had never before experienced, nor is ever likely to experience again.

Tonya Harding, born November 12, 1970, grew up in Portland, Oregon. Her young life was challenging; her father was physically disabled, which often made it difficult for him to earn a living. Harding alleges that her mother was physically abusive. In spite of these and other hardships, she showed promise as a skater at an early age. Her career began in the mid-1980s when she placed sixth in the 1986 U.S. Figure Skating Championships. In 1991, at the U.S. Championships, Harding became the first woman to land a triple axel during a competition. She also earned the competition's first perfect 6.0 score for technical merit, along with the event's title. At the subsequent World Championships Kristi Yamaguchi edged out Harding for the gold, but with her second-place finish

American figure skaters Nancy Kerrigan, left, and Tonya Harding work out during an Olympic practice session at Hamar Olympic Amphitheater, Tuesday, February 22, 1994, Hamar, Norway. (AP Photo/Doug Mills.)

the powerful skater seemed to have a promising career ahead of her.

On the other side of the country, Nancy Kerrigan was also making a name for herself. Born October 13, 1969, in Woburn, Massachusetts, she began skating after spending time at the ice rink with her hockey-playing older brothers. By 1987 she placed fourth in the Junior U.S. Figure Skating Championships. Three years later, competing at the senior level, she placed third at the National Championships and subsequently won bronze at the World Figure Skating Championships. Placing above her in a U.S. sweep of the medals were Kristi Yamaguchi in first place and Tonya Harding, who came in second. In 1992, Kerrigan won the silver, again bested by Yamaguchi, who retired in 1993 leaving Kerrigan and Harding to vie for the top spot.

With the 1994 Lillehammer Olympics just a month away, both Harding and Kerrigan were training hard for the U.S. Figure Skating Championships, for the top two finishers would represent the United States at the Games. On the afternoon of January 6, 1994, Kerrigan was training at the Cobo Arena in Detroit, Michigan. As she left the ice, satisfied with her preparation for the impending competition, a man named Shane Stant entered the arena and struck Kerrigan in the right leg with a collapsible police baton. The injury was not career ending, though her thigh was bruised severely enough to force her to withdraw from the championships, where Harding captured the title. Despite Kerrigan's inability to qualify for the 1994 Games, her competitors, along with the United States Figure Skating Association (USFSA), agreed that she should earn one of the spots in Lillehammer. This left the second-place finisher, Michelle Kwan, off the Olympic team.

Kerrigan soon recovered and trained arduously for the upcoming Games. Her fame skyrocketed and she signed lucrative endorsement deals in the wake of the scandal. As her star began to rise, Harding's soon started to plummet. Within days of the attack, a police investigation determined that Stant was a hired thug employed by Harding's husband, Jeff Gillooly, and her bodyguard, Shawn Eckhardt, to break Kerrigan's leg. Harding denied any prior knowledge of the attack but conceded, "I am responsible, however, for failing to report things I learned about the assault." Despite her confession, the USOC permitted her to compete in the 1994 Olympic Winter Games. The controversy proved good for television ratings and women's figure skating drew the largest audience as 120 million viewers watched the two women face off. Magazines such as *Newsweek* and *Time* helped hype the event, featuring the two athletes on their covers. The U.S. media largely treated Kerrigan as its darling, casting her as America's golden girl. Harding, on the other hand, became primarily characterized as the villain.

The scandal made women's figure skating the biggest draw of the Winter Olympics. More than 120 million people tuned in to watch the two skaters compete and the broadcast became one of the most watched events in television history. Kerrigan, by then fully

---

Triple Axel Jump

When Tonya Harding successfully landed a triple axel she gained entry into a very small and exclusive group of female figure skaters. First completed by Vern Taylor in 1978, the triple axel is a jump that requires a skater to leap from the right foot, complete three complete body rotations in the air, and land on the left foot. Although the jump has become commonplace in men's figure skating, only Midori Ito, Ludmila Nelidina, Yukari Nakano, Mao Asada, and Harding have successfully landed the jump in female competition.

---

recovered, skated brilliantly, earning a silver medal. Harding finished a disappointing eighth. Taking the gold medal was the underestimated Ukrainian athlete, Oksana Baiul.

The scandal raged on. Gillooly, Stant, Eckhardt, and Derrick Smith, who drove the getaway car, were all convicted for their roles in the attack and sentenced to prison time. Gillooly testified against his wife as part of a plea bargain and Harding, in an attempt to avoid jail time, pleaded guilty to hindering the prosecution. She was sentenced to three years' probation, 500 hours of community services, and a $160,000 fine. The USFSA, after an internal investigation, determined that Harding knew of the attack before it took place and had acted unethically and in conflict with its bylaws. The organization stripped her of her 1994 U.S. title and banned Harding from all of its future events. A pariah in the figure skating community, Harding was unable to earn a living in the sport to which she had devoted her life.

Kerrigan retired from figure skating competitions following the 1994 Olympics but still performs in ice shows. She has worked as a broadcaster for skating events, has published a successful instructional book on figure skating technique, and was inducted into the United States Figure Skating Hall of Fame in 2004. Tonya Harding, on the other hand, has not fared as well. Plagued by controversy, she has not shied away from the public eye and remains one of sport's most tragic tales, the butt of jokes, and a derisive reference in music, movies, television, and even in a speech delivered by Barack Obama. In the end, no matter what the two women accomplish, they will always be remembered for the ugly incident that forever tethers them to each other.

Sara Roser-Jones and Jaime Schultz

Suggested Resources

Baughman, Cynthia. *Feminist Essays on the Tonya Harding/Nancy Kerrigan Spectacle.* New York: Routledge, 1995.

Smolowe, Jill, et al. "Figure Skater Tonya Harding: Tarnished Victory." January 24, 1994. http://www.time.com/time/magazine/article/0,9171,980013,00.html. Accessed November 29, 2011.

Torres, Dara (1967–)

American swimmer Dara Torres became the oldest swimmer to compete at the Olympic Games when she represented the United States in three events at the 2008 Olympics in Beijing. As a 41-year-old athlete competing in her fifth Olympic Games, in addition to winning three silver medals, she set a record for most Olympic appearances by a female swimmer. Winning her first Olympic medal in Los Angeles in 1984 as a 17-year-old swimmer, Torres went on to compete at the 1988, 1992, 2000, and 2008 Olympic Games, winning medals each time for a total of four gold, four silver, and four bronze medals. Torres has gained fame promoting the message that you do not need to put an age limit on winning or dreams. She has emerged as a role model for women interested in taking up new sports in their 30s and 40s, and remaining competitive after having children. In interviews, she describes herself as "pathologically competitive" and states that her success stems from her hatred of losing.

Torres grew up in Beverly Hills, California, with four brothers and a younger sister. When she was five years old, her parents divorced but remained on good terms. Her mother, former model Marylu Kauder, taught the children to swim in their backyard pool, while her father, Edward Torres, spent considerable time in Las Vegas as an owner and manager of hotels, including the Fremont, Riviera, and Aladdin. The family had strong ties to the Hollywood area as her paternal grandfather worked for Paramount Pictures in the 1940s and won two Academy Awards for sound.

As a child, Torres participated in tennis, soccer, basketball, and cycling, but excelled at swimming from a young age. She broke her first American age-group record when she was 12 and set her first world record when she was 15 years old. She attended the Westlake School for Girls and accepted an athletic scholarship to the University of Florida. As a student-athlete, she won 28 NCAA All-American swimming awards, which is the maximum a swimmer can win.

After competing in her second Olympic Games in 1988 at age 22, Torres retired from swimming and claims to have avoided swimming, even recreationally, for several years. Equipped with a bachelor's degree in telecommunications, she moved to New York City in 1990 and immersed herself in her work, eventually working her way up to the job of production assistant at NBC Sport. While watching taped footage of figure skater Brian Boitano's comeback in 1991 as a 27-year-old athlete, and in light of a younger swimmer breaking her 100-meter freestyle American record, Torres decided to stage a comeback. She left New York City to join the University of Florida Gators swimming program. As a student-athlete training under the tutelage of coach Randy Reese, Torres struggled with bulimia. She attributes her disordered eating patterns to many sources: a coaching philosophy that required athletes to weigh-in weekly and encouraged extremely lean physiques, a desire to please her coach, her extreme competitiveness, and family pressures. A condition of her acceptance to rejoin the swim program, imposed by new coach Mitch Ivey, was that she first overcome her eating disorder by seeing a psychiatrist.

After a successful performance at the 1992 Olympics where she won a gold medal as part of the 4x100-meter freestyle relay, Torres retired from swimming for the second time. During her second retirement she worked on televisions shows aired on ESPN2 and the Discovery Channel, filmed infomercials for Tae Bo, and worked as a sports model, most notably as the first athlete featured in the *Sports Illustrated* swimsuit issue. This retirement was also short-lived. In 1999, despite pressure from her father to marry and have children, she decided to attempt to qualify for the 2000 Olympics, and she began training at Stanford

University with Coach Richard Quick. After collecting another five Olympic medals in Sydney, including her first individual Olympic medals in the 50-meter freestyle, 100-meter freestyle, and 100-meter butterfly, as well as another two medals in relays, Torres retired for the third time.

At the time of her third retirement, Torres vowed to only swim again as a form of light exercise if she were to become pregnant. Medical advice at the time discouraged intensive training while pregnant, so Torres reasoned she could handle swimming for enjoyment and exercise if she were medically constrained from attempting to race. Hence, when Torres was seven weeks pregnant in 2005, at the age of 38 after a long struggle with infertility, she started swimming at the nearby Coral Springs (Florida) Aquatic Club. The Coral Springs Aquatic Club was the home base of legendary swimming coach Michael Lohberg, whose swimmers have qualified for every Olympic Games since 1984. Despite her plan to swim recreationally and at low intensity during pregnancy, Torres found it very difficult not to race the fittest swimmers in the pool. She began training with Ray Antonov, who represented Bulgaria at the 2004 Olympics in the 100-meter freestyle, and only four weeks after giving birth to a daughter, Tessa, she competed in a master's swim meet. She qualified for the 2008 Olympic Trials at the World Masters Championship less than four months after her child's birth. Not long after, Torres was permitted to leave the master's group to join Lohberg's high-performance training group, which consisted of swimmers as young as 15 years old.

Lohberg's individualized training plan for Torres involved frequent monitoring of lactic acid levels via blood drawn from behind the ear and a substantial decrease in the number of training hours and miles compared to her previous training regiments. To facilitate optimal performance, Torres prepared as thoroughly as possible, avoiding caffeine and alcohol, and ensuring she got adequate rest and sleep. She used unconventional methods, such as consulting psychics and bringing her personal trainers with her to major competitions to help her stretch and recover, to help achieve her Olympic dreams. She carried her swim gear in a rolling bag instead of a backpack like her

Oldest Olympians

At age 33, Dara Torres set the record for being the oldest female swimmer to compete for the United States at the Olympics. She broke this record again in 2008 at age 41. However, Torres is far from achieving the title of oldest Olympian. In Beijing, American sailor John Dane was 58 years old and American shooter Libby Callahan was 56 years old. Taking the title of oldest 2008 Olympian was dressage rider Hiroshi Hoketsu, 67, of Japan, who is still two Olympiads away from breaking Swedish shooter Oscar Swahn's record of competing at the 1920 Olympics at age 72.

fellow swimmers, to protect her shoulders and avoid unnecessary strain; consumed a carefully developed cocktail of amino acids to aid recovery; and was a strong advocate of resistance stretching. Her commitment to optimal nutrition led her to invest in the company Living Fuel, which produces nutrition shakes.

Torres qualified for the 2008 United States Women's Olympic swimming team by winning the 50-meter and 100-meter freestyle races at the U.S. Olympic Trials. In addition to Torres, seven other athletes on Lohberg's team competed at the 2008 Olympics, but he was unable to attend due to medical reasons. With the help of a sport psychologist, Torres put aside her worry about Lohberg's health to win three silver medals, missing the gold medal in the 50-meter freestyle by just 0.01 second and placing second in both the 4x100-meter medley and 4x100-meter freestyle relays.

One of Torres's defining features is her extremely lean and muscular physique. While she is very popular among people who praise her role in demonstrating that women can compete at the highest levels of sport in their 40s, she has experienced a backlash from people who attribute her continued success in swimming to doping. Torres has never failed a doping test and volunteered for the United States Anti-Doping Agency's enhanced drug-testing program leading up to the Beijing Olympics, yet she is plagued by persistent allegations that she uses banned substances. In response, she claims that the reason many women stop competing at the highest level is due to lifestyle choices rather than genetics. Further speculation about Torres's success in the pool stems from her association with Anthony Galea, a physician renowned for his innovative healing methods, but also for being caught transporting banned performance-enhancing drugs across the Canada-U.S. border. Not all of her teammates on the U.S. national swim team welcomed her multiple comebacks. Notable tensions included an icy reception at the University of Florida by then–100-meter freestyle U.S. record holder Nicole Haislett and lasting tensions with rival Jenny Thompson, which forced Torres off the Stanford team when their rivalry in practice began hurting them both physically and mentally.

Torres is supported financially by several sponsors and is managed by the Premier Management Group. She has endorsed products by Toyota, Speedo, NXT Nutritionals, BP Products, Sleep Innovations, and Tae Bo, among others. Her charitable work includes raising money for cancer and autism research. Torres works hard to challenge people's beliefs about middle-aged female athletes, and since her success at the 2008 Olympics she has been awarded several honors and recognitions, including the trophy for the Best Comeback at the ESPY Awards. Since the 2008 Olympics, in addition to training and recuperating from knee surgery, Torres has worked as a feature correspondent on *Good Morning America*, coauthored two books, and provided commentary for several television networks. She qualified for the 2012 Olympic Trials and battled for the chance to represent the United States at the Olympic Games for the sixth time, but finished fourth in the 50-meter race and failed to qualify.

Sarah J. Teetzel

See also ESPY Awards; 1984 Olympic Games, Los Angeles; Sports and Drugs/Doping

Suggested Resources
Anderson, Kelli. "One for the Aged." August 25, 2008. http://sportsillustrated.cnn.com/vault/article/magazine/MAG1144308/index.htm. Accessed May 1, 2011.

Dara Torres Website. http://daratorres.com/. Accessed May 1, 2011.

Torres, Dara, and Billie Fitzpatrick. *Gold Medal Fitness: A Revolutionary 5-Week Program.* New York: Broadway Books, 2010.

Torres, Dara, and Elizabeth Weil. *Age Is Just a Number: Achieve Your Dreams at Any Stage in Your Life.* New York: Broadway Books, 2009.

Trevino, Lee (1939–)

Lee Buck Trevino is a Mexican American professional golfer. He was born December 1, 1939, in Dallas, Texas, and is a great source of pride for Mexican Americans and Latinos. Frequently referred to as "The Merry Mex" or "Supermex," Trevino captured a total of six major championships over the course of his illustrious career. Trevino is known for his humor and personality, his self-taught golf swing, an unrivaled creativity in terms of shot making and execution, as well as being one of Jack Nicklaus's main rivals during the 1970s. He amassed 89 professional wins, including 29 on the PGA Tour and 29 on the Champions Tour.

His mother, Juanita Trevino, and his grandfather, Joe Trevino, raised Lee. He did not know his father, Joseph Trevino, who left the family when Lee was just a small boy. At the age of five, Trevino began working in cotton fields to help support his family and attended school occasionally. He was introduced to the game of golf when his uncle gave him a golf club and a few golf balls. From there, he began sneaking into local country clubs where he would practice his craft. He began caddying at Dallas Athletic Club, where he eventually went to work full-time after leaving school at the age of 14. As a caddie, Lee would practice hitting balls every day after work and frequently has told of times when he would hustle competitive golfers for money, sometimes using nothing more than a shovel and a makeshift golf club that he made from a can of Dr. Pepper.

At the age of 17, Trevino enlisted in the United States Marine Corps. He served four years, eventually earning the rank of lance corporal, a promotion that he would later claim was aided by his golf prowess and play, which he demonstrated playing golf with Marine officers. During his time as a Marine, he played in many successful armed forces golf events. One of his peers at the time, Orville Moody, would eventually follow in Trevino's footsteps, becoming a PGA Tour professional golfer.

Following his military career, he began working as a golf club professional in El Paso, Texas. He became known as a money player, frequently entering and winning many head-to-head matchups as a club professional. In 1965, he won the Texas State Open,

Lee Trevino holds his good luck coin at Oak Hill Country Club as he arrives for the final round of the 68th U.S. Open golf championship in Rochester, New York, June 16, 1968. (AP Photo.)

which he successfully defended the following year, becoming the first repeat champion of the tournament. His stint as a club pro didn't last long. Soon after being discharged from the Corps, he began playing on the PGA Tour in 1967. He experienced immediate success on the PGA Tour, where he earned enough money in the 1967 U.S. Open to secure his status for the rest of year on the tour. *Golf Digest* named him Rookie of the Year the same year. In 1968, Trevino captured his first major championship by winning the U.S. Open at the Oak Hill Country Club in Rochester, New York. Jack Nicklaus came in second.

After notching his first PGA Tour win (U.S. Open) in 1968, Trevino went on to claim victory that same year in the Hawaiian Open. In 1969, he won at the Tucson Open Invitational by a margin of seven strokes. In 1970, Trevino recorded two more PGA Tour victories by winning again at the Tucson Open Invitational and the National Airlines Open Invitational, with both wins coming in playoffs. His two wins in 1970 propelled Trevino toward his most successful season on the PGA Tour the following year. In 1971, Trevino won six events including his second U.S. Open

victory, beating Jack Nicklaus in a playoff, and his first British Open Championship title. Also that year, Trevino won the Tallahassee Open Invitational, Danny Thomas Memphis Classic, the Canadian Open, and the Sahara Invitational.

In 1972, Trevino won four times, including successfully defending his British Open Championship title from the year before, gaining his fourth major championship as a PGA Tour golf professional. He also recorded wins at the Danny Thomas Memphis Classic, the Greater Hartford Open Invitational, and the Greater St. Louis Golf Classic in 1972. Lee added two more wins the following season in 1973, claiming victory at the Doral-Eastern Open and the Jackie Gleason Inverrary–National Airlines Classic. In 1974, Trevino won twice more, including his first PGA Championship, bringing his major championship total to date to five, and the Greater New Orleans Open. Over the next five years, from 1975 to 1979, Trevino won once each year. He notched victories at the Florida Citrus Open (1975), Colonial National Invitational (1976), Canadian Open (1977), Colonial National Invitational (1978), and Canadian Open (1979).

Lee won three times in 1980, marking his last multiple win season on the PGA Tour. He beat fellow Texan Ben Crenshaw in the Tournament Players Championship by one stroke. He also won his third Danny Thomas Memphis Classic title and the San Antonio Texas Open. In 1981, Trevino edged out Raymond Floyd in the MONY Tournament of Champions. He won his final tournament on the PGA Tour in 1984, claiming his second PGA Championship and sixth major championship title. The following year, in 1985, Trevino won on the European Tour claiming victory at the Dunhill British Masters, his second European Tour win (1978 Benson & Hedges International Open). Trevino also won the 1975 Mexican Open as a professional while on the PGA Tour.

Trevino's 29 PGA Tour wins place him in a tie for 19th among all-time leading winners on the professional tour. He has more wins than Gary Player (24), Raymond Floyd (22), and Johnny Miller (25). His six major championships on the PGA Tour place him tied for 12th (Nick Faldo) of all-time major championship winners, one behind Bobby Jones (7) and one ahead of Byron Nelson (5).

Lee Trevino also had tremendous success on the Champions Tour as a professional golfer. His 29 total Champions Tour wins place him second on the list of all-time winners, behind only Hale Irwin (45). He also won four Champions Tour major championships including the U.S. Senior Open (1990) over Jack Nicklaus by two strokes, The Tradition (1992) over Jack Nicklaus by one stroke, and the PGA Seniors' Championship (1992, 1994).

Trevino began his Champions Tour career after turning 50 in 1989. It didn't take him long to make his mark as a rookie on the tour. He claimed his first Champions Tour victory in 1990 at the Royal Caribbean Classic. He notched six more titles that year at the Aetna Challenge, Vintage Chrysler Invitational, Doug Sanders Kingwood Celebrity Classic, NYNEX Commemorative, U.S. Senior Open, and Transamerica Senior Golf Championship. Trevino then went on to record four more multiple-win seasons in a row from 1991 to 1995. In 1991, Trevino was victorious again at the Aetna Challenge, at Vantage at The Dominion, and at Sunwest Bank Charley Pride Senior Golf Classic. In 1992, he won Vantage at The Dominion, The

Tradition, PGA Senior Championship, Las Vegas Senior Classic, and Bell Atlantic Classic. In 1993, Trevino added three more Champions Tour wins at Cadillac NFL Golf Classic, Nationwide Championship, and Vantage Championship. In 1994, Trevino had his most successful Champions Tour season since his rookie season, claiming victory five times, including Royal Caribbean Classic, PGA Senior Championship, Paine Weber Invitational, Bell Atlantic Classic, BellSouth Senior Classic at Opryland, and Northville Long Island Classic. Over the next five years, Trevino earned five more Champions Tour victories at the Northville Long Island Classic (1995), The Transamerica (1995), Emerald Coast Classic (1996), Southwestern Bell Dominion (1998), and Cadillac NFL Golf Classic (2000) before retiring from full-time play in 2001.

Trevino earned numerous distinctions and awards as a professional golfer. He was the first player to shoot four consecutive subpar rounds (all in the 60s) in a U.S. Open, a feat he accomplished winning the major championship in 1968 to claim his first professional title. He made the Ryder Cup team six times and earned an impressive 17–7–6 record. Trevino was inducted into the World Golf Hall of Fame in 1981, becoming the first person of Latino descent to receive the honor. He won five Vardon trophies given to the players with the lowest scoring average in a season. In 2000, *Golf Digest* ranked Trevino as the 14th greatest golfer of all time. He coauthored his autobiography, titled *They Call Me Supermex*. He has also established numerous scholarships in support of Mexican Americans in Texas and across the country.

Trevino's influence goes beyond the game of golf and reaches into the depths of popular culture. He has been featured on the television series *The Simpsons* in an episode called "Marge Be Not Proud." He has had Nintendo games named after him. He was featured in the film *Happy Gilmore* (1996), where he played himself as a professional golfer.

Trevino is known as much for his loveable, likeable, and often laughable personality. He was known as a joker who had a tendency to bring pleasure and laughter into the most pressure-filled golf situations. He also excelled while bringing his own form of humor into those situations, frequently beating his rivals on the course while all the while telling jokes.

He has credited his wife, Claudia, as his inspiration. He famously quipped in 1975 after being struck by lightning that if he were ever on the course again in a storm, he would hold his one iron and point it to the sky, "because not even God can hit the 1-iron."

Lee Trevino's rags-to-riches story, his immense skills in golf, and his good faith and humor place him among the all-time greats in the game of golf and in sports in general.

David A. Fuentes

See also *Happy Gilmore*; Nicklaus, Jack

Suggested Resources

"Lee Trevino." Champions Tour. http://www.pgatour.com/golfers/002213/lee-trevino/. Accessed May 3, 2012.

"Lee Trevino." Gold Legends. http://www.golflegends.org/lee-trevino.php. Accessed May 3, 2012.

"Lee Trevino." World Golf Hall of Fame. http://www.worldgolfhalloffame.org/hof/member.php?member=1116. Accessed May 3, 2012.

Trevino, Lee, and Sam Bair. *They Call Me Supermex: The Autobiography of Lee Trevino.* New York: Random House, 1982.

Triple Crown

The Triple Crown is the American series of spring classic races for three-year-old Thoroughbred racehorses, consisting of the Kentucky Derby, the Preakness Stakes, and the Belmont Stakes. Only 11 horses have swept the Triple Crown and no horse has won the series since Affirmed in 1978. Each of the three races evolved separately and was not recognized collectively as the Triple Crown until the 1930s. *Daily Racing Form* writer Charles Hatton coined the term "Triple Crown" in his articles when referring to the spring classic races. The Thoroughbred Racing Association officially recognized the Triple Crown in 1950. America's Triple Crown is also modeled on the British classic races for three-year-olds, the English Derby, the Two Thousand Guineas, and the St. Leger Stakes.

The first race in the Triple Crown, the Kentucky Derby, has been run at Churchill Downs in Louisville, Kentucky, since 1875. Held on the first Saturday in May, the Derby is 1¼ mile in length.

The Preakness Stakes is held two weeks later at Pimlico Race Course in Baltimore, Maryland. At 1³/₁₆ miles, it is slightly shorter than the Derby. The Preakness has not always been run at this distance; from its inception through 1888, it was held at 1½ miles, then at 1¼ miles in 1889, and back to 1½ miles in 1890. After a three-year hiatus from 1891 to 1893, it was run at three different distances during the period from 1894 to 1910 from 1 to 1¹/₁₆ miles. In 1911, the Preakness was lengthened to 1¹/₈ miles, where it remained until 1925, when another furlong was added.

Survivor won the inaugural Preakness Stakes in 1873 at Pimlico in Baltimore. The Preakness was named for Milton Holbrook Sanford's horse who won the Dinner Party Stakes at Pimlico on the track's opening day on October 20, 1870. In 1890, the Preakness took place at Morris Park in the Bronx, New York, and from 1894 to 1908, at Gravesend Course in Brooklyn, New York, returning to Baltimore in 1909. The original Preakness trophy is the silver Woodlawn Vase, made by Tiffany and Company in 1860 for the Woodlawn Racing Association, and at $1 million it is the most valuable in American sports. Five fillies have won the race: Flocarline (1903), Whimsical (1906), Rhine Maiden (1915), Nellie Morse (1924), and Rachel Alexandra (2009). Tank's Prospect (1985) and Louis Quatorze (1996) share the fastest official winning time (for 1³/₁₆ miles) of 1:53²/₅.

The final and longest race in the series at 1½ miles, the Belmont Stakes occurs three weeks after the Preakness at Belmont Park in Elmont, New York. The Belmont was named for August Belmont I (1816–1890), the president of the Jockey Club. The Belmont's inaugural running in 1867 at Jerome Park in New York was won by the filly Ruthless at the distance of 1⁵/₈ miles. The length of the race varied considerably during its first half-century. Contested at its present distance of 1½ miles for the first time in 1874, the Belmont was run at the subsequent distances during these years: 1890–1892, 1895, and 1904–1905, 1¼ miles; 1893–1894, 1¹/₈ miles; 1896–1903, 1906–1925, 1³/₈ miles. Since 1926, the Belmont has remained at 1½ miles.

The Belmont Stakes was moved to Morris Park in 1891 and then to its present home at Belmont Park in 1905. Aqueduct hosted the stakes from 1963 to 1967 during the construction of Belmont Park's new

Whirlaway is draped with the floral tribute in the winner's circle at Belmont Park, New York, on June 7, 1941, after winning the Belmont Stakes race of the Triple Crown with jockey Eddie Arcaro. Trainer Ben Jones holds the bridle. (AP Photo.)

grandstand. In addition to Ruthless, two other fillies—Tanya in 1905 and Rags to Riches in 2007—have won the Belmont. Secretariat (1973) holds the record for the fastest Belmont ever at 2:24 at the 1½ distance.

Sir Barton (chestnut colt by Star Shoot x Lady Sterling by Hanover, 1916–1937), the first winner of the Triple Crown in 1919, failed to win a race as a two-year-old, but Commander J. K. L. Ross saw promise in the colt and purchased him from breeder John E. Madden. Trainer Guy Bedwell employed Sir Barton as a workout partner for Billy Kelly, Ross's most promising colt. Entered in the Kentucky Derby as an afterthought, Sir Barton, under jockey Johnny Loftus, led

the entire way, beating his stablemate by five lengths. In the Preakness, he triumphed by four lengths, and he completed his Triple Crown in the Belmont, defeating two rivals. Sir Barton raced at four, setting a track record for 1¼ miles in the Saratoga Handicap while beating the legendary gelding Exterminator. Man O' War trounced the Triple Crown winner by seven lengths in a match race, the $75,000 Kenilworth Gold Cup at Kenilworth Park in Ontario, Canada. Sir Barton was a mediocre sire, with Kentucky Oaks winner Easter Stockings his best offspring.

The next two Triple Crown winners, Gallant Fox (bay colt by Sir Gallahad III x Marguerite by Celt,

1927–1954) and his son Omaha (chestnut colt out of Flambino by Wrack, 1932–1959) emerged from William Woodward's Belair Stable in Bowie, Maryland. Both horses were trained by James "Sunny Jim" Fitzsimmons. Gallant Fox showed promise as a two-year-old, winning two stakes, but had his best season at three. Gallant Fox so impressed veteran jockey Earl Sande that he came out of retirement to ride the colt. In 1930, the Fox captured the Preakness eight days before winning the Kentucky Derby. "The Fox of Belair" completed his triple in the Belmont, prevailing by three lengths over Whichone. Racing fans were stunned that summer when a 100–1 long shot named Jim Dandy defeated Gallant Fox in the Travers Stakes at Saratoga. But Gallant Fox rebounded to win the 1¾-mile Saratoga Cup, the Lawrence Realization Stakes, and the two-mile Jockey Club Gold Cup. When the champion developed a fever following the Gold Cup, Woodward retired him to stud at Claiborne Farm in Kentucky. Gallant Fox had an inconsistent record as a stallion but sired Horses of the Year Flares and Granville, in addition to Omaha.

Omaha was a slow-developing two-year-old but improved tremendously at three, winning the Kentucky Derby under jockey Willie Saunders after only two preparatory races. Omaha easily prevailed by six lengths in the Preakness before a record crowd of 45,000 fans. He completed his crown in the Belmont beating four rivals. Following the Belmont, Omaha ran the fastest 1¼ miles (at that time) by a three-year-old in 2:01²/₅ in the Arlington Classic in Chicago, but missed the rest of the season due to lameness. He distinguished himself at four by making the transatlantic trip to England, where he captured two stakes on the turf while training for the Ascot Gold Cup. He was the only Triple Crown winner to compete in Europe. In the Gold Cup, Omaha narrowly lost by a nose to the filly Quashed in the grueling 2½-mile race. Omaha retired in 1937 to Claiborne Farm, but did not sire any offspring of note.

The 1937 Triple Crown winner, War Admiral (brown colt by Man O' War x Brushup by Sweep, 1934–1959), failed to resemble his great sire in looks or stature, measuring 15.3 hands in height and colored a nondescript shade of brown in contrast to Man O' War's burnished red chestnut coat. The Admiral

was bred and owned by Samuel D. Riddle (Man O' War's owner), trained by George Conway, and ridden by Charles Kurtsinger. War Admiral won three out of six races during his juvenile season. Despite Riddle's prejudices against running horses in the Kentucky Derby that had kept Man O' War on the sidelines for the 1920 edition, Riddle decided to enter War Admiral in the 1937 Derby. The Admiral handily defeated 19 rivals, beating second-place Pompoon by 1¾ lengths. Just one week later in the Preakness, the Admiral prevailed over Pompoon again, this time by a short head. War Admiral then emulated Man O' War in capturing the Belmont Stakes, despite stumbling at the start and gashing his foreleg. Although he trailed blood the whole 1½-mile length of the race, the Admiral won by three lengths and shaved ¹/₅ second off his sire's track record of 2:28⁴/₅.

In 1938, War Admiral won 9 of 11 starts, including the Widener Handicap at Hialeah (Florida); the Saratoga and Whitney Handicaps and the Saratoga Cup; and the Jockey Club Gold Cup at Belmont. War Admiral lost by four lengths to Seabiscuit in a widely publicized match race, the Pimlico Special in Baltimore, on November 1, 1938. After two more victories, War Admiral retired. He was a successful stallion and Man O' War's best son at stud, siring 40 stakes winners, including Busher, Blue Peter, and Busanda, the dam of the great Buckpasser.

The 1940s brought a record four Triple Crown winners: Whirlaway (1941), Count Fleet (1943), Assault (1946), and Citation (1948). Whirlaway (chestnut colt, Blenheim II x Dustwhirl by Sweep, 1938–1953) and Citation (bay colt, Bull Lea x Hydroplane II by Hyperion) both hailed from the racing dynasty of Mr. and Mrs. Warren Wright's Calumet Farm. Whirlaway was trained by Ben E. Jones and Citation by Ben's son, Jimmy Jones. The charismatic Italian American jockey Eddie Arcaro rode both of Calumet's Triple Crown winners.

Whirlaway, an idiosyncratic colt nicknamed "Mr. Longtail," competed in 60 races during his career and finished out of the money only four times. He won three stakes as a two-year-old, but exhibited the bad habit of bearing out in the homestretch. Thus, trainer Ben Jones fitted Whirlaway with a one-eyed set of blinkers to keep him focused and hired the experienced

Arcaro to ride him. Whirlaway responded by winning the Kentucky Derby by a record-equaling eight lengths in a track record 2:01²/₅. He followed with a Preakness win by 5½ lengths and defeated three rivals in the Belmont. Whirlaway won five more major stakes in 1941, including the Travers. As a four-year-old, Whirlaway captured 12 of 22 races, including the Brooklyn Handicap and the Jockey Club Gold Cup. Whirlaway became the first Thoroughbred racehorse to surpass $500,000 in earnings. He lost a match race to Alsab by a scant nose at Narragansett Park in Rhode Island, but returned in 1943 as a five-year-old, yet failed to win. Retired to stud, Whirlaway sired several good fillies, including Scattered and Going Away. Breeder Marcel Boussac bought the stallion in 1950 and exported him to stand in Normandy, France, where he died in 1953.

Citation, the second Calumet Triple Crown winner, was one of racing's greatest champions and also its first millionaire. For more than three decades, he held the North American record for winning 16 races in succession.

Count Fleet (brown colt, Reigh Count x Quickly by Haste, 1940–1973) was foaled at Stoner Creek Farm in Kentucky, which belonged to Yellow Cab Company magnate John D. Hertz. Legendary rider Johnny Longdon convinced Hertz not to sell the colt, and Count Fleet won 10 of 15 starts as a two-year-old and his division title. After capturing the 1942 Champagne Stakes, Count Fleet never again tasted defeat and won all his prep races for the Kentucky Derby, including the Wood Memorial. Count Fleet emulated his sire, 1928 winner Reigh Count, in capturing the Derby and swept the Preakness by eight lengths. Winning the one-mile Withers in preparation for the Belmont, he plucked the last jewel from the Crown by an astounding 25 lengths. Unfortunately, the colt suffered a career-ending injury necessitating his retirement to stud. Count Fleet sired 1951 Derby winner Count Turf, Horses of the Year Counterpoint and One Count, and champion filly Kiss Me Kate. He was also the broodmare sire of five-time Horse of the Year Kelso. Count Fleet was also the longest-lived of all Triple Crown winners, passing away at age 33 in 1973.

Assault (chestnut colt, Bold Venture x Igual by Equipoise, 1943–1971) was foaled at Robert J. Kleberg Jr.'s mammoth King Ranch in Kingsville, Texas. As a weanling, Assault stepped on a stake, which pierced the hoof of his right foreleg, causing a permanent malformation of the foot and an awkward gait. However, Assault's injury did not prevent him from racing. Max Hirsch trained Assault, and the colt won two of nine races as a juvenile. During the spring of 1946 as a three-year-old, Assault won the Wood Memorial but lost the Derby Trial. His Kentucky Derby was a spectacular accomplishment as he thundered home by eight lengths, tying Old Rosebud (1914), Jamestown (1939), and Whirlaway (1941) for the widest winning margin. Assault narrowly won the Preakness, holding off Lord Boswell's late charge by a neck, but drew away commandingly in the Belmont by three lengths. Assault raced nine more times in 1946, trouncing the top handicap horse Stymie in the Pimlico Special. Assault went undefeated in 1947 in five stakes and won at least one race in each subsequent season from 1948 to 1950, including the 1949 Brooklyn Handicap. Assault proved sterile at stud and failed to sire any Thoroughbred foals, but sired a few foals when mated with quarter horse mares.

Racing fans waited a quarter-century after Citation for the arrival of the next Triple Crown winner, Secretariat, in 1973. Fortunately, the 1970s was a bountiful decade for Triple Crown winners, with Seattle Slew and Affirmed following Secretariat.

Seattle Slew (dark bay or brown colt, Bold Reasoning x My Charmer by Poker, 1974–2002) was foaled at Ben Castleman's White Horse Acres near Lexington, Kentucky. Seattle Slew came from modest, unfashionable bloodlines (although he was a great-grandson of Bold Ruler) and was extremely ungainly as a youngster. Castleman sold him as a yearling at the Fasig-Tipton sales for a modest $17,500. The buyers of Seattle Slew, Mickey and Karen Taylor and Dr. James Hill, were newcomers to racing. Karen Taylor nicknamed the awkward colt "Baby Huey" after the clumsy cartoon duck. Placed in the hands of trainer Billy Turner, Seattle Slew did not make his first start until September 20, 1976, which he won easily under jockey Jean Cruguet. Slew captured an allowance race and the prestigious Champagne Stakes and won the Eclipse Award for Champion Two-Year-Old colt. Slew won his three prep races in the spring of 1977 leading up to the Derby. Despite "washing out" (sweating profusely) in the postparade at Churchill Downs prior to the Kentucky Derby, Slew prevailed by 1¾ lengths. Slew easily won the Preakness in 1:54²/₅, equaling Secretariat's time and just ²/₅ second shy of Canonero II's 1971 record. Seattle Slew led the entire way in the Belmont Stakes, winning by two lengths on a muddy track. Following the Triple Crown, Slew finished fourth to J. O. Tobin in the Swap Stakes at Hollywood Park in California. The Taylors and Hill rested him for the remainder of the 1977 season.

While preparing in Florida for his four-year-old season with a new trainer, Doug Peterson, Slew contracted a bacterial infection, ran a fever, and nearly died. For a while, the Taylors and Hill considered retiring him and syndicated the colt for a record $12 million. But when Slew recovered, they decided to keep him in training. Slew won three stakes in 1978—the Woodward, the Marlboro Cup (in which he beat 1978 Triple Crown winner Affirmed), and the Stuyvesant Handicap. Although he lost the Jockey Club Gold Cup by a nose to Exceller, fans celebrated Slew's courage in defeat. Slew retired to Spendthrift Farm and was moved in the mid-1980s to Three Chimneys Farm. He sired Horse of the Year A. P. Indy, 1984 Kentucky Derby winner Swale, Slew o' Gold, Landaluce, Vindication, and Surfside. Seattle Slew was the most important progenitor of the Bold Ruler sire line and still exerts a great influence on racing today through his grandsons, the leading sires Pulpit, Bernardini, and Malibu Moon (all sons of A. P. Indy). Seattle Slew is also the broodmare sire of Hall of Fame and two-time Horse of the Year Cigar, the first horse to equal Citation's record of 16 consecutive wins.

The 11th and last Triple Crown winner was the Florida-bred colt Affirmed (chestnut colt, Exclusive Native x Won't Tell You by Crafty Admiral, 1975–2001). Affirmed was born and raised at Louis Wolfson's Harbor View Farm and was placed with trainer Lazaro "Laz" Barrera, who had trained 1976 Kentucky Derby winner Bold Forbes. As a two-year-old, Affirmed commenced his rivalry with Calumet Farm's colt, Alydar. In six meetings at two, Affirmed won four of their contests and Alydar two, with Affirmed receiving the Eclipse Award for Champion Two-Year-Old of 1977.

Affirmed and Alydar renewed their rivalry during the 1978 Triple Crown. Of all the Triple Crown

---

Recent Attempts at the Triple Crown

For more than three decades, racing fans have awaited another Triple Crown winner, yet have been disappointed time and time again. Before a stunned crowd, Spectacular Bid faded in the last quarter mile at Belmont. Following the race, Bid's connections discovered that he had an infection of the laminae, the sensitive tissue within his hoof, caused from stepping upon a safety pin during Belmont week.

In 1989, Sunday Silence and his rival Easy Goer were so closely matched in the Preakness that they mirrored each other stride-for-stride in the homestretch, with Sunday Silence nosing out his rival at the wire. But Easy Goer turned the tables on him in the Belmont, triumphing by eight lengths. In 1997, Silver Charm seemed a sure thing to win the Belmont, only to be passed by Touch Gold in the stretch. Real Quiet came nearest to capturing the Crown, but was nipped by a nose at the wire in the 1998 Belmont by Victory Gallop. In 2004 Smarty Jones seemed destined for glory, but was beaten by Birdstone in the Belmont. The last Derby-Preakness winner to lose the Belmont was Big Brown in 2008.

Several factors may explain the Triple Crown drought. During racing's heyday in the 1940s, most horses raced more frequently than the modern Thoroughbred and did not have extended periods of downtime between races. Some contend that today's Thoroughbred has become inbred and riddled with predispositions to injury. Others point to the increasing emphasis during the past two decades on preparing horses to compete for lucrative stakes purses as two-year-olds. The lack of a Triple Crown winner during the past three decades only underscores the series' difficulty and shows the extraordinary courage and athletic prowess of the 11 winners.

---

winners, perhaps no horse had to work as hard as Affirmed for his crown. Ridden by 18-year-old riding sensation Steve Cauthen, Affirmed captured the Derby over Alydar by 1½ lengths. Alydar shortened Affirmed's winning margin in the Preakness to a scant neck. In the Belmont Stakes, the two gallant horses turned in one of the greatest performances in racing's history. The two chestnut colts battled the length of the Belmont homestretch with Affirmed prevailing over the gallant Alydar by a head.

Returning in 1979 for his four-year-old season, Affirmed won seven of nine races and defeated top three-year-old Spectacular Bid in the Jockey Club Gold Cup. Affirmed set a then-record for lifetime earnings of just under $2.4 million. Syndicated for $14.4 million, Affirmed retired to Spendthrift Farm and was later moved to Calumet Farm, where he and Alydar occupied adjoining stalls in the stallion barn. Affirmed finished his stud career at Jonabell Farm. Although not as successful as Seattle Slew or Alydar at stud, Affirmed sired several good horses, including Canadian Triple Crown winner Peteski, Hall of Fame turf mare Flawlessly, Mossflower, Charley Barley, and Affirmed Success.

Since Affirmed won the Triple Crown in 1978, no horse has succeeded in winning the series, although 17 horses between 1979 and 2008 have been victorious in two out of the three races. In 1985, the connections of Kentucky Derby winner Spend a Buck decided to bypass the Preakness in favor of the Jersey Derby at Garden State Park, which offered a $2 million bonus to the horse that could win both Derbies. In response to Spend a Buck's defection, Triple Crown Productions was incorporated in 1985 to promote the

Horses Winning Two Legs of the Triple Crown, 1979–2008

Kentucky Derby and Preakness Stakes
Spectacular Bid (1979)
Pleasant Colony (1981)
Alysheba (1987)
Sunday Silence (1989)
Silver Charm (1997)
Real Quiet (1998)
Charismatic (1999)
War Emblem (2002)
Funny Cide (2003)
Smarty Jones (2004)
Big Brown (2008)
I'll Have Another (2012)

Preakness and Belmont Stakes
Risen Star (1988)
Hansel (1991)
Point Given (2001)
Afleet Alex (2005)

Kentucky Derby and Belmont Stakes
Swale (1984)
Thunder Gulch (1995)

series. The organization sought corporate sponsorship, and Chrysler Motors stepped up, offering a $5 million bonus to the horse that could sweep the series. In 1996, the credit card company Visa took over the $5 million bonus sponsorship, but discontinued it in 2006.

Elizabeth M. Tobey

See also Citation; Kentucky Derby; Man O' War; Secretariat

Suggested Resources

Belmont Stakes Website. http://www.belmontstakes.com. Accessed January 31, 2012.

Bowen, Edward. *War Admiral*. Thoroughbred Legends 17. Lexington, KY: Eclipse Press, 2002.

Boyd, Eva Jolene. *Assault*. Thoroughbred Legends 23. Lexington, KY: Eclipse Press, 2004.

Capps, Timothy. *Affirmed and Alydar*. Thoroughbred Legends 15. Lexington, KY: Eclipse Press, 2002.

Drager, Marvin. *The Most Glorious Crown: The Story of America's Triple Crown Thoroughbreds from Sir Barton to Secretariat*. New York: Winchester Press, 1975.

Haskin, Steve. *Tales from the Triple Crown*. Lexington, KY: Eclipse Press, 2008.

Kentucky Derby Website. http://www.kentuckyderby.com. Accessed January 31, 2012.

Magee, Michael, and Pat Bayes. *Champions*. New York: William Morrow, 1980.

Mearns, Dan. *Seattle Slew*. Thoroughbred Legends 5. Lexington, KY: Eclipse Press, 2000.

Preakness Website. http://www.preakness.com. Accessed January 31, 2012.

Robertson, William H. P. *The History of Thoroughbred Racing in America*. New York: Bonanza Books, 1964.

Turner Broadcasting System (TBS)

Turner Broadcasting System, Inc., originally named Turner Communications Group, was officially launched in 1970 by Ted Turner when Turner purchased Atlanta UHF channel 17, WJRJ. Turner then debuted the first national cable television network in 1976, which he named SuperStation. This was the first station to transmit its signal via satellite and then be distributed by cable to consumers.

Before founding Turner Communications Group, Turner inherited Turner Advertising, a firm focused on billboard marketing, from his father in 1963. In 1965, the federal government passed the Highway

Actor David Arquette, left, shares a laugh with Edgar Lopez, during a taping for TBS's *Lopez Tonight* show before the NBA Western Conference basketball finals between the Los Angeles Lakers and the Phoenix Suns in Los Angeles, May 19, 2010. (AP Photo/Jae C. Hong.)

Beautification Act, which forced the removal of outdoor advertising from federal highways except in commercial and industrial areas. Turner, understanding that his current business model was becoming obsolete, began to look for alternatives, and decided to model his company after Metromedia and Combined Communications. Both these companies diversified their advertising options portfolio though television and radio in addition to outdoor advertising opportunities. After raising the necessary funds, Turner purchased five radio stations: one in Norfolk, Virginia; one in Chattanooga, Tennessee; two in Charleston, South Carolina; and one in Jacksonville, Florida.

Turner never found the same passion for radio as he did for billboards due to the competitive nature of the market and the many personal issues, often drug related, that plagued many of his radio employees. He became determined to continue to expand Turner Advertising. Seeking to enter the television market and wanting to get more presence in Atlanta, headquarters

for Turner Advertising, Turner changed the name of his company to Turner Communications Group and purchased UHF channel 17 in January 1970. At the time UHF 17, now renamed WTCG, was an independent station, meaning that it had no commitments to national networks (ABC, NBC, and CBS) and so had flexibility in its programming options. Turner would look to see what the competition was airing, then air what they were not; when the major networks showed talk shows at night, he aired movies. Turner would continue to utilize this strategy as he expanded his company.

Turner purchased a second television station in Charlotte, South Carolina, in 1971, which he renamed WRET for his initials, and began to sell off some of his billboard and radio assets, focusing more on television. In 1973, WATL, Turner Communications Group's largest direct competitor, went out of business and WTCG became the only independent television station in Atlanta, which Turner leveraged into securing additional programming from the major networks, as they tried to balance their own programming schedule.

Turner purchased the rights to the Atlanta Braves as he continued to grow Turner Communications Group. He had already purchased professional wrestling from ABC and was even producing the events in-house when in 1971 he managed to secure the rights to 60 Braves games for the 1972 season. He soon secured the rights to the Atlanta Hawks, the Atlanta Flames (a hockey franchise that moved to Calgary, Canada, in 1980), and a soccer team from the now-defunct North American Soccer League (NASL). The Braves by far received the highest ratings and the greatest interest, but the other sports helped to grow the popularity of the station.

The acquisition of the rights to Braves games had a profound impact on the growth of Turner Communication Groups. Approximately 100,000 people in Atlanta soon purchased UHF receivers to watch the telecasts, not only driving the ratings for the sports broadcasting, but increasing viewership across the board as more consumers gained access to the station. The Braves in the early part of the 1970s did not experience a lot of success on the field, which was the only limit to Turner's advertising sales; companies want the association with winners. However, the relationship that he had built with the Braves ownership eventually allowed him to purchase the team in 1976. He became one of two owners in baseball who controlled both the team and its broadcast station.

Turner, now the owner of the Braves, again looked to expand the reach of Channel 17. The only independent channel in 1975 that occupied a major southeastern market, not including Florida, was Channel 17. CATV or cable television was a new product on the market that allowed viewers to gain access to additional programming outside their own markets with a better picture than what traditional broadcasts could provide. Turner eventually moved Channel 17 to cable and created the first regional television station in the process. However, Turner found that companies did not want to purchase advertisements on a regional scale. Most companies only wanted to make local or national buys and the regional option did not fit their advertising model. The Turner Communications Group introduced the infomercial as a way to secure the revenue lost to the lack of traditional advertisement sales.

Turner Communications Group did not want to limit their market to the southeast region; they wanted to go national. The opportunity quickly presented itself and, through a partnership with HBO, Turner began to broadcast not from just land-based transmitters but satellites in 1976. Turner Communications Group changed its name again to Turner Broadcasting System (TBS) to signify that the company now competed nationally. Channel 17 also got rebranded as the "SuperStation TBS" or the SuperStation for short.

Many local stations voiced concerns with the government that the SuperStation violated rules about the redistribution of local TV signals. Since the SuperStation was beamed directly into their territory with shows for which they owned the license, TBS violated the local stations' exclusivity rights. The NBA and MLB voiced their own concerns that because the SuperStation carried both Braves and Hawks games into other teams' markets that had their own local teams, this created unnecessary competition for viewership. However, the Federal Communications Commission eventually ruled that the SuperStation engaged in no violations and the existing entities would have to learn to adapt to the changing market conditions. With this victory in hand, TBS began to call the Braves "America's Team."

In 1980, Turner created Cable News Network (CNN), a 24-hour cable news network. TBS then launched CNN2, which later was renamed Headline News (HLC), to expand their market presence before competitors could try to disrupt their new channel. Turner continued to expand his media empire when, in 1984, he launched Cable Music Channel to compete with MTV. The channel failed but helped to mold VH1. In 1986 Turner purchased the entire film library of the movie studio Metro-Goldwyn-Mayer (MGM) after an unsuccessful attempt to acquire CBS. He used this collection of titles as the foundation for TNT, launched in 1988. TBS launched TNT with the goal of creating a one-stop channel dedicated to entertainment. Turner wanted a channel that aired the top 100 top events on television.

From 1984 to 1986, TBS purchased the rights to select nationally televised games for $10 million a year. These contracts were renewed until 1988, paying an additional $2.5 million a year more. With the introduction of TNT in 1988, Turner Sports was officially created as a division inside Turner Broadcasting System and both the SuperStation and TNT aired basketball games until 1990. TBS paid $50 million dollars to secure those rights. The contact costs grew exponentially over the next 20 years. From 1990 to 1994 TBS paid nearly $70 million each year to secure the rights to NBA games. From 1994 to 1998 games returned to both TBS and TNT for the rights fee of nearly $100 million a year. The cost for the rights to the NBA games continued to nearly double every four years. The 2007–2008 season cost Turner Sports almost $400 million a year.

TBS continued to expand its platforms when in 1991 Turner purchased Hanna-Barbera Entertainment Co., which led to the creation of the Cartoon Network in 1992. Turner Classic Movies (TCM) launched in 1994. In 1996 Turner Broadcasting System merged with Time Warner, which accelerated its growth, allowing the company to soon broadcast to over 200 countries and territories worldwide.

In 2000, Time Warner merged with AOL. During this process, Ted Turner, who, since the merger between TBS and Time Warner, had had control over the cable networks, effectively was phased out of a leadership position during a restructuring even though he remained the largest single shareholder.

Since 2010, TBS has continued to grow in the baseball market. They continued to broadcast postseason games. For the 2012 postseason, MLB awarded them the exclusive rights to cover all four MLB League Division Series and the American League Championship Series.

Also in 2010, Turner Sports entered into a 14-year, $10.8 billion partnership with CBS to broadcast the NCAA Men's Basketball Tournament. TBS and TNT will cover most of the early rounds until the Sweet Sixteen. In 2016, TBS/TNT will air the regional finals, Final Four, and national championship. This will continue in every even year for the remainder of the television rights contract with the NCAA.

Chett Miller

See also Final Four: National Basketball Association; NCAA; Turner, Ted

Suggested Resources

Auletta, Ken. *Media Man: Ted Turner's Improbable Empire*. New York: W. W. Norton, 2005.

Bibb, Porter. *Ted Turner: It Ain't As Easy As It Looks: A Biography*. Boulder, CO: Johnson Books, 1997.

O'Connor, Michael. *Ted Turner: A Biography*. Westport, CT: Greenwood Press, 2009.

Ted Turner Website. www.tedturner.com. Accessed September 13, 2011.

Turner, Ted, and Bill Burke. *Call Me Ted*. New York: Grand Central, 2008.

Turner, Ted (1938–)

Robert Edward "Ted" Turner III is an American media mogul worth approximately $2.1 billion who, during his infamous career, greatly influenced sailing, advertising, cable television, sports broadcasting, sports team ownership, cable news, and global philanthropy. His forays into the sporting world include owning the Atlanta Braves, Atlanta Hawks, and World Championship Wrestling, and creating the Goodwill Games.

Turner was born November 19, 1938, in Cincinnati, Ohio, to parents Robert Edward "Ed" Turner II and Florence Turner. His sister, Mary Jane Turner, was born three years later. Turner had a tempestuous relationship with his father, Ed. Turner's biography indicates that during his childhood Ed was often on the road for work and when he was home he was drunk and angry. In various interviews Turner has stated that he was often beaten and humiliated by his father. During World War II Ed joined the navy and moved the family (minus Turner) to the Gulf Coast. Turner stayed in Cincinnati with his grandmother and later attended boarding school there.

Turner's family moved south to Savannah, Georgia, when he was nine years old. Turner suggests that Ed felt he needed more discipline and decided to send him to the Georgia Military Academy in Atlanta and then to a military program in Chattanooga, Tennessee. Regardless of their turbulent relationship, Turner repeatedly tried to impress his father. By age 12 Turner was actively competing in sailing events at the local yacht club and in high school Turner won a state high school debate championship.

Atlanta Braves owner Ted Turner is seen wearing a headdress on the baseball field before the start of the Braves' home opener in Atlanta, Georgia, on April 14, 1976. (AP Photo.)

Tragedy hit the family when Turner's sister, Mary Jane, contracted systematic lupus erythematosus and died of the immune disease before he left for college. In 1957, when Turner left for college, Ed Turner divorced his wife, Florence, and remarried.

Turner attended college at Brown University, an Ivy League college in Providence, Rhode Island. He initially majored in classics but later switched to economics at his father's insistence. While at Brown Turner was a member of the Kappa Sigma fraternity, vice president of the debate team, and captain of the sailing team. Turner was expelled from Brown University before earning his degree for having a girl in his dorm room. He then returned to Georgia and became a general manager at the Macon branch of his father's business, Turner Outdoor Advertising, which owned the majority of billboard advertising in the South.

After a large business deal where Ed financed over $4 million to purchase rights to billboard companies throughout the South, he became so despondent that he decided to end his life. Turner's father committed suicide in 1963, leaving 24-year-old Ted to take over the family business. The billboard advertising company had fallen into debt due to the large loan and it was up to Ted to either sell it or turn it around. Turner decided to focus on building the business into the largest advertising company in the Southeast and eventually into a global business, Turner Advertising.

In the 1960s, Turner used revenue from his growing advertising empire to purchase radio stations in Chattanooga, Tennessee; Jacksonville, Florida; and Charleston, South Carolina. Turner sold the radio stations in 1970 to fund his purchase of Atlanta's UHF Channel 17 (changing the call letters from WJRJ to WTCG). At the time of the sale the channel was in last place in the Atlanta UHF station ratings. The channel did not create any original programming; furthermore, UHF stations were not yet popular with audiences. However, Turner foresaw a time when audiences would want more viewing choices. At the outset, WTCG primarily aired 1930s–1950s movies and syndicated shows such as *Bugs Bunny*, *Gilligan's Island*, *I Love Lucy*, and *Star Trek*. In just three years' time, Turner managed to use this content to garner an audience—successfully launching the first "SuperStation" by turning the channel around from last place in the ratings to first.

Turner went on to purchase several other UHF stations and in 1976 began using a satellite to transmit local channel content to national cable television providers. Initially, Turner's channels were carried free on cable television and as audience numbers grew, so did advertising revenue. Turner was not content with that success, however, seeking new content to build a bigger viewing audience. Convinced that people would flock to televised sporting events, Turner decided to purchase the Atlanta Braves baseball and Atlanta Hawks basketball teams. Both teams provided sports content for the WTCG channel. This was a first for the sports industry as previously audiences only had access to local sports via radio or VHF television channels. This move effectively made the Braves and Hawks household names throughout the nation. It didn't hurt that the Braves went to the World Series five times in the 1990s and won the World Series championship in 1995. Their success helped increase

TBS's audience size as well as advertising revenue. Since 1997, the Braves have played on Turner Field (originally Centennial Olympic Stadium, built for the 1996 Summer Olympics, but later converted to a baseball stadium).

To make the leap from local television to national cable Turner had to gain Federal Communications Commission (FCC) approval. Against him were the broadcast networks, local television stations, Hollywood studios, and professional sports teams. Each had a stake in the content that Turner would be airing. The broadcast networks and local TV stations suggested that Turner owned too many stations. However, the loudest complaints came from the Hollywood studios and professional sports teams, which suggested that Turner wasn't paying fair prices for their content—paying local television prices, then broadcasting shows to a national audience. Turner convinced the FCC that he was trying to provide the public with inexpensive program choices, and the government agreed to let the stations become national cable channels. Turner's station holdings became an overnight cable empire.

Convinced that he needed to grow his brand, in 1978 Turner paid $50,000 for the WTBS call sign to MIT (who owned the Technology Broadcasting System radio station). Thus, Turner began the "SuperStation" brand with WTCG (renamed WTBS) under the banner of the Turner Broadcasting System.

Turner further ventured into the sports broadcasting arena by founding (and televising) the Goodwill Games. The Goodwill Games were an international sports competition established in 1986 when due to Cold War tensions the United States and other Western nations boycotted the 1980 Summer Olympics held in Moscow and the Soviets and other Eastern nations boycotted the 1984 Summer Olympics held in Los Angeles. Turner saw the Goodwill Games as a way to bring East and West together in the spirit of friendly competition. He once suggested in an interview that if we were busy training for the games, we were less likely to try to bomb each other.

Despite being known for providing entertainment, Turner found himself questioning news content. He was concerned with media bias and what he felt was consistently negative reporting. To address this, Turner founded the Cable News Network (CNN) in

1980 and created the first 24-hour cable news channel. On June 1, 1980, when the network launched, Turner himself announced what was to become the mission statement of CNN:

> We won't be signing off until the world ends. We'll be on, and we will cover the end of the world, live, and that will be our last event . . . and when the end of the world comes, we'll play "Nearer, My God, to Thee" before we sign off.

The broadcast networks, still upset that Turner had been able to get FCC approval for his "Super-Station," snubbed CNN by not allowing the station to adequately cover White House events. In retaliation, Turner did three things: (1) filed a federal lawsuit against the broadcast networks and the Reagan Administration citing First Amendment and antitrust violations, (2) sought the support of Congress by telling them that CNN's 24-hour news cycle would mean more air time for them, and (3) installed cable into each Congress member's office as well as a satellite dish for the White House. Congress overwhelmingly began supporting CNN and Turner won his federal case. CNN immediately became the leader in world news. Over the years CNN has proved itself a global leader in news, broadcasting the space shuttle *Challenger* disaster, the rescue of baby Jessica McClure, Jimmy Carter's press conference live (while giving a report from the Middle East) and in-depth coverage of the 1991 Gulf War (which cost the station an estimated $20 million to produce).

Turner spent the remainder of the 1980s and early 1990s adding to his global broadcasting empire. In 1986, Turner created Turner Entertainment Co. and tried a hostile takeover of the Columbia Broadcasting System (CBS) to the tune of $5.4 million. After failing in that acquisition Turner Entertainment Co. purchased Metro Goldwyn Mayer and United Artists (MGM/UA) including their film and television library (which included several RKO shows) for over $11 million. Both MGM/UA were later sold to Lorimar Pictures though Turner managed to retain the film and television library holdings. Turner Network Television (TNT) was added in 1988, the Cartoon Network in 1992, and Turner Classic Movies (TCM) in 1994.

TNT initially broadcast syndicated television shows and old movies (*Gone with the Wind* was its first broadcast) but later added original programming as well as Turner's 1988 sports purchase, World Championship Wrestling (WCW), to its lineup, thereby attracting a very different audience to the station. The WCW successfully competed with the World Wrestling Foundation (WWF) owned by Vince McMahon for a number of years and the WCW's Monday-night broadcasts were ratings contenders against *Monday Night Football*. The WWF later purchased the WCW during the AOL–Time Warner merger in 2001.

Meanwhile, TCM broadcast old movies from the MGM and RKO libraries and the Cartoon Network aired Warner Brothers (WB) favorites *Looney Tunes* and *Merrie Melodies* (WB was part of the MGM library). Turner also purchased Hanna-Barbera Productions in 1992 and used their animation library to provide content for the Cartoon Network. During this time Turner pushed for colorizing old black-and-white movies. The first colorized picture, *Yankee Doodle Dandy*, aired on TNT in 1985. Turner went on to colorize the majority of his film library holdings, playing colorized versions on TNT and original black-and-white versions on TCM. In 1991, Turner was named *Time Magazine*'s Man of the Year, the first time a media figure was honored with the award.

Turner did not limit his broadcast empire to national holdings. In 1993 he joined Russian journalist Eduard Sagalejev in purchasing the Moscow Independent Broadcasting Corporation (Russian channel 6), founded by Russian press baron Vladimir Gusinsky.

In 1990 Turner, in a joint venture with Scripps Howard and Liberty Media, launched Turner South, a Southeast network that aired professional sport teams such as the Atlanta Braves, Atlanta Hawks, Atlanta Thrashers, and Charlotte Hornets in addition to major sports such as auto racing, college football, golf, tennis, volleyball, and World Championship Wrestling. The cable channel was available to residents of Alabama, Georgia, Kentucky, Mississippi, North Carolina, South Carolina, and Tennessee. The network was sold to Fox Sports in 2006 and renamed SportSouth.

After joining forces in the early 1990s to try to purchase Paramount Pictures and the National Broadcasting Company (NBC), Time Warner, Inc., and Turner Broadcasting System became uneasy partners. During this time Turner tried different ways to separate Time Warner and TBS. The sticking point in the deal seemed to be CNN as Time Warner wanted control of the station (to brand it with their magazine offerings). After six months of negotiations, Turner finally decided to sell the company. In 1996 Turner Broadcasting System merged with Time Warner, Inc., which added E! Entertainment Network and Comedy Central to the cable lineup. Following the purchase Turner remained part of the merged company, first as head of cable networks, then as vice chairman (2003), and later as a member of the board of directors (2006).

Time Warner was purchased by America Online (AOL) in early 2001 —a move initially supported by Turner. At the time of the merger AOL Time Warner was valued at $165 billion and was touted as the largest corporate merger to date. Turner's share was 4 percent of the company, a vice presidency, and a seat on the board. By late 2001, however, AOL Time Warner stock fell more than 30 percent as the dot.com bubble burst, leading to changes in AOL Time Warner leadership. As Time Warner's largest stockholder, Turner lost more than $7 billion in the collapse. Turner remained with the company, however, though criticized by many who disregarded his "cut spending" approach to management. The two companies were separated again by 2009. Time Warner and Turner differ in their accounts regarding Turner's "firing" from the company, but regardless Turner is no longer in a leadership position at Time Warner, which controls all of the Turner Broadcasting System's former holdings.

In addition, Turner has also taken turns producing and acting. In 1993 he appeared as Colonel Waller T. Patton in *Gettysburg* and reprised the role in 2003 in *Gods and Generals*. Turner was a producer for both TV series. Turner's latest venture has been to produce the animated series *Captain Planet and the Planeteers*.

Throughout his career Turner has been highly controversial and never afraid to speak his mind. Often referred to as "Terrible Ted," "Captain Outrageous," and "The Mouth of the South," Turner is known for imprudent comments about Christianity, abortion, sex, global warming, cannibalism, and taxing the rich. During the CNN versus Fox News ratings wars Turner even called Fox News owner Rupert

Ted Turner is an accomplished athlete in his own right. In 1964 Turner, who had been competing in sailing events since age 12, participated in the Olympic sailing trials. Turner skippered the yacht *Courageous* in the 1977 America's Cup, defeating Australia 4–0 to win the cup.

Two years later Turner competed in the Fastnet Race (the final race of the five-race Admiral's Cup Competition), which was so plagued by storms that only 89 yachts of the 306 that began the race finished—194 retired and 24 were abandoned while 15 sailors died during the race. Turner, skippering his yacht *Tenacious*, was the corrected-time winner of the Fastnet Race.

Turner was named America's Cup Yachtsman of the Year four times, was inducted into the America's Cup Hall of Fame in 1993, and was inducted into the Sailing Hall of Fame in 2011.

Murdoch "Hitler" and challenged him to a televised Las Vegas boxing match.

Turner has been married three times: Judy Nye (1960–1964), Jane Shirley Smith (1965–1988), and Jane Fonda (1991–2001). He has five children: Laura Lee Turner (mother, Judy Nye), Robert Edward Turner IV (mother, Judy Nye), Rhett Turner (mother, Jane Smith), Beauregard Turner (mother, Jane Smith) and Jennie Turner (mother, Jane Smith). Turner's biography describes his private life as being marred by infidelities, drinking, depression, and desire to control the lives of his wives and children.

Today, Turner is a philanthropist and businessman focusing most of his efforts on his five foundations: the Turner Foundation (founded in 1990), the Captain Planet Foundation (founded in 1990), the Turner Endangered Species Fund (founded in 1997), the United Nations Foundation (founded in 1997), and the Nuclear Threat Initiative (founded in 2001). Turner recently donated $1 billion to the United Nations where he serves as chairman of the board of directors of the UN Foundation. He also provides funding for the National Forensic League and the Crossfire Debate (also known as the Public Forum Debate).

Turner owns almost two million acres of land at his 15 ranches in Kansas, Montana, Nebraska, New Mexico, Oklahoma, and South Dakota, making him one of the top five largest individual landowners in the United States. Turner has also raised the largest bison herd in the world (over 50,000 head) on his Montana ranch, which he uses in his restaurant chain, Ted's Montana Grill.

Jensen Moore

See also Fox Sports; *Monday Night Football*; 1984 Olympic Games, Los Angeles; 1996 Olympic Games, Atlanta; Turner Broadcasting System; World Wrestling Entertainment

Suggested Resources
Auletta, Ken. *Media Man: Ted Turner's Improbable Empire*. New York: W. W. Norton, 2005.
Bibb, Porter. *Ted Turner: It Ain't As Easy As It Looks: A Biography*. Boulder, CO: Johnson Books, 1997.
O'Connor, Michael. *Ted Turner: A Biography*. Westport, CT: Greenwood, 2009.
Ted Turner Website. www.tedturner.com. Accessed September 13, 2011.
Turner, Ted, and Bill Burke. *Call Me Ted*. New York: Grand Central Publishing, 2008.
Williams, Christian. *Lead, Follow or Get Out of the Way: The Story of Ted Turner*. New York: Times Books, 1981.

2002 Olympic Games, Salt Lake City

The 2002 Olympic Winter Games in Salt Lake City, Utah, held in February 2002, displayed both the triumph of the Olympic ideals and the darker side of staging the prestigious international competition. Despite a bid scandal, judging controversies, and fears of terrorism, the Games were considered largely successful.

In the 1960s, 1970s, and 1980s, organizers in Salt Lake City tried to secure the Olympic Winter Games for their city. Although the United States Olympic Committee (USOC) named it as the country's candidate city in bids for the 1972 and 1998 Games (and the proposed replacement city after Denver surrendered the 1976 Games), it wasn't until the 1990s that Salt Lake City won the right to host the Winter Olympics. The International Olympic Committee (IOC) awarded the XIX Winter Games, to be held in early 2002, to Salt Lake City on June 16, 1995. Over the next 6½ years, the preparations for the Games would be overshadowed by two major issues: the bribery scandal surrounding Salt Lake City's successful bid and the

Michelle Kwan of the United States performs during the 2002 Winter Olympics figure skating exhibition at the Salt Lake Ice Center, February 22, 2002. (AP Photo/Lionel Cironneau.)

fear that the Games would be controlled by Salt Lake City's prominent religious organization, the Church of Jesus Christ of Latter-day Saints.

In November 1998, a Salt Lake City newspaper reported that members of the Salt Lake City Organizing Committee (SLOC) had acted improperly in securing a university scholarship for the daughter of an IOC member. The report alleged that the scholarship was offered as a "gift" to secure the IOC member's vote for

Salt Lake City to host the 2002 Games. Other allegations of wrongdoing soon materialized. In addition to internal inquiries by the IOC, USOC, and SLOC, the United States Department of Justice launched an investigation in December 1998. Eventually, the investigation determined that the Salt Lake City organizers had provided over $1 million of improper benefits to IOC members and their relatives. These benefits included cash payments, college tuition, no-work jobs, vacations, payment of credit-card bills, a purebred dog, and a mayoral campaign in Chile. As U.S. federal investigators built their case, the IOC cleaned its own house by expelling or accepting resignations from 10 members. The IOC quickly adopted several reforms, including restrictions on individual IOC member visits to candidate cities and a new Ethics Commission. In December 1999, a year after news of the scandal surfaced, IOC president Juan Antonio Samaranch (1920–2010) appeared before members of the United States Congress to read a statement and to answer questions about corruption and the bidding process. Samaranch, who would not seek reelection as IOC president in 2001, assured the U.S. Congress and the world at large that the IOC had effectively reformed itself. Seven months later, in July 2000, a grand jury indicted two former SLOC executives (Thomas Welch and David Johnson) on charges related to conspiracy, fraud, and racketeering. In December 2003, nearly two years after the 2002 Games had concluded, both men were acquitted on all charges for lack of evidence.

As the bid scandal escalated in early 1999, several key executive members of the SLOC resigned, jeopardizing the timeline for the preparations for the Games. In the midst of this leadership crisis, the SLOC's board of trustees appointed an outsider, Willard "Mitt" Romney, as its new CEO on February 11, 1999. Romney's appointment highlighted the close relationships between the Games' organizers and the leadership of the Church of Jesus Christ of Latter-day Saints, a relationship that came under increasing scrutiny.

It was the members of the Church of Jesus Christ of Latter-day Saints, commonly called the LDS or Mormon church, who settled Salt Lake City in the 1840s and the LDS church maintains its worldwide headquarters in downtown Salt Lake City. The LDS church had historically placed a strong emphasis on proselytizing, and critics feared the LDS church would use the Olympic Games as a platform to send its missionary message to the world. Soon after the Games were awarded to Salt Lake City in 1995, pundits throughout the world labeled the Games the "Mormon Olympics" or "Mo-lympics."

As early as 1998, the LDS church established the Church Olympic Coordinating Committee to assist the SLOC in recruiting volunteers for the Games. Although in 2002 over half of Salt Lake City's residents were not affiliated with the LDS church, the church's reputation was inextricably linked with that of the city. When the bid scandal disrupted the preparations for the Games, the LDS church felt a strong sense of urgency to help.

It was Robert Hales, an LDS apostle and the chief liaison between the LDS church and the SLOC, who recommended hiring Mitt Romney to the SLOC. The hiring of Romney, an LDS bishop, prompted speculation about the church's influence over the SLOC. Romney did little to defuse the speculations when he asked Merrill Bateman, an LDS general authority and president of the LDS-owned Brigham Young University in Provo, Utah, to close the school during the Olympic Games so that its students, many of whom had learned foreign languages as LDS missionaries abroad, could volunteer for the Games. In addition, the LDS church donated the use of several parcels of land as park-and-ride lots and provided a large parking lot to be used as the Olympic Medals Plaza. City officials feared that the proximity of this parking lot to the picturesque LDS temple and the church administration building would draw undue attention to the city's most prominent religion.

In the midst of growing criticism, LDS officials scaled back their overt efforts to support the struggling SLOC and focused on its own public relations, rather than proselytizing. The church encouraged its members to volunteer for the organizing committee, scheduled several free performances by the Mormon Tabernacle Choir, and produced an elaborate musical event called "Light of the World: A Celebration of Light" to emphasize Mormon heritage and values. In February 2002, to further distance itself from the appearance of unwelcome evangelizing, LDS church president Gordon Hinckley (1910–2008) suspended Mormon proselytizing efforts on the streets of Salt Lake City for the duration of the Games.

Less than five months before the scheduled opening of the 2002 Olympic Winter Games, the terrorist attacks of September 11, 2001, on New York City and Washington, D.C., forced the IOC, the SLOC, and the United States government to reevaluate the security plans for the Games. Since the tragic outcome of a terrorist attack at the 1972 Olympic Games in Munich had left 11 Israeli athletes and coaches dead, security had been a fundamental concern in Olympic planning. In September 2001, despite being authorized by the IOC to cancel, move, or make other emergency decisions about the 2002 Games, new IOC president Jacques Rogge (b. 1942) urged Salt Lake City's Organizing Committee to continue its plans to stage the Games on time. With help from the U.S. government, the Organizing Committee and the State of Utah assembled the most comprehensive security plan for any Olympics to date, stressing the importance of implementing security while adhering to tight event schedules. The efforts of 7,000 military, police, and security personnel allowed the Games to proceed with only minimal inconvenience to athletes, officials, and spectators. The price tag for Olympic security during the 17-day festival topped $300 million. In addition, 14 nations brought their own security forces to Salt Lake City. The threat of terrorism had permanently altered the business of staging the Games.

The 2002 Olympic Winter Games opened on February 8, 2002, to the fanfare, pageantry, and spectacle typical of the modern Olympic movement. Its theme, "Light the Fire Within," was highlighted by the lighting of the Olympic Cauldron at the stadium by members of the 1980 United States Olympic hockey team. In addition to honoring the athletes and their home countries, the ceremonies paid homage to the tragedies of September 11, 2001, with the display of an American flag from the site of the World Trade Center, and in the remarks of IOC president Jacques Rogge. U.S. president George W. Bush officially opened the Games.

These Winter Games featured 2,399 athletes (of whom 886 were women) from 77 countries competing in 78 events (41 for men, 34 for women, 3 mixed), 10 more than were held at Nagano, Japan in 1998. The skeleton, this time for men and for women, was reintroduced after a 54-year hiatus, and 2002 marked the first time women were able to compete in the bobsled (two-person only).

There were several notable performances in the Salt Lake Winter Olympics. Sampaa Lajunen (b. 1979) from Finland became the first athlete to win three gold medals in one Games in the Nordic combined events. Georg Hackl (b. 1966) of Germany won silver in the singles luge, becoming the first person to win a medal in the same individual event in five straight Olympic Games (Summer or Winter). In addition to these achievements, the 2002 Games witnessed a growing diversity in winter sport. On February 19, Vonetta Flowers (b. 1973) became the first black athlete (and the first African American) to win gold in the Winter Games. A few days later, Jarome Iginla (b. 1977) became the first male black athlete to win Olympic gold as a member of Canada's hockey team. China and Australia won their nations' first gold medals in the Winter Olympics. In addition, Croatia and Estonia won their first Olympic medals in the Winter Games, with four medals and three medals, respectively. At a national level, the United States also celebrated its growing diversity of racial and ethnic participation and success in the Winter Olympics. Besides Flowers's bobsled win, Derek Parra (b. 1970), a Mexican American, and Apolo Anton Ohno (b. 1982), a Japanese American, both won medals in speed skating events.

Besides these achievements and accomplishments, the Games witnessed some darker moments. Near the conclusion of the Games, Olympic officials revealed that three cross-country skiers, Johann Muehlegg of Spain and Russian women Larissa Lazutina and Olga Danilova, had tested positive for darbepoetin, a performance-enhancing drug that increased red blood cells. Muehlegg lost his gold medal in the 50-km classical cross-country ski race and Lazutina lost the gold medal she had won in the women's 30-km race. All three skiers kept other medals they had won earlier in the Games, since earlier tests had proven negative. Besides the pall of doping, ethical scandals and allegations of impropriety erupted in the judged events.

On February 11, Canadian figure skaters Jamie Sale (b. 1977) and David Pelletier (b. 1974) finished second in the pairs figure skating competition, behind Elena Berezhnaya (b. 1977) and Anton Sikharulidze

(b. 1976) of Russia. Despite an obvious technical mistake by the Russian skaters, the 5–4 judges' vote awarded the gold medals to Berezhnaya and Sikharulidze. Shocked and outraged fans, media, and Canadian Olympic officials asked the International Skating Union (ISU) to investigate. When it was revealed that the judges from France, Russia, and Ukraine had all awarded identical scores (5.9) to both pairs for technical merit, despite the Russian couple's obvious mishaps, attention quickly focused on the judge from France, Marie-Reine Le Gougne. Le Gougne confessed that she had succumbed to pressure to favor the Russian pair in exchange for a high score for a pair of French ice dancers (who won the gold medal), although she later recanted. After an emergency meeting of the ISU on February 14, the ISU and IOC agreed to award a second pair of gold medals to Sale and Pelletier on February 17. Russian Olympic Committee officials decried the decision as diminishing the accomplishments of their skaters. They accused the IOC of changing the competition's rules after the fact, since the decision to award dual gold medals circumvented established procedures under the Court of Arbitration in Sport. The aftermath of the judging scandal was long lasting. Allegations connected a Russian businessman with suspected links to organized crime to the score fixing. In August 2002, a U.S. grand jury issued an indictment against Alimzhan Tokhtakhounov. Although he was arrested in Italy, Italian officials refused to extradite Tokhtakhounov and released him. In May 2002, the ISU banned Le Gougne from judging for three years and for the next Olympic Winter Games. Later, it adopted a code of ethics for its judges in 2003 and instituted a new international judging system in 2004.

Besides the scandal in figure skating, judging controversies marred the men's short-track 1,500-meter race. South Korean officials launched a protest after a South Korean skater, Kim Dong-Sung (b. 1980), was disqualified after he crossed the finish line first. Officials ruled that the South Korean had impeded the progress of U.S. skater Apolo Anton Ohno and awarded the gold medal to the American. Angry South Korean Olympic officials threatened to boycott the closing ceremonies of the Games, as did the Russian delegation, smarting from the doping allegations against its women cross-country skiers and the figure skating judging scandal. Despite these threats to skip events, IOC president Jacques Rogge managed to calm the aggrieved parties, and both the South Korean and Russian delegations participated in the closing ceremonies.

The XIX Olympic Winter Games closed on February 24, just hours after Canada's men's hockey team won its first gold medal in 50 years, soundly defeating the U.S. squad. The silver medal in men's hockey pushed the U.S. medal total to 34, decisively breaking its previous Winter Games record of 13. In his closing remarks, Rogge thanked Salt Lake City for reminding the world that its people can live together peacefully. After the performances and speeches, American performer Willie Nelson sang "Bridge over Troubled Waters," fitting as a plea to remember the unifying nature of the Olympic festival rather than the divisive judging and doping scandals.

As the Games came to a close, organizers, officials, and media members expressed relief. The Games had exceeded most expectations and run smoothly and effectively with minimal disruptions. Visa, a credit-card company sponsor of the 2002 Olympic Winter Games, reported a 31 percent increase in transactions in the Salt Lake City area over the same period in 2001. NBC, the television network that paid $545 million to televise the Games in the United States, enjoyed the second-highest ratings of all televised Winter Olympics to date, with a 19.2 average for the 17 days of the Games (behind only Lillehammer, Norway, in 1994). Less than two weeks after the conclusion of the Olympic Winter Games, Salt Lake City hosted the 2002 Paralympics, a 10-day festival for athletes with disabilities.

There are several reasons for the success of Salt Lake City in staging the Olympic Winter Games. The population of Salt Lake City's metropolitan area, at 1.5 million people in 2002, was larger than any previous host of the Winter Games. This concentration of people provided access to an international airport, freeways, and the hotel amenities of a sizeable city, and allowed the city to welcome the world in resplendent style. In addition, the SLOC's ability to overcome the negativity of the bid scandal and heightened security concerns after September 11, 2001, demonstrated

The Shea Legacy

When he won the gold medal in the men's skeleton in the 2002 Winter Games, Jim Shea (b. 1968) became not only the first American to win the event but also the first American to compete as a third-generation Winter Olympian. Shea's grandfather Jack had competed in the 1932 Games at Lake Placid, winning two gold medals in speed skating. Shea's father, James, was a Nordic skier in the Innsbruck Games in 1964. Both Sheas played integral roles in Salt Lake City's opening ceremonies, with Jim administering the Olympic oath to the gathered athletes and James participating in the torch procession.

Tragically, the 91-year-old Jack Shea died in a car accident less than a month before the opening of the 2002 Games. On February 19, as Jim Shea sped down the skeleton course at around 80 miles per hour, he carried in his helmet the funeral card from his grandfather's services. When he reached the end of the course, Jim saw his final time and jubilantly pulled out his grandfather's card to show the crowd. He had won the gold medal by a margin of .05 second.

In the wake of the bid scandal that preceded the Games and amid the discord about figure skating and speed skating judging, Shea's gold medal run provided one of the most memorable and compelling human-interest stories of the 2002 Olympic Winter Games.

remarkable resilience and dedicated leadership. After such a rocky start, the Games themselves were received as a great success for Salt Lake City, the United States, and the spirit of the Olympics.

David Lunt

See also Miracle on Ice; Ohno, Apolo

Suggested Resources
Atkinson, Michael, and Kevin Young. "Terror Games." *Olympika: The International Journal of Olympic Studies* XI (2002): 53–78. Available at www.la84foundation.org/SportsLibrary/Olympika/Olympika_2002/olympika1101c.pdf. Accessed October 24, 2011.
Barney, Robert K., Stephen R. Wenn, and Scott G. Martyn. *Selling the Five Rings: The International Olympic Committee and the Rise of Olympic Commercialism.* Salt Lake City: University of Utah Press, 2002.
Gerlach, Larry R. "The 'Mormon Games.'" *Olympika: The International Journal of Olympic Studies* XI (2002): 1–52. Available at http://www.la84foundation

.org/SportsLibrary/Olympika/Olympika_2002/ olympika1101b.pdf. Accessed October 24, 2011.

Le Gougne, Marie-Reine. *Glissades à Salt Lake City*. Paris: Editions Ramsay, 2002.

Paralympic Movement Website. http://saltlake2002.paralympic.org/. Accessed October 24, 2011.

Salt Lake City 2002 Website. http://www.olympic.org/salt-lake-city-2002-winter-olympics. Accessed October 24, 2011.

"Winter Olympics History. Utah.com. http://www.utah.com/olympics/history.htm. Accessed October 24, 2011.

2008 Redeem Team

The so-called Redeem Team refers to the 2008 U.S. men's Olympic basketball team, who won the gold medal in the Bejing Olympics to reclaim American supremacy in basketball, after the United States won bronze in 1988 and 2004.

Basketball in the Olympics began in 1936 at the Games in Berlin and the United States began a string of winning that extended to 1972 in Munich. The United States had invented and perfected the game and it took decades for the rest of the world to even come close to defeating a U.S. team, even though they were composed of college, AAU, or military players, all amateurs, and the top teams in the Eastern bloc were all professionals, despite their ostensible standing as amateurs.

In 1972 in a famous finish that consisted of three different replays of the last five seconds, the United States was declared the loser to the Soviet Union by a disputed score of 51–50, breaking the gold medal run of the United States at seven Olympic Games championships in a row. The United States returned to dominance in 1976, boycotted the 1980 Games, then won handily in 1984. The world, however, was beginning to catch up to the United States in basketball.

In 1988, the United States lost to the Soviet Union in the semifinals of the Seoul Games, then salvaged the bronze medal by overpowering Australia, but the sting and the feeling of international betrayal because of the definition of "amateur" and "professional" lingered. FIBA then dropped the amateur sham and declared the Games to be open to all for 1992. With that the United States put together the "Dream Team" that destroyed all comers in coasting to the 1992 Olympic title in Barcelona. Led by Michael Jordan, Magic Johnson, Hakeem Olajuwon, Larry Bird, Charles Barkley, and David Robinson, the team won its eight contests by an average of 44 points, the closest being the championship where they won by 32 over Croatia.

In 1996 it was more of the same with a spotless record, highlighted by a 27-point victory over Yugoslavia in the gold medal game. It appeared that the United States was back on top in the game that it had invented and pioneered. In Sydney for the 2000 Games, questions were raised, however. Despite going 8–0 once again and winning the championship, the United States stumbled in edging Lithuania in the semis, 85–83, and in the championship game against France, winning by a score of 85–75.

Those questions became concerns in 2002, when the U.S. team finished sixth in the FIBA world championships, and were further exacerbated when the 2004 Olympic team never seemed to come together as a unit and played poorly throughout the tournament in Athens. First they were shocked in the opening round, losing by 92–73 to Puerto Rico; then they lost again, this time to Lithuania, 94–90. They did manage to sneak into the medal round, despite their 3–2 record, but there they lost in the semifinals by a score of 89–81 to Argentina. In the bronze medal game for third, they managed to recapture a bit of their pride by defeating Lithuania in a rematch, 104–96. Nevertheless, the damage was done and there were no rules that could be altered to help the United States recapture their prominence.

In 2006 at the FIBA world championships in Japan, the United States seemed to have righted the ship when they captured their first seven games, but then in the semifinals lost to Greece and won only a bronze medal in the tournament. A long-term plan was necessary to regain Olympic and world respect for 2008.

A new commitment on the part of players, coaches, and USA Basketball would be needed to prepare the 2008 men's Olympic team to win in Bejing. This would start by a much earlier naming of a coach and then a series of tryouts with the top American players. First, however, USA Basketball created a new position, managing director, and they appointed Jerry

Colangelo, a Chicago native who had played basketball at Illinois before becoming an executive with the Chicago Bulls, then the general manager of the Phoenix Suns.

Colangelo met with a number of knowledgeable people to gain their advice on how to create a winning team and attitude for the USA Basketball team. These included Hall of Fame and former Olympic players Jerry West, Michael Jordan, and Larry Bird, among others. Using their input and that of others, he determined that the two best candidates for the coach of the U.S. team were Greg Popovich of the San Antonio Spurs and Mike Krzyzewski of Duke University. Popovich was wary of the long-term commitment, but Krzyzewski embraced it, and he took over as coach in 2006.

The next step was rebuilding the team. A number of 2004 players were not interested in being considered for the 2008 squad and some would not be at the peak of their games in two or three years because of injuries or prior commitments, so they were not invited to continue. The core of the team would be its four returning players, Carmelo Anthony, Kobe Bryant, LeBron James, and Dwyane Wade. Carlos Boozer also returned from the 2004 team. The remainder of the team was filled out over the next year, but they had only begun to play together as a unit under Coach K when the world championships were held in 2006. The third-place finish was disappointing, but it helped to solidify their resolve. Following the loss to Greece, the last pieces of the team were added and the squad would be together practicing in the summers until the Games in 2008.

The United States had to qualify in the Americas tournament in 2007 to become eligible for the 2008 Games, and they won that FIBA tournament with 8 of the 12 players who would constitute the 2008 team. The roster was finalized in June 2008.

Krzyzewski appointed three assistant coaches, one from the college ranks—Jim Boeheim of Syracuse—and two NBA coaches—Mike D'Antoni of the Knicks and Nate McMillan of Portland. The team had no seven-footers, but Chris Bosh at 6'10" and Dwight Howard at 6'11" were fierce rebounders and defenders.

From the time the NBA season ended in May–June 2008, the players began working out in the weight rooms and on the court, both individually and as a team. The Games would open in August and the team had long practices and some tough intersquad scrimmages as the month grew closer.

The last scrimmage on American soil was against the Canadian team in Las Vegas in late July and the United States ran them out of the gym. The Americans then flew to China and arrived to play for more exhibitions in different parts of the country against four other national teams. The games against Turkey and Lithuania were not close and the third, against Russia, was also surprisingly easy. The last game was against Australia in Shanghai and the United States did not play well. The Australians held the Americans to 3 of 18 shooting from beyond the arc and the U.S. players hurt themselves by shooting just 60 percent from the free throw line. The 87–76 victory for the United States was almost seen as a loss and a source of concern.

The American team arrived in Bejing in time for the amazing opening ceremony, then later toured the Olympic village to greet other American athletes. The team was mobbed and it was clear why they had arranged to stay off-site at a hotel with better security. Nevertheless, the American team wanted to make clear that they were part of the Olympic contingent, and this was well appreciated by the other American athletes who strongly supported the American basketball team. It was also clear that the American basketballers were the "rock stars" of the Games, basketball being the most widely played sport in China and because of shoe endorsements by many American players, including Kobe, LeBron, and Wade.

The United States played its first game before a capacity crowd that included President George Bush and his father, former president Bush. An estimated one billion people watched on television and saw the United States, led by Dwyane Wade's 19 points, topple China, 101–70. Two nights later, Wade again had 19 points to lead the Americans to an easy victory over Angola, 97–76.

The third opponent was Greece, the team that had defeated them in 2006 in the FIBA semifinals in Tokyo. The United States got a measure of revenge with a 92–69 victory, led by Kobe and Chris Bosh with 18 points each. The U.S. players shot poorly from the line and the three-point arc, but their defense

2008 Olympic Men's Basketball Roster and Scoring Averages	
Carmelo Anthony	11.5
Carlos Boozer	3.3
Chris Bosh	9.1
Kobe Bryant	15.0
Dwight Howard	10.9
LeBron James	15.5
Jason Kidd	1.6
Chris Paul	8.0
Tayshaun Prince	4.3
Michael Redd	3.1
Dwyane Wade	16.0
Deron Williams	8.0
Team	106.2

was tenacious and indicated that even when shooting poorly, the Americans would be strong enough to beat most teams.

The next opponent was Spain, the team that had triumphed in the FIBA championships, defeating Greece for the title. Spain had size in the Gasol brothers, Pau and Marc, as well as a number of other current and future NBA players. The U.S. team, however, was simply too fast and too team oriented as every player on the U.S. roster scored. LeBron had 18 points, eight assists, five rebounds, and four steals. Carmelo had 16 points and six rebounds, totals matched by Wade. As a team the United States forced 17 turnovers in the first half alone and won going away, 119–82.

On August 18, the United States finished the preliminary round with a 106–57 destruction of Germany with Dirk Nowitski and Chris Kamen (whose great-grandparents had lived in Germany) unable to staunch the bleeding. The United States was now a heavy favorite for the gold medal, but they would have to continue to play team basketball and stay focused, things that Coach K had emphasized from the first practice in 2006 and which were finally being adhered to.

The first team that the United States faced in the medal round was Australia, a team that they had stumbled against earlier in the month, making this game a bit more tense than would have been expected. This time there was no need for worry as the Americans came to play, and play well, defeating the Aussies, 116–85. Five players scored in double figures, led by Kobe's 25.

The semifinal opponent was defending Olympic champion Argentina, led by NBA stars Manu Ginobli, Luis Scola, and Andres Nocioni. The American team hardly noticed, sprinting to a 34–13 first-quarter lead, but then letting the Argentines back into the game, when they closed to 46–40 near the end of the first half. The second half was never close and the United States ran to a 101–81 victory. Carmelo Anthony made 13 of 13 free throws in garnering 21 points, James had 15, and Wade, Chris Paul, and Kobe each had 12. Chris Bosh had 11 points and 10 rebounds and Dwight Howard had 10 points and nine rebounds. The United States looked ready to claim the gold, but they would have to defeat Spain for a second time, since they had beaten Lithuania in the other bracket.

The United States played well, but so did Spain. They minimized their turnovers, played a tough zone defense against the Americans, and shot well. At the half, the United States led by just 69–61, and the second half remained just as close. With 3:32 left in the game, Spain pulled to 104–99 on a basket by Pau Gasol, but then Kobe Bryant made a three-pointer and drew a foul on Rudy Fernandez, his fifth, who fouled out with 22 points to lead Spain. Bryant's four-point play gave the United States a nine-point margin. Spain then closed to four, but Wade hit his fourth three-pointer to extend the lead to seven with 2:04 left. The final score was 111–104. Wade, the leading American scorer for the Games, had 27, Bryant 20, and James 14 with six rebounds. Both Paul and Anthony had 13. The United States led in most team categories and was clearly the class of these Olympic Games. The coach and the players continually emphasized what a team effort it had been.

The Redeem Team had done what it had set out to do. Few American victories at the Bejing Games were as satisfying to the nation. In addition, being part of the U.S Olympic team was now more coveted than ever and the carryover to the Olympics in London in 2012 seemed obvious.

Murry R. Nelson

See also Bird, Larry; Bryant, Kobe; Dream Team; James, LeBron; Jordan, Michael; Krzyzewski, Mike; West, Jerry

Suggested Resources

Bickley, Dan. *Return of the Gold: The Journey of Jerry Colangelo and the Redeem Team.* Hampton, VA: Morgan James, 2009.

Cunningham, Carson. *American Hoops: U.S. Men's Olympic Basketball from Berlin to Bejing.* Lincoln: University of Nebraska Press, 2009.

USA Basketball. http://www.usabasketball.com/mens/national/moly_2008.html. Accessed December 29, 2011.

Tyson, Mike (1966–)

In the 1980s, Mike Tyson emerged as the youngest man ever to become heavyweight boxing champion of the world. The story of his life is, one sense, the classic American tale of rags to riches: From incredibly hard beginnings, Tyson rose to the top, achieving all his dreams through hard work and single-minded determination and focus. But his is also the story of too much, too soon. Having achieved greatness, fame, and wealth at such a young age, Tyson found he had absolutely no idea what to do with himself.

He made millions of dollars in boxing, and he squandered millions. His wealth and fame may have enabled him, but it also made him a target. Tyson enjoyed seemingly an endless string of second chances and advantages, even as so many others took parasitic advantage of him.

On June 30, 1966, Tyson was born in Brooklyn. Tyson was raised by a single mother. His father left the family when he was two. He spent his early teen years in the Brownsville section of New York City. While it is difficult to take a direct or exact measure of such things, by all accounts Brownsville was one of the toughest, most dangerous inner-city neighborhoods in the country.

As a child, Tyson was overweight, fearful, and extremely shy. He had an unusual manner of speech—a gentle, almost feminine lisp—and he often hesitated, stopped himself, before words suddenly came out all in a rush. He was a target for bullies and repeatedly got in fights with older kids. At some time in his early teens, he participated in his first mugging, with many more to follow. Tyson later described how much he enjoyed overpowering his victims.

He was arrested for theft and other petty crimes over 30 times. At age 13, he was sent to the Tryon School for Boys in upstate New York. It was there that he took up boxing, which was offered as way to teach boys discipline and as an outlet for aggression. The facility's resources were rough, the training sometimes less than expert, but Bobby Stewart, a retired boxer and a counselor at the school, saw something in Tyson and thought he had great potential. Stewart worked with Tyson for months, and then introduced him to the aging Cus D'Amato. D'Amato had trained and managed the champions Floyd Patterson and Jose Torres, and now operated a gym in the nearby Catskills. D'Amato had been playing with the idea that he might find and train one last great fighter. When D'Amato watched the very raw Tyson in the ring, he saw incredible possibility in the combination of speed and angry power Tyson had and decided this was the one.

D'Amato took Tyson home, removing him to the large country house in the Catskills where D'Amato lived with his wife. It was a completely different and isolating environment for Tyson, but that was part of D'Amato's idea: Remove all distractions, remove all opportunities to find trouble. If you broke curfew, if you ran away in the middle of the night, there was nowhere, really, to go. Tyson was one of a few boys who lived at the house—D'Amato hedged his bets and so had many possible candidates for boxing greatness—but Tyson quickly distinguished himself as the most promising. D'Amato became Tyson's legal guardian at age 16, after the death of Tyson's mother. Soon D'Amato, first with in-ring trainer Teddy Atlas and then with Kevin Rooney, was focusing all his energies on Tyson. A longtime D'Amato associate, Bill Cayton, provided the financial backing for Tyson's training and career.

Tyson was not tall, but he was quick, and he hit very, very hard. D'Amato schooled Tyson in the "peek-a-boo" style: With chin down and both hands raised in front of his face, the fighter ducks and bobs his head from side to side, never truly presenting a stationary target, even as he comes straight on at the opponent. It was an unusual, old-school style, hard to learn and even harder to maintain in the ring, and not much taught anymore. It was perfect for Tyson, as it turned his lack of height into an advantage and

Mike Tyson celebrates his victory over Tony Tucker at the coronation gala following his world boxing heavyweight championship fight in Las Vegas, August 2, 1987. (AP Photo/Jeff Widener.)

allowed him to make the most of his quickness and short-armed power.

D'Amato became a surrogate father for Tyson. Part of Tyson's training was a serious education in boxing history, and in D'Amato's basement film room, Tyson watched all the great heavyweights again and again. He grew particularly fascinated and later came to empathize with Jack Johnson, the first black heavyweight champion, a man who flaunted his wealth and status at a time when white men were rarely prosecuted for participating in lynchings.

Tyson began his career as an amateur in 1981, competing in the 1981 and 1982 Junior Olympic Games and winning two gold medals. He won every fight by knockout. Very powerful but still something

of a work-in-progress, he lost to Henry Tillman twice (Tillman won the gold at the 1984 Summer Olympics in Los Angeles). The losses to Tillman didn't much worry D'Amato. He maintained, simultaneously, both a long and a short view: Tyson, he said, would surely be the youngest heavyweight champion ever.

Tyson turned pro in March 1985, fighting Hector Mercedes and winning by first-round knockout. A quick succession of bouts followed, about one a month. D'Amato and Tyson's handlers wanted him fighting, wanted to keep him on a constant upward curve, with no down periods, no breaks from training or opportunities for distraction. In November 1985, Cus D'Amato, who had struggled with his health for years, died, and Tyson just kept fighting. He won his first 19 fights by knockout, 12 of these in the first round. In 1986, Jesse Ferguson managed to last to the sixth round before being knocked out—the longest anyone had gone against Tyson. Perhaps his most frustrating opponent in these early years was Mitch "Blood" Green, who went the distance with Tyson in May 1986 but still lost unanimously. Tyson defeated the promising Marvis Frazier, the son of the great Joe Frazier, by knockout in the first round in July 1986, and then knocked out Jose Ribalta (10th round) and Alonso Ratliff (2nd) to earn a WBC title fight with Trevor Berbick. He was 27–0 with 25 knockouts.

Tyson's knockouts were devastatingly impressive, the punches exploding suddenly and seemingly out of nowhere. As he gained increased media attention and television exposure, it may have been easy for casual fans, at least, to perceive Tyson as an unskilled, brutal force. But the young Tyson was a disciplined fighter, and a tactical one. His unusual, energetic defense and his underrated jab enabled him to quickly find gaps to deliver a swarm of crushing uppercuts and short hooks.

The Berbick title fight took place in November 1986. It stands as probably the best example of the sheer impact of Tyson's power, on how it impressed itself on both his opponents and audiences. In the second round, Tyson hit Berbick with a right, and Berbick went down. As the referee counted, Berbick got to his feet, then lost his balance and fell down. Berbick pounded his glove on the mat in frustration, managed to get to his feet again, only his legs would not hold still. As Tyson watched impassively from a neutral corner, Berbick careened helplessly across the ring and fell down again. He was counted out. Tyson had knocked Berbick down three times with one punch.

Tyson went on a quest to claim all the title belts. He fought James "Bonecrusher" Smith for the WBA title in March 1987, winning by decision (Smith hugged and clutched Tyson throughout the fight, unwilling to risk being knocked out and, in some quarters, earned himself a new nickname: "Bonehugger"). He knocked out Pinklon Thomas in the sixth round in May 1987, then took the IBF title from Tony Tucker by decision. He became the first fighter to own all the heavyweight belts at the same time.

On June 27, 1988, Tyson was scheduled to face Michael Spinks. Michael Spinks was the son of Leon Spinks, who had once defeated Muhammad Ali for the heavyweight championship. Spinks was an excellent fighter, expected to be the biggest challenge in Tyson's career. Spinks had won the world championship from Larry Holmes—no small feat, as Holmes had held the all-time winning streak for heavyweight champions at the time. Spinks had never been beaten (his title belt had been stripped after some contractual gerry-mandering), and many considered him the legitimate champion. Tyson simply steamrolled him. He charged into Spinks like a bull, backed him up, and knocked him through the ropes and out in 91 seconds flat.

The victory over Spinks was the pinnacle of Tyson career. D'Amato had long ago been proven right. But with D'Amato's death, the rigid structure and routine that had been built up around Tyson had slowly begun to erode. In the weeks leading up to the Spinks fight, Tyson contracted gonorrhea, which went untreated. As his fame and fortune grew, he was slowly losing the discipline.

Early in his career, Tyson had been shielded from the influence of Don King, the powerfully charismatic but notoriously shady ring promoter who had put to-gether many of Muhammad Ali's greatest fights. With D'Amato's death, King had his opening, which he slowly began to exploit. Tyson finally separated from longtime manager and D'Amato's financial partner Bill Cayton in 1988, and fired Kevin Rooney as his trainer.

The signs of a coming fall were there. Tyson had married actress Robin Givens on February 7, 1988.

Soon after, the two appeared in commercials for Diet Pepsi, in which Givens playfully "whipped" Tyson into line with a towel and he smiled indulgently. But early in the marriage, police were called to Tyson's mansion and he was hospitalized after he ran his car into a tree, an incident that was initially reported as a suicide attempt. In September 1988, the two appeared in a joint interview with Barbara Walters on ABC Television's 20/20, with Givens discussing incidents of domestic abuse and identifying Tyson as violently manic depressive. Tyson sat stone-faced during the interview and said nothing. The two separated and eventually divorced in February 1989. True or not, the public's general perception was that she had sought publicity and Tyson's money all along.

Tyson defended his championship, but he fought less and less frequently, with just two fights in 1989. In August 1989, he encountered former opponent Mitch "Blood" Green outside a Harlem clothing store and punched Green in the face. Tyson broke his hand, de-laying a scheduled fight for several weeks. Tyson may have been continuing to win, and convincingly so, but the sense of total domination was slipping. He stopped working the peek-a-boo defense and moved his head less and less. He abandoned combinations and used his short, smart jab infrequently. He came to rely, in-stead, on trying to land the single knockout punch.

Most of his opponents were too intimidated to no-tice, much less take advantage of, his increasing slop-piness. The British fighter Frank Bruno improbably managed to hurt Tyson early in a fight in February 1989, but Bruno seemed as surprised as anyone and proved unable to capitalize. Bruno was knocked out in the fifth.

Tyson had a longstanding contract with HBO tele-vision, which had broadcast all his fights. King—who was now acting both as Tyson's manager and pro-moter—planned to move Tyson strictly to pay-per-view. In Tyson's last contracted fight for HBO, he was scheduled to meet James "Buster" Douglas in Tokyo on February 11, 1990. Douglas was a journeyman. While he was a fighter of some talent, Douglas had never much distinguished or (by his own admission) applied himself. It was assumed that Tyson would quickly dispatch Douglas and move on to better, more lucrative fights on pay-per-view.

The recent death of Douglas's mother, though, drove him to prepare and train hard for Tyson. Douglas was also exactly the kind of fighter most likely to give Tyson trouble: very tall, with a long reach and a strong jab. Over the first few rounds, Douglas demonstrated that he was not intimidated. Tyson lurched after him, trying to land that one big punch, but Douglas kept him at bay, pounding Tyson's eye with jabs and straights. The eye began to swell, and Tyson's new corner man (who had replaced Kevin Rooney) proved too inexperienced and unprepared to offer much help beyond encouraging Tyson to hit Douglas back. Tyson did manage a wild, out-of-nowhere knockdown of Douglas in the 8th, but Douglas recovered and, in the 10th, he landed a series of five straight punches to Tyson's head, putting him down. Tyson numbly scrabbled after his mouthpiece on the canvas and was counted out.

It was one of the greatest upsets in boxing history. Don King initially challenged the decision, arguing that the referee had miscounted and given Douglas extra time to recover when he had been knocked down in the seventh. But those protests came off as so desperate and disingenuous—even for King, who had built a career out of being somehow winningly disingenuous—that King was quickly forced to drop the matter. Tyson was gracious in defeat, but insisted he would win the title back one day.

It was not to be. Tyson fought a string of number two and number one contender matches in preparation for a title fight (this time with Evander Holyfield, who had by now beaten Buster Douglas), but in July 1991, he was arrested and charged with rape. Desiree Washington, Miss Black Rhode Island, said he had invited her to his Indianapolis hotel room and then attacked her. Tyson was found guilty on February 10, 1992. Tyson was sentenced to 10 years in the Indiana Youth Center.

Tyson ultimately served three years in prison, where he became a convert to the Nation of Islam. When he was released, he began his boxing career again, beating Peter McNeeley, an unknown who posed little actual threat to Tyson's comeback, in August 1995. A short string of pay-per-view bouts followed, each one featuring less-than-impressive competition but raking in good money. Tyson won a token title belt by knocking out Frank Bruno again in March 1996.

The apparent idea was to reestablish Tyson's fighting reputation and set him for a big fight with Evander Holyfield, without exposing him to a loss that might diminish the eventual payday.

While this strategy worked and made Tyson (and King) millions, it did little to re-sharpen Tyson's actual skills or to prepare him for Holyfield. The two met in November 1996. Tyson made a good early showing, but eventually the rust became evident, and Holyfield slowly started to dominate. In an upset, Holyfield won by knockout when the referee stopped the fight in the 11th round.

In their second fight in June 1997, Holyfield picked up where he had left off, smothering, shoving, and manhandling Tyson. Holyfield repeatedly head butted his smaller opponent, something Tyson had complained about during their first fight. Whether Holyfield continued to do this by design or by accident is unclear, but in the third round, Tyson bit off a portion of Holyfield's ear, tearing the lobe's outer edge loose as he pushed out of a clench. When Holyfield jumped up and down, stamping his feet and clutching at his ear in obvious and considerable pain, the referee paused the fight. He issued Tyson a warning and let it resume. Tyson then bit off a portion of Holyfield's other ear.

Tyson was disqualified and to a large extent disgraced. He was fined, banned, given a psychological evaluation, and then reinstated less than a year later. The simple fact was: There was still money to be made with Mike Tyson in boxing. In the years that followed Holyfield, Tyson's public behavior became ever more extreme even as his skills diminished with age and neglect. His press conferences degenerated into sometimes humorous, sometimes violent, but almost always colorfully vulgar affairs. He publicly threatened to sexually assault a male reporter, told an interviewer after another fight that he desperately wanted to eat another fighter's heart and to consume his children. Some of Tyson's "madman" persona was clearly manufactured or staged to maintain his place in the public's imagination (and to keep making money). In any event, he had clear and ongoing personal problems: In the year 2002, he was charged once again with sexual assault and later faced charges for multiple incidents of assault, drunken driving, and possession of cocaine.

Mike Tyson's Boxing Career

A quick survey of Mike Tyson's boxing record demonstrates just how often he fought in the early years of his career (he fought John Alderson and Larry Sims, for example, practically in the same week) and the sensational results. It also shows the gradual slowdown leading to his first defeat to James "Buster" Douglas, and beyond that, as age and his lifestyle took their toll.

Key: Overall record, opponent name, result and round, date, location, and title won/lost.

1985

1–0	Hector Mercedes	W TKO 1	March 6	Albany, NY	
2–0	Trent Singleton	W TKO 1	April 10	Albany, NY	
3–0	Don Halpin	W KO 4	May 23	Albany, NY	
4–0	Ricardo Spain	W KO 1	June 20	Atlantic City, NJ	
5–0	John Alderson	W KO 2	July 11	Atlantic City, NJ	
6–0	Larry Sims	W KO 3	July 19	Poughkeepsie, NY	
7–0	Lorenzo Canady	W KO 1	August 15	Atlantic City, NJ	
8–0	Michael Johnson	W KO 1	September 5	Atlantic City, NJ	
9–0	Donnie Long	W KO 1	October 9	Atlantic City, NJ	
10–0	Robert Colay	W KO 1	October 26	Atlantic City, NJ	
11–0	Sterling Benjamin	W TKO 1	November 1	Latham, NY	
12–0	Eddie Richardson	W KO 1	November 13	Houston, TX	
13–0	Conroy Nelson	W TKO 2	November 22	Latham, NY	
14–0	Sammy Scaff	W TKO 1	December 6	Felt Forum, NY	
15–0	Mark Young	W TKO 1	December 27	Latham, NY	

1986

16–0	David Jacob	W TKO 1	January 11	Albany, NY	
17–0	Mike Jameson	W TKO 5	January 24	Atlantic City, NJ	
18–0	Jesse Ferguson	W TKO 6	February 16	New York, NY	
19–0	Steve Zouski	W KO 3	March 10	Uniondale, NY	
20–0	James Tillis	W 10	May 3	Glen Falls, NY	
21–0	Mitch Green	W 10	May 20	Madison Square Garden, NY	
22–0	Reggie Gross	W TKO 1	June 13	Madison Square Garden, NY	
23–0	William Hosea	W KO 1	June 28	Madison Square Garden, NY	
24–0	Lorenzo Boyd	W KO 2	July 11	Swan Lake, CA	
25–0	Marvis Frazier	W KO 1	July 26	Glen Falls, CA	
26–0	Jose Ribalta	W TKO 10	August 17	Atlantic City, NJ	
27–0	Alonzo Ratliff	W KO 2	September 6	Las Vegas, NV	
28–0	Trevor Berbick	W TKO 2	November 22	Las Vegas, NV	Won WBC title

1987

29–0	James Smith	W 12	March 7	Las Vegas, NV	Won WBA title
30–0	Pinklon Thomas	W TKO 6	May 30	Las Vegas, NV	
31–0	Tony Tucker	W 12	August 1	Las Vegas, NV	Won IBF title
32–0	Tyrell Biggs	W TKO 7	October 16	Atlantic City, NJ	

1988

33–0	Larry Holmes	W TKO 4	January 22	Atlantic City, NJ	
34–0	Tony Tubbs	W TKO 2	March 21	Tokyo, Japan	
35–0	Michael Spinks	W KO 1	June 27	Atlantic City, NJ	

1989

36–0	Frank Bruno	W TKO 5	February 25	Las Vegas, NV	
37–0	Carl Williams	W TKO 1	July 21	Atlantic City, NJ	

1990

37–1	James Buster Douglas	L KO 10	February 11	Tokyo, Japan	Lost WBA, WBC, IBF titles
38–1	Henry Tillman	W KO 1	June 16	Las Vegas, NV	
39–1	Alex Stewart	W TKO 1	December 8	Atlantic City, NJ	

(continued)

Mike Tyson's Boxing Career (Continued)

1991					
40–1	Donovan Ruddock	W TKO 7	March 18	Las Vegas, NV	
41–1	Donovan Ruddock	W 12	June 28	Las Vegas, NV	
1995					
42–1	Peter McNeely	W DQ 1	August 19	Las Vegas, NV	
43–1	Buster Mathis, Jr.	W KO 3	December 16	Philadelphia, PA	
1996					
44–1	Frank Bruno	W TKO 3	March 16	Las Vegas, NV	Won WBC title
45–1	Bruce Seldon	W TKO 1	September 7	Las Vegas, NV	Won WBA title
45–2	Evander Holyfield	L TKO 11	November 9	Las Vegas, NV	Lost WBA title
1997					
45–3	Evander Holyfield	L DQ 3	June 28	Las Vegas, NV	
1999					
46–3	Francois Botha	W KO 5	January 16	Las Vegas, NV	
46–3	Orlin Norris	NC 1	October 23	Las Vegas, NV	
2000					
47–3	Julius Francis	W TKO 2	January 29	Manchester, England	
48–3	Lou Savarese	W TKO 1	June 24	Glasgow, Scotland	
48–3	Andrew Golota	NC 3	October 20	Auburn Hills, MI	
2001					
49–3	Brian Nielson	W RTD 7	October 13	Copenhagen, Denmark	
2002					
49–4	Lennox Lewis	L KO 8	June 8	Memphis, TN	
2003					
50–4	Clifford Etienne	W KO 1	February 22	Memphis, TN	
2004					
50–5	Danny Williams	L KO 4	July 30	Louisville, KY	
2005					
50–6	Kevin McBride	L TKO 6	June 11	Washington, DC	

In June 2002, he fought champion Lennox Lewis. Overmatched and looking tired almost from the opening bell, Tyson went down in the eighth round. Later, he admitted the only reason he had agreed to the fight was to pay off his debts. After Lewis, Tyson fought a number of desultory bouts, losing most of them. In his last pro fight in 2005, he was either unable or refused to get off his stool before the start of the seventh round and lost to journeyman Kevin McBride.

Tyson's financial fortunes declined, as he had spent wildly and inappropriately for years. He took Don King to court, accused him of siphoning off millions of dollars. Tyson filed for bankruptcy in 2003.

Besides Givens, Tyson has been married to two other women. He married Monica Turner in 1997. They had two children and divorced in January 2003.

In June 2009, he married Lakiha Spicer, with whom he has two children. Tyson's four-year-old daughter, Exodus, died in an accident involving a treadmill in May 2009. He has seven children, total.

In recent years, Tyson has reemerged as a more thoughtful, stable, and even complex public figure. He lives a quiet, suburban existence with his wife and children. He is comfortable enough to poke fun at his public persona, making a memorable appearance in the 2009 comedy smash, *The Hangover*, and the sequel in 2011. He has appeared on women's daytime talk shows to discuss his bankruptcy, his struggles with weight, and his adoption of a vegan lifestyle. In film and print interviews, Tyson has been willing to discuss frankly and candidly almost any part of his life or past history.

Ultimately, Tyson will be remembered as one of the most fearsome boxers of all time. At his all-too-brief peak, it seemed he might even surpass all-time legends like Muhammad Ali and Joe Louis. But his legacy, if not quite a tragic one, is a mixed bag. He enjoyed many triumphs, but may have wasted even more opportunities.

Michael Smith

See also 1984 Olympic Games, Los Angeles; Ali, Muhammad; Johnson, Jack

Suggested Resources

Barich, Bill. "In Prime Time." August 29, 1988. http://www.newyorker.com/archive/1988/08/29/1988_08_29_068_TNY_CARDS_000350447 Accessed November 15, 2011.

Heller, Peter. *Bad Intentions: The Mike Tyson Story*. New York: Da Capo Press, 1995.

Junod, Tom. "Mike Tyson: The Father's Kiss." May 27, 2009. http://www.esquire.com/features/ESQ0699-JUN_TYSON. Accessed November 15, 2011.

Layden, Joe. *The Last Great Fight: The Extraordinary Tale of Two Men and How One Fight Changed Their Lives Forever*. New York: St. Martin's Press, 2007.

Merkin, Daphne. "Mike Tyson Moves to the Suburbs." March 15, 2011. http://www.nytimes.com/2011/03/20/magazine/mag-20Tyson-t.html?pagewanted=all. Accessed November 15, 2011.

O'Connor, Daniel, and George Plimpton. *Iron Mike: A Mike Tyson Reader*. New York: Thunder's Mouth Press, 2002.

U

UCLA Basketball

One of the great things about sports is the debate it triggers among fans. Who's the greatest NFL team of all time? The Steelers or Cowboys? How about the Patriots? Don't forget about the Packers. Who's better, the Celtics or Lakers? Mario or Gretsky? Ali or Frazier? There are no right or wrong answers to these questions and others like them. Your answer usually depends on who you root for. When it comes to identifying the most dominant college basketball program of all time, however, there is no debate. None. The University of California at Los Angeles (UCLA) stands alone atop the college basketball world. Their success is unmatched. And it's not even close.

By any measure, UCLA reigns supreme. Since its first season in 1919–1920, the Bruins have won 11 national titles. Kentucky is runner-up with seven. UCLA has advanced to the NCAA Final Four 18 times and played in 13 national championships. North Carolina also has 18 Final Four appearances, but the Tar Heels moved onto the title contest on only half of these occasions, winning five crowns. How about winning streaks? The Bruins reeled off 88 consecutive victories from January 1971 to January 1974. The University of San Francisco ranks second—28 games off UCLA's mark—with 60 straight wins during the mid-1950s. Consecutive national titles for UCLA? Seven straight from 1967 to 1973. No other program has won more than two in a row.

Given its unmatched success, many assume UCLA has always been a force on the hardwood. The Bruins, however, were not a powerhouse from day one. During the program's first 29 years (1919–1948), UCLA posted just 13 winning seasons. When Wilbur Johns resigned as the team's head coach to assume athletic director responsibilities at the school following the 1947–1948 season, coaching responsibilities were turned over to a mild-mannered midwesterner named John Wooden. A former All-American player at Purdue, Wooden had led the Boilermakers to the 1932 national championship. After graduating from Purdue, he taught English and coached basketball at Dayton (Kentucky) and South Bend (Indiana) Central high schools. Following a two-year stint as head coach at Indiana State (1946–1948), he took over a UCLA squad that had finished last in the Pacific Coast Conference in 1947–1948 and returned no starters.

Wooden immediately put his stamp on the Bruins program. He stressed the importance of conditioning, fundamentals, and discipline. He installed an up-tempo offense and a pressure defense. His practices were grueling tests of endurance and the approach paid dividends. After winning just 12 games in 1947–1948, UCLA posted a school-record 22 victories in Wooden's first season and captured the Pacific Coast's Southern Division title. It was the first of four straight divisional crowns and the start of something special. In 1949–1950, UCLA guard Ralph "Bifocal" Joeckel launched a buzzer-beater from just beyond midcourt in the first game of a best-of-three series against Washington State for the Pacific Coast championship. Joeckel's half-court heave banked off the glass and in at UCLA's Westwood Gym and the Bruins were 60–58 winners. A 52–49 victory the following night clinched the program its first conference title and NCAA Tournament bid.

In Wooden's first 15 seasons in Westwood (1948–1963), UCLA won 18 or more games 11 times. His teams pushed the basketball when most of the other schools in the Pacific Coast Conference and around the

UCLA's Walt Hazzard, tournament Most Outstanding Player, carries the NCAA basketball championship trophy as the team arrives from Kansas City to Los Angeles on March 23, 1964. (AP Photo/Harold Matosian.)

nation played a ball-control game. Wooden's squads utilized full-court, man-to-man pressure, while others played half-court defense. It was his implementation of a full-court zone press in 1967–1968, however, that propelled UCLA to greatness. Up to this point, Wooden's teams were effective pushing the ball on offense and creating turnovers with full-court, man-to-man pressure on defense, but they were unsuccessful in achieving the coach's primary objective—speeding up the tempo of the game. While UCLA scored its points quickly, most of its opponents slowed the pace when they had the ball. Wooden wanted his tempo to be forced on the other team. The Bruins' man-to-man,

full-court pressure was effective at forcing turnovers, but it actually slowed the pace of the game because most teams tried to dribble through the press. Wooden wanted to force opponents to pass—not dribble—the ball against UCLA's full-court defense. The zone press—in which each player was assigned a "zone" of the court to defend, instead of an opposing player—achieved this objective. Wooden had used the zone press as a high school coach and experimented with it at Indiana State, but he was unsure whether or not it could be effective at the major college level.

The 1963–1964 season confirmed that the zone press could be effective. Positioning Gail Goodrich and

Fred Slaughter under the UCLA basket, Walt Hazzard and Jack Hirsch near midcourt, and Keith Erickson at the far end of the floor to protect the opponent's goal, the Bruins' 2–2–1 press created fits for the opposition. It worked—literally—to perfection. UCLA posted a 30–0 record in 1963–1964 and captured the first of 10 national titles in a 12-year span. Hazzard (18.6 points per game) was voted college basketball's Player of the Year and Goodrich averaged a team-high 21.5 points per game. The effectiveness of the zone press was on display in the 1964 national title game against Duke. Trailing 30–27 with just over seven minutes remaining in the first half, UCLA used the press to outscore the Blue Devils 16–0 in a span of less than three minutes. The run proved the difference in a 98–83 victory.

The Bruins made it back-to-back titles a year later, repeating as NCAA champs in 1964–1965 with a 91–80 finals win over Michigan. In a performance Wooden described as the most spectacular he had ever seen, Goodrich scored 42 points against the Wolverines. The smallest player on the court at six feet tall, the senior guard had already scored 40 points in the opening round of the NCAA Tournament against Brigham Young. He averaged 24.6 points per game for the season, a school record for guards. After an 18–8 season in 1965–1966—the first for the Bruins in their new arena, Pauley Pavilion—UCLA began the most impressive streak in the history of collegiate sports. The Bruins won the first of seven straight national titles in 1966–1967. Behind 7'2" sophomore center Lew Alcindor (now Kareem Abdul-Jabbar), UCLA posted a 30–0 mark, defeating Dayton, 79–64, to capture its third national championship. Alcindor scored 20 points and grabbed 18 rebounds in the title game against the Flyers and finished the season averaging 29.0 points per game, including a 61-point outburst against Washington State in February. Even more impressive was his NCAA single-season record 66.7 field goal shooting percentage.

The Bruins rolled to a 29–1 record and another national title in 1967–1968, despite the NCAA's new no-dunking rule, which most believed was instituted to neutralize Alcindor. UCLA's only loss of the season—in a game in which Alcindor was nursing an eye injury—came in a 71–69 setback to Houston and its star, Elvin Hayes. The Bruins and Cougars met again in the 1968 NCAA semifinals, with UCLA posting a 101–69 runaway victory. Wooden employed a diamond-and-one defense to slow down Hayes in the rematch. The following night, his Bruins walloped North Carolina, 78–55, to claim their fourth NCAA crown in five years. Another title followed in 1968–1969, Alcindor's senior season. Big Lew averaged 24.0 points per game in his final season in Westwood and poured in 37 in a 92–72 thumping of Wooden's alma mater, Purdue, in the 1969 championship game. Alcindor closed his collegiate career with 2,325 points (26.4 per game), 1,367 rebounds (15.5 per game), an 88–2 record, and three national titles.

With Alcindor in the middle of the Bruins' lineup, Wooden had slowed his team's pace and played more of a traditional half-court offense to take advantage of his All-American center. With his seven-footer off to the NBA, he returned to the up-tempo style that had been the trademark of his first two national championship squads. Behind the high-octane play of guards John Vallely and Henry Bibby, UCLA averaged 92 points per game in 1969–1970, going 28–2 and defeating Jacksonville, 80–69, in the national title contest for its sixth NCAA crown. One of the team's regular-season wins that year was a 133–84 victory at Pauley Pavilion over LSU and its super-scorer, "Pistol" Pete Maravich. Wooden had Bibby and Vallely double-team Maravich all over the floor and the Bruins "held" the Tigers star to 38 points on 14 of 42 shooting. The 133 points for UCLA is a school single-game record.

National title number seven followed in 1970–1971, with 6'8" Sidney Wicks leading the way. A showman who would flex his muscles during time-outs, the senior led the Bruins in scoring (21.2 per game), rebounding (12.7 per game), and clutch plays. Time and time again, Wicks delivered the key basket or rebound for Wooden's squad, which posted a 29–1 mark and upended Villanova, 68–62, in the 1971 title game. The lone loss of the season was an 89–82 setback at Notre Dame. It marked the last time UCLA would lose a game in three years.

The 1971–1972 season marked the coming-out party for UCLA's precocious, outspoken, 6'11" sophomore center Bill Walton. Walton was the player other teams loved to hate. Strong, quick, heady, and arguably the greatest player the college game has ever seen, Walton averaged 21.1 points in 1971–1972 and tied Alcindor's single-season school record by grabbing 466 rebounds. The "Walton Gang" scored more than 100 points in each of the first seven games of 1971–1972 and outscored its opponents on the season by an average of 30.3 points per game, cruising to a 30–0 record. Only two teams managed to stay within six points of the Bruins on the scoreboard that season, one of them being Florida State in the 1972 NCAA championship game. Behind 24 points from Walton, however, UCLA made it six straight titles with an 81–76 victory over the Seminoles.

In 1972–1973, it was another 30–0 season for UCLA, another national title, and plenty more from Walton. The San Diego native broke the Bruins' single-season school record for rebounds he had tied a year earlier, collecting 506 boards. He averaged 20.4 points per game, 16.9 rebounds per game, and made 66.5 percent of his shots. An unselfish player who enjoyed setting up his teammates as much as he did scoring, Walton dished out 5.6 assists per game, the most for a front-court player in school history. Against Memphis State in the 1973 national title game, he sank 21 of 22 shots from the floor, scoring 44 points in an 87–66 victory. Walton and the Bruins also broke the NCAA record for consecutive victories in 1972–1973, winning their 61st straight game in an 82–63 thumping of Notre Dame in January. The victory over the Irish eclipsed the mark of 60 straight wins posted by the San Francisco Dons (1955–1957).

To say that UCLA was a marked team entering the 1973–1974 season would be an understatement. Seven straight national titles. Two consecutive undefeated seasons. Seventy-five straight victories. Walton, the two-time national Player of the Year, returning for his senior season. Wooden and the Bruins would see each of these streaks snapped. The winning streak ended at 88 games at Notre Dame in January, as the Irish forced five missed shots by the Bruins in the final 21 seconds to hang on for a 71–70 win. For Walton, it was his first loss in 140 games, dating back to his scholastic career at Helix High School. The string of seven straight NCAA titles ended two months later, when UCLA fell to North Carolina State, 80–77, in double-overtime in the national semifinals. Walton netted 29 in the loss to the Wolfpack. He claimed his

third consecutive Naismith Player of the Year award, averaging 19.3 points and 14.7 rebounds per game. Walton departed Westwood with 1,767 points (20.3 per game) and a school-record 1,370 rebounds (15.7 per game).

When Walton graduated, few viewed UCLA as one of the favorites to contend for the national crown in 1974–1975. With senior forward David Meyers the team's lone returning starter, Wooden turned to a pair of sophomores to bolster his front line and Richard Washington and Marques Johnson did not disappoint. The two combined to average 27.5 points a game, complementing Meyers's team-leading 18.3 points per contest. The Bruins reeled off a dozen straight victories to open the season before falling at Stanford. And while the first season of the post-Walton era featured many close games—something the Bruins were unaccustomed to—at season's end, UCLA was again conference champs and primed for another run at a national crown. The Bruins disposed of Michigan, Montana, and Arizona State in the first three rounds of the NCAA Tournament. Following a 75–74 overtime win over Louisville in the national semifinals, Wooden shocked the college basketball world, announcing he would retire after his team's next game, a championship showdown with Kentucky. Wooden played just six players against the Wildcats in the 1975 title game, with four of them playing all 40 minutes. Meyers (24 points, 11 rebounds), Washington (28 points, 12 rebounds), and junior Ralph Drollinger (10 points, 13 rebounds) all posted double-doubles and the Bruins edged Kentucky, 92–85. Wooden retired with 10 national championships and a 620–147 record (.808 winning percentage) in 27 seasons at UCLA.

Following Wooden's retirement, Gene Bartow (1975–1977), Gary Cunningham (1977–1979), and Larry Brown (1979–1981) each spent two seasons coaching the Bruins. Under Brown's direction, UCLA returned to the national finals in 1980, falling to Louisville and its coach, former Bruin guard and Wooden assistant Denny Crum. It was the most unlikely run to a national title game in UCLA's storied history. After opening the season with an 8–6 mark, Brown's team caught fire and carried a 22–9 record into the championship against the Cardinals. Leading 54–50, with four and a half minutes remaining in the finals, the

Bruins were outscored by Louisville 9–0 the rest of the way in a 59–54 setback.

Brown coached the Bruins for one more season before leaving Westwood for a coaching opportunity in the NBA. Larry Farmer (1981–1984) and Walt Hazzard (1984–1988) followed, but neither was able to get UCLA past the NCAA round of 32. When Jim Harrick arrived in 1988, the program had gone through five coaches in 13 seasons following Wooden's 27-year tenure. Harrick's teams never won fewer than 21 games in his eight seasons (1988–1996) and his 1994–1995 team hung a national championship banner of its own in Pauley Pavilion. And it took arguably the greatest play in school history to capture title number 11, the first in the post-Wooden era.

Facing a 74–73 deficit against Missouri in the second round of the 1995 Big Dance, the Bruins' 5'10" point guard Tyus Edney took an inbounds pass from Cameron Dollar, dribbled nearly the length of the court, and banked in a four-foot shot at the buzzer to give Harrick's team a 75–74 victory. UCLA, which had rallied from an eight-point halftime deficit against the Tigers, moved on and defeated Mississippi State and Connecticut to advance to the Final Four. The Bruins dismissed Oklahoma State, 74–61, in the semifinals before knocking off defending national champion Arkansas, 89–78. UCLA finished the season with a school-record 32 wins against just one loss. Senior Ed O'Bannon poured in 30 points and grabbed 17 rebounds against the Razorbacks in the title game and finished the season as his team's leader in scoring (20.4 per game) and rebounding (8.3 per game).

Steve Lavin (1996–2003) succeeded Harrick as the top man at UCLA in 1996, leading the team to an Elite Eight appearance in his first season. The Bruins, however, failed to get past the NCAA round of 16 over the next five years and Ben Howland took over as head coach in 2003. In 2005–2006, he returned UCLA to the national title game, where his Bruins fell to Florida, 73–57. The 2005–2006 team matched the school record with 32 victories, posting a 32–7 final mark. Point guard Jordan Farmar scored a game-high 18 points in the 2006 title game against the Gators and finished the season averaging 13.2 points and 5.3 assists per game. Farmar's backcourt mate, Arron Afflalo, led the team in scoring at 15.8 points per game.

Following the 2006 title game appearance, UCLA advanced to back-to-back Final Fours in 2007 and 2008. Howland entered his ninth season at the helm of the UCLA program in 2012–2013, having signed some of the top freshmen in the country.

In 1976, the Los Angeles Athletic Club introduced the John R. Wooden Award. It is presented annually to the nation's most outstanding college basketball player. In 1999, Wooden was named the greatest coach of the 20th century by ESPN. In July 2003, he was presented the Presidential Medal of Freedom, the nation's highest civilian honor. In December 2003, the basketball floor at Pauley Pavilion was named the "Nell and John Wooden Court." Wooden died in June 2010 at the age of 99.

Pat Farabaugh

See also Abdul-Jabbar, Kareem; Final Four; Maravich, Peter "Pete"; March Madness; Walton, Bill; Wooden, John

Suggested Resources
Bruin Basketball Report. http://www.bruinbasketballreport.com/. Accessed November 27, 2011.
Chapin, Dwight, and Jeff Prugh. *The Wizard of Westwood: Coach John Wooden and His UCLA Bruins*. Boston: Houghton Mifflin, 1973.
Harrick, Jim, John McGill, and Tom Wallace. *Embracing the Legend: Jim Harrick Revives the UCLA Mystique*. Chicago: Bonus Books, 1995.
Howard-Cooper, Scott. *The Bruin 100: The Greatest Games in the History of UCLA Basketball*. Lenexa, KS: Addax, 1999.
Medley, H. Anthony. *UCLA Basketball: The Real Story*. Los Angeles: Galant Press, 1972.
UCLA Basketball Website. http://members.tripod.com/ucla_hoops/Bruin%20History.htm. Accessed November 27, 2011.
Wooden, John, and Swen Nater. *John Wooden's UCLA Offense*. Champaign, IL: Human Kinetics, 2006.

Uecker, Bob (1935–)

Bob Uecker is a former major league catcher who has gained much more fame from his announcing of baseball games, a recurring role in all three *Major League* films, and his role in a television series, *Mr. Belvedere*.

Robert George Uecker was born January 26, 1935, in Milwaukee, Wisconsin, although he claims

Bob Uecker, Cardinals catcher, clowns around during a workout by playing tuba near the bleachers at Busch Stadium before the start of the second game of the World Series against the New York Yankees, October 8, 1964, in St. Louis. (AP Photo.)

the majors until 1962 at the age of 27. In 33 games, he hit .250, the highest average that he would attain as a big leaguer. The next year he played in just 13 games, spending most of the season in the minors, and was traded to the St. Louis Cardinals in April 1964. The Cardinals had a top catcher in Tim McCarver and Uecker was his backup for two years, hitting .198 and .228, but making a reputation as an excellent fielder and handler of pitchers. The Cards won the 1964 championship, beating the Yankees in seven games, but Uecker did not appear in the series. He then hit .228 in 1965 in 53 games.

In late October 1965, Uecker was the "throw-in" as Dick Groat and Bill White were traded to the Phillies for Alex Johnson, Art Mehaffey, and Pat Corrales. He played in 78 games in 1966, hit .208, and had his top power year with seven homers and 30 runs batted in. In mid-season of 1967 he was shipped to the Atlanta Braves for Gene Oliver. He hit .150 combined in 80 games and was released in October 1967 at the age of 32 by the same team that had initially signed him.

Unlike many marginal ball players, Uecker found a way to stay in the game. The Braves hired him to do public relations through their speakers' bureau and color commentary on their games. Through the intervention of his friend Al Hirt, the great trumpet player, Uecker was asked to be a guest on the *Tonight Show with Johnny Carson* and he was an instant hit for his zany humor.

In 1971, he was offered a position on the Milwaukee Brewers radio broadcast team by owner (now baseball comissioner) Bud Selig. After a number of regular *Tonight Show* appearances and his glibness on the Brewers' telecasts, Uecker was hired to be part of the original broadcast team for *Monday Night Baseball* on ABC in 1976, along with Warner Wolf and Bob Prince. Uecker continued with ABC baseball and other sports telecasts through 1983. He was still doing Brewer games and was rapidly becoming a folk hero in Wisconsin.

In 1985, Uecker began a six-season run as the head of a middle-class family in Beaver Falls, Pennsylvania, that hires an English butler named Mr. Belvedere. The series was based on a 1947 novel, later made into a series of films in the late 1940s and early 1950s. Uecker's character was a sportswriter, and over

that he was actually born on Highway 41 as his parents made an oleo run to Illinois. This illustrates the unusual humor of Uecker, who has gained his greatest fame as a comic commentator. He attended Boys Technical High School (now Lynde and Harry Bradley Technology and Trade School), graduating in 1954, then enlisted in the army. It was there at Fort Leonard Wood that he began playing baseball more seriously and was signed by the Milwaukee Braves for a small bonus when he left the service in 1956.

Uecker had grown up a big fan of the Milwaukee Brewers, a minor league team of the Boston Braves. In 1953, the Braves relocated from Boston to Milwaukee and became the darlings of the city. Uecker was thrilled to be a part of that, but he didn't make it to the life of the series, he becomes a sportscaster and his three children go from high school and elementary school to law school, college, and high school, respectively.

During this period of time, Uecker also starred in the film *Major League* (1989) as a baseball announcer named Harry Doyle. The part was written for him and his crazy humor and he was one of the many reasons why the film was so successful. Two sequels followed in 1994 and 1998; these were far less popular, justifiably.

In the 1980s Miller Lite Beer ran a series of humorous commercials with a variety of sports celebrities. Some of the best starred Uecker and one contributed to a catch phrase that has continued today. Uecker is getting help finding his seats at the ballpark and says, "I must be in the front row," after which he is seated in the upper reaches of the stadium. He then comments on his great seats and yells critical comments at the umpire about missing the call. As a result many ballparks have referred to such "nosebleed" seats as "Uecker seats." The commercials were instrumental in getting Uecker the *Major League* role.

Uecker also broadcast World Wrestling on pay-per-view and in one match in Wrestlemania was actually gotten in a headlock by Andre the Giant. He was inducted into the Celebrity Wing of the WWE Hall of Fame in 2010. He also was voted into the Wisconsin Athletic Hall of Fame in 1998, the Radio Hall of Fame in 2001, and received the 2003 Ford C. Frick Award from the Baseball Hall of Fame, awarded each year to a broadcaster.

In April 2010, Uecker underwent heart surgery and missed broadcasting until mid-season as he recuperated. He returned to the booth for WTMJ radio and the Brewers' television network in July. In October, he had a second heart surgery to replace a tear from a previous valve replacement. He recovered and was able to broadcast the Brewers' games as they won the Central Division championship of the National League. It was Uecker's 41st season of broadcasting.

Murry R. Nelson

See also Baseball Hall of Fame; St. Louis Cardinals; Selig, Bud; World Series

Suggested Resources

"Bob Uecker." Baseball-Reference.com. http://www.baseball-reference.com/players/u/ueckebo01.shtml. Accessed November 8, 2011.
"Bob Uecker." IMDb. http://www.imdb.com/name/nm0879902/. Accessed November 8, 2011.
Uecker, Bob, and Mickey Herskowitz, *Catcher in the Wry*. New York: Jove Books, 1982.

Ultimate Fighting Championship (UFC) and Mixed Martial Arts (MMA)

Ultimate fighting is a generic term that describes a genre of combat sport that involves two competitors who utilize a combination of ground-based wrestling and jiu-jitsu as well as stand-up striking skills to submit or knock out the opponent. These events, while increasingly popular in the United States, Brazil, Japan, the UK, and Australia, are often mired in controversy due to the public perception of extreme violence and brutality that once led U.S. senator John McCain to infamously brand the sport "human cockfighting." While there are many organizations worldwide promoting what are known as mixed martial arts (MMA) contests, it is the American promotion, the Ultimate Fighting Championship (UFC), perhaps more than any other that helped to introduce this sporting contest to the masses.

So-called no-holds-barred fighting competitions have been held since at least the seventh century BCE. In ancient Greece, the *pankration*, regarded as one of the first "fighting systems" and the ancient precursor to the modern-day sport of MMA, was a skillful combination of stand-up striking and ground-based wrestling that employed a number of sophisticated joint-locks. *Kato Pankration*, which was added to the

33rd Olympiad in 648 BCE, had been traditionally said to be founded by the mythical hero Theseus, who used a combination of boxing and wrestling to defeat the minotaur in the labyrinth.

While it can be argued that no-holds-barred contests have existed since at least the time of the Greeks, the contemporary fighting practice known as mixed martial arts (MMA), and in particular, the brand-name fighting organization called the Ultimate Fighting Championship (UFC), can trace its more recent lineage to the streets of Brazil.

The genesis of the UFC began in Brazil, when Carlos Gracie, the descendant of Scottish immigrants, began teaching a modified version of traditional Japanese jiu-jitsu and adapted it to feature ground-based grappling and efficient submission holds like chokes and joint-locks. The Gracies were a wealthy diplomat family who relocated from Scotland to Brazil in the late 1800s and eventually helped to arrange the settlement of Japanese immigrants in Brazil. To show his appreciation for helping to settle his fellow countrymen and women, former Japanese jiu-jitsu champion Mitsuyo Maeda offered to teach Gastão Gracie's eldest son, Carlos, jiu-jitsu. Carlos and his brother Helio are credited with modifying the traditional jiu-jitsu to capitalize on leverage rather than sheer strength. Moreover, these modifications were found to be more effective in "free-fighting" contests, dubbed *vale tudo*, that were often conducted between martial arts academies of various styles. Through a series of successful promotions and the highly publicized success of the slightly built Helio the Gracie name would become synonymous with the hybrid form known as Brazilian jiu-jitsu (BJJ).

By the late 1980s, having moved to the United States, Helio's son Rorion, in an attempt to expand and market the Gracie fighting system, issued a series of challenges in martial arts magazines and in a 1989 *Playboy* article entitled "Bad," offered money to any challenger who could beat one of his brothers in a no-rules fight. Shrewdly, Rorion began videotaping these challenges, which often pitted various martial arts disciplines against Gracie jiu-jitsu. Rorion marketed the videotapes, dubbed *Gracies in Action*, that demonstrated the superiority of the Gracie system over the flashy yet ineffective martial arts styles that were wildly popular in the United States at that time.

Rorion Gracie had an idea to help promote the Gracie style of jiu-jitsu in the United States modeled after the anything-goes, style-vs.-style *Vale Tudo* contests popular in Brazil since the 1950s. His grand idea would come to be known as the Ultimate Fighting Championship (UFC), a fighting promotion that held its inaugural event in Denver, Colorado, in 1993. Billed as a battle of various fighting styles, including karate, kickboxing, judo, standup striking, wrestling, and jiu-jitsu, the contest was ultimately a vehicle to showcase the Gracie system of fighting. The early UFC promotion used the catchphrase "There are no rules!" to differentiate it from boxing, full contact karate, and other mainstream combat sports of the day. While this marketing ploy helped to initially generate interest and eventually pay-per-view buys that would rival boxing and professional wrestling in the mid-1990s, the brand was marked as a brutal oddity.

With the growing success of videotape sales and increasing numbers of students that Rorion was teaching in his converted California garage, interest was picking up significantly after the publication of the *Playboy* article. In fact, with the success of the "Gracie Challenge," Rorion was able to open a new school in Torrance, California. The *Playboy* article intrigued Art Davie, an advertising industry worker, and he set about tracking down Rorion at his new school to try to pitch a promotion idea. The meeting resulted in Davie quitting his job at the advertising agency and going to work for the Gracies trying to broker a deal that would capitalize on the growing curiosity in Brazilian jiu-jitsu. The idea to put on a tournament showcasing the superior effectiveness of Gracie jiu-jitsu suited Rorion's larger plan of promoting Gracie academies throughout the United States. Davie began shopping the idea for a tournament event tentatively called the "War of the Worlds" with little success until he met with executives from Semaphore Entertainment Group (SEG). Trusting his staff, president and *King Biscuit Flower Hour* creator Bob Meyrowitz, with limited knowledge of martial arts, green-lighted the project since SEG had been looking for a successful new pay-per-view (PPV) event.

The inaugural UFC event itself was notable for its lack of professional presentation. Despite hiring NFL star Jim Brown, karate champion Bill "Superfoot" Wallace, and former kickboxing champion Kathy Long, the lack of familiarity with this novel event left the commentators struggling to make sense of the contest unfolding before their eyes. The rules for the first UFC were simple: no biting and no eye gouging. There were no weight classes and no gloves, no time limits, and no judges. Twenty-six seconds into the first bout, Dutch kickboxing champion Gerard Gordeau had knocked down 410-pound sumo champion Teila Tuli and, according to Howard Rosenberg's November 15, 1993, *Los Angeles Times* account, "sent a tooth flying and blood pouring from his mouth" with a savage kick. While the tournament appeared chaotic and barbaric to many outsiders, the matchups were carefully controlled by Gracie and SEG. Since the larger aim of the tournament was to demonstrate the superior fighting technique of the Gracie system, it was important to ensure that Royce Gracie, the smallest competitor in the contest, would be able to showcase his Brazilian jiu-jitsu skills.

Despite eventual rule changes and the financial success of the UFC, public scrutiny was growing due to the violent nature of the events. Arizona's U.S. senator, John McCain, then-chairman of the Senate Commerce Committee, began to exert significant pressure on cable operators who carried the UFC, which was constantly mired in controversy, especially following the ban on MMA competitions in New York State (which is still in place). The rationale for cable operators to pull the controversial sport seemed, on the surface, quite clear. Indeed, while McCain's publicly stated reasons for pressuring the major PPV providers revolved around the issue of violence, as showcased in a broadcasted debate on no-holds-barred fighting on the *Larry King Live* show in December 1995, it is interesting to note that McCain, himself a vocal supporter of boxing, a major competitor of the UFC, had close family ties to Anheuser-Busch, one of the largest corporate sponsors of boxing in the United States. Considering the pressure being exerted on cable operators, the future of the UFC looked bleak indeed.

In many ways, the UFC was reborn in 2001 when Zuffa Sports Entertainment bought the struggling

Dan Miller, bottom, in action against John Salter during their UFC fight at the TD Garden on August 28, 2010, in Boston, Massachusetts. (AP Photo/Gregory Payan.)

promotion. The new UFC owners had big plans to elevate the promotion in the eyes of the public and they would implement a sophisticated strategy to reposition the UFC brand as a legitimate sporting event. The new owners were Frank and Lorenzo Fertitta, Las Vegas casino business owners who had ties to the Nevada State Athletic Commission. Lorenzo, in fact, had served on the commission since 1996 and in 1999 was invited, at the request of SEG, to attend UFC XXI in Iowa and was impressed with the level of professionalism and athleticism that competitors displayed. Upon resigning his post on the Nevada State Athletic Commission (NSAC), the idea to buy out the UFC began to emerge. The Fertitta brothers along with longtime friend Dana White, who was appointed president, began to outline how to promote and popularize the controversial sport. The new business was named Zuffa (Italian for "to scrap" or "to fight") and set out on a significant promotional campaign to educate state athletic commissioners, television cable companies, and the public alike. By highlighting significant rule changes—many of which had been implemented by the end of SEG's ownership—including the introduction of rounds, mandatory gloves, weight classes, and the prohibition of head-butting, the UFC hoped to reposition itself as a legitimate sporting practice. The first Zuffa-promoted event took place at the Trump Taj Mahal casino on the boardwalk of Atlantic City, New Jersey, on February 23, 1999, and while the event was not broadcast on PPV, it would take less than a year from Zuffa's purchase to achieve that significant milestone.

In what would become the most important business move since Zuffa's UFC buyout, the UFC secured a television deal with the Spike television network in 2004. Spike purchased the rights to air a Zuffa-produced reality television show, *The Ultimate Fighter* (TUF), which featured two teams of relatively unknown fighters vying for a chance to win a UFC contract. The contestants lived in a lavish house and trained under two of the UFC's marquee fighters, Chuck Liddell and Randy Couture. The show not only generated a record number of viewers, it served as a season-long buildup for the anticipated rematch of Couture and Liddell. Not only was the show an unqualified hit for the Spike TV network (winning the coveted male ages 18–35 audience convincingly), the very fact that an MMA show of any type was available on cable signaled nothing short of a coup for the UFC. In five short years the brand had resourcefully repositioned itself through the familiar genre of reality television.

The popularity and appeal of MMA contests are perhaps at an all-time high as demonstrated by a 2011 landmark seven-year television deal with Fox Media Group worth a reported $100 million per year. For the first time in the company's history, the UFC will broadcast live bouts on network television, thereby significantly extending the reach of the UFC brand into the lucrative sports-media marketplace. While the Ultimate Fighting Championship and mixed martial arts in general only garner a small percentage of the revenue generated by popular American sport leagues

such as the NFL, MLB, and the NBA, shrewd promotion, greater public acceptance, as well as multimedia distribution are poised to position the unique sporting event as the "new and safer boxing" and the "sport of the future."

Matthew A. Masucci

Suggested Resources

Gentry, Clyde. *No Holds Barred: The Complete History of Mixed Martial Arts in America.* Chicago: Triumph Books, 2011.

Krauss, Erich, Bret Aita, and Bob Shamrock. *Brawl: A Behind-the-Scenes Look at Mixed Martial Arts Competition.* Toronto: ECW Press, 2002.

Mayeda, David, and David Ching. *Fighting for Acceptance: Mixed Martial Artists and Violence in American Society.* Bloomington, IN: iUniverse, 2008.

Mixed Martial Arts. ESPN.com. http://espn.go.com/mma/. Accessed January 13, 2012.

Mixed Martial Arts Weekly. http://mmaweekly.com/. Accessed January 13, 2012.

Poliakoff, Michael. *Combat Sports in the Ancient World: Competition, Violence, and Culture.* New Haven, CT: Yale University Press, 1986.

Shamrock, Ken, and Erich Krauss. *Beyond the Lion's Den: The Life, the Fights, the Techniques.* North Clarendon, VT: Tuttle, 2005.

Sherdog.com. http://www.sherdog.com/ Accessed January 13, 2012.

Unitas, John (1933–2002)

John Unitas, also known as "Johnny U," the "Golden Arm," or "Mr. Clutch," was one of the best quarterbacks ever to play professional football. Unitas played the bulk of his 18-year career with the Baltimore Colts, and when he retired in 1973, he held eight career passing records including most wins by a starting quarterback (118), most pass attempts (5,186), most completions (2,830), most yardage (40,239), and most touchdown passes (290). He was the first quarterback to reach 40,000 passing yards in a career as well as the first to throw at least 30 touchdown passes in a season (32 in 1959). His record 47 straight games with a touchdown pass (1956–1960) is often compared to Joe DiMaggio's 56-game hitting streak and, like DiMaggio's record, has never been seriously threatened. Unitas received many accolades after his retirement including, in 1999, being selected number 32 in ESPN's "SportsCentury: 50 Greatest Athletes of the 20th Century," being named best quarterback of all time by the *Sporting News* in 2004, and being enshrined in the NFL Hall of Fame in 1979. As football has evolved into a more passing-oriented game, many of his records have since been surpassed, but Unitas set the bar by which future NFL quarterbacks were judged.

Despite his eventual success, Unitas's legendary career almost never got started. He grew up in Pittsburgh, raised by his mother (his father died when John was four). As a sophomore, Unitas took over as the starting quarterback of his high school team only after the regular starter was injured. Despite a successful high school career, Unitas's dream school, Notre Dame, was concerned that his small size would hinder his success. Instead, Unitas went to the University of Louisville, where as a freshman, he recorded a 4–1 record as a starter to lead the Cardinals to a 5–5 record that season. However, the rest of his career at Louisville was marred by losing records and an injury in his senior season that prevented him from playing most of the year. The Pittsburgh Steelers still selected Unitas in the ninth round of the 1955 draft, but cut him before the season started. After this disappointment, Unitas started working various construction jobs and played for a Pittsburgh semipro team, the Bloomfield Rams. In 1956, the Baltimore Colts and their Hall of Fame coach, Weeb Ewbank, signed Unitas as a backup quarterback for $7,000. In the fourth game, Unitas got his chance, replacing starter George Shaw who went down with an injury. While he got off to a rocky start as his first NFL pass was intercepted and returned for a touchdown, Unitas set a rookie record for completion percentage and led the Colts to upset victories over the Green Bay Packers and Cleveland Browns. In the final game of the 1956 season, Unitas started his streak of 47 consecutive games throwing a touchdown pass.

As the starting quarterback, Unitas led the Colts to new heights. In 1957, the Colts achieved their first winning record (7–5) and Unitas earned the Most Valuable Player (MVP) award from the Newspaper Enterprise Association (NEA). During the 1958 and 1959 seasons Unitas established himself as the face of the NFL. In 1958, he led the Colts to a 9–3 record and the West Division title, earning them a game against

Johnny Unitas holds the Jim Thorpe Memorial Trophy awarded him when he was chosen the National Football League's outstanding player of 1967. (AP Photo/William Smith.)

the New York Giants in the NFL championship game. Toward the end of the hard-fought contest, the Colts got the ball on their own 14-yard line with 2:20 left, trailing the Giants 17–14. Unitas calmly led the Colts on a 13-play drive that ended with Steve Myhra's 20-yard, game-tying field goal with seven seconds remaining. In the first overtime playoff game in NFL history the Giants won the coin toss and received the ball, but were quickly stopped and punted to the Colts, who took over on their own 20-yard line. Once again, Unitas drove the Colts down the field with running back Alan Ameche putting the finishing touches on the 23–17 victory with a one-yard plunge for the game-winning touchdown. On the day, Unitas threw for a championship game–record 349 passing yards, but it was his two drives at the end of the game that made Unitas a legend. This 1958 championship game was dubbed "The Greatest Game Ever Played" and is partially responsible for the NFL's increased popularity during the 1960s. The first championship game to be nationally televised (by NBC), it was seen by over 45 million people who tuned in to witness Unitas's game-winning heroics, helping turn professional football into one of the most popular sports in America.

While this championship game vaulted Unitas into the public consciousness, he continued his successful and winning play the following year. In 1959, Unitas won the AP MVP by leading the NFL in passing yards, touchdowns, and completions. He also led the Colts to their second straight title, again defeating the Giants in the championship game, 31–16. In this game, Unitas passed for 265 yards and accounted for three touchdowns (two passing, one rushing). The Colts slumped to several mediocre seasons between 1960 and 1963 as several key players suffered injuries. Unitas maintained a high level of personal achievement during these down years, passing for over 3,000 yards in both 1960 and 1963. In 1964, Unitas once again won the Most Valuable Player award in leading the Colts back to the NFL championship game. But both he and the Colts struggled and were upset by the Cleveland Browns, 27–0. The Colts remained on the cusp of greatness over the next few seasons as they finished tied for first in the Western Division in both 1965 and 1967, but did not make the playoffs in either year, first losing to the Green Bay Packers in 1965 for the right to go to the NFL title game and then losing to the Los Angeles Rams in the last game of the 1967 season to miss the playoffs.

On the heels of his third AP MVP award in 1967, Unitas and the Colts looked forward to a special season in 1968. But Unitas tore a muscle in the preseason and appeared in only five games that year. Behind NFL MVP Earl Morrall, the Colts put together a 13–1 record and were considered by many to be one of the best teams in football history. As it turned out, this "title" was prematurely applied as the American Football League's New York Jets and their star quarterback Joe Namath upset the heavily favored Colts in Super Bowl III. Morrall started the game, but Unitas came on in the fourth quarter to try to spark a Colts comeback.

John Unitas Honors

In recognition of his playing ability, impact on the game, and generosity in his postplaying life, Unitas has been honored with several different memorials. Unitas's number 16 is still the only retired number at the University of Louisville and his number 19 is retired by the Colts and by the Ravens. Since 1987, the best senior college quarterback is given the Johnny Unitas Golden Arm Award in recognition of his abilities that season. Unitas has several buildings named after him including a residence hall at the University of Louisville and the football stadium at Towson University. After his death, Unitas was memorialized in a statue and banners in M&T Bank Stadium, the home of the Baltimore Ravens. Unitas is also a member of the Ravens Ring of Honor. Finally, a statue of Unitas was erected in the north end zone of the Papa John's Cardinal Stadium at the University of Louisville, and it is a tradition for all Louisville football players to touch the statue as they make their way down to the field.

His efforts were not enough as the Jets, behind former Colts coach Weeb Ewbank, held on for a 16–7 victory. In commentary both before and after the game Unitas and Namath were both held up as symbols of two different sides of the 1960s culture clash. Unitas was the embodiment of the conservative establishment against the liberal youth represented by Namath. In this view, the Jets' victory was a symbol of the growing strength of the counterculture.

Despite this setback, Unitas led the Colts back to the Super Bowl only two years later. After the AFL-NFL merger in 1970, the Colts joined the American Football Conference (AFC) and Unitas led them to an 11–2–1 record that included two victories over their new division rival, the New York Jets. After impressive playoff wins over the Cincinnati Bengals and Oakland Raiders, the Colts earned the trip to Super Bowl V where they would take on the Dallas Cowboys. After falling behind 6–0 early in the game, Unitas connected with John Mackey on a Super Bowl–record, 75-yard touchdown pass to tie the game. Unfortunately, Unitas was injured in the first half and had to watch as Earl Morrall helped lead the Colts to their first Super Bowl victory on Jim O'Brien's last-second, game-winning field goal. In 1971, Unitas led the Colts to the verge of a second consecutive Super Bowl, but the Miami Dolphins, led by former Colts head coach Don Shula, ousted them in the AFC championship game. That was the closest Unitas would come to his former glory as he was a part-time starter for the Colts in 1972 and was traded to the San Diego Chargers, playing in five games for them in 1973 before retiring.

Following his playing career, Unitas remained active in the football and Baltimore communities. He worked as a color commentator for CBS during the 1970s and was a successful fundraiser for Towson University in Baltimore, which some of his children attended. Unitas was an avid Baltimore supporter and bitterly opposed Colt owner Robert Irsay's decision to move the team to Indianapolis in 1984. He cut ties with the Colts, and in 1996 when the Cleveland Browns moved to Baltimore and became the Ravens, Unitas supported the new team and often appeared on the sidelines during games. Unitas left a legacy as one of the most prolific quarterbacks in NFL history. His reputation as a fierce competitor, cool under pressure, and intelligent provided the model for the NFL's quarterback position. In an era when most teams emphasized the running game, Unitas revolutionized the quarterback's passing role and his success also contributed to the exploding popularity of the game during the 1960s.

Unitas suffered a fatal heart attack while working out and died on September 11, 2002, at the age of 69.

Jeffrey T. Ramsey

See also ESPN Channels; Namath, Joe; 1958 NFL Championship Game; Pro Football Hall of Fame and Museum; *Sports Illustrated*; Super Bowl

Suggested Resources
Callahan, Tom. *Johnny U: The Life and Times of John Unitas*. New York: Crown Publishers, 2006.
"Johnny Unitas." Pro Football Hall of Fame. http://www.profootballhof.com/hof/member.aspx?PlayerId=219&tab=Bio. Accessed December 1, 2011.
Johnny Unitas Website. http://www.johnnyunitas.com/. Accessed December 1, 2011.
Sahadi, Lou. *Johnny Unitas: America's Quarterback*. Chicago: Triumph Books, 2004.
Towle, Mike. *Johnny Unitas: Mr. Quarterback (Great American Sports Legends)*. Nashville, TN: Cumberland House, 2003.

V

Valenzuela, Fernando (1960–)

Fernando Valenzuela was a major league pitcher, most notably for the Los Angeles Dodgers, from 1980 to 1997. He later became a broadcaster of the Dodger games on Spanish-language radio stations.

Valenzuela seemingly burst onto the Dodger scene in the fall of 1980, appearing in 10 games, pitching just over 17 innings, and allowing no earned runs. The Dodgers were edged by one game for the National League Western Division title, so Valenzuela's stats, though impressive, were overshadowed by the tight pennant race. In 1981, however, this was not the case.

Valenzuela won his first eight decisions, making him 10–0 as a major leaguer, and he was the talk of the baseball world for a number of reasons. Besides his startling statistics, Valenzuela had a most unorthodox pitching delivery. During his windup, his eyes looked skyward and it seemed impossible that he could pitch with any consistent control; yet he did. In 192 innings pitched that year, he allowed just 61 walks while striking out 180 batters; both his innings pitched and strikeouts led the league.

More vital to many fans was that Valenzuela was Mexican, the first big star from that country who played for the Dodgers. With Los Angeles just two hours away and the largest number of Mexican immigrants in the Southern California area, Valenzuela was a marketing phenomenon for the Dodgers' appeal to their Latino base.

Valenzuela seemed to be a perfect example of a common man for thousands of Mexican immigrants. He was born in 1960 in Navoja in the state of Sonora, one of 12 children, raised in a small village of adobe huts called Ethcohuaquila. His father was a farmer and Fernando somehow learned to pitch well at a young age.

Signed at age 17 by Dodger scout Mike Brito from a Mexican League professional team, Valenzuela moved swiftly through the Dodger minor league chain. At Lodi (California) of the Class A level, he learned to throw a screwball and that became his "money pitch." He debuted with the Dodgers at 19.

A fascinating question was Valenzuela's age. He had a baby face and looked like a teddy bear at 5'11", 195 pounds, but seemed too mature for his 20 years of age. Rumors were that he was older, but those subsequently proved to be untrue. He also seemed to speak no English and always spoke to the media through a translator, adding an air of mystery to his demeanor. All of these factors—age, heritage, unusual delivery, mystery—became vital when major league players went on strike on June 12. The strike lasted until July 31 and made a mess of the playoff determinations. Many fans boycotted the rest of the season and vowed to no longer follow the game. Valenzuela's outsize personality and performance drew fans back almost immediately to the game in August. He became the center of what was referred to as "Fernandomania." The games in which he pitched were almost all sell-outs, both at home and on the road.

For the year Valenzuela went 13–7 with an ERA of 2.48. Besides leading the league in strikeouts and innings pitched, he also led in complete games (11) and shutouts (8). He was tied for second in victories behind Tom Seaver's 14 wins. Valenzuela was voted Rookie of the Year, *Sporting News* Pitcher of the Year, Major League Player of the Year, and won the National League Cy Young Award as top pitcher.

Los Angeles Dodgers rookie pitching sensation Fernando Valenzuela autographs baseballs for a group of Catholic school teachers in May of 1981. (AP Photo/Ramussen.)

In the convoluted playoff system that was implemented, the Dodgers, who won the first half of the season in the West, defeated the Houston Astros, who won the second half, three games to two. In that series Fernando pitched two games and won his only decision, 2–1. Then the Dodgers defeated the Montreal Expos, who won the Eastern Division, in five games with Fernando winning one and losing one. The Dodgers then defeated the New York Yankees in the World Series, four games to two, to claim their first world championship since 1965. Fernando won his only start in the series.

After the many awards that Valenzuela received for his great season he was hailed as a national hero in Mexico and a star throughout the United States, but especially among Chicanos in Southern California. Expectations were high for 1982 for both the world champion Dodgers as well as for Fernando. He did not disappoint, winning 19 games, but the Dodgers fell a

game short in the Western Division and had no post-season play.

Fernando's salary for 1983 jumped to $1 million, quite a rapid rise, and he won another 15 games in 1983, tied for the team lead. The Dodgers won the Western Division, but lost to the Phillies in the playoffs, three games to one. Fernando pitched the only Dodger victory, 4–1.

The year 1984 was another Dodger down year, as well as for Fernando, who went 12–17, but had a fine ERA of 3.03. Both he and the Dodgers came back to top performances in 1985 as he went 17–10 and the Dodgers won the Western Division. In the playoffs, the Dodgers were defeated by the St. Louis Cardinals in six games. Fernando won game one by a 4–1 score, but got no decision in a 3–2 Dodger loss in game five.

The next year (1986) the Dodgers were terrible, finishing fifth in the division, but Fernando was 21–11 with an ERA of 3.14. He led the league with 20 complete games, as well as victories, but finished second in Cy Young voting to Mike Scott of the Astros.

Over the next four years Valenzuela was bothered by occasional arm problems, probably because of the great stress that a screwball places on the arm, as well as the enormous number of innings that he was pitching, over 250 for six seasons in a row. The Dodgers were surprise pennant and World Series winners in 1988, but Fernando missed much of the season with his injuries and ended up just 5–8 for the year.

After he went 13–13 in 1990, the Dodgers abruptly released him and Valenzuela was both shocked and hurt. He pitched briefly for the California Angels in 1991, but was still ailing, then played all of 1992 back in the Mexican League with Jalisco, where he was a national hero.

In 1993, he was given another opportunity to pitch in the majors with the Baltimore Orioles, where he went 8–10 for an Oriole squad that finished third in a tough division. He became a free agent at the end of the year and signed with the Philadelphia Phillies in June 1994, where he was 1–2 in 45 innings of work. The next year he was on the move again, this time going to San Diego as a free agent. He had two fine years for the Padres, going 8–3 in 1995 and 13–8 in 1996.

Then, in 1997, Valenzuela was just 2–8 when he was traded in June to the St. Louis Cardinals, where he went 0–4 and was released at the end of the season. His major league career was over at the age of 36, but he returned to Mexico and continued to pitch into his 40s in the Mexican winter leagues. Fernando was 173–153 in his career as a major leaguer, but his impact on attendance and popularizing baseball was enormous. He was featured in articles in *Newsweek* and other national magazines, in addition to the various pieces in *Sports Illustrated* and the *Sporting News.*

In 2003, the Dodgers offered him a position with their Spanish-language broadcast team and Valenzuela has been with the club since then. He has demonstrated great insight into the game as well as a wry sense of humor. He is now fully bilingual, but prefers to speak in Spanish and occasionally still uses a translator, just to make sure his comments are recorded correctly. Fernando remains one of the few baseball players who

---

All-Around Fernando

Despite his appearance Valenzuela is a fine all-around athlete. He won a Gold Glove Award in 1986 for being the best-fielding pitcher of that year, tied with Greg Maddux, who won 18 years in a row. Fernando made only 30 errors in 17 seasons. He also won two Silver Slugger awards as best-hitting pitcher in 1981 and 1983. Valenzuela hit .304 one year, had more than 20 hits three times in a year, and was occasionally used as a pinch hitter.

---

had a phenomenon named for him and retains legendary status in the game.

Murry R. Nelson

Suggested Resources

"Fernando Valenzuela." Baseball-Reference.com. http://www.baseball-reference.com/players/v/valenfe01.shtml. Accessed July 19, 2011.

Freedman, Lew. *Latino Baseball Legends: An Encyclopedia*. Westport, CT: Greenwood Press, 2010.

Wendel, Tim, and Jose Luis Villegas. *Latino Baseball Players in America*. Washington, DC: National Geographic, 2008.

VanDerveer, Tara (1953–)

Tara VanDerveer is the Hall of Fame coach for the Stanford University women's basketball team, and is widely regarded as one of the best basketball coaches of all time. Through the 2011–2012 basketball season, VanDerveer compiled an outstanding 861–200 career coaching record at Stanford, Ohio State, and Idaho. She has won two NCAA national championships at Stanford (1990 and 1992) and has been named national Women's Coach of the Year three times. VanDerveer is also well known as the coach of the 1995–1996 United States National Women's Basketball Team. In this capacity, she led the U.S. women to a gold medal in the 1996 Summer Olympic Games in Atlanta, Georgia. VanDerveer is widely respected as an ambassador for women's basketball and has promoted its spread among America's youth. Along with other legendary coaches, such as Pat Summitt and Geno Auriemma, VanDerveer is often given credit for popularizing women's basketball in the United States.

USA women's head coach Tara VanDerveer, right, hugs Ruthie Bolton, as Venus Lacey watches the action on the court during the final moments of the gold medal women's basketball game against Brazil at the Summer Olympic Games in Atlanta, August 4, 1996. (AP Photo/ Eric Draper.)

Tara VanDerveer was born on June 26, 1953, in Boston. After her childhood in upstate New York, she played guard for three years at Indiana University, graduating in 1975 as a Dean's List scholar. In 1978, VanDerveer was named head coach at the University of Idaho, where she led the Vandals to the AIAW Division II National Tournament in 1980.

VanDerveer left Idaho to become the head coach at Ohio State University (OSU) for the 1980–1981 season. Just as she did at Idaho, VanDerveer took over a mediocre program at OSU and raised it to national-contender status. In her five years at Ohio State, VanDerveer's Buckeye teams won 20 games or

more four times and captured three Big Ten championships. The pinnacle of her success at OSU came in 1984–1985, when the Buckeyes went 28–3 and advanced to the 1985 NCAA Women's Basketball Tournament, barely losing to eventual national champion Old Dominion in the quarterfinals.

VanDerveer made another career change in May 1985, when she accepted the women's basketball head coaching position at Stanford University. Though the Cardinal struggled at times during her first two seasons as head coach, VanDerveer soon built Stanford into one of the nation's most successful college basketball programs. In her 26 seasons at Stanford (through the 2011–2012 season), VanDerveer's teams made the NCAA Tournament every year but her first two. The Cardinal have won 20 Pac Ten regular-season championships during her tenure, as well as eight Pac Ten tournament titles. VanDerveer has led the Cardinal to the NCAA Women's Final Four nine times, including three straight appearances in 1990–1992 and five straight from 2008 to 2012.

VanDerveer's first truly successful season at Stanford came in 1987–1988, when the Cardinal went 27–5 and were invited to the NCAA Women's National Championship Tournament. Stanford improved a bit the next year, going 28–3 and advancing to the NCAA quarterfinals. However, the 1989-1990 season marked Stanford's arrival on the national scene for good, as the Cardinal lost only a single game all year and defeated Auburn to win the NCAA championship. After returning to the Final Four in 1991, Stanford overcame some regular-season struggles in 1992 and ended the season playing its best basketball of the year. The hot streak lasted into the tournament, and the Cardinal thrashed Western Kentucky for its second national title in three years.

Though it fell short of its national championship aspirations, Stanford's 1994–1995 team reached its fourth Final Four in six years, a run of success that thrust VanDerveer into the women's basketball national spotlight. After the season, VanDerveer agreed to serve as the head coach for the United States Women's Basketball Team through the 1996 Summer Olympic Games. VanDerveer had previously coached the national team in 1994, leading them to a 7–1 record and a bronze medal at the 1994 FIBA World Championships. After turning Stanford head coaching duties over to Marianne Stanley and Amy Tucker, VanDerveer and her 1995–1996 national squad embarked on a grueling travel schedule, playing 60 games over the course of the next year.

The U.S. women's team was favored going into the 1996 Summer Games, since it was 52–0 in warm-up matches and was going to be playing in Atlanta, on U.S. soil. However, victory is never a sure thing, and the previous U.S. women's Olympic team had come in third in 1992. Brazil, the defending FIBA world champions, was expected to be a particularly tough challenge for the host Americans. Both the United States and Brazil won their respective pools with little trouble, but the Americans struggled against Japan in the quarterfinals, while Brazil easily defeated Cuba—a team that had given the United States its toughest game in pool play. As expected, both teams won their semifinal games, setting up what promised to be a dogfight in the gold medal game.

However, in one of the best coaching efforts of her career, VanDerveer got her team to play its best game against Brazil, and the United States trounced the world champions, 111–87. Though her team was stocked with excellent players (such as Lisa Leslie, Sheryl Swoopes, Rebecca Lobo, and Dawn Staley), VanDerveer received a lot of credit from fans and players alike. The 1996 gold medal effort did much to popularize women's basketball in the United States, since it happened in Atlanta, was widely publicized, and came against a Brazilian team that was frequently dominant. This upswing in popularity helped to further establish the fledgling Women's National Basketball Association, which was founded earlier in the year and began play in 1997.

After her yearlong sabbatical with the national team, VanDerveer made a successful return to Stanford, leading the Cardinal to a 34–2 record and a third straight Final Four appearance. Over the next 10 years, however, while Stanford continued to dominate the Pac Ten and appear in the NCCA Tournament, the Cardinal failed to advance in the postseason any higher than the quarterfinals. The 1997–1998 season witnessed a particularly low point for VanDerveer professionally; the injury-plagued Cardinal became the only number one seed in college basketball history to lose to a number 16 seed, when Harvard shocked Stanford at

home in the first round of the NCAA Tournament. The Cardinal dropped to 18–12 the following year (one of only four times when a VanDerveer-led Stanford team has failed to win at least 20 games), came in third in the Pac Ten, and was again bounced in the first round of the NCAA Tournament, this time by Maine.

VanDerveer worked hard during this relatively unsuccessful period to bring Stanford back to the status of a national championship contender. Through patient teaching and solid recruiting, VanDerveer brought the Cardinal back to the NCAA quarterfinals in 2004 for the first time since 1997. Stanford would reach the quarterfinals again in 2005 and 2006, before going on a run of four consecutive Final Four appearances from 2008 to 2011. Though the Cardinal lost in the national championship game to Tennessee in 2008 and Connecticut in 2010, VanDerveer's program was clearly back on the national stage.

In 2002, VanDerveer was acknowledged as one of the best coaches in women's basketball history through her election to the Women's Basketball Hall of Fame in Knoxville, Tennessee. This honor was extended to include the wider basketball community in August 2011, when VanDerveer was inducted into the Naismith Memorial Hall of Fame in Springfield, Massachusetts. On December 22, 2010, she joined a select club after securing her 800th career victory in a game against the University of San Francisco, just the fifth women's college coach to reach that milestone. She has been selected as National Women's Coach of the Year four times and was named conference Women's Coach of the Year twice while at Ohio State and 11 times at Stanford, through the 2010–2011 season.

VanDerveer is also well known as an accomplished piano player and as coauthor (with journalist Joan Ryan) of a highly regarded account of her tenure as U.S. National Team head coach titled *Shooting from the Outside: How a Coach and Her Olympic Team Transformed Women's Basketball* (1997).

Matt DeFraga

See also Auriemma, Geno; Leslie, Lisa; Naismith Memorial Basketball Hall of Fame; 1996 Olympic Games, Atlanta; Summitt, Pat; Swoopes, Sheryl; Women's National Basketball Association

Suggested Resources

Grundy, Pamela, and Susan Shackelford. *Shattering the Glass: The Remarkable History of Women's Basketball.* Chapel Hill: University of North Carolina Press, 2007.

Skaine, Rosemarie. *Women College Basketball Coaches.* Jefferson, NC: McFarland, 2001.

"Tara VanDerveer." Naismith Memorial Basketball Hall of Fame. www.hoophall.com/hall-of-famers/tag/tara-vanderveer. Accessed January 17, 2012.

"Tara VanDerveer." Stanford Website. www.gostanford.com/sports/w-baskbl/mtt/vanderveer_tara00.html. Accessed January 17, 2012.

"Tara VanDerveer." Women's Basketball Hall of Fame. www.wbhof.com/tara.html. Accessed January 17, 2012.

VanDerveer, Tara, and Joan Ryan. *Shooting from the Outside: How a Coach and Her Olympic Team Transformed Women's Basketball.* New York: Avon Books, 1997.

Veeck, Bill (1914–1986)

Unpredictable, wild, creative, half-crazy—not words normally associated with a baseball executive, but commonly connected to any discussion of Bill Veeck, a man born into a baseball family who spent his life as a baseball owner and showman.

William L. "Bill" Veeck Jr. was born in Chicago, September 1, 1914, the son of William Veeck Sr., a former sportswriter and president of the Chicago Cubs, and was raised, so he claimed, at Wrigley Field. Certainly he spent much of his youth there, observing the business and the exploits of baseball. He began working for the Cubs shortly after the death of his father in 1933 and was responsible for two of the iconic portions of the landmark stadium. First, he completed the work on the center field scoreboard, which displayed not only the Cubs' game data, but also inning by inning scores of every game in the majors with the pitchers in each game denoted by their numbers carried in the scorecards sold at the stadium. The former "cutting-edge" scoreboard remains today, still hand-operated for scores, but also electrified for batter data and scoring decisions. The second innovation was growing ivy on the walls of the outfield to cover the bricks. This didn't provide a lot of padding for outfielders, but it did make the park more beautiful and created a sense of adventure whenever a ball was hit into the ivy.

In 1941, Veeck partnered with Charlie Grimm, a retired Cub first baseman and their manager on three different occasions (1932–1938, 1944–1949, and 1960), to purchase the Milwaukee Brewers, a top minor league franchise of the Detroit Tigers. The Brewers had been a part of the American Association since 1902, but had become a dull, losing franchise at the time of Veeck's purchase. Veeck provided most of the money and the general management and Grimm was the manager. In his first effort at ownership, Veeck showed the creativity and unpredictability that would mark the remainder of his baseball career. The Brewers played some games at 8:30 a.m. (serving coffee and doughnuts, as well as cornflakes and milk) to accommodate wartime workers who were finishing night shifts; he gave away live animals and held weddings at home plate. The fans turned out and Veeck acquired excellent players whom Grimm molded into a winning team.

Veeck joined the marines in 1944 and served in the Pacific Theater, where he suffered a crushed leg in combat. After a series of unsuccessful operations that failed to heal the damaged and infected leg, it was amputated in 1946. This failed to discourage Veeck and, in fact, often served as a source for various comic actions that Veeck took such as dancing on one leg, things that others might find a bit odd, if not macabre. In 1944, when the Cubs rehired Grimm, he recommended Casey Stengel as his successor. Stengel had been a losing manager for the Brooklyn Dodgers and Boston Bees/Braves in the 1930s and 1940s, but he had great success in Milwaukee and became the manager of the Yankees in 1949, leading them to seven World Series titles. Since Veeck was in the Pacific, Stengel was hired and the Brewers won the 1944 pennant, following Grimm's success in 1943. In 1945 Veeck sold the Brewers for a large profit (for the time) of $275,000. He then attempted to buy the Philadelphia Phillies with the intention of stocking it with talent from the Negro Leagues. Since baseball was still segregated, his efforts to buy the team were quickly rebuffed.

In 1946, Veeck purchased the Cleveland Indians from the longtime owners, the Bradley family.

Bob Feller talks about his 1948 contract with the Cleveland Indians. Feller, left, grabs one end of the unsigned paper while Bill Veeck, the Indians' president and owner holds the other. (AP Photo.)

Cleveland had not won a pennant since 1920, but Veeck made a number of clever baseball moves to provide the team the personnel for a pennant run in 1948. Veeck was the first American League owner to sign African American players. In mid-1947 he signed the second African American in the major leagues, Larry Doby, and in 1948 he signed the ageless wonder and pitching star of the Negro Leagues, Satchel Paige. Despite Paige's age (anywhere from 40 to 44), he was still capable and won six games for the Indians, including two shutouts.

The Indians won 97 games, edged Boston by a game for the pennant, then defeated the Braves for the world championship, the last time the Indians won the title, as of 2012. The team also drew over 2.5 million fans, leading the majors, as Veeck moved the team from their old ballpark to cavernous Municipal Stadium, which sat 78,000. The Indians finished third in 1949, but still drew 2.2 million, but it was not enough

for Veeck to retain control of the team. After a messy divorce from his wife of nearly 14 years, Veeck needed money to finalize a settlement in the divorce and his only real asset, the Indians, were sold. Within a year he had remarried to Mary Frances Ackerman.

In 1951, Veeck returned to the baseball scene by purchasing the hapless St. Louis Browns, who had finished at the bottom of the American League for the previous five years after winning their only pennant in 1944. Between their poor play and the city's great fondness for the Cardinals, the Browns drew fewer than 250,000 for the years prior to Veeck's purchase. He tried lots of gimmicks to draw crowds since the team played too poorly to attract fans interested in quality baseball. Veeck signed Satchel Paige as a free agent in July 1951 and he went on to be the best Browns pitcher in 1952, going 12–10 with a 3.07 ERA at the age of 45 (or so). Veeck's antics did not endear him to his fellow owners. Despite getting St. Louis attendance over 500,000 in 1952, he saw no future for the Browns in St. Louis and tried to move the team to Milwaukee. The owners blocked the move, Veeck again ran into financial problems, and he was forced to sell the Browns in 1953. The next season the owners allowed the team to be relocated to Baltimore, where they became the Orioles.

In 1959, Veeck purchased the Chicago White Sox from the Comiskey family. There had been family feuding for a number of years within the family, whose patriarch, Charles Comiskey, had founded the club, a charter member of the American League when it formed in 1900. Comiskey was an early star of Major League Baseball in the late 1800s and a manager into the early 1900s. The White Sox had not won a pennant since the ill-fated 1919 "Black Sox" team, but they had a great mix of veterans and young players. These included Nellie Fox, Luis Aparicio, Early Wynn, and Sherman Lollar. In a down year for the perennially powerful Yankees, the White Sox snared the 1959 pennant as Fox was voted Most Valuable Player and Wynn took the Cy Young Award. Veeck and the city of Chicago were ecstatic, despite the fact that the Dodgers defeated the White Sox in six games in the 1959 World Series.

Veeck brought in Hank Greenberg, the Hall of Famer who had worked with him in Cleveland, as a vice president, as well as Mary Frances Veeck, who charmed the city as Veeck amused it. He added an exploding scoreboard to Comiskey Park, which erupted after each White Sox homer, which certainly annoyed opposing pitchers and teams. This only added to Veeck's "outsider" position among owners, but fans loved his innovations and within 10 years, most teams had some sort of fireworks response when a homer was hit or a game won by the home team. Veeck put the players' names on the backs of uniforms, as big an innovation as had been the case when the Yankees first added numbers to the backs of their uniforms in the late 1920s.

Veeck worked constantly, appearing at various functions throughout the city, handling many front office duties and sometimes sitting in the bleachers at games. The fans loved him, but his health suffered from his heavy smoking and long work days. He was forced to sell the team to maintain his health in 1961 and he disappeared from baseball for a time. He and

Veeck's "Little" Joke

For a game in 1952, Veeck signed a midget named Eddie Gaedel to a contract and he appeared in a game as a pinch hitter. He walked on four pitches since he had almost no strike zone once he went into a crouch for his hitting stance. He wore uniform number 1/8. He was immediately removed for a pinch runner.

Mary Frances Veeck managed Suffolk Downs, a racetrack outside of Boston, in 1969–1970. Veeck wrote a book about this experience entitled *Thirty Tons a Day*, in which he detailed the many zany promotions there that continued to characterize his career.

In 1975, the White Sox were not drawing, since the Cubs were the city's darlings, despite their record of not getting into a World Series in 30 years. There was consideration of moving the Sox to St. Petersburg, their spring training home, but Veeck stepped in and bought the White Sox once again with the promise of keeping the team in Chicago. As usual Veeck was short on cash and his response to the new reality of free agency was to rotate players in when they were on the verge of free agency and out when he could not meet the financial demands of the free agents. During this period the Sox finished last in 1976; then the 1977 team won 90 games, but finished third in the Western Division. In 1978 and 1979, the Sox were fourth, then fifth in the seven-team division. The 1975 Sox drew 750,000, but in 1977 the team drew over 1.6 million, then 1.4 and 1.2 million in the next two years. In July 1979, the White Sox had a Disco Demolition Night and the result was a disaster, with the field being declared unplayable and the White Sox forfeiting the second game of a doubleheader.

Veeck's health again was an issue in 1980 and he sold the team for $20 million, a tidy profit from the $7 million that he had paid when he purchased the club. Veeck continued to show up at the ballpark and sit in the stands with the Wrigley Field "bleacher bums" for a few years before his health problems became too severe. He died on January 2, 1986, of congestive heart failure. Five years later, the maverick owner was elected to the Baseball Hall of Fame.

In 2000, Pat Williams, the former general manager of the Chicago Bulls and the Orlando Magic, published a paean to Veeck entitled *Marketing Your Dreams*.

Murry R. Nelson

See also Baseball Hall of Fame; Black Sox Scandal: Chicago Cubs; Cleveland Indians; Disco Demolition Night; Greenberg, Hank; Negro Leagues; Paige, Satchel; Wrigley Field

Suggested Resources
Acocella, Nick. "Baseball's Showman." August 20, 2006. http://espn.go.com/classic/veeckbill000816.html. Accessed December 12, 2011.
Eskenazi, Gerald. *Bill Veeck: A Baseball Legend*. New York: McGraw-Hill, 1987.
Veeck, Bill, with Ed Linn. *Thirty Tons a Day*. Lanham, MD: Ivan R. Dee, 2009.
Veeck, Bill, with Ed Linn. *Veeck, as in Wreck*. Chicago: University of Chicago Press, 2001.
Williams, Pat, with Michael Winereb. *Marketing Your Dreams: Business and Life Lessons from Bill Veeck, Baseball's Marketing Genius*. Champaign, IL: Sports Publishing, 2000.

Vick, Michael (1980–)

In the early 21st century, few other professional athletes have elicited such strong and polarizing opinions as Michael Vick. While many superstar athletes whom people idolize have tarnished their names in sex scandals or gotten caught using banned substances, for example, Vick's conviction for animal cruelty remains among the most controversial topics regarding professional athletes. To his fans, Vick is a once fallen hero who seems to have redeemed himself. To scholars in sociology, cultural anthropology, and psychology, for example, Vick has been an interesting case study in a variety of ways. To the public at large, he remains a topic of polarizing discussion for his actions both on and off the football field.

Michael Dwayne Vick was born to Brenda Vick and Michael Boddie in Newport News, Virginia, on June 26, 1980, the second oldest of the four Vick children—Christina, Michael, Marcus, and Courtney. His parents were only teenagers and unmarried at the time of his birth, living in a small three-bedroom apartment in the Ridley Circle housing project in Newport News, known for low socioeconomic status and crime. Vick

Philadelphia Eagles quarterback Michael Vick talking to children in February of 2010, as part of the Humane Society of the United States' "End Dogfighting" outreach program, at the Overtown Youth Center in Miami. (AP Photo/Wilfredo Lee, File.)

became passionate about football at a very young age, and his success started early in his career, too. As a freshman at Homer L. Ferguson High School he threw for 433 yards and four touchdowns in one game. As the school was closed in 1996, Vick and his coach, Tommy Reamon, moved to Warwick High School, also in Newport News. At Warwick, he was a three-year starter, passing for 4,846 yards with 43 touchdowns over his high school career. After his stellar high school career, he chose in-state Virginia Tech as his college.

Vick's first game at Virginia Tech continued the successful story he had started to write for himself on the football field when he scored three rushing touchdowns in just over one quarter of play against James Madison. He went on to lead the Hokies to an 11–0

Financial Roller Coaster

When Michael Vick was drafted to the NFL in 2001, he signed a six-year, $62 million contract with the Falcons. Throughout the years, his endorsements have included many global corporations, such as Nike, Reebok, Coca-Cola, EA Sports, and Powerade. In 2005 he was ranked 33rd among *Forbes's* Top 100 Celebrities and in 2006 he landed number 10, according to *Sports Illustrated*, on the list of the richest American athletes. When he re-signed with the Atlanta Falcons in 2007, his 10-year contract for $130 million included a $37 million signing bonus, making him the highest paid professional football player of all time. In July 2008, while he was serving his sentence in prison, Vick filed for bankruptcy stating assets of $16 million and liabilities of $20.4 million; in less than a year, he went from being the highest paid player in the NFL to a broke prison inmate with a 12 cents/hour job. After his release from prison, Vick first signed a one-year, $1.6. million contract with the Philadelphia Eagles, but after his successful reentry to the highest level of professional football, the Eagles signed him to a six-year, $100 million contract, making him one of the highest paid players in the league again.

regular season and the BCS national title game against Florida State, the Hokies' first appearance on such a large national stage. Vick led the NCAA in passing efficiency that year, set an NCAA passing record for a freshman quarterback, and established several single-season school records. Overall, he won numerous awards and recognitions during his time at Virginia Tech, including finishing third in the voting for the Heisman Trophy in 1999. After two phenomenal years in college football, Vick announced he was entering the NFL draft in 2001.

After being drafted by the Atlanta Falcons, Vick immediately donated $1 million to Virginia Tech athletics and Michael Vick Hall, a prominent hall located within Virginia Tech's Merryman Athletic Center, was named in his honor. Virginia Tech later retired Vick's jersey in 2002 and his likeness can be found throughout the university's athletic facilities.

When the Falcons drafted Vick first in the NFL draft, he became the first African American quarterback ever to be selected number one overall. After a solid but not stellar rookie year, Vick became Atlanta's starting quarterback in the fall of 2002 and quickly established himself as an MVP candidate. He started all 15 games he played in the 2002–2003 season and was named to his first Pro Bowl. He also set numerous team and league records for quarterbacks. In the years between 2002 and 2007, Vick established himself as one of the most popular and successful players in the NFL. In 2006, he started The Vick Foundation, a nonprofit organization to support at-risk youth and after-school programming in the Metro Atlanta and Hampton Roads areas. His generosity and altruism even led to him being featured in a book titled *A Hand to Guide Me: Legends and Leaders Celebrate the People Who Shaped Their Lives*, along with Hank Aaron, Muhammad Ali, Phil Jackson, Colin Powell, and former president Bill Clinton, for example, which speaks volumes about his public image and social status at the time.

In early 2007, Michael Vick seemed to have everything a professional athlete could hope for. According to the Harris Poll, football has been the most popular sport in the United States since 1965, with a fan base about equal to the next four highest professional sports in the poll combined. As a successful All-Pro NFL quarterback with several records in the books and the highest salary in the league, Vick was on top of his professional career.

In April 2007, the arrest of Vick's cousin, Devon Boddie, for marijuana possession led the law enforcement officers to one of Vick's houses in Suffolk, Virginia, and consequently to the discovery of kennels containing pit bulls in the woods behind the property. This prompted a new investigation for dog fighting. During the police search on the property, law enforcement and animal control staff found dozens of dogs in general bad health, scarred and malnourished, with evidence of a dog-fighting operation on the site. Authorities gathered enough evidence to serve Vick with federal indictments charging that Vick and three of his friends were the founders of a dog-fighting venture named Bad Newz Kennels. Vick was charged with traveling to dog fights and sponsoring fights on his property. On August 24, 2007, he filed plea documents with the federal court and in December of the same year he was sentenced to 23 months in federal prison. In a statement made at a news conference following his guilty plea, Vick took full responsibility for his

Michael Vick—Records and Achievements

College Awards and Recognitions

- 1999—Big East Rookie of the Year; Big East Offensive Player of the Year
- 1st player in Division I history to win a conference rookie of the year award and offensive player of the year award in the same season
- 1999—3rd in voting for the Heisman Trophy
- 2000—Best College Football Player ESPY Award; Runner-up in Associated Press Player of the Year
- 2001—Toyota Gator Bowl MVP
- Freshman of the Year by *The Sporting News*
- First-team Freshman All-America teams by TSN and *Football News*
- First team All–Big East
- ECAC All-Star team

NCAA records for a freshman and single-season school records in 1999

- Highest yards passing per completion (20.4)
- Highest yards passing per attempt (12.1)
- Highest completion percentage (59.2)
- Most yards per play (9.3)
- Led all Division I-A teams in passing efficiency (180.37)

NFL Awards

- 2001—No. 1 draft pick
- 2002, 2003, and 2004—Pro Bowl Selection (7th QB to be voted in during his first year as a starter since 1970)
- 2003—Best NFL Player ESPY Award

NFL Records (for Quarterbacks):

- Highest average per carry in a single season (8.45 in 2006)
- Most rushing yards in a single game (173 in 2002)
- Best two-game rushing total (225 in 2004)
- 1st to throw for more than 250 yards and rush for over 100 yards in the same game (2004)
- 1st to rush for over 1,000 yards during the regular season (1,039 in 2006)
- 2nd to throw for 3,000 yards, run for 500 yards, and maintain a 100+ passer rating in only 12 games in 2010
- 1st to pass for 300 yards and four touchdowns and rush for 50 yards and two touchdowns in a single game (against the Redskins in 2010)

actions, admitted to his mistakes and bad judgment, and promised to "redeem himself." Vick was released on July 20, 2009, after serving 18 months.

Vick's return to the NFL was by no means a smooth one, as most teams stated they wanted nothing to do with him. Eventually, it was the Philadelphia Eagles that signed him to an initial one-year deal worth $1.6 million. With his hard work ethic, a chance partially offered due to Donovan McNabb's and Kevin Kolb's injuries, and his subsequent success on the field, Vick ended up earning the starting QB position with the Eagles by the beginning of the 2010 season. After a career year in passing in 2010, the Eagles signed him to a six-year, $100 million contract that made him, once again, one of the highest paid players in the NFL.

On the whole, at the age of 31, Michael Vick has experienced and achieved far more than most athletes do in a lifetime. Throughout his time in prison, he kept a journal, reflected on his past, studied the game more, realized how he could become an even better quarterback than he had ever been, and found the way to persevere and make a successful comeback. Whether he ever manages to completely redeem himself in the eyes of the public remains to be seen, but on the football field, what he has achieved already sets him apart from legions of peers; few will ever have a chance to change a sport as much as Michael Vick may have done with changing the quarterback position in football.

Mika T. Elovaara

See also EA Sports; National Football League; Nike, Inc.

Suggested Resources

"Michael Vick." hokiesports.com. http://www.hokiesports.com/vick. Accessed October 30, 2011.

1416 | Videogames

Reiter, Ben. "Masked Man." August 24, 2009. http://sports illustrated.cnn.com/vault/article/magazine/MAG1159240/index.htm. Accessed November 11, 2011.

Vick, Michael. *Finally Free: An Autobiography*. Brentwood, TN: Worthy, 2011.

Wertheim, L. Jon, and Jack McCallum. "What's Next for Michael Vick?" July 13, 2009. http://sportsillustrated.cnn.com/vault/article/magazine/MAG1157660/index.htm. Accessed November 11, 2011.

Videogames

Since the start of the videogame era in the late 1970s, sport has been a popular genre among gamers. Some videogame publishers, such as EA Sports, produce nothing but sport titles. Sports have been represented in popular series, such as *Madden NFL* and *NBA Live*, and Take-Two's *2K* franchise. The Big Three American sports have featured predominantly throughout videogame history. Starting with the Atari 2600, sports videogames have progressed into lifelike representations. While this entry focuses on American sport in videogames, it is important to note that the vast majority of other major sports have been made into videogames. Soccer games, for example, such as the *FIFA* series and *Pro Evolution Soccer*, largely dominate the sports videogame market outside the United States.

While the first successful sport videogame was arguably 1972's *Pong*, American sports were portrayed in both arcade and handheld videogames during the 1970s. The arcade had been popularized through the late 1970s with the financial success of machines such as *Gunfight*, *Sea Wolf*, and *Space Invaders*. In 1978, Atari released *Football*, played using a trackball. Two players squared off against each other in an offense versus defense match. *Football*, along with *Space Invaders*, has been credited by historians as a central reason behind the growth of the arcade in the late 1970s.

American sports were also prominent in the handheld market. In June 1977, Mattel released *Football*, featuring a single small screen. The player controlled three athletes on a nine-yard field. *Football* was sold through the Sears catalogue. By mid-February 1978, *Football* was selling half a million units per week. Mattel's *Football*, along with Coleco's *Electronic*

Quarterback, were the main American sport handhelds during this period.

American sports moved into the home with the production of the videogame console. While home consoles had existed since the middle of the 1970s with the Magnavox Odyssey, Coleco Telestar, and Channel F, the most successful was the Atari 2600. Released in October 1977, the 2600 was the first console to have a joystick and it featured over 100 games by 1982. Not to be confused with the arcade version, Atari released *Football* in 1978. *Football* was released at an opportune time in American sports history. The recent success of *Monday Night Football* on television had galvanized the popularity of the NFL. Atari's *Football* barely resembled the actual sport. Each team had only three players and there were no field goals, fumbles, or even end zones. The actual players themselves looked more like refrigerators than human beings. Yet *Football* was a financial success mainly due to the lack of competition. The only other football videogames were the aforementioned handhelds and arcade machines. Within the home, Atari's *Football* was the only videogame based on the sport.

The year 1978 also heralded Atari's *Baseball* and *Basketball*. In a similar fashion, *Baseball* also featured three blocklike fielders. *Basketball* featured two players and a block as the ball. Yet Atari's console faced competition from the Mattel Intellivision, ColecoVision, the Magnavox Odyssey, and Channel F II. Mattel's Intellivision became the main competitor for Atari in terms of sports videogames. In 1980, Mattel released *NFL Football*. The game was a massive improvement over Atari's offering. The players resembled human beings and end zones were present, as were field goals and interceptions. Mattel's *NFL Football* was ported to the Atari 2600 in 1982 as *Super Challenge Football*. Yet it did not completely match the real sport as each team only featured five players. In a similar fashion, *Super League Baseball* on the Intellivision was also ported to the 2600 as *Super Challenge Baseball*. The ColecoVision continued the sports theme by releasing *Super Action Football* in 1983. *Super Action Football* was the first to portray the sport in an isometric view, similar to a television broadcast. It was also the first football videogame to have all the standard rules present. Yet *Super Action*

Camille McClaren, eight, right, of Philadelphia, watches Seattle Supersonics Kevin Durant, center, play Dallas Mavericks Reyshawn Terry, left, as they play the *NBA Live 08* videogame, July 27, 2007, at the MSG Training Center in Tarrytown, New York. (AP Photo/Frank Franklin II.)

Football required players to purchase a new "Super Action Controller." The necessity of buying such peripherals ensured that *Super Action Football* did not match the success of its rivals.

The home console industry in the United States was virtually eliminated by the crash of 1983. In December 1982, Atari, largely dominating the industry, announced an increase in sales of 10 to 15 percent. Industry commentators had expected it to be closer to 50 percent. Stocks in Warner Communications, owner of Atari, collapsed by almost 17 points. Several problems had caused the crash. A glut of consoles competed for dominance in the American market. By 1982, there were seven different consoles for consumers to choose from. Low-quality games, such as the famous *E.T.*, also contributed to the downfall of the industry. In early 1983, the market for videogames in the United States collapsed. Atari buried millions of game cartridges in

the New Mexico desert and announced a loss of over $500 million in 1983. For a while, American sports in console videogames were almost nonexistent.

Although the home console industry collapsed, the market for computers still remained. The Commodore 64 and Apple II were still an option for those wanting to experience sports. Electronic Arts, founded in 1983 by Trip Hawkins, released *Dr. J and Larry Bird Go One on One*. Played on the Apple II, the basketball game featured Bird and Julius Erving battling it out for victory. The animated players were far superior to those in any other basketball game and the players could perform slam dunks. The legacy of *Dr. J and Larry Bird*, however, is in the use of athletes to promote videogames. The use of recognized names in a game's title would increase its appeal to gamers. Such a tactic continued with EA and other publishers readily using athletes to advertise their videogames.

While *Dr. J and Larry Bird* later morphed into 1988's *Jordan vs. Bird*, other series have become inseparable from their namesakes. It would be hard to imagine EA Sport's yearly football game without John Madden's name adorning the packaging.

Although the American videogame industry was languishing, its salvation would come from Japan. The Nintendo Famicom had sold half a million units in Japan in only two months. Wary of the American market, the Famicom, rebranded as the Nintendo Entertainment System (NES), had a limited release in Christmas 1985. Sales far outperformed expectations and production was quickly extended to the entire country. By 1986, the NES had sold three million units in a single year. Despite its Japanese origins, the NES became a popular platform for American sports. For the football aficionado, there was 1989's *Tecmo Bowl* and its 1991 follow-up, *Tecmo Super Bowl*. The former possessed the NFL Players Association license, spread across 12 fictional teams. The latter amended this by introducing a season mode and almost the entire NFL roster. Basketball was represented by *Double Dribble* and *Tecmo NBA Basketball*. *Double Dribble* offered a five-on-five game and a halo above the player signifying the optimum release for shots. But it was baseball that was the winner on the NES. The NES boasted the first fully licensed baseball videogames with *RBI Baseball* and *Major League Baseball*, both released in 1988. Two of the more popular baseball videogames on the NES were *Baseball Stars* and *Bases Loaded*. *Baseball Stars* was more of an arcade version of the sport while *Bases Loaded* aimed to simulate the sport with statistics. This period is generally known as the Golden Age of baseball videogames.

During the late 1980s, one of the longest-lasting videogame franchises was created. Following a meeting between Trip Hawkins and John Madden in 1986, Madden agreed to lend his name to a realistic football simulation. Hawkins had initially proposed a 7-a-side game. Madden refused to endorse the product unless it was 11-a-side, however. Forced to return to the drawing board, *John Madden Football* was released on the Apple II computer in 1989. Although the game did not possess the license for all NFL teams, nor the names of players, it was 11-a-side football. The subsequent release, *John Madden Football 92*, possessed all the NFL teams as well as realistic weather. Renamed *Madden NFL* in 1994, there has been a yearly update ever since. Although challenged by Take-Two's *NFL 2K* series in the early 21st century, *Madden* has seen off all challengers to become the dominant football videogame.

The Sega Genesis was released in America in 1989. The Genesis was twice as powerful as the NES. Until 1989, Nintendo controlled over 90 percent of the American console market. The Genesis, however, was marketed to a different audience than the NES. With the creation of *Sonic the Hedgehog* in 1991, Sega created a new style of mascot that appealed to the American teenager. Whereas Nintendo was often considered to be for children, Sega tapped into the older market. This was best epitomized with the release of *Mortal Kombat* in 1993. *Mortal Kombat* featured the now famous "fatality moves," which involved the brutal and bloody death of the opponent. The Genesis version outsold the Nintendo release, which significantly toned down the blood, by three to one. The Genesis also became renowned for its sports games. The *John Madden Football* series was first released on the Genesis in 1992. Yet the Genesis was also the home of *Madden*'s main console competitor in the early 1990s: *Joe Montana Football*. The original game was an update of *Great Football*, released on the Genesis's predecessor, the Master System. The sequel, *Joe Montana II: Sports Talk Football,* followed in 1991. It was the first football game to feature audio commentary and multiple human players. With Sega's acquisition of the NFL license, the game changed to *NFL Sports Talk Football Starring Joe Montana*. This was eventually shortened to just *NFL*. The series, facing overwhelming competition from the *Madden* franchise, was canceled in 1997. Basketball was represented on the Genesis by Electronic Arts' *Lakers vs. Celtics and the NBA Playoffs*, released in 1990. This morphed into the *NBA Live* series in 1994, which has been its namesake ever since. *World Series Baseball* was released on the Genesis in 1994 and introduced the "catcher-cam." *World Series Baseball* was the first game in the Sega Sports line. After several successful iterations, the franchise was sold to Take-Two in 2005. With these games and a larger install base, Sega emerged as a challenger for Nintendo's crown in America.

In response to the Genesis, Nintendo released the Super Nintendo Entertainment System (SNES) in 1991. In an attempt to shake off its child image, Nintendo even supported the full blood version of *Mortal Kombat 2*. Yet, despite this, it still heavily sold staple games featuring Mario and Luigi, the famous Italian plumbers. Nintendo was unable to move away from its core "child" games. Despite this, the SNES offered *Ken Griffey Jr. Presents Major League Baseball* in 1994. It was one of the first console games to offer the player the chance to edit character likenesses. This option, albeit more advanced, now comes as standard in most sports videogames in the 21st century. This game was followed by *Ken Griffey Jr.'s Winning Run* in 1996. Nintendo, however, bowed out of the licensed baseball games in 1999. Along with the Genesis, the SNES offered a popular arcade version of basketball: *NBA Jam. NBA Jam* removed the referees and offered bullet passes and extreme dunks. Despite this, the Genesis outpaced the SNES in terms of sports videogames.

Both Sega and Nintendo produced next-generation consoles only to be outdone by a newcomer. Sony, previously separate from the console market, released the PlayStation in 1995. Although Sega and Nintendo released the Saturn and N64, respectively, Sony vastly outsold the competition. After the September 1995 North American release of the PlayStation, Sony sold more consoles in two days than Sega had since the Saturn's release. On the PlayStation and Saturn, the *Madden NFL* series was still as popular as ever. For basketball fans, the *NBA Live* series was the favorite on the PlayStation. Baseball videogames, however, started to become less popular. EA Sports, developer of both *Madden* and *NBA Live*, have steered clear of a baseball franchise. Despite this, the *All-Star Baseball* series started in 1998.

The next generation of videogame consoles saw the death of one and the emergence of another. Sega produced their Dreamcast console, which massively undersold. In 2001, Sega announced it would concentrate solely on software. The Nintendo Gamecube was released in 2000, but was unable to produce the success previously garnered by the company. The star of

Mario and Sonic at the Olympic Games

During the early 1990s, Sonic and Mario were the mascots for two competing consoles. Mario, an Italian plumber, had represented Nintendo since the release of *Super Mario Bros.* in 1985. *Sonic the Hedgehog* was created in response to the success of Mario. The speedy blue hedgehog was designed with "attitude" so as to appeal to the teenage market. Nintendo had a reputation, especially with characters such as Princess Peach, for focusing on the children's market. Yet it is Mario that has been the most successful of the pair. Sonic has been unable to reproduce its early success in later console generations. With Sega's withdrawal from the market in 2001, Sonic has repeatedly undersold on other consoles. Yet Sonic would find an unlikely home on the Nintendo Wii and DS. In preparation for the Beijing 2008 Olympics, Sega was offered the opportunity by the International Olympic Committee to create a videogame that would promote competitive sportsmanship. Sega received approval from Nintendo to use characters from the Mario series for such an endeavor. Titled *Mario and Sonic at the Olympic Games*, it was released in November 2007. The game was successful and resulted in a sequel: *Mario & Sonic at the Winter Olympic Games*. That two adversaries could come together to produce a videogame promoting the IOC's message of sportsmanship could be a positive example to youngsters as well as professional sportsmen and women.

the new generation was Sony's PlayStation 2. Unlike its competitors, it was backwards compatible and played DVDs. It was also far more powerful than either the Dreamcast or Gamecube. Microsoft, seeing the success of Sony's move into the home entertainment market, announced the production of the Xbox. With the success of Bungie's *Halo* series, the Xbox became the main competitor for the PlayStation 2. It was during this generation that EA Sports became the dominant force in sports videogames. Take-Two's *2K* series had become the main challenger to the *Madden* franchise. *NFL 2K* had been first released on the Dreamcast in 1999 but was eventually released annually on both the PlayStation 2 and Xbox. In an attempt to become the main football franchise, Take-Two announced in 2004 that *NFL 2K5* would cost only $19.95 and would be released two weeks prior to *Madden NFL 05*. In response to this unexpected challenge, EA announced a five-year deal with the NFL in December 2004 to be the sole publisher of licensed videogames. Shortly after, they also revealed a 15-year deal with ESPN. Without the official NFL license, the *NFL 2K* series died. EA Sports had secured such extensive deals for other sports, such as soccer and basketball, to increase their share of the market.

The next generation quickly emerged with Microsoft's release of the Xbox 360 in 2006. Sony revealed their competition with the PlayStation 3. However, it was Nintendo that emerged from the dark to challenge both Sony and Microsoft. Understanding that it could not match the other consoles in terms of power, Nintendo introduced motion detection on the Wii. The players did not have a controller in the typical sense. Players instead used a "wand," which was detected by the console and produced movement on the screen. The Wii was a success in the casual gaming market with people who had never used a console before. The Wii also revealed a possible new direction for sports videogames. *Wii Sports* allowed players to use the wand to play baseball. While *Madden* and EA Sports still boasted graphical superiority and realism, *Wii Sports* allowed unprecedented player involvement in sports videogames. While typical sports videogames did not transfer to the Wii due to its nonconventional controller, it produced a possible new avenue for such games to explore. Both Sony and Microsoft subsequently released Move and Kinect, respectively, to compete with Nintendo's unexpected dominance of the casual videogame market.

From the beginning of the videogame era in the 1970s, sports have been a popular choice for players. Starting with *Pong*, sports videogames have progressed in realism and graphical quality right into the 21st century. Although EA Sports retains dominance in the market, other videogames, such as *Wii Sports*, have shown that new directions can be explored. The future of sports videogames is as bright as its past.

Matthew Bentley

See also Bird, Larry; Boston Celtics; EA Sports; Erving, Julius; Griffey, Ken, Jr.; Jordan, Michael; Los Angeles Lakers; *Madden NFL*; *Monday Night Football*; World Series

Suggested Resources

Hall of Fame History of Baseball Video Games. http://www.gamingtarget.com/article.php?artid=8514. Accessed September 1, 2011.

"The History of Football Games." uk.gamespot.com. http://uk.gamespot.com/features/6130897/index.html. Accessed September 1, 2011.

Kent, Steven L. *The Ultimate History of Video Games*. New York: Three Rivers Press, 2001.

UGO Entertainment Website. www.ugo.com/channels/sports/features/basketball/games.asp. Accessed September 1, 2011.

Violence, Guns, and Sport

Violence is not something new in sport; in fact, many sports are built around the inherent violence in the game. There may be a question of excessive or inappropriate violence, but, violence is not unusual in many contests. Historically, it is easy to examine and trace forward the violence that was part of the sports of ancient Greece and Rome as well as the violence that characterizes other cultures close to the United States, such as England, Italy, Spain, and Germany. In our contemporary world, a number of countries have become infamous for soccer riots, both inside the stadium and on the streets of the city where a match is played. England has been the scene of such events at least as far back as the late 1800s, but in recent years, violent soccer riots have occurred in Italy, Spain, Egypt, Belgium, France, Germany, Argentina, and Syria, to name just some of the most prominent. Few countries are immune as fans so strongly identify with their teams and the group that it represents that the fans feel that they must take a personal hand in the efforts at "winning." This fanaticism reflects the origin of the word "fan," short for "fanatic."

What is of most concern in this entry is violence that has arisen in the major spectator sports, football, basketball, baseball, and hockey, and the "extracurricular" manner in which that violence has been perpetrated. Of the four sports, two, football and hockey, have violence and rough contact inherent in their games. The question in hockey is not whether one can check an opponent, but what constitutes a legal check, how many strides can be taken before barreling into an opponent, and does a player leave his feet or not in the process of administering a check. Other points of contact that involve the boards or the stick, especially as a weapon, also are seen as violence not condoned by the game's arbiters.

Over the past few years, the dramatic increase in concussions in the sport have caused reexaminations of the rules, as well as the equipment and the manner of identifying concussions. When big stars like Sid Crosby are forced to miss most of a season with "concussion-like symptoms," it hurts not just Crosby and the Pittsburgh Penguins, but the popularity and ratings of the game itself.

In previous generations there was less concern about this, despite the fact that helmets were not worn on a regular basis until the 1960s and were not mandatory in the National Hockey League until 1979. So, too, with the masks that all goaltenders now wear. Jacques Plante first wore a mask of his own design in 1959, then refined it and wore a mask for the rest of his playing days, which ended in 1975. The last goalie to go barefaced was in 1974.

Football has always had poundings of players, but violence in the form of plays like the flying wedge was outlawed because the likelihood of severe injury was too great. Football's violence nearly led to a national ban on college football (there was no pro football at the time) during the presidency of Theodore Roosevelt, and the need for national control led to the creation of the National Collegiate Athletic Association (NCAA) in 1906. As in hockey, football has continued to develop better equipment to protect the players from "legal" violence. Increased sizes and numbers of pads, as well as better material for absorbing force have been instrumental in allaying injuries to some extent, but the greatest need has been for a better, more stress-absorbent helmet. Amazingly, most players did not even use helmets until the 1920s, and even then they were generally just thick pieces of leather. The plasticized helmet was created in the 1940s and that base has continued to be improved. The major problem has been the increased weight and strength of the players, which couples with greater speed to create greater force that the head must absorb.

Over the past few years, football has also seen more concussion-related injuries, although part of that is the more cautious attitude toward "getting one's bell rung," which used to mean one sat on the bench until one's head cleared, then one was often sent back into the fray. No longer. The injury potential, at least in professional football, was raised by "bounties," which were associated with the New Orleans Saints' defense and defensive coach in 2012 for incidents that occurred at least two and three years previously. Players were provided with rewards for knocking key opponents out of the game. When this was exposed, the coaches involved and the team were fined and/or suspended, but there was discussion that such actions, though inappropriate, were not as rare as some might have believed.

The violence of football and guns is more localized and relates to those football players who have used guns in some manner off the field. The most recent perpetrator has been Plaxico Burress, a former All-American wide receiver at Michigan State, who was a top receiver in the NFL for the New York Giants. In November 2008, Burress and teammate Antonio Pierce went to a New York nightclub, but were denied entry because Burress was carrying a gun. He managed to hide the Glock pistol in the waistband of his sweatpants, but once in the club, the pistol began sliding down his leg. In attempting to retrieve the pistol, Burress accidently discharged the gun and shot himself in the thigh. After a brief hospitalization, Burress was suspended by the Giants and later charged with two counts of criminal possession of a weapon (he was licensed to carry in Florida, but not in New York) and one count of reckless endangerment. Burress accepted a plea agreement, entered prison in September 2009, and was released in June 2011. Since that time he has worked with the Brady Center to Prevent Gun Violence while resuming his pro football career.

Baseball violence both in the stands and on the field has been around for more than 100 years. Players like Ty Cobb were known for sharpening their spikes to deter infielders from stepping into the base path to take a runner. Cobb also famously left the field to attack a man in the stands who had been riding him in a series of games in Detroit. Cobb was suspended and his teammates walked out in protest, but eventually returned when Cobb asked them to do so, despite his suspension.

In 1920 Roy Chapman was struck in the head by a ball pitched by Carl Mays and Chapman died later from the blow. Throwing at a player to brush him back from digging in at the plate had been a part of the game for decades, but because of increased fighting and retaliatory beanings the umpires now usually stop the back-and-forth attacks before they get into retaliation. These events, beanings and brushbacks, are often the catalyst for brawls between teams. In 1957, one of the most famous brawls between the New York Yankees and the Chicago White Sox resulted in an iconic picture of Yankee outfielder Enos Slaughter leaving the field with his shirt torn off and his cap knocked backward on his head.

In 1960, Reds infielder Billy Martin, the fiery future manager of the Yankees and A's, was brushed back by Cubs pitcher Jim Brewer. On the next pitch, Martin let the bat fly toward the mound as he swung. In retrieving the bat, Brewer and Martin exchanged words and that precipitated a fight that resulted in Martin smashing Brewer in the face and shattering his right orbit bone.

A more unusual beginning to a brawl occurred in August 1962 when the Giants and Dodgers, traditional rivals, were engaged in a tight pennant race. Juan Marichal knocked down both Maury Wills and Ron Fairly, but Sandy Koufax would not retaliate; Koufax feared that his fastball would kill someone and would not throw brushbacks. John Roseboro, the Dodger catcher, decided he'd do the brushback, so when Marichal came to bat, he twice threw close to him when returning the ball to Koufax. Marichal was incensed and slammed Roseboro on the head with his bat, opening a wound that required 14 stitches and setting off a major brawl.

In the 1990s and early 2000s the increased use of steroids was seen as causing more aggressive actions in some baseball games; one often cited is Roger Clemens's action in game two of the 2000 World Series when, after pitching inside to Mike Piazza (whom he had hit in a game in July), he "fielded" Piazza's shattered bat and threw it toward the first-base line, resulting in both benches clearing.

An off-the-field incident was the shooting of Eddie Waitkus, a Phillies infielder, who had played for the Cubs for a number of years. Waitkus was shot in the chest in the Edgewater Beach Hotel by a deranged girl, but lived to play seven more years in the majors. The incident was the impetus for Bernard Malamud's novel *The Natural*, later made into a film with Robert Redford.

Violence in basketball probably is the most jarring because the players have absolutely no protection from injury and the fans can see everything that happens on the court and the sidelines. Nevertheless, basketball violence has a long history, at least as far back as the 1920s when teams were identified with ethnic groups or employers and the battles were seen as more than just basketball. Two kinds of violence should be noted; the first, on the court, is more common in small doses, usually a push, a shove, a punch, and a suspension, but there are occasions when things have gotten totally out of hand. The most noted may be the 1977 brawl between the Houston Rockets and the Los Angeles Lakers in which Kermit Washington of the Lakers threw a punch, accidentally blindsiding Rudy Tomjanovich of the Rockets, shattering his face, and nearly killing him. Washington was suspended for 60 games, heavily fined, and never was the same player again. Tomjanovich eventually recovered, played three more years, but also never displayed the same aggressiveness that he had before.

In December 1997 Latrell Sprewell, during a practice session, attacked, punched, and tried to choke his coach on the Golden State Warriors, P. J. Carlesimo. Sprewell was suspended for the remainder of the season and fined. Sprewell, who also had poor relationships with teammates, was eventually traded to the New York Knicks and played until 2005 without further incidents of violence on the court.

In 2003 Kobe Bryant was accused of raping a woman in a hotel in Eagle, Colorado. He denied the rape, saying the sex was consensual, but the case continued, eventually being dropped because the accuser would not testify in the criminal hearing. A civil suit was also filed against Bryant and it was settled out of court with Bryant issuing a statement of apology for his actions.

The most well-known perpetrator of violence over the past 10 years has been Ron Artest, who changed his name in 2011 to Metta World Peace. In 2004, Artest and his Indiana Pacers teammates were involved in an on-court brawl with the Detroit Pistons at the

Palace of Auburn Hills, Michigan. As the brawl wound down, a fan tossed a cup of ice and soda at Artest and he vaulted into the stands, attacked the fan, and provoked a larger melee between fans and players. Nine players were suspended without pay for a total of 146 games (Artest received 73 of those games plus 13 in the playoffs). Five players and five fans were arrested. The players received a year of probation and community service; the fans were barred from attending Pistons home games for life.

In 2010 Gilbert Arenas of the Washington Wizards and teammate Javaris Crittendon reportedly drew guns on each other over gambling debts. Crittendon was waived and signed with a couple other teams before being charged in August 2011 with a murder in Atlanta. He was out on bond as of May 2012. Arenas was suspended for the rest of the year, then traded to Orlando, and subsequently waived. In April 2012 Artest (now World Peace) was suspended for seven games for throwing a vicious elbow that hit an unsuspecting James Harden in the back of the head, causing a concussion.

Sport clearly involves rough, aggressive behavior, often resulting in sanctioned or unsanctioned violence. Fans have long been catalysts for some of this violence and the involvement of guns has become easier because of many states passing concealed carry laws. Most leagues have tried to deter violence with tighter and swifter enforcement and greater crowd control, but the very nature of the events will continue to foster smoldering relations that can spark into violence.

Murry R. Nelson

See also Bryant, Kobe; Clemens, Roger; Concussion; Koufax, Sandy; *The Natural*

Suggested Resources

Abdal-Haqq, Ismat. "Violence in Sports." 1989. http://www.ericdigests.org/pre-9214/sports.htm. Accessed April 27, 2012.

Feinstein, John. *The Punch: One Night, Two Lives and the Fight that Changed Basketball Forever.* Boston: Little, Brown, 2002.

Goldstein, Jeffrey H., ed. *Sports Violence.* New York: Springer-Verlag, 1983.

Jamieson, Lynn M., and Thomas J. Orr. *Sport and Violence: A Critical Examination of Sport.* Burlington, MA: Butterworth-Heinemann, 2009.

Kerr, John. *Rethinking Aggression and Violence in Sports.* New York: Routledge, 2004.

McGran, John. *World's Greatest Sports Brawls.* Atlanta: Longstreet, 1998.

Vitale, Richard J. (Dick) (1939–)

Dick Vitale, known affectionately to millions as "Dickie V," is the premier men's college basketball analyst for ESPN. Vitale joined ESPN during the 1979–1980 season—just after the network's September 1979 launch—following several years of coaching at the high school, college, and NBA levels. In 2008, Vitale received the sport's ultimate honor when he was selected as an inductee into the Naismith Memorial Basketball Hall of Fame as a contributor (after being named a finalist in 2004, 2006, and 2007). His enthusiasm and personal connection with fans, unique use of language and catchphrases, and in-depth knowledge of the game have helped promote and grow the sport, his persona, and ESPN's college basketball franchise.

Because he lost the sight in his left eye at age four, after mistakenly poking it with a pencil, Vitale never played organized basketball. He even missed his junior year of high school due to complications with his eye. However, his hard-working Italian Catholic parents, especially his mother, Mae, instilled a never-give-up, make-something-of-yourself attitude in the young "Richie" that led Vitale, instead, into coaching basketball and has been his driving force as a professional and as a person ever since. Vitale often says that he owes much of his success to his parents' encouragement, work ethic, and family togetherness. He even credits his love of sports to many Sundays as a young boy spent listening to his uncles argue about the popular sports figures of the day.

Vitale was born June 9, 1939, in Passaic, New Jersey. After graduation from high school and then Seton Hall University in 1963, Vitale began teaching elementary school in East Rutherford, New Jersey. While teaching at Franklin Junior High there from 1964 to 1971, he led the East Rutherford High School varsity basketball team to four state sectional championships, back-to-back state championships in 1969 and 1970, and 35 consecutive victories.

Dick Vitale looks skyward during a court dedication in his honor at the University of Detroit in Detroit, December 5, 2011. (AP Photo/Carlos Osorio.)

He joined Rutgers University in 1971 as an assistant coach, and in 1973 he joined the University of Detroit as head coach, later taking on the duties of athletic director following the 1977 season. His last season in 1977 was his best, as Detroit beat eventual national champion Marquette during a 21-game winning streak that propelled Detroit into the NCAA Tournament. He resigned as Detroit's coach with a 78–30 record.

Vitale left the University of Detroit in 1978 to become head coach of the NBA's Detroit Pistons. He coached one full season and part of a second before being dismissed in November 1979 as the Pistons began a housecleaning that eventually led the franchise to multiple NBA titles in the 1980s and 1990s. He finished with a record of 34–60.

And then came the phone call that changed televised college basketball coverage forever. ESPN, then a brand-new cable sports network headquartered in Bristol, Connecticut, asked Vitale to announce their first-ever NCAA basketball game—Wisconsin at DePaul—on December 5, 1979. He was reluctant to accept the assignment, but decided to have some fun with the experience and stay with it until another coaching job became available. Vitale never coached again and has called close to a thousand college basketball games, the NBA Finals, and the 1992 Summer Olympics with ESPN and ABC Sports. Vitale just completed his 31st year with ESPN and has a contract that goes to 2015.

Starting with that very first telecast in 1979, Vitale has developed a broadcasting style unlike anyone else. He has capitalized on an innate knowledge of basketball, a gregarious personality, and a childlike enthusiasm to create the Dickie V brand—and an instantly recognizable vocabulary of "Vitale-isms" that he uses in his commentary. These catchphrases even have their own website (http://dickvitaleonline.com/about-dickie-v/dick-vitales-dictionary.html) and include such gems as "awesome baby," "diaper dandy" (sensational freshman), "M&Mer" (a mismatch), "PTPer" (prime-time player) and "trifecta" (three-point basket).

Vitale has developed his talents far beyond just enthusiastic game announcing. Along the way, he has often stepped away from the court and made significant contributions to the various ESPN media platforms. During the college basketball season, he is used constantly across all of ESPN's cable channels and news programs to provide expert analysis and insight on breaking basketball news and events. Vitale provides commentary on a variety of topics in his weekly *Dick Vitale's Fast Break* segment on ESPN's *SportsCenter*. He is heard each Monday on ESPN Radio's *Mike & Mike in the Morning* show giving his take on college basketball and the breaking sports news of the moment. He's also a regular writer and contributor to *ESPN The Magazine*. Vitale's weekly ESPN.com column is one of the website's most popular features, and, of course, he has his own website—www.dick vitaleonline.com.

Off the ESPN grid, Vitale serves as a columnist for the monthly college-only basketball magazine *Basketball Times*, and since 1991, as a guest columnist for *USA Today*. He is also a highly sought-after motivational speaker, spokesperson (e.g., Hooters, Bridgestone Tires, DiGiorno Pizza), and fundraiser. Represented by IMG and a member of the Washington Speakers Bureau, Vitale is listed in the highest-priced speaker category that commands one-time speaking fees of $40,000 and above. His talks often focus on what he knows best, "winning the game of life," while motivating audiences toward achieving their individual and organizational goals using lessons from the sports world, his own personal struggles, and the journeys of everyday individuals who have exhibited his can-do attitude.

Vitale's brand has extended into popular culture as well. He has written or cowritten nine books, including one children's title, *Dickie V's ABC's and 1-2-3's* (2010). Other recent titles include *Dick Vitale's Fabulous 50 Players and Moments in College Basketball* (2008) and an autobiography, *Living a Dream: Reflections on 25 Years Sitting in the Best Seat in the House* (2003). Two of his motivational speeches for high school basketball players, *The Game of Life* and *Game Plan for Life*, were televised by ESPN in 1991 and 1994. He provided commentary for EA Sports *NCAA Basketball* video game series. His Vitale-isms were even used as part of the 1995 multiplatinum music CD *Jock Jams*, which is still played in arenas today.

Yet there is no difference between his college basketball professional persona and Vitale's attitude and dedication in two areas for which he cares deeply: cancer research and children. Serving as an active member of the board of directors of the V Foundation, a nonprofit organization dedicated to finding a cure for cancer, founded in 1993 by ESPN and the late Jim Valvano, Vitale has helped raise $1,000,000 or more a year primarily through the Dick Vitale Gala for Cancer Research, a celebrity event held annually in his hometown of Sarasota, Florida. The foundation honors Valvano, a friend of Vitale's who died of cancer in April 1993 after successful careers as a college basketball coach (1983 national champion at NC State) and an ESPN analyst.

Similarly, Vitale actively supports the Boys and Girls Club of Sarasota County, whose mission to help children work hard to overcome the challenges they face daily is exactly the message he continually tries to communicate to youth—to use sports intelligently and to be the best they can be not only in the game, but in their lives. He emphasizes the importance of self-responsibility in reaching goals and of making good life decisions. Vitale has donated thousands of dollars in scholarships to the Boys and Girls Clubs of Sarasota County and has helped raise more than $1 million for the organization.

In addition to these and a number of other charitable works in which Vitale takes part, he and his family have endowed the Dick Vitale Family Scholarship at the University of Notre Dame. The scholarship is presented annually to an Irish undergraduate who participates in Notre Dame sports or activities and does not receive financial aid. Past recipients of the scholarship have included the school's leprechaun mascot, cheerleaders, and band members. Vitale's two daughters attended Notre Dame and played tennis, a sport Vitale also actively plays and endorses.

Vitale is also a member of the advisory boards for the American Sportscasters Association, the Harlem Globetrotters, and the Henry Iba Citizen Athlete Awards. He participates on the selection committees for three prestigious annual college basketball awards: the Atlanta Tipoff Club's Naismith Award, the Los Angeles Athletic Club's John R. Wooden Award, and the Basketball Hall of Fame's Bob Cousy Award. Additionally, Vitale is a member of the Associated Press weekly voting panel for the Top-25 college basketball teams.

During his 29th season as an ESPN college basketball analyst, Vitale faced the extreme highs and lows of life himself. First, after experiencing trouble with his throat, which had originally been diagnosed as reflux, Vitale got the news that he had ulcerated lesions on his left vocal cord that could threaten his life and career. But, following his own advice, Vitale battled back, after successful surgery in December 2007, to rejoin ESPN back on the court in February 2008. Then, two months later, Vitale was selected for induction into the Naismith Memorial Basketball Hall of Fame Class of 2008 as a contributor to the sport. Hall of Fame contributors are described as those who have made significant contributions to the game and its growth. Calling it his ultimate honor, Vitale credited his Hall of Fame induction to hard work, good fortune, and the support of family and friends along the way.

As one might suspect, Vitale has received numerous other honors in addition to his Hall of Fame recognition. One of the most "permanent" additions to Vitale's legacy was the 2011 naming of the basketball court at the University of Detroit in his honor. He has been inducted into eight other halls of fame, including the National Collegiate Basketball HOF (2008), the Five-Star Basketball Camp HOF (2003), and the Florida Sports HOF (1996). Additional recent awards include the John Wooden Pyramid of Success Award in 2009, the 2010 Ronald McDonald House Man of the Year Award of Excellence, and the 2010 Make-A-Wish Chris Greicius Award for exceptional dedication to helping grant the wishes of children with life-threatening medical conditions.

Ted Carlin

See also Cousy, Bob; EA Sports; ESPN Channels; Harlem Globetrotters; Naismith Memorial Basketball Hall of Fame; Wooden, John

Suggested Resources

Dick Vitale Index. ESPN.com. http://espn.go.com/espn/dickvitale/. Accessed April 10, 2012.

Dick Vitale Website. http://dickvitaleonline.com/about -dickie-v/dickie-v-biography.html. Accessed April 10, 2012.

Miller, James Andrew, and Tom Shales. *Those Guys Have All the Fun: Inside the World of ESPN*. New York: Little, Brown, 2011.

Vitale, Dick, and Dick Weiss. *Dick Vitale's Living a Dream: Reflections on 25 Years Sitting in the Best Seat in the House*. Champaign, IL: Sports Publishing, 2003.

Vitale, Dick, and Dick Weiss. *Holding Court: Reflections on the Game I Love*. Indianapolis, IN: Masters Press, 1995.

W

Walker, Herschel (1962–)

Definitely one of the most difficult sports stars to classify satisfactorily, he has been a figure in the public eye for over 30 years now, making a name in various fields such as football, mixed martial arts, bobsledding, and as a spokesperson for mental illness.

Since he broke onto the scene in 1980 as a record-breaking freshman running back and eventual Heisman Trophy winner for the University of Georgia, Herschel Walker has been a consistent focus for the national sports media.

Along the way, the fitness guru has intermittently been involved in the headlines of the day, from his amazing touchdown run against Tennessee as a freshman to later exploits in the fledgling UFSL to more recent publicity in the mental health realm. There has seldom been a dull moment in the life of this native of Wrightsville, Georgia.

Voted the national Player of the Year in 1979 at Johnson Co. High, Walker rushed for 3,167 yards that senior season and helped the Trojans to the state football championship. Then he was off to Athens, where a unique combination of speed and strength allowed him to explode on the scene immediately with 1,616 yards as the Bulldogs won the national championship.

At 6'1", 225 pounds, Walker merged a trackman's speed with a weightlifter's power on the field, and at once gained recognition for an intense workout regimen that, ironically, eschewed the traditional weight-room drill in favor of massive numbers of daily situps and pushups.

However he prepared, it was obvious that number 34 was one of the greatest runners to ever hit the college football scene, and he earned the Heisman in 1982, becoming the first player to finish in the top three in voting for the prestigious award three times. His electrifying 16-yard TD run against the Vols, on which he ran over future NFL safety Bill Bates, became instantly famous, and the call by legendary Tennessee broadcaster Larry Munson is still replayed thousands of times a year on YouTube.

When it was patently obvious that the onrushing Walker had nothing more to prove on the college level, he took advantage of an NCAA loophole and turned pro after his junior campaign, landing with the New Jersey Generals of the new United States Football League, doing more than his part in putting the NFL's rival circuit on the radar. Walker won the league rushing title in 1983 and 1985 for the short-lived USFL, compiling a professional record of 2,411 yards in 18 games during the 1985 season.

When the league went bankrupt, Walker moved on to the NFL, playing for Dallas, the team that had drafted him on a whim in 1985.

Though he enjoyed some outstanding years with the Cowboys, including Pro Bowl seasons in 1987 and 1988, the disappointment in him began in earnest with the trade in 1989. At the height of his pro career, the bruising speedster was dealt from Dallas to Minnesota for a total of five players and numerous future draft picks. As the Vikings floundered and Dallas became a three-time NFL champ in the early 1990s, the trade and its one-sided result acted as a brand that Walker could not avoid. Soft-spoken to a fault and not given to the self-aggrandizement that by then seemed to come with the big-league territory, the former Georgia star quickly became a

Dallas Cowboy Tommie Agee grabs for Philadelphia Eagles Herschel Walker (34), December 6, 1993. (AP Photo/ Eric Gay.)

punch line and a punching bag, a lightning rod for criticism.

He went from the Vikings to Philadelphia (1992–1994) to the New York Giants (1995) and back to Dallas (1996–1997), carving out a niche as a dangerous receiver and dependable return man, but never truly found his niche as a feature back again.

Walker's pro legacy is thus considered a disappointing one by many observers, who often note that despite his incredible fitness, speed, and strength, the inability to make quick-hipped cuts left him a step beyond the greats of the game. Backers would argue that his 8,225 yards in 12 NFL seasons (13,787 including the USFL years) place him among the best of the best. His total of 18,168 combined yards including returns ranked second all-time upon retirement in 1997 and he's still the only player to amass at least 4,000 yards rushing, receiving, and returns.

But the fact that he never played on an NFL champion, only rushed for 1,000 yards twice in the NFL, and is still maligned for jumping to the rebel pro league way back when have all conspired against a more favorable assessment by pundits and fans alike.

As a member of the Cowboys in 1988, Walker danced with the Fort Worth Ballet and has exhibited a flair for the esoteric his whole life. He earned a spot on the U.S. bobsled team that competed in the 1992 Winter Olympics, worked his way to a fifth-degree black belt in tae kwan do, and even took a turn on the popular TV show *Celebrity Apprentice* a few years back.

Life after football for Walker saw him involved in that diverse range of activities, including a successful debut in MMA competition in 2009. But it was his 2008 book, *Breaking Free*, that made as big a media splash. In it, the gridiron great revealed that he had been suffering from dissociative identity disorder (formerly known as multiple personality disorder) for many years.

He quickly became fodder for gossipy, snarky Internet message boards; however, the admission met with a positive response from the mental health community, which welcomed the telling of a tale involving the courage of a professional athlete and his struggle against a debilitating disease. It also marked a way to raise awareness and credibility about the situation.

At the current time, Walker continues to work as a spokesman on mental health issues while perfecting mixed martial arts as he once did the game of football. Always in the news, one of the finest physical specimens ever to play the game is in tremendous condition as he enters his 50s, and even hinted recently at an NFL comeback.

Greg Selber

See also Dallas Cowboys; National Football League

Suggested Resources

Benagh, Jim. *Sports Great Herschel Walker*. Hillside, NJ: Enslow, 1990.

Hayes, Thomas C. "Walker Balances Bulk with Ballet." April 11, 1988. http://www.nytimes.com/1988/04/11/sports/walker-balances-bulk-with-ballet.html. Accessed October 7, 2011.

Kirkpatrick, Curry. "Walker: A Renaissance Man." October 3, 2007. http://sportsillustrated.cnn.com/vault/article/magazine/MAG1115704/index.htm. Accessed October 7, 2011.

Walker, Herschel. *Herschel Walker's Basic Training*. Garden City, NY: Doubleday, 1985.

Walker, Herschel, with Gary Brozek and Charlene Maxfield. *Breaking Free: My Life with Dissociative Identity Disorder*. New York: Simon and Schuster, 2008.

Walton, Bill (1952–)

Bill Walton was a top high school, college, and professional basketball player who led or contributed to a number of teams that won national titles in the 1970s and 1980s. He also did color commentary on basketball telecasts in the 1990s and into the next century and was known for his outspokenness.

William Theodore Walton III was born in La Mesa, California, on November 5, 1952. His father worked for San Diego County and his mother was a librarian. Walton was both an avid reader and basketball player as a youngster and his dedication to the game was nicely augmented by his height (he was 6'10" in high school). He led Helix High of La Mesa to the San Diego Section Championships of the California Interscholastic Federation in both 1969 and 1970, achieving *Parade Magazine* All-American status in his senior year, when the Highlanders went 33–0. Walton set a state record for rebounds that year and was heavily recruited by every top basketball program in the country, including UCLA. The Bruins had won four national championships in a row in 1970 and Walton agreed to enroll there and play under legendary coach John Wooden.

Freshmen were not eligible for varsity play and Walton joined the UCLA varsity in the fall of 1971 after they had won a fifth national championship in a row and seventh in eight years. He immediately stepped into a starting and starring role for UCLA, having grown another inch to 6'11" and weighing 235 pounds. Led by senior Henry Bibby, junior Larry Farmer, and two other sophomores, Greg Lee and Keith Wilkes, the Bruins went undefeated with Walton leading in scoring with 21 points and rebounds with 15.5 per game. He only shot 12 times a game, but was a 64 percent shooter.

The NCAA Tournament had only 25 teams and UCLA drew a bye before beating Weber State and Long Beach State to advance to the NCAA Final Four, held in Los Angeles that year. The Bruins disposed of Louisville by 19, then struggled before beating Florida State by five, 81–76, for the NCAA title. Walton was named Most Outstanding Player (MOP) in the NCAA tourney, as well as Player of the Year by the AP, UPI, *Sporting News*, Helms Foundation, and U.S. Basketball Writers Association, and he won the Naismith Award.

The next year the Bruins returned four starters and were ranked number one all season long. Walton averaged just over 20 points and just under 17 rebounds a game as the Bruins were again undefeated when they entered the NCAA tourney. They defeated Arizona State and San Francisco to advance to the Final Four in St. Louis. There they defeated Indiana, coached by

UCLA center Bill Walton (32) shoots for two of his record 44 points against Memphis State in the final game of the NCAA Tournament in St. Louis, March 26, 1973. (AP Photo, File.)

Bobby Knight, by 11, then faced Memphis State in the championship game. There, Walton played a nearly flawless game, hitting 21 of 22 shots and scoring 44 points, and UCLA won by a score of 87–66. Walton was named MOP for the NCAA Tournament, as well as every other individual honor in college basketball, just as he had done in the prior season.

These were turbulent times on college campuses and there were anti–Vietnam War rallies and protests throughout the nation. Walton became caught up in these and was arrested at least once for demonstrating at a peace rally. He became close friends with Jack Scott, a sports activist who was later linked to Patty Hearst, who had been kidnapped and then became a part of the Symbionese Liberation Army (SLA). Coach Wooden told Walton that he was free to do

whatever he wished as a student demonstrator, but he would have to separate himself from the basketball team because of the interference. Walton chose to dial back his activism for the rest of his college years, although he returned to activism following his senior season.

During Walton's senior year, the Bruins defeated North Carolina State early in the year. The Wolfpack had been ineligible for the NCAA Tournament the previous year, despite going undefeated. In 1973–1974 they went through the rest of their schedule undefeated. The Bruins had their 88-game winning streak broken in January when they lost to Notre Dame, then absorbed two more defeats in the Pacific 8 Conference to Oregon State and Oregon to enter the NCAA tourney at 24–3. Walton averaged 19.3 points and 14.7 rebounds for the year. In the NCAA tourney, the Bruins won the West regional, defeating Dayton and San Francisco. In the Final Four they faced NC State once again, and the Wolfpack avenged their one loss with an 80–77 victory over UCLA. Despite the disappointing end to Walton's college career, UCLA was 86–4 with Walton and he was POY for three straight years in nearly every poll or award given.

Walton graduated in 1974 with a degree in history and was selected as the number one pick in the NBA draft by the Portland Trailblazers, an expansion franchise, which in their four years of existence had never won more than 29 games. In Walton's rookie season, the four returning starters improved and Walton was a big help in his limited time on the court. In what would be a recurring problem, mostly because of Walton's high arches, which were very susceptible to stress fractures, he played in only 35 games, but averaged just under 13 points and 13 rebounds per game as the Blazers went 38–44, their best year ever. The next season Walton was able to play in 51 games, averaging 16 points and 13.4 rebounds per game. The Blazers declined slightly to 37–45, but they would be aided by the agreement with the ABA that allowed four teams to join the NBA and the players from the other teams to be distributed among the NBA teams. The Blazers signed Dave Twardzik as a free agent and obtained Maurice Lucas in the dispersal draft.

With Twardzik and Lucas joining Walton, Lionel Hollins, and Bob Gross in the starting lineup, the

Blazers were a young, aggressive team with dominating inside defenders in Lucas and Walton. Walton played in 65 games and led the league in both rebounds (14.4) and blocks (3.25) per game, while scoring at an 18.6 points per game clip and was Second-Team All-NBA. The team of "strangers" quickly learned to play together and ended the year 49–33, four games behind L.A. in the Pacific Division. They closed the year in a rush and their superior playing carried over into the playoffs. First they defeated the Chicago Bulls in a best of three series and followed that with an upset of Midwest Division winner Denver, defeating them in six games. In the Western Conference finals against UCLA alum Kareem Abdul-Jabbar and the favored Lakers, the Blazers were dominant, sweeping the series in four straight. In the NBA Finals, the Blazers faced the Philadelphia 76ers with their tandem of Julius Erving and George McGinnis. After losing the first two games, the Blazers swept the next four to become NBA champions. Walton was voted MVP of the finals. Overall in the playoffs, he averaged 18 points, 15 rebounds, and 5.5 assists per game, and also led all players in total rebounds, assists, and blocks.

Walton continued to miss games with foot problems, but in 1977–1978 he played 58 games and was in the top six in rebounds and blocks, while achieving his highest scoring average (18.9) and assist average (5.0). The Blazers finished with the best record in the league (58–24) and Walton was voted the league's MVP. Unfortunately, he was injured once again, and he managed to play in just two playoff games, as the Blazers lost in the first round to the Seattle Supersonics, four games to two.

Due to stress fractures and bone spurs, Walton missed all of the 1978–1979 season and Portland decided not to re-sign him for 1979–1980. Walton signed as a free agent with the San Diego Clippers, envisioning a great homecoming, but was only able to play in 14 games in his first season with the Clippers. He missed both 1980–1981 and 1981–1982 with his injuries. The next year (1982–1983) he played in just 33 games as the Clippers continued their mediocre status in the league. He finally played nearly a full season in 1983–1984, but injuries had made him slower and not able to jump as quickly. The Clippers had sunk to last in the Pacific Division

---

Grateful Red

Bill Walton, the "Big Redhead," is an unabashed Grateful Dead fan, a Dead Head, having seen the band, in his own estimation, at least 600 times, including on a tour of Egypt where he played drums briefly with the band. On his radio show, *One More Saturday Night*, heard on SiriusXM Radio, he plays many rock bands, but none more than the Dead.

---

and they improved only slightly in 1984–1985. An encouraging sign for Walton was his ability to play in 67 games, the most he had ever done. Playing about 24 minutes each game, he averaged 10 points and 9 rebounds a game. Going nowhere with him, the Clippers (now playing in L.A.) traded Walton in September 1985 to the Boston Celtics for Cedric Maxwell and a top draft pick in 1986. In Boston, Walton managed to have one last hurrah.

Walton was part of a strong bench that helped the Celtics with their great frontline of Larry Bird, Kevin McHale, and Robert Parish to 67 victories, tops in the league. Walton played in 80 games, averaging 19 minutes per game. In that time he averaged 7.6 points and 6.8 rebounds a game and won the NBA's Sixth Man Award. In the playoffs, he maintained those averages as the Celtics lost only one game in surging to the Eastern Conference championship, then defeated Houston in six games to win the NBA Finals.

Walton played in only 10 games the next year, but returned to play 12 games in the playoffs for the Celtics, who lost in the NBA Finals. Walton then chose to retire at age 34. In 1990 he had surgery to fuse the bones in his ankles, making basketball, even recreationally, impossible. Instead he pursued what would have once seemed unlikely, a career in broadcasting. Walton had been a stutterer since childhood, but with the help of Cincinnati broadcaster Mart Glickman, a former sprinter on the 1936 Olympic team, Walton learned to overcome his stutter and began a successful career as a commentator for CBS's coverage of college basketball and then for NBC and for various stations covering the NBA in the late 1990s and early 2000s. All four of his sons played college basketball and one, Luke, also played in the NBA.

Murry R. Nelson

See also Abdul-Jabbar, Kareem; Bird, Larry; Boston Celtics; Final Four; Knight, Bobby; Scott, Jack; UCLA Basketball; Wooden, John

Suggested Resources

"Bill Walton." Basketball-Reference.com. http://www.basketball-reference.com/players/w/waltobi01.html. Accessed October 27, 2011.

"Bill Walton." SR/College Basketball. http://www.sports-reference.com/cbb/players/w/waltobi01.html. Accessed October 27, 2011.

Bill Walton Website. http://billwalton.com/. Accessed October 27, 2011.

Scott, Jack. *Bill Walton: On the Road with the Portland Trailblazers*. New York: Crowell, 1978.

Walton, Bill, with Gene Wojciechowski. *Nothing but Net: Just Give Me the Ball and Get Out of the Way*. New York: Hyperion Books, 1995.

Weissmuller, Johnny (1904–1984)

Johnny Weissmuller was a champion swimmer in the 1920s, winning five Olympic medals, holding no fewer than 52 national championships, and setting 67 world records before taking on the film role of Tarzan in 1931. Weissmuller invented the stroke referred to as the American crawl with six beats of the legs for every two arm strokes, and it brought him great success, as well as fame and fortune.

Weissmuller was born in 1904 to German parents in a part of Austria-Hungary that is now Serbia and near the Romanian border, but came to the United States while still an infant. The family lived briefly with relatives in Windber, Pennsylvania, which Weissmuller (to get an American passport) later claimed as his birthplace, before the family moved to Chicago where Weissmuller grew up. He attended elementary school and, briefly, Lane Technical High School, dropping out to help support his family after his father abandoned them.

He learned to swim in Lake Michigan and a local pool and his prowess was recognized by a noted swimming coach, William "Big Bill" Bachrach of the Illinois Athletic Club, where Weissmuller worked as an elevator operator. In his first national competition at the National Amateur Athletic Union Championships in Duluth, Minnesota, he won the 50-yard freestyle and went on to set records regularly. By July 1923,

Johnny Weissmuller, freestyle swimming champion, and Aileen Riggin, women's professional diving champion, pose poolside after participating in an international swim meet in Paris, France, in 1930. (AP Photo.)

when he broke the world record for the 500-meter freestyle, he had set more than 50 world records. He was named the American Swimmer of the Year for 1923 by the Helms Athletic Foundation.

The 1924 Olympics were to be held in Paris and Weissmuller was an obvious choice for the U.S. team, except that he had never received American citizenship. Thus, he traded birth dates and identities with his younger brother, who was born in the United States soon after their family had arrived in the United States. This was all sorted out years later.

In the 1924 Games, Weissmuller won three gold medals and one bronze, setting Olympic records in the 100-meter freestyle (defeating Duke Kahanamoku) and the 400-meter freestyle. He was part of the winning

4x200-meter freestyle relay team and the bronze-winning water polo team. He was named Helms World Athlete of the Year for 1924. Weissmuller continued to swim and set records for the next four years, then went to the 1928 Olympics in Amsterdam and won two more gold medals in the 100-meter freestyle and the 4x200-meter freestyle relay. At those Games, he carried the American flag in the opening ceremonies. He then retired from amateur swimming in 1929. Soon afterward, he signed an endorsement contract with BVD, manufacturer of swimsuits and men's underwear. He was reportedly paid $500 a week, an unheard-of sum for such activities at the time.

Weissmuller appeared in some swimming documentaries and had a cameo appearance in a major film before writing a book on his life and swimming techniques, published in 1930. It included a series of photographs on his techniques and an extensive list of his various swimming records. In 1931 Weissmuller was asked to do a screen test by MGM studios and then was offered the part of the Edgar Rice Burroughs hero, Tarzan of the Apes.

In 1932 *Tarzan the Ape Man* was released, which began a successful series of Tarzan films for Weissmuller. Maureen O'Sullivan, a lovely young actress under contract to MGM, was Jane, his "mate." Over the next 16 years Weissmuller swam, swung on vines, dived off cliffs, and made his fearsome call as Tarzan in 11 more films.

He also appeared in other films of a similar genre, most notably as Jungle Jim Bradley, a "great white hunter," guide, and explorer in the jungles of Africa. These were all made by Weissmuller's own production company. The Jungle Jim series included 13 films between 1947 and 1954. These were B movies, that is, the second show of a double feature, and swiftly became part of Saturday matinees. In 1955–1956 a syndicated *Jungle Jim* television show was produced and distributed in over 100 U.S. and 30 world markets. Some of the episodes took Bradley (Weissmuller) to Asia and South America. The character was based on a popular comic strip, presaging the spate of popular movies in today's popular culture. The television series was rerun for many years after the initial broadcasts.

For a six-month period in 1939–1940 Weissmuller appeared in Billy Rose's *Aquacade* with Eleanor Holm,

then Esther Williams, at the World's Fair in Flushing, New York. During the Second World War he raised funds for war bonds and trained marines in San Pedro, California, in techniques of diving from airplanes as well as how to swim in water engulfed in flames.

Weissmuller emulated a common Hollywood cultural pattern, multiple marriages. He married five times to, among others, a singer, a socialite, an actress, and a golfer. These lasted from 1 to 14 years, but his last marriage, to German-born Maria Bauman Brock, endured for over 20 years, until his death. He had three children.

In 1949, Weissmuller was elected to the Helms Swimming Hall of Fame and the next year he was voted by the Associated Press the Greatest Swimmer of the Half Century. He was also elected to the United States Olympic Hall of Fame in 1983, the first year inductees were honored by the Hall. Weissmuller was also instrumental as founding chairman of the International Swimming Hall of Fame in Fort Lauderdale, Florida, where he and his wife moved in 1965. He was one of the Hall's first inductees and worked to raise funds and awareness of that institution. Weissmuller was involved in a number of business ventures, including swimming pools, but none were very successful.

Weissmuller left Florida in 1973 after another failed business deal and he and his wife moved back to California and Nevada. He worked for a time as a

---

Tarzan Saves Johnny

A story, possibly apocryphal, focused on Weissmuller, who loved to play golf, being on a golf course in the Havana, Cuba, area in 1958. At this time, the Cuban rebels, led by Fidel Castro, were waging a guerrilla war with the government of Cuba under dictator Fulgencio Batista. A cadre of rebels appeared on the golf course where Weissmuller was playing and intended to kidnap the players and hold them for ransom. Weissmuller, thinking quickly, unleashed one of his famous Tarzan yells, which the rebels immediately recognized. The rebel soldiers recognized his call and said, "Tarzan, Tarzan," and were thrilled to meet him. They then accompanied the group to a safe area of the region. At Weissmuller's funeral a recording of his famous yell was played, at his request, as the coffin was lowered into the ground.

greeter at the MGM Grand Hotel and Casino in Las Vegas. His health began to decline in 1974 when he broke his hip and his leg. Then in 1977 he suffered a stroke that weakened him further. He was hospitalized in the Motion Picture and Television Country House and Hospital in Woodland Hills, California, in 1979 for a number of weeks. Upon release, he and his wife moved to Acapulco, Mexico. On January 20, 1984, Weissmuller died at home as a result of pulmonary edema and was buried at Valle de la Luz Cemetery in Acapulco. He was inducted into the Body Building Guild Hall of Fame in 1976.

In December 2011, Weissmuller was back in the news for a most unexpected reason. An aged chimpanzee had died at a primate sanctuary in Florida and claims were made that he was 80 years old and was Cheetah of Johnny Weissmuller's *Tarzan* films. Most primatologists dismissed the claims as nearly impossible, but it did lead to old stock photos of Weissmuller and Cheetah being reprinted in the newspapers and articles quoting some of Weissmuller's children regarding their father's feelings toward his chimpanzee co-star.

Weissmuller's enormous number of national and international swimming records makes him one of the greatest, if not the greatest, swimmer in American history. Amazingly, he never lost a race in competition from 1923 until he retired after the 1928 Olympics. His acting career, which made him much more a figure of popular culture, was limited to three roles, Tarzan, Jungle Jim, and Johnny Weissmuller. He found that career wonderful and easy.

Murry R. Nelson

See also Kahanamoku, Duke

Suggested Resources

Fury, David A. *Johnny Weissmuller, Twice the Hero.* New York: Artists Press, 2000.

"Johnny Weissmuller." IMDb. http://www.imdb.com/name/nm0919321/. Accessed July 11, 2011.

Onyx, Narda. *Water, World and Weissmuller, a Biography.* Washington, DC: Vion, 1964.

Schmidt, John R. "Chicago's Own Olympic Superstar." Johnny Weissmuller." July 11, 2011. http://www.wbez.org/blog/john-r-schmidt/2011-07-11/chicagos-own-olympic-superstar-johnny-weissmuller-88775. Accessed July 11, 2011.

Weissmuller, Johnny, with Clarence Bush. *Swimming the American Crawl.* New York: Grosset & Dunlap, 1930.

Weissmuller, Johnny, Jr., William Reed, and W. Craig Reed. *Tarzan, My Father.* Toronto: ECW Press, 2008.

West, Jerry (1935–)

Jerry West was an All-American basketball player who starred for many years with the Los Angeles Lakers before becoming a coach and general manager in the NBA. The NBA uses the profile of West dribbling as their logo.

Jerry West was born on May 28, 1935, in Chelyan, near Cabin Creek, West Virginia, leading to one of his nicknames, "Zeke from Cabin Creek." Cabin Creek is located on the Kanawha River about 20 miles south of Charleston in Kanawha County, in the coalfields of the state. His father was an electrician in the mines. West was always playing basketball and in his senior year led East Bank High School to the 1956 state basketball championship. He was the first to score 900 points in a high school career in that state.

Inundated with offers of basketball scholarships, he decided to remain in-state and enrolled at West Virginia University, coached by Fred Schaus. In his freshman year, his freshmen team was undefeated and he was an immediate starter on the varsity in the fall of 1957 on a team that had been 25–4 the prior year. West averaged 17.8 points per game and West Virginia went 25–1, losing only to Duke, before accepting an invitation to the NCAA Tournament, where they were upset in the first round by Manhattan, 89–84. The next year, West played nearly 36 minutes per game and led the team with a 26.6 points and 12.3 rebounds per game average, despite his 6'3" stature. West Virginia went 25–4 in the regular season, then won three games to take the East Regional title of the 1959 NCAA Tournament and advance to the Final Four. There, they swamped Louisville, 94–79, before being edged by California in the title game. West had early foul trouble and had to sit more than he and Coach Schaus would have liked, but he still scored 28 points and had 11 rebounds in the championship game. For the five games of the tournament, West scored 162 points (32.4 ppg) and had 61 rebounds (12.2 rpg) to earn the MOP of the tournament.

The next year West Virginia was 24–4 and won the Southern Conference once again and then played Navy in the first round of the NCAA Tournament. They easily dispatched the Middies, but were upset by NYU, 82–81, before topping St. Joe's 106–101 to capture third in the East Regional. West averaged 29.3 points per game for the season, but upped that to 35 points per game for the three NCAA games. He was a unanimous All-American in both 1959 and 1960.

West was the Lakers' (recently moved from Minneapolis to Los Angeles) first pick of the 1960 draft (second overall), but before signing a contract he played for the 1960 U.S. Olympic basketball team in Rome, considered one of the best teams ever. West was joined by Oscar Robertson, Terry Dischinger, Jerry Lucas, Walter Bellamy, and Bob Boozer on a team that went 8–0 and whose closest contest was a 24-point victory over the USSR, in which West led the team with 19 points. West averaged 13.8 points, third to Robertson's and Lucas's 17.0 points per game.

The Lakers had been 25–50 in 1959–1960, despite the presence of young superstar Elgin Baylor. West quickly became a starter, sending veteran Bob Leonard to the bench, and averaged 17.6 points his rookie year, helping the Lakers to an improvement to 36–43, second in the Western Division. They defeated Detroit in the first round of the playoffs, but lost to St. Louis, four games to three, after leading three games to two. West upped his average to 22.9 in the playoffs, a portent of the future. In 1961–1962, West exploded for 30.8 points per game, fourth in the league in scoring, and seventh in assists. The Lakers won the West with a record of 54–26 with the same team they fielded the prior year. In the playoffs the Lakers defeated Detroit to advance to the NBA Finals, but were beaten by the Celtics in seven games, the last going to overtime. West scored 31.5 in the playoffs. The Lakers added Dick Barnett as West's running mate at guard for 1962–1963 and the team was 53–27. West missed 25 games with a leg injury, but still averaged 27.1 points and 5.5 assists per game. In the playoffs, the Lakers defeated the Hawks, but lost to the Celtics in the NBA Finals once again.

In 1963–1964 West was third in the league in scoring and assists, but the Lakers, lacking a strong center, fell to 42–38 and lost in the first round of the playoffs. L.A. improved to 49–31 the next year and

West Virginia University basketball star Jerry West in 1959. (AP Photo.)

won the West once more. West averaged 31.0 points to finish second in scoring as well as fourth in field goal percentage, fifth in free throw percentage, and sixth in assists. For the fourth year in a row, West was First-Team All-NBA, but the Lakers lost in the NBA Finals to their nemesis, the Celtics. Baylor's knee injury in 1965–1966 put more pressure on West to score and he continued to do so, finishing second in the league once again with a 31.0 average. He also was in the top 10 in free throw percentage, field goal percentage, and assists and was First-Team All-NBA. The Lakers won the West, but were edged by Boston in seven games in the finals, with the last a 95–93 margin.

In 1966–1967 the Lakers and West were only 36–45, barely making the playoffs and being eliminated in the first round by the San Francisco Warriors. West with his 28.7 average was still a first-team pick, but the losses added to his depression, only revealed in a 2011 autobiography. West played only 51 games the next year, averaging 26.3 points, but the Lakers, with a stronger bench and better defense, won 52 games, then defeated Chicago and San Francisco before falling to Boston in the NBA Finals again. Over the summer, the Lakers and 76ers made a blockbuster trade and the Lakers finally got a powerful center, Wilt Chamberlain. With West, Baylor, and Chamberlain all scoring over 20 points per game, the Lakers were strong, but after winning the Western Division, they were edged in seven games by the Celtics for the title.

Bad luck struck the Lakers in 1969–1970 as both Chamberlain and Baylor missed a large number of games and West had to pick up the slack. Again he did, averaging 31.2 points per game to lead the league and finishing fourth in assists. Both Baylor and Chamberlain returned for the playoffs, but were a bit rusty. Still, led by West and his 31.2 ppg in the playoffs, the Lakers went back to the NBA Finals before losing to the New York Knicks in seven games. West was First-Team All-NBA, once more, but losing in the finals was gnawing at him.

The NBA had expanded to four divisions for 1970–1971 and the Lakers won the Pacific by seven games. Baylor retired because of knee problems and West missed 13 games with his own knee injury. He still averaged 26.9 points and 9.5 rebounds, sixth and second, respectively, in the league in average. West missed the playoffs and the Lakers edged Chicago, but lost to Milwaukee. At 32, there was concern for his future. Showing no signs of injury, West came back in 1971–1972 to lead the league in assists and finish seventh in scoring with 25.8 points per game. Gail Goodrich, his partner at guard, averaged 25.9 and Wilt led the league in rebounding as the Lakers ran off 33 wins in a row (an NBA record) on the way to a 69–13 record (another NBA record, subsequently broken by Michael Jordan and his Bulls in 1995–1996). The Lakers then won three playoff series, dropping only three games total, and were finally the NBA champions. Jerry West had proven he was a champion after years of being a runner-up. He also was named First-Team All-NBA for the third year in a row.

In 1972–1973 West was first team again, despite missing 13 games. The Lakers won the Pacific Division and went to the finals, but were defeated, in surprisingly easy fashion, by the Knicks in five games.

Mr. Clutch

One of Jerry West's nicknames was Mr. Clutch and it was well deserved. When the game was on the line, he wanted the ball, and he delivered. In game three of the 1962 NBA Finals against the Celtics, he sank two jumpers in the waning minutes to tie the game, stole an inbounds pass, and drove the lane to score for a 117–115 Laker win. In 1965 he scored 50 points in a playoff game after breaking his nose. His most famous clutch shot was in game three of the 1970 finals when he sank a shot from 63 feet to tie the game as the clock ran out, sending the contest into overtime. It is often replayed during the NBA playoffs.

West played in only 35 games in 1973–1974 and 14 minutes in the Lakers' playoff loss to Milwaukee. West averaged 20.3 points per game, but he was through. The injuries and the grind had caught up to the 35-year-old.

West retired with over 25,000 points in the NBA, which was then third all-time. He averaged 27.0 points per game over his nearly 14 full seasons, as well as 6.7 assists and 5.8 rebounds. He was an All-Star every year and either First- or Second-Team All-NBA for 12 of his 14 seasons, only missing in his first and last years.

In 1976, West became the Lakers' coach and had a three-year coaching record of 145–101, making the playoffs each year. After a change in ownership in 1979, West resigned, but was rehired in 1982 as the general manager of the Lakers. He remained in that position through 2000 and presided over championships in 1982, 1985, 1987, 1988, and 2000. He drafted Magic Johnson, traded for Kobe Bryant, and signed Shaquille O'Neal; he was the architect of the first of the Laker three-peats in 2000, 2001, 2002.

In 2002, West agreed to be general manager of the Memphis Grizzlies and turned a woebegone franchise into a playoff team. He retired in 2007. In May 2011, West agreed to be a head consultant to the new ownership group that had purchased the Golden State Warriors; he also received a minority ownership in the team. West was voted into the Naismith Memorial Hall of Fame in 1979 and named one of the 50 greatest NBA players ever in 1997.

Murry R. Nelson

See also Boston Celtics; Bryant, Kobe; Chamberlain, Wilt; Chicago Bulls; Johnson, Earvin "Magic"; Jordan, Michael; Los Angeles Lakers; Naismith Memorial Basketball Hall of Fame; O'Neal, Shaquille; Robertson, Oscar

Suggested Resources

"Jerry West." Basketball-Reference.com. http://www.bas ketball-reference.com/players/w/westje01.html. Accessed October 18, 2011.

"Jerry West." SR/College Basketball. http://www.sports -reference.com/cbb/players/w/westje01.html. Accessed October 18, 2011.

Lazenby, Roland. *Jerry West: The Life and Legend of a Basketball Icon*. New York: ESPN, 2010.

West, Jerry, and Jonathan Coleman. *West by West: My Charmed, Tormented Life*. New York: Little, Brown, 2011.

Westminster Kennel Club/ Westminster Dog Show

It is impossible to discuss the Westminster Dog Show without discussing the Westminster Kennel Club, as the two are intertwined. The Westminster Kennel Club and the Dog Show are of interest to society due to the longevity of the club and the show, use of media, donations, gender-breaking milestones, and America's love of dogs. The Westminster Kennel Club Dog Show is the United States' second-longest continuously held sporting event, behind only the Kentucky Derby.

There are two accounts about how the Westminster Kennel Club was named. One account tells of sporting men meeting at their favorite hotel bar in the 1870s. They had just formed a club and needed a name for it. After hours in the bar, they could not agree, and the suggestion was made to name it after the bar, which was housed in the Westminster Hotel in New York. The other account claims that the club was named after the Duke of Westminster, who did import dogs to America. However, this account has been disclaimed as none of the duke's dogs appeared at the first show.

The Westminster Kennel Club had a clubhouse in New Jersey in the late 1800s. In the late 1800s and early 1900s, kennel clubs were involved with owning and breeding dogs. For this reason, kennel clubs were large and included land for the dogs. The Westminster

Kennel Club's clubhouse was a mansion with kennels located in an area rich in game. The members (all men) were sport hunters, and most of the dogs were pointers, including Sensation, the pointer who is the symbol of the Westminster Kennel Club. After two years in New Jersey, the club moved to Long Island (and then other locations). The pointers were used in the hunt tests on the club grounds until 1907, when the Westminster Kennel Club stopped having its own kennels.

The first members of the club held their first show seven months before their first official meeting. It should be noted that the club members did meet prior to this time, the difference being that formal notes and club formalities were not used until late 1887. The first president of the club was General Alexander Stewart Webb, a Civil War general and president of the College of the City of New York. Interestingly, he was not active in dog shows or as a hunter. But he did own a pointer and was able to guide the kennel club, and he was elected as president for the first 11 years of the club.

The "First Annual New York Bench Show of Dogs, Given Under the Auspices of the Westminster Kennel Club" was held in 1877. The show was held at the Hippodrome in New York City and had an entry of 1,201 dogs. The first show awarded ribbons for placements (blue, red, white). Anyone could give "special prizes" to different breeds. There was not a Best in Show placement offered at this show, and uniformed attendants took all entries into the ring. The show was popular, with attendance between 6,000 and 8,000 the first day. The second and third day each drew an attendance of 20,000. The Westminster Kennel Club gave a percentage of the show proceeds to the ASPCA to establish a home for stray and disabled dogs. The check sent to the ASPCA was for $1,295.25. The show was covered in the magazine *Forest and Stream* that year and for many years afterward.

The third show was eventful because the Premium List (show application) contained the show rules and regulations. The rules and regulations were adopted by the Westminster Kennel Club and the Philadelphia Kennel Club, and a Board of Appeals was created for the show. This was the first time a set of rules was written for a dog show, as there was not a national governing body.

Scottish deerhound Hickory poses for photographers with his handler Angela Lloyd, right, and judge Paolo Dondina after Hickory won Best in Show during the 135th Westminster Kennel Club Dog Show in February of 2011. (AP Photo/Mary Altaffer, File.)

The Westminster Dog Show began with attendants bringing the dogs into the ring. In 1881, owners brought the dogs into the ring for the first time. But it was a change in 1884 that would have a huge significance for the sport. For the first time, in 1884 there were two shows. There was a fall show for nonsporting dogs known as the "Forgotten Show." Five hundred and ninety dogs were entered. Although this was the first and last time for a fall show, during the second night of the show, the event of significance was the formation of a national dog organization, the American Kennel Club (AKC). Bylaws were written, and kennel clubs would now have delegates to the AKC.

The Westminster Kennel Club was the first club to be admitted to the AKC.

In 1888, Anna H. Whitney became the first woman to judge at Westminster. Whitney was one of the first approved by the AKC as a licensed judge in 1889, and she judged until 1918. An additional change occurred in 1888. The AKC had 30 member clubs at this time and was seen as too small to represent individual breeders who were not members of clubs. The individual breeders started the National Dog Club of America. Because of the new organization, the AKC proposed new rules to provide for associate membership, which would allow individual breeders to elect

AKC delegates (1 for every 100 associates). This proposal passed. The National Dog Club disbanded after two years, and the American Kennel Club is still the premier organization in the United States for all dog-related sports.

For spectators, the judging was hard to follow because they did not know which dogs were in the ring and placing. In 1904, arm cards were used for the first time. The arm card had the catalog number of the dog on it so that spectators could follow the judging and know which dogs were in the ring. Arm cards (known as arm bands) are still used today.

A major change in 1907 that has continued to today is the award for Best in Show (BIS). This ushered in a new era of the Westminster Dog Show, as Best in Show is the award that the breeders strive to achieve, as it brings international recognition to the winner.

A woman was part of a panel of five judges to judge Best in Show in 1928, and in 1933, a woman judged Best in Show alone. A woman showed a dog for Best in Show for the first time in 1935. Today, men and women handle their dogs in the same classes. During these years, the Junior Handler class was offered for the first time as "Children's Handling classes" in 1934. Learning sportsmanship was a high priority for these young exhibitors.

The media has played an important role in the history of the Westminster Kennel Club and Dog Show. There are motion picture shorts from 1921 and newsreel coverage in the 1930s. In the 1940s, there were lengthier films created about the show, and television coverage began in 1948. Television created a sizable new dog show audience in less than three years. Over the years, the television audience and television sponsorship has increased. In 1996 and 1998, the Dog Show was aired by USA Network and was seen in over 2.8 million homes each night (a 4.0 rating). The 2000 show had the second-highest rating for any show on cable. The Dog Show held its own in 2002 when it aired opposite the Winter Olympics with a 3.4 rating (2.9 million households).

In 1935, the Dog Writers Association of America was established. Today it has an annual writing and photography competition in print and nonprint media, and it also runs the Dog Writers Educational Trust for scholarships for young people.

Media Coverage and the Westminster Kennel Club (2011)

The Westminster Kennel Club has excelled at using all forms of printed, televised, and social media. The 2011 show drew over 3.5 million viewers on the USA channel. Their website for the two show days and the day after had 10.2 million page views from 1.04 million visits. Video streaming was used 937,000 times. There were 772,090 Facebook users and 2,716 Twitter users. In terms of magazine and newspaper coverage, over 500 media passes were distributed for the event, representing 20 countries and including the Associated Press.

In addition to the magazine reporting in *Forest and Stream* magazine, the show had coverage from *Harper's Bazaar* (including cover drawings) and the *New York Times*. *Time* magazine put the show on the cover in 1938. In 1950, the Dog Show was the lead story in a radio and television column in the *Times*. One writer for the *Times*, Fletcher, wrote about the show from 1969 to 1996. The Westminster Dog Show is now written about in the sports section of the *New York Times* (among many other media and online sources).

The Westminster Kennel Club has continued to utilize new forms of media. In 2005, streaming video with same-day coverage of breed judging highlights was made available for the first time on the Westminster website. It was an immediate and huge hit.

The Westminster Kennel Club has continued the practice of giving donations every year of its existence to various charities. In 1918 and 1919, donations were given to the American Red Cross in the amounts of $2,500 and $4,000. In 1940, 1941, and 1942, $5,000 donations were given to the New York Chapter of the American Red Cross. Other recipients included Dogs for Defense and War Bonds ($500,000 raised); Take the Lead, a charitable foundation for members of the dog show family; and veterinary scholarships at six veterinary medical schools: Cornell, Tufts, Penn, Michigan State, Tuskegee, and UC Davis.

Brenda A. Riemer

Suggested Resources

American Kennel Club Website. http://www.akc.org. Accessed September 6, 2011.

Bengtson, B. *Best in Show*. Irvine, CA: BowTie Press, 2008.

Byron, J., and A. Yunck. *Competitive Obedience: A Balancing Act*. Ann Arbor, MI: JABBY Productions, 1998.

Crufts Dog Show Website. http://www.crufts.org.uk/. Accessed September 6, 2011.

The Kennel Club Website. http://www.thekennelclub.org.uk/. Accessed September 6, 2011.

Stifel, W. F. *The Dog Show: 125 Years of Westminster*. Guilford, CT: Lyons Press, 2003.

United Kennel Club Website. http://ukcdogs.com. Accessed September 6, 2011.

Westminster Kennel Club Website. http://www.westminsterkennelclub.org/. Accessed September 6, 2011.

WGN Television

WGN is a Chicago television station that was one of the first two stations to pay to have their signal transmitted by communications satellite in 1978, thus becoming a "superstation" and having their station accessible throughout the country. With the change of TBS exclusively to cable, WGN is the only remaining superstation of this type.

WGN started in 1948 as a joint affiliate of CBS and the Dumont Broadcasting Company. Like many early call letters, WGN's actually stood for something, other than just being a placeholder. Owned largely by the *Chicago Tribune*, WGN Radio and Television initially stood for World's Greatest Newspaper, the banner for the *Chicago Tribune*. (Other noted "meaningful" call letters include WTMJ—the *Milwaukee Journal* in Milwaukee; WLS in Chicago, owned by Sears—world's largest store; WNYC in New York, owned initially by the city; WCFL in Chicago, begun by the Chicago Federation of Labor.)

In 1953 WGN lost its CBS affiliation and in 1956, when Dumont went out of business, WGN (Channel 9) became an independent station. The station began doing live broadcasts in color in 1957. The station became famous and successful, largely through its original children's programming and its enormous coverage of Chicago sports, including the Cubs, the White Sox, the Bulls of the National Basketball Association, and the Blackhawks of the National Hockey League. They also picked up the syndicated Big Ten basketball games in the 1960s, packaged by the Great Plains Sports Network, among other sports packages.

Jack Brickhouse, with color from Lloyd Pettit and Vince Lloyd, announced most of the baseball and basketball games. Pettit was the lead anchor for professional hockey coverage. WGN Radio had been carrying Cubs and Sox broadcasts since the early 1930s with Bob Elson announcing. The WGN television coverage of the Cubs began as early as 1948, the year that the station began, and eventually, beginning in the 1950s, WGN carried all of the Cubs' home games and a few road games. The fact that the Cubs played only day games meant that any prime-time coverage would not be interfered with and the station had built-in daytime exclusives. During the late 1950s WGN began to televise selected White Sox games, but that affiliation ended in the 1960s as the White Sox switched to WFLD, a UHF station, for a time. Without cable in Chicago, most viewers only received VHF broadcasts until newer television incorporated UHF possibilities. The White Sox returned to WGN in 1990 after an eight-year absence. The Cubs' relationship with WGN was greatly enhanced by the Tribune Company's purchase and ownership of the team from 1981 to 2009.

Much of the success of the sports programming has been directly linked to the two Hall of Fame broadcasters who announced the Cubs from 1948 to 1981 (Brickhouse) and 1981 to 2007 (Harry Caray). Brickhouse, a Peoria native, had begun his broadcasting career there doing Bradley University basketball and Three-I League baseball games, but in 1940, Bob Elson recommended him for a position at WGN, which he was able to obtain after an audition.

For more than 40 years, Brickhouse was the voice of sports (and many other things) on WGN television and on many radio broadcasts. Before the NFL had a regular television package, Brickhouse was the WGN radio announcer (Irv Kupcinet, a columnist for the *Chicago Sun-Times*, did the color) for the Chicago Bears' games and he maintained that position on radio until his retirement. On television he did all the Cubs' home games and some road games, then all the games when the team began televising all of its games in the late 1960s.

WGN also did the Chicago Blackhawks games in the 1960s (1961–1975, then starting in 2009 through at least 2016, but limited to the Chicago broadcast area) and then began covering the Chicago Bulls shortly after

From left, Jack Brickhouse, WGN TV sportscaster, Arch Ward, sports editor of the *Chicago Tribune*, Rocky Marciano, heavyweight champion of the world, and Al Weil, Marciano's manager, as they appear before the television camera at WGN TV studios in Chicago on March 18, 1953. (AP Photo.)

the team was formed in 1966. All of these games could be viewed only by Chicago regional customers until October 1978 when WGN began broadcasting nationally on cable via satellite. This made the Chicago teams nationally seen on a regular basis. The opportunity to view Michael Jordan regularly from 1984 to 2003 made the Bulls' games highly sought after for advertisers, increasing WGN's revenue stream. The Bulls are now limited to broadcasting 15 games a year on WGN America because of NBA restrictions. But the Bulls and Blackhawks only had some of their games on WGN; the Cubs had all of them and millions of new fans became enthralled with the loveable losers and their great broadcasters. First was Brickhouse with his distinctive "hey hey" for a home run or exciting play. Brickhouse broadcast over 5,000 games in his career, almost all on WGN, plus at least one World Series (1959).

After his retirement in 1981, the Cubs unexpectedly convinced Harry Caray to move from the Chicago White Sox across town to the Cubs. Caray had been a broadcaster with the Cardinals from 1945 to 1969 when he was abruptly fired, then worked for the Oakland A's for a year. In 1971 he went to the Chicago White Sox and then in 1982 to the Cubs. Caray had begun leading the crowd in the singing of "Take Me Out to the Ballgame" during the seventh-inning stretch when he was the White Sox announcer and he continued that practice with the Cubs. Now, however, he had a national audience on cable and he became as renowned and adored nationally as he had been in St. Louis and Chicago. Caray was kept on past the WGN retirement age and continued broadcasting through 1997. Caray died in February 1998, but his legacy was continued on WGN from 1998 through 2004 in the person of Chip Caray, his grandson, who was the Cubs announcer until he left to broadcast the Atlanta Braves.

In 1993, WGN became affiliated with the WB Network and carried many of their shows, but this had little effect on the primacy of the station's sports programs. In 1999 the station split itself in regard to programming into a regional and superstation (WGN America). The superstation did not carry the WB programs. In 2006, when the WB combined with UPN to form the CW Television Network, the superstation did not carry these programs, but the regional channel did.

WGN America began airing WWE Superstars as part of a deal with World Wrestling Entertainment in April 2009, but dropped the show in April 2011. With Atlanta's TBS moving all Atlanta Braves games to local channel WPCH in Atlanta, WGN is now the only superstation broadcasting local sports.

In November 2010, WGN-TV began broadcasting Chicago Bears games not aired by a broadcast network, but these are only regional, not shown on WGN America. WGN-TV broadcasts a number of news shows during the day and at least two are also carried, at different times generally, on WGN America. Thus, both sports and Chicago's local news are televised and popular nationwide.

Murry R. Nelson

See also Caray, Harry; Chicago Bears; Chicago Bulls; Chicago Cubs; Jordan, Michael; St. Louis Cardinals; "Take Me Out to the Ballgame"; World Wrestling Entertainment (WWE)

Suggested Resources

Petterchak, Janice. *Jack Brickhouse: A Voice for All Seasons*. Chicago: Contemporary Books, 1996.

Stone, Steve, with Barry Rosner. *Where's Harry?* Dallas: Taylor, 1999.

WGN America Sports. http://www.wgnamerica.com/sports/. Accessed August 16, 2011.

Wheaties—The Breakfast of Champions

Wheaties is a brand of cereal produced by General Mills. It was first sold in the United States in 1924. It is important to American popular culture and sports history because Wheaties cereal brand was one of the first corporate sponsors of radio and television and its parent company, General Mills, was a pioneer in sports marketing. Wheaties' tagline, "The Breakfast of Champions," and its classic orange box, complete with sports endorsements and photos of celebrity athletes, are American cultural icons.

Wheaties cereal was created by accident in 1922 when an employee of the Washburn-Crosby Company accidentally dropped wheat bran on a hot stove in one of the grain processing mills. The Washburn-Crosby Company had its origins in 1856 in a series of mills along the Mississippi River in Minnesota. Following the accidental discovery of Wheaties, Washburn-Crosby's head miller took the next two years to experiment with recipes that would perfect the cereal so that it could be packaged in its current flake form. It was first sold in November 1924 as "Washburn's Gold Medal Whole Wheat Flakes." When the company held an employee contest to rename the cereal, "Wheaties" was selected over "Nutties" and "Gold Medal Flakes." This new name had been suggested by Jane Bausman, wife of Washburn-Crosby's export manager.

Launching Wheaties cereal was part of an overall company transformation. In 1924, Washburn-Crosby purchased a Twin Cities radio station and renamed it with the company's initials, WCCO. The first Wheaties radio commercial was broadcast on WCCO on December 24, 1926. The Wheaties commercial had its own lyrics and was sung to "She's a Jazz Baby." The following spring and summer of 1927, Wheaties became the official sponsor of the Minneapolis Millers

Home run king Hank Aaron poses with a Wheaties box featuring his photograph outside Turner Field in Atlanta, January 23, 2002. (AP Photo/John Bazemore.)

minor league baseball team. It paid for broadcasting the Millers' games on WCCO and in return received advertising space on a large billboard and on the walls inside the Millers' home baseball field at Nicollett Park in Minneapolis. The now famous tagline, "Wheaties—The Breakfast of Champions," was coined by a Minneapolis advertising agent as an ad to be displayed on the Nicollett Park billboard.

In 1928, Washburn-Crosby merged with 26 other mills to create General Mills. Following this consolidation, Wheaties' sponsorship programs grew exponentially over the next two decades. Wheaties increased its presence in baseball with new team sponsorships. At the same time, General Mills began using athlete endorsements in its radio and print ads. Wheaties

expanded its marketing beyond baseball to a variety of other sports such as rodeo, automobile racers, hunting, aviation, and football. Athlete endorsements were broadcast on hundreds of radio stations and printed directly on the now iconic orange Wheaties box. The year 1934 marked some "first" advertising milestones for the Wheaties box ads including the first athlete, Lou Gehrig; the first woman, aviator Elinor Smith; and the first woman athlete, golfer Babe Didrikson. The year 1936 marked the first depiction of an African American athlete, Jesse Owens.

In 1937, Wheaties helped launch the career of Ronald Reagan, future California governor (1967–1975) and U.S. president (1981–1989). Wheaties sponsored a contest looking for America's most popular Wheaties radio sports announcer. Ronald Reagan, a radio sports announcer in Des Moines, Iowa, won the award for his enthusiastic rendition of Wheaties commercials during play-by-plays of Chicago Cubs baseball games. His all-expense trip to the Chicago Cubs' training camp in Southern California included a Warner Brothers screen-test, which led to his studio acting career in Hollywood and eventually to a successful career in politics.

Wheaties had a big year in 1939. At the All-Star baseball game 46 out of 51 players endorsed Wheaties. Then, on August 29, 1939, Wheaties became the first TV commercial sponsor of a televised sports broadcast. The commercial was aired on NBC during the Cincinnati Reds versus Brooklyn Dodgers game. Sports announcer Red Barber made the play-by-plays to a limited audience of approximately 500 TV sets.

In the 1950s, the sports marketing costs skyrocketed and General Mills decided to change its Wheaties advertising campaign. It switched from a focus on sports to children's radio and television programming. Sponsorship was given to television shows such as *The Lone Ranger* and *The Mickey Mouse Club*. Overall, the new strategy failed. Adult purchases of Wheaties declined and sales were not replaced by the outreach into the children's market. As Wheaties sales declined, so did General Mills' overall profits.

In 1958, General Mills decided to return to its historical sports marketing strategy. Efforts were refocused on: (1) new TV commercial and sponsorship programs; (2) creation of the Wheaties Sports Federation; and (3) the appointment of an official brand spokesperson. In the TV sponsorship program, Wheaties pioneered the concept of pregame and postgame shows. Sponsorships were reconfigured to match the mission of the new Wheaties Sports Federation. This was responsible for creating educational and instructional videos that promoted athletic training and physical education. Support was given to Olympic education programs and Jaycee Junior Champ track-and-field meets.

Between 1958 and 1977, Wheaties' first spokesperson was Bob Richards. Richards won two Olympic gold medals in pole vaulting at the 1952 Helsinki Games and the 1956 Melbourne Games and an Olympic bronze medal at the 1948 London Olympics. He also had two gold medals from the 1951 Buenos Aires

and 1955 Mexico City Pan American Games. In 1956, in addition to being on the U.S. Olympic pole vaulting team, he came in 13th place in the decathlon.

Bruce Jenner was the Wheaties spokesperson from 1977 to 1983. He won a gold medal for the decathlon at the 1976 Montreal Olympic Games. Achieving this feat at the height of the Cold War made him an American hero because a Soviet athlete had won the previous Olympic gold medal in the decathlon in 1972. In 1981, while serving as the Wheaties spokesperson, he was also a regular on the popular TV series *CHiPs*. This was a TV show produced by NBC and MGM about two motorcycle police officers with the California Highway Patrol.

Between 1984 and 1985, Mary Lou Retton was the first female Wheaties spokesperson. She won five medals (one gold, two silver, and two bronze) in gymnastics at the 1984 Los Angeles Olympics. Her gold medal for all-around gymnast was significant because it broke a tradition of the medal being awarded to Eastern Europeans. According to a 1993 Associated Press sports study, Retton along with Olympian Dorothy Hamill is considered the most popular athlete in the United States. Since her work with Wheaties, she has done commercial endorsements with Revco and Dairy Queen. She has made numerous guest appearances in TV shows and movies, and continues to appear on television as a sports commentator for gymnastics.

American football running back Walton Payton was the Wheaties spokesperson in 1986. He played for the Chicago Bears in the National Football League (NFL) and in 1985 led this team to victory in Super Bowl XX. He was inducted into the Pro Football Hall of Fame in 1993, College Football Hall of Fame in 1996, and the Black College Football Hall of Fame in 2010. Payton passed away in 1999 at age 45 from a rare liver disease. His legacy includes a growing public awareness about organ donations and two football awards including the Walter Payton Award (Division I college football) and the Walter Payton Award of the Year (awarded to an NFL player for outstanding voluntary and charity work).

Professional tennis player Chris Evert became the Wheaties spokesperson in 1987. Between 1976 and 1981 she was the number one–ranked player in the world five times. Overall, she has the best career win-loss record in singles of any professional tennis player (89.96 percent, 1,309–146). Between 1974 and 1986, she won 18 Grand Slam singles championships, seven French Open championships, and a record six U.S. Open championships. In 1980, she was named by *People Magazine* as the "Sexiest Female Athlete." She appears regularly on television as a tennis commentator.

Michael Jordan was the Wheaties spokesperson between 1988 and 1998. He is a former professional basketball player for the Chicago Bulls and part-owner of the professional basketball team the Charlotte Bobcats. The National Basketball Association has called him "the greatest basketball player of all time." Known as "Air Jordan" and "His Airness" for his ability to slam dunk, he helped the Chicago Bulls win NBA titles in 1992, 1993, 1996, 1997, and 1998. He appeared 18 times on the Wheaties box, holding the number one spot for most depictions. Since 1985, he has been the official spokesman for Nike's line of sneakers known as Air Jordans. He has appeared in numerous movies and TV shows including *Space Jam* (1996), *Michael Jordan: Air Time* (1993), *Michael Jordan: Above and Beyond* (1996), *MJ: His Airness* (1999), and *Michael Jordan to the Max* (2000).

Since 1998, the Wheaties spokesperson has been professional golfer Tiger Woods. He has been on the Wheaties box 14 times, coming in second after Michael Jordan for the number of depictions on the box. In 2010, he was ranked as the highest-paid professional athlete in the world, receiving an estimated $90.5 million from playing golf and from sports endorsements. He has won 14 professional major golf championships and 71 Professional Golf Association (PGA) events. He has been named the PGA Player of the Year a record 10 times. Beside Wheaties, Tiger's other endorsements include Buick Rendezvous SUV, Rolex, Titleist, American Express, Accenture, Nike Golf, TAG Heuser, Electronic Arts, and Gatorade.

References to Wheaties in American popular culture abound. For example, in 1973, fiction writer Kurt Vonnegut wrote *Breakfast of Champions*. That same year, Cheech and Chong's parody of ABC's *Wide World of Sports* (1973) made references to this same Wheaties tagline. In 1977, *Saturday Night Live* comedian John Belushi imitated Wheaties spokesman Bruce Jenner. In 1993, in the movie *Cool Runnings*

about the 1988 Jamaican Olympic bobsled team, reference is made to being depicted on the Wheaties box.

Some first appearances on the Wheaties box are significant firsts in American popular culture. These include the 1987 World Series champion Minnesota Twins, the first team photo; the 1991 Stanley Cup champion Pittsburgh Penguins, the first professional ice hockey team photo; in 1992, the first nonorange Wheaties box was colored red and black to honor the Chicago Bulls; the first NASCAR race driver was Dale Earnhardt in 1997; and the first women's professional sports team was the Sacramento Monarchs in 2005.

Margaret Carroll Boardman

See also *Cool Runnings*; Didrikson, Babe; Evert, Chris; Gatorade; Gehrig, Lou; Hamill, Dorothy; Jenner, Bruce; Jordan, Michael; Nike, Inc.; 1984 Olympic Games, Los Angeles; Payton, Walter; Retton, Mary Lou; *Space Jam;* Woods, Tiger

Suggested Resources

Forsythe, Tom, Anne Brownfield Brown, and Sarah Huesing. *General Mills: 75 Years of Innovation, Invention, Food and Fun*. Minneapolis: General Mills, 2003.

Webster, Maurie. *And Now, a Word from Our Sponsor: 40 Years of Notable Radio Advertising*. New York: Columbia Special Products, 1960.

"Wheaties History." Wheaties Website. http://www.wheaties.com/pdf/wheaties_history.pdf. Accessed July 9, 2012.

White Men Can't Jump (1992)

White Men Can't Jump is an American film written and directed by Ron Shelton, released in 1992. The comedy is the story of Billy Hoyle (Woody Harrelson) and Sidney Deane (Wesley Snipes), two street basketball players who decide to join forces to make money on the playgrounds of Los Angeles.

The movie begins on the Venice Beach playgrounds where Billy, recently arrived from Louisiana, shows up—basketball under his arm, tie-dyed cap on backwards, wearing a surf shirt and shorts. He sits watching the frenzy of all-black teams playing street ball, pretending to be the stereotypical goofy and naive white player. Of course, no one wants to pick this "slow white geeky chump" for his team. Billy is finally chosen to play against Sidney's team. He wins the game, and then an impromptu shooting contest against Sidney. "This is like the luck of the Irish," says Billy. But Sidney, the classical muscular, fast-mouthed, streetwise black man, acknowledges Billy's talent and suggests they make money playing two-on-two basketball games around the city.

Their plan soon becomes a well-oiled basketball hustle: Sidney proposes a high-stakes game to two opponents and lets them pick his teammate to encourage them to bet as much money as he. Inevitably, the black opponents choose Billy, who they think is "the worst player here." Billy and Sidney win several games like this.

Their plan works so well that this significant source of new-found cash helps Billy and Sidney solve their family financial problems. But the partnership collapses after a severe defeat and the loss of hundreds of dollars. Billy's girlfriend, Gloria, and Sidney's wife, Rhonda, manage to bring them back together for the Two-On-Two For Brotherhood Basketball Tournament, worth $5,000 in prize money. They win the tournament and the much-needed cash.

On their way home, Billy maintains that he can dunk the ball. "I don't jam in a game," he says, "because it's showboating for the sake of showboating. . . . A white man wants to win first, look good second. A black man wants to look good first, win second." Billy bets Sidney his prize money that he can dunk. He tries and fails twice. Embarrassed, Sidney explains that "white men can't jump"—only black men can—and urges Billy to forget about the bet. But Billy fails a third time and loses all his money. Finally, during their last big pickup game, he catches Sidney's alley-hoop pass and slam dunks the ball, proving that white men really can jump.

Ron Shelton's *White Men Can't Jump* was one of the very first street basketball movies. Thanks to its realistic basketball scenes, its fast-paced "your mama" teasing and endless trash talking, its straightforward dealing with racial stereotypes, and its friendly ambiance, the movie was a huge commercial success. It was the top money-making movie in the United States in the first two weeks after its release in late March and early April 1992. The movie would eventually gross more than $76 millions.

White Men Can't Jump was released during a period marked by the increasing public fear about violence and crime in inner cities across the United States. Large ghettos like Watts in Los Angeles had come to be viewed as characteristic of the deindustrialized, impoverished, and violent black 'hoods. From the 1980s on, more and more movies—like John Singleton's *Boyz N the Hood*, released one year before *White Men Can't Jump*—depicted L.A. as the backdrop for bleak inner city tales. In May 1992, the Los Angeles riots, triggered by the acquittal of four white police officers accused of the beating of black motorist Rodney King, reinforced the anxiety about the likelihood of peaceful race relations in the country.

For the general public, the 1980s also marked the final transformation of basketball into a "black sport," with the commercial rise of the NBA and NCAA and their global marketing of the black style of basketball. For instance, during the 1991–1992 season, the controversial Michigan Fab Five reached the NCAA Division I finals, 75 percent of the players of the NBA were black, Michael Jordan was elected MVP for the third time, and his Chicago Bulls won the NBA title for the second year in a row. Three months after the Los Angeles riots, the U.S. men's basketball team, the famous Dream Team, competed at the 1992 Olympic Games in Barcelona, giving the world the most tangible image of basketball perfection and good race relations.

The success of *White Men Can't Jump* should be placed in relation to this troubled context. The harmonious racial climate in the movie allows Ron Shelton to play with political correctness to debunk stereotypes from a comical perspective. Many scenes contain crude but funny jokes about violence, armed robberies, and hustling in the black ghetto, about white and black people's supposed cultural peculiarities, or black men's alleged predatory sexual appetite. But at the same time, Sidney embodies a caring and supportive black father, who tries hard to start a construction business to "put food on the table" for his family.

The movie's eye-catching title exposes an enduring stereotype about whites' "natural" physical inferiority. But the end of the story, which seeks to demonstrate the absurdity of this cliché, is not convincing. Rather, the general impression given by the film is that racial differences in athletic ability do exist and can only be acquired by very few exceptional individuals of the other, allegedly less gifted race. A stereotype in itself, the final message of the movie seems to be that the biological racial divide between humans should not prevent them from working toward brotherhood and equality across racial lines, and that sport is the perfect place for this.

Nicolas Martin-Breteau

See also Chicago Bulls; Dream Team; Fab Five; Jordan, Michael; Shelton, Ron

Suggested Resources

Brooks, Scott. *Black Men Can't Shoot*. Chicago: University of Chicago Press, 2009.

Hoberman, John. *Darwin's Athletes: How Sport Has Damaged Black America and Preserved the Myth of Race*. Boston: Houghton Mifflin, 1997.

Marks, Jonathan. *What It Means to Be 98% Chimpanzee: Apes, People, and Their Genes*. Berkeley and Los Angeles: University of California Press, 2002.

White Men Can't Jump. IMDb. http://www.imdb.com/title/tt0105812/. Accessed October 9, 2011.

The White Shadow

The White Shadow was a dramatic television series running on CBS from 1978 to 1981. It centered on a white basketball coach mentoring and shaping the lives of his players in a largely ethnic, lower-middle-class Los Angeles high school. While never a ratings success, the critically acclaimed series enjoyed a healthy life in syndicated reruns, launched several prominent careers in the television industry, and remains fondly recalled by Generation X viewers.

Ken Howard starred as Ken Reeves, a journeyman Chicago Bulls player whose career prematurely ended because of a knee injury. His former college roommate Jim Willis (portrayed in the series by Ed Barnard), presently the principal at Carver High School in Los Angeles, offered him the basketball coaching job. Against the advice of his sister (and at a considerable reduction in salary), Reeves took the job and moved west. Reeves quickly commanded the respect of his players, threatening to be their "white shadow" throughout their time at school, and eventually became not only a disciplinarian but their confidant and an outspoken defender on their behalf.

The Carver High basketball team was composed of star center Warren Coolidge (Byron Stewart), guards Morris Thorpe (Kevin Hooks) and James "Hollywood" Heyward (Thomas Carter), guard Milton Reese (Nathan Cook), forward C. J. Jackson (Erik Kilpatrick), guard Mario "Salami" Pettrino from New York City (Timothy Van Patten), forward/center Abner Goldstein (Ken Michelman), and guard Ricardo "Go-Go" Gomez (Ira Angustain). Carver's vice principal Sybil Buchanan (Joan Pringle), who would be promoted to principal by the series' end, frequently butted heads with Reeves over school matters but developed a grudging respect for the coach and his players.

The White Shadow drew strong critical approval upon its premiere in November 1978. "Bok" with the show-business journal *Variety* enthused that "the debut episode made its best points on the basketball floor, where the coach earned the respect he needed to get his team turned around by physical dexterity— a universal proving ground that recognizes no social or cultural barrier. . . . The team players are more realistically portrayed than the usual run of high school–age youngsters on the tube."

The *Variety* reviewer presciently concluded that "CBS may have another well-made hour-long show on its schedule, but its rating strength is somewhat hard to ascertain—considering its tough timeslot." Indeed, *The White Shadow* debuted opposite NBC's established hit *Little House on the Prairie*. During its two-and-one-half-year run, in fact, *The White Shadow* would switch time slots no fewer than five times.

The plots included genuine melodrama. During the series one basketball recruit collapsed and died while running punishment laps, while Kilpatrick's C. J. Jackson character was shot dead during a liquor store robbery on the eve of a championship game. *The White Shadow* also made effective use of celebrity cameos. Watching his players getting arrogant during a lengthy winning streak, Reeves scheduled a pickup game between them and a team of gentlemen he introduced as carwash workers, who proceeded to

---

Ken Howard or Ken Reeves?

Ken Howard was actually nicknamed "the White Shadow" by the local press as the only white starter on the Manhasset (New York) High School basketball team. His teammates called him "Stork." Reeves is 6'6" and played at Division III Amherst College, captaining the squad in his senior year.

---

showboat and humiliate them—the upstarts then revealed themselves to be the Harlem Globetrotters.

The series received the ultimate compliment with a parody on the November 3, 1979, broadcast of *Saturday Night Live*, titled "The Black Shadow," as guest host/Hall of Fame center Bill Russell played an African American basketball coach at an all-white high school.

The series began to fade during the end of its second season. While other youth-based TV shows often kept its characters perpetually in school, *The White Shadow* acknowledged reality by having several of the basketball stars graduate from Carver High, and Reeves was obligated to recruit new players. ESPN.com commentator Bill Simmons would write, "CBS wouldn't stop tinkering with the show. Responding to lukewarm ratings instead of the critical groundswell, they quietly started softening the show for Middle America (against Paltrow's objections). First, the players started singing in the shower. Another white guy (Salami's cousin, a New Yorker) joined the cast. Every show started to feature an 'After-School Special'–type theme (somebody does PCP, somebody does speed, somebody's getting beaten up by their dad, somebody has an affair with a teacher). You could feel the wheels coming off."

Mark Tinker, one of the series' producers (*The White Shadow* was an MTM production, founded by his then-stepmother, Mary Tyler Moore), told an interviewer that CBS "probably thought the show was a little too heavy from time to time and wanted it to be lighter in tone. We agreed to do that in the last season [1980–1981] and I think the last season suffered for that very reason. The shows got fluffy and light and often silly, and I think we sort of lost sight of the gritty reality that we had in the early episodes that the network thought may have been too heavy."

The White Shadow was created by Bruce Paltrow (1942–2002), father of Academy Award–winning actress Gwyneth Paltrow. Howard had performed with Paltrow's wife, Blythe Danner, in the Broadway and Hollywood versions of the musical *1776* as Thomas and Martha Jefferson. After its cancellation in 1981, the series continued to resonate in popular culture. Paltrow subsequently created *St. Elsewhere*, one of the 1980s' most popular and lauded TV dramas, famous for its inside jokes about television history. In several episodes of that series, Byron Stewart reprised his role as Warren Coolidge, now an orderly at St. Eligus Hospital; he usually wore a Carver High School T-shirt. In one episode where Timothy Van Patten appeared as a character different from Salami, Coolidge did a double-take when looking at him. Van Patten went on to direct episodes of *The Wire* and *Boardwalk Empire*; in addition to frequently directing *The Sopranos*, he co-wrote one of that series' signature episodes, "Pine Barren."

ESPN anchor Dan Patrick, in his 1997 book, *The Big Show* (coauthored with Keith Olbermann), irreverently named Reeves as one of the 10 greatest athletes of all time. "If not for that tragic knee injury," Patrick dryly wrote, "he could've been Michael Jordan. Coach Reeves, strong to the hole—he was the next Mark Olberding, maybe Mark Iavaroni. He could do it all. But he did something AFTER the injury that not many athletes are capable of doing: blending into society, giving something back. And he ran that Carver High Basketball team to perfection—trying to keep Coolidge under wraps, making sure Salami knew how to go to his left. He made us proud. He made us want to play for Carver High, to wear the orange of Carver." Around the same time Howard appeared as Coach Reeves in one of ESPN's memorable "This is *SportsCenter*" promotional commercials, walking through the ESPN offices in Bristol, Connecticut, and begging the anchors to cover the Carver High team.

Howard, who went on to further TV success on *Dynasty*, *The Colbys*, and *Melrose Place*, became president of the Screen Actors Guild in 2008. While making a publicity appearance at the Basketball Hall of Fame in 2011, he said he has no problem with being known as Coach Reeves. "We had a great time putting the show together," he told a reporter. "We got it on the air and it lasted a while. It still has a good following and I'm proud to have been a part of it."

Andrew Milner

See also Chicago Bulls; Harlem Globetrotters; Jordan, Michael; Russell, Bill

Suggested Resources
Feuer, Jane, Paul Kerr, and Tise Vanimagi. *MTM: Quality Television*. London: BFI, 1984.
Ford, Jake. "'White Shadow' Ken Howard Roams the Basketball Hall of Fame." May 27, 2011. http://www.masslive.com/sports/index.ssf/2011/05/white_shadow_ken_howard_roams.html. Accessed October 30, 2011.
Patrick, Dan, and Keith Olbermann. *The Big Show: A Tribute to ESPN's* SportsCenter. New York: Pocket Books, 1997.
Simmons, Bill. "Genius in the 'Shadow.'" October 4, 2002. http://proxy.espn.go.com/espn/page2/story?page=simmons/021004. Accessed October 31, 2011.

White, Shaun (1986–)

Shaun White is most known for his dominating performances on the snowboarding circuit. However, White is also a champion in skateboarding. The media has given White many nicknames, including "Future Boy" (a reference to being the future of the sport when he first began), "Senor Blañco," "The Egg," "The Flying Tomato" (given to him during the 2006 Olympics in reference to his long red hair), and "Animal" (a reference to Jim Henson's Muppet that wildly plays the drums). White became a professional snowboarder in 2000. In 2003 he also became a professional skateboarder as well. White has not only become a role model for young snowboarders but sets the standard over and over again for fellow competitors.

White was born in San Diego, California, in 1986. As a baby he suffered from tetralogy of Fallot, a heart condition affecting the oxygen levels in the blood, and had two heart surgeries before the age of three. He recovered and began competing in all types of sports with his older brother, Jesse, whom he admired. The family spent winter weekends at Big Bear Mountain, three hours north. This is where White began snowboarding at the age of six. He first learned from his father. His mother made him ride backward on the snowboard so she could keep up and also in an attempt to keep him from going too fast.

Shaun White does a frontside heel flip during skateboard vert practice for X Games Twelve, August 2, 2006, in Los Angeles. (AP Photo/Mark J. Terrill.)

White won his first amateur snowboarding contest in 1993 at the age of seven. This qualified him for the United States Amateur Snowboard Association National Championships where he placed 11th. He went on to win five different national titles at the amateur level in the under-12 division. His family spent a lot of money on equipment and travel expenses for Shawn; they often slept in their van, nicknamed "Big Mo," at events because they did not always have enough money for a hotel room.

White became a professional snowboarder at age 13 so he could earn prize money and gain endorsements. To date, he is sponsored by Burton Snowboards, Target, goggle-maker Oakley, game-maker Ubisoft, Stride Gum, Red Bull, BF Goodrich Tires, AT&T, and Park City Mountain Resort. He has his own line of snowboard equipment with Burton and two lines of fashion apparel—Shaun White 4 Target and White Collection. White also has his own sunglasses with Oakley. He has appeared in a commercial for Stride Gum and has a video game entitled *Shaun White Snowboarding: Road Trip.* White also released a DVD titled *The Shaun White Album* in 2004; it is a biography of his life. *Forbes Magazine* named White the highest paid athlete of the 2010 Winter Olympics. Critics assert that earning million-dollar sponsorships such as Shaun does has moved extreme sports away from the underground roots with which they began.

Among White's charitable acts is, most notably, his involvement with the Target House, a long-term housing facility for children and their families at St. Jude Children's Research Hospital in Memphis, Tennessee. White created the Shaun White Great Room. It is a game room complete with foosball table, flat-screen television, and videogames.

White participated in the 2002 Winter X Games, a competition of extreme sports such as snowboarding, and took the silver medal for slopestyle, performing tricks on a downhill obstacle course, and superpipe, a large, extended halfpipe structure with walls at least 16 feet high that allows riders to do tricks. In the 2003 Winter X Games he won gold in the same two events. He was the youngest person to ever win the U.S. Open Slopestyle Championship at age 17. From 2003 to 2011 he has won a gold medal in the superpipe seven times. He was unable to compete in the 2004 Winter X Games because of surgery on his knee. He would return to compete in the 2005 Winter X Games and win a gold medal in slopestyle. From 2003 to 2010 he won gold in slopestyle six times and won bronze once (2008). During the 2005 Winter X Games White won gold in both superpipe and slopestyle, marking the second time he would medal in two events during the X Games. White holds the record for most Winter X Games medals with 15 through 2010.

White missed qualifying for the 2002 Winter Olympic team by 0.3 point. As a professional snowboarder he would go on to later win two Olympic gold medals for the men's halfpipe competition in both the 2006 and 2010 Winter Olympics. During the 2010 Olympics in Vancouver, White had the highest score of any of his competitors during the qualifying run. He

was the last to go for the final run and he had already won the competition. White completed his final half-pipe "victory lap," as it would become known, faster, higher, and with more tricks, including the Double McTwist 1260, than any other snowboarder that day. The Double McTwist 1260 is three and a half twists with two head-over-heel flips; White was the first to land one in competition. He scored 46.8 in the qualifying run and 48.2 in the final run out of a possible 50 points per run, receiving the highest score of anyone in the event. White is able to soar up to 23 feet into the air above the halfpipe, which is taller than the halfpipe itself. The record for the highest halfpipe jump is held by Peter Olenick at 24 feet 11 inches. White uses what is known as pumping, crouching and lifting the body up, and hitting the pipe at an 85-degree angle, all of which serve to increase his height and speed.

Shaun White met professional skateboarder Tony Hawk when he was nine years old. Hawk, a legend in skateboarding, has won more titles and created more new tricks than anyone else. Hawk convinced White to become a professional skateboarder. White placed fourth in the 2003 Slam City Jam North American Skateboarding Championship and placed sixth in the vert competition, a halfpipe structure that resembles the side and bottom of a swimming pool used in skateboarding, in the 2003 Summer X Games. White became the first athlete to compete in both the Summer and Winter X Games. He then won an Espy for the Best Action Sports Athlete for his performances in both snowboarding and skateboarding. White won a silver medal in the 2005 Summer X Games on the skateboard vert, becoming the first athlete to ever medal in both the Summer and Winter X Games. White won his first Espy award in 2003 for Best Male Action Sports Athlete after participating in both the Summer and Winter X Games. White has won a total of seven Espy awards for Best Male Action Sports Athlete, the most recent in 2011. Both *TransWorld Snowboarding* and *TransWorld Skateboarding* magazines named White Rider of the Year in 2006. As of 2008 he was the only skateboarder to land a body varial frontside 540.

White not only participates in the Summer X Games but in both the summer and winter Dew Tours, a four-month traveling competition. He won one summer Dew Tour Competition in 2005 but ranked ninth

Shaun White's Private Red Bull Superpipe

The Red Bull Superpipe was created for Shaun White in a remote location near Silverton, Colorado, to keep media and competitors from knowing what tricks White was working on to prepare for the 2010 Vancouver Winter Olympics. The superpipe was only accessible by helicopter, followed by a snowmobile ride into the mountains. There White perfected his McTwist 1260. He also completed a series of tricks—Frontside 720, Cab Double Cork, Frontside Double Cork, and Cab 1080—that had never been done before.

The superpipe was constructed by dynamiting snow, causing an avalanche that piled the snow up. World-renowned superpipe architect Frank Wells then carved the superpipe. Using real snow instead of man-made snow meant that the pipe would not chunk off after being used. A foam pit was trucked in over 1,000 miles and transferred to skids for the last seven miles. The foam pit allowed White to practice and land safely.

Location: 7 miles from Silverton, Colorado
Altitude: 12,000 feet
Cost: $1 million
Length: 550 feet
Amount of Snow Used: 250,000 cubic feet (almost three Olympic-sized swimming pools)
Dynamite Used: 30 boxes weighing 25 pounds each
Foam Pit: Contained 7,000 foam blocks; 20 feet wide, 30 feet long, 8 feet deep; weighed 4 tons

that season overall in skateboarding. He won the Dew Cup for skateboarding vert in 2007. He has participated in the Dew Tour through the 2011 season. He is the first person to ever win both a summer and winter Dew Cup.

White began snowboarding at a time when extreme sports were just beginning. The 1998 Winter Olympics marked the first time snowboarding was incorporated into the Games. At this time extreme sports were still regarded as something that daredevils did. People were not sure whether to consider extreme athletes as real athletes. Shaun White became both a celebrity and a hero during the 2006 Olympics when he won gold in the men's halfpipe competition. His gold medal was widely covered by the media and pushed the sport into the mainstream, making it an accepted

sport. Both Shaun White and Tony Hawk have helped to pave the way for extreme sports, allowing society to view and accept them as "real sports" like football, basketball, and baseball. Part of White's appeal is that he is from what many consider a good family, with caring and supportive parents, brother, and sister, and he appears as the everyday American guy turned hero. White enjoys music and cars; when not on his board, he prefers hanging out with friends rather than celebrities, making him the guy next door that everyone wants to hang with. This has helped him push extreme sports into acceptance.

White is also responsible for not only creating tricks that others copy, but taking current tricks and tweaking them to make them his own. This has helped to push the sport forward and change the sport as it was known. According to Bud Keene, the U.S. Snowboard coach, Shaun White can match anyone but do it bigger and better; since the Vancouver Olympics, White has become an innovator in the sport. Red Bull, one of White's sponsors, built him a private and hidden 500-foot superpipe in Colorado so he could perfect his tricks. There he perfected his versions of the Front Double Cork 1080, a Cab Double Cork 1080, and created the McTwist 1080, which would later become a McTwist 1260. Shaun White sets the bar in snowboarding.

See also ESPY Awards; Hawk, Tony; Skateboarding; 2002 Olympic Games, Salt Lake City; X Games

Kelly Poniatowski

Suggested Resources
Alli Sports. www.allisports.com. Accessed July 26, 2011.
Doeden, M. *Shaun White.* Minneapolis: Lerner Publications, 2011.
Kennedy, M. *Today's Superstars: Shaun White.* Pleasantville, NY: Gareth Stevens, 2010.
Shaun White Website. www.shaunwhite.com. Accessed July 26, 2011.
X Games. ESPN.com. www.espn.go.com/xgames. Accessed July 26, 2011.

White, Willye Bertha (1939–2007)

Willye White was one of the world's top long jumpers spanning three decades and competed in five different Olympic Games (1956, 1960, 1964, 1968, 1972).

Born December 31, 1939, White was the oldest of five children born to Willie and Johnnie White. Her father was a disabled veteran of World War II. White was raised by her maternal grandmother.

White attended a segregated elementary school in Greenwood, Mississippi. By the age of 10, White was competing with her cousin on the high school track-and-field team. She was also a member of the high school basketball team. During her high school years, she ran a number of sprint events, including the 50-yard dash, 50-yard hurdles, and 75-yard dash. She also anchored the 300-yard relay and participated in the running long jump, which would become her best event. White's high school team competed against other African American high schools in the South.

White began attending Tennessee Agricultural & Industrial State University, also known as Tennessee State, during the summer of 1956. She was 16 years old and still in high school. Coach Ed Temple hosted a summer track-and-field program for high school girls and his women's team at Tennessee State. The girls' team and senior division team competed in the Amateur Athletic Union national championships every year. In August 1956, the national championships were held in Philadelphia, Pennsylvania, and White, along with Temple and her Tigerbelle teammates, won their first national AAU title. White jumped 18 feet 6 inches, setting a record in the girls' division and earning her a trip to the Olympic Trials in Washington, D.C. At the Trials, White finished second to Margaret Mathews with a jump over 19 feet and earned a position on the U.S. Olympic team. White, with several of her Tigerbelle teammates, competed in the 1956 Olympic Games in Melbourne, Australia. White continued her success in the event in Australia, setting a new American record in the long jump with a leap of 19 feet 11½ inches and winning a silver medal.

White returned as an Olympic medalist to the United States and her high school. She continued to attend Temple's summer program at Tennessee State. In the summer of 1957, White won the broad jump event in the girls' division, but was injured before the start of the senior division. The Tigerbelles won their second team championship title. The next summer, White jumped 20 feet 2½ inches in Warsaw, Poland, beating Margaret Mathews's new record by an inch

and one-half. White attended Temple's summer camp until 1959, when she decided to compete as a member of Mayor Daley's Youth Foundation team out of Chicago.

As a member of Mayor Daley's team, White competed in the 1960 Olympic Trials, making her second Olympic team with a winning jump of 20 feet 5 inches. She finished a disappointing 16th place in Rome. Though she continued to train for her track-and-field career, White became a nurse in Chicago after attending the Board of Education School of Nursing. Because she was no longer affiliated with Tennessee State, she no longer had the same kind of access to coaching, training, and financial support.

Despite White's poor showing at the 1960 Olympic Games, she returned to form the next year, winning the AAU national long jump title, running the first leg of the winning 440-yard relay, and finishing third in the 100-yard dash. Her two victories contributed to Mayor Daley's team beating Temple's Tigerbelles by 44 points for the team title. Two weeks later, White was selected to compete on the American team in a series of European meets including a dual meet in Moscow. At the U.S.-USSR meet, White set an American record in the long jump with a leap of 20 feet 11¾ inches, as well as running on the winning 400-meter relay, anchored by her former teammate at Tennessee State, Wilma Rudolph. White bested her American record a few days later in a meet held in Stuttgart, Germany, where she jumped 21 feet ¼ inch. In an amazing display of athletic excellence, White broke her newly established record at the next meet in London, jumping 21 feet 1¾ inches. Along with her great summer performances in the long jump, she continued to run on the winning relay teams and competed in the 100-meter dash at each meet, winning the race in London.

White continued her dominance in the long jump, winning the AAU indoor and outdoor titles in 1962, and claiming second in both events in 1963, losing both times to Tennessee State's Edith McGuire. White also participated on the American team at dual meets, including both the 1962 meet against the USSR in Palo Alto, California, and in Moscow in 1963.

During the Olympic year, 1964, White found herself in first place again at the AAU outdoor championships in Hanford, California, with a jump of 21 feet

7 inches. Two weeks later, White and her American teammates competed against the USSR in Los Angeles. White jumped a personal best of a wind-aided 21 feet 7¾ inches, finishing second in the event to the USSR's Tatanya Schelkanova. In early August, the Olympic Trials were held in Randalls Island, New York, where White won with a jump of 21 feet 4 inches, qualifying for her third Olympic Games. Though White did not leave Tokyo empty-handed (she won a silver medal as a member of the 400-meter relay team), she finished a disappointing 12th place in the long jump with a jump of 19 feet 1i inches.

In the years between 1964 and the 1968 Olympic Games in Mexico City, White continued to compete in the AAU indoor and outdoor championships, and on American teams in dual meets versus European teams as well as the USSR-U.S. dual meet. White won the AAU outdoor long jump title in 1965 and 1966. Another highlight of 1965 for White was winning the international "fair play" trophy.

Despite winning the AAU outdoor title in 1968, White did not win the event at the Olympic Trials, finishing second to Tennessee State's Martha Watson. At the 1968 Olympic Games, Watson and White finished one place apart, in 10th and 11th, respectively. She returned to win the AAU outdoor title in the long jump in 1969 and 1970, finishing second in 1971.

White's final year of competition was marked by her fifth trip to the Olympic Games. She won the AAU outdoor jump title in 1972, and then finished second in the event at the Olympic Trials, bested again by Martha Watson, competing for the Los Angeles Track Club. In Munich, White jumped 20 feet 7 inches, finishing in 11th place and marking the end of her Olympic competition. White, however, was not completely finished in track and field. She placed second in the long jump at the AAU outdoor championships in 1973 and 1974, finishing behind Watson both times.

Even as she continued to compete in track and field, White maintained employment in the city of Chicago. In addition to working as a nurse, she worked as a health administrator for the city, served as a recreational director, and offered sport programming for girls who resided in low-income housing. She started the Willye White Foundation in 1991 to help young girls develop self-esteem.

White remains the only American—male or female—to compete in five Olympic Games. She made the long jump finals in all five and won two silver medals, in the long jump in 1956 and as a member of the 400-meter relay in 1964. For 10 consecutive years beginning in 1958, White competed as a member of the American contingent in the U.S.-USSR dual meets. She was inducted into the Black Hall of Fame in 1975 and into the National Track and Field Hall of Fame in 1981, just two of the 11 halls of fame to which she was inducted. White died from pancreatic cancer on February 6, 2007. In 2008, the Chicago Park District named a park in the Rogers Park district in honor of White and her longtime link to the city.

See also 1968 Olympic Games, Mexico City; Rudolph, Wilma Glodean

Maureen Smith and Rita Liberti

Suggested Resources
Davis, Michael D. *Black American Women in Olympic Track and Field: A Complete Illustrated Reference*. Jefferson, NC: McFarland, 1992.
The History Makers Website. http://www.thehistorymakers.com/biography/biography.asp?bioindex=190. Accessed December 24, 2011.
Tricard, Louise Mead. *American Women's Track and Field, A History, 1895 through 1980*. Jefferson, NC: McFarland, 1996.

"Who's on First?"

"Who's on First?" was a routine developed and perfected by Abbott and Costello in the 1940s, first in their vaudeville act and later shown on their syndicated television show in the 1950s. The routine has been repeated innumerable times and the title has almost become a cultural icon itself.

William "Bud" Abbott (1895–1974) was the straight man of the duo. He was born in Asbury Park, New Jersey, to parents who both worked for Barnum and Bailey Circus. He was doing jobs in show business as early as 13 and toured on the vaudeville/burlesque circuit with his wife through the 1920s and early 1930s. It was here that he met Lou Costello (born Louis Cristello in 1906 in Paterson, New Jersey) and they teamed up beginning in 1936.

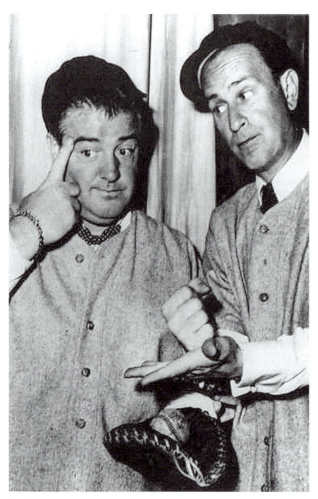

Bud Abbott, right, and his partner, Lou Costello, do their famous baseball sketch. (AP Photo.)

The "Who's on First?" routine became part of their act sometime in the late 1930s, but gained its most fame when they did an abbreviated version in the 1940 film, *One Night in the Tropics.* In 1945 a longer version was done in the film *The Naughty Nineties,* where Abbott is the owner of the St. Louis Wolves, and Costello's character wants to meet the team. The duo would perform the routine at times as part of their radio show on the NBC and, later, the ABC radio networks in the 1940s. In the 1950s the team had stints as guest hosts on a number of television variety shows before landing their own *Abbott and Costello Show* on syndicated television from 1952 to 1954. It remained on television in reruns for many years afterward. It was here that most viewers saw the "Who's on First?" routine, done at the end of the show in front of a bare curtain. Reading the patter of the skit is funny, but it was the verbalizations and physical actions of Costello that made the routine hilarious.

The skit involves Costello quizzing Abbott on the names of the players on his baseball team, which includes a first baseman named "Who," a second baseman named "What," and "I Don't Know" as the third baseman.

Sports announcers today refer to it briefly in the course of games that have many substitutions with a singular "who's on first?" quip. The routine can be found on YouTube. The routine plays on a continuous loop at the Baseball Hall of Fame and the two were honored with a plaque in that museum, one of the few honoring nonplayers.

In 1957, Abbott and Costello ended their partnership after years of acrimony. Costello died in 1959 and Abbott in 1978.

Murry R. Nelson

See also Baseball Hall of Fame

Suggested Resources

Anobile, Richard, ed. *Who's on First? Verbal and Visual Gems from the Films of Abbott and Costello.* New York: Darien House, 1972.

Mulholland, Jim. *The Abbott and Costello Book.* New York: Popular Library, 1975.

"Who's on First?" Baseball Almanac. http://www.baseball-almanac.com/humor4.shtml. Accessed March 12, 2012.

"Who's on First?" YouTube.com. http://www.youtube.com/watch?v=wfmvkO5x6Ng. Accessed March 12, 2012.

Williams, Doug (1955–)

The twin roles of race and football intertwined frequently in the life of Doug Williams, who was an accomplished collegiate and professional football player as well as a racial pioneer. Despite his many groundbreaking efforts on and off the field, Williams remains a cultural icon as the only African American quarterback to ever win a Super Bowl and because of a question leading up to that game that was never actually asked.

Williams was born August 9, 1955, in Zachary, Louisiana, the sixth of eight children in his family. His father, Robert, was wounded in the attack on Pearl Harbor and spent his postwar life as a construction worker and a nightclub manager. His mother was a cook at an area school. He was a star at Chaneyville High School, throwing for 1,180 yards and 22 touchdowns his senior year. In spite of this, only Southern University and Grambling University recruited him. Williams chose to play at Grambling State University under legendary coach Eddie Robinson.

As Grambling was one of the nation's historically black colleges and universities, Williams was able to continue his path as a quarterback unimpeded by the racism that permeated many college programs of that era. He led the Tigers to three straight Southwestern Athletic Conference championships and finished fourth in the voting for the 1977 Heisman Trophy.

The Tampa Bay Buccaneers used the 17th pick in the 1978 draft to select Williams, who helped lead the team to the playoffs in three of his first four years. Prior to Williams's arrival in the NFL, only 12 black men had played quarterback in the league, dating back to Fritz Pollard's work in the 1920s. After Williams's selection, no black quarterback would enter the league for another five years.

In 1979, Williams led the Buccaneers to the NFC championship game, marking the first time the 1976 expansion team had gone that far in the playoffs. Williams was drastically underpaid during his tenure in Tampa, making less money than every other starting quarterback in the league and less than at least 12 backups. After a protracted contract dispute with Tampa owner Hugh Culverhouse, Williams left for the Oklahoma expansion franchise of the upstart United States Football League. Had it not been for the entry of Vince Evans in the 1983 season, the NFL would have been without a single black quarterback that year.

During the 1984 and 1985 seasons, the Outlaws failed to have a winning record, while the Buccaneers slid to 2–14 and failed to make the playoffs for a 14-year span. When Evans followed Williams's path to the USFL, the NFL would have been without a black quarterback again, had it not been for the arrival of Warren Moon from the Canadian Football League.

After the USFL dissolved, Washington Redskins coach Joe Gibbs lobbied for the team to sign Williams, who served as a backup for starter Jay Schroeder. Due to several injuries Schroeder sustained, Williams substituted for him throughout the 1987 season. When the

Washington Redskins quarterback Doug Williams passing in Super Bowl XXII against the Denver Broncos in San Diego, January 31, 1988. (AP Photo/Elise Amendola.)

team made the playoffs, Williams was selected as the starting quarterback. He led the Redskins to a 42–10 route over the Denver Broncos in Super Bowl XXII, throwing for 340 yards and four touchdowns while earning the game's MVP award.

Despite his early success with Tampa Bay and his remarkable performance in the Super Bowl, Williams retired from the NFL in 1989 with a 42–45–1 record as a starter (including playoffs) and a quarterback rating of 69.4, both below-average numbers. The importance of Williams is often related to his position as a trailblazer and his decency in dealing with issues of race.

While race has always been a component of sport, several incidents brought the issue to a head in advance of the Super Bowl. In an April 6, 1987, interview, Los Angeles Dodgers general manager Al Campanis made comments about the intellectual inferiority of minorities. He stated that blacks "may not have some of the necessities to be, let's say, a field manager or perhaps a general manager." Later in that interview, he noted that blacks were poor swimmers because they "don't have the buoyancy" of whites.

Two weeks before the game on January 16, 1988, Jimmy "The Greek" Snyder, a football commentator on CBS's popular pregame show, gave an interview in which he made several comments regarding the natural superiority of black athletes. Snyder attributed this to the pre–Civil War era, in which a slave owner "would breed his big black to his big woman so that he could have . . . a big black kid."

While both men were subsequently fired as a result of the fallout from these incidents, their comments highlighted an undercurrent of sentiment among some Americans: Blacks were required to rely on innate physical gifts while learned skills and intelligence remained the realm of whites.

The two-week span between the end of the playoffs and Super Bowl XXII allowed a media frenzy to envelop Williams. He was to become the first African American quarterback to start a Super Bowl and that thread ran through the stories leading up to the game. According to an apocryphal story, a media representative asked Williams, "How long have you been a black quarterback?" Williams's answers were supposed to have ranged from "I've been a quarterback since high school; I've been black all my life" to "I don't think the football cares."

In years following the game, multiple journalists have debunked the myth regarding that question. Michael Wilbon of the *Washington Post*, however, had tracked the questions that involved race that were asked, which included the following:

- "Do you feel like Jackie Robinson?"
- "Would it be easier if you were the second black quarterback to play in the Super Bowl?"
- "Why haven't you used the first black quarterback as a personal forum for yourself?"
- "Are you upset about all the questions about your being the first black quarterback in the Super Bowl?"

According to all reports, Williams responded to these questions with grace and dignity, never resorting to ridicule or anger.

The following year, Williams was often injured and lost his starting job to Mark Rypien. Both men showed respect for each other and the situation, going as far as to wear "United We Stand" T-shirts. Williams wore an "I'm for Mark" shirt while Rypien wore an "I'm for Doug" shirt. Williams served as a backup for Rypien for one more year after that before retiring in 1989.

Williams continued his career through various jobs at multiple levels of football. He worked throughout his home state of Louisiana, coaching and serving as the athletic director at Pointe Coupee Central High School in 1991 and as the head coach at Northeast High School in 1993. He moved into college coaching in 1997 at Morehouse State University before moving back to his alma mater, Grambling, to replace the retiring Robinson. He spent five years (1998–2003) as the coach before departing. In 2011, he returned to take the head coaching job at Grambling once again.

He worked in various capacities in professional football, including stints as a scout for the Jacksonville Jaguars and the director of professional scouting for the Buccaneers. He also worked as the offensive coordinator for the Scottish Claymores of the World League of American Football and as the general manager of the Virginia Destroyers of the United Football League.

Williams and James "Shack" Harris created a foundation named after the pair that provides economic opportunities to disadvantaged youth via after-school programs, mentoring opportunities, and higher education assistance. Harris, who also attended Grambling and became the first black quarterback to lead a team to the playoffs, played for the Buffalo Bills, the Los Angeles Rams, and San Diego Chargers from 1969 to 1981. The foundation also was instrumental in creating the Black College Football Hall of Fame, which honors players and coaches from historically black colleges and universities who have made substantial contributions to the game. In 2010, the Black College Hall of Fame inducted its first set of members and in 2011 Williams was

Barrier and Start in the NFL. Kearney, NE: Cross Training, 2002.

Doug Williams Website. www.dougwilliams17.com. Accessed September 20, 2011.

Rhoden, William C. *Third and a Mile: From Fritz Pollard to Michael Vick: An Oral History of the Trials, Tears and Triumphs of the Black Quarterback*. Bristol, CT: ESPN, 2007.

Ross, Charles. *Outside the Lines: African Americans and the Integration of the National Football League*. New York: NYU Press, 2001.

Williams, Doug, and Bruce Hunter. *Quarterblack: Shattering the NFL Myth*. Los Angeles: Bonus Books, 1990.

"So, Doug, how long have you been a black quarterback?"

The person purported to have asked this question of Doug Williams prior to Super Bowl XXII was Butch John, who was a sportswriter for the Jackson (Mississippi) *Clarion-Ledger*.

According to recent media accounts, John was with a group of more than a dozen reporters who kept finding new ways to ask the Williams the same question. After it was clear Williams was tiring of "first black quarterback" questions, John asked a question meant to make a point. Williams had noted earlier in the year that his status as a black quarterback was never really an issue until he reached the NFL. With that in mind, John's actual question to Williams was: "Doug, it's obvious you've been a black quarterback all your life. When did it start to matter?"

Williams misheard the question and repeated what he thought he was asked: "What? How long have I been a black quarterback?" From this misquote, an item trickled into media reports of the day and the myth began to grow.

---

enshrined. In 2001, he was enshrined in the College Football Hall of Fame.

In the years after Williams retired from the NFL, black quarterbacks have become more common, although they still lack representation equal to that of the overall racial makeup of the league. In the first week of the 2011 NFL season, 6 of the 32 teams (or approximately 19 percent) started a black quarterback. A 2008 article by Judd Spicer of *City Pages* found the same percentage among starting quarterbacks in that year. Of the 766 players who started at any position in that examination, 75.8 percent were black. Of all the positions on the field, only placekickers (100 percent) and punters (97 percent) had a worse representation of black players.

Vincent F. Filak

See also Heisman Trophy; Pro Football Hall of Fame and Museum; Robinson, Eddie G.; Robinson, Jackie; Super Bowl

Suggested Resources

Briscoe, Marlin, and Bob Schaller. *The First Black Quarterback: Marlin Briscoe's Journey to Break the Color*

Williams, Serena (1981–)

Serena Jameka Williams ranks among the top American women tennis players of all time, with 29 Grand Slam titles and four Olympic gold medals. She held number one rankings with the Women's Tennis Association (WTA) at two different times in her professional tennis career. Beginning with her 1998 Grand Slam debut at the Australian Open, Serena demonstrated her power and dominance in the sport, and she earned additional attention among tennis fans and the general public through her extracurricular interests, including clothing design and acting. Serena once famously declared, "I am not a tennis superstar, I am a superstar."

Childhood

Born in 1981 in Saginaw, Michigan, Serena is the second of two daughters born to Richard Williams and Oracene Price, and she was Oracene's fifth daughter. As the youngest child in the family, Serena looked up to her older sisters and they doted on her. She admired her sister Venus the most and tried to emulate her. Serena's family noticed this and when she was a child, her parents insisted that Serena order her meal first when they went to a restaurant; otherwise, Serena would order whatever Venus was having.

As a child, Serena's favorite thing was to look at herself and to have others look at her. Her mother explained that one of Serena's hobbies was looking in the mirror, and her biography on the WTA website

Serena Williams of the U.S. returns a shot during a tennis match in Istanbul, Turkey, October 28, 2012. (AP Photo.)

once listed her favorite place to visit as the mirror in her house.

Serena, who made it a ritual to do her nails before a game, also believed that she must look good to play great tennis. She once explained to talk show host Oprah Winfrey, "I'm a firm believer, if you don't look good, you won't play well. And if you look bad, and your hair's messed up, or your clothes [are] wrinkled, if you don't look good, you don't play well. And that's why we play very well."

As the youngest sister, Serena always faced comparisons with her older sisters, particularly Venus. She was three inches shorter than Venus, but Serena more than made up for this difference in height with her powerful build and sheer strength. Even though she worked out regularly at the gym, Serena seemed to have a natural athleticism and build. Of course her athletic build and talent contributed enormously to her success on the tennis court.

Serena began to play tennis when she was four years old. She entered 49 tournaments by age 10 and won all but 3 of them. When the Williams family moved to Florida in 1991, Serena attended Rick Macci's prestigious tennis academy in DelRay, Florida, for four years with her sister Venus. Under Macci's tutelage, the girls played tennis six hours a day, six days a week. When they stopped attending the academy, Richard Williams became their primary coach and the sisters spent less time on the court. Richard had a tremendous influence on both of his daughters' professional tennis careers and other pursuits. He insisted that they set aside time for their education and other interests, and he would not allow them to focus only on tennis.

Tennis

Serena began to play tennis professionally when she was 14 years old. At her first pro event, the Bell Challenge in Quebec, she was unseeded and largely unnoticed and lost in less than an hour of play. In 1996, Serena did not play any tournaments. Then, after failing to qualify for several tournaments in early 1997, Serena played in a tournament in Russia, but was defeated in an early round. After this, she seemed to gain some momentum and entered the Ameritech Cup in Chicago. Although she was ranked 304th by the WTA, she defeated Mary Pierce and Monica Seles before falling in the semifinal against Lindsay Davenport. She was the lowest ranked player ever to defeat two top 10 players in the same tournament. After the Chicago victories, Serena rose quickly through the ranks of women's tennis, finishing her first full season at 99th.

Serena became known for her powerful, aggressive baseline game and consistent serves that some felt were the best in the game. These traits quickly propelled her to the top of women's tennis. Serena finished 1999, her second full year on the tour, ranked fourth in the world. One highlight among her many victories was winning the U.S. Open, earning the distinction of being the second African American woman to win a Grand Slam singles title (Althea Gibson was the first). She seemed unstoppable when teamed in doubles tournaments with her sister Venus, winning Olympic gold in Sydney. By 2001, she had earned the WTA number one singles ranking, a title she held for 57 weeks. Only Steffi Graf, Martina Navratilova, Chris Evert, Martina Hingis, and Monica Seles have held this ranking for longer.

Serena claimed her most memorable experience was winning Wimbledon in 2002, which followed a victory at the French Open, and preceded her wins at the 2002 U.S. Open and 2003 Australia Open. Her victory in Australia completed the "Serena Slam" as she won four consecutive Grand Slam tournaments in one year's time, three in the same calendar year (2002). Only five other women, including Margaret Court, Maureen Connolly, Steffi Graf, and Monica Seles, had won three Grand Slams in the same year. To win each of these tournaments, Serena faced and defeated Venus in the finals. Although she didn't play the Australian Open in 2002, Serena returned in 2003 to win the event, defeating Venus in three sets (7–6, 3–6, 6–4). She was only the sixth woman to complete a career Grand Slam, and the fifth woman to hold all Grand Slam titles simultaneously.

In 2003, Serena also captured the singles titles at Open Gaz de France, the Sony Ericsson Open, and Wimbledon. Then she spent the remainder of the year and the early part of 2004 recovering from a knee surgery. Some people began to wonder if Serena was losing interest in the sport, but she reached the final at Wimbledon, losing to Maria Sharpova, and the final at the JP Morgan Chase Open in Los Angeles, where she lost to Lindsay Davenport. She competed in the 2004 U.S. Open, but lost in the quarterfinal round. Serena finished the year ranked seventh, even though she did not win a single Grand Slam tournament.

Serena seemed to begin 2005 strong when she won the Australian Open, but she did not reach the finals for any of the following five tournaments she played. She seemed to struggle with injuries and illness throughout the year, suffering particularly with a recurring knee injury. By April 2006, Serena was no longer among the top 100 on the WTA rankings, her lowest position since 1997.

Serena returned to the courts with what seemed like renewed commitment to the game in 2007, and she was able to reach several quarterfinal and semifinal matches, even though she did not win a major tournament. In 2008, she won a Tier II tournament in Bangalore, India, followed by a Tier I singles title in the Sony Ericsson Open and a Tier I singles title at the Family Circle Cup. Serena met Venus at the finals of Wimbledon, but lost in straight sets before teaming with her sister to win the doubles title at the same event. When she defeated Jelena Jankovic to win the U.S. Open, Serena finally returned to her world number one ranking.

Serena continued to play well in 2009, winning the Australian Open and Wimbledon. Serena lost at the U.S. Open, however, amid a controversial call about a foot fault that resulted in a shouting match with the chair umpire when she was defending a match point. She finished the year ranked number one and was named Female Athlete of the Year by the Associated Press.

Serena began 2010 with a singles title at the Australian Open and a doubles title with Venus. Then she was forced to withdraw from several tournaments due to a leg injury, but after struggling through some smaller tournaments, she returned to win Wimbledon. Shortly after this, Serena stepped on broken glass when leaving a bar in Munich, Germany. The injury turned out to require surgery and forced Serena off the court for several months. During this time she also suffered a hematoma and a pulmonary embolism.

Because of these health problems, Serena did not return to a WTA tournament for an entire year. She lost in the fourth round at Wimbledon to Marion Bartoli, whom she defeated at Stanford to win the singles title in the next major tournament. She followed with a singles victory at the Rogers Cup. She then faced Samantha Stosur in the finals at the U.S. Open, but she lost 6–2, 6–3 in a set that included Serena yelling at the lineswoman and verbally abusing her when she disagreed with a call. It was Serena's last tournament of the year, due to unspecified health problems.

In 2012, however, Serena won her fifth Wimbledon title and 14th singles title in Grand Slam events, defeating Agnieszka Radwanska of Poland, 6–1, 5–7, 6–2; she also broke her own Wimbledon record with 102 aces in the tourney. Serena then joined her sister Venus to win the Wimbledon doubles title, 7–5, 6–4. Serena and her sister repeated these titles on the same court at the 2012 London Olympics, Serena as singles champion and the two as women's doubles champions.

Clothing Lines and Business Ventures

Serena has been known for her fashion on and off the court, and she designed many of the styles she wore to play tennis. Sometimes her outfits brought public attention and scrutiny, from the braided hair and beads she wore as a youth to the black, skin-tight Puma catsuit she sported at the U.S. Open in 2002.

Just prior to the 2004 U.S. Open tournament, Serena released a new line of tennis outfits she designed for Nike in a deal worth $40 million. She debuted the line at the Open, appearing for her first match clad in a denim tennis skirt, a black studded tank top, a matching

denim jacket with a rhinestone-studded "SERENA" on the back, and black knee-high "boots" (a Lycra legging zipped off her legs when she was ready to play). She described her choice of clothing as her "rebel" look, explaining that she would prefer to look good rather than to be comfortable. Major news media from the *New York Times* and *Washington Post* to the *Xinhua News Agency* in China reported extensively on this outfit, and the others that followed, including a micro-mini skirt she wore during her second round. After winning her second round at the U.S. Open in 2004, Serena explained to a reporter, "I always considered myself as an entertainer. I remember always thinking of myself as a broader picture as opposed to just your normal athlete. I don't think I've ever been your normal athlete. I've always had something different going on in my life." In response to a question about the controversy her clothing choices evoked, Serena replied, "I just think I represent all females out there who believe in themselves. It doesn't matter what you look like, it's all about having confidence in you. That's not necessarily having to wear some short shorts or extremely small top, it's just about believing in yourself. I think, like, I represent that woman that believes in herself and has confidence in herself and to be unique."

That same year, she began her own fashion line called Aneres, which is her name spelled backward, and in 2009 she began a signature jewelry and handbag collection for the Home Shopping Network. She also was involved with a nail collection for Hair Tech. Serena and Venus became part owners of the Miami Dolphins football team in 2009. They were the first African American women to have ownership in an NFL franchise.

Serena is a published author. She published an autobiography, *On the Line*, in 2009, which she dedicated to her father. She also coauthored several books with Venus about playing tennis. These were intended for young people.

Acting and Modeling

When she was 20 years old, Serena began to dabble in professional acting. Her first experience was in 2001 when she made a guest appearance with Venus as a voice on the animated television show *The Simpsons*. She signed with the William Morris casting agency and began to do more television roles than film because of the time commitment involved in film roles. Television seemed to be easier to fit around her tennis schedule.

In 2001, Serena made a cameo appearance in Martin Lawrence's movie *Black Knight*. After this, Serena appeared as a schoolteacher in *My Wife and Kids*, which stars Damon Wayans, on ABC-TV in October 2002. On October 22, 2003, Serena appeared in a dramatic role on a Showtime episode of *Street Time*. Then during the summer of 2003, Serena filmed a part for the upcoming movie *Beauty Shop* starring Queen Latifah (a spinoff of the box-office hit *Barbershop* that starred Ice Cube).

Serena has posed for the swimsuit issue of *Sports Illustrated* magazine, and she has appeared as a guest on MTV's *Punk'd*, *ER*, *Law and Order: Special Victims Unit*, and in the rapper Common's music video "I Want You."

Philanthropy

Serena is an active philanthropist. She participated in a number of clinics to help teach urban youth how to play tennis, and she made numerous appearances at schools and for charitable and community organizations, particularly those that target programs for at-risk youth. There is a Venus and Serena Williams Tutorial/Tennis Academy in Los Angeles to help inner-city kids have academic and tennis resources that would allow them to attend the college of their choice. The academy includes after-school programs, summer camps, mentorship programs, and more.

Serena served as an advocate for ovarian and breast cancer research and the homeless. She was also a spokesperson for the American Library Association's Celebrity READ campaign. This campaign conveyed a simple message, "read," through posters and bookmarks that showed celebrities with books.

She helped to raise money for the victims of the 2010 earthquake in Haiti and has been actively involved with UNICEF. In 2006, she traveled to Ghana with UNICEF to assist with a major health campaign. She helped to immunize children and distribute free mosquito bed nets. In 2008, Serena helped to support the construction of the Serena Wiliams Secondary School in Matooni, Kenya. In 2011, Serena was appointed UNICEF Goodwill Ambassador to assist with the Schools for Africa and Schools for Asia programs.

In June 2011, *Time* magazine named Serena among the "30 Legends of Women's Tennis: Past, Present and Future." Whatever her future in the sport may hold, she clearly has made her mark and will remain among the legends of women's tennis.

Jacqueline Edmondson

See also Evert, Chris; Gibson, Althea; Navratilova, Martina; Nike, Inc.; *Sports Illustrated*; Williams, Venus

Suggested Resources

Edmondson, Jacqueline. *Venus and Serena Williams: A Biography*. Westport, CT: Greenwood Press, 2005.

"Serena Williams." ESPN.com. http://espn.go.com/tennis/player/_/id/394/serena-williams. Accessed October 16, 2011.

Serena Williams Website. http://www.serenawilliams.com. Accessed October 15, 2011.

Venus and Serena Williams Tutorial/Tennis Academy. http://www.venusserenatennisacademy.org/. Accessed October 16, 2011.

Williams, Serena. *On the Line*. New York: Grand Central, 2009.

Williams, Venus, and Serena Williams. *How to Play Tennis*. New York: DK Publishers, 2004.

Williams, Ted (1918–2002)

Ted Williams was a Major League Baseball player for the Boston Red Sox from 1939 to 1960, one of the few players in history to play in four different decades. He was called by many as the greatest hitter that ever played the game.

Theodore Samuel Williams was born in San Diego on August 30, 1918, named Teddy after President Roosevelt and Samuel after his father. He later changed his name to Theodore. Williams was raised in San Diego and learned to play baseball from his mother's brother, a former semipro player and manager. He attended Herbert Hoover High School where he was the star of the team, as both a pitcher and outfielder. Ted was 6'3" and weighed under 150 pounds and his slender size scared off some scouts. Nevertheless, many major league teams pursued him, but his mother refused to cosign a contract for the 17-year-old unless he received at least $1,000, which no team would offer; instead she encouraged him to stay closer to home and he agreed to a contract with the San Diego Padres, a team in the independent AAA Pacific Coast League, who had moved from Hollywood the previous year and had played as the Hollywood Stars. Williams signed with the Padres in June 1936, having used up his high school eligibility, although he did not graduate until February 1937, being a "splitter" (i.e., having enrolled in mid-year as a youngster, when that was a common school practice).

The Padres had many talented future major leaguers on their squad, such as Bobby Doerr and Vince DiMaggio, as well as former big leaguers hoping to stay in the game, so Williams didn't play that much as a 17-year-old. He hit just .271 in 42 games, with no homers, but he was playing at a level highly unusual for one so young. He was expected to do more for the club in 1937 and he did not disappoint, hitting .291 with 23 homers and 98 runs batted in. The Padres, after finishing third in the league, surprised both of their playoff opponents to win the Pacific Coast League title.

Both the Boston Red Sox and the Boston Braves were bidding to purchase Williams from the Padres and the former obtained him for two mediocre players and $35,000. Although initially unimpressed with being signed by a middle-of-the road team (the Red Sox had finished fourth, sixth, and fifth in the previous three years), he changed his tune after meeting Eddie Collins, the Red Sox general manager and Hall of Famer who had played against Babe Ruth, Lou Gehrig, and Lefty Grove. Williams was impressed by Collins's courtly manner, his experience and knowledge.

For a variety of reasons, Williams reported late to spring training in 1938, then wasn't able to crack the starting lineup and was sent instead to the Red Sox affiliate in Minneapolis to begin the 1938 season. There he battered American Association pitching, leading the league in batting average (.366), home runs (43), and runs batted in (142). Just 20 years old, Williams would be starting for the Red Sox in 1939.

Williams adjusted to major league pitching almost immediately, hitting .327 with 31 homers, a league-leading 145 runs batted in, and 344 total bases. Williams was an immediate hit with the Boston press (who dubbed him "the Splendid Splinter") and fans. He was fourth in Most Valuable Player voting and surely would have been Rookie of the Year, had such an award been in place then (it began in 1940 as one award and expanded to one per league in 1947). The Red Sox went from also-rans to a solid second-place team, although the Yankees won the pennant by 17 games.

The next year Williams and the Red Sox closed the gap on the Yankees to six games, but New York had finished in third behind the Tigers and the Indians, relegating Boston to fourth place. Ted dropped a bit in power numbers to 23 homers and 113 runs batted in, but improved his average to .344 and he led the league in runs scored with 134. That year he was also switched from right to left field, where he would play for the rest of his career. A new center fielder, Dom DiMaggio (Joe's brother), was fast and smart, making up for any slowness of foot that Ted might have. Williams was criticized by some for not having more power that year and he became angry with the local press and fans, leading to frosty relations that persisted for much of his career.

Williams reported late to spring training, which may have bred some resentment toward him on the part of fans and players, but that was forgotten once the season started. Williams had a bone chip in his ankle and didn't play regularly until the end of April, then had a 23-game hitting streak; he hit .436 for the month of May and .477 from May 17 to June 17.

Meanwhile Joe DiMaggio was dominating the sports pages with a 56-game hitting streak from May 15 until July 17 when the Indians held him hitless. He hit .409 during that streak, although Williams, during the same period, hit .412. By the All-Star break, Ted was hitting .405 for the season with 62 runs batted in, despite missing a dozen games. The Red Sox were solidly in second, but the Yankees again ran away with the pennant by 17 games, winning 101 to the Red Sox's 84. DiMaggio ended the season with a .357 average, leading the league with 125 runs batted in and 348 total bases. Williams finished with a .406 average after going six for eight on the final day of the season in a double header in Philadelphia. He also led the league in home runs (37), runs scored (135), walks (147), and

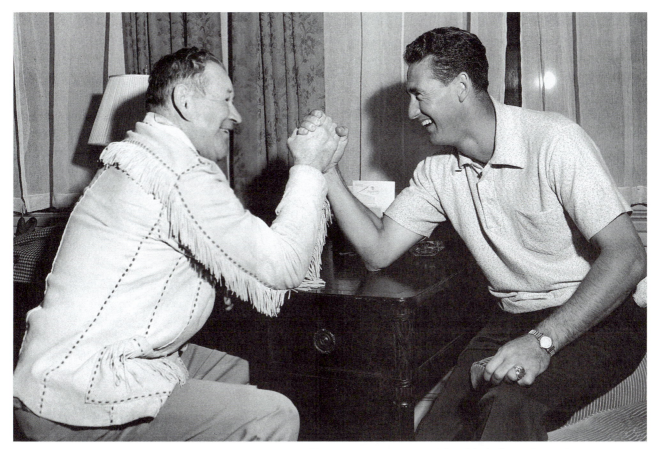

Ted Williams, right, tries his arm leverage against Jim Thorpe as they meet at New York City's Savoy Plaza Hotel, on February 1, 1952. (AP Photo/Harry Harris.)

slugging (.735), but finished second to DiMaggio in MVP balloting.

Hitting .400 was impressive, but no one realized that it would be the last time it was done since it had been done eight times since 1920, the last being 1930, when Bill Terry had hit .401 for the New York Giants. Today it is shocking that Williams was not voted MVP, but readers today have the advantage of historical perspective, plus the voters for the award were the baseball writers, whose relationship with Ted was already frayed. Williams, however, was not upset over DiMaggio's award, seeing his record hitting streak, in the midst of a hot summer, unbelievable.

After the Japanese bombing of Pearl Harbor and the entrance of the United States into World War II, there was a rush by many men to join the war effort, but Williams initially had his draft classification as exempt because he was the sole support of his mother. Williams was criticized by many fans and media people for this and, although he felt justified, decided to enlist in the naval aviation program in May 1942, but did not have to report for duty until the fall, allowing him to complete the 1942 season. He led the league in almost every hitting category—batting average, home runs, runs batted in, runs scored, slugging, walks, and total bases—but again finished second in MVP voting, this time to Joe Gordon of the pennant-winning Yankees, who were their top hitter (.322), but was third on the team in RBIs. The vote was very close, but the writers who disliked Williams carried the day.

In November Williams reported for active duty and underwent extensive training in Massachusetts, North Carolina, Indiana, and Florida before being shipped to San Francisco and Hawaii. He was there when the war ended in August 1946, having not seen actual combat, but having missed three full seasons of baseball.

Williams returned to the Red Sox for the 1946 season; during his three years the team had finished seventh, fourth, and seventh, but the return of so many servicemen made the team and the league a much different entity. The Red Sox came out of spring training going 41–9 and easily led the league by the All-Star break, when Williams was hitting .347 with 23 home runs. Williams finished the year at .342 and led the league in runs scored, walks, and total bases, while also hitting 38 home runs and 123 runs batted in. The Red Sox won the pennant by nine games (their first title since 1918) and Williams was voted Most Valuable Player easily. In the World Series against the St. Louis Cardinals and Stan Musial, both future Hall of Famers were disappointments. Williams had five singles and hit .200 with one run batted in; Musial hit .222 with four doubles and a triple among his six hits. In addition, the Cardinals were victorious in seven games when Enos Slaughter raced home with the winning run from first base on a double to left center. Williams was distraught, but he would have been even more devastated if he had known that he would never play in another World Series.

In 1947 Williams won another Triple Crown by hitting .343 with 32 homers and 114 runs batted in, as well as leading the league in walks, runs scored, slugging, and total bases. The Red Sox slipped to third as the Yankees returned to the top. Joe DiMaggio, with 20 homers, 97 RBIs, and a .315 average was MVP, a result of anti-Williams feeling and Joe's iconic status. The next year Williams would lead the league in hitting with .369, as well as slugging, walks, and doubles, but would finish third in MVP voting to Lou Boudreau, whose Indians won the pennant, and DiMaggio. The Red Sox finished in second after a one-game playoff loss to Cleveland.

The 1949 season was almost as frustrating for the Sox as they lost by one game to the Yankees, after the New Yorkers beat the Bosox in the final two games of the season. Williams led the league in home runs, runs batted in, slugging, walks, runs scored, and total bases, and his .343 batting average was the same as George Kell's until it was carried out to four places with Kell at .3429 and Williams at .3427. By that much Ted was deprived of another Triple Crown, although he did win the Most Valuable Player award for the second and final time.

The next season was a great disappointment for Ted and the Red Sox as he broke his left elbow in the All-Star Game and was forced to miss more than 50 games, finishing with 97 runs batted in, despite playing only 89 games. The Red Sox finished third, but Ted's injury lasted a lifetime as he claimed he was never able to get more than 90 percent extension of that arm ever again. Nevertheless Williams returned in 1951 in what was his last really full season of play to hit .318 with 30 homers and 126 runs batted in and led the league in walks, total bases, and slugging. The Red Sox finished in third once again, eleven games behind the Yankees.

In June 1950, North Korea invaded South Korea and the Korean conflict began. Foreign troops supported both sides with the United States supplying most of the South Korean support. In January 1952, Williams was told that his reserve unit would be recalled into active duty. He started the season with the Red Sox, but was only able to play six games before being called up. He would return for just 37 games of the 1953 season, when he batted .407 with 13 homers, 34 runs batted in, and a .901 slugging percentage for just 91 at-bats.

During the war Williams was now able to use his combat flying skills, which he had perfected in training for World War II. He flew a total of 39 combat missions and survived one crash landing. He contracted pneumonia and was sent to Hawaii to recover, then discharged in mid-season of 1953, making his first appearance in a game on August 6. The Red Sox finished in fourth, but Ted's return at age 34 buoyed their hopes for the next year.

The next season was filled with difficulties for Williams; his wife filed for divorce, he broke his collarbone in spring training, and the Red Sox won only 69 games, finishing deep in fourth, 42 games out of first. Ted finished with a respectable season, hitting .345 with 29 homers and 89 runs batted in, while leading the league in walks and slugging, despite playing only 117 games. Williams was exhausted at season's end and intimated that he was going to retire at age 36.

When spring training opened in 1955, Williams was not there and the speculation regarding retirement was rampant, but no rumors were addressed by Williams or the team. Finally, the news broke that his divorce had reached a settlement, which had included examinations of his other business enterprises. With the settlement, Williams called the Red Sox and said he was returning, which he did in mid-May. Despite his late start, Williams hit .356 and had 28 homers and 83 RBIs in 98 games. He managed to place fourth in the MVP voting (behind Yogi Berra, Al Kaline, and Al Smith) for the fourth-place Bosox, who did finish at a respectable 84–70.

At the age of 37 (he turned 38 near the end of the season) Williams played in 136 games, hit .345, and drove in 82 runs, while leading the league in on-base percentage. The Red Sox, in the midst of what would be another failed youth movement, finished in fourth with the same record as the previous year. The next season did not seem to bode better results, although Williams had an amazing year. He played 132 games, had 38 homers, and led the league in batting with an incredible .388 mark, the best by anyone since his .406 campaign of 1941. He also led the league in on-base percentage and slugging, impressive enough to gain him second place in MVP voting to Mickey Mantle of the pennant-winning Yankees. The *Sporting News* disagreed, naming Williams its Player of the Year.

Williams came back for another year in 1958 at the age of 39 as defending batting champion and proceeded to uphold his title, hitting 60 points less (.328), but still leading the league, and also doing so in on-base percentage. He had 26 homers and 85 RBIs in just 129 games. The Red Sox were again a distant third and speculation was that Williams would retire. Instead, Williams returned, but his numbers went into a sharp decline. He played in 103 games, but managed only 10 homers and hit .254. In early spring training Williams had wrenched his neck swinging the bat before warming up and the problem persisted throughout the year. He was on the disabled list until May 12, was benched at times, and demanded a pay cut at the end of the season. Williams was angry and embarrassed and was not about to retire after such a horrid season.

So, at age 41, Williams began the 1960 season, the fourth decade in which he had played. He played in 10 more games than in 1959 and was as good as he could be for a player over 40. The Red Sox were terrible, finishing seventh, but Ted led the team in home runs with 29 and was second to Pete Runnels in batting, .320 to .316, which was also the league order, although Williams didn't have enough plate

---

Williams's Last At-Bat

John Updike, one of the most famous men of American letters, wrote a piece for *The New Yorker* that both immortalized Ted's last at-bat, but also indicated how his persona extended beyond baseball to a kind of Greek drama. Updike wrote of Ted's demeanor, the fans' reaction, the overall atmosphere and the glory of September 28, 1960. After walking in the first, then flying out twice, Williams took a 1–2 pitch to right field for a home run. He circled the bases to a standing ovation, but would not tip his cap to the cheering throng, then refused to come out of the dugout for a bow, despite the entreaties of teammates, umpires, and team administrators. In Updike's famous words, "Gods do not answer letters." In 2010 the article was reprinted in book form.

---

appearances to qualify for the title. Williams's 29 home runs pushed him past 500, making him just the fourth player in history to reach that standard (now there are 25). Despite the good year, Williams was beset by nagging injuries, the result of his age, and it was becoming clear to him that he would retire at the end of the season.

Williams decided to end his career in Fenway Park and not make the last three-game road trip to New York that ended the season. He wanted to keep his intentions secret, but word leaked out and there were a number of dignitaries at the game. The Red Sox honored Williams by retiring his uniform number in a brief ceremony on a cold dark day, before a sparse crowd of just over 10,000. Williams homered in his final at-bat in the majors, bringing the crowd to its feet for a standing ovation, as the Red Sox won, 5–4.

In retirement Williams remained active, continuing to hunt and fish, his favorite activities; for a time he held a record for the biggest black marlin ever caught. He also continued to be deeply involved with the Jimmy Fund, a Boston-based fund at the Dana-Farber Cancer Institute focusing on young people with cancer and also supported by the Red Sox.

In 1966 Williams was elected to the Baseball Hall of Fame on the first ballot with just over 93 percent of the votes. It was hard to understand how someone could not vote for Williams, whose lifetime batting average of .344 was seventh all-time. In 1969 he agreed to manage the Washington Senators, a perpetual also-ran. During his tenure the team moved from Washington to Texas and became the Rangers. In his first year he took the team from 30 games below .500 to 10 games above, and he was named American League Manager of the Year. In 1970, they fell back to 70–92, then were even worse in 1971. The first year in Texas the Rangers went 54–100 and Williams resigned with one year left on his contract.

Williams had a series of health problems that plagued him in the 1990s and his condition continued to deteriorate. On July 2, 2002, Williams died of cardiac arrest. Rather than having a peaceful repose, his body was fought over by his children, one of whom said his last will and testament expressed a desire to be cremated, while two others said that he wanted to be cryonically frozen to preserve his DNA, in the event that he could be "revived" if scientists found a way to do so in the future. The fight played out in the media and was the subject of comedy routines on late-night shows like those of Letterman and Leno. Eventually, the courts decided for the latter "solution" when his daughter dropped her fight because of financial problems. Part of Ted Williams's body is now frozen in a facility in Arizona, an ignominious end for such a fabulous ballplayer.

Murry R. Nelson

See also Berra, Yogi: Boston Red Sox; DiMaggio, Joe; Fenway Park; Mantle, Mickey; Musial, Stan "The Man"; New York Yankees; *The Sporting News*; World Series

Suggested Resources

Markusen, Bruce. *Ted Williams, A Biography*. Westport, CT: Greenwood Press, 2004.

Montville, Leigh. *Ted Williams: The Biography of an American Hero*. New York: Doubleday, 2004.

Seidel, Michael. *Ted Williams: A Baseball Life*. Chicago: Contemporary Books, 1991.

"Ted Williams." Baseball-Reference.com. http://www.baseball-reference.com/players/w/willite01.shtml. Accessed March 20, 2012.

Ted Williams Website. http://www.tedwilliams.com/. Accessed March 20, 2012.

Updike, John. *Hub Fans Bid Kid Adieu: John Updike on Ted Williams*. New York: Library of America, 2010.

Williams, Ted, with David Pietrusza. *Teddy Ballgame: My Life in Pictures*. Toronto: Sport Classic Books, 2002.

Williams, Venus (1980–)

Venus Williams was one of the most notable women in American sport at the turn of the 21st century. When she first competed on the Women's Tennis Association (WTA) tour in 1994, few could have predicted the tremendous influence she would have on the sport and American culture. Venus broke and set records for fastest serves, won three gold medals in the Olympics, and was the first African American woman to hold the WTA number one ranking in more than 50 years. Beyond her personal accomplishments, Venus helped to fight for and win equal pay for men and women in Grand Slam tournaments. Across her professional tennis career, Venus held record endorsement deals, completed art school, started her own business and clothing line, and enjoyed tremendous celebrity as she forged new ground in the sport with great power, beauty, and determination.

Childhood

Venus Ebony Starr Williams was born in Lynwood, California, in 1980, the fourth of her mother Oracene Price's five daughters, and the first child born to Oracene and Richard Williams. Venus spent her early years in the ghetto in Compton, California, always keeping a protective eye on her younger sister, Serena (1981–). As a young child, Venus always seemed to have a serious disposition, and she often appeared to be lost in thought. She was an avid reader and always loved to learn new things. In spite of this serious side, Venus enjoyed a good laugh and was always ready to share a joke with her sisters and her mother.

Venus began to play tennis as a very young child when her father took her to the tennis courts in Compton, California. The four-year-old loved tennis as soon as she held a racquet in her hand. She returned volley after volley to her dad as he served hundreds of balls to her from a grocery store cart, and she would often cry when it was time to go home. At one point, Richard even took her tennis racquet from her for a year because he feared she loved the game too much. This began the trend of on-again, off-again time with tennis. Tennis would not be the only thing in her life. Richard wanted Venus to have other interests, to be

Venus Williams holds the trophy after winning the Mexico Tennis Open in Acapulco, Mexico, February 28, 2009. (AP Photo/Alexandre Meneghini.)

well-balanced, and, most importantly, to have a good education. In fact, there were times when Venus would not be permitted to practice, even after she was a well-known champion, if Richard felt her grades in school were not as high as they should be.

When Venus was 10 years old, her family moved to West Palm Beach, Florida, so that she and Serena could attend Rick Macci's tennis academy. Macci helped Richard to coach the girls for approximately five years, and then Richard resumed as the sole coach for his daughters.

At 15 years of age, Venus turned pro, making her professional debut by winning her first match against Shaun Stafford at the Bank of the West Classic in Oakland, California. In 1995, the WTA rules were changing in light of criticism about athletes' age and the amount of play they could engage in. In part, this had to do with controversy surrounding young players, including Tracy Austin, a tennis prodigy plagued

by injury at an early age, and, more recently, Jennifer Capriati, who turned pro at age 13. Capriati was the youngest player to reach a professional tennis final, but she left the tennis scene amid much personal turmoil. Beginning in 1995, players were required to be 16 years of age to turn professional, and they were only permitted to play a limited number of tournaments until they were 18 years old. In 1994, Venus needed to decide whether to turn pro right away before the WTA change took effect, or to wait until she was older to play on the pro circuit.

Venus graduated from the Driftwood Academy in Lake Park, Florida, in 1997, two years after entering the professional tennis circuit, bringing to a close the first phase of her education, which included a mixture of public, private, and home-schooling experiences. After her high school graduation, Venus enrolled at the Art Institute in Florida, and then went on to earn a certificate in interior design from Palm Beach Community

College. To complete the requirements for this certificate, Venus took courses that taught her about color, design, the history of interior design, and more. She did the majority of her coursework during the 11-week fall semester at the school, which ran between October and December each year, and through online study. The school did not make special exceptions for Venus, so if she was playing tennis, she needed to arrange it around her school schedule and online course work. After completing her certificate, she continued her education by studying for a bachelor's degree in interior design.

Early Major Victories

Venus Williams's win over Lindsay Davenport in straight sets (6–3, 7–6) at Wimbledon in the year 2000 was the realization of her childhood dream. When she was 12 years old, Venus watched as Zina Garrison made the finals, the first African American woman to play a Grand Slam final since Althea Gibson's historic 1957 championship. A Williams would hold Wimbledon victories for the next four years. Venus won in 2000 and 2001, followed by Serena, who defeated her sister for the title in 2002 and 2003. Overall, Venus won five Wimbledon titles, which placed her eighth on the all-time list (a position that is tied with two other women).

Venus's victory at the 2000 Wimbledon championship began a 35-match winning streak that included wins in the finals against Lindsay Davenport at a tournament in Stanford, California, and Monica Seles at tournaments in San Diego, California, and New Haven, Connecticut. Venus then competed and became the champion at the U.S. Open, defeating Martina Hingis (ranked number one at the time) and Davenport (ranked number two at the time). Venus followed this by winning gold in the singles of the Olympics in Sydney, Australia, and gold in the doubles where she competed with her sister Serena. Venus finished the year ranked third by the WTA.

Venus continued to play quite well into 2001, but faced public controversy when she was accused of defaulting a semifinals match to her sister Serena in a tournament at Indian Wells, California. Venus was suffering from tendinitis in her knee, but the fans assumed she did not want to compete against her sister.

Venus was booed as she sat with her father in the stands to watch the tournament finals, and Serena was booed during the final and trophy presentation. Neither Venus nor Serena competed in this tournament again.

Williams won Wimbledon for the second time in 2001. She successfully defended her title at the U.S. Open, where she met her sister Serena for the first time in a Grand Slam final. Venus was only the sixth woman in the history of tennis to win these two tournaments in two consecutive years.

By February 2002, Williams was ranked number one in the world. She was the first African American woman to earn this ranking. Venus met Serena in the final of the French Open, but this time the younger sister won. Serena then defeated Venus at Wimbledon and the U.S. Open. Venus finished the year ranked number two, and Serena ended the year with the number one ranking.

The pattern of Serena defeating Venus in major tournaments continued in 2003. Venus met her sister in the finals at the Australian Open and Wimbledon. Venus struggled with an abdominal injury and personal losses after her older sister Yetunde Price was murdered in September. She finished the year ranked number 11.

Injuries and Setbacks

Venus's play was inconsistent at best throughout 2004 and by the time of the Wimbledon tournament, many wondered if her professional tennis career was over. Venus, who still ranked eighth in the WTA when Wimbledon began, had not won a Grand Slam in three years. Injuries, including a torn abdominal muscle and hurt ankle, contributed to her absence from the tennis court at major events. Venus was bounced out in Wimbledon's second round by Karolina Sprem (ranked 30th), her earliest exit from a Grand Slam tournament since her first-round loss at the French Open in 2001. The Wimbledon fall came amid controversy concerning an umpire's miscall that awarded a point to Sprem, yet Venus recognized that this was not the sole cause of her loss. Venus accepted her defeat with great composure and sportsmanship, acknowledging that Sprem played well and deserved to win. Venus's ranking plummeted from 8th to 15th.

In 2005, Venus's play remained inconsistent until she reached the grass courts at Wimbledon. After defeating Mary Pierce in the quarterfinals and Maria Sharpova in the semifinals, Venus beat Lindsay Davenport to win her third Wimbledon singles title and her first Grand Slam victory since 2001. Venus did not have any other major victories that year. Venus suffered a wrist injury that interfered with her playing throughout most of 2006.

Venus seemed to be on a comeback in 2007 when she won her first singles title since 2005 at the Cellular South Cup in Memphis, Tennessee. At Wimbledon, she ranked number 31 going into the event, but won her fourth singles title at the event when she defeated Marion Bartoli. Venus was diagnosed with exercise-induced asthma, which did not respond to medication, and she struggled with anemia, yet she was clearly still quite powerful, setting a Grand Slam record serve at 129 mph at the U.S. Open. At the Open, she advanced to the semifinal, but lost to Justine Henin.

In 2008, Venus won Wimbledon again, defeating Serena in the finals (the first time this had happened since 2001). She also won gold for doubles play with her sister Serena at the Olympics in Beijing, although she lost in the quarterfinals of the singles tournament. She finished the year with a singles victory at the Zurich Open and the 2008 WTA Tour Championship at Doha, Qatar.

By 2009, Venus seemed to be playing more strongly and her rankings improved. She began the year as the sixth seed in the Australian Open, but lost in the second round. She won the doubles tournament with Serena, their eighth title as a duo. Venus was victorious in the Premier 5 Dubai Tennis Championship, where she defeated Serena in the semifinals before winning against Virginie Razzano in the finals. This victory placed Venus in the WTA top five for the first time since 2003. Venus was seeded third at Wimbledon, but lost in the final round to Serena. The sisters were victorious in their doubles tournament.

In early 2010, the Williams sisters returned to number one and two rankings, with Venus at number two. She returned to the Dubai championship and successfully defended her title, a feat she replicated when she won her second consecutive tournament at Abierto Mexcio Telcel in Acapulco, Mexico. While playing in the Sony Ericsson Open in Florida, Venus suffered a knee injury, which forced her to miss several tournaments in 2010 and 2011.

Venus seemed to struggle with illness and injury in 2011. Finally, at the U.S. Open, after winning in straight sets in a strong opening match against Vesna Dolonts, Venus announced she was suffering from an autoimmune disorder called Sjögren's syndrome. The syndrome is characterized by dry eyes and mouth, extreme tiredness, and difficulty breathing. Venus was hopeful that medication would help to alleviate her symptoms and she would be able to return to competitive play in the near future. She has continued to struggle with her singles game, but she joined with her sister Serena to win the 2012 women's doubles title at Wimbledon in July. They repeated the feat at the 2012 London Olympics, winning the gold medal.

Legacy

Venus holds 43 career tennis titles, 21 of which are Grand Slam titles: 7 singles, 12 doubles, and 2 mixed doubles. Venus competed against her sister Serena in 23 professional matches since 1998, defeating her 10 times. The sisters played against each other in eight Grand Slam singles finals, and Venus won two of these. Venus and Serena also competed together in doubles matches, winning 12 Grand Slam doubles titles.

Gender Equity in Sport

Venus is a well-known and effective advocate for equal pay for men and women tennis players, something former players like Billie Jean King unsuccessfully struggled to achieve. In 2005, Venus met with officials from the French Open and Wimbledon, and while she left a favorable impression, she was unsuccessful in her bid for equal pay. In 2006, Venus wrote an essay published in *The Times* in advance of the Wimbledon tournament where she argued again for equal pay for men and women. Her comments received support from British prime minister Tony Blair and members of Parliament, and later in the year Venus led the WTA-UNESCO Gender Equity Program's efforts to promote gender equity in tennis. At the beginning of 2007, it was clear their efforts had made a difference.

Wimbledon and the French Open both announced they would pay men and women equally. Venus was the first woman to benefit from this announcement when she won Wimbledon later that year.

Professional Interests and Further Accomplishments

In addition to her professional tennis accomplishments, Venus opened and successfully ran an interior design business, V Starr Interiors, and she developed a clothing line called EleVen, which offered a range of activewear for women. She was named *Glamour* magazine's Woman of the Year in 2005 and is a four-time ESPY award winner. She coauthored books for young people with her sister Serena about playing tennis, and her 2010 book with coauthor Kelly E. Carter entitled *Come to Win: Business Leaders, Artists, Doctors and Other Visionaries on How Sports Can Help You Top Your Profession* went to a top five position on the *New York Times* best sellers list. Venus was named among the "30 Legends of Women's Tennis" by *Time* magazine in 2011.

Venus has also been quite active in philanthropy and charity work, participating in a number of tennis and celebrity events to benefit children. The Venus and Serena Williams Tutorial/Tennis Academy in Los Angeles is intended to help inner-city youth have academic and tennis resources that would allow them to attend the college of their choice. Venus has also supported the Great Ormond Street Hospital and the OWL foundation, which addresses learning problems for young people at risk for academic failure.

Venus Williams has left an indelible mark on the sport and American culture. She has provided hope, inspiration, and more to aspiring young athletes around the world, and will continue to do so whether on or off the court.

Jacqueline Edmondson

See also Williams, Serena

Suggested Resources

Edmondson, Jacqueline. *Venus and Serena Williams: A Biography*. Westport, CT: Greenwood Press, 2005.
Venus Williams Website. www.venuswilliams.com. Accessed September 28, 2011.
Williams, Venus, and Serena Williams. *How to Play Tennis*. New York: DK, 2004.
Williams, Venus, and Serena Williams. *Venus and Serena: Serving from the Hip: 10 Rules for Living, Loving, and Winning*. San Anselmo, CA: Sandpiper Press, 2005.

The Winning Team (1952)

The Winning Team stars Ronald Reagan as baseball pitcher Grover Cleveland Alexander and Doris Day, who received top billing, as Alexander's wife, Aimee. The release of *The Winning Team* coincided with an era of increased production of baseball films in the years following World War II. The biopic, directed by Lewis Seiler two years after Alexander's death, portrays Alexander as a tragic hero, a depiction epitomized when he joins the House of David barnstorming baseball team after his successful career in the big leagues is cut short by bouts of dizzy spells and subsequent self-medication through alcohol. But as the film's title suggests, Alexander emerges victorious.

The film's plot follows closely the description on Alexander's National Baseball Hall of Fame plaque. The plaque serves to frame the film with a shot of the bronze monument prior to the opening scene and again after the final scene. The plaque's phrase "final crisis," which refers to action on the field during the 1926 World Series, takes on added meaning, suggesting Alexander overcame his final dizzy spell and proved a winning combination with both Aimee in the stands and his St. Louis Cardinal teammates on the field.

The Winning Team begins with Alexander's early adulthood in Elba, Nebraska. A team of barnstorming professionals comes through the town, and Alexander is persuaded to take the mound for the locals. His dominating performance earns him a roster invitation on the barnstorming team, and it is with them that he is hit in the head while running the bases by an attempted double-play throw. The throw knocks him unconscious for almost three days, and when he awakes a doctor diagnoses him with diplopia, setting the stage for the narrative conflict.

The film's title, *The Winning Team*, is a double entendre. The first meaning derives from Aimee's support of her husband's first love, baseball. The second meaning emerges from a plot twist in which "Alex" rises from the depths of humiliation after a stint first with the House of David's barnstorming baseball team and then traveling as a sideshow with a flea circus to make a heroic comeback in Major League Baseball. Upon his triumphant return, he leads the 1926 Cardinals to World Series victory.

Hollywood, however, took great artistic license in manipulating the sequence of events to produce the film's namesake. Alexander, indeed, participated in the 1926 World Series, striking out New York Yankee Tony Lazzeri to avert the "final crisis" in the seventh inning of the game. But this defining moment of Alexander's career occurred before he took the mound for the House of David, rather than as his triumphant comeback to capstone his career and provide the film's climatic conclusion. In actuality, Alexander played several more years in Major League Baseball (until 1930) before he took the mound for the House of David, for whom he played as his final "winning team."

Warner Brothers, which produced *The Winning Team*, received criticism for their avoidance in identifying Alexander's double vision and dizzy spells as epilepsy. They likewise downplayed his alcoholism as exaggerations by paparazzi reporters anxious to fill gossip columns. The film instead presents a clear linear progression of cause and effect. Alexander's beaning to the head causes double vision; his service as a World War I gunnery sergeant in the trenches of Germany intensifies the effects; his doctor's postwar prognosis that his "affliction" is incurable prompts his inroad into speakeasies. Meanwhile, the baseball field provides the stage for Alexander to overcome each obstacle.

The Winning Team is among an upsurge of baseball films released after World War II. As a post–World War II production of an interwar period, the focus is on a consensus attitude exemplified in the radio broadcaster's voiceover explanation that St. Louis player/manager Rogers Hornsby (played by Frank Lovejoy) "has literally lifted his weak but scrappy team by its bootstraps." This message is not only that with effort and determination anything can be accomplished, but also that there is increasingly less room for actions outside the status quo.

Ronald Reagan and Doris Day in *The Winning Team*, a 1952 biopic of pitcher Grover Cleveland Alexander. (AP Photo.)

Aimee Alexander served as a technical advisor on the Warner Brothers production set. Cameos made by big league players include Bob Lemon, Jerry Priddy, Peanuts Lowrey, George Metkovich, Irving Noren, Hank Sauer, Al Zarilla, and Gene Mauch.

Joshua Fleer

See also Baseball Hall of Fame; New York Yankees; St. Louis Cardinals; World Series

Suggested Resources

Dickerson, Gary E. *The Cinema of Baseball: Images of America, 1929–1989*. Westport, CT: Meckler, 1991.

Erickson, Hal. *The Baseball Filmography: 1915 through 2001*. Jefferson, NC: McFarland, 2002.

The Winning Team. IMDb. http://www.imdb.com/title/tt0045332/. Accessed January 24, 2012.

Women's National Basketball Association (WNBA)

The Women's National Basketball Association (WNBA) tipped off in the summer of 1997 with the distinction of being the first professional women's basketball league to receive the full financial and promotional backing of the NBA. Riding a wave of popularity left over from the 1996 Olympic gold medal–winning U.S. women's basketball team, the league immediately captured a niche audience. However, the WNBA has since struggled to expand its fan base and has remained on the fringe of cultural relevance.

The NBA board of governors announced the formation of the league on April 24, 1996. It began with eight teams, a TV deal, and the catchy slogan "We Got Next." The Charlotte Sting, Cleveland Rockers, Houston Comets, and New York Liberty in the Eastern Conference, and the Los Angeles Sparks, Phoenix Mercury, Sacramento Monarchs, and Utah Starzz in the Western Conference comprised the league, while a limited TV agreement with NBC, ESPN, and Lifetime Network was the league's initial lifeline.

United States national team members Rebecca Lobo, Sheryl Swoopes, and Lisa Leslie were the first players signed by the WNBA and were positioned on geographically significant teams. For example, Swoopes, a native of Texas and college star at Texas Tech, became the face of the Houston Comets. As would be the case for the next several seasons, the teams were owned by their NBA counterparts and competed in the same arenas during the NBA offseason.

With much fanfare, NBC broadcast the first game on June 21, 1997, when the Sparks hosted the Liberty at the Great Western Forum before 14,284 fans. Sparks guard Penny Toler scored the first basket in WNBA history, but the Liberty defeated the hosts, 67–57.

Though Swoopes missed most of the inaugural season due to pregnancy, her Houston Comets defeated Lobo's New York Liberty in one game for the first WNBA championship. The Comets were led by Most Valuable Player Cynthia Cooper, who had played internationally for a decade before the advent of the WNBA. Cooper would win back-to-back MVP honors and lead the Comets to four consecutive league titles. She retired in 2000 after becoming the first WNBA player to score 500, 1,000, 2,000, and 2,500 career points.

The inaugural campaign saw an average of 9,669 fans in attendance and it was considered a success. Because of its short three-month season, many popular and successful players opted to play for the American Basketball League (ABL), a grassroots league that operated independently from 1997 to 1999. The ABL initially competed with the WNBA for the top talent out of U.S. universities, but the WNBA held more appeal for international players, like Australian guard Michele Timms and 7'2" Polish center Margo Dydek. These players took advantage of the short summer season and many continued to train with their national teams or played outside of the United States the remainder of the year.

The league expanded in each of its next three seasons with the additions of the Detroit Shock and Washington Mystics (1998), and the Minnesota Lynx and Orlando Miracle (1999). For the 2000 campaign, the league doubled from its original size with four more teams—the Indiana Fever, Miami Sol, Portland Fire, and Seattle Storm—joining the fold. It also got a shot in the arm with a major influx of talent after the ABL folded prior to the 1999 season.

Four-time All-American Chamique Holdsclaw out of the University of Tennessee was the number one draft pick by the Mystics in 1999, but ABL stars, including the Sacramento Monarchs' number two pick Yolanda Griffith, comprised the bulk of the draft picks that year. Griffith was named the league MVP for the 1999 season after averaging 18.8 points and 11.3 rebounds per game.

By its third year, the WNBA was receiving the full professional treatment and its attendance spiked in 1998 at 10,869 per game. A collective bargaining agreement between players and the league was signed. That marked a first in women's professional sports. The championship teams visited the White House. The first All-Star Game was played in 1999 before a sellout crowd at New York's Madison Square Garden where pop sensation Whitney Houston sang the national anthem. However, the league struggled to improve its status on the professional sports landscape.

As Leslie led the Sparks to back-to-back championships in 2001 and 2002, the NBA restructured its relationship and sold the WNBA teams to their NBA

The Indiana Fever celebrate after winning the WNBA basketball finals against the Minnesota Lynx in Indianapolis, October 21, 2012. (AP Photo/Michael Conroy.)

counterparts in the same city, different cities, or to nonaffiliated third parties. The Connecticut Sun became the first franchise to operate independently of an NBA entity when the Mohegan Sun casino in Uncasville purchased the Orlando franchise. The Utah Starzz were relocated to San Antonio, and the Miami and Portland franchises folded outright as their NBA counterparts chose not to sponsor the teams. Further complicating the WNBA's go of it was a reluctance of international stars to stay with their WNBA commitments as opposed to playing overseas and training with their national teams in anticipation of the 2004 Olympics.

Still, the league proved it was not going away and it persisted on a conscious level in the media. The league played a central role in the 2000 Hollywood film *Love & Basketball* starring Sanaa Latham and Omar Epps. Leslie became the first woman to dunk in a game on July 12, 2002, and the clip ran repeatedly on ESPN's *SportsCenter*.

The WNBA gained some street cred when former Detroit Pistons champion and "bad boy" Bill Laimbeer took over the Detroit Shock, led the team from worst to first, and won the 2003 title. (He would guide the team to the 2006 and 2008 championships as well.) The Seattle Storm won the 2004 and 2010 championships led by likeable personalities such as former University of Connecticut point guard Sue Bird and the colorful Australian sensation Lauren Jackson. The Phoenix Mercury, led by five-time scoring leader Diana Taurasi, also won two titles in three years (2007 and 2009).

The league was thrust into the mainstream press in October 2005 when Swoopes, a five-time MVP and one of the league's founding players, came out as a lesbian to become the most high-profile team athlete to do so publicly.

Staying in the public's mind and getting people in seats proved to be separate issues, though. Attendance declined each season from 2002 to 2008. With the inception of the Atlanta Dream, Chicago Sky, and Tulsa Shock (relocated from Detroit) and their small, non-NBA arenas, average attendance again dipped in 2010. The Mystics have continued to be one of the WNBA's leaders in attendance since the team launched in 1998, but it slowed over the next decade. In 2011, the average attendance was roughly 8,000 fans per game with the Los Angeles Sparks the only team to top the 10,000 per game average mark.

The WNBA's finances and promotion continue to be a mixed bag as the league's popularity seems to have plateaued. In 2010, the league announced that its TV ratings improved for the fourth consecutive year, but those numbers still remained small at about half of the viewership of prime-time National Hockey League coverage. There were an average of 269,000 viewers in 2009 on ESPN, up 8 percent from 2008. The league found new revenue sources in 2010 by cashing in on new marketing deals with Coca-Cola, Pirate's Booty snack foods, and Jamba Juice. Further, four teams struck primary sponsorship deals that included logos on the fronts of jerseys for the Los Angeles, New York, Phoenix, and Seattle teams.

Some of the league's best players have landed individual sponsorship deals, while others—like Phoenix's Taurasi and Seattle's Jackson—have graced the cover of *ESPN the Magazine* and shined in *Sports Illustrated*'s swimsuit issue. Despite this, these players have not proven to be iconic superstars. Pundits predicted the popularity of college stars like Candace Parker and Maya Moore would transcend into the professional game, but while the two have succeeded on the court, their endorsement potential and face recognition remains minimal.

In 2010, *SI* columnist Jeff Pearlman called the WNBA a "fringe entity" and compared the league to the NBA by writing: "If the NBA feels larger than life, the WNBA feels like, well, life. Nice, solid, pedestrian life."

The WNBA may exist on the fringe because it delivers to a diverse and unique audience. In-arena, the gender breakdown is approximately 70–30 female-male with a large percentage of that female demographic being lesbian. The TV audience, according to the league, is about 50–50 female-male with a large percentage of nonadult viewers. But, 15 years in, the WNBA has surpassed the success of all other women's sports professional leagues. Its survival will continue to hinge on the subsidies it receives from its NBA counterparts, and the league may always be holding on for dear life, pedestrian or not.

See also Cooper, Cynthia; ESPN Channels; Leslie, Lisa; *Love & Basketball*; National Basketball Association; 1996 Olympic Games, Atlanta; *Sports Illustrated*; Swoopes, Sheryl; Taurasi, Diana

Molly Yanity

Suggested Resources

Chambers, Alex. *13 Teams: One Man's Journey with the WNBA*. Phoenix: Team Effort Productions, 2011.

Gundy, Pamela, and Susan Shackelford. *Shattering the Glass: The Remarkable History of Women's Basketball*. Chapel Hill: University of North Carolina Press, 2007.

Sepic, Matt. "WNBA Has Higher Ratings but Uncertain Future." October 5, 2011. http://www.npr.org/2011/10/05/141013682/wnba-has-higher-tv-ratings-but-uncertain-future. Accessed January 10, 2012.

Terzieff, Juliette. *Women of the Court: Inside the WNBA*. Los Angeles: Alyson Books, 2008.

WNBA Website. http://www.wnba.com. Accessed January 10, 2012.

Women's Professional Basketball League (WBL)

The Women's Professional Basketball League (WBL) was the first women's professional basketball league in the United States. Although the league lasted only three seasons, its legacy includes many prominent figures in women's basketball today, as well as the "women's" basketball used in all organized games today. The WBL also confronted for the first time the enduring question of how to market women's basketball—as basketball players who happen to be women, or women who happen to play basketball?

Until the Women's National Basketball Association (WNBA), the WBL was the first and longest-lasting attempt at professional women's basketball in the United States. It was the brainchild of a sports fan and dreamer in Columbus, Ohio, named William J. "Bill" Byrne. In 1977, when Byrne first raised the idea of professional women's basketball, his friends dismissed the idea as crazy. After all, women had quite recently been required to play six-on-six half-court, nothing like the five-person full-court game played by men at the time (and by girls and women today). Most high schools and colleges had not even offered basketball programs for women.

But Byrne had watched the situation evolve after Congress passed Title IX of the Education Amendments of 1972. In just five years since the enactment of Title IX, participation of girls and women in athletics programs had grown more than 500 percent. Some colleges were beginning to offer athletic scholarships to women. Women's basketball had been accepted as an Olympic sport in 1976.

In women's basketball, Byrne saw something that might grow in value like the National Basketball Association or the National Football League. (Ironically, however, the continued survival of the NBA was itself in doubt at the time. One 1979 *New York Post* headline exclaimed, "[Commissioner] O'Brien Denies NBA is Kaput.") Byrne placed an ad in the *Wall Street Journal* seeking investors, and a year later, the first women's professional basketball game tipped off in Milwaukee, Wisconsin, on December 9, 1978.

Women's professional basketball was a new animal for most people, including sportswriters. Even before the first season began, controversy arose as to whether men would be allowed into WBL locker rooms. A year earlier, a federal judge had ordered Major League Baseball to let a female reporter into its locker rooms—did it cut both ways? Yes and no—some WBL teams said no; some welcomed any reporter anywhere.

Finding owners for the new venture was not easy. Most WBL owners (all men, except one) had never even seen a women's basketball game. Several were tax lawyers, suggesting to outsiders that the league was a cleverly disguised tax shelter. Other owners were just optimists—a funeral home director, a liquor store owner, a car dealer—hoping to get in on the ground floor of something big. Although the league later attracted a few wealthy investors, such as actors Alan Alda (*M*A*S*H*) and Mike Connors (*Mannix*) and San Francisco mayor Willie Brown, most owners were not rich.

Recruiting players was not always easy, either. With no inkling of a professional career, many prospects had settled into normal jobs, working in retail stores, or as security guards, or teaching. Others were hoping to compete in the 1980 Olympics, which required them to maintain amateur status at the time. The league did attract much of the available talent, however, including All-Americans, Olympians, and dozens of players later inducted into their college's hall of fame.

The first player enlisted to promote the new league was Karen Logan. As a member of the All-American Redheads—a traveling Harlem Globetrotters–type team, but with women players—Logan was among the best-known women's basketball players of the 1970s. She had, among other things, defeated NBA star Jerry West in a nationally televised game of H-O-R-S-E.

Debate arose immediately as to how professional women's basketball should be both played and marketed. Should referees call fouls closely, to keep the game more "ladylike?" Should teams like the Houston Angels (called the Houston "Muggers" by opponents) be banned from using a swarm defense? Should comparisons with the NBA be encouraged or discouraged? No one really knew; no one had tried to sell women's basketball like this before.

In one experiment still talked about today, the WBL team California Dreams tried to give players a more refined media image by sending them to the John Robert Powers charm school. The Iowa Cornets sold posters of All-Star Molly Bolin reclining in a swimsuit, a highly controversial—and successful—promotional campaign. New Orleans Pride players put on makeup before games. Some teams were given feminine-sounding names, such as the Angels, the Milwaukee Does, and the New Jersey Gems. The WBL logo itself was strategically curvy.

Some teams set ratios of white to African American players, hearing rumors that a predominance of black players in the NBA was contributing to that league's struggles. All teams wanted to win, but many owners hoped to do so with "attractive" or "feminine" players who might appeal to male fans. (To their frustration, WBL teams could never get women to come to games in significant numbers.)

Owners also tried to add excitement to WBL games in other ways. The league adopted the same

24-second shot clock and three-point shot as in the NBA. Player Karen Logan's proposal for a smaller "women's" ball was also embraced by the league. A ball more proportional to the size of women's hands would increase scoring, WBL owners hoped, and perhaps bring the coveted dunk to women's basketball. (It did, eventually. 5'6" WBL player Cardte Hicks often dunked during warm-ups, and when the WBL-sized ball was later adopted by colleges and the WNBA, dunking began to occur at those levels as well.)

Once the WBL season began, living and training conditions were sometimes primitive compared to today. To save on electricity, games might be played in a gymnasium with no heat. Players might travel to a game by bus (driven by the coach), riding for eight hours, playing the game, then climbing back into the bus for the trip home. For road games, up to six players might cram into one hotel room, and players might get to an arena by hitchhiking. The Washington Metros practiced outdoors on a tennis court in the middle of winter. Most teams did not have trainers or workout facilities, and players often wore the same shoes they had worn in college. Practices were set at 6 a.m. or 7 p.m., so that players could hold second jobs.

Women could join or leave WBL teams at any time during a season, and often did. (The Minnesota Fillies went through 22 players in a single season.) Iowa Cornets player Nancy Wellen was traded to an opposing team 45 minutes before a game, for example, switching uniforms and playing against her former team that same night.

Over its three years, significant changes occurred in the league. Hoping for even an indirect association with the NBA, several teams hired well-known ex-NBA figures as coaches, such as Butch van Breda Kolff, Jim Loscutoff, Larry Costello, and Dean Meminger. The lack of women coaches (and referees) in the women's league became a topic of some ridicule. Women coaches were said to be not only rare, but expendable: Candace Klinzing, who coached the Milwaukee Does in the very first WBL game, was fired when the Does lost that game by five points.

Several big-name players also joined the WBL league after its first season, beginning with Ann Meyers. A year earlier, Meyers had famously signed with an NBA team, the Indiana Pacers, rather than the

WBL. After being cut from the Pacers during training camp, Meyers agreed to join a WBL team, but only if it matched her NBA salary—$50,000, five times greater than the average WBL salary. That led to the "Annie Meyers Syndrome," with other star players such as Nancy Lieberman and Carol Blazejowski demanding Meyers-like salaries the following season.

Camaraderie was high on most WBL teams, and there were positive signs for the league at times. Television station WGN reported that several WBL Chicago Hustle games had drawn better ratings than NBA Chicago Bulls games. A Dallas Diamonds WBL game had higher attendance than an NBA Dallas Mavericks game played the same night. Fans were often passionate (police had to be called at one Chicago game when dozens of fans rushed the court in protest of an officiating call.) The title games in all three WBL seasons drew large crowds; the 1981 championship game

"Machine Gun" Molly

Both the accomplishments and the risks of being a pioneer were illustrated by WBL player Molly Bolin. Nicknamed "Machine Gun" Molly by a *Washington Post* reporter because of her prolific shooting ability, three-time All-Star and All-WBL player Bolin set several lasting records in women's professional basketball, including single-game scoring (55) and single-season scoring average (32.8). As the sole wage-earner for her family, the attractive blonde also provided a marketing boost to her two teams, the Iowa Cornets and the San Francisco Pioneers, allowing photographs of herself in a swimsuit to be sold as posters and printed in newspapers.

A year after the WBL folded, those photographs and Bolin's professional career itself were used against her in a historic custody battle in Iowa. Allowing herself to be featured in the poster and leaving her family to play in road games showed that Molly put her career above her child, her ex-husband's lawyer argued. But it was unfair to punish a professional female athlete for traveling in her job when male athletes had been doing it for years, Molly and her lawyer pointed out. The trial judge disagreed, and Molly was devastated when he awarded custody of her son to her ex-husband. The Iowa Supreme Court later overturned the ruling, finding that Molly was a wholesome and loving parent, and ordering that custody be returned to her.

between the Diamonds and the Nebraska Wranglers in Omaha was delayed more than an hour to accommodate an overcapacity crowd, some of whom ended up sitting on the court.

The 1980 Olympic Games in Moscow were expected to give a major boost to women's basketball, much as the 1996 United States gold medal team led to the formation of the WNBA and a competing league, the American Basketball League. To crank up the publicity for the WBL, an investment banker and part-owner of the financially stable San Francisco Pioneers rounded up a pool of investors, planning to fly to the Soviet Union and sign either Lieberman or Blazejowski to the first $1 million contract in women's basketball.

The Soviet Union later invaded Afghanistan, and in protest the United States boycotted the 1980 Olympics. That decision killed the WBL, many league officials felt. Although the boycott unquestionably deprived the WBL of much-needed publicity, other factors also caused the league's dissolution after the 1980–1981 season.

Most WBL owners simply did not have enough staying power. The NBA had taken three decades to develop and, until revitalized by players Larry Bird and Earvin "Magic" Johnson beginning in 1979, was still on shaky ground. Stiff salaries extracted by some WBL players in the third season hurt. Renting NBA-quality facilities such as the Superdome and Madison Square Garden, while lending an air of credibility, was costly. Expansion from the original 8 teams, all of which were east of the Mississippi, to 14 teams across the country, drove up travel costs. Attendance flagged, and sponsors were uneasy. Media coverage was spotty; some owners complained that the only time they got ink was when a player was murdered (Connie Kunzman) or players were not getting paid. A strike by unpaid Minnesota Fillies players near the end of the third season was widely reported, adding to the impression that the league's days were numbered.

The WBL officially folded after three full seasons. In addition to the "women's" basketball, the charm school and makeup experiments, and broader lessons learned in marketing women's basketball, the WBL's legacy also includes many players and coaches who went on to prominent roles in women's basketball,

including future WNBA president Donna Orender, future Women's Basketball Coaches Association president Doug Bruno, future NCAA Division I championship coach Muffet McGraw, and several coaches and managers in the WNBA and NCAA.

Karra Porter

See also Blazejowski, Carol; Dunk; Harlem Globetrotters; Lieberman, Nancy; National Basketball Association; Title IX; West, Jerry; Women's National Basketball Association

Suggested Resources

Grundy, Pamela, and Susan Shackelford. *Shattering the Glass: The Remarkable History of Women's Basketball.* Chapel Hill: University of North Carolina Press, 2007.

Porter, Karra J. *Mad Seasons: The Story of the Women's Professional Basketball League.* Lincoln: University of Nebraska Press, 2006.

Women's Basketball Hall of Fame Website. http://www .wbhof.com/. Accessed August 1, 2011.

Women's Basketball Museum Website. http://womens basketballmuseum.com/. Accessed August 1, 2011.

Women's Basketball Online. http://www.womensbasket ballonline.com/history/index.html. Accessed August 1, 2011.

Women's Tennis Association (WTA)

The Women's Tennis Association, or WTA, is the organizing group of the professional women's tennis circuit. The association was founded in 1973 by women's tennis champion Billie Jean King and serves as the female counterpart to the men's professional tennis group, the ATP (Association for Tennis Professionals). The WTA headquarters is presently located in St. Petersburg, Florida, with additional locations in London, England, and Beijing, China.

The WTA grew out of a need for an organizing body to put together tournaments and professional events for female tennis players in the 1970s. Billie Jean King saw the desire for an organizing body for women in tennis because there were wide disparities in the prize amounts awarded to men and women. In the early 1970s, the ratio of male prize amounts to female was 2.5:1. At more well-known tournaments,

Tennis stars Billie Jean King, left, and Tracy Austin don hats for photographers at a press conference in New York on August 23, 1978, to announce that Avon Products Inc. will take over sponsorship of the Women's Tennis Association's major tour. (AP Photo/Dave Pickoff.)

that ratio was at one time as large as 8:1. One of the more well-known incidents of the pay differences between men and women was evidenced in 1970 when Australian Margaret Smith Court won all four Grand Slam tournaments (and was the first woman to do so). As a result of this achievement, Court was entitled to additional prize money, but a female player would earn only an additional $15,000 while a man who accomplished the same feat could win $1 million.

That same year, tennis star Jack Kramer announced that he would direct the Pacific Southwest Championships in California and that the prize ratio for men to women would be 12:1. This led several female players, including Billie Jean King, to boycott the event.

With the support and direction of *World Tennis* magazine founder Gladys Heldman, the women who boycotted Kramer's tournament played in the Houston Women's Invitation, the first all-female invitation-only tournament with prize money. Heldman invited

nine of the best female tennis players to Houston, Texas, in September 1970; this group of females became known as the Original Nine. This group included Billie Jean King, Rosie Casals, Nancy Richey, Kristy Pigeon, Peaches Bartkowicz, Julie Heldman, Valerie Ziegenfuss, Judy Tegart Dalton, and Kerry Melville Reid. American Rosie Casals won that first female event. This group signed one-dollar contracts with Heldman to become part of the Virginia Slims Series. The Original Nine were champions of women's right to participate in sporting events in the same way as men. Their achievement in 1970 occurred two years prior to the passage of Title IX in the United States, demanding equity in sports for females.

That first event led to the creation of a women's tour that was independent from the existing women's tour that was part of the International Tennis Federation. The tour for the Original Nine was sponsored by cigarette company Virginia Slims and became known as the Virginia Slims Circuit. This included 19 tournaments in the

United States and prize money totaling over $300,000. This tour is the basis for the WTA.

A week before the 1973 Wimbledon Championships, Billie Jean King organized a meeting of female tennis players at the Gloucester Hotel in London and the Women's Tennis Association was born. The efforts of the WTA paid off quickly; that year, the United States Tennis Association (USTA) offered equal prize money to the men's and women's champions at the U.S. Open.

The league was able to increase its visibility in 1974 when it reached a television deal to televise the WTA tournaments on CBS. Virginia Slims continued to sponsor the tournament but Colgate sponsored the tour from April to November 1976. In 1979, the WTA dropped Virginia Slims for Avon to sponsor the winter season of the women's tour. Avon's sponsorship in that year also brought the largest prize for a women's tournament to that time at the Avon Championships, where the top female could take home $100,000. Colgate and Avon were able to both be sponsors because Colgate-sponsored events were mostly held in international locations, while Avon events were mostly in the United States. By 1980, there were over 250 professional female tennis players in the WTA and prize money for the various events surpassed $7 million.

In 1981, Toyota became the new sponsors of the international WTA events, replacing Colgate. In 1983, Virginia Slims became the sponsor of the entire WTA tour, both international and domestic, and events sanctioned by the WTA were named Virginia Slims World Championship Series. In 1995, the WTA merged with the Women's Tennis Council and formed the WTA Tour. With additional corporate sponsors, the championship at the end of the season had a prize of $2 million.

The Women's Tennis Association allowed for equity in women's tennis, but also was a trailblazer in the field of women athletics in general. A governing body that provided opportunities for females to excel in the sport of tennis allowed for more opportunities within tennis to become available, but showed the wider athletic community that when given the opportunity, women players could excel just as well as men and deserved their fair share of prize winnings, sponsorships, and endorsement deals as their male athletic counterparts.

With the supervision of the WTA, female tennis players excelled in tournaments previously not open to women and were able to participate in more events with one another. Chris Evert was the first female athlete ever to earn over $1 million in career earnings, an achievement she earned in 1976. Martina Navratilova was the first woman to make a million dollars in one single tennis season, in 1982. The efforts of the WTA and the Original Nine players were important in making equity in prize winnings a priority for the tennis world; despite their hard work, equal prize earnings for men and women was not achieved at all the major events so quickly. It was not until 2007 that the Grand Slam events at Wimbledon and the French Open awarded the same amount of money to the men's and women's championship. Over 30 years after Billie Jean King began the fight for prize equity, all four major Grand Slam tournaments offered the same prize money to the men's and women's champions.

Kristen Costa

See also Evert, Chris; King, Billie Jean; Navratilova, Martina; Title IX

Suggested Resources

Ware, Susan. *Game, Set, Match: Billie Jean King and the Revolution in Women's Sports*. Chapel Hill: University of North Carolina Press, 2011.

Women's Tennis Association Website. http://www.wtatennis .com/page/AboutTheTour/0,,12781,00.html. Accessed November 25, 2011.

WTA Championships. http://www.wtachampionships.com/ page/Home. Accessed November 25, 2011.

Women's United Soccer Association (WUSA)

The Women's United Soccer Association (WUSA) was a women's professional soccer league that operated for three seasons (2000–2003) in eight cities across the United States. The WUSA was founded on February 15, 2000, when major U.S. media companies and individual investors joined forces with the members of the 1999 U.S. Women's World Cup team. Investors included Cox Communications, Comcast Corporation, and Time Warner Cable, among others. John Hendricks, chairman and CEO of Discovery

Atlanta Beat's Cindy Parlow (12) goes high against Carolina Courage's Brooke O'Hanley (12) and Tiffany Roberts, front, during the first half of a WUSA game, July 4, 2003, in Cary, North Carolina. (AP Photo/Karl DeBlaker.)

Communications, spearheaded the investors' efforts and pledged $40 million to fund a minimum of eight teams and the league's administration for the first five years of operations. The eight teams were:

Atlanta Beat
Bay Area CyberRays (changed to San Jose
    CyberRays in 2002)
Boston Breakers
Carolina Courage
New York Power
Philadelphia Charge
San Diego Spirit
Washington Freedom

In May 2000, each member of the 1999 World Cup–winning U.S. National team was divided among the eight teams. Several months later, 16 of the best international players were signed to WUSA contracts as well. Officials staged drafts in December 2000 and February 2001 to fill their rosters. By opening day of the first season in spring 2001, each team consisted of 20 players (including three U.S. National team players and four foreign players) and operated under a salary cap of $800,000. The WUSA was the first fully professional soccer league for women in the world and boasted nearly all of the sport's best talent.

The WUSA's inaugural game was held in Robert F. Kennedy Stadium in Washington, D.C., on April 14, 2001. A crowd of 34,148 people watched as Mia Hamm's Washington Freedom beat Brandi Chastain's Bay Area CyberRays, 1–0. The CyberRays recovered from a slow start to the season, though, and ultimately won the initial WUSA Founders Cup, named after the U.S. National team's "founding players." The CyberRays and the Atlanta Beat played in the final in Foxboro Stadium to a 3–3 draw in regulation. The CyberRays won the game in a penalty kick shootout in front of a crowd of approximately 24,000 spectators. The first season eclipsed attendance projections by about 25 percent with average crowds just under 9,000. However, operations were much more expensive than predicted and the league began to struggle financially despite fan turnout. The investor group pledged another $60 million and the league searched for stable corporate sponsorship.

The 2002 season saw the same talent level, but more financial difficulties for the young league. Sponsorships and TV viewership did not meet expectations and attendance, while still relatively strong by most standards, began to drop off. The 2002 Founders Cup final took place in Atlanta's Herndon Stadium in front of 15,000 fans. The Carolina Courage won Founders Cup II, 3–2, over Mia Hamm's Washington Freedom with a thrilling game-winning goal for the Courage by German star Birgit Prinz.

Going into the 2003 season, hoping to save the floundering league, players voluntarily took a 30 percent pay cut and some of the founding players reportedly agreed to even greater salary reductions. Average

Founding Players

The 20 members of the U.S. National team that won the 1999 World Cup became the WUSA's "founding players" and together forged a legacy unmatched in American sports. They entered into negotiations and stood as one against efforts by U.S. Soccer to derail the formation of the WUSA. They each made personal sacrifices in hopes of making the league sustainable. In a first in American sports, a group of athletes stuck together and refused larger paychecks to make the league more viable for all. In the end, the founding players' unselfishness won over their adversaries at U.S. Soccer. In 2001, former president of U.S. Soccer Alan Rothenberg finally said about them, "They are a unique group. Some of the things they've done in setting up this league, leaving money on the table with no guarantee of future profit, is unheard of in this day and age. When you look at what big-time sports is today, they're really a shining light."

The WUSA founding players were the following:

Julie Foudy	Carla Overbeck
Mia Hamm	Kristine Lilly
Brandi Chastain	Michelle Akers
Briana Scurry	Joy Fawcett
Tiffeny Milbrett	Cindy Parlow
Danielle Fotopoulos	Shannon MacMillan
Saskia Weber	Tiffany Roberts
Christy Pearce (Rampone)	Sara Whalen
Kate Sobrero (Markgraff)	Tisha Venturini
Lorrie Fair	Tracy Ducar

attendance stayed relatively strong in year three, averaging close to 7,000 fans per game, but TV ratings were almost nonexistent and investor excitement for the league dwindled. The 2003 season proved to be the WUSA's last. That year Mia Hamm's Washington Freedom won the Founders Cup in a 2–1 victory over the Atlanta Beat in Torero Stadium in San Diego in front of 7,106 fans. New superstar Abby Wambach scored both Freedom goals.

The WUSA folded on September 15, 2003, just five days before the start of the 2003 Women's World Cup in the United States. Owners and players in the WUSA held out hope that the world's premier event would create another infusion of excitement for women's soccer and that new investors and sponsors would resurrect the WUSA or start a successor league as soon as 2005. After much deliberation, a new league did form with a much more conservative business model. Women's Professional Soccer (WPS) began operations in 2009 and is still in existence today.

Ann Cook

See also Chastain, Brandi; Hamm, Mia: 1999 FIFA Women's World Cup

Suggested Resources

Lisi, Clemente A. *The U.S. Women's Soccer Team: An American Success Story*. Lanham, MD: Scarecrow Press, 2009.

Michaelis, Vicki. "WUSA Ceases Operations After Three Years." September 16, 2003. http://www.usatoday.com/sports/soccer/wusa/2003-09-15-wusa-folds_x.htm. Accessed January 19, 2012.

Silver, Michael. "Playing for Keeps." 2001. http://sports illustrated.cnn.com/siforwomen/2001/july_august/playing_for_keeps/. Accessed January 19, 2012.

Weiner, Richard. "WUSA: Creating a Legacy." April 14, 2001. http://www.usatoday.com/sports/soccer/wusa/stories/2001-04-13-cover.htm. Accessed January 19, 2012.

Wooden, John (1910–2010)

John Wooden was a basketball player and coach who had the unique distinction of being the only person elected to the Naismith Memorial Basketball Hall of Fame in two categories—player (1961) and coach (1973). (Since then Lenny Wilkins and Bill Sharman have also been so honored.)

Wooden was born in 1910 in rural Hall, Indiana, one of six children of Joshua and Roxie Rothrock Wooden. The family moved to Martinsville, Indiana, when Wooden was 14 and he attended high school there, lettering four years in basketball and excelling as a student. In three straight years he led his team to the Indiana state championship game, winning in 1927 and finishing second in 1926 and 1928. Wooden was named an all-state basketball player all three years. In the fall of 1928 he enrolled at Purdue University where he majored in English and received a teaching certificate.

UCLA basketball coach John Wooden wears a basketball net around his neck after his team won the NCAA basketball championship over Kentucky, 92–85, in San Diego, California, on March 31, 1975. (AP Photo.)

In Wooden's three years of varsity basketball he was an All–Big Ten and All-American player under Coach Ward "Piggy" Lambert. Purdue went 13–1, 12–5, and 17–1 in Wooden's three varsity years. There were no national tournaments, but Purdue was named by most writers and the Helms Athletic Foundation as the nation's top team for 1931–1932. Wooden was named the Helms Foundation Player of the Year.

Upon graduation Wooden married his high school sweetheart, Nell Riley, and began teaching English at Dayton High School in northern Kentucky. In 1934, Wooden went to teach at South Bend Central High School in northern Indiana, where he remained until

1943. He also played professional basketball for the Indianapolis Kautskys. In 1935 the Kautskys joined the newly formed Midwest Conference at a time when pro basketball was hardly a national sport. Wooden received $50 per game, was a big drawing card for the league, and ended up leading the league in scoring. Wooden was fast, aggressive, and intelligent; he was a good shooter and passer. At one point Wooden made 134 free throws in a row. The next season, 1936–1937, he was forced to miss a number of games because of his teaching and coaching.

In 1937, Wooden was on the Whiting (Indiana) Ciesars in the National Basketball League, which had succeeded the Midwest Conference and was a much more formal league. He also continued at South Bend Central as English teacher and basketball coach. These duties continued to interfere with his pro playing, although he still was one of three players to average in double figures in the 1937–1938 NBL season. In 1938–1939 the team moved to Hammond, very close to Whiting, but Wooden played less and less as his coaching and teaching demanded more of his time. He retired as a player following that season, at the age of 28.

Wooden coached and taught until 1943 when he entered the navy. At Dayton, his coaching record was 21–14 and at South Bend Central he was 197–28. Wooden served until 1946, leaving the service with the rank of lieutenant. He then chose to accept an offer to be the head coach at Indiana State Teachers College in Terre Haute, Indiana. The job also included being athletic director, baseball coach, and an English instructor. Wooden's two-year record at Indiana State was 45 wins and 15 losses. At that time Indiana State competed in the National Association of Intercollegiate Athletics (NAIA) tournament and his Sycamores finished second to the University of Louisville in 1948.

Wooden then decided that he would seek a position at a larger, more prominent university and he applied for positions at the University of Minnesota and the University of California at Los Angeles (UCLA). The former was his preferred position since it was in the Big Ten and he felt most comfortable in the Midwest. He interviewed there and hoped to be offered the position, but it was not immediately forthcoming. Eventually, Minnesota did offer him the head coach position, but by that time, he had interviewed at UCLA and had been offered and accepted the position as head coach.

UCLA had been 12–13 in 1947–1948, but Wooden turned the program around almost immediately, going 22–7 in 1948–1949, then winning 20 or more games for the next three years. Wooden also had to win over a largely indifferent population of students and fans while maintaining the program on a minimal budget. The big sport at UCLA was football, and basketball made do with limited office space, lack of a home gymnasium, and recruiting sanctions against the university because of violations by the football staff. Nevertheless, Wooden had a respectable record into the 1960s with no losing seasons and a record of 271–116 at the end of the 1962 season, after 14 years at UCLA. His team had played in the NCAA Tournament in 1950 (fourth in the West regional), 1952 (fourth in the regional), and 1956 (third in the regional), until 1961 brought a new level of talent to UCLA.

At that point Wooden was able to recruit more nationally known talent, rather than just West Coast stars. The most notable was Walt Hazzard, nicknamed "East Coast," from Philadelphia, who joined with Gail Goodrich and Keith Erickson to lead the Bruins to National Collegiate Athletic Association (NCAA) championships in 1964. Hazzard was the MVP of the NCAA tourney and was the first draft selection in the NBA draft by the Los Angeles Lakers in 1964. In 1965 the Bruins repeated as national champions as Goodrich, Erickson, and Edgar Lacey led the team. UCLA also finished fourth in the NCAA Tournament in 1962 and fourth in the regional in 1963. Both the 1964 and 1965 teams finished undefeated in the Pacific Eight Conference and the 1964 team was undefeated for the year.

The dominance of UCLA under Wooden was a late event in his long career with his first national title coming at the age of 53. The 1965 team lost a lot of talent and the next year the team went only 18–8 and failed to make the NCAA Tournament, since only league champions and top independents were invited at that time and just 22 teams were in the field that year. The UCLA varsity even lost the annual game to the UCLA freshmen, 75–60, that year, but that loss was deceptive. Wooden had managed to attract an unprecedented class of talented players, most notably Lew Alcindor (who converted to Islam and changed

his name to Kareem Abdul-Jabbar in 1972) and Lucius Allen, a cat-quick guard from Kansas City. Alcindor was convinced by Ralph Bunche, a UCLA alumnus and United Nations ambassador, to attend the university because of its strong academic programs and its welcoming atmosphere for black students, in addition to the coaching of John Wooden.

The 1966–1967 UCLA Bruins were voted the top college team of all time in a 2011 poll conducted by *The Sporting New*s. That team, led by Alcindor and Allen, as well as Mike Warren and Kenny Heitz, went undefeated in 30 games, winning the third NCAA championship for UCLA and Coach Wooden. Wooden was also voted Coach of the Year for the second time. (He had previously won the award in 1964.)

The next year UCLA was favored to repeat as national champions and, possibly, go undefeated again. The biggest obstacle was the University of Houston which was led by All-American Elvin Hayes. The two teams met in the Houston Astrodome on January 20, 1968. This was a precedent-setting site, presaging the present-day NCAA championships played in enormous stadia. The week before the game Alcindor suffered a scratched cornea and there were fears that he would not be able to play. He was fitted with special goggles (which he ultimately wore as he continued to play for many years) and an eye patch; he could not see as well as normal. The game attracted over 52,000 fans and was the first nationally televised regular-season college basketball game. Houston edged UCLA, 71–69, 39 by Hayes, to end the 47-game winning streak of UCLA.

The Bruins proceeded to win the rest of the games and continued winning into the NCAA Tournament where they met the University of Houston in the national semifinals. UCLA held Hayes to 10 points and they romped over the Cougars, 101–69. The championship game was only slightly closer as UCLA gave Wooden his fourth championship by a score of 78–55. Alcindor's senior year was similar. The Bruins lost one game in the Pacific Eight Conference, then swept through the NCAA tourney, defeating Purdue, Wooden's alma mater, by a score of 92–72 in the championship game. Wooden was named Coach of the Year for the third time.

With the graduation of Alcindor and Allen, there was a consensus that UCLA would have a down year because of the obvious hole at the center position. The Bruins had become the top team in the country, not just through talent, but from conditioning that allowed them to implement a full-court press (really a ¾-court press) and apply it through much of a game to build a lead. The quickness, conditioning, and coaching of the players had been instrumental in the 1964 and 1965 NCAA titles. Then, with the addition of Alcindor, the guards could gamble on defense even more, because of the presence of Alcindor at the defensive basket on the press. The loss of the big man caused other teams to think that 1969–1970 would be the year that UCLA could be beaten.

Wooden inserted Steve Patterson, Alcindor's backup at center, then built another team on speed and quickness led by Sidney Wicks, Curtis Rowe, Henry Bibby, and John Vallely to go 12–2 in conference play, which was best in the Pacific Eight. In the NCAA Tournament, UCLA drew a bye in the first round, pounded Long Beach and Utah State to win the West Regional, then went on to the NCAA Final Four in College Park, Maryland. There they defeated New Mexico State before toppling Jacksonville and their giant center, Artis Gilmore, 80–69, to win their fourth title in a row and sixth of Wooden's career. He was voted Coach of the Year for the fourth time.

Patterson was a senior the next season, with freshman Bill Walton set to play for the varsity in 1971. This was a time of great societal unrest in the country. Wooden tried to be responsive to the interests of his players, but maintained his rules amid a time of rule breaking becoming common in the nation. The Bruins still had a powerful team as they returned most of their starters from the previous year, then went 29–1, going undefeated in the conference and winning another NCAA championship. The tournament was much tougher in 1971 as UCLA edged Long Beach, 57–55, in the regional finals, defeated Kansas by eight in the national semifinals, then Villanova by six, 68–62, in the championship match. (Later, Villanova's NCAA run was vacated because of the use of an ineligible player, Howard Porter, MOP of the tournament, who had signed with an agent prior to the end of his college career.)

After UCLA's win in 1971, the team was favored to win the NCAA title the next three years with Bill Walton as their center. They did not disappoint as Wooden kept them focused on their task. In both 1971–1972 and 1972–1973 the Bruins went undefeated, 30–0, both seasons. In 1972 they breezed through the tournament with only the championship game against Florida State (81–76) closer than 16 points. In 1973, their closest tournament game was an 11-point victory over Indiana (70–59) in the national semifinals, followed by a victory over Memphis State, 87–66. In that game Walton made 21 of 22 from the field and scored 44 points to be the tourney's MOP. Wooden won his sixth and final Coach of the Year award in 1972.

Wooden's Bruins had now won seven national championships in a row and nine in the previous 10 years. They also took an 88-game winning streak into an early-season game against Notre Dame. In an amazing comeback, in South Bend, the Irish won 71–70 on January 19, 1974. UCLA was still favored to win another championship in 1973–1974, but lost three games, two in the conference that year. In the NCAA tourney, they won the West Regional, then faced North Carolina State in the semifinals, a team that UCLA had beaten by 18 in the third game of the season. N.C. State was led by All-Americans David Thompson and Tommy Burleson, who was 7'4". In a double overtime game, the Bruins lost to eventual national champion N.C. State, by a score of 80–77. UCLA defeated Kansas easily to finish third in the tournament.

With the loss of both Walton and Keith Wilkes, Wooden's Bruins seemed likely to have difficulty winning the Pacific Eight, let alone the NCAA title. But, led by returnee Dave Myers, Marques Johnson, Richard Washington, and Pete Trgovich, the Bruins went 12–2 in the conference, then won the West Regional to play in the Final Four of the tournament once again. In the semifinals, the Bruins played Louisville, coached by Denny Crum, who had been Wooden's top assistant until 1971, when he accepted the position of head coach for the Cardinals. In a tight contest, UCLA edged the Cardinals and their All-American, Junior Bridgeman, by a 75–74 score. In the finals, the Bruins, led by Washington's 28 points, topped the Kentucky Wildcats, who were led by Kevin Grevey's 34, by a 92–85 score. It was Wooden and UCLA's 10th NCAA title, all won in a 12-year period.

John Wooden became 65 in October 1975 and retired at that time, following UCLA regulations, which

John Wooden's Seven Rules for Living

1. Be true to yourself.
2. Make each day your masterpiece.
3. Help others.
4. Drink deeply in good books.
5. Make friendship an art.
6. Build a shelter against a rainy day.
7. Pray for guidance and give thanks for your blessings every day.

required retirement at that age. (Such a mandatory retirement has since become a violation of the law, but was not at that point.) Wooden was saddened by having to retire, but looked forward to being a spectator and enjoying new adventures with his wife, Nell. Unfortunately, Nell died in 1985 after a long illness.

Wooden had authored or coauthored a number of books on basketball techniques, as well as life philosophy and leadership, both during his coaching career and afterward. His autobiography, *They Call Me Coach*, was widely read and his *Practical Modern Basketball*, first published in 1966, went through at least three editions and became a kind of bible for new coaches in the 1970s and beyond.

Wooden's overall coaching record at Indiana State and UCLA was 664–162, a percentage of .804. Because of his amazing record as a coach the John Wooden Award is presented each year (starting in 1977 for men, 2004 for women) to the outstanding college basketball players in the nation by the Los Angeles Athletic Club. In addition, a Legends of Coaches Award, also named after Wooden and a California High School Player Award are given each year.

Wooden was inducted as a coach in the Naismith Memorial Basketball Hall of Fame in 1973. Following retirement he continued to give speeches, mostly on leadership and highlighting his Pyramid of Success with its seven basic rules. In 2003 UCLA named its basketball court the Nell and John Wooden Court. He continued to attend UCLA games, but tried to be unobtrusive. When various injuries (hip replacement, knee replacement) made attending games difficult, he watched UCLA games regularly at home on television.

In 2003, Wooden received the Presidential Medal of Freedom from President George W. Bush. In 2006,

he was one of five inaugural members elected to the National Collegiate Basketball Hall of Fame, along with Oscar Robertson, Dean Smith, Bill Russell, and Dr. James Naismith. In 2008 he fell at home and broke his wrist and collarbone and spent weeks in rehabilitation. In late May 2010, he was hospitalized, and he died at UCLA Medical Center on June 4, 2010, at the age of 99.

Wooden's success was legendary and he became an iconic figure of basketball dominance as well as Christian principles. His records of NCAA dominance are unlikely ever to be approached, let alone broken. He is seen as almost a mystical figure in popular American culture.

Murry R. Nelson

See also Abdul-Jabbar, Kareem; Final Four; Naismith Memorial Basketball Hall of Fame; NCAA; Robertson, Oscar; Russell, Bill; *The Sporting News*; UCLA Basketball; Walton, Bill

Suggested Resources
John Wooden Website. http://www.coachwooden.com/. Accessed August 27, 2011.
Litsky, Frank, and John Branch. "John Wooden, Who Built Incomparable Dynasty at UCLA, Dies at 99." June 4, 2010. http://www.nytimes.com/2010/06/05/sports/ncaabasketball/05wooden.html. Accessed August 30, 2011.
Wooden, John. *Practical Modern Basketball*. Upper Saddle River, NJ: Benjamin Cummings, 1998.
Wooden, John, and Jay Carty. *Coach Wooden's Pyramid of Success: Building Blocks for a Better Life*. Ventura, CA: Regal, 2009.
Wooden, John, with Jack Tobin. *They Call Me Coach*. New York: McGraw-Hill, 2003.

Woods, Tiger (1975–)

As far back as he can remember Tiger Woods has always loved to play golf. In fact, even before his mother gave birth she claims his restlessness would stop whenever she walked onto a golfing green. A child prodigy, Tiger appeared on numerous television shows to exhibit his incredible talents, which included meeting Johnny Carson on *The Tonight Show* and putting with Bob Hope on *The Mike Douglas Show*.

Professional golfer Tiger Woods. (Shutterstock.)

With this in mind, it is no surprise that Eldrick "Tiger" Woods grew up to be one of the greatest golfers of all time. The long hours at the driving range and countless trips up and down the links helped prepare him for the rigors of professional golf, but nothing could prepare Tiger for his role in the public spotlight as an African American playing a game traditionally reserved for white men. Not only must Tiger Woods navigate being perhaps the most recognizable athlete in the world, but because of his ethnically diverse racial background the media has also charged him with the responsibility of representing minority athletes across the country—a task Tiger has experienced with varying levels of comfort throughout his career. Despite these difficulties, however, Tiger Woods has established his legendary status as an icon of golf. Although Tiger's run as the number one–ranked golfer in the world came to an end in 2010 after the details of his very public divorce

from Elin Nordegren came to light, his tenacity and determination to overcome the odds will continue to lead him to success.

Born Eldrick Tont Woods on December 30, 1975, Tiger gravitated toward golf from the beginning. His parents, Earl and Kultida Woods, say all of their earliest memories of their child in some way involve the game. Playing an extremely significant role in shaping the person Tiger has become, Earl and Kultida have both instilled lessons that continue to influence how he handles problems on and off the golf course. Although much has been made about the methods Earl Woods employed in training his young son—characterizing the relationship between Earl and Tiger as less father and son and more coach and pupil, or even drill sergeant and military recruit—none of the people close to the situation report anything but positive, fatherly support from Earl. His parents claim they simply supported Tiger's unusual attraction to the game of golf, and that if he would had wanted to collect stamps, for instance, they would have supported that instead. Because Tiger owes so much of who he is to his parents, knowing their background offers a telling portrait of Tiger himself.

One of the great traumas in Tiger's life was when his father, Earl Woods, died on May 3, 2006, at the age of 74 after losing his battle with prostate cancer. A major source of inspiration, instruction, and motivation, Earl Woods was determined to provide a positive upbringing for his son. Feeling the pains and regrets from an earlier marriage that produced two other children, Earl would not let himself make the same mistakes with Tiger. Born into modest conditions in 1932, Earl grew up in Manhattan, Kansas, raised mainly by his eldest sister, Hattie, after he lost both his mother and father to strokes at a young age. Even though he did not get much time with his parents, their influence on him lasted his entire life. Earl's father, Miles Woods, worked as a brick mason and instilled in Earl the value of a hard day's work. Miles was an ambitious young man and always had dreams of playing professional baseball. Earl's mother, Maude Woods, instilled the value of proper etiquette and a college education, an extremely rare achievement for an African American woman during this time period in the United States. Maude had earned her college degree and made sure

Earl understood the importance of higher education before her untimely death. Although Miles and Maude both died too young, Earl would internalize their messages and incorporate both in his own life.

With an appreciation for the value of both an education and demanding manual labor, Earl continued to honor his parents' wishes and made choices in his life that he believed would have made his parents proud. Because Miles always dreamed of playing professional baseball and because Maude held higher education in such esteem, Earl decided to continue those dreams and accept an athletic scholarship at nearby Kansas State University to play baseball. As his son would do years later in a different sport, Earl also established a couple of racial firsts, becoming not only the first African American baseball player at Kansas State, but the first in the entire Big 12 Conference (known then as the Big 7). Although his career as a baseball player would be short-lived, Earl's decision to join the ROTC program at Kansas State would have a far bigger impact on his life.

Earl's time in the army was volatile. Serving two tours of duty in Vietnam—from 1962 to 1963 and from 1970 to 1971—he received Special Forces training as a member of the elite army unit known as the Green Berets. During his second tour of duty in Vietnam, the army stationed Earl in South Vietnam. His assignment had been to visit relocation villages championing democracy over communism. In his travels, Earl met someone who would prove to be a great influence in his life. Lieutenant Colonel Vuong Dang Phong and Earl became fast friends after meeting in Vietnam. Developing a strong bond while overseas, Earl and Col. Phong faced many harrowing experiences, and on more than one occasion Col. Phong saved Earl's life. Nicknaming him after the most ferocious animal in the jungles of Vietnam, Earl dubbed Col. Phong "Tiger" after one of these occasions, and when Saigon fell in 1975, Earl promised Col. Phong that he would name his next-born son Tiger in his honor.

Although Earl had already been married and had three children by the end of his first tour in Vietnam, his home life had not been as fulfilling as he had hoped. After he divorced his first wife, Earl met Kultida Punsawad during a stopover in Thailand. Playing a much more behind-the-scenes role than Earl, Kultida's influence on Tiger is nonetheless apparent. Characterized by spiritual tranquility and an even temper, Kultida taught Tiger the Buddhist lessons she grew up with in Thailand, and this surely had a profound impact on Tiger's ability to quiet his internal dialogue and achieve a mental calm on the golf course. During a trip to Thailand when he was nine years old, Kultida brought Tiger to a Buddhist temple. After analyzing a chart that Kultida had been keeping on Tiger, the Buddhist monk declared, unaware of the attention Tiger had already received for his golfing, that Tiger was a very special child and would be a leader in whatever he chose to do.

Although the exact date is not known, Earl and Kultida married sometime in 1969, and by 1973 they moved to New York City where Earl was stationed at nearby Fort Hamilton. After only a year at Fort Hamilton, Earl retired from the military. Desiring to live closer to his children from his first marriage, Earl and Kultida moved to California; a year later Kultida gave birth to Tiger.

In deciding on a name for their newborn son, Earl and Kultida wanted a name representative of them both. They chose Eldrick because the "E" at the beginning represented Earl and the "K" at the end stood for Kultida. Remembering his promise to Col. Phong, however, Earl began calling his son "Tiger" at a very young age. The nickname stuck and soon everyone knew him as Tiger. Tiger's birth gave both Earl and Kultida something to pour their hearts and souls into. Both of his parents made huge sacrifices in supporting Tiger. Traveling from tournament to tournament, making sure he had the best equipment and could play at quality courses cost Tiger's parents a significant amount of time and money. In addition, Tiger and his parents endured many instances of social derision for having an interracial child playing on golf courses that typically saw only white players. Aside from their financial and emotional support, however, Tiger's parents contributed heavily to the skills he used to become the best golfer in the world.

Looking at Tiger the golfer, it is easy to see the influences both his parents have had. The capacity to work hard, persevere, and do whatever it takes to get the job done is clearly evidenced in Earl's approach to life, all values that were passed down from his own father. Although Earl was never a great golfer, he did achieve a high level of skill in the game and was able to instruct Tiger on the basic mechanics of a golf swing. Kultida taught Tiger the internal composure that has become a hallmark of his game. The inner game of golf is arguably the most important aspect of the game. Without the ability to calm one's mind and block out any external distractions, proper swing mechanics are meaningless. Kultida's background in Buddhist teachings undoubtedly provided a rich source from which to draw while instructing Tiger through his developmental years. Though each parent contributed mightily to Tiger's success, perhaps the biggest contribution from his parents came from the unwavering support each of them showed throughout Tiger's early playing career. Their unconditional love and support undeniably supplied Tiger with a wealth of determination, self-assurance, and the confidence to make mistakes without fearing reprisal.

As a baby not yet able to walk, Tiger was taken by Earl out to the garage to sit in a car seat and watch his father practice his golf swing. Entranced by this, Tiger would sit for hours and watch his father hit golf balls into a net. As soon as he could walk Tiger started swinging his own golf club, and he accompanied Earl to the driving range. Apparent from an early age, Tiger exhibited prodigy-like tendencies. His motivation and concentration were highly abnormal when compared to other children his age. At the driving range, people would stop their play to watch young Tiger strike the ball with more precision and gain more distance than most of the adult golfers at the range. Earl could not help but notice Tiger's talents and, knowing that his own instruction could bring Tiger only so far, began looking for a professional teacher. In what would eventually become known as "Team Tiger," his first coach, Rudy Duran, saw Tiger swing a golf club and knew he was a special young player. Over the next decade Earl would expose Tiger to a bevy of professional golf instructors, aiding him in achieving success on an international level, winning two Junior World Championships by the age of 10. The success of Tiger's junior career was unsurpassed to that point. His achievements on the golf course began to draw notice from the national media; *Sports Illustrated* featured a 14-year-old Tiger in its "In the Crowd" section

in a September 24, 1990, issue. Although he claims that his adolescence maintained a relatively normal structure, Tiger chose not to participate in any other sports growing up because it would have taken time away from golf practice. At the conclusion of middle school, Tiger began his high school career at Western High School in California.

Equally as dominant as his junior high career, Tiger's high school career featured four years of varsity golf and four state titles. Not to have his academic career outdone by his golfing successes, Tiger was perennially on the honor roll and became a member of the National Honor Society. In 1993 he was named the Dial High School Athlete Scholar of the United States. As early as age 13 Tiger began receiving recruiting letters from colleges across the country. By the time Tiger hit his senior year at Western High he had narrowed his list of potential colleges to two, Stanford and University of Nevada–Las Vegas. Again, the influence of Tiger's parents can be said to have had a huge impact on the school he chose. Kultida, an ever-present figure looming over her son, valued high-quality education. It is likely that Stanford's outstanding academic reputation and their track record of consistently graduating an extremely high percentage of student-athletes became the determining factor in Tiger's decision. Aside from the incredible accolades he garnered playing for Stanford's golf team, Tiger's college career represented his official coming-out party on a national pop-culture level.

Although Tiger accomplished something significant when he qualified for the 1992 and 1993 USGA Amateur Championships, he bowed out early in each of those contests. At the 1994 Amateur Championships, however, Tiger proved he belonged in the conversation about the brightest up-and-coming stars in golf. In fact, some say Tiger's run of three consecutive Amateur Championship titles from 1994 through 1996 resurrected the failing amateur golf tour. In the years leading up to Tiger's appearance on the amateur scene, the USGA amateur tour had experienced declining attendance and dwindling interest. The professional game has taken center stage in the golf world, and not since the likes of Arnold Palmer had the public been interested in amateur competition, preferring matches featuring the best players in the game, regardless if their play is motivated by monetary rewards or not. The popularity of amateurism—of those who play purely for the love of the game—waned in postwar America. But following Tiger's third consecutive Amateur Championship, the public's interest in amateur golf was reinvigorated; people could not wait to see Tiger tee off on the Professional Golfers Association (PGA) Tour.

While Tiger's success at every level of golf turned him into a national celebrity, each step of the way was marred by racial conflicts. Starting as early as age four, when Earl and Kultida brought their son to play golf at the country clubs, Tiger has endured the harsh spotlight of having an ethnically mixed appearance in a traditionally white game. Although the game of golf began in Scotland and was played mostly by the working class, upon its arrival in the United States in the mid-19th century the game quickly became an amateur pastime for elite, white-collar Americans, who looked down their noses at the "professionals"—mainly European immigrants who played tournaments for money. As the ethos surrounding golf's subculture slowly evolved into a country club sport catering to rich, white males, women and minorities found themselves on the outside looking in—as they did in so many other aspects of American life at that time. Even the PGA, which formed in 1916, maintained bylaws that prevented nonwhite players from becoming professionals. It was not until 1961 that the PGA of America removed their restriction on racial participation.

Though African Americans maintained a presence in the sport of golf since its beginning stages in the United States, they occupied mostly caddy roles on the nation's golf courses. Ironically, however, the first American-born professional golfer was an African American. As the growth of the PGA of America spread throughout the country, their exclusionary policies prompted the development of African American–owned golf courses to fuel the rising demand. Shady Rest Golf Club, perhaps the most well known and influential of these African American–owned courses, began in 1921 and catered to the more well-to-do African Americans of the time. Located in Scotch Plains, New Jersey, the course's close proximity to New York City made it a popular destination for African American celebrities such as W. E. B. Du Bois, Ella Fitzgerald, Duke Ellington, and Althea Gibson.

Shady Rest functioned as an escape from the injustices and inequalities they faced in everyday life for many working-class and professional men and women. Despite these few and far between oases, the discrimination exhibited by the PGA of America kept countless African Americans from ever having the chance to perform on a professional level. The world will never know the greatness of those players who were denied the opportunity to play. Upon the completion of his first Masters Tournament victory, the most prestigious tournament in North America, Tiger lamented this travesty and believed his triumph at the 1997 Masters provided at least a modicum of vindication for those who never had the chance to play.

Because of golf's volatile history concerning minorities and the elitist, country club aura that surrounds the game, Tiger's emergence as the odds-on favorite to become the next great golfer was met in the media with amplified publicity. An unprecedented anticipation of Tiger's professional career led to many different corporations being interested in signing Tiger to endorsement deals. Of course, by 1997 there had been many African American athletes that crossed over into mainstream pop culture, such as Bo Jackson and Michael Jordan, but the fact that he played golf made Tiger's situation unique. Prior to Tiger the public had not seen a truly dominant African American golfer, and his announcement that he would seek entry into the PGA of America and to play on the PGA Tour—foregoing his amateur status—was met with mixed reactions. Exemplifying the uncertainty about how Tiger would be received by the public—how a black man playing golf would be received by the public—the *Wall Street Journal* printed a three-page ad featuring text ending with the quote: "There are still golf courses in the United States that I cannot play on because of the color of my skin. I'm told I'm not ready for you. Are you ready for me?"

An inescapable issue for Tiger, the makeup of his racial background occupied much of the public discourse in the early part of his career. Not all child prodigies end up realizing their great potential, but Tiger defied these odds time after time. In 1996–1997, his first year as a professional, Tiger shattered many records and set precedents that astounded onlookers. Tiger took top honors in six PGA Tour events, became the youngest player to ever win the Masters tournament with a record-setting 12-stroke margin of victory, was named PGA Tour Rookie of the Year, Associated Press Male Athlete of the Year, and the ESPY Male Athlete of the Year, and led the list of PGA money earners with $2,440,831 in winnings. Although accolades such as these were nothing new to Tiger, his victory at the 1997 Masters not only set the margin of victory record but also made Tiger the first major champion of African or Asian descent. A brief review of the media coverage after Tiger's improbable victory shows that the issue of race receives at least a mention in a vast majority, often comparing him in some way to Jackie Robinson.

At times Tiger embraced his status as a role model, providing a positive example for other African American children to emulate. For example, the Tiger Woods Foundation has assisted with the proliferation of golf among inner-city minority youth through financial and emotional support since 1997. At other times the pressure of representing all black Americans took its toll. Attempting to deflect some of the responsibility to the African American population, Tiger began identifying himself as not only of African, but also of Asian descent, citing his mother's Thai background. Referring to his ethnic heritage as "Cablinasian"—a mix of Caucasian, African, Indian, and Asian—Tiger ultimately wanted to be known simply as an American. His extraordinary success early in his career, however, continued to thrust him and his racial background into the national spotlight.

Throughout the remainder of the 1990s and the better part of the 2000s Tiger Woods dominated the field. To date Tiger has won 71 PGA Tour events, placing him third on the all-time wins list behind only Sam Snead and Jack Nicklaus. He has won 14 major tournaments (the Masters four times, the U.S. Open three times, the British Open Championship three times, and the PGA Championship four times); he has been named PGA of America and PGA Tour Player of the Year eight times; and he has been the PGA Tour leading money winner nine times throughout his illustrious career. Tiger was ranked number one on and off during his career, but established a new record for consecutive weeks at number one with 281 weeks

between 1999 and 2005. As astounding and prolific as Tiger's accomplishments, victories, and professional successes are, they have been well documented in available literature. As with anyone at the pinnacle of one's profession, however, Tiger's unprecedented success, coupled with the fact that his success came in a sport traditionally reserved for white men, led to an acute level of interest in his personal life that few (inter)national celebrities have experienced.

In an ostensibly storybook love affair Tiger met Elin Nordegren at the 2001 Open Championship. Nordegren, a Swedish model, and Tiger wed in 2004 on the island of Barbados. Giving birth to their first child in 2007, a daughter named Sam Alexis Woods, Tiger and Elin seemed poised to become pop-culture's next "It Couple." Because of his success on the golf course there has always been interest in Tiger on a cultural level, but after his marriage to Elin, tabloids and celebrity paparazzi could not get enough of him and his beautiful new bride. Being a naturally private person—evidenced by the name he christened his yacht: *Privacy*—Tiger shied away from the extreme media coverage, choosing instead to focus on his family. From the outside looking in, Tiger had it all: a loving family, a hugely successful professional life, and enough money to never have to worry about not having money. However, shortly after the birth of their second child in 2009, a son named Charlie Axel Woods, rumors began to surface about Tiger's involvement in extramarital affairs.

In an awkward and befuddling turn of events, Tiger Woods—once golf's golden boy and mentor to young African American golfers around the country—fell from his pedestal and came crashing back down to Earth. It began on November 25, 2009, with a *National Enquirer* story claiming Tiger cheated on his wife with a New York nightclub employee named Rachel Uchitel. Although Uchitel denied these reports, two days after this story went to print Tiger inexplicably crashed his vehicle into a hedge and a fire hydrant less than a mile from his home in Orlando, Florida. After he was treated for minor lacerations, the police issued Tiger with a citation for careless driving, and he offered no immediate explanation for why it happened. This incident fueled the ensuing firestorm as nearly every media outlet aired it as their top story. In the days that followed this bizarre episode, many more reports came in from women all across the country claiming that they too had engaged in sexual activity with Tiger, some claiming that their illicit relationship lasted for over two years. As Tiger's personal life began to unravel before the nation's eyes, he announced that he would be taking an indefinite leave of absence from the PGA Tour, even bowing out of his own charity event in 2009, the Chevron World Challenge. These events had a humanizing effect on him for many onlookers. Prior to this, the nation viewed Tiger as unbeatable, both in golf and in life. Many critics even wondered if he was harmful to the game because he was too good, too dominant. Following these events, however, Tiger's mythic invincibility had been shattered.

After more than a dozen women emerged as accusers, Tiger and Elin announced their plans to divorce. Tiger made a public admission and apology on national television, announcing his plans to seek treatment for a sexual addiction. With that stunning admission and apology, the descent of Tiger's fall from grace had been completed. The once great promoter of all things consumer product–related had his endorsement deals from Gillette, Accenture, TAG Heuer, AT&T, General Motors, and Gatorade, among others, either canceled outright or not renewed. Once the brutal storm front had passed, the wreckage included over 120 women over a span of five years. Tiger's malfeasance resulted in the loss of his family, his career, and a large portion of his fortune. Detailing every gruesome aspect, the media covered these events feverishly as Tiger stepped down from his place among the PGA Tour's best golfers.

Never one to let the pressures of a situation get the best of him, Tiger's poise on the golf course would need to carry him through this part of his life as well. Taking some time off from the game, Tiger did not return to tournament play until April 2010 when he made an impressive fourth-place finish at the Masters. Following this, however, Tiger battled a series of injuries, failing to win a single tournament in that season for the first time in his career. Dropping to a low of number 58 in the world golf rankings, Tiger did not give up or give in to the pressure. Although, by his own standards,

2011 proved to be an unsuccessful campaign, he did manage a third-place finish at the Emirates Australian Open and finally broke through to the winner's circle at the 2011 Chevron World Challenge in December—working his way back up the rankings to number 25 after his first win in over two years. In March 2012, Tiger won his first PGA tournament since 2009, winning the Arnold Palmer in Florida and taking home just over $1 million. Then in May, he won the Memorial in Ohio, before finishing in the U.S. Open in a tie for 21st, but finishing 3rd at the British Open. Nevertheless, his popularity continues as he ranked number one among athletes in the *Forbes* ranking of the top 100 celebrities for the 11th consecutive year.

Like any great American saga, Tiger Woods's life has been mixed with jubilant highs and agonizing lows. His unparalleled success in a sport traditionally reserved for white men generated an intense interest in his sporting career among the national media outlets, and his subsequent fall from grace only fanned the fires. Now playing the role of underdog, his pursuit of once again reaching the top will be watched and documented with similar zeal. Regardless of whether or not he returns to the level of dominance he demonstrated in the early part of his career, he will continue to captivate audiences and defy stereotypes. Although Tiger's story is yet unfinished, his status as a fixture of American pop culture has been cemented.

Jarrod Jonsrud

See also Advertising and Sport; ESPY Awards; Gatorade; Jackson, Bo; Jordan, Michael; The Masters; Nicklaus, Jack; Palmer, Arnold; Robinson, Jackie; *Sports Illustrated*

Suggested Resources

Clary, Jack. *Tiger Woods*. Twickenham, England: Tiger Books International, 1997.
Londino, Lawrence. *Tiger Woods: A Biography*. Westport, CT: Greenwood Press, 2006.
"Tiger Woods." PGA Tour. http://www.pgatour.com/golfers/008793/tiger-woods/. Accessed January 23, 2012.
Tiger Woods Website. http://web.tigerwoods.com/index. Accessed January 23, 2012.
Woods, Earl, and Pete McDaniel. *Training a Tiger: A Father's Guide to Raising a Winner in Both Golf and Life*. New York: HarperCollins, 1997.

World Series

There is no sports event in the United States with the tradition, the memories, and the excitement of the World Series. The Super Bowl is the biggest one-day event in sports, but it has only been around since 1966. The NCAA Tournament was played in relative obscurity until the 1960s and didn't become fully televised and followed until the 1980s. The World Series, however, combines over 100 years of tradition with high drama and a mélange of memories from everyone who has ever followed American sport.

Baseball, or base ball, as it was originally known, was played in various forms and under various names in the earliest days of the American republic. The Civil War served as a kind of sports "melting pot," allowing the diverse forms to be synthesized and many rules standardized as soldiers from different parts of the country came together in the armies and played versions of baseball in their down time.

In 1869 the first professional baseball team, the Cincinnati Red Stockings, were formed and played games around the country. As other teams were formed, professional leagues began and the first successful and long-lasting major league, the National League, was formed in 1876. Over the next 24 years, other major leagues came and went until, in 1900, the American League, which had changed its name and scope from the Western League in 1894, became recognized as a legitimate major league, at least by the American League and its initial president, Ban Johnson.

The American League then began raiding the National League for players and in 1902 the two leagues agreed to a truce. That included a moratorium on raiding, an agreed-upon set of rules, and the formation of a national commission to serve as the governing body of the major leagues. Although there was no provision for a series between the two league champions at the end of the season, the two owners of the 1903 champions, the Boston Pilgrims of the American League and the Pittsburgh Pirates of the National, agreed to a nine-game, end-of-season series. The Pilgrims won in eight games, but in 1904, John McGraw, the manager of the New York Giants, the National League champions, refused to play a season-ending series against the AL champs, the Boston Pilgrims, noting that his Giants were the champions of the only real major league.

Thus, in 1905, the first fully league-sanctioned World Series was played, pitting the Giants and their ace, Christy Mathewson, against the Philadelphia A's of Connie Mack. One important part of the official agreement was that the players would receive a percentage of the gate from the first four games only, thus ensuring that players would not try to extend the game through poor play to maximize their pay. At that time, pitchers routinely pitched on three or two days' rest and complete games were the rule, rather than the exception. Nevertheless, Mathewson's record in the 1905 Series of winning three games, all shutouts, in six days was astounding even for the time and pitcher. Since that time, a few other pitchers have won three games in a series, but always in a seven-game series, with travel days included. Mathewson's and the Giants' performances made John McGraw's taunts of the prior year seem accurate. However, the next year, 1906, the heavily favored Cubs, who had won 116 of 154 games and who sported the famous infield combination of Tinker to Evers to Chance, lost to their cross-city rivals, the Chicago White Sox, in six games. The powerful Cubs, however, came back to take the next two World Series in 1907 and 1908. As of 2012, the Cubs had gone 104 years without another World Series victory.

The next "dynasty" was that of Connie Mack's Philadelphia A's, winning the World Series in 1910, 1911, and 1913. In the 1911 series, John Baker earned the moniker "Home Run" Baker by hitting two homers in two days, a highly unusual feat in the dead-ball era when the season home run leader in the major leagues failed to exceed 21 until 1911, then not again until 1915, when the leader hit 24. The A's failed to win in 1914 when the "Miracle Braves" of Boston came from last place in July and won 68 of their last 87 games to capture the National League pennant. They then swept the A's in four games for the title.

The other Boston team, formerly the Pilgrims, now the Red Sox, captured three of the next four World Series with their dynamic pitcher-outfielder, Babe Ruth, leading them to victory. In the 1918 World Series, Ruth set a record by pitching 29⅔ consecutive scoreless innings, a record that would stand until 1961 when it was

Baseball teams and fans, including President Calvin Coolidge, await the start of the last game of the World Series between the Washington Senators and the New York Giants on October 10, 1924. (Library of Congress.)

broken by Whitey Ford of the New York Yankees. A year after setting that record, Ruth was sold to the New York Yankees, beginning the greatest baseball dynasty of all time. Before that, however, the 1919 Series between Cincinnati and the Chicago White Sox nearly destroyed baseball as eight players from the favored Sox were later exiled from the game for taking or not reporting bribes to throw the Series, which they lost to the Reds, five games to three. Those White Sox have been known as the Black Sox ever since.

Beginning in 1921, the World Series was strictly a New York affair for three straight years with the Giants winning the first two years and the Yankees breaking through for their first pennant in 1923. After two more years the Yankees returned to the Fall Classic in 1926, but were defeated by the Cardinals and their Hall of Fame player-manager, Rogers Hornsby. The 1927 Yankees, who came to be known as Murderers' Row, won the pennant by 19 games, then swept the Pirates in four games. They repeated in 1928, but were denied another World Series title until 1932. In between the Philadelphia A's won back-to-back championships and lost in the Series in 1931 before Mack, always in need of money, broke the team up and sold most of the stars; the A's did not get back to the World Series

until 1972, after franchise moves from Philadelphia to Kansas City and then on to Oakland in 1968.

The St. Louis Cardinals and their "Gas House Gang" were champions in 1931 and 1934 with the latter squad getting all four wins from the Dean brothers, Jay (Dizzy) and Paul (Daffy). In the climactic seventh game, Joe "Ducky" Medwick hit a triple and slid into third base, sending the Detroit Tiger third baseman sprawling. The Detroit fans, angry over their impending loss of game seven and the Series, as well as Medwick's perceived rough play, pelted him with fruit and vegetables when he resumed his outfield position. The commissioner, Kenesaw Mountain Landis, ordered him removed from the game to maintain order, making Medwick the only player to be ejected from a World Series game by a commissioner.

The 1932 Series was the last for 37-year-old Babe Ruth, but he added to his legend by seeming to call his own home run in the third game of the Series in Wrigley Field. The Yankees swept the Cubs, powered more by Lou Gehrig, who drove in eight runs in the four games, than Ruth.

Yankee dominance returned in 1936 as the Bronx Bombers won four World Series championships in a row and six in eight years under manager Joe

McCarthy. The Cincinnati Reds won in 1940 and the St. Louis Cardinals in 1942. The Cards had a great decade in the 1940s, also winning in 1944 and 1946. In 1944 the only all–St. Louis series was staged with the Cards defeating the Browns in six games. The Browns moved to Baltimore and became the Orioles, ending the Missouri rivalry. In 1946 the Cardinals, led by Hall of Famer Stan Musial, defeated the Boston Red Sox in fellow Hall of Famer Ted Williams's only World Series appearance. Neither excelled in this classic, Musial hitting .222 and Williams .200.

In 1947, a tense rivalry between the Yankees and the Brooklyn Dodgers in World Series play heated up, but the Yankees almost always came out on top. The Yanks had won in 1941, then edged the Dodgers in seven games in 1947. The most exciting game was the fourth game when Bill Bevans of the Yankees took a no-hitter into the ninth inning, but with two outs, Cookie Lavagetto of the Dodgers doubled off the wall to spoil the no-hitter, drive in two runs, and give the Dodgers the victory. There would be no no-hitters in the World Series for another nine years. Also in 1947, Jackie Robinson became the first African American to appear in a World Series, getting seven hits for the Dodgers in a losing cause.

The Cleveland Indians interrupted the Yankees' latest win skein in 1948, topping the Boston Braves in six games. The Indians have not won a World Series title since. Beginning in 1949, the Yankees bested their record of the 1930s, winning five championships in a row, led by Joe DiMaggio, then by his successor in center field, Mickey Mantle. Casey Stengel was the manager and made all the right moves in pennant drives and World Series games. In three of those years the Dodgers were the victims, but in the other two, the Whiz Kid Philadelphia Phillies were beaten (1950) and the New York Giants were the losers (1951), both times after defeating the Dodgers in playoffs to get into the Series.

The Indians again broke the Yankee winning streak in 1954 as they won 111 games and the pennant, but they then lost to Willie Mays and the New York Giants in four straight games. The Yankees and Dodgers met for the next two years and both were memorable, the former because the Dodgers, for the first and only time in Brooklyn history, won. The next year, the Yankees

won in seven games, but in game five, Don Larsen pitched a perfect game, the only one in Series history. The Yankees met the Milwaukee Braves in the next two World Series with the Braves winning in 1957 and the Yankees reversing the result in 1958.

In 1958 the unthinkable happened when the Dodgers and the Giants abandoned New York for the West Coast. The Dodgers fell to seventh in 1958, but managed to win the pennant in 1959 and face the surprising Chicago White Sox in their first World Series appearance since 1919. The Dodgers played in the Memorial Coliseum, an enormous edifice much more suited for track or football and built for the 1932 Olympics. It seated over 90,000 and World Series attendance records were shattered during this Fall Classic, which the Dodgers won in six games.

In 1960 the Pirates were in the Series for the first time since 1927 and they were rocked in three games by the Yankees, but managed to win three others to send the Series to a seventh game. In what was the first World Series ended by a walk-off homer, Bill Mazeroski broke a 9–9 tie to win the game and the Series for the Pirates.

The Yankees won the next two Series, but were beaten in 1963 by the Dodgers. The Dodgers won again in 1965, topping the Twins, who were in the series for the first time, then were upset by the Orioles in 1966, Sandy Koufax's last games as a player. He had been the MVP of both the 1963 and 1965 Series, striking out 52 in the two classics, but the Dodgers were swept in 1966.

In 1969 the New York Mets, an expansion franchise begun in 1962, stormed to the National League pennant, then surprised the favored Orioles in five games to win the Series. Beginning in 1972, the Oakland A's had a mini-dynasty, winning three straight titles, led by Reggie Jackson and a great pitching staff, led by Jim "Catfish" Hunter.

It was during the 1970s that the World Series began playing more games at night. Previously all games had been during the day and schoolchildren would have to either beg their teachers to allow them to listen to the games in school or they would sneak the first transistor radios into school to listen through earphones, covertly. As the Series became more and more a night event, many schoolchildren would be shut out from viewing all or most of the games.

The 1975 World Series seemed to revive interest in baseball, which had been slowly declining. The Reds defeated the Red Sox in seven games, but game six is still seen as one of the greatest contests in Series history, won by a home run in the 12th inning by Carlton Fisk of the Red Sox. The Reds and their Big Red Machine repeated in 1976. For the next two years, the Yankees-Dodgers rivalry resumed with the Yankees winning both times, highlighted by Reggie Jackson's five homers, three in one game, in 1977.

After the Phillies won in 1980, for the first time ever, the Dodgers returned to the Series in 1981 and beat the Yankees. Over the next nine years, there were nine different World Series champions, illustrating the new parity of Major League Baseball. For some of these teams, it was their first title ever and these included the Kansas City Royals in 1985 and the Minnesota Twins in 1987. They repeated in 1991.

In the 1988 Series, the Dodgers met the heavily favored Oakland A's. In game one, the game was tied in the bottom of the ninth and Manager Tommy Lasorda sent an injured Kirk Gibson to the plate against Hall of Fame reliever Dennis Eckersley, who had led the league with 45 saves. With two outs and the A's up, 4–3, Eckersley walked Mike Davis, then faced Gibson, who limped to the plate. After going 0–2, Gibson worked the count to 3–2, then muscled a pitch over the fence to win the game, 5–4. This image is often shown during the season and during the playoffs and is readily available at a variety of Internet sites.

In 1992 and 1993 the World Series champion was not a team from the United States; the Toronto Blue Jays captured the title, highlighted by a Series-ending home run by Joe Carter in the bottom of the ninth of game six. Baseball made a large error in 1994, allowing a strike to end the season early and cancel the World Series for the first time since McGraw's refusal to play in 1904. It would take a while to win back the fans, and two new teams in the 1995 Series made an effort, but it was a forgettable Series as the Atlanta Braves defeated the Indians in six games.

The year 1996 saw the return of the New York Yankees to some dominance, winning the Series in

The Rarities

The two most rare events in a game are a triple play or a perfect game. The history of the World Series has one of each. In 1920, the Cleveland Indians played the Brooklyn Robins (the Dodgers had changed their name to honor Wilbert Robinson for a time). In game 5 of the Series, the Dodgers had runners on first and second in the fifth inning with no one out. Clarence Mitchell hit a line drive that was snared by shortstop Bill Wambsganss. Both runners had been running on the play and Wambsganss stepped on second for the second out, then tagged the runner coming from first for the third out. Not only was it a triple play, but an unassisted triple play.

In 1956 Don Larsen of the New York Yankees took the mound for game five after being rocked by the Brooklyn Dodgers in game two. In the second inning, Jackie Robinson hit a line drive that caromed off the third baseman's glove, but right to the shortstop, who threw out Robinson. In the fifth, Gil Hodges hit a deep drive to center, but Mickey Mantle was able to make a running, back-handed catch to preserve the no-hitter. The last batter, Dale Mitchell, was called out on a high outside pitch for strike three. Catcher Yogi Berra raced to the mound and jumped into Larsen's arms, one of the most famous of World Series shots ever made.

1996, 1998, 1999, and 2000. The latter Series was the first Interborough Series since the Dodgers had left New York, but there was little real excitement as the Yankees won in five games. The one exception to the Yankee run was 1997, when the Florida Marlins were champions, defeating the Cleveland Indians, who lost for the second time in three years. Florida returned to the Series in 2003, winning once again.

In between those Marlin triumphs were a number of notable Series highlights. In 2001, the Arizona Diamondbacks upset the Yankees in seven games; in 2002 the Anaheim Angels won their first Series, beating the Giants in an all-California series.

Since the sale of Babe Ruth in 1919, the Red Sox had been thwarted by what was referred to as the Curse of the Bambino, failing to win a World Series. It looked to be more of the same in 2004 as they were down three games to none to the Yankees in the American League Championship Series. But then, the seemingly impossible occurred as the Red Sox won four games in a row to top the Yankees, then followed that with four straight wins against the Cardinals to win the World Series. They then repeated their victory in 2007.

Another seemingly cursed team, the Chicago White Sox, who had not won the World Series since 1917, made it two sweeps in a row as they beat the Houston Astros in four games in 2005. The Cardinals were the winners in both 2006 and 2011, the latter being the most amazing, since the Cards didn't even make the playoffs until the end of the last day of the season. They defeated the Texas Rangers, who had also lost in 2010, that time to the Giants, who won their first title in San Francisco. The Giants repeated as champions in 2012.

The year 2008 saw the Philadelphia Phillies win, then lose in six games in 2009 to the Yankees. Both teams expected to return to the Series the next two years, but lost in the playoffs.

As of 2012 the New York Yankees have had 27 titles in 40 appearances, the most, by far, of any team. The St. Louis Cardinals have had 11 titles in 18 appearances. Of the original franchises, the Chicago Cubs now carry the longest streak without a World Series victory, with their last one in 1908.

Murry R. Nelson

See also "Baseball's Sad Lexicon"; Big Red Machine; Black Sox Scandal; Boston Red Sox; Brooklyn Dodgers; Chicago Cubs; Cincinnati Reds; Cleveland Indians; Dean, Dizzy; Gehrig, Lou; Hunter, Jim "Catfish"; Jackson, Reggie; Koufax, Sandy; Landis, Kenesaw Mountain; Los Angeles Dodgers; Mays, Willie; Mazeroski Homer, Game Seven, 1960 World Series; Murderers' Row; Musial, Stan "The Man"; New York Mets; New York Yankees; 1975 World Series Sixth Game; Oakland A's; Robinson, Jackie; Ruth, Babe; St. Louis Cardinals; Williams, Ted; Wrigley Field

Suggested Resources

Fimrite, Ron. *The World Series*. New York: Sports Illustrated, 1993.

Honig, Donald. *The World Series: An Illustrated History from 1903 to the Present*. New York: Crown, 1986.

Leventhal, Josh. *The World Series: An Illustrated History of the Fall Classic*. Darby, PA: Diane, 2002.

"World Series." Baseball Almanac. http://www.baseball-almanac.com/ws/wsmenu.shtml. Accessed January 9, 2012.

World Wrestling Entertainment (WWE)

World Wrestling Entertainment (WWE) is the most recent incarnation of the sport known as professional wrestling. If someone brings up the subject of professional wrestling at the office water cooler, in a dorm room bull session, or in a middle school lunchroom, a more lively discussion is likely to ensue than had the topic been politics or religion. Is it real or fake? Is it combat or just show? Is it competition or theater?

Although wrestling as an ancient martial art has been around since ancient Greece, professional wrestling traces its roots to the traveling carnival strong man who would challenge anyone to beat him in the ring or even to last 10 minutes. Challengers almost never won the prize money, since the strong man had carnies that would cheat to guarantee his victory. In the late 1800s, promoters put such wrestling events in arenas much like boxing. In 1901, a loose organization was formed called the National Wrestling Association (NWA).

After World War II, the NWA divided wrestling into regional leagues. A gentlemen's agreement kept the federations from stealing talent from one another or from expanding into another league's region. However, the World Wide Wrestling Federation (WWWF), which operated in the northeast, tended to be a maverick. Started in the early 1960s by Vince McMahon Sr., the WWWF came under the ownership of his son, Vince McMahon Jr., in the 1970s. The younger McMahon changed the name to World Wrestling Federation (WWF) and ignored the gentlemen's agreement. He competed directly with the regional leagues, stealing their talent, scheduling arena shows in their areas, and securing lucrative cable TV contracts.

Unable to compete, the old regional NWA leagues disappeared. By the 1980s, only one was still in existence, operating in the Southeast. Ted Turner, the Atlanta-based media mogul, purchased this league and changed its name to World Championship Wrestling (WCW). Turner's televised events competed directly with McMahon's, and for a time the WCW drew the best talent away from the WWF and beat McMahon in the ratings. Thanks in part to poorly conceived story lines and a federal investigation into steroid use, which eventually cleared McMahon, the WWF declined in popularity. However, McMahon adopted new creative approaches and hired young, talented wrestlers, and the WWF revived. In 2001, McMahon purchased the WCW, gaining control of all of its wrestlers, trademarks, and video library. In 2002, the WWF became World Wrestling Entertainment, Inc. (WWE), a change made in response to a lawsuit by the World Wildlife Fund.

Today, the WWE is a publicly traded, privately controlled sports entertainment company dealing primarily in professional wrestling with major revenue sources also coming from film, music, product licensing, and direct product sales. It is the largest professional wrestling company in the world, reaching 14.4 million viewers in the United States and broadcasting its shows in 30 languages to more than 145 countries.

Typically, matches are staged between a protagonist (an audience favorite or "the good guy or gal") and an antagonist (a villain with arrogance, a tendency to break the rules, or other despicable qualities).

Among the more recognizable "superstars" of the male wrestlers, over the past 75 years, are Buddy "Nature Boy" Rogers (Herman Rohde), Gorgeous George (George Wagner), Vern Gagne, Andre the Giant (Andrzej Renat Russimow), Ric Flair (Richard Fliehr), Hulk Hogan (Terry Bollea), Jesse Ventura (wrestler turned governor of Minnesota), the Rock (Dwayne Johnson, wrestler turned movie star), Stone Cold Steve Austin (Steven Anderson), the Undertaker (Mark Calaway), Randy Orton, and John Cena.

The Women's Division of professional wrestling has maintained a recognized World Champion since 1937, when Mildred Burke (Mildred Bliss) won the World Women's title. She then formed the Women's Wrestling Association in the early 1950s and recognized herself as the first champion. Perhaps the most famous female wrestler was the Fabulous Moolah (Mary Lillian Ellison) who claimed the Women's Championship in 1958. More recent "divas" of the past 25 years include Chyna (Joan Marie Laurer), Torrie Wilson, Beth Phoenix (Elizabeth Carolan), and Mickie James.

Fans of professional wrestling have their own subculture. Many collect trading cards and autographs of wrestlers that they have come to know and revere on the WWE weekly shows, *RAW* and *Smackdown*, or the

WWE star The Great Khali, left, faces off with television personality Johnny Knoxville on October 13, 2008, at the Honda Center in Anaheim, California. (Chris Weeks/AP Images for WWE.)

pay-per-view events such as Wrestlemania, King of the Ring, or the Royal Rumble.

There are those that disdain pro wrestling because it is scripted. Certainly, professional wrestlers are exceptional athletes. They exercise and train for years to learn the moves and to practice how to implement them safely while still making it look dangerous. Sometimes, however, the performance goes awry and the injuries are real, even fatal.

On May 23, 1999, professional wrestler Owen Hart died tragically while attempting a dramatic ring entrance from the rafters of the Kemper Arena in Kansas City. Hart was in the process of being lowered

The German Provocateur

Although the late Baseball Hall of Fame sports announcer Jack Brickhouse was best known for his broadcasts on WGN radio and television for the Cubs, the White Sox, and the Bears, some followers of professional wrestling remember him best for his Saturday night show, *Live from the Marigold Arena!* on Chicago's North Side. During the course of his long career, Brickhouse interviewed thousands of people, from presidents to skid row bums, from potentates to prostitutes, but the interview that drew the greatest response was with professional wrestling villain Hans Schmidt at Marigold on a Saturday night in the early 1950s.

On that night, Schmidt made the following statements on network television: "I am going to win the championship and take it back to Germany where it belongs. I will never give an American a crack at it. People who teach sportsmanship to their children are crazy. The only answer is to win at any cost. I don't like the fans. As a matter of fact, I hate them."

Brickhouse had heard enough. He brought an abrupt end to the interview. Within 48 hours, WGN received over 5,000 letters and phone calls, all but a handful of them violently opposing Schmidt's tirade. The attorney general of the United States received calls demanding Schmidt's deportation as an undesirable alien.

The FBI dispatched an agent, Gus Kayne, to check out the whole story. What Kayne learned was that Hans Schmidt was not a German after all. He was a French Canadian whose real name was Guy LaRose who was not drawing very well as a wrestling attraction in Minneapolis, so his promoter said: "You don't look Canadian. From now on, you are a German villain and your name is Hans Schmidt!" LaRose/Schmidt became a $100,000 a year pro wrestler, big money for the early 1950s. Sport or entertainment?

or the show. This is not a sensationalistic attempt to leave a mark on this event. This is real life."

It is true that the plots are predetermined, the moves are choreographed, and the outcome is known to the participants before the bell is sounded. It is true that professional wrestlers are not really trying to injure each other. Sometimes, the bitterest enemies in the ring are really best friends and, often, the outlandish stories surrounding the characters and the rivalries are only the fantasies of scriptwriters; but to call wrestling "fake" is like calling an action movie fake. When people watch a movie, they know that the actor did not really die in that flaming wreck on an exploding bridge. Stunt people and special effects crews make those scenes seem real. Their work is very impressive and frequently earns them the accolades of the public and their peers. Pro wrestling is like that. That is why the corporation is known as World Wrestling Entertainment!

Harry Strong

See also Baseball Hall of Fame; WGN Television

Suggested Resources

Beekman, Scott. *Ringside: A History of Professional Wrestling in America.* Santa Barbara, CA: Praeger, 2006.

Brickhouse, Jack. *Thanks for Listening.* South Bend, IN: Diamond Communication, 1986.

Guttman, James. *World Wrestling Insanity: The Decline and Fall of a Family Empire.* Toronto, ON: ECW Press, 2006.

Mazer, Sharon. *Professional Wrestling: Sport and Spectacle.* Jackson: University Press of Mississippi, 1998.

Professional Wrestling. http://prowrestling.about.com/. Accessed November 1, 2010.

WWE Website. http://www.wwe.com/. Accessed November 1, 2010.

with a harness and grapple line when the equipment failed. He fell 78 feet into the ring below. He was pronounced dead on arrival at Truman Medical Center as a result of internal bleeding from a severed aorta. During the ominous silence in the arena while paramedics treated Hart (in his caped wrestling persona known as the Blue Blazer), ringside announcer James Ross ad-libbed to the pay-per-view audience: "Owen Hart has been terribly injured in this live broadcast. This is not a wrestling angle. This was not a part of the story line

Wrigley Field

Wrigley Field, which stands at 1060 West Addison Street on the north side of Chicago, Illinois, has been home to the Chicago Cubs baseball team since 1916. It is the oldest ballpark in the National League and the second-oldest active major league ballpark, after Fenway Park (1912) of the Boston Red Sox. Wrigley Field is nicknamed "The Friendly Confines," a phrase popularized by Cubs legend Ernie Banks, and

Wrigley Field, Chicago, Illinois. (Library of Congress.)

it stands as one of the last remaining monuments to a bygone era.

It was the first park to allow fans to keep foul balls. It was the first to have an organist. It was the first to build a permanent concession stand. It was the first to draw over one million fans in a single season. At the same time, it was the last major league ballpark to install lights. It has refused to replace its iconic manually operated scoreboard with a Jumbotron. There are no hidden bullpens concealed under the outfield stands. There are no costumed animal mascots or between-inning contests to deter fans from focusing on the fact that they are there to watch a Major League Baseball game. Wrigley is also known for its large art deco–style red marquee over the main entrance and for the unusual wind patterns off nearby Lake Michigan, less than a mile to the east, which can impact games dramatically.

It is somewhat ironic that the man who built Wrigley Field, Chicago lunchroom magnate Charles Weeghman, initially tried to destroy the Chicago Cubs.

Weeghman was the owner of the Chicago Whales of the old Federal Baseball League, a third major professional league that was only in operation for two years, 1914–1915. Weeghman knew that to compete in Chicago with the Cubs and the White Sox he needed a top-rate facility, so he hired renowned architect Zachary Taylor Davis to design Weeghman Park. Davis had also designed Comiskey Park for the White Sox on the south side of Chicago. Weeghman purchased a vacant lot in the middle of a residential neighborhood from Chicago Lutheran Theological Seminary. The irregularly shaped lot was bounded by West Waveland Avenue, Seminary Avenue, North Clark Street, West Addison Street, and North Sheffield Avenue. The ballpark was constructed in six weeks at a cost of $250,000. By the end of 1915, Weeghman had accomplished his goal. His Whales were the king of Chicago baseball, averaging over 10,000 fans per game, while the Cubs and White Sox combined were lucky to approach half that number.

Nevertheless, after the 1915 season, the Federal League folded. Every franchise except the Chicago Whales was losing money. Part of the settlement with the American and National Leagues was to allow Weeghman and nine colleagues to purchase the Cubs, merge them with the Whales, and play their games at Weeghman Field.

Among Weeghman's partners in buying the Cubs was a chewing gum entrepreneur named William Wrigley Jr., who used to boast that he could sell pianos to armless men in Borneo. Expelled from school in Philadelphia at age 12, Wrigley had left home and managed to survive by selling newspapers in New York City and soap in rural Pennsylvania. In 1891, he made his way to Chicago and soon after, at age 30, he got into the chewing gum business. In 1915, he collected addresses out of phone books all over the country and mailed four free sticks of chewing gum to 1.5 million people. He did the same thing again in 1919 with a bigger mailing list: seven million. This marketing ploy must have been a huge success, because Wrigley purchased the Cubs from Weeghman that very same year.

Over the next 20 years, Wrigley oversaw a number of major renovations to the ballpark, which was renamed Cubs Park that same year. He moved the grandstand and playing field 60 feet to the southwest between the 1922 and 1923 seasons. In 1926, he removed the left field bleachers and added a second deck to the grandstand, increasing the seating capacity to 38,143, and the Cubs' home was christened Wrigley Field. The current capacity is 41,160, making Wrigley the 10th smallest baseball venue in the major leagues.

The famous ivy was planted at the base of the brick outfield walls in 1937. It is not uncommon for a batted ball to become lost in the ivy. Special Wrigley rules allow an outfielder to raise both arms when a ball is lost, permitting the batter to be awarded a ground-rule double by the umpiring crew. Although the ivy appears to cushion the bricks, it is of little use as padding. Many an outfielder has staggered or been carried from the playing field as a consequence of losing a collision with Wrigley's unforgiving outfield wall.

The center field scoreboard, constructed in 1937, remains the biggest throwback in Wrigley Field. It is operated by hand as if the scoreboard were located at an old-time baseball or softball diamond in one of thousands of small towns across the country. When it was built by Bill Veeck, head of promotions in 1937, it was state-of-the-art. Now it is just "art," and somewhat primitive art at that. Most other scoreboards in major league parks feature huge screens that provide instant replays, pictures of fans, and commercials. But the way the Cubs see it, if people wanted to watch the game on television, they would have stayed home. They came to Wrigley to see it all in person.

The scoreboard looms invincibly over the intersection of Waveland and Sheffield, never having been hit by a baseball in a game. Two players came close, Pittsburgh Pirate Hall of Famer Roberto Clemente missing to the left and Cub outfielder Bill "Swish" Nicholson missing to the right. In a pregame stunt in 1951, golfer Sam Snead teed up a ball on home plate and *did* hit the scoreboard! One accommodation to modern technology, added in 1982, is a small electronic message board that briefly provides players' statistics, wishes happy birthday to fans, and announces upcoming game promotions. But the line scores of the game at hand and from other games (though not all) from around the country are hung the same way they have always been—by men and women who wander amid the bowels of the beast, putting up five-pound green metal plates with white or yellow numbers.

As previously mentioned, Wrigley Field was the last major league park to install lights. The Cubs held out for day baseball until August 8, 1988, when, despite the objections of fans, neighbors, and some city administrators, the Cubs played their first night game against the Philadelphia Phillies. Some allege that the gods of baseball were also against night baseball at Wrigley, because the game was rained out after just 3½ innings. However, the next night the Cubs defeated the New York Mets, 6–4, on a dry field, and the gods of baseball were mentioned no more, at least not in the context of cursing night baseball at Wrigley Field. What few fans may realize is that the Cubs were planning to install lights between the 1941 and 1942 seasons, but, following the attack on Pearl Harbor, the lights were donated to the war effort.

Wrigley Field has a "party room" with unreserved seating and unreserved enthusiasm as well: it is called "the bleachers." The bleachers comprise the modest seating area (no chairs, only benches) that extends from the left field foul pole around and above the outfield wall to the right field foul pole. Strange things take place out there in home run territory. For example, back in 1920, the Cubs asked the police to break up gambling in the bleachers, so officers disguised themselves as sailors, soldiers, farmers, and ice wagon drivers and raided the place, arresting 24 bettors. In the late 1950s and early 1960s, the bleachers were populated by a combination of teenage greasers in leather jackets and an organization called the Right Field Bleacher Choir. The Choir would sing during the seventh-inning stretch and also carried out brazen plots to smuggle beer into the ballpark. Once a Choir member sat in a wheelchair with a pony keg hidden under a blanket while other choristers wheeled him to his seat. On another occasion, the Choir also managed to hoist cases of beer by rope over the right field wall.

The most famous bleacher group of all appeared in the mid-1960s. They were known as the Bleacher Bums. The original Bums were 10 fans who sat in the left field bleachers. Their name was coined when two fans from Morton Grove, Illinois, known as Ma Barker and Big Daddy, held up a bed sheet transformed into a sign with a hole in the middle. A fan stuck his head through the hole encircled by the caption, "Hit the Bleacher Bum." The group's legend was expanded by a popular play, *Bleacher Bums*, written in 1977 by Chicago's Organic Theater Company, including Joe Mantegna and Dennis Franz, who later attained national fame in the television series *Criminal Minds* and *NYPD Blue*.

On hot summer days, popular Cub television broadcaster Harry Caray would sometimes abandon his booth in the press box and offer the play-by-play in the middle of some of his greatest admirers, the fans in the bleachers. The flamboyant Caray pioneered singing "Take Me Out to the Ballgame" during the seventh-inning stretch and he was not above lifting a cup of beer with his buddies in the bleachers as he directed the Wrigley faithful in song. Harry, who died in 1998, was the total personification of Wrigley Field. Big crowds, cold beer, and good baseball—it's what they both were all about.

Beginning in 1937, a flag with either a "W" (win) or "L" (loss) was hoisted on the scoreboard or foul pole to announce the results of the day's game. In 1982, the retired number of Ernie Banks (14) was

---

Vin Scully Pays Homage

In 1989, as the baseball world turned its eyes toward Chicago for game one of the National League playoffs, Hall of Fame broadcaster Vin Scully paid homage to Wrigley Field (The Lady) with this memorable tribute:

> She stands alone on the corner of Clark and Addison, this dowager queen, dressed in basic black and pearls, 75 years old, proud head held high and not a hair out of place, awaiting yet another date with destiny, another time for Mr. Right.
>
> She dreams as old ladies will of men gone long ago. Joe Tinker. Johnny Evers. Frank Chance. And those of recent vintage like her man Ernie. And the Lion [Leo Durocher]. And Sweet Billy Williams.
>
> And she thinks wistfully of what might have been [shots of the Cubs losing to the Padres in 1984], and the pain is still fresh and new, and her eyes fill, and her lips tremble, and she shakes her head ever so slightly. And then she sighs, pulls her shawl tightly around her frail shoulders, and thinks—this time, this time will be better.

But, alas, as any Cub fan knows, 1989 would *not* be better. Nor would 1998, 2003, 2007, or 2008, when the Cubs made the playoffs, but not the World Series. And still, The Lady waits.

---

mounted on the left field foul pole. In 1987, Billy Williams's number (26) was added to the right field foul pole. More recently, other players were honored with similar flags: Ron Santo (10), Ryne Sandberg (23), Ferguson Jenkins and Greg Maddux (both 31).

Although Wrigley Field has been the home of the Cubs since 1916, it has yet to see the Cubs win a World Series. It has hosted several (1923, 1929, 1932, 1936, 1938, and 1945, the last time the Cubs made it to the World Series); however, the last World Series win by the Cubs (1908) took place when the Cubs called the old West Side Park their home.

Wrigley Field has served as a venue for other sports beside baseball. The Chicago Bears of the National Football League (NFL) played their home games at Wrigley from 1921 to 1970 before relocating to Soldier Field. Wrigley Field once held the record for most NFL games played in a single stadium (365); however, that record was surpassed in 2003 by Giants

Stadium in New Jersey. The Northwestern Wildcats and the Illinois Fighting Illini of the Big Ten played a collegiate football game at Wrigley Field on November 20, 2010. It was the first collegiate football game at Wrigley since DePaul University played its regular season games there in 1938.

The Chicago Sting of the North American Soccer League (NASL) used Wrigley, along with Comisky Park, for their home matches in the late 1970s and early 1980s. On January 1, 2009, the National Hockey League played its 2009 Winter Classic at Wrigley, featuring the Chicago Blackhawks hosting the Detroit Red Wings.

In recent years, Wrigley Field has opened its doors, again over the objections of many of its neighbors, to a variety of concerts, including Jimmy Buffett (2005), the Police (2007), Elton John and Billy Joel (2009), Rascal Flatts (2009), and the Dave Matthews Band (2010).

Hollywood has featured Wrigley Field in a plethora of films, including *The Blues Brothers* (1980), *Ferris Bueller's Day Off* (1986), *A League of Their Own* (1992), *Rookie of the Year* (1993), and TV shows such as *ER*, *Crime Story*, *Chicago Hope*, *Prison Break*, *Perfect Strangers*, *My Boys*, and even the animated comedy *Family Guy*.

The Wrigley family sold the ballpark and the Chicago Cubs franchise to the (Chicago) Tribune Company in 1981. The new owner chose not to rename the Cubs home and found other ways to generate corporate sponsorship for the ballpark. Then, on October 27, 2009, Thomas S. Ricketts officially assumed 95 percent ownership of the Chicago Cubs, Wrigley Field, and 20 percent ownership of Comcast SportsNet Chicago. The Tribune retained 5 percent ownership. Ricketts has expressed no interest in selling the naming rights to Wrigley Field, preferring that it retain the name Cub fans have revered since 1926.

Harry Strong

See also Banks, Ernest "Ernie"; Baseball Hall of Fame; Caray, Harry; Chicago Bears; Chicago Cubs; Clemente, Roberto; National Football League; New York Mets; Philadelphia Phillies; Scully, Vin; "Take Me Out to the Ballgame"; Veeck, Bill

Suggested Resources

Gentile, Derek. *The Complete Chicago Cubs.* New York: Black Dog & Leventhal, 2002.

Jacob, Mark, and Stephen Green. *Wrigley Field.* Columbus, OH: McGraw-Hill, 2002.

Peterson, Paul Michael. *Chicago's Wrigley Field.* Mount Pleasant, SC: Arcadia, 2005.

Shea, Stuart. *Wrigley Field: The Unauthorized Biography.* Dulles, VA: Potomac Books, 2006.

Wrigley Field Website. http://cubs.com//ballpark. Accessed October 1, 2010.

X

X Games

X Games are a series of extreme sports contests begun in the mid-1990s, initially by young men, but now no longer limited by gender nor, at times, by age.

Many young men and women can still vaguely remember watching the first X Games, then called the Extreme Games. Members of the so-called Generation X were the main target audience for this made-for-television, Olympics-like sporting event, which featured a collection of risk-taking activities performed mainly, but not exclusively, by young white men who fancied themselves as athletic outsiders previously ignored and shunned by the gatekeepers of the American sports establishment.

An early experience—watching "The Condor," Mat Hoffman, catch "big air" on his BMX bike in a halfpipe, or Arlo Eisenberg follow suit on his inline skates, or street lugers repeatedly crashing into the bales of hay that lined the sides of the hilly street courses they attempted to traverse—instantly captured the fascination of many of these Gen Xers, glued to the television, spellbound by the daredevil antics, athletic audacity, and antiestablishment rebel style that marked these participants as different from the stereotypical image-conscious, highly processed, conformist, mainstream American athlete-celebrity that was often criticized by sport pundits. It seemed as if something new was certainly in the "big air."

The first iteration of the X Games took place in 1995. Staged in Newport, Rhode Island, and Mount Snow, Vermont, the event drew approximately 22,000 fans per day to the various sites of this four-day event. A modest average of 307,000 households tuned in to ESPN2 to watch what was billed as the Olympic games for "extreme sports." The original events held that year were aggressive inline skating, bicycle stunt riding, bungee jumping, extreme adventure racing, skateboarding, skysurfing, snowboarding, sport climbing, street luge racing, and wakeboarding. While some derided ESPN for attempting to recast these unusual fringe athletic activities that had been largely unfamiliar to most Americans as a new form of extreme sports, the network instantly trumpeted the event as a huge success. In retrospect, who could argue? Today, it is hard to imagine the American sports media landscape without thinking about extreme sports.

After rebranding the event a year later as the X Games, the second event was also held in Rhode Island, this time at venues in Newport and the capital city of Providence. Subsequently, ESPN made the decision to hold the X Games in other sites around the United States in an effort to broaden the appeal of the event. In 1997–1998, the X Games were held in San Diego. In 1999 and 2000, they were staged up the California coast in San Francisco. For the following two years, the X Games were held across the country on the East Coast in the city of brotherly love, Philadelphia. In 2003, ESPN/Disney decided to have Los Angeles become the permanent home of the United States edition of the X Games.

The Winter X Games was added to the X Games brand in 1997. Originally staged in Big Bear Lake Resort, California, the event was later moved to sites in Colorado and Vermont, before permanently making Aspen, Colorado, the home of the Winter X Games in 2002.

Since the turn of the 21st century ESPN has made several efforts to globalize the X Games brand. In 2003, it tested the appeal of nationalism to X Games

Clifford Adoptante performs a jump during his practice prior to the freestyle motorcross competition at the X Games in San Francisco, June 29, 1999. The San Francisco–Oakland Bay Bridge can be seen in the background. (AP Photo/ Adam Turner.)

audiences when it created the X Games Global Championships. This event imagined competitors not simply as individuals, but as representatives of nations and continents. In the event, individuals from five continents competed in 11 disciplines that could be found in both the original and the Winter X Games. Subsequently, ESPN decided to scrap the Global Championships idea, preferring instead to expand the X Games brand through a global regionalization strategy whereby the Latin, Asian, and Euro X Games were created. In 2011, ESPN/Disney provided an opportunity for cities across the globe to bid for a spot to host various X Games events for three years. In 2012, ESPN/Disney awarded events to Barcelona, Spain; Munich, Germany; and Foz do Iguaçu, Brazil.

X Games VIII was the most-watched X Games ever as nearly 63 million people tuned in on ESPN, ESPN2, and ABC Sports. In 2006, X Games XII was ESPN's highest-rated X Games ever among young men in the 18–34, 18–49, and 25–54 age groups. That year, for the first time, the X Games was aired 24 hours each day of the event using the media platforms ESPN, ESPN2, ABC, ESPN Classic, EXPN.com, ESPN360, Mobile ESPN, and ESPN International.

With this viewership and television ratings, it is clear to see how the X Games franchise currently stands as a multimillion-dollar asset for ESPN. Indeed, in creating and owning the concept of the X Games, ESPN achieved an ideal form of vertical integration of a sporting event as it controls the production, media representation, licensing, and merchandising of all the X Games materials and products and thus optimally profits from each of these links in the X Games commodity chain. Yet, to far less fanfare and media attention, ESPN's monopolistic control over the means of producing the X Games has not gone unnoticed by X Games competitors. Participants of the 2004 Winter X Games spoke out about the minimal amount of prize money ESPN offered competitors, $576,000 in total for 250 participants, considering the millions the company makes from these events.

From the very start, the X Games were created in a top-down manner as a corporate vehicle to be the flagship program ESPN used to launch its new cable channel, ESPN2. Indeed, today many people forget that ESPN was ridiculed and considered to have taken an enormous risk by launching a second television channel, especially one that rested its future on appealing to a younger male demographic of 13–34-year-olds who were imagined as being bored by the traditional "big three" American sports of baseball, football, and basketball featured on ESPN. As *Time* magazine's Kate Pickert recalls, "One especially snarky *USA Today* columnist called the X Games the 'Look Ma, No Hands Olympics,' adding, 'Apparently—and it's possible I'm misinterpreting a cultural trend here—if you strap your best friend to the hood of a '72 Ford Falcon, drive it over a cliff, juggle three babies and a chain saw on the way down and land safely while performing a handstand, they'll tape it, show it and call it a new sport.'"

ESPN's move was also driven by what, at the time, was a widespread corporate interest in generational marketing that "discovered" that members of the so-called Generation X were responsible for millions in personal and family spending. Despite how successful ESPN has been in coopting the outsider, nonconformist, and rebellious ethos of the participants in these previously largely invisible alternative sport subcultures, it is important to realize that ESPN always imagined the X Games as a media product driven by the economic interests of its advertisers rather than the grassroots desires and values of the athletic participants.

As ESPN and its various corporate sponsors coopted these activities it constituted as extreme sports, there existed a widespread tension between members of these sporting subcultures and the producers of these televised events over whether these activities would be driven by the logic of art or commerce. In the wake of the enormous expansion of extreme sports in American mainstream culture generally and the X Games brand specifically, it is easy to forget the way in which the first few X Games telecasts were contested terrains over the values that would be associated with these activities as they became constituted as extreme sports and gained much greater visibility in American media culture at large.

One must keep in mind that prior to 1995, most of these sporting activities were performed in relative obscurity by small subcultures of performers who participated in the activities out of a pure joy and love for the embodied experience of riding a skateboard or skydiving or riding a street luge and for being a part of a small, alternative community. So, on one hand, many of the participants in these activities were skeptical of ESPN's newfound interest in promoting their activities, considering the way in which these activities were long ignored and even ostracized by the American sporting mainstream. Skateboarders, BMX riders, street lugers, and others had defined their activities through values that were antithetical to the values of mainstream organized sports like hypercompetition, winning and being the best, materialism, and even nationalism. Instead, they strongly valued participant control, cooperation among participants, progress based on individual goals, athleticism as art, participating for the love of the activity versus playing only to win or to be the best, and nonconformity to middle American norms. Many were suspicious about how ESPN would represent them and their athletic subcultures as ESPN repackaged them as extreme sports. And their concern proved to be justified.

Early telecasts of the X Games often revealed the uneasy relationship between the participants in these athletic subcultures and their paternalistic corporate patron as ESPN attempted to sell extreme sports to audiences by downplaying the values participants associated with their activities. Instead, ESPN announcers frequently imbued the sports and athletes with the values often associated with mainstream, organized American sports like hypercompetition, winning and being the best, materialism, and even nationalism. Conscious of the possibility that ESPN might attempt to coopt the values and meanings associated with their activities, athletes like inline skater Arlo Eisenberg and BMX rider Mat Hoffman purposefully resisted some of the rules of the competitions.

For example, it was not unusual for skaters and BMX riders to challenge the authority of the X Games organizers and assert their own sense of control over the competition by continuing their rides long after the horn sounded marking the end of their competitive turn. Tony Hawk's historic landing of his first 900 in a competition at X Games V in 1999 came about because he simply refused to give up on the trick long after time had expired on his official run. Urged on by his fellow skating brethren who lined the top of the halfpipe, Hawk asserted his control over the competition by repeatedly attempting the trick until he finally landed it on his 11th try. That same year, Travis Pastrama famously rode his motocross bike into San Francisco Bay on his second run as an act of challenging the corporate and competitive boundaries of the X Games. These are just a few of the examples of how early X Games participants embodied their subcultural outsider values of riding for the love of the activity and challenging corporate control of their sports rather than for fame or fortune.

Additionally, participants would also often challenge ESPN2's on-air commentators' efforts to frame extreme sports with some of the values often associated with mainstream American sports like winning, competition against others, and materialism as goal and purpose of participation. For example, Arlo Eisenberg, like some other winning participants in the first Extreme Games, would use postcompetition interviews to subvert broadcasters' hyperbolic focus on winning by proclaiming that they could care less about their victory. Then, they would proceed to give credit to their fellow participants' personal bests, talk about the artistry of the activity, or focus on the joy of the embodied sensation of risk or speed they experienced in participation even as broadcasters kept awkwardly trying to emphasize their victory and individual superiority or supposed greatness.

Today, it seems as though many of the activities now defined as extreme sports have been thoroughly swallowed up by the whale that is the corporate American sports-media complex. The values of mainstream American organized sports—competition, winning, being the best, and using sport to accumulate personal wealth—now thoroughly saturate the rhetoric and aspirations of most extreme sports professionals and X Games telecasts and marketing materials even as all participants attempt to maintain the illusion of their outsider authenticity and mitigate against the slur of their "selling out" to corporate America.

Most sports industry experts explain the genesis of the X Games as simply the brainchild of then–director of programming for ESPN2 Ron Semiao, who sought to create much-needed programming content for the new channel, a hip, edgier version of ESPN, intended to draw and sell products to a young male audience whose purchasing power was said to be $700 billion in individual and familial spending, according to a November 1998 article in *Time* by Karl Greenfeld.

But, this economic explanation can only partially explain the widespread cultural interest in the X Games in the United States from the mid-1990s to the present. To truly understand how the X Games and extreme sports became a pervasive cultural phenomenon, they must be understood as products of their social and historical times.

Social and cultural analysts have explained the creation and subsequent popularity of the X Games and extreme sports, more generally, as a product of a number of social and historical forces. First, sociologists have noted the rise of a "risk society" that demands social conformity, increased surveillance, and punishment of deviance, as well as the aversion of a host of risks in daily life for its citizens. From this view, the X Games are imagined as appealing to participants and viewers by offering examples of performers who resist social conformity, embrace deviance from dominant social norms, and value taking the types of risks with their bodies that are too often being eliminated from public life.

Others have noted that the X Games could only be created within a media landscape marked by the logic of creating or finding niche media/audiences/markets and the corresponding increase in the number of channels on television in order to reach these smaller niche audiences/markets. From this perspective, the X Games are an outgrowth of the dominant logic of niche marketing and programming that organizes media production at the turn of the 21st century.

Still others have tried to make sense of the rapid manner in which extreme or action sports have been mainstreamed and embraced by corporate America since 1995, especially considering how the cultural values of these activities seemed at first glance to be antithetical to those of mainstream American society. These studies have attempted to understand how these activities have undergone a radical redefinition from strange, fringe athletic subcultural activities performed by young people who were very often perceived as "alien" others to acceptable activities performed by sturdy American men firmly grounded in the American mainstream whose proclivity for taking risks, pushing boundaries, and achieving individual progress was suddenly interpreted as echoing the same core, traditional values cherished and embraced by the founding fathers and frontiersmen of the United States.

This resignification of extreme sports as unquestionably American and masculine activities that would appeal to average, youthful American white men is interpreted as an imagined solution to the racial and gender anxieties that American white men were said to be experiencing in a historical moment when multiculturalism was challenging the idea of whiteness as the unspoken racial norm of American culture and society. The idea of extreme sports and the X Games as an antidote to the destabilization of the position of white men on the professional sporting stages of the United States athletic mainstream is best evidenced in a 1997 *Sports Illustrated* cover story titled, "Whatever Happened to the White Athlete?" In this article, extreme sports were cast as the refuge of young and youthful white males who were said to be quitting basketball, football, and (to a lesser extent) baseball and developing an inferiority complex in sports because of the athletic superiority of black male athletes. A *US News and World Report* cover story of the same year subtly revealed the gender and racial meanings being attached to extreme sports when it explained the appeal of extreme athletes as resembling "the romantic heroes of spaghetti Westerns or Indiana Jones–style adventures and thus pique the imaginations of those secretly wishing to put that Man With No Name swagger in their step—if not full time, at least for a few brief moments on Saturday or Sunday."

Finally, the cultural impact of the X Games might also be measured by acknowledging how it has helped to usher in new ways of covering sports on television.

The sky diving events in the first Extreme Games were the first to make the camera operator a part of the actual competitive activity, as she or he would dive alongside and synchronize with his or her competitor. Later, this move to have cameras closer to the action, on the field of play, or even attached to players' equipment in order to enable viewers to better experience a sporting activity can be witnessed in telecasts for the National Football League, National Basketball Association, and even the Olympic Games. The X Games also increased the mainstream sports media complex's appropriation of slicker production values first popularized on MTV like quick, rapid cuts, close-up "in your face" camera shots, along with the infusion of popular music scores in sporting telecasts. Today, these impacts can be witnessed in the increasingly blurred line between the imagery of music videos, sport game telecasts, Hollywood sport films, and even daily sport reporting on ESPN's *SportsCenter*.

Kyle Kusz

See also ESPN Channels; Hawk, Tony; *Sports Illustrated*

Suggested Resources

Gutman, Bill, with Shawn Frederick. *Being Extreme: Thrills and Dangers in the World of High-Risk Sports.* New York: Citadel Press, 2003.
Price, S. L. "What Ever Happened to the White Athlete?" December 8, 1997. http://sportsillustrated.cnn.com/vault/article/magazine/MAG1011593/index.htm. Accessed June 1, 2012.
Tomlinson, Joe. *In Search of the Ultimate Thrill.* Richmond Hill, Ontario: Firefly Books, 2004.

XFL

The XFL was a professional American football league that was created in 2001 through a joint venture between World Wrestling Federation (now World Wrestling Entertainment) chairman Vince McMahon and the National Broadcasting Company (NBC). XFL unofficially stood for the Xtreme Football League but officials of the league stated that the X did not stand for anything. The league only played for one full season before ceasing operations. While the XFL was able to garner a strong initial audience for its first week of

Memphis Maniax running back Beau Morgan (32) tries to gain yardage through Los Angeles Xtreme's Errick Herrin (59), Leomont Evans and Chad Pegues, right, April 1, 2001. (AP Photo/Lance Murphey.)

competition, the league failed to maintain that audience throughout the 2001 season.

Upon creation of the XFL, McMahon promised that this new football league would be a viable alternative to the National Football League. The XFL differed from the NFL in many ways. The most obvious distinction was the design of the game ball. The football used in the XFL was designed by Spalding. The ball was colored black opposed to the traditional brown used in the NFL and NCAA. The ball also possessed red stripes that crested the XFL logo. The XFL logo itself was a large black X with the letters X, F, and L in red.

The time frame and length of the season also differed. The XFL played a 10-week schedule that began one week after Super Bowl XXXV between the Baltimore Ravens and the New York Giants. The choice to play games beginning in February 2001 was to avoid any direct competition the XFL would have with the NFL, repeating a tactic that startup leagues have used in the past. The season would conclude in April with the XFL championship game entitled "The Big Game at the End." This would later be changed to the Million Dollar Game due to the prize of $1 million being split among the winning team.

The XFL's inaugural season was comprised of eight teams divided into two divisions. The Eastern Division contained the New York/New Jersey Hitmen, Orlando Rage, Birmingham Thunderbolts, and Chicago Enforcers. The Western Division was occupied by the Los Angeles Xtreme, San Francisco Demons, Memphis Maniax, and Las Vegas Outlaws. Instead of each franchise being individually owned, the league operated as a single business unit. This structure was used in order to avoid any overspending issues that have corrupted startup leagues in the past.

The payment of players was unique. Most players received a standard compensation of $45,000 for the 10-game season. Quarterbacks received $50,000 while kickers brought $35,000 home. In order to further compensate players, a $100,000 bonus was given to the winning team of each game, being split among the team's players, as well as the aforementioned $1,000,000 prize for winning the XFL championship.

In addition to the payment schedule, the XFL employed some relatively dramatic rule changes that differed from the NFL. To help create these changes, the XFL looked to Hall of Fame linebacker and Chicago Bear great Dick Butkus. Butkus was initially hired as the Chicago Enforcers head coach but was immediately named the XFL director of football competition in order to provide legitimacy to the league. His knowledge of professional football combined with the vision McMahon had for the league helped create some of the famous rules that helped the XFL differ from the NFL.

First, all XFL teams were required to play in grass stadiums. No domed stadiums, artificial turf stadiums, or retractable roof stadiums were allowed. Full bump-and-run coverage was allowed early in the XFL season. However, this rule was later changed to the modern five-yard rule employed in the NFL in order to increase offensive production. Fair catching on a punt or kickoff was also illegal and was paired with a five-yard zone excluding kick coverage players from interfering with returners catching the ball before the ball hit the ground. The XFL also allowed forward motion for one offensive player to move toward the line of scrimmage once he was outside the tackles.

One of the most obvious changes occurred before a game even began. Instead of a coin toss to decide possession, the XFL implemented an opening scramble between two players from the opposing teams. Both players lined up side by side on the 30-yard line with the ball sitting at midfield. When ready, both players would sprint toward the ball to gain possession. The player acquiring the ball was allowed to choose whether or not his team wanted possession for the first half. This opening scramble also led to the first XFL injury as Orlando Rage free safety Hassan

Shamsid-Deen separated his shoulder in the scramble during the league's opening weekend. Shamsid-Deen would miss the entire season due to this injury.

Teams were not allowed to kick for an extra point after a touchdown. League officials made this rule due to a perception that the kick was a "guaranteed point." To earn the additional point, teams ran a single offensive down from the two-yard line. When postseason play began, two- and three-point conversions were allowed as teams could attempt these conversions further away from the goal line.

Overtime rules resembled current NCAA rules with at least one possession for each team, starting from the 20-yard line. To differ, there were no first downs as teams had to score on four downs or less. If a team happened to score in fewer than four downs, the second team would only have the same number of downs to match or beat the score. If tied after one overtime period, the team that had played offense second in the first overtime would be on offense first for the second overtime.

The XFL's opening game occurred on February 3, 2001, the same weekend of the NFL Pro Bowl. The first game was between the New York/New Jersey Hitmen and Las Vegas Outlaws at Sam Boyd Stadium in Las Vegas. The game itself was very lackluster, ending in a 19–0 victory for the Outlaws. During this contest, NBC made the decision to switch to the other contest of the evening between the Orlando Rage and Chicago Enforcers, a much closer contest. Despite the result of the game, the league was able to attract an estimated 14 million viewers and earn an impressive 9.5 Nielsen rating for its first week of the season.

While earning better than expected ratings and viewership, the audience declined heavily as ratings dropped from 9.5 to 4.6 after one week. This can be attributed to many things. Because of McMahon's involvement with the league, the media ridiculed the league due to McMahon's professional wrestling ties. This stigma also impacted American football fans. Many fans believed that endings of games were scripted in advance, although there was no evidence to support this claim.

On April 21, 2001, the Million Dollar Game was played between the San Francisco Demons and the Los Angeles Xtreme. The championship game

"He Hate Me"

One of the XFL's infamous players ushered in the league with the phrase "He Hate Me." In most sport organizations, players were allowed to put their given surname or first initial and surname on the back of their jersey. However, the XFL permitted players to replace their surname with whatever words they chose.

Rod Smart, a running back for the Las Vegas Outlaws, replaced the name on his jersey with the phrase "He Hate Me." Smart discussed the origin of the phrase in 2004 with the *Milwaukee Journal Sentinel*. Smart stated that the other team would hate him for his success on the field through personal and team accolades.

This phrase was also parodied further when the Outlaws played their division rival, the Los Angeles Xtreme. Two Xtreme players put the phrases "I Hate He" and "I Hate He Too" on their jerseys to express their hatred for Smart. The parody was continued further as the same Xtreme players changed their jerseys once again to "Still Hate He" and "Still Hate He Too."

Smart led the Outlaws in rushing and finished second in the league with 555 yards. After the league's collapse, Smart signed with the Carolina Panthers as a special teams ace and contributed to the Panthers' Super Bowl run in 2003. Smart was one of seven players from the XFL to play in the Super Bowl.

was another lackluster affair as the Xtreme defeated the Demons, 38–6. The major highlight of the game was Xtreme quarterback Tommy Maddox, who was named the league's only Most Valuable Player. Maddox, a former first-round draft choice of the Denver Broncos, would later sign with the Pittsburgh Steelers and become the starter in the 2001 season, leading the Steelers to an AFC North Division crown.

Though paid attendance to XFL games was respectable, the XFL ceased operations due to low television ratings. One of the lowest-rated televised games occurred on March 31 when a game between the Chicago Enforcers and New York/New Jersey Hitmen earned a 1.5 rating. At the time, this was considered the lowest rating for a weekend prime-time first-run sports program in the United States. The agreement with NBC was to broadcast league games for two years and also own half of the league. Nevertheless, NBC announced it would not broadcast the XFL's second season.

McMahon intended to keep the league-maintained broadcast outlets with the National Network (now Spike TV) and UPN (now the CW). McMahon also reviewed the possibility of expanding the league to 10 teams, with Washington, D.C., and Detroit as potential locations. However, UPN executives would only agree to broadcast a second season if McMahon would cut the WWF's *Smackdown* program from two hours to one and a half. McMahon refused to meet this demand and announced the closure of the league on May 10, 2001. Since its demise, the XFL has been considered one of the biggest television blunders of all time.

Dylan Williams

See also Butkus, Dick; Chicago Bears; World Wrestling Entertainment

Suggested Resources

Ackles, Bobby. *Water Boy: From the Sidelines to the Owner's Box: Inside the CFL, the XFL, and the NFL.* Mississauga, Ontario: John Wiley & Sons Canada, 2007.

Forrest, Brett. *Long Bomb: How the XFL Became TV's Biggest Fiasco.* New York: Crown, 2002.

Higley, Cheryl H., Roland Laxenby, Larry Mayer, and Julian L. D. Shabazz. *Extreme Football: XFL: All You Need to Know About the League, Teams, and Players.* Chicago: Triumph Books, 2000.

Parks, Greg. *It Was Football Stupid: The Untold Story of the XFL.* Baltimore: Publish America, 2010.

XFL Website. http://www.all-xfl.com/xfl/. Accessed December 1, 2010.

Y

Yankee Stadium

Located at East 161st Street and River Avenue in the New York City borough of the Bronx, Yankee Stadium was home to Major League Baseball's New York Yankees from 1923 to 2008, with the exception of 1974 and 1975 when it was extensively rebuilt. In 2009, a new stadium with the same name opened on adjacent public parkland and demolition of the original Yankee Stadium began. If the first stadium was "The House That Ruth Built," so called for Yankee slugger Babe Ruth whose home run hitting heroics had caused the tenant Yankees to wear out their welcome when they outdrew the New York Giants in the nearby Polo Grounds, the new ballpark could well be nicknamed "The House That George Built" for Yankee owner George Steinbrenner, whose money and authoritarian ownership style had revived the American League club's fortunes after years in the doldrums. Barnstorming Negro League teams also used the original stadium beginning in 1930, and the New York Black Yankees of the Negro National League played home games there in 1946 and 1947. Not a facility limited to baseball, the old ballpark was home to other sports as well. College and pro football, most notably the New York Giants of the National Football League (1956–1973), soccer, and boxing all had their day. The stadium also served as a venue for concerts and religious events, hosting Jehovah's Witness conventions, masses celebrated by three Popes, and a Billy Graham crusade. Thirty-seven World Series were held at old Yankee Stadium, and it served as a site for games of three Negro League World Series and hosted four Major League All-Star Games and four Negro League East-West games. Three pre-Super Bowl NFL championship games took place there, as well as 30 championship fights. The new stadium quickly followed suit, hosting the Fall Classic in its first year, and the initial title bout was held there in 2010.

When (at Manager John McGraw's insistence) Giants owner Charles Stoneham told the Yankees to move out of the Polo Grounds, the upper Manhattan ballpark they had shared with his club since 1913, Yankees owners Col. Tillinghast L'Hommedieu Huston and Col. Jacob Ruppert decided to build a new facility, one that would be not a mere ballpark but rather a stadium like those in ancient Greece and Rome. They ultimately settled on a site in the Bronx just across the Harlem River from their rented home on Coogan's Bluff. The spot had been a farm before the American Revolution, and more recently a lumberyard owned by William Waldorf Astor, which the colonels purchased from his estate for $675,000. The Osborn Engineering Company of Cleveland completed their plans in January 1921 before the land was purchased, and construction of the reinforced concrete and structural steel edifice began in May 1922 with the White Construction Company of New York as the prime contractor. The three decks familiar to later baseball fans were part of the original design, though the upper deck was uncovered and not as extensive; renovations made between 1936 and 1938 would complete the stadium's classic configuration. An especially strong concrete developed by Thomas Edison was used for the walls. The original seating capacity was 58,000. The initial dimensions were 280.58 feet to left, 395 to the bullpen gate in short left center, 460 to deep left center, 490 to center field, 429 to deep right center, and 294.75 to right. Completed at a cost of $2.4 million, Yankee Stadium officially opened on April 18, 1923, with the attendance announced as 74,217; though the figure was later said to have been exaggerated, it still was easily an all-time record. An army band led by John Phillip Sousa played the national anthem, and Governor Alfred E. Smith threw out the first pitch. The Yankees, coming off two consecutive AL pennants followed by losses to the Giants in the Series, rose to the occasion, defeating the Boston Red Sox, 4–1, as Ruth hit a three-run homer into the right field stands. They would go on to win their third straight pennant and finally defeat the Giants in the inaugural World Series played in their new home.

The seating capacity of Yankee Stadium fluctuated over the years, as did the dimensions of the field of play. The largest crowd to attend a Yankee game at the stadium was 85,625 on September 9, 1928, versus the Philadelphia Athletics, and the highest paid attendance was 81,841 versus the Red Sox on May 30, 1938. After the 1974–1975 renovations, the capacity shrank considerably to 54,028, but was gradually raised again to its final configuration at 57,545. The size of the field shrank as well, though the foul lines were extended, finally settling at 318 feet to left, 379 feet to short left center, 399 feet to left center, 408 feet to center field, 385 feet to right center, and 314 feet to right. Perhaps the most distinctive design feature of Yankee Stadium was the façade, actually a 15-foot-deep art deco frieze that ran along the roof of the upper deck. It was made of copper, which eventually weathered and developed a patina. It was painted white in the 1960s, then removed during the 1970s renovations, with a small portion being saved and placed on top of the center field bleachers. The monuments in center field were another distinguishing feature. Originally a stone memorial stood in front of the flagpole, part of the field of play, placed there in 1929 to honor Manager Miller Huggins, who had died during the season. It was a block of red granite with a bronze plaque on it, and it resembled a tombstone. Similar memorials to Lou Gehrig and Babe Ruth were placed there after their deaths. Bronze plaques were awarded to the still-living Mickey Mantle and Joe DiMaggio in 1969, and hung on the center field wall behind the monuments. After the 1970s stadium remodeling, the area was enclosed and removed from the field of play as part of the shortening of the playing surface. This created

the area that came to be known as Monument Park, and the Mantle and DiMaggio plaques were removed from the wall and placed on red granite blocks, joining the original three. Over the years other plaques were mounted to honor living and deceased players and other personnel. The former Yankee players so honored were Thurman Munson, Elston Howard, Roger Maris, Phil Rizzuto (also a broadcaster), Billy Martin, Lefty Gomez, Whitey Ford, Bill Dickey, Yogi Berra, Allie Reynolds, Don Mattingly, Reggie Jackson, Ron Guidry, and Red Ruffing. Martin, Dickey, and Berra were also Yankee managers. Jackie Robinson was the only non-Yankee so honored. The nonplayer plaques belong to owner Jacob Ruppert, General Manager Ed Barrow, managers Joe McCarthy and Casey Stengel, broadcaster Mel Allen, and public address announcer Bob Sheppard.

Many baseball highlights occurred in old Yankee Stadium over the years, as the New York Yankees were far and away the most successful team in the major leagues. Babe Ruth in 1927 and Roger Maris in 1961 were greatly aided by the stadium's friendliness to left-handed hitters as they set single-season major league home run records. Happy events such as the 26 World Series victories by the Yankees were tempered by more somber moments, notably the farewell addresses by Lou Gehrig in 1939, fatally stricken though young and appearing healthy, and Babe Ruth in 1948, prematurely aged and obviously dying. Mickey Mantle hit some prodigious home runs there, including one in 1963 that would have left the stadium on the fly if it had not struck the façade. No fair balls officially left the ballpark, and one supposedly hit out by Negro League slugger Josh Gibson in the 1930s cannot be verified by any written account. In his book *Green Cathedrals*, researcher Phil Lowry quotes Mantle and Yankee left fielder Roy White as stating that Frank Howard of the Washington Senators hit a fair ball inside the left field foul pole that left the stadium on a rainy and foggy day in the 1960s, which the umpires miscalled as foul.

The New York football Giants, though they would win the NFL championship only in their first season at Yankee Stadium after moving from the Polo Grounds, provided thrills aplenty for their fans. The best-remembered contest was one they would sooner forget,

Yankee Stadium in the Bronx, home of the New York Yankees from 1923–2009. (Corel.)

an overtime title game loss to the Baltimore Colts on December 28, 1958, that has been called by more objective observers the greatest game ever played and has been credited with being responsible for the rise of the NFL to national prominence. Only one unsuccessful bowl game was played at the stadium, with college football being mainly noted for the Army–Notre Dame game contested there annually from 1925 to 1947 and occasionally in later years. Additionally, Bronx schools NYU and Fordham played many games there, with generally favorable results. Pro circuits that unsuccessfully tried to break the NFL's stranglehold on major league status found homes for their New York franchises at Yankee Stadium, beginning with the New York Yankees of the 1926 American Football League, the league and team both created to showcase the skills of Red Grange. The Yankees joined the NFL for the 1927 and 1928 seasons after the AFL folded, but were permitted to play only a limited number of games at their namesake stadium before the team, too, faded into history. The 1936–1937 AFL's team of the same

name played some of their home games at Yankee Stadium and a 1940–1941 AFL placed another New York Yankees there in 1940, with a name change to the New York Americans the following season. A New York Yankees team in the more successful All-America Football Conference played at the stadium from 1946 through 1949, and many of its players moved on to an NFL team that took to the Yankee Stadium turf as the New York Yanks in 1950 and 1951; that franchise also disappeared after an unsuccessful move to Dallas.

The first soccer team to play home games at Yankee Stadium was the New York Yankees of the American Soccer League in 1931. Exhibition games were played there over the following decades involving Jewish teams from Palestine playing U.S. all-star teams and teams from Europe and South America playing each other, as well as some friendly matches involving the U.S. national team. The New York Americans of the American Soccer League lost in the finals of the Lewis Cup at Yankee Stadium in 1952. The New York teams of the ASL played the first five

---

Curse of the Bambino

While the new Yankee Stadium was being built, a construction worker who was a fan of the New York Yankees' archrival, the Boston Red Sox, buried a jersey under the visitors dugout that was a replica of the one worn by David Ortiz, the Red Sox star known as Big Papi, allegedly to place a curse on the Yankees similar to the one that supposedly befell the Boston club when owner Harry Frazee sold Babe Ruth to New York in 1919. Yankee fans among his co-workers exposed the deed, and the humiliated worker was forced to help dig up the offending uniform top. The Yankees donated the now-famous and presumably valuable jersey to the Jimmy Fund, a Boston-based charity long supported by the Red Sox.

Undeterred by his exposure, the same worker then claimed to have buried, at a location under the stadium turf which he refused to disclose, a program from the 2004 American League Championship Series, in which the Red Sox overcame a three games to none deficit to beat the Yankees en route to exorcising the "Curse of the Bambino" and winning their first World Series since 1918. His hard work failed to pay off, however, as the Yankees won the Series in their first year at the new ballpark.

---

weeks of the 1952–1953 season there in an attempt to raise the league's profile. The New York Skyliners of the United Soccer Association (actually Cerro F.C. of Uruguay) and the New York Generals of the competing National Professional Soccer League each played their home games at the stadium in 1967, and when those two leagues merged to form the North American Soccer League in 1968, the team kept the name New York Generals and played one season in Yankee Stadium before folding. Their successor in the NASL, the New York Cosmos, evolved into the most successful soccer team that ever played in the United States, hiring big-name talent from Europe and South America. The Cosmos called Yankee Stadium home during their first season in 1971 and again in 1976 when they featured Pelé, the world's greatest player.

Between 1923, when Benny Leonard defended his lightweight title with a decision over Lou Tendler, and 1976, when Muhammad Ali defended his heavyweight crown with a come-from-behind decision over Ken Norton in the only title fight held there after the 1950s, many historic boxing matches took place at old Yankee Stadium. Heavyweight champions Gene Tunney, Max Schmeling, Joe Louis, Ezzard Charles, Rocky Marciano, and Ingmar Johansson also won or defended their crowns there. Many nontitle fights were held there as well. The African American Louis fought for the heavyweight title at Yankee Stadium eight times, most famously defending his crown in 1938 with a first-round knockout in a politically charged rematch with the German Schmeling, who had won his own title there in 1930 on a foul by Jack Sharkey and had knocked out the Brown Bomber in a 1936 stadium bout.

New York Yankees owner George Steinbrenner had begun to campaign for a new home for his ballclub in the 1980s after his deep pockets had allowed the team to buy players who would return them to respectability, alleging unsafe conditions at the old ballpark and with an eye to the potential income from the incorporation of luxury boxes and suites into a new stadium. Options considered included moving to the West Side of Manhattan or across the Hudson River to New Jersey. Mayor Rudolph Giuliani of New York announced plans before he left office in December 2001 that would have financed new stadiums for the Yankees and their National League counterpart New York Mets with taxpayer money paying for half of each, as well as for transportation improvements to the new venues. Giuliani's successor Michael Bloomberg said this would be a bad investment for the city and used an escape clause in the agreements to back out of the deals. In the case of Yankee Stadium, New York City agreed to pay only for infrastructure improvements, with the New York state legislature authorizing $1.5 million toward the $320 million cost of parking garages. The city offered substantial tax incentives as its contribution, which turned out to be much the same share as was agreed to in the original deal. The overall cost of more than $2.3 billion included nearly $1.2 billion in taxpayer subsidies. Planning to build the new Yankee Stadium at its location across 161st St. from the existing ballpark on the site of what was Macombs Dam Park began in 2004, with ground broken on the anniversary of Babe Ruth's death, August 16, 2006, and construction completed in time for the opening exhibition game with the Chicago Cubs, a 7–4 Yankee victory on April 3, 2009. The first regular-season game was a 10–2 Yankee loss to the Cleveland Indians on April 16. The design by the architectural firm Populous, formerly known as HOK Sport, was intended to be very similar to the old stadium, right down to the original frieze. Even the field dimensions replicated the final configuration of its predecessor, 318 feet to left, 399 to left center, 408 to center field, 385 to right center, and 314 to right, with the bullpens in the same locations. Monument Park was moved intact to the area behind the center field fence, with a new stone monument honoring George Steinbrenner added by his family following the owner's death in 2010. The new stadium seats approximately 51,000, with a capacity including standing room of 52,325.

The new ballpark still favored left-handed power hitters, as the old ballpark had since its original 1923 layout was tailored to Babe Ruth's home run stroke. Although the foul lines were later moved out, the first stadium continued to cater to lefties with its invitingly close right field porch, and since the dimensions were reproduced, it was assumed the new stadium would do the same. What was unforeseen was the ease with which hitters of all persuasions were able to reach the seats nearly at will. The record for most home runs hit in a season at the old stadium was surpassed in the 73rd game (of 81) of the first season in the new one. There seemed to be a wind tunnel effect, which pushed the ball away from home plate, and after the demolition of the old ballpark was completed early in the 2010 season, the number of four-baggers hit in the new park was dramatically reduced. In addition to the Yankees winning the World Series in its first year, other events in the new Yankee Stadium recalled the traditions of the original ballpark. The first religious event was held in 2009, and the first concert took place the following year. College football returned in 2010 in the form of Army versus Notre Dame, their first meeting in the Bronx since 1969, with Army to play additional games against other opponents in future seasons. The inaugural Pinstripe Bowl was played later that year in the hope that it would become an annual event, unlike the ill-fated Gotham Bowl at the old stadium, which had been canceled due to lack of interest after making its Bronx debut in 1962. Boxing also returned in 2010, with Yuri Foreman losing the first fight at the new stadium, as

well as his light middleweight title, to Miguel Cotto via technical knockout in the ninth round. Soccer made its debut in 2012, as the new ballpark hosted international friendly matches featuring some of the world's great clubs, kicked off by Paris Saint-Germain and European champion Chelsea FC of London.

The first baseball park built on a grand enough scale to be called a stadium, Yankee Stadium in all of its incarnations has remained the iconic symbol of Major League Baseball to fans and nonfans around the world. Loved and hated, the stadium's feature attraction has always been and will continue to be the New York Yankees baseball club. By virtue of their performance on the field, the Yankees have mostly lived up to the high expectations that come with the territory.

David C. Skinner

See also Ali, Muhammad; Berra, Yogi; DiMaggio, Joe; Gehrig, Lou; Grange, Red; Jackson, Reggie; Louis, Joe; Negro Leagues; New York Yankees; Notre Dame Fighting Irish Football; Robinson, Jackie; Ruth, Babe; Stengel, Casey

Suggested Resources

Durso, Joseph. *Yankee Stadium: 50 Years of Drama*. Boston: Houghton Mifflin, 1972.

Green Gridirons. North Huntington, PA: Professional Football Researchers Association, 1990.

Lowry, Philip J. *Green Cathedrals*. Reading, MA: Addison Wesley, 1992.

Sullivan, Neil. *The Diamond in the Bronx: Yankee Stadium and the Politics of New York*. New York: Oxford University Press, 2001.

Weintraub, Robert. *The House That Ruth Built: A New Stadium, the First Yankees Championship, and the Redemption of 1923*. Boston: Little, Brown, 2011.

"Yankee Stadium." ballparksofbaseball.com. http://www.ballparksofbaseball.com/al/YankeeStadiumII.htm. Accessed December 2010.

Yankee Stadium History. http://newyork.yankees.mlb.com/nyy/ballpark/stadium_history.jsp. Accessed December 2010.

Yao Ming (1980–)

Yao Ming's entry into the NBA powerfully demonstrates how truly globalized and internationalized the league had become. Yes, there had certainly been successful foreign players before Yao established himself. In the late 1980s and 1990s, Eastern Europeans like Vlade Divac (who had a long career with the Los Angeles Lakers and Sacramento Kings) and the late Drazen Petrovic (New Jersey Nets) had proved to be solid, if not spectacular, pros. France's Tony Parker and Spain's Manu Ginobli helped the San Antonio Spurs win the NBA title in 2003. Germany's Dirk Nowitzski, too, had been in the league for many years before Yao. Today, Nowitzki can reasonably lay claim to being not only the greatest foreign player in history, but one of the best NBA players ever.

None of them compare, in global scale, to the phenomenon that was Yao. First of all, he was Asian, not European. And coming from China, he had the collective weight and hopes of his country—the world's largest population—behind him. He came into the league, too, just at a time when China was seeing the seeds of a long, steady modernization project bear fruit. By slowly democratizing its markets, China had firmed up its place as a dominant economic power in the world. Along with this, the explosion in communication technologies and media set the stage for China to become less isolated. While the government maintained control over the Internet by blocking Web pages and limiting access, it was no longer feasible or, indeed, economically desirable for China to attempt to keep all doors into and out of the culture closed.

Sports, and basketball in particular, was one such door, and Yao walked through it. He was born September 12, 1980, in Shanghai. His father and mother had both played professional basketball in China (his father played in a pro league in Shanghai, while his mother had captained the woman's national team), and both were extraordinarily tall—his father 6'7", his mother 6'3". He started playing basketball before the age of 10 and attended one of China's junior sport schools, a communist leftover that was designed to identify, focus, and develop athletic talent from an early age. As a teen, he played for the junior group of the Chinese Basketball Association's Shanghai Sharks before moving to the professional team's seniors at age 17.

Yao played five years in the CBA league. During his time with the team, the Sharks played for the CBA championship twice, losing both times. His best year was 2002, his last with the team, when he averaged 32 points and nearly 20 rebounds per game on 72 percent shooting. For his CBA career, Yao averaged 23 points, 15 rebounds, with a field goal percentage of 65 percent. While the quality and depth of China's professional league was somewhat suspect—China's teams and players had never really proven much of a force in international competition—a buzz about Yao was slowly accumulating in the West. He played for China in the 2000 Summer Olympics in Sydney, Australia, and while the team lost in the preliminary round, finishing 10th, Yao distinguished himself early in a game against the U.S. team, blocking a number of shots by NBA players.

Physically, too, he was impossible to ignore. Yao had extraordinary height—by the time of those Olympics, he was approaching 7'6"—but he also moved with a surprising grace. While there had been NBA players that tall, or even taller—the Sudanese Manute Bol and the Romanian Georghe Muresan had each measured 7'7"—they tended to be physically awkward, alternatively clumsy and plodding or long and light as a kite. Yao, in contrast, was smooth and well proportioned. In the post, he clearly possessed promising basketball skills, with good hands and tidy footwork. In December 2000, he was featured on the cover of *ESPN* magazine's annual "NEXT" issue, dedicated to identifying athletes who might one day revolutionize their sport. By then, it was apparent that Yao was coming to the NBA, though it was unclear when.

In 2001, Yao led the Chinese national team to the FIBA Asian Championship, winning the MVP (the Chinese would win again in 2003 and 2005, with Yao again taking the MVP both times). That same year, negotiations that would allow for his entry to the NBA began. Yao's CBA rival and Olympic teammate Wang Zhizhi had actually beaten Yao into the NBA by a year, becoming the league's first Chinese player. While the 7'1" Zhizhi had been drafted by the Dallas Mavericks in 1999, he was denied permission to play in the United States until 2001. Yao's own negotiations were made much more difficult when Zhizhi later refused to return to China and play for the national team. As a result, the Chinese wanted some ironclad guarantees: first, that whoever drafted Yao wouldn't allow him to do what Zhizhi had done (it was taken as a great national embarrassment) or else face serious financial repercussions; and second, that Yao would be drafted with the first pick in the draft.

Yao needed a large, unusual team of financial advisors and experts—a Chinese negotiator, his agent in China, his agent in the United States, his NBA and marketing agents, even a University of Chicago economics professor—to help maneuver him through the political and business permutations and strike an eventual deal with the Houston Rockets. In 2002, Yao Ming became the first international player to be taken number one overall in the NBA draft.

Perhaps because of these prolonged negotiations, and because Yao was contractually obligated to play for China's national team and skipped the Rockets' preseason and training camp, there was some skepticism surrounding Yao heading into the 2002–2003 season. He did not score a point in his first NBA game, and many commentators said he appeared intimidated. He played less than 15 minutes a game for his first few weeks in the NBA, averaging well under 10 points. A breakthrough of sorts came when he scored 20 points against the Lakers in mid-November, going 9 for 9 from the field and 2 for 2 at the line.

There was some basic racial insensitivity, too, to go along with the skepticism. In an early-season game in Miami, the Heat handed out fortune cookies to the crowd (it is somewhat unclear whether the intention was to mock Yao with a stereotype or to celebrate his arrival). When asked how he felt about the cookies, Yao disarmed the situation by suggesting he had never seen such things before and just assumed they were an American delicacy. In the weeks and years ahead, whenever he was confronted with some messy clash of cultures or stereotyping, Yao fell back on this brand of barely detectable, gentle, and ambiguous humor, which incorporated his audience's sense of "Is he joking with me or is he serious or is he just foreign and naïve?" to carry him through. When, for example, Shaquille O'Neal insulted Yao and then spoke in garbled mock Chinese during a television interview, Yao indicated he could empathize with the Lakers center, since he, too, had had a great deal of trouble learning the language.

Yao gradually improved during his rookie season, finishing with averages of 13.5 points, 8.2 blocks, and placing second in the Rookie of the Year voting. The

Houston Rockets Yao Ming shoots over Phoenix Suns Amare Stoudemire, January 15, 2003, in Houston. (AP Photo/David J. Phillip.)

Rockets did not make the playoffs, but Yao was elected to the 2003 NBA All-Star Game and was actually voted in as a starter above O'Neal, a perennial candidate for the league's Most Valuable Player award who was now at the peak of his powers, having just won three consecutive NBA titles. The NBA actually printed ballots in Chinese, and the vote was a strong indicator of just how wide the league's appeal could reach.

The next year, Yao continued to improve, finishing with averages of 17.5 and 9 rebounds a game, and again starting at center for the West in the NBA's All-Star contest. The Rockets made the playoffs, but lost to the Lakers in five games, with Yao averaging 15 points and 7.4 rebounds going head to head with O'Neal.

In the off-season, Yao returned to China and played for his country's team in the 2004 Olympics in

1518 | Yao Ming (1980–)

Jeremy Lin

In early 2012, the New York Knicks signed a 10-day contract with Jeremy Lin, a second-year player from Harvard, who had initially played briefly with both the Golden State Warriors and the Houston Rockets. The Warriors thought that Lin's roots (he had played at Palo Alto High School in the San Francisco Bay Area) would be good for drawing more local fans, especially Asian Americans, but he was cut after playing just 29 games and averaging 2.6 points per game in about 10 minutes per game. With the Knicks, Lin exploded as a starter, scoring more than 25 points per game in his first five games. "Lin-mania" soon followed. Unlike Yao Ming, Lin is an American, but his parents were born in Taiwan and he is the first Asian American star in the NBA. How long his success and possible stardom will continue is still problematic. His success led to the Knicks being unable to afford to sign him again, and he accepted a free agent contract with the Houston Rockets for $25.1 million for three years.

Athens. He carried the Chinese flag for his country's delegation in the opening ceremonies. The team made the quarterfinals—its best showing in the Olympics—and defeated Serbia and Montenegro's world champion squad along the way, Yao averaging 20.7 points and 9.3 rebounds on 55 percent shooting.

After a blockbuster trade with Orlando in which they acquired a host of new players including superstar Tracy McGrady, the 2004–2005 Rockets won 51 games, and Yao was again named the West's starting center for the All-Star Game. Yao was elected with the highest vote tally in history, breaking the record held by Michael Jordan. Yao was now, inarguably, a global and iconic force. Owing to his fans in China, he was the most popular and most watched basketball player in the world, and he had become a brand in his own right, with shoe and clothing endorsements, a film documentary, and numerous books being written about him. He finished the season averaging 22.3 points and 10.2 rebounds, but in the playoffs, the Rockets fell to the Dallas Mavericks in seven games. In the series, Yao averaged 21 points and shot 65 percent from the floor.

It was around this point that Yao began the long, frustrating battle with chronic foot and ankle injuries that would eventually end his career. He had broken his foot as a junior player, and he lost most of his 1998 season with Sharks after suffering the same injury. In the 2005–2006 season, he missed 21 games to a toe injury and surgery in December. He rehabbed and returned, only to break his foot at the very end of the seasons. His season (22.3 points and 10.2 rebounds) was in keeping with his career averages. Yao had again made the All-Star team, but the Rockets missed the playoffs. His broken foot took six months to heal.

He was again injured in 2006–2007, breaking his right knee in December. At the time, Yao had been having his best statistical season, with career-high averages in points, rebounds, and blocks. After missing 34 games, he returned in time for the playoffs, but the Rockets were eliminated in the first round by the Utah Jazz.

The next season, Yao played in 55 games before breaking a bone in his foot in February. Yao needed yet another surgery, and he was done for the season. This injury was especially devastating, as it threatened Yao's ability to play in the 2008 Summer Olympics in Beijing. For Yao, the symbolic and real importance of participating in those Olympics cannot be overstated. He had been China's most prominent citizen in the West, filling not just the role of basketball player but also serving as a kind of a quietly dignified ambassador for his entire culture. His nation's basketball team needed him to play, of course. But China itself needed him there, as both leader and as a kind of validating figure.

He carried the Olympic torch into Tiananmen Square and again carried the flag for his country's Olympic delegation. With Yao averaging 19 points and 8.2 rebounds, the Chinese made it into the quarterfinals of the basketball tournament, losing to Lithuania. Yao hit the very first basket of the Olympics, an unlikely (for Yao, a center) but remarkable three-pointer in a game against the United States.

Yao returned to play a full season in 2008–2009, averaging 19 points and nearly 10 rebounds a game. The Rockets won 53 games. He made the All-Star team (he had done so every year), and Yao led the team past the Portland Trailblazers and into the second round against the Lakers. After Yao scored 28 points in the first game to win, the Rockets dropped the next two. After game three, he was diagnosed with an ankle sprain. Yao was done for the series, and the Rockets lost in seven games.

It was later revealed that Yao had suffered yet another fracture in his foot, and he missed the entirety of the 2009–2010 season. He attempted a return in 2010–2011 and played well in limited minutes, but he broke his foot yet again in December. He retired from basketball in July 2011, announcing his decision in Shanghai.

It is unclear how much Yao's injuries were the result of his size, or his punishing schedule. He returned to China to play more basketball at the end of each NBA off-season, and so his body was never truly given a chance rest. The human foot, too, is not really designed to absorb the punishment that comes when a 7'6" and 300 pound person jumps repeatedly up and down. His too-early retirement is most likely a combination of both.

Yao's entry into the NBA was driven by economics. It was, simply put, no longer in China's best interests to keep him for itself—there was just too much money to be made, too much benefit for all sides. In that sense, his success in the league could be considered a triumph of capitalism, where the promise of new markets and revenue streams encourages very different cultures to engage with one another and to get along.

Michael Smith

See also Jordan, Michael; National Basketball Association; O'Neal, Shaquille

Suggested Resources

Abrams, Jonathan. "The Legacy of Yao." July 12, 2011. http://www.grantland.com/story/_/id/6760779/the-legacy-yao. Accessed November 15, 2011.

Chin, Oliver. *The Tao of Yao: Insights from Basketball's Brightest Big Man*. Mumbai: Frog Books, 2003.

Hessler, Peter. "Home and Away: Yao Ming's Journey from China to the NBA, and Back." December 1, 2003. http://www.newyorker.com/archive/2003/12/01/031201fa_fact_hessler. Accessed November 15, 2011.

Kang, Jay Caspian. "Can I Write Check?" July 12, 2011. http://www.grantland.com/story/_/id/6764541/can-write-check. Accessed November 15, 2011.

Larmer, Brook. *Operation Yao Ming: The Chinese Sports Empire, American Big Business, and the Making of an NBA Superstar*. New York: Gotham Books, 2005.

Ming, Yao, and Ric Bucher. *Yao: A Life in Two Worlds*. New York: Hyperion, 2004.

Z

Zaharias, Babe Didrikson

See Didrikson, Babe

Selected Bibliography

Aamidor, Abraham. *Chuck Taylor, All Star*. Bloomington, IN: University of Indiana Press, 2006.

Abdul-Jabbar, Kareem, and Peter Knobler. *Giant Steps*. New York: Bantam, 1987.

Alexander, Charles. *Breaking the Slump: Baseball in the Depression Era*. New York: Columbia University Press, 2002.

Alexander, Charles. *Our Game: An American Baseball History*. New York: Fine Communications, 1997.

Allen, Maury. *All Roads Lead to October: Boss Steinbrenner's 25-Year Reign over the New York Yankees*. New York: St. Martin's, 2001.

Angell, Roger. *Late Innings: A Baseball Companion*. New York: Ballantine, 1983.

Anobile, Richard, ed. *Who's on First? Verbal and Visual Gems from the Films of Abbott and Costello*. New York: Darien House, 1972.

Araton, Harvey. *Alive and Kicking: When Soccer Moms Take the Field and Change Their Lives Forever*. New York: Simon & Schuster, 2001.

Ardell, Jean Hastings. *Breaking into Baseball: Women and the National Pastime*. Carbondale: Southern Illinois Press, 2005.

Armstrong, Lance, with Sally Jenkins. *Every Second Counts*. New York: Broadway, 2003.

Ashe, Arthur. *A Hard Road to Glory: A History of the African-American Athlete*. New York: Amistad, 1993.

Auerbach, Red, and John Feinstein. *Let Me Tell You a Story: A Lifetime in the Game*. New York: Little, Brown, 2004.

Auletta, Ken. *Media Man: Ted Turner's Improbable Empire*. New York: W. W. Norton, 2005.

Axthelm, Pete. *The City Game: Basketball from the Garden to the Playground*. Lincoln: University of Nebraska Press, 1999.

Baker, William. *Jesse Owens: An American Life*. New York: Free Press, 1986.

Bass, Anne. *Not the Triumph but the Struggle: The 1968 Olympics and the Making of the Black Athlete*. Minneapolis: University of Minnesota Press, 2002.

Beekman, Scott. *Ringside: A History of Professional Wrestling in America*. Santa Barbara, CA: Praeger, 2006.

Betts, John R. *America's Sporting Heritage: 1850–1950*. Reading, MA: Addison-Wesley, 1974.

Bird, Larry, Ervin Johnson, and Jackie McMullan. *When the Game Was Ours*. New York: Houghton Mifflin Harcourt, 2009.

Bjarkman, Peter. *The Biographical History of Basketball*. Chicago: Masters Press, 2000.

Bogumil, Mary L. *Understanding August Wilson*. Columbia: University of South Carolina Press, 1999.

Bowen, Edward L. *The Jockey Club's Illustrated History of Thoroughbred Racing in America*. Boston: Bulfinch Press, 1994.

Bowen, Edward. *Man O' War*. Lexington, KY: Eclipse, 2000.

Boyd, Todd. *Young, Black, Rich and Famous: The Rise of the NBA, the Hip Hop Invasion, and the Transformation of American Culture*. New York: Doubleday, 2003.

Brake, Deborah L. *Getting in the Game: Title IX and the Women's Sports Revolution*. New York: New York University Press, 2010.

Brennan, Joseph L. *Duke: The Life Story of Duke Kahanamoku*. Honolulu: Ku Pa'a, 1994.

Briley, Ron, Michael Schoenecke, and Deborah A. Carmichael. *All Stars and Movie Stars: Sports in Film and History*. Lexington: University of Kentucky Press, 2008.

Briley, Ron. *The Baseball Film in Postwar America: A Critical Study, 1948–1962*. Jefferson, NC: McFarland, 2011.

Britton, Wesley. *Beyond Bond: Spies in Fiction and Film*. Westport, CT: Praeger, 2005.

Bryant, Jill. *Amazing Women Athletes*. Toronto: Second Story Press, 2003.

Buford, Kate. *Native American Son: The Life and Sporting Legend of Jim Thorpe*. New York: Alfred Knopf, 2010.

Burgos, Adrian, Jr. *Playing America's Game: Baseball, Latinos and the Color Line*. Berkeley: University of California Press, 2007.

Cahn, Susan K. *Coming on Strong: Gender and Sexuality in Twentieth-Century Women's Sport*. New York: Free Press, 1994.

Callahan, Tom. *Johnny U: The Life and Times of John Unitas*. New York: Crown, 2006.

Canseco, Jose. *Juiced: Wild Times, Rampant 'Roids, Smash Hits and How Baseball Got Big*. New York: Regan, 2005.

Carroll, Bob. *When the Grass Was Real: Unitas, Brown, Lombardi, Sayers, Butkus, Namath and All the Rest: The Best Ten Years of Pro Football*. New York: Simon & Schuster, 1993.

Carroll, Brian. *When to Stop the Cheering? The Black Press, the Black Community and the Integration of Professional Baseball*. New York: Routledge, 2007.

Carroll, John. *Red Grange and the Rise of Modern Football*. Urbana: University of Illinois Press, 1999.

Cayleff, Susan. *Babe: The Life and Legend of Babe Didrikson Zaharias*. Urbana: University of Illinois Press, 1995.

Chamberlain, Wilt, and David Shaw. *Wilt: Just Like Any Other 7-Foot Black Millionaire Who Lives Next Door*. New York: Macmillan, 1973.

Chambers, Thomas A. *Drinking the Waters: Creating an American Leisure Class at Nineteenth-Century Mineral Springs*. Washington, DC: Smithsonian Institution Press, 2002.

Chapin, Dwight, and Jeff Prugh. *The Wizard of Westwood: Coach John Wooden and His UCLA Bruins*. Boston: Houghton Mifflin, 1973.

Chew, Peter. *The Kentucky Derby: The First 100 Years*. Boston: Houghton-Mifflin, 1974.

Chivers Yochim, Emily. *Skate Life: Re-imaging White Masculinity*. Ann Arbor: University of Michigan Press, 2010.

Cocchiarale, Michael, and Scott Emmert, eds. *Sports in American Literature*. Westport, CT: Praeger, 2004.

Coenen, Craig R. *From Sandlot to the Super Bowl: The National Football League, 1920–1967*. Knoxville: University of Tennessee Press, 2005.

Cohen, Stanley. *The Game They Played*. New York: Carroll & Graf, 2001.

Concannon, Dale. *Complete Illustrated History of the Ryder Cup: Golf's Greatest Drama*. Chicago: Triumph Books, 2006.

Conner, Dennis, and Michael Levitt. *The America's Cup: The History of Sailing's Greatest Competition in the Twentieth Century*. New York: St. Martin's, 1998.

Coppage, Keith. *From Roller Derby to RollerJam: The Authorized Story of an Unauthorized Sport*. Santa Rosa, CA: Squarebooks, 1999.

Corbett, Theodore. *The Making of American Resorts: Saratoga Springs, Ballston Spa, Lake George*. New Brunswick, NJ: Rutgers University Press, 2001.

Costas, Bob. *Fair Ball: A Fan's Case for Baseball*. New York: Broadway, 2001.

Creamer, Robert. *Babe: The Legend Comes to Life*. New York: Simon & Schuster, 1974.

Creamer, Robert W. *Stengel: His Life and Times*, New York: Simon & Schuster, 1984.

Davies, Richard O. *Sports in American Life: A History*. New York: Blackwell, 2007.

Davis, Michael D. *Black American Women in Olympic Track and Field*. Jefferson, NC: McFarland, 1992.

Davis, Seth. *When March Went Mad: The Game That Transformed Basketball*. New York: Times Books, 2009.

Davis, Timothy, and Kenneth L Shropshire. *The Business of Sports Agents*. 2nd ed. Philadelphia: University of Pennsylvania Press, 2008.

Derderian, Tom. *Boston Marathon: The First Century of the World's Premier Running Event*. Champaign, IL: Human Kinetics, 1996.

Dickey, Glenn. *The History of Professional Basketball Since 1896*. New York: Stein and Day, 1982.

Didinger, Ray, and Glen Macnow. *The Ultimate Book of Sports Movies: Featuring the 100 Greatest Sports Films of All Time*. Philadelphia: Running Press, 2000.

Drager, Marvin. *The Most Glorious Crown: The Story of America's Triple Crown Thoroughbreds from Sir Barton to Secretariat*. New York: Winchester Press, 1975.

Dunnavant, K. *The Fifty-Year Seduction: How Television Manipulated College Football from Birth of the Modern NCAA to the Creation of the BCS*. New York: St. Martin's, 2004.

Dyreson, Mark. *Making the American Team: Sport, Culture and the Olympic Experience*. Urbana: University of Illinois Press, 1998.

Edelman, Rob. *Great Baseball Films: From* Right Off the Bat *to* A League of Their Own. New York: Citadel Press, 1994.

Edgerton, Gary T. *Ken Burns' America*. New York: Palgrave, 2001.

Edgington, K., Thomas L. Erskine, and James Michael Welsh. *Encyclopedia of Sports Films*. Lanham, MD: Scarecrow Press, 2011.

Edwards, Harry. *The Revolt of the Black Athlete*. New York: Free Press, 1969.

Einhorn, Eddie, and Ron Rapoport. *How March Became Madness: How the NCAA Tournament Became the Greatest Sporting Event in America*. Chicago: Triumph, 2006.

Erickson, Hal. *The Baseball Filmography, 1915 through 2001*. Jefferson, NC: McFarland, 2002.

Evensen, Bruce. *When Dempsey Fought Tunney*. Knoxville: University of Tennessee Press, 1996.

Evey, Stuart. *Creating an Empire: ESPN—The No-Holds-Barred Story of Power, Ego, Money, and Vision That Transformed a Culture*. Chicago: Triumph Books, 2004.

Fainaru-Wada, Mark, and Lance Williams. *Game of Shadows: Barry Bonds, BALCO, and the Steroids Scandal*

That Rocked Professional Sports. New York: Gotham Books, 2006.

Feuer, Jane, Paul Kerr, and Tise Vanimagi. *MTM: Quality Television*. London: BFI Publishing, 1984.

Fidler, Merrie. *The Origins and History of the All-American Girls Professional Baseball League*. Jefferson, NC: McFarland, 2010.

Fitzpatrick, Frank. *And the Walls Came Tumbling Down: The Basketball Game That Changed American Sports*. New York: Simon & Schuster, 1999.

Fountain, Charles. *Under the March Sun: The Story of Spring Training*. New York: Oxford University Press, 2009.

Fox, Stephen. *Big Leagues: Professional Baseball, Football and Basketball in National Memory*. New York: William Morrow, 1994.

Freedman, Lew. *Dynasty, the Rise of the Boston Celtics*. Guilford, CT: Lyons Press, 2008.

Freedman, Lew. *Latino Baseball Legends: An Encyclopedia*. Westport, CT: Greenwood Press, 2010.

Freeman, Mike. *Jim Brown: The Fierce Life of an American Hero*. New York: HarperCollins, 2000.

Frommer, Harvey. *Baseball's Greatest Rivalry: The New York Yankees and Boston Red Sox*. New York: Atheneum, 1982.

Gardner, Joe. *Speed, Guts and Glory 100 Unforgettable Moments in NASCAR History*. New York: Warner Books, 2006.

George, Nelson. *Elevating the Game: Black Men and Basketball*. Lincoln: University of Nebraska Press, 1999.

Ginsburg, Daniel E. *The Fix Is In: A History of Baseball Gambling and Game Fixing Scandals*. Jefferson, NC: McFarland, 1995.

Golenbock, Peter. *Fenway: An Unexpurgated History of the Boston Red Sox*. New York: G. P. Putnam's Sons, 1992.

Gorn, Elliott, and Warren Goldstein. *A Brief History of American Sports*. Urbana: University of Illinois Press, 2004.

Goudsouzian, Aram. *King of the Court: Bill Russell and the Basketball Revolution*. Berkeley: University of California Press, 2010.

Gould, William B. *Bargaining with Baseball: Labor Relations in an Age of Prosperous Turmoil*. Jefferson, NC: McFarland, 2011.

Gray, Frances Clayton, and Yanick Rice Lamb. *Born to Win: The Authorized Biography of Althea Gibson*. Hoboken, NJ: John Wiley & Sons, 2004.

Green, Ben. *Spinning the Globe: The Rise, Fall, and Return to Greatness of the Harlem Globetrotters*. New York: Amistad, 2005.

Guttmann, Allen. *Women's Sports: A History*. New York: Columbia University Press, 1991.

Halberstam, David. *Playing for Keeps: Michael Jordan and the World He Made*. New York: Broadway Books, 1999.

Harper, William. *How You Played the Game: The Life of Grantland Rice*. Columbia: University of Missouri Press, 1999.

Heaphy, Leslie. *The Negro Leagues: 1869–1960*. Jefferson, NC: McFarland, 2003.

Heisler, Mark. *Kobe and the New Lakers Dynasty*. Chicago: Triumph, 2009.

Hillebrand, Laura. *Seabiscuit: An American Legend*. New York: Random House, 2001.

Hoberman, John. *Darwin's Athletes: How Sport Has Damaged Black America and Preserved the Myth of Race*. Boston and New York: Houghton Mifflin, 1997.

Hogshead-Maker, Nancy, and Andrew Zimbalist, eds. *Equal Play: Title IX and Social Change*. Philadelphia: Temple University Press, 2007.

Hollander, Zander. *Madison Square Garden: A Century of Sport and Spectacle on the World's Most Versatile Stage*. New York: Hawthorn Books, 1973.

Hollister, Geoff. *Out of Nowhere: The Inside Story of How Nike Marketed the Culture of Running*. Aachen, Germany: Meyer & Meyer Fachverlag und Buchandel, 2008.

Holway, John B. *Josh and Satch: The Life and Times of Josh Gibson and Satchel Paige*. New York: Meckler, 1991.

Howard, Johnette. *The Rivals: Chris Evert vs. Martina Navratilova: Their Epic Duels and Extraordinary Friendship*. New York: Broadway Books, 2005.

Hyatt, Wesley. *Kicking Off the Week: A History of Monday Night Football on ABC Television*. Jefferson, NC: McFarland, 2007.

Inabinett, Mark. *Grantland Rice and His Heroes*. Knoxville: University of Tennessee Press, 1994.

Isaacs, Neil. *A History of College Basketball*. New York: Harper and Row, 1984.

Jackson, Jonathon. *The Making of* Slap Shot: *Behind the Scenes of the Greatest Hockey Movie Ever Made*. Mississauga, Ontario: John Wiley and Sons, 2011.

Jenner, Bruce, and Phillip Finch. *Decathlon Challenge: Bruce Jenner's Story*. Englewood Cliffs, NJ: Prentice-Hall, 1977.

Johnson, Mary. *Make Them Go Away: Clint Eastwood, Christopher Reeve and the Case Against Disability Rights*. Louisville, KY: Avocado Press, 2003.

Judd, Ron C. *The Winter Olympics: An Insider's Guide to Legends, Lore and Events of the Games*. Seattle: Mountaineer Books, 2009.

Kalinsky, George. *Garden of Dreams: Madison Square Garden 125 Years*. Introduction by Pete Hamill. New York: Stewart, Tabori and Chang, 2004.

Katz, Donald. *Just Do It: The Nike Spirit in the Corporate World*. New York: Random House, 1994.

Katz, Harry. *Baseball Americana: Treasures from the Library of Congress*. New York: HarperCollins, 2009.

Kent, Steven L. *The Ultimate History of Video Games*: New York: Three Rivers Press, 2001.

King, Richard, and Charles Fruehling Springwood, eds. *Team Spirits: The Native American Mascot Controversy*. Lincoln: University of Nebraska Press, 2001.

Klima, John. *Willie's Boys: The 1948 Birmingham Black Barons, the Last Negro League World Series and the Making of a Legend*. New York: Wiley, 2009.

Koppett, Leonard. *Koppett's Concise History of Major League Baseball*. Philadelphia: Temple University Press, 2003.

Lanctot, Neil. *Negro League Baseball: The Rise and Ruin of a Black Institution*. Philadelphia: Temple University Press, 2004.

Leavy, Jane. *The Last Boy: Mickey Mantle and the End of America's Childhood*. New York: HarperCollins, 2010.

Leavy, Jane. *Sandy Koufax: A Lefty's Legacy*. New York: HarperCollins, 2002.

Levenson, Barry. *The Seventh Game: The 35 World Series That Have Gone the Distance*. New York: McGraw-Hill, 2004.

Levine, Peter. *Ellis Island to Ebbets Field: Sport and the American Jewish Experience*. New York: Oxford University Press, 1992.

Light, Jonathan F. *The Cultural Encyclopedia of Baseball*. 2nd ed. Jefferson, NC: McFarland, 2005.

Lowry, Philip J. *Green Cathedrals*. Reading, MA: Addison Wesley, 1992.

Madden, John, with Peter Kaminsky. *John Madden's Ultimate Tailgating*. New York: Viking, 1998.

Maguire, James. *American Bee: The National Spelling Bee and the Culture of Word Nerds*. Emmaus, PA: Rodale, 2006.

Maraniss, David. *Clemente: The Passion and Grace of Baseball's Last Hero*. New York: Simon and Schuster, 2006.

Martin, Charles. *Benching Jim Crow: The Rise and Fall of the Color Line in Southern College Sports, 1890–1980*. Urbana: University of Illinois Press, 2010.

McCallum, Jack, Mel Greenberg, Blair Kerkoff, et al. *Hoops Heaven: Commemorating the 50th Anniversary of the Naismith Memorial Basketball Hall of Fame*. Overland Park, KS: Ascend Books, 2009.

McCallum, Jack. *Dream Team*. New York: Ballantine Books, 2012.

McCambridge, Michael. *The Franchise: A History of Sports Illustrated Magazine*. New York: Hyperion, 1997.

McGimpsey, David. *Imaging Baseball: America's Pastime and Popular Culture*. Bloomington: Indiana University Press, 2000.

McGinn, Bob. *The Ultimate Super Bowl Book: A Complete Reference to the Stats, Stars, and Stories Behind Football's Biggest Game—Why the Best Team Won*. Minneapolis: MVP Books, 2009.

McGuiggan, Amy Whorf. *Take Me Out to the Ball Game: The Story of the Sensational Baseball Song*. Lincoln: University of Nebraska Press, 2009.

Margolies, John, Barbara Garfinkel, and Maria Reidelbach. *Miniature Golf*. New York: Abbeville Press, 1987.

Mead, Chris. *Joe Louis: Black Champion in White America*. New York: Dover Publications, 2010.

Mead, William, and Paul Dickson. *Baseball, the Presidents' Game*. Washington, DC: Farragut, 1993.

Moffi, Larry. *The Conscience of the Game: Baseball's Commissioners from Landis to Selig*. Lincoln, NE: Bison Books, 2006.

Most, Marshall G., and Robert Rudd. *Stars, Stripes and Diamonds: American Culture and the Baseball Film*. Jefferson, NC: McFarland, 2006.

Muskat, Carrie. *Banks to Sandberg to Grace*. Chicago: Contemporary Books, 2002.

Myers, Gary. *The Catch: One Play, Two Dynasties, and the Game That Changed the NFL*. New York: Random House, 2009.

Nelson, Murry. *Encyclopedia of Sports in America: A History from Foot Races to Extreme Sports*. Westport, CT: Greenwood Press, 2009.

Nelson, Murry. *The National Basketball League: A History, 1935–1949*. Jefferson, NC: McFarland, 2009.

Nowlin, Bill, and Bill Prime. *100 Years of Fenway Park: A Celebration of America's Most Beloved Ballpark*. Champaign, IL: Sports Publishing, 2012.

O'Connor, Ian. *Arnie and Jack: Palmer, Nicklaus and Golf's Greatest Rivalry*. Boston: Houghton Mifflin, 2008.

Oriard, Michael. *Brand NFL: The Making and Selling of America's Favorite Sport*. Chapel Hill: University of North Carolina Press, 2010.

Oriard, Michael. *King Football: Sport and Spectacle in the Golden Age of Radio, Newsreels, Movies and Magazines, the Weekly and the Daily Press*. Chapel Hill: University of North Carolina Press, 2001.

Owens, Jesse, and Paul G. Neimark. *Blackthink: My Life as Black Man and White Man*. New York: Morrow, 1970.

Palmatier, Robert A., and Harold L. Ray. *Sports Talk: A Dictionary of Sports Metaphors*. Westport, CT: Greenwood Press, 1989.

Patrick, Dan, and Keith Olbermann. *The Big Show: A Tribute to ESPN's SportsCenter*. New York: Pocket Books, 1997.

Pennington, Bill. *The Heisman: Great American Stories of the Men Who Won*. New York: It Books, HarperCollins, 2005.

Peterson, Robert. *Cages to Jump Shots: Pro Basketball's Early Years*. New York: Oxford University Press, 1990.

Posnanski, Joe. *The Machine: A Hot Team, a Legendary Season, and a Heart-Stopping World Series: The Story of the 1975 Cincinnati Reds.* New York: William Morrow, 2009.

Prager, Joshua. *The Echoing Green: the Untold Story of Bobby Thomson, Ralph Branca and the Shot Heard 'Round the World.* New York: Pantheon Books, 2006.

Rader, Benjamin G. *Baseball: A History of America's Game.* 3d ed. Urbana: University of Illinois Press, 2008.

Regalado, Samuel O. *Viva Baseball! Latin American Players and Their Special Hunger.* Champaign: University of Illinois Press, 2008.

Reston, James, Jr. *Collision at Home Plate: The Lives of Pete Rose and A. Bartlett Giamatti.* New York: HarperCollins, 1991.

Ribowsky, Mark. *A Complete History of the Negro Leagues, 1884 to 1955.* Toronto: Citadel Press, 1995.

Riess, Steven A., ed. *Sports in America: From Colonial Times to the Twenty-First Century.* Armonk, NY: Sharpe Reference, 2011.

Roberts, Randy. *Joe Louis: Hard Times Man.* New Haven, CT: Yale University Press, 2012.

Roberts, Randy. *Papa Jack: Jack Johnson and the Era of White Hopes.* New York: Free Press, 1983.

Robinson, Eddie, and Richard Lapchick. *Never Before, Never Again: The Stirring Autobiography of Eddie Robinson, the Winningest Coach in the History of College Football.* New York: St. Martin's Press, 1999.

Rosen, Daniel M. *Dope: A History of Performance Enhancement in Sports from the Nineteenth Century to Today.* Westport, CT: Praeger, 2008.

Rovell, Darren. *First in Thirst: How Gatorade Turned the Science of Sweat into a Cultural Phenomenon.* New York: American Management Association, 2006.

Russell, Bill, with Taylor Branch. *Second Wind.* New York: Random House, 1979.

Rust, Art, Jr., and Edna Rust. *Art Rust's Illustrated History of the Black Athlete.* Garden City, NY: Doubleday, 1983.

St. John, Allen. *The Billion Dollar Game: Behind the Scenes of the Greatest Day in American Sport—Super Bowl Sunday.* New York: Anchor Books, 2009.

Sammons, Jeffrey. *Beyond the Ring: The Role of Boxing in American Society.* Urbana: University of Illinois Press, 1988.

Savage, Jim. *The Encyclopedia of the NCAA Basketball Tournament: The Complete Independent Guide to College Basketball's Championship Event.* New York: Dell Publishing, 1990.

Scheft, Bill. *America's Gift to Golf: Herbert Warren Wind on The Masters.* Greenwich, CT: The American Golfer, 2011.

Schleppi, John. *Chicago's Showcase of Basketball: The World Tournament of Professional Basketball and the College All-Star Game.* Haworth, NJ: St. Johann Press, 2008.

Schulz, Charles. *My Life with Charlie Brown.* Jackson: University of Mississippi Press, 2010.

Shapiro, Michael. *Bottom of the Ninth: Branch Rickey, Casey Stengel, and the Daring Scheme to Save Baseball from Itself.* New York: Times Books, 2009.

Shea, Stuart. *Wrigley Field: The Unauthorized Biography.* Dulles, VA: Potomac Books, 2006.

Simon, Mary, and Mark Simon. *Racing Through the Century: The Story of Thoroughbred Racing in America.* Mission Viejo, CA: Bowtie Press, 2003.

Smelser, Marshall. *The Life That Ruth Built: A Biography.* New York: Quadrangle, 1975.

Smith, Anthony F., and Keith Hollihan. *ESPN the Company: The Story and Lessons Behind the Most Fanatical Brand in Sports.* Hoboken, NJ: John Wiley & Sons, 2009.

Smith, Ronald. *Play-by-Play: Radio, Television and Big-Time College Sport.* Baltimore: Johns Hopkins University Press, 2001.

Sperber, Murray. *Shake Down the Thunder: The Creation of Notre Dame Football.* New York: Henry Holt, 1993.

Spink, Al. *The National Game.* 2nd ed. Carbondale: Southern Illinois University Press, 2000.

Sporting News. *Saturday Shrines: College Football's Most Hallowed Grounds.* St. Louis: The Sporting News, 2005.

Springwood, Charles Fruehling. *Cooperstown to Dyersville: A Geography of Baseball Nostalgia.* Boulder, CO: Westview Press, 1995.

Stansfield, Dean, *Images of America (Lake Placid, New York).* Mount Pleasant, SC: Arcadia, 2002.

Stark, Douglas. *The SPHAS: The Life and Times of Basketball's Greatest Jewish Team.* Philadelphia: Temple University Press, 2011.

Stout, Glenn. *The Dodgers, 120 Years of Dodgers Baseball.* Boston: Houghton Mifflin, 2004.

Stout, Glenn, and Richard A. Johnson. *Yankees Century: 100 Years of New York Yankees Baseball.* Boston: Houghton Mifflin, 2002.

Telander, Rick. *Heaven Is a Playground.* 3rd ed. Lincoln: University of Nebraska Press, 2008.

Thomas, Ron. *They Cleared the Lane: The NBA's Black Pioneers.* Lincoln, NE: Bison Books, 2004.

Thornley, Stew. *The History of the Lakers: Basketball's Original Dynasty.* Minneapolis: Nodin Press, 1989.

Tudor, Deborah V. *Hollywood's Vision of Team Sports: Heroes, Race, and Gender.* New York: Garland, 1997.

Tye, Larry. *Satchel: The Life and Times of an American Legend.* New York: Random House, 2009.

Tygiel, Jules. *Baseball's Great Experiment: Jackie Robinson and His Legacy.* New York: Oxford University Press, 1983.

Voigt, David Q. *American Baseball, Vol. 3: From Postwar Expansion to Electronic Age.* University Park: Pennsylvania State University Press, 1983.

Vorwald, Bob. *Cubs Forever: Memories from the Men Who Lived Them.* Chicago: Triumph Books, 2008.

Washburn, Patrick. *The African American Newspaper, Voice of Freedom.* Evanston, IL: Northwestern University Press, 2006.

Ware, Susan. *Game, Set, Match: Billie Jean King and the Revolution in Women's Sports.* Chapel Hill: University of North Carolina Press, 2011.

Watterson, John S. *The Games Presidents Play: Sports and the Presidency.* Baltimore: Johns Hopkins University Press, 2006.

Webster, Maurie. *And Now, a Word from Our Sponsor: 40 Years of Notable Radio Advertising.* New York: Columbia Special Products, 1960.

Wendel, Tim, and Jose Luis Villegas. *Latino Baseball Players in America.* Washington, DC: National Geographic, 2008.

Wenner, Lawrence A., and Steven J. Jackson, eds. *Sport, Beer, and Gender: Promotional Culture and Contemporary Social Life.* New York: Peter Lang, 2009.

Wheaton, Belinda. *Lifestyle Sport: The Cultural Politics of Alternative Sports.* London: Routledge Press, 2012.

Wiggins, David K., and R. Pierre Rodgers. *Rivals: Legendary Matchups That Made Sports History.* Fayetteville: University of Arkansas Press, 2010.

Wilner, Barry, and Ken Rappoport. *The Big Dance: The Story of the NCAA Basketball Tournament.* Lanham, MD: Taylor, 2012.

Wood, Stephen C., and J. David Pincus. *Reel Baseball: Essays and Interviews on the National Pastime, Hollywood and American Culture* Jefferson, NC: McFarland Press, 1994.

Yarbrough, Roy. Mascots: *The History of Senior College and University Mascots/Nicknames.* Lynchburg, VA: Bluff University Communications, 1998.

Zacchino, Narda, ed. *The Los Angeles Lakers: 50 Amazing Years in the City of Angels. Revised and Expanded Edition—Updated for 2009–10 NBA Championship Season.* San Leandro, CA: Time Capsule Press, 2009.

Zucker, Harvey Marc, and Lawrence J. Babich. *Sports Films: A Complete Reference.* Jefferson, NC: McFarland, 1987.

About the Editor and Contributors

EDITOR

Murry R. Nelson is an Emeritus Professor of Education and American Studies at Penn State University. He received both doctorate and master's degrees from Stanford University and has held Senior Fulbright lectureships at the University of Iceland (1983) and the Norwegian Ministry of Education (1990–1991) and held the Laszlo Orszagh Distinguished Chair in American Studies at the University of Debrecen (Hungary) in 2007–2008. He is the author of Greenwood Press/ABC-CLIO biographies of Bill Russell (2005), Shaquille O'Neal (2007), and the Rolling Stones (2010), as well as histories of the original New York Celtics (1999), the National Basketball League (2009), and the American Basketball League (2013).

CONTRIBUTORS

Dean Allen, PhD, is currently based in Cape Town, South Africa, as a Senior Lecturer at Cape Peninsula University of Technology. Having lectured at universities in the UK, Ireland, and Australia, Dr. Allen is widely published in the area of sport history and sociology.

Lauren Applebaum is a PhD candidate in the Art History department at the University of Illinois at Urbana-Champaign. She specializes in 20th-century American art, material culture studies, and mass market illustration.

Sarah D. Bair received her doctorate in Curriculum and Instruction from Penn State University and is currently an Associate Professor of Education at Dickinson College.

Kelly Balfour earned her doctorate in Kinesiology and Sport Studies with a concentration in sociocultural studies of sport from the University of Tennessee–Knoxville. Her research interests include gender issues in sport, as well as understanding the experiences of female fans of men's professional sports.

David Barney has coached interscholastic athletics for more than half a century in the United States, achieving the status of National Honor Coach. He is a frequent lecturer and contributor to various sports history organizations and journals.

Robert K. Barney is Professor Emeritus in the School of Kinesiology, Faculty of Health Sciences, at Western University in London, Ontario, Canada. He has "lived and died" as a fan of the Red Sox since the third grade in Massachusetts in 1939, Ted Williams's first year in "the Bigs."

Nick Bascom received a master's degree in English from Penn State. He is a contributing writer for *Science News*, based in Washington, D.C.

Joy A. Bauer is completing graduate studies at the University of Maryland in Kinesiology (Physical Cultural Studies specialization) and Women's Studies. A retired gymnast and lifelong fan of the sport, she has taught courses on gender and sport, and her research interests include visual representations of girls and women in sport and bodily practices in sporting cultures.

Becky Beal is a Professor of Kinesiology at California State University, East Bay in Hayward, California, where she teaches courses in the sociology and philosophy of sport. Her research interests are centered on issues of social justice in sport and physical activity. Beal also serves as the Associate Director of the Center for Sport and Social Justice.

John Beauge has covered the Little League World Series as a photographer, writer, and editor since 1957. He has a bachelor's degree from Penn State, a master's from Northwestern University, and is a correspondent for the *Harrisburg Patriot-News*.

Matthew Bentley is an Associate Tutor at the University of East Anglia. His research interests include the history of sport, masculinity, the American West, and American Indian history.

Adam P. Berg is from State College, Pennsylvania. He is currently a PhD candidate at Penn State University where he studies the history and philosophy of sports.

Ulrika Billme is a Swedish student with a bachelor's degree in Pedagogics and Health Promotion. She is studying to achieve a master's degree in Sport Psychology at Halmstad University, Sweden, in spring 2013.

Margaret Carroll Boardman is Managing Director of Global Food Strategies LLC and was a Visiting Scholar at the University of Notre Dame's Reilly Center for Science, Values & Technology in 2011–2012. She has a PhD in History from UCLA (1999) in the fields of international history and American diplomatic history.

Ron Briley has taught American history and film studies for the last 35 years at Sandia Preparatory School in Albuquerque, New Mexico. In addition to publishing numerous scholarly articles on film and sport, Ron is an author or editor of *Class at Bat, Gender on Deck, and Race in the Hole* (2003), James T. Farrell's *Dreaming Baseball* (2007), *All-Stars and Movie Stars* (2008), *The Politics of Baseball* (2010), and *The Baseball Film in Postwar America* (2012). Ron's teaching has been honored by the Organization of American

Historians, American Historical Association, Society for History Education, National Council for History Education, and New Mexico's Golden Apple.

Dean Bring grew up in Columbus, Ohio, and graduated from Denison University in 2005 with a BA in Economics. He then graduated from Capital University Law School in Columbus with a JD. In 2012 he graduated from Ohio State with an MA in Sports Humanities. He currently works at Perio, Inc. (Barbasol Brands).

Scott J. Bukstein is an Instructor, Assistant Director, and Program Coordinator within the DeVos Sport Business Management Program at the University of Central Florida.

O. Richard Bundy, PhD, has earned degrees from Pennsylvania State University and the University of Michigan. He performed professionally as a trombonist and taught in the Iroquois (Pennsylvania) School District before joining the Penn State School of Music faculty in 1983 where he currently is a Professor of Music Education and Director of Athletic Bands. Under his leadership, the Penn State Blue Band received the 2005 Sudler Trophy presented annually by the John Philip Sousa Foundation to recognize college marching band programs with sustained histories of excellence.

Christopher Busey is an alumnus of the University of Florida in Gainesville, Florida, and an avid college football fan. He is also a PhD candidate in Social Science Education at the University of Central Florida.

Ted Carlin, PhD, is a Professor of Electronic Media and New Communication technology at Shippensburg University of Pennsylvania. Dr. Carlin is the station operator for WSYC-FM and Executive Producer for the Red Raider Sports Network.

Megan Chawansky earned her PhD from The Ohio State University in 2008. Her research examines gender and sexuality in various sporting contexts. She was Northwestern University Athlete of the Year in 2001.

Yeomi Choi is a doctoral student pursuing sociohistorical studies in the Department of Kinesiology at the University of North Carolina at Greensboro.

Craig R. Coenen is a Professor of History at Mercer County Community College in West Windsor, New Jersey. He obtained a PhD in History from Lehigh University, wrote *From Sandlots to the Super Bowl: The National Football League, 1920–1967* (Knoxville: University of Tennessee Press, 2005), and co-edited *American Presidential Campaigns and Elections* (M. E. Sharpe, 2003).

R. Dawn Comstock holds a PhD in Epidemiology and Public Health from the joint program at the University of California–San Diego and San Diego State University. She is an Associate Professor at The Ohio State University College of Medicine and a Primary Investigator at Nationwide Children's Hospital.

Ann Cook is currently the Associate Head Women's Soccer Coach at Pennsylvania State University as well as an Assistant Director of Soccer Without Borders, a nonprofit that uses soccer as a vehicle for positive change in the lives of marginalized youth. She played in the WUSA for the three years of its existence—two years with the Bay Area CyberRays and a year with the Washington Freedom.

Will Cooley is an Assistant Professor of History at Walsh University. He studies race and social mobility in the United States.

Kristen Costa is a museum curator at the Newport Restoration Foundation in Newport, Rhode Island, and an independent scholar with a specialization in American sports and cultural history. She previously held curatorial positions at the National Baseball Hall of Fame and Museum and International Tennis Hall of Fame.

Rosarita Cuccoli is a published author on sports in various countries, with a 25-year combined work experience in international organizations, research, and business. An Italian-born Parisian, with degrees from the universities of Cambridge and Bologna, she is the founder and CEO of Stadio Novo, a consulting firm based in France and operating internationally that provides sport-based learning solutions to companies and schools.

Matt DeFraga holds a BA in History from UC Santa Barbara and two MAs in History from UCSB and San Francisco State University. A former editor for ABC-CLIO's *America: History and Life*, Matt works for the federal government and teaches history part-time for the University of Phoenix.

Natalie Deibel received a doctorate in History from George Washington University and has taught history at a number of levels.

Charlie Deitrich teaches in the History program at the College of Southern Nevada.

Ari de Wilde, PhD, is an Assistant Professor of Sport Management at York College of Pennsylvania. His main research interests lie in the business history of sport, the North American bicycle racing industry, and sport management studies research methodologies.

Joshua Dickhaus earned his PhD at the University of Alabama in 2011. Dr. Dickhaus joined the Bradley University faculty in the fall of 2011 as Professor of Sports Communication.

Richard Diem is Professor of Education and Dean of the Honors College. He is a lifelong baseball fan since seeing his first big league game at the Polo Grounds in 1951 when the New York Giants beat the Cincinnati Red Legs, 8–2. He does have the scorecard to prove it.

Lyndy Doran graduated from the University of Central Florida in 2011 and was a Research Assistant in the Paul Robeson Research Center for Academic and Athletic Prowess during her senior year.

Mark Dyreson is Professor of Kinesiology and Affiliate Professor of History at Penn State. He is the author of numerous books and articles on the history of sport, an academic editor for the *International Journal of the History of Sport*, the co-editor of the *Sport in Global Society: Historical Perspectives* book series for Routledge Press, and a former president of the North American Society for Sport History.

Jacqueline Edmondson is Associate Dean of Undergraduate and Graduate studies in the College of Education at Pennsylvania State University. She is also editor of *Music in American Life: An Encyclopedia of the Songs, Styles, Stars and Stories That Shaped Our Culture*.

Mika T. Elovaara is an author, teacher, coach, a former professional athlete, and a lifelong sport enthusiast. He has taught classes in Sport Sociology for undergraduate and graduate students and currently enjoys full-time coaching and independent research.

Beth Emery was a graduate of North Carolina State University where she was a 19-time AIAW and NCAA All-American in women's swimming from 1980 to 1983. She received her master's degree at Ohio State and was completing doctoral studies in Sports Humanities when she died suddenly in April 2012.

Colleen English is a graduate student at Penn State University pursuing her doctorate in Sport Philosophy and History.

Amy Essington is a Lecturer at California State University, Long Beach. Her dissertation was on the racial integration of the Pacific Coast League, the minor baseball league on the West Coast (Claremont Graduate University).

Pat Farabaugh is an Assistant Professor of Communication Arts at Saint Francis University (Pennsylvania). Before entering academia, he worked in athletic media relations at Slippery Rock, Bucknell, and Saint Francis universities. His first book, *Carl McIntire and His Crusade Against the Fairness Doctrine*, was published in 2010.

Rory Faust is a Lecturer in the School of Communication at Northern Arizona University. He has covered the NFL, Major League Baseball, NASCAR, and numerous other high-profile events in nearly two decades of work as a sports journalist.

Sarah K. Fields is an Associate Professor in Sport Management at The Ohio State University. She holds a JD from Washington University in St. Louis and a PhD in American Studies from the University of Iowa.

Vincent F. Filak is an award-winning teacher, scholar, and college media adviser. He currently works as an Associate Professor of Journalism at the University of Wisconsin–Oshkosh where he also advises the *Advance-Titan*, the university's student newspaper.

Joshua Fleer is a PhD candidate in Religious Studies at Florida State University. He teaches the course Religion and Sport at Florida State University, and he is Associate Editor of *Communal Societies: Journal of the Communal Studies Association*.

David A. Fuentes is an Assistant Professor in the department of Elementary and Early Childhood Education at William Paterson University of New Jersey. He teaches courses aimed at preparing inquiring educators for teaching in diverse settings, as well as courses that examine the historical and philosophical foundations of education in the United States. His current research focuses on understanding the relationship between race, culture, ethnicity, and identity in a variety of school settings.

Gary Gershman is Associate Professor of History and Legal Studies in the Division of Humanities at Nova Southeastern University.

Chris B. Geyerman is an Associate Professor of Communication Studies in the Department of Communication Arts at Georgia Southern University, where he also serves as the NCAA Faculty Athletics Representative.

John Gleaves is an Assistant Professor of Kinesiology at California State University, Fullerton. He specializes in historical and philosophical aspects of sport and is currently preparing an edited book on the legacy of the 1984 Los Angeles Olympic Games.

Zackary A. Goncz is enrolled in a joint graduate degree in law and international affairs at Penn State University.

Kieran Gordon is a sport scholar and coach. He is dedicated to a holistic approach to sport education through his experience as a practitioner and academician.

Chip Greene is a Society for American Baseball Research (SABR) member and regular contributor to the SABR Biography Project. Additionally, he has contributed to several SABR book projects, as well as *Yankees Yearly* magazine. A management consultant, he lives in Waynesboro, Pennsylvania.

Kevin Hagopian teaches film studies and media studies at Penn State University, University Park. His research specialty is the cultural history of the American cinema.

C. Keith Harrison is Associate Professor at the University of Central Florida and President of Scholar-Baller, a nonprofit organization sponsored by the NCAA. He is a former NCAA football scholar-athlete.

James Hashek is a visiting scholar in English at the University of New Orleans where he teaches journalism classes.

Steven Herb is the head of the Education and Behavioral Sciences Library at Penn State University and the Director of the Pennsylvania Center for the Book, an affiliate of the Center for the Book at the Library of Congress.

Amanda Leigh Higgins is a PhD candidate in American History at the University of Kentucky. Her dissertation project investigates the intersections of black power, anti–Vietnam War, and welfare rights activism.

Karen E. Holleran has been published in encyclopedias, dictionaries, and academic books. She has presented papers on baseball, women in sports, medieval literature, and 18th-century literature. She teaches classes online for Robert Morris University, Coraopolis, Pennsylvania. She is studying public history at West Virginia University and is a member of SABR.

Katherine M. Jamieson, PhD, is an Associate Professor in Kinesiology at the University of North Carolina in Greensboro. She earned her PhD at Michigan State University under the direction of Yevonne Smith (Kinesiology) and Maxine Baca Zinn (Sociology) and conducts scholarly work around social difference, cultural power, and structural inequalities in sporting spaces, especially in a post–Title IX and post–9/11 set of social conditions.

Ric W. Jensen is an Assistant Professor in the Department of Marketing at Montclair State University in Montclair, New Jersey. He teaches Sports Marketing and related courses. Previously, he taught public relations and mass communication courses at the University of South Dakota and Ashland University (Ohio).

Claude Johnson is an author, a historian, and an entrepreneur as the founder/CEO of BlackFives .com, a leading resource in honoring, promoting, preserving, and teaching about the pre-1950 history of African American basketball teams, as well as advocating for the recognition of its pioneers. He tweets @ claudejohnson.

Jarrod Jonsrud attends Pennsylvania State University as a doctoral student focusing his studies in the history and philosophy of sport. His areas of research include ethics in sport and the history of basketball.

Charles Kaufman, Editor and Publisher of *Sweet Spot* (www.sweetspotnews.com), a publication devoted to vintage and autographed sports memorabilia, is a member of the journalism and mass communication faculty at Texas State University–San Marcos. His 18-year newspaper career includes work at the *Arkansas Gazette* and the *Austin American-Statesman*. Mr. Kaufman has authored or co-authored two textbooks and chapters for two others. He is a graduate of the University of Texas at Austin with a master's degree from Northwestern University.

Mark Kissling is an Assistant Professor in the College of Education at Penn State University. He received his PhD from Michigan State University.

Brad Klypchak, PhD, teaches courses in Liberal Studies at Texas A&M University–Commerce. His scholarship reflects his interdisciplinarity including works in film, theater, sport, performance, mass media studies, and, his particular emphasis, heavy metal music.

Susannah Kaye Knust completed her PhD in Sport Psychology and Motor Behavior from the University of Tennessee. She is originally from Grand Rapids, Michigan.

Kyle Kusz is an Associate Professor of Physical Cultural Studies at the University of Rhode Island. His research, best captured in the book *Revolt of the White Athlete: Race, Media, and the Emergence of Extreme Athletes in America* (Peter Lang, 2007), focuses on the politics of cultural representations of white masculinity produced at the intersection of sport, film, and popular culture.

Rita Liberti is a Professor in the Department of Kinesiology at California State University, East Bay. Her primary research interest centers on African American women's 20th-century sport history.

Andrew Linden received a bachelor's degree in History and a master's degree in Sports Humanities at Ohio State and is currently a doctoral student in Kinesiology at Penn State.

Amy Lively is an independent scholar and writer from Phoenix, Arizona. She holds an undergraduate degree in Behavioral Science and a master of arts in American History. Her background includes nonprofit management and higher education.

Ryan Lizardi received his doctorate from Penn State University. His dissertation examined contemporary nostalgic media. Similarly, his research focuses on the creation of ideological connections to our collective and individual pasts through new and traditional media.

Matthew P. Llewellyn is an Assistant Professor in the Department of Kinesiology at California State University, Fullerton. He is the author of *Rule Britannia: Nationalism, Identity and the Modern Olympic Games* (Routledge Press, 2011). Matthew earned a PhD from Pennsylvania State University in the History and Philosophy of Sport.

David Lunt received his PhD in History from Penn State in 2010. He currently works as the Director of Interdisciplinary Studies at Southern Utah University.

Patricia Macales, Los Angeles Unified School District, former secondary education specialist. Award-winning poet—*Victory Day.*

Rich Macales, UCLA, former senior writer and public information officer. Citation: University Extension Task Force on Diversity. Awards (partial): Public Relations Society of America (PRSA) and National University Continuing Education Association (NUCEA).

Joe Marren is an Associate Professor and the Chair of the Communication Department at Buffalo State College. Prior to academia, he was a newspaper reporter and editor for 18 years at various community dailies and business newspapers in western New York. He is the author of numerous academic journal articles, book chapters, and several books; and he was also a stringer for the Associated Press and did commentaries on the Buffalo-area NPR station.

Nicolas Martin-Breteau is a Lecturer in U.S. History, University of La Sorbonne, Paris, France. He is also a doctoral candidate in U.S. History, Ecole des hautes études en sciences sociales (EHESS), Paris, France.

Fred Mason is an Associate Professor in the Faculty of Kinesiology at the University of New Brunswick, teaching history and sociology of sport. His research focuses on media, disability, and sport in literature and film.

Matthew A. Masucci is an Associate Professor of Sport Studies and Sport Philosophy in the Department of Kinesiology at San Jose State University in San Jose, California. Matthew's recent research activities include a critical multidisciplinary investigation of mixed martial arts (MMA), a World Anti-Doping Agency (WADA)–sponsored study of doping knowledge among female triathletes, and a series of projects exploring the creation and meaning of alternative bicycle communities.

Lindsey Mauro graduated from Michigan State University and is currently a Graduate Assistant at the DeVos Sport Business Management Program at the University of Central Florida and Paul Robeson Research Center for Academic and Athletic Prowess.

Kathy McCleaf is an Associate Professor in the School of Social Science, Business and Global Studies at Mary Baldwin College. Dr. McCleaf teaches Sexuality and Gender Studies courses including a class focused on Gender and Sport. Inquiries can be made at kmccleaf@mbc.edu.

Bryan A. McCullick is a Professor in the Department of Kinesiology at the University of Georgia. His research targets issues germane to teacher and coach development and expertise. He has presented his work to scholarly societies worldwide, is an Associate Editor for *RQES*, a Fellow in the Research Consortium, and on the editorial board for *JTPE* and the *Annual Review of Golf Coaching*.

Clint McDuffie is a doctoral student at the University of Missouri–Kansas City in American History. His area of focus is in sports in the United States from 1850 to 1920, particularly college football, and the issues of race, masculinity, performance, and everyday life.

Chett Miller recently graduated from The Ohio State University. He is currently working in entertainment sports in the Los Angeles area and is continuing his education in sociology.

Andrew Milner contributed entries to *Sports in America from Colonial Times to the Twenty-First Century* (M. E. Sharpe, 2011) and *The St. James Encyclopedia of Popular Culture* (St. James, 1999) and original research to *Our Times: The Illustrated History of the 20th Century* (Turner, 1995). He is a member of

the Society for American Baseball Research and is a regular contributor to the Philadelphia *City Paper*, *The Sondheim Review*, and *Base Ball: A Journal of the Early Game*.

Jensen Moore is an Assistant Professor of Strategic Communication at the Manship School of Mass Communication at Louisiana State University. Moore's professional experience included working as a public relations director and advertising executive for minor league teams the Grand Rapids Hoops (CBA) and the St. Paul Saints Professional Baseball team.

Michael D. Murray is University of Missouri Board of Curators Distinguished Professor on the University of Missouri's St. Louis campus, where he also currently serves as Chairman of the Faculty Senate and the University Assembly.

Daniel A. Nathan is an Associate Professor of American Studies at Skidmore College and the author of the award-winning *Saying It's So: A Cultural History of the Black Sox Scandal* (2003). The President-elect of the North American Society for Sport History, Nathan has served as the Film, Media, and Museum Reviews editor for the *Journal of Sport History*.

David Naze, PhD, is Associate Professor of Communication at Prairie State College in Chicago Heights, Illinois. He received his PhD from Indiana University, Bloomington in Communication and Culture.

Caryn E. Neumann is a Lecturer in Integrative Studies and History at Miami University of Ohio. She holds a PhD in History from The Ohio State University.

Bill Nowlin is author of over 30 books on baseball, as well as a former professor of political science who has recently begun teaching again, in courses tied into baseball. He is a co-founder of Rounder Records and longtime Vice President of the Society for American Baseball Research.

Elsa A. Nystrom is a Professor of History at Kennesaw State University. She teaches social and cultural history, including a course with a focus on auto racing.

Ellie Odenheimer is completing her PhD in Kinesiology and Sport Studies at the University of Tennessee. Her research interests include sport sociology, health and wellness, and the intersection of physical activity, religion, and spirituality.

Adam G. Pfleegor is a Sport Management doctoral candidate at the Louisiana State University. His main research focus is ethical issues in sport and sport management primarily concerned with NCAA intercollegiate athletics.

Benjamin P. Phillips is a PhD candidate in American Studies at Michigan State University. His research interests include modern U.S. history, popular culture, and sports culture—especially college football and issues of the amateur ideal.

Lindsay Parks Pieper is an Assistant Professor at Lynchburg College in Sport Management.

Kelly Poniatowski is an Assistant Professor in the Department of Communications at Elizabethtown College. Her research interests include gender, race, and nationality in mediated sports, particularly the Olympics.

Karra Porter is the author of *Mad Seasons: The Story of the First Women's Professional Basketball League 1978–1981*, and an attorney in Salt Lake City, Utah.

Mark Previte is an Associate Professor of Secondary Education (Social Studies) at the University of Pittsburgh at Johnstown. His research interests include issues centered on education, historical foundations of social studies, and the democratic classroom.

Jeffrey T. Ramsey is a doctoral candidate in History at Marquette University. His research interests include the intersection of popular American sports and gender. His dissertation is focused on the reaction and resistance to Title IX from Big Ten universities.

Caleb J. Rebarchak is a conductor, musician, and educator. He received his bachelor of science in Music Education and master of Music in Band/ Wind Ensemble Conducting from Pennsylvania State University.

Arthur Remillard is Assistant Professor of Religious Studies at Saint Francis University (Loretto, Pennsylvania). He is author of *Southern Civil Religions: Imagining the Good Society in the Post–Reconstruction Era*.

Brenda A. Riemer is an Associate Professor of Sport Management at Eastern Michigan University. Brenda and her canine companions are active participants in competitive dog sports, including obedience.

Katelyn Rockenbach is a biomechanist with a master's of science degree from the University of Tennessee. Katelyn will be attending medical school to pursue a career and lifetime dream as an orthopedic surgeon.

Sara Roser-Jones is a sport historian with special interest in the history of African Americans in sport during the 20th century.

Alexandra Schierer received her undergraduate degree in English Literature from Chestnut Hill College and her master's degree in Broadcasting, Telecommunications, and Mass Media from Temple University. She has been working in the professional sports industry for five years.

Jaime Schultz is an Assistant Professor in the Department of Kinesiology at Penn State University. She received her PhD from the University of Iowa.

Chad Seifried, PhD, is a J. Franklin Bayhi Endowed Professor for the College of Human Sciences and Education at the Louisiana State University and graduate coordinator for the Sport Management program and School of Kinesiology. Dr. Seifried's research interests primarily center on sport facilities but also utilize history as means to contextualize contemporary management decisions in sport.

Greg Selber, PhD, is Professor of Communication at the University of Texas–Pan American in South Texas and has 25 years of experience in the media business, in print and broadcast. He won the state's Putt Powell Award in 2011 for top sportswriter of the year and published *Border Ball* in 2009, a history of high school football in the Rio Grande Valley.

Jack Selzer, a native Cincinnatian, has been an active member of the Society for American Baseball Research (SABR) since 1978. On the side he is an English professor at Penn State.

Brooke Sherrard is an Instructor of Religion and History at William Penn University in Oskaloosa, Iowa. She earned her PhD in American religious history from Florida State University in 2011.

Stefanie Shimansky is a senior at the University of Central Florida and a recipient of the Blair Thomas Book Scholarship for Women in Sport Business Management.

Ronald Shook is Associate Professor of English and Technical Communication at Utah State University. A lifelong motoring enthusiast, he has recently written a history of racing on the Bonneville Salt Flats.

David C. Skinner has published numerous articles on Cuban and Negro League baseball. He lives in Arizona, where he formerly taught history at Cochise College.

Lauren Reichart Smith is an Assistant Professor in the Department of Communication and Journalism at Auburn University. Her research focuses on sports media and has been published in the *Journal of Sports Media* and the *International Journal of Sports Communication.*

Maureen Smith is a Professor in the Department of Kinesiology and Health Science at California State University, Sacramento, where she teaches sport history and sport sociology. She is a graduate of Ithaca College and The Ohio State University. Smith is a past president of the North American Society for Sport History.

Michael Smith is an Associate Professor in the School of Writing, Rhetoric & Technical Communication at James Madison University. He has worked as a newspaper reporter, a business and medical writer, and in a German delicatessen.

Lyle Spatz is the Chairman of the Society for American Baseball Research's Baseball Records Committee. He has authored and edited numerous baseball books and articles.

Karyn K. Spencer has been an educator for 30 years, teaching at all levels from pre-K to doctoral students. Her experiences include teaching in Alabama, Louisiana, Idaho, Hawai'i, Tennessee, and Utah. She obtained her doctorate in kinesiology in 1988 and has published two books and over 40 research articles, obtained over $150,000 in grant funds, and made hundreds of research presentations.

Jennifer Sterling received her PhD in Physical Cultural Studies (Kinesiology) from the University of Maryland. Her current research interests focus on the articulations of visual and physical culture, including (but not limited to) art, museums, scientific imaging, and visual methodology.

Harry Strong grew up in the shadow of Wrigley Field in Chicago and is currently serving as Pastor of a flock of Lutheran, Methodist, Presbyterian, and United Church of Christ folks in Ridgway, Colorado.

Richard Strong is a graduate of Towson University and teaches physical education at Jemicy Middle School in Owings Mills, Maryland. During the summer he directs sports camps in the Baltimore area. He also boasts the only hole-in-one in history on the par 4, 343-yard 15th hole at the Dinosaur Mountain course at Gold Canyon Resort in Arizona.

Philip C. Suchma received his doctorate from Ohio State University and currently teaches history at Lehman College, St. John's University, and Fordham University in New York City. His research centers on the meaning of sport in urban centers and he has several publications on professional sport and urban decline in postwar Cleveland.

Sarah J. Teetzel is an Assistant Professor in the Faculty of Kinesiology and Recreation Management at the University of Manitoba in Winnipeg, Canada. Her research in applied ethics in sport, performance enhancement, and gender issues in sport has recently been funded by the Canadian Centre for Ethics in Sport, the World Anti-Doping Agency, and the IOC Olympic Studies Centre.

Dain TePoel completed his master's degree in Sport Humanities at Ohio State University in 2012. He is currently a PhD student in Sport Studies at the University of Iowa.

Stephen D. Thiel is a graduate student in the dual-degree DeVos Sport Business Management program at the University of Central Florida. He also serves as the Graduate Assistant to the undergraduate sport business management minor at UCF.

Elizabeth M. Tobey earned her doctorate in Italian Renaissance art history from the University of Maryland in 2005. Tobey worked for the National Sporting Library and Museum in Middleburg, Virginia, from 2007 to 2010, a research library dedicated to the history of equestrian and field sports. Most recently she has worked for the Smithsonian American Art Museum in Washington, D.C. Tobey was born and raised in Hingham, Massachusetts, and currently lives in Greenbelt, Maryland.

Grant Tracey, an English Professor at the University of Northern Iowa and long-suffering Toronto Maple Leafs fan, has published three collections of stories and edits *North American Review*.

Robert Trumpbour is Associate Professor of Communications at Penn State Altoona. He is author and editor of two texts, *The New Cathedrals: Politics and Media in the History of Stadium Construction* (Syracuse University Press) and *Cathedrals of Sport: The Rise of Stadiums in the Modern United States* (Routledge). He has published in other venues and prior to entering the teaching profession, Trumpbour worked at CBS in New York for the television and radio networks.

Brian Turner is an Associate Professor in Sport Management at The Ohio State University. He received his PhD from Ohio State and is a North American Society for Sport Management (NASSM) Research Fellow.

Cathy Van Ingen is an Associate Professor in Kinesiology at Brock University. She is also a member of the International Boxing Research Organization (IBRO).

Darin H. Van Tassell is an Associate Professor in the Center for International Studies at Georgia Southern University. He served as the Competition Director for the International Baseball Federation in the 2008 Beijing Olympics and the 2004 Athens Olympics. He became the youngest head coach in Olympic history when he coached the Nicaraguan baseball team to the bronze medal game in the 1996 Olympics in Atlanta.

Theresa Walton, PhD, an Associate Professor in Sport Administration at Kent State University, draws on critical cultural studies to investigate power relationships within mediated sport narratives. In particular, she has examined media discourse of Title IX and sport, women's amateur wrestling, and elite distance running.

Dylan Williams is a second-year PhD student at Louisiana State University under Dr. Chad Seifried. He is a licensed CPA in Louisiana and has research interests in accounting policies and taxation in sport.

Melissa C. Wiser is a doctoral candidate and Lecturer in Sport Humanities at The Ohio State University. Her research focuses on the construction of gender in the rules and governance of women's lacrosse.

Ying WuShanley, PhD, is Professor of Wellness and Sport Sciences at Millersville University of Pennsylvania and a former council member of the North American Society for Sport History. His major publication is *Playing Nice and Losing: The Struggle for Control of Women's Intercollegiate Athletics, 1960–2000* (Syracuse University Press, 2004).

Molly Yanity served as a sportswriter for the *Seattle Post-Intelligencer* from 2000 to 2009 where she primarily covered college football. She earned a PhD in Mass Communication from Ohio University in May 2013 and, at the time of publication, was searching for a job in academia where she could continue her research on sports media and political economy.

Vincent W. Youngbauer is an Assistant Professor of Curriculum & Instruction at the University of South Dakota where he teaches a variety of education courses for future social studies teachers. Dr. Youngbauer has a professional interest in how media and popular culture influence education. Having grown up near Pittsburgh, he has been a lifelong fan of the Steelers.

Index

AAGPL. *See* All-American Girls Professional Baseball League (AAGPL)

Aaron, Henry, **1–5,** 2 (image), 13–14, 103, 169, 600, 781, 1169, 1255 (image), 1443 (image); childhood of, 1–3; election to the Baseball Hall of Fame, 4; institution of the Hank Aaron Award by Major League Baseball, 5; major records and accomplishments, 4 (box); as member of the Atlanta Braves, 1, 3; as member of the Milwaukee Braves, 3; as member of the Milwaukee Brewers, 3; in the minor leagues, 3; as the object of racial hatred, 1, 3; winning of the World Series, 3

AAU (Amateur Athletic Union) Basketball, **5–9,** 6 (image); annual champions of, 8 (table); different types of teams involved in its annual tournament, 6–7; final tournament of, 9; formation and early history of, 5–6; as a marketing opportunity for small businesses, 7; and the Olympics, 6, 7. *See also* National Industrial Basketball League (NIBL)

Abbott, Bud, 1453–1454

Abdul-Jabbar, Kareem, **9–14,** 21, 158, 227, 243, 731, 732, 863, 1078, 1393, 1483; as an actor, 10–11; childhood of, 11; as a coach, 13; college career of at UCLA, 10; conversion to Islam, 11; critics of, 11; desire to be known as more than just a basketball player, 9, 10; influence of on the slam dunk, 9, 364–365; love of music, 12; as member of the Los Angeles Lakers, 10; as member of the Milwaukee Bucks, 9–10; NBA championships won by, 9; records and accomplishments of, 13 (box)

Abdul-Khaalis, Hamaas, 12

Abdullah, Kulsoom, 1237

Adams, Franklin P., 113–114

Adidas (Adidas Group), **14–17,** 15 (image), 18, 21, 1050; international presence of, 16–17; purchase of by Bernard Tapie, 16; purchase of Reebok by, 16

Advertising, and sport, **17–23;** and "ambush marketing," 21 (box); and athlete contracts, 19; and celebrity endorsements, 21–22; and ESPN, 20–21, 22; influence of Wheaties on, 17–18; and the major television networks, 19; and NASCAR, 20, 21, 22; sporting events bringing in the largest advertising dollars, 20; and the Timex Company, 19

Affirmed, 1367–1368

AFL. *See* American Football League (AFL)

African Americans, and tennis, 71 (box)

Agassi, Andre, **23–26,** 24 (image), 957 (box); career Grand Slam of, 25; as a celebrity, 26 (box); childhood of, 23; comeback of, 24–25; dominance of, 24; drug test failure of, 24; Grand Slam finals of, 25; marriages of, 26; Olympic gold medal of, 25; personal style of, 24; philanthropy of, 26; refusal to appear at Wimbledon, 23; rivalry with Pete Sampras, 23, 24, 25, 1150–1151, 1151 (box)

Agee, Arthur. See *Hoop Dreams* (1994)

Aikman, Troy, 287, 316, 317

Akeelah and the Bee (2006), 1211, 1212–1213

Alcindor, Ferdinand Lewis, Jr. *See* Abdul-Jabbar, Kareem

Alda, Alan, 1000 (image), 1001, 1001 (box)

Alderson, Sandy, 829

Alexander, Grover Cleveland, 1470–1471

Alford, Steve, 669, 670

Ali, Laila, **26–29,** 27 (image); advertising campaign with her father, 28 (box); defeats of Jacqui Frazier-Lyde and Christy Martin, 28–29; television appearances of, 29; undefeated record of, 29; world titles of, 27–28

Ali, Muhammad, 26, 27 (image), **29–35,** 31 (image), 192 (image), 226 (image), 297, 1095, 1310, 1343 (image); bouts with Joe Frazier, 30, 753; bouts with Sonny Liston, 32; childhood of, 31–32; as a conscientious objector to the Vietnam War, 33; defeat of George Foreman to regain the world title, 34; defeat of Ken Norton, 33, 34; and Don King, 33–34; fame and popularity of, 30; illness of (Parkinson's disease), 30; lighting of the Olympic torch at the 1996 Olympic

Low Vision Rehabilitation

A Practical Guide for Occupational Therapists

Low Vision Rehabilitation

A Practical Guide for Occupational Therapists

Mitchell Scheiman, OD, FCOVD, FAAO
Director of Pediatric and Binocular Vision Programs
Pennsylvania College of Optometry
Philadelphia, PA

Maxine Scheiman, MEd, OTR/L, CLVT
Visual Function Rehabilitation Associates
Bala Cynwyd, PA

Steven Whittaker, OTR, PhD, CLVT
Vision Rehabilitation Consulting
Southampton, PA

Contributing Authors:

Paul B. Freeman, OD, FAAO, FCOVD
Diplomate Low Vision
Chief of Low Vision Services
Allegheny General Hospital
Pittsburgh, PA

Debra A. Sokol-McKay, MS, CVRT, CDE, CLVT, OTR/L
Consultant in Vision Rehabilitation & Diabetes Self-Management
Adjunct Faculty, Pennsylvania College of Optometry
Chair, Disabilities/Visual Impairment Specialty Practice Group
American Association of Diabetes Educators
Philadelphia, PA

Medical Illustrators:
Barbara A. Steinman, OD, PhD
Software in Motion
Memphis, TN

Scott B. Steinman, OD, PhD, FAAO
Professor, Southern College of Optometry
Memphis, TN

SLACK®
INCORPORATED

Delivering the best in health care information and education worldwide

www.slackbooks.com

ISBN-10: 1-55642-734-4
ISBN-13: 978-1-55642-734-3

The procedures and practices described in this book should be implemented in a manner consistent with the professional standards set for the circumstances that apply in each specific situation. Every effort has been made to confirm the accuracy of the information presented and to correctly relate generally accepted practices. The authors, editor, and publisher cannot accept responsibility for errors or exclusions or for the outcome of the material presented herein. There is no expressed or implied warranty of this book or information imparted by it. Care has been taken to ensure that drug selection and dosages are in accordance with currently accepted/recommended practice. Due to continuing research, changes in government policy and regulations, and various effects of drug reactions and interactions, it is recommended that the reader carefully review all materials and literature provided for each drug, especially those that are new or not frequently used. Any review or mention of specific companies or products is not intended as an endorsement by the author or publisher.

SLACK Incorporated uses a review process to evaluate submitted material. Prior to publication, educators or clinicians provide important feedback on the content that we publish. We welcome feedback on this work.

Published by: SLACK Incorporated
                   6900 Grove Road
                   Thorofare, NJ 08086 USA
                   Telephone: 856-848-1000
                   Fax: 856-853-5991
                   www.slackbooks.com

Contact SLACK Incorporated for more information about other books in this field or about the availability of our books from distributors outside the United States.

Library of Congress Cataloging-in-Publication Data

Scheiman, Mitchell.
    Low vision rehabilitation : a practical guide for occupational therapists / Mitchell Scheiman, Maxine Scheiman, Steven Whittaker.
       p. ; cm.
    Includes bibliographical references and index.
    ISBN-13: 978-1-55642-734-3 (alk. paper)
    ISBN-10: 1-55642-734-4 (alk. paper)
    1. Low vision--Patients--Rehabilitation. 2. Low vision--Patients --Services for.   I. Scheiman, Maxine. II. Whittaker, Steven.
III. Title.
    [DNLM: 1. Vision, Low--rehabilitation. 2. Vision, Low. 3. Occupational Therapy--methods.
WW 140 S319L 2006]
  RE91.L69 2006
  617.7'12--dc22
                                        2006025883

Printed in the United States of America.

Last digit is print number: 10   9   8   7   6   5   4   3   2   1

DEDICATION

To our children for their love, patience, and understanding.

MMS and MTS

To my parents, Trudy and Whit, for their lifelong love of discovery, of people, and of each other.

SW

CONTENTS

Printable forms discussed in this book are available online at http://www.slackbooks.com/otvisionforms

ACKNOWLEDGMENTS

My thanks to the following persons who have had such a strong influence on my professional development:

Dr. Jerome Rosner, who was instrumental in teaching me how to teach.

Drs. Nathan Flax, Irwin Suchoff, Jack Richman, Martin Birnbaum, and Arnold Sherman, who have been outstanding role models.

Drs. Mel Wolfberg, Tom Lewis, and Tony Di Stefano from the Pennsylvania College of Optometry who gave me the opportunity to be an optometric educator and created an environment that has allowed me to succeed in this position.

I want to thank Barbara and Scott Steinman for their outstanding work in designing many of the illustrations used in this book, and the editorial staff at SLACK including Amy McShane, Kim Shigo, and Debra Toulson for their help and guidance through the challenging process of writing this book.

My special thanks to my wife Maxine who has always patiently allowed me to pursue my professional goals.

MMS

When I started in this field I did not fully realize the extent of influence certain people would have on my career. To the faculty at Pennsylvania College of Optometry I would like to offer many thanks for having taught me and guided me in my pursuit of low vision rehabilitation skills. Many thanks to my mentor Maureen Duffy, who went the extra mile and enabled me to begin my second career. Above all, I would like to thank my husband Mitch, for without him none of this would be possible.

MTS

So many have consistently and patiently nurtured my interest in low vision rehabilitation over many years, in particular, Jan Lovie-Kitchin, Roger Cummings, and Gale Watson. I thank the staff at the William Feinbloom Low Vision Center who taught me so much, especially Almeda Ruger and Sarah Appel. It was the faculty at Thomas Jefferson department of Occupational Therapy and Carlos Moreno, OT, who taught me that vision rehabilitation was much more than about vision. Finally, I not only appreciate the emotional support of Jan, Nora and Sean, but the compelling questions, great ideas and hearty laughs.

SGW

About the Authors

Mitchell Scheiman, OD, FAAO, FCOVD

Dr. Mitchell Scheiman is a nationally known optometric educator, lecturer, author, and private practitioner. He is the author of *Understanding and Managing Visual Deficits: A Guide for Occupational Therapists*, published by SLACK Incorporated. Dr. Scheiman has a long and close relationship with occupational therapists. He works closely with occupational therapists in his practice comanaging patients, and more than 5,000 occupational therapists have attended his workshops on Understanding and Managing Vision Deficits. He has specialized in vision rehabilitation of children and adults for the past 30 years. Dr. Scheiman is currently a Professor of Optometry at the Pennsylvania College of Optometry. He is a Diplomate in Binocular Vision and Perception and a Fellow in the College of Optometrists in Vision Development.

Maxine Scheiman, MEd, OTR/L, CLVT

After working as a learning disabilities specialist for many years, Maxine decided to change careers and in 1988 graduated from Temple University in Philadelphia as an occupational therapist. She has been practicing as an occupational therapist for about 18 years and has worked in many different settings including acute care and rehabilitation hospitals, school occupational therapy, early intervention, and low vision rehabilitation. In 2000, Maxine became interested in low vision rehabilitation and she attended the Rehabilitation Teaching program at the Pennsylvania College of Optometry in Philadelphia. After becoming certified as a low vision therapist, she has worked as a low vision rehabilitation therapist helping patients with visual impairment. She is currently owner of Visual Function Rehabilitation Associates and is a certified low vision therapist.

Stephen G. Whittaker, PhD, FAAO, OTR/L, CLVT

Involved in low vision rehabilitation for over 25 years as a researcher, educator, and practitioner, Dr. Steve Whittaker currently serves as a member of the Low Vision Certification committee of the Academy of Certification of Vision Rehabilitation Professionals. He has numerous scientific publications, has received grants from the National Eye Institute and NASA, and lectures internationally on low vision rehabilitation. With a doctorate in experimental psychology, and postdoctoral training in visual neurophysiology, Dr. Whittaker began studying eye movements and reading with macular degeneration while he served on the faculty of the Pennsylvania College of Optometry as a researcher and educator for 20 years. He, along with Dr. Jan Lovie-Kitchin, published a seminal work on the visual requirements for reading that later earned the Gordon Clay award as the most influential paper published in an optometric journal over a 5-year period. He served as coordinator of the low vision technology service at the William Feinbloom Low Vision Rehabilitation Center. Dr. Whittaker earned his masters in Occupational Therapy at Thomas Jefferson University. He currently provides outpatient services including low vision rehabilitation at Moss Rehabilitation Hospital in the Philadelphia area.

About the Contributors

Paul B. Freeman, OD, FAAO, FCOVD

Dr. Paul B. Freeman, optometrist, is an internationally known lecturer, author, and private practitioner. He is the coauthor of *The Art and Practice of Low Vision*, published by Butterworth/Elsevier. Dr Freeman is chief of low vision services at Allegheny General Hospital in Pittsburgh, Pennsylvania and consults to a number of rehabilitation settings, where he works closely with occupational and physical therapists as well as others on the rehabilitative team. He has limited his practice to the care and rehabilitation of visually impaired, brain injured, and multi-handicapped individuals of all ages.

Debra A. Sokol-McKay, MS, CVRT, CDE, CLVT, OTR/L

Debbie Sokol-McKay graduated from Temple University's occupational therapy program in 1982, and received her masters degree in Rehabilitation Teaching (Vision Rehabilitation Therapy) from the Pennsylvania College of Optometry (PCO) in 1999. Debbie is adjunct faculty in the Graduate Low Vision Rehabilitation program at PCO. She has practiced as an occupational therapist for more than 20 years, and in the fields of vision rehabilitation and diabetes education for more 10 years. She holds certifications as a vision rehabilitation therapist, low vision therapist, and diabetes educator. Debbie is the immediate past chairperson of the Disabilities/Visual Impairment Specialty Practice Group of the American Association of Diabetes Educators (AADE) and was a member of AOTA's expert low vision certification panel. She serves as AADE's liaison to the National Eye Institute. Debbie has published professional articles in all three fields and presented at the national conferences of AOTA, AADE, and the Association for the Education and Rehabilitation of the Blind and Visually Impaired.

PREFACE

The emergence of three separate factors over the past two decades has vaulted the profession of occupational therapy into the mainstream of low vision rehabilitation. These three factors are the high prevalence of vision impairment in the elderly, which is the fastest growing segment of our population; chronic underfunding and the lack of availability of treatment for the elderly through the current structure called the "blindness system"; and the inclusion of low vision as a disability under Medicare Guidelines in the early 1990s. Because of these three factors, occupational therapists now have a primary role to play in this field.

In addition, there are four other very strong arguments for occupational therapy to play a more prominent role in vision rehabilitation.

1. While the elderly comprise the majority of the low vision population, they are the most underserved by existing state, charitable, and private programs. Because of the lack of availability of services and treatment through the current system, rehabilitation may be delayed and these individuals are likely to become socially isolated, depressed, and dependent. Involvement of occupational therapists through the healthcare system provides significantly greater access to low vision rehabilitation for the elderly.

2. Two-thirds of older persons have at least one other chronic condition, in addition to low vision, that limits their independent functioning. Occupational therapists are already primary providers for older clients with other chronic conditions.

3. Occupational therapists are trained in the physical, cognitive, sensory, and psychological aspects of disability and aging, and therefore, may be the natural choice to work with older persons whose limitations in daily living are a result of a combination of deficits.

4. Occupational therapists are more evenly distributed throughout the United States than other vision rehabilitation professionals, who tend to be located in larger metropolitan areas. Low vision services can be more widely disseminated through the healthcare delivery system.

The challenge at this time is for occupational therapists to achieve competency in this field. This will require a combination of independent study and reading, clinical experience, and in some cases,

postgraduate education. This textbook is designed to provide a practical and clinically oriented guide to enable occupational therapists to begin this process of independent study and reading in order to seize this opportunity and the responsibility of joining the team of professionals that cares for this population.

We have established three objectives for this book. The first is to present our viewpoint of the role of occupational therapy in the field of low vision rehabilitation. Low vision rehabilitation is a relatively young, developing discipline and occupational therapy is the newest professional addition to this field. A number of other professions have been involved in this area of care for decades, and the challenge is for occupational therapy to define a role within the established system that will augment current service delivery rather than factionalize service delivery into competing services. In Chapter 1, we present our ideas about various current roles of the occupational therapist regarding low vision as well as a suggested "ideal" role. We consider how these practice settings fit into current service delivery systems as well as the cost-effectiveness of these roles.

Our second objective for this book is to create a resource for occupational therapists to independently learn about low vision rehabilitation for the older adult in preparation for providing these services in clinical practice. While there are several excellent books on vision rehabilitation written for other professionals involved in this field, to our knowledge there is currently no stand-alone textbook written specifically for occupational therapists on this topic.

Our third objective is to create a resource that can be used by occupational therapists to prepare for certification examinations such as that offered by the Academy for Certification of Vision Rehabilitation and Education Professionals (ACVREP) and the AOTA Specialty Certification in Low Vision.

This book was not designed to cover vision rehabilitation in the pediatric population. We decided that trying to cover both populations in one book would not do justice to either population. While the needs of children with vision impairment are significant, occupational therapists are much more likely to be called upon to help the elderly population because of the current insurance reimbursement system. Thus, we chose to devote this book entirely to the adult client with vision impairment.

The book is divided into four sections with 17 chapters, Appendices, and a companion website.

Section I contains six chapters that are designed to provide background information about epidemiology,

history, roles of various professionals, anatomy of the eye and visual system, eye diseases that cause vision impairment, optics of lenses and magnification, and psychosocial issues related to vision impairment. Section II is devoted to the evaluation of clients with vision impairment. In Chapter 7, Dr. Paul Freeman, a nationally recognized optometric expert in low vision rehabilitation, reviews the optometric low vision rehabilitative examination. The objective of this chapter is to provide enough information so that occupational therapists will be able to understand the examination process and common terminology used in reports they are likely to see from eyecare providers. In Chapter 8, we describe our recommendations for the occupational therapy low vision evaluation.

The third and largest section of this book is devoted to low vision rehabilitation. In Chapter 9, we begin with an overview of the entire process and suggest an organized, seven-step treatment process. Individual chapters are devoted to the use of therapeutic activities, modification of environment, the use of nonoptical assistive devices, teaching clients how to use optical devices, incorporating computer technology in low vision rehabilitation, and an entire chapter on adaptive diabetes self-management tools and techniques written by Debra Sokol-McKay, a well-known occupational therapist and certified diabetes educator who writes and often lectures about this topic.

The book concludes with a section devoted to practical issues and practice management. All three of us have had extensive experience presenting workshops for occupational therapists about low vision rehabilitation. During these workshops, numerous practical questions have been asked about how to get started in the field of low vision rehabilitation. Some of the questions that have often been asked include:

1. What are the educational requirements for an occupational therapist to provide low vision rehabilitation services?

2. Is certification necessary to provide low vision rehabilitation services?

3. How does the occupational therapist interact with other vision rehabilitation professionals?

4. What practice opportunities are available?

5. How do I market my services as a provider of low vision rehabilitation services?

6. Are low vision rehabilitation services provided by occupational therapists covered by Medicare and other insurance?

7. How do I properly bill insurance for low vision rehabilitation services?

8. Are optical aids and other devices covered by insurance?

9. What equipment do I need to get started in the field of low vision rehabilitation?

Chapter 16 is designed to provide answers to these important questions. We also included a short chapter designed to provide some guidance about writing goals for low vision rehabilitation.

The book is accompanied by a website that contains evaluation forms and other documents referred to in the book, plus a list of many of the key resources about low vision and rehabilitation services currently available, including general information, large-print and audio resources, computer technology, community resources, and low vision equipment vendors.

This book is a collaboration of occupational therapists and optometrists. Just as collaboration was important for the completion of this book, collaboration between these two professions, as well as ophthalmologists, vision rehabilitation therapists, orientation and mobility specialists, and social workers, is vital for insuring quality care for clients with vision impairment. It is our hope that this book will become an important resource for occupational therapists entering this exciting field, which the American Occupational Therapy Association has identified as one of the top ten emerging fields in occupational therapy in the next millennium.

We have built a model of practice on a foundation of evidence, or theory derived from empirical science. This text will provide the professional with a starting point, an evaluation methodology, and tools and procedures that have been shown to be effective. With accumulating experience, the professional will challenge our suggestions and assumptions. Professionals will continue to search for published peer-reviewed research on low vision rehabilitation and perform careful clinical observation to build something better, and, finally, tell us about their discoveries.

Section I

Introduction and Background Information

Epidemiology, History, and Clinical Model for Low Vision Rehabilitation

The objectives of this chapter are to establish the importance of low vision rehabilitation for the practice of occupational therapy and to review the definitions, epidemiology and history of low vision and low vision rehabilitation in the United States. We will also present a model of clinical care with suggested roles for the various professions involved with low vision rehabilitation.

WHY SHOULD OCCUPATIONAL THERAPISTS BE INTERESTED IN THE FIELD OF LOW VISION REHABILITATION?

Effect of Visual Impairment on Activities of Daily Living

Mrs. Smith is a 75-year-old woman who recently developed age-related macular degeneration (AMD). Other than her vision problem, she has no other significant medical conditions. She has always been an active woman, working until age 67 as a real estate agent and raising her family of three children. After retirement, she became active as a volunteer in both her church and local civic organizations. She has been an avid recreational tennis player and continued to play tennis twice a week with friends until recently. Thus, she was actively involved in many activities, looking after herself and her family, enjoying life, and contributing to the social and economic fabric of her community.

Two years ago, however, she developed AMD in both eyes. Her vision deteriorated rapidly and affected almost every aspect of her life. She can no longer safely drive and this creates difficulty in many everyday activities such as shopping, doctors' visits, visiting her grandchildren, maintaining her role as a volunteer at church, and playing tennis. Because of her vision impairment, she has trouble taking care of her personal needs as well. Her color perception has deteriorated, so she cannot select clothes on her own and putting on her makeup is no longer possible. Household tasks such as cooking, washing dishes, and finding ingredients for recipes have become very frustrating and difficult to perform. Mrs. Smith had managed the monthly task of paying bills and balancing the checkbook, but can no longer perform

these activities. Of course, she also has great difficulty reading for pleasure, as well as for everyday, essential reading tasks.

Mrs. Smith's vision impairment has also impacted on her social life. She now hesitates to go to meetings, parties, and other social events because she is unable to identify people's faces. Even if she can identify the person by his or her voice, she is unable to see facial expressions, and this makes it challenging to interact in a meaningful manner. This devastating combination of loss of independence in many essential activities of daily living (ADL), along with the negative impact on her social life, has led to secondary depression and lack of desire and motivation to deal with her new disability.

This history is typical of the effects of AMD on the life of a client with this very common ocular disease. As a result, she is no longer able to perform daily life activities and participate in desired roles and life situations at home and in the community. Of course, since its inception, the focus and mission of the profession of occupational therapy has been to care for people with precisely these needs. In 2002, the American Occupational Therapy Association (AOTA) published the *Occupational Therapy Practice Framework* to reaffirm and articulate occupational therapy's "unique focus on occupation and daily life activities and the application of an intervention process that facilitates engagement in occupation to support participation in life."[1]

The Occupational Therapy Practice Framework outlines the language and constructs that define the profession's focus.[1] This *Framework* states that "Engagement in occupation to support participation in context is the focus and targeted end objective of occupational therapy intervention".[1] The authors go on to state: "Occupational therapists assist individuals to link their ability to perform daily life activities with meaningful patterns of engagement in occupations that allow participation in desired roles and life situations in home, school, workplace, and community."[1]

Given this *Framework*, it is clear that the client described above, and others with low vision, require occupational therapy services. In this case, the specific type of intervention an occupational therapist would provide is called low vision rehabilitation. The following discussion of the definition, prevalence, and incidence of low vision and the shortage of available resources emphasizes the need for occupational therapy involvement in low vision rehabilitation.

DEFINITIONS AND EPIDEMIOLOGY

Definition of Blindness and Low Vision

A commonly quoted prevalence figure for vision impairment in the United States is that one in six adults (17%) age 45 and older, representing 13.5 million Americans, report some form of visual impairment.[2] Massof[3] argues that this figure is inaccurate and a significant overestimation of the prevalence of low vision in the United States. There are a number of problems with determining the prevalence of blindness and visual impairment.[3,4] These problems include differences in criteria to define visual impairment, differences in study methodology, variation in method of assessing visual acuity, and differences in the age range of the oldest category.

Differences in Criteria to Define Visual Impairment

The criteria used to define blindness and low vision vary from study to study. In the United States, the standard definition of legal blindness is 20/200 or worse in the better eye. There is much more variability, however, in the definition of low vision. The World Health Organization (WHO) proposed a classification system that is now accepted as the international standard. The definition of blindness is a visual acuity of worse than 20/400 in the better eye with best correction or a visual field diameter of less than 10 degrees in the widest meridian in the better eye. The WHO definition for low vision is worse than 20/60 in the better eye with best correction.[5] Another commonly used criterion by epidemiologists is to define low vision as corrected visual acuity worse than 20/40 in the better eye with correction.[6] This criterion is based on the ability to obtain an unrestricted driver's license. Finally, Medicare carriers have adopted the International Classification of Diseases, Clinical Modification (ICD-9-CM) coding system definition of low vision, which is worse than 20/60 visual acuity in the better-seeing eye, as the eligibility criterion for coverage of low vision services. Because different authors have used varying definitions of blindness and low vision, it is easy to understand the difficulty in establishing the prevalence of these conditions. The practitioner needs to be vigilant to changing definitions of low vision and blindness because this debate will lead to changes in the criteria Medicare, Medicaid,

government payers, and insurance companies use for reimbursable rehabilitation services.

Table 1-1 is an attempt to help the reader appreciate the relationship among visual acuity loss, functional visual problems, and definitions of blindness and visual impairment.

The definition of low vision that will be used in this book is summarized in Sidebar 1-1. We define low vision as a condition caused by eye disease in which the vision is 20/70 or poorer in the best eye and the vision cannot be improved with eyeglasses. It is important to remember that this is not necessarily the definition that has been used in prevalence studies. However, it is a definition that makes sense in the everyday practice of low vision rehabilitation by occupational therapists. This is the definition that is currently used by Medicare to establish medical necessity for low vision rehabilitation.

The use of this definition also does not preclude treating clients with visual acuity better than 20/70. 20/40 acuity, for example, can create significant disability for a client who values reading or occupations that require detail vision, such as fine needlepoint. We believe that early intervention is critical for success. Once a patient's visual acuity deteriorates to 20/70, he or she may have already started to disengage from many ADL, leading to potential depression. The primary impediment to routinely initiating therapy when visual acuity is better than 20/70 is lack of reimbursement. Services are not covered by Medicare until visual acuity declines to 20/70.

Sidebar 1-1: Definition of Low Vision

Low vision is a condition caused by eye disease in which vision is 20/70 or poorer in the better-seeing eye and the vision cannot be improved with eyeglasses.

Differences in Study Methodology

The two main study methods to evaluate prevalence of low vision have been self-assessment surveys and population-based vision screening studies. The Lighthouse study quoted above was a telephone survey of 1,219 people over the age of 45 years.[2] Data were not available about refractive error (nearsightedness, farsightedness, or astigmatism) or eye disease for the people surveyed. Massof[3] argues that some of the criteria used in the survey to determine if a person had low vision could simply reflect inadequate eyeglass correction at the time of the survey. For example, the

Baltimore Eye Study found that if they used presenting visual acuity only as a criterion for defining low vision, they found a prevalence of about 10.25 million people. However, 7.5 million people in this group would not actually have low vision because with new eyeglasses their visual acuity reached normal levels. Thus, the main problem with estimating low vision prevalence from self-assessment surveys is that the cause of the reduced visual acuity is unknown.

In contrast to the self-assessment methodology, a number of population-based prevalence studies have been performed in the United States.[6-10] All of these studies measured visual acuity with refractive errors corrected and determined if eye disease was present. The results of these studies indicate that the prevalence of low vision is much lower than the estimate based on self-assessment surveys. However, even among these studies, there are differences in estimates because the studies differ in their definitions of low vision (visual acuity cutoff that determines if client has low vision) and methodology of performing the visual acuity assessment.

Variation in Method of Assessing Visual Acuity

Generally, measures of distance visual acuity have been used to define significant vision loss and there are two important sources of variation in the current literature when trying to categorizing persons into affected and nonaffected groups. These include the type of acuity chart used and the visual acuity criteria used to define the condition.[4] There is no standardized method of assessing visual acuity in clinical practice. Various charts such as Landolt C, Snellen charts, and Sloan letters are commonly used. In recent years, a standardized visual acuity chart was developed for research studies called the Early Treatment of Diabetic Retinopathy Study acuity chart (ETDRS) and is now the standard for research involving visual acuity measurements.[11] However, this chart has not been widely used in the low vision prevalence literature. Only three of the five population-based studies of low vision in the United States referred to above used the ETDRS chart as the method for assessing distance visual acuity. Even in those studies using the ETDRS chart, the distance at which testing occurred and the method for determining the final visual acuity differed among the studies.

Differences in the Age Range of the Oldest Category

All studies, regardless of methodology, agree that the prevalence rate of low vision and blindness increases sharply with age. Various studies, however,

Table 1-1.

Relating Visual Acuity Loss, Functional Problems, and Definitions of Blindness/Low Vision

Best Corrected Visual Acuity	Functional Problems	Standards Met for Legal Blindness or Visual Impairment
6/150 (metric) 20/500 (Imperial)	Can barely read newspaper headlines at 40 cm	WHO criteria for blindness
6/60 (metric) 20/200 (Imperial)	Can barely read newspaper bylines or chapter headings at 40 cm	USA criteria for blindness, eligible for all services by State, Federal agencies and Veterans Administration
6/18 (metric) 20/60-20/70 (Imperial)	Can barely read newsprint	Eligible for Medicare reimbursed services, and receive limited services from State, Federal and Veterans administration. Many states prohibit driving.
6/12 (metric), 20/40 (Imperial)	Reading normal print and street signs is slower and more difficult	Impaired Visual Acuity becomes disabling. Legal criteria for unrestricted driving in most states

have categorized the age brackets differently. This creates difficulty in comparing one study to another.

Prevalence of Low Vision and Blindness in the United States

In this section, we review the prevalence and incidence of low vision and blindness in the United States. This research is important to someone planning to develop a new low vision service. The planner combines these statistics with published census data to estimate the potential need for services in a given area. Prevalence refers to the current number of people suffering from an illness in a given year. This number includes all those who may have been diagnosed in prior years, as well as in the current year. For example, if the prevalence of a disease is 80,000, it means that there are 80,000 people living in the United States with this illness.

Incidence refers to the frequency of development of a new illness in a population in a certain period of time, normally 1 year. When we say that the incidence of a disease has increased in past years, we mean that more people have developed this condition year after year, eg, the incidence of thyroid cancer has been rising, with 13,000 new cases diagnosed this year.

While many studies have used less than 20/40 visual acuity in the better-seeing eye as the criterion for low vision, from a practical standpoint it is reasonable for occupational therapists to be interested in the 20/70 or worse criterion that has been adopted by Medicare carriers. Medicare is the main source of reimbursement for low vision rehabilitation for occupational therapists and the ICD-9-CM coding system definition of low vision is worse than 20/60 visual acuity in the better seeing eye.

Massof[3] analyzed the data from all five population-based studies of vision impairment in the United States. He used the 20/70 or worse criterion as the definition of low vision along with the 2000 census data. Based on these parameters, he estimated that 1,275,000 whites and 230,000 blacks over age 45 have low vision. Looking only at the Medicare eligible population (65 years and older), he estimates that 1,120,000 whites and 135,000 blacks have low vision. It is important to note that even these numbers are an overestimation because they include many potentially correctable cases of cataract (about 15% to 20%). Although these prevalence rates are certainly significant, they are only about one-tenth the number cited by other authors.[2,12]

The most up-to-date estimates of the prevalence of visual impairment in the United States were published by the Eye Diseases Prevalence Research Group in 2004.[13] Because of the difficulty and expense of implementing an appropriate sampling scheme, few population-based studies of a national scope have been carried out in the United States to estimate the prevalence of visual impairment.[13] To meet this need for prevalence data, principal investigators from eight population-based vision studies agreed to standardize definitions and methodology so that their data could be analyzed together. Age- and race/ethnicity-specific prevalence of blindness and low vision were calculated based on eight different studies. These estimates were then applied to the population of the United States as reported in the 2000 census to estimate the number of visually impaired persons nationally. Projections of prevalence in 2020 were also made based on census projections for the US population in that year. The definition of blindness used was 20/200 or worse in the better-seeing eye and for low vision 20/40 or worse in the better-seeing eye.

Using this approach, the authors found that in 2000 there were an estimated 937,000 blind Americans older than age 40, a prevalence of 0.78%. The number of persons with low vision was estimated to be 2.4 million (1.98% prevalence). This number is significantly higher than the estimate from Massof of about 1.5 million. The main reason for the difference is likely the definition of low vision used in each study. Massof[3] used 20/70 or worse in the better-seeing eye as the criterion, versus 20/40 or worse in the better-seeing eye used in this recent study. Because occupational therapists in the United States function within the healthcare system and depend primarily on Medicare funding for reimbursement of low vision rehabilitation, the lower estimate is more representative of the need for occupational therapy services for low vision rehabilitation in the United States.

Incidence of Low Vision and Blindness

The only published incidence data (new cases of low vision each year) for the United States are from the Beaver Dam Eye Study.[14] The number of new cases of low vision and blindness is greatest for people over the age of 65 years, and based on the Beaver Dam Eye Study data, Massof[3] estimated the incidence to be about 250,000 cases per year in 2000 and 500,000 new cases per year in 2025.

The prevalence and incidence of low vision in the United States are high, and experts predict a large increase over the next two decades because the prevalence of low vision increases sharply in persons older than 65. In the study by Congdon et al, persons older

than 80 years made up only 7.7% of the population but accounted for 69% of the severe visual impairment.[13] It is this group that is the fastest-growing segment of the US population. Prevalence and incidence clearly depend on ethnicity, age, and socioeconomic variables. Someone planning to develop services should look to the most recent published research and census data to develop more precise estimates of need by considering age and ethnic and socioeconomic composition of the region being studied.

LEADING CAUSES OF VISUAL IMPAIRMENT IN THE UNITED STATES

The leading cause of severe visual impairment among white Americans in 2000 was AMD, which accounted for 54% of visual impairment with cataract (9%). Diabetic retinopathy (6%) and glaucoma (5%) were the next most common causes[13] (Table 1-2). These conditions are described in detail in Chapter 4.

The leading causes of severe visual impairment in black persons were cataract (37%), diabetic retinopathy (26%), glaucoma (7%), and AMD (4%). Among Hispanics, glaucoma was the most common cause (29%), followed by AMD (14%), cataract (14%), and diabetic retinopathy (14%).

It is surprising that there is such a high prevalence of low vision due to cataract, since it is generally a treatable condition. Surgical treatment of cataract has been shown to be a very effective procedure. A national study of cataract surgery investigators found that 96% of the clients were improved based on Snellen visual acuity and 89% reported improvement and satisfaction based on a 14-item instrument designed to measure functional impairment. Since cataract surgery is so successful, it is questionable whether it should even be included as a cause of low vision, because low vision is defined as a loss of vision that cannot be treated with lenses or any other medical/surgical treatment. There are, of course, some situations in which cataracts cannot be treated surgically because of other coexisting medical or ocular conditions. In such cases, cataracts could indeed be a cause of low vision. Evans and Rowlands[15] reviewed the literature to determine the prevalence of correctable visual impairment in the United Kingdom. Many of their findings apply to the United States. They reported that between 20% to 50% of older people have undetected reduced vision and the majority of these had correctable vision problems such as refractive error and cataracts. The Baltimore Eye Study found that almost 70% of people reporting low vision based on reduced visual acuity alone

Table 1-2.

Causes of Blindness (Visual Acuity <20/200) by Race/Ethnicity

	Age-Related Macular Degeneration	Cataract	Glaucoma	Diabetic Retinopathy	Other
White Persons	54.4%	8.7%	5.4%	6.4%	9.7%
Black Persons	4.4%	36.8%	7.3%	26%	25.6%
Hispanic Persons	14.3%	14.3%	28.6%	14.3%	28.6%

Adapted from Congdon N, O'Colmain B, Klaver CC, et al. Causes and prevalence of visual impairment among adults in the United States. *Arch Ophthalmol.* 2004;122(4):477-485.

would not actually have low vision because with new eyeglasses their visual acuity reaches normal levels.[6] Correctable vision impairment is associated with poorer general health, living alone, and lower socioeconomic status.[15] Often the therapist becomes the first person to identify correctable impairment and initiate appropriate referral to an ophthalmologist or optometrist. In the meantime, when correctable vision loss is encountered, the therapist needs to have available relatively inexpensive, short-term interventions that enable clients to maintain their occupations and routines until the underlying problem is corrected.

Most studies have indicated that AMD is the leading cause of low vision in developed countries.[16,17] The prevalence of AMD in low vision clinics has been reported to be between 23% and 44%.[18] Warren[19] reported on her experience as an occupational therapist working in a low vision program in an ophthalmology department. Thirty-seven percent of the clients referred for occupational therapy (low vision rehabilitation services) had AMD, 9% diabetic retinopathy, 7% glaucoma, 3% neurological problems, and 44% had other miscellaneous conditions. Thus, low vision caused by AMD is the condition that occupational therapists will be most likely to treat. Note that because people with stroke and resulting hemianopia or oculomotor problems do not meet the criteria for low vision, the current estimates of low vision associated with neurological problems likely are underestimated. In these cases, the underlying condition can be still be treated by an occupational therapist using the neurological diagnostic codes.

PROFESSIONS INVOLVED WITH LOW VISION CARE

Low vision rehabilitation is a relatively young, developing discipline and occupational therapy is the newest professional addition to this field. The various professions and their roles are listed in Table 1-3. At the end of this chapter, we present our ideas about the roles and relationships for these various professions in the field of low vision rehabilitation.

Ophthalmologists

Ophthalmologists are physicians who, after graduating from medical school, specialize in the diagnosis and treatment of eye disease by completing a residency in ophthalmology. Many ophthalmologists also complete a fellowship program to further specialize in an area of ophthalmology. A number of specialty areas exist, including cataract, glaucoma, retina, cornea, pediatric ophthalmology, and neuro-ophthalmology. Considering that the most common causes of low vision are retinal and neurological pathology, the main sources of potential referrals for low vision rehabilitation are ophthalmologists specializing in retinal disease and neuro-ophthalmologists. There is no specific subspecialty of low vision in the profession of ophthalmology. Occasionally, ophthalmologists specialize in low vision rehabilitation. There are currently about 16,000 practicing ophthalmologists in the United States.

Typically, the primary areas of interest and responsibility of ophthalmologists are the diagnosis and

---

Table 1-3.

Low Vision Professionals and Their Roles

Profession	Role
Ophthalmologists	Examination and diagnosis of eye disease Treatment of eye disease Medication Surgery
Optometrists	Low vision examination Treatment of refractive error Eyeglasses Contact lenses Treatment of low vision Optical magnification Modification of lighting and contrast
Occupational Therapists	Low vision rehabilitation examination Low vision rehabilitation
Vision Rehabilitation Therapists (Formerly Rehabilitation Teachers)	Low vision rehabilitation examination Low vision rehabilitation, Braille reading instruction
Orientation and Mobility Specialists	Orientation and mobility examination Orientation and mobility
Teachers of the Visually Impaired	Special education of children with low vision and blindness
Low Vision Therapist	Low vision rehabilitation examination Low vision rehabilitation
Social Worker	Individual and group counseling, facilitate access to resources and support services

---

treatment of eye disease. Treatment modalities generally involve the use of medication and surgery. Thus, clients often see the ophthalmologist first because of a perceived significant change in vision. The ophthalmologist attempts to restore normal visual function by treating the eye disease. In some cases this fails, or in other cases the vision can never be restored to normal and the client is now faced with permanent low vision. It is at this point that the ophthalmologist should refer the client with low vision to other professionals for further evaluation and rehabilitation.

Optometrists

After graduating from a 4-year college program, optometrists complete 4 years of additional education at one of the 17 colleges of optometry in the United States. During this 4-year program, optometry students learn to diagnose and treat vision and eye health problems. Treatment modalities include the use of eyeglasses, contact lenses, eye drops and other medication, vision therapy, and low vision rehabilitation. After graduating from optometry school, some optometrists complete residency programs in specialty areas such as low vision, vision therapy, pediatrics, contact lenses, and primary care optometry.

Trying to locate a qualified low vision optometrist for a client can be challenging because the profession of optometry does not recognize specialties. Therefore, any optometrist can provide low vision services, regardless of his or her experience in this area. However, the American Academy of Optometry Low Vision Section has a Diplomate program for interested optometrists. To become a Diplomate in

Low Vision, an optometrist must pass a written test, an oral examination, and a practical low vision examination. As of 2006, there were only about 45 practicing Low Vision Diplomats worldwide. A current list of optometrists that have successfully completed this process can be found at the website for the American Academy of Optometry (www.aaopt.org).[20] The American Optometric Association also has a Low Vision Section. Although there is no testing program required to become a member of this section, optometrists who have joined are likely to have a strong interest in the area of low vision. Some low vision optometrists have completed a residency program and/or a masters degree in low vision rehabilitation while others have chosen to specialize in this area and have acquired additional knowledge and clinical skills through continuing education and independent learning. Currently there are about 36,000 optometrists in the United States and there are about 1000 members in the Low Vision Section of the American Optometric Association.

Optometrists who specialize in low vision help those with vision problems see better, even if surgery, medications, and conventional glasses can no longer improve sight. They design and prescribe low vision devices (eg, optical, nonoptical, electronic) and make recommendations about lighting, contrast, and other environmental factors that influence vision. Low vision optometrists often work along with low vision therapists such as occupational therapists, vision rehabilitation therapists, and orientation and mobility specialists who teach clients how to use these assistive devices in ADL and assist with orientation and mobility issues.

Occupational Therapists

According to the AOTA's *Practice Framework*, occupational therapists focus on assisting people to engage in daily life activities or occupations that they find meaningful and purposeful. Occupational therapists' expertise lies in their knowledge of occupation and how engaging in occupations can be used to affect human performance and the effects of disease and disability.[1] Occupational therapists work with individuals who have conditions that are mentally, physically, developmentally, or emotionally disabling, including low vision.

Occupational therapists may work exclusively with individuals in a particular age group or with particular disabilities. In schools, for example, they evaluate children's abilities, recommend and provide therapy, modify classroom equipment, and help children participate as fully as possible in school programs and activities. Occupational therapy also is beneficial to the elderly population. Therapists help the elderly

lead more productive, active, and independent lives through a variety of methods, including the use of adaptive equipment.

Occupational therapists in mental-health settings treat individuals who are mentally ill, developmentally disabled, or emotionally disturbed. To treat these problems, therapists choose activities that help people learn to engage in and cope with daily life. Activities include time management skills, budgeting, shopping, homemaking, and the use of public transportation. Occupational therapists also may work with individuals who are dealing with alcoholism, drug abuse, depression, eating disorders, or stress-related disorders.

Currently, a bachelor's degree in occupational therapy is the minimum requirement for entry into this field. Beginning in 2007, however, a master's degree or higher will be the minimum educational requirement. All states and the District of Columbia regulate the practice of occupational therapy. To obtain a license, applicants must graduate from an accredited educational program and pass a national certification examination. The National Board for Certification in Occupational Therapy, Inc. (NBCOT®) is a not-for-profit credentialing agency that provides certification for the occupational therapy profession. Those who pass the exam are awarded the title, Occupational Therapist Registered (OTR).

As of 2006, entry-level education was offered in about 40 bachelor's degree programs, three postbaccalaureate certificate programs for students with a degree other than occupational therapy, and about 85 entry-level master's degree programs.

Occupational therapists have been peripherally involved in the rehabilitation of clients with low vision since the early days of the profession in 1917.[19] Their involvement, however, was never as the main caregiver for low vision clients. Rather, if a client with other disabilities also happened to have low vision, the occupational therapist would attempt to take care of these needs as well. Until recently, low vision rehabilitation was rarely the primary focus of occupational therapists. This all changed in 1990, when the Health Care Finance Administration (HCFA) expanded the definition of physical impairment to include low vision as a condition that can benefit from rehabilitation. With this change, physicians could specifically refer clients with only low vision to occupational therapists for low vision rehabilitation services.[19]

Occupational therapists are currently the only therapists among the group described in this chapter that are licensed and can function independently in the Medicare reimbursement program. Thus, occupational therapists have a unique opportunity to make an impact as providers for the older client with low vision in the United States. Three other professions

have been providing rehabilitation services for people with low vision for decades.

In 2006, the AOTA introduced a program in which an occupational therapist or occupational therapy assistant who has substantial clinical experience may achieve certification in low vision rehabilitation. The certification does not require a test. Rather, certification is based on a review of a reflective professional development portfolio and a series of narrative reflections.

Vision Rehabilitation Therapists

Recently, the name for rehabilitation teachers has been changed to vision rehabilitation therapists. According to Crews and Luxton:[21]

Rehabilitation Teachers constitute a cadre of university-trained professionals who address the broad array of skills needed by individuals who are blind and visually impaired to live independently at home, to obtain employment, and to participate in community life. As a discipline, Rehabilitation Teaching combines and applies the best principles of adaptive rehabilitation, adult education, and social work to the following broad areas: home management, personal management, communication and education, activities of daily living, leisure activities, and indoor orientation skills.

Vision rehabilitation therapists provide instruction and guidance in adaptive independent living skills, enabling individuals who are blind and visually impaired to confidently carry out their daily activities. Historically, vision rehabilitation therapists have emphasized use of nonsighted strategies, although they have certainly employed low vision techniques as well. Vision rehabilitation therapists are also qualified to teach Braille. They are active members of multidisciplinary and interdisciplinary service teams and provide consultation and referrals through the utilization of community resources. Vision rehabilitation therapists provide services in a variety of settings: agencies serving people who are blind and visually impaired, community-based rehabilitation teaching services, centers for people with developmental disabilities, state vocational rehabilitation services, hospital and clinic rehabilitation teams, residential schools, and local school districts.[22]

There are currently about 10 colleges and universities in the United States, Canada, central Europe, and New Zealand that provide either a bachelor's or master's degree or a certificate in vision rehabilitation therapy. Six of these universities are located in the United States.[22]

There is currently no state licensing for vision rehabilitation therapists; however, there is a national certification process administered by the Academy for Certification of Vision Rehabilitation and Education Professionals (ACVREP). When a vision rehabilitation therapist becomes certified, he or she can use the initials CVRT (Certified Vision Rehabilitation Therapist) with his or her signature.

Certified vision rehabilitation therapists are currently not eligible Medicare providers. A recent policy change by the Centers for Medicare & Medicaid Services (CMS) also prevents ophthalmologists and optometrists from billing for services provided by vision rehabilitation therapists who are salaried to work with their clients. However, a CMS sponsored, 5-year demonstration program started in April 2006. This project (Pub 100-19, Transmittal 25 CR 3816, June 7, 2005) is designed to extend coverage under Medicare B for the same services to treat vision impairment that would be payable when provided by an occupational or physical therapist if they are now provided by a vision rehabilitation professional under the general supervision of a qualified physician. Only vision rehabilitation professionals certified by the ACVREP are eligible to participate in this demonstration project.[23]

Orientation and Mobility Specialists

Orientation and mobility specialists (O&Ms) are professionals who specialize in teaching travel skills to persons who are visually impaired, including the use of sighted guides, canes, and electronic devices. They may also teach skills that will prepare their clients to travel with a dog guide. The goal of orientation and mobility instruction is to enable individuals with visual impairments to travel safely, efficiently, confidently, and independently throughout their environment. O&Ms are prepared to work with individuals of all ages, including young children.

To become an O&M, one must attend an undergraduate or graduate program accredited by the Association for Education and Rehabilitation of the Blind and Visually Impaired (AER). At present, there are approximately 19 programs that prepare O&Ms.[22] The majority of O&M programs are at the graduate level and attract students with diverse backgrounds, including the social and physical sciences, art and music therapy, and general education.

O&Ms are also currently not eligible Medicare providers, but are part of the CMS Low Vision Rehabilitation Demonstration Project that began in April 2006.

Teachers of the Visually Impaired

The profession that takes care of the needs of children with low vision is the Teacher of Children with Visual Impairments (TVI). These individuals generally acquire the common core of knowledge and skills

essential for all beginning special education teachers in addition to the specialized body of knowledge required for teachers of students with visual impairments.[22] TVIs work with blind and visually impaired infants, children and youth of all ages, including those with multiple disabilities. They apply low vision and blindness adaptive equipment and strategies, and, like vision rehabilitation therapists, are qualified to teach Braille. TVIs often operate as itinerant teachers, traveling from school to school to serve children where they are located. They serve as the child's primary case manager in school, and may solicit the expertise of additional therapists to develop specific goals and objectives that comprise the child's Individualized Education Plan (IEP).

TVIs are prepared in accredited higher education programs recognized by the AER in the United States and Canada. At present, there are approximately 40 institutions of higher learning offering special education programs for teacher preparation in the area of blindness and low vision.[22] TVI programs often recommend or require prior degrees or certification in elementary, secondary, or special education. TVIs are certified through their appropriate state's Department of Education.

Low Vision Therapists

In recent years, a more generic term has developed to describe therapists who engage in low vision rehabilitation and have been certified by the ACVREP as Certified Low Vision Therapists: CLVT. This term is actually trademarked and can only be used by someone who has been certified by the ACVREP. An individual who has been certified as a low vision therapist by the ACVREP will have the initials CLVT after his or her name and degree. There are currently two university programs that offer a degree in low vision therapy (Pennsylvania College of Optometry and University of Alabama, Birmingham). However, the term is also being used in the low vision field to describe any therapist engaged in low vision rehabilitation. To become a low vision therapist, one must pass a national certification examination administered by the ACVREP. To be eligible for this examination, one must possess a bachelor's degree. Thus, a vision rehabilitation therapist, an O&M, a teacher of the visually impaired, an occupational therapist, a physical therapist, and a nurse would all be qualified to take this examination. There is no licensure for a low vision therapists and such a person would not be eligible for Medicare reimbursement as an independent practitioner, with the exception of the occupational or physical therapist. These two professionals would be eligible because they are already part of the healthcare and Medicare systems. Many occupational therapists also have become certified low vision therapists with additional continuing education, by passing a certification exam, and also completing supervised clinical training.

Social Workers

Social workers help people function optimally in their environment, deal with their relationships, and solve personal and family problems. Social workers often see clients who face a life-threatening disease or a social problem, such as inadequate housing, unemployment, a serious illness, a disability, or substance abuse. Social workers also assist families that have serious domestic conflicts, sometimes involving child or spousal abuse. Social workers often provide social services in health-related settings that now are governed by managed care organizations.

In regard to low vision rehabilitation, social workers provide individual and group counseling and facilitate consumer access to appropriate community-based services, including public assistance programs, rehabilitation programs, senior centers, hospitals, and clinics.[24] They use self-help techniques to assist blind and visually impaired adults who may be economically, physically, mentally, or socially in need of vision-related rehabilitation services.[24] Because of the significant psychosocial problems related to vision impairment, social workers play a key role in the field of vision rehabilitation.

Although a bachelor's degree is sufficient for entry into the field, an advanced degree has become the standard for many positions. A master's degree in social work (MSW) is typically required for positions in health settings and is required for clinical work as well. As of 2004, the Council on Social Work Education (CSWE) accredited 442 BSW programs and 168 MSW programs. All states and the District of Columbia have licensing, certification, or registration requirements regarding social work practice and the use of professional titles. Most states require 2 years (3,000 hours) of supervised clinical experience for licensure of clinical social workers. In addition, the National Association of Social Workers (NASW) offers voluntary credentials. Social workers with an MSW may be eligible for the Academy of Certified Social Workers (ACSW), the Qualified Clinical Social Worker (QCSW), or the Diplomate in Clinical Social Work (DCSW) credential, based on their professional experience.

HISTORY OF LOW VISION

General History

Eyecare professionals have been treating correctable vision problems such as myopia (nearsightedness), hyperopia (farsightedness), and astigmatism for

centuries using eyeglasses and, more recently, contact lenses and refractive surgery. However, attempts to help people with permanent vision loss secondary to eye disease is a relatively new phenomenon.[25] Earlier in this chapter, we demonstrated that the incidence and prevalence of low vision is currently quite high, and as the population ages, these numbers are expected to grow significantly. However, until the mid-20th century, the prevalence of low vision was not significant and most of the care provided was for children with blindness and visual impairment. We know that the most common causes of low vision—macular degeneration, diabetic retinopathy, glaucoma, and cataract—are all diseases related to the aging process. Given the fact that age is the single best predictor of low vision,[25] and that longer life expectancy has characterized the 20th century, it is not surprising that more attention has been given to low vision rehabilitation in the past 50 years.

Goodrich has written extensively about the history of low vision[25-29] and divided low vision history into a number of stages that are summarized in Table 1-4.[26] In the following summary, we have modified his five stages into four.

Pre-1950

This was a time period during which low vision rehabilitation for adults essentially did not exist. Most services were provided for blind children and little distinction was made between those children who were blind and those who had low vision. A common belief at the time was that it was important to prevent further loss of vision in these children by restricting the use of their eyes. By the end of the 1940s, about 17 residential schools for the blind had been established with specially equipped classrooms for children with low vision. While some schools began to question whether blind children should be separated from those with low vision, the principle of sight conservation prevailed in the majority of schools.[26] This was the era in which the rehabilitation teachers and teachers of the visually impaired became defined as professions.

In 1934, the American Medical Association (AMA) defined legal blindness as visual acuity 20/200 or worse in the better-seeing eye. This definition was adopted for establishing eligibility for special services and benefits for the blind in the Social Security Act of 1935. This stage of low vision history was also the era in which William Feinbloom, an optometrist and pioneer in low vision, began to develop numerous optical devices for people with low vision. Some of the earliest journal articles about low vision were written by William Feinbloom.[30,31] Nevertheless, the field of low vision rehabilitation was in its infancy.

1950s to 1970s

From the 1950s to 1970s, low vision rehabilitation for adults finally became a priority for the various professions involved in low vision care. With the return of veterans from World War II and with the increasing life expectancy of the population, the number of people with low vision increased, leading to a greater demand for low vision services. This lead to the development of a low vision service delivery system that has been called the "blindness system," the educational rehabilitation model, or the nonmedical vision rehabilitation system.[29] This system is a comprehensive nationwide network of services consisting of state, federal, and private agencies serving children and adults with blindness and low vision.[32] Table 1-5 lists the four components of the blindness or nonmedical rehabilitation system in the United States.

One of the key components in this system of care has been the Veteran's Administration (VA). In the 1950s, the VA was among the first organizations to establish comprehensive low vision care and has served as a model for others.[33] Two well-known private agencies also started comprehensive low vision programs in the 1950s. The Industrial Home for the Blind began in 1953 and the Lighthouse (New York Association for the Blind) in 1955. The professionals working in the blindness system included optometrists, ophthalmologists, rehabilitation teachers, O&M specialists, and teachers of the visually impaired. The blindness system is separate from the traditional healthcare system in the United States and services provided are not reimbursed by Medicare or any other type of health insurance. Occupational therapists have generally not been part of this system of care.

The blindness system has been chronically underfunded. As a result, agencies have had to prioritize their services, generally favoring children and young adults of working age. In addition, the limited number of rehabilitation professionals in the blindness system primarily work in metropolitan areas. Thus, for many older clients and for those not living in large metropolitan areas, low vision rehabilitation has not been readily available through the blindness system.[34]

This is also the time period in which educators developed new methods for teaching children with low vision how to more effectively use their vision, rather than trying to conserve their vision. This movement was lead by Barraga, who developed a visual efficiency scale and a set of sequential learning activities designed to develop visual efficiency in children with low vision.[35,36]

Finally, this was the era in which a number of influential books on low vision care were published, when a variety of professional organizations devoted significant time at conferences to low vision, and new

Table 1-4.
History of Low Vision – Five Stages

Stage	*Key Issues/Developments*
Stage 1: Pre 1950	• No distinction between blindness and low vision • Almost all services provided to children • Commonly believed that children with poor vision needed to restrict the use of their eyes to prevent further loss (sight-saving programs) • Residential schools for the blind established (by the end of the 1940s, 17 schools established) • In 1934 the AMA defined legal blindness • 1930s William Feinbloom (optometrist) began developing optical devices for people with low vision
Stage 2: 1950s to 1970s	• Various professional disciplines developed knowledge bases for treating people with low vision • Beginning of "Blindness System" for low vision rehabilitation with adults • Emphasis on sight-saving for children replaced by concept of low vision rehabilitation • Optometrist and ophthalmologists developed reliable tools for assessment of vision and new optical devices for the treatment of low vision • Optometrists and ophthalmologists develop low vision practices
Stage 3: Mid-1970s to Mid-1980s	• Concept of team approach to low vision care developed • Low vision becomes more prevalent as life expectancy increases • Expansion of low vision rehabilitation programs • Significant increase in low vision research
Stage 4: Mid-1980s to Mid-1990s	• Significant increase in low vision research continues • Significant expansion of the interdisciplinary approach • Professionals of each discipline become more familiar with philosophies, skills, and techniques of associated disciplines
Stage 5: Present	• Important changes in Medicare leads to changes in delivery system for low vision rehabilitation including occupational therapists for the first time • Significant increase in low vision research continues

Adapted from Goodrich GL, Sowell V. Low vision: A history in progress. In: Corn AL, Koenig AJ, Eds. *Foundations of Low Vision: Clinical and Functional Perspectives.* New York: American Foundation for the Blind; 2000.

testing equipment and optical devices, including the first video magnification units, were developed.

1970s to 1990s

From the 1970s to the 1990s, the team approach to low vision care gained momentum as professionals from various disciplines became more familiar with the philosophies, skills, and techniques of associated disciplines.[26] As life expectancy continued to increase, the prevalence of low vision in the elderly population grew and fueled the expansion of low vision programs. This era also saw a significant increase in the quantity and quality of research on low vision. This started with a National Eye Institute initiative in the mid-1980s and the growth in low vision research continues to grow today with publications in major

Table 1-5.

Four Major Subsystems of the Blindness System

1. Federal and state vocational rehabilitation system administered by the Rehabilitation Services Administration (RSA) of the US Department of Education, Office of Special Education and Rehabilitative Services, which serves primarily adults
2. The US Department of Veterans Affairs
3. The Private nonprofit sector, which serves both children and adults
4. The Office of Special Education Programs which primarily serves children through its educational services

Adapted from Ponchillia PE, Ponchillia SV. *Foundations of Rehabilitation Teaching with Persons Who are Blind or Visually Impaired.* New York, NY: American Foundation for the Blind; 1996:3-21.

vision and vision rehabilitation journals throughout the world. Starting with maybe a dozen publications before 1950, the number of publications has doubled every decade to approximately 3700 between 1990 and 2000.[28]

1990s to Present

"The last decade of the twentieth century produced what is perhaps the greatest change in vision rehabilitation since the 1950s."[25] Beginning in the late 1980s, the federal government dramatically reduced funds for programs that provided services to individuals who were blind or visually impaired. Subsequently, in 1991 the HCFA, which administered Medicare, amended its definition of physical impairment to include visual impairment. This change allowed Medicare coverage for the first time by licensed healthcare providers for low vision rehabilitation with vision loss as the primary diagnosis when prescribed by a physician. This amendment also set the stage for the involvement of occupational therapy in the field of low vision rehabilitation.

This delivery system of low vision rehabilitation service is sometimes referred to as the "health care system" in contrast to the blindness system described above. Because Medicare does not recognize vision rehabilitation therapists or O&M specialists as licensed healthcare providers, these professionals are not reimbursed for their services through Medicare. While these changes were certainly welcomed by occupational therapists, other professionals such as rehabilitation therapists, O&M specialists, and low vision therapists were concerned about being left out of this alternative system for providing low vision rehabilitation. In addition, some vision rehabilitation therapists even expressed concern about the ability of occupational therapists to provide low vision rehabilitation care as indicated in the following statement from a report of the American Foundation

for the Blind's National Task Force on General and Specialized Services, Working Group on Allied Health Professional Relationships:

Professionals in the vision field are demonstrating a heightened awareness of a concern about the increasing number of allied health professionals (ie, occupational therapists) who are providing vision-related services that have been traditionally administered by trained and certified rehabilitation teachers, teachers of students with visual impairments, O&M specialists, and low vision therapists.[37]

Orr and Huebner go on to state that "the concern of professionals in the vision field is that allied health professionals may not have the specialized knowledge base and skills needed to work with this population because they have not received university training in rehabilitation teaching and/or O&M."[37]

There have been several failed attempts in which legislation has been introduced into the US Congress to provide Medicare coverage for vision rehabilitation professionals other than occupational therapists. These efforts are ongoing and at this time it is difficult to predict the results of these efforts. The topic of Medicare coverage for low vision rehabilitation will be covered in detail in Chapter 16.

History of Occupational Therapy Involvement in Low Vision Rehabilitation

The impetus for occupational therapy's involvement in the area of low vision rehabilitation was the 1991 amendment by the HCFA that allowed Medicare coverage for the first time for licensed healthcare providers for low vision rehabilitation. Since that time,

efforts have been made at the national, state, and local levels to enable occupational therapy to play a primary role in low vision rehabilitation.

Mary Warren has been a strong advocate of occupational therapy involvement in low vision rehabilitation. She has lead the way with significant publications,[12,19,34,38-40] national leadership,[40] presentation of many continuing education courses, clinical work as an occupational therapist treating clients with low vision,[19] and helping to establish a university-based training program in low vision rehabilitation for occupational therapists at the University of Alabama, Birmingham. In 1995, she stated "Although occupational therapists have been involved in the rehabilitation of persons with vision loss since the inception of the profession in 1917, we never played an extensive role in low vision rehabilitation."[38] Occupational therapists have indeed always played a role in low vision rehabilitation because nearly two-thirds of older adults with low vision have at least one other chronic medical condition that may interfere with ADL and require occupational therapy.[41] Thus, in the context of providing care for other chronic conditions, occupational therapists routinely manage issues related to low vision in their elderly clients.

However, with the inclusion of low vision as a disability under Medicare guidelines in the early 1990s, occupational therapists now have a primary role to play in this field. This sudden involvement by occupational therapists in low vision rehabilitation has lead to some controversy. The primary basis for this controversy was a perception that the impetus for occupational therapy's entrance into the low vision arena was not a change in education and preparation of its practitioners. Rather, it was purely based on reimbursement issues. Thus, other vision rehabilitation therapists have raised questions about occupational therapists' qualifications, education, and clinical experience in the area of low vision. For example, Lambert[42] raised the following concerns about occupational therapists:

- They may be unfamiliar with the various disciplines in the field, and thereby fail to appropriately refer clients for other needed services.
- They have inadequate knowledge or specialized training in low vision.
- Clinics may favor occupational therapy in the delivery of low vision services even though more disability-specific professionals may be the most appropriate provider.

As discussed earlier, similar concerns were raised by Orr and Huebner in 2001[37] when they expressed their unease about occupational therapists' lack of specialized knowledge base and skills needed to work with the low vision population.

Others have argued that there are a number of important reasons why the occupational therapist should play a primary role in low vision rehabilitation.[38,43] These reasons are listed below:

1. Although the elderly comprise the majority of the low vision population, they are the most underserved by existing state, charitable, and private programs. Because of the lack of availability of services through the blindness system, rehabilitation may be delayed and these individuals are likely to become socially isolated, depressed, and dependent. Involvement of occupational therapists through the healthcare system provides significantly greater access to low vision rehabilitation for the elderly.[43]

2. Two-thirds of older persons have at least one other chronic condition, in addition to low vision, that limits their independent functioning. Occupational therapists are already primary providers for older clients with other chronic conditions.[38,43] Occupational therapists are trained in the physical, cognitive, sensory, and psychological aspects of disability and aging, and therefore, may be the natural choice of professionals to work with older persons whose limitations in ADL are a result of a combination of deficits.[38]

3. Occupational therapists are more evenly distributed throughout the United States than O&Ms and vision rehabilitation therapists, who tend to be located in larger metropolitan areas. Low vision services can be more widely disseminated through the healthcare delivery system.[38]

Occupational therapy as a profession, as well as individual therapists, have reacted in a positive way to this debate. In the past 15 years, many occupational therapists have gained the knowledge base and clinical skills necessary to provide excellent care to clients requiring low vision rehabilitation. This has been accomplished through a variety of learning formats, including independent study, continuing education courses, clinical internships, and university-based training. In addition, many occupational therapists have completed the same national certification program that other low vision rehabilitation therapists must complete. This certification process is run by the ACVREP, which was established in January 2000. It is an independent and autonomous legal certification body governed by a volunteer Board of Directors. ACVREP's mission is to offer professional certification for vision rehabilitation and education professionals in order to improve service delivery to persons with vision impairments. As of January 2006, there were

approximately 2,100 certified O&M specialists, 600 certified vision rehabilitation therapists, and 300 certified low vision therapists. Although ACVREP does not release data on how many occupational therapists are certified, it is likely that many of the 300 who are certified low vision therapists are occupational therapists.

In 1995, the AOTA devoted its entire October issue to the topic of low vision and in 1998 developed the *Occupational Therapy Practice Guidelines for Adults with Low Vision*. In recent years, the AOTA has listed low vision rehabilitation as one of the "10 emerging areas" of clinical practice for occupational therapists. The AOTA has also created a low vision panel to develop a set of competencies by which occupational therapists and occupational therapy assistants can achieve specialty certification from the AOTA, indicating that they have acquired the knowledge and skills to be specialists in low vision intervention.[44]

Fifteen years in the history of a profession is a relatively short time. Yet within this timeframe, occupational therapy has made dramatic strides toward becoming a primary care provider in the area of vision rehabilitation. With the need for these services growing significantly as the US population grows older, there is a need for many more occupational therapists to become involved in this exciting area of practice. As occupational therapists become involved, it is critical to be aware of the history of low vision rehabilitation in the United States, the various professions involved, and some of the sensitivities and important political issues described above.

CLINICAL MODEL

Although the blindness system or educational model of low vision rehabilitation has been the dominant system since the 1950s, the four factors listed below challenge the continued viability of this model of care.

1. Growing demand for low vision services: The demand for low vision services is expected to grow rapidly in the next decade. The population of the United States is aging and the prevalence of eye disease that causes low vision is greatest in people 65 years of age and older. More therapists are needed to meet this demand.

2. Poor distribution of vision rehabilitation providers: Vision rehabilitation therapists and O&M specialists are not well distributed throughout the country. They tend to be located in larger metropolitan areas. As a result, large numbers of people requiring low vision

rehabilitation could not be served within this model.

3. Decrease in funding for the blindness system: There have been significant budget cuts, creating funding problems and limited availability of services for the older population.

4. Changes in Medicare: Changes over the past decade in Medicare policy now allow occupational therapists to provide low vision rehabilitation in medical settings such as hospitals, outpatient clinics, nursing homes, and in client's homes.

Massof[45] proposed a practice model for standardizing low vision rehabilitation as a healthcare service (Table 1-6). He and others have emphasized the similarities between physical medicine and rehabilitation (PM&R) and low vision rehabilitation.[45-47]

According to Fishburn,[47] the aims of PM&R are to prevent injury or frailty, minimize pathology, prevent secondary complications, enhance function of involved systems, and develop compensatory strategies. She argues that these are essentially the same aims of low vision rehabilitation. In addition, many clients now being served within the PM&R system have low vision as a secondary disability. The primary reason for their rehabilitation might be physical, neurologic, or cognitive impairments caused by stroke, diabetes, brain injury, or demyelinating disease.[47] Thus, low vision rehabilitation should be part of the larger rehabilitation system. We agree with this approach and believe that this model addresses each of the four issues listed above.

When designing a model for vision rehabilitation, it is also important to review the WHO vocabulary defining impairment and disability. In 1980, the WHO proposed four terms that should be used when defining impairment and disability.[5] This terminology is illustrated in Figure 1-1.

- A *disorder* is an anatomical deviation from normal and can be congenital or acquired. Examples of visual disorders causing low vision are AMD, diabetic retinopathy, glaucoma, and cataract.

- *Impairment* is a loss or abnormality in function. The impairment can be either physiological or psychological. Visual impairments include decreased visual acuity, reduced contrast sensitivity, central scotomas (blind spots in the center of the visual field), and constricted visual fields.

- *Disability* refers to a restriction or an inability to perform a task in the normal way. Examples are difficulty reading newspaper print, recognizing faces, and driving a car.

Table 1-6.

Low Vision Rehabilitation in the United States Healthcare System Service Delivery Model

Physical Medicine and Rehabilitation Professional	Role	Low Vision Rehabilitation Professional
Physiatrist	Responsible for evaluating the client, diagnosing functional disabilities, planning therapy, coordinating health care and performing procedures that are within the purview only of a licensed physician	Ophthalmologist Optometrist
Occupational Therapist	Specializes in the rehabilitation of daily living and other functional activities	Occupational Therapist Vision Rehabilitation Therapist
Physical Therapist	Specializes in mobility training, joint mobilization and muscle strengthening exercises	Orientation and Mobility Specialist
Social Worker	Helps the client and family cope with psychosocial issues related to disabilities and to identify and use resources	Social Worker

Based on model proposed by Massof RW, et al. Low vision rehabilitation in the U.S. health care system. *J Vis Rehab.* 1995;9(3):3-31.

Definition	Term	Examples
Anatomical deviation from normal, whether congenital or acquired	**Disorder**	Cataract, Age-related macular degeneration, Glaucoma
Loss or abnormality of function, whether phsyiological or psychological	**Impairment**	Visual acuity loss Reduced contrast sensitivity Constricted visual field
Restriction or inability to perform a task in a manner considered normal	**Disability**	Inability to read Inability to recognize faces Inability to drive a car
Disadvantage that prevents or limits fulfillment of a role that the individual would consider normal	**Handicap**	Inability to work Restricted social interaction Giving up hobbies

Figure 1-1. World Health Organization terminology for impairment and disability. WHO. *International classification of impairments, disabilities, and handicaps: A manual of classification relating to the consequences of disease.* Geneva: WHO; 1980.

Table 1-7.
Optometric Low Vision Evaluation
Case History Distance Visual Acuities Near Visual Acuities Central Visual Field Testing Color Vision Testing Visual/Mobility Field Testing Contrast Sensitivity Testing Refraction Eye Health Evaluation Magnification Evaluation

- *Handicap* is a disadvantage that prevents or limits the fulfillment of a role that is normal for the client. Examples are the inability to work or engage in hobbies, and restricted social interactions.

In the model presented below, the ophthalmologist and optometrist are primarily interested in the disorder and impairment, while the occupational therapist manages the disability and handicap, although there may be overlap in some areas.

Role of the Ophthalmologist

The role of the ophthalmologist is to diagnose and treat the eye disease. This might involve the use of medication or surgery. When it is clear that vision has been permanently impaired due to the eye disease, the ophthalmologist refers the patient to a low vision optometrist for evaluation and treatment.

Role of the Low Vision Optometrist

The optometric low vision examination is described in detail in Chapter 7. The evaluation includes the components listed in Table 1-7.

The role of the optometrist is to evaluate the patient and determine whether a change in the traditional eyeglass prescription might be of benefit. The optometrist also performs a detailed evaluation of distance and near visual acuity, contrast sensitivity, assessment of central scotomas, and peripheral visual field. Based on the results of this evaluation and the case history, the optometrist begins the process of determining the magnification needs of the client for various ADL and selects and prescribes appropriate low vision optical aids. The optometrist then refers the client to the occupational therapist for training in the use of the prescribed devices for various ADL.

Although the scenario described above represents current thinking about the interaction between the optometrist and occupational therapist, we suggest that to provide optimal care for clients, the ideal working relationship could be modified as detailed in the section below.

Role of the Occupational Therapist

The role of the occupational therapist is to determine the cognitive, psychosocial, and physical needs of the client to resume meaningful roles, routines, and occupation. The occupational therapist performs a comprehensive evaluation of the client's performance areas such as ADL and instrumental activities of daily living (IADL), education, work, play, leisure, and social participation.[1] According to the AOTA *Practice Framework*, ADL refers to activities that are oriented toward taking care of one's own body, such as: bathing, bowel and bladder management, dressing, eating, feeding, functional mobility, personal device care, and personal hygiene.[1] IADL refers to activities that are oriented toward interacting with the environment and are generally optional in nature, such as: care of others, child rearing, communication device use, community mobility, financial management, health management, and meal preparation.[1] The occupational therapy low vision evaluation includes review of the reports from the ophthalmologist and low vision optometrist, and further evaluation of the impairment as needed to identify what client and environmental factors might limit performance. This evaluation is described in detail in Chapter 8.

Based on the results of the optometric low vision evaluation and the occupational therapy evaluation, the therapist designs a vision rehabilitation treatment program to enable the client to achieve the established performance goals. The rehabilitation program should

include education about the functional implications of visual impairment, management of psychosocial issues, referral to community resources, teaching the client visual scanning skills that optimize the use of remaining vision, the use of both optical and nonoptical assistive devices in ADL, and environmental modifications including management of lighting, contrast, and glare. In most states, a physician must approve and periodically review the occupational therapy treatment plan. The physician approving the plan should be a low vision optometrist even in states in which approval is not required. Effective low vision rehabilitation requires the specialized expertise of a low vision optometrist because rehabilitation requires integrated management of the visual effects of the disease, refractive error, and the optical demands of a task. The occupational therapist will need to refer the client back to the low vision optometrist if it becomes apparent that the prescribed optical devices are not as effective as desired. Other potential referrals include orientation and mobility and social work.

An important issue is how the occupational therapist interacts with eyecare providers. In the sections above, we described a typical model where the ophthalmologist will generally refer the client to a low vision optometrist for further evaluation and treatment. Then the optometrist refers to the occupational therapist. There are exceptions to this standard of practice. When an ophthalmologist has advanced training in low vision, a direct referral might be made to the occupational therapist, along with collaboration with the occupational therapist in evaluation and treatment of the visual impairment. Many occupational therapists practice in educational, home care, or other settings in which a low vision optometrist is not physically present. In these settings, eyecare providers not specializing in low vision rehabilitation or other physicians may refer clients directly to the occupational therapist. In such cases, we propose that following the initial occupational therapy evaluation, the occupational therapist refers the patient to a low vision optometrist before implementation of the treatment plan.

However, it is our belief that an alternative model should be considered. We believe that the ideal practice situation would be for an occupational therapist to play a role in the final determination of the appropriate optical devices. In this model, after the optometrist performs the optometric low vision examination and determines the approximate ideal magnification based on visual acuity, the client would be examined by the occupational therapist. The role of the occupational therapist would be to assess the client's goals and to determine the physical limitations that might impact on the optometrist's final decision about optical aids and magnification selection. The therapist

would convey this information to the optometrist, who would then determine and write the final prescription. Of course, to be effective this would have to be an ongoing and interactive process in which the optometrist and occupational therapist work together to determine the appropriate optical devices for a client. Under either model, ultimately, the optometrist would prescribe all recommended optical devices.

The primary support for this model is that occupational therapists routinely observe their clients engaged in various occupations and ADL. This creates an ideal situation to help determine the type of device and magnification that will work best for the client in the ADL most important to the client. In every other area of practice, occupational therapists routinely include measurement of physical function as part of the evaluation. When an occupational therapist with advanced training in low vision rehabilitation works with a low vision optometrist, an occasion may present in which the occupational therapist may be asked to measure acuity, visual fields, and contrast sensitivity. Optometrists, with their specialized understanding of optics, refractive error, and the functional effects of disease and progression of disease, must insure that all optical device options are considered and that the optical devices and prescribed eyeglasses work together. This model highlights the strengths of each profession and allows both the occupational therapist and low vision optometrist to provide complementary and essential components of the rehabilitation process. This model would also be a cost-effective collaboration, with the occupational therapist performing many of the time-consuming procedures typically required in a low vision evaluation, thereby decreasing the time required by the eyecare provider.

SUMMARY

This chapter was designed to establish the importance of low vision rehabilitation for the practice of occupational therapy and to review the definitions, epidemiology and history of low vision and low vision rehabilitation in the United States. We also presented a model of clinical care with suggested roles for the various professions involved with low vision rehabilitation.

REFERENCES

1. American Occupational Therapy Association. Occupational Therapy Practice Framework: Domain and Process. *Am J Occup Ther.* 2002;56(6):609-639.
2. The Lighthouse National Survey on Vision Loss. *The Experience, Attitudes, and Knowledge of Middle-Aged and Older Americans.* New York: The Lighthouse; 1995:11.

3. Massof RW. A model of the prevalence and incidence of low vision and blindness among adults in the US. *Optom Vis Sci.* 2002;79(1):31-38.

4. Tielsch JM. The epidemiology of vision impairment. In: Silverstone B, Lang MA, Rosenthal B, Faye EE, eds. *The Lighthouse Handbook on Vision Impairment and Vision Rehabilitation.* New York: Oxford University Press; 2000: 5-17.

5. World Health Organization. *International classification of impairment, disabilities, and handicaps: a manual of classification relating to consequences of disease.* Geneva, Switzerland: WHO; 1980.

6. Tielsch JM, Sommer A, Witt K, Katz J, Royall RM. Blindness and visual impairment in an American urban population. The Baltimore Eye Survey. *Arch Ophthalmol.* 1990;108(2):286-290.

7. Kahn HA, Leibowitz HM, Ganley JP, et al. The Framingham Eye Study. I. Outline and major prevalence findings. *Am J Epidemiol.* 1977;106(1):17-32.

8. Klein R, Klein BE, Linton KL, De Mets DL. The Beaver Dam Eye Study: visual acuity. *Ophthalmology.* 1991;98:1310-1315.

9. Dana MR, Tielsch JM, Enger C, Joyce E, Santoli JM, Taylor HR. Visual impairment in a rural Appalachian community. Prevalence and causes. *JAMA.* 1990;264(18):2400-2405.

10. Rubin GS, West SK, Munoz B, et al. A comprehensive assessment of visual impairment in a population of older Americans: The SEE study. *Invest Ophthalmol Vis Sci.* 1997;38:557-568.

11. Ferris FL, Kassoff A, Bresnick GH, Bailey I. New visual acuity charts for clinical research. *Am J Ophthalmol.* 1982;94:91-96.

12. Warren M. Lesson 1: An overview of low vision rehabilitation and the role of occupational therapy. In: Warren M, Ed. *Low Vision: Occupational Therapy Intervention with the Older Adult.* Bethesda, MD: American Occupational Therapy Association; 1992:3-21.

13. Congdon N, O'Colmain B, Klaver CC, et al. Causes and prevalence of visual impairment among adults in the United States. *Arch Ophthalmol.* 2004;122(4):477-485.

14. Klein R, Klein B, Lee KE. Changes in visual acuity in a population: The Beaver Dam Eye Study. *Ophthalmology.* 1996;103:1169-1178.

15. Evans BJ, Rowlands G. Correctable visual impairment in older people: a major unmet need. *Ophthalmic Physiol Opt.* 2004;24(3):161-180.

16. Schmidt-Erfurth U, Miller JW, Sickenberg M, et al. Photodynamic therapy with verteporfin for choroidal neovascularization caused by age-related macular degeneration: results of treatments in a phase 1 and 2 study. *Arch Ophthalmol.* 1999;117:1177-1187.

17. Schwartz SD. Age-related maculopathy and age-related macular degeneration. In: Silverstone B, Lang MA, Rosenthal B, Faye EE, eds. *The Lighthouse Handbook on Vision Impairment and Vision Rehabilitation.* New York: Oxford University Press; 2000.

18. Lovie-Kitchin J, Bowman KJ. *Senile Macular Degeneration: Management and Rehabilitation.* Boston, MA: Butterworth; 1985.

19. Warren M. Providing low vision rehabilitation services with occupational therapy and ophthalmology: a program description. *Am J Occup Ther.* 1995;49(9):877-883.

20. American Academy of Optometry. *American Academy of Optometry Low Vision Section List of Low Vision Diplomates.* 2005.

21. Crews JE, Luxton L. Rehabilitation teaching for older adults. In: Orr AA, Ed. *Vision and Aging.* New York: American Foundation for the Blind; 1992:233-253.

22. Duffy MA, Huebner K, Wormsley DP. Activities of daily living and individuals with low vision. In: Scheiman M, Ed. *Understanding and Managing Vision Deficits: A Guide for Occupational Therapists.* Thorofare, NJ: SLACK Incorporated; 2002: 289-304.

23. Center for Medicare and Medicaid Services. Low Vision Rehabilitation Demonstration. CMS Manual System Pub 100-19 Demonstrations 2005 [cited August 28, 2005]; Available from: http://www.cms.hhs.gov/manuals/pm_trans/R25DEMO.pdf.

24. Graboyes M. Psychosocial implications of visual impairment. In: Brilliant RL, Ed. *Essentials of Low Vision Practice.* Boston, MA: Butterworth-Heinemann; 1999:12-17.

25. Goodrich GL, Bailey IL. A history of the field of vision rehabilitation from the perspective of low vision. In: Silverstone B, Lang MA, Rosenthal B, Faye EE, eds. *The Lighthouse Handbook on Vision Impairment and Vision Rehabilitation.* New York: Oxford University Press; 2000:675-715.

26. Goodrich GL, Sowell V. Low vision: A history in progress. In: Corn AL, Koenig AJ, Eds. *Foundations of Low Vision: Clinical and Functional Perspectives.* New York: American Foundation for the Blind; 2000.

27. Goodrich GL, Arditi A. An interactive history: the low vision timeline. In: Stuen C et al, Eds. *Proceedings of the Vision '99 Conference, Vision Rehabilitation: Assessment, Intervention and Outcomes.* Lisse: Swets & Zeitlinger; 2000:3-9.

28. Goodrich GL, Arditi A. A trend analysis of the low-vision literature. *Br J Vis Impair Blind.* 2004;22(3):105-196.

29. Mogk L, Goodrich G. The history and future of low vision services in the United States. *J Vis Imp Blind.* 2004(Oct):585-600.

30. Feinbloom W. Introduction to the principles and practice of subnormal vision correction. *J Am Optom Assoc.* 1935;6:3-18.

31. Feinbloom W. Report of 500 cases of subnormal vision. *Am J Optom Arch Am Acad Optom.* 1938;22:238.

32. Ponchillia PE, Ponchillia SV. *Foundations of Rehabilitation Teaching with Persons Who are Blind or Visually Impaired.* New York, NY: American Foundation for the Blind; 1996:3-21.

33. Goodrich GL. Low vision services in the VA: an "aging" trend. *J Vis Rehab.* 1991;5(3):11-17.

34. Warren M. An overview of low vision rehabilitation and the role of occupational therapy. In: Warren M, Ed. *Low Vision: Occupational Therapy Intervention With the Older Adult.* Bethesda, MD: American Occupational Therapy Association; 2000:3-21.

35. Barraga NC. *Increased Visual Behavior in Low Vision Children* (Research Series No. 13). New York, NY: American Foundation for the Blind; 1964.

36. Barraga NC. Learning efficiency in low vision. *J Am Optom Assoc.* 1969;40(8):807-810.

37. Orr AL, Huebner K. Toward a collaborative working relationship among vision rehabilitation and allied health professionals. *J Vis Imp Blind.* 2001;95(8):468-482.

38. Warren M. Including occupational therapy in low vision rehabilitation. *Am J Occup Ther.* 1995;49(9):857-860.

39. Warren M. *Low Vision: Occupational Therapy Intervention with the Older Adult.* Bethesda, MD: American Occupational Therapy Association; 2000.

40. Warren M. Occupational therapy practice guidelines for adults with low vision. In: Lieberman D, Ed. *The AOTA Practice Guidelines Series.* Bethesda, MD: American Occupational Therapy Association; 2001:1-25.

41. Elliott DB, Trukolo-Ilic M, Strong JG, Pace R, Plotkin A, Bevers P. Demographic characteristics of the vision-disabled elderly. *Invest Ophthalmol Vis Sci.* 1997;38:2566-2575.

42. Lambert J. Occupational therapists, orientation and mobility specialists and rehabilitation teachers. *J Vis Imp Blind.* 1994;88:297-298.

43. McGinty Bachelder J, Harkins D. Do occupational therapists have a primary role in low vision rehabilitation? *Am J Occup Ther.* 1995;49(9):927-930.

44. Sokol-McKay DA. Facing the challenge of macula degeneration: therapeutic interventions for low vision. *OT Practice.* 2005;10(9):10-15.

45. Massof RW, et al. Low vision rehabilitation in the U.S. health care system. *J Vis Rehab.* 1995;9(3):3-31.

46. Wainapel SF. Low vision rehabilitation and rehabilitation medicine: A parable of parallels. In: Massof RW, Lidoff L, Eds. *Issues in Low Vision Rehabilitation.* New York: AFB Press; 2001:55-60.

47. Fishburn MJ. Overview of physical medicine and rehabilitation. In: Massof RW, Lidoff L, Eds. *Issues in Low Vision Rehabilitation.* New York: AFB Press; 2001:61-70.

Review of Basic Anatomy, Physiology, and Development of the Visual System

BASIC ANATOMY AND PHYSIOLOGY

This chapter is designed to provide a review of the basic anatomy and physiology of the visual system. Space limitations prevent a comprehensive discussion of this topic. Readers requiring more in-depth information about these topics should review the texts listed in the Bibliography of this chapter.

Orbit, Eyelids, and Eyeball

A traditional method of describing the anatomy of the eye is to begin with the outermost structures and move inward. The orbit of the eye, which is a bony recess in the skull, contains a number of major structures, including the eyeball, the optic nerve, the muscles of the eye, and their nerves and blood vessels. The eyeball, which is about 2.5 cm long, is suspended in the orbital cavity in such a way that the six extraocular muscles can move it in all directions.

The eyelids protect the eyes from injury and excessive light and keep the cornea moist. As illustrated in Figure 2-1, the upper eyelid partially covers the iris, whereas the entire inferior half of the eye is normally uncovered. The eyelids are covered internally by the highly vascular palpebral conjunctiva. The palpebral conjunctiva continues onto the eyeball and is called the bulbar conjunctiva. Inflammation of either the bulbar or palpebral conjunctiva is referred to as con-junctivitis, commonly called pink eye. Conjunctivitis can be secondary to bacterial, viral, or allergic etiology. Infection of the conjunctiva is generally self-limiting, but occasionally conjunctivitis can lead to inflammation of the cornea as well.

The bulbar conjunctiva covers the white portion of the eye called the sclera. The sclera is the external coat of the eye and is a white tissue covering the posterior five-sixths of the eye. The anterior one-sixth of the outer coat of the eye is the transparent structure called the cornea (Figure 2-2). The cornea is an extremely important structure of the eye because it is the key optical component responsible for refraction of light that enters the eye. It is an unusual tissue because it is clear and has no blood vessels. The cornea is susceptible to infection from bacterial, viral, fungal, or allergic causes, and inflammation of the cornea is referred to as keratitis. Severe inflammation, a corneal burn due to exposure to toxic substances, or trauma to the cornea can all lead to scarring and loss of transparency of the cornea. This can then lead to a loss of vision if the scarring is located in the central portion of the cornea. Reduced visual acuity secondary to central corneal scarring is a condition that may be encountered by occupational therapists in clients who have experienced head trauma. Other common age-related problems of the anterior part of the eye that affect vision and cause discomfort include blepharitis (chronic inflammation of the lids) and dry eye. These can be managed medically but with varying success.

Figure 2-1. The upper eyelid partially covers the iris, whereas the entire inferior half of the eye is normally uncovered (Steinman).

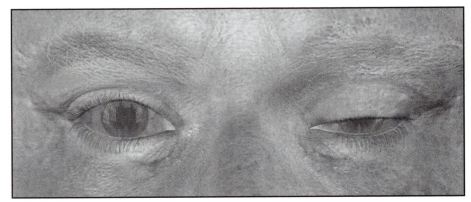

Figure 2-2. Cross-section of the eye. The anterior one-sixth of the outer coat of the eye is the transparent structure called the cornea (Steinman).

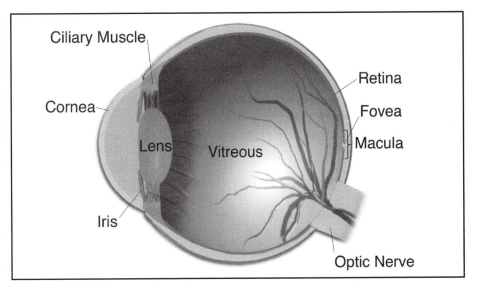

Directly behind the cornea is a clear, watery fluid called the aqueous humor, which is produced in the posterior chamber and fills the anterior chamber of the eye (Figure 2-3). The aqueous is continuously produced by the ciliary body and provides nutrients for the avascular cornea and lens. After passing through the pupil from the posterior chamber into the anterior chamber, the aqueous is drained off through canal of Schlemm (Figure 2-3).

Lens

The lens is a transparent, flexible structure that is held in position by zonular fibers (see Figure 2-3). It is located posterior to the iris and anterior to the vitreous humor. Like the cornea, the lens is both transparent and avascular and is another key part of the refractive system of the eye. To accommodate or focus on objects, the lens must change shape. The ciliary muscle contracts, and this allows the lens to thicken, enabling the individual to focus. As an object moves away, the ciliary muscle relaxes, the lens becomes thinner, and the focusing system relaxes. The lens of the eye is the structure that gradually loses its transparency as a person ages. This loss of transparency and development of opacities is referred to as cataracts.

Vitreous

The vitreous body is located behind the lens (see Figure 2-3). It consists of a jelly-like substance called vitreous humor, in which there is a meshwork of collagen fibrils. Vitreous humor is a colorless, transparent gel. It consists of 99% water and forms four-fifths of the eyeball. In addition to transmitting light, it holds the retina in place and provides support for the lens. Unlike the aqueous humor, it is not continuously replaced.

Choroid

The eyeball has three concentric coats. The first or outermost coat, the sclera, was described above. The middle coat is a heavily pigmented, vascular layer consisting of the iris, ciliary body, and the choroid. The iris, which is the colored portion of the eye (Figure 2-4), is located between the cornea and the lens. The eye color depends on the amount and distribution of pigment in the iris. The iris is a contractile diaphragm that has a central, circular aperture for transmitting light called the pupil. The size of the iris continually varies to regulate the amount of light entering the eye through the pupil. The ciliary body lies between the

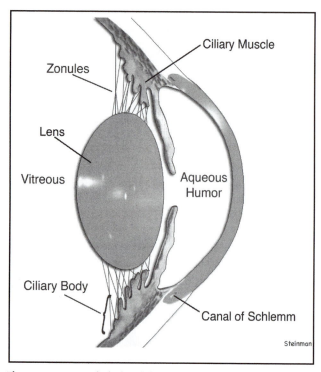

Figure 2-3. Directly behind the cornea is a clear, watery fluid called the aqueous humor. Aqueous is drained off through the Canal of Schlemm (Steinman).

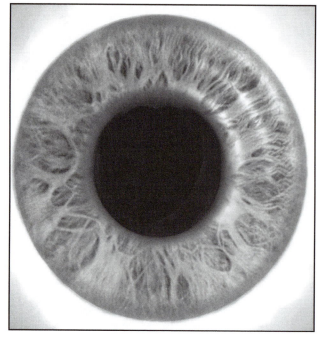

Figure 2-4. The iris is the colored portion of the eye located between the cornea and the lens (Steinman).

iris and the choroid (see Figure 2-3). This structure secretes aqueous humor. The ciliary body also contains the ciliary muscle, which can contract or relax to permit accommodation or focusing of the eye. The choroid is a dark brown membrane and is also part of this middle coat of the eye. It continues from the ciliary body and covers the entire posterior portion of the eye. The choroid attaches firmly to the retina and contains the venous plexus and layers of capillaries that are responsible for nutrition of the retina.

Retina

The most internal coat of the eye is the retina, which is a thin, delicate membrane. The retina is the posterior portion of the eye and there is a circular depressed area called the optic disc (Figure 2-5). This is where the optic nerve enters the eye and its fibers spread out in the neural layer of the retina. Because it contains nerve fibers and no photoreceptor cells, the optic disc is insensitive to light. For this reason, it is sometimes referred to as the blind spot. Another very important structure just lateral to the optic disc is the fovea (see Figure 2-5). The fovea is the part of the eye that contains the area of most acute vision. Whenever we look at an object, we must aim the eye so that the image of the object is focused on the fovea. Smooth eye movements, called pursuits, and jump eye move-

ments, called saccades, are both designed to allow the individual to use the fovea.

The retina is composed of 10 layers, including the pigmented epithelium, which is closest to the choroid and the photoreceptors (cones and rods).

Beneath the pigmented epithelium of the retina are these four layers (Figure 2-6) from the outside (furthest from the retina) to the inside (closest to the retina):

1. Sclera (white part of the eye)
2. Large choroidal blood vessels
3. Choriocapillaris
4. Bruch's membrane (separates the pigmented epithelium of the retina from the choroid).

Note that light must pass through all layers of the retina to reach the photoreceptors, where the visual process begins. Diseases such as macular degeneration or diabetic retinopathy that affect the clarity of retina, or swelling that affects the shape of the retina, will have a profound effect on vision.

Photoreceptors (Cones and Rods)

Light causes a chemical reaction in cones and in rods, beginning the visual process. Activated photoreceptors stimulate bipolar cells, which in turn stimulate

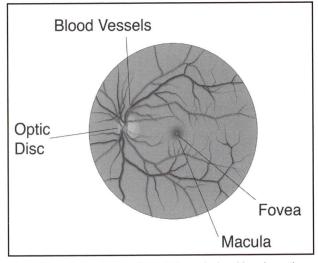

Figure 2-5. The retina as viewed through the dilated pupil: the optic disc is a circular depression in the posterior portion of the retina. This is where the optic nerve enters the eye and its fibers spread out in the neural layer of the retina. The fovea is lateral to the optic disc (Steinman).

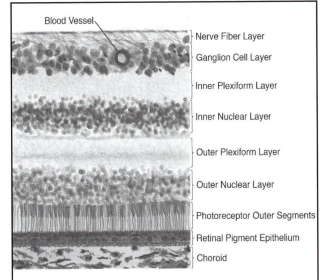

Figure 2-6. Ten layers of the retina (Steinman).

ganglion cells. The impulses continue into the axons of the ganglion cells, through the optic nerve, and to the visual cortex at the occipital lobe of the brain.

There are about 6.5 to 7 million cones in each eye, and they are sensitive to bright light and to color. The highest concentration of cones is in the macular. The center of the macular contains only cones and no rods. The highest concentration of rods is in the peripheral retina, decreasing in density up to the macular. Rods are used for night vision and do not detect color, which is the main reason it is difficult to tell the color of an object at night or in the dark. Defective or damaged cones results in color deficiency. Defective or damaged rods result in problems seeing in the dark and at night.

Muscles of the Orbit and Their Innervation

Six extraocular muscles attach to each eye and allow movement in all directions of gaze. There are four rectus muscles—the superior, inferior, lateral, and medial recti muscles—and two oblique muscles called the inferior and superior oblique muscles.

Each of the six muscles has one position of gaze in which it exerts the main influence on eye position. Figure 2-7 illustrates the various positions of gaze that are evaluated clinically. The diagram also displays the muscle that is primarily responsible for movement into each position of gaze. This diagram is the basis for the clinical evaluation of eye muscle problems. For example, if a client has difficulty moving his eyes down and to the right, the two possible muscles

involved would be the right inferior rectus and the left superior oblique. The left superior oblique moves the left eye down and to the right and the right inferior rectus moves the right eye down and to the right. To determine which of the two remaining muscles is at fault requires additional clinical testing.

Three cranial nerves supply innervation to the six extraocular muscles. The third cranial nerve innervates the superior, inferior, medial recti, and the inferior oblique muscle. The fourth cranial nerve supplies innervation to the superior oblique, and the sixth cranial nerve innervates the lateral rectus.

Diplopia, or double vision, is a very common symptom of clients treated by occupational therapists, particularly after cerebrovascular accident or head trauma. Diplopia occurs when the object at which the individual is looking stimulates the fovea of one eye and a nonfoveal part of the retina of the other eye. Thus, diplopia suggests misalignment of the eyes. There are a number of disorders that can lead to diplopia. Brain injury from stroke or trauma that affect the midbrain or cerebellum area often affect both balance and eye movements. Among the more common problems are cranial nerve palsies. The most common nerve palsies seen by occupational therapists are sixth and fourth nerve palsies.

The most common causes of fourth nerve palsy are head trauma and vascular problems. Fourth cranial nerve palsy can be unilateral or bilateral and can affect the superior oblique muscle. Bilateral fourth nerve palsy is often seen following vertex blows to the head, such as those that occur in motorcycle accidents. The presence of a fourth nerve palsy causes the eye

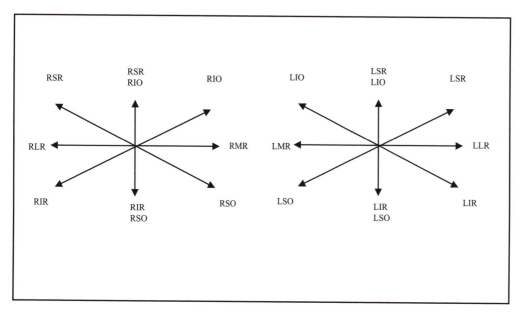

Figure 2-7. Positions of gaze that are evaluated by clinicians when testing the extraocular muscles.

with the affected muscle to drift upward. The client has difficulty looking down and to the right if it is a left superior oblique problem, and down and to the left if it is a right superior oblique problem.

Sixth cranial nerve palsies are the most frequently reported ocular motor nerve palsies. The nerve has the longest intracranial course of any nerve and is often subject to damage with raised intracranial pressure. The causes include vascular disease, trauma, elevated intracranial pressure, and neoplasm. The sixth nerve innervates the lateral rectus. A sixth nerve palsy will interfere with the client's ability to abduct the eye (move the eye away from the nose).

Visual Pathways

One of the most common vision problems occupational therapists encounter after acquired brain injury is visual field deficits. A right or left field loss is referred to as an homonymous hemianopsia. To understand why a client would lose vision on just one side, it is necessary to understand how visual information travels from the retina to the visual cortex. Vision begins with the capture of images focused by the optical media on photoreceptors of the retina. The fibers from the upper half of each retina enter the optic nerve above the horizontal meridian, and those from the lower half enter below the horizontal meridian. Fibers from the periphery of the retina lie peripherally in the optic nerve, and fibers from the fovea lie centrally. This arrangement persists throughout the entire course of the visual pathways from the optic nerve through the chiasm, the optic tracts, and optic radiations.

Visual information from the right field strikes the nasal half of the retina of the right eye and the temporal half of the retina of the left eye. Similarly, visual information from the left field strikes the nasal half of the retina of the left eye and the temporal half of the retina of the right eye (Figure 2-8). When the fibers from each optic nerve reach the optic chiasm, a semi-decussation or partial crossing takes place. The fibers from the temporal part of the retina remain on the temporal or outside aspect of the chiasm and are called uncrossed fibers. The nasal fibers of the retina cross over in the chiasm and are called crossed fibers. After leaving the chiasm, the fibers form the optic tract. Thus, all visual information originating from the right field travels in the left optic tract, and all visual information originating from the left field travels in the right optic tract. The fibers in the upper half of the tract originate from the upper half of the two retinas, and the fibers from the lower half of the tract come from the lower half of the two retinas. The fibers from the optic tract synapse in the lateral geniculate body. The cells of the lateral geniculate body give rise to new fibers, which form the optic radiation. These fibers then proceed to the cells of the visual cortex (Figure 2-9). Any lesion that affects the visual pathway on only the right or left side after this decussation takes place will affect either the left visual field or right visual field.

Vision Areas of the Brain

The brain is divided into several different lobes. Starting anteriorly are the frontal lobes, which are responsible for decision making, planning ahead, emotional tone, abstract thinking and carrying out intentions. Immediately behind them and in front of the motor area is the prefrontal cortex, which is involved in organizing and sequencing complex

Figure 2-8. The right visual cortex receives information from the left visual field and the left visual cortex receives information from the right visual field.

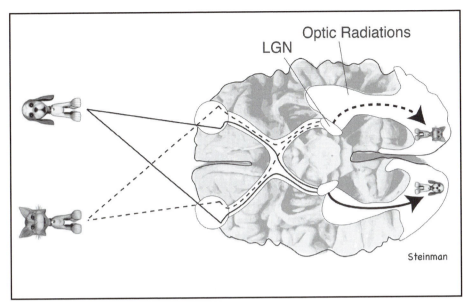

Figure 2-9. Visual pathway from the optic nerve to the visual cortex.

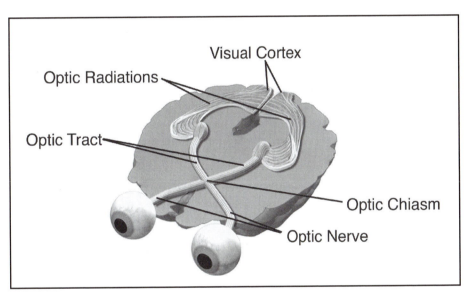

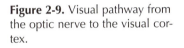

motor behavior. The temporal lobes are associated with hearing and also provide some contribution to vision. The parietal lobes are responsible for tactile recognition. Parietal lobe injury commonly results in perceptual deficits that disrupt ambulation and self-care activities. Hemi-sensory neglect is a common problem in clients with a lesion in the posterior parietal cortex.

The occipital lobe contains the visual cortex, with nerve pathways leading to higher centers in the parietal and temporal lobes, where visual sensations acquire meaning. Lesions in the visual cortex and in associated areas can produce visual and perceptual problems.

All of the visual fibers end in the striate area of the cortex, which is called area 17. Area 17 is considered to be the primary visuosensory area in man. Outside of area 17 and closely following its contours are two other areas that are concerned with visual reactions as well. These are called areas 18 and 19. Most physiologists agree that vision is a function of higher parts of the brain than just the visual cortex. The message relayed to area 17 enables a person to see. It does not enable a person to recognize what he or she sees or to recall things that have been seen. These functions are dependent on other parts of the brain. In order for a person to be able to interpret the sensory information reaching area 17, the message must be sent on to the two secondary visual areas and areas 18 and 19. Area 18 is concerned exclusively with the recognition of objects, animate or inanimate, but is not concerned with the recognition of written or printed symbols

of language. Area 19 is concerned with the recall of visual memory relating to objects but not to language symbols. In general, occipital areas are involved with spatial relations while temporal occipital areas are involved with object and letter recognition.

Two parallel routes carry visual information from the occipital lobe to the prefrontal lobe and the frontal eye fields. Fibers from these two routes distribute fibers to many other areas along each route before terminating in the prefrontal cortex and in the frontal eye fields. The first route is the superior route via the parietal and frontal lobes. The other route is the inferior route via the temporal and frontal lobes.

The cerebellum integrates the smooth coordination of muscular activity. If it is damaged, general motor clumsiness occurs. This may interfere with manual dexterity and other forms of fine muscular performance, as well as eye movement control. Dysfunction within the cerebellum yields problems with equilibrium, motor control, body image, laterality, and sometimes with reading and speech.

SUMMARY

Since low vision is a condition in which visual acuity is reduced because of eye disease, it is important to have a basic understanding of the anatomy and physiology of the eye and visual system. We urge readers who feel a need for more detail to refer to the Bibliography provided at the end of this chapter.

BIBLIOGRAPHY

Moore KL. *Clinically Oriented Anatomy*. Baltimore, MD: Williams and Wilkins; 1980.

Moses RA. *Adler's Physiology of the Eye*. 7th ed. St. Louis, Mo: CV Mosby Co; 1981.

Solomon H. *Binocular Vision: A Programmed Text*. London: William Heinemann Medical Books Ltd; 1978.

Visual Acuity, Contrast Sensitivity, Refractive Disorders, and Visual Fields

VISUAL ACUITY

Definition

Visual acuity is a measure of the smallest high-contrast detail that one can resolve. Visual acuity usually is measured with letters or words: the detail is 1/5th the size of the letter or about the stroke width or the gap in a C. Most people are familiar with the concept of 20/20 visual acuity. An individual with "20/20" acuity is considered to have normal ability to see small detail at the distance tested. The numerator refers to the testing distance at which the subject recognizes the stimulus. The denominator refers to the letter size. Letter size is described as the distance at which the letter being viewed could be identified by a client with normal visual acuity. Since larger letters can be seen further away, a larger number in the denominator indicates a larger size letter on the eye chart. For an example, we will use a client with 20/100 acuity. This indicates that he or she was tested at 20 feet and the smallest letter the client could see was large enough so that someone with normal visual acuity could identify the letter presented at a distance of 100 feet. A letter that could be seen at 100 feet is 5X larger than a letter

seen at 20 feet. The client in our example could only see this letter at 20 feet, indicating that the visual acuity is reduced 5X relative to the normal finding. This method of recording visual acuity is routinely used in the United States and the units in feet are referred to as "imperial units". In other countries, in the research literature, and in some clinics in the United States, meters rather than feet are used to express distance visual acuity using the M system described below. For example, 6/6 is equivalent to 20/20 acuity (6 meters is about 19 feet), 6/60 is equivalent to 20/200 acuity, and 6/30 is equivalent to 20/100 acuity.

In traditional vision screenings, visual acuity below the level of 20/30 to 20/40 is considered cause for referral. However, clinically, any deviation from 20/20 is considered a problem, and in the course of the vision evaluation the clinician must determine the basis for the loss of visual acuity.

The meaning of 20/20 visual acuity can also be expressed based on a mathematical concept. Someone with 20/20 visual acuity is able to recognize a letter that subtends a visual angle of 5 minutes of arc at the eye (Figure 3-1); the critical detail is 1 minute of arc. As illustrated in Figure 3-1, this means that if you draw a line from the top of a 20/20 letter to the eye and another line from the bottom of the letter to the

Figure 3-1. Definition of 20/20 visual acuity (Steinman).

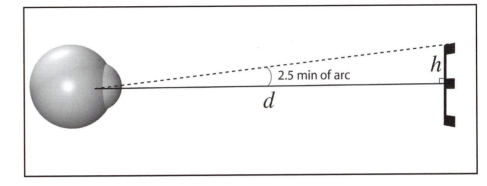

eye, the size of the angle at the intersection of these two lines at the eye is 5 minutes of arc.

When measuring near visual acuity, the convention is based on the "meter system" or "M" notation. In this system, a 1 M letter will subtend 5 minutes of arc at 1 meter. To compare acuity at distance and near, it is important to be able to convert from one measurement system to the other. The formula for converting metric acuity to imperial notation is as follows:

D/S = 20/X

where D = the test distance in meters, and S = the letter size in M units. One would solve for X by cross-multiplying DX = 20S, then solve for X. X = 20S/D

Be careful that the numerator and denominator are the same units.

Example: What is the Snellen equivalent to 1M acuity at 40 cm?

If the metric acuity was 1.0 M at 0.4 meters (40 cm), the formula would be 0.4/1 M = 20/X
   cross multiply,
   X = 20S/D, S = 1, D = 0.4
   X = 20/0.4
   X = 50
Answer: 0.4/1 M = 20/50 acuity

Another way to approach the problem is to multiply the numerator by a number that results in 20. Then multiply the denominator by the same number.

A short cut method is to divide the numerator and denominator in half so it equals 0.2/0.5, then multiply by 100 to 20/50. Since the test distance was not actually 20 feet, 20/50 would be called equivalent visual acuity.

Table 3-1 can also be used to convert common visual acuity findings from one notation system to another.

Often, metric visual acuity charts provide equivalent Snellen acuity on the chart so one does not need to make the calculation. It is very important to note that equivalent acuity is only valid at the recommended test distance for the chart. Another number listed next to each line on some acuity charts is "logMAR". This is a measure of the angular subtense of the critical detail of the letter at the recommended test distance, and is used for research (not clinical) purposes.

Clinical Assessment

Visual acuity testing is a critical aspect of a vision evaluation and is performed by every type of eye care professional and is repeated at every eye examination. The standard Snellen Acuity Chart (Figure 3-2) is the most common method of testing visual acuity.

The Snellen visual acuity chart has a number of flaws that make it an inappropriate chart for clients with low vision. As Figure 3-2 illustrates, there is only one letter at 20/200, two letters at 20/100, and three at 20/70. On the other hand, as visual acuity approaches 20/20, the number of letters per line increases and the gradations become smaller (ie, 20/40, 20/30, 20/25, 20/20). The construction of this chart is ideal for clients with 20/20 visual acuity and allows the eye doctor to precisely examine clients with normal visual acuity requiring standard eyeglasses. In most offices today, these charts are not hung on the wall; rather, the chart is projected on the wall using a special visual acuity projector. Projected acuity charts commonly used also suffer from low luminance and poor contrast and are not typical of everyday objects someone might try to resolve. The contrast also varies with the age of the projector bulb. Thus, although the standard Snellen visual acuity chart is widely used, it is not an acceptable chart for the low vision client.

Low vision clients, however, have visual acuity poorer than 20/70. To examine such an individual, the chart should have small gradations in the poorer visual acuity range. Instead of 20/200, 20/100, and 20/70 that are large gradation changes, the chart should have smaller increments, such as 20/400, 20/350, 20/300, 20/275, and 20/250. Visual acuity charts for low vision clients should have letters that start at

Table 3-1.
Near Visual Acuity Equivalents at 40 cm Near Test Distance

Snellen Equivalent	Meter System "M" Notation	Point	Usual Type Size
20/250	5.00	40	Newspaper Headlines
20/200	4.00	32	Newspaper subheadlines
20/100	2.00	16	Large-print material
20/80	1.60	12	Children's books
20/60	1.20	10	Magazine print
20/50	1.00	8	Newspaper print
20/40	0.80	6	Paperback print
20/25	0.50	4	Footnotes
20/20	0.40	3	————

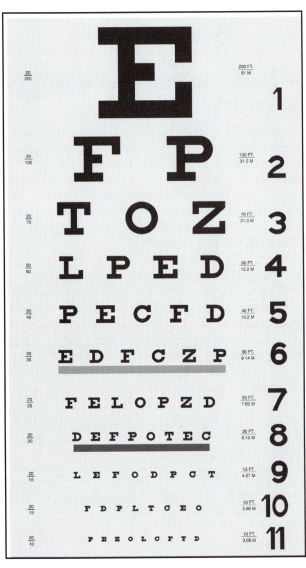

Figure 3-2. The standard Snellen Acuity Chart (Steinman).

Figure 3-3. Feinbloom Chart (Steinman).

much higher acuity levels, such as 20/700, 20/800, and 20/1000. In addition, the chart should have an equal number of letters at each acuity level. When only one or two letters are available on a line, the client could memorize the line, guess the letter(s) correctly, and the clinician could not be sure that the visual acuity obtained was accurate and reliable. Current standards for near and distance acuity charts standardize the letters and space all lines at the same 25% difference in size, corresponding to a mathematical progression of 1/10th (0.1) of a logarithmic unit. Log spacing enables more precise and repeatable measurements and also enables the experienced practitioner to more easily perform calculations at nonstandard test distances and estimate magnification. Charts adhering to this standard are referred to as *Log* charts.

Any therapist who has been involved with low vision rehabilitation will relate to the following scenario. A client is referred for low vision rehabilitation with a medical diagnosis of macular degeneration. The referral also indicates the best-corrected visual acuity as: right eye 20/200, left eye: counting fingers. What does *counting fingers* mean and how does the therapist use this information to properly code for Medicare documentation and reimbursement? Generally, the term counting fingers means that the eye doctor used the standard projected Snellen chart for the visual acuity examination. The client was unable to see even the large letter "E" at the top of the chart. The eye doctor, therefore, held up his hand and waved it, showing anywhere from 1 to 5 fingers, and asked the client "How many fingers do you see?" This is obviously not an appropriate assessment of visual acuity and indicates that the eye doctor simply did not have the proper equipment to complete the examination and did not use an acceptable method for the visual acuity assessment. In such cases, the therapist will need to repeat visual acuity testing using an appropriate target and technique described below.

Because of these issues special visual acuity eye charts have been developed. There are a number of excellent visual acuity charts that are available for the low vision client. In this chapter we will review three visual acuity charts that are effective and widely used.

LOW VISION DISTANCE VISUAL ACUITY CHARTS

Original Distance Test Chart for the Partially Sighted

This chart (Figure 3-3) is often called the Feinbloom Distance Test Chart and is widely used and considered the gold standard by some authorities.[1] The advantage is that the chart has numeric optotypes at the following visual acuity levels: 20/700, 20/600, 20/400, 20/350, 20/300, 20/225, 20/200, 20/180, 20/160, 20,140, 20/120, 20/100, 20/80, 20/60, 20/40, 20/30, 20/25, 20/20, 20/10.

The chart was calibrated for 20 feet, but is typically used at a 10-foot distance, which means the acuity values listed above would be doubled. This means that at a 10-foot distance, the acuity range extends from 20/1400 to 20/20.

Freeman and Jose[1] discuss the advantages of performing this test at 10 feet and include the following:

- Doubles the number of lines the client can attempt compared to a standard visual acuity chart.

- Decreases the background confusion because the numbers are not spaced as close together as with a standard visual acuity chart.

- Allows for better lighting and less glare.

- Elicits a more positive response than a standard visual acuity chart.

If a client cannot even see the large "7" at 10 feet, the chart can be moved to 5 feet. At this distance, the acuity range is extended from 20/1400 to 2800 because

each time you decrease the distance by half, you double the denominator.

Another major advantage of this visual acuity chart is that because of the large visual acuity range that can be assessed, almost all clients with low vision will be able to read at least some letters on the visual acuity chart. This is important from a psychological standpoint. Many clients with low vision have had negative experiences during visual acuity testing (being unable to even see the large "E"). This can be depressing. The client feels that there is no hope if he or she could not see the eye chart at all. With the Feinbloom chart, however, most clients are able to read quite a few lines on the chart, leading to a much more positive experience.[1,2]

A major advantage of the Feinbloom chart is portability. For this reason, the Feinbloom chart is recommended for home-based evaluation. The Feinbloom chart is also valuable because it can be used to assess eccentric viewing. This technique is often required when an occupational therapist is assessing eccentric viewing, and is reviewed in detail in Chapter 8.

One major problem with the Feinbloom chart is that it does not have an equal number of optotypes per acuity level. There is only one number at the 20/700, 20/600, 20/400, 20/350, 20/300, and 20/225 levels, and only three per line from 20/200 to 20/60. Another problem is the letters are not standard, so acuity measured with the Feinbloom chart may not match acuity measured with another chart. Because of these shortcomings, the Feinbloom Chart should be supplemented with one of the two described below, if possible.

Early Treatment Diabetic Retinopathy Study Chart

Using a design developed by Lovie-Kitchen and Bailey,[3] this Log chart provides five letters per line and also standardizes the separation between letters. A unique aspect of the Early Treatment Diabetic Retinopathy Study Chart (ETDRS) is its geometric progression of size differences between lines, referred to as logMAR progression (Figure 3-4). Optotypes on each line are 0.1 log unit or 25% larger than the previous line. This format results in every three lines representing a halving or doubling of visual acuity at any given viewing distance, eg, if one starts at 100 and goes down three steps (step 1 = 80, step 2 = 80 to 63, and step 3 = 63 to 50), which is one-half of 100. These characteristics allow for consistent and accurate evaluation of visual acuity. This chart is considered the gold standard for accurate, repeatable measurement. However, the ETDRS chart is large and cannot be easily carried for home healthcare. Thus, it may not be practical for home health practice.

The standard test distance is 4 meters, but for low vision evaluations the test distance is usually halved to 2 meters to insure that a client can read the largest letters. This also makes conversion to Snellen equivalent easy. One just adds a zero to the numerator and denominator. For example, a 2/10 acuity measurement in M units becomes 20/100 in imperial notation.

Chronister Pocket Acuity Chart

The Chronister Pocket Acuity Chart (CPAC) is very similar to the Feinbloom chart (Figure 3-5). It has many acuity gradations, from 20/220 to 20/10 when used at 20 feet, from 20/449 to 20/20 at 10 feet, and from 20/880 to 20/40 at 5 feet. The major advantage is that it can be held in one hand and carried in one's pocket. Therefore, it is easy for an occupational therapist to carry this chart when providing care in a client's home, hospital room, or nursing home room. It does share the same shortcoming as the Feinbloom chart, having only two letters per visual acuity level from 20/220 to 20/40, and then four letters per visual acuity level from 20/30 to 20/10.

LOW VISION NEAR VISUAL ACUITY CHARTS

A common goal of clients with low vision is to be able to read again. Therefore, the evaluation of near visual acuity is essential because this visual acuity testing is performed at the reading distance. Generally, near visual acuity should be measured with words or continuous text because word acuity better predicts the visual requirements for reading than letter acuity.[4,5] Near visual acuity testing differs from distance visual acuity testing in two ways.

1. In addition to testing the client's ability to read single letters or numbers, charts with phrases and sentences are also used to evaluate reading ability.

2. The meter system of notation is often used for near visual acuity testing as mentioned earlier in this chapter (see Table 3-1).

Three commonly used near visual acuity charts are described below.

Lighthouse Near Acuity Test (Meter System)

The Lighthouse Near Acuity Test (LHNV-1) letter chart is illustrated in Figure 3-6 and shows that the card has both Snellen equivalent and meter system notation. Near visual acuity testing is typically performed at 40 cm with clients with normal vision. If

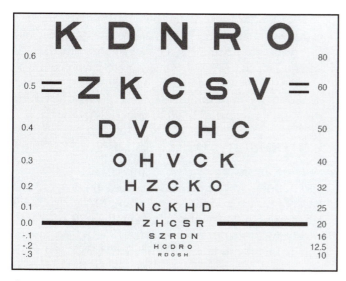

Figure 3-4a. ETDRS Visual Acuity Chart (Steinman).

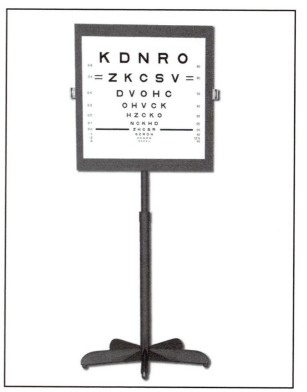

Figure 3-4b. ETDRS Visual Acuity Chart (Steinman).

Figure 3-5. Chronister Pocket Acuity Chart (Gulden Ophthalmics) (Steinman).

a client with low vision is unable to see the largest letters at 40 cm, the testing can be performed at any distance. When recording the result, it is important to record the distance at which the testing occurred as well as the visual acuity achieved. For example, if a client can see the 4 M print at 25 cm, it would be recorded as 0.25/4 M.

A typoscope is often useful when testing near visual acuity. It enables the examiner to isolate one line at a time and tends to simplify the task for the client (Figure 3-7).

A shortcoming of this chart is the limited number of optotypes with the larger size letters.

Lighthouse Reduced ETDRS Chart

The same advantages that were described above for the ETDRS visual acuity chart apply to the reduced ETDRS near visual acuity chart illustrated in Figure 3-8. The chart also has both Snellen and metric system notation and can be administered at any distance. Recording should include the distance at which the test was administered. The major disadvantage of this chart is that it only presents individual symbols. In the low vision evaluation, we are more interested

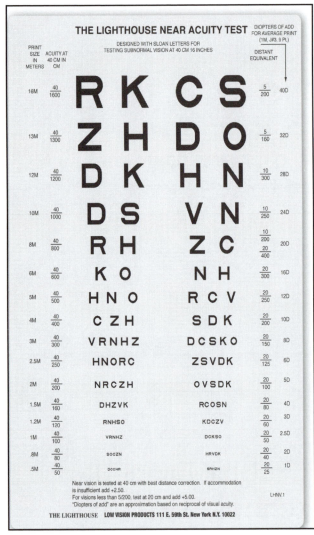

Figure 3-6. Lighthouse Near Visual Acuity Chart (Steinman).

Figure 3-7. Typoscope (Steinman).

in the client's ability to read words, not letters. If an ETDRS test was used at distance, the Lighthouse Reduced ETDRS Chart will allow the therapist to compare distance and near acuity. Differences of more than one line between letter and word acuity may indicate severe restriction in central visual fields or distortions in vision (discussed below).

Minnesota Low-Vision Reading Test (MN Read Test)

One of the major differences between distance visual acuity and near visual acuity testing is the use of charts with phrases or sentences for near visual acuity. This is recommended because of the importance of reading in our society. If a client is going to regain independence in activities of daily living (ADL), he or she will need to be able to read again. We know that near visual acuity for single letters is often considerably better than near visual acuity for reading phrases and sentences. Therefore, to better understand the impact of low vision on reading, it is important to assess both single letter and continuous text near visual acuity.

A popular test for assessing continuous reading acuity is the Minnesota Low-Vision Reading Test (MN Read Test) illustrated in Figure 3-9. An advantage of using this test is that it not only provides an assessment of near visual acuity with continuous text, it also allows us to evaluate the client's reading speed. Unlike visual acuity, which is not expected to improve with vision rehabilitation, reading speed is one function that can be improved. Thus, reading speed is one of the areas for which the occupational therapist may be able to document improvements with treatment and justify additional vision rehabilitation in Medicare documentation.

Figure 3-8. Lighthouse Reduced ETDRS Chart (Steinman).

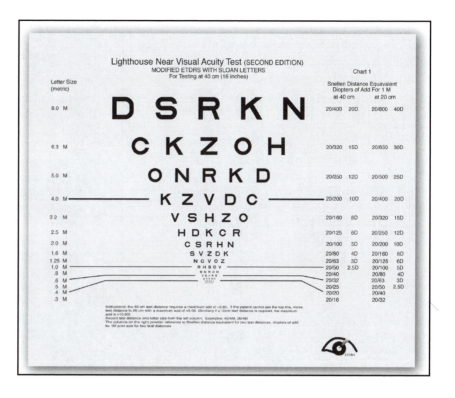

Figure 3-9. MN Read Near Visual Acuity Test (Steinman).

The MN Read acuity chart has been validated and can be used to provide a sensitive and reliable measure of reading acuity.[6] Each sentence has 60 characters, which corresponds to 10 standard length words, assuming a standard word length of 6 characters (including a space). The reading levels of the passages are approximately the same, about a 3rd to 4th grade difficulty. An estimate of reading acuity is given by the smallest print size at which the client can read the entire sentence without making significant errors. (Usually reading performance deteriorates rapidly as the acuity limit is approached, and it is easy to determine the level where reading becomes impossible.) The examiner uses a stopwatch to record the time required to read each paragraph and this allows a determination of reading speed.

SIGNIFICANCE OF VISUAL ACUITY IN LOW VISION REHABILITATION

As we reviewed in Chapter 1, the definition of low vision is based on either distance visual acuity or visual field. Thus, visual acuity is a critical assessment in low vision care. The definition used to determine Medicare eligibility is 20/70 or worse in the better-seeing eye with best correction. In the United States, visual acuity is used to categorize a person as legally blind (20/200 or worse in better-seeing eye with best correction). This entitles the individual to a number of entitlements and benefits, such as property tax exemptions, an extra income tax exemption, reduced fares on public transportation, access to social security disability, and books on tape. Visual acuity is also used by the low vision optometrist to estimate the magnification needs of a client. The optometrist determines the actual visual acuity and divides that value by the desired acuity level. Let's say a client's visual acuity is 20/200 and the client needs to see 20/50 print for the desired ADL. One would divide 200 by 50, yielding an estimate of 4X enlargement needed to achieve this task.

The difference between target size and acuity threshold is acuity reserve, estimated by dividing the target size being viewed by target size at acuity threshold. If a person with normal vision wishes to read 1M print (typical of newspaper) at 40 cm, he or she requires better than 0.5 M acuity threshold at the same distance. Print size must be twice acuity threshold for fluent, comfortable reading (see Chapters 7 and 9).

CONTRAST SENSITIVITY

Definition

An important topic that is related to visual acuity is contrast sensitivity. While visual acuity tests enable the therapist to estimate how well someone can see small high-contrast objects, contrast sensitivity testing enables the therapist to estimate how well someone can see larger low-contrast objects. Contrast sensitivity is related to visual acuity, but provides information that is not as well captured by visual acuity measurement.[7] Contrast sensitivity is strongly associated with reading performance,[8] mobility,[9,10] driving,[11,12] face recognition,[12,13] and ADL.[13,14] Contrast sensitivity testing tells us about the quality of the available vision when viewing larger objects. For instance, it is possible for a client to have reasonably good visual acuity, but still complain of problems such as dim, foggy, or unclear vision or sensitivity to bright light. Visual acuity only allows us to evaluate one limited aspect of the person's ability to see. Contrast sensitivity is a measure of how faded or washed out an image can be before it becomes indistinguishable from a uniform field. A person with impaired contrast sensitivity might describe the problem by saying "it is like looking through a dirty windshield when I drive". People with reduced contrast sensitivity often are very particular about lighting. They usually are glare sensitive or can see best over only a very narrow range of light intensity.

Contrast sensitivity determines the lowest contrast level that can be detected by a client for a given size target. Contrast can vary from no contrast (0%) to highest contrast (100%). For example, high-quality print has 85% to 95% contrast, while paper currency has only 55% to 60% contrast. Another term that is used is contrast threshold. Contrast threshold is defined as an object with the lowest contrast that a client can recognize. A client with normal vision can usually see objects with as little as 2% to 3% contrast. If the contrast of an object is less than the contrast threshold of the client, the object cannot be seen. Table 3-2 shows the contrast of some common everyday objects. This table indicates that the contrast of most objects is considerably higher than the normal contrast threshold of 2% to 3%. The difference between the contrast of objects and a client's contrast threshold is contrast reserve, expressed as a ratio of object contrast divided by contrast threshold. For fluent reading and presumably quick identification of objects, contrast reserve must be greater than 10:1 (10 times threshold), and ideally greater than 20:1 (see Chapter 9).

Table 3-2.
Contrast of Common Everyday Objects

Contrast (%)	Object
5	Maroon chair on maroon carpet
74	Maroon chair on gray carpet
80	Illuminated Red Exit sign
82	Black automobile on sunny street
32	Gray automobile on shady street
55-60	US currency
71-75	Daily newspaper
76-80	Paperback books
88-93	Glossy periodicals

Adapted from Brilliant RL. *Essentials of Low Vision Practice.* Boston, MA: Butterworth-Heinemann; 1999:48-49.

Contrast sensitivity is the reciprocal of the contrast at threshold, ie, one divided by the lowest contrast at which forms or lines can be recognized. If a person can see details at very low contrast, his or her contrast sensitivity is high, and vice versa. A client with a contrast threshold of 2% has higher contrast sensitivity (1/2 = 50) than a client with a contrast threshold of 10% (1/10 = 10).

Examples of Low Contrast in Activities of Daily Living

- Communication: The faint shadows on people's faces carry the visual information related to facial expressions.
- Orientation and mobility: We need to see low-contrast forms such as the curb, faint shadows, and the last step of carpeted stairs when walking. When driving, seeing in dusk, rain, fog, snow fall, and at night are challenging tasks requiring good contrast sensitivity.
- Reading and writing: Poor quality copies, newsprint, an old Bible.
- Kitchen tasks: Cutting chicken, onion or other light colored objects on a white or light colored cutting board, pouring a glass of water.

Why Is Contrast Sensitivity Important to Measure?

In all conditions where visual acuity is reduced, contrast sensitivity is reduced as well. However, in some conditions that reduce acuity, contrast sensitivity is reduced more than expected based upon the visual acuity alone. This means that if visual acuity only is tested, the visual disability of the person with relatively reduced contrast sensitivity will be underestimated. People with impaired contrast sensitivity often are sensitive to lighting. They are more sensitive to glare, and often see best over a narrow range of light—sometimes bright, sometimes dim light. There is mounting evidence in the literature that suggests that contrast sensitivity may be a sensitive indicator of disease and disease progressions.[15-18] Contrast sensitivity should be assessed when a client's performance does not match the expected results,[19] eg, if a client reports difficulty seeing on a cloudy day or a very bright day and visual acuity testing shows no change from previous visits. Another example: if a client can read enlarged print well but cannot read with equivalent magnification with an optical device (assuming all other factors such as visual acuity and working distance are the same), the therapist should consider contrast sensitivity testing. Optical devices degrade print contrast and create lighting problems. In our clinical experience, people with impaired contrast sensitivity (higher than 5%) often are very sensitive to glare from reflections from optics, degraded contrast from optics, and problems with lighting.

Clinical Assessment of Contrast Sensitivity

Contrast sensitivity has traditionally been measured with gradings (Figure 3-10) that measure the ability to see low contrast over a full range of object sizes. In recent years, however, letter contrast sensitivity testing has become the preferred method in clinical settings because it is easy to administer and clients are familiar with the use of letters to test vision.[20] The Pelli–Robson Contrast Sensitivity Chart has been a popular method of testing letter contrast sensitivity.[21] The Pelli-Robson Contrast Sensitivity Chart (Figure 3-11) is a large wall-mounted chart, 59 cm wide and 84 cm high, that consists of 16 triplets of letters, each

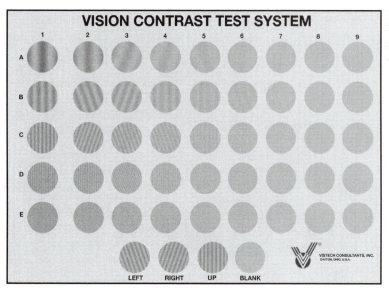

Figure 3-10. VisTech Contrast Sensitivity Testing. The client is instructed to begin with the top row and identify the orientation of as many of the circular patches as possible (Steinman).

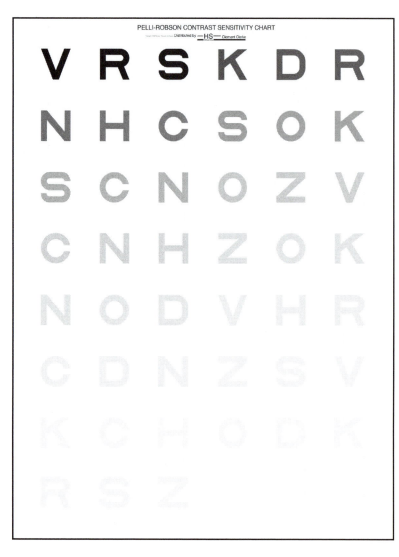

Figure 3-11. Pelli-Robson Contrast Sensitivity Test (Steinman).

Figure 3-12. Mars Letter Contrast Sensitivity Test (reprinted with permission from the Mars Perceptrix Corporation).

subtending 2.8 degrees at the intended 1 M test distance, arranged in eight rows of two triplets each. The three letters within each triplet have constant contrast, whereas the contrast across triplets, reading from left to right, and continuing on successive lines, decreases in contrast. The client reads the letters across and down the chart, as in standard letter acuity measurement. Instead of the letters decreasing in size, however, they decrease in contrast. The final triplet in which the client reads two of three letters correctly determines the Log contrast sensitivity.

Although widely used by researchers, it has not been widely used by clinicians for a variety of reasons.[20] First, it is inconvenient for testing in small clinical spaces, as it requires a large amount of wall space. Second, it is difficult to arrange lighting that will uniformly illuminate such a large area. Third, a wall-mounted chart is difficult to keep clean and free of defects.[20]

Recently, Arditi[20] reported on a new letter contrast sensitivity test called the Mars Letter Contrast Sensitivity Test (Figure 3-12). It is similar to the Pelli-Robson, but has greater accuracy due to its finer contrast decrements and scoring procedure. It is handheld, with a recommended viewing distance of 50 cm, and is portable. These advantages may make this chart more desirable in a clinical setting.

Either test involves instructions to test at a set distance based on near normal vision. For low vision, one must be careful that testing was performed at a distance where the letters were larger than letter size at acuity threshold. This can be easily done by first finding the distance where the high contrast letters on the chart are barely visible, and then decreasing the test distance by one-half and then one-half again.

Significance of Disorders of Contrast Sensitivity for Occupational Therapy

As indicated above, contrast sensitivity testing provides us with information about the clients' visual function that is not available from standard visual acuity testing. Because contrast sensitivity is closely associated with reading, mobility, driving, and other ADL, it is particularly important for occupational therapists.

In vision rehabilitation, occupational therapists can help clients with contrast sensitivity problems by increasing the contrast of objects being viewed. Methods of modifying contrast include the environmental modifications that enhance contrast or add color contrast, lighting modifications that eliminate glare, mobility instruction, and the use of closed circuit televisions.[19] These interventions are described in detail in Chapters 10 and 14.

REFRACTIVE DISORDERS

Definition

Refraction is the term used to describe the evaluation of the optical system of the eye. We use the term *refractive error* to describe any disorder of refraction. When the optometrist performs the refraction, he or she determines whether the individual is emmetropic (absence of refractive error), myopic (nearsighted), hyperopic (farsighted), or astigmatic. The refraction

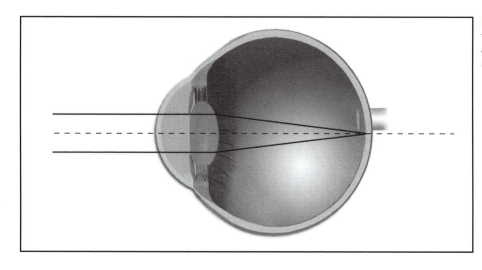

Figure 3-13. Light rays entering the eye are perfectly focused on the retina in emmetropia (Steinman).

is the examination procedure used to determine if a client will benefit from glasses and the exact prescription that is appropriate.

Classification of Refractive Conditions

Emmetropia

This term is used to describe the condition in which there is an absence of refractive error. In *emmetropia,* the light rays entering the eyes focus right on the retina. Figure 3-13 illustrates how the light rays entering the eye are perfectly focused on the retina in emmetropia. In such a case, the client is neither nearsighted nor farsighted and does not have astigmatism. Emmetropia is not necessarily considered normal, expected, or desirable. In fact, the average person is slightly hyperopic.

Myopia (Nearsightedness)

Myopia is a condition in which the light rays entering the eye focus in front of the retina. In myopia, the vision is blurred at distance but clear at near. Figure 3-14 shows why a client with myopia experiences blurred vision. The light rays entering the eye are focused in front of the retina because the optics of the eye are too strong relative to the length of the eye. The myopic eye has a longer axial length than the emmetropic or hyperopic eye. The human eye can make no internal adjustment to overcome the optical problem associated with myopia. An individual with myopia can squint, which actually does allow improved vision, but this is generally considered an unacceptable way to regain clarity because it can cause discomfort and is cosmetically unacceptable. Squinting helps compensate for the blur associated with myopia because it creates a pinhole effect. A pinhole effect occurs when

an individual views an object through a small opening in front of the eye. This setup will bring an object into focus on the retina regardless of refractive error. Any attempted focusing adjustment by the lens of the eye (accommodation) will simply make the blurred vision worse. Thus, a client with myopia will have to move closer to the object he/she is trying to view. A person who has myopia ("nearsightedness") will have better visual acuity at near than at distance if he or she is not wearing correction.

Hyperopia (Farsightedness)

Hyperopia is a condition in which light rays entering the eye focus behind the retina and the individual must accommodate to see clearly. This need to accommodate requires the use of muscular effort. The amount of effort necessary is greater when the individual looks at near. Figure 3-15 illustrates that to see clearly, a person with hyperopia must contract the ciliary muscle to change the shape of the lens in the eye and regain clarity. Contraction of the ciliary muscle leads to a change in focus and is referred to as *accommodation.* The effort that is necessary to accommodate is directly related to the degree of hyperopia. A very high degree of hyperopia requires so much muscular effort that it cannot be overcome and results in blurred vision. Moderate degrees of hyperopia can be overcome using accommodation. The constant need for accommodation, however, requires the use of muscular effort and leads to signs and symptoms, such as blurred vision, eyestrain, tearing, burning, inability to concentrate and attend, avoidance of visual tasks, and the need to move the object of interest closer or farther away. In younger people, small degrees of hyperopia are generally successfully overcome without symptoms. Remember that a low degree of hyperopia is considered normal, expected, and desirable. An older person with hyperopia (older than 45 to 50 years of

Figure 3-14. The light rays entering the eye are focused in front of the retina in myopia causing blurred vision (Steinman).

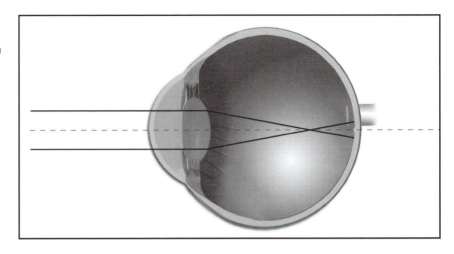

Figure 3-15a. To see clearly, a person with hyperopia must contract the ciliary muscle to change the shape of the lens in the eye and regain clarity (Steinman).

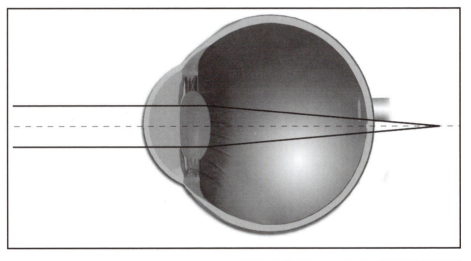

Figure 3-15b. After contracture of the ciliary muscle, the shape of the lens changes and light rays are now focused on the retina (Steinman).

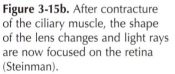

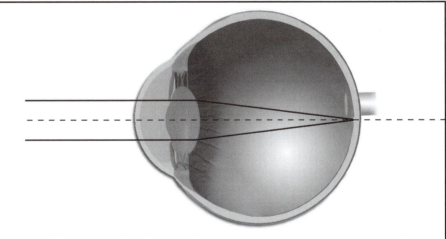

age) cannot accommodate well enough to compensate for the hyperopia and will, therefore, have better acuity at distance than at near. A younger person with hyperopia who can compensate with accommodation might have normal acuity at near but complain of eyestrain or blurry vision at near when tired.

Astigmatism

Astigmatism is a condition in which vision is blurred and distorted at both distance and near. An astigmatic eye is not spherical. Rather, it has an oval shape, and this causes the light rays entering the eye to focus at two different points. Figure 3-16 illustrates the

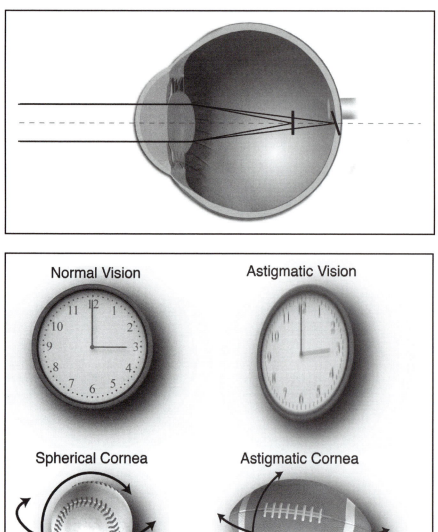

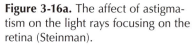
Figure 3-16a. The affect of astigmatism on the light rays focusing on the retina (Steinman).

Figure 3-16b. Distortion caused by uncorrected astigmatism (Steinman).

effect that astigmatism has on the light rays focusing on the retina. In order to see clearly, a person with astigmatism will attempt to accommodate. While accommodation may improve clarity in one direction (eg, vertical lines), accommodation never completely clears an image with astigmatism, and the effort that is necessary to accommodate may lead to discomfort. As discussed above for hyperopia, the degree of accommodation necessary is related to the degree and type of astigmatism. In some cases of astigmatism, accommodation has no beneficial effect on clarity. A very high degree of astigmatism generally cannot be overcome and results in blurred vision. If not corrected early, such problems can lead to amblyopia (loss of vision) and difficulty interacting with the environment. Moderate degrees of astigmatism can sometimes be overcome using accommodation. The constant need for accommodation, however, requires the use of muscular effort and leads to signs and symptoms, such as blurred vision, eyestrain, tearing, burning, inability to concentrate and attend, avoidance of visual tasks, and the need to move the object of interest closer or farther away. Small degrees of astigmatism are common and are generally successfully overcome without symptoms. A person with astigmatism will have reduced acuity at both distance and near, and may see stripes in one direction more clearly than stripes in another, so some letters may be easier to see than others.

Figure 3-17. The phoropter, an instrument used to find the combination of lenses that will provide the best possible vision for any client being examined (Steinman).

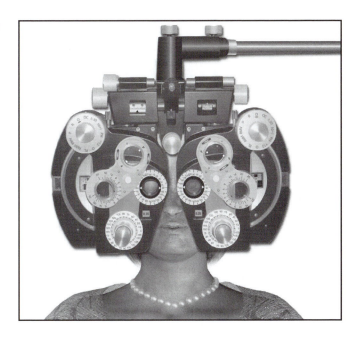

Clinical Assessment of Refractive Error

Refraction is a test that is performed by all eyecare professionals. There are two general methods of evaluating the refractive status of the eye: objective and subjective. Subjective tests can only be successfully performed with cooperative, attentive clients with reasonable cognitive ability. Objective testing, however, can be successfully performed at any age and for virtually any client.

Subjective Refraction Techniques

Most adults have had an eye examination at least once in their lives, and if so they are likely to remember the subjective refraction portion of the examination. The instrumentation used is illustrated in Figure 3-17. This instrument, called the *phoropter*, contains numerous lenses and allows the optometrist to find the combination of lenses that will provide the best possible vision for any client being examined. The procedure is very subjective and the optometrist will ask questions such as "Which is better, choice one or choice two?" or "Does this lens make the letters look clearer or just blacker and smaller?" This subjective approach works well for most of the population, but is generally not used with children under the age of 6 or 7 or with clients who have attention problems, perceptual and cognitive disorders, or other special needs.

Objective Refraction Techniques

The instrument illustrated in Figure 3-18 is called a *retinoscope*. This instrument permits the optometrist to accurately and objectively assess refractive status in virtually any client. The optometrist directs the light from the retinoscope into the client's eye and views the light that is reflected out of the eye. As the optometrist moves the retinoscope from side to side, he or she interprets the movement of the reflected light. Lenses are used to alter the movement of light and help the clinician determine the refraction and necessary eyeglass prescription. The procedure generally requires less than 1 minute per eye. It can be performed with or without eye drops. Using objective refraction, the optometrist or ophthalmologist is able to identify and correct refractive error in infants and patients who are unable to communicate.

Screening for Refractive Error

One can quickly screen for potential problems with refractive error when glasses are not available by having the patient look through a pinhole. The therapist can create this pinhole by simply punching a small hole in an index card. The pinhole bypasses the optics of the eye and focuses an image on the retina regardless of refractive error. The pinhole will greatly reduce the amount of light but will improve acuity regardless of the refractive error if the chart is illuminated enough. If reduced visual acuity improves with a pinhole, vision can usually be improved with eyeglasses.

Significance of Refractive Disorders for Occupational Therapy

It is important that significant refractive errors be treated by an eyecare practitioner before low vision

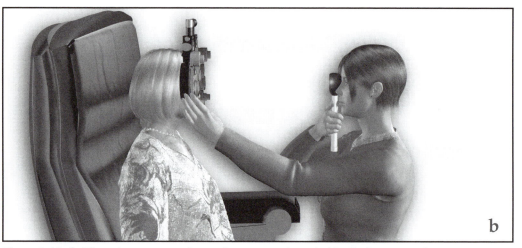

Figure 3-18a,b. The retinoscope can be used to accurately and objectively assess refractive status in virtually any client (Steinman).

rehabilitation is initiated. Some might feel that a small amount of refractive error might not significantly affect functional vision in someone who has severe vision loss. However, a good refraction should always be the very first step in the treatment of any low vision client, even with severe vision loss. Researchers have been surprised at the high prevalence of uncorrected refractive errors in the elderly population. The Baltimore Eye Study found that almost 70% of people reporting low vision based on reduced visual acuity alone actually only needed new eyeglasses.[22] Correctable vision impairment is associated with poorer general health, living alone, and lower socioeconomic status.[23]

VISUAL FIELD DISORDERS

Definition

The term *visual field* describes how much of the visual world an individual can see while looking straight ahead at a point of fixation. When a client has a normal visual field, he or she can see everything from the fixation point superiorly about 50 degrees, inferiorly about 70 degrees (Figure 3-19a), tempo-rally (toward the ear) about 90 degrees, and nasally (towards the nose) about 60 degrees (Figure 3-19b). Thus, with only one eye open, a client has a horizontal visual field of about 150 degrees and vertically about 120 degrees. This is true for each eye. Note that with both eyes open, the horizontal field only increases by about 30 degrees. While only the object being viewed directly is seen clearly, the client is able to see this entire area peripherally and can perceive movement and the presence of objects in the entire visual field. As indicated in Chapter 1, the definition of low vision includes not only visual acuity, but visual field as well. A person is said to be legally blind if the visual field is 20 degrees or less in the better-seeing eye. Therefore, an individual could have perfect 20/20 visual acuity and still have low vision. For Medicare, a diagnosis of a significant visual field deficit would qualify the client for low vision rehabilitation even if visual acuity is normal. Although visual requirements for driving vary from state to state, in most states the field requirement for driving is 120 degrees horizontally.

Causes of Visual Field Loss

Visual field loss is usually classified as central versus peripheral visual field loss. As described above and in Figure 3-19, the visual field is 150 degrees horizontally and about 120 degrees vertically. The central

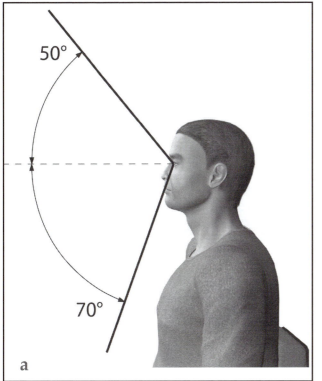
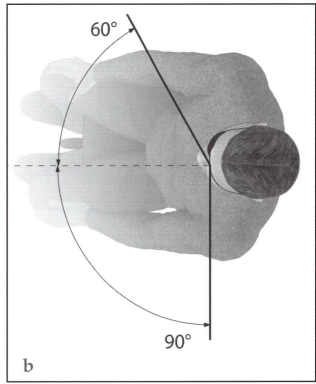

Figure 3-19a,b. Normal visual field (Steinman).

10 to 20 degrees are referred to as *central visual field*. Outside this central 20 degrees is referred to as *peripheral visual field*. We use these terms to classify visual field loss as central or peripheral visual field loss. The "rule of thumb" is that the thumb at arm's length is about 2 degrees; a fist is about 10 degrees wide.

Peripheral Visual Field Loss

Peripheral visual field problems are associated with many eye diseases and diseases that affect the brain, such as acquired brain injury, glaucoma, and retinitis pigmentosa (described in detail in Chapter 4). One of the most common peripheral visual field disorders is a right or left field loss, referred to as an *homonymous hemianopsia*. To understand why a client would lose vision to just one side, it is necessary to understand how visual information travels from the retina to the visual cortex (Figure 3-20a). Vision begins with the capture of images focused by the optical media on photoreceptors of the retina. The fibers from the upper half of each retina enter the optic nerve above the horizontal meridian, and those from the lower half enter below the horizontal meridian. Fibers from the periphery of the retina lie peripherally in the optic nerve, and fibers from the fovea lie centrally. This arrangement persists throughout the entire course of the visual pathways from the optic nerve through the chiasm, the optic tracts, and optic radiations.

Visual information from the right field strikes the nasal half of the retina of the right eye and the temporal half of the retina of the left eye. Similarly, visual information from the left field strikes the nasal half of the retina of the left eye and the temporal half of the retina of the right eye (see Figure 3-20a). When the fibers from each optic nerve reach the optic chiasm, a decussation takes place. The fibers from the temporal part of the retina remain on the temporal or outside aspect of the chiasm and are called *uncrossed fibers* (see Figure 3-20a). The nasal fibers of the retina cross over in the chiasm and are called *crossed fibers*. After leaving the chiasm, the fibers form the optic tract. Thus, all visual information originating from the right field travels in the left optic tract, and all visual information originating from the left field travels in the right optic tract. The fibers in the upper half of the tract originate from the upper half of the two retinas, and the fibers from the lower half of the tract come from the lower half of the two retinas. The fibers from the optic tract synapse in the lateral geniculate body. The cells of the lateral geniculate body give rise to new fibers, which form the optic radiation. These fibers then proceed to the cells of the visual cortex (see Figure 3-20a). Any lesion that affects the visual pathway on only the right or left side after this decussation takes place in the optic chiasm will affect either the left visual field or right visual field in both eyes. For example, Figure 3-

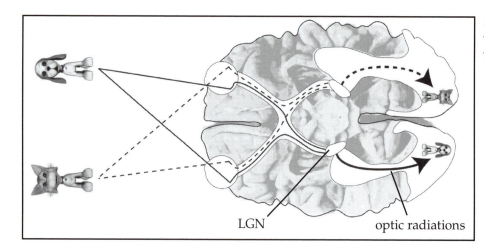

Figure 3-20a. Illustration of visual pathway from eye to visual cortex.

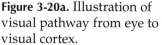

LGN   optic radiations

Figure 3-20b. If there is no lesion in the visual pathway, the individual sees both the cat and the dog.

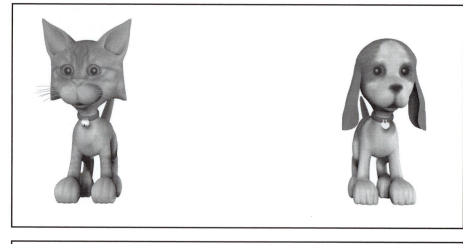

Figure 3-20c. If there is a lesion in the right side of the cortex, the individual will only see information from the right visual field (the dog only).

20b illustrates what a client with normal visual fields would see. Figure 3-20c illustrates a lesion on the right side of the brain and in this case the individual would only see the dog. Any damage to the eye or optic nerve will affect one eye. Any damage to the optic chiasm itself often affects both eyes, with a different effect on each eye. For example, the left field of the right eye and right field of the left eye may be affected. Brain injury associated with trauma or stroke often leads to this type of visual field loss and may require vision rehabilitation by occupational therapists.

Glaucoma is a disease that causes progressive peripheral field loss that could eventually lead to total loss of vision. A person with peripheral visual field loss due to glaucoma loses field in all directions, not just the left or right side. Thus, as the field loss progresses, it is like looking through a tube (Figure 3-21). Retinitis pigmentosa causes peripheral field loss that is similar to the loss caused by glaucoma.

Figure 3-21. Illustration of peripheral visual field loss characteristic of glaucoma (Steinman).

Central Visual Field Loss

The most common visual field loss that an occupational therapist is likely to encounter is central visual field loss associated with diseases of the macula, such as macular degeneration. This type of visual field loss is referred to as a *central scotoma*. A scotoma is defined as an island of absent or reduced vision in the visual field, surrounded by an area of normal vision.

Clinical Assessment of Visual Field Disorders

Peripheral visual field testing is generally performed in the office of the optometrist or ophthalmologist who refers the client for low vision rehabilitation. Standard field testing requires that a client maintain a steady fixation eye position. With people who have gaze instability, or severe attention deficits, visual field testing becomes more of an art. As a therapist teaches a client to function with gaze instability, he/she often combines field testing with instruction on controlling gaze position and may provide critical data on a client's visual fields. Central field testing is best performed using a simple screen set at 1 M (Tangent Screen) (Figure 3-22a,b), or using more expensive computerized visual field testing (Figure 3-22c). Unless one has a bowl perimeter, testing can be done using confrontation field testing methods described in Chapter 7. This requires no special equipment and can easily be performed by an occupational therapist.

Central visual field testing can be performed using a device called the Amsler Grid Test. The stan-dard Amsler Grid consists of a square grid of white horizontal and vertical lines on a black background (Figure 3-23). The client views this target with one eye open at a distance of about 13 inches. The client is asked to fixate the central dot and report if all the corners are visible, if the grid is uniform, and if any areas of the grid are distorted or missing.

Central field testing becomes more difficult to administer and interpret if people have central field loss because when they attempt to look directly at the fixation target in the center of the field test, the target disappears from view. As a result, people may look to the side of a target to see it, or some with recent vision loss just keep generating random searching eye movement trying to look at a fixation target. By adapting the standardized procedure, the eyecare practitioner or low vision therapist can not only describe a client's central fields, but also his or her fixation eye movements (see Chapter 10).

Significance of Visual Field Disorders for Occupational Therapy

The status of the visual field is an important measure of visual function that must be considered by the occupational therapist when developing a low vision rehabilitation treatment plan. In some cases, the visual field disorder is a secondary issue and in others it is the primary reason for the client's disability. Central field loss is the most common cause of low vision, and managing unstable fixation that results from central field loss presents a critical challenge in treatment. It

Figure 3-22a. Tangent screen (Steinman).

Figure 3-22b. Tangent screen (Steinman).

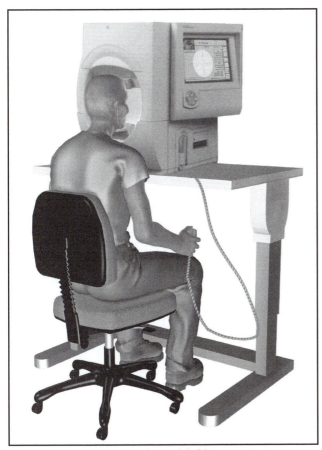

Figure 3-22c. Computerized visual field testing (Steinman).

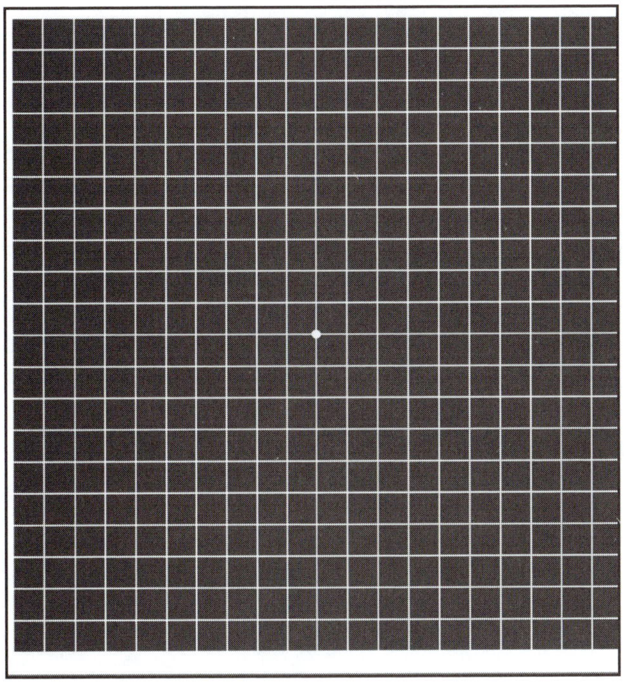

Figure 3-23. Amsler Grid (Steinman).

is important to remember that a client could have perfect visual acuity in both eyes and yet still have low vision based on a deficit in visual field that does not involve central vision.

SUMMARY

It is important for occupational therapists to understand visual acuity, contrast sensitivity, visual refraction, and visual field disorders. This chapter reviewed definitions, test procedures, and the significance of these problems in low vision clients.

REFERENCES

1. Freeman PB, Jose RT. *The Art and Practice of Low Vision.* 2nd ed. Boston: Butterworth-Heinemann; 1997.
2. Brilliant RL. *Essentials of Low Vision Practice.* Boston: Butterworth-Heinemann; 1999.
3. Bailey IL, Lovie JE. New design principles for visual acuity letter charts. *Am J Optom Physiol Opt.* 1976;53:740-745.
4. Sloan LL. New test charts for the measurement of visual acuity at far and near distances. *Am J Ophthalmol.* 1959;48:807-813.
5. Bailey IL, Lovie JE. The design and use of a new near-vision chart. *Am J Optom Physiol Opt.* 1980;57:378-387.
6. Legge GE, Ross JA, Luebker A, LaMay JM. Psychophysics of reading. VIII. The Minnesota Low-Vision Reading Test. *Optom Vis Sci.* 1989;66(12):843-853.
7. Haegerstrom-Portnoy G, Schneck ME, Lott LA, Brabyn JA. The relation between visual acuity and other spatial vision measures. *Optom Vis Sci.* 2000;77:653-662.
8. Whittaker SG, Lovie-Kitchin J. Visual requirements for reading. *Optom Vis Sci.* 1993;70(1):54-65.
9. Marron JA, Bailey IL. Visual factors and orientation: Mobility performance. *Am J Optom Physiol Opt.* 1982;59:413-426.
10. Kuyk T, Elliott JL. Visual correlates of mobility in real world settings in older adults with low vision. *Optom Vis Sci.* 1998;75:538-547.
11. Wood JM. Elderly drivers and simulated visual impairment. *Optom Vis Sci.* 1995;72:115-124.
12. Owsley C, Sloane ME. Contrast sensitivity, acuity, and the perception of "real-world" targets. *Brit J Ophthalmol.* 1987;71:791-796.
13. West SK, Rubin GS, Broman AT, Munoz B, Bandeen-Roche K, Turano K. How does visual impairment affect performance on tasks of everyday life? The SEE Project. Salisbury Eye Evaluation. *Arch Ophthalmol.* 2002;120(6):774-780.
14. Rubin GS, Roche KB, Prasada-Rao P, Fried LP. Visual impairment and disability in older adults. *Optom Vis Sci.* 1994;71(12):750-760.

15. Alexander KR, Derlacki DJ, Fishman GA. Visual acuity vs. letter contrast sensitivity in retinitis pigmentosa. *Vision Res.* 1995;35:1495-1499.

16. Elliott DB, Hurst MA. Simple clinical techniques to evaluate visual function in patients with early cataract. *Optom Vis Sci.* 1990;67:822-825.

17. Hawkins AS, Szlyk JP, Ardickas Z, Alexander KR, Wilensky JT. Comparison of contrast sensitivity, visual acuity, and Humphrey visual field testing in patients with glaucoma. *J Glaucoma.* 2003;12:134-138.

18. Rubin GS, Adamson IA, Stark WJ. Comparison of acuity, contrast sensitivity, and disability glare before and after cataract surgery. *Arch Ophthalmol.* 1993;111:56-61.

19. Cummings RW, Muchnick BG, Whittaker SG. Specialized testing in low vision. In: Brilliant RL, Ed. *Essentials of Low Vision Practice.* Boston, MA: Butterworth-Heinemann; 1999:47-69.

20. Arditi A. Improving the design of the letter contrast sensitivity test. *Invest Ophthalmol Vis Sci.* 2005;46:2225-2229.

21. Pelli DG, Robson JG, Wilkins AJ. The design of a new letter contrast chart for measuring contrast sensitivity. *Clin Vis Sci.* 1988;2:187-199.

22. Tielsch JM, Sommer A, Witt K, Katz J, Royall RM. Blindness and visual impairment in an American urban population. The Baltimore Eye Survey. *Arch Ophthalmol.* 1990;108(2):286-290.

23. Evans BJ, Rowlands G. Correctable visual impairment in older people: a major unmet need. *Ophthalmic Physiol Opt.* 2004;24(3):161-180.

Eye Diseases Associated With Low Vision

INTRODUCTION

This chapter reviews only the eye diseases that are the leading causes of low vision in the adult population and includes description, prevalence, risk factors, effect on vision, and treatment of each condition. The leading causes of severe visual impairment among white Americans in 2000 were age-related macular degeneration (AMD), accounting for 54% of visual impairment, with cataract (9%), diabetic retinopathy (6%), and glaucoma (5%) the next most common causes.[1] The leading causes of severe visual impairment in black persons were cataract (37%), diabetic retinopathy (26%), glaucoma (7%), and AMD (4%). Among Hispanics, glaucoma was the most common cause (29%), followed by AMD (14%), cataract (14%), and diabetic retinopathy (14%).[1] Therefore, while the relative prevalence may differ depending on race and ethnicity, the primary eye diseases that the occupational therapist will encounter when dealing with adult patients with low vision are AMD, diabetic retinopathy, glaucoma, and cataract.

AGE-RELATED MACULAR DEGENERATION

Description

AMD is a degenerative, acquired disorder of the central retina called the macula, which usually occurs in patients over age 55, and results in progressive, sometimes significant, irreversible loss of central visual function from either fibrous scarring or atrophy of the macula. It is the leading cause of vision loss in the adult population.

The macula is located roughly in the center of the retina and is a small and highly sensitive part of the retina responsible for detailed central vision. The fovea is the very center of the macula. The normal macula has a characteristic appearance and is more heavily pigmented than the surrounding retina (Figure 4-1). The macula allows us to appreciate detail and perform tasks that require central vision, such as reading, writing, recognizing faces, and driving.

To understand this disease, it is important to have an understanding of the anatomy of the retina and

Figure 4-1. The normal macula has a characteristic appearance and is more heavily pigmented than the surrounding retina (Steinman).

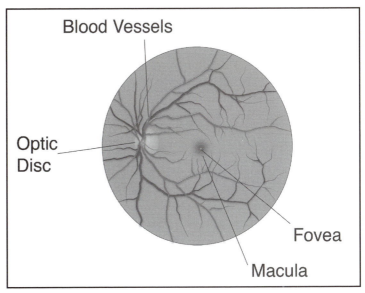

adjacent structures of the eye, which was reviewed in Chapter 2. As a brief review, the retina is composed of 10 layers. Two of the important layers that become an issue in AMD are the retinal pigment epithelium that is closest to the choroid, and the photoreceptors (cones and rods) (Figure 4-2). Beneath the retinal pigment epithelium of the retina are four additional layers (see Figure 4-2) ranging from the outside (furthest from the retina) to the inside (closest to the retina):

1. Sclera (white part of the eye)
2. Large choroidal blood vessels
3. Choriocapillaris
4. Bruch's membrane (separates the pigmented epithelium of the retina from the choroid)

The underlying etiology of AMD is poorly understood and no cure currently exists. The International ARM Epidemiological Study Group defined AMD in 1995.[2] AMD typically occurs in adults over the age of 50 and is characterized by any of the following problems:

1. Drusen: Drusen are discrete, round, slightly elevated whitish-yellow spots in the macular area and elsewhere in the retina. Drusen are one of the earliest signs of AMD and are typically clustered in the macular area. They may change in size, shape, color, and distribution over time.
2. Hyperpigmentation: Hyperpigmentation refers to areas of increased pigmentation and may not be associated with drusen.
3. Hypopigmentation: Hypopigmentation refers to depigmentation and is typically associated with drusen.

AMD is classified as either dry (nonexudative) or wet (exudative).

Dry AMD

Dry (nonexudative or atrophic) AMD accounts for 90% of all patients with AMD in the United States.[3] The disorder results from a gradual breakdown of the retinal pigment epithelium (RPE), the accumulation of drusen deposits, and loss of function of the overlying photoreceptors (Figure 4-3). Most patients with dry AMD experience gradual, progressive loss of central visual function. This loss of vision is more noticeable during near tasks, especially in the early stages of the disease. In an estimated 12% to 21% of patients, dry AMD progresses to cause vision levels of 20/200 or worse.[4,5] Neovascularization is not present in dry AMD.

Wet AMD

Although wet (exudative) AMD accounts for only 10% of patients with AMD, 90% of the AMD patients with significant vision loss have this form of the disease.[4,6] Wet AMD is characterized by the development of neovascularization in the choroid, leading to leakage of blood and subsequent elevation of the RPE (Figure 4-4). Patients with wet AMD tend to notice a more profound and rapid decrease in central visual function. The leakage of blood from the new choroidal vessels causes distorted vision, central scotoma, and blurred vision.[7] As the blood in the vitreous dissipates, vision might improve somewhat.

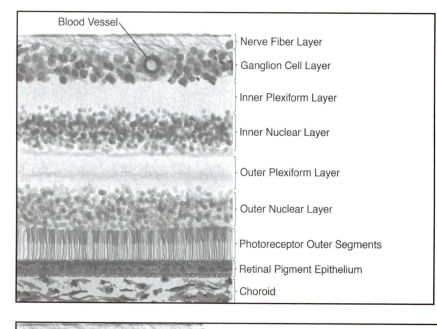

Blood Vessel

Nerve Fiber Layer

Ganglion Cell Layer

Inner Plexiform Layer

Inner Nuclear Layer

Outer Plexiform Layer

Outer Nuclear Layer

Photoreceptor Outer Segments

Retinal Pigment Epithelium

Choroid

Figure 4-2. Layers of the retina (Steinman).

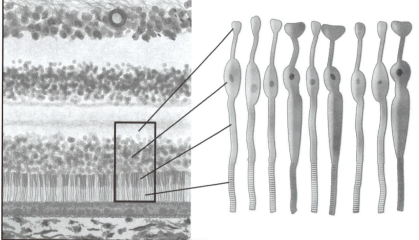

Figure 4-3. Photoreceptors (Steinman).

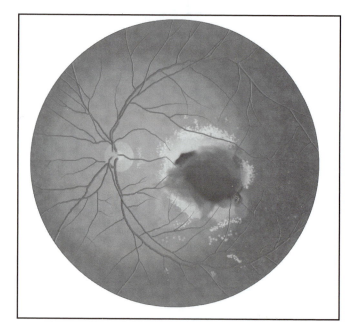

Figure 4-4. Wet AMD (Steinman).

Table 4-1.
Risk Factors Associated with Age-Related Macular Degeneration
Age
Smoking
Genetics
Female gender
Race (higher prevalence in whites)
High intake of fats
Elevated levels of serum cholesterol
Hypertension
Cardiovascular disease
Ultraviolet light exposure
Obesity
Cataract surgery

Prevalence

Most studies have indicated that AMD is the leading cause of low vision in developed countries.[8,9] The prevalence of AMD increases with age, and about 30% of patients 75 years of age and older are affected.[3,10] While AMD is the leading cause of visual impairment among white Americans (54%), it is less prevalent in black persons (4%) and Hispanics (14%).[1] Warren[11] reported on her experience as an occupational therapist working in a low vision program in an ophthalmology department. Thirty-seven percent of the patients referred for occupational therapy (low vision rehabilitation services) had AMD. Thus, low vision caused by AMD is the condition that occupational therapists will be most likely to treat.

Risk Factors

Table 4-1 lists the risk factors associated with AMD. Age is the most significant risk factor and clearly increases the risk of both developing AMD and of progressing to the late stages of the disorder.[12] Although age is a strong risk factor, AMD and vision loss do not inevitably occur with advancing age. People with an AMD-affected first-degree relative have a 50% lifetime risk of experiencing advanced AMD and vision loss, and tend to develop it earlier than those without a family history.[13] Smoking is associated with a fourfold increase in the risk of AMD and visual loss and, again, tends to promote earlier occurrence.[14] Studies have consistently implicated female gender as a risk factor. In the Framingham Eye Study, females with AMD outnumbered males by 50%, but this may have reflected the increased proportion of women in the older age groups. In the Beaver Dam Study, results controlling for age showed a twofold higher incidence of AMD in women than in men in the 75-

year and older group.[15] A relationship seems to exist between increased cumulative exposure to sunlight and ultraviolet radiation and wet AMD.[16] However, strong epidemiologic evidence is lacking. Weaker associations have been found with obesity, hypertension, macrovascular disease, raised cholesterol, and cataract surgery.

Dietary associations have also been found both with the signs of AMD and with progression to vision loss.[17-19] In a well-conducted prospective study, dietary fat intake was systematically analyzed after correcting for other risk factors.[18] Vegetable fat intake had the strongest relationship with AMD progression, with a relative risk of 3.82 for the highest fat-intake quartile compared with the lowest quartile. Higher intakes of total fat and of saturated, monounsaturated, polyunsaturated, and transunsaturated fats all raised the relative risk of AMD progression about twofold. Weekly fish intake and eating nuts two to three times a week were mildly protective. The implication is that a large shift away from vegetable oils, margarine, and fat-containing processed foods might reduce this epidemic of blindness in the elderly.

There is also evidence from a randomized controlled trial that high-dose dietary supplements of the antioxidants vitamin C, vitamin E, beta-carotene, and zinc can reduce the risk of progression from large or soft drusen to advanced AMD and visual loss by about 20% compared with controls over 6 years.[20] However, high-dose zinc can cause gastric irritation or anemia, and beta-carotene may possibly be associated with an increased risk of lung cancer among smokers. Uncontrolled studies suggest the antioxidants selenium, lutein, and zeaxanthin, which localize in the normal macula, may also help. There are as yet no studies to show whether dietary supplements are protective in patients in the early stages of dry AMD or in the 20% of patients who are at genetic risk.

Figure 4-5. The effect of macular scotoma in age related macular degeneration (Steinman).

It is not yet known whether major dietary adjustment and/or introduction of dietary supplements for large numbers of elderly people will be justified in terms of preventing blindness. On present evidence, we should identify people at increased risk of AMD, encourage them to stop smoking, and promote a diet that includes vegetables, fish, and nuts and reduces fatty foods laced with vegetable oils. Antioxidant supplements may be recommended if a fresh diet is impractical and if retinal signs of progression are present. Clients should not attempt to treat themselves with vitamin therapy and should be encouraged to ask the eyecare practitioner who is treating the retinal disease.

Effect on Vision

Visual acuity varies with the extent of the degeneration and includes distortion, blurred vision (especially at near), and central scotoma. With dry AMD, visual acuity can range from 20/20 to 20/400. Visual acuity with wet AMD is generally worse than 20/400. All patients with only AMD have central visual field defects with normal peripheral vision. Patients with AMD almost never go totally blind. However, if AMD occurs in both eyes, the visual acuity loss along with the central scotoma significantly impair a person's ability to engage in activities of daily living and quality of life. High-resolution tasks such as reading, writing, sewing, telling time, taking care of financial issues, driving, and distinguishing colors and facial

expressions usually become severely impaired. The consequences of AMD lead to loss of independence, lowered self-esteem, decreased mobility, increased risk of injury due to falls,[21,22] and depression.[23] Figures 4-5 and 4-6 illustrate what a patient might see with AMD and a macular scotoma.

Some patients with AMD have a phenomenon called Charles-Bonnet Syndrome or visual hallucinations.[24] This is an occasional complaint of patients with bilateral AMD and may occur spontaneously with no known external cause.

Treatment

Treatment of AMD includes various medical procedures to slow the progression of the disease, low vision rehabilitation including optical and nonoptical devices, environmental changes, education, support groups, and training in eccentric viewing, scanning, and reading.

Dry AMD

There is no medical treatment for dry AMD that can restore vision loss. Patients who have early retinal changes such as small drusen or mild pigmentation changes may experience no symptoms or may notice slowly progressive changes in visual function. These patients are generally seen by an eye doctor every 6 months. The eye doctor should educate the patient to look for signs of decreased vision, scotoma, and distortion by covering each eye and assessing visual

Figure 4-6a. The effect of macular scotoma in age-related macular degeneration (Steinman).

Figure 4-6b.

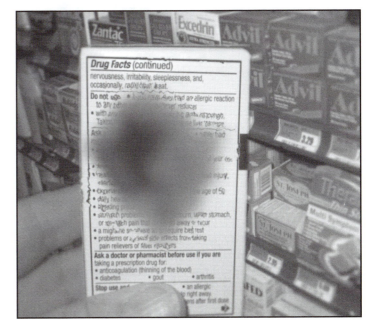

Figure 4-6c.

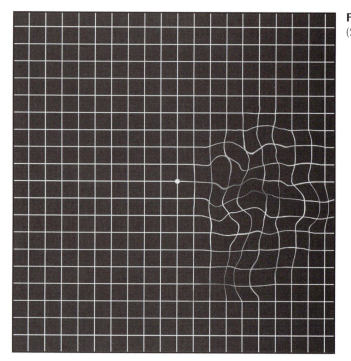

Figure 4-7. Amsler Grid. Distortion reported by patient (Steinman).

function monocularly. Some eye doctors give the patient an Amsler Grid (Figure 4-7) for self-assessment at home. The patient is able to see changes in the pattern of blur, distortion, and scotoma using the Amsler grid. Patients are instructed to return for further examination within 24 hours of the onset of new symptoms because 10% of patients with dry AMD progress to wet AMD. Studies have shown that early treatment of wet AMD may limit the extent of damage and vision loss.

Wet AMD

The principal aim of treatment of wet AMD is to preserve visual acuity and reduce the risk of additional severe vision loss for as long as possible. This goal can be accomplished by destroying the choroidal neovascularization without causing serious damage to the retina. There are several treatments for wet AMD that have proved effective in large-scale randomized clinical trials. These include laser photocoagulation, photodynamic therapy with verteporfin, and injection of drugs called angiogenesis inhibitors. None of these treatments is a cure for wet AMD and they do not improve vision. Each treatment may slow the rate of vision decline or stop further vision loss, but the disease and loss of vision may progress despite treatment. Sometimes treatments may result in an immediate decline in vision, in order to maximize vision in the long run. Treatments may also create blind spots around the central most part of vision, so that, for example, one or two letters in a word might be missing.

Laser Surgery

In the 1990s, most AMD treatment research focused on laser photocoagulation. The Macular Photocoagulation Study Group showed that laser photocoagulation was effective in the treatment of neovascularization if the vessels were not too close to the fovea.[25,26] This procedure uses a laser to destroy the fragile, leaky blood vessels. A high-energy laser beam is aimed directly onto the new blood vessels and destroys them, preventing further loss of vision. However, laser treatment also may destroy some surrounding healthy tissue and some vision. Therefore, laser surgery is more effective if the leaky blood vessels have developed away from the fovea. Only a small percentage of people with wet AMD can be treated with laser surgery, because in most patients the disease is near the center of the macula.[27] The risk of new blood vessels developing after laser treatment is high. Repeated treatments may be necessary. In some cases, vision loss may progress despite repeated treatments.

Photodynamic Therapy

A light-activated drug called verteporfin (Visudyne, Novartis Pharmaceuticals Corporation, East Hanover, NJ) is injected intravenously and travels throughout the body, including the new blood vessels in the eye. The drug tends to "stick" to the surface of new blood vessels. Low power, nonthermal laser light is shined into the patient's eye for about 90 seconds and activates the drug. The activated drug destroys the new blood

vessels and leads to a slower rate of vision decline. Unlike laser surgery, this drug does not destroy surrounding healthy tissue. Because the drug is activated by light, the patient must avoid exposing his or her skin or eyes to direct sunlight or bright indoor light for 5 days after treatment.

Photodynamic therapy has been shown to be effective in selected patients with certain types of wet AMD and slows the rate of vision loss.[28,29] It is important to understand how "success" or "effectiveness" is defined in these studies. In photodynamic therapy investigations, the researchers compare the risk of losing 15 or more letters (3 lines) of vision with the treatment versus placebo treatment. The studies demonstrating "success" reduced the risk of losing 15 letters from 61% in the placebo group to 33% in the verteporfin-treated group.[29] Thus, this treatment does not totally stop vision loss or restore vision in eyes already damaged by AMD. Rather, the treatment slows the progression of vision loss. Treatment results often are temporary and may need to be repeated as often as every 3 months.

Another important finding from these studies is that the greatest benefits of photodynamic therapy can be achieved if the diagnosis is made early and patients receive therapy before the disease causes too much destruction of the macula.[30]

Injections

In December 2004, the Food and Drug Administration (FDA) approved the latest treatment available for wet AMD, called Macugen (Eyetech Pharmaceuticals Inc. and Pfizer Inc., New York, NY). Macugen (pegaptanib) is a vascular endothelial growth factor (VEGF) inhibitor. When Macugen is injected into the vitreous humor of the eye, it has the capability of neutralizing a specific growth factor that promotes the growth of abnormal new blood vessels in eyes with wet AMD. The result is a decrease of the vascular growth and leakage that are together responsible for the visual loss in wet AMD. Macugen has demonstrated prevention of visual loss as compared with previous "standard of care" treatments that include photodynamic therapy.[31] Macugen has broad implications for treatment because it is effective in management of all types of new-onset wet AMD. In fact, Macugen has shown that it can prevent severe visual loss (defined as loss of three lines of visual acuity on the Snellen eye chart) in as many as 70% of the treated patients during the period of follow-up.[32] Unfortunately, Macugen only has a temporary effect and must be readministered approximately every 6 weeks. Furthermore, only 6% of patients experienced gains in visual acuity and the average patient in the study still lost visual acuity over the 2 years of treatment. Nevertheless, Macugen ther-

apy represents a major advance against AMD. It will prevent severe vision loss in the majority of appropriately selected patients with new-onset wet AMD and has opened the door to further investigation in the management of this potentially devastating disease.

Antioxidants

In a clinical trial called the Age-Related Eye Disease Study (AREDS), researchers found that high levels of antioxidants and zinc significantly reduce the risk of advanced AMD and its associated vision loss.[33] In this study, patients at high risk of developing advanced stages of AMD lowered their risk by about 25% when treated with a high-dose combination of vitamin C, vitamin E, beta-carotene, and zinc. In the same high-risk group, the nutrients reduced the risk of vision loss caused by advanced AMD by about 19%. For those study participants who had either no AMD or early AMD, the nutrients did not provide an apparent benefit.[33] It is important to understand that these nutrients are not a cure for AMD, nor will they restore vision already lost from the disease. However, they may delay the onset of advanced AMD.

The specific daily amounts of antioxidants and zinc used by the study researchers were 500 milligrams of vitamin C, 400 international units of vitamin E, 15 milligrams of beta-carotene (often labeled as equivalent to 25,000 international units of vitamin A), 80 milligrams of zinc as zinc oxide, and 2 milligrams of copper as cupric oxide. Copper was added to the AREDS formulation containing zinc to prevent copper deficiency anemia, a condition associated with high levels of zinc intake. People who are at high risk for developing advanced AMD should consider taking the formulation under the supervision of a retinal specialist.

It is also important to understand that there is no evidence that this AREDS formulation is effective for those diagnosed with early-stage AMD. The study did not find that the formulation provided a benefit to those with early-stage AMD.

Low Vision Rehabilitation

Although vision loss cannot be restored with medical treatment, low vision rehabilitation is an effective treatment that enables patients with dry AMD to function more effectively in activities of daily living (ADL) and regain independence in spite of the visual deficit. The occupational therapist's role in low vision rehabilitation includes instruction in the use of optical and nonoptical assistive devices; modification of lighting, contrast, and other environmental factors; treatment to learn adaptive eye movement patterns, scanning, and reading skills; education; and involvement in support groups.

Many patients with AMD may not have had a recent examination and may benefit from a change in eyeglass prescription. If prescribed in conjunction with low vision rehabilitation, most patients with AMD respond well to magnification at both distance and near (see Chapter 9). This is especially true with people who have the dry type of AMD. Because the loss of vision is gradual, these individuals may disengage from occupations such as reading for pleasure or sewing because the tasks become difficult, and are often not referred because the condition has not stabilized. These clients may develop depression, yet intervention may be as simple as instruction about lighting and a new set of reading glasses. These treatments are discussed in detail in Chapters 10 through 12.

DIABETIC RETINOPATHY

Description

Diabetic retinopathy is the most serious vision-threatening complication of chronic diabetes mellitus. Although there has been extensive research over several decades, knowledge about the etiology of diabetic retinopathy is still incomplete. Diabetes mellitus is a chronic, incurable disease with major medical and social implications. Diabetes occurs when the pancreas does not produce enough insulin or when the body cannot effectively use the insulin it produces. The vascular complications of diabetes involve all organ systems, including the eye. Diabetes is a heterogeneous group of diseases with different etiologies and clinical features. The two major categories of diabetes are insulin-dependent diabetes mellitus and noninsulin-dependent diabetes mellitus.

Insulin-Dependent Diabetes Mellitus

Insulin-dependent diabetes mellitus (IDDM), or type 1, or juvenile onset diabetes mellitus, occurs at any age but most often before the age of 30 years. It has an abrupt onset that requires medical treatment. Only approximately 10% of the patients with diabetes mellitus have type 1 diabetes and the remaining 90% have type 2 diabetes mellitus.

Noninsulin-Dependent Diabetes Mellitus

Noninsulin-dependent diabetes mellitus (NIDDM), or type 2, occurs at any age but most often in adults. It has an insidious onset and a subtle progression of

symptoms. People with NIDDM are frequently obese and sedentary.

Diabetes can affect the retinal blood vessels and cause hemorrhaging and abnormal growth of new blood vessels into the vitreous (Figure 4-8).

Diabetic retinopathy has four stages:

1. Mild Nonproliferative Retinopathy. At this earliest stage, microaneurysms occur. They are small areas of balloon-like swelling in the retina's tiny blood vessels.

2. Moderate Nonproliferative Retinopathy. As the disease progresses, some blood vessels that nourish the retina are blocked.

3. Severe Nonproliferative Retinopathy. Many more blood vessels are blocked, depriving several areas of the retina of their blood supply. These areas of the retina send signals to the body to grow new blood vessels for nourishment.

4. Proliferative Retinopathy. At this advanced stage, the signals sent by the retina for nourishment trigger the growth of new blood vessels. These new blood vessels are abnormal and fragile. They grow along the retina and along the surface of the clear, vitreous gel that fills the inside of the eye. By themselves, these blood vessels do not cause symptoms or vision loss. However, they have thin, fragile walls. If they leak blood, severe vision loss and even blindness can result. Proliferative diabetic retinopathy is the more advanced form of the disease, and in this condition the new blood vessels hemorrhage and grow into the vitreous. The vitreous may then pull away from the retina, causing additional hemorrhage into the vitreous. This blocks transmission of the light through the normally transparent vitreous, causing significant vision loss. Floaters or debris in the vitreous may follow along with retinal detachment and additional loss of vision. Fluid can also leak into the center of the macula, the part of the eye where sharp, straight-ahead vision occurs. The fluid makes the macula swell, blurring vision. This condition is called *macular edema*. It can occur at any stage of diabetic retinopathy, although it is more likely to occur as the disease progresses. About half of the people with proliferative retinopathy also have macular edema. Macular edema can cause significant loss of vision along with distortion of vision.

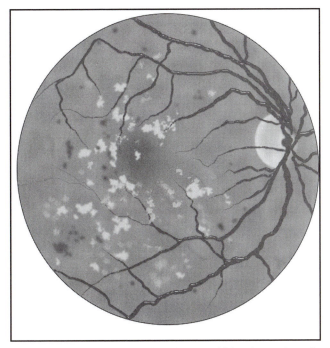

Figure 4-8. Diabetes can affect the retinal blood vessels and cause hemorrhaging and abnormal growth of new blood vessels into the vitreous (Steinman).

Prevalence of Diabetes and Diabetic Retinopathy

Diabetes mellitus affects 18 million people (about 6.3% of the population) in the United States.[34] An estimated 5.2 million people in the United States have diabetes and do not know it. Diabetes is the third leading cause of death in the United States after heart disease and cancer.[34] The prevalence of diabetes varies by age as indicated in Figure 4-9. Men and women are equally affected. About 1.3 million people aged 20 years or older are diagnosed per year with new cases of diabetes mellitus.[34]

Diabetic retinopathy is the leading cause of new blindness in the 20- to 64-year-old population in the United States. It accounts for about 12% of all new cases of blindness each year. In a recent study of US adults 40 years and older known to have diabetes, the estimated prevalence rates for retinopathy and vision-threatening retinopathy were 40.3% and 8.2%, respectively.[1] The estimated US general population prevalence rates for retinopathy and vision-threatening retinopathy were 3.4% (4.1 million persons) and 0.75% (899,000 persons).[1] Future projections suggest that diabetic retinopathy will increase as a public health problem, both with aging of the US population and increasing age-specific prevalence of diabetes over time.[1] The prevalence of diabetic retinopathy among patients with diabetes is more dependent on the duration of the disease than the patient's age.[35,36]

Risk Factors

Having diabetes (whether type 1 or type 2) puts an individual at risk of retinopathy. The risk of diabetic retinopathy increases the longer the person has the disease. The Wisconsin Epidemiologic Study of Diabetic Retinopathy found that after having diabetes for 20 years, almost all people with IDDM and more than 60% of those with NIDDM have some degree of retinopathy.[37-39] The duration of the diabetes is also the major determinant of the severity of retinopathy and progression. Other risk factors for diabetic retinopathy include poorly controlled blood sugar levels, high blood pressure, high blood cholesterol, pregnancy, obesity, and kidney disease.

Effect on Vision

Patients with diabetic retinopathy experience decreased, fluctuating, or distorted vision; focusing problems; loss of color vision; and floaters.[40] They frequently have impaired contrast sensitivity (because of cataracts), cloudy vitreous and retinal edema, are very glare sensitive, and are particular about lighting. They may also have a central scotoma due to effects of the diabetes on the macular area (maculopathy), loss of peripheral vision, and difficulty in dim light. Treatments (described below) often leave clients with a small island of good vision. They may see individual numbers or letters but not words. The treatments also produce scotomas in the periphery, or "swiss cheese" vision. Figure 4-10 illustrates the visual problems of a patient with diabetic retinopathy.

Treatment

During the first three stages of diabetic retinopathy, no treatment is needed, unless macular edema is present. The current approach in these early stages emphasizes the early recognition of retinopathy, vigorous control of blood glucose, and direct therapy with laser photocoagulation and vitreous surgery.[41]

Proliferative retinopathy is treated with laser surgery. This procedure is called laser photocoagulation treatment. Laser photocoagulation treatment helps to shrink the abnormal blood vessels. The ophthalmologist places 1,000 to 2,000 laser burns in the areas of the retina away from the macula, causing the abnormal blood vessels to shrink. Because a high number of laser burns are necessary, two or more sessions usually are required to complete treatment. Although the patient may lose some peripheral vision, scatter laser treatment can save central vision.

Laser photocoagulation treatment works better before the fragile new blood vessels have started to hemorrhage. Thus, patients with diabetic retinopathy

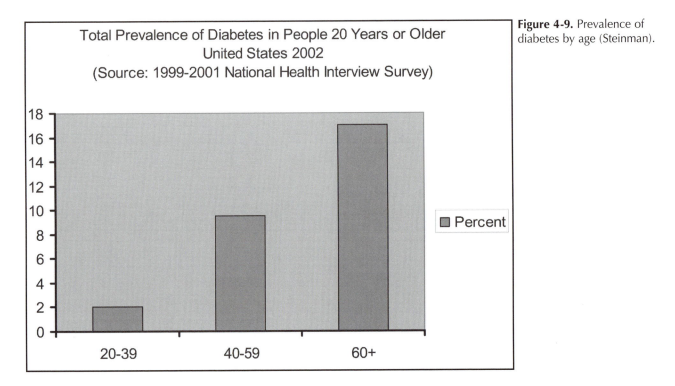

Figure 4-9. Prevalence of diabetes by age (Steinman).

Figure 4-10. Illustration of visual problems of a client with diabetic retinopathy (Steinman).

should be seen frequently for follow-up appointments. Even if hemorrhaging has begun, laser treatment may still be possible, depending on the amount of bleeding.

If the hemorrhaging is severe, the patient may need a surgical procedure called a *vitrectomy*. During a vitrectomy, blood is removed from the vitreous of the eye. During this procedure, the ophthalmologist inserts a small instrument into the vitreous of the eye and removes the vitreous that is clouded with blood. The vitreous is replaced with a salt solution.

Effectiveness of Treatment

Both laser surgery and vitrectomy are effective in reducing vision loss.[42,43] People with proliferative retinopathy have less than a 5% chance of becoming blind within 5 years when they get timely and appropriate treatment. Although both treatments have high success rates, they do not cure diabetic retinopathy. Once a patients has proliferative retinopathy, he or she will always be at risk for new hemorrhages.

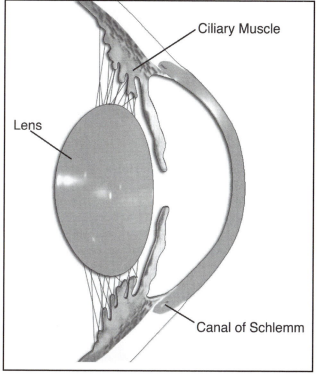

Figure 4-11a. Illustration of the front of the eye called the anterior chamber (Steinman).

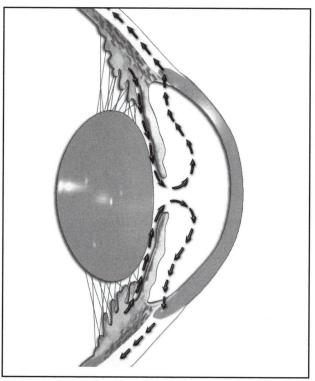

Figure 4-11b. Aqueous fluid flowing into anterior chamber (Steinman).

Low Vision Rehabilitation

The first step in low vision rehabilitation is an accurate refraction by the low vision optometrist and modification of the patient's eyeglasses, if required. One of the unique problems that occurs with diabetes is fluctuation of vision due to changes in refractive error and vitreous debris. This examination may need to be repeated if blood sugar levels are unstable. Visual acuities should be frequently remeasured. Because diabetes is often associated with other conditions treated by occupational therapists, the occupational therapist should routinely screen for vision loss, the onset of retinal edema with Amsler grid, and insure the patient has a thorough retinal examination by a eyecare practitioner every 6 months. In managing any client with diabetes, even those without diagnosis of low vision, the occupational therapist should always be vigilant for visual changes and frequent eye examinations.

A hallmark of diabetic vision changes is impaired contrast sensitivity. The low vision optometrist may prescribe special tinted lenses that block blue wavelengths in an attempt to improve contrast, eliminate glare, and reduce sensitivity to light (photophobia).[40] Patients often require multiple optical devices for various ADL. Because of their fluctuating vision, these individuals usually respond well to electronic magni-

fication, where contrast can be enhanced and magnification varied. The occupational therapist must often work with the patient to improve eccentric viewing if the macula is involved in the disease. Nonoptical devices such as a glucose monitor and insulin-syringe aids are helpful to the patient.[40] Chapter 15 covers the rehabilitation of the diabetic patient in detail.

GLAUCOMA

Description

Glaucoma is not a single clinical entity, but a group of ocular diseases with various etiologies that cause an elevation of pressure in the eye (intraocular pressure [IOP]), ultimately leading to progressive optic nerve damage and loss of peripheral visual function.

Figure 4-11a is an illustration of the front of the eye, called the *anterior chamber*. The ciliary body is the structure that produces *aqueous fluid*. This fluid is produced on a daily basis and flows to the front of the eye as illustrated in Figure 4-11b. Because the eye is a closed structure, if new fluid is produced on a daily basis, an equal amount of fluid must drain out of the eye to maintain the proper IOP. Under normal conditions, the amount of aqueous fluid that is produced

is equivalent to the amount that drains out on a daily basis, maintaining equilibrium and normal IOP. In glaucoma, this equilibrium is disrupted. There are a number of reasons why a person may develop glaucoma; however, regardless of the cause, the ultimate problem is loss of this equilibrium, which causes a rise in IOP. When the IOP rises, the nerve fibers exiting the eye through the optic nerve are compressed and damaged. The fibers that are generally affected in the beginning of the disease are those that carry information about our side vision (peripheral vision). Thus, in the initial stages of the disease, glaucoma leads to a gradual loss of peripheral vision. In most cases of glaucoma, the disease is painless because the rise in pressure is very gradual. As a result, a person with glaucoma may be unaware of the problem until the loss of vision is advanced. Thus, routine eye examinations are important to rule out this disease, and are the best way to avoid the consequences of glaucoma.

Glaucoma is classified as *primary* open-angle glaucoma when it is not related to another underlying condition, and *secondary* when the cause of the glaucoma is another ocular or systemic disease, trauma, or the use of certain drugs. Primary open-angle glaucoma represents about 70% of all glaucoma and is a chronic, progressive disease causing optic nerve damage and subsequent visual field loss. It occurs primarily in adults and generally affects both eyes, although one eye can have more advanced disease than the other. The majority of persons with primary open-angle glaucoma have elevated IOP. As described above, the elevated IOP observed in primary open-angle glaucoma usually results from decreased outflow of aqueous fluid from the eye. The cause of this decreased outflow is not well understood, but may be due to acceleration and exaggeration of normal aging changes in the area of the eye responsible for drainage of aqueous fluid (anterior chamber angle).[44,45]

How Is Glaucoma Diagnosed?

Several tests can help the eyecare professional detect glaucoma. Individuals at high risk for glaucoma should have a dilated pupil eye examination at least every 2 years. High risk factors for glaucoma include being an African American over 40, having a family history of the disease, or for the general population, being over 60. Those who are very nearsighted, have a history of diabetes, have experienced eye injury or eye surgery, or take prescription steroids also have an increased risk of developing glaucoma. Japanese ancestry is a risk factor for normal-tension glaucoma. Tests involved in the diagnosis of glaucoma include:

1. Tonometry: Measures the fluid pressure inside the eye. There are several methods for measuring eye pressure. The Schiotz and applanation tonometer measure eye pressure by directly applying pressure on the cornea. The tonometer is gently placed against the eyeball and a pressure reading is then taken from the instrument. These methods require anesthetic drops in both eyes. Eye pressure can also be measured by sending a puff of air onto the eyeball. No anesthetic eyedrops are required for this method.

2. Pupil dilation: Special eyedrops are used to temporarily enlarge the pupil so that the eyecare specialist can obtain a better view of the inside of the eye.

3. Visual field: This measures the entire area that can be seen when the eye is looking forward to document straight-ahead (central) and/or side (peripheral) vision. The test measures the dimmest light that can be seen at each spot tested. The test consists of responding by pressing a button every time a flash of light is perceived.

4. Visual acuity: This measures how well the person sees at various distances. While seated 20 feet away from an eye chart, the person is asked to read standardized visual charts with each eye. The test is performed with and without corrective lenses.

5. Pachymetry: This procedure uses ultrasonic waves to help determine corneal thickness.

Prevalence

Glaucoma is an incipient disease, and can progress to significant loss in peripheral visual function before the patient is aware that there is a problem. An estimated 2.5 million Americans have open-angle glaucoma,[46] although at least half of all cases may be undiagnosed.[47] Primary open-angle glaucoma represents about 70% of all adult glaucoma cases.[48] The Baltimore Eye Survey estimated the prevalence of glaucomatous blindness to be 1.7 per 1,000 in the general population, of which more than 75% was due to primary open-angle glaucoma.[49] Over 11% of all blindness and 8% of all visual impairment may be due to glaucoma.[48] Primary open-angle glaucoma is 6.6 to 6.8 times more prevalent and accounts for about 19% of all blindness among African Americans, compared with 6% of blindness in Caucasians.[49]

Risk Factors

Risk factors for glaucoma include general and ocular factors (Table 4-2). Age is a major risk factor for the development of glaucoma. The prevalence of glaucoma is 4 to 10 times higher in the older age groups

Table 4-2.		
Risk Factors for Primary Open Angle Glaucoma		
General	*Ocular*	*Nonocular*
Age	Elevated or asymmetric levels of IOP	Diabetes mellitus
Race	Diffuse or focal enlargement of cup	Vasospasms
Family history	portion of optic nerve	Systemic hypertension
	Diffuse or focal narrowing of	
	neuroretinal rim	
	Asymmetry of cup-to-disc ratios >0.2	
	Myopia	

Figure 4-12. Reduction in visual field caused by glaucoma (Steinman).

than in persons in their 40s.[50,51] Race is another major risk factor for primary open-angle glaucoma. African Americans develop the disease earlier, do not respond as well to treatment, are more likely to require surgery, and have a higher prevalence of blindness from glaucoma than Caucasians.[51] Finally, a family history of glaucoma is also a significant risk factor. Ocular factors include high IOP, thinness of the cornea, and abnormal optic nerve anatomy.

Effect on Vision

Left uncorrected, glaucoma causes a reduction in visual field (Figure 4-12), which may progress to total blindness. Central vision is generally unaffected until the end stage of the disease.[40]

Treatment

Treatment of glaucoma usually begins with medications (pills, ointments, or eyedrops) that help the eye either drain fluid more effectively or produce less fluid. Several forms of laser surgery can also help fluid drain from the eye.

Laser Trabeculoplasty

In this procedure, a high-intensity beam of light is aimed at the area of the anterior chamber of the eye responsible for drainage of the aqueous fluid. Several evenly spaced burns are used to stretch the drainage holes and allow the fluid to drain better. Laser trabeculoplasty is a common treatment if topical medication is not effective. The long-term benefits of this treatment of glaucoma remain controversial because its effectiveness diminishes over time.[52]

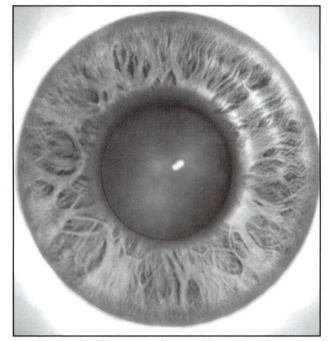 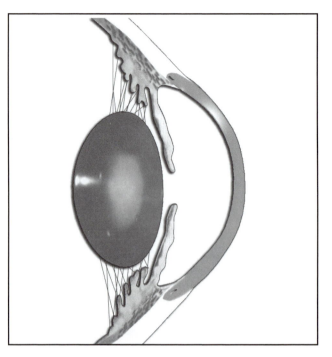

Figure 4-13a,b. Illustrations of a cataract (Steinman).

Conventional Surgery

Conventional surgery makes a new opening for the fluid to leave the eye. This often is done after medicines and laser surgery have failed to control pressure.

Conventional surgery is about 60% to 80% effective at lowering eye pressure. If the new drainage opening narrows, a second operation may be needed. Conventional surgery works best if the patient has not had previous eye surgery, such as a cataract operation.

Surgical intervention, the third level of treatment for primary open-angle glaucoma, is required in many moderate or advanced glaucoma patients to lower the pressure if other treatments have not been successful. This surgery is also designed to improve the drainage of aqueous from the eye. Filtration surgery usually results in a dramatic and stable reduction in IOP. [53] Although long-term control of IOP is often achieved, many patients must remain on medications and may require additional surgery.

Low Vision Rehabilitation

Many patients with AMD may not have had a recent examination and may benefit from a change in eyeglass prescription. For patients with intact central visual acuity and peripheral visual field loss, optical devices that minify the visual field can be used. This is the opposite approach used for macular degeneration. Visual scanning strategies to compensate for an overall field loss, similar to techniques used with field cuts associated with stroke, are used as well. Severe visual field loss associated with end-stage glaucoma can create problems with orientation and mobility and referral to an orientation and mobility (O&M) specialist is often required.[40] Electronic magnification may be useful because it allows for increased contrast and brightness.[40] The occupational therapist's role in low vision rehabilitation includes medication management, especially if eyedrops are used; instruction in the use of optical and nonoptical assistive devices; modification of lighting, contrast, and other environmental factors; referral for orientation and mobility; education; and involvement in support groups. Chronic glaucoma usually responds well to treatment if the patient consistently administers eyedrops. For this reason, the occupational therapist should carefully evaluate medication management if a patient experiences vision loss with chronic glaucoma.

CATARACT

Description

A cataract is an opacification or clouding of the lens in the eye that affects vision. Cataracts are very common in older people and can occur in either or both eyes. Figure 4-13 is an illustration of a cataract.

Age-related cataracts develop in two ways:

1. *Clumps of protein reduce the sharpness of the image reaching the retina.* The lens consists mostly of water and protein. When the protein clumps up, it clouds the lens and reduces the light that reaches the retina. The clouding may become severe enough to cause blurred vision. Most age-related cataracts develop from protein clumpings. When a cataract is small, the cloudiness affects only a small part of the lens. Over time, the cloudy area in the lens may get larger, and the cataract may increase in size.

2. *The clear lens slowly changes to a yellowish/brownish color.* The clear lens slowly changes color with age. At first, the amount of tinting may be small and may not cause a vision problem. Over time, increased tinting may make it more difficult to read and perform other routine activities. This gradual change in the amount of tinting does not affect the sharpness of the image transmitted to the retina. With advanced lens discoloration, a person may have difficulty identifying colors.

How Is a Cataract Diagnosed?

A cataract is easily detected in the course of any routine eye examination. The eyecare provider finds reduced visual acuity that cannot be improved by modifying the patient's prescription. After dilating the pupil, the eye doctor uses instruments that provide views of the lens under a variety of magnified conditions. This direct examination of the lens allows the eyecare provider to detect and diagnose the condition.

Prevalence

Eye Diseases Prevalence Research Group completed a research study in 2004 designed to determine the prevalence of cataract in the United States and to project the expected change in these prevalence figures by 2020.[54] They collected data from major population-based studies in the United States. They found that an estimated 20.5 million (17.2%) Americans older than 40 years have cataract in either eye. Women have a significantly higher age-adjusted prevalence of cataract than men in the United States. The total number of persons who have cataract is estimated to rise to 30.1 million by 2020. They concluded that the number of Americans affected by cataract and undergoing cataract surgery will dramatically increase over the next 20 years as the US population ages.[54]

Risk Factors

The main risk for developing cataracts is aging. By age 65, about half of all Americans have developed some degree of lens clouding, although it may not impair vision. Other significant factors are diabetes, a family history of cataracts, previous eye injury or inflammation, previous eye surgery, prolonged use of corticosteroids, excessive exposure to sunlight, and smoking.

Effect on Vision

A cataract usually develops slowly and causes no pain. As a result, most people are unaware of its development until it begins to interfere with everyday activities. Symptoms of a cataract include:

- Blurry vision
- Increasing difficulty with vision at night
- Sensitivity to light and glare
- Poor contrast sensitivity
- Halos around lights
- The need for brighter light for reading and other activities
- Frequent changes in eyeglass or contact lens prescription
- Fading or yellowing of colors
- Double vision in a single eye

Figure 4-14 illustrates the effect of cataract on vision.

Treatment

The only effective treatment for a cataract is surgery to remove the clouded lens and replace it with a clear lens implant. The lens implant can correct refractive error as well. In some cases, one eye is corrected to focus at near and the other to focus at distance. Cataracts cannot be cured with medications, dietary supplements, exercise, or optical devices. However, in the early stages of cataract development, the symptoms may be improved with new eyeglasses, brighter lighting, antiglare sunglasses, or magnifying lenses. When these measures are no longer effective, surgery is necessary. Ophthalmologists treat cataract surgically when vision loss interferes with a person's activities, such as working, driving, reading, or watching TV. Typically, if a person requires surgery on both eyes, the surgery is performed on each eye at separate times, usually about 4 to 8 weeks apart.

Cataract removal is one of the most common, safest, and most effective types of eye surgery. More than 1.5 million cataract operations are performed

Figure 4-14. Illustration of visual problems of a client with a cataract (Steinman).

each year. In a study of about 18,000 patients, Desai et al reported that 92% of patients without other eye disease achieved 20/40 or better visual acuity.[55] The main risk indicators associated with visual outcomes and complications related to surgery were age, other eye diseases, diabetes, and stroke. Other studies have reported similar results.[56,57]

There are two types of cataract surgery. The most common procedure is called *phacoemulsification*. During this procedure, the surgeon removes the cataract but leaves most of the outer layer (lens capsule) in place. The capsule helps support the lens implant when it is inserted. During phacoemulsification, the ophthalmologist makes a small incision where the cornea meets the conjunctiva and inserts a needle-thin probe. The surgeon then uses the probe, which vibrates with ultrasound waves, to break up (emulsify) the cataract and suction out the fragments. The lens capsule is left in place to provide support for the lens implant. This procedure is sometimes referred to as *small incision cataract surgery*. The other procedure is called *extracapsular surgery*. This technique is generally used if the cataract has advanced beyond the point where phacoemulsification can effectively break up the clouded lens. This procedure requires a larger incision where the cornea and sclera meet. Through this incision, the ophthalmologist opens the lens capsule, removes the nucleus in one piece and vacuums out the softer lens cortex, leaving the capsule in place. With either procedure, after the lens has been removed, it is replaced with an artificial lens, called an intraocular

lens (IOL). An IOL is a clear, plastic lens that requires no care and becomes a permanent part of the person's eye. If a person cannot have an IOL because of some other eye disease or problems during surgery, a soft contact lens, or glasses that provide high magnification, would be required to obtain clear vision.

Although cataract surgery is one of the most effective surgical procedures, there are potential risks, including inflammation, infection, bleeding, swelling, retinal detachment, and glaucoma. Occasionally, cataract surgery fails to improve vision because of conditions such as glaucoma or macular degeneration.

Another potential complication of cataract surgery is a condition called *posterior capsule opacification*. Common terms for this condition are second cataract or after cataract. This condition occurs when the back of the lens capsule (the part of the lens that isn't removed during surgery) eventually becomes cloudy and blurs the client's vision. Posterior capsule opacification can develop months or even years after cataract surgery and occurs about 25% of the time. Treatment for posterior capsule opacification involves a technique called YAG laser capsulotomy, in which a laser beam is used to make a small opening in the clouded capsule to let light pass through. This is a quick and painless outpatient procedure that usually takes less than 5 minutes.

Low Vision Rehabilitation

Because visual impairment from cataracts can be corrected, cataracts rarely are the primary diagnosis

of moderate or severe vision loss. As normal lens changes in the eyes of clients over 80 years old involve mild cataracts, in most cases of cataracts, low vision rehabilitation involves managing the mild impairment in contrast sensitivity, light sensitivity, and visual acuity in older patients with a nonvisual primary diagnosis. In some cases, especially when other visual pathologies are present, if a client is medically fragile or refuses the surgery, more severe cataracts are not removed. When moderate cataracts are involved, treatment focus is on management of glare, careful control of lighting, and environmental interventions and electronic devices to maximize contrast of reading material and objects with good results. Severe cataracts left untreated will result in profound vision loss.

SUMMARY

It is important for the occupational therapist specializing in low vision rehabilitation to keep updated about the latest research regarding eye pathology and treatment. In a multidisciplinary low vision rehabilitation setting, the occupational therapist often is involved in helping clients with medication management. With clients who have active pathology, a treatment plan usually includes instructing the client about how to self-monitor for vision changes and educating the client regarding the cause, treatment, and prognosis associated with eye diseases. In a home care, general outpatient, or inpatient setting where the occupational therapist does not practice with eyecare providers, the occupational therapist who specializes in low vision plays an active role in insuring that patients are receiving appropriate eyecare and insuring appropriate referrals. In inpatient settings with older persons who typically also have nonvisual primary diagnoses, the occupational therapist often is the first to identify the need for a referral to a low vision optometrist. In these settings, the occupational therapist may provide stop-gap, nonoptical, low vision interventions necessary to maintain a rehabilitation program while the patient is waiting for an eye examination.

REFERENCES

1. Congdon N, O'Colmain B, Klaver CC, et al. Causes and prevalence of visual impairment among adults in the United States. *Arch Ophthalmol.* 2004;122(4):477-485.
2. Bird AC, Bressler NM, Bressler SB, et al. An international classification and grading system for age-related maculopathy and age-related macular degeneration. *Surv Ophthalmol.* 1995;39:367-374.
3. Klein R, Klein BEK, Linton K. Prevalence of age-related maculopathy. The Beaver Dam Study. *Ophthalmology.* 1992;99:933-943.
4. Hyman LG, Lilienfeld AM, Ferris FL 3rd, Fine SL. Senile macular degeneration: a case control study. *Am J Epidemiol.* 1983;118:213-227.
5. Murphy RP. Age-related macular degeneration. *Ophthalmology.* 1986;93:969-971.
6. Ferris FLI, Fine SL, Hyman LA. Age-related macular degeneration and blindness due to neovascular maculopathy. *Arch Ophthalmol.* 1984;102:1640-1642.
7. Fine AM, Elman MJ, Ebert JE, Prestia PA, Starr JS, Fine SL. Earliest symptoms caused by neovascular membranes in the macula. *Arch Ophthalmol.* 1986;104:513-514.
8. Schmidt-Erfurth U, Miller JW, Sickenberg M, et al. Photodynamic therapy with verteporfin for choroidal neovascularization caused by age-related macular degeneration: results of treatments in a phase 1 and 2 study. *Arch Ophthalmol.* 1999;117:1177-1187.
9. Schwartz SD. Age-related maculopathy and age-related macular degeneration. In: Silverstone B, et al, Eds. *The Lighthouse Handbook on Vision Impairment and Vision Rehabilitation.* New York: Oxford University Press; 2000.
10. Leibowitz HM, Krueger DE, Maunder LR, et al. The Framingham Eye Study monograph: An ophthalmological and epidemiological study of cataract, glaucoma, diabetic retinopathy, macular degeneration, and visual acuity in a general population of 2631 adults, 1973-1975. *Surv Ophthalmol.* 1980;24(Suppl):335-610.
11. Warren M. Providing low vision rehabilitation services with occupational therapy and ophthalmology: a program description. *Am J Occup Ther.* 1995;49(9):877-883.
12. Hirvela H, Luukinen H, Laara E, Sc L, Laatikainen L. Risk factors of age-related maculopathy in a population 70 years of age or older. *Ophthalmology.* 1996;103(6):871-877.
13. Klaver CC, Wolfs RC, Assink JJ, van Duijn CM, Hofman A, de Jong PT. Genetic risk of age-related maculopathy. *Arch Ophthalmol.* 1998;116:1646-1651.
14. Klein R, Klein BE, Franke T. The relationship of cardiovascular disease and its risk factors to age-related maculopathy. The Beaver Dam Eye Study. *Ophthalmology.* 1993;100(3):406-414.
15. Klein R, et al. The five-year incidence and progression of age-related maculopathy: The Beaver Dam Study. *Ophthalmology.* 1997;104:7-21.
16. Newsome D. Medical treatment of macular diseases. *Ophthalmol Clin North Am.* 1993;6:307-314.
17. Cho E, Hung S, Willett WC, et al. Prospective study of dietary fat and the risk of age-related macular degeneration. *Am J Clin Nutr.* 2001;73(2):209-218.
18. Seddon JM, Cote J, Rosner B. Progression of age-related macular degeneration: association with dietary fat, transunsaturated fat, nuts, and fish intake. *Arch Ophthalmol.* 2003;121(12):1728-1737.
19. Seddon JM, Rosner B, Sperduto RD, et al. Dietary fat and risk for advanced age-related macular degeneration. *Arch Ophthalmol.* 2001;119(8):1191-1199.
20. Age-Related Eye Disease Study Research Group. A randomized, placebo-controlled, clinical trial of high-dose supplementation with vitamins C and E, beta carotene, and zinc for age-related macular degeneration and vision loss: AREDS report no. 8. *Arch Ophthalmol.* 2001;119(10):1417-1436.
21. Ivers RQ, Cumming RG, Mitchell P. Visual impairment and risk of falls and fracture. *Inj Prev.* 2002;8(3):259.
22. de Boer MR, Pluijm SM, Lips P, et al. Different aspects of visual impairment as risk factors for falls and fractures in older men and women. *J Bone Miner Res.* 2004;19(9):1539-1547.

23. Brody BL, Gamst AC, Williams RA, et al. Depression, visual acuity, comorbidity, and disability associated with age-related macular degeneration. *Ophthalmology*. 2001;108(10):1893-1900; discussion 1900-1.

24. Siatkowski RM, Zimmer B, Rosenberg PR. The Charles-Bonnet syndrome. *J Clin Neuroophthalmol*. 1990;10:215-218.

25. Argon laser photocoagulation for neovascular maculopathy. Five-year results from randomized clinical trials. Macular Photocoagulation Study Group. *Arch Ophthalmol*. 1991;109(8):1109-1114.

26. Krypton laser photocoagulation for idiopathic neovascular lesions. Results of a randomized clinical trial. Macular Photocoagulation Study Group. *Arch Ophthalmol*. 1990;108(6):832-837.

27. Ciulla TA, Danis RP, Harris A. Age-related macular degeneration: a review of experimental treatments. *Surv Ophthalmol*. 1998;43(2):134-146.

28. TAP Study Group. Photodynamic therapy of subfoveal choroidal neovascularization in age-related macular degeneration with verteporfin: one-year results of 2 randomized clinical trials—TAP report. Treatment of age-related macular degeneration with photodynamic therapy. *Arch Ophthalmol*. 1999;117(10):1329-1345.

29. Verteporfin therapy of subfoveal choroidal neovascularization in age-related macular degeneration: two-year results of a randomized clinical trial including lesions with occult with no classic choroidal neovascularization—verteporfin in photodynamic therapy report 2. *Arch Ophthalmol*. 2001;131(5):541-560.

30. Bressler NM. Early detection and treatment of neovascular age-related macular degeneration. *J Am Board Fam Pract*. 2002;15:142-152.

31. Gragoudas ES, Adamis AP, Cunningham ET Jr, Feinsod M, Guyer DR; VEGF Inhibition Study in Ocular Neovascularization Clinical Trial Group. Pegaptanib for neovascular age-related macular degeneration. *N Engl J Med*. 2004;351(27):2805-2816.

32. Azab M, Benchaboune M, Blinder KJ, et al. Verteporfin therapy of subfoveal choroidal neovascularization in age-related macular degeneration: meta-analysis of 2-year safety results in three randomized clinical trials: Treatment of Age-Related Macular Degeneration With Photodynamic Therapy and Verteporfin in Photodynamic Therapy Study Report no. 4. *Retina*. 2004;24(1):1-12.

33. AREDS. A randomized, placebo-controlled, clinical trial of high-dose supplementation with vitamins C and E, beta carotene, and zinc for age-related macular degeneration and vision loss: AREDS report no. 8. *Arch Ophthalmol*. 2001;119(10):1417-1436.

34. National Institute of Diabetes and Digestive and Kidney Diseases. *National Diabetes Statistics Fact Sheet: General Information and National Estimates on Diabetes in the United States*, 2003. Bethesda, MD: US Department of Health and Human Services, National Institutes of Health; 2003.

35. Klein R, Klein BE, Moss SE, Davis MD, DeMets DL. The Wisconsin Epidemiologic Study of Diabetic Retinopathy. X. Four-year incidence and progression of diabetic retinopathy when age at diagnosis is 30 years or more. *Arch Ophthalmol*. 1989;107(2):244-249.

36. Klein R, Klein BE, Moss SE, Davis MD, DeMets DL. The Wisconsin Epidemiologic Study of Diabetic Retinopathy. IX. Four-year incidence and progression of diabetic retinopathy when age at diagnosis is less than 30 years. *Arch Ophthalmol*. 1989;107(2):237-243.

37. Klein R. The epidemiology of diabetic retinopathy: findings from the Wisconsin Epidemiologic Study of Diabetic Retinopathy. *Int Ophthalmol Clin*. 1987;27(4):230-238.

38. Klein R, Klein BE, Moss SE, Davis MD, DeMets DL. The Wisconsin epidemiologic study of diabetic retinopathy. II. Prevalence and risk of diabetic retinopathy when age at diagnosis is less than 30 years. *Arch Ophthalmol*. 1984;102(4):520-526.

39. Klein R, Klein BE, Moss SE, Davis MD, DeMets DL. The Wisconsin epidemiologic study of diabetic retinopathy. III. Prevalence and risk of diabetic retinopathy when age at diagnosis is 30 or more years. *Arch Ophthalmol*. 1984;102(4):527-532.

40. Brilliant RL. *Essentials of Low Vision Practice*. Boston: Butterworth-Heinemann; 1999.

41. Horowitz A, Leonard E, Reinhardt J. Measuring psychosocial and functional outcomes of a group model of vision rehabilitation services for older adults. *J Vis Impairment & Blind*. 2000;94(5):328-338.

42. Early Treatment Diabetic Retinopathy Study Research Group. Photocoagulation for diabetic macular edema. Early Treatment Diabetic Retinopathy Study report number 1. *Arch Ophthalmol*. 1985;103(12):1796-1806.

43. Smiddy WE, Feuer W, Irvine WD, Flynn HW Jr, Blankenship GW. Vitrectomy for complications of proliferative diabetic retinopathy. Functional outcomes. *Ophthalmology*. 1995;102(11):1688-1695.

44. Alvarado J, Murphy C, Juster R. Trabecular meshwork cellularity in primary open-angle glaucoma and nonglaucomatous normals. *Ophthalmology*. 1984;91:564-579.

45. Grierson I. What is open angle glaucoma? *Eye*. 1987;1:15-28.

46. Quigley HA. Models of open-angle glaucoma prevalence and incidence in the United States. *Invest Ophthalmol Vis Sci*. 1997;38:83-91.

47. Prevent Blindness America. *Vision Problems in the U.S.* Schaumburg, IL: Prevent Blindness America; 1994.

48. Leske MC, Rosenthal J. The epidemiologic aspects of open-angle glaucoma. *Am J Epidemiol*. 1979;109:250-272.

49. Sommer A, Tielsch JM, Katz J, et al. Racial differences in the cause-specific prevalence of blindness in East Baltimore. *N Engl J Med*. 1991;325:1412-1417.

50. Hollows FC, Graham PA. Intraocular pressure, glaucoma, and glaucoma suspects in a defined population. *Br J Ophthalmol*. 1966;50:570-586.

51. Tielsch JM, Sommer A, Katz J, Royall RM, Quigley HA, Javitt J. Racial variations in the prevalence of primary open-angle glaucoma. The Baltimore Eye Survey. *JAMA*. 1991;266:369-374.

52. Baez K, Spaeth GL. Argon laser trabeculoplasty controls one third of patients with progressive, uncontrolled open-angle glaucoma for five years. *Trans Am Ophthalmol Soc*. 1991;84:47-58.

53. Werner EB, Drance SM, Schulzer M. Trabeculectomy and the progression of glaucomatous visual field loss. *Arch Ophthalmol*. 1977;95:1374-1377.

54. Congdon N, Vingerling JR, Klein BE, et al. Prevalence of cataract and pseudophakia/aphakia among adults in the United States. *Arch Ophthalmol*. 2004;122:487-494.

55. Desai P. The National Cataract Surgery Survey: II. Clinical outcomes. *Eye*. 1993;7(Pt 4):489-494.

56. McGwin G Jr, Scilley K, Brown J, Owsley C. Impact of cataract surgery on self-reported visual difficulties: comparison with a no-surgery reference group. *J Cataract Refract Surg*. 2003;29(5):941-948.

57. Desai P, Reidy A, Minassian DC, Vafidis G, Bolger J. Gains from cataract surgery: visual function and quality of life. *Br J Ophthalmol*. 1996;80(10):868-873.

Optics of Lenses, Refraction, and Magnification

INTRODUCTION

Optical devices are an important part of low vision rehabilitation and help clients compensate for impaired visual acuity and see objects more effectively at near, intermediate, and far distances. These optical devices include handheld magnifiers, spectacle magnifiers, stand magnifiers, and telescopes. The low vision eyecare practitioner ultimately prescribes these devices. The occupational therapist contributes to the selection of the device, evaluates these devices with the tasks the client wishes to perform, and plays the key role in teaching the client how to use the optical aids in various activities of daily living (ADL). To teach a client how to effectively utilize these devices, however, requires an understanding of the basic principles of lenses, optics, accommodation, and refraction. The objective of this chapter is to review these principles so that an occupational therapist can function comfortably in this role. Chapter 13 provides details about the devices and instructional methods that can be used to teach clients how to use these aids.

LENSES

Three types of lenses are used for eyeglass prescriptions and low vision optical devices: convex, concave, and cylindrical.

Convex Lens (Plus Lens)

A convex lens is thicker in the middle and thinner at the edges (Figure 5-1) and is also referred to as a plus lens, because when an optometrist writes a prescription for a convex lens the symbol "+" is used. Convex lenses are used by eye doctors when prescribing glasses for hyperopia (farsightedness), as described in Chapter 2.

A typical prescription for a client with hyperopia (farsightedness) would look like this:

OD: +1.50
OS: +1.50

In this case, the acronym OD is used to designate the right eye, or oculus dextrus, and OS is the acronym for the left eye, or oculus sinister. Occasionally,

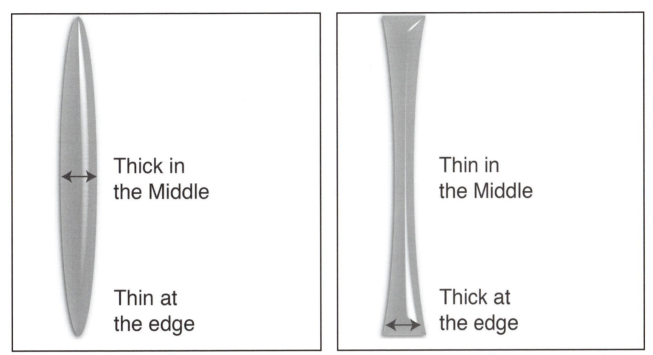

Figure 5-1. A convex lens is thicker in the middle and thinner at the edges (Steinman).

Figure 5-2. A concave lens is thicker at the edges and thinner in the middle (Steinman).

you will see the acronym OU used. This is used to refer to both eyes, or oculus uturque.

Convex lenses are also used in most low vision optical devices such as handheld magnifiers, stand magnifiers, spectacle magnifiers, and telescopes (Chapter 13). The therapist can quickly check to see if a client has been prescribed a plus lens for hyperopia by looking through it. If distance objects are blurred and near objects clear, it is a convex lens. Note that because the lens compensates for hyperopia, it will have an effect opposite to the refractive error, making objects clear at near.

Concave Lens (Minus Lens)

A concave lens is thinner in the middle and thicker at the edges (Figure 5-2) and is also referred to as a minus lens. When an optometrist writes a prescription for a convex lens, the minus symbol is used. Concave lenses are used by eye doctors when prescribing glasses for myopia (nearsightedness), as described in Chapter 2.

A typical prescription for a client with myopia (nearsightedness) would look like this:

OD: -1.50
OS: -1.50

The therapist can quickly check to see if a client has been prescribed a concave lens for myopia by looking through it. If distance objects look smaller and

are clear, it is a concave lens, opposite to the effect of myopia.

Cylindrical Lens (Astigmatic Lens)

While a convex or concave lens has only one uniform power throughout the lens, a cylindrical lens has two powers and is used for the treatment of astigmatism. Most clients have a combination of hyperopia and astigmatism or myopia and astigmatism. The occupational therapist can easily determine if a client has astigmatism by looking at his or her eyeglass prescription. A typical prescription for a client with astigmatism and myopia (nearsightedness) would look like this:

OD: -1.50 - 1.25 x 180
OS: -1.50 - 1.50 x 180

This would be read as: Right eye, minus 1.50 with -1.25 axis 180 and left eye, minus 1.50 with -1.50 axis 180.

An example of a prescription for a client with astigmatism and hyperopia (farsightedness) would look like this:

OD: +2.50 - 2.25 x 180
OS: -2.00 - 1.75 x 180

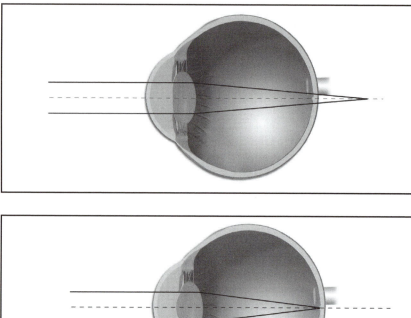

Figure 5-3. Cross-section of the human eye showing the lens and the ciliary muscle in its relaxed state (Steinman).

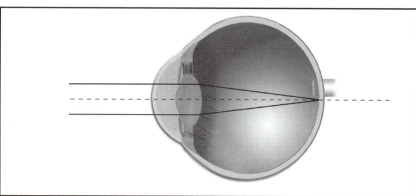

Figure 5-4. Ciliary muscle has contracted and allows the light rays to focus on the retina (Steinman).

The therapist can quickly check to see if a client has been prescribed a cylindrical lens for astigmatism by looking through it and slowly turning the lens clockwise or counterclockwise. If the object being viewed changes shape as it is rotated, the correction has a cylindrical component to correct for astigmatism.

ACCOMMODATION

Definition and Description

Assuming that any refractive error has been corrected with eyeglasses, the human visual system is physiologically focused for objects at distances of 20 feet and greater. If an object is brought closer than 20 feet, a focusing adjustment must be made or the object will appear blurred. This focusing adjustment is referred to as accommodation. Accommodation is the ability to change the focus of the eye so that objects at different distances can be seen clearly. Accommodation occurs by stimulating the smooth muscle of the ciliary body in the eye to contract, thereby enabling the lens to change its shape to become more convex. Optically, therefore, accommodation is identical to putting a variable plus-lens in front of the eye. Figure 5-3 is a cross-section of the human eye showing the lens and the ciliary muscle in its relaxed state. The light rays

entering the eye are focused behind the retina, which would cause blurred vision. In Figure 5-4, the ciliary muscle has contracted and allows the light rays to focus on the retina.

The accommodative ability of an individual is inversely related to age. We use the term accommodative amplitude to refer to the total amount of accommodation available for a particular client. Young children have very large amplitudes of accommodation, and this declines with age. This relationship between age and accommodative amplitude is so consistent across the population that it is possible for an optometrist to predict a client's age within several years simply by measuring the amplitude of accommodation. The accommodative amplitude declines gradually with age, and by 40 to 45 years of age the decline is significant enough to interfere with the ability to see small print held at a normal reading distance of 40 cm or 16 inches. This is referred to as presbyopia.

Presbyopia is a condition in which near visual acuity is decreased because of an age-related decline in accommodative ability. All adults after the age of 45 or so have this condition, and require reading glasses or some modification of their eyeglasses to account for it. Reading glasses that supplement accommodation position plus lenses in front of each eye. Bifocals are lenses that add extra plus to a person's distance prescription, referred to as reading addition or by the shorthand term add. Since most clients will be older,

occupational therapists working in the field of low vision rehabilitation of adults usually deal with clients who have presbyopia and require a reading addition to focus at near.

In the report from an eyecare practitioner, the reading addition is specified as the number at the end of the prescription for refractive error. It always follows a plus sign, but should not be confused with the correction for hyperopia. An example for a correction for 1 diopter (D) of hyperopia, 2.25 D of astigmatism, with 2.50 D of reading addition to compensate for presbyopia would be as follows:

OD: +1.00 – 2.25 x 180, +2.50
OS: +1.00 – 2.25 x 180, +2.50

Significance of Accommodation for Low Vision Rehabilitation

When working with optical aids, it is important to consider accommodation and how it may impact on the client's ability to use the device. With some optical devices, the client is required to accommodate and with others accommodation is not required. To determine if a client must use accommodation, one must consider a number of factors, including the working distance, or the distance from the eye to the material being viewed. The working distance is the distance at which the object being viewed is held from the eye, always specified in metric units. If an object is held at 20 feet (~6 meters), no accommodation is required. As the object is brought closer, more and more accommodation is required. We determine the amount of accommodation required by using the following formula:

Accommodation Demand = 100/working distance in centimeters

Example 1

If a client holds the reading material at 40 cm, the amount of accommodation required is:

Accommodation Demand = 100/distance (cm)
Accommodation Demand = 100/40 = 2.50 D

Example 2

If a client holds the reading material at 10 cm, the amount of accommodation required is:

Accommodation Demand = 100/distance (cm)
Accommodation Demand = 100/10 = 10 D

Thus, close working distances require a considerable amount of accommodation. In the adult population over the age of 40 years, the ability to accommodate has declined significantly. The optometrist must consider this when prescribing the optical aid and the occupational therapist must always be aware of the issue of accommodation when instructing clients in the use of optical devices.

If a client is experiencing difficulty using an optical device, one of the issues to consider is accommodation. This will be reviewed in detail in Chapter 13.

OPTICS OF LENSES

Manufacturers use two different methods to label the power or magnifying capability of optical devices. Some designate the device or lens by its actual power, while others label the device using the term magnification. This information, in whichever format provided, tells the therapist how to position the device and to instruct the client how to use the optical device. It is, therefore, important to understand various parameters of lenses, such as focusing power, focal distance, and magnification.

Focusing Power of a Lens

The unit of measurement of the focusing power of a lens is called a diopter (D). The definition of a 1 D lens is one that will focus parallel light rays entering the lens from a distant object to a point focus 100 cm away (Figure 5-5). We refer to this as a 1 D lens. As the power of a lens increases, it focuses parallel rays of light closer and closer to the back surface of the lens.

We use the following formula to determine the power of a lens:

D = 100/d (cm)

Examples

1. A lens focuses parallel light at 1 meter - D = 100/100 = 1 D
2. A lens focuses parallel light at 50 cm - D = 100/50 = 2 D
3. A lens focuses parallel light at 33 cm - D = 100/33 = 3 D
4. A lens focuses parallel light at 25 cm - D = 100/25 = 4 D
5. A lens focuses parallel light at 10 cm - D = 100/10 = 10 D (Figure 5-6)

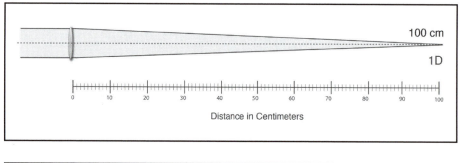

Figure 5-5. A 1 D lens will focus parallel light rays entering the lens from a distant object to a point focus 100 cm away (Steinman).

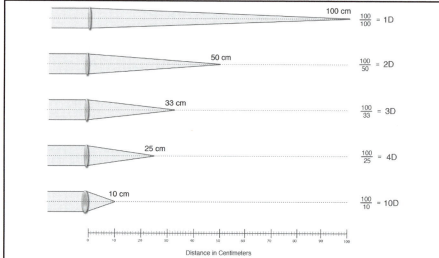

Figure 5-6. Five examples of convex lenses of varying power (Steinman).

Many of the optical devices that the occupational therapist will use with clients will have the power of the device designated in diopters. Note that the formula for accommodative demand is the same because it measures the required focusing power.

Focal Distance (Length) of a Lens

Another important term used in optics is the focal distance of a lens. The focal distance of a lens is the distance at which the lens brings parallel rays to a sharp focus (Figure 5-5). It is the distance between the lens and the point focus. The point or plane at which the lens focuses light is called the focal point of the lens. The focal distance of the lens is determined by the power of the lens in diopters.

The focal distance of a lens is computed using the following formula:

Focal Distance (cm) = 100/D

Thus, the focal distance of a lens is the reciprocal of the dioptric power. The greater the power of the lens, the closer the image is focused to the back of the lens.

Examples

1. The focal length of a 1 D lens - = 100/1 = 100 cm
2. The focal distance of a 2 D lens - = 100/2 = 50 cm
3. The focal distance of a 3 D lens - = 100/3 = 33 cm
4. The focal distance of a 4 D lens - = 100/4 = 25 cm
5. The focal distance of a 10 D lens - = 100/10 = 10 cm

Knowledge of the focal distance is critical for the occupational therapist because it determines the distance at which the client needs to hold the optical device from the working material. We will refer to this distance as the lens-to-object distance.

For example, a client is using a 10 D handheld magnifier to read a label on a can of soup. How far from the can of soup should the client hold the magnifier to achieve most magnification with a sharp focus? To determine lens-to-object distance of this magnifier, use the formula:

Lens-to-object distance = 100/D, lens-to-object distance = 100/10 = 10 cm

In this case, the occupational therapist would instruct the client to hold the magnifier 10 cm from the can of soup. Thus, if the dioptric power of the lens is known, the therapist can determine the appropriate lens-to-object distance of the optical device.

Optics of Magnification

One method of describing a low vision optical device lens is by its dioptric power as described above. For example, a handheld magnifier may have a power of 6 D, 10 D, or 20 D. Another method used by manufacturers to describe an optical device is by its degree of magnification. A device might be labeled as a 5X or 10X magnifier, for example. Unfortunately, the convention used to calculate magnification is inconsistent.

The most common formula used to relate the power of a lens to its magnifying ability is:

$M = D/4$
where M = Magnification

Examples

A lens has a power of 20 D. What is its magnifying power?

$M = D/4$
$M = 20/4 = 5X$

Other manufacturers may use the formula:

$M = D/4 + 1$

Others may use the formula:

$M = D/2.5$

Thus, the actual magnification of a device marked as 4X may differ between manufacturers depending on the definition used to determine the magnification. In addition, for other devices such as telescopes and video magnifiers, magnification is described as how much the image viewed through the optical device is enlarged. For example, a 4X telescope implies that the object size as viewed through the telescope is 4 times larger than the same object viewed without the telescope. This inconsistency in terminology is a source of great confusion for therapists. Because of this inconsistency, in this text we use the term magnification only in a general qualitative sense, as in "to make something appear larger."

Fortunately, one general convention has emerged in low vision care that helps resolve this problem. The magnification of any near device can be described as the power "equivalent" to the power of the near reading addition. This is referred to as equivalent power (EP).[1] All major manufacturers now list the EP of their devices. In order to understand how EP relates to magnification, one must first understand the various ways that an object can be magnified to compensate for impaired visual acuity.

Methods of Achieving Magnification

One of the primary ways to compensate for impaired visual acuity is to magnify the object of interest. All methods of magnification enlarge the retinal image of an object. There are four methods of achieving this goal. These four methods are actually variations of either relative distance or relative size magnification. The relationship between relative size and relative distance magnification forms the foundation for understanding all interventions, optical and nonoptical, that involve magnification of the object of interest to compensate for inadequate visual acuity.

Relative Size Magnification

In relative size magnification, the actual size of the object is increased. To avoid confusion with the many other definitions of magnification, the convention is to call size magnification "enlargement." The concept is quite simple. If the size of the object is doubled, the size of the retinal image is doubled. To achieve 2X enlargement, therefore, we simply enlarge the object twofold. If a client has trouble reading 8 point font, but can fluently read the 16 point font typical of large print books, the therapist could print a document on the computer using 16 point font or use large-print books typically printed with 16 point letters, as long as the eye-to-object distance remained the same.

This approach is relatively easy and can be an inexpensive option that is generally well-accepted because the client does not require any optical aids and can read at a normal distance. However, as the magnification demands grow and the print size for books is increased, the size and weight become issues. This method of magnification, therefore, is generally best suited for clients with mild to moderate loss of vision. It is also used in combination with other methods of magnification.

Relative Distance Magnification

Another simple means of achieving magnification of an object is to move closer to it. As an object

is moved closer to the eye, the retinal image of the object increases. If the distance is halved, the retinal image size doubles and 2X magnification is achieved. To achieve 4X magnification, the therapist would decrease the distance by one-fourth. If a client is having trouble seeing a 20-inch television at a distance of 12 feet, the therapist can suggest that the client move to 6 feet away. This would double the size of the retinal image of the television and magnify the image twofold.

If a client is having difficulty reading a newspaper at 40 cm, bringing the newspaper closer to 10 cm distance would magnify the print 4X. However, moving the newspaper this close creates another problem. Recall the discussion above about accommodation. The closer an object is brought to the eye, the more accommodation is required. Although decreasing the working distance from 40 cm to 10 cm achieves 4X magnification, the client would experience blurred vision if he/she is unable to accommodate for that distance. While a young child would be able to accommodate even at 25 cm, this would not be possible for an adult, particularly an adult age 40 and older. To solve this problem in adult clients with limited accommodation, the eyecare practitioner prescribes a reading addition or other optical device that focuses the light on the retina. In this example, the amount of additional plus required to read at 25 cm can be calculated using the formula described above.

Power (Diopters) = 100/D (cm) = 100/25 = 4 D.

The amount of relative distance magnification can, therefore, be described in terms of the additional plus power required to see something at a given distance, otherwise called equivalent power.

Angular Magnification

Angular magnification is the magnification experienced when a person looks through a device like a telescope. Angular magnification also increases the size of the retinal image just like relative size and relative distance magnification. The advantage of angular magnification is that it can be used when moving closer to an object or enlarging it is impractical or impossible. Viewing a sporting event is an example of such a situation. If an individual sits far from the action, neither relative distance nor relative size magnification is possible. However, the use of a telescope or binoculars will magnify the object of interest. When viewing objects further than 20 feet, angular magnification is an optical method of achieving size magnification, and the magnification specification can be described as an enlargement ratio. A 4X telescope produces the same effect as enlarging an object 4X.

Projection Magnification

Projection magnification refers to enlarging an object by projecting on a screen; this is the same as size magnification. Electronic devices like closed circuit televisions (CCTV) increase the size of the image to be viewed through the projection process, and like size and angular magnification may be described as an enlargement ratio. A 4X enlargement on a CCTV screen means that the 1.5 mm high, 8 point newsprint being viewed under the camera of the CCTV will be enlarged 8X to 12 mm on the screen. A CCTV can be used to project printed and graphic materials to increase their size.

In low vision care rehabilitation, the type of magnification used is dependent on many factors that will be discussed in Chapter 13. It is not unusual to use a combination of magnification systems. For example, the eye doctor may prescribe a magnifier and the therapist may suggest the use of larger print. How to combine magnification will be discussed in the advanced optics section of Chapter 13.

Lovie-Kitchin and Whittaker compared the effect on reading rates of adults using relative distance versus relative size magnification.[2] They found that the reading rates of the subjects with low vision did not differ significantly with the two methods of providing magnification if the magnification provided was adequate. They also concluded that for most tasks, it is more practical to enlarge the image optically, rather than to enlarge the reading material physically.[2]

FIELD OF VIEW

Field of view refers to the size of the area that can be viewed through a lens, magnifier, or telescope. Typically, when we are reading a book, we are able to see the entire page at once. Although only the words we are looking at are clear, the rest of the sentence, paragraph, and page are visible in our peripheral vision. This is important because it is this peripheral vision that helps us know where to move our eyes next to continue to effectively gather visual information. When introduced to an optical device for the first time, clients often are pleased that they can now see detail better but complain about the reduced field of view. A common question is "Can't I find a magnifier with a larger field of view?" The answer, unfortunately, is simple. When a client uses an optical device, the field of view will always be smaller; the stronger the magnification, the smaller the field of view. Magnification is like enlarging on a copy machine when the paper size cannot be changed. If the page is doubled in size, only half the original page will fit onto the copy. At times, a client may only be able to see a few words or

Table 5-1.	
Factors Affecting the Field of View	
Factor	*Effect on Field of View*
Diameter of the magnifier	A wider diameter lens will have a wider field of view. The diameter is related to the power of the lens. Stronger lenses have smaller diameters.
Power of the magnifier	The greater the power, the smaller the field of view.
Distance between eye and lens	The field of view becomes larger the closer the client is to the lens.

even just a few letters at a time. This, of course, makes reading difficult, interfering with speed, fluency, and comprehension. The reason that larger size handheld magnifiers enable people to see with a larger field of view is generally because larger diameter lenses generally have less magnification.

When using optical devices, a number of factors affect the field of view through the device. These are listed in Table 5-1. Stronger magnifiers have smaller fields of view because they must be made with smaller diameters and must be held closer to the material being viewed. The field of view also becomes smaller if the client moves his or her eyes away from the magnifier.

SUMMARY

The use of optical devices is an integral part of low vision rehabilitation. Occupational therapists will routinely need to educate and instruct clients about the use of these devices in ADL. In this chapter, we reviewed the basic concepts that occupational therapists must know to comfortably work with optical devices.

REFERENCES

1. Bailey IL. Equivalent viewing power or magnification? Which is fundamental? *The Optician.* 1984;188:14-18.
2. Lovie-Kitchin J, Whittaker S. Relative-size magnification versus relative-distance magnification: Effect on the reading performance of adults with normal and low vision. *J Vis Impairment & Blind.* 1998;16:433-446.

Psychosocial Issues Related to Visual Impairment

INTRODUCTION

An enduring irony of low vision rehabilitation is that potential beneficiaries of services often resist participation. It is not uncommon to find that once clients discover that interventions do not restore vision, they drop out of treatment, even though compensatory low vision rehabilitation is available that may restore nearly all activities of daily living (ADL), most instrumental activities of daily living (IADL), and many leisure and vocational occupations. We feel that this resistance occurs because psychosocial and cognitive effects of adventitious (later onset) vision loss can present unique and substantial complications that extend beyond functional vision problems.[1] It is critical, therefore, that occupational therapists attend to the cognitive and emotional impact of the vision loss and the client's ability to cope when providing low vision rehabilitation. Clients who do not cope or adapt well to vision impairment are at risk for depression, which may have a negative impact on rehabilitation. One of the very important issues in low vision rehabilitation is the high prevalence of depression and psychosocial problems associated with vision impairment.[2] Occupational therapists are very aware that engagement in occupations and in daily life activities can be influenced by cognitive and psychosocial factors.[3] In the field of low vision rehabilitation, depression and other psychosocial problems are important client factors that must be considered in intervention. Profound or peripheral vision loss that requires focus on nonvisual compensatory strategies presents additional cognitive demands as well. As with other disabilities, occupational therapists address all aspects of performance (physical, cognitive and psychosocial, and contextual) when providing low vision intervention[3] and this includes consideration of the psychosocial problems commonly associated with vision impairment. This chapter is designed to provide background information about the psychosocial issues related to vision impairment.

FACTORS AFFECTING ADJUSTMENT TO VISION IMPAIRMENT

Clinical reports and mostly retrospective descriptive research indicates a number of factors that affect the client's adjustment to vision loss and suggests that information about these factors should be gathered

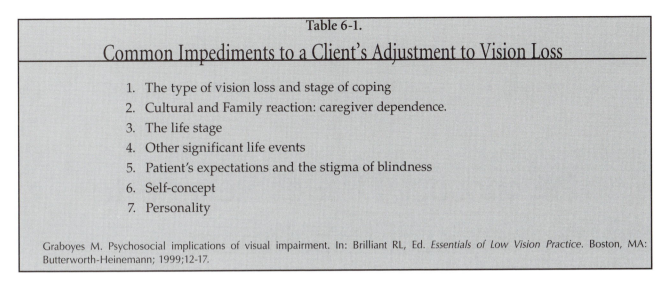

Table 6-1.

Common Impediments to a Client's Adjustment to Vision Loss

1. The type of vision loss and stage of coping
2. Cultural and Family reaction: caregiver dependence.
3. The life stage
4. Other significant life events
5. Patient's expectations and the stigma of blindness
6. Self-concept
7. Personality

Graboyes M. Psychosocial implications of visual impairment. In: Brilliant RL, Ed. *Essentials of Low Vision Practice*. Boston, MA: Butterworth-Heinemann; 1999;12-17.

during the history and while watching the client engaged in occupation and activities.[1,4-7] These factors are listed in Table 6-1, are briefly explained below, and should be considered in every evaluation. Issues related to any of these factors have the potential to limit the overall outcome for a client.

Type of Loss

An important issue is whether the vision loss is congenital, adventitious and longstanding or adventitious and recently acquired. Tuttle and Tuttle's review[7] uncovered a sequential pattern of coping with vision loss (Table 6-2). A review of phenomenological studies revealed that these stages often overlap and may occur in a different sequence.[5] Clients with recently acquired vision loss who are in denial may still be hopeful for a cure that will restore their vision. Many will also be in stages of mourning or depression. As will be discussed below, many will become "stuck" in a stage of clinically significant depression. The lack of initiation, memory impairment, and decreased activity level associated with depression will invariably have a negative impact on rehabilitation designed to teach the client how to adapt to vision impairment. Gradual loss of vision caused by dry macular degeneration may be easier to adapt to than the sudden loss of wet macular degeneration, especially if early rehabilitation intervention enables a client to maintain habits, routines, and occupations.[4]

Cultural and Family Reaction

The family's reaction to the person's vision loss can have a significant effect on the client's adjustment. This reaction will vary with different cultures. For example, vision loss may cause role changes within the household, causing anger and resentment.[1] Stigmas associated with vision loss, perceptions of

disability, and expectations of family for recovery of roles and functions vary with different cultures. Since cultural diversity exists within broad ethnic groups, we find the best strategy is to explore such expectations by careful interview of the client and the family. Sometimes interpreters can help. Vision impairment often leads to social problems such as nonacceptance, difficulty sustaining relationships, and attitudes of pity and overprotection by family members.[8]

Life Stage

The life stage of the client at the onset of the visual impairment and at the time of intervention has implications for psychological adjustment. For example, the older adult already faces challenges related to aging and these challenges can be compounded by vision impairment. Low vision rehabilitation involves hard work and stress. Many older individuals consider themselves as having retired from stress and hard work. Vision loss may interfere with many of the leisure activities that a retiree expected to enjoy in the retirement years, and for an elderly person living alone, vision impairment can lead to the end of independence.

Significant Life Events

Older age involves many stresses, especially the loss of loved ones, other illnesses and the dependence of others. Interestingly, older adults appear more resilient than their younger counterparts in adapting to stressful events, a resilience that appears to relate to social support.[5] It is important to determine if there have been recent stressful life events. A client who has recently been challenged to deal with other stressful situations may not have the energy to adjust to the vision impairment and embark on a vision rehabilitation program.[9]

Table 6-2.
Tuttle and Tuttle's Stages of Coping
Trauma: physical and social Shock and denial Mourning and withdrawal Succumbing and depression Coping and mobilization Self-acceptance and self-esteem

Patient Expectations

During the occupational profile/case history (see Chapter 8), the occupational therapist should ask about the client's goals and expectations from vision rehabilitation. Clients who have advanced to later stages of coping (see Table 6-2) begin to understand the nature of their problem and will have reasonable goals and expectations. For individuals who have initiated adaptation, vision rehabilitation has a better chance of success. Clients still in denial, who have not fully accepted the vision loss, may still be seeking the special pair of glasses that will suddenly restore their vision. If the client presents with unrealistic objectives, it is important to accept the need to advance through the stages of coping and focus. This advance can be facilitated by external routines, roles, and social demands that gently encourage recovering performance of occupation accompanied by a rehabilitation focus on more highly valued, enjoyed, and easily attained goals.

Self-Concept or Perceived Locus of Control

A person's self-concept may be impacted in a negative way by a vision impairment.[1] It is not unusual for a person with vision impairment to get the message from others that he or she is unable to perform certain activities and the implied message is that the person is unable to be independent anymore. People differ in their perception of their own ability to control outcomes.[4,5] A loss of self-esteem and loss of sense of control is observed behaviorally as lack of initiation, especially when problem-solving is required. For example, a client may "give up" when a handheld magnifier that has enabled reading does not seem to work, rather than try different magnifier positions or experiment with lighting. Self-perception and self-concept often are altered by a disability. We feel that locus of control or hardiness can be learned.[5] The effective strategy to restore a person's "hardiness" is to provide positive feedback when the individual exhibits a suc-

cessful attempt at adaptation, even if a better solution to the problem might exist. Avoid corrective feedback and errors by focusing on easily attained goals at first. Educate family and friends to do likewise.

Personality

Each client will react to vision loss in a different manner. As will be discussed below, older individuals with vision loss are at high risk for depression. Any other factor that predisposes a person to depression, therefore, would impact on low vision rehabilitation outcomes. For example, those people with an anxious personality prone to depression will react differently from an independent, motivated individual.[4]

Occupational therapists should evaluate the seven factors listed in Table 6-1 and this information should be considered when developing a treatment plan.

VISION IMPAIRMENT AND COGNITIVE FUNCTION

Treatment planning to address disability from visual impairment involves consideration of cognition as either a support or barrier to a successful performance outcome. Evaluation of cognitive function and interventions involving consideration of cognitive function[10] have been an integral part of the repertoire of skills an occupational therapist brings to any rehabilitation team. Critical for success, a review of cognitive evaluation and treatment is beyond the scope of this book and these topics have been covered elsewhere.[10] Low vision and blindness present some unique cognitive demands, including dependence on higher-order processing of other senses, auditory localization and processing, and hepatic processing. Although some people who are blind have developed near normal spatial processing abilities, in general, spatial perception based on touch and sound is not as accurate as spatial perception based on vision. Examples of spatial-perceptual tasks include: recall-

ing where a glass is located during a meal, finding the door that one entered when leaving a room, recalling where a throw rug was located in an unfamiliar location, determining by touch if a seam being sewn is straight, or finding the dominoes on a table. People with adventitious peripheral vision loss acquired after adolescence or profound blindness where high contrast landmarks cannot be seen have the greatest difficulty with spatial perception.[6]

People with long-duration blindness tend to move fewer joints when scanning an environment, whereas people with recent blindness move the whole arm and hand.[6] This suggests that a strategy for teaching someone to locate objects by feel should include careful, stereotypic arm positioning. An example is pressing the elbows to the body and keeping the wrists rigid so the hand is moved only by shoulder rotation, and then incremental, careful shoulder flexion to reposition the elbow on a table for a reach. If possible, only the hand or digits should be moved to scan smaller areas. By decreasing the joints involved, we suspect, spatial localization can become more accurate.

Adaptive strategies include use of high-contrast markers to help someone orient to a room or objects on a table. If someone has full visual fields but profound visual acuity loss, small bright lights, bright windows, table lamps, and streetlights work very well as markers. Careful organization of objects in the living space becomes a critical adaptive strategy.

The therapist needs to be careful to respect individual organization schemes and carefully evaluate a person's ability to locate objects after performance has been evaluated to see if someone can find given objects. The stacks of paper and jumble of objects on a table might actually be positioned according to a person's premorbid organization scheme; any change could devastate performance. Family needs to be carefully instructed not to alter the environment of a person with visual impairment in any way without directly involving the person in moving each object. Low tables or throw rugs that are normally considered hazards may not present a safety hazard to someone who is familiar with the location of these items. Indeed, the client may use these objects as markers in orienting to a room.

During mobility training, a person with low vision can be alerted to sounds and smells associated with landmarks, such as a food cart, reception desk, escalator, or busy doorway.

Learning to use other senses to perform tasks provides a considerable cognitive challenge to someone who has lost vision later in life. For this reason, we suspect individuals with recent vision loss may find use of visual devices or visual markers more helpful than a counterpart who has lived with impaired vision for many years. Care must be taken to intro-

duce someone with low vision to searching, scanning and localization tasks that may, to a normally sighted person, be very easy.

VISUAL IMPAIRMENT AND DEPRESSION

There is a significant body of literature demonstrating a relationship between visual impairment and depressive illness in adulthood and later life.[2,11-18] Horowitz and Reinhardt suggest two possible reasons for this relationship.[4,18] The first factor is the relationship between chronic illness of any type and functional disability.[19,20] This concept suggests that it is not the chronic illness itself that causes the depression. Rather, it is the loss of independence in ADL caused by the chronic illness that leads to depression. Studies have demonstrated that adults with visual impairment are more functionally disabled in ADL than those without vision impairments.[4,21-25] Williams et al interviewed 86 patients with age-related macular degeneration (AMD) and found severe disabling effects of the disease.[25] Patients rated their quality of life substantially lower than people with intact vision. These patients were eight times more likely to have trouble shopping, 13 times more likely to have difficulty managing finances, four times more likely to have problems with meal preparation, nine times more likely to have difficulty with light housework, and 12 times more likely to have trouble using the telephone. Rovner et al[16] found that depressive symptoms are more prevalent and persistent among low vision patients and appear more highly correlated to the disability than to the actual visual acuity loss. Brody et al[14] also found that in the group of patients they studied, visual acuity had little correlation with the severity of the depressive symptoms. In a study of 144 subjects, Tolman et al[17] examined psychological adaptation to vision loss and its relationship to depressive symptomatology in older adults. Their findings support the contention that depressive symptomatology is mediated by one's perceived sense of individual control as it relates to intrapersonal factors underlying adaptation to vision loss.

There is also evidence that vision impairment may have a more severe impact than other physical disabilities on everyday functioning.[4] Furner et al found that vision impairment and stroke are the most significant in their effect on instrumental activities of daily living.[26] Ford et al identified vision impairment as second only to arthritis as a cause of disability in the elderly.[27] Thus, there is convincing evidence demonstrating that vision impairment interferes with occupational performance, causing loss of indepen-

dence. It is this loss of independence that may be a key factor in explaining the high prevalence of depression in clients with visual impairment.

The second factor that may explain the relationship between visual impairment and depressive illness is the subjective characteristics of vision impairment.[4] Horowitz and Reinhardt[4] suggest that the most unique characteristic of vision impairment is that it is a particularly feared disability. In 1995, the Lighthouse surveyed adults 45 and older and found that blindness was more feared than other disabilities.[28] A public opinion poll found that blindness ranks fourth, following only AIDS, cancer, and Alzheimer's disease, as the illness most feared by Americans.[29] The results of a Gallup survey in 1988 showed that blindness was the most feared disability by 42% of adults polled.[30] Thus, adults who become visually impaired may have internalized this attitude, which influences their reaction and adaptation to vision loss.[4] Ainlay suggests that older adults may assume that vision loss invariably leads to a loss of independence, which then leads to self-imposed social isolation.[31]

Another important issue is that vision impairment has a negative impact on driving and reading, two activities that are very highly valued by most people.[18,32,33] For older adults, the inability to drive affects their sense of autonomy, self-worth, and independence.[18] Losing the ability to drive has been identified as one of the most feared aspects of vision impairment.[33]

Thus, the emotion elicited by vision impairment plus the relationship between vision loss and functional disability combines to increase the client's susceptibility to develop clinically significant depression.

PREVALENCE OF DEPRESSION IN ADULTS WITH VISION IMPAIRMENT

In a small pilot study using a convenience sample of 70 patients at a low vision clinic, Rovner et al found that 38.7% of the patients were clinically depressed.[16] In another study, Rovner et al prospectively studied a group of 51 older patients with recently acquired bilateral AMD using a depression scale and found clinically significant depression in 33% of the cohort.[34] Brody et al performed a similar study and found that 32.5% of the 151 elderly with AMD were found to have a depressive disorder.[14] Higher levels of depression have been associated with more recent onset of the vision impairment.[25]

These studies indicate that it is reasonable to expect one out of every three older adult clients with visual impairment to have a significant level of depression that could interfere with rehabilitation. Occupational therapists should consider the use of easily and quickly administered questionnaires to assess clients for depression during the low vision evaluation. A brief overview of the assessment of depression and available screening tests is reviewed below.

MEASURES OF DEPRESSION

Definition and Background

The gold standard for a research diagnosis of depression is the Structural Clinical Interview (SCID), a clinical interview that uses the DSM-III-R criteria for illness.[35,36] However, because of the time and level of experience required to administer a clinical interview, self-report questionnaires have been developed that can be used by clinicians who are not in the mental health professions. Three of the most popular self-report measures are the Center for Epidemiological Studies Depression Scale (CES-D), the Beck Depression Inventory (BDI), and the Geriatric Depression Scale (GDS).

The Beck Depression Inventory

The Beck Depression Inventory (BDI) is a list of 21 symptoms and attitudes that are each rated in intensity.[37] Examples include: mood, pessimism, sense of failure, lack of satisfaction, guilt feelings, self-dislike, etc. It is scored by summing the ratings given to the 21 items. Although originally designed to be administered by trained interviewers, it is most often self-administered and takes 5 to 10 minutes.

The Center for Epidemiologic Studies Depression Scale

The Center for Epidemiologic Studies Depression Scale (CES-D) was designed to measure current level of depressive symptomatology, and especially depressive affect.[38] The 20 items were chosen to represent all major components of depressive symptomatology. These include: depressed mood, feelings of guilt and worthlessness, feelings of helplessness and hopelessness, loss of appetite, sleep disturbance, and psychomotor retardation. Each item is rated on 4-point scales indicating the degree of occurrence during the last week. The scales range from "rarely or none of the time" to "most all of the time."

The Geriatric Depression Scale

The Geriatric Depression Scale (GDS) is a self-report scale designed to be simple to administer and does not require the skills of a trained interviewer.[39] Each of the 30 questions has a yes/no answer, with the scoring dependent on the answer given. A shorter 15-item version of the GDS has been devised and is probably the most common version currently used.[40]

For an example of the The Geriatric Depression Scale, see www.slackbooks.com/otvisionforms

As depression responds well to medication and counseling, if an occupational therapist suspects a client is depressed, the client should be referred to a mental health professional for treatment, and this professional should collaborate in treatment planning.

Rehabilitation and Depression

Depressed clients may be less likely to use optical devices and less likely to benefit from vision rehabilitation.[41] It is, therefore, important to try and address the psychosocial needs of clients as well as intervention aimed at improving occupation and ADL. Davis et al reported that despite vision rehabilitation, persons with long-standing AMD are likely to still show psychosocial dysfunction well after the onset of vision loss.[42] They recommend that therapists should continue to assist clients with their psychosocial adjustment as a follow-up to previous intervention because vision rehabilitation at the time of vision loss does not fully meet the client's needs. In another study designed to evaluate the importance of addressing the psychosocial needs of the client, Horowitz et al provided vision rehabilitation to 395 older adults with vision impairment.[43] They used a program called the Adaptive Skills Training Program. The goal was to help clients maintain themselves independently using a group intervention model. After attending this program, participants demonstrated significant improvement in adaptation to vision loss and life satisfaction and significantly less sadness or depression. The study had some design limitations, such as the use of unmasked examiners, short follow-up, and lack of a control group. Nevertheless, the study suggests the importance of addressing broad goals of rehabilitation to include not only specific functional skills, but fostering global well-being and a better quality of life for persons with visual impairment.[43]

Brody et al conducted a randomized clinical trial of 92 elderly patients with AMD.[41] The purpose of the study was to assess whether a self-management group intervention would improve mood, self-efficacy, and activity in people with central vision loss due to AMD. The intervention involved six weekly 2-hour group sessions providing education about the disease, group discussion, and behavioral and cognitive skills training to address barriers to independence.[41] Half of the patients were assigned to this group, while the other half were assigned to a "waiting list" and received no intervention during the 6 weeks. They used a variety of questionnaires and inventories to assess the patients before and after intervention. The results demonstrated the value of a brief, behavioral self-management group in reducing distress, enhancing self-efficacy, and improving adaptation. In a larger, randomized clinical trial of 252 older adults with AMD, Brody et al again studied the effectiveness of a self-management program. Patients were followed for 6 months after receiving a 12-hour self-management program, a series of 12 hours of tape-recorded health lectures, or a waiting list. The primary outcome measure was the score on the Profile of Mood States. At the 6-month follow-up visit, participants in the self-management group reported significantly less emotional distress compared with control subjects. The incidence of clinical depression at the 6-month follow-up was significantly lower in the self-management group than the control group.[44]

In addition to interventions that specifically address an underlying depression, Table 6-3 lists several general treatment strategies we have found help clients continue to participate in a rehabilitation program until performance goals are attained. In general, we have found that a good strategy to encourage resumption of activity is to ask the patient to start an activity according to a routine but stop anytime when tired or feeling frustrated. Remember, low vision rehabilitation presents considerable challenges if someone has even mild cognitive limitations.

SUMMARY

This chapter was designed to provide background information about the psychosocial issues related to vision impairment. The information provided suggests that an occupational therapist engaged in vision rehabilitation must attend closely to the psychosocial status of his/her client. Goals should be established to address this issue in rehabilitation. If a therapist suspects that a client is significantly depressed, use of one of the simple questionnaires should be considered, along with referral to a mental health practitioner.

REFERENCES

1. Graboyes M. Psychosocial implications of visual impairment. In: Brilliant RL, Ed. *Essentials of Low Vision Practice*. Boston, MA: Butterworth-Heinemann; 1999;12-17.

Table 6-3.

Intervention Strategies to Avoid/Address Depression

Speak with family when the client is present and included.

Provide family instruction on "courtesies" with people with low vision:
    Always speak directly to the client.
    Do not raise your voice.
    Always ask before helping and accept "no" for an answer.
    Do not leave without telling someone you are leaving.
    Describe your feelings, do not use gestures or facial expressions to communicate.
    Always introduce people who arrive, sometimes by just saying "Hello Jim".

Provide family instruction to use proper sighted guide techniques.

Provide family instruction to praise success and initiation of activity and to avoid any negative feedback, comments or reference to premorbid activities.

Recommend specific activities that a person can resume, encourage family to gently but firmly encourage resumption of these activities and roles at home.

Encourage family involvement in shared activity, reading aloud, family members describing a TV show, games that all can play like Bingo.

Recommend resumption of premorbid routines and spiritual activities.

Smile, joke, and tease. Encourage the family to do the same.

2. Casten RJ, Rovner BW, Tasman W. Age-related macular degeneration and depression: a review of recent research. *Curr Opin Ophthalmol.* 2004;15(3):181-183.
3. American Occupational Therapy Association. Occupational Therapy Practice Framework: Domain and Process. *Am J Occup Ther.* 2002;56(6):609-639.
4. Horowitz A, Reinhardt JP. Mental health issues in vision impairment. In: Silverstone B, et al, Eds. *The Lighthouse Handbook on Vision Impairment and Vision Rehabilitation.* Oxford: Oxford University Press; 2000:1089-1109.
5. Ringering L, Amaral P. The role of psychosocial factors in adaptation to vision impairment and rehabilitation outcomes for adults and older adults. In: Silverstone B, et al, Eds. *The Lighthouse Handbook on Vision Impairment and Vision Rehabilitation.* Oxford: Oxford University Press; 2000:1029-1048.
6. Hollins M. Vision Impairment and cognition, In: Silverstone B, et al, Eds. *The Lighthouse Handbook on Vision Impairment and Vision Rehabilitation.* Oxford: Oxford University Press; 2000:339-358.
7. Tuttle DW, Tuttle NR. *Self-Esteem and Adjusting with Blindness.* 2nd ed. Springfield, IL: Charles Thomas; 1996.
8. Steffens MC, Bergler R. Blind people and their dogs. In: Wilson CC, Turner DC, Eds. *Companion Animals in Human Health.* Thousand Oaks, CA: Sage; 1998:149-157.
9. Kobasa SCO, Puccetti MC. Personality and social resources in stress resistance. *J Pers Soc Psychol.* 1983;45(4):839-850.
10. Zoltan B. *Vision, Perception and Cognition: A Manual for the Examination and Treatment of the Neurologically Impaired Adult.* 3rd ed. Thorofare, NJ: SLACK Incorporated; 1996:211.

11. Shmuely-Dulitzki Y, Rovner BW. Screening for depression in older persons with low vision. Somatic eye symptoms and the Geriatric Depression Scale. *Am J Geriatr Psychiatry.* 1997;5(3):216-220.
12. Wells KB, Stewart A, Hays RD, et al. The functioning and well-being of depressed patients. Results from the Medical Outcomes Study. *JAMA.* 1989;262(7):914-919.
13. Shmuely-Dulitzki Y, Rovner BW, Zisselman P. The impact of depression on function in low vision elderly patients. *Am J Geriatr Psychiatry.* 1996;3:325-329.
14. Brody BL, Gamst AC, Williams RA, et al. Depression, visual acuity, comorbidity, and disability associated with age-related macular degeneration. *Ophthalmology.* 2001;108(10):1893-1900; discussion 1900-1.
15. Rovner BW, Shmuely-Dulitzki Y. Screening for depression in low-vision elderly. *Int J Geriatr Psychiatry.* 1997;12(9):955-959.
16. Rovner BW, Zisselman PM, Shmuely-Dulitzki Y. Depression and disability in older people with impaired vision: a follow-up study. *J Am Geriatr Soc.* 1996;44(2):181-184.
17. Tolman J, Hill RD, Kleinschmidt JJ, Gregg CH. Psychosocial adaptation to visual impairment and its relationship to depressive affect in older adults with age-related macular degeneration. *Gerontologist.* 2005;45(6):747-753.
18. Horowitz A. The prevalence and consequences of vision impairment in later life. *Topics in Geriatric Rehab.* 2004;20:185-195.
19. Williamson GM, Schulz R. Physical illness and symptoms of depression among elderly outpatients. *Psychol and Aging.* 1992;7:343-351.

20. Zeiss AM, Lewinsohn PM, Rohde P, Seeley JR. Relationship of physical disease and functional impairment to depression in older people. *Psychol and Aging*. 1996;11:572-581.
21. Branch LG, Horowitz A, Carr C. The implications for everyday life of incident self-reported visual decline among people over age 65 living in the community. *Gerontologist*. 1989;29(3):359-365.
22. Gillman AE, Simmel A, Simon EP. Visual handicap in the aged: Self-reported visual disability and the quality of life of residents of public housing for the elderly. *J Vis Impairment & Blind*. 1986;80:533-590.
23. Heinemann AW, Colorez A, Frank S, Taylor D. Leisure activity participation of elderly individuals with low vision. *Gerontologist*. 1988;28(2):181-184.
24. Salive M, Guralnik J, Glynn RJ, Christen W, Wallace RB, Ostfeld AM. Association of visual impairment with mobility and physical function. *J Am Geriatr Soc*. 1994;42(3):287-292.
25. Williams RA, Brody BL, Thomas RG, Kaplan RM, Brown SI. The psychological impact of macular degeneration. *Arch Ophthalmol*. 1998;116:514-520.
26. Furner SE, Rudberg MA, Cassel CK. Medical conditions differentially affect the development of IADL disability: Implications for medical care and research. *Gerontologist*. 1995;35:444-450.
27. Ford AB, Folmar SJ, Salmon RB, Medalie JH, Roy AW, Galazka SS. Health and function in the old and very old. *J Am Geriatr Soc*. 1988;36:187-197.
28. *The Lighthouse National Survey on Vision Loss: The Experience, Attitudes, and Knowledge of Middle-Aged and Older Americans.* New York: The Lighthouse; 1995:11.
29. National Society for the Prevention of Blindness, Survey '84: Attitudes towards blindness prevention. *Sight-Savings*. 1984;53:14-17.
30. Augusto CR, McGraw JM. Humanizing blindness through public education. *J Vis Impairment & Blind*. 1990;93:397-400.
31. Ainlay SC. Aging and new vision loss: Disruptions of the here and now. *J Social Issues*. 1988;44:79-94.
32. Ryan EB et al. Coping with age-related vision loss in everyday reading activities. *Educ Gerontol*. 2003;29:37-54.
33. Corn AL, Sack SZ. The impact of nondriving on adults with visual impairments. *J Vis Impairment & Blind*. 1994;88:53-68.
34. Rovner BW, Casten RJ, Tasman WS. Effect of depression on vision function in age-related macular degeneration. *Arch Ophthalmol*. 2002;120(8):1041-1044.
35. Williams JB, Gibbon M, First MB, et al. The Structured Clinical Interview for DSM-III-R (SCID). II. Multisite test-retest reliability. *Arch Gen Psychiatry*. 1992;49(8):630-636.
36. Spitzer RL, Williams JB, Gibbon M, First MB. The Structured Clinical Interview for DSM-III-R (SCID). I: History, rationale, and description. *Arch Gen Psychiatry*. 1992;49(8):624-629.
37. Beck AT, Steer RA, Garbin MG. Psychometric properties of the Beck Depression Inventory: Twenty-five years of evaluation. *Clinical Psychology Review*. 1988;8:77-100.
38. Ensel WM. Measuring depression: The CES-D scale. In: Lin N, Dean A, Ensel WM, Eds. *Social Support, Life Events, and Depression*. New York: Academic Press; 1986.
39. Yesavage JA, Brink TL, Rose TL, et al. Development and validation of a geriatric depression screening scale: a preliminary report. *J Psychiatr Res*. 1982;17(1):37-49.
40. Shiekh J, Yesavage JA. Geriatric Depression Scale: recent findings in development of a shorter version. In: Brink J, Ed. *Clinical Gerontology: A Guide to Assessment and Intervention*. New York: Howarth Press; 1986.
41. Brody BL, Williams RA, Thomas RG, Kaplan RM, Chu RM, Brown SI. Age-related macular degeneration: a randomized clinical trial of a self-management intervention. *Ann Behav Med*. 1999;21(4):322-329.
42. Davis C, Lovie-Kitchin J, Thompson B. Psychosocial adjustment to age-related macular degeneration. *J Vis Impairment & Blind*. 1995;88:16-27.
43. Horowitz A, Leonard E, Reinhardt J. Measuring psychosocial and functional outcomes of a group model of vision rehabilitation services for older adults. *J Vis Impairment & Blind*. 2000;94(5):328-338.
44. Brody BL, Roch-Levecq AC, Thomas RG, Kaplan RM, Brown SI. Self-management of age-related macular degeneration at the 6-month follow-up: a randomized controlled trial. *Arch Ophthalmol*. 2005;123(1):46-53.

Section II

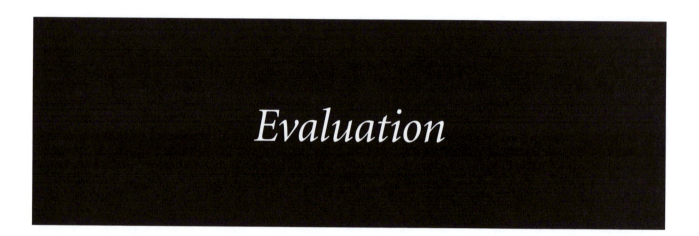

Evaluation

Overview and Review of the Low Vision Evaluation

Paul B. Freeman, OD, FAAO, FCOVD, Diplomate, Low Vision

OPTOMETRIC LOW VISION EXAMINATION

It is imperative for occupational therapists involved in low vision rehabilitation to be familiar with the low vision examination. The following is a description of the optometric low vision evaluation (Table 7-1). This evaluation can be performed in a variety of settings, including a professional office, a rehabilitative facility, or a personal care facility.

Case History

The history of a visually impaired patient, as with any other history, is a snapshot of the patient up to the time of questioning. The general areas that this history should cover are listed in Table 7-2. This information may be obtained from a number of sources, including the patient, family, friends, caregivers, therapists, and doctors. Among the most common chief visual complaints of visually impaired patients is the inability to see conventional size print, the inability to drive, and the inability to recognize people.

It is always important to determine the date and results of the last eye examination. In many cases,

individuals who believe they are visually impaired may simply require an eye examination and conventional eyeglasses. This was demonstrated in the Baltimore Eye Survey, which found that "the acuity of about three-fourths of the visually impaired whites and two-thirds of the visually impaired African Americans could have been corrected to better than 20/40 with only eyeglasses."[1]

Once it is established, however, that the patient has a bona fide decrement in visual acuity that cannot be corrected by conventional eyewear, the remaining questions explore the impact of this visual deficit on the patient's ability to visually interact with the environment and the challenges faced. During the case history, the doctor can obtain information about the patient's understanding of the impact of the visual impairment, cognitive level, motivation, support systems, and previous attempts at vision rehabilitation.

Visual Acuity Information

Visual acuity information is generally communicated as a fraction, which can be in either feet (Snellen) or metric notation. The numerator signifies the actual or calculated testing distance and the denominator the actual or calibrated target size. For example, 10/200 should be recorded if the physical testing distance was

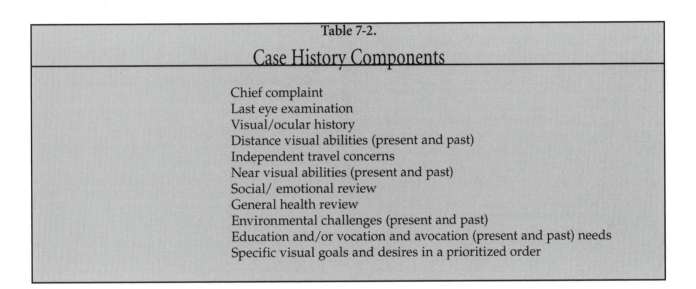

Table 7-1.

Components of Optometric Low Vision Evaluation

Case history
Distance visual acuities
Near visual acuities
Amsler grid testing
Color vision testing
Visual/mobility field testing
Contrast sensitivity testing
Refraction
Binocular vision evaluation
Eye health evaluation
Magnification evaluation

Table 7-2.

Case History Components

Chief complaint
Last eye examination
Visual/ocular history
Distance visual abilities (present and past)
Independent travel concerns
Near visual abilities (present and past)
Social/ emotional review
General health review
Environmental challenges (present and past)
Education and/or vocation and avocation (present and past) needs
Specific visual goals and desires in a prioritized order

10 feet and the smallest target size correctly identified was a 200 size letter. Any of the modifiers listed in Table 7-3 should be included if there is anything unusual or pertinent about the manner in which the acuity was measured. These findings are typically obtained for each eye independently, if possible, both with and without the patient's current eyeglass or contact lens prescription.

DISTANCE VISUAL ACUITIES

Distance visual acuities are measured to establish the patient's baseline ability to see at a specific distance. Specially designed charts (which allow for better quantification of reduced acuity levels) other than the standard Snellen projected chart can be used, but when doing so, the specific chart used and actual testing distance should be noted (Figure 7-1). Other factors that should be considered, including expressive and receptive language skills and cognitive functioning that can also affect this measurement when assessing visual acuity at distance, are listed in Table 7-3.

There are occasions when a person cannot recognize, identify, or match symbols. In these instances, there are other ways the practitioner can establish what a patient can see. In these cases, a more functional approach can be used. For instance, a patient's ability to fixate and follow a light and/or localize a specific sized target (without the actual ability to identify it) at a specific distance can be used to indirectly assess visual acuity.

Table 7-3.
<u>Factors to Be Considered When Assessing Visual Acuity</u>
Lighting Contrast Specific chart used Numbers of targets at each acuity level Spacing of the targets Difficulty of the targets being identified (ie, letters, numbers, pictures, etc) Single letter versus reading acuity Type of letters (block, serif, etc) Ease with which the targets are identified Expressive as well as receptive language skills Cognitive functioning Eccentric viewing (body positioning, eye/head posture)

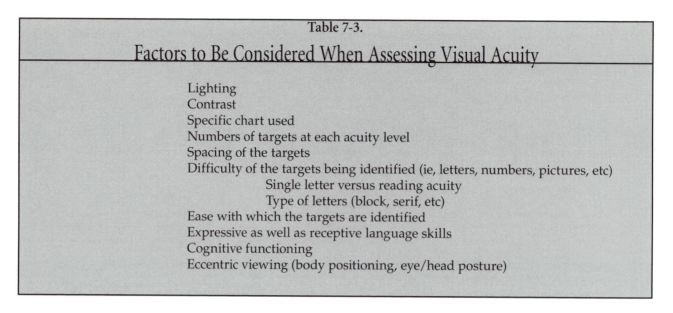

Figure 7-1. Specially designed charts for testing visual acuity in visually impaired patients.

NEAR VISUAL ACUITIES

The vast majority of activities for which visually impaired patients require assistance revolve around near work. Therefore, a measure of visual acuity should be done at near as well as distance. This information will not only help the occupational therapist when trying to determine an appropriate sized target to work with, but also helps the optometrist to evaluate the consistency between distance and near acuity measurements. As with distance visual acuity measurement, all pertinent information about the test (see Table 7-3) should be made available to anyone reviewing the data. Additionally, knowing whether the target size was based on identification (discrimination) acuity or actual reading acuity is important, as there can be a difference. The ability to recognize a letter does not always equal the ability to actually read.

Figure 7-2 illustrates some of the commonly used near visual acuity charts.

Amsler Grid Testing

Using an Amsler grid (Figure 7-3) can help to determine whether a patient is experiencing distortion or has (multiple) areas of scotoma. A scotoma is defined as "an isolated area of absent vision or depressed sensitivity in the visual field, surrounded by an area of normal vision or of less depressed sensitivity."[2] The Amsler grid measurement can provide information used to identify the onset of a pathology, monitor a pathology, or modify the ultimate optical device(s) that might be needed by a patient for a specific task. Functionally, the results can also give guidance as to whether a patient eccentrically views or needs to learn to do so. Figure 7-4 illustrates an example of the distortion of the Amsler grid that can be experienced by a patient with macular degeneration.

Figure 7-2. Commonly used near visual acuity charts.

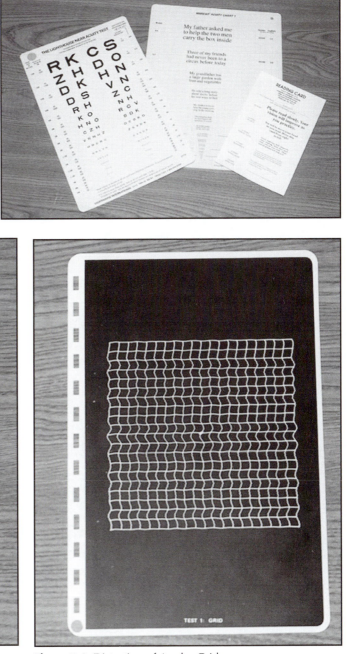

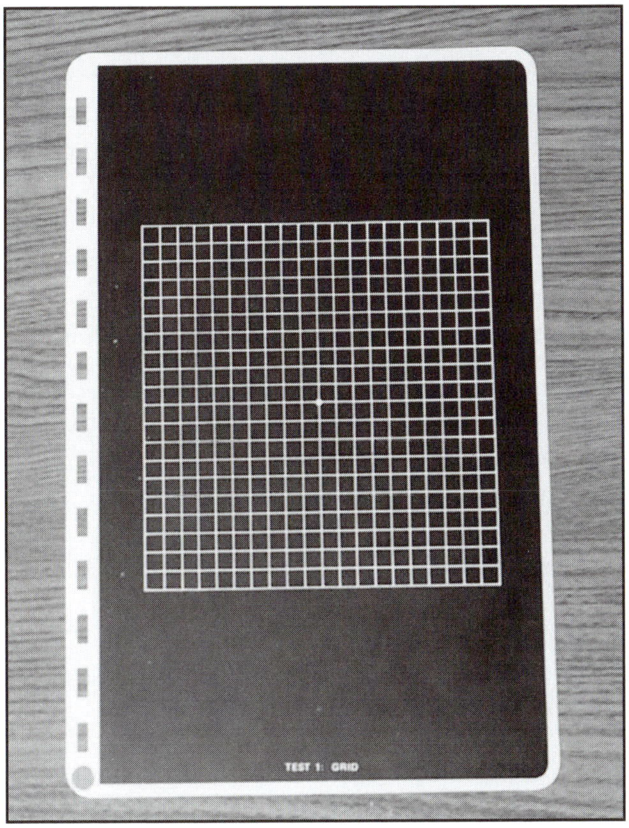

Figure 7-3. Amsler Grid.

Figure 7-4. Distortion of Amsler Grid.

COLOR VISION TESTING

Several tests are available for assessing color vision (Figure 7-5). The results of color vision testing can be used to identify the onset of a pathology, monitor a pathology, or alert a therapist to color deficits that might impact a therapeutic regimen for the patient. Color vision deficits are generally not as detrimental to functioning as other losses such as visual acuity, visual field, or contrast. However, knowing the patient's color vision status can be important in educational, vocational, and social planning or training.

VISUAL/MOBILITY FIELD TESTING

Perimetry or visual field testing is designed to evaluate the depth and breadth of an individual's peripheral vision. Visual field loss can be either absolute or relative. An absolute visual field loss is one in

Figure 7-5. Several tests available for color vision testing.

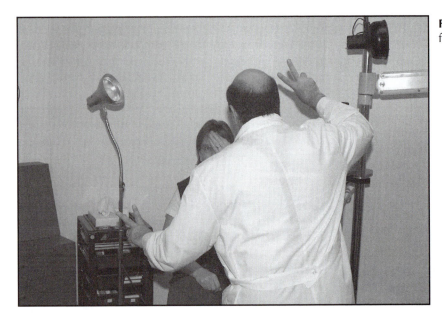

Figure 7-6. Illustration of confrontation field testing.

which no matter how large and bright the target is, it will not be seen within the blind area. A relative visual field loss, on the other hand, is dependent on the size, brightness, and contrast of the target relative to the environmental background. This translates functionally into variations of visual field awareness consistency based on environmental conditions. For example, a person with a relative peripheral visual field loss might function better under bright illumination than under dim lighting conditions or at night. There are several instruments that can formally quantify the extent of the visual field. However, for initial screening, confrontation field testing (Figure 7-6) is the method of choice. It is typically carried out by the doctor sitting opposite the patient, each covering the eye on the same side, and having the patient then demonstrate awareness of when the doctor's (or a third person's) hands (or object) are brought in from the periphery. As in other testing, notations about environmental conditions should be made (see Table 7-3). This type of testing will uncover gross peripheral visual field deficits and is very useful for determining the presence of a hemianopia (which is absolute). Confrontation field testing is not as sensitive for subtle peripheral field loss or for central visual field disturbances.

To accurately quantify visual field loss, a formal visual field study must be performed. Typically,

Figure 7-7. Manual visual field apparatus.

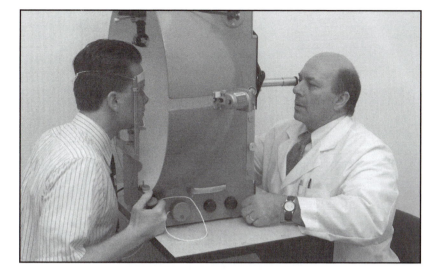

a computerized visual field apparatus is used for this purpose (Figure 7-7). However, for purposes of determining visual disability from a medical-legal standpoint, a manual Goldmann visual field test is required.[3]

CONTRAST SENSITIVITY TESTING

Contrast sensitivity testing determines the patient's ability to distinguish borders, eg, a gray car against a foggy background or coffee in a dark cup. It is a method of assessing the qualitative aspects of visual functioning. This is particularly important when following a patient's progress over multiple visits. Patients sometimes report that their sight has changed, but on a standard eye chart (which has a maximum contrast of black and white) there may be no measured difference. These are patients who are noticing real functional difficulties, even though their measured visual acuity has not changed. In these cases, contrast sensitivity may demonstrate a qualitative change in vision that confirms the patient's report. This test is also valuable when it is difficult to pinpoint a visual complaint, especially with patients with "good" visual acuities. Proper lighting is integral to this testing.

REFRACTION

Refraction is the term used to describe the evaluation of the optical system of the eye. We use the term refractive error to describe any deviation from emmetropia. When the optometrist performs the refraction, it can be determined whether the eye is emmetropic (absence of refractive error), myopic (nearsighted), hyperopic (farsighted), or astigmatic.

The refraction is the examination procedure used to determine if a patient has a refractive error that needs to be corrected, as well as the exact lens prescription that is appropriate. A phoropter or a trial frame with loose lenses is used to perform the refraction. When a patient is visually impaired, the optometrist must also use information about the refractive error when designing low vision optical devices.

As noted previously, we sometimes encounter patients who appear to be visually impaired or legally blind, but a thorough refraction indicates that the patient simply requires an updated eyeglass prescription to regain normal vision. I cannot emphasize enough the importance of performing a careful refraction before initiating any low vision rehabilitation activity. For example, a patient who needs a bifocal correction and is not wearing it, may not be able to see clearly through a "simple" stand magnifier. A misleading conclusion might be that the patient is unable to cognitively handle the task, when in fact it is simply the omission of the appropriate refractive prescription.

BINOCULAR VISION EXAMINATION

Binocular vision is the ability of the visual system to fuse or combine the information from the right and left eyes to form one image. For binocular vision to occur, the information arriving from each eye must be identical, with approximately equal vision in both eyes. To satisfy these requirements, the two eyes must be aligned so that they point at the same object at all times, and the visual acuity, optics, or refractive error of the two eyes must be approximately equal. Therefore, it is understandable that many patients

---

Table 7-4.

Classification of Strabismic Binocular Vision Disorders

Direction

Esotropia	An eye turns in toward nose
Exotropia	An eye turns out temporally
Hypertropia	An eye turns up

Each of these conditions is also classified based on the following characteristics:

Frequency

Intermittent esotropia or constant esotropia
Intermittent exotropia or constant exotropia
Intermittent hypertropia or constant hypertropia

Laterality (which eye turns)

Right esotropia, left esotropia, or alternating esotropia
Right exotropia, left exotropia, or alternating exotropia
Right hypertropia, left hypertropia, or alternating hypertropia

Comitancy

Comitant
Noncomitant

---

with vision impairment do not have normal binocular vision because they lack approximately equal visual acuity in both eyes.

It is not uncommon for an older adult with low vision to lose binocular vision, which can cause a misalignment of the eyes; referred to as strabismus. When strabismus occurs, the eyes may drift in, out, up, or down. Table 7-4 lists some of the common terms associated with binocular vision problems that an occupational therapist may encounter in a low vision examination report.

Clinical Assessment of Binocular Disorders

Some of the common tests used to evaluate binocular vision in patients with low vision include the cover test and tests to assess fusion. Using the cover test procedure, an optometrist can determine many key binocular vision characteristics, including the direction, magnitude, frequency, and comitancy of the strabismus.

Direction of Strabismus

This refers to whether the eyes turn in, out, up, down, or a combination of these directions. Table 7-5

lists the various possibilities, including esotropia (eyes turn in), exotropia (eyes turn out), and hypertropia (one eye turns up).

Magnitude of Strabismus

This refers to the amount of the eye turn. When an eye turn is large, it is quite obvious, even to a nonprofessional. However, it is important to be aware that the magnitude of a strabismus may be moderate or small and in such cases the eye turn may be not be visible or detectable without special testing. The magnitude of the strabismus is recorded in prism diopters. For example, you might see the following notation in an optometric report:

25 pd esotropia (or 25Δ)
where pd = prism diopters.

Frequency of Strabismus

Frequency of the strabismus refers to the amount of time the eye turns in, out, up, or down (see Table 7-4). For example, it is possible for the eye turn to be present 100% of the time and this would be called a constant strabismus. In contrast, the strabismus may

	Table 7-5.

Commonly Used Abbreviations in Eye Examinations

Abbrev	*Term*
VA	Visual acuity
OD	Right eye (oculus dexter)
OS	Left eye (oculus sinister)
OU	Both eyes (oculus uterque)
XP	Exophoria
EP	Esophoria
XT	Exotropia
ET	Esotropia
AA	Accommodative amplitude
VF	Visual field
PERRL	Pupil equal, round, respond to light
WNL	Within normal limits

occur only part of the time and would be called an intermittent strabismus.

For example, you might see the following notation in an optometric report:

25 pd (or 25Δ) intermittent esotropia, or
15 pd (or 15Δ) constant esotropia

Comitancy of Strabismus

The final variable is referred to as comitancy and refers to the uniformity of the size of the strabismus from one position of gaze to another. A strabismus is called comitant if it is the same size regardless of where the patient looks (left, right, up, or down). If there is a significant difference from one position to gaze to another, it is called a noncomitant strabismus.

For example, if a patient's eyes are aligned when looking straight ahead but deviate when looking to the right, it is called a noncomitant strabismus.

Additional tests may be used to evaluate the patient's ability to "fuse" or use information from both eyes in a coordinated way. A popular probe of sensory fusion is stereopsis testing. In this test (Figure 7-8), the patient wears special polaroid glasses and is asked if any of the figures on the page appear to be floating off the page in 3D. Another commonly used test is called the Worth 4 Dot test. This test is used to determine if the patient has double vision or is suppressing the vision of one eye.

The low vision optometrist should provide information about binocular vision to the therapist. This information will help the occupational therapist to understand why an optical device was prescribed for just one eye versus both eyes.

EYE HEALTH EVALUATION

An eye health evaluation can include but is not limited to the following tests: observation of the external structures of the eye and adnexa, intraocular pressure (IOP) measurement, evaluation of the anterior structures of the eye, and evaluation of the internal structures of the eye through a dilated pupil (unless contraindicated). The goal of the eye health evaluation is to determine the underlying basis for the visual acuity, contrast sensitivity, and/or visual field loss. There are many good texts available for a detailed description of these procedures.[4,5] An ocular health evaluation is indicated prior to beginning any low vision rehabilitation, or if any change in vision or functioning is noticed by the patient, family, or therapist, and periodically as indicated by the patient's primary eyecare doctor.

MAGNIFICATION EVALUATION

Determining the magnification necessary for the patient to see desired materials is another prerequisite for beginning a vision rehabilitation program. Magnification refers to the process of enlarging the image on the retina. Magnification of an object can be accomplished using four different methods: relative size magnification, relative distance magnification, angular magnification, or electronic magnification.

Relative Size Magnification

Relative size magnification refers to enlarging the target. This is similar to taking conventional size print

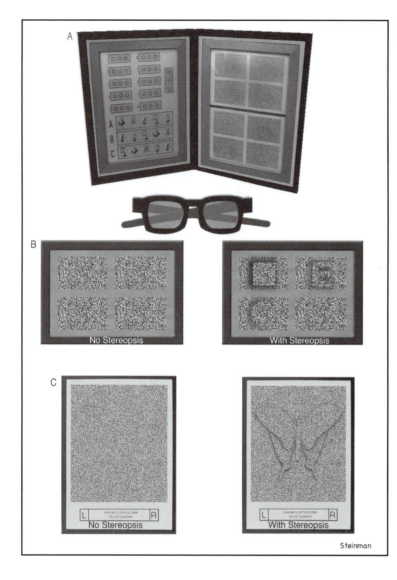

Figure 7-8. Stereopsis test – Random Dot Stereogram (Steinman).

and enlarging it to fit on a billboard. When viewing targets at distance, the patient's appropriate refractive correction should always be in place. When viewing objects at closer distances, a compensatory lens for a specific viewing distance must be considered. This concept is reviewed in detail in Chapter 5. Therefore, even when using large print, conventional glasses or bifocals may be needed to see the print clearly, even before other forms of optical magnification are considered.

Relative Distance Magnification

This is accomplished by bringing the object of interest closer. It might be considered similar to "airplane magnification," where at 10,000 feet houses look small, but the closer one gets to the ground, the larger the houses appear. Similarly, a target at 2 inches will give the appearance of being 8 times larger than the same target at 16 inches. Remember that when objects

are held at a closer working distance, the patient must exert additional "muscular" effort (if possible) to accommodate (focus). This effort can lead to discomfort and eyestrain after short periods of time. Additionally, many older patients are unable to exert this effort and, along with discomfort, will not see clearly. Thus, an appropriate powered lens must be used for the target to be seen clearly at that distance. This lens minimizes or eliminates the need for the patient to accommodate (or focus) the eyes.

Angular Magnification

Angular magnification is the magnification experienced when a person looks through a device like a telescope. This form of magnification is typical of a stand magnifier or a telescope where the relationship between lenses in the system creates an enlarged image. Angular magnification also increases the size of the retinal image just like relative size and relative

distance magnification. The advantage of angular magnification is that it can be used when moving closer to an object or enlarging it is impractical or impossible. Viewing a sporting event is an example of such a situation. If an individual sits far from the action, neither relative distance nor relative size magnification are possible. However, the use of a telescope or binoculars will magnify the object of interest. Telescopic lenses must be focused properly. To see clearly through a telescope, the refractive error must be corrected or compensated for in some manner. This can be done by using glasses or contact lenses, or by adjusting the telescope for the refractive error. It should be noted that focusing the telescope for an uncorrected eye may modify the power (or magnification) of the telescope, even though the image will be clear.

Electronic or Projection Magnification

This form of magnification uses electronic equipment and is basically a combination of relative size and relative distance magnification considerations. Once again, the application of lenses for the near focusing demand must be considered; otherwise the target may be made large enough to see, but will be out of focus. Big and blurry is not as easy to see as big and clear. In some instances, a clearer image can be recognized with less magnification (ie, smaller on the screen), thereby allowing more information to be displayed on the screen at one time.

DETERMINING MAGNIFICATION

When an individual cannot see to perform a task, magnification may be necessary. Simply stated, the magnification required is determined by dividing the patient's actual acuity level by the desired acuity level. For example: An individual has 20/200 distance visual acuity, sees the 20/200 near target at 16 inches (with appropriate glasses), and would like to see 20/50 size print at near. That requires 4X magnification, and can be calculated a number of ways:

1. Using "billboard" magnification (relative size magnification), the target (print size) can be made four times larger.

2. If the 20/200 target is at 16 inches initially, it can be brought four times closer ("airplane" or relative distance magnification) to approximately 4 inches, which would require a lens, or accommodation, of approximately +10.00 D.

3. A combination of relative size and relative distance magnification could be provided with electronic equipment like a closed circuit television (CCTV). For example, the target can be made physically larger on the CCTV monitor, and the patient can sit closer (or farther) than 16 inches, with the appropriate glasses.

If this individual needed to see the 20/50 sized target at a 20 foot measured distance, a 4X telescope, or electronic equipment that could magnify four times at distance, could be used. The limiting physical and optical factors of these as well as near devices are the weight, appearance, field of view, and lighting constraints that these systems impose.

These are generalities and should be reviewed with the optometrist who has prescribed the devices in relationship to what the occupational therapist has identified as the visual requirements necessary for the task.

CONCLUSION

This chapter reviewed the low vision examination that an occupational therapist should expect to be performed by the eyecare provider. We have also included a sample report from a low vision optometrist, and Table 7-5 provides a list of common abbreviations used in a low vision examination record or report. When receiving such a report, if the occupational therapist has questions about terminology, test results, or any other issues, it is best to contact the referring optometrist. The team effort stressed in this book is one that will benefit clients with vision impairment who most need the integrated services of both the low vision optometrist and the occupational therapist.

REFERENCES

1. Tielsch JM. Prevalence of visual impairment and blindness in the United States. In: Massof RW, Lidoff L, Eds. *Issues in Low Vision Rehabilitation: Service Delivery, Policy, and Funding.* New York: American Foundation for the Blind; 2001:13-26.
2. Cline D, Hofstetter HW, Griffin JR. *Dictionary of Visual Science.* Newton, MA: Butterworth-Heinemann; 1997.
3. United States Social Security Administration. Code of Federal Regulations. 1992.
4. Spalton DJ, Hitchings RA, Hunter PA. *Atlas of Clinical Ophthalmology.* London, England: Gower Medical Publishing; 1984.
5. Harley RD. *Pediatric Ophthalmology.* Vol I and II. Philadelphia, PA: W.B. Saunders Co.; 1983.

Occupational Therapy Low Vision Rehabilitation Evaluation

INTRODUCTION

The objective of this chapter is to present an organized evaluation approach for the adult low vision client. In 2002, the American Occupational Therapy Association (AOTA) published the *Occupational Therapy Practice Framework: Domain and Process*.[1] The *Framework* was developed to articulate occupational therapy's unique focus on occupation and daily activities and the application of an intervention process that facilitates engagement in occupation to support participation in life.[1] In regard to the occupational therapy evaluation, the *Framework* states that "the evaluation process is focused on finding out what the client wants and needs to do and on identifying those factors that act as barriers to performance".[1] The evaluation that we present below follows these guidelines.

OVERVIEW

In the model of low vision care we proposed in Chapter 1, the ophthalmologist diagnoses and treats the eye disease responsible for the vision loss. The low vision optometrist evaluates the client once it is determined that additional medical/surgical treatment will not be useful. The role of the optometrist is to try and maximize the client's visual function using a combination of traditional eyeglasses plus low vision optical devices. The occupational therapist's role is to determine what the client wants and needs to do, identify factors that act as barriers to performance, and develop a treatment plan to meet the client's specific needs. It is also important for the occupational therapist to interact with the low vision optometrist. The occupational therapist can provide important information to the optometrist about the client's physical capabilities, living environment, and needs. This information can then be used by the optometrist to determine the appropriate low vision optical aids.

Thus, although the occupational therapist's examination screens for changes in an underlying pathology, the occupational therapy evaluation is not designed to be diagnostic in terms of identifying the disorder. This information should be available from the ophthalmologist and optometrist. Rather, the objective of the occupational therapy low vision rehabilitation evaluation is to understand the client's functional ability before the vision loss, to define his/her current goals, to evaluate the client's ability to participate in

activities of daily living (ADL), leisure, work, play, and social and spiritual occupations. In addition, the occupational therapist evaluates social, cultural, and physical context as well as client factors other than vision, including musculoskeletal process and mental/cognitive factors. Although the low vision optometrist typically provides the initial device selection and estimation of magnification, the occupational therapist evaluates devices in the context of occupational performance and may recommend magnification and different devices. The low vision therapist may need to estimate the magnification required for performance of some tasks. It is also important to remember that under Medicare Part B guidelines, the initial evaluation completed by the occupational therapist is used to determine whether there is medical necessity for low vision rehabilitation.[2]

To accomplish these goals, the occupational therapy vision rehabilitation evaluation consists of four components:

1. Occupational profile/case history
2. Evaluation of visual factors
3. Environmental evaluation
4. Evaluation of occupational performance

Of course, some clients may have other physical disabilities/issues that need to be addressed and the traditional occupational therapy evaluation procedures should be used to assess these problems.

The Veterans Affairs Low-Vision Visual Functioning Questionnaire [VA LV VFQ-48] and an evaluation form can be found on www.slackbooks.com/otvisionforms

OCCUPATIONAL PROFILE/CASE HISTORY

The occupational therapy evaluation of an adult who is suspected of having low vision begins with the occupational profile/case history. The occupational profile/case history is the formalized process of asking relevant questions to elicit information that will contribute to an understanding of the client's problems. Specifically, the objectives of this part of the evaluation are to gather information about the client's vision and health status, previous eyecare and low vision treatment, to understand the client's functional ability before the vision loss, and to define his or her current goals.

An integral part of the evaluation, the occupational profile/case history offers a rich source of data for case formulation that is not available from other forms of assessment. The occupational profile/case history will shape the evaluation strategy, development of the management plan, and the formulation of the rehabilitation prognosis. In addition to contributing to better diagnostic and therapeutic decisions, the foundation for a good client-therapist relationship is established during this time.

One important issue for occupational therapists is time management. In almost all clinical settings, the amount of time available for the occupational therapy evaluation is limited to about 1 hour. This limitation may be based on high client census or insurance guidelines and protocols. It is, therefore, important to design an evaluation that can be completed in a reasonable period of time. To facilitate this objective, we suggest the use of a low vision visual functioning questionnaire. Visual functioning questionnaires include a series of questions that assess the performance of ADL.[3] Stelmack et al recently described a self-report questionnaire designed to measure the difficulty visually impaired persons have performing ADL.[4] The questionnaire, called the Veterans Affairs Low-Vision Visual Functioning Questionnaire (VA LV VFQ-48), was found to be a valid and reliable measure of visual ability in low-vision clients with moderate to severe vision loss. This questionnaire is not only used to measure performance ability, but can also be used to tailor rehabilitation programs to meet individual client needs and to measure outcomes of rehabilitation programs.[4] The VA LV VFQ-48 has a strong research basis and its validity and reliability have been established. The questionnaire can be scored and the occupational therapist can, therefore, obtain a number that can be compared to normative data. This score can be used to document the need for rehabilitation. In addition, the VA LV VFQ-48 can be readministered at each reevaluation to document functional improvement. Thus, in addition to streamlining the evaluation, it is an effective tool for Medicare documentation.

The VA LV VFQ-48 can be administered over the phone or can be sent to the client, and the client is asked to bring the completed form to the occupational therapy low vision rehabilitation evaluation. The questionnaire was not designed for the low vision client to complete independently. Rather, a family member or friend would have to help the client complete this questionnaire because it is not available in large print size. The occupational therapist can review the questionnaire and elaborate on pertinent issues raised by the client's responses using the Low Vision Rehabilitation Evaluation form included in the appendix. It is important, however, to understand that the VA LV VFQ-48 is not a substitute for interaction with the client. The Occupational Profile/Case History interview is an excellent time to establish rapport with the client, to demonstrate interest in the client as

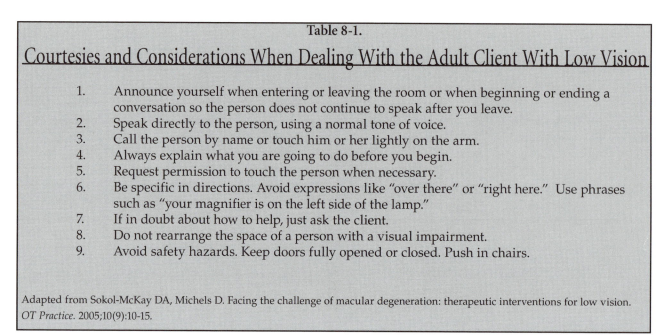

Table 8-1.

Courtesies and Considerations When Dealing With the Adult Client With Low Vision

1. Announce yourself when entering or leaving the room or when beginning or ending a conversation so the person does not continue to speak after you leave.
2. Speak directly to the person, using a normal tone of voice.
3. Call the person by name or touch him or her lightly on the arm.
4. Always explain what you are going to do before you begin.
5. Request permission to touch the person when necessary.
6. Be specific in directions. Avoid expressions like "over there" or "right here." Use phrases such as "your magnifier is on the left side of the lamp."
7. If in doubt about how to help, just ask the client.
8. Do not rearrange the space of a person with a visual impairment.
9. Avoid safety hazards. Keep doors fully opened or closed. Push in chairs.

Adapted from Sokol-McKay DA, Michels D. Facing the challenge of macular degeneration: therapeutic interventions for low vision. *OT Practice.* 2005;10(9):10-15.

a person, and thereby to establish a basis for effective communication.

Interviewing the Client

The rapport established between the occupational therapist and client will influence the accuracy of the information obtained during the interview as well as the client's confidence in the assessment and his/her response to later recommendations. Therefore, the occupational therapist's attitude should be one of interest, willingness to listen, and empathetic concern. A manner that is friendly and informal will lessen any anxiety associated with the visit. A hurried, indifferent, detached, or unempathetic presence is a barrier to effective communication, which in turn may have a deleterious effect on the interview process.[5] Breakdowns in communication frequently result in failure to comply with a professional's recommendations.[6] Because of the client's visual impairment, interaction is different from that typical of a case history with a normally sighted person. Sokol-McKay[7] emphasized the importance of implementing certain courtesies and considerations when evaluating an adult client with low vision. Examples of these courtesies are announcing yourself when entering or leaving the room or when beginning or ending a conversation, speaking directly to the person, using a normal tone of voice, and requesting permission to touch the person when necessary. Table 8-1 is a list of these suggested courtesies.

Using the VA LV VFQ-48 as a basis for exploration of particular areas of concern, the occupational therapist can begin with broad-based questions with a progression to more focused inquiries. The strategy is to scan potentially important areas and focus in when appropriate, while maintaining sensitivity and flexibility in listening and pursuing.[5]

The key areas to be investigated are listed in Table 8-2 and included in the Low Vision Rehabilitation Evaluation form. These are only suggested starting points. The occupational therapist will need to ask additional questions based on the client's initial responses.

The Low Vision Rehabilitation Evaluation form can be found on www.slackbooks.com/otvisionforms

Important Areas to Be Addressed in the Occupational Profile/Case History

Vision History

It is important to determine the client's understanding of his or her eye disease and vision problem. The therapist should ask questions about onset (when did the problem begin), duration (how long has the client been visually impaired), the date of the last examination, and questions to probe the client's understanding of the diagnosis, prognosis, and effects on performance (Table 8-3). Even if a complete report is available from the referring doctor, it is worthwhile to gather this information from the perspective of a client. A client's answers to these questions will indicate stage of coping, expectations, and many aspects of cognitive functioning. One of the critical factors determining the effectiveness of vision rehabilitation is a motivated, educated client. The more the cli-

Table 8-2.

Suggested Additional Questions for Occupational Profile/Case History

Living Situation

- Prior Level of Function
- Marital Status
- Description of residence
- Assisted living
- Nursing home
- One floor/multifloor

Prior Level of Function

(Goal is to determine how client functioned in home/work prior to visual impairment)
- Driving
- Meal preparation
- Finances
- Cleaning home
- Leisure activities
- Shopping
- Mobility

Medical History

- Hearing loss
- Hearing Aid
- Diabetes
- Dialysis
- Stroke
- Hypertension
- Angina
- Cardiac problems
- Arthritis
- Respiratory problems
- Cognitive and emotional health
- Medications

ent knows and understands about his or her vision problems, the more likely rehabilitation will be effective. After discussing the onset and duration, ask the client about previous and current treatment. We are primarily interested in the treatment of the resulting disability, not the impairment or eye disease itself. By definition, this client has been sent to the therapist because the underlying eye disease has caused permanent vision loss.

We need to know the optical or nonoptical devices that have been prescribed or purchased by the client on his or her own, and if the client is able to use these devices. Have there been any previous attempts at vision rehabilitation? If so, who provided these servic-

es and were these services helpful? It is also important to determine if the client is aware of support groups and other opportunities in the community to receive help, support, and education about low vision.

Health History

The health history is an important component of the occupational profile/case history. An understanding of the client's other medical problems is necessary when planning vision rehabilitation. Nonoptical and optical device selections are contingent on the client's physical and health status. Common examples include: peripheral sensation problems secondary to diabetes that limits the use of tactile devices, hand

Table 8-3.

Suggested Initial Questions About Vision Loss for Occupational Profile/Case History

What happened and why are you here?
Do you know the name of the eye disease that has caused your vision loss?
Can you tell me when this eye disease first became a problem for you?
What are some things you cannot do now that you did before your vision loss?
What do you miss the most?
How long have you experienced trouble seeing?
Do you know your visual acuity?
What is most difficult to see?
Do people treat you differently now than before the vision loss?
Have you ever had a low vision evaluation? When? Where?
Do you use any magnifiers or special glasses?
Who gave the magnifiers or special glasses to you?
Have you had any previous vision rehabilitation services? If so, describe.

tremors that might interfere with the use of optical devices, hearing problems that may preclude the use of assistive devices such as liquid level alert and books on tape, and arthritis that may limit movement and, therefore, the ability to use certain optical devices.

Of course, most occupational therapists will not be treating clients with only low vision problems. Because the population of clients seen by the occupational therapist will generally be the older adult, many clients will have multiple medical conditions requiring occupational therapy. It is, therefore, important to question the client about general health status. The occupational profile/case history, therefore, should include questions about hearing loss, diabetes, dialysis, previous stroke, hypertension, cardiac problems, arthritis, and respiratory ailments.

It is also important to obtain a complete list of the client's medications. The therapist should review the medications for potential side-effects that might be important when planning vision rehabilitation. Some drugs affect pupil size and function and can cause blurred vision and photophobia (sensitivity to light).

Premorbid Occupational Performance and History

The importance of occupational history has been summarized in the AOTA *Practice Framework*.[1] A person's expectations about vision rehabilitation are often closely associated with his/her previous level of activity, occupation, habits, routines, and roles. Clients typically want vision to be the way it was before the eye disease caused the vision loss, rather than focus on lost occupation and roles. In some cases, improvement in vision may be possible using optical devices with

mild vision loss, or lighting changes, but treatment often focuses on compensatory strategies, assistive devices, and vision rehabilitation that enable occupational performance using different sensory modalities or strategies. In most cases, therefore, the client will need to realize that some significant changes will be required in lifestyle. Information should be gathered about work, sports, and leisure activities.

To understand a client's expectations and to insure that the client's chief concern will be addressed, one should begin with a general question such as: "Why are you here? What is it you want us to do for you?"

Typical responses include the following:

- "I have something wrong with my eyes and want to see better" (the focus is on the impairment).

- "I have macular degeneration, I can't read, I want to use a computer again" (the focus is on occupation).

- "My [doctor, daughter] sent me here" (no clear goals, client education needs, psychosocial impairment with coping, cognitive impairment, or family/caregiver education needs).

The client's initial response will indicate education needs, level of insight, as well as the general stage of coping with the disability. Since the most effective interventions are often compensatory, a skilled clinician will focus this segment of the evaluation on recovery of occupational performance with questions such as: "What did you do before you vision loss that you can't do now?" "What do you miss the most?" "Do people treat you differently now?" These questions will begin to reveal important occupational

Table 8-4.

List of Questions to Determine a Client's Goals for Vision Rehabilitation

Close-up Vision

As you go about your daily household chores, what do you need to read (mail, cooking controls, medical prescriptions, etc)?
How many of these chores are essential for continuing the same level of independence you currently experience?
What, if any, are you professional reading requirements (journals, magazine, memos, computer work)?
What are your leisure reading activities?
Which of these activities are important for your continued happiness?
What other daily household chores require close-up vision (sorting laundry, housecleaning, preparing meals)?
What chores could you confidently perform without sight?
Name your recreational activities that require close-up vision (cards, sewing, and music).
Which of these could you perform without sight?

Distance Vision

Name the daily distance tasks you do that require sight (driving, seeing signs, lights, landmarks). Which of these activities could you confidently undertake if your vision deteriorates?
Which of your leisure activities require good distance vision (television, attending shows, movies, sporting events)? Which of these activities could you perform without good vision?

---

goals and lost roles that could be restored using compensatory strategies.

Client's Needs and Goals

Finally, it is important to let the client tell you what he/she hopes to achieve through vision rehabilitation. As discussed above, it is not unusual to hear some unrealistic expectations from clients. Remember that the prior experience of this client was that new glasses always restored clear vision. Clients often expect the same result even when the vision loss is caused by disease. They either fail to understand that the vision loss is permanent or refuse to accept this prognosis. By the time the client is being examined by the occupational therapist, he/she may have had numerous examinations with an ophthalmologist and perhaps a low vision optometrist. The client has been told that there are no miracle glasses, devices, or drugs that will restore normal vision. Yet, it is not unusual for the client to say, "I want to be able to see well again" or "I am hoping you can prescribe glasses that will help me see well again".[8]

Low vision treatment and vision rehabilitation are designed to help clients with low vision fulfill realistic vision-related goals.[8] Freeman indicates that the two primary ingredients that determine success or failure are: 1) the client's acceptance of the need to use optical and nonoptical assistive devices, and 2) motivation to take an active role learning how to use his or her remaining vision.[8]

Table 8-4 lists a series of questions modified from a "personal eyesight evaluation" developed by Paul Freeman, OD. These questions allow the therapists to help the client systematically develop a list of realistic goals for vision rehabilitation. Before moving on to the next part of the evaluation, the therapist must have a list developed by the client of his or her goals for vision rehabilitation.

Examples of common, realistic performance goals are:

- I want to be able to read the sports page.
- I want to be able to follow a recipe and cook meals for my family.
- I want to be able to enjoy a movie in a movie theater.
- I want to be able to find products myself at the supermarket.
- I want to be able to write letters to my grandchildren and read their responses.
- I want to be able to independently read mail, write checks, and handle my finances.

Visual Function	Recommended Technique Home Health Setting	Recommended Technique Hospital/Nursing Home/Outpatient Settings
Visual acuity at distance	Feinbloom Distance Test Chart	ETDRS Chart
Reading acuity at near	MN Read test	MN Read test
Peripheral visual field	Confrontation Field Testing	Confrontation Field Testing
Contrast sensitivity	Mars Letter Contrast Sensitivity Test	Mars Letter Contrast Sensitivity Test
Scotoma assessment	Clock Face scotoma assessment	Tangent Screen
Reading assessment/ reading speed	Pepper Test, MN Read test	Pepper Test, MN Read test

Table 8-5.
Recommended Test of Visual Function

Psychosocial and Cognitive Issues

Vision loss is one of the most emotionally devastating physical problems that one can experience, and its impact extends beyond functional vision problems to many psychosocial issues.[9] It is critical, therefore, that occupational therapists attend to the emotional impact of the vision loss and the client's ability to cope when providing low vision rehabilitation. In Chapter 7, we outlined seven key factors[9] that should be reviewed by the occupational therapist during the occupational profile/case history. These include: the type of vision loss, the family's reaction to the vision loss, the client's life stage, significant life events, the client's expectations, the client's self-concept, and personality. In addition, if the occupational therapist is concerned about the client's mental health, we suggest using one of the self-report questionnaires described in Chapter 7. Three of the most popular self-report measures are the Center for Epidemiological Studies Depression Scale (CES-D), the Beck Depression Inventory (BDI), and the Geriatric Depression Scale (GDS). We recommend using the GDS because it can be easily administered in a very short period of time. There is no cost for this test because it was developed with federal funds.

Low vision, especially severe and profound vision loss, creates unique and substantial cognitive demands, especially with spatial perception and use and interpretation of other senses. A person with a long-standing visual impairment may have developed an ability to interpret vision differently, eg, using a hairline and a person's gait to recognize him, or using blobs of color to orient in a room. These skills are sometimes informally called "blur interpretation." Introducing visual devices (optical or electronic) may confuse individuals with long-standing visual impairment at first, but acceptance might follow with repeated practice.

EVALUATION OF VISUAL FACTORS

For the occupational therapist to determine the needs of a client and develop a treatment plan, he or she must have a thorough understanding of the client's visual status. Important visual factors include: visual acuity at distance and at near; the specific eye disease; visual field; contrast sensitivity; presence, size, and location of the central scotoma; reading skill; and reading speed. Depending on the occupational therapist's practice setting, much of this information may be readily available from the referring ophthalmologist or optometrist. Occupational therapists working in an ophthalmology office, a low vision practice, or any other facility in which an ophthalmologist and/or an optometrist is working, will have full access to the client's eye records and the required information. Even if the occupational therapist is not working directly with an eyecare professional, this information can be requested from the referring doctor. We have included a form in the Appendix that can be used for this purpose. However, there may be situations in which the necessary data are just not available. In such cases, the occupational therapist will need to perform specific testing to gather this information. The recommended areas and tests are listed in Table 8-5. Background information for these tests is reviewed in Chapter 3. It should be noted that visual acuity testing should be repeated every session to monitor for changes in vision and in cases of active pathology.

Figure 8-1. Feinbloom Distance Acuity Chart.

One additional issue that will determine the actual test selection is the therapist's practice setting. Therapists working in the client's home will need portable tests that can easily be transported and set up in a variety of home settings. Therapists working in hospitals, nursing homes, and outpatient settings should be able to establish some dedicated space in which all of the necessary equipment is permanently set up and available. Thus, in the following discussion and in Table 8-5 we make recommendations based on practice settings.

Visual Acuity at Distance—Feinbloom Chart

Practice Setting

Recommended for home health setting or any setting in which portability is important.

Equipment Required

Feinbloom Distance Test Chart
Occluder

Description

This chart (Figure 8-1) is widely used.[10] The characteristics of the chart are reviewed in Chapter 3. The Feinbloom chart was calibrated for 20 feet but is typically used at a 10-foot distance, which means the acuity values listed above would be doubled. At a 10-foot distance, the acuity range extends from 20/1400 to 20/20.

If a client cannot even see the large "7" at 10 feet, the chart can be moved to 5 feet. At this distance, the acuity range is extended from 20/1400 to 2800 because each time you decrease the distance by half you double the denominator.

Another major advantage of this visual acuity chart is that because of the large visual acuity range that can be assessed, almost all clients with low vision will be able to read at least some letters on the visual acuity chart. This is important from a psychological standpoint. Many clients with low vision have had negative experiences during visual acuity testing if they were unable to even see the large "E." This can be depressing. The client feels that there is no hope if he or she couldn't see the eye chart at all. With the Feinbloom chart, however, most clients are able to read quite a few lines on the chart, leading to a much more positive experience.[10,11]

Setup and Procedure

1. The client should wear his/her usual glasses. The examiner should be careful to make sure glasses are clean (clean with cotton cloth and water) and adjusted so the client is looking through the top half of the lens for distance testing.

2. The Feinbloom chart is positioned 10 feet away and the client's left eye is covered with the occluder.

3. The occupational therapist opens the chart to the largest number (number 7 = 20/1400 at 10 feet) and asks the client to call out the number.

4. The occupational therapist proceeds until the client can no longer read the numbers correctly at 10 feet and records the last level at which the client can read more than 50% of the numbers.

5. The occluder is then held before the client's right eye and then neither eye so that binocular visual acuity is tested.

6. If the client is unable to see the largest number at 10 feet, the chart should be moved to 5 feet and testing should be attempted again.

7. If the client is still unable to see the largest letter, test at a 2.5 foot distance.

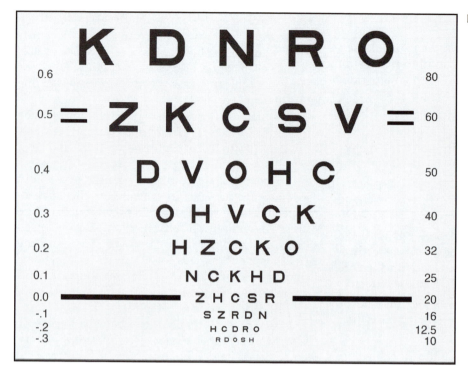

Figure 8-2. ETDRS Chart.

Interpretation

The visual acuity should be recorded as 10 (testing distance)/last size number identified. For example, if the testing was performed at 10 feet and the client could identify the 350 size numbers, the visual acuity would be reported as 10/350. To convert this to the more traditional 20/20 notation, the clinician multiplies both the top and bottom of the equation by 2. Thus, 10/350 is equivalent to 20/700.

It is appropriate to encourage guessing, eye movements, and eccentric viewing to see the numbers[10] as a means of determining the prognosis for rehabilitation. However, when determining the visual acuity for Medicare documentation and coding, the chart should be placed at 20 feet and eccentric viewing and turning of the head should not be permitted.

Shortcomings of the Feinbloom Chart

One major problem with the Feinbloom chart is that it does not have an equal number of optotypes per acuity level. There is only one number at the 20/700, 20/600, 20/400, 20/350, 20/300, 20/225 levels, and only three per line from 20/200 to 20/60. Also, the letters are not standard, so acuity measured with the Feinbloom chart may not match acuity measured with another chart. Because of these shortcomings, the Early Treatment Diabetic Retinopathy Study Chart (ETDRS) described below should be used when the therapist can establish a permanent work area.

Visual Acuity at Distance—ETDRS Chart

Practice Setting

Recommended for any setting in which the equipment can be setup permanently.

Equipment Required

ETDRS Chart
Occluder

Description

This chart provides five letters per line and also standardizes the separation between letters (Figure 8-2). A unique aspect of this chart is its geometric progression of size differences between lines, referred to as logMAR progression. Optotypes on each line are 0.1 log unit or 25% larger than the previous line. This format results in every three lines representing a halving or doubling of visual acuity at any given viewing distance, for example, if one starts at 100 and goes down three steps (step 1 = 80, step 2 = 80 to 63, and step 3 = 63 to 50), which is one-half of 100. These characteristics allows for consistent and accurate evaluation of visual acuity.

The standard test distance is 4 meters, but for low vision evaluations the test distance is usually halved to 2 meters to insure a client can read the largest letters.

Setup and Procedure

1. The client should wear his or her usual glasses. The examiner should be careful to make sure the glasses are clean (clean with cotton cloth and water) and adjusted so the client is looking through the top half of the lens for distance testing.

2. The ETDRS chart is positioned at 4 meters and the client's left eye is covered with the occluder.

3. The occupational therapist asks the client to call out the letters on the top line.

4. The occupational therapist proceeds until the client can no longer read the letters correctly at 4 meters and records the last level at which the client can read more than 50% of the letters.

5. The occluder is then held before the client's right eye and neither eye so that binocular visual acuity is tested.

6. If the client is unable to see the largest letters at 4 meters, the chart should be moved to 2 meters and testing should be attempted again.

Interpretation

Testing distances are typically 2 meters or 4 meters. At the 2-meter working distance, the acuity obtained can easily be converted to standard Snellen 20-ft notation by just adding a zero to the numerator and denominator. For example, a 2/10 acuity measurement becomes 20/100; an acuity of 32 M at 2 meters corresponds to a 20-ft equivalent of 20/320.

As with the Feinbloom chart, it is appropriate to encourage guessing, eye movements, and eccentric viewing to see the numbers as a means of determining the prognosis for rehabilitation.

Reading Acuity (Visual Acuity at Near With Continuous Text)

Practice Setting

Appropriate for any practice setting.

Equipment Required

Minnesota Low-Vision Reading Test (MN Read Test)

Description

If a client is going to regain independence in ADL, he or she will need to be able to read again. We also know that near visual acuity for single letters (letter acuity) is often different than near visual acuity for reading phrases and sentences (reading acuity). Therefore, to better understand the impact of the low vision on reading, it is important to assess both letter and reading acuity. While low vision specialists routinely administer both types of tests, most eye doctors only evaluate near letter visual acuity. Thus, the occupational therapist may need to evaluate reading acuity at near.

A popular test for assessing continuous reading acuity is the Minnesota Low-Vision Reading Test (MN Read Test) illustrated in Figure 8-3. An advantage of using this test is that it not only provides an assessment of near visual acuity with continuous text, it also allows the therapist to evaluate the client's reading speed. Unlike visual acuity, which is not expected to improve with vision rehabilitation, reading speed is one function that can be improved. Thus, reading speed is one of the areas for which the occupational therapist may be able to document improvements with treatment and justify additional vision rehabilitation in Medicare documentation.

The MN Read acuity chart can be used to provide a sensitive and reliable measure of reading acuity. Each sentence has 60 characters, which correspond to 10 standard length words, assuming a standard word length of 6 characters (including spaces). The reading level of each line is controlled as well. An estimate of reading acuity is given by the smallest print size at which the client can read the entire sentence without making significant errors. (Usually reading performance deteriorates rapidly as the acuity limit is approached, and it is easy to determine the level where reading becomes impossible). The examiner uses a stopwatch to record the time required to read each paragraph and this allows a determination of reading speed. A modified graph that can be used for recording results can be found in the Appendices.

The therapist's goal with this test is to determine the best print size for reading at a given distance. Typically, there are two distances at which clients often must read. The most common distance for continuous text reading is 16 inches or 40 cm. The second common distance is about 32 inches or about 80 cm (arm's length), the usual distance of stovetop dials and shelf labels.

Two endpoints should be noted with this test:
1. Continuous text reading acuity: This is the smallest print the client can read.
2. Critical print size: The print size just before reading starts to slow, ie, the smallest print that results in maximum reading rate.

Setup and Procedure

1. The client should wear his or her usual reading glasses. The examiner should be careful to make sure the glasses are clean (clean with cotton cloth and water) and adjusted so the client is looking through the bottom half of the

Figure 8-3. MN Read Visual Acuity Chart.

lenses for near testing if it is a bifocal or progressive lens (no-line bifocal) design. A client is usually tested under binocular conditions if he or she typically reads with both eyes, or with the better eye if he or she reads with one eye.

2. The usual distance for the MN Read chart is 40 cm from the eyes. If the patient is reading with stronger reading glasses, the test should be measured at the correct distance for the prescribed glasses. This can be calculated from the reading addition in the report from the eyecare provider (see Chapter 13). This information must be accurate before testing proceeds. Make sure the test distance is maintained throughout the testing.

3. Allow the client to move the card side to side, but be careful to prevent the client from bringing the chart closer as the print size becomes smaller.

4. Instruct the client to begin reading the paragraphs from top to bottom of the chart. Note the critical print size, the print size just before the line where reading starts to slow.

5. As the client reads smaller print, encourage him to keep reading until he starts making mistakes. The smallest print at which the client can read with no more than one error is continuous text reading acuity.

6. Using a stopwatch, the examiner also records how long it takes to read each paragraph. This information is used to determine the client's reading speed. The MN Read Test comes with a conversion table that allows the examiner to convert the stopwatch measurement into words per minute.

Interpretation

The critical print size is the last paragraph read before reading starts to slow. This is recorded using "M" notation. The client continues reading even if he or she slows down, and the smallest print at which the client can read with no more than one error is continuous text reading acuity. This would also be recorded using "M" notation as above. Typically, critical print size is 3 lines above continuous test acuity. If distance visual acuity indicated that the vision in the left eye was better than the vision in the right eye, the left eye should be tested separately. If the last paragraph read

before reading starts (critical print size) was 1 M at a test distance of 40 cm, the result would be recorded as:

Critical print size: 0.4/1 M (OS) or "1 M at 40 cm"
Acuity: 0.4/ 0.5 M (OS) or "0.5 M at 40 cm"

Note that acuity, reading performance, and critical print size must always include a specification of test distance as well as target size.

Peripheral Visual Field

Practice Setting
Appropriate for any practice setting.

Equipment Required
None.

Description
Visual field testing is designed to evaluate an individual's peripheral vision. Visual field loss can be either absolute or relative. An absolute visual field loss is one in which no matter how large and bright the target is, it will not be seen within the blind area. A relative visual field loss, on the other hand, is dependent on the size, brightness, and contrast of the target, relative to the environment. This translates functionally into variations of visual field consistency based on environmental conditions. For example, a person with a relative peripheral visual field loss might function better under bright illumination than under dim lighting conditions or at night. There are several instruments that can formally quantify the extent of the visual field. These instruments are expensive and the testing is time consuming. A good alternative for the occupational therapist is confrontation field testing. No equipment is necessary for this testing. The examiner sits opposite the client, and the client has to indicate when he or she can see the examiner's fingers or hands brought in from the periphery.

When eye doctors assess a client's visual field, the testing is done monocularly, first with the right eye and then with the left eye alone. However, for the occupational therapist performing peripheral field testing under normal viewing conditions with both eyes open is more practical. The occupational therapist is trying to determine if a visual field deficit exists under normal seeing conditions and how it might affect ADL.

Setup and Procedure
Part 1 – Testing for a Hemianopsia (Field Cut)
1. The examiner sits an arm's length away from the client, or about 80 cm (32 inches).
2. The examiner's hands should be half the distance between him and the client, or about 40 cm (16 inches).
3. The examiner and the client will see the same thing, except the examiner's right is the client's left.
4. The examiner instructs the client to "look directly into my eye and tell me how many fingers you see out of your side vision. Do not look at my hands, only at my eye".
5. Make sure the background is not cluttered. For example, a uniform wall or curtain should be behind the examiner.
6. The examiner positions her fingers about 40 cm from the client and presents 1, 2, or 3 fingers together, one hand at a time, until the client counts them reliably.
7. The examiner tests the client's peripheral vision using three positions on the right and three positions on the left (ie, presenting his fingers at 2, 4, 6, 8, and 10 o'clock positions).

Interpretation
A visual field loss is indicated if the client is unable to see the target on one side. If the client is unable to see the target when presented on the right side until the target is essentially at the midline, the deficit is called a right hemianopsia. The same problem on the left side is called a left hemianopsia.

Contrast Sensitivity and Lighting Evaluation

Practice Setting
Appropriate for any practice setting.

Equipment Required
Mars Letter Contrast Sensitivity Test.

Description
The Mars Letter Contrast Sensitivity Test is a set of letter charts for testing peak contrast sensitiv-

ity (Figure 8-4). The more familiar visual acuity test assesses the ability to see small, high-contrast objects or print. Symbol contrast sensitivity with symbols that are well above acuity threshold relates to a person's ability to see large, lower contrast objects such as magnified but lower contrast print, or larger lower contrast shapes like the last step on carpeted stairs. As such, it is a useful instrument in the clinician's arsenal of assessment tools. The test consists of three printed charts for independent left eye, right eye, and binocular testing. The three forms are identical except for the sequence of letters chosen. Figure 8-5 is a sample score sheet.

The test itself consists of 48 letters arranged in eight rows of six letters each. The contrast of each letter gradually decreases reading from left to right, and continuing on successive lines. The client simply reads the letters across lines and down the chart, as in standard letter acuity measurement. Instead of the letters decreasing in size, however, they decrease in contrast.

Setup and Procedure

1. For best results, the chart should be illuminated uniformly. The patient is tested with both eyes or the preferred eye as with near acuity.
2. The viewing distance should be selected to insure that the letters are at least 2 times acuity threshold and more. This is easily done by starting far away and moving the chart closer until the client can barely recognize the darkest letter. Move the chart half that distance and start testing.
3. Clients should wear their appropriate eyeglass correction for the test distance and an occluder or patch on the untested eye.
4. To speed up test time, have the patient read down the left side of the chart. When reading slows, ask the client to read the letters from left to right across each line of the chart. If the client responds with a letter other than C, D, H, K, N, O, R, S, V, or Z, do not score the response as incorrect. Instead, inform the client of the restricted letter set, and ask for another response.
5. Encourage the client to guess, even when the letters seem too faint.
6. On the score sheet (see Figure 8-5), mark in the grid corresponding to the chart form used, an X for each letter incorrectly identified. Stop testing only when the client makes two consecutive errors or reaches the end of the chart
7. Do not terminate the test because the client has given up and has stopped responding. If

this happens, encourage the client to guess, and score the guesses as ordinary responses. This will help to insure that the score is based on what the client can see and not on what the client believes he or she can see.

8. The score is given by the contrast sensitivity value of the lowest contrast letter just prior to two incorrectly identified letters, minus a scoring correction.
9. The letter just prior to the two consecutive misses is called the final correct letter.
10. If the client reaches the end of the chart without making two consecutive errors, then the final correct letter is simply the final letter correctly identified.
11. If the client does not achieve contrast threshold of 2% or better after the lighting modifications described below, decrease the distance in half once again, and start testing at the last line tested above. Record the results as contrast threshold at 4X acuity.

Interpretation

Table 8-6 is used to determine the contrast sensitivity for the client. This can then be converted to contrast threshold. Contrast threshold is defined as an object with the lowest contrast that a client can recognize. A client with normal vision can usually see objects with as little as 2% to 3% contrast. If the contrast of an object is less than the contrast threshold of the client, the object cannot be seen. Contrast sensitivity is the reciprocal of the contrast at threshold, ie, one divided by the lowest contrast at which forms or lines can be recognized. If a person can see details at very low contrast, his or her contrast sensitivity is high and vice versa. A client with a contrast threshold of 2% has higher contrast sensitivity (1/2 = 50) than a client with a contrast threshold of 10% (1/10 = 10).

On this test, the contrast of the final letter before which the client misidentifies two consecutive letters, with a correction for earlier incorrect responses, determines the log contrast sensitivity. Normal values of monocular log CS are about 1.8 (1.6% contrast) in children and young adults, and about 1.68 (2.0% contrast) for older adults (over 60 years of age). Table 8-7 can be used to interpret the results of contrast sensitivity testing.

Effect of Lighting

For patients with vision impairment, lighting can have a significant effect on performance. Therefore, when performing these visual acuity or contrast sensitivity tests, it is useful to modify the lighting conditions and determine the effects of these changes.

Figure 8-4. Mars Letter Contrast Sensitivity Test (reprinted with permission from the Mars Perceptrix Corporation).

Figure 8-5. Sample Scoring Sheet from Mars Letter Contrast Sensitivity Test (reprinted with permission from the Mars Perceptrix Corporation).

The Mars Letter Contrast Sensitivity Test

Score Sheet

Patient _____   Administered by _____

Date _____   Correction _____   Test distance _____

Comments _____

Quick Instructions: Instruct patient to read letters left to right for each line, from top to bottom of the chart. Mark misses with an "X." Stop test on 2 consecutive misses.

Important: Allow *only* the letters C D H K N O R S V Z as responses.

FORM 1   Left eye ☐   Right eye ☐   Binocular ☐

C☐ 0.04	H☐ 0.08	V☐ 0.12	O☐ 0.16	S☐ 0.20	N☐ 0.24
D☐ 0.28	S☐ 0.32	Z☐ 0.36	N☐ 0.40	R☐ 0.44	K☐ 0.48
N☐ 0.52	D☐ 0.56	R☐ 0.60	H☐ 0.64	V☐ 0.68	Z☐ 0.72
C☐ 0.76	S☐ 0.80	O☐ 0.84	N☐ 0.88	K☐ 0.92	H☐ 0.96
K☐ 1.00	N☐ 1.04	V☐ 1.08	D☐ 1.12	S☐ 1.16	R☐ 1.20
Z☐ 1.24	R☐ 1.28	D☐ 1.32	K☐ 1.36	H☐ 1.40	O☐ 1.44
H☐ 1.48	Z☐ 1.52	C☐ 1.56	V☐ 1.60	R☐ 1.64	K☐ 1.68
S☐ 1.72	C☐ 1.76	Z☐ 1.80	D☐ 1.84	V☐ 1.88	O☐ 1.92

Value of final correct letter: _____

Number of misses prior to stopping _____ X 0.04   = _____

Subtract

log Contrast Sensitivity _____

FORM 2   Left eye ☐   Right eye ☐   Binocular ☐

K☐ 0.04	S☐ 0.08	H☐ 0.12	O☐ 0.16	N☐ 0.20	C☐ 0.24
Z☐ 0.28	D☐ 0.32	C☐ 0.36	R☐ 0.40	V☐ 0.44	O☐ 0.48
C☐ 0.52	K☐ 0.56	O☐ 0.60	N☐ 0.64	R☐ 0.68	S☐ 0.72
N☐ 0.76	S☐ 0.80	Z☐ 0.84	K☐ 0.88	H☐ 0.92	D☐ 0.96
H☐ 1.00	N☐ 1.04	C☐ 1.08	O☐ 1.12	R☐ 1.16	Z☐ 1.20
V☐ 1.24	K☐ 1.28	S☐ 1.32	N☐ 1.36	D☐ 1.40	R☐ 1.44
K☐ 1.48	R☐ 1.52	V☐ 1.56	Z☐ 1.60	O☐ 1.64	S☐ 1.68
V☐ 1.72	Z☐ 1.76	C☐ 1.80	D☐ 1.84	V☐ 1.88	H☐ 1.92

Value of final correct letter: _____

Number of misses prior to stopping _____ X 0.04   = _____

Subtract

log Contrast Sensitivity _____

FORM 3   Left eye ☐   Right eye ☐   Binocular ☐

H☐ 0.04	R☐ 0.08	Z☐ 0.12	V☐ 0.16	C☐ 0.20	N☐ 0.24
S☐ 0.28	O☐ 0.32	K☐ 0.36	D☐ 0.40	R☐ 0.44	S☐ 0.48
K☐ 0.52	D☐ 0.56	C☐ 0.60	V☐ 0.64	O☐ 0.68	H☐ 0.72
N☐ 0.76	S☐ 0.80	O☐ 0.84	Z☐ 0.88	C☐ 0.92	D☐ 0.96
R☐ 1.00	H☐ 1.04	N☐ 1.08	K☐ 1.12	Z☐ 1.16	O☐ 1.20
C☐ 1.24	R☐ 1.28	S☐ 1.32	V☐ 1.36	K☐ 1.40	N☐ 1.44
S☐ 1.48	K☐ 1.52	R☐ 1.56	N☐ 1.60	H☐ 1.64	D☐ 1.68
C☐ 1.72	V☐ 1.76	H☐ 1.80	D☐ 1.84	O☐ 1.88	Z☐ 1.92

Value of final correct letter: _____

Number of misses prior to stopping _____ X 0.04   = _____

Subtract

log Contrast Sensitivity _____

mars perceptrix

Table 8-6.

Converting Log Contrast Sensitivity to Contrast Values (From the Mars Letter Contrast Sensitivity Test Manual)

log CS	Contrast	log CS	Contrast	log CS	Contrast	log CS	Contrast	log CS	Contrast	log CS	Contrast
0.04	0.912	0.08	0.832	0.12	0.759	0.16	0.692	0.20	0.631	0.24	0.575
0.28	0.525	0.32	0.479	0.36	0.437	0.40	0.398	0.44	0.363	0.48	0.331
0.52	0.302	0.56	0.275	0.60	0.251	0.64	0.229	0.68	0.209	0.72	0.191
0.76	0.174	0.80	0.158	0.84	0.145	0.88	0.132	0.92	0.120	0.96	0.110
1.00	0.100	1.04	0.091	1.08	0.083	1.12	0.076	1.16	0.069	1.20	0.063
1.24	0.058	1.28	0.052	1.32	0.048	1.36	0.044	1.40	0.040	1.44	0.036
1.48	0.033	1.52	0.030	1.56	0.028	1.60	0.025	1.64	0.023	1.68	0.021
1.72	0.019	1.76	0.017	1.80	0.016	1.84	0.014	1.88	0.013	1.92	0.012

Procedure

1. To determine the effect of lighting, place the Mars Letter Contrast Sensitivity Test at a distance at which the letters are at least 2 times the visual acuity threshold.

2. If at this distance the contrast threshold is worse than 4%, vary the amount of light to determine the range of light levels and type of light that produces contrast threshold at better than 4%.

3. We recommend the use of an illuminometer, which is an inexpensive device that measures light levels in units called Lux or footcandles. This allows the therapist to reproduce acceptable light levels accurately under various treatment situations and make appropriate home modifications.

4. To systematically modify lighting, the therapist first finds the type of light (fluorescent, incandescent, natural light) that produces best vision.

5. Once the best type of lighting is determined, the therapist varies the intensity by varying the distance of the light from the material being viewed.

6. If an illuminometer is unavailable, report type of light, wattage, and range of distances that produce contrast threshold better than 4% to 5%.

7. If contrast threshold better than 4% to 5% cannot be achieved, decrease test distance to the 4X distance.

8. Decreasing test distance is equivalent to increasing magnification of the print. If acceptable contrast threshold is achieved by relative distance magnification, this indicates the client will not only require careful control of lighting, but may require more magnification than is typical of someone with his or her visual acuity.

9. If contrast threshold never improves to a level better than 7%, this indicates that electronic magnification that enhances contrast may be more effective than optical magnification.

10. A severe loss (contrast threshold worse than 10%) indicates that fluent reading is unlikely even under optimal visual conditions.

This lighting assessment provides an excellent opportunity to determine the effect of usual glare sources, and educate the client. For example, the therapist can move the light source so that it shines directly into the client's eyes and measure any changes in contrast threshold, as well as directly illustrate to the client the effects of bad lighting.

Sunlens Evaluation

Someone walking outside on a sunny day, driving into the sun, or trying to recognize a familiar place in a brightly lit fluorescent dining hall must try to optimize lighting using sunglasses or sunlenses. An important component of the occupational therapy evaluation, therefore, involves having the client try on and select sunlenses under simulations of the conditions that cause problems. The general approach

Table 8-7.	
Interpreting Contrast Sensitivity Test Results	
Mars Log Contrast Sensitivity Score	*Interpretation*
0.60 or less	25% or higher—severe loss in contrast sensitivity Reading unlikely unless contrast enhanced and with very careful light control.
0.64 to 1.00	10% to 24%— oderate/severe loss in contrast sensitivity Fluent reading unlikely
1.04 to 1.28	5% to 9%—moderate loss in contrast sensitivity Contrast enhancement (electronic magnification) usually more effective than optical devices. Lighting evaluation indicated.
1.40 to 1.60	2.5% to 4%—mild loss in contrast sensitivity Increased sensitivity to light intensity level and glare
1.64 or greater	1.25% to 2.4%—normal contrast sensitivity

to a sunlens evaluation involves a trial-and-error approach under simulated conditions. The "getting started" evaluation equipment for a therapist should include an assortment of wrap-around style sunlenses to demonstrate (see Chapter 16).

The sunlens evaluation involves selecting the style, density and color of the sunlenses. In general, the best style of sunlens wraps tightly above and around the eyes (www.noir-medical.com) to block glare and reflections around the lenses. Relatively inexpensive or more stylish models can be purchased to fit over conventional eyeglasses. With standard commercial sunglasses, this glare can be blocked with a hat brim or visor.

The density of the sunlens describes the amount of light transmitted through the lens, usually described as a light transmittance percentage where 100% is clear and 0% would be completely opaque. Typically, the lightest sunlenses have transmittance values of 50% to 60%; very dense sunlenses have transmittance values of approximately 10%. Sunlenses also vary in color. Most clients will respond best to polarized yellow or orange sunlenses that decrease glare, or color neutral lenses (Polaroid Gray). Some, however, prefer green hues, and occasionally red and blue. Colored lenses will degrade color vision, but the yellow hues will improve perceived contrast and decrease glare.

The sunlens evaluation is time consuming and will require about 30 minutes in a separate session. One must wait for a sunny day, and evaluate the lens by having the client attempt to identify an object or person next to a glare source, such as reflections off of a

car. The therapist provides lenses in pairs for the client to compare and choose which is better, taking care to allow the client to adjust after he dons each sunlens. To save time, the lighting evaluation should reveal the approximate sunlens density required. If a light meter is used, one can hold the meter behind the lens to quickly locate those lenses that will provide best light levels in a given environment; otherwise the therapist may use gray sunlenses first and then compare colors at the selected transmittance values. One should also perform a sunlens evaluation indoors under lighting conditions where the client has a problem, typically in brightly lit fluorescent rooms with shiny tile floors. One might also use the selected high transmittance sunlens to cut glare during reading, or with a white on black CCTV.

Assessment of Central Scotoma/ Eccentric Viewing

There are several ways to evaluate the central scotoma and eccentric viewing. The complexity, cost of equipment, and accuracy varies dramatically from one technique to another. For example, the most accurate method uses an instrument called the scanning laser ophthalmoscope. The scanning laser ophthalmoscope takes a picture of the patient's retina, and is able to map exactly where scotomas exist and which areas are used for fixation. The benefits of this procedure are its accuracy and that it does not rely on the client's responses. However, it is very expensive and usually only used in large eye clinics. Most private practice

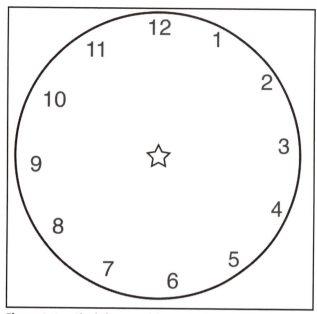

Figure 8-6a. Clock face used for evaluation of central scotoma/eccentric viewing.

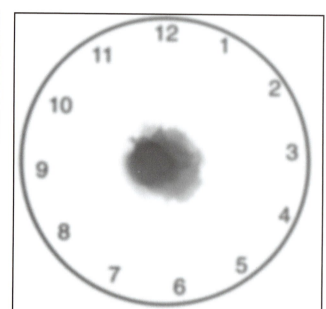

Figure 8-6b. Clock face used for evaluation of central scotoma/eccentric viewing with scotoma covering central star.

ophthalmologist and optometrists would not have this instrument available.

Fortunately, less expensive techniques requiring minimal equipment are available. We recommend that the therapist use either the clock face technique or the Tangent screen.

Clock Face Technique

Practice Setting

Recommended for home health setting or any setting in which portability is important.

Equipment Required

Clock drawn on 8.5 by 11-inch sheet of paper.

Description

As described in Chapter 4, macular degeneration is almost always associated with a macular scotoma or a blind spot in the center of the visual field. This creates major difficulty for the client when engaged in any ADL requiring vision. During vision rehabilitation, the occupational therapist will teach the client how to look off to the side or to eccentrically view to improve performance. Therefore, it is important during the evaluation to determine if there is a scotoma and the best position for eccentric viewing.

Setup and Procedure

Wright and Watson[12] describe the following technique used to teach clients how to eccentrically view.

We believe that this is also a valuable evaluation tool.

1. Draw a clock (numbers 1 to 12) with a star in the middle with a black marker on a sheet of paper (Figure 8-6a).

2. Occlude the client's left eye and place the clock about 2 feet away from the client.

3. If the client has eyeglasses, these should be worn for this procedure.

4. Ask the client to look at the clock and so that the scotoma or unclear area is obscuring the star in the middle of the clock (Figure 8-6b). The star should either be unclear or missing at this point.

5. While the client maintains this position, he or she should see that some of the numbers on the clock are clearer than the star in the middle (Figure 8-6c).

6. Instruct the client to move his or her eye so that the star is most clear. The client should do this systematically by looking up and toward the right at the number 1 on the clock, and continue clockwise. The client should be able to find at least one position in which the star is now clearer than when looking straight ahead.

7. Once this position is established, instruct the client to look directly at the star again and notice that it is now blurred or disappears. Then repeat either eye movement required to regain better clarity.

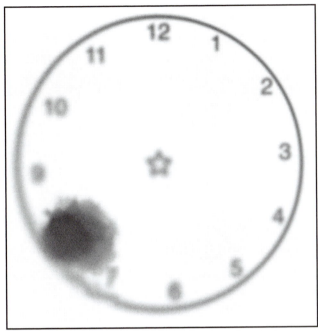

Figure 8-6c. Clock face used for evaluation of central scotoma/eccentric viewing with central star visible and scotoma down and to left.

Interpretation

- A scotoma below fixation can present a safety problem, as clients might miss small obstacles, trip, and fall.

- A scotoma to the right of fixation may impair reading.

- Inconsistent responses indicate inconsistent fixation and the need for instruction on eccentric fixation (see Chapter 10). Inconsistent fixation often results soon after a client has a central scotoma. These individuals will see something out of the corner of their eye, only to have it disappear when they look at it, a frustrating experience. Client education and use of other senses are the best immediate interventions. Training someone to develop adaptive eccentric viewing is an important aspect of low vision rehabilitation.

Tangent Screen

Practice Setting

Recommended for any setting in which the equipment can be setup permanently.

Equipment Required

Tangent screen

Description

The tangent screen method is less convenient, takes more practice to become skilled, and is not possible to do in every setting, but is more sensitive to small scotomas that could be missed with the Clock Face technique and actually permits the scotoma to be measured.[13] Eyecare providers use the Tangent screen to evaluate the central visual field of patients. It is a black piece of felt with a white fixation target mounted on a wall (Figure 8-7). The screen usually has circles of black thread stitched into it to indicate the degrees from the center of the fixation target.

The procedure we suggest combines testing for scotomas with instruction, so that scotoma awareness and eccentric viewing training are combined. This procedure is discussed in more detail in Chapter 10. The results of Tangent Screen testing are useful diagnostically and indicate how to begin the eccentric viewing training.

Procedure

1. The tangent screen method involves first positioning the fixation target in the center of a 1-meter-square tangent screen. The fixation target is usually a letter large enough for a patient to recognize in the center of a felt board (see Figure 8-7). The letter is positioned in the center of a large cross.

2. It is important for the therapist to be positioned to allow careful observation of the patient's eyes.

3. The client is asked to "look at the letter so that it is the clearest." It is important that the client continue to hold the eye in this position during testing. Individuals who have had central field loss for several months or more may have already started developing eccentric viewing or fixation. If so, the client may position his or her eyes so that the eyes appear to be looking above, below, or to one side of the letter and the client reports seeing the whole letter. This behavior is acceptable as long as the client maintains this eye position throughout the testing.

4. While watching carefully that the eyes do not move, the therapist moves a 5-mm white testing spot at the end of long black wand around the fixation area in an attempt to find a scotoma. At this stage, the therapist is empirically trying to find the location of the scotoma.

5. When the white spot enters the scotoma, the client will report that it disappears. When this occurs, the therapist explains to the client that the scotoma has been found and its size will now be measured.

6. To measure the size of the scotoma, the white target is moved until it is first seen and the edge of the scotoma is marked with a low-contrast mark or pin (not visible to the client), and

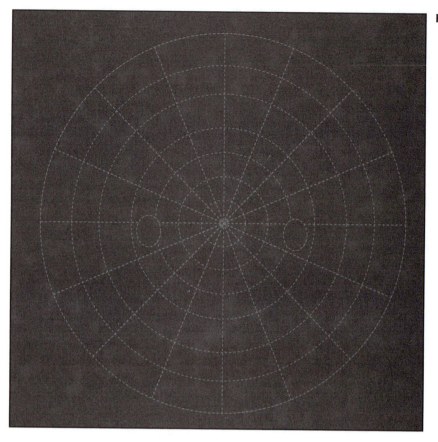

Figure 8-7. Tangent screen (screen only).

quickly moved from nonseeing to seeing and the border of the scotoma is marked several times. Typically, the clinician maps at least 4 points: 12 o'clock, 6 o'clock, 3 o'clock, and 9 o'clock (Figure 8-8).

7. Some clients may shift fixation, eg, from looking above to looking below the fixation letter. The therapist can detect these shifts by looking at the eyes and noting inconsistency in where the target is seen. It is important to instruct the client to try not to shift the position of his or her eyes.

8. When the scotoma is mapped, the edges are more clearly marked (with white yarn wrapped around the push pins in the felt board). The patient is instructed to move his or her eyes to see the outlined scotoma (Figure 8-9).

9. The therapist should instruct the client to look into different positions and with another letter or the wand, to demonstrate where the scotoma has moved.

10. The client may be coaxed with verbal instructions ("look further to the right"). Sometimes one needs to give the client a target to look towards, such as waving the testing spot to the right of the fixation target to encourage eccentric fixation to the right.

In Chapter 10, we describe the use of this procedure to teach eccentric viewing, which is often incorporated into this testing procedure.

Reading Assessment/Reading Speed

Practice Setting
Appropriate for any practice setting.

Equipment Required
The Pepper Visual Skills for Reading Test (Pepper VSRT)

Description
The Pepper VSRT is a test in which clients read unrelated words aloud (Figure 8-10). The words increase in length as the reader reads down the chart. The examiner records reading rate and also the occurrence and type of errors. When comparing reading performance with different optical devices, or monitoring changes in reading performance after vision rehabilitation, the Pepper VSRT is the reading evaluation instrument of choice. The Pepper test has exceptional test-retest reliability and is very sensitive to small changes in reading performance in clients

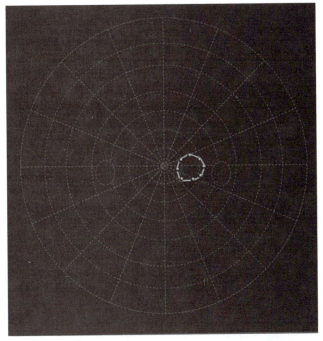

Figure 8-9. Tangent screen showing white yarn used to outline the scotoma.

Figure 8-8. Tangent screen showing therapist holding the target, client viewing the screen, and 4 pins showing size of scotoma, which is to the right of fixation.

with a 9th grade or higher reading level. A change in reading rate of about 10 words per minute is statistically significant when measured by the Pepper test. In addition, many compound words are used, so readers may miss either the beginning or end of the words. This would lead to certain error patterns. The examiner can make inferences about underlying visual impairments on the basis of the error patterns based on an analysis of these errors. For example, a tendency to omit the end of words indicates a scotoma in the right field.

The Pepper VSRT engages the client in reading processes that depend solely, or in part, on visual sources of information, including: word recognition ability, saccade control, return-sweep eye movement control, and scotoma placement while reading.[14]

One of the three forms of the Pepper VSRT is illustrated in Figure 8-6. Word recognition ability is required because unrelated letters and words are presented. The absence of contextual information forces clients to rely on vision to identify the items presented. The test becomes increasingly more difficult from top to bottom because line delineation and spacing, word length, and word spacing change as the client reads successive lines. Both saccadic and return sweep eye movements are also increasingly more difficult because of systematic decreases in either spac-

ing between successive items on a single line or the spacing between successive lines.

Setup and Procedure

1. The examiner should select the appropriate test size based on the reader's acuity. The appropriate VSRT size is at least one size larger print than the reader's acuity. The authors recommend using two sizes larger or more than acuity for best performance. Therefore, if the reader's acuity is 2 M, the 3 M test is appropriate, but 4 M may give better reading ability.

2. If the reader is using an optical device to read the test, then the appropriate test size is one or two sizes larger than the aided acuity. That is, if the reader is using a 5X microscope with an aided acuity of 0.8 M, the 1 M or 1.5 M test should be administered.

3. To stimulate the reader to do his or her best, and to reduce the stress of the testing situation, encouragement can be given consistently at the end of each line read, or when the reader asks for feedback. Such comments as, "Good, keep going," "You are doing well," or "That's fine" are effective. However, praise can be overdone. Most adults know when they are beyond their skills. The sensitive examiner will strive to

Figure 8-10. Pepper VSRT.

Form III

			# correct # item	percent correct
Line				
1	x g a j p m u l c d s b r h o		_____/15	_____ %
2	f w z i t b k e n q v y a m r		_____/15	_____ %
3	yes so j pop sat d at c am h in so		_____/12	dummy
4	oh of n to am g k in u do of s b		_____/13	_____ %
5	fire side past gold fish own sky help		_____ /8	_____ %
6	advice badger slide anyone table mirror		_____ /6	_____ %
7	understudy sportsman campground fenders		_____ /4	_____ %
8	bad z navy specific g show dog amber		_____ /8	dummy
9	narrow today penny cream hopped honest		_____ /6	_____ %
10	meantime upbringing summertime splendid		_____ /4	_____ %
11	quick sand spiteful outlast stops winds		_____ /6	_____ %
12	side walk tracking readily overshadow employ		_____ /6	_____ %
13	story milk bunny college crayons idea gotten		_____ /7	dummy

---

- Total Number Correct   (add lines 1-13)= _____
- Mean Percent Correct   (sum of percentages/10)= _____ %
- Total Test Time=_____ min _____ sec   (Time in Minutes)= _____
- Corrected Reading Rate =   Total # Correct/Total Time (in min)= _____

-Error Codes-

Misidentification .... substitution written above item .... e.g.
Repetition .... wavy line placed below item repeated .... e.g.
Spells Word .... "sp" placed above word item spelled .... e.g.
Omission .... circle item omitted .... e.g.
Insertion .... caret placed where insertion occurs .... e.g.
Connects Words .... line underneath indicating connection .... e.g.
Separates Words .... slash indicating separation .... e.g.
Changing Word Order .... arrow to where item was read .... e.g.
Line Skip .... arrow to skipped line ➝

Test Termination .... 1. 10 consecutive errors   3. fatigue of reader
                                                          2. skipped line twice   4. exceeded time limit

---

learn the appropriate amount of encouragement to elicit maximum performance from a particular reader.

4. Before the test is begun, the examiner should tell the reader that the test cannot be discussed until it is completed, and it is important that the reader keep reading until the test if finished. These procedures are important both to motivate the reader, and to allow spontaneous changes in answers, which are accepted. The examiner should be as responsive and positive with incorrect as with correct responses.

Also, the examiner should be careful not to let the reader know when she is right or wrong either by a glance, expression, tone of voice, or the sound of the mistake being marked on the score sheet.

5. The reader should be handed the appropriate test, provided the best illumination, and instructed to call the letters and words aloud. If the reader is using a low vision device, insure that he or she knows the correct focal distance before administering the VSRT. The client should be instructed to hold the card as

close or far away as needed to see the symbols clearly. If necessary, the examiner should point out the beginning of the first line as a localization clue.

6. The examiner should say to the reader:

"I am going to show a card to you with unrelated letters and words on it. The letters and words are not sentences; they have no meaning when read together. The first line has a black border around it as a visual guide, but the rest of the lines do not. I would like you to say the letters and words aloud as you see them. Please read the entire test. The first two lines will be letters, and on the third line there will be words. When you see a word, please say the word, do not spell it. While you are reading the test, I cannot answer questions about how you are doing, but as soon as you finish, we will talk about how you did. Do you have any questions before we begin?"

7. Timing for speed using a stopwatch begins as soon as the reader has the card in focus and is fixing on the beginning letter.

If a reader asks about the correctness of an answer or how she is doing on the test, the examiner should give an ambiguous, noncommittal response, such as, "You are doing a fine job, keep going."

9. The test has a coding scheme for recording errors. For example, if the reader spells the first word instead of saying the word, the instructor should indicate that the item is a word and asked the reader to pronounce the word instead of spelling it. If the reader is able to pronounce that word, no error is scored. After this, however, if the reader spells the word instead of saying it, the examiner should score a "spells word" error.

Readers should be encouraged to guess test items if they are not immediately recognizable. If there is no response to an item after 10 seconds, the examiner should say, "Even if you are not sure, just tell me what it looks like". If the reader is still struggling, made such a remark as, "That is difficult, go to the next item". If the reader did not read the item, it is considered an omission error and is scored as such (check score sheet).

The last answer given is the one that is scored. Thus, if the reader spontaneously corrects an incorrect answer, even after leaving the item, credit is given. Also, if the reader changes to a wrong answer, the item is scored as incorrect.

12. The VSRT should be administered in one sitting. There is a maximum time limit. It is not useful to administer the test in more than one sitting. If the reader is tired, or for any other reason unable to finish the test, the examiner should decide whether to readminister the test at another time (because of extenuating circumstance), or score the remainder of the test as errors and count the administration as the pretest, and indicative of the reader's best performance at the time.

13. As soon as the reader pronounces the last word on the test, or the test is terminated, the timing of the test is completed.

Interpretation

At the end of the scoring, the examiner should have a profile of the reader's performance that contains the following:
- Accuracy of performance (mean percent correct)
- Reading rate (number correct words/minute)
- Line mastery for symbol length, symbol spacing, line spacing

The reading rate measure has exceptional test-retest reliability and sensitivity to small changes in performance; change in reading rate of about 10 words per minute is statistically significant. Four forms of the test are available to enable repeated testing. This test has been used, therefore, to document improvement in performance with therapy or provide justification for the effectiveness of reading devices using an objective measure of performance.

An evaluation of both the accuracy and rate scores for each reader can provide the clinician with information to make a preliminary categorization of the reader's reading performance. Typically, low vision readers will be reading:
- inaccurately and slowly
- accurately but slowly
- with both speed and accuracy

The VSRT suggests guidelines that may aid the low vision therapist in making these categorizations. Observations of the VSRT performance of individuals with macular disease suggest that accuracy scores below 75% correct may be indicative of inaccurate performance and rate scores below 20 words/minute may be considered slow performance

The VSRT scoring manual also has an extensive discussion of interpretation and analysis of common reading errors, line mastery issues, problems with word length, symbol spacing, omissions, insertions,

repetitions, jumping or changing word order, and a variety of other important issues.

ENVIRONMENTAL EVALUATION

Even a well-developed treatment plan will fail unless the therapist considers the location where the client will habitually perform the goal performance in question. For example, a client may successfully perform a task in an office setting using an optical device, while sitting at a desk with a task light and a reading stand. However, when the client takes the prescribed device home and sits in his favorite chair with inadequate lighting, poor support for materials, and disabling glare, he may be unable to perform the identical task. Fortunately, outpatient low vision rehabilitation is a covered service under Medicare B and occupational therapists can provide these services in the client's home. This allows the therapist to evaluate the client's environment.

As individuals age, they often tend to perform tasks in the same place, eg, bill paying is performed on the dining room table, knitting and reading in the stuffed chair in the living room. Indeed, as people age, the space within which they perform most activities decreases to a favorite chair, referred to as the "personal surveillance zone."[15] This is a sacred place. Individuals resist moving from this place or changing the layout of the space. An environmental assessment, therefore, should focus on the preferred living spaces. Careful consideration should be given to:

- The available lighting and glare sources
- Possible positioning of task lights, reading stands, and tables
- Possible organizational schemes
- Placement and storage of devices
- Ergonomics when performing a task
- Escape and emergency response

EVALUATION OF OCCUPATIONAL PERFORMANCE

The final portion of the occupational therapy low vision rehabilitation evaluation is designed to evaluate occupational performance. Occupational performance is defined as the ability to carry out activities of daily life, including basic and personal ADL, instrumental activities of daily living (IADL), education, work, play, leisure, and social participation.[1] Table 8-8 summarizes these activities. During the evaluation

process, the performance skills and patterns used in performance are identified, and other aspects of engaging in occupation, such as client factors, activity demands, and context are assessed.[1] The occupational performance evaluation involves discussion, observation, and evaluation of the client's use of vision in ADL and IADL.

The occupational profile/case history assessment establishes what the client wants and needs to do. This part of the evaluation is designed to identify deficits in performance or specific disabilities. By considering the results of the above evaluation of visual and non-visual client factors, the therapist then identifies client factors that act as barriers to performance—performance limiting factors. The performance evaluation combines questioning the client as well as observing the client engaged in the activities of interest. This information will be used to develop a treatment plan that attempts to remove the barriers and enable occupational performance, thus meeting the client's specific needs.

An excellent starting point for this phase is the evaluation driven by the client's results on the Veterans Affairs Low-Vision Visual Functioning Questionnaire (VA LV VFQ-48). As discussed earlier in this chapter, this has been found to be a valid and reliable measure of visual ability in low vision clients with moderate to severe vision loss. After reviewing this questionnaire, the therapist should evaluate the client's actual performance in the areas of concern and also concentrate on what the client has identified as important goals. If paying bills is an important goal for the client, the therapist should have the client demonstrate where and how he or she pays the bills. The therapist should carefully observe lighting, contrast, glare, and other environmental issues.

It is also wise to routinely ask clients to perform several basic activities that are almost uniformly necessary for all individuals, such as pouring liquid, reading labels on medicine bottles, food containers, reading the newspaper, reading mail, or using the microwave.

The location of the evaluation is an important issue to consider. Ideally, the occupational performance evaluation should take place in the client's home or current living situation. This allows the therapist to explore the various areas of occupation and actually observe the client engaged in these activities in the client's real environment (performance context). This is particularly important because for the low vision client, context issues such as lighting, contrast, glare, home design, appliance setup, and organization are so critical to an analysis of occupational performance. In addition, one should observe performance of familiar tasks under somewhat unfamiliar circumstances to

Table 8-8.

Areas of Occupation Assessed in OT Low Vision Rehabilitation Evaluation

Activities of Daily Living (ADL): These activities are oriented toward taking care of one's own body.

Bathing, showering
Bowel and bladder control
Dressing
Eating
Feeding
Functional mobility
Personal device care
Personal hygiene and grooming
Sexual activity
Sleep/rest
Toilet hygiene

Instrumental Activities of Daily Living (IADL): Activities that are oriented toward interacting with the environment and that are often complex and generally optional in nature.

Care of others
Care of pets
Child rearing
Communication device use
Community mobility
Financial management
Health management and maintenance
Home establishment and maintenance
Meal preparation and cleanup
Safety procedures and emergency responses
Shopping

Education: Includes activities needed for being a student ands participating in a learning environment.

Formal educational participation
Exploration of informal personal educational needs or interests
Informal personal education participation

Work: Includes activities needed for engaging in remunerative employment or volunteer activities.

Employment interest and pursuits
Employment seeking and acquisition
Job performance
Retirement preparation
Volunteer exploration
Volunteer participation

Play: Any spontaneous or organized activity that provides enjoyment, entertainment, amusement, or diversion.

Play exploration
Play participation

Continued

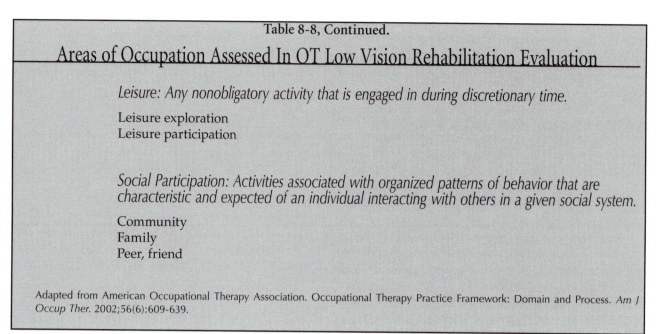

Table 8-8, Continued.

Areas of Occupation Assessed In OT Low Vision Rehabilitation Evaluation

Leisure: Any nonobligatory activity that is engaged in during discretionary time.

Leisure exploration
Leisure participation

Social Participation: Activities associated with organized patterns of behavior that are characteristic and expected of an individual interacting with others in a given social system.

Community
Family
Peer, friend

Adapted from American Occupational Therapy Association. Occupational Therapy Practice Framework: Domain and Process. *Am J Occup Ther.* 2002;56(6):609-639.

evaluate cognitive functions such as problem solving, insight, reasoning, and frustration tolerance.

Another important issue to consider when evaluating the client's performance is how much effort and energy is expended. Warren states that the primary issues to consider regarding performance of ADL are safety and effort.[16] She states that most people with vision loss are technically independent, but expend a great deal of mental and physical effort with questionable safety and little margin for error. They perform at their maximum capability at all times, leaving them with little energy to enjoy what else life has to offer.[16]

ASSESSMENT OF REHABILITATION POTENTIAL

As the therapist performs the evaluation described in this chapter, he or she is not simply gathering bits of unrelated information to be analyzed at the very end of the evaluation. Rather, during the evaluation process, the therapist is already thinking about how this information relates to rehabilitation potential and the actual treatment plan. Experienced clinicians tend to follow a basic clinical reasoning process, which we have outlined below:

To determine rehabilitation potential, the basic reasoning process is as follows:

1. Define the specific performance goal.

2. Look first to evidence-based research and then to clinical experience to ascertain the visual and nonvisual requirements to perform the goal task.

3. Consider visual performance of the task and ascertain if the visual, movement, and cognitive requirements can be met by available devices or interventions to enhance vision.

4. Consider nonvisual performance of the task and ascertain if other modalities, movement, and cognitive requirements can be met by available devices or interventions.

5. Evaluate and document the pre- and postmorbid specific performance deficits or disability.

One must be careful to consider visual and nonvisual options and keep the focus on what the client requires to recover roles, essential function, and quality of life, rather than just visual criteria. For example, arranging for a sighted reader or books on tape for someone who wishes to read again is a successful rehabilitation outcome even if the client is unable to read visually. Too often, a clinician may be so focused on the visual aspects of the task and visual solutions, that he or she ignores a much more simple nonvisual adaptation or solution.

After completing the evaluation, the therapist must make a decision about the client's rehabilitation potential. The information gathered from all four compo-

nents of the evaluation should be used to make this decision. Ultimately, almost any client with low vision has the potential for improving his or her ability to more effectively engage in ADL. To make the determination of rehabilitation potential, however, the therapist must first define the specific performance goal and then follow the other four steps listed above.

DETERMINING THE PRIMARY DIAGNOSIS

After determining that the client has the potential to benefit from vision rehabilitation, the therapist must determine the primary diagnostic code that will be used for billing Medicare. Medicare considers low vision rehabilitation services reasonable and necessary only for clients with a clear medical need. To establish this need, clients must have a moderate visual impairment or worse not correctable by conventional eyeglasses and clients must have a clear potential for significant improvement in function following rehabilitation over a reasonable period of time.

Please note that the primary diagnosis is not the eye disease that caused the vision loss. The occupational therapist does not treat macular degeneration or diabetic retinopathy. Rather, it is the visual disability that is treated. Table 8-9 can be used to determine the primary diagnosis. These codes periodically change and it is important for therapists to check frequently for updates.

Step one: Relate the visual acuity in each eye to one of the categories in the left hand column.
Example:
Visual Acuity:
Right Eye 20/300
Left Eye OS 20/800

20/300 falls into the category of severe impairment (20/200 to 20/400)

20/800 falls into the category of profound impairment (20/500 to 20/1000)

Step two: Find the intersection between the two categories.

Begin in the left column and locate the row that corresponds to the right eye acuity (severe impairment). Move left to right across that row until it intersects with the column corresponding to the left eye acuity (profound impairment). In this case, the primary diagnostic code would be 369.14.

Four other codes that can be used relate to visual field loss and include:

368.41—Visual field defects, scotoma involving central area

368.45—Visual field defects, generalized contraction or constriction

368.46—Homonymous bilaterial field defects

368.47—Heteronymous bilateral field defects

In some cases, visual acuity may be better than 20/60 but field loss may be present and the field loss codes apply. The secondary code is determined based on information received from either the ophthalmologist or optometrist. Some of the common codes are listed in Table 8-10.

SUMMARY

The objective of the occupational therapy low vision rehabilitation evaluation is to understand the client's functional ability before the vision loss, to define his or her current goals, to evaluate the client's ability to participate in ADL, and assess the his or her social and emotional health. In this chapter, we described an evaluation consisting of three components, including the occupational profile/case history, the evaluation of visual factors, and the evaluation occupational performance.

Table 8-9.

ICD-9CM Codes for Visual Impairment – Primary Disability (Hart, 2000)

	Normal vision	Near normal vision	Moderate impairment	Severe impairment	Profound impairment	Near total impairment	Total impairment
Normal vision 20/20- 20/25			369.76	369.73	369.69	369.66	369.63
Near normal vision 20/30–20/60			369.75	369.72	369.68	369.65	369.62
Moderate impairment 20/80–20/160	369.76	369.75	369.25	369.24	369.18	369.17	369.16
Severe impairment 20/200- 20/400 or VF =<20 degrees	369.73	369.72	369.24	369.22	369.14	369.13	369.12
Profound impairment 20/500- 20/1000 or VF <=10 degrees	369.69	369.68	369.18	369.14	369.08	369.07	369.06
Near total impairment 20/1250–20/2500 or VF<=5 degrees	369.68	369.65	369.17	369.13	369.07	369.04	369.03
Total impairment NLP (no light perception)	369.63	369.62	369.16	369.12	369.06	369.03	369.01

Table 8-10.

Secondary Diagnostic Codes

362.01 — Diabetic retinopathy, background
362.02 — Diabetic retinopathy, proliferate
362.35 — Central retinal vein occlusion
362.51 — Macular degeneration, dry
362.52 — Macular degeneration, wet
362.74 — Retinitis Pigmentosa
365.10 — Glaucoma, open angle, unspecified
365.20 — Glaucoma, primary, angle-closure, unspecified
366.10 — Cataract, senile, unspecified
368.46 — Field deficit homonymous, bilateral
377.10 — Optic nerve atrophy
377.41 — Optic neuritis

Sidebar 8-1: Resources for Equipment

Equipment	Company	Contact Information
Feinbloom Visual Acuity Chart	Lighthouse Professional Products	800-826-4200 www.lighthouse.org/prodpub_procat.htm
MN Read Test	Lighthouse Professional Products	800-826-4200 www.lighthouse.org/prodpub_procat.htm
Mars Contrast Sensitivity test	MARS Perceptrix	www.marsperceptrix.com/
Tangent screen	Bernell Corporation	800-348-2225 www.bernell.com/
Pepper Test	Lighthouse Professional Products	800-826-4200 www.lighthouse.org/prodpub_procat.htm
Veterans Affairs Low-Vision Visual Functioning Questionnaire (VA LV VFQ-48)		See www.slackbooks.com/otvisionforms
Geriatric Depression Scale		See www.slackbooks.com/otvisionforms

REFERENCES

1. American Occupational Therapy Association. Occupational Therapy Practice Framework: Domain and Process. *Am J Occup Ther.* 2002;56(6):609-639.
2. Warren M. Providing low vision rehabilitation services with occupational therapy and ophthalmology: a program description. *Am J Occup Ther.* 1995;49(9):877-883.
3. Massof RW, Rubin GS. Visual function assessment questionnaires. *Surv Ophthalmol.* 2001;45(6):531-548.
4. Stelmack JA, Szlyk JP, Stelmack TR, et al. Psychometric properties of the Veterans Affairs Low-Vision Visual Functioning Questionnaire. *Invest Ophthalmol Vis Sci.* 2004;45(11):3919-3928.
5. Cotter SA, Scharre JE. Optometric assessment: case history. In: Scheiman M, Rouse M, Eds. *Optometric Management of Learning Related Vision Problems.* St. Louis, MO: C.V. Mosby; 1994.
6. Korsch BM, Negrete VF. Doctor patient communication. *Sci Am.* 1972;227:66-74.
7. Sokol-McKay DA. Facing the challenge of macula degeneration: therapeutic interventions for low vision. *OT Practice.* 2005;10(9):10-15.
8. Freeman P, Mendelson R. *Believing Is Seeing: Hope for Those Victimized by Macular Degeneration and Other Conditions that Cause Low Vision.* 1st ed. Pittsburgh, PA: Freeman and Mendelson; 1996.
9. Graboyes M. Psychosocial implications of visual impairment. In: *Essentials of Low Vision Practice.* Brilliant RL, Ed. Boston, MA: Butterworth-Heinemann; 1999:12-17.
10. Freeman PB, Jose RT. *The Art and Practice of Low Vision.* 2nd ed. Boston, MA: Butterworth-Heinemann; 1997.
11. Brilliant RL. *Essentials of Low Vision Practice.* Boston: Butterworth-Heinemann; 1999.
12. Wright V, Watson GR. *Learn to Use Your Vision for Reading Workbook.* Lilburn, GA: Bear Consultants; 1995.
13. Greer R. Evaluation methods and functional implications: children and adults with visual impairments. In: Lueck AH, Ed. *Functional Vision: A Practitioner's Guide to Evaluation and Intervention.* New York: American Foundation for the Blind; 2004.
14. Watson GR, Baldasare J, Whittaker S. The validity and clinical uses of the Pepper Visual Skills for Reading Test. *J Vis Impairment & Blind.* 1990;84:119-123.
15. Rowles GD. Beyond performance: being in place as a component of occupational therapy. *Am J Occup Ther.* 1991;45(3):265-271.
16. Warren ML, Lampert J. Assessing daily living needs. In: Fletcher DC, Ed. *Ophthalmology Monographs: Low Vision Rehabilitation: Caring for the Whole Person.* San Francisco, CA: American Academy of Ophthalmology; 1999:89-125.

Section III

Treatment

9

Overview of Treatment Strategy

MODEL OF CARE FOR LOW VISION REHABILITATION

In Chapter 1, we reviewed our proposed model of care for low vision rehabilitation and included a discussion of the four terms for defining impairment and disability proposed by the World Health Organization (WHO).[1] This terminology is illustrated in Figure 9-1.

A *disorder* is an anatomical deviation from normal and can be congenital or acquired. Examples of visual disorders causing low vision are age-related macular degeneration (AMD), diabetic retinopathy, glaucoma, and cataract.

Impairment is a loss or abnormality in function. The impairment can be either physiological or psychological. Visual impairments include decreased visual acuity, reduced contrast sensitivity, central scotomas, and constricted visual fields.

Disability refers to a restriction or an inability to perform a task in the normal way. Examples are difficulty reading newspaper print, recognizing faces, and driving a car.

Handicap is a disadvantage that prevents or limits the fulfillment of a role that is normal for the client. Examples are the inability to work or engage in hobbies, and restricted social interactions.

In the low vision rehabilitation model presented below, the ophthalmologist and optometrist are primarily interested in the disorder and impairment, while the occupational therapist and other vision rehabilitation professionals manage the disability and handicap, although there may be overlap in some areas.

Role of the Ophthalmologist

The role of the ophthalmologist is to diagnose and treat the eye disease. This might involve the use of medication or surgery. When it is clear that vision has been permanently impaired due to the eye disease, the ophthalmologist refers the client to a low vision optometrist for evaluation and treatment. In many cases, optometrists manage diseases with medical interventions as well.

Role of the Low Vision Optometrist

The role of the optometrist is to evaluate the patient and determine whether a change in the traditional eyeglass prescription might be of benefit. The low vision optometrist also performs a detailed evaluation of distance and near visual acuity, contrast sensitivity,

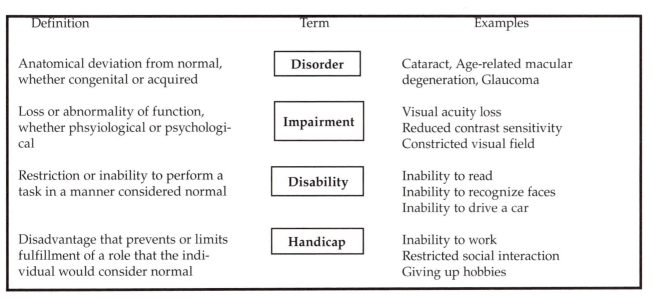

Definition	Term	Examples
Anatomical deviation from normal, whether congenital or acquired	**Disorder**	Cataract, Age-related macular degeneration, Glaucoma
Loss or abnormality of function, whether phsyiological or psychological	**Impairment**	Visual acuity loss Reduced contrast sensitivity Constricted visual field
Restriction or inability to perform a task in a manner considered normal	**Disability**	Inability to read Inability to recognize faces Inability to drive a car
Disadvantage that prevents or limits fulfillment of a role that the individual would consider normal	Handicap	Inability to work Restricted social interaction Giving up hobbies

Figure 9-1. World Health Organization terminology for impairment and disability. WHO. *International classification of impairments, disabilities, and handicaps: A manual of classification relating to the consequences of disease.* Geneva: WHO; 1980.

assessment of central scotomas, and peripheral visual field. Based on the results of this evaluation and the case history, the optometrist begins the process of determining the magnification needs of the client for various activities of daily living (ADL) and selects and prescribes appropriate low vision optical aids. The optometrist then refers the client to the occupational therapist for training in the use of the prescribe devices in various ADL. A few ophthalmologists specialize in low vision rehabilitation as well.

Although the scenario described above represents current thinking about the interaction between the optometrist and occupational therapist, we suggest that to provide optimal care for clients, the ideal working relationship could be modified as detailed in the section below.

Role of the Occupational Therapist

The role of the occupational therapist is to determine the cognitive, psychosocial, and physical needs of the client. The evaluation process described in Chapter 8 allows the occupational therapist to evaluate visual and nonvisual client factors, history, roles, physical environment, and occupational performance.

Based on the evaluation, the occupational therapist designs a vision rehabilitation program to teach the client how to function more effectively in ADLs in spite of the vision loss. Rehabilitation includes education about low vision, managing the psychosocial issues, referral to community resources, teaching the client how to eccentrically view and read more effec-

tively, the use of both optical and nonoptical assistive devices in ADLs, and in some cases sensory substitution. Management of lighting, contrast, and glare are also critical roles. The occupational therapist may need to refer the client back to the low vision optometrist if he/she finds that the prescribed optical device is not as effective as desired. Other potential referral sources include professionals such as the orientation and mobility (O&M) specialist, a psychologist or psychiatrist, and the social worker.

Other Vision Rehabilitation Professionals

In Chapter 1, we described the background, education, and history of vision rehabilitation therapists, O&M specialists, and teachers of the visually impaired. Until 1990, these three professions supplied all of the vision rehabilitation services in the United States through the chronically underfunded blindness system. This system has had to prioritize services generally favoring children and young adults of working age. In addition, the limited numbers of rehabilitation professionals in the blindness system primarily tend to work in metropolitan areas. Thus, for many older clients and for those not living in large metropolitan areas, low vision rehabilitation has not been readily available through the blindness system.[2] Teachers of the visually impaired work with children and are not involved in the care of the older client with low vision. However, vision rehabilitation therapists and O&M specialists will continue to be actively involved in low vision rehabilitation of the older adult. Although these

two professions are unable to bill Medicare or other insurers directly for their services, in the spring of 2006 the Centers for Medicare and Medicaid Services (CMS) initiated a 5-year Low Vision Rehabilitation Demonstration Project that will allow these two professions to provide these services under the supervision of a physician.

Thus, we can expect that in the traditional medical settings in which occupational therapists currently work (acute care hospitals, rehabilitation hospitals, long-term care facilities, home health, outpatient rehabilitation), occupational therapists will provide the bulk of the vision rehabilitation. In other settings, such as private practices of ophthalmologists and optometrists, large eye clinics, and state-funded agencies, occupational therapists, low vision therapists, vision rehabilitation therapists and O&M specialists may compete as service providers. One strategy for occupational therapists to avoid competition is to join the ranks of these other professionals. Just as many occupational therapists continue their education to become certified hand therapists, many occupational therapists have acquired a dual professional certification and become low vision therapists (see Chapter 16 for certification requirements).

A typical collaborative continuum of care would be as follows. The occupational therapist would begin the vision rehabilitation process working in a medical rehabilitation outpatient setting or home-care setting, collaborating with a low vision optometrist from a distance. Often occupational therapists work in the offices of low vision optometrists as well, sometimes with other low vision therapists who are not occupational therapists. As part of this initial intervention, the occupational therapist would encourage the client who meets eligibility criteria to apply immediately to state and regional blind associations and vocational rehabilitation services, often staffed by vision rehabilitation teachers and O&M specialists. These agencies and organizations often provide equipment and additional services as well. A client who has severe vision loss may benefit from Braille instruction and intensive instruction on blind techniques and would be best served by a vision rehabilitation teacher. A client who might require instruction on use of a white cane, guide dog, or mobility instruction should be referred to a certified O&M specialist. As a result of such collaboration, the services available to a client with visual impairment might be greatly extended and the costs of assistive devices funded.

Role of the Social Worker

The social worker can play an important role in both the evaluation and treatment of the client with low vision. Social workers can participate in the psychosocial assessment, and help assess the client's coping and adaptation to the vision loss. Studies show that we can expect about one of three older adults with vision impairment to be clinically depressed.[3-5] Thus, an important role for the social worker in rehabilitation is to provide counseling services to these clients. The social worker is also knowledgeable about community and government resources as well as potential financial assistance. Providing guidance and education about these issues may lead to more effective adaptation and coping with the vision impairment.

LOW VISION REHABILITATION— GENERAL CONCEPTS

Remediation

Professionals involved in low vision rehabilitation know that the loss of visual acuity and visual field is related to a disease process that is almost always irreversible. Although remediation may be an integral part of physical, psychosocial, and cognitive rehabilitation, vision rehabilitation generally is not designed to improve visual acuity or visual field. Rather, the goal of the occupational therapist is to provide therapeutic intervention to enable the client to function effectively in spite of the presence of the disability. While this essential concept is well known by low vision professionals, clients with low vision often have difficulty understanding and accepting this idea. In the client's previous experiences with blurred vision and other vision disorders, the problems were always solved quite easily with a new set of eyeglasses. It is easy to understand the clients asking "Why can't the doctor just prescribe stronger lenses?", or "Why can't the doctor just give me a different eye drop?" This difficulty accepting the chronic nature of vision loss is one of the most significant obstacles to successful low vision rehabilitation.[6]

Many clients spend years looking for a miracle that will restore their vision and valuable time is lost. Studies show that vision rehabilitation tends to be more successful when initiated soon after the vision loss and when visual acuity or visual field are not too severely impaired.[7] There is no doubt that you will encounter the frustration of clients who do not enthusiastically embrace your attempts at vision rehabilitation because they simply have not yet accepted the fact that the vision loss is permanent. In such situations, the role of the occupational therapist is to provide understanding, education, and guidance through

the stages of coping discussed in Chapter 6. One of the most effective ways to deal with this issue is to encourage the client to attend local support groups. These support groups not only have educational presentations, but also provide opportunities for the person to interact with other people who have lived with low vision for many years.

The one area where remediation is possible is reading rehabilitation (see Chapter 10). Patients with low vision generally struggle with reading, particularly when the underlying disease affects the macula and causes a central scotoma. Effective reading is very closely linked to the ability to fixate and make accurate, rapid eye movements called *saccades*. Both fixation and saccadic ability are negatively affected after macular disease such as AMD. Studies demonstrate, however, that in spite of the permanent visual acuity loss and central scotoma, reading speed and comprehension can indeed improve, even though the visual characteristics of the print or a person's visual acuity does not improve. Indeed, as clients develop skills in using their remaining vision in functional tasks, many areas of visual performance improve considerably with practice. Although some clients might claim their vision improves, these improvements are likely higher order perceptual changes or visual scanning skills, not changes in basic sensory function such as visual acuity, contrast sensitivity, or visual fields.

Compensatory Approaches

Low vision rehabilitation has been successfully practiced for many years with an emphasis on compensatory techniques. Compensatory rehabilitation strategies include the use of optical and nonoptical devices; treatment of visual skills such as fixation, eccentric viewing, saccades, and scanning; modification of the environment; and education. The research supporting low vision rehabilitation is reviewed below.

Early Intervention Is Critical

One of the key factors in the success of low vision rehabilitation is early intervention.[7] When treatment is initiated earlier in the disease process, visual acuity and visual field loss are generally less severe. With better visual acuity, lower magnification optical aids can be prescribed and it is easier for clients to learn how to use lower power devices because the working distance is closer to normal and the field of view is wider. In addition, the use of nonoptical assistive devices is more effective because less magnification is required and a wider variety of appropriate devices are available. Simple rehabilitation strategies such as organization of the environment, improved lighting and contrast, and elimination of glare are more effec-

tive in the early stages of visual loss. Even if the client eventually progresses to more serious vision loss, he or she has already experienced success in low vision rehabilitation and is more likely to be motivated to continue treatment. As a result, early intervention encourages people to begin applying relatively easy compensatory techniques to maintain occupations, routines, and roles.

McIlwaine et al[7] found that there was a relationship between age and success with low vision aids. In their study, there was a significant difference in use of aids between clients less than 65 years and those greater than 65 years old. Over one-third of clients over the age of 65 never used their low vision aids, compared with only one-sixth of clients under the age of 65 years.[7]

The obstacle to early intervention, however, is that many clients are not emotionally ready for rehabilitation after initially sustaining visual loss.[6] They may still not accept that the vision loss is permanent. Patients often schedule appointments with other doctors for additional options, hoping that there may be a conventional way of restoring vision.

Determine Patient Goals

It is important to have the client actively involved in development of the specific performance goals of the treatment plan. This process actually occurs during the low vision rehabilitation evaluation. As we stated in Chapter 8, the objectives of the occupational profile/case history part of the evaluation are to gather information about the client's vision and health status, previous eyecare and low vision treatment, and understand the client's functional ability before the vision loss to define his or her current goals. We suggest the use of the Veterans Affairs Low-Vision Visual Functioning Questionnaire (VA LV VFQ-48).[8] This questionnaire not only measures performance ability, but can also be used to tailor rehabilitation programs to meet individual client needs.

Of course, it is important for the therapist to guide the client through the process of establishing goals. Patients will typically require guidance because they may not know what rehabilitation strategies are possible.[9,10] Quillman and Goodrich state that people with recent and severe vision loss may not have been able to think about vision goals as yet.[10] They state that "It is never a good idea for a practitioner to set a goal for a client; it is appropriate to help the client set his or her own goals." Watson suggests using checklists or performance assessment systems to negotiate between felt needs and ascribed needs.[9] In some cases, the client may be depressed and reluctant to establish his or her own goals. In such cases, it is critical for the therapist to acknowledge that a significant

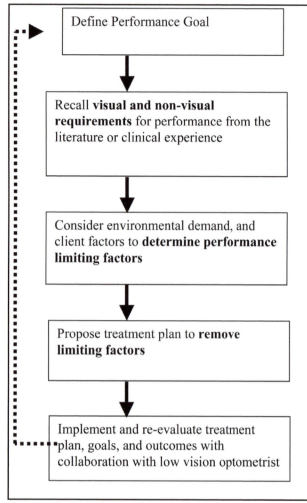

Define Performance Goal

Recall **visual and non-visual requirements** for performance from the literature or clinical experience

Consider environmental demand, and client factors to **determine performance limiting factors**

Propose treatment plan to **remove limiting factors**

Implement and re-evaluate treatment plan, goals, and outcomes with collaboration with low vision optometrist

Figure 9-2. Clinical reasoning process.

then to clinical experience to ascertain the visual, cognitive, and other physical requirements to perform the goal task. In the case of Ms. Jones, the visual requirements for fluent reading are presented in Chapter 10. One then considers context, social and environmental context, visual function, motor skills, cognitive and communication skills in order to define performance-limiting factors. Performance-limiting factors may include environmental components (available print size) and client factors (visual acuity). In the case of Ms. Jones, the evaluation of visual and nonvisual factors reveals inadequate visual acuity to read the 1.2 M print novels, and mild contrast sensitivity impairment also limits reading performance. In addition, she has no social support and has a severe hearing impairment. The proposed treatment plan addresses the limiting factors by physical and social environmental modification and prescription and instruction to use assistive devices. In the case of Ms. Jones, the treatment plan includes moving the chair or shading the window to eliminate glare, adding a task light, consideration of regular size and large print books, and referral to a low vision optometrist for recommended trial optical magnification devices to try in order to read 1.2 M (regular print) and 2 M (large print). The treatment plan includes instruction first under controlled clinical conditions with different devices and finally in a simulation of her home context, with a report and recommendations for a final device prescription.

loss has occurred, while encouraging the client about proper intervention and motivation. Much can be done to help the client become more independent in ADL.[10] Once the goals are established, the sequential treatment program outlined below can be planned and initiated.

Clinical Reasoning Process

The occupational therapist uses the results of this four-part evaluation to develop a treatment plan, which is described in detail in Chapter 8. We suggest the clinical reasoning process illustrated in Figure 9-2. Performance goal definition involves consideration of occupational history, habits, roles and culture context, demand, and finally, the results of current occupational performance assessment.[1] It is important to define observable and measurable performance goals within context, not in the clinic. For example, Ms. Jones, a 72-year-old, wishes to read a novel fluently and comfortably in her favorite chair by the window. One then refers first to evidence-based research and

SEQUENTIAL TREATMENT APPROACH

The seven-step sequential treatment approach for low vision rehabilitation is summarized in Table 9-1, and each phase of this treatment approach is described in detail in Chapters 10 through 15.

Recall that many clients begin therapy skeptically and need to be convinced of the value of therapy. The therapist should always begin the rehabilitation program with a careful discussion of performance goals and, if possible, demonstrate to the client that achievement of a performance goal is possible. Sometimes this might be done during an initial evaluation. The therapist will spend time discussing the client's particular eye disease and the expected course of the disease, but care must be taken not to discourage the client. The goal is to encourage the client to focus on the end, a performance goal, rather than the means. For example, a client with AMD might hope for the day when she will be able to read mystery novels again. This client is expecting to read visually. As will be discussed in Chapter 10, fluent visual reading is

---

Table 9-1.

Vision Rehabilitation: Seven-Step Sequential Treatment Plan

Education

Nature of eye disease
Outlook for the future
Expectations of vision rehabilitation

Therapeutic Activities

Eccentric Viewing

Scanning
Reading skills

Environmental Modifications

Lighting
Contrast
Glare

Nonoptical Assistive Devices

Visual
Tactile
Auditory

Optical Magnification

Computer Technology in Low Vision Rehabilitation

Resources/Handouts

---

usually not possible with AMD, although spot reading is possible after considerable instruction. In the first session, one might introduce the client to a tape recorder and an audiotape from Recordings for the Blind (a free service) as a place to start, emphasizing that normally sighted people use books on tape and that with rehabilitation she will likely read again but it will be very difficult at first. The therapist might also show the client how to perform a simple cooking activity, dial a phone, or find the right cell in her medication dispenser---a task that requires little or no vision to perform.

A large percentage of the clients seen in vision rehabilitation have AMD and, therefore, have a central scotoma. When dealing with a client with a central scotoma, it is best to begin therapy with eccentric viewing techniques. Once the client is comfortable with eccentric viewing, he or she can use these skills throughout the rest of the rehabilitation.[10] Eccentric viewing, scanning, eye movement training, and reading skills training are covered in depth in Chapter 10.

One of the easiest and most economical treatment approaches is the use of environmental modifications. A client can often achieve substantial gains with improved lighting, contrast and elimination of glare. Therapists will need to evaluate these aspects of the client's environment, educate the client about the importance of optimal lighting and contrast, and then demonstrate the possible improvements by making appropriate changes. Other strategies, such as changing the working distance and enlarging

target size, are used in this phase of the rehabilitation. These approaches are described in Chapter 11. If one is providing services in an outpatient setting, at least one home visit early in the treatment is highly recommended not only for treatment planning, but also because several simple home modifications can be highly effective and easy to implement. One often finds that removing glare and seating a client closer to the TV will easily enable one performance goal to be met.

Occupational therapists just becoming involved in the field of low vision are sometimes intimidated by the need to develop a knowledge and understanding of low vision optical devices. New terminology, an understanding of optics, and the impression that there are so many aids available can potentially create an obstacle to getting involved. We feel that it is important to understand that the use of low vision optical devices, although very important, is just one aspect of low vision rehabilitation. In many cases, very simple environmental modifications and the use of nonoptical assistive devices can be of great benefit to a client. These nonoptical assistive devices include visual devices and also devices that utilize sensory substitution, such as tactile and auditory assistive devices. Occupational therapists should acquire the various catalogs that are available and include a wide variety of available nonoptical assistive devices. This topic, along with information about resources, is covered in Chapter 12.

Optical Magnification

The use of optical magnification is, of course, critically important in low vision rehabilitation. Almost all clients with low vision will be able to perform better with the prescription of appropriate optical aids. These aids will typically be prescribed by the low vision optometrist. In the ideal professional environment, however, the occupational therapist will also be involved in the early phase of selection of optical aids. The occupational therapist can assist in this process by providing critical information about the clients' ADL problems and goals. If the client has other physical problems that could interfere with the use of some types of aids, the therapist can make suggestions about optical aids selection based on these needs as well. Chapter 13 covers this topic.

Just as computer technology has become important in so many aspects of our lives, it is also gaining importance in the field of low vision rehabilitation. Every year, more elderly present in the clinic with premorbid familiarity with computers. For some, computer use is as familiar an activity as cooking. Once a specialty skill, every low vision therapist now needs to understand how to adapt computers for use by people with low vision. Computers themselves have become important assistive devices that enable shopping, leisure, and functional written communication regardless of the level of vision loss. This generation will want and need to continue using computers and will feel comfortable with computer-assisted technology for low vision rehabilitation. Thus, the use of computer technology will become a vital part of the sequential rehabilitation treatment plan and is described in detail in Chapter 14.

REVIEW OF RESEARCH ON LOW VISION REHABILITATION

Research studies have been published reporting on the effectiveness of low vision rehabilitation. However, this research has been impeded by a lack of standardized measurement tools, and a lack of quality research.[11,12] Some of the design flaws in the available research include retrospective design, lack of placebo groups, the use of unmasked examiners, lack of standardized measurement tools, and small sample size. Most of the available research is limited to investigation of the use of low vision aids with limited training sessions,[7,13,14] and the use of low vision aids with additional training.[15-23] Few studies have reported on the benefits of other services such as occupational therapy and O&M training.[24,25] One study reported on the effectiveness of a self-management intervention program for clients with AMD.[26]

An interesting problem when designing research to study the effectiveness of low vision rehabilitation is what to use as an outcome measure, or how to measure the effectiveness of treatment. Various strategies have been used, including measurement of reading speed,[14-17,19,23] duration,[15,19] and comprehension;[19] administration of questionnaires that assess quality of life;[20,21,23] compliance with the use of low vision aids;[7,13,14,22,26] satisfaction with treatment;[7,16-18] independence in ADL;[13,20,21,24-26] and psychological adjustment to vision loss.[20,26] Even among studies that have used questionnaires as outcome measures, the actual questionnaires have differed from one study to another. These significant variations in study design are problematic and make it challenging to compare the results of one study to another. Nevertheless, the research that is available generally suggests that low vision rehabilitation is indeed beneficial and allows clients to read faster and for longer periods of time, and leads to improvement in independence in ADL and psychological adjustment to the vision loss.

There are numerous studies that demonstrate that the use of low vision aids is helpful when actually used by clients.[13-19,22-24] Of critical importance, however, is the finding that many clients either never use the low vision aids that have been prescribed or fail to use them properly. Humphry[27] studied a sample of visually impaired clients who received low vision devices with no training and found that 75% reported that they never used them. Another study[7] found that 33% of clients who were prescribed aids without training never used their devices. Training or rehabilitation designed to teach clients how to use prescribed aids in ADL may, therefore, be an important component of low vision rehabilitation.

The outstanding question is one of dosage. How many therapy sessions are necessary? The number of training sessions required to achieve maximum effectiveness is an important question because of its implications for healthcare costs. Several studies have been designed to compare limited to more extensive training.[7,15-19,28] Goodrich et al[19] performed two experiments and all clients received eccentric viewing training before starting the research. In the first experiment, they found that five sessions of optical device training were as effective in improving reading speed as 10 sessions of training, and seven sessions of training to read with a CCTV were as effective as 15 sessions. In the second experiment, they compared very short training typically used in private practices (one session of optical device training) to five sessions, and two sessions of CCTV training to seven sessions of CCTV training. In this study, the shorter number of sessions was not as effective as the longer treating approach for improving reading speed. They concluded that extended training sessions beyond what is typically provided in private practice is beneficial

for the rehabilitation of reading ability in clients with central vision loss. However, they also found that a moderate amount of training (five sessions versus 10 sessions with optical aids, and seven sessions versus 15 sessions with a CCTV) was as effective as longer amounts of training. A problem with this study was that the outcome examination was not performed by a masked examiner. A similar study was performed comparing 1 hour to 5 hours of low vision device training.[23] The outcome measures were reading speed and accuracy and quality of life measures. This study also used an unmasked examiner who knew the clients' treatment assignments. They found that the extended training time made a significant difference in reading ability as well as the clients' perceptions of the quality of their lives.

In contrast to these studies, a randomized clinical trial with masked examiners was performed comparing the effectiveness of conventional low vision rehabilitation, conventional low vision rehabilitation enhanced with home training sessions, and a control group.[20] The conventional low vision rehabilitation included demonstration of low vision aids, use and handling of low vision aids, advice about lighting, providing large print materials with information about lighting, use of low vision aids, and other services. The enhanced group also received this basic care plus three home visits from a rehabilitation therapist. During these visits, the rehabilitation therapists provided additional training with the low vision aids, demonstrated additional or alternative low vision aids, and provided additional client support. Patients assigned to the control group received the same conventional care plus three home visits from a community care worker. This individual did not provide any low vision rehabilitation. Instead he or she discussed the client's ability to cope with daily activities, leisure activities, and any other problems raised by the participant. The trial found no evidence of benefit from enhanced low vision rehabilitation. The authors conclude that researchers should be cautious about advocating modified or supplemental interventions without more in-depth evidence of their effectiveness.

La Grow[21] also compared traditional community-based treatment from private optometrists or ophthalmologists to enhanced treatment. The enhanced or comprehensive treatment consisted of training in the use of low vision aids (1.5 to 2 hours) and nonoptical assistive devices. The results revealed no significant differences between the two groups on visual function questionnaires, quality of life questionnaires, and measures of independence in ADL.

Thus, there is no consensus at this point in the literature about the benefits of additional training visits and more research is necessary to clarify this issue.

Nevertheless, conventional wisdom suggests that clients are more likely to use prescribed optical aids and perform more effectively in ADL when they receive additional rehabilitation from a low vision therapist.

Because occupational therapy has only recently become involved in the field of low vision rehabilitation, there is limited research in which occupational therapists played a significant role in the treatment.[24] A study conducted at the Massachusetts Eye & Ear Infirmary tested the hypothesis that vision rehabilitation using optometry, occupational therapy, and social work services increases clients' functional ability. The study also investigated whether involving families in the intervention resulted in more successful outcomes. Ninety-seven subjects were studied and were randomized into either individually focused or family focused intervention. Table 9-2 lists the services provided by each profession.

All clients received the services listed in Table 9-2. For those clients assigned to the individual protocol, their family members were excluded from all sessions. Rehabilitation intervention focused solely on the client. If the family had questions, these were answered in the waiting room or hallway as the client was entering or leaving the service. In contrast, the family focused group had family members included with the client in all stages of the rehabilitation process. A functional assessment questionnaire and a functional vision performance test were used to measure the outcome of the study.

The results of the study demonstrated that a vision rehabilitation plan involving optometry, occupational therapy, and social work services increased the client's level of function as measured by both an objective observation of performance of daily tasks and a self-report of difficulty and independence in performing ADL and social activities. The gains in function applied to even predominantly frail elderly clients. The study did not support the hypothesis that family involvement in vision rehabilitation increases the level of functional improvement.

SUMMARY

This chapter presented an overview of the seven-step sequential treatment plan for vision rehabilitation as well as a review of the research on the effectiveness of low vision rehabilitation. There is an urgent need for additional research to study the importance and effectiveness of occupational therapy intervention for low vision impairment. This need should be a priority for the profession of occupational therapy.

Table 9-2.

Services Provided by Profession

Optometry Services

- History
- Assessment of visual acuity, contrast sensitivity, visual field, color vision, glare sensitivity, refraction
- Recommendations for rehabilitation
- Education and emotional support
- Determination of optical and nonoptical systems
- Follow-up to ensure progress

Occupational Therapy Services

Evaluation and training in:
- Prescribed optical devices
- Nonoptical devices
- Adaptive techniques
- Environmental modifications
- Vision substitution techniques
- Systematic organization
- Energy conservation
- Work simplification
- Postural alignment
- Joint protection

Social Work Services

- Psychosocial assessment
- Supportive counseling
- Referral to community services
- Registration with state agencies
- Referral for financial assistance
- Advocacy

Adapted from McCabe P, Nason F, Demers Turco P, Friedman D, Seddon JM et al. Evaluating the effectiveness of a vision rehabilitation intervention using an objective and subjective measure of functional performance. *Ophthalmic Epidemiol.* 2000;7(4):259-270.

REFERENCES

1. World Health Organization. *International classification of impairment, disabilities, and handicaps: a manual of classification relating to consequences of disease.* Geneva, Switzerland: WHO; 1980.
2. Warren M. An overview of low vision rehabilitation and the role of occupational therapy. In: Warren M, Ed. *Low Vision: Occupational Therapy Intervention With the Older Adult.* Bethesda, MD: American Occupational Therapy Association; 2000:3-21.
3. Brody BL, Gamst AC, Williams RA, et al. Depression, visual acuity, comorbidity, and disability associated with age-related macular degeneration. *Ophthalmology.* 2001;108(10):1893-1900; discussion 1900-1901.
4. Rovner BW, Zisselman PM, Shmuely-Dulitzki Y. Depression and disability in older people with impaired vision: a follow-up study. *J Am Geriatr Soc.* 1996;44(2):181-184.
5. Rovner BW, Casten RJ, Tasman WS. Effect of depression on vision function in age-related macular degeneration. *Arch Ophthalmol.* 2002;120(8):1041-1044.
6. Graboyes M. Psychosocial implications of visual impairment. In: Brilliant RL, Ed. *Essentials of Low Vision Practice.* Boston, MA: Butterworth-Heinemann; 1999:12-17.
7. McIlwaine GG, Bell JA, Dutton GN. Low vision aids: is our service cost effective? *Eye.* 1991;5:607-611.
8. Stelmack JA, Szlyk JP, Stelmack TR, et al. Psychometric properties of the Veterans Affairs Low-Vision Visual Functioning Questionnaire. *Invest Ophthalmol Vis Sci.* 2004;45(11):3919-3928.

9. Watson GR. Older adults with low vision. In: Corn AL, Koenig AJ, Eds. *Foundations of Low Vision: Clinical and Functional Perspectives*. New York: American Foundation for the Blind; 2000:363-390.

10. Quillman RD, Goodrich GL. Interventions for adults with visual impairments. In: Lueck AH, Ed. *Functional Vision: A Practitioner's Guide to Evaluation and Intervention*. New York: AFB Press; 2004:423-474.

11. Stelmack J. Emergence of a rehabilitation medicine model for low vision service delivery, policy, and funding. *Optometry*. 2005;76(5):318-326.

12. Vision rehabilitation: care and benefit plan models. Literature review. 2002 [cited 2005 October 7, 2005]. Available from: http://www.ahrq.gov/clinic/vision/.

13. D'Allura T, McInerney R, Horowitz A. An evaluation of low vision services. *J Vis Impairment & Blind*. 1995;89:487-493.

14. Leat SJ, Fryer A, Rumney NJ. Outcome of low vision aid provision: The effectiveness of a low vision clinic. *Opt Vis Sci*. 1994;71:199-206.

15. Goodrich GL, Mehr EB, Quillman RD, Shaw HK, Wiley JK. Training and practice effects in performance with low-vision aids: a preliminary study. *Am J Optom Physiol Opt*. 1977;54(5):312-318.

16. Nilsson UL, Nilsson SE. Rehabilitation of the visually handicapped with advanced macular degeneration. A follow-up study at the Low Vision Clinic, Department of Ophthalmology, University of Linkoping. *Doc Ophthalmol*. 1986;62(4):345-367.

17. Nilsson UL. Visual rehabilitation of patients with advanced diabetic retinopathy. A follow-up study at the Low Vision Clinic, Department of Ophthalmology, University of Linkoping. *Doc Ophthalmol*. 1986;62(4):369-382.

18. Nilsson UL. Visual rehabilitation with and without educational training in the use of optical aids and residual vision. A prospective study of patients with advanced age-related macular degeneration. *Clin Vis Sci*. 1990;6:3-10.

19. Goodrich GL. Goldilocks and the three training methods: a comparison of three models of low vision reading training on reading efficiency. *Vis Impairment Res*. 2004;6:135-152.

20. Reeves B, Harper RA, Russell WB. Enhanced low vision rehabilitation service for people with age-related macular degeneration: a randomised controlled trial. *Br J Ophthalmol*. 2004;88:1443-1449.

21. La Grow SJ. The effectiveness of comprehensive low vision services for older persons with visual impairments in New Zealand. *J Vis Impairment & Blind*. 2004;98:679-692.

22. Shuttleworth GN, Dunlop A, Collins JK, James CR. How effective is an integrated approach to low vision rehabilitation? Two year follow-up results from south Devon. *Br J Ophthalmol*. 1995;79:719-723.

23. Scanlan JM, Cuddeford JE. Low vision rehabilitation: a comparison of traditional and extended teaching programs. *J Vis Impairment & Blind*. 2004;98:601-611.

24. McCabe P, Nason F, Demers Turco P, Friedman D, Seddon JM. Evaluating the effectiveness of a vision rehabilitation intervention using an objective and subjective measure of functional performance. *Ophthalmic Epidemiol*. 2000;7(4):259-270.

25. Pankow L, Luchins D, Studebaker J, Chettleburgh D. Evaluation of a vision rehabilitation program for older adults with visual impairment. *Topics in Geriatric Rehab*. 2004;20(3):223-232.

26. Brody BL, Williams RA, Thomas RG, Kaplan RM, Chu RM, Brown SI. Age-related macular degeneration: a randomized clinical trial of a self-management intervention. *Ann Behav Med*. 1999;21(4):322-329.

27. Humphry RC, Thompson GM. Low vision aids: evaluation in a general eye department. *Trans Ophthalmol Soc UK*. 1986;105:296-303.

28. Watson GR, De l'Aune W, Stelmack J, Maino J, Long S. National survey of the impact of low vision device use among veterans. *Optom Vis Sci*. 1997;74(5):249-259.

Foundation Skills and Therapeutic Activities

COMPENSATING FOR CENTRAL FIELD LOSS

This chapter includes the foundation skills for low vision rehabilitation. In Chapter 9, we stressed the general rule that rehabilitation for vision impairment is not remedial. Low vision rehabilitation improves performance of activities that typically depend on vision, rather than improve vision itself. The one important exception to this rule is the area of reading and localization of objects in space. Clients with low vision generally struggle with reading, particularly when the underlying disease affects the macula and causes a central scotoma. Clients with peripheral field loss or unilateral field loss struggle with spatial localization, finding and localizing objects in their immediate surroundings, and avoiding tripping hazards. Effective reading and scanning of one's environment is very closely linked to the ability to fixate and make accurate, rapid eye movements called *saccades*. One often must relearn saccade control and scanning in order to recover reading and localization of objects in space. Studies demonstrate, however, that in spite of the permanent visual acuity loss and central scotoma, a person can learn to fixate more accurately and make more accurate saccades after vision rehabilitation. Thus, reading and localization of objects in space

can indeed improve after vision rehabilitation as the client learns to more effectively use the remaining vision. This chapter is designed to present a systematic approach to rehabilitation of eccentric viewing, fixation, scanning, and reading and is the second step of the seven-step sequential treatment approach for low vision rehabilitation that was summarized in Table 9-1.

In occupational therapy, occupation is used as a means for developing necessary foundation skills and abilities. For example, reading and finding an object in a store provide engaging activities that help build foundation visual scanning skills for other activities as well. In occupational therapy, the development of meaningful occupation is not only a means, but an end, the ultimate outcome. Towards this end, the occupational therapist will readily consider nonvisual as well as visual solutions to enable someone to enjoy a book or find something in a store.

Central Field Loss and Macular Degeneration

Macular degeneration ranks as the most common cause of low vision in developed countries.[1] As the disease progresses to the end stage, macular degeneration usually restricts damage to the central visual field, the macula and immediately surrounding area,

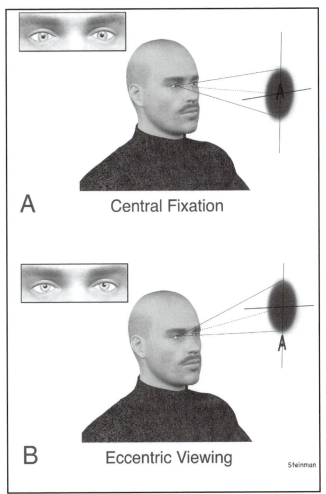

A   Central Fixation

B   Eccentric Viewing

Steinman

Figure 10-1. A. Illustration of central viewing. B. Eccentric viewing w/ Neillson technique added. The letter "A" is the fixation target and the cross indicates the scotoma center (Steinman).

scotomas or islands of vision rather than one large central scotoma. With exudative macular degeneration, onset of vision loss occurs suddenly with more extensive vision loss at first due to hemorrhaging at the retinal level. As blood in the vitreous dissipates, the measured scotoma will stabilize and shrink and contrast sensitivity will improve somewhat. *Atrophic* (dry) macular degeneration usually begins with a *relative scotoma*, ie, an area of reduced visual acuity. This area gradually increases in size and density, allowing the affected individual to adapt to loss of central vision. In some cases, people will experience active hallucinations in the scotoma, referred to as the Charles Bonnet syndrome.[3] Medical treatment for macular degeneration due to retinal pathology, at best, slows the progression of the disease; rarely is vision improved.[1] The functional problems associated with central field loss, however, have responded well to rehabilitation interventions.

Learning Eccentric Viewing

Vision loss is usually restricted to a relatively small percentage of visual field; however, unmanaged macular or central field loss severely disables performance of most visual tasks that require resolution of detail, such as reading, finding objects in a room, or recognizing a face. This is because the macula represents the region of our retina that provides the best resolution of detail and color. Someone with a macular scotoma often does not visualize the scotoma as a dark spot and may not even be aware of a central blind spot. For example, someone might see a person normally in his or her peripheral vision, then look over at the person only to find that the face, or part of the face seems to disappear. Indeed, people with recent onset central field loss often complain that "things appear and disappear." If the macular problem is left unmanaged, reading becomes impossible, as even with magnified text, words or parts of words appear and disappear. Not surprisingly, nearly one out of four of those with this frustrating and confusing impairment develop clinically significant depression.[4-7]

Several studies and clinical experience indicate that a person with central field loss can learn to use his or her peripheral vision rather than central vision to view objects (Figure 10-1). Research indicates that people who have adapted to central field loss will prefer to use one or more patches of functioning retina outside of macula called Preferred Retinal Loci or PRL.[8-15] Someone using a PRL rather than the fovea will appear to be looking above, below, or to the side of a target rather than directly at it. Many use the terms *eccentric viewing* or *eccentric fixation* to describe how a person's eyes appear when he or she uses a PRL (eccentric means "off center"). Learning to use a new

creating a central scotoma. A *scotoma* is a "blind spot," an island in the visual field with reduced or no vision that is surrounded by better vision. The central portion of our visual field, the macula, comprises the central 15 to 20 degrees of visual angle, an area about twice the width of a fist at arm's length.[1] With macular degeneration, this central region is damaged and creates a central scotoma surrounded by functioning more peripheral retina. Investigators have measured scotoma sizes to about 30 degrees,[2] an area about the size of three fist widths. In addition to macular degeneration, central field loss also occurs with untreated diabetic retinopathy and cortical blindness. With these conditions, the central field loss might be larger than the central field loss associated with macular degeneration.

There are two types of macular degeneration. With the *exudative* (wet) type of macular degeneration, retinal swelling might distort the shape of objects being viewed and the person might have multiple

Table 10-1.

Eccentric Viewing (EV) Instructional Sequence

1. Scotoma awareness training, and evaluation of scotoma and eccentric viewing skills.
2. If no or inconsistent eccentric viewing. Eccentric viewing training with central fixation cue that is faded out and replaced with verbal cues.
3. If consistent eccentric viewing. Verify client can shift eccentric viewing positions with verbal cues.
4. Eccentric viewing training under natural viewing conditions—without central fixation cue. Identify the best eccentric viewing position.
5. Patient ready for device evaluation and preliminary recommendation by optometrist.
6. Reading training with the scrolling technique and introduction to magnification device.
7. Final prescription of magnification device—home program with device.
8. Tracking with and without a handheld device.
9. Scanning without optical devices.
10. Finding the best eccentric viewing position.

patch of retina to see something develop is much like relearning a tennis or golf swing after many years of using another technique. Learning the new task is conscious and clumsy at first, becoming automatic and smooth later after considerable practice with feedback. At first, if someone sees something to the side and quickly looks directly at it using the fovea, it will disappear. With practice, people with central field loss will learn to directly look at something using the PRL, but not as quickly or efficiently as someone with intact central vision.[16] People also can learn to use different eccentric viewing positions that optimize vision for different conditions.[17]

Instructional protocols have been shown to rather quickly and effectively teach a person with central field loss to develop a PRL that substitutes for loss central retinal function.[18-20] These instructional procedures have improved functional reading as well as clinical measures of viewing performance. The methods described below are a blend of those reported by Nilsson with methods developed by Gale Watson[21,22] and personal clinical experience. How the therapist teaches eccentric viewing depends on the client's level of skill when started, as many learn some eccentric viewing without instruction. These steps are summarized in Table 10-1.

Scotoma Awareness Instruction and Evaluation of Vision and Skills

The first and most important step in eccentric viewing training has two objectives. The first objective is to determine if the client has already developed adaptive eccentric viewing or still has nonadaptive central fixa-

tion. The second goal is to teach the client to become aware and in some cases visualize the central scotoma. As this instruction is best done by demonstration, the therapist can instruct the client and evaluate eccentric viewing and scotoma size at the same time. The client also requires education regarding the expected prognosis and reassurance that by learning a new way of looking at things, vision will once again become more predictable, although magnification will be required to read and recognize faces and TV again. Learning to eccentrically fixate is difficult and can be frustrating. Care must be taken to carefully grade activities to insure early success, to be positive, and to keep training sessions short.

Often the visual system "fills in" the central scotomas; the person with a central scotoma cannot see the blind area but can be instructed to become aware of it. When asked to look at a target "so you can see it clearly," the beginner who has not yet developed eccentric viewing will tend look directly at the target and it will disappear, but he or she can still see objects to the side. Scotoma awareness training requires demonstration combined with explanation. At the end of scotoma awareness training, the client should be able to describe the shape of his central blind spot and why things appear and disappear. At the end of eccentric viewing training, the client will voluntarily move the blind spot to make isolated targets disappear as well as to position his eye to see an object most clearly. The client who has developed eccentric viewing will be able to position the eye eccentrically, that is looking above, below, or to the side so the target that is straight ahead can be visualized. One case that illustrates this skill involves an attractive young woman who had adapted to a juvenile macular degeneration

Figure 10-2. Clock face for EF instruction. A. Central fixation with numerals of best acuity indicated to the client's left. B. Rightward eccentric viewing.

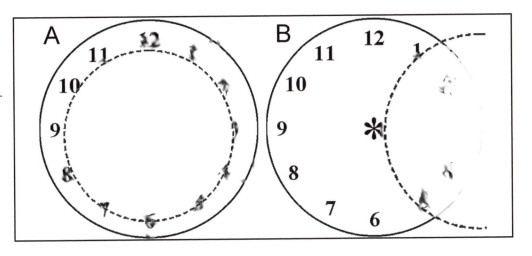

she acquired at age 16. She described one advantage of macular degeneration: at a party she could make unattractive guys "go away" just by looking at them, while checking out the cute ones from the "corner of her eye." One might say she had mastered scotoma awareness.

There are several methods to approach scotoma awareness training. We describe two useful procedures, the tangent screen and clock face methods. Ideally, instruction should include both techniques. The clock face method is quickly administered; the tangent screen method might require approximately 5 minutes. Early in the instructional sequence, a larger tangent screen is required and may not be practical in a home-based therapy setting.

The Clock Face Method

Wright and Watson developed methods available in a workbook that provides excellent worksheets and resources for eccentric viewing instruction.[21] The clock face method involves the use of a picture of a clock (Figure 10-2) with a star at the center of the clock. The therapist tells the client to "look at the center of the clock so that you can see it." If the client still has central fixation tendencies, the client will report that center star will disappear and that all of the numbers can be seen. If the client cannot see the numerals, the therapist can move the clock closer until the numeral shapes can be seen, or use a larger picture of a clock. If the client has developed eccentric viewing, when asked to describe the shape at the center of the clock, the client will report that a star can be seen but that some of the numbers are missing. The missing numbers will indicate the location of the scotoma and direction of eccentric viewing. For example, if the numbers 2, 3, and 4 are missing, the client is eccentrically fixating to the right (see Figure 10-2). If all of the numbers can be seen and the client reports seeing the star, then one of three possibilities exist. One is that no scotoma exists. The most likely option is that the client is not steadily fixating; rather, the client is looking around with searching eye movements. The therapist should carefully observe the client's eyes to insure viewing is stable. If the client has steady viewing, the third possibility is that the scotoma might be small or might be a relative scotoma (reduced central vision but enough vision to see shapes). In this case, the therapist moves the clock further away until the client reports that the star fades from view (central fixation) or some numbers disappear (eccentric viewing). During this testing, scotoma awareness training involves explaining to the client about the center "blind spot" and pointing out how it can be moved by looking in different directions.

The Tangent Screen Method

The tangent screen method (see Figure 10-3 and Chapter 8) also can be used to combine central field testing and eccentric viewing evaluation with scotoma awareness training. The viewing target is usually a letter large enough for a client to recognize in the center of a felt board. The tangent screen method involves first positioning the viewing target in the center of the 1-meter square tangent screen. The letter is placed in the center of a large cross. The client is instructed to "look at the letter so that you can see it most clearly." With a large screen, the therapist is able to sit or stand between the client and the screen to carefully observe the client's eyes. The client who has not developed eccentric viewing and is still centrally fixating will fixate the center of the cross and report that the letter disappears. The person with adaptive eccentric viewing will report that she sees the letter in the center of the cross and if the scotoma is large, eccentric viewing should be evident by looking at the eyes. If the client generates random searching type movements, gently instruct the client to "look directly at the center of the cross—don't worry about the letter." If the client centrally fixates the cross, the letter will disappear into the scotoma.

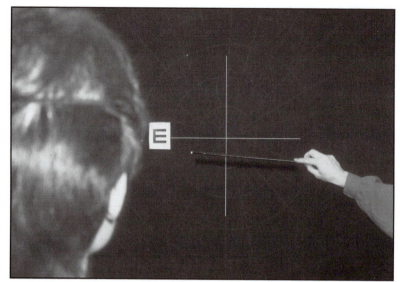

Figure 10-3. Tangent screen method. The E is the eccentric viewing target. The client is looking at the center of the cross, the central fixation cue. The client reports when the dot stimulus at the end of the wand appears and disappears. Often the cross is eliminated to simplify the task visually.

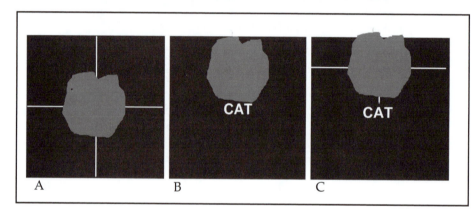

Figure 10-4. A. Tangent screen with scotoma with central fixation. B. Upward viewing with word stimulus without a central fixation cue. C. Upward viewing with a central fixation cue.

If the client has nonadaptive central fixation, while the client continues to fixate and position the scotoma in the center of the cross, move a dot attached to the end of the wand away from the center until the client sees it (Figure 10-4). Mark the spot where the wand dot "appears" with a pin, and then start at the center and quickly move to the edge of the scotoma in all directions. The pins should be small or low contrast so they are not visible. Once all of the pins are in place, a thick high-contrast yarn can be placed around the pins to illustrate the size and location of the scotoma.

Individuals who have had central field loss for several months or more may have already started developing eccentric viewing. The client who has already developed stable eccentric viewing will position the eyes to be looking above, below, or to one side of the letter and the client will report seeing the whole letter. The client may also move his head. The therapist should be able to predict where the scotoma is expected to be located based on where client's eyes appear to be looking, observing the eyes and not the head because often the head is moved in the direction opposite to the eyes. Based on this prediction,

the therapist moves a white testing spot at the end of a long black wand to where the client appears to be looking (see Figure 10-3). It is essential that the therapist carefully watch the client's eyes to be sure that he does not move during this procedure. When the white wand dot enters the scotoma, the client will report that it disappears. Explain to the client that you have found the scotoma and that you will now be measuring how large it is. Move the wand dot until it is first seen and mark the edge of the scotoma with a low-contrast mark or pin (not visible to the client). Quickly move from nonseeing to seeing and mark the border of the scotoma so that it is mapped in a couple of minutes. The outline of the scotoma should be above, below, or to the side of the letter indicating the direction of eccentric viewing and the size of the scotoma.

It is not unusual for a client with eccentric viewing to shift eye position, for example, from looking above to looking below the viewing letter. The therapist can detect these shifts by looking at the eyes and noting inconsistency in where the target is seen on the screen. If this occurs, illustrate the new location of the scotoma by positioning the white spot in the scotoma's

new location. This demonstrates to the client that the scotoma moved. Gently coax the client back to his original position and complete mapping. When the scotoma is mapped, more clearly mark the edges (with white yarn wrapped around the push pins in the felt board) and have the client move his eyes to see the outlined scotoma.

Eccentric Training With a Central Fixation Cue

This phase of instruction should be done with clients who have not developed adaptive eccentric viewing (see Table 10-1). The purpose of this instruction is to teach the client to look in a particular direction above, below, or to the side of a target, ie, to eccentrically fixate in order to see a target that is positioned at the center of the screen. Note that to avoid confusion we use the term *eccentric viewing target* as the word or shape that the client is trying to see using eccentric viewing. The term *central fixation cue* refers to targets used to encourage the client to look in a particular direction. Central fixation cues are used with beginners who have not yet developed eccentric viewing, and still tend to look directly at objects using the macula even though the macula no longer functions. The central fixation cue is used in conjunction with an eccentric viewing target to stimulate the client to position the eyes in a particular direction so that the client might better see the eccentric viewing target. For example, when asked to identify the letter E on the screen, the beginner will tend to look directly at it and will report that the E disappears. To encourage eccentric viewing, the therapist asks the client to look at the cross above the E using a large cross as a central fixation cue. When the client then looks at the cross, the center of the cross disappears, but the E now can be visualized and recognized using eccentric viewing (Figure 10-4C). Since the client intends to identify the letter E, it is an eccentric viewing target. The cross is a central fixation cue. Note that clients who have become well adapted to a central scotoma will automatically eccentrically fixate even if instructed to look directly at a target.

Clock Face Method

The client is asked to first look at the center of the clock where a star is positioned. If the client tends to centrally fixate, then the client will report the center star disappears. The clock distance should be positioned so the shapes of all of the numbers can be seen, bringing it closer if the numbers cannot be seen. The therapist then directs the client to "look at" different clock numerals; the clock numerals act as central fixation cues. When the client directs central fixation to a numeral, he should report that the numeral

disappears and the center target appears. Using the disappearing numerals on a clock face for feedback, the client becomes aware of the direction of eccentric viewing as well as how to control the scotoma position in order to see the central star.

Now ask the client which numerals can be seen most clearly while he fixates at the middle of the clock. This report indicates the area if the retina with best visual acuity. Moving the eye in the direction opposite to the numeral most easily seen (area of best vision) will bring the retinal locus of best vision to the center and the star or shape in the center of the clock will be seen most clearly (see Figure 10-2). Again, note that the therapist needs to vary the distance of the clock face from the eye depending on the expected size of the central scotoma. For those with better vision and a smaller scotoma the clock should be held further away.

Tangent Screen Method

Frennesson, Jakobsson, and Nilsson[23] described a different method that is well-suited for a person in the early stages of adaptation with a strong tendency to centrally fixate. This method keeps the eccentric viewing target, a letter or number, stable in the center of the screen and uses a computer program to move the cross above, below, or to the side of the letter on a computer screen. A high-contrast cross made out of thin dowels attached to the end of a wand might work as well with a tangent screen. The client is instructed to always direct central fixation and the scotoma to the center of the cross. The cross is then moved until the client reports being able to see the letter. By moving the cross above, below, or to the side of the eccentric viewing target, the therapist encourages the client to redirect the line of gaze eccentrically so that the letter can be seen with side vision (see Figure 10-4C). One might think of this technique as enabling the therapist to slowly drag the client's gaze into a desired position. The letters may be replaced with three to four letter words placed in the center of the screen and different eccentric positions attempted until the eccentric viewing position that produces the best word recognition is found.

Fading Out the Central Fixation Cue and Introducing Natural Eccentric Viewing Targets

This step is quickly performed with individuals who have demonstrated eccentric viewing during initial evaluation. It should be used to verify that the client can voluntarily adopt different eccentric viewing positions in response to verbal instruction. With cognitively or linguistically impaired individuals, one might just empirically determine the best viewing

Table 10-2.	
Instruction on Compensatory Scanning	
Compensatory scanning:	*If also unilateral inattention, add the following:*
Search tasks for expected objects.	Forced fixation on the side of the deficit.
Search with unexpected objects.	Cued fixation to the side of the deficit.
Behavior modification of right–left scanning.	
Holding fixation in the direction of the deficit.	Use cued fixation to the side of the deficit.

position, and instruct the client to always adopt this one position.

Tangent Screen Method

In this stage of instruction, the tangent screen method is most suitable. The purpose of this step of the instruction sequence (Table 10-2) is to enable the client to follow verbal instructions to look to each side of the target or above and below the eccentric viewing target without a central fixation cue. Instruction begins with a central fixation cue that is faded out and replaced by verbal cues or no cues. During this instruction, different meaningful eccentric viewing targets are used—three to four letter words for someone who wishes to read, pictures of loved ones, or a TV. Thus, during instruction, the therapist can ascertain the eccentric viewing position that is best for a particular goal task. At first, a central fixation cue is used such as a cross at the end of a wand or a laser spot to encourage the person to eccentrically view in a particular direction. The central fixation cue is positioned at different points around the eccentric viewing target, encouraging eccentric viewing above, below, and to each side of the eccentric viewing target with verbal instruction. The therapist should place a word on the tangent screen and instruct the client to "look at the center of the cross (the central fixation cue) until it disappears" and determine the position that allows the words to be seen clearly. Then repeat the movement without the wand. As one teaches the client to move in different positions, one will determine the position most suitable for reading. Occasionally, one finds a client with one PRL with a larger field of view more suitable for reading, and another PRL that allows isolated letters to be seen more clearly. This tangent screen method could be performed on a computer screen or any near card. Variations on the tangent screen can be improvised by using a wall, laser pointer, and a drawn or real life eccentric viewing target. The eccentric fixation target is centered and a central fixation cue (laser spot) is positioned as needed to the side and

eventually faded out so a client can follow directions such as "look up" and eventually eccentrically fixate a centered target without any cues.

Another therapeutic activity that can be used at this stage of training with either the tangent screen or the clock involves the use of a telescope or small diameter tube. The client looks through a tube of about 1 cm (0.5 inch). If the person with a central scotoma centrally fixates through the tube, nothing will be seen. If the person eccentrically views, then something will be seen. This exercise may be done with a telescope and provides salient feedback as to whether adaptive eccentric viewing has been achieved or not.

Clock Face Method

Recall that during the initial evaluation, when the client with adaptive eccentric viewing was asked to look at the center star he would report seeing the center star and that some clock numerals would disappear. At this point, the client who has just received completed instruction should also be able to do the same.

Eccentric Viewing Under Natural Viewing Conditions

Home exercise or practice also may be performed with pairs of large-print playing cards positioned so that while "looking at" one card, the other card becomes visible. Computer programs that act like flash cards might also help a client practice eccentric viewing by themselves (Magnimaster, Hunstad Magnimaster Reading Improver SMC, Paradis, Norway). The fixation tube, computer program, and clock face may also be sent home for practice as a home exercise program. At this stage of instruction, the client should be able to practice by watching TV, taking care to insure the TV is close enough to see.

During this training, a client may turn his head. This head turn may be in the direction opposite the direction to which the client moves the eyes to eccentrically view. There is no evidence that head turning presents

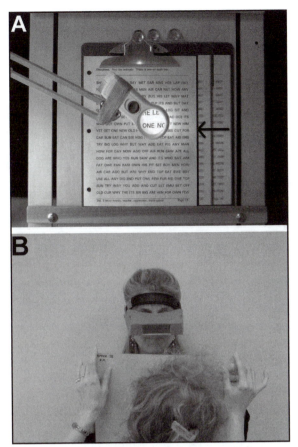

Figure 10-5. A. Steady eye technique at a reading stand with mounted handheld magnifier. B. Steady eye technique seated with hand-over-hand assistance.

most cases, looking above the line is best for reading. Once the client can see the word, slowly scroll the text from right to left while he tries to keep the eye in the same position. The eye and the head should not move. Watson calls this the *steady eye technique.*[21] Starting with hand-over-hand assistance, the client holds the text affixed to a clipboard and scrolls the text (Figure 10-5). In addition to reading lines of text, the client needs to learn to return to the beginning of the line. This is accomplished by marking the beginning of the line with a finger and following the line just read back to the beginning and moving down. This is called the *retracing technique.* The therapist gradually withdraws assistance until the client is able to read without assistance. The client can practice scanning multiple lines and finally more complex activities such as reading bills and bank statements. The key to this technique is that the client slowly moves the material being read from right to left rather than the eyes and head.

People with more normal visual acuity read by generating left to right eye movements (saccades) to look from one word to the next. Visually guided saccades are compromised in people without central vision.[24] When using the steady eye technique, a person with central field loss can more easily shift gaze from word to word using a reflexive eye movement, the quick phase of optokinetic nystagmus rather than visually guided saccades.[25]

Tracking and Viewing Through a Handheld Magnifier

After the client has demonstrated good steady viewing and mastered reading scrolled text, tracking and scanning techniques are used along with magnification devices. The procedure begins with steady viewing. The client attempts to identify playing cards as the therapist pulls each card off the top of the deck. Index cards with numbers and short words (four letters or less) can also be used. Once the client can perform well with steady viewing, the therapist should add movement to the procedure. To do so, the therapist holds the cards while carefully observing the client's eyes. The stack of cards is then slowly moved and the client should track the cards. Maintaining viewing with a slowly moving target with a predictable motion is relatively easy. Recovering eccentric viewing when viewing is lost presents the greater difficulty, especially if the target disappears into the scotoma. If the client loses visibility of the target during this procedure, the therapist should stop until he recovers and then continues. At first the characters should be at least three times the client's visual acuity. Starting from the card position that allows most consistent eccentric viewing, slowly move the cards in various

a problem except to the therapist trying to observe eye position. Head turning may present ergonomic problems and clients can be taught to eccentrically view without head turning during advanced instruction. Research needs to be done to better understand the effect of head position. However, eccentric viewing is a difficult skill to learn, and we feel that focusing too much on technique may be discouraging.

Reading With Scrolled Text

Once the client demonstrates the ability to eccentrically view and identify a single stationary object like playing cards or short word cards, large-print text should be used. The print size used should be at least twice the visual acuity level of the client. The client might also require a microscope (strong reading glasses), a mounted handheld magnifier, or a closed circuit television (CCTV) for this training period. When practicing with printed text, the client should be sitting at a table in front of a reading stand with the text mounted on a card that slides horizontally on the lip of the stand (see Figure 10-4A). The client is then directed to eccentrically view the first word. In

directions (up and to the right, down and to the right, up and to the left, down and to the left), starting with movement away from the scotoma because movement toward the scotoma will present the most difficulty. Increase task difficulty by increasing the speed of the target movement and then moving the tracking stimulus unpredictably. To further increase the level of difficulty of the task, decrease print size. Note that people will sometimes switch from one eccentric viewing position to another. Let your client know when you observe this happening. Rapid alternation between eccentric viewing positions slows reading and should be discouraged for reading; this strategy, however, may be adaptable when scanning during mobility.

A practical extension of tracking a large stimulus is to have the client read through a handheld magnifier or stand magnifier held at about 20 to 40 cm (16 inches) from the eye. Begin with the client seated, and once he can master reading while seated instruct the client to attempt reading through a handheld magnifier or stand magnifier while standing. Recall that the handheld magnifier and the head should rotate together with the lateral movement of the head as the magnifier moves across the page, as if an imaginary rod connects the magnifier through the eye and the head. Scanning with telescopic magnification can also be introduced at this point in the therapy.

Localizing and Scanning

The most advanced task is to have the client scan a room using saccadic eye movements. The goal of scanning training is to enable the client to make an accurate saccade to an object seen peripherally without the object disappearing into the scotoma. Although this is a simple task for a person without a central scotoma, this type of saccadic control is irreversibly compromised with the loss of central vision. A person with a central scotoma requires increased time to make a saccade to an object seen peripherally because these eye movements are inaccurate and several saccades may be required to scan from one object to the next.[8] To practice scanning, a large, high-contrast eccentric viewing target can be presented in the periphery such as a waving hand, a person, or a light in regular, predictable positions at first. Eventually the targets should be presented in unpredictable positions. A laser light, flashlight, or flash card works well as an eccentric viewing target at this stage.

A more advanced technique used by individuals learning to use optical devices is *localization*. With localization, the client scans a room or page of text until he fixates a spot where he expects to see something of interest. Without breaking eccentric viewing, the client positions a magnification device in front of the eye so that the object of interest is magnified. For example, he might scan a bill and localize where some

numbers are printed that are likely to be the amount due by the layout of the text. The client then positions the magnification device in front of the eye to read the number. Localization will be described in detail in Chapter 13 when discussing optical devices.

Researchers have found that some well-adapted people with central vision loss use different eccentric viewing positions after saccades.[8] This advanced technique can be taught if the evaluation reveals different functional ability for various eccentric viewing positions, such as one PRL that has better acuity, and another with a larger horizontal field of view for reading.

Finding the Best Eccentric Viewing Position

To teach people to use different PRLs, the therapist should select targets that are typically involved in real-life tasks. Targets should be carefully selected so that a different visual skill is required to best identify the chosen target. For example, one target might be more easily identified with a PRL that works well with longer words, while another target (picture of a face) might be more easily identified with a PRL that has better acuity. Often different PRLs have different visual acuity ability, requiring a change in required magnification. It is important to understand that for mobility, the use of inferior viewing is dangerous because a scotoma in lower central field puts people at risk for tripping on objects on the floor.[26] Positioning the scotoma above the text is generally thought to be better for reading.

Equipment for Eccentric Viewing Training and Home Exercise Program

Ideally, eccentric viewing instruction involves a display for stimuli and a method for the therapist to view the client's eye while he is attempting to eccentrically fixate. A 1 meter (3 foot) felt screen that will accept pins will work for most techniques, although smaller and improvised tangent screens may become necessary when a large tangent screen is not practical.

A computer can also be used for eccentric viewing training. The therapist can generate a graphics display on a computer screen using a draw program such as the draw feature in Microsoft Word. One draws the four lines of a cross and then uses the "group" feature to connect them so that one can click on one line and drag all four. One or two viewing letters or words might be written in a "text box" that can be dragged and placed anywhere on the screen with the mouse. Template word documents are provided in the Appendices.

The procedures described above using playing cards or the clock face can easily be performed at home. Workbooks are available that provide a sequence of progressively more challenging home exercises for reading.[21] Indeed, even if reading is not the client's primary goal, the skills developed for reading should transfer to other tasks as well. The Magnimaster is a computer program that flashes magnified words on a screen for a limited period of time for a client to identify, functioning much like the deck of cards in training steady eccentric viewing. The client can be set up to work on this program without one-on-one assistance as well.[27]

Another challenge is providing the client with a magnification device sufficient to identify the targets or text used to practice the steady eye technique. Several options have been developed to provide magnification. Handheld magnifiers that are relatively inexpensive are often prescribed and dispensed for spot reading tasks. These devices can be mounted to allow the client to practice the scrolled text technique described above. A CCTV is ideal because the magnification can be adjusted as the client's skill improves. Another option includes a "loaner" program where full field microscopes or loupes can be loaned to the client during the exercise program, although this is costly to equip and difficult to manage. A final option is to have the client attend office-based treatment sessions and practice before or after the scheduled therapy session in the clinic with a borrowed device.

Eccentric Viewing With Cognitive Impairment

Learning to eccentrically view requires considerable practice even in clients with normal cognitive function. Eccentric viewing training proceeds much more easily if the client understands complex, multistep instructions, can perform ideational problem solving, and has good semantic as well as procedural memory. If a client is capable of following one-step commands and demonstrates learning with practice, eccentric viewing training may proceed if a helper is present who understands the process and can assist with practice. This client is unlikely to learn how to shift eccentric viewing with verbal cues, but might learn one eccentric viewing position with training. One should skip trying to teach this client how to voluntarily shift eccentric viewing positions and use multiple PRLs.

Compensating for Peripheral Field Loss

Basic Functions of Peripheral Vision

A key to the rehabilitation of clients with peripheral field loss is an understanding of the three basic functions of peripheral vision: organization of visual scanning, warning, and night vision.

Organize Visual Scanning

The first basic function of peripheral vision is to help an individual organize visual scanning. When someone with normal visual function "looks at" a larger scene or area such as a room or a restaurant menu, he generates a sequence of quick saccades at a rate of three to four saccades per second. Each saccade ends with a period of viewing on some part of the scene. During this viewing, the visual system samples a different area within the scene. During the approximately one-quarter second fixation period, the visual system uses the macula with its high resolution and color rendition to collect detail about some patch of the immediate surroundings. Using this sequence of saccades, the visual system rapidly pieces together a detailed and complex perception of the scene or area. For example, when a person with normal visual function enters an unfamiliar room for the first time, his peripheral vision with its lower acuity detects larger, higher contrast and moving objects. The person may detect people moving to the left and glance over to see who they are, then check the doors, signs, tables, and chairs seen in the periphery. Within a few seconds, using three to four saccades per minute, this person has gathered critical information that will allow him to interact with the other people, know where the doors are located, avoid obstacles in the room, as well as read the sign that indicates which doorway to enter. Organization of visual scanning involves not only peripheral vision, but also memory and other sensory modalities. A person entering a room may glance over to a radio playing music, or to the person talking to her left. The next time this person enters the room, she can use memory of the room layout, and may look directly to the door that leads to the desired destination and eventually could navigate the room, and even know where to look for the faint outline of obstacles if the lights are out. If this person developed a field cut, she may become aware that she is not seeing on

one side just as one is generally aware of the limits of typical visual fields.

However, damage to the parietal cortex and certain areas in the frontal cortex may compromise this scanning process.[28] This problem may manifest as a unilateral visual inattention or visual neglect. For example, a client named Mary has had a right cerebral vascular accident. We assume she has an intact left field because she responds to a bright light, a waving hand, or a ball thrown to her on the left. However, she does not spontaneously glance in that direction or notice signs to her left when looking around the room or when her attention is divided. We would conclude that Mary has intact visual fields but a unilateral inattention or visual neglect. In some cases, people will have both a unilateral inattention and unilateral field loss. These individuals cannot see anything on one side and are not aware of the vision loss or that objects exist on the side of the vision loss. Note that with unilateral field loss or inattention, the pattern of eye movements will be abnormal, but basic eye movement control such as saccade control by itself is not necessarily compromised. The abnormal pattern of saccades is secondary to a basic deficit in the neurophysiological and/or the sensory system that organizes the pattern of saccades required for scanning eye movements. The focus of therapy, therefore, should be on the visual and attention deficit, not directly on the eye movements themselves.

Use of the Visual Periphery as a Warning System

The second basic function of peripheral vision is the use of the visual periphery as a warning system. This is important for driving, walking in crowds, or mobility in general in busy areas. Our ability to respond to high-contrast moving objects is a phylogenically ancient system that allows creatures to detect and respond to high-contrast moving objects approaching from the side. That flash of fear we all experiences when something unexpected darts rapidly in from the side illustrates this warning system. In humans, this orienting response includes a saccade toward the suspected threat.[29] In our modern era, these threats may be a child running in front of the car, a car suddenly approaching an intersection that we are trying to cross, suddenly noticing and avoiding a rolling ball, or an animal running in front of us. These events may occur very quickly while we are looking somewhere else. If a client has a peripheral field loss and is looking straight ahead, the early warning system will not alert him or her to unexpected danger.

Role of Peripheral Vision in Night Vision

The final basic function of peripheral vision is the role peripheral vision plays in night vision. The peripheral retina has much greater sensitivity to dim light than central retina. Loss of peripheral vision, therefore, leads to night blindness, a severe loss of vision when the light levels drop.[30] A person with an overall peripheral vision loss due to advanced glaucoma or retinitis pigmentosa, for example, may report little problem during the day but severe visual disability at night.

Overall Field Loss

The retinal conditions that lead to overall visual field loss or "tunnel vision" usually have a gradual onset, allowing the client to progressively adapt with compensatory scanning. If someone with restricted visual fields reports problems bumping into objects or difficulty finding things, he should be taught compensatory scanning (Figure 10-6), described below. The usual progression includes searching tasks for objects graded from salient objects, such as bean bags on a table, to searching for objects in a cluttered area, such as a room. The common challenge in managing people with peripheral loss is addressing the loss of the "warning system." Even when using good scanning technique, a person with an overall peripheral field loss will miss an unexpected, quickly moving hazard from the "blind side." People with overall peripheral vision loss often experience night blindness. As peripheral visual field loss has a gradual onset, these clients may deny functional problems because of occupational disengagement. People with peripheral visual field loss may not go out at night, may avoid crowds or new environments, and may be in denial if the prognosis is total blindness. The best compensation for loss of the warning system is to use a white cane or guide dog, at least to signal to others to be careful. Mobility training, especially if it involves the use of a white cane, should be performed by a certified orientation and mobility (O&M) specialist. The vision rehabilitation therapist, however, can and should introduce the client to sighted guide techniques, use of nonvisual cues, environmental adaptations, and trailing techniques (sliding the back of the hand along a wall while walking), and convince the client to seek training on the use of the white cane. The denial process that occurs with recent onset low vision complicates the introduction of techniques associated with blindness.[7] The therapist often must subtly introduce blindness strategies. Better accep-

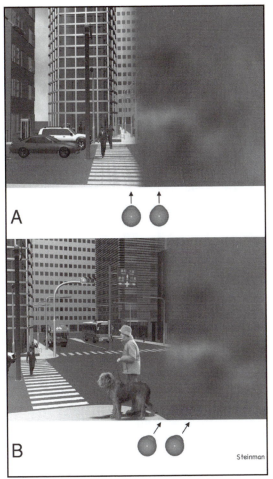

Figure 10-6. Compensatory scanning left-right with homonymous hemianopia (Steinman).

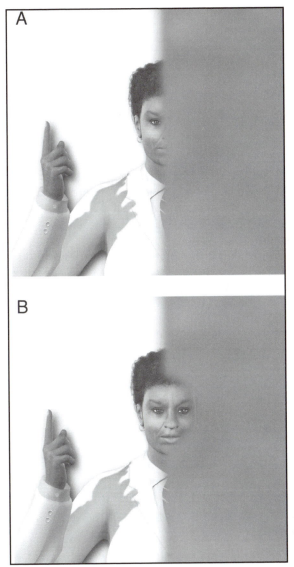

Figure 10-7. Unilateral field loss with and without central sparing during confrontation field testing (Steinman).

tance might be expected if the therapist introduces a sighted guide or the need for a white cane for "walking at night" when the client is less likely to deny the problem. People will gradually become accustomed to the advantages of using the methods, and begin using many of these techniques at all times and when vision further declines.

Unilateral Field Loss

Unilateral field loss results from brain injury to tracks or cortical areas post optic chiasm, often associated with cerebral vascular accident. Damage to the right side of the brain may lead to blindness in the left visual field of both eyes. Damage to the left side of the brain may lead to blindness in the right visual field of both eyes. If the blind area comprises nearly half of the visual field, starting approximately at the midline of both eyes, the condition is called *homonymous hemianopia* (Figure 10-7). If a quarter of the visual field is affected, the condition is called *homonymous quadrantanopia*.

To develop effective treatment, sensory deficits must be differentiated from perceptual, attention,

linguistic and other cognitive deficits. Brain injury affects a variety of cognitive and linguistic functions that might affect visual function such as letter identification and reading. People may have difficulty reading because of damage to linguistic processing areas. They may not respond to objects in the periphery because of impaired visual attention or unilateral inattention and neglect.[28,31] Since unilateral field loss in often associated with unilateral inattention, the treatments often address unilateral attention as well as unilateral field loss.

Unilateral field loss usually does not cut the field down the middle but rather leaves central vision intact, called *central sparing* (see Figure 10-7). Functionally, an individual with a unilateral field loss with central sparing will see most of a person's face at about 1 meter (3 feet), but see nothing to one side or the other of the face. People with field cuts and central sparing

usually have normal acuity and only minor problems with reading. These individuals will read a single line of text normally but might lose their place when reading, or may have difficulty scanning a page for information. In some cases, people have a unilateral field loss that also bisects the central field (see Figure 10-7). These individuals will report that one half of the examiner's face can be seen during field testing. People with "split central fields" will only see half of a letter or words they are trying to identify as well. The resultant loss of basic shape, letter, and face recognition may be confused with higher-order perceptual deficits. People with a right unilateral field loss with a split central field will have severe problems with reading, even though other linguistic functions are intact.

Functionally, people with unilateral field loss will present with disabled visual scanning and peripheral warning system, often with the functional effects compounded by an overlay of unilateral visual inattention. In addition, a person with unilateral field loss may present with "wayfinding deficits," and often cannot even retrace his steps. A person may have basic problems with wayfinding, primarily due to a unilateral field loss rather than cognitive deficit. For example, if a client with a left field loss walks down a hall for the first time, he will see one side of the hall to his right. When he turns around to retrace his steps, the formerly right side of the hall will now be to his blind, left visual field. The side of the hall that is now in his intact right field would never have been seen before. In effect, he has never seen the route he is retracing. This problem is exacerbated for people who have split central fields and/or unilateral inattention.

Damage to the optic chiasm, most often associated with pituitary tumor but sometimes associated with traumatic injury, will cause field loss that causes binasal or bitemporal field loss. With binasal deficit, the client cannot see objects nasal to the fixation objects with each eye and the temporal fields are intact. With bitemporal field loss, the client cannot see temporal to the fixation target in each eye and the nasal fields are intact. If one overlaps the visual fields, it appears that the fields are full because one eye will see what the other does not. For example, with binasal defects, the left (temporal) field of the left eye is intact, and the right (temporal) field of the right eye is intact. At least in theory, if the two eyes look at the same fixation target, the client has an intact right and left field and should have full binocular fields. There are, however, subtle but disabling problems. A person with binasal deficits will not see some objects closer than the fixation target because closer objects might fall into the nasal field of each eye. One can demonstrate this by positioning a finger at arm's length and another a few inches from the nose on the midline.

Fixate the far finger with both eyes, then close each eye to see how the proximal finger falls into the nasal field of each eye. If a client had a binasal field deficit, he would not see the closer object. With bitemporal defects, one will not see some objects further than the fixation target, which can be dangerous. If central vision is cut, a client will also have difficulty fixating an object with both eyes at the same time and will report double vision.

Remediation

One training technique has been reported to actually decrease the size of the blind area[32] 5 to 10 degrees in people with a presumably stable field loss of 18 months to several years. This instructional technique involved having clients detect flashing lights presented at the edge of the scotoma for 1 hour for 3 or more days a week for 3 to 6 months as part of a home program involving specialized training equipment. The results have not been replicated in studies controlling for compensatory scanning eye movements.[33] Therefore, the evidence for this procedure is questionable at this time.

The method that seems to produce the largest and functionally greatest increase in peripheral awareness is called *compensatory visual scanning*. In this technique, the therapist teaches the client to look with quick saccades in the direction of the blind hemifield.[32] Compensatory visual scanning does not actually increase the size of the intact field.

Compensatory Visual Scanning

To compensate for a unilateral field loss, the client must change habitual eye movement patterns. Normally we look at an object and depend on our peripheral vision to see on either side. Compensatory visual scanning involves frequently and consistently looking in the direction of the blind hemifield, much like a driver uses a rear-view and side-view mirrors when driving to get a sense of what is going on around the car and beyond the range of peripheral vision. As with any therapeutic intervention, the client must be educated about the deficit and provided with an explanation for the compensatory strategy. Understanding and verbalizing the problem or demonstrating improved performance during instructional protocols is not sufficient. The client must demonstrate compensatory scanning as an ingrained habit during real-life activities when attention is on the activity, not the eye movement.

Scanning With Expected Then Unexpected Objects

We suggest a three-step sequence for teaching this skill.

Figure 10-8. Two techniques to facilitate adaptive scanning into an affected hemifield. A. Partial lens occlusion forces the eye to look into the affected hemifield. B. The Sarah Appel technique uses a colored translucent filter to cue the client when he is looking in the correct direction (Steinman).

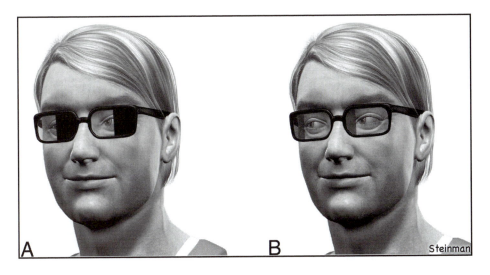

1. Step One

   The first stage in treatment is to engage the client in various search tasks: looking for specified objects in a room, looking for cooking or self-care items, simple puzzles, dominoes, or completing cancellation and drawing tasks. Examples of these treatment strategies have been well described in the occupational therapy literature.[31,34] This step is quickly mastered by people with intact visual attention, and less easily recovered with clients who have attention deficits. When grading the activities, easier tasks should be familiar and meaningful activities such as brushing teeth. Using tasks with expected objects (the brush, toothpaste, and glass) will encourage the client to continue looking until all the components in the visual task are found.

   To remediate inattention deficit, first one might force fixation to the side where there is inattention by smearing Vaseline or taping one-half of each lens on the intact side with translucent tape (Figure 10-8). This forces the client to look past the midline in the direction of the visual field loss, if the head is straight ahead. Nonvisual or extravisual cues might be added to direct attention to the affected side as well. A classic strategy is to place a brightly colored line and tactile marker down the edge of the page or field being scanned and cueing the client to keep looking until the line is seen. The next stage in this step is to use a method described by Appel[35] that involves placing a colored filter on one-half of each lens or cutting the lenses of inexpensive sunglasses (see Figure 10-8). When the client looks in direction of the field loss he will see a color change (see Figure 10-8A). The client is instructed to look

in the direction of the field loss until he sees the color (see Figure 10-8B). This cues the client that he is looking in the correct (compensatory) direction. Once the client can consistently scan for objects even with less familiar tasks, the searching and scanning function has been restored.

2. Step Two

   Step two involves having the client scan a room where unexpected objects might be found, eg, trying to find hazards in a kitchen or picking up objects on the floor.

3. Step Three

   Step three re-establishes the warning function of the peripheral retina. This step presents a greater challenge because responding to approaching objects from the affected side usually requires performance during divided attention, which is often impaired with brain injury or in older individuals. One approach we have successfully used involves behavior modification of scanning eye movements. The goal is to establish the habit of frequently and quickly looking in the direction of the field defect. Computer programs and equipment has been developed that allow the client to be set up to perform this task independently. This author has found any number of computer games where objects fly in unexpectedly from all directions (eg, "Squares," which is a free game found on the Web) that provide an engaging opportunity for home-based practice as well.

   Laser tag transitions the client to more real-life situations. The therapist and client each hold a laser pointer. The therapist presents the laser spot on a surface such as an uncluttered wall.

The client responds by pointing to the light and tagging the spot with his laser pointer. At first, the light is flashed at two predictable points in the right and left field. The task is graded to become more challenging and realistic by moving from predictable positions in an uncluttered area to unpredictable locations in a cluttered area. To further increase difficulty, the laser spot targets can be presented at different distances. Finally, the task is performed when the client's attention is divided, such as in a visually busy environment with people walking around. During this task, the therapist gradually decreases the frequency of presentations and varies the interval between laser spot presentations as well, pausing up to a minute or two between presentations. At this point, the client should be walking with frequent automatic glances into the affected hemifield, so that when the light eventually appears, she detects it within 2 seconds. This instructional sequence should result in the client frequently and habitually looking in the direction of the field deficit.

Holding fixation in the direction of the deficit is another strategy that provides early warning in the direction of the field loss. In this procedure, the client must look over and maintain fixation in the direction of the field deficit, using peripheral vision in the intact field to look straight ahead and to see into the unaffected hemifield. The sunglasses procedure or a colored filter on glasses (see Figure 10-8) can be used effectively to cue the client to look and maintain the eye in one direction. The client could be encouraged to play two-on-one ball games such as soccer or basketball, practice walking in crowds, practice crossing intersections with supervision, and when walking down the street, a partner might intermittently and unexpectedly veer into the client and playfully bump shoulders if not detected. Success is achieved if the client automatically maintains most of the fixation between straight ahead and the affected side so as to detect an approaching target within a second or two.

Instructional Strategies With Central Field Cut

A person with a central field cut needs to develop eccentric viewing in the direction of the field deficit and use side vision to expand the field of view. Since the region of highest visual acuity has been compromised, some magnification, usually under 2X or 5 D

of equivalent power, is required. Strategies for reading rehabilitation with central field cut are discussed below.

Field Expansion Devices

The use of field mirrors and prism have been advocated for many years and purportedly work as an early warning system, allowing clients to detect the approach of something on the affected side.[36-38] Prism, usually Fresnel-type prisms (see Figure 10-8), are pressed onto one spectacle lens with the base of the prism in the direction of the field defect. The prism displaces an image away from the base toward the point of the prism. (Think of the prism wedge as an arrow that points in the direction in which the person's view will move.) This prism is attached to one lens so that when the client looks into the blind hemifield or to the edge of the blind area, double vision will be experienced. One image is the normal view as seen by the eye looking through the plain lens. The eye looking through the prism will see the other image, actually a scene displaced from the blind area by the prism usually by no more than about 20 degrees.

A major problem with the use of prism is that it causes double vision, and we have found it might discourage compensatory scanning toward the affected side. To minimize this problem, Peli suggested that the prism be attached in the superior field above the pupil so the double vision is seen peripherally where it is less bothersome (Figure 10-9).[38] In theory, the client should detect objects in the blind field before the object enters the intact visual field.

READING

People with low vision often present upon initial evaluation with performance goals that involve reading. The visual requirements and performance demands of a reading activity vary considerably depending on the particular task. Reading a medicine bottle, finding the total on a credit card invoice, meditating on a very familiar passage in the Koran alone during morning prayer, reading the Torah in Hebrew in front of synagogue, locating a sign on the street corner, and enjoying the latest Tom Clancy novel involve substantially different assistive devices, motor skills, and visual demands. School systems, state offices of vocational rehabilitation, and medical insurance companies must recognize literacy as medically, vocationally, and educationally necessary. Not surprisingly, reading has become the cornerstone therapeutic activity as one develops a treatment plan for a variety of visual impairments and performance goals. Reading

Figure 10-9. The position of the Fresnel prism on spectacles and a simulation of the visual effects. Note the double image of a potential obstacle approaching from the blind hemifield becomes visible before contact (Steinman).

is so often the focus of treatment because the skills apparently transfer to other tasks as well.

Although reading is almost universally identified as a visual task, successful rehabilitation requires the therapist to move beyond the process of typical reading to appreciate the meaning of reading as an "occupation" to each individual. The act of reading might be viewed as purely functional, the process of transmitting information from the printed page into the brain. From this functional perspective, whether the reader uses vision, hearing, or touch to "read" becomes less significant. A person can acquire the information printed in a newspaper visually with an optical device, tactilely using a Braille transcription, listening to someone read, or as auditory reading using a computer equipped with a screen-reader that reads Web pages aloud. For students, those employed with productivity demands, people who want to read quickly, or people who read for pleasure, even with moderate vision loss, the most efficient solution often is text-to-speech. For many, however, the performance goal might focus on the process. How one reads a spiritual text often becomes a focus in religious ritual, as with unison recitations in a church or synagogue, the reading of a young man during his bar mitzvah, or the recitation of the Divine Office by a priest. Productivity might be less important than the process, or *how* we read. In this case, treatment planning should consider the process as well as speed and efficiency of information acquisition.

Reading Evaluation

Overview

The steps for evaluation and treatment for reading rehabilitation are summarized Table 10-3. The evaluation begins with consideration of the context in which the reading will occur and the instruction ends in the natural context. If one does not consider context, a successful demonstration of good reading performance in the clinic will not carry over into the home or workplace. The evaluation of context begins with the physical and social settings. Then one considers the font characteristics of the reading material and availability in other media. Is the material available in large print or as a recording of someone reading the text? Next one considers the task demand. Does the client need to read a few words on a label, or relax and enjoy a novel? Does a lawyer need to scan and read hundreds of pages all day long?

Once the task demand has been ascertained, it is usually advisable to discuss the nonvisual options first, as text-to-speech options often are the easiest to implement. The use of sighted assistants or Recordings for the Blind can quickly enable the goal task while the more difficult rehabilitation of visual reading is undertaken. Next the therapist performs an evaluation and with the consulting low vision optometrist decides if the visual requirements for reading can be met, and if so how. The evaluation identifies

> **Table 10-3.**
>
> ## Steps for Reading Rehabilitation
>
> *Evaluation*
>
> - Determine reading context (lighting, glare, seating, ergonomics).
> - Determine font characteristics and availability of alternative media (Braille and recordings).
> - Ascertain reading task demand (duration, rate, comprehension requirements).
> - Consider and present available nonvisual options to client.
> - Evaluate visual requirements for reading: identify performance limiting factors to address in treatment.
> - Evaluate reading performance.
>
> *Treatment (if visual requirements can be met)*
>
> - Address performance-limiting factors:
>   - Inadequate acuity reserve, use assistive devices
>   - Inadequate contrast reserve, use assistive devices
>   - Inadequate field of view
>   - Central field loss and compensatory scanning strategies
> - Provide initial instruction under idealized settings.
> - Transition to natural context and perform necessary environmental modifications.

the visual impediments that must be addressed in the treatment. Instruction begins out of context, in a setting where ergonomics and visual conditions can be carefully controlled to remove the impediments, meeting the visual requirements. For example, in home-based therapy, reading is often best started on a table. If one performs all of the instruction in the preferred context, such a person's favorite easy chair, the therapist will not be able to demonstrate environmental modifications that might make reading easier. The final phase of instruction moves to the client's preferred context, where environmental modifications permitted by the client are performed.

Context

In general, one first ascertains where each goal reading task will be performed: reading tags in a grocery store, reading a novel in a favorite chair in the living room, or managing medications at a table in the bathroom. The therapist usually starts instruction on a table that encourages good posture, and support for the upper body required for finely controlled movement of text, optical devices, and the head. A table also provides for easy repositioning of a directional task light. During this phase, the therapist must reassure the client that the task will eventually be adapted to his preferred, habitual context. As the therapist transi-

tions from the ideal setting to the habitual setting, the client will become aware of the effects environmental changes have on reading ability. For example, a client might stubbornly refuse to move his chair so that it does not face a window. Once the client has recovered reading in the clinic with directional lighting from the side, and then struggles in a simulation of the position of his favorite easy chair in the clinic, he appreciates the impact of glare on performance. The client might now accept the therapist's suggestion and move the chair. Evaluation of context should include attention to lighting and potential glare sources, the potential for mounting reading stands or positioning assistive devices, and ergonomics. Often, optical devices for reading are more easily used if the client stabilizes the material being read and his upper body on a table.

Font Characteristics and Availability of Alternative Media

Once goals for treatment of reading problems have been developed, the occupational therapist should establish the media and formats in which the reading material is available (Table 10-4). For example, most bills, checks, legal documents and many magazines and books are available in large (2 M or 14-16

Table 10-4.

Typical Print Sizes and Acuity Requirements[41]

Text Size	Sample		Text Acuity Usually Required
N scale (points)	M scale	Approximate; point size varies with font type	
3 pt	0.4 M	NORMAL acuity threshold at 40 cm	——
4 pt	0.5 M		——
5 pt	0.6 M	Ads, bibles	0.3
6 to 8 pt	0.8 M	Telephone book	0.4
8 to 10 pt	1.0 M	Newspaper	0.5
10 to 12 pt	1.25 M	Magazines, books, computer	0.6
12 to 14 pt	1.6 M	Books, typewriter	0.8
16 to 18 pt	2.0 M	Child & large print	1.0
18 to 20 pt	2.5 M	Large print	1.2

point) print. Information is also available as speech, for example, telephone companies and utilities must provide information by phone at no additional charge if a client can certify his disability. Automated Teller Machines (ATMs) have jacks for headphones so users can hear as well as see the display. Books, magazines, and daily newspapers are available in Braille, on tape, or on CD in a listening format by free services such as Radio Services for the Blind, and the National Library for the Blind. Major newspapers and magazines are available on the Web and are accessible by Web browsers equipped with software that reads the display aloud, magnifies the print, and improves contrast.

Font characteristics must be considered. Print size is expressed in N notation (points) or M notation. The M scale refers to the test distance in meters where the lower case letter with no extender (eg, x or m) subtends 5 minutes of arc on the retina, approximately the distance where the print is barely seen with normal vision. N notation refers to the printer's standard for sizing print where 1 point equals 1/72 of an inch; however, the actual print size in points varies from font to font because it dates to the days when lead type was set and refers to the "slug" size, not the letter itself. Mehr and Fried's[37] survey of fonts found N8 (8 pt) lower case and N5 (5 pt) upper case to be approximately equivalent to 1 M. Print characteristics also influence reading.

Font characteristics include type of font (Times New Roman, Arial), font size (discussed above), boldness, spacing between characters, and spacing between lines. Font characteristics significantly affect the visibility of individual letters (Figure 10-10). Unfortunately, the earliest research on the effects of font characteristics on visibility of print did not report how distance was controlled, if at all. More recent, controlled research has revealed one general finding: increasing letter spacing increased the visibility of individual letters.[39,40] Different font types can be categorized as serif and sans serif (no serif). Serifs are little enhancements in letters (illustrated in Figure 10-10). The effects of using serif versus sans serif fonts have not been found to consistently affect the visibility of print, although as with the use of colored filters, we have found strong individual preferences. Figure 10-10 also demonstrates how the same size font (in points) can have different visibility by varying font characteristics. Computer systems and newer screen reading electronic systems allow font characteristics to be modified (see Chapter 14).

Reading Task Demand

The visual requirements for reading vary depending on the fluency demands.[41] The performance goal might be categorized as spot reading, low fluent and high fluent reading. Reading a few words such as a label or short passage requires "spot reading", reading about 40 wpm. Reading a longer passage such as a letter or instructions requires "fluent reading of 80 wpm". High fluent reading of 160 wpm is an average

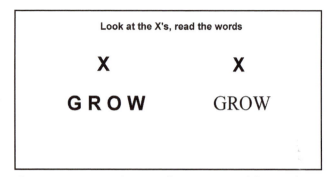

Look at the X's, read the words

X   X

GROW   GROW

Figure 10-10. Fixate the Xs and attempt to read the word below. Font characteristics in san serif (Arial) with heavy stroke width and increased print spacing (left) is more visible than with regular serif font type (Times New Roman) and typical spacing.

sixth grade reading rate. Normal reading rates are approximately 250 wpm.[42]

One must consider the required reading rate, endurance, and comfort. Reading for pleasure requires that a person read comfortably for a relatively long time, enabling endurance. Speed is an individual preference. Students and many professionals often also need to read for long periods of time and at speeds consistent with the normal visual reading. Some may need to skim and scan for critical information, such as a purchasing agent scanning a catalog for products. Others may wish to read slowly and carefully, such as an actor memorizing lines or someone reading poetry. People, even older individuals with moderate hearing loss, can read from slower to normal reading rates, quickly and comfortably with text-to-speech (listening to someone with normal vision or a computer read a newspaper).[43]

Nonvisual Options

It is generally advisable to introduce text-to-speech options first. For someone with a vision impairment, fast, comfortable "reading" is usually easily achieved by listening to the passages being read. Sighted assistance should be considered if the client is socially isolated. People with long-standing visual impairment often have not read for a long time, and have lost basic literacy skills from disuse. People with poor literacy skills will benefit more from text-to-speech systems, at least at first.

Books on tape, and CD and Braille transcriptions of printed material are free and easily accessed services through the National Library for the Blind and Visually Handicapped and the private organization Recordings for the Blind, and can be easily located by a Web search. Note that these services are available to anyone who has a physical or cognitive disability that might disable visual reading. Tape recorders are provided at no cost. Recordings are mailed with postage-free return boxes that are easy for someone to handle, even if totally blind. The tape recorders, however, have various settings that are not used in conventional tape recorders and often require careful instruction to learn. Using computer software that magnifies and reads the display aloud requires considerable skill and practice, but can be relatively easy to start using if someone has premorbid familiarity with computers and can touch-type. Chapter 14 presents a variety of electronic systems that will read Web pages, computer screens, even print aloud to individuals or convert the text into printed Braille or a Braille display.

The text-to-speech options should be presented prior to the evaluation and incorporated throughout the evaluation. Indeed, it is our practice to introduce Recordings for the Blind to anyone who is eligible, even those who have an excellent prognosis for recovering fluent visual reading. Clients should be reminded that normally sighted people often listen to books on tape and CD, and these options can be used as an addition to visual reading, not a substitution. Introducing these options at the end of the session as "a last resort" after attempts to read visually have been rejected or failed tends to discourage clients from using nonvisual options.

Although the focus of this book is on vision rehabilitation with people who have usable vision, federal law requires that one consider nonvisual options such as Braille for younger people who are unlikely to acquire fluent reading visually. Braille reading has become an important rite of passage into the culture of the blind. Associations and federations by and for blind people are communities interwoven into other cultures around the world that have and will continue to fortify people who have "different" rather than "low" vision with a network of friends, leisure activities, employment opportunities, and a sense of pride. Introduction of Braille to a client requires specialized certification as a vision rehabilitation teacher or a certified educator for the blind. The occupational therapist however, should have a sample of the Braille alphabet and numbers in order to assess whether a client with hand impairment or cognitive impairment might have the capacity to learn Braille. Braille is typically read scanning left to right with one, two, or sometimes three fingers. Good tactile sensitivity is required. We have had adults and teens pursue Braille literacy, although this is not common in our experience.

Evaluation of Visual Requirements

The occupational therapy evaluation is described in detail in Chapter 8. What follows is a brief review with a focus on special considerations for a reading assessment. Evaluation of central and peripheral field loss, and secondary oculomotor dysfunction was described previously in this chapter. The therapist must know or measure the reading acuity, letter contrast sensitivity, and visual fields in order to undertake reading rehabilitation (see Chapters 7 and 8).

Visual Acuity and Critical Print Size Assessment

Under a common practice model, clients may have already been prescribed a magnification device by the low vision optometrist. Reading speed with different print sizes must be evaluated with an assistive device that may be used, such as strong reading glasses or a handheld magnifier without an optical device. If the device is not providing the predicted magnification (Chapter 13), or if visual acuity tends to fluctuate as it does with diabetes, reading acuity and critical print size should be frequently re-evaluated.

The evaluation and treatment for reading requires an appropriate near reading acuity chart. An appropriate reading acuity chart includes a logarithmic progression of print sizes starting at 0.4 M up to 8 to 10 M. A log progression is as follows: 0.4, 0.5, 0.63, 0.8, 1.0, 1.25, 1.5, 1, 3.2, 4 M, etc. A chart design must control linguistic difficulty (reading level) of the text, maintaining a level that is relatively easy (third to fifth grade level). Several popular near charts are not suitable for a functional reading evaluation because the passages used with smaller print are at a higher reading level. More difficulty reading smaller print, therefore, might be due to vision or comprehension. Estimates of critical print size will directly indicate the magnification required for fluent reading (see below). With the appropriate reading chart, the therapist can measure critical print size by having the client read down the chart without magnification, then predict reading speed for print sizes on or above critical print size using the principles described in Chapter 7.

When the therapist evaluates functional reading with a continuous text reading test, the client begins reading with the largest print. The client reads each line as quickly as possible. Fluent reading of the first line quickly establishes basic literacy, and a good prognosis for recovering fluent visual reading. Normally, reading will remain relatively stable as print size decreases, then reading speed will slow as the decreasing print size approaches acuity threshold, usually about 3 lines above threshold print size. The smallest print size just before reading slows is the *critical print size*. This is the smallest print size that should be used with the client who wishes to read fluently. As an additional significant convenience, charts such as the MNRead have been designed so that each line is of the same length.[44] With a stop watch, the therapist times how long it takes to read each line (reading time) and quickly determines the critical print size as the smallest print size before reading time begins to increase. In cases where a person has a restricted field of view, reading speed will be slower with larger print, then increase in speed somewhat, then decrease again when print size approaches acuity threshold. Table 10-3 indicates the print size of different reading materials and the visual acuity threshold that is typically required in order to read these materials fluently. Instruction should begin with print that is a line or two above critical print size.

Case Study

In an illustrative case, Ms. Jones was diagnosed with early atrophic macular degeneration and aspired to read the newspaper fluently as she always had in her big chair by the window. In the clinic, testing was conducted at 20 cm (8 in) rather than the usual 40 cm because her optometrist had suggested that stronger reading glasses be tried and used at 20 cm. A table was used and cues provided to encourage her to maintain the test distance. The client read the largest size (8 M) in a few seconds with recommended reading glasses, indicating a good prognosis for recovering fluent reading visually. The client read the successive lines on the chart at about the same speed. At 1.2 M print size, the reading time increased, indicating that reading slowed, and she started to stumble over words. The critical print size was 1.6 M at 40 cm (0.4/1.6 M), the last line read at the maximum reading rate. The client continued to read until at 0.8 M reading was slow and one word was missed. The reading acuity threshold was 0.8 M at 40 cm (0.4/1 M). Because fluent reading was achieved with print magnification, and the critical print size was about three to four lines above acuity threshold, typical of normal reading, the therapist concluded that no other visual impediments existed. Since fluent reading was achieved with print magnification alone, additional visual testing was unnecessary. During instruction, the therapist varied lighting to determine the best lighting for reading.

In this example, reading instruction began with print that was 2.0 to 2.5 M to insure early success. As instruction progressed, the print size was reduced and reading acuity testing repeated at the smaller print sizes to see if critical print size might change with practice. It is wise to retest reading near visual acuity after a few sessions. If after instruction critical print size was 1.2 M, the therapist would recommend additional magnification or larger print.

Table 10-5.

Typical Print Contrast and Contrast Threshold Requirements[41]

Contrast Threshold Requirements

Text contrast of reading material	Uses	Severe loss (10:1 contrast reserve). Cannot fully compensate	Moderate loss Can usually fully compensate with optimized lighting
>95%	Computer and CCTV display with no reflections	Greater than 10% contrast threshold	5% to 10% contrast threshold
85-95%	Good quality print	Greater than 8% contrast threshold	4% to 8% contrast threshold
60-70%	Newsprint, telephone directory, paperback books	Greater than 5% contrast threshold	2.5% to 5% contrast threshold
50%	Cash register receipts, US paper money	Greater than 2.5% contrast threshold	1.2% to 5% contrast threshold

This client returned a year or two later with complaint of difficulty reading even with newer, stronger glasses. The reading acuity test was performed at a closer working distance and revealed that reading began to slow at 6.3 M and progressively slowed until reading acuity was achieved at 1.6 M, although she could make out a few words at 1.2 M. This result indicated a reduction in visual acuity, and also a need to test for the other possible visual impediments to reading, such as impaired contrast sensitivity or a central scotoma.

Contrast Threshold Assessment

For reading, contrast sensitivity should be measured with a letter contrast chart. For functional reading testing, the most relevant results are measured with the test distance chosen so that letter size is at about 2X to 4X acuity threshold (see Chapter 7). Table 10-5 indicates the contrast of typical reading that we have measured in a survey, and the contrast threshold requirements to read these different materials. In the cases of more advanced atrophic macular degeneration, glaucoma, or diabetes, often contrast sensitivity is impaired as well as acuity, indicating a need for higher contrast print, and careful evaluation of lighting.

Assessment of Field of View

If a client has a reduced field of view, the therapist should estimate and monitor field of view throughout treatment.[45] During an evaluation of central visual fields described above, the therapist can assess the characteristics of eccentric viewing, and the size and location of the central scotoma. Field of view can be directly measured by having the client attempt to read using words of different lengths while fixating the first letter of the word. It is important to select the font size the client intends to read. Alternatively, the client can fixate the first letter on a row of a near visual acuity chart and measure how many adjacent letters can be identified at once without shifting fixation. A therapist can infer field restrictions from actual reading performance. Clients with restricted fields will tend to spell words or hesitate or omit the end of longer words, or miss the last letters on a line when reading a near visual acuity chart. The Pepper Visual Skills for Reading Test (see Chapter 8) was designed to enable users to measure reading speed with different word lengths and score errors to estimate field restrictions and scanning problems.[46] It is important to attempt to estimate field of view during reading because people with central field loss may use different viewing positions for reading words rather than individual letters because these retinal positions may have different fields of view.

The Visual Requirements for Reading

The visual requirements for reading depend on the visual demand of the task and font characteristics.[41] The performance goal might be categorized as spot reading, low fluent, and high fluent reading. Reading a few words such as a label on a medicine bottle or short passage requires spot reading—reading about 40 wpm. Reading a longer passage such as a letter or

Table 10-6.
The Visual Requirements for Reading

The Visual Requirements for Various Reading Rates

Visual Factor	Reading Rates			
	Spot (40 wpm)	Fluent (80 wpm)	High Fluent (160 wpm)	Maximum
Acuity Reserve	1:1 (0 lines)	1.25:1 (1 line)	1.5 to 2.5:1 (2 to 4 lines)	2.0 to 3.0:1 (3 to 5 lines)
Contrast Reserve	3:1	4:1	10:1	>30:1
Field of View	1 character	2 to 5 cha.	5 to 6 cha.	16 to 20 cha.
Scotoma Size	No limit defined	<22°	<4°	No scotoma

instructions requires fluent reading of 80 wpm. High fluent reading of 160 wpm is an average sixth grade reading rate, with normal reading speed at about 250 wpm.

The visual requirements for each reading rate depend on the client's visual function and characteristics of the print. For example, the print size required for a particular reading rate depends on the client's visual acuity and the print size being read. In order to take both the client factor and print characteristics into account, the size print required to read at a given rate is specified as *acuity reserve* (see Figure 10-10). Acuity reserve is a ratio of the actual print size being read divided by the print size at threshold. Typically, a person with 20/20 acuity, 0.4 M threshold at 40 cm, reads newsprint, 1M with a 2:5:1 acuity reserve, or print that is 2½ times acuity threshold. A 2:1 acuity reserve means that the print size is twice threshold. If someone with low vision can barely read regular newsprint, he likely has an acuity threshold of 1 M (8 point) at 40 cm (16 in), reading large print, 2 M (16 point), provides an acuity reserve of 2:1, usually sufficient for fluent reading (Tables 10-3 and 10-6). If a logarithmic acuity chart is used, reserve can be specified more simply in terms of lines on the chart. With a 2:1 acuity reserve, a person is reading a print size that is 3 lines above threshold. Table 10-5 indicates the acuity reserve requirements for different reading rates. Table 10-4 indicates an approximation of the visual acuity requirements to read different common print sizes. In general, someone can read slowly and with difficulty print that is at threshold or 1 line above acuity threshold. If a client needs to read fluently, the print size should be at least 3 lines above threshold, or a 2:1 acuity reserve. Additional acuity reserve is required for those with macular degeneration, media opacities like cataracts, and individuals whose acuity might be expected to fluctuate (diabetic retinopathy).

Table 10-5 indicates the contrast threshold required for different reading rates. For fluent reading, print contrast must be at least 10 times contrast threshold (>10:1). High quality print is about 90% contrast. Contrast threshold must be better than 9%. For contrast enhanced print with an electronic device, print must be better than 10%.

A surprising finding in our review of the research on vision and reading is that people can read fluently with a rather narrow five to six character field of view.[41] This assumes that the client is reading by scrolled text, slowly moving the line of print from right to left while looking straight ahead—the steady eye technique— (described earlier) rather than scanning left to right with typical eye movement patterns. When someone reads with magnification, he typically moves scrolled text from right to left in front of the narrow field of a magnification device or under a CCTV. The major problem created by a restricted field of view is with scanning a page for relevant information, and losing one's place when reading. Once the line of text is found, however, it can still be read fluently as long as acuity and contrast reserve are high enough. Based on this concept, electronic and computer-based devices have been developed that scan several lines of text and present the text as one continuously scrolling line (like the marquee on Times Square) in front of the eye so that the client does not have to look from line to line. These devices are discussed in Chapter 13.

Central field loss, generally resulting from macular degeneration, has a particularly devastating effect on visual reading. Although people with any level of central field loss can recover visual spot reading sufficient for activities of daily living (ADL) with appropriate magnification, recovery of high fluent reading cannot be recovered with significant central scotoma unless nonvisual reading strategies are used (see Table 10-6).

Clients with visual impairment generally benefit most from increased magnification. Increased magni-

fication enables the acuity reserve and contrast reserve requirements to be met, usually without approaching the field of view limitations of a few characters. As described below, clients can be taught to compensate for a narrower field of view resulting from higher magnification, but cannot progress to faster reading if inadequate magnification is prescribed. Clients with central field loss larger than 4 degrees (about 2 to 3 fingers' width at arm's length) cannot recover high fluent visual reading and must use text-to-speech or Braille to read fluently.

Possible Nonvisual Impediments

There are other nonvisual requirements for reading. Good motor skills are required to precisely move the text and position the devices. These requirements depend on the device being used (see Chapter 12). The cognitive and linguistic requirements are certainly a consideration, and these aspects are often the focus of treatment by educators for college and high school students, and speech therapists for adults treated in medical rehabilitation settings. People with longstanding visual impairment often have not read for a long time, and have lost basic literacy skills from disuse. If it has been established that someone must read visually, a reading evaluation requires that one establish premorbid literacy and the cognitive ability to read. This can be easily done with larger, high-contrast print that is easy for the client to see.

Evaluation of Reading Performance

Performance is evaluated before and during treatment and as part of an ongoing evaluation of intervention strategies. It is useful to have numerous short reading passages of relatively easy to read, engaging reading material for nonstandardized evaluation during this process (see Appendices). The Pepper Visual Skills for Reading Test is valuable for a standardized reading[46] evaluation (see Chapter 8). This test uses unrelated words that increase in length and line spacing. This test has exceptional test-retest reliability, has been validated, and might, therefore, be used to document changes in reading performance as a benchmark test for documenting the efficacy of devices and therapeutic intervention. The test also has diagnostic value in revealing scanning difficulties in people with central field loss. Also designed for adults with low vision, the Morgan Test of Reading Comprehension allows one to document literacy limitations using a validated instrument.[47-49]

Finally, one might need to compare reading performance with optical devices and electronic devices. It becomes essential to provide objective performance data to agencies or insurance companies to justify purchase of devices. One compares reading speed after the devices have been configured for maximum reading performance. Since devices often must be purchased with justification before instruction on use of the device can commence, the user is also provided with assistance to insure performance is only limited visually, not by his familiarity with the device, which will improve with training using the device. In the Appendices, we have included a continuous text reading test that allows one to compare reading with text-to-speech, with print reading using paragraphs.[43] To evaluate text-to-speech reading, one must play a recording of the MP3 files. The different paragraphs are of approximately the same visual and phonological length, and linguistic difficulty (fifth to sixth grade level). The recording will read the paragraph at increasing speeds until comprehension drops below two out of three questions correct. Likewise, clients read paragraphs silently as quickly as possible, with comprehension validated at the same level or higher. The Pepper test is recommended to compare visual reading using a test with better sensitivity to small changes in performance.

Re-evaluation

Once the visual requirements are met, clients often require special instruction to recover reading skills. Often people with low vision have not read for a long period of time. The client may need additional instruction with a new device or the new device might create problems with lighting or glare. When people with low vision use optical and electronic devices, the appearance of text, eye movement scanning strategies, and the ergonomics of the reading task change substantially.

Strategies for Meeting the Visual Requirements for Reading

Once performance-limiting factors have been identified, one must develop treatment plans to address these impediments to reading.

Inadequate Acuity Reserve: Magnification

The most common method to increase acuity reserve involves a magnification assistive device. An assortment of optical devices are available to magnify the image of print on the retina (see Chapter 12), including handheld devices and strong reading glasses that enable relative distance magnification. Under the more common practice management model, the low vision optometrist may have already been prescribed these devices. Ideally devices are recommended, and not prescribed until after the occupational therapy

evaluation and instruction has begun. If magnification (acuity reserve) appears inadequate, then the therapist should compensate by first enlarging the print used for instruction. After instruction with a device, its effectiveness might increase, at which time the print size can be reduced to the font characteristic of the expected goal reading task. If the goal reading task cannot be met with the recommended device, the client should be referred back to the low vision optometrist for re-evaluation. Electronic devices both increase print size and enhance contrast (see Chapter 13), increasing contrast reserve as well.

Inadequate Contrast Reserve: Lighting and Print Contrast

Contrast reserve can be improved by improving contrast sensitivity (threshold) or increasing print contrast. Both visual acuity and contrast sensitivity can be improved by optimizing lighting.[50,51] Retinal pathology and optic nerve degeneration appears to have variable, often unpredictable and idiosyncratic effects on performance. Always minimize glare. Although people with low vision vary in the sensitivity to glare, glare always impairs visual acuity and contrast sensitivity. Directing light from the side, using a black mask with window cut out for the print (Figure 10-13) decreases reflection off of a white page. Reversing contrast to light letters on a dark background reduces glare as well. One should carefully evaluate the work setting to insure that glare light sources do not interfere with the client's performance. The therapist can sit where the client sits to determine if there are reflections off of screens, shiny surfaces, bright windows, and improperly positioned lights. If optical devices are used, lights often reflect off of the lenses, producing disabling glare as well. With CCTVs or computer screens, the lights used to illuminate the pages can also become glare sources. Sometimes colored overlays, different lights, or tinted lenses seem to increase subjective measures of reading comfort. Note that although most people with low vision perform best with increased directional light, some perform better with decreased light. A lighting evaluation should always be performed (see Chapter 7) to determine optimum light levels, and then reproduced during the functional reading evaluation and treatment. The easiest and most effective way to modify light levels is to vary the distance of the light source rather than change the wattage of the bulb. A handout for clients and family to use for glare avoidance is included in the Appendices.

Increasing print contrast also will generally improve acuity, and, as a result, acuity reserve. For clients who present with restricted visual fields, often due to advanced glaucoma, retinitis pigmentosa, or laser-treated diabetic retinopathy, increasing acuity reserve by magnification of print is not possible. For these clients, electronic systems that enhance contrast and reverse print contrast should be the treatment focus (see Chapter 13). As many of the conditions that lead to restricted fields progress to total blindness, these individuals benefit from computer systems where the display contrast is enhanced and maybe magnified slightly, but also with text-to-speech screen readers that will become more functionally significant as vision deteriorates.

Peripheral/Unilateral Field Loss

People with intact central fields rarely have difficulty reading unless they also have impaired visual acuity that requires print magnification. They may have difficulty scanning a page for information because they cannot see the whole page. People with central field loss might eccentrically fixate to the right, positioning the central scotoma in the right field. Others might have scotoma in the right field. People with field loss due to stroke or brain injury usually have intact central fields. Individuals with a split central field need to be managed like someone with central field loss. People with left hemisphere stroke with right field loss who have split central fields will have significant reading disability.

Right Visual Field Loss

If a client has a right visual field loss, reading is severely compromised because only the left half of the character fixated can be seen. The letters to the right of the viewing position cannot be seen as well. When trying to read a word, the client will have difficulty recognizing letters and if reading is possible, reading is very slow and often involves spelling words. Reading can be quickly recovered by first reorienting reading material so the client is reading vertically. For a right field loss, the client learns to rotate the page 90 degrees clockwise so the beginning of the lines should be on top (see Figure 10-11). The client is reading down and to the left. In addition, the therapist must teach the client to eccentrically view to the right of the letters being read so entire letter can be visualized. Because the client is now eccentrically viewing, acuity will be reduced and print must be enlarged somewhat to 1.6 M (14 pt). Inexplicably, we have noticed clients quickly recover reading, but with practice begin slowly moving the text around back to a typical horizontal position, usually on a diagonal. If the client holds the text and scrolls the text from right to left in front of the eye, the field of view requirements for fluent reading will decrease and reading sometimes is better than when stationary text is read.

Figure 10-11. The client's view of text being read using the vertical scrolling technique. The client has a right field cut and would normally not see anything to the right. The client has been instructed to fixate to the right of the letter (eccentrically viewing) to see the entire letters and to read from top to bottom. Try reading this way. Vertical reading is relatively easy for someone with good reading ability. (Reprinted from Wright V, Watson GR. *Learn to Use Your Vision for Reading.* [LUV Reading Series]. Lilburn, GA: Bear Consultants; 1996.)

Left Visual Field Loss

With left visual field loss, the client often loses his place when reading and has difficulty finding the beginning of a line of text. A commonly used strategy is to place a brightly colored straightedge along the left margin of the page. The client will know that he has to make a saccade back to the bright line when making the return sweep. An even more effective technique is to use a sandpaper or a Velcro strip along the left margin. The client places a finger on this strip and can "feel" the left margin. The client quickly learns to use this tactile awareness as a cure for the required eye movement at the end of each line. Retrace strategies described above for eccentric viewing will also help someone read with a left unilateral or overall field loss.

Central Field Loss and Eccentric Viewing

When people with normal vision read, they use the fovea/macula area of the retina in which visual acuity is at its highest level. People who have lost more than about 4 to 5 degrees of central vision, lose the ability to read at rates approaching normal fluency with vision. Nonvisual modalities should always be considered in cases of central field loss.

People with central field loss must be taught eccentric viewing and then the scrolled reading technique. Reading becomes a critical therapeutic activity in meeting a number of goals with people who have central field loss. Recovery of spot reading is common.

Treatment: Instructional Strategies

Teach Setup for Reading

Reading instruction should proceed from carefully controlled, ideal circumstances with assistance to a setting more typical of the natural environment in which the reading activities will occur. During this instruction, if reading in the natural environment is inadequate, the therapist should demonstrate how easy it is to read under the new method. Such demonstrations may convince the client to allow environmental modifications.

Learning to read with low vision can be difficult and stressful. Recovery of reading resembles recovery of ambulation after a stroke. At first, the client is insecure and compensation for this insecurity can significantly impede progression and recovery of normal movement patterns. Likewise, with reading, people often regress to painstaking, word by word reading, where typical readers often skip words when reading a passage.[42] The reader might also overreact emotionally to every stumble. The therapist should first instruct the client on relaxation strategies, and then provide frequent rest breaks. When practicing at home, the client should have assistance if possible. A

Table 10-7.

Reading Instructions With Magnification Devices

1. Teach setup for reading.

2. Use text easy to see and read. Assist with device.

3. Teach how to use the device.

4. Teach how to scan successive lines of text.

5. Begin home-based exercises.

6. Grade the text being read from easier and larger to smaller and more difficult.

7. Teach localization and scanning techniques.

---

good strategy is to schedule longer treatment sessions with frequent rest breaks. Recommended graded steps for reading instruction are summarized in Table 10-7.

Use Text Easy to See/Read and Assist With Device

If a client has low frustration tolerance or is easily fatigued, do not begin reading instruction with complicated instruction on how to use the assistive optical devices. The therapist should setup the device and provide hand-over-hand assistance so that the reader is using the device correctly. A good starting point is to use text that is easy to understand with single sentences written at a third grade level, and more than 2X the visual acuity level. Examples that are included in the Appendices can be printed in different font sizes. More advanced exercises, in a progression of easier to see and understand to smaller print and higher grade level, are provided by the LUV reading series workbook, which is highly recommended.[21] This text uses exercises that are very engaging that make the otherwise tedious practice enjoyable to most clients.

Teach Use of the Device

Reading instruction with optical devices or electronic devices like CCTVs should begin with the client seated at a table with feet firmly on the floor. A reading stand and height adjustment that insures posture appropriate for the client (usually 90-90-90) should be used. The client should be instructed how to identify and correct lighting problems. Refer to Chapters 12 and 13 for additional information about environmental setups for optical and electronic devices. The ideal reading surface should be a stand with a lip on the bottom against which the reading material rests (Figure 10-12), and which allows the page on a clipboard to easily slide left and right along a straight horizontal line.

Teach Scanning Successive Lines of Text

With a magnification device, often only a word or two can be seen at a time. One of the first skills a client must master is staying on the line being read and scanning back to the beginning of the next line. Sliding or moving the text horizontally on a reading stand facilitates staying on a line. To find the beginning of a line, use of a ruler, or having the client position his finger at the beginning of the line being read, provide effective cues. A retrace technique involves having the client first read a line, then at the end of the line follow it backward to the beginning and then move down to the next line to continue. Finally, if a reading stand is not available at home, the client should learn to read multiple lines on a table or holding the reading material.

Home Exercises and Transition to the Goal Task

The client is now ready to practice at home. Setup for reading including use of devices and lighting that will be used at home should be practiced. Using graded exercises described below, the client can practice.

At this point, the client should be able to identify and correct a problem with the setup for reading, poor lighting, poor positioning of the material being read or improper use of a device. Once these obstacles have been overcome, the client can practice alone or with distance supervision and with additional practice progress rapidly through the rehabilitation process.

Grade the Text Being Read

The progression of practice reading has traditionally started with single word identification. Tasks include searching for words or categories of words such as counting or circling the names of plants or

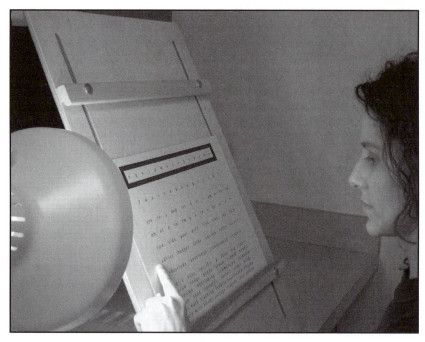

Figure 10-12. A client reading the Pepper Test using her left finger to cue the beginning of a line on a reading stand that encourages good ergonomics and, as a result, improved visual-motor control.

toys on a page. Then the client should be presented with simple sentences. An excellent method that is often used at this stage in therapy is a traditional reading instructional approach called the *cloze strategy*. The cloze strategy is a technique in which a person tries to read a sentence with some words or parts of words missing. For example, "You can lead a horse to water but you ____ make him drink." To succeed, the individual must rely on grammatical and linguistic cues. This is useful with clients with central scotomas because the scotoma causes parts of words or whole words to disappear. To use the close strategy in vision rehabilitation treatment, the client is taught to skip words not immediately understood and rely more on context to understand the content. Using this strategy, clients can still read with better than 90% accuracy. Reading then progresses to smaller print, and longer passages with questions about content. The reading difficulty of the material can be advanced as well. These exercises written for adults are available in workbook form.[21]

Localization and Scanning Skills

Finding the starting place is the next skill that the client must master and this is accomplished using localization techniques. When a reader uses a magnification device that allows the words to be recognized and read, the device often restricts field of view, sometimes to just a word or two. Localization techniques are used to compensate for restricted field of view in order to find a place on a page to start reading. The reader first views the unmagnified or minimally magnified page, then estimates where he wishes to read (the target) by the general layout of the text. The

reader then positions the text so the target will be centered under the magnifier and then magnifies the text to read the individual words or places the magnifier in front of the eye while looking at the target. For example, a reader can see where lines begin and end without a magnifier. The page is repositioned so that beginning of the line is directly in front, and then while continuing to look at the beginning of the line, the magnifier is positioned in front of the eye. This increases magnification so the reader can now recognize the word. These specific techniques for spotting and navigating with high magnification are described for each magnification device in Chapters 12 and 13.

Reading as a Multidisciplinary Effort

Reading rehabilitation should be a multidisciplinary effort if possible. In a typical medical rehabilitation model, the occupational therapist focuses on environmental modifications, adaptations to social roles, use of assistive devices, ergonomics, and the mechanics of reading. Speech therapists, if available, may work on developing reading strategies such as the cloze procedure, as well as providing an opportunity for practice. The occupational therapist should provide in-service to these other professionals on ergonomics and device use.

Writing Strategies

Handwriting with low vision is often problematic. A basic strategy to help a client with writing problems is to recommend the use of a black pen with a wide point using special paper with heavy lines.

Figure 10-13. Picture of writing devices: A. writing guide. B. low power stand magnifiers with lens that can be tilted. C. a typoscope or signature guide (photo courtesy of Eschenbach Optik of America, Ridgefield, CT).

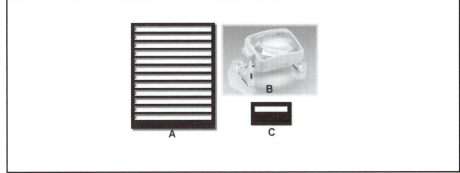

Large-print checks and dark lined paper are available as well. A person who loses vision later in life and retains good motor coordination will be able to sign her name or fill out a check by hand without seeing as long as she has a guide to help stay on the line (Figure 10-13). But filling out forms, applications, and other commercially available materials often requires smaller writing that cannot be easily accomplished by the client with low vision. Writing guides, overlays with cutouts, and signature cards (see Figure 10-13) are flat black plastic, metal, or cardboard with spaces cut out to, for example, fit over a check, form, or piece of paper. The user of these devices can feel the space in which he can write by feeling it with the other finger while writing. Since the overlays are black, the white paper can be more easily seen through the window of the overlay, so often the client can see the space in which he must write. These devices are described in more detail in Chapter 11. Some optical devices such as lower power stand magnifiers, handheld magnifiers, and telemicroscopes (see Chapter 12) allow a person to see while writing. People can also write near normal size lettering using electronic magnification devices like CCTVs (see Chapter 13).

For an individual with low vision who needs to write long letters and passages, the best option is to learn to touch type. Most people can master this process practicing 15 minutes a day for a few weeks. Programs like Talking Typing Teacher (MarvelSoft Enterprises, Inc, Abbotsford, British Columbia) have been developed that teach people who are blind to type on a computer. The Hadley School for the Blind (www.hadley-school.org) has a correspondence typing course for people who are blind. As will be discussed in Chapter 13, the instability and complexity that discourages people from computer use can be overcome. Once a client can type, he can use personal organizers to keep notes, maintain a calendar, and even write emails. Personal organizers were actually developed and used widely by blind people before these devices become popular among sighted people.

These are available with a standard size keyboard and speech output (no display), allowing the user to type in and retrieve notes, appointment schedules, names and addresses. Personal organizers can be used as simple word processors as well.

Instructional Materials

The materials for reading include a chair, table, and reading stand with adjustable height so the client's posture can be optimized. A variety of directional lights should be available including fluorescent, standard incandescent, and a spectrally balanced light. The low vision rehabilitation therapist needs to have a computer equipped with adaptive software and a CCTV, preferably one that allows color contrast to vary. Black overlays with cut outs, paper with darkened lines and extra space between lines, felt tip pens, and signature guides should be available to give to the clients.

Evaluation materials should include a continuous text reading chart like the MNRead Chart, the Pepper Visual Skills for Reading Test, and a workbook with reading exercises.[21]

ORIENTATION AND MOBILITY ON FOOT OR IN A WHEELCHAIR

Clients with vision impairment often require assistance with orientation and mobility. Clients with these needs should be referred to a certified O&M instructor for comprehensive help. However, it is important for occupational therapists to be familiar with some basic principles so that they can help clients while they wait for O&M services.

Visual Strategies

The general principles described below apply to either ambulation with and without an assistive

device, and wheelchair use. The following strategies can be used with individuals who have some useable vision.

- Teach the client to look common for high-contrast stationary landmarks. Common highly visible landmarks are lights in the ceiling, windows along a wall, and the baseboard where the floor and wall meet. The baseboard is an excellent cue because it allows a client to see when steps might begin or slopes in a walkway.

- With the exception of the first and last step, steps are often less of a problem than anticipated unless someone is mobility impaired. Properly installed, the rise and tread of each step is always the same in a set of steps. After the first step, people often can continue without looking at their feet.

- The therapist should make modifications to insure the first and last steps are clearly marked in an environment, especially where someone occasionally walks. In a home environment, the layout is often well memorized. Curbs often create a hazard.

- In a room, the client can usually see doors, baseboards, large contrasting furniture, and exit signs. Low-contrast furniture or patterns on patterns can be difficult to see.

- Teach the client to recognize restroom labels.

- Orient the client to sounds and smells. A busy doorway can often be identified by sound.

Nonvisual Strategies

If people have profound vision loss, the following strategies should be considered. Navigation with a guide dog, by sighted guide, a white cane, or by feel requires the use of at least one hand. People in manual wheelchairs, using crutches or walkers, therefore, must depend on vision or consider another mobility device. In these cases, power wheelchairs or canes would be preferred.

- Trailing techniques involve the client dragging her hand along the wall to walk in a straight line. People often use this when walking around the house in the dark, eg, when getting up at night to use the bathroom. The client should drag the back of her hand along a wall with the fingers pointed behind and the wrist in front of the fingers. This strategy helps the client avoid jamming a finger against a door jam or edge.

- Never dispense or recommend a long white cane. Using a cane requires specialized training by an O&M specialist. If it is used incorrectly, a false sense of security might put the client at a greater a risk for trips and falls than if no cane were used.

- A white support cane might be recommended. If a patient has had a CVA and has a unilateral field cut and inattention, a white support cane might be appropriate. The white cane only serves to alert others and motorists to be particularly careful. It also may help the client avoid a fall if he trips.

- A white support cane should only be used for support. The client should not use a support cane to feel around in front for obstacles. A client who needs both a cane for support and another to compensate for visual impairment will hold a support cane in one hand and a long cane in the other.

Driving Strategies

Some people with visual impairment, even legal blindness due to acuity loss, are allowed to drive in some states. These individuals require specialized instruction on driving. As driving rehabilitation is a practice area for occupational therapists, the low vision occupational therapist might consider obtaining additional training in driving rehabilitation as well. This topic is beyond the scope of this book but some important points apply for all low vision therapists.

People with visual impairment sometimes continue to drive illegally. The occupational therapist is responsible for convincing the client to stop driving and should notify the physician if a person continues to drive. The occupational therapist should know the laws regarding the visual requirements for driving that vary from state to state and test to insure the client can legally drive. In some states, driving with reduced visual acuity is legal if the person uses an assistive device such as a spectacle-mounted telescope. In such cases, the telescope is mounted high on glasses so the driver can look through the telescope to spot something or read a road sign, much like a rearview mirror is used. If drivers compensate by driving more slowly, mild to moderately reduced visual acuity (20/100) presents a measurable but relatively small risk for drivers unless there is also a loss in contrast sensitivity.[52] Field restrictions and decreased peripheral attention create a high risk for driving with hemianopia, presenting a significantly higher

risk than quadrantanopia.[53] The low vision therapist should be aware that meeting the state requirements does not necessarily indicate a safe driver. Another important predictor of increased risk for driving is decreased peripheral visual attention, associated with older drivers.[54] The best general strategy is to encourage legal drivers to take on-road driving tests to evaluate safety rather than depend on state criteria.

SUMMARY

For someone with central field loss, development of eccentric viewing and scanning provides foundational skills for reading and finding the face of a loved one in a room. Reading as an activity builds and solidifies eccentric viewing and scanning skills. For someone with peripheral field restriction, development of compensatory scanning provides the foundation for orientation and mobility. Shopping as an activity builds and solidifies compensatory scanning. We as occupational therapists relish the discovery of therapeutic occupations that continue to teach long after we have formally discharged our client. Yet the occupational therapist must still have the wisdom to appreciate that the ultimate goal of therapy is not just about fixing vision and visual function, it is about using all available resources—touch, smell, and hearing—to help someone find, once again, that flow of living.

REFERENCES

1. Berger JW, Fine SL, Maguire MG, eds. *Age-Related Macular Degeneration*. Philadelphia, PA: Mosby; 1999.
2. Cummings RW, Whittaker SG, Sinclair SH. Scotoma characteristics and reading performance in patients with central and paracentral vision loss. *Invest Ophthalmol Vis Sci*. 1991;32(4):816.
3. Siatkowski RM, Zimmer B, Rosenberg PR. The Charles-Bonnet syndrome. *J Clin Neuroophthalmol*. 1990;10:215-218.
4. Rovner BW. Depression and increased risk of mortality in the nursing home patient. *Am J Med*. 1993;94(5A):19S-22S.
5. Rovner BW, Zisselman PM, Shmuely-Dulitzki Y. Depression and disability in older people with impaired vision: a follow-up study. *J Am Geriatr Soc*. 1996;44(2):181-184.
6. Rovner BW, Ganguli M. Depression and disability associated with impaired vision: the MoVies Project. *J Am Geriatr Soc*. 1998;46(5):617-619.
7. Horowitz A, Reinhardt JP. Mental health issues in vision impairment: research in depression, disability and rehabilitation. In: Silverstone B, Lang MA, Rosenthal B, Faye EE, Eds. *The Lighthouse Handbook on Vision Impairment and Vision Rehabilitation*. Oxford: Oxford University Press; 2000:1089-1109.
8. Whittaker SG, Cummings RW, Swieson LR. Saccade control without a fovea. *Vision Research*. 1991;31:2209-2218.
9. Whittaker SG, Cummings RW. Eccentric eye movements with loss of central vision. In: Johnston M, Ed. *Low Vision Ahead II*. Melbourne: Association for the Blind; 1990:67-73.
10. Whittaker SG, Cummings RW, Carroll J. Slow saccades in alert humans. *Invest Ophthalmol Vis Sci*. 1989;30:397.
11. Whittaker SG, Cummings RW. Foveating saccades. *Vision Research*. 1990;30(9):1363-1366.
12. Timberlake GT, Mainster MA. Reading with a macular scotoma: I. Retinal location of scotoma and fixation area. *Invest Ophthalmol Vis Sci*. 1986;27:1137-1147.
13. Whittaker SG, Budd JM, Cummings RW. Eccentric fixation with macular scotoma. *Invest Ophthalmol Vis Sci*. 1988;29(2):268-278.
14. Timberlake GT, Peli E, Essock EA, Augliere RA. Reading with a macular scotoma: II. Retinal locus for scanning text. *Invest Ophthalmol Vis Sci*. 1987;28(8):1368-1374.
15. Timberlake GT, Mainster MA, Peli E, Augliere RA, Essock EA, Arend LE. Reading with a macular scotoma: I. Retinal location of scotoma and fixation area. *Invest Ophthalmol Vis Sci*. 1986;27(7):1137-1147.
16. Whittaker SG, Cummings RW, Sweison LR. Saccade control without a fovea. *Vision Research*. 1991;31(12):2209-2218.
17. Lei H, Schuchard RA. Using two preferred retinal loci for different lighting conditions in patients with central scotomas. *Invest Ophthalmol Vis Sci*. 1997;38(9):1812-1818.
18. Nilsson UL. Visual rehabilitation with and without educational training in the use of optical aids and residual vision. A prospective study of patients with advanced care-related macular degeneration. *Clinical Vision Sciences*. 1990;6(1):3-10.
19. Nilsson UL, Nilsson SE. Rehabilitation of the visually handicapped with advanced macular degeneration. A follow-up study at the Low Vision Clinic, Department of Ophthalmology, University of Linkoping. *Documenta Ophthalmologica*. 1986;62(4):345-367.
20. Nilsson UL, Frennesson C, Nilsson SE. Location and stability of a newly established eccentric retinal locus suitable for reading, achieved through training of patients with a dense central scotoma. *Optom Vis Sci*. 1998;75(12):873-878.
21. Wright V, Watson GR. *Learn to Use Your Vision for Reading* (LUV Reading Series). Lilburn, GA: Bear Consultants; 1996.
22. Watson GR, Jose RT. A training sequence for low vision patients. *J Am Optom Assoc*. 1976;47(11):1407-1415.
23. Frennesson C, Jakobsson P, Nilsson UL. A computer and video display based system for training eccentric viewing in macular degeneration with an absolute central scotoma. *Documenta Ophthalmologica*. 1995;91:9-16.
24. Whittaker SG. A cost-effective design and implementation of a computer learning centre. *Optometry and Vision Science*. 1992(Dec):173-174.
25. Cummings RW, Whittaker SG, Swieson LR. Individuals with maculopathies use OKN to scan text during unconstrained reading. *Invest Ophthalmol Vis Sci*. 1989;30:398.
26. Lovie-Kitchin JE, Mainstone J. What areas of the visual field are important for mobility in low vision patients? *Clinical Vision Sciences*. 1990;5:249-263.
27. Hunstad E. The Magnimaster Gold. 2005 [cited 2005 Dec 2005]; Available from: www.magnimaster.com.
28. Trobe JD. *The Neurology of Vision*. Contemporary Neurology Series. Vol. 60. Oxford: Oxford University Press; 2001:451.
29. Whittaker SG, Cummings RW. Foveating saccades. *Vision Research*. 1990;30(9):1363-1366.
30. Moses RA, Hart WM. *Adler's Physiology of the Eye: Clinical Application*. 8th ed. Philadelphia, PA: Mosby; 1987.
31. Zoltan B. *Vision, Perception and Cognition: A Manual for the Examination and Treatment of the Neurologically Impaired Adult*. 3rd ed. Thorofare, NJ: SLACK Incorporated; 1996:211.
32. Heikki HA, Julkunen LA. Treatment of visual field deficits after a stroke. *Advances in Clinical Neuroscience and Rehabilitation*. 2004;3(6):17-18.

33. Reinhard J, Schreiber A. Does visual restitution training change absolute homonymous visual field deficits? A fundus controlled study. *Br J Ophthalmol.* 2005;89:30-35.

34. Pedretti W, Zoltan B, eds. *Occupational Therapy: Practice Skills for Physical Dysfunction.* Philadelphia, PA: Mosby; 1996.

35. Appel S. Use of color filter to cue direction of gaze. Personal communication, December 2004.

36. Brilliant R, ed. *Essentials of Low Vision Practice.* 1st ed. Boston, MA: Butterworth Heinemann; 1999:409.

37. Mehr EB, Freid AN. *Low Vision Care.* Chicago, IL: Professional Press; 1975.

38. Peli E. Field expansion for homonymous hemianopia by optically induced peripheral exotropia. *Optometry and Vision Science.* 2000;77:453-464.

39. Liu L, Arditi A. How crowding affects letter confusion. *Optometry and Vision Science.* 2001;78:50-55.

40. Leat SJ, Wei L, Epp K. Crowding in central and eccentric vision: The contour interaction and attention. *Invest Ophthalmol Vis Sci.* 1999;40:404-512.

41. Whittaker SG, Lovie-Kitchin J. Visual requirements for reading. *Optom Vis Sci.* 1993;70:54-65.

42. Carver RP. *Reading Rate: A Review of Research and Theory.* San Diego, CA: Academic Press; 1990.

43. Hensil J, Whittaker SG. Comparing visual reading versus auditory reading by sighted persons and persons with low vision. *J Vis Impair Blind.* 2000;94(12):762-770.

44. Mansfield JS et al. A new reading-acuity chart for normal and low vision. In: *Noninvasive Assessment of the Visual System Technical Digest.* Washington, DC: Optical Society of America; 1993.

45. Lovie-Kitchin JE. Reading performance of adults with low vision. PhD Thesis. Brisbane, Queensland: Queensland University of Technology; 1996.

46. Watson GR, Baldasare J, Whittaker SG. The validity and clinical uses of the Pepper Visual Skills for reading test. *J Vis Impair Blind.* 1990;84(2):119-123.

47. Watson GR, Whittaker SG, Steciw M. *Pepper Visual Skills for Reading Test* (revised). Lilburn, GA: Bear Consultants, Inc.; 1995.

48. Watson GR et al. A low vision reading comprehension test. *J Vis Impair Blind.* 1996;90(6):486-494.

49. Watson GR, Wright V, De l'Aune W. The efficacy of comprehension training and reading practice for print readers with macular loss. *J Vis Impair Blind.* 1992;86(1):37-43.

50. Fosse P, Valberg A. Lighting needs and lighting comfort during reading with age-related macular degeneration. *J Vis Impair Blind.* 2004;98:389-409.

51. Fosse P, Valberg A. Contrast sensitivity and reading in subjects with age-related macular degeneration. *Vision Impairment Research.* 2001;3:111-124.

52. Higgins KE, Wood JM. Predicting components of closed course driving performance from vision tests. *Optom Vis Sci.* 2005;82(8):647-656.

53. Racette L, Casson EJ. The impact of visual field loss on driving performance: evidence from on-road driving assessment. *Optom Vis Sci.* 2005;82(8):668-674.

54. Clay O et al. Cumulative meta-analysis of the relationship between useful field of view and driving performance in older adults: Current and future implications. *Optom Vis Sci.* 2005;82(8):724-731.

Patient Education and Modification of the Environment

INTRODUCTION

When one thinks of low vision rehabilitation, the images that commonly come to mind are optical devices such as magnifiers and telescopes. This image can be somewhat intimidating to the therapist just developing an interest in this field because the occupational therapist generally requires development of a new knowledge base in optics and magnification and hands-on experience with these devices. While the use of optical devices is an essential element in low vision rehabilitation, it is important to emphasize that it is only one of the seven components of the sequential treatment approach we suggest in this book. Table 11-1 lists these seven components in the order in which we believe they should be applied.

In Chapter 10, we discussed the various therapeutic activities that should be included in a low vision rehabilitation plan, particularly when a client has a central scotoma. This chapter is designed to present a systematic approach to client education and modification of the environment to maximize the client's function. The suggestions described in this chapter are not remedial. Rather, they are designed to improve a client's functional ability despite of his or her visual impairment.

EDUCATION

Studies have shown that despite the best efforts of low vision rehabilitation providers, a proportion of clients achieve less than satisfactory results.[1] In addition to visual factors, the success of vision rehabilitation has been shown to be related to a number of psychosocial factors, such as depression, satisfaction with life, social support, self-esteem, stress, and motivation.[2-4] Brody et al demonstrated that intervention that includes education about the underlying cause of the client's low vision, increased access to support groups, home modifications, and treatment of depression improves outcomes.[5] Therefore, to optimize the effectiveness of a vision rehabilitation program, the therapist generally should start the process by educating the client about the cause of his/her low vision, the goals of rehabilitation, outlook for the future, available resources, support groups, and expected rehabilitation outcomes.

Watson stresses that any instruction in the use of vision and visual skills must be preceded by a thorough discussion with the client about his or her vision.[6] She recommends that client education include the following seven elements:

Table 11-1.

Vision Rehabilitation: Seven-Step Sequential Treatment Plan

1. Education

Nature of eye disease
Outlook for the future
Expectations of vision rehabilitation

2. Therapeutic Activities

Eccentric Viewing
Scanning
Reading skills

3. Environmental Modifications

Size
Distance
Color
Lighting
Contrast
Glare

4. Nonoptical Assistive Devices

Visual
Tactile
Auditory

5. Optical Magnification

6. Computer Technology in Low Vision Rehabilitation

7. Resources/Handouts

1. The name of the disease or condition, and the part of the eye that is affected.

2. The functional implications of the condition.

3. The functional implications of the visual acuity, contrast sensitivity, and visual field loss.

4. The refractive error and why eyeglasses that previously corrected the client's vision are still important but will no longer restore vision.

5. Discussion of any devices recommended by the low vision optometrist.

6. The ways in which any recommended devices will help the client achieve his/her performance goals.

7. Illumination needs, preferences, and problems indoors and outdoors.

At the end of this phase of rehabilitation, the client should have a good understanding of all of these components. The use of written materials and explanations should be considered to allow the client to review this information at home.

MODIFICATION OF THE ENVIRONMENT

Duffy et al[7] stress the importance of a careful environmental assessment before attempting to modify the environment. They describe environmental assessment as the process of systematically analyzing the area and surroundings in which individuals with low vision will be living, working, or attending school. To be effective, the environmental evaluation should encompass two broad areas: the individual's general environment and surroundings, and specific tasks that the individual will be performing within those environments.[7]

Table 11-2.
__Factors That Can Be Manipulated to Modify the Environment__
1. Size of the object being viewed
2. Distance between the object and the client
3. Color
4. Contrast
5. Illumination
6. Figure-ground
7. Angle of viewing

While discussing modification of the environment, Watson states that loss of visual function such as reduced contrast sensitivity or color sensitivity cannot be resolved by prescribing an optical device.[8] She indicates that treatment of these problems requires environmental enhancement and suggests seven factors that can be manipulated to make the environment more "client friendly".[8] These factors are listed in Table 11-2 and discussed below.

MODIFICATION OF SIZE

In Chapter 5, we discussed four methods of achieving magnification, including relative size, relative distance, angular, and projection magnification. The first two methods simply require modification of the client's environment.

Relative Size Magnification

In relative size magnification, the actual size of the object is increased. The concept is quite simple. If the size of the object is doubled, the size of the retinal image is doubled. To achieve 2X magnification, therefore, we simply enlarge the object twofold. If a client has trouble reading 12-point font, we could print a document on the computer using 24-point font and double the retinal image size. Large print phone dials, large print microwave time on frozen meals, or noting phone messages on a large pad with a marker are simple and effective applications of size magnification.

This approach is a relatively simple and inexpensive option, and is generally well accepted because the client does not require any optical aids and can read at a normal distance. However, as the magnification demands grow and the print size for books is increased, size and weight become issues. This method of magnification, therefore, is generally best suited for clients with mild to moderate loss of vision.

It is also used in combination with other methods of magnification.

Examples of the use of relative size magnification are listed in Table 11-3 and illustrated in Figures 11-1 through 11-6.

MODIFICATION OF DISTANCE BETWEEN THE OBJECT AND THE PATIENT

Relative Distance Magnification

Another simple means of modifying the environment to achieve magnification of an object is to move closer to it. As an object is moved closer to the eye, the retinal image of the object increases. If the distance is halved, the retinal image size doubles and 2X magnification is achieved. To achieve 4X magnification, you would decrease the distance by one-fourth. If a client is having trouble seeing a 20-inch television at a distance of 12 feet, the therapist can suggest that the client move to 6 feet away. This would double the size of the retinal image of the television and magnify the image twofold.

If a client is having difficulty reading a newspaper at 40 cm, bringing the newspaper closer to a 10 cm distance would magnify the print 4X. However, moving the newspaper this close creates another problem. Recall the discussion in Chapter 5 about accommodation. The closer an object is brought to the eye, the more accommodation is required. Although decreasing the working distance from 40 cm to 10 cm achieves 4X magnification, the client would experience blurred vision if he or she is unable to accommodate for that distance. While young children would be able to accommodate even at 10 inches, this would not be possible for an adult, particularly an adult from the age of 40 years and older. To solve this problem in adult

Table 11-3.

Examples of Using Relative Size Magnification to Modify Environment

Kitchen/Cooking

- Bold, black, large letters on 3 x 5 inch index cards to label household supplies
- Bold, black, large letters on spice bottles
- Kitchen timer with large numerals
- Large-print recipes and cookbooks
- Large-print measuring cups/spoons

Bathroom

- Bold, black, large letters on 3 x 5 inch index cards to label bathroom supplies

Medications

- Ask pharmacist to make large-print labels for each medication
- Store medication in pill boxes with large print

Dressing

- Bold, black, large letters on 3 x 5 inch index cards to label clothing

Financial Management

- Large-print calendar
- Large-print address book
- Large-print checks

Leisure

- Large-print magazines/newspaper (*Reader's Digest, NY Times*)
- Large-print Bingo cards
- Large-print playing cards

Figure 11-1. Bold, black, large letters on spice bottles.

Figure 11-2. Kitchen timer with large numerals (reprinted with permission from LS&S Products).

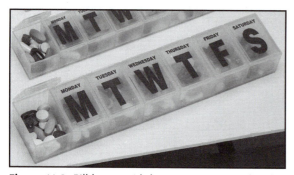

Figure 11-3. Pill boxes with large print (reprinted with permission from LS&S Products).

Figure 11-4. Large-print address book (reprinted with permission from LS&S Products).

Figure 11-5. Large-print Bingo cards.

Figure 11-6. Large-print playing cards (reprinted with permission from LS&S Products).

clients with limited accommodation, the optometrist prescribes a convex lens or other optical devices that focuses the light on the retina.

Lovie-Kitchin and Whittaker compared the effect on reading rates of adults using relative distance versus relative size magnification.[9] They found that the reading rates of the subjects with low vision did not differ significantly with the two methods of providing magnification if the magnification provided was adequate. They also concluded that for most tasks, it is more practical to enlarge the image optically, rather than to enlarge the reading material physically.[9] Nevertheless, in clients with mild to moderate loss of vision, these relatively simple environmental modifications should always be tried and may be used in combination with other forms of magnification.

MANIPULATION OF COLOR

Color is a key factor to consider when assessing and modifying the environment.[7,8] Patients who are visually impaired may have difficulty distinguishing between groups of colors, such as navy blue-brown-black, blue-green-purple, and pink-yellow-pale green. By paying careful attention to color, however, it is still possible to use color to enhance physical safety, accessibility, and independent participation in activities of daily living (ADL).[7] The three characteristics of color that must be considered are defined in Table 11-4.

Duffy recommends the following general principles for manipulating color in environments to help clients with low vision: [7]

Table 11-4.
Characteristics of Color
Hue: A color's "hue" describes which wavelength appears to be most dominant. The terms "red" and "blue" for example, are primarily describing hue.
Saturation: A fully saturated color is one with no mixture of white. Pink may be thought of as having the same hue as red but being less saturated.
Brightness: How luminous or full of light the color appears.

- Bright colors are generally the easiest to see because of their ability to reflect light.
- Solid bright colors, such as red, orange, and yellow, are usually more visible than pastels because they are more saturated.
- Lighting can influence the perception of color: dim light can "wash out" some colors; bright light can intensify others Colors can be best seen using more recent "natural" lamps that simulate sunlight.
- Color can also provide important safety cues: an indicator of change in surface or level; a warning for potential hazards, such as steps or construction; a means of coding for location or identification; and a crucial factor in judging depth perception.

Examples of the manipulation of color to help clients with low vision are listed in Table 11-5.

MODIFICATION OF LIGHTING

Before discussing the assessment and modification of lighting, it is important to understand that in people with normal vision, light levels can change considerably from shade to bright sunlight on a snowy day, without significantly affecting visual function. One effect of most eye diseases that cause low vision is to narrow the range of light over which someone has best vision. There is no ideal or best lighting solution for all people with low vision.[10,11] Different causes of low vision create different sensitivities to different aspects of lighting. Sometimes people with the same diagnosis respond differently to light, especially macular degeneration and diabetic retinopathy.[12] Therefore, the appropriate modification of lighting will vary from individual to individual.

There are two aspects of lighting to consider: the amount of light (brightness, illumination or luminance) and glare. Glare, which should always be avoided, generally results when light scatters within the eye so the light from one object interferes with one's ability to see another object. For example, a bright light or reflection from a window in the room off of the screen might interfere with someone's ability to see a television. Unfortunately, increasing the brightness of an object also increases glare. To create the largest change in brightness, one should change the distance of the light source. To minimize glare, the light source should be a directional, have a shade, and be directed from the side. Light behind or above tends to reflect off of the material being viewed.

Boyce and Sanford stress the concept that various causes of low vision may affect the significance or benefits from modification of lighting.[10] These causes include diseases that:

- Reduce transmission of light and require more light to see best
- Diseases that cause scatter within the eye or sensitivity to glare (cataract and optic atrophy)
- Diseases in which there is minimal effect on transmission of light but destruction of parts of the retina and neural transmission (retinitis pigmentosa)
- Diseases that are a combination of both (macular degeneration).

Generally, the lighting of the visual environment will always be important in determining how well a client can use his or her remaining vision when the cause of low vision alters the optical characteristics of the eye, such as with cataract. When the cause of the low vision primarily affects the retina and neural transmission, changes in lighting are less likely to be helpful.[10] Finally, in situations where there is a

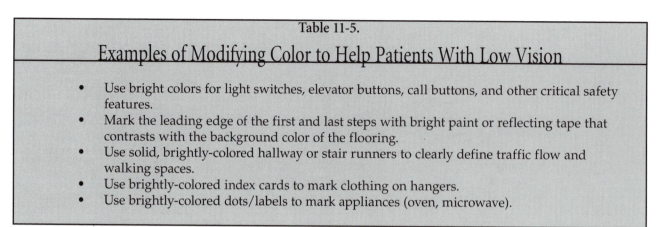

Table 11-5.

Examples of Modifying Color to Help Patients With Low Vision

- Use bright colors for light switches, elevator buttons, call buttons, and other critical safety features.
- Mark the leading edge of the first and last steps with bright paint or reflecting tape that contrasts with the background color of the flooring.
- Use solid, brightly-colored hallway or stair runners to clearly define traffic flow and walking spaces.
- Use brightly-colored index cards to mark clothing on hangers.
- Use brightly-colored dots/labels to mark appliances (oven, microwave).

combined effect, such as macular degeneration, careful attention to lighting will be helpful.[13] Boyce and Sanford, however, emphasize that this distinction between causes of low vision and the importance of lighting should be used only as a guideline.[10] Lighting modifications should always be attempted and will generally lead to some improvement in function. In an experiment to determine the effect of lighting on object perception, investigators found that all subjects, regardless of the cause of low vision, showed improvement in ability to recognize objects as illuminance was increased. However, the amount of illuminance at which improvement ceased varied significantly among subjects.[11,12] This again suggests that there is no optimal amount of light for all individuals. Rather, clinicians must empirically determine the optimal lighting for each client.

Visual acuity, contrast sensitivity, and color discrimination improve as the amount of light increases, but only up to a point. At a certain level, functional improvement plateaus and further increases in the amount of light may be detrimental. Too much light (glare) can cause discomfort or even disrupt vision. Glare is usually divided into two categories: discomfort and disabling glare.

Discomfort Glare

Discomfort glare refers to the sensation one experiences when the overall illumination is too bright, and commonly results from excessive amounts of illumination and/or reflections within the visual field. Surroundings including sand, water, snow, or polished surfaces can produce discomfort glare. Discomfort glare does not generally degrade vision; however, it is distracting and may cause discomfort and eye fatigue.

Disability Glare

Disability glare refers to reduced visibility of a target due to the presence of a light source elsewhere in the field. It occurs when light from the glare source is scattered by the ocular media. This scattered light forms a veil of luminance that reduces the contrast and thus the visibility of the target. An example of disability glare would be the familiar experience of being bothered by oncoming headlights while driving at night. One form of disability glare, called starburst glare, is particularly disabling when someone is viewing white objects against a dark background. A light against the dark tends to almost explode like a starburst. Oncoming headlights in the fog at night also simulate a starburst glare effect.

Assessment of Lighting

The occupational therapist should perform an evaluation of the lighting in the client's general living environment while the client is engaged in specific ADL within that environment. In many cases, it will become apparent that the amount of light or type of light available is not appropriate for the client. It is not uncommon to find that the home of an elderly person with low vision is poorly illuminated even for a person with normal vision. As stated above, some clients benefit from additional lighting while others require less, and the therapist must empirically determine what will be best for each client. Table 11-6 lists the lighting requirements and light sensitivity expected for clients with common eye diseases causing low vision in the elderly population.

A light meter is an instrument that provides information about the illumination coming from a light source to the task and can be used by the therapist to accurately assess the amount of light available in the client's environment.[14] A light meter is very useful because it is very difficult for someone with normal vision to judge absolute brightness. The therapist can evaluate lighting during the occupational therapy low vision evaluation during contrast sensitivity or visual acuity testing as described in Chapter 8. The therapist varies lighting by varying the distance of a directional

Table 11-6.

Lighting Requirements and Light Sensitivity for Clients With Common Eye Diseases

Eye Disease	Preferred Lighting	Sensitivity to Light
Cataract	High	High
Diabetic Retinopathy	Moderate	Moderate
Glaucoma	Moderate	Moderate
Macular Degeneration	Varies usually Brighter	High
Retinitis Pigmentosa	Moderate to bright	High

Modified from Flom R. Appendix: Visual consequences of most common eye conditions associated with visual impairment. In: Lueck AH, Ed. *Functional Vision: A Practitioner's Guide to Evaluation and Intervention.* New York: AFB Press; 2004:475-481.

task light from the task and uses a light meter to measure the range of illuminance that produced best contrast sensitivity or visual acuity. This same light level can then be reproduced in the clinic or the home. In addition, once the therapist finds the best brightness for one task, it can be measured and used to guide lighting with similar tasks. The final test will be the client's performance and preference in context, as the best light may be task specific as well. Using a light meter, however, will save considerable time.

After a general assessment of lighting conditions in the house or living environment, it is important to observe the client performing various ADL. Observe activities such as reading, check writing, reading mail, reading medicine bottles, cooking, grooming, sorting and folding clothing, selecting clothing, etc. For each activity, make observations about the amount of lighting, contrast, and glare. After this assessment, the therapist should alter the lighting conditions by changing locations for the task, increasing brightness by changing bulbs, moving the light source closer, reducing glare, and improving contrast.

There are five different types of light that should be considered when evaluating and modifying the environment.[7,15] Table 11-7 lists the different types of light and their advantages and disadvantages. To properly evaluate and modify lighting, the therapist will typically have to bring an assortment of bulbs and various desk and floor lamps to the clients' living environment. The therapist can try different combinations of lamps and bulbs while the client is engaged in various ADL. Examples of some of the popular types of lamps are illustrated in Figures 11-7 to 11-9.

Regardless of the type of lighting used, one of the very important concepts that is used routinely when modifying lighting is the inverse square law.[14] This law states that the intensity of light observed from a light source falls off as the square of the distance from the object.

$I = 1/d^2$
I = intensity of light
d = distance from the bulb to the working surface

Thus, if a therapist decreases the distance of a 75-watt bulb by one-half, he or she will increase the intensity four times the bulb's original value. Thus, the intensity of the bulb becomes 300 watts instead of 75 watts simply by halving the distance. This law is the foundation for the very effective environmental modification of moving the light source closer to the client's reading material, rather than increasing the wattage of the bulb.

Figures 11-10 and 11-11 illustrate two common examples of possible use of lighting to enhance a client's ability to participate in ADL. In Figure 11-10, the client is working on finances at his desk and a gooseneck lamp is placed very close to the client's work. In Figure 11-11, a floor lamp with a combination bulb is place behind the shoulder of the better-seeing eye while the client is reading.

MODIFICATION OF CONTRAST

When we discuss contrast, we often use the term contrast sensitivity. This topic is discussed in detail in Chapter 3. While visual acuity tests measure the smallest high-contrast object that can be recognized, contrast sensitivity measures the lowest contrast an object or pattern must have to be recognized. Contrast and contrast sensitivity are important factors to consider because they are intimately related to performance in ADL and provide information that is not as easily captured by visual acuity measurement.[16] For example, contrast sensitivity is strongly associated with reading performance,[17] mobility,[18,19] driving,[20,21] face recognition,[21,22] and ADL.[22,23] In vision rehabilitation, occupational therapists can help clients

Table 11-7.

Contrast of Common Everyday Objects

Type Of Light	Advantages	Disadvantages
Natural Light	Most natural type of light Appropriate for most tasks	Inconsistent Creates glare Creates shadows
Incandescent	Readily available in a large variety of wattages Newer full-spectrum incandescent bulbs (Chromalux bulbs) are closer to natural sunlight Light is concentrated Better for "spot" lighting on near tasks Light does not "flicker" like fluorescent light	Not recommended for general room lighting Can create shadows and glare As wattage increases, heat also increases
Fluorescent	Better for general room lighting Illuminates a wider area than incandescent light Does not create shadows Cooler than incandescent New compact fluorescent bulbs fit into regular lamp sockets with less heat and use less energy	Light is not stable; can flicker Can't be dimmed as easily as incandescent light
Combination Incandescent and Fluorescent	Most natural and comfortable type of artificial light Approximates natural light Some lamps come with socket for both types of bulbs	May require the purchase of additional lamps Specialized lighting fixtures can be expensive
Halogen	Brighter than incandescent light Gives more illumination and uses lower wattage More energy-efficient than regular incandescent light bulbs	Light is hotter, more focused, and requires a shield Not recommended for prolonged close work Bulbs need to be replaced frequently and are more expensive than comparable incandescent lights May be dangerous for low vision clients because of potential for burns

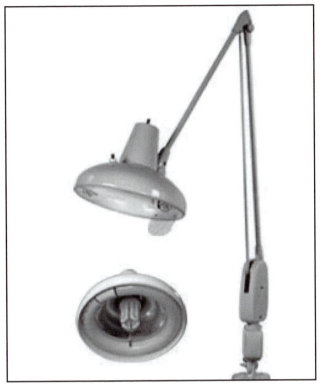

Figure 11-7. Combination fluorescent and incandescent table lamp (reprinted with permission from LS&S Products).

Figure 11-8. Floor lamp (reprinted with permission from LS&S Products).

Figure 11-9. Swing lamp (reprinted with permission from LS&S Products).

with contrast sensitivity problems by increasing the contrast of objects being viewed. Methods of modifying contrast include environmental modifications and lighting modifications.[24]

Generally, increasing the contrast between an object and its background will make the object more visible. Enhancing contrast between elements of the environment is one of the simplest and most effective modifications to implement in most home, work, and recreational environments.

SUGGESTED CONTRAST AND LIGHTING MODIFICATIONS BY ROOM/ACTIVITY

The following list of potential modifications is not meant to be comprehensive. Rather, it is a selection of ideas from a number of excellent resources to provide guidelines for potential environmental modifications. Please refer to the references provided for more detail and additional ideas for environmental modifications. The book entitled *Making Life More Livable*, by Maureen Duffy, a vision rehabilitation therapist, is the best available resource and guide for environmental modifications and should be part of every occupational therapist's library.

Kitchen

- Lighting should be spread out evenly throughout the room.[25]
- Attach lights to the underside of cabinets.[26]

Figure 11-10. Example of lighting/lamp setup at desk (Steinman).

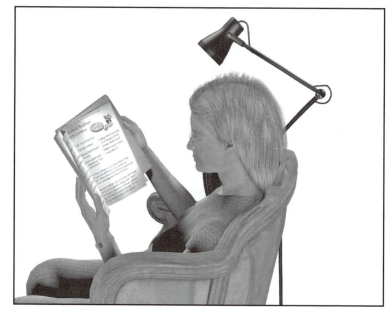

Figure 11-11. Example of lighting/lamp setup while reading (Steinman).

- A strip of bright, contrasting tape on the edge of a cabinet door makes it easier to see when it is left open.[26]

- Each workstation should have its own light source.[7,25,26]

- There should be areas of light and dark on countertops and walls to provide contrast when chopping and pouring ingredients when cooking.[15,25]

- Glassware should have a pattern or color.[25]

- Dials on often-used temperature settings, lines on measuring cups, and timers should be marked with colored tape or raised bumps.[25-27]

- Use a kitchen timer with large print or tactile markings.[26]

- Mount a reading stand that can be swiveled on a counter.[25]

- Place light-colored food items on dark plates.[28]

- Cut dark-colored foods on light-colored cutting boards.[8,28]

- Pour dark liquids (like coffee) into a light-colored cup and light liquids (like milk) into a dark cup.[28]

- Wrap plastic tape of a contrasting color around pot handles.[26]

- Use trays to create contrasting background on a kitchen counter.[28]
- Color code recipe cards (one color for meat dishes, one for poultry, another for desserts).[28]
- Rewrite favorite recipes in large print with thick, black felt-tipped pen.[26,28]

Finances

- Install a swing-arm lamp and gooseneck lamps in areas where client will be paying bills, reading, and writing.[7,26]
- Write with medium to wide felt-tip pens on lined white paper.[28]
- Color code household files and documents with fluorescent sticky notes.[26]
- If desk is shiny, cover it with a desk pad.[26]
- Order large-print checks with black print on yellow background.
- Use large-print calendar.
- Use large-print address book.

Bathroom

- Experiment with different light bulbs, such as full spectrum incandescent bulbs or compact fluorescent bulbs, or increase wattage of bulbs.[26]
- Install swing-arm lamps for additional lighting.[7,15,26]
- Use magnifying mirrors to help when shaving or applying makeup.[28]
- When choosing a shower curtain, clear plastic (with design) allows more light to be transmitted than an opaque solid color.[28]
- Circle the handle of a transparent plastic hairbrush with brightly colored electrical tape.[28]
- Lighting should be spread out evenly throughout the room.[25]
- Toothbrushes, cups, and bottles should be brightly colored.[25]
- When towels, washcloths, and bath mats need replacement, purchase solid colors that contrast with the tub, floor, and wall tile.[7]
- One wall should be dark, another light to provide contrast for different tasks.[15,25]
- Place items such as combs and brushes on a contrasting colored tray.

- Wrap the grab bar with bright tape to create a barber pole effect.[7]
- To avoid glare, use low-gloss or flat paint.[15]

Dining Room

- The color of the furniture should contrast the color of the floor and walls, and the colors of table and chairs should contrast.[25]
- Food, dishes, and the tabletop should contrast with each other.[15,25]
- A white dinner plate is more visible against a brown or navy blue table covering.[7,28]
- If the tabletop is dark, use light-colored placemats or dishes.[28]
- Use a tablecloth that contrasts with tableware.[28]

Living Room

- Mini-blinds or vertical shades control direct sunlight, and can be adjusted for variable lighting conditions according to the weather and time of day.[7,15]
- Lighting should be spread out evenly throughout the room.[25,26]
- Light fixtures that provide little overall light and create bright spots and shadows should be avoided.[25,26]
- The door frames should be in a color that contrasts with the wall color.[15,25]
- Space should be provided for the person to move closer to the television.[25,26]
- A large-screen television should be considered.
- Use of a flexible-arm lamp for auxiliary lighting for crafts or reading.[7,15,25,26]

Safety

- Place colored tape around a wall socket.[28]
- Lighting should be bright and spread evenly.[7,25]
- Walls and steps should be free of clutter.[25]
- Use solid, brightly colored hallway or stair runners to clearly define traffic flow and walking spaces.[7]
- Put contrasting strips of tape on the bottom and top of steps on a flight of stairs.[7,8,25,28]
- Outline electrical outlets with masking tape of a contrasting color.[7,28]

SUMMARY

In this chapter, we emphasized the importance of environmental modifications. In our experience, these modifications, along with the use of nonoptical assistive devices described in Chapter 12, should be attempted very early in the rehabilitation process and in many cases will be more effective in enabling recovery of more home-based activities than optical devices. In addition, most of the suggestions presented in this chapter are easy and inexpensive to implement and are rehabilitation strategies that all occupational therapists can begin using with their clients with vision impairment.

REFERENCES

1. Davis C, Lovie-Kitchin J, Thompson B. Psychosocial adjustment to age-related macular degeneration. *J Vis Impairment & Blind.* 1995;88:16-27.
2. Greig DE, West ML, Overbury O. Successful use of low vision aids: visual and psychological factors. *J Vis Impairment & Blind.* 1986;80:985-988.
3. Ringering L, Amaral P. Vision loss in the elderly: psychosocial repercussions and interventions. In: *Low Vision Ahead II: Proceedings of the International Conference on Low Vision. Melbourne, Australia: Association for the Blind.* Vision Victoria; 1990.
4. Robbins H, McMuray N. Psychosocial and visual factors in low vision rehabilitation of patients with age-related maculopathy. *J Vis Rehab.* 1988;2(1):11-21.
5. Brody BL, Williams RA, Thomas RG, et al. Age-related macular degeneration: a randomized clinical trial of a self-management intervention. *Ann Behav Med.* 1999;21(4):322-329.
6. Watson GR. Using low vision effectively. In: Fletcher DC, Ed. *Low Vision Rehabilitation: Caring for the Whole Person.* San Francisco: American Academy of Ophthalmology; 1999:61-87.
7. Duffy MA, Huebner K, Wormsley DP. Activities of daily living and individuals with low vision. In: Scheiman M, Ed. *Understanding and Managing Vision Deficits: A Guide for Occupational Therapists.* Thorofare, NJ: SLACK Incorporated; 2002:289-304.
8. Watson GR. Functional assessment of low vision for activities of daily living. In: Silverstone B, Lang MA, Rosenthal B, Faye EE, Eds. *The Lighthouse Handbook on Vision Impairment and Vision Rehabilitation.* New York: Oxford University Press; 2000:869-884.
9. Lovie-Kitchin J, Whittaker S. Relative-size magnification versus relative-distance magnification: effect on the reading performance of adults with normal and low vision. *J Vis Impairment & Blind.* 1998;16:433-446.
10. Boyce PR, Sanford LJ. Lighting to enhance visual capabilities. In: Silverstone B, Lang MA, Rosenthal B, Faye EE, Eds. *The Lighthouse Handbook on Vision Impairment and Vision Rehabilitation.* New York: Oxford University Press; 2000:617-636.
11. Cornelissen FW, Bootsma A, Kooijman AC. Object perception by visually impaired people at different light levels. *Vis Res.* 1995;35:161-168.
12. Fosse P, Valberg A. Lighting needs and lighting comfort during reading with age-related macular degeneration. *J Vis Impair Blind.* 2004;98:389-409.
13. Eldred KB. Optimal illumination for reading in patients with age-related maculopathy. *Opt Vis Sci.* 1992;69:46-50.
14. Carter K. Assessment of lighting. In: Jose RT, Ed. *Understanding Low Vision.* New York: American Foundation for the Blind; 1999:403-414.
15. Kern T, Miller ND. Occupational therapy and collaborative interventions for adults with low vision. In: Gentile M, Ed. *Functional Visual Behavior in Adults: An Occupational Therapy Guide to Evaluation and Treatment Options.* Bethesda, MD: AOTA Press; 2005:127-165.
16. Haegerstrom-Portnoy G, Schneck ME, Lott LA, Brabyn JA. The relation between visual acuity and other spatial vision measures. *Optom Vis Sci.* 2000;77:653-662.
17. Whittaker SG, Lovie-Kitchin J. Visual requirements for reading. *Optom Vis Sci.* 1993;70(1):54-65.
18. Marron JA, Bailey IL. Visual factors and orientation: mobility performance. *Am J Optom Physiol Opt.* 1982;59:413-426.
19. Kuyk T, Elliott JL. Visual correlates of mobility in real world settings in older adults with low vision. *Optom Vis Sci.* 1998;75:538-547.
20. Wood JM. Elderly drivers and simulated visual impairment. *Optom Vis Sci.* 1995;72:115-124.
21. Owsley C, Sloane ME. Contrast sensitivity, acuity, and the perception of "real-world" targets. *Brit J Ophthalmol.* 1987;71:791-796.
22. West SK, Rubin GS, Broman AT, Munoz B, Bandeen-Roche K, Turano K. How does visual impairment affect performance on tasks of everyday life? The SEE Project. Salisbury Eye Evaluation. *Arch Ophthalmol.* 2002;120(6):774-80.
23. Rubin GS, Roche KB, Prasada-Rao P, Fried LP. Visual impairment and disability in older adults. *Optom Vis Sci.* 1994;71(12):750-760.
24. Cummings RW, Muchnick BG, Whittaker SG. Specialized testing in low vision. In: Brilliant RL, Ed. *Essentials of Low Vision Practice.* Boston: Butterworth-Heinemann; 1999:47-69.
25. Watson GR. Older adults with low vision. In: Corn AL, Koenig AJ, Eds. *Foundations of Low Vision: Clinical and Functional Perspectives.* New York: American Foundation for the Blind; 2000:363-390.
26. Duffy MA. *Making Life More Livable.* New York: American Foundation for the Blind; 2002.
27. Inkster W. *Rehabilitation Teaching for Persons Experiencing Vision Loss.* 2nd ed. New York: CIL Publications and Audiobooks of VISIONS; 1997.
28. Quillman RD, Goodrich GL. Interventions for adults with visual impairments. In: Lueck AH, Ed. *Functional Vision: A Practitioner's Guide to Evaluation and Intervention.* New York: AFB Press; 2004:423-474.
29. Flom R. Appendix: Visual consequences of most common eye conditions associated with visual impairment. In: Lueck AH, Ed. *Functional Vision: A Practitioner's Guide to Evaluation and Intervention.* New York: AFB Press; 2004:475-481.

Nonoptical Assistive Devices

INTRODUCTION

This chapter continues our presentation of the seven components of the sequential vision rehabilitation treatment plan reviewed in Table 12-1, and is designed to present a systematic approach to the use of nonoptical assistive devices to maximize a client's ability to engage in occupational performance.

The suggestions described in this chapter are not remedial. Rather, they are designed to improve a client's functional ability in spite of his or her visual impairment. Some of the nonoptical assistive devices are designed on the principle of relative size magnification, some provide better contrast, and others are a combination of the two. In addition, this chapter reviews some of the available resources that utilize sensory substitution. In some cases, it is more efficient for a client with visual impairment to use the tactile and auditory sensory modalities to accomplish a visual task.

ORGANIZATION OF RESOURCES/ MATERIALS

As suggested in previous chapters, the occupational therapist will typically visit the client's living environment to both assess and treat the client. This may be in the client's home, nursing home, hospital environment, or an assisted living facility. It is important to have samples of the various nonoptical assistive devices available for demonstration in the client's environment. We suggest the use of the following organizational scheme that allows the therapist to efficiently provide low vision rehabilitation care. Divide the various nonoptical assistive devices into the following categories:

1. Writing and communication

2. Kitchen

3. Self-care and leisure

4. Labeling

These materials can be organized by placing them in large plastic bins that can easily be transported to the client's living environment, or can be easily accessed in a practice or hospital setting (Figure 12-1). This is in addition to a similar plastic bin with a variety of lightbulbs discussed in Chapter 11.

Please be aware that there are frequent new additions to the available nonoptical assistive devices. This chapter is designed to introduce the reader to a selection of commonly used and popular devices, but is by no means comprehensive. Occupational therapists should order the catalogs listed in Sidebar 12-1. These catalogs will provide therapists with a comprehensive resource of available devices for low vision rehabilita-

Table 12-1.

Vision Rehabilitation: Seven-Step Sequential Treatment Plan

1. Education
    Nature of eye disease
    Outlook for the future
    Expectations of vision rehabilitation
2. Therapeutic Activities
    Eccentric Viewing
    Scanning
    Reading skills
3. Environmental Modifications
    Size
    Distance
    Color
    Lighting
    Contrast
    Glare
4. Nonoptical Assistive Devices
    Visual
    Tactile
    Auditory
5. Optical Magnification
6. Computer Technology in Low Vision Rehabilitation
7. Resources/Handouts

Sidebar 12-1: Resources

Independent Living Aids, Inc.	800-537-2118	www.independentliving.com
Lighthouse International	800-829-0500	www.lighthouse.org
LS&S Group, Inc.	800-468-4789	www.lssgroup.com
Maxi Aids Catalog	800-522-6294	www.maxiaids.com

Figure 12-1. Plastic bins to organize nonoptical assistive devices.

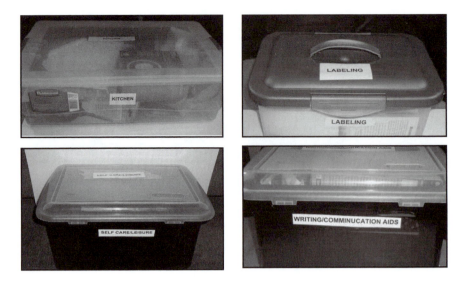

tion and the ability to remain up-to-date. To remain current, it is also useful to sign up for the email updates from each company.

There are also two other essential resources that should be part of every low vision therapist's library:

1. *Making Life More Livable: Simple Adaptations for Living at Home After Vision Loss.*[1]

   This book is designed as a resource for adults with vision loss. It is filled with practical tips and has numerous illustrations showing people how to continue living independent, productive lives on their own. The author stresses the use of nonoptical devices and environmental adaptations such as print size, lighting, and contrast.

2. *Rehabilitation Teaching for Persons Experiencing Vision Loss.*[2]

This book is designed to be used by low vision rehabilitation therapists and its format makes it quite valuable in everyday practice. The authors focus on common ADL and break down various activities (eg, cooking) into smaller parts, such as: placing a pot on a burner, setting the gas stove controls, determining the readiness of food, heating food on a burner, frying foods, using a toaster oven, using a microwave, etc. For each task, the authors organize the presentation, providing specific objectives, and detailed step-by-step techniques.

Tables 12-2 through 12-5 summarize some of the commonly prescribed nonoptical assistive devices, subclassified into the four categories listed above.

WRITING AND COMMUNICATION

Organization

When a client is visually impaired, organization is an important part of vision rehabilitation. Duffy recommends the guidelines in Table 12-6 for getting organized.[1] Organizing materials to be used for a task, establishing a work area with proper lighting, and storing necessary items in an accessible and organized manner, all go a long way towards improving effectiveness.

For writing and communications, it is important to establish a consistent work area with proper lighting and contrast and no glare. Materials to be used for this aspect of occupational performance should be organized in a meaningful way so that everything is readily accessible when needed.

Writing and Communication

Writing and communication are essential activities if a person is going to continue to live independently. These skills are important for managing finances; paying bills; reading and responding to written communication; interacting with friends, relatives, businesses; shopping; reading and writing recipes, etc. Most of these activities take place at a desk or table with the client viewing materials at a near distance. Before providing nonoptical assistive devices for this category, it is important to work with the client to

---

Table 12-2.

Nonoptical Assistive Devices: Writing and Communication

- Writing guides
  - Signature guides
  - Letter guides
  - Check-writing guides
- Bold line paper
- Felt-tip pens
- Enlarged print
- Reading stands
- Telephone/computer
- Large-button phones
- Talking watches/clocks

Table 12-3.

Nonoptical Assistive Devices: Kitchen

Eating/Meal Preparation Aids

Large-print timers
Boil Alert
Liquid level indicators
Measuring cups/spoons
Cutting boards
Talking kitchen scale
Long oven mitts
Bright Dish Brush
Large-print recipes

---

improve eccentric viewing, scanning, and reading skills as discussed in Chapter 10. In addition, it is essential to first insure that lighting and contrast are optimized.

Table 12-2 lists some of the nonoptical assistive devices commonly used for writing and communication. A simple approach for helping the client with low vision to perform writing tasks is the use of writing guides illustrated in Figure 12-2. These guides provide better contrast and also work on the principle of sensory substitution. The client can use his/her tactile sense to substitute for poor vision. The popular guides illustrated in Figure 12-2 include a signature guide, a letter-writing guide, and a check-writing guide. The use of bold-lined paper and thick felt-tip pens are also

useful for helping a person with low vision to write more effectively (Figure 12-3).

The use of reading/writing stands is important for clients with low vision for two reasons (Figure 12-4). The use of a stand frees the hands so that the person can hold the low vision optical device being used. It also makes it easier to provide consistent and appropriate illumination for the task at hand by creating stability and an appropriate viewing angle.

For people who intend to write extensively, typing or word processing should be considered because computer systems can be simplified and adaptive software employed to enable the client to see or hear what is being typed (see Chapter 14).

Table 12-4.

Nonoptical Assistive Devices: Self-Care/Leisure

Personal Care

Sock holders
Iron Guides
Jumbo plastic pill box
Talking Rx
Magnifying pill cutter
Magnifying clippers
Double-sided lighted makeup mirror
Tweezer magnifier
Item locator
Iron safety guide
Talking Scale
Needle threader

Leisure

Large Bingo
Large symbol playing cards
Giant print Bible
New York Times large-print crossword puzzles
Large remote
Playing card holder

Table 12-5.

Nonoptical Assistive Devices: Labeling

Labels/Identifiers

Bump on tactile markers
Loc dots
Spot and liner
Buttons for labeling
Index cards
Vegetable/fruit identifiers
Puffy paint/Hi Marks

Table 12-6.

Getting Organized

- Organize belongings and items into predictable groupings.
- Store equipment, supplies, and other items near the activity for which they are used.
- Always return things to the same place.
- Eliminate clutter whenever possible by disposing of unnecessary items.
- Establish a comfortable workplace for each activity.
- Establish good lighting and contrast at each workplace.

Adapted from Duffy MA. *Making Life More Livable*. New York: American Foundation for the Blind; 2002.

Figure 12-2. Writing guides (reprinted with permission from LS&S Products).

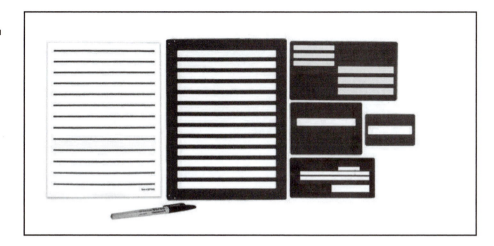

Figure 12-3. Bold paper and felt tip pen (reprinted with permission from LS&S Products).

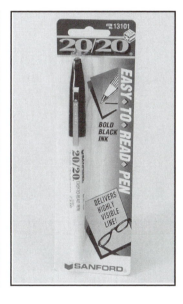

Figure 12-4. Reading stand (reprinted with permission from LS&S Products).

Figure 12-5. Large-print check register (reprinted with permission from LS&S Products).

Figure 12-6. Change purse (reprinted with permission from LS&S Products).

Figure 12-7. Billfold (reprinted with permission from LS&S Products).

Finances

Paying Bills

It is helpful to suggest the use of large-print materials such as a large-print check register (Figure 12-5) and large-print checks with raised lines. Most banks provide large-print checks with raised lines to clients with low vision at no additional charge. Some other services often offered by banks for customers who are visually impaired are reader services, information reformatting including monthly statements in large print, Braille, audiocassette or computer disk, and talking automatic teller machines (ATMs). Clients should also be advised that some utility companies provide large-print bills on request. After working for a period of time in a community, therapists will know which companies provide this service and can share this information with clients. The telephone is another viable option for paying bills and is now an available option with many companies and should be proposed as an option by the occupational therapist.

Handling and Distinguishing Currency

For people with low vision, distinguishing among bills of different denominations and determining the authenticity of a bill can be difficult or impossible. All of the features present in currency design either to help the user verify the legitimacy of a particular banknote or to indicate its value are visual clues, although it is possible to learn to identify coins using the sense of touch.

The therapist should teach the client that the quarter and dime have milled, or ridged edges as opposed to the smooth edges of a penny or nickel. This difference, combined with the size difference, can be used to distinguish coins. Therapists should also be aware of assistive devices such as special change purses (Figure 12-6) with separate compartments for each type of coin, and billfolds that have separate sections for each denomination (Figure 12-7). Another strategy is to fold each denomination in different ways. For example, one might keep one denomination of notes (such as $1 bills) unfolded, then fold $5 bills in half, fold $10 bills in fourths, and fold $20 bills in half lengthwise. Anything larger might be folded into a triangle. When giving money to another person, such as a store cashier, it is common practice for people who are visually impaired to state the denomination of the bill as they hand it to the other person. Others recommend avoiding the use of large bills altogether, so that only $1 bills and coins that are readily identified are received as returned change.

Another nonoptical assistive device is a note identifier. These are fairly small electronic devices that allow one to insert a bill into a slot and run it over a scanner. The unit then scans the bill and reads its denomination out loud through an earphone worn by the user. These units are popular with blind vendors and other business people who must be able to receive money and make change regularly. They work fairly well in many situations. However, the quality of their performance is influenced heavily by the quality of the bill inserted into the unit, as well as the ability of the user to hear the sound coming from the unit.

The currency designs of other countries attempt to address the problems of blind people and those with low vision by identifying the value of a banknote with a variety of features. A common technique is to make bills of different values different sizes. Using a size template or, with some practice, by feel, a visually impaired person can differentiate among bills of various denominations by size alone. The use of different colors for different denominations is also common in currency outside the United States and is of use

Figure 12-8. Large numeral in lower right hand corner of US currency.

Figure 12-9. Large numeral telephone (reprinted with permission from LS&S Products).

to many with low vision. In Canada, the bills have Braille markings to help the visually impaired.

Within the United States, there is a long history of groups advocating changes to the US banknotes to make them more user-friendly. However, minimal changes have been made to make paper currency more accessible. At this time, the features that have been designed to help visually impaired people are the addition of different colors for different denominations and a large dark-colored numeral identifying the note's denomination in the lower-right corner of the back of the bill. The size of this numeral is about 20/300 to 20/400 (Figure 12-8). Notes also include a denominating feature readable by special devices designed to help those who are blind verify denominations.

Finally, bank debit cards or credit cards may be used as a substitute for using cash. The client needs to always carry a signature guide and ask the cashier to position the guide. The store and card receipts can be folded together and verified later by a sighted assistant.

Telephone

Another important aspect of communication is the telephone. An obstacle for the client with low vision is being able see the numerals and then dial the telephone number. One of the trends in technology is to make new models smaller and more portable. Of course, this is problematic for clients with low vision. Fortunately, telephones with large numerals/letters (Figure 12-9) are still available in the catalogs listed in Sidebar 12-1. These telephones not only have large print, but high contrast as well. It is important to teach

the client who has sufficient tactile sensitivity to find telephone buttons by feel because this will enable this client to use any telephone.

One important benefit of new technology is programmable telephones that allow people to program a large number of commonly used phone numbers. Phones are also available that allow the individual to program numbers and use a photograph of the person when selecting the number. This is ideal for clients with low vision. They would simply need to program all the numbers commonly used and then use a one- or two-number combination to call the telephone number. The therapist, a family member, or friend could program the telephone numbers for the client. In 2006, newer mobile phones and telephones were available with voice recognition systems that allowed the dialer simply to say the name of a person in their directory, and the phone repeats the name of the person dialed and dials the number. Certain brands of mobile phones and caller ID systems also had features that announce the name of the caller. As this technology rapidly changes, one will need to search for the latest technology with these features.

For persons who are visually impaired, most telephone companies offer a service in which the person simply speaks the name of the person or business and the number is dialed for the person. This is useful for those clients with significant loss of vision and is an example of sensory substitution.

It is important for the therapist to know that Congress amended US telecommunications law in 1996 to require telephones and telephone services to be more accessible. They enacted Section 255 to ensure that new telephones would be designed for use by

Figure 12-10. Alarm clock for clients with low vision (reprinted with permission from LS&S Products).

people with disabilities, including people who are blind or visually impaired. Section 255 applies to all telephone equipment and services.

Section 255 requires companies to do all that is "readily achievable" to make each product or service accessible. As phones become more complex, Section 255 ensures that clients with low vision should be able to use cordless, wireless, business, or traditional telephones to manage telephone calls just like sighted users can. Telephone manufacturers and service providers are legally required to be able to explain access features. The therapist can help by determining an appropriate contact number for the client. The Federal Communications Commission (FCC), Consumer & Governmental Affairs Bureau maintains a web page with contact information for most manufacturers and service providers. The websites in Sidebar 12-2 contain a list of available equipment. Use the search terms to find service providers.

Computers

The use of computer technology for communication, learning, gathering information, and recreation is a topic of great importance. Although only a small percentage of clients with low vision currently use computers, this number will grow dramatically in the near future. The use of computers has become so commonplace that the next generation of elderly with low vision will require compensatory solutions that will enable them to continue to use computers and the internet. We have, therefore, devoted Chapter 14 to this topic.

Telling Time

Telling time can also be challenging for clients with low vision. Relative size magnification, contrast, and sensory substitution can all be used to help clients. Clocks and watches are available from catalogs with high contrast and large numerals. In addition, sensory substitution using talking watches and clocks is an excellent compensatory approach. These watches and clocks are readily available, and inexpensive. Figure 12-10 illustrates an example of an alarm clock that is available for clients with low vision.

KITCHEN

The ability to prepare meals and eat independently are ADL that are essential for a client's ability to function independently, and many nonoptical assistive devices are available.

Figure 12-11. Magnetic labels for cans (reprinted with permission from LS&S Products).

Organization

Organization is particularly important in the kitchen and dining room. The food pantry, refrigerator, spices, pots and pans, flatware, and cooking utensils should all be well organized. This not only allows the client to know where to find necessary items, it also enables the client to keep track of inventory and develop shopping lists (see Table 12-6). Remember to be respectful of the client's familiar organization scheme; if it is changed, care must be taken to teach the new scheme.

Labeling pantries, drawers, the refrigerator, spices, and food items can be very helpful. Magnetic labels are available (Figure 12-11) and other labeling approaches are discussed later in this chapter.

Meal Preparation

Large-print recipes and cookbooks can be found at any bookstore or online through the Internet. In a recent Internet search, we were able to find 15 popular titles in large-print simply by searching for "large-print cookbooks." When clients have favorite family recipes, a family member or the therapist can copy the recipe onto a large index card using large print, or print it out using a computer and a font of 16 point or larger. These cards can then be laminated. When using these recipes or cookbooks, it is best to place them on a cookbook holder or reading stand. The use of a gooseneck lamp positioned near the reading stand will further improve the client's ability to read the recipes.

Nonoptical devices can be helpful with food preparation tasks, such as measuring, pouring, weighing, cutting, boiling liquid, and washing utensils and dishes. Some of the more commonly used devices are illustrated in Figures 12-12 through 12-16 and include: large-print timers (Figure 12-12), Boil Alert (Figure 12-13), liquid level indicators (Figure 12-14), large-print measuring cups/spoons (Figure 12-15), dark- and light-colored cutting boards (Figure 12-16) to improve contrast, a talking kitchen scale (Figure 12-17), long oven mitts, and a bright dish brush.

Knowing when water or other liquid is boiling can be a challenge. It is dangerous to get too close to the stove to make this determination, and if the client's hearing is impaired, listening for the sound of boiling water may not be effective. A device illustrated in Figure 12-13 called Boil Alert can be used. The Boil Alert solid disk marker rattles against the sides of the pan when liquid is boiling. When pouring liquids, it may be difficult for a client to know when to stop pouring. The Liquid Level Indicator (Figure 12-14) is a device that easily determines when a container of liquid is filled to within approximately 1 inch of the top. The device is hung over the lip of the cup, glass, or container. When the liquid reaches the alert height, a buzzer sounds and the unit vibrates. Another simple method of monitoring liquid levels for cold liquids is the use of a ping-pong ball.[3] The ping-pong ball is placed in the cup and the client can feel the ball when the liquid rises to about an inch from the top of the cup. A client pouring for herself might simply place her finger over the side of the cup and feel when the top is reached.

Figure 12-12. Large-print timer (reprinted with permission from LS&S Products).

Figure 12-13. Boil Alert.

Figure 12-14. Liquid level indicator (reprinted with permission from LS&S Products).

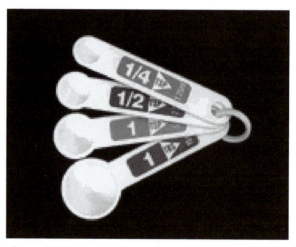

Figure 12-15. Large-print measuring cups/spoons (reprinted with permission from LS&S Products).

Large-print measuring cups/spoons (Figure 12-15), dark- and light-colored cutting boards (Figure 12-16), and a bright dish brush make use of the concepts of relative size magnification and contrast to help the client. A client may benefit from having both light-colored and black measuring spoons and cups. Dry measuring cups designed to level off to the top can be used with liquids as well without need to visually align a liquid level to a mark. The cup is filled over something that will catch the spill. Another aid for measuring is a talking kitchen scale, as illustrated in Figure 12-17.

Duffy suggests attaching light and dark sheets of contact paper to the counter or on the wall near the food preparation area,[1] or use cutting boards that are light on one side and dark on the other. The client can hold up dark ingredients against light-colored sheets and light ingredients against dark to improve contrast and the ability to measure things.

The use of flame retardant, elbow-length oven mitts when removing pots and pans from the stove or oven makes sense from a safety standpoint.[1]

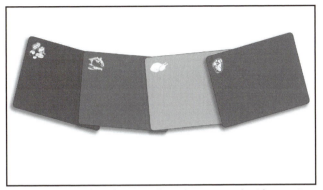

Figure 12-16. Colored cutting boards (reprinted with permission from LS&S Products).

Figure 12-17. Talking kitchen scale (reprinted with permission from LS&S Products).

Figure 12-18. Washing machine marked with bump dots.

SELF-CARE AND LEISURE

Organization

As stated before, organizing materials to be used for various self-care and leisure activities is essential, along with establishing a work area with proper lighting. Organization of items used for grooming, cleaning, and dressing can go a long way towards making these ADL less stressful (see Table 12-6).

Self-Care

Laundry

A challenge with laundry is being able to read and set the dials of the washer and dryer. Installing an adjustable swing-arm light and marking the dials can be helpful.[1] The dials can be marked with "bump dots" (Figure 12-18) or pieces of Velcro. This enables the client to feel when the dials point to the correct setting. Before washing items such as socks, the client may use sock holders (Figure 12-19) to keep pairs together. This minimizes the need to pair the socks after they are washed and dried, as pairing socks can be problematic because of color contrast problems. When ironing, the use of a guide that fits over the iron minimizes the likelihood of burns.

Medication

Although clients often receive medical information in writing, many people with low vision are unable to read the instructions for their treatment, particularly instructions on medicine bottles. A study was recently published investigating the ability of people with visual impairment to read instructions on a bottle of eyedrops.[4] The researchers found that clients whose visual acuity was 20/80 or worse were significantly less able to read the instructions on bottles. Patients whose acuity was 20/80 or worse preferred 16-point type, 18-point type for the 20/120 group, and 22-point type for the 20/200 group.

Since most clients with low vision will have visual acuity worse than 20/80, occupational therapists providing low vision rehabilitation will have to insure that their clients are able to read medicine bottle

Figure 12-19. Sock holders.

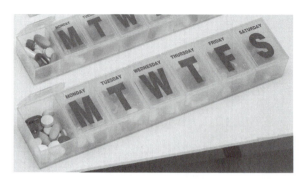

Figure 12-20. Jumbo pill boxes (reprinted with permission from LS&S Products).

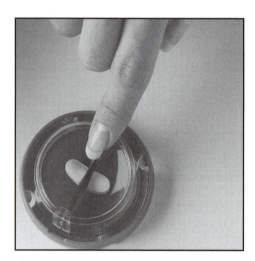

Figure 12-21. Magnifying pill cutter (reprinted with permission from LS&S Products).

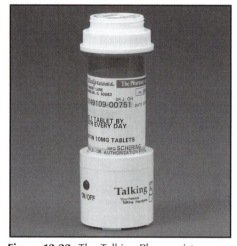

Figure 12-22. The Talking Pharmacist (reprinted with permission from LS&S Products).

labels. Clients need to be able to take the correct and safe dose of medicine. Some of the nonoptical assistive devices that can be used to help clients manage their medications include jumbo plastic pill boxes (Figure 12-20), a magnifying pill cutter (Figure 12-21), and the Talking Rx device (Figure 12-22).

The Talking Rx is a device that tells the person exactly how many pills to take, how to take the medication, potential side effects, and what to do if a dose is missed. The pharmacist, therapist, or family member records the prescription information right into the Talking Rx. The pharmacist can record up to 60 seconds of instructions when dispensing the medication. A simple, inexpensive approach is to have the client use the large plastic pill organizer. Using this device, the client can find the next appropriate cell by feel if the cover is left open after the medication has been taken. A sighted helper can sort the medications into the dispenser cells. Medications can also be organized in alphabetical order, separated by location (morning pills in the kitchen, nighttime pills in the bedroom).[1] Therapists can also use large print to relabel bottles.

For a detailed discussion of adaptations available for the medical needs of clients with diabetes, refer to Chapter 15.

Dressing and Grooming

A significant complaint of clients with low vision is that they feel uncomfortable going out of their homes because they are unable to manage grooming and dressing activities. Organization can be very helpful when dressing. Clothing items can be separated by season, type of outfit (suit, shirt, slacks), and color of items. There are commercially available labels with

Figure 12-23. Braille clothing identifiers (reprinted with permission from LS&S Products).

Figure 12-24. Electronic color identifier (reprinted with permission from LS&S Products).

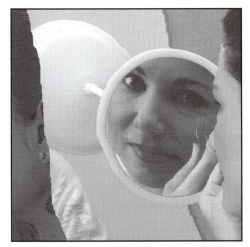

Figure 12-25. Lighted makeup mirror (reprinted with permission from LS&S Products).

large print and Braille (Figure 12-23). Alternatively, a therapist can make labels using colored index cards to correspond to the color of the garment. These tags and labels are attached to the hanger. Another option is an electronic color identifier. This electronic unit (Figure 12-24) distinguishes different color shades, with distinctions such as light red and vivid red.

Bureaus can also be organized by type of garment (socks, underwear, shirts, and sweaters). There are a number of useful nonoptical assistive devices available to help clients with other grooming activities, including magnifying clippers and tweezers, and lighted makeup mirrors (Figure 12-25). These special mirrors are very helpful for shaving, applying makeup, and other grooming tasks. An excellent strategy

for shaving is to have the client feel for where the face has been shaved.

Miscellaneous

Many people with normal vision have occasional difficulty finding common items such as keys, telephone receivers, and remote control devices for televisions, DVD players, or VCRs. It is not surprising that this problem is more common with clients who also have low vision. Thus, the use of locator systems can be very helpful. These devices can be attached to commonly misplaced household items. If an item is misplaced, the client simply presses a button on the locator system and will hear a tone and find the item by locating the sound.

Finally, for clients who must monitor their weight, reading a traditional scale may be difficult. Talking scales can be used to overcome this problem.

Leisure

Numerous options are available today that allow people with low vision to engage in leisure activities. The wide availability and decreasing prices of large-screen televisions, computer screens, and video projectors enables many clients with low vision to watch television and movies and use computers just using the concept of relative size magnification. If this is combined with relative distance magnification, the effects can be further enhanced. Chapter 14 covers the topic of technology in detail.

Many nonoptical assistive devices are available for leisure activities, including: large-print Bingo cards (Figure 12-26); large-symbol playing cards (Figure

Figure 12-26. Large-print Bingo cards (reprinted with permission from LS&S Products).

Figure 12-27. Large-symbol playing cards (reprinted with permission from LS&S Products).

Figure 12-28. Large remote for television (reprinted with permission from LS&S Products).

Figure 12-29. Hi-Marks 3D Marker or Spot'n Line Pen (reprinted with permission from LS&S Products).

12-27); playing card holders; large-print Bibles, newspapers, and books; large-print crossword puzzles; and large remotes for television (Figure 12-28). These devices are all available from the catalogs listed in Sidebar 12-1. It is wise to keep updated copies of these catalogs because new products are often introduced.

LABELING

An important role of the occupational therapist is to help the client label and mark household items to make them more visible. Labeling and marking is useful to identify food items, clothing, medication, cleaning products, and appliances. Labeling can be very simple, such as using a rubber band to differentiate one can from another, or placing a dot on one type of medication.[1,2] For example, a rubber band could

be placed on an orange juice container, but not on the milk container, or one band on mushroom soup, two bands on tomato soup.[2] Figure 12-11 illustrates the use of commercially available magnetic labels for labeling cans.

Index cards can be used along with a black wide-tip marker to label food items and cleaning supplies. Other commonly used labeling materials include brightly colored electrical tape, safety pins, Velcro, iron-on patches, and craft paint. There are marking and labeling products such as Hi-Marks 3-D Marker or Spot'n Line Pen (Figure 12-29) in the catalogs listed in Sidebar 12-1.

Marking appliances is an important function for the low vision therapist. Common appliances with dials or push buttons that require marking include the stove, oven, microwave, toaster-oven, refrigerator dials, washing and drying machines, and the thermo-

Figure 12-30. Bump dots (reprinted with permission from LS&S Products).

Figure 12-31. Dials marked on oven.

Figure 12-32. Dials marked on microwave.

stat. Newer appliances with touch pads create a particular problem because the user cannot find the buttons by feel. Materials for marking include liquids that can be squeezed out of a container directly onto the appliance and harden over time, and pre-shaped dots that stick on the dials (Figure 12-30). To mark appliances, determine the most frequently used settings. It is preferable not to mark more than two settings on a dial, as too many markings can cause confusion.[2] Figures 12-31 and 12-32 illustrate examples of an oven dial and a microwave oven that have been marked to improve accessibility for the client with low vision. With microwaves, often only the "add minute" button and stop button need to be marked. A person sets minutes by pressing the button a number of times.

SUMMARY

In this chapter, we described the use of nonoptical assistive devices to maximize a client's ability to engage in ADL. These devices are readily available and in many cases inexpensive. While most people think of optical devices as the primary method of assisting clients with low vision, nonoptical assistive devices can be just as important and effective. Of course, in most cases the occupational therapist will need to use all of the available rehabilitation tools discussed in this book to maximize success.

REFERENCES

1. Duffy MA. *Making Life More Livable*. New York: American Foundation for the Blind; 2002.
2. Inkster W, Newman L, Stormweiss D, Yeadon A. *Rehabilitation Teaching for Persons Experiencing Vision Loss*. 2nd ed. New York: CIL Publications and Audiobooks of VISIONS; 1997.
3. Duffy MA. *Course Notes: Independent Living Skills - Home Management*. Pennsylvania College of Optometry: Rehabilitation Certificate Course: Philadelphia, PA; 2000.
4. Drummond SR, Drummond RS, Dutton GN. Visual acuity and the ability of the visually impaired to read medication instructions. *Br J Ophthalmol*. 2004;88(12):1541-1542.

Optical Devices and Magnification Strategies

INTRODUCTION

Impaired visual acuity is the most common visual impairment encountered by the low vision rehabilitation therapist. Optical magnification devices such as strong reading glasses or microscopes (Figure 13-1), handheld magnifiers (Figure 13-2), stand magnifiers (Figure 13-3), telescopes (Figure 13-4), and telemicroscopes (Figure 13-5) compensate for visual acuity that is inadequate to perform a particular task. Optical devices compensate by magnifying the retinal image of whatever the client is viewing, allowing the detail to be resolved. People use optical devices for many everyday tasks such as reading, needle working, bird-watching, watching television, enjoying theater or a sports event, repairing appliances, managing medications, and reading package labels.

Recommendation or prescription of any optical device, even a handheld magnifier, requires the collaboration of an optometrist or ophthalmologist (eyecare provider) with the vision rehabilitation therapist. In Chapter 1, we presented two potential collaborative models, which are reviewed below.

1. The standard model involves an eyecare provider with advanced skills in low vision rehabilitation working with a therapist who has basic skills. The first section of this chapter provides detailed information required by the occupational therapist working under this

standard model. In this model, the low vision optometrist takes the primary responsibility for recommending and prescribing the optical devices. The therapist performs an occupational therapy low vision evaluation (see Chapter 8) and provides information about client goals, such as the specific task requirements, and nonvisual impairments such as a hand-tremor or low frustration tolerance, to the low vision optometrist. The therapist may also suggest types of devices that seem appropriate. The therapist conveys this information to the low vision optometrist, who recommends devices to try, and eventually prescribes the devices. The occupational therapist configures the environment and instructs the client about use of the recommended device to achieve the performance goals. If the client has difficulty performing the required tasks with a recommended device, the therapist consults with the low vision optometrist, who recommends different devices or other solutions.

2. The advanced model requires that the therapist have advanced understanding of principles of magnification and optical devices. In this second collaborative model, the occupational therapist takes a more active role in recommending device magnification, selecting devices, and problem solving. The occupational therapist

Figure 13-1. Reading with a full field high power microscope.

Figure 13-3. An illuminated stand magnifier.

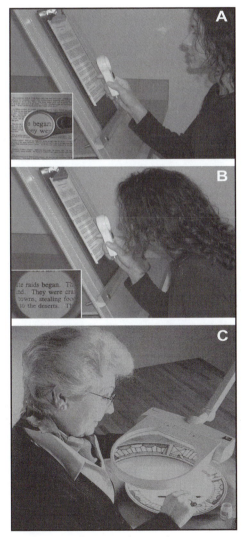

Figure 13-2. Illuminated magnifier. A. Handheld at distance (shopping). B. Handheld at near. C. Mounted for hands-free use.

Figure 13-4. Telescopes. A. spectacle mounted. B. Handheld Keplerian telescope. C. Galilean telescope (designed for spectacle mount) with near cap in place for close work (Photos courtesy of Eschenbach Optik of America, Ridgefield, CT).

Figure 13-5. Spectacle-mounted telemicroscope (Beecher-Mirage telescope with a near cap).

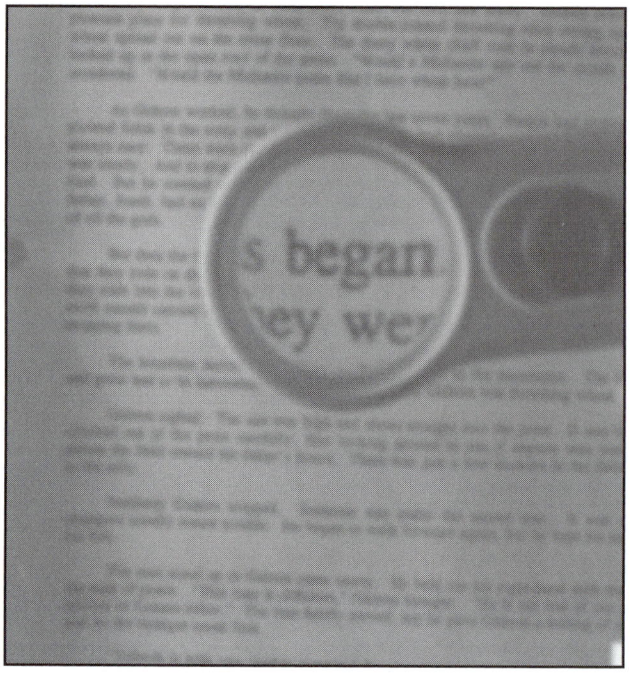

Figure 13-6. Simulated impaired visual acuity of a client as seen with and without an optical magnification device.

must understand how to estimate the optical device magnification required to perform a task, as well as how optical devices work, and how to identify the limiting visual factor when they do not work as predicted.

This chapter is divided into three sections. The first section describes what an occupational therapist needs to understand about optical magnification devices to perform low vision rehabilitation therapy in the standard collaborative model. The second section is advanced and describes additional principles required for the occupational therapist to perform low vision rehabilitation therapy under the advanced model. Finally, some clients with visual impairment also have reduced visual fields. Optical devices have been developed to help compensate for visual field problems. These "field expansion devices" are discussed in the final section of this chapter. All of these sections include the knowledge of optical devices required for the certification examination for the ACREP certified low vision therapist.

In the seven-step sequential treatment approach for low vision rehabilitation described in Chapter 9, optical devices are used following several interventions, including environmental modifications, consideration of nonoptical devices, and instructional interventions. With more severe vision loss, optical devices are

difficult to learn to use and usually provide a fixed magnification, and should be recommended after less complicated solutions have been considered and incorporated in the treatment plan. Environmental modification or nonoptical interventions affect the type of device and magnification of the device required. Often, referring physicians and clients assume that optical devices are central in the low vision rehabilitation process, leading to an unfortunate expectation by many clients that a device or intervention exists that will remediate and restore clear vision. Unlike a pair of eyeglasses designed to correct refractive error and make vision clear and sharp again, optical magnification devices magnify objects to compensate for inadequate acuity. Rather than clear vision, the client experiences an enlarged but still fuzzy view of the object (Figure 13-6).

THE BASIC PRINCIPLES (THE STANDARD MODEL)

Often low vision optometrists recommend, and some might even prescribe, optical devices for magnification before the therapist has started treatment. When possible, final prescription of optical devices should be discouraged until after instruction has begun and the client has had an opportunity to try

Table 13-1.

Recommended "Getting Started" Optical Devices

- Illuminated handheld devices with bright white LED type lights at approximately 5, 6, 8, 10, 12, 16, 20, 25, and 32 D.
- Illuminated stand magnifiers from 10, 12, 16, 25, and 32 equivalent D.
- Open stand magnifier for writing at 5 and 8 D.
- A low-power horizontal bar magnifier.
- Hooded visors or loops at 5, 6, 8, 10, and 12 D that can be worn on the head, with or without eyeglasses.
- Microscopes at 16, 20, 25, or 32 D.
- 1.5X, 2.5X, 3X sports glasses, Eschenbach TV-max (2x).
- 4X, 6X, and 8X handheld Keplerian handheld telescope.
- 1 set of 6X and 8X Beecher Mirage head-mounted telescope with two 2.5 D caps.
- A metric tape measure, reading stand, lap tray. Typoscopes, continuous text reading card, and directional task light with extension cord. Tape and clipboard to secure the reading material.

the devices. This will increase client satisfaction and decrease the possibility that a device will need to be returned or exchanged. With either model, the occupational therapist should have an assortment of optical devices available that will approximate the devices recommended by the low vision optometrist (Table 13-1).

The Collaborative Model for Evaluation and Treatment With Optical Devices

The following seven steps outline our recommended sequence for device selection and implementation (Table 13-2). As described previously, a client should be under the care of an eyecare provider and be referred with a diagnosis, prognosis, visual acuity, and a current pair of glasses whose optics are fully described before being evaluated by the occupational therapist. Ideally, the final prescription of a low vision device should occur later in the sequence. The following steps provide an overview of the process of selecting, providing instruction, and evaluating optical devices. The first four of the seven steps have been described as part of the occupational therapy evaluation in Chapter 8. In the remainder of this section, we describe the basis for selecting devices, and instructional procedures.

1. Defining the Goal Tasks and Performance Requirements

The first step in selecting devices is to define the tasks that the client needs to perform, along with observable and measurable performance goals.

Performance goals are often implicit in a goal task and need not be specified. For example, a goal to read labels is a "spot task," whereas reading a newspaper or watching television is an "extended task". The goals need to be written on the referral to the low vision optometrist. The information to be conveyed to the low vision optometrist is summarized in Table 13-3.

Goal definition often requires detective work. For example, Ms. Jason, an 86-year-old retired accountant with atrophic macular degeneration, initially denied that she had goals but she and her husband agreed they had been fighting a lot lately. An examination of her history and interview with her husband revealed medication management errors and frequent arguments about how he manages the bills and checkbook, a job she had been performing for the 43 years of her marriage. She also used to perform cross-stitch. She had not performed this activity for years and did not identify this as a goal because she did not think cross-stitch was possible. She continued to "watch" television but reported that she could not see the screen very well. Based on this information, four goals might be: 1) identify people on a television screen, 2) locate amount due and write check for bills and balance a checkbook, 3) read medication labels and identify pills, and 4) perform cross-stitch independently.

2. Perform Environmental and Task Analysis

In order to recommend magnification, the low vision optometrist needs to know the required print or object size that someone must see in order to perform each goal task. The therapist can specify this information on the referral form and include this

Table 13-2.

The Standard Collaborative Model for Evaluating Optical Devices

1. Define the Goal Task and Performance Goal.
2. Perform an Environmental and Task Analysis.
    2.1. Working distances?
    2.2. Hands-free device required?
    2.3. Illuminated device required?
    2.4. Work surfaces available?
3. Identify nonvisual impairments.
    3.1. Tremors and impaired fine motor control.
    3.2. Cognitive impairments, impaired problem solving, impaired procedural memory/learning, and impaired frustration tolerance.
4. Identify visual impairments.
    4.1. Functional visual acuity.
    4.2. Contrast sensitivity and optimum lighting.
    4.3. Field restrictions, central scotoma and fixation and scanning performance.
    4.4. Binocular vision problems, if any.
5. Recommend type of optical device(s) for all tasks.
6. In-clinic instruction and device evaluation and final prescription by an optometrist.
7. Instruction in context.

Table 13-3.

Information to Include on Referral to Low Vision Optometrist for a Device Evaluation

- Specific Goal Task and performance requirement (device used for spotting or sustained use; do high productivity requirements exist).
- Specify what the client is trying to see. Specify print sizes, size of television, or have client bring sample.
- Specify special working distance requirements that are not obvious by task description.
- Specify if a task requires both hands.
- Specify tremors, ataxia, or other motor impairments and if a table is available.
- Specify if a device requires built-in illumination.
- Specify significant cognitive and psychosocial impairments.
- Include visual findings such as continuous text acuity, contrast sensitivity, fields, best lighting and, if field loss, visual scanning performance.
- Recommend types of devices to consider.

with the performance goal. Although eyecare providers should have continuous text near acuity charts, few eyecare providers will have real-life objects like cross-stitch patterns. In such cases, the therapist needs to encourage the client to bring in a sample of the object or print she is trying to see. The therapist needs to consider how the device will be held if two hands are required to perform the task, the demand on fine motor skills, and whether a table is available for support. Hands-free optical magnification devices are available that can be mounted on spectacles, or on a table. The required working distances may be obvious to the consulting optometrist from the list of goal tasks, but should be specified if not obvious. In the environmental analysis, the therapist needs to consider if lighting can be controlled; if not, an illuminated device might be recommended. A summary of information that should be included on a referral can be found in Table 13-3. In the case of Ms. Jason, she would be encouraged to bring her cross-stitch to the optometrist, along with samples of bills and medications. The print size required would be specified as "1 M preferred, 2 M possible" because large-print bills and checks may be obtained.

The environmental evaluation revealed that Ms. Jason preferred to do her cross-stitch and watch television in her favorite easy chair, and sort her medication into dispensers as well as pay bills at the kitchen table. In these settings, reading novels and reading bills can be done at any distance, but cross-stitch and writing in the check register cannot be done closer than about 15 cm (8 to 9 inches). She could use one hand to hold a device for most tasks except cross-stitch. She will require a hands-free device for this task.

3. Evaluate Nonvisual Factors

Clients with tremors and impaired fine motor control require devices with support, such as stand magnifiers, and spectacle-mounted rather than handheld magnifiers. Clients with cognitive impairments such as apraxia, impaired problem solving, impaired procedural memory/learning, and impaired frustration tolerance require simple devices with which they had premorbid familiarity, such as low power handheld magnifiers. They require gradual introduction of stronger magnification and are generally poor candidates for handheld telescopes, stand-magnifiers, and microscopes. In the case of Ms. Jason, she was cognitively intact and very detail-oriented with low frustration tolerance and had compensated in past years by structuring her routine and environment and avoiding challenging activities. She was resistant to change. For example, she refused to move her chair or television so she could decrease her viewing distance to the television. The therapist summarized all of the information and shared it with the eyecare provider

who performed the clinical low vision evaluation (see Table 13-3).

4. Evaluate Visual Factors

In the standard model, the eyecare provider should perform most of the visual testing. The therapist may also perform some or all of the following tests (Chapter 8).

- Distance visual acuity, continuous text acuity, and critical print size.
- Contrast sensitivity and the light levels (using a light meter) that produce best contrast sensitivity or acuity. In general, if someone has severe contrast sensitivity impairment, electronic magnification devices (see Chapter 14) are preferred because optical devices degrade contrast, while electronic devices increase contrast.
- Visual fields and description of adaptive visual scanning or eccentric fixation if the client has a central or peripheral field loss.
- Determination of whether the client performs the task more effectively with both eyes open or by patching one eye.

In the case of Ms. Jason, the therapist might specify:

- At 40 cm, 4 M print acuity (0.4/4 M) with her left eye and 0.4 M/8 M critical print size to read fluently and comfortably.
- With letters 4X acuity threshold, she has a moderate loss in contrast threshold (7%) with improvement to mild loss (5%) when light levels were increased to greater than 500 Lux.
- Using the tangent screen method, she was found to have stable superior eccentric fixation with a scotoma size of approximately 15 degrees.

5. Recommend Devices

In the referral to the low vision optometrist, the therapist might recommend specific devices based on the occupational therapy evaluation described above. A summary of the applications of different types of devices is listed in Table 13-4 and will be explained later in this section. In the case of Ms. Jason, for example, the therapist might recommend consideration of a spectacle-mounted telescope for television watching and an objective lens cap to turn the telescope into a telemicroscope for near work for sewing. The therapist might also recommend an electronic table-mounted closed-circuit television (CCTV) for reading and bill paying. The low vision optometrist might then determine the magnification for the telescope, and lower power full field reading glasses to use with the CCTV at 30 cm (10 inches) to allow her to use it more easily. The optometrist also might suggest

Table 13-4.

Magnifier Devices and Typical Applications

Device	Up Close	Far Distance	Arm's Length	Hands-Free	Example
Handheld	Spot	No	Spot	Possible with table and mount	Reading labels, menus, fixing something
Stand	Extended	No	No	No	Reading a letter or catalog
Spectacle reading addition	Extended	No	No	Yes	Reading a book or newspaper
Telescope	No	Yes	Spot with cap	Yes, if mounted on spectacles	Fixing something, reading music, watching TV
Electronic	No	Extended if remote camera is used	Yes	Yes, if worn on head	Reading book, seeing blackboard

short duration—spot, long duration—extended

that Ms. Jason may be able to use a 10 D illuminated handheld device to write large-print checks and keep a register, and since she is already nearsighted, she could hold it to her eye without her glasses for extra magnification, if needed.

6. Grade the Task: The Success-Oriented Approach

In the success-oriented approach, evaluation and initial instruction should emphasize successful performance of a goal task.[1] Starting with the device most likely to enable successful task performance, have the client try the device in a situation that requires little if any learning or skill on the part of the client and with maximum assistance if necessary. This will convince the client that success is possible from the beginning.

The client should experience what it is like to perform the task with a device before facing the challenging task of learning to use it. In the example of

Ms. Jason, before trying needlepoint, the therapist might begin by having her watch television with the telescope since this is easier to accomplish and generally successful. Bill paying would be started with the CCTV because success is more likely, and then a handheld device could be attempted later because it is more difficult to use.

If the result with a particular device is unsuccessful, attempt to identify other performance-limiting factors such as lighting or other visual or physical impairments. Ideally, the eyecare provider participates in this problem solving. In the case of Ms. Jason, if her initial attempts to use the telescope were unsuccessful, larger stitches with less magnification and better lighting might be attempted. During this process, the client is often able to decide if she wants the device. The therapist should try to find one device that meets several needs. In the case of Ms. Jason, with task modification (using larger stitches) she could use the

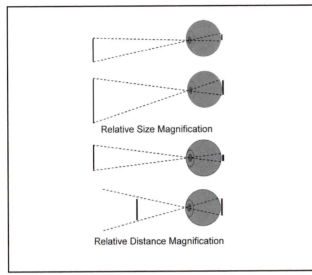

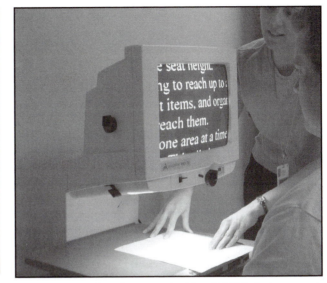

Figure 13-7. Increasing retinal-image size with relative size magnification and relative distance magnification.

Figure 13-8. A closed-circuit television (CCTV) device magnifies, enhancing contrast by reversing and increasing contrast.

same telescope to watch television and perform cross-stitch in a favorite easy chair.

7. Instruct in Natural Context: From Ideal to Real

Once a device is selected and successful performance is accomplished in a controlled instructional setting, the therapist provides instruction in the actual setting or a simulation of the actual setting in which a task will be performed. A client who might insist on a particular seating or environment at first may be inspired to change after experiencing how much easier it is to perform a task under an ideal setup. If a device has been prescribed, the client can practice in her most comfortable setting and report problems to the therapist during scheduled sessions. At this point, sessions can be scheduled less frequently with more emphasis on a home program.

An Overview of Magnification Strategies and Devices

Relative Size and Distance Magnification

Many devices and strategies can magnify objects to compensate for impaired visual acuity. The term magnification has many definitions, but ultimately magnification refers to changing the size of the image of an object on the retina. The most straightforward magnification method to increase the size of an image on the retina is enlargement, or relative size magni-

fication and relative distance magnification (Figure 13-7). Relative size magnification can be accomplished with large print books, enlarging objects on a copy machine, using larger stitches in a needlepoint task or using electronic devices such as the CCTV system illustrated in Figure 13-8 (more fully described in Chapter 14). If a device being used does not have sufficient magnification, the therapist can compensate by enlarging the material being viewed.

Another strategy the therapist can use if device magnification is not sufficient is relative distance magnification, which is moving a client closer to the material being viewed. However, one must be careful using relative distance magnification with near devices; usually a different device must be used if a person needs to move closer to the object. Handheld magnifiers, spectacle near reading addition, and stand magnifiers must be used at prescribed distances. Telescopes, however, can be refocused at different distances, so if a telescope is not strong enough, the client can move closer and refocus to achieve increased overall magnification. With some devices like telescopes, magnification depends on how far the device is positioned from the object being viewed—the device-to-object distance.

Magnification and Field of View

Clients ideally want a device that will allow magnification while maintaining a large field of view and a normal working distance. Unfortunately, regardless of the optical device used, there are some universal trade-offs. As magnification increases, field of view necessarily decreases (Figure 13-9). This is easy to

Figure 13-9. Three views through a 10 D handheld magnifier held with a 40 cm eye-to-lens distance (top), a closer eye-to-lens distance (middle). Lens-to-paper distance did not change. Note magnification does not change but field of view does change. Eye-to-lens distance in the middle and bottom pictures are the same. Field of view increases only because magnification decreases from the middle lens to the bottom lens.

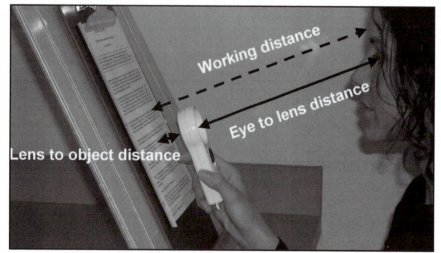

Figure 13-10. An illustration of working distance, eye-to-lens distance and lens-to-object (page of text) distance.

understand, because as the image is enlarged, less of it will fit in the person's visual field. Secondly, the field of view through a device also depends on the eye to lens distance.

Positioning a Device

When using devices, the following important distances must be carefully considered (Figure 13-10).

1. Lens-to object-distance is the distance of the lens from the object or page being viewed. The lens-to-object distance determines if the object is in focus or not and with some devices magnification is affected by lens to object distance. With a stand magnifier, a stand holds the lens at a fixed distance from the page being viewed to control the lens-to-object distance.

2. Eye-to-lens distance is the distance of the eye from the lens, or in the case of a telescope or multilens system, the distance from the lens closest to the eye (the ocular) and the eye. In general, eye-to-lens distance affects field of view: the closer the lens is to the eye, the larger the field of view.

3. Working or viewing distance refers to how far the eye is from the object being viewed.

Depth of focus describes how much one might change the lens distance and still keep the object in focus. As near optical devices become more powerful, the working distance and depth of focus decreases. For example, someone using a 5 D handheld magnifier may vary 20 to 30 mm from the 20 lens distance without significant defocus. With a 20 D magnifier, a change of 5 to 7 mm will produce significant defocus. Telescopes and telemicroscopes may vary in depth of focus depending on design and focus distance.

Figure 13-11. Top view through a simple lens. The bottom view is through the Clear Image Lens (courtesy of Designs for Vision) that is designed to decrease optical aberrations.

Light Transmittance, Contrast Degradation, and Chromatic Aberration

When a client looks through some optical devices, especially telescopes, light decreases significantly. Lenses also pick up reflections from extraneous lights, such as overhead lights in a room, and poorer quality lenses will scatter light and degrade the contrast of objects being viewed. Antireflective coatings, the use of visors, shielding the lens from light, and positioning light from the side so it does not reflect off of the lens will greatly improve lens performance. Very strong, simple lenses act like prisms and turn white light into component colors at the edges and blur the image (Figure 13-11). This is called chromatic aberration. Newer, often more expensive, compound lenses have not only become thin and light but they have included layers of refraction and defraction-type optics that eliminate chromatic aberration. Clients differ in their sensitivity to chromatic aberration. It is

reasonable to suspect that clients who are sensitive to glare and have impaired contrast sensitivity will be more sensitive to reflections off of the lenses, defocus, and chromatic aberrations.

Movement

Devices not only magnify the size of objects being viewed but also magnify the motion of objects being viewed by the same amount. We all have experienced how difficult it is to hold a pair of powerful binoculars steady, as the motion greatly degrades what is being viewed. Stronger magnifiers require higher levels of fine motor control and visual motor coordination, or external supports and bracing to reduce this movement. Motion sickness can sometimes result from this movement magnification.

Properties of Optical Devices

High Near-Addition (Full Field Microscopes) and Loupes

A client young enough to accommodate (focus his eyes) at a close viewing distance might use relative distance magnification, simply moving his eye closer to the text or objects being viewed. An older adult will require microscopes, also called NVO (near vision only) reading glasses, to read up close (see Figure 13-1). A near add is essentially plus power lens "added" to a person's distance correction. A near addition or lenses that focus at near may take the form of bifocals, or variable focus lenses (progressive lenses or no-line bifocals) in the bottom segment of spectacle lens. In some cases, the plus lenses are actually mounted in front of a person's eyes or eyeglasses in the form of loupes or visors (Figure 13-12). Half-eyes or NVO glasses are used only for near work or reading. Low vision practitioners often refer to high add NVO glasses as microscopes (see Figures 13-1 and 13-11). NVO glasses are generally preferred over bifocals with higher adds because with high add a client's distance view through the bottom segment becomes defocused at near and might impair his or her ability to see objects directly in front while walking. In addition, NVO glasses enable a broader field of view than bifocals. Progressive or variable focus lenses can be prescribed by the eyecare professional for clients working on machinery, or doing repair work, crafts, fine furniture, or other tasks in which the client must focus at various distances.

Loupes are plus lenses that clip onto spectacles. Loupes in the form of visors fit on someone's head in front of the eyes or spectacles (see Figure 13-12). Some have multiple lenses, allowing one to change add depending on the task. The head visors are a favorite

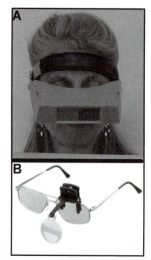

Figure 13-12. A. Visor loupe magnifier generally provides some glare control. B. A spectacle-clip loupe for near magnification (photo courtesy of Eschenbach Optik of America, Ridgefield, CT).

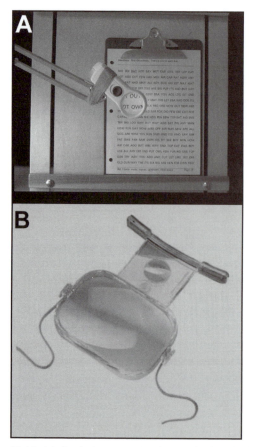

Figure 13-13. Methods for mounting lenses for hands-free use. A. "Gerry-rigged" holder for a magnifier from an old lamp stand. B. Chest magnifier (courtesy of Eschenbach Optik of America, Ridgefield, CT). See also Figure 13-2C.

because they easily flip up out of the way, and the shroud blocks extraneous light from producing glare. For users working in a shop, these devices afford some degree of eye protection as well. These are stronger than typical reading glasses.

Relative distance magnification and microscopes require that the client learn to perform a task at a closer than normal working distance. Stronger microscopes also require precise motor control or some external support to maintain the lens-to-object distance and to carefully move the material being read.

Important Properties of High Near Addition or Microscopes

- High reading addition, microscopes, and loupes are often preferred to a handheld magnifier for extended reading.

- If the client is unable to accommodate (focus at near), lens-to-object distance in centimeters is fixed. A person younger than 40 can bring an object closer to achieve additional magnification and still keep it in focus.

- With higher magnification, working distance is a few inches and the object can go out of focus if not held at the exact distance. External support or good fine motor skills are required.

- With higher magnification, maintaining good lighting becomes more of a problem.

- Because the lens is close to the eye, the client's visual field through the device is not restricted by optics.

- If a handheld magnifier is held against the reading addition, the power of the lenses will add together.

Handheld Magnifiers

Most clients will be familiar with handheld magnifiers (see Figure 13-2), more commonly called magnifying glasses. Handheld magnifiers are the least expensive and most versatile magnification device. Handheld magnifiers might also be mounted to a table or on a string around the neck to allow a client to use both hands (Figure 13-13). A client can hold the magnifier at any distance from the eye, bringing it closer to increase the field of view. When held close to the eye, the handheld magnifier functions just like a microscope. Like the microscope, the stronger handheld magnifier requires a close lens-to-object distance, and good fine-motor control to maintain this distance and to control the position of the magnifier to avoid losing one's place.

Handheld magnifiers are usually used for short periods of time. Examples include spot reading, such

as reading price tags, bills and labels, checking medication, checking skin or fingernails, or reading menus. For sustained tasks, the user often quickly fatigues because the magnifier must be held at the precise distance from the objects being viewed. For more sustained work, such as sewing, using near addition, spectacle clip-ons, visors, or stand magnifiers is preferred.

Important Properties of Handheld Magnifiers

- Handheld magnifiers are usually used for spotting rather than extended use.
- Lens-to-object distance is fixed and can be determined by lifting the lens away from a page until it focuses the image of a distant light onto the page, or maximizes magnification and focus of an object viewed through the lens. If the power of the device is known, lens-to-object distance in centimeters also can be estimated as 100 cm/D. For example, a handheld magnifier labeled as a 20 D lens would have a lens-to-object distance of $100/20 = 5$ cm.
- Decreasing eye-to-lens distance increases the field of view (see Figure 13-9).
- If the magnifier is held away from the eye, the client looks through the distance (upper) segment of eyeglasses, or without glasses if he or she does not wear correction for distance.
- The client looks through the bifocal addition or reading addition if the lens is held close to the eye. The combined effect of reading addition and the magnifier will increase overall magnification.
- A lens with a larger diameter has a lower power. Larger diameter lenses have a larger field of view, mostly because of lower power. Rectangular magnifiers are available to increase horizontal field of view, but these are available only for low power magnification.
- Lower power handheld devices are quite forgiving if not positioned correctly; higher power devices are not forgiving and should not be used for people with tremors, apraxia, incoordination, or if hand function is limited by problems such as severe arthritis.
- Lighting should ideally be directed from the side and aimed between the magnifier and the material/object being viewed.
- Illuminated handheld magnifiers with built in LED light sources are generally recommended, especially with stronger magnifiers. Therapists are cautioned to avoid inexpensive illuminated handheld magnifiers with poor switches or regular bulbs and should caution users against

them. Broken switches and problems with batteries easily consume considerable clinical time, disable performance, and irritate everyone involved.

Stand Magnifiers

A stand magnifier (Figure 13-3) can be used if a client does not have the endurance or fine motor control to hold the handheld magnifier at the correct distance. Stand magnifiers usually require that the client work on a table or hard surface. Stand magnifiers are used for reading. One simply rests base of the stand magnifier on the page and the stand itself maintains the correct object-to-lens distance. The stand magnifier, however, is not as versatile as the handheld magnifier. Stand magnifiers require a flat surface. These devices are usually designed so that user can easily maintain a given distance from the magnifier to keep the print in focus.

Important Properties of Stand Magnifiers

- The client looks through the bottom half of bifocals or reading eyeglasses with the stand magnifier positioned at a prescribed eye-to-lens distance. The prescribing optometrist should provide information about eye-to-lens distance and what reading glasses to use. Calculating these distances is addressed in the Advanced section of this chapter.
- These devices are generally preferred if someone with impaired motor control needs to use a higher magnification.
- These devices are generally preferred over handheld magnifiers for extended reading.
- Higher magnification devices should have built-in illumination. Lower power stand magnifiers (Figure 13-14) are available as bar readers or some are adapted for writing as well as reading.

Telescopes and Telemicroscopes

Devices that are used for seeing sports events, theater, the television at distance or recognizing faces or reading signs are distance devices. Telescopes and binoculars can be handheld or spectacle-mounted (see Figures 13-4 and 13-5). Spectacle-mounted telescopes may also be mounted on the top of the lens so the client can look through the bottom half of the lenses while moving about, then stop and look through the lens to read a sign or identify someone. This is referred to as a bioptic mount (Figure 13-15). In many states, people with low vision can legally drive with bioptic-mounted telescopes. Spectacle-mounted telescopes stabilize the device and allow both hands to be free. Spectacle mounting, however, positions the telescope further from the eye and, thus, reduces the field

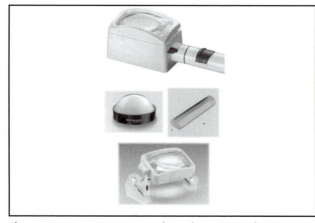

Figure 13-14. An assortment of stand-type magnifiers. Illuminated stand magnifier (top), bright field and bar magnifier (middle), and magnifier designed for writing (photos courtesy of Eschenbach Optik of America, Ridgefield, CT).

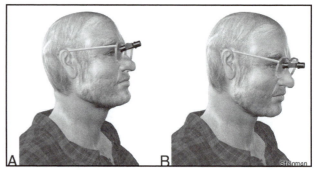

Figure 13-15. Bioptic mount. Someone looking through the carrier lens for a full-field view and the telescope for a magnified view of a target (Steinman).

of view. Various mounting strategies and devices are available that allow the eyecare practitioner to mount the ocular closer to the eye and incorporate correction into the ocular of the telescope. Furthermore, the devices should be mounted to maintain telescopic alignment with the optical axis of the eye. For these reasons, telescopic systems should only be dispensed by an optometrist or ophthalmologist.

Telescopes can be fitted with an extra removable lens that fits over the lens farthest from the eye (the objective lens) to enable the telescope to focus at near (see Figure 13-4). A telescope that focuses at near is called a telemicroscope (see Figure 13-5). As anyone who has used binoculars might attest, telescopes and telemicroscopes require good coordination, adaptable visual motor skills, and good fine motor control to focus and use effectively. Spectacle mounting stabilizes the telescope or binocular and makes it much easier to use, but creates cosmetic problems.

Under controlled laboratory circumstances, image motion seems to be the major impediment to the use of telescopes;[2] however, cost and cosmesis are certainly important factors as well. A person seen by the public looking through a telescope at other people may be viewed as spying or nosy. Spectacle-mounted devices may be perceived as odd looking. Imagine a young man or woman with low vision at a party trying to discreetly "check out" someone across the room with a telescope. Imagine an elderly person with low vision watching people out of the front window in her neighborhood through a telescope.

Often telescopes are dispensed to be handheld, as these are cosmetically the most acceptable and are least expensive (see Figure 13-4). These devices may be worn around the neck or can be worn as a ring.

If the user wants to see something, he holds the telescope in front of his eye. A more stable view is usually achieved by holding the telescope in the webspace (Figure 13-16A) so that the hand hides the telescope from the view of others. More cosmetically acceptable spectacle-mounted devices are mounted above the glasses, having a box shape that can be hardly identified as a telescope (see Figure 13-16C). This and other devices may be further hidden under the brim of a hat that also shields the optical elements and client's eyes from light glare (see Figure 13-16B). Someone watching television in the privacy of his own home or watching a sports event often prefers center-mount devices. Clip-on telescopes may be clipped onto spectacles that correct refractive error (Figure 13-17). Recall that a simple alternative to the center-mount device that enables someone to maintain a full field of view, is to use relative distance magnification (bring the television screen closer or sit closer to the action), a simpler alternative that always should be considered before telescopes are recommended. Inexpensive, lightweight telescopes with good optics are now available for watching television (see Figure 13-17).

Important Properties of Telescopes

- The closer the ocular lens is to the eye, the larger the field of view.

- Viewing through eyeglasses or mounting on eyeglasses generally results in a smaller field of view than holding the ocular lens to the eye.

- For people with myopia or hyperopia without significant astigmatism, the telescope can be focused to compensate for the refractive error and held against the eye.

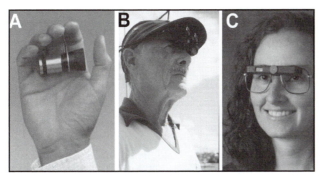

Figure 13-16. Various telescope configurations that are more cosmetically accepted. A. Handheld, note clip between index and long finger (courtesy of Eschenbach Optik of America, Ridgefield, CT). B. Beecher-Mirage using a hat for glare control and to hide the device from others during sailing competition. C. An Ocutech Keplerian telescope in a bioptic (photo courtesy of Ocutech).

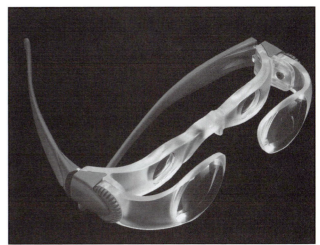

Figure 13-17. Lower power spectacle telescope ideal for TV watching (photo courtesy of Eschenbach Optik of America, Ridgefield, CT).

- For people with significant astigmatism, the telescope should be viewed through corrective eyeglasses or contact lenses, or special telescopes can be made to correct refractive error.

- For those with tremor, arthritis, or impaired fine motor control, telescopes should be mounted on eyeglasses or a headband.

- Galilean type telescopes have magnifications up to about 4X, are smaller, lighter, and have a smaller field of view.

- Keplerian type telescopes have magnifications greater than 3X, are often larger and heavier, and have a larger field of view.

- Telescopes reduce the amount of light. The larger the objective lens (far lens), the more light is transmitted through the telescope.

- Telescopes can be focused closer to about 1 M. A special cap can be purchased that fits over the objective lens to allow the telescope to focus closer, turning it into a telemicroscope.

Electronic Devices

Electronic versions of several optical magnification devices are emerging in the marketplace. Examples discussed in Chapter 14 include head-mounted CCTV devices that focus at distance and near like telescopes. Handheld devices act much like stand magnifiers, except the magnified image is displaced on a screen on top of the device. The advantage of electronic devices is the potential to enhance contrast as well as magnify the object being viewed.

Instruction on Device Use

General Strategies for Success-Oriented Instruction

- Complete eccentric fixation training or training on specific compensatory scanning strategies (see Chapter 9) before recommending devices or providing instruction with those devices. Often a person's functional visual acuity will change as a result of this instruction. In some cases, devices may be used as part of eccentric fixation instruction.

- It is often, but not always, advisable to begin instruction at the full magnification that the client will eventually be required to use. Grading the activity by gradually increasing device power requires that working distance, focusing, and lighting strategies be relearned as well. Grade the activity by gradually withdrawing assistance with the manipulation of the device or materials. If the client resists the magnification, consider modifying the task to decrease magnification demand, using large print for example. One might later return to the more demanding task and increased magnification once the skills with a lower power device are mastered.

- Instruction is not complete unless the client is taught not only how to use the device for a goal task, but how to maintain the device, store it for ready access, and solve common problems with a device such as how to change batteries.

Figure 13-18. Scrolling technique where the reading material is moved from right to left in a smooth continuous motion in front of a stationary optical magnification device such as a mounted magnifier (shown) or full-field microscope (see Figure 13-1).

With all devices, the training activities[3] from easier to most difficult are as follows.

- *Align, focus and fixate.* Have the client align the device, focus the device, and keep a single letter or word in focus. The client keeps the device steady while the therapist moves the material in front of the magnification device. Position playing cards in front of the device or move a line of text from right to left in front of the device (Figure 13-18). Intentionally change the focus and alignment of the device until the client self-corrects consistently.

- *Manage lighting.* Instruct the client to adjust lighting to avoid glare and reflections off of the optical surfaces (Figure 13-19).

- *Localization and spotting.* Have the client find an object that is large enough to see unaided with the magnification device. For example, with a telescope, the client carefully fixates the shape of someone standing across the room. While maintaining fixation on the person, the user positions the telescope in front of his eye to see the details (Figure 13-20). With an electric bill, for example, even if she cannot read individual words, a client might see where the lines of print begin and end without the device. The client then looks where he or she thinks a total might be located using the overall layout of the text and without averting gaze, positions a handheld or stand magnifier over the spot to read the total.

- *Tracking.* Slowly move the object being fixated and have the client follow the movement, gradually increasing the movement speed. Challenge the client's ability to correct focus and device alignment and not lose the target.

Figure 13-19. Poor (top) and good (bottom) posture using a handheld magnifier. Top: Working tabletop encourages poor posture and a tilted positioning of the magnifier relative to the eye and object, as well as exacerbates optical reflections (see insert) and shadows from overhead light. Bottom: Use of a reading stand encourages better posture and correct positioning of the device (perpendicular to the line of sight). The hat brim reduces glare from room lights and directional light is used rather than overhead lights to eliminate lens reflections. The typoscope decreases glare from the page.

- *Scanning and tracing.* Scanning and tracing are methods to skim a space to look for something. With a handheld device or stand magnifier, the client learns to move the magnifier from left to right over a line of text while maintaining gaze at the center of the device, in coordinated

head and hand movement. In some cases, the clients skim text by quickly following lines of text, stopping and reading a couple of words at a time, then skimming over several words until the information they are looking for is found. Scanning and tracing with a telescope requires the client to recognize and follow contours, such as following a sign-post up to the top where the street sign can be read.

- *Moving.* An advanced technique is to have the client practice using a device on an unstable surface, holding the object of interest in one hand while standing. Clients may also need to learn to spot through a bioptic telescope while driving a wheelchair or car, or while walking without stopping.

Specific Strategies for Near Additions, Microscopes, Visors, and Loupes

Ergonomics and Common Applications

Ergonomics becomes a significant issue with closer lens distances that require people to lean forward, and requires precise maintenance of lens distance. This is especially true for a client who is somewhat deconditioned or frail because fatigued muscles become unstable and lose precise control. In general, the therapist should attempt to maintain the approximately 90-90-90 posture for maximum stability and minimum muscle strain during reading. If the client reads or works at a table, the use of a reading stand and directional lighting will enable the client to hold the material steady and sit up straight (see Figures 13-14 and 13-19). If the user leans forward, one hand might be used to support the head with an elbow on the table to relieve neck and back strain. Users often prefer to read with these devices in a favorite easy chair. Lap trays may be used and other forms of elbow support might help the client steady the material and maintain support for the head and spine as one transitions from the artificial instructional setup to a simulation of the client's home situation.

Optimize lighting by turning off overhead lights. Introduce directional lighting from the side aimed between the lens and paper, being careful to avoid reflections and glare. Use a hat brim or visor to eliminate reflections from the optical surfaces of the glasses from overhead lights.

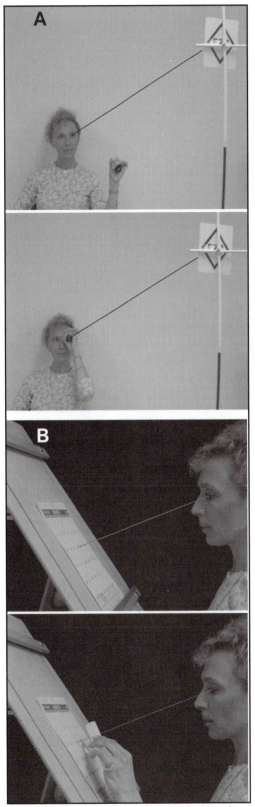

Figure 13-20. Spotting technique with a handheld telescope (A) and a handheld magnifier (B).

Overall Instructional Strategy

If the client wishes to recover continuous reading, use graded materials in available workbooks such as the LUV reading series (see Chapter 9). A typical instructional sequence might include the following:

1. Setup and light. Start in an artificial work setting most likely to produce successful task performance and allow sufficient control to identify specific impediments. Have the client sit at table with good (90-90-90) posture using a reading stand (see Figure 13-14). Use a typoscope (a black card with a window cut out or contrasting ruler to help the client keep his place and reduce glare). Teach the client how to position the light.

2. Grade the activity. Begin with enlarged samples of the materials that the client wishes to read with an uncluttered layout. Use playing cards, numbers, or single short words. When reading, use a scrolling or steady-eye technique. The head is kept steady while staring straight ahead. Move a line of text from right to left in front while the client stares straight ahead so the words move to the point on the page where a client is looking. This strategy is most effective if someone with maculopathy is trying to maintain eccentric fixation (see Figure 13-18).

3. Align, focus, and fixate. Instruct the client to control lens-to-object distance and keep alignment of the lens to paper parallel. This is done by intentionally positioning the paper incorrectly and having the client correct the problem. For example, the therapist can purposely begin with the device too close or far from the object. The client adjusts the eye-to-paper distance until the object is in focus. Next, have the client perform controlled rotations of the working material held in his hand so that the lens is no longer parallel to the paper, then correct the problem so the paper is parallel to the lens.

4. Localization and spotting is possible with half-eyes because a client can look over the lens to approximate where to begin reading, then bring the paper to the correct distance, and while still maintaining fixation on the target, tilt her head up to look through the device. With full field microscopes this is more difficult.

5. Scrolling. To instruct the client about how to scan, begin with hand-over-hand assistance. Slowly scroll the print from left to right in front of the microscope at the correct distance. To minimize fatigue, the client should move the paper rather than his head. Loose paper should be attached to a clipboard. Gradually withdraw assistance and finally increase task demand by performing tracing/skimming type tasks such as finding the total number of simple words (eg, "the", "it") in a paragraph or a number in a phone book.

6. Writing and nonreading tasks. If the device is to be used with nonreading tasks or writing, these tasks should be introduced after reading instruction.

7. Natural context. Once good performance has been achieved under controlled circumstances, begin changing the situation to match the home environment. Change seating, external supports, and lighting according to the client's preferred task environment and educate the client regarding the effects of each change. Help the client develop changes in positioning and introduce supports to enable task performance. Consider hats to eliminate reflections on optical surfaces and glare. To decrease light or the effect of uncontrollable glare sources, consider lightly tinted wraparound sunlenses.

8. Home program. Once the device has been prescribed, develop a home program with materials graded in size, duration, and task difficulty.

Common Difficulties and Solutions

The client never sees the object or reads print as predicted

- Using large high-contrast letters or thick lines, check focus by having the client hold the print against the glasses, then gradually increase lens-to-object distance until the image appears to clear.

- Make sure the client is looking through the center of the lens.

- With high magnification lenses, use a support or a spacer between the lens and paper to maintain focal distance.

- Turn off overhead lights, adjust lighting wearing a brimmed hat.

- Recheck near acuity.

- With certain conditions such as with vitreous floaters, acuity may vary within a session, or with diabetes, from session to session.

- Try larger letters, as the device may have insufficient magnification.

Intermittent object or print recognition

- Check lighting.

- Check for central scotomas or floaters.
- Check to make sure the client is viewing through center of lens.
- Consider lenses with less distortion.
- The client with macular scotoma may require additional eccentric fixation practice.

Cannot maintain focal distance

- Rest head on hand with elbow on the table using a reading stand to bring the material closer to the lens.

Inadequate light

- Bring the light source closer and aim the light toward the page from the side.
- Be careful to avoid glare and reflections from the surface of the lenses.

Distortion

- Use better quality optics with less distortion.
- Look through the center of the lens at a closer distance.
- Move it closer to the object being viewed.

Quick fatigue and complaints of headache

- Stop immediately, give the client a rest, and change the task.
- Check to make sure lens is at correct distance from the page.
- At close working distances, a change in distance of a few millimeters may significantly change accommodative demand, and in a younger client, stress the accommodative system.
- Rule out inadequate magnification by enlarging print and rechecking.
- Patch the eye with the poorer vision to rule out binocular problems.
- Check posture.
- Task stress may increase blood pressure.
- The client may be developing hypotension, a precursor to motion sickness.

Motion sickness

- If the client starts to perspire, reports a sudden headache, reports feeling cold, or has a measurable drop in blood pressure, stop immediately. These symptoms are precursors to nausea associated with motion sickness.
- Decrease field of view by using a handheld device.
- Reduce head motion during reading.
- Reduce irregular image motion such as a shaking image by stabilizing the material being viewed on a reading stand.

Loses place when reading

- Use a typoscope, dark ruler, or finger to keep one's place.

Specific Strategies for Handheld Devices

Most clients have prior familiarity with lower power handheld devices, and thus must be carefully instructed if higher power devices are prescribed. Handheld magnifiers are used at about arm's length when spotting, reading a label, or checking skin or nails, or up close to the eye to maximize the field of view for more sustained reading.

Ergonomics and Lighting

Start in an artificial work setting that optimizes vision and ergonomics. Have the client sit at a table with good (90-90-90) posture using a reading stand. Provide support for the hand to help maintain working distance. Optimize lighting by turning off overhead lights and introduce directional lighting from the side. Vary illumination until the best reading speed is achieved. Demonstrate the effects of glare and overhead lights. Reflections on optical surfaces are a common problem with handheld devices. Teach the client to identify offending lights, then position the body or a hat brim to block reflections from overhead lights. If a client is glare sensitive, consider lightly tinted wraparound sunlenses and antireflective coatings on optics.

Ancillary Equipment

- A reading stand or lap tray.
- A directional light with a deep shade so it directs light to a very specific location under the lens of the magnifier.
- A typoscope, dark ruler, or straight edge.
- Firm pads on which the wrist or an arm might rest.
- Tape or clipboard to secure the reading material.
- A clamp stand or chest stand to hold a handheld magnifier, allowing hands-free use.

Interaction With Corrective Lenses

When reading through the bottom half of bifocal (the near segment of the lens) or reading glasses, bringing a handheld magnifier closer will not only increase field of view, power will increase as well. When the eye-to-lens distance increases, the user should look through the top half of the glasses, the distance segment of the lens. If the user does not wear glasses for distance, then glasses should not be worn when using the handheld magnifier. If the user holds the handheld magnifier further than about 40 cm from the eye, looking through the lower half of bifo-

cal lenses or reading glasses will actually decrease magnification when compared with looking through the upper distance segment of the lens.

Stand magnifiers are usually designed to be used at an intermediate distance while the client is looking through the reading addition or bottom half of bifocals.

Device Stabilization Strategies

For clients who wish to perform craft or sewing activities, table-mounted magnifiers, usually with light incorporated, are available commercially. Weak handheld devices are readily available in sewing stores that can be hung around the neck to enable hands free use (see Figure 13-13). Smaller, stronger lenses are often incorporated into the larger lens. Commercially available devices are usually low power (under 5 D).

Mounts for handheld devices are limited, however, only by the creativity of the therapist. The low vision clinic should be equipped with a bin of salvaged table clamps, flexible arms and tubing, and splinting material (see Figure 13-13). With a hot glue gun, the therapist can quickly develop a prototype of a lens mount, customized to a client's particular application. Hot glue can be peeled off to modify a design but is not usually durable enough for permanent use. The final product could be fabricated using splinting material to hold the handle of the device to the arm.

Instruction for Handheld Magnifiers

1. Set up and lighting. Start in an artificial work setting most likely to produce successful task performance and allow sufficient control to identify specific impediments. Have the client sit at a table with good (90-90-90) posture using a reading stand. Use a typoscope. Teach the client how to position the light.

2. Grade the task. Begin with enlarged samples of the materials that the client wishes to read and use an uncluttered layout. Initially provide hand-over-hand assistance. Start by laying the lens on the material and providing a slow, controlled increase in lens-to-object distance to well beyond the focal distance and describing the visual effect.

3. Align, focus, and fixate. Instruct the client to control lens distance and align his or her line of sight with the center of the optics. Intentionally position the magnifier incorrectly and have the client correct the problem. Since handheld magnifiers are often used under varied, uncontrolled situations such as shopping, the client should be taught how to solve problems with these devices. To teach the client to hold the device parallel to the paper, have him or her perform controlled rotations of the lens so that it is no longer parallel to the paper. Demonstrate how failure to view through the center of the lens produces optical distortions. Contrive incorrect lens-eye-material positioning and have the client correct the positioning.

4. Device management. Gradually withdraw hand and wrist supports. If such support is necessary, consider stand magnifiers or head-mounted devices such as loupes or microscopes.

5. Spotting/localizing. Instruct the client on how to spot information with the device. Orient the client to the lines of print or borders of columns and ask him/her to estimate where the information might be by first looking where it is expected to be located and then, without averting his gaze, placing the magnifier over that spot (see Figure 13-20).

6. For scanning, start with hand-over-hand assistance. Slowly have the client scan a line of text with a coordinated hand and head movement from left to right. Gradually withdraw assistance and finally increase task demand by performing tracing/skimming type tasks such as finding the total number of simple words (eg, "the" or "it") in a paragraph, a number in a phone book, or a dosage on a medicine label.

Common Difficulties and Solutions with Handheld Magnifiers

The client never resolved the object or read print as predicted

- Check focus by checking alignment of glasses, and determine whether the client views through distance segment.
- Check the focus of the handheld device by gradually lifting it from the page to a little less than the focal distance.
- Check for optical distortion, and try better quality optics.
- Turn off overhead lights and adjust lighting.
- Recheck near acuity.
- With certain conditions, such as vitreous floaters, acuity may vary within a session or with diabetes, from session to session.

Intermittent object or print recognition

- Check lighting.
- Check for central scotomas or floaters.
- Check to make sure the client is viewing through center of lens.

- Consider a lens with less distortion.
- The client with macular scotoma may require additional eccentric fixation practice.

Inadequate field of view
- Decrease eye-to-lens distance.
- Consider a microscope.

Inadequate light
- Switch to an illuminated magnifier.
- Direct light between the lens and the paper.

Quick fatigue and complaints of headache
- Stop immediately, give the client a rest, and change the task.
- Rule out inadequate magnification by enlarging print and rechecking.
- Check that the lens-to-object distance is at the focal distance.
- Patch the eye with poorer vision to rule out binocular problems.
- Check posture.
- Task stress may increase blood pressure.
- The client may be developing hypotension and precursor to motion sickness.

Motion sickness
- If the client starts to perspire, reports feeling cold, or has a measurable drop in blood pressure, stop immediately. These symptoms are precursors to nausea associated with motion sickness.
- Decrease field of view by increasing eye-to-lens distance.
- Reduce head motion during reading.
- Reduce irregular image motion, a shaking image, by working on a firm surface and using a handheld magnifier.

Loses place when reading
- Use a typoscope, contrasting ruler, or finger to keep one's place.

Specific Strategies for Stand Magnifiers

Instruction is identical to instruction for the handheld magnifier except the client does not need to be instructed how to align and position the lens relative to the paper being read.

Instruct the client to keep the stand firmly against the page being read. You do not need to teach the client how to control lens-to-object distance and position.

The client looks through the reading glasses and at a prescribed eye-to-lens distance. Demonstrate the effects of viewing at various distances or without the

reading glasses prescribed for the device. In some cases, these effects will be minimal.

Common Difficulties and Solutions With Stand Magnifiers

The client never resolved the object or read print as predicted
- Check focus by checking alignment of glasses, and determine whether the client views through the bifocal or reading glasses.
- Check for optical distortion, and try better quality optics.
- Turn off overhead lights and adjust lighting.
- Recheck near acuity.
- Enlarge the print.
- With certain conditions, such as vitreous floaters, acuity may vary within a session, or with diabetes, from session to session.

Intermittent object or print recognition
- Check lighting.
- Check for central scotomas or floaters.
- Check to make sure the client is viewing through center of lens.
- Consider a lens with less distortion.
- The client with macular scotoma may require additional eccentric fixation practice.

Inadequate field of view
- Decrease eye-to-lens distance.
- Consider a microscope.

Inadequate light
- Switch to an illuminated magnifier.
- Direct light between the lens and the paper.

Quick fatigue and complaints of headache
- Stop immediately, give the client a rest, and change the task.
- Check to make sure magnifier is at correct distance or the client is at the correct distance from a stand magnifier.
- Rule out inadequate magnification by enlarging print and rechecking.
- Patch the eye with poorer vision to rule out binocular problems.
- Check posture. Use a reading stand.
- Task stress may increase blood pressure.
- The client may be developing hypotension and precursor to motion sickness.

Motion sickness
- If the client starts to perspire, reports feeling cold, or has a measurable drop in blood pres-

sure, stop immediately. These symptoms are precursors to nausea associated with motion sickness.

- Reduce head motion during reading.
- Reduce irregular image motion, a shaking image, by working on a firm surface and using a handheld magnifier.

Loses place when reading
- Use a typoscope, contrasting ruler, or finger to keep one's place.
- Slide the device along a straightedge, and secure page being read.

Specific Strategies for Telescopes

Overall Instructional Strategy

In general, users of telescopes or binoculars, whether handheld or mounted, should be warned to always stop moving before looking through the device. These devices are more stable if someone stops and supports the device or his head. For example, if a client is spotting a street sign, he could lean against something while spotting. As an exception to this rule, users may be taught how to use a bioptic during driving or power wheelchair use as a special advanced technique. A person wearing center-mount "sports glasses" to watch television often reduces motion through the telescope if he reclines slightly and rests his head on a headrest. Again, ergonomics is critical for near tasks. For example, Ms. Jason would perform her needlework more comfortably if the work were on a raised table so she could sit up straight. The head is more stable if aligned with the spinal column, and she would be more comfortable and the device more stable.

1. Setup. Reassure the client that the task will eventually be adapted to the preferred work environment. Start in an artificial work setting most likely to produce successful task performance and allow sufficient control to identify specific impediments. Have the client sit at a high table with good (90-90-90) posture, resting the elbows on the table while holding the telescope in front of the eye. The user should face a large board with lines of sequential numbers that are large enough to be seen through the telescope. Without the telescope, the client should ideally see the numbers as blobs. The poster board should be positioned against a contrasting wall with an uncluttered background at a distance greater than 3 M (9 feet) from the user. This allows the user to locate the object if out of focus and identify

where the telescope is pointed. If quick learning is anticipated, a television can be substituted for the poster board.

2. Lighting. As telescopes often reduce light, the target should be well lighted. Instruct the client to use a hat brim or visor to shade optical surfaces of the glasses and telescope from overhead lights.

3. Device familiarization. Have the client learn to identify the ocular, objective lens, the focusing knob and whether it is focused all the way to distance or near without looking through it. If used with glasses, fold the eye cup back so it can be pressed against the lens of the glasses. Have the client describe a strategy for storing and cleaning the device. Have the client set the focus for distance before starting.

4. Align. The user should first master alignment and positioning. The ocular end of the telescope should be held in the webspace, not the fingertips, for maximum stability. It should be held as close to the eye as possible to maximize field of view. If properly aligned, the telescope should have a round view, as a crescent view indicates misalignment. With a light shining on the eye, the therapist should be able to look through the objective lens and visualize the user's eye looking back through the telescope--if the telescope is aligned with the eye. Note that a client with macular scotoma may report no view because he or she is not eccentrically viewing properly; central fixation will result in no vision. Mastery of this step requires the client bring the telescope to the eye, quickly align it, and report what he is viewing.

5. Focus and fixate. Begin with the telescope focused at distance. By changing the distance from a board with high-contrast letters, have the client refocus after he has aligned the telescope with the board.

6. Localization/spotting with real life tasks. Ask the client to look to the spot where he would expect to find a particular number on the board without the telescope (see Figure 13-18). The therapist can assist the client by pointing, then having the client bring the telescope in front of the eye without averting gaze and focus the telescope. When the client masters this procedure, the therapist can begin training with real-life goal tasks such as spotting and recognizing people, a television screen, and a piece of furniture at different distances. Repeat these tasks with the client using hearing to estimate the location of a target.

7. Tracking. Have the client look at someone or something in your hand and continue to follow it as it moves. Then have the client localize and track someone walking in the room.

8. Grading the task. Have the client perform the tasks described above while seated and leaning on the elbow of the hand holding the device, then without elbow supports, and finally, while standing. When standing, the client should stabilize the telescope by holding the elbow against the body. The client should lean against something to avoid body sway. If the client cannot stabilize the handheld telescope, consider a spectacle-mounted device. At this point, the device can be dispensed and practice at home can begin.

9. Tracing and scanning. This difficult step should begin only after all procures listed above have been mastered. Starting in a familiar space, have the client follow contours such as baseboards, room corners, ceiling edges, door frames, curbs, or signposts to find signs and objects in the room. Have the client do the same to check out other people and discuss discretion. Finally, have the client perform systematic scanning techniques such as scanning a blackboard for a word, a poster of a group of people for a familiar face, or a room for a particular object such as car keys or a misplaced coffee cup using a left-right or vertical scan pattern.

10. Moving with bioptics. Now have the client localize and spot objects while walking or moving as a passenger in a car. These spotting maneuvers should be completed in less than a second, like glancing in a rearview mirror of a car, and are appropriate only if a bioptic device is prescribed.

Common Difficulties and Solutions

The client never resolves object detail or reads print as predicted

- Check telescopic alignment.
- Make sure it is focused at distance.
- If client has macular scotoma, reassess eccentric fixation.
- Check for change in visual acuity.
- Intermittent object or print recognition
- Check alignment, lighting, and eccentric fixation.
- Check for central scotomas or floaters.
- Increase field of view (see below).

Inadequate field of view

- Use a Keplerian type telescope to maximize field of view.
- Bring the ocular closer to the eye.
- If client wears glasses, and has simple spherical refractive error, have client remove glasses to bring the ocular cup to the eye and refocus to compensate.
- Refer to eyecare provider for special spectacle mounts or an ocular lens with refractive correction.
- Consider a lower magnification device and moving closer to the object being viewed.

Loses objects and difficulty tracking

- Practice.
- Increase field of view (above), evaluate visual motor coordination, and consider spectacle mounts.

Cannot focus

- Practice with high-contrast edges.
- Estimate focus by feel (length of telescope) or place tactile or visible marks on focusing apparatus to provide starting point.
- Consider an auto focus device.

Inadequate light

- Typically, light with distance tasks cannot be controlled.
- Head visors, hats with brims, or body positioning will decrease disabling glare.
- If light is inadequate with a real-life goal task, consider a telescope with a larger diameter objective lens or lower magnification.

Distortion

- Use better quality optics with less distortion.
- Quick fatigue and complaints of headache
- Stop immediately, give the client a rest and downgrade the task.
- Check focus.

Motion sickness

- If the client starts to perspire, reports a sudden headache, reports feeling cold, or has a measurable drop in blood pressure, stop immediately. These symptoms are precursors to nausea associated with motion sickness.
- Avoid scanning and tracing tasks.
- Stabilize telescope using spectacle mounting.
- Move it further away to decrease field of view.

Specific Strategies for Telemicroscopes

Telemicroscopes (see Figures 13-4 and 13-5) allow a user to perform tabletop tasks, repairs, sewing, playing cards, or reading music. These devices are widely used by people with more typical vision who need to work with very small objects at near, such as biologists, surgeons, or electronic technicians and are thus generally available in a binocular mount. Because they have a narrow field of view, telemicroscopes are not as suitable for reading as microscopes, handheld devices, or CCTVs. If carefully fit by an eyecare practitioner, the telemicroscope does not require the user to align the device. Telemicroscopes also do not need to be focused. Rather, if the user usually works with a three-dimensional object, then the client usually compensates if out of focus by moving his head closer or further from the object being viewed until the correct distance is achieved. Otherwise, the training program is similar to that used for telescopes. Instead of a large poster board with numbers, a smaller paper is used on a table for initial alignment, focus, and practice. Practice localizing, tracking, scanning, and tracing may be performed with tabletop activities as well. In general, if clients intend to use the device for a particular task, they should bring in the materials to simulate the actual work situation, as many tasks do not require all of the skills required for telescopic use.

ADVANCED CONCEPTS/ TECHNIQUES: MAGNIFICATION DEVICES

How therapists and eyecare providers collaborate varies considerably from practice to practice. Often an occupational therapist does not have access to an eyecare practitioner who specializes in low vision. General practitioners may be more willing to see low vision patients and prescribe devices if a therapist performs preclinical visual testing and makes specific recommendations regarding devices and magnification. In a busy eye clinic where reimbursement to the physician is based on procedure rather than time spent with the client, eye doctors might expect the occupational therapist to recommend initial device selection prior to the formal clinical examination. A therapist may need to problem solve when a recommended device does not work as predicted. In such cases, the therapist must understand the principles of optics and magnification, and how the devices actually work.

The clinical reasoning remains as illustrated in Table 13-2 except that in step 5, where the therapist recommends optical devices, the therapist would also recommend magnification. To recommend magnification, the therapist must understand the various formal definitions of magnification, strategies for estimating how much magnification is required to perform a task, how to select devices that have comparable magnification, and how the final amount of magnification depends on interaction with the client's refractive error.

What follows is the general strategy for determining the magnification of an optical device.

- Estimate the magnification demands of the task
- Understand the interaction of magnification devices with refractive error
- Select devices with equivalent magnification

Estimating the Magnification Demands of the Task

Definition of Magnification

Specifying magnification has been complicated by the varied definitions of magnification and different methods for specifying the magnification of different types of devices. In low vision rehabilitation, although magnification has a common general definition ("an increase in the apparent size of an object"), the precise mathematical definition of magnification varies significantly.

Ultimately, the low vision practitioner is interested in enlarging the size of a retinal image. For example, visual acuity describes the size of the retinal image where the critical detail is just resolvable. Retinal image size is increased either by relative size or relative distance magnification (see Figure 13-7). In the scientific literature, retinal image size is reported directly as the retinal image size of the critical detail called Minimum Angle of Resolution (MAR). MAR is 1/5th the size of a letter in minutes of arc. Trigonometry is required to calculate MAR; it is not practical to use in the clinic. In the low vision clinic, the emerging convention is to describe magnification at a distance greater than about 1 M in terms of enlargement ratio. Magnification at closer distances is described using equivalent power (EP) in diopters.[4-7,9]

Relative Size Magnification

Increasing the size of the letter or object (see Figure 13-8) enlarges the size of the image of an object on the retina. The relationship between object size and retinal image size can be approximated as a simple proportion. Enlargement ratio (ER) refers to the ratio of two object sizes (S1 and S2), ER = S2/S1.[4] Increasing

the size of print from 1 M (8 point) to 2 M (16 point) at a given distance will increase the ER "2 times (2X)". The definition of ER is virtually the same as projection magnification or relative size magnification, terms that have also been used widely in the low vision literature since the 1970s.[1] If you double the size of an object, you double the retinal image size of the object. Estimating required object or print size for a task is very direct and no calculations are required. In the case of Ms. Jason, for example, functional visual acuity testing revealed that critical print size was 8 M, so she required print size be increased from 1 M to at least 8 M (64 point) to read fluently, an ER = 8X. A CCTV was used to enlarge the print to the same 8 M (1/2 inch letter) size used on the acuity chart. One may also use a telescope focused at distance (optical infinity) to produce virtual enlargement. To see faces on a television, a 3X telescope might be prescribed to enlarge the image to an equivalent of a large screen television 3 times larger. This is similar to the definition of angular magnification given in Chapter 3. ER is used to specify the magnification of devices that are used at a distance greater than 1 M, such as a telescope or changes in a sign lettering.

Relative Distance Magnification

The retinal image may also be enlarged by relative distance magnification, which is decreasing the distance from the object to the eye (see Figure 13-7). The relationship between object distance and retinal image size is approximated as a negative proportion. If you halve the distance of the object to the eye, you double the size of the retinal image. If you decrease the distance by 25%, you increase the retinal image size by 25%. Relative distance magnification by moving a television screen from 8 feet to 4 feet is equivalent to doubling the size of the television screen.

Overall magnification (M_{OA}) at distances greater than about 1 meter can be calculated by simply multiplying relative distance and relative size magnification as follows:

$$M_{OA} = S_2/S_1 * d_1/d_2$$

where S_1 and d_1 are the original object size and distance and S_2 and d_2 are the new object size and distance.

If, for example, a therapist found a client needed to decrease the distance from the television screen from 8 feet to 2 feet to see the screen and the client rejected 2 feet distance as too close, the telescope that provided a 2X enlargement could be used in combination with decreasing the television distance from 8 feet to a more acceptable 4 feet would achieve the same overall magnification of 4X.

With distances less than about 1 M, a client must focus his eyes to see clearly and near type devices that

focus light must be used that insure the client can see the object clearly. The amount of focus is specified as "power". The emerging convention is to specify the magnification of near devices in terms of equivalent power (EP).

Equivalent Power

If someone has refractive error, the eyecare provider prescribes corrective lenses (distance correction) to focus objects that are far away on the retina (see Chapter 3). Even with correction for distance, when someone looks at an object up close, the eye must accommodate, and the lens becomes thicker and acquires more power, which is the equivalent power of adding a plus lens in front of the distance correction (see Chapter 3). This additional need to focus or accommodate for near objects is called accommodative demand. As people age, they lose the ability to accommodate and this decreases the ability to focus at near. This loss of focusing ability related to the aging process is called presbyopia. Reading glasses are plus lenses that are added to distance correction that allow people with presbyopia to focus at a closer distance. These reading glasses are also called near vision additions.

The power (P) of accommodative demand is expressed as diopters (D), referred to by the shorthand "add". The formula that relates eye-to-object distance (d) in cm to the power (P) of required add for reading or working on tasks at near is as follows:

$$P(Diopters) = 100/d(cm)$$

The typical reading distance is 40 cm (16 in). Using the above formula, 2.5 D of add are required for objects held at 40 cm. This is called accommodative "demand" because the accommodative demand is not necessarily the same as the addition prescribed in the glasses. This additional power might be generated by accommodation or a change in the lens in the eye that allows focus at near. In the case of a younger client who can accommodate on his own, the addition would not be prescribed because the person can focus (accommodate) without the use of lenses. The accommodative demand of a person reading at 40 cm would always be 2.5 D whether addition was prescribed or not. How much addition is required for reading addition requires consideration of a number of factors, including a person's age, and should be determined by an eyecare provider.

The use of handheld magnifiers, microscopes, telemicroscope, enlargement, the CCTV or just working at a close distance without glasses are all potential magnification strategies for achieving better performance at near. To compare devices, the therapist must be able to calculate the equivalent magnification for a client to perform a variety of near goal tasks such as needle

point, clipping fingernails, bill paying, and reading a book. The EP is a universal term that describes the magnification of all near devices as well as strategies for near work. The term "equivalent power" describes the magnification as "equivalent" to the accommodative demand required for particular eye-to-object distance. For example, a manufacturer might specify the magnification of a stand magnifier used with 20 cm eye-to-lens distance, as "20 D of equivalent power". This means that the stand magnifier has magnification "equivalent" to someone using a 20 D of near add with a lens-to-object distance of 5 cm, even though the actual power of the lenses and distances may differ. This now allows us to use the same term for describing the magnification of all near devices. Essentially, the term equivalent power describes magnification that is equivalent to the accommodative demand at a particular distance.

The formula for EP is different from the formula for accommodative demand above. Magnification requires that we also consider enlargement of the object being viewed. As described above, the therapist might enlarge print or use larger objects, as well as decrease working distance. Some devices, such as telemicroscopes or stand magnifiers, enlarge the appearance of objects as well as the distance of an object. EP can be calculated by simply multiplying the accommodative demand (100/d) by the enlargement ratio (ER). The formula for calculating EP is as follows:

$$EP(Diopters)=100/d(cm) * ER$$

This important formula can be used to approximate the EP of all optical devices or viewing situations at near. For example, if a client requires that regular print be doubled from 1 M (8 point) to 2 M large print (16 point) to read comfortably, the ER is 2.0. If he is reading at the customary reading distance of 40 cm, the accommodative demand is 100/VD or 2.5 D, and this would be multiplied by an ER of 2 to calculate the EP of 5 equivalent diopters. This would be equivalent to reading the 1 M print at 20 cm, a distance at which the actual accommodative demand is 5 D. Note that even when print is simply enlarged or a CCTV is used at a normal reading distance, EP increases even though reading addition or optical devices do not change.

In the case of Ms. Jason, she wished to read and pay bills. Initially, the therapist found with a continuous text she required 8 M print to read fluently at 40 cm. To read 1.0 M print fluently, she required an ER = 8X. She would use the 2.5 D bifocal in her regular reading glasses to view the card at 40 cm (16 in). EP would equal 2.5 D multiplied by 8 or 20 D. One strategy would be to keep the print size at 1 M, and enlargement ratio of 1.0 and recommend a 20 D reading addition or use a 20 D handheld device. Ms. Jason could

not maintain the precise working distance of 5 cm and was too close to write. One could double the working distance from 5 to 10 cm, decreasing the accommodative demand (100/10cm) to 10 D. The therapist could also double the size of the print from 1 M to 2 M (standard large-print checks and books), increasing the ER from 1X with regular print to 2X with large print. The EP would be 10 D multiplied by 2X, preserving an EP of 20 D.

In summary, for working distances less than about 1 M, the magnification of any optical device or just a change in object size can both be described as equivalent power (EP) using equivalent diopters (ED) as the measurement units. Knowing EP allows one to compare several different methods of magnification without changing the overall magnification. Equivalent diopters is calculated using relative size magnification and relative distance magnification.

A Shorthand Approach

To apply the above formulas to estimate EP would typically require the therapist use a calculator to multiply and divide. Table 13-5 describes an alternative way to perform the calculations that allow one to more easily perform these calculations without a calculator by adding and subtracting.

Estimating Required Magnification

To estimate the magnification required for a task, the general strategy is to use relative size and relative distance magnification to magnify text or an object until the client is able to perform the task. If it is a near task, performed at less than about 1 M or 3 ft, one would use the formula for EP to describe the magnification required to perform the task. The therapist must generally perform an evaluation to determine magnification needs at distance by changing the size of the object. At distances greater than about 1 M, the therapist can usually estimate the required enlargement by changing the distance of objects.

Estimating Required Magnification at Near

The occupational therapist estimates the required magnification at near by changing the size of the object or text being viewed. In general, an occupational therapist does not have the ability to correct for different working distances at near because such changes require a different near correction. It is essential that the image be in focus on the retina, ie, that the client is wearing corrective eyeglasses for the specific working distance. For reading, one can maintain near test distance using a continuous text reading card where sentences are printed at a progression of print sizes (see Chapters 8 and 9). The client starts reading

Table 13-5.
A Shorthand Approach for Performing Magnification Calculations

This approach can save considerable time, because as a low vision rehabilitation therapist, one frequently performs these calculations. The following method allows one to more easily calculate print size, distance, or changes in the power of magnification optics. For example, if a reading evaluation indicated that 1M print is needed to magnify to 5 M for best reading at 40 cm, one could quickly calculate the decrease in distance from 40 cm that would provide the equivalent magnification, as well as the equivalent diopters (D) required by simply counting steps rather than multiplying or dividing. Adding or subtracting the "steps" of a logarithmic progression of a number sequence is equivalent, respectively, to multiplying and dividing numbers that fall on a standard arithmetic progression.

The first step is to memorize 10 steps of a logarithmic progression from 1 to 10. Note that these numbers correspond to the numbers on a log near acuity chart so one can easily refer to an acuity chart to recall this progression. The 10-step logarithmic progression: 1.0, 1.25, 1.6, 2.0, 2.5, 3.2, 4.0, 5.0, 6.4, 8, (10). The progression of letter sizes in a log near acuity chart will typically be as follows:

Print Size: 0.32 M, 0.4 M, 0.5 M, 0.6 M, 0.8 M, 1.0 M, 1.25 M, 1.6 M, 2.0 M, 2.5 M, 3.2 M, 4.0 M, 5.0 M, 6.4 M, 8 M.

Note that 10 steps from 1 to 10 equal a 10-fold increase. Note that 3 steps equal a 2X increase and that each step is 1.25X larger than the previous step. Note in Table 13-6 we can put print size, power, and distance on this same progression by shifting the decimal place.

To trade working distance (relative distance magnification) against ER (size magnification) involves counting steps and maintaining the same total number of steps.

Round to the nearest step and count the steps from S1 to S2. Using the above example, there are 7 steps from 1 M to 5 M, 1.25, 1.5, 2.0, 2.5, 3.2, 4, 5. To calculate the decrease in eye to print distance that would provide a magnification equivalent to increasing print size 5X, we count 7 steps starting at the test distance of 40 cm to 8 cm. To calculate equivalent diopters, we start at 2.5 D accommodative demand at 40 cm and count 7 steps up to 16 D of equivalent power. This allows us to easily trade size increase against decreasing distance. For example, 1 step increase in size is equivalent to 1 step decrease in distance. If we use large 2 M print, then we count 3 steps from 1 M to 2 M, and would decrease distance from 40 cm for the remaining 4 steps to 15 cm, a total of 7.

Print size											
(M)	1	1.25	1.6	2.0	2.5	3.2	4.0	5.0	6.4.	8	10
Distance (cm)	4.0	5.0	6.4	8	10	12.5	16	20	25	32	40
Demand (D)	25	20	16	12.5	10	8	6.4	5.0	4.0	3.2	2.5

at the largest print size and reads down the chart until reading starts to slow. The smallest print size before reading slows is critical print size. The smallest print that someone can read and still understand the text is reading acuity threshold. The required magnification depends on the task demands and available print size. If a client wishes to read print fluently, one calculates EP by dividing critical print size by the desired print size. If someone desires only spot reading, then the ER can be somewhat smaller. One then uses the formula for EP and multiplies the ER by accommodative demand of the test distance, 100/d.

For example, assume a client wants to read 1M newsprint fluently, and the measured critical print size at 40 cm is 4 M. The required equivalent power would be calculated by dividing 4 by 1 and multiply

4 by 100/40 or 2.5 to estimate a required magnification of 10 D of EP. For spot reading, where speed and endurance are less important, less magnification might be acceptable.

For nonreading tasks, estimating magnification required becomes more of a challenge because it is not easy to enlarge real-life objects. One approach involves using a color CCTV that can magnify virtually anything at a fixed distance using a color view. One would enlarge the image on the screen until the client can identify a critical feature, then calculate the ER by dividing the enlarged size by the actual size. For example, one might display a family snapshot where the heads of the subjects were about 1 cm on a CCTV. The client might recognize the faces when they were enlarged to 5 cm on the screen at 40 cm away. One could then calculate the EP. The ER is 5 cm/1 cm = 5X. The accommodative demand at 40 cm of (100/40) equals 2.5 D. EP is 5 times 2.5 D or 12.5 D. Using a 12 D loupe or handheld magnifier should work about as well to enable this client to see the pictures in this family photo. Another approach is to have photographs or actual samples of different size objects.

A therapist might also try using a succession of handheld magnifiers (see Table 13-1). The therapist should carefully hold the magnifier at the correct lens-to-object distance and have the client look through the distance correction (the upper half of eyeglasses if worn). It is also important to control lighting. The therapist should increase magnification until the object can be seen. In this case, the estimated magnification in equivalent diopters is directly estimated by the power of the device. The problem with this approach is that it is very difficult to correctly position the magnifier if the client is not familiar with the device.

In general, it is much easier to be working in close collaboration with a low vision optometrist who can quickly prescribe trial lenses for a given working distance with the normal objects being used.

Estimating Required Magnification for Distance

It is an unfortunate tradition to prescribe telescopes to general criterion visual acuity such as 20/40 acuity. In general, estimating the required ER should based on the relative distance magnification required to perform real tasks that are meaningful to the client. At the very least, involving the client in the actual task that he wishes to perform will be more engaging than an acuity chart. The visual requirement to perform the tasks, the required ER, can be estimated by first bringing an object of interest (a television, a street sign, or person's face) close enough to the client so that the client can reliably and quickly discern the critical features, and the required distance (d_r). The therapist

then estimates the distance at which the client prefers the preferred distance (d_p). One then divides the preferred distance (d_p) by required distance (d_r) to estimate the required telescopic ER (ER = d_p/d_r).

For example, using an actual street sign, a client can quickly read the sign at 2 M (6 ft) but needs to read it just as well across a wide street, about 12 M (40 ft). The required ER would be 12/2 = 6X. A similar strategy might be used for face recognition. For example, if a client requires someone be 2 M (6 ft) to reliably discriminate facial expressions, but wants to be able to do this when someone is 3 M (9 ft) away, an ER of about 1.3X is required.

In another example, a client wants to watch television and it is determined in the clinic that he can see the television at 3 ft (1 M). At home, the television is 9 ft away (3 M). In this case, the minimum ER for this task is 9/3 = 3X.

Selecting Devices

Fortunately, the manufacturers of optical devices specify the magnification in EP, or in the case of telescopes, as ER. The therapist needs only to look up the EP in a specification sheet or read it off of the device. Actually estimating the magnification of different devices is beyond the scope of this text and is well described elsewhere.[5-11] Since the convention for magnification can vary, alternative conventions for describing magnifications will be briefly discussed. Some special considerations regarding optical devices are described below.

How Manufacturers Specify Magnification

The emerging convention is to describe the magnification of devices using ER or EP. ER describes magnification of devices that use size magnification alone, such as a telescope focused to distance. EP describes the magnification of devices that focus at near, such as handheld magnifiers, stand magnifiers, telescopes focused at near (telemicroscopes), or CCTVs used at near. Manufacturers have in the past used different and inconsistent conventions for describing the magnification of near devices.

Describing the magnification property of a device requires reference to the size of one object relative to another. When one reads the "magnification" of a handheld magnifier as "2X", one must ask, "magnification of what compared to what?" For example, when we set the magnification on a copy machine to 2X, this implies the copy will be twice as large as the original. Yet, manufacturers might imprint 2X magnifier on the handle of a handheld magnifier, leaving the consumer of such a device with no idea what is being magnified compared with what. For example, at 40 cm a client might require print to be enlarged from 1M to 8M to read. This is an enlargement of 8/1 = 8X. If she read

at 40 cm with her reading glasses, the accommodative demand would be 100/40 or 2.5 D. The EP would be 8 times 2.5 or 20 D. One might not know whether an "8X" handheld magnifier should enable Ms. Jason to read the 1 M fine print on her medicine bottle. On the other hand, if the manufacturer imprinted 16 D on the device, one would immediately know that it would not have enough power. One could use the above formulas for EP to find a 20 D magnifier.

The convention of some manufacturers is to calculate magnification of a handheld magnifier or microscope by dividing the power of the lens by 4, others divide power of the lens by 4 then add 1, so a 4X from one manufacturer might be equivalent to a 5X from another. These same devices might have different angular magnification, depending on how far they were held from the object being viewed and whether a person was wearing reading glasses while using the device. Rather than attempt to describe the assortment of conventions used by manufacturers we will describe how to estimate EP for each near device. If the prescribed device does not fit the task requirements, using the formula for EP, the therapist can select different devices with the same magnification. Fortunately, manufacturers of optical devices have generally adopted the convention of also including EP, or the information that allows the therapist to calculate EP, into the specifications for a device.

Special Considerations: Near Addition, Microscopes, and Loupes

Interaction With Refractive Error and Presbyopia

A person who is already myopic (nearsighted) will require a weaker near addition lens to achieve a required EP of magnification if the myopia is not corrected (client is not wearing corrective glasses). Uncorrected myopia is equivalent to wearing a plus lens in front of the eye. For example, if a client has 5 D of myopia without his distance glasses, he needs only an additional 5 D to achieve 10 D of EP. People with high myopia sometimes are able to focus up close by taking off their glasses. If wearing glasses for distance, however, the minus lens acts like a reverse telescope, minifying the image and reducing visual acuity. For these individuals, wearing a contact lens correction for distance will result in better visual acuity than wearing glasses.

A client with uncorrected hyperopia (farsightedness) has insufficient plus in his or her lens and cornea and extra plus must be added to achieve an EP if the client does not wear his spectacle correction.

Distance correction in glasses in someone with significant hyperopia will have just the opposite effect as the minus lens in myopia. If someone has hyperopia, corrective spectacles will act as a weak telescope and provide distance magnification. In some cases, when clients use near addition lenses and view binocularly (both eyes open), binocular vision (eye muscle) problems may occur and cause eye strain or double vision. If occluding one eye relieves these symptoms, the eyecare provider should be informed. The eyecare provider may address this issue when prescribing near addition lenses for low vision by adding prism to the lens.

Special Considerations With Handheld Magnifiers

Most clients are familiar with handheld magnifiers or "magnifying glasses". Handheld magnifiers are simply plus lenses mounted in a handle. Better magnifiers include thin lens optics and special compound lenses that reduce chromatic aberration that occurs around the edges of the lens. Many have built-in light so they can be used to read menus or price tags in a dark store.

Since the therapist often must estimate the power of handheld magnifiers that clients have obtained from a variety of sources, the method for calculating the power of the magnifier will be discussed.

In theory, if the magnifier is held at the focal distance from the page of text being read, or object being viewed, the magnification will not change as the client moves closer to the magnifier (see Figures 13-2, 13-9). Thus, one need only specify the magnification of the handheld magnifier like the spectacle add or microscopes described above as diopters (D).

The emerging convention is to include dioptric value of a handheld magnifier on the handle of the device with other specifications. Calculating EP is very simple and the power of plus lens can be measured as follows. The therapist should look at an object and move the magnifier forward and backward until the object appears to be in focus. Measure the distance between the object and the back of the lens and use the following formula from Chapter 5 to determine the power:

$$D = 100/d \text{ (cm)}$$

For example, if the object being viewed is in focus when the magnifier is held at 10 cm, the power would be:

$$D = 100/d \text{ (cm)}$$

$$D = 100/10 = 10 \text{ D}$$

In general, since most users hold handheld magnifiers away from the eye for spotting, the general rule is to teach the client to look through distance correction (upper half of bifocals) or without glasses if they do not require glasses for distance. The client should not use reading glasses and handheld magnifiers at the same time because using both when the lenses are far apart actually decreases magnification.[11] If, on the other hand, the handheld magnifier is held close to the eye, then looking through the reading glasses or lower segment of bifocals actually increases magnification. To explore these types of multilens interactions, trial and error with working distance seems to be the best strategy for solving task-related problems. If someone has stronger reading glasses and a handheld magnifier, one strategy for providing a client with an extra high magnification is to teach him or her to use the two together with the magnifier against the lens of the reading glasses.

Special Considerations With Stand and Bar Magnifiers

Unlike handheld magnifiers, stand magnifiers are designed to be used at a more typical reading distance while someone looks through reading glasses or the lower half of bifocals designed for a particular distance. A stand magnifier is essentially a handheld magnifier set into a stand that rests on the page being read to maintain the lens distance. A bar magnifier (see Figure 13-14) is a low power stand magnifier that magnifies vertically. Some stand magnifiers maintain the lens distance (the distance from the lens to the page) at the focal length of the magnifying lens; like handheld magnifiers, these are used while someone is looking through distance correction. Most stand magnifiers, however, maintain a lens distance that is somewhat shorter than the focal distance of the lens. For a perfectly focused image, one must view the device within a prescribed range of distance and, if presbyopic, through reading glasses prescribed for a particular distance.[10,11] In some cases, stronger reading glasses will require that the eye-to-lens distance decreases, with an increase in magnification and field of view.

How Magnification Is Specified

One would first look at the manufacturer's specification for the ER of the device. This simply describes the "apparent" size or angular size of an object viewed through the device (S2) when compared to the angular size of the object without the device (S1), ER = S2/S1. Note that ER is often different than the manufacturer's magnification specified on the handle. The stand magnifier also optically increases the apparent distance of the object. Even though the actual distance of the object might be 3 cm from the lens, the optical

distance might be 20 cm. The optical distance is specified as "L" by the manufacturer. One then estimates how far the client will be holding the lens of the magnifier from the eye and adds this eye-to-lens distance to the value of L, an equivalent to the eye-to-object distance (d). Using the now general formula for EP described above for all devices, one calculates EP of the device as follows.

$$EP(Diopters) = 100/d(cm) * ER$$

In the example above where a client was reading with a 20 D stand magnifier set 4 cm from the page, the ER provided in the specification sheet is 5X. The value of L = 20 cm. If the client holds the magnifier 20 cm from his reading glasses, the total viewing distance (d) is 40 cm. Using the above formula, the EP would be 100/40*5= 12.5 D. This device will interact with a client's refractive error much like a handheld magnifier. In general, these devices are designed for use with a client's near addition, which, of course, fully corrects for this error. If the client places his eye against the magnifier, EP will increase to 25 D. However, without correction for a 20 cm viewing distance, the image will be somewhat blurry (if this client cannot accommodate), although the amount of blur is insignificant.

Specific Considerations for Telescopes and Telemicroscopes

When focused at distance, the telescope has no power and therefore, unlike the other devices and reading situations above, magnification cannot be specified in terms of EP. Telescopes are described in terms of ER. The convention is that the ER is described by the magnification specification etched on the device as, for example, 2X. When focused closer than 1 M, a telescope technically becomes a telemicroscope and power can be specified in terms of EP using the general formula for ER and thus directly compared to other near devices (see Figure 13-5).

Two types of telescopes exist: Galilean and Keplerian (see Figure 13-19). Both telescopes have two lenses. The lens closest to the eye is called the ocular and the lens at the other end is the objective. Galilean telescopes are simpler and less expensive with only two lenses. Keplerian systems involve two plus lenses spaced further apart than Galilean telescopes. In addition to the two lenses, a prism or mirror must be incorporated into the telescope to "right" the image. Galilean telescopes have a smaller field of view than a Keplerian telescope of the same magnification. Typically, the smaller and less expensive Galilean telescopes are prescribed for magnification up to 4X.

Since the late 1950s, telescopes have decreased in size and weight, while optical quality has improved.

Miniature telescopes can be mounted on spectacles, allowing hands-free, easier use and a decrease in movement.

Normally, just like a set of binoculars or a camera, the user must refocus a telescope when looking at objects at different distances. As with binoculars and cameras, an auto focus feature is available with some telescopes. Because electronic auto focus often becomes "confused" and might focus at a different distance than the user intends, auto focus is only recommended if there is a manual override and the user has the ability to "lock" the focus at a given distance.

Although telescopes have become smaller and lighter, the necessary cost of miniaturization is a decrease in the amount of light through the telescope. Light transmission depends on the diameter of the objective lens. The convention is to specify the size of the objective after the ER. For example, a 7X50 has an ER of 7X and the size of the objective lens is 50 mm.

Telescopes can also be mounted in the bottom of lenses where the bifocal segment is located (see Figure 13-5). The telemicroscope is focused at near, allowing one to look down to perform a near task with magnification while maintaining a normal working distance. The cost of this greater working distance, however, is a narrower field of view than can be achieved by a simple microscope (near add). Note that most telescopes can be converted to telemicroscopes by purchasing caps that are plus lenses that fit over the objective (far) lens of the telescope. Like near reading add, the value of the cap in diopters is calculated using the formula for accommodative demand:

$$D = 100/d$$

where D is the value of the cap in diopters, and d is the distance from the telescope to the object in centimeters.

Typically, 2 to 2.5 D caps are used.

Since the working distance used with telemicroscopes is less than about 1 M, magnification is specified in terms of EP. To calculate the EP of a microscope, one uses the general formula for EP. The ER is specified on the telescope as, for example, 4X. To calculate EP, ER is multiplied by accommodative demand for the particular distance (d) that the telescope is being used. Accommodative demand in diopters is 100/d (cm). If a 4X telescope were used at 40 cm, the EP would be 4 multiplied by 2.5 D, or 10 D of EP.

Special Considerations

Restricted Visual Fields

Magnification by any means might limit performance because the client sees a smaller piece of the text or object being viewed. For example, a client with a visual field restricted to 4 degrees would read text magnified to 1 degree letters more slowly because she would see just about 4 letters at a time. In people with normal visual fields, field of view is limited by the optical device (see Chapter 3). In some cases, retinal or neurological disease restricts a client's visual field to less than the field through the device. Too much magnification might slow reading because fewer letters can be seen at one time. Using a continuous text reading acuity test without a magnification device, a clinician can estimate the magnification at which performance is limited by a client's visual field. Normally, reading slows as the print decreases in size to approach acuity threshold. With significant field restriction, reading also slows as the print is enlarged beyond a given size. One needs to select an optical device magnification based on the print sizes or object that produce maximum reading rate because too much magnification might impair performance as much as too little magnification.

Clients with field restrictions often have progressive diseases such as retinitis pigmentosa or glaucoma. When these diseases progress to the point that visual acuity is impaired, the residual field of view is often very small. Contrast sensitivity often is impaired as well. In general, these individuals benefit more from electronic devices than optical devices because electronic devices enhance contrast and optimize lighting, allowing acceptable performance with less magnification. Computer systems that afford text to speech, allow contrast enhancement and controlled lighting, and the future capability to use nonsighted strategies are ideal methods to introduce as alternatives to optical devices with clients who often resist nonvisual strategies.

Central Field Loss

People with central field loss will present with inconsistent reading and visual performance, even with enlarged text rather than an optical device. This condition should be evaluated and the client should be taught compensatory scanning and viewing techniques such as eccentric viewing before optical devices

are prescribed. Learning eccentric viewing is difficult and complicates learning new optical devices. As with introduction of any new technique, learned eccentric viewing strategies may regress with fatigue. A client who has successfully completed eccentric viewing instruction and is learning to use a telescope for the first time may suddenly complain that nothing can be seen through the telescope because he has regressed to central fixation. Although use of optical devices might be incorporated into the instruction, these devices often are different than the device that will eventually be prescribed. Chapter 9 provides detailed instructions about eccentric viewing strategies.

Poor Contrast Sensitivity

In general, people with impaired contrast sensitivity as well as impaired acuity will benefit more from electronic magnification where contrast of print may be enhanced as well as magnified. Avoidance of glare and reflections from lenses becomes essential if someone with impaired contrast sensitivity uses an optical device. Careful control of lighting becomes critical as well; too much light will produce glare. Use of a typoscope where the client reads through a window cut out of a black card will decrease glare reflecting off of a white page. Matte rather than high gloss paper will reduce glare as well. Tinted lenses or colored overlays may enhance visual function as well.

Cognitive Impairment

Use of optical devices generally require the short-term memory sufficient to learn new materials, and the capacity to problem solve. As with any rehabilitation program with someone with impaired memory and problem solving, one must consider a person's premorbid skills and historical roles and activity. A typically complicated low vision computer system may be relatively easy to someone who worked with computers for 30 years. With assistance, often people may use devices such as telescopes to watch television or a gradual increase in reading add as a visual impairment progresses. Clients often have premorbid familiarity with low powered handheld devices that may enhance learning if similar devices are prescribed, but complicate learning to use stronger magnifiers or stand magnifiers. In general, simple size magnification (using large black marker on a large yellow pad) or relative distance magnification (moving closer to a television) usually are the best solutions. Use of sighted assistance, eg, someone to read a book, provides the client with socialization as well as an easy way for two people to spend time together.

Impaired Fine Motor Control

People with tremor or incoordination, in general, respond better to stand magnifiers, external mounted handheld magnifiers, and spectacle-mounted telescopes. Computer systems with screen magnification and modified keyboard input become excellent alternatives to optical devices for reading and writing tasks (see Chapter 13).

FIELD ENHANCEMENT DEVICES

A variety of optical devices have been developed to help people with restricted or narrow fields compensate for a reduced field of view. Reverse telescopic arrangements minify a view of the world, but also lead to greater difficulty seeing details.[12-14] Use of fresnel prisms mounted on half of the lens (on the affected side) of spectacles have been attempted that move the view through the prism toward the apex of the prism that is pointed nasally. In theory, the prism moves the visual scene from the blind field into the sighted field.[15,16] If the client scans toward the affected size into the prism, the client experiences double vision---the displaced view superimposed on the normal view. This allows him or her to see something approaching unexpectedly from the blind side. Although these interventions have expanded clinical measurement of the client's visual field, performance-based improvements (obstacle avoidance) remain unconvincing. This author has observed the opposite effect: clients avoid scanning into a fresnel prism to avoid diplopia, thus discouraging adaptive compensatory scanning. Rather than using optical devices, use of compensatory scanning techniques are thus generally recommended for peripheral field loss (see Chapter 9).

REFERENCES

1. Mehr EB, Freid AN. *Low Vision Care*. Chicago, IL: Professional Press; 1975.
2. Demer JL, Porter FI, Goldberg J, et al. Predictors of functional success in telescopic spectacle use by low vision patients. *Investigative Ophthalmology and Visual Science*. 1989;30(7): 1652-1665.
3. Beliveau M, Smith A. Training for visual efficiency without low vision aids. In: Beliveau M, Smith A, Eds. *The Interdisciplinary Approach to Low Vision Rehabilitation*. Stillwater, OK: National Clearinghouse of Rehabilitation Training Materials: University of Oklahoma; 1980:224-256.
4. Bailey IL. Equivalent viewing power or magnification? Which is fundamental? *The Optician*. 1984;188:14-18.

5. Bailey IL. Principles of near vision telescopes. *Optom Monthly.* 1981;(Aug): 32-34.

6. Bailey IL, Bullimore MA. Specifying the magnification performance of optical aids for near vision. Paper presented at the International Conference on Low Vision, Groningen; July 1993.

7. Bailey IL, Bullimore MA, Greer RX. Low vision magnifiers: their optical parameters and methods for prescribing. *Optometry and Vision Science.* 1994;71:689-698.

8. Brilliant R. Magnification in low vision aids made simple. *J Vis Impair Blind.* 1983;77(4):169-171.

9. Bailey IL. Prescribing low vision reading aids: a new approach. *Optometric Monthly.* 1981(Jul):6-8.

10. Bailey IL. The use of fixed-focus stand magnifiers. *Optometric Monthly.* 1981(Aug):37-39.

11. Brilliant R, Ed. *Essentials of Low Vision Practice.* 1st ed. Boston: Butterworth Heinemann; 1999.

12. Bailey IL. Field expanders: Choosing the best field expander for increased depth and decreased distortion and loss of acuity. *Optometric Monthly.* 1978(Aug):130-133.

13. Cohen JM. An overview of enhancement techniques for peripheral field loss. *J Am Optom Assoc.* 1993;64(1):60-68.

14. Krefman RA. Reversed telescopes on visual efficiency scores in field-restricted patients. *American Journal of Optometry and Physiological Optics.* 1981;58(2):159-162.

15. Hoppe E, Perlin RR. The effectivity of Fresnel prisms for visual field enhancement. *J Am Optom Assoc.* 1992;64(1):46-53.

16. Perlin RR, Dziadul J. Fresnel prisms for field enhancement of patients with constricted or hemianopic visual fields. *J Am Optom Assoc.* 1991;62(1):58-64.

Computer Technology in Low Vision Rehabilitation

OVERVIEW OF TYPES AND APPLICATIONS OF ELECTRONIC ASSISTIVE DEVICES

Case Study 1

The train was late. Dan quickly checked the time, then advanced to the next email in his personal organizer. A flurry of emails always seemed to descend from the Internet the day before a critical meeting. Fortunately, Dan transferred his emails to his organizer before he left for the train that morning and started reviewing the messages on the train. As he entered the building three blocks from the train station, Dan finished his last email. One advantage of a talking personal organizer is that the user can walk and read at the same time. Dan was a little concerned, however. His coworkers all knew that they should correspond with him by computer and describe charts and graphs in emails so that he could easily process the information, but Dan expected a bundle of printed material from another office. As he entered his office, he gratefully noticed the office secretary feeding pages into the scanner of his document reader. He

handed her a cup of her favorite latté. Dan smiled and began looking at the graphs and charts on his CCTV while listening to the computer read the memos that had just been scanned into it.

By habit, Dan arrived 10 minutes before the meeting began. He no longer did so to insure seating close to the projection screen, because he now had a portable device. He used the extra time to hook the camera up to his notebook computer and point it at the projection screen so that he could also see a magnified view on the screen of his laptop. As an additional advantage, Dan could perform screen captures, allowing him to review more complicated graphics later. When the CEO arrived, she handed him the meeting agenda. He flipped the camera attached to his notebook down toward the document on the table, refocused it, and photographed the memo to display and magnify it on his notebook screen with enhanced contrast. When the meeting began, Dan was ready.

Dan could be any young, rising executive. Thirty years ago, someone with juvenile macular degeneration and a maximum visual reading rate of 80 to 100 wpm would not have been able to keep up with the paperwork required of someone in Dan's position. Today, with electronic assistive devices, a person with low or no vision can read text-to-speech[1] and process

Table 14-1.

Types of Electronic Devices

1. Closed Circuit Televisions (CCTV)
   a) Table top—camera and display in one unit
   b) Component—separate camera and display
   c) Computer component—camera is hooked through computer that can process image
   d) Split screen—both computer and CTTV share display but CCTV camera does not connect to computer
2. Computer systems
   a) Screen magnifiers: magnify and enhance computer display
   b) Screen-reader: reads display aloud or converts to refreshable Braille
   c) Combined screen magnifiers and screen readers
3. Document readers: reads printed documents aloud
4. Personal organizers: portable devices with text-to-speech or Braille output, keyboard or Perkins-Braille input
5. Books on tape or MP3 player: read books aloud from audio tape, CD, or digital files
6. Digital readers: read books aloud from digitized files that include natural voice and text

numerical information as quickly as someone with more typical vision.

Case Study 2

Ms. Wassel refused to move in with her daughter. She loved her house, and the morning walk to the coffee shop. She was close to her family in spirit, but they had all moved away and were living in various locations around the world. Ms. Wassel had always loved to write, and even published a short book of poems after she retired. As this 80-year-old woman painstakingly read a handwritten note from her best friend, she momentarily missed the flow and beauty of handwriting. She still added a word or two in her own handwriting before signing her printed letters. How she struggled to learn that "darn computer"! Now with the daily emails from friends and family, Ms. Wassel was able to keep in touch with her network of family and friends. This benefit had made the effort worthwhile. Ms. Wassel had macular degeneration, but unlike many with her condition, with the help of a therapist who had simplified computer access and the computer class organized by her therapist, she could once again read and write.

Historically, electronic assistive devices for blindness and low vision included closed circuit television (CCTV) systems and computer-based systems (Table 14-1). The CCTV systems modify a video image. A typical CCTV (Figures 14-1 and 14-2) allows the user to vary the image magnification, and to increase and reverse the image contrast so that the faded black print on a newspaper can be seen as large bright white letters on a dark black page. The user must move the material being read under the camera, and can easily lose place with a slip of the hand. CCTVs usually are packaged with special tables that can be moved horizontally and vertically under the camera, enabling the reader to move along a line of text or down a column of numbers with relative ease. Color CCTVs allow users to see images in natural color and add color contrast enhancements that soften glare, such as using light yellow letters on a dark blue background.

Once only available as tabletop devices, CCTVs have become smaller and lighter and are nearly as portable as optical devices (Figure 14-3). The cameras can be pointed at distant objects, such as a blackboard, converting the CCTV into a telescopic system, and can even be head-mounted with the image displayed on a miniature screen in front of the client's eyes (Figure 14-3A). Some CCTVs have split screens and two cameras so that the user can quickly move from one image to another, avoiding the time consuming process of scanning with high magnification to find information (Figure 14-5).

Screen magnifier computer programs provide the same enhancements as a CCTV with the display on a computer screen (Figure 14-6). In addition to CCTV features, a screen magnifier can modify the fonts or font spacing and include a variety of features to allow

Figure 14-1. Conventional CCTV (Telesensory Alladin), with curtain feature turned on to reduce glare from screen. Other advantages: excellent controls such as lever controls for magnification on control of contrast features (not visible). The XY table has margin stops, and controlled resistance to movement. Disadvantages: The illumination of the XY table creates glare, the device requires manual focus, and the monitor cannot be moved.

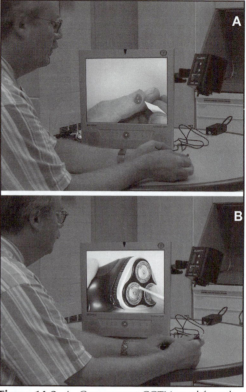

Figure 14-2. A. Component CCTV used for taking a blood sample. B. Component CCTV used for small appliance repair.

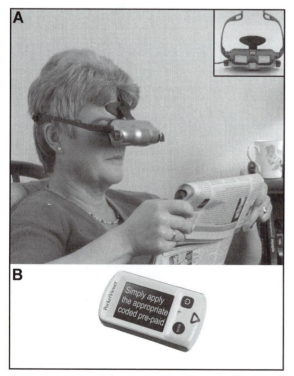

Figure 14-3. Portable CCTV systems. A. Head-mounted CCTV. B. Handheld CCTV (courtesy of Eschenbach Optik of America, Ridgefield, CT).

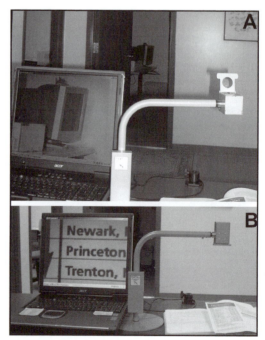

Figure 14-4. Notebook system with remote camera. A. Camera positioned for telescopic viewing at distance (the monitor in the adjoining room) with near-cap up. Note luminance enhancement. B. Camera positioned down for reading with near-cap in place.

Figure 14-5. A workstation designed for good ergonomics for someone with severe vision impairment. The display stand is height and distance adjustable to allow a closer working distance without compromising posture. The seat should be fully adjustable as well. The CCTV XY table and keyboard have been positioned to minimize rotation of the trunk and neck. The same monitor is used for CCTV and computer display by switching between CCTV and computer or splitting the display. Most importantly all of the components can be repositioned to vary body positioning. Earphones are for text-to-speech (Steinman).

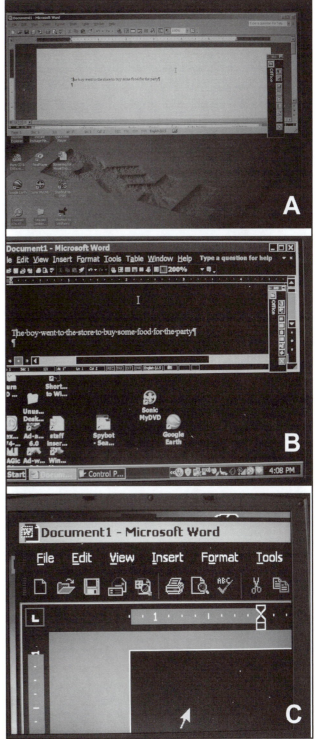

Figure 14-6. A. Computer screens with no enhancement. Active accessibility features in Microsoft Windows enables contrast enhancement and magnification up to about 2X with full screen view—components only are enlarged. B. A screen magnifier program enlarges a portion of the display with much greater magnification (4X is illustrated) and also provides text-to-speech to read displayed text aloud.

Figure 14-7. Personal organizers (Type Lite and Braille Lite) with standard typewriter and Perkins Braille input. The notebook displayed has a refreshable Braille strip just under the keyboard at the bottom of the device (courtesy of Freedom Scientific).

the user to scan a document or quickly jump from place to place on the screen such as from space to space on a data entry form. A screen reader reads the text displayed on a computer screen aloud or converts the text to a Braille display of moveable raised dots for people who are totally blind (Figure 14-7). Instead of using a mouse, the blind individual uses key combinations to quickly navigate a screen and read text. A major breakthrough for people with low vision, screen magnifiers and screen readers have combined to allow people with low vision to navigate a page and read with vision enhancement, as well as appreciate the ease and comfort of hearing longer passages read aloud. With these combined systems, people with progressive vision loss can gradually transition from dependence on vision to read, to a screen reader, and gradually learn the more difficult keyboard control required of someone who is totally blind.

Document readers (also called document scanners) are used to scan printed pages, display the print with magnification and enhancement, and convert the text to speech or Braille. Once very expensive and cumbersome, document readers are now easily packaged with personal computers to read printed material aloud, as well as display the text and figures using screen magnification features. Document readers are also packed as stand-alone units that are easy to use. Finally, personal organizers are portable devices that were developed for blind people before they became popular with the general public. The information is presented as computer speech or Braille rather than on a visual display. Personal organizers either have keyboards or Perkins-Braille input. The Perkins-Braille input is a standard 9-key input used by people to type in Braille (see Figure 14-7). Personal organizers effectively act as notepads and address books, allowing people with

vision impairment to keep personal information, names and addresses, and an appointment book.

Newer devices enable recorded books to be more easily read. Recordings for the blind are currently evolving from tape recordings that require the user to fast-forward through the tape to find a section of interest to read, to digital devices that allow the user to more quickly scan material for an article or passage of interest. The digital devices also allow the user to vary the speaking speed without distorting the tone of the reader. Older tape readers have a tone distortion, a "Mickey Mouse effect," when the speaking speed on a tape is increased. Because electronic assistive devices are evolving so rapidly, whole product lines have appeared and disappeared in a few years. In this chapter, we avoid mention of specific products, but rather provide guidance about important features in this technology.

Before selecting an electronic assistive technology, the therapist must consider the cost and complexity of the devices. For a person with recent vision loss, even simple activities such as grooming, dressing, cooking, and eating become complicated. As a result, such individuals may not welcome the additional complication of a high-technology assistive device. Even the newer CCTVs with auto focus features and simpler controls still require relearning complex visual motor coordination, such as moving a book on a tablet under a camera while looking straight ahead at the screen. As with optical devices, electronic devices should be introduced in the context of a task that the client deems important. Hand-over-hand assistance should be provided to enable the client to quickly achieve success when performing the goal task with the device before confronting more challenging tasks. With repetition and instruction, the assistance can be gradually reduced.

With computer systems, the client must have intact cognitive function and the ability to touch type. Software programs are available that teach typing/keyboarding and an introduction to computer assistive technology, and prepare the client for use of the Web.

EVALUATION

The Success-Oriented Clinical Reasoning Process for Electronic Devices

The evaluation for electronic devices closely resembles the evaluation for optical devices described in Chapter 13. It is important to anticipate which cli-

Table 14-2.

The Success-Oriented Clinical Reasoning Process for Electronic Devices

1. Define goals and task performance requirements.
2. Evaluate context and ergonomics.
3. Consider optical and nonoptical devices with eyecare provider.
4. Determine the display enhancement.
5. Evaluate performance with all necessary assistance.
6. Consider cosmetic, social, financial, prognosis, and ergonomics.
7. Provide or arrange for instruction.
8. Consider cost.

Table 14-3.

Ancillary Devices for CCTV and Computer Use

- Privacy screen
- Monitor stand – variable height, distance and lateral positioning
- Adjustable office chair on wheels
- Corner desk with swivel chair if using more than one display
- Glare screen, Velcro (translucent yellow plastic with Velcro)

ents might benefit from electronic devices and present these options concurrently with optical devices. Starting with optical devices, and moving on to the more expensive electronic devices if the optical devices fail, may discourage a client from considering the CCTV. If the initial evaluation indicates that an electronic device may be more effective than an optical device in enabling the client to achieve his or her goals, then the therapist should demonstrate the CCTV system first. The client will be encouraged at first just by performing a desired task and developing some basic skills and will be pleasantly surprised if a less expensive optical device is later found to be sufficient.

Special considerations associated with the low vision evaluation for electronic devices include the following (Table 14-2).

Goals and Performance Requirements

What is the task the client wishes to perform? Examples include correspondence, viewing pictures or graphs, reading short or long passages, and searching for information. What are the performance requirements? Examples include normal fluent reading (for a student or someone working) for >1 hour, skimming, and scanning.

Context and Ergonomics

This includes the range of tolerable working distances for different goal tasks. Are two hands required to perform the task or can the client perform the task holding a device with one hand? Where will the client sit to perform the task? What is the closest possible working distance? Ancillary devices such as monitor stands and antiglare screens should be considered (Table 14-3).

Optical Devices and Prognosis

A prescription for a device from a physician will support requests for external funding. Moreover, the client should have proper eyeglasses for the expected working distance from the monitor. In some cases, special prescription for a closer working distance will enable the user to more easily use the electronic device.

Display Enhancement Settings

Include an estimation of the optimum object/print size, contrast, and color contrast optimum for reading. Determination of the optimum magnification for reading is generally easier than for optical devices. The therapist determines the critical print size (smallest print that produces fast, comfortable reading on a near reading chart), and as a starting point, duplicates the same print size on the screen of a CCTV or computer at the same distance used with the reading chart.

With objects, one simply magnifies the image with the device until the user is able to easily identify critical features. For object identification, the most natural color and contrast settings are used. For reading, if the client has impaired contrast sensitivity, performance is expected to improve with reverse contrast or various color contrast enhancements.

To select an ideal screen magnification, as well as contrast for reading, the therapist first determines the best contrast and color contrast settings. To compare normal, reverse contrast, and different color contrasts, the therapist should measure reading speed with print size in between acuity threshold and critical print size. This can be done quickly by decreasing the magnification until reading slows significantly—being careful to maintain the same working distance. The therapist should then try reverse contrast and different color contrast combinations to determine if reading speed and reported comfort increases. Informed of the performance effects, the client's subjective preferences and objective performance will tend to agree. After best contrast is ascertained, the therapist should remeasure reading speed with different magnifications until an optimum print size is found using timed reading. With contrast enhancements, critical print size for reading often decreases.

This testing is most easily performed with different sentences of the same length on the CCTV. Test sentences are included in the Appendices. During testing, the therapist should provide hand-over-hand assistance moving the text to insure reading speed is only limited visually and not by the client's ability to manipulate the device. Just having the client adjust the magnification and contrast to "what looks right" without an objective performance evaluation is not acceptable and often results in the client choosing what is familiar rather than more efficient. After performance is evaluated objectively and the client is informed of the results, the client should now be willing to select the configuration that produces the best performance in the long run. With computer systems, several other characteristics of display presentation may be modified as well. Again, some performance measures, such as how quickly someone performs a task, should be combined with subjective preferences in order to decide on the preferred setup.

Evaluate Performance

Begin with the device most likely to be successful. This step is essential if the medical necessity of the more expensive device and instructional program needs to be justified to an agency. In the success-oriented approach, the first experiences attempting to perform a goal task should be successful. Often, performance with a new device is impaired not only by vision, but also by a client's lack of skill using the device. Learning to use a device often is an expensive and difficult process. Moreover, the client also must obtain the device to practice using it. One must convince the client and any agency funding the program that at the completion of instruction, the client will be able to perform the goal task once instruction is completed. The therapist should provide as much assistance as necessary to manipulate the device; all the client needs to do is read or perform the visual task. In this supported setting, the therapist should compare reading speed and comfort using various options, such as less expensive optical solutions, electronic displays, or text-to-speech.

We recommend that the therapist obtain easy-to-understand paragraphs of the same length and compare reading time with the various options. With text-to-speech, the computer can read the passages aloud at different speeds. Comparison of visual performance with optical devices versus electronic devices can be performed with the Pepper Test, which will be more sensitive to smaller differences. As with optical devices, if performance is not well predicted by vision testing, the therapist, in collaboration with the low vision optometrist, should attempt to identify other performance limiting factors, such as lighting and other visual impairments.

Cosmetic and Social Considerations

Often, the final selection of a device depends on how it looks or affects a client's social interaction. Does the client require seating away from coworkers? Will the client be working in a public area and be required to deal with stares and questions? These important considerations should follow the performance evaluation because a significant performance enhancement might persuade a client to tolerate these problems.

Instruction

An electronic device should never be recommended unless instructional needs are addressed. Instruction for CCTV systems or basic word processing for writ-

ten communication can generally be provided by a therapist in the context of medical rehabilitation. Shopping on the Web, using email, spreadsheets, database, or proprietary software requires considerable instruction that is generally beyond the scope of "medical necessity" and the skill of most therapists. Vocational rehabilitation and college-level educational programs are often available to provide such instruction, although these programs may be expensive and require the client pay for the instruction. It is the responsibility of the therapist to arrange for such instruction before a device is recommended for such vocational goals.

Affordability

The client ultimately selects a preferred device if he is paying for it. If an agency, school system, or insurance pays, the therapist must provide objective performance evaluations and work within the agency requirements.

Electronic devices are expensive. Young adults under 21 who have not yet graduated high school or vocational programs are eligible for what remains the best resource for instruction and equipment—the public school system. If the client is enrolled in a public school system, the school is required by Federal Law I.D.E.I.A. (12/04) to provide devices necessary for education, including electronic and optical devices. A request for such a device must include clear performance data in support of the recommendation, with data relating the device to the educational objectives as stated in the student's Individual Educational Program (IEP). The parents should make such a request with the help of the special education teacher who provides low vision services. Many states have Blind and Vocational Rehabilitation Services that pay for assistive devices for adults with vocational goals, including primary homemakers and caregivers. These agencies, however, have budget limitations. Thus, letters with objective performance data must provide a convincing argument that a device is necessary to perform an essential task for a particular job or to live independently. There has been limited success obtaining reimbursement from Medicare, Medicaid, and other medical insurance for assistive devices for low vision and blindness. However, a therapist should at least try to help the patient obtain reimbursement. When documenting the need for devices, it is essential to justify medical necessity. For the CCTV, for example, the justification might be for medication management, diabetic management, and self-care functions such as skin checks or catheter management.

ELECTRONIC DISPLAY DEVICES: EDD VERSUS CCTV

CCTVs are comprised of three basic features: the camera that focuses on the material being read, the display of the enlarged image of the material being read, and the table on which the user rests the material being viewed. The more conventional term CCTV has been used in this text. Evolving technology has been replacing the "TV" or televideo components with digitally based components, rendering the term CCTV a technical misnomer. Figure 14-1 illustrates a classic tabletop CCTV system. The display is a video monitor using a CRT tube, sometimes a conventional TV set.

Newer display systems use the lighter and more portable LCD displays that could have critical visual characteristics that are often inferior to the CRT-type monitors. Newer digital CCTVs also use digital cameras that may likewise have inferior visual display characteristics when compared to older videocameras. Note that the material being viewed is on an XY table that can be moved horizontally and vertically under a fixed camera. Figure 14-2 illustrates some various uses of a component CCTV system, where the camera can be detached and positioned for a variety of tasks and the monitor moved as well. The tabletop CCTV has been used for grooming and small appliance repair as well. The detachable camera on a component CCTV can be set up like the tabletop system, but the component systems are considerably more versatile. Figure 14-3 illustrates the head-mounted and handheld systems that are the most portable and versatile but may have smaller and inferior display characteristics compared to tabletop CCTVs and may, therefore, be more difficult to use.

Some component systems allow the camera to be moved manually or electronically to scan as well and use an XY table accessory (see Figure 14-4). The most popular use of the CCTV is for reading and writing activities.[2] These activities can easily be performed with the less expensive tabletop CCTVs. CCTVs are available that share the display monitor with a computer (see Figure 14-4), allowing the user to quickly switch back and forth from the display of some printed material or information on a screen and the display of a word-processor or some other application. These may be used with two cameras as well and can display information from the two sources on the same monitor (see Figure 14-5). Split-screen CCTVs are generally the products of choice in vocational rehabilitation with users in typical white-collar jobs who also use computers, such as Dan in Case Study 1.

Table 14-4.
__Important Properties of a CCTV__

- Ease and use of controls
- Levers rather than knobs
- Magnification is easy to reach
- Easy focus or auto focus
- 1-step switch between natural and contrast enhanced display
- Magnification between 1X to 3X
- High and stable contrast with moving text (low smear)
- Ergonomic flexibility
- Table characteristics, (adjustable horizontal and vertical resistance, margin stops, locking capability).
- Low glare from table illuminator
- Portability
- Color
- Camera stability (component system)
- Product support and integrity of vendor

Consider how a person with low vision typically uses a CCTV. To read, the user will take the page or book and place in on the XY table, center the book, and position it by feel up against a lip so that it is perfectly horizontal on the XY table. When starting, the user must setup and focus the unit. After the setup, the user rarely touches any control except the magnification and a switch between normal view and reading-enhanced view.

The setup is as follows. For a reading-enhanced view, the user first sets up the color of the display and the contrast. The client might choose high-contrast light yellow text on a dark blue background, for example. Sometimes horizontal or vertical guidelines on the screen are displayed to help the user stay on a line or column. To focus the unit, the person increases the magnification to maximum, and then adjusts the focus until the letters appear clearest. The CCTV will then keep the focus throughout the range of magnification as long as the thickness of the reading material does not change. Sometimes a clear plastic overlay must be used to hold the reading material flat to stay in focus. The user will then decrease magnification and either adjust the margin stops or place a finger or move the book so that the table stops at the beginning and end of the lines or column displayed. Finally, the user increases magnification until the text can be read. The reader then can start reading by moving the book from left to right under the camera of the CCTV. At the end of the line, the user will quickly move the table back over the line just read, and then up slightly until the beginning of the next line is seen.

For viewing pictures, the client will adjust the CCTV to use natural color and contrast. For writing, the user will lock the table or increase the drag so it does not move as easily and move the table to where the user wishes to write. For three-dimensional objects (trimming fingernails, taking a blood sample, or fixing an appliance), the user must readjust the focus to the correct depth plane. Focusing on lower-contrast objects is difficult. It is often helpful to have high-contrast focusing targets for the client to use.

Once the focus is set, it is often easier to move the object being viewed closer or further from the camera to maintain focus, than to readjust focus. For an experienced user, CCTV setup can be completed in a few seconds, with focus being the hardest part. A beginning user might find the setup tedious and overwhelming.

Carrying electronic devices such as CCTVs and monitors presents a problem for those doing home-based or workplace-based low vision practice. For CCTV evaluation, the therapist may schedule a demonstration by a vendor who will provide the device at the same time a treatment session is scheduled. For instruction, a rental may be arranged. The choice of which devices to demonstrate to clients will depend on the willingness of vendors to provide such support.

Important Properties of CCTVs

The following features of CCTVs have significant functional impact (Table 14-4). Ideally, several models should be available for the client to try and evaluate, but often the therapist must arrange demonstrations for users by sales representatives. The therapist must, therefore, anticipate which models will be acceptable and suggest two or three devices for a sales representative to demonstrate.

Ease of Use and Controls

Ease of use is not just about positioning the control. It also reflects the intuitive nature of the control—how easy it would be for someone with cognitive impairment to learn.

- In general, levers are better than knobs, and button controls to adjust magnification should be avoided. Digital button controls are the least intuitive for users less familiar with digital technology, but may be easier than knobs for those with motor impairment. Consider hand dominance and manual disability and rule out devices where controls cannot be reached.

- The magnification control is most frequently used and should be positioned lower and closer to where the hand must be positioned during the task.

- Focus should be easy and accessible or use auto focus. Learning to focus the camera and make manual adjustments is difficult. It is easier to read a book that does not lay flat with auto focus. An auto focus feature is valuable; however, a focus lock button should be available if the user is using the CCTV for grooming, or examining three-dimensional objects.

- Switching between color and reading modes must be quick and easy. A person using a color CCTV will most often switch between two configurations. The setting for reading might have contrast enhancement or reversed (white on black) contrast not suitable for viewing pictures or objects. A natural color mode is suitable for viewing pictures and objects, or grooming. Avoid units where switching between these two setups is more than one step and is complicated.

Magnification

Often higher magnification is used as a selling feature. In fact, the ability to achieve lower magnification from 1X to 3X is a most important and useful feature. To scan and locate information, the client uses lower magnification to view as much of a whole page as pos-

sible. The user estimates where critical information might be located, using a spotting technique similar to that used with optical devices. Once this location is found, the user centers the target and zooms up magnification. People with field restrictions and poor contrast sensitivity appreciate the contrast enhancement features and perform best with lower magnification. Rarely do users set magnification greater than 10X. The visual evaluation should indicate the ideal range of magnification for an individual. With higher magnification, CCTVs are easier to use if linear magnification is combined with relative distance magnification. A user can effectively double the magnification of the display by decreasing the working distance from 40 cm (16 in) to 20 cm (8 in), enabling a 5X setting on the CCTV to be used rather than a 10X setting.

High and Stable Contrast With Image Motion (Low Smear)

A major advantage of a CCTV over optical systems is the ability to increase print contrast. This advantage can be negated by smear or ghosting. To evaluate smear, set a CCTV to reverse contrast and decrease the magnification, and then move the page under the camera quickly. Note that the letters will fade when the page is moved. With some CCTVs, especially those using digital technology, smear appears quite significant. Smear becomes functionally very important in people with poor contrast sensitivity who are reading with lower magnification, such as someone with diabetic retinopathy, advanced glaucoma, or retinitis pigmentosa. With more magnification, smear is less of a problem. In general, users appreciate the highest contrast possible. If illumination creates glare, eg, from a bright white letter on a black background, consider one or more of the following additional CCTV features:

- Turn down monitor brightness (or have the user wear lightly tinted polarized or yellow sunlenses).

- Use a color unit with different color contrasts (the most popular is light yellow on a dark blue background).

- Use normal black-on-white contrast with a curtain feature (see Figure 14-1) that darkens all but the line being used, like a typoscope.

- Wear light (indoor) sunlenses while using the device.

Ergonomic Flexibility

A component system provides the most ergonomic flexibility but is more difficult to setup and more expensive than tabletop models. For example, a detachable

monitor can be set up and positioned at any distance or height with a monitor stand. Newer product lines have display monitors that can be moved. This is an important feature for those requiring higher magnification, where relative distance magnification is used in combination with relative size magnification on the screen. With a closer working distance, one often must bring the monitor closer and raise it to enable an upright posture. With a separate monitor, the user can put the monitor on an adjustable stand and change the elevation and working distance to achieve a comfortable posture (see Figure 14-5).

Table Characteristics

For someone with motoric impairment, low frustration tolerance, and/or incoordination, table characteristics become the most important features of a CCTV. A table should at least have a lip against which the material can be rested to insure it is positioned horizontally. The table should have greater resistance to movement vertically than horizontally to help the user stay on the same line. The table should have tab stops to stop movement when the beginning and end of a line is reached. The table should have a locking mechanism or mechanism for increasing drag if someone plans to use the CCTV for viewing and working on objects or writing.

Glare From Table Illumination

Since the CCTV is often most useful for people with impaired contrast sensitivity, glare from the light illuminating the material being read becomes a significant problem. Fabricating and positioning a glare shield between the display monitor and the XY table where the light is shining can solve this problem. The shield often can be attached with Velcro without invalidating a product warranty. Ideally, the shield could be made from a clear, colored plastic so the client can still see how the page or book is positioned under the CCTV camera.

Portability

CCTV systems in general have become smaller and lighter. Currently, relatively inexpensive handheld cameras can be purchased. Some use any TV, others can use a computer monitor, and most can be purchased with a portable display monitor. The handheld cameras are difficult to use and these systems afford limited control over magnification. When considering a portable monitor or use of a laptop display, one must consider the effect of the usually smaller display on relative size magnification and ergonomics. Component systems are now available that work through a computer and may be used with a portable notebook computer (see Figure 14-4). An important advantage of head-mounted displays, the proximity of the screen to the eye enables the same range of magnification possible with a conventional CCTV. Head-mounted systems and handheld systems package the camera and display together (see Figure 14-3) and are portable, but decrease the display area. When compared with stand or handheld magnifiers, handheld electronic devices afford enhanced contrast and magnification adjustment and a somewhat greater field of view at distance. One must recall that a simple, relatively inexpensive, illuminated handheld optical device affords comparable magnification to a handheld electronic device, good illumination under varied lighting magnification conditions, and greater potential field of view and magnification if the eye-to-lens distance is decreased.

Color

Color features add cost and complexity. Color only enhances reading if the user appreciates color contrast features, such as yellow letters on a dark blue background, to decrease glare. Otherwise, color becomes useful to those using the CCTV to enjoy pictures, read tables, graphs, and maps, and color illustrations.

Camera Stability and Rotational Camera Adjustment

With component CCTV systems (see Figure 14-2), the camera often attaches to an arm that might easily bounce and magnify any movement of the table on which it rests. Likewise, when a camera is pointed at a target from an oblique angle, the object will be viewed as rotated on the screen. Some units allow one to rotate the camera to compensate. For those using the CCTV for skin inspections, or to work in a shop, one also should consider how the camera might be mounted. A camera with a conventional camera screw mount is an advantage, as one might be able to use the assortment of relatively inexpensive camera mounting systems, including table and tube clamp mounts and tripods, available in a photography store.

Product Support/Integrity of Vendor

Unlike optical devices that only can be prescribed by an eyecare provider, CCTV devices can be sold and dispensed without any special qualifications. Moreover, most low vision services cannot afford to stock and maintain the plethora of expensive and ever-changing product lines. A good relationship between a vendor of such products and a therapist becomes essential to effective delivery of low vision rehabilitation services. The therapist can provide the vendor with valuable advice as to what products will

Table 14-5.

Instructional Strategies for CCTV

1. Setup
2. Use of XY Table

    Begin with activity of interest to patient

    Horizontal and vertical scanning
3. Reading and Writing

    Successive horizontal lines of print

    Sentences or sequenced words

    Random words and numbers
4. Practice Writing

    Learn to find the pen tip

    Begin with thick felt-tip pen, thick-lined paper

    Start with signature, proceed to writing

    Completion tasks
5. Localization training

    Spotting strategies

    Locate sequential numbers in the corner of page

    Practice finding and naming the first word in successive paragraphs

    Locate byline or headline

    Reading a picture caption
6. Skimming and Scanning

    Magnify text perform systematic left-right and vertical scanning. Search text for particular words or numbers
7. Grooming, skin inspections, and working with three-dimensional objects

sell, and provide a vendor with an opportunity to sell their products. If a vendor is frequently demonstrating and selling products at a site, the vendor is often willing to provide demonstration units at no charge for the therapist to demonstrate and use for training. Outpatient therapists may depend on vendors to correctly configure a device in a client's home and provide some home-based instruction. Therapists can educate therapists as to instructional strategies. Vendors can keep therapists abreast of new technological developments and train therapists in how to use new equipment. If a vendor is unwilling to support his or her product, oversells expensive features, and fails to respond to queries from consumers, the therapist often must provide the additional support a client requires. The therapist has a responsibility to carefully document complaints by consumers regarding vendors and report unethical behavior first to the distributors and manufacturers of the product, and possibly to regulatory agencies. Fortunately,

manufacturers and distributors of electronic devices are keenly aware of maintaining a good reputation among a group where word of mouth can make or break a company.

Instructional Strategies

Generally with a CCTV, one begins instruction with use of the XY table, setup of the device, reading, writing, and finally other special applications suited to an individual client's interest (Table 14-5). To motivate an ambivalent or resistant client, or someone who is expected to find learning the CCTV difficult, the therapist should begin with an activity that directly addresses a client's interest or individual goal, teaching actual use of the device before the therapist instructs the client on setup. We have presented an order of instruction used for a client with recent vision loss who is resistant to change and is expected to find learning an electronic device difficult. If setup

is taught later, however, the client cannot practice at home or independently until demonstrating competency with setup and basic trial and error problem solving. The therapist might try to instruct a helper on setup if someone is available. Indeed, for the reluctant client, the therapist should not recommend purchase of the device until competency with task performance has been demonstrated or a helper can setup the device and solve problems. For a client who is willing and able, setup instruction should be first. Indeed, with younger vocationally-aged clients and students, instruction can often be completed in one session. For the reluctant client, expect instruction to require several sessions. Rolf Lund and Gale Watson have described a detailed, excellent instructional program for the CCTV, as well as a detailed account of CCTV design and use[3] as part of the *Learn to Use Your Vision for Reading (LUV)* series.

One challenge in providing CCTV instruction is gaining access to these expensive devices. A well-equipped clinic will have at least one CCTV system, preferably a color system with most extras that can be set up to simulate a less expensive system. All of the instructions described below, except for the setup, will rather easily transfer to another CCTV as long as the design of the XY table is similar. In the case of the reluctant client, to avoid transfer of learning issues, the therapist should recommend the device available for instruction in the clinic.

Setup

If a client finds learning a CCTV challenging, teaching a client how to setup a CCTV requires access to the unit the client will be using after discharge. The client must be taught to use the following features in the recommended order:

1. On/off switch and initial setup. Turn it on, turn all settings to natural view, and minimize magnification by feel.

2. After prefocusing the system, teach operation of the magnification setting.

3. Teach focus if auto focus is not available. Place a high-contrast target like a letter so that it is centered in the display screen. Maximize magnification. Adjust focus. Minimize magnification again. If auto focus is used, demonstrate how it might be confused and corrected.

4. Teach contrast polarity and color contrast settings to select ideal reading enhanced view as determined by the evaluation.

5. Teach the user to switch quickly from natural view to reading enhanced view.

6. Teach adjustment of contrast, screen brightness, and aperture settings (these are not changed very often and may even be taped in particular position to avoid accidental change).

Use of the XY Table

In the success-oriented approach, the first activity a client performs with a difficult device should be of interest, and part of a stated goal. Reading is the most common goal, but if the client had hoped for the day when she could perform cross-stitch again, then the demonstration material should be a photograph of cross-stitch, and the task might be "looking for missed stitches". The well-equipped service will have life-size photographs of a variety of nonreading activities for such clients as a starting point. Photographs will be much easier to manipulate at first, then three-dimensional objects. If a client has central field loss, the following instruction can be incorporated into eccentric viewing training (see Chapter 9) as the "steady eye technique" once development of eccentric fixation of isolated fixation targets has been mastered.

The change in the visual motor demands of reading or any task presents the greatest challenge with the CCTV. Typically, people are accustomed to directly looking at whatever they wish to see. For this reason, optical devices are more natural to use. With a CCTV, the user must look at a display positioned above or to the side of the object being viewed. When someone tries to locate something under a CCTV, the beginning user will often first try to look directly at the book or material on the XY table, rather than at the display.

Before this instruction begins, the therapist should set up the CCTV with the appropriate focus and natural color and the lowest magnification setting. The therapist positions the client's hand to point to something on a paper and instructs the client to "find the tip of your finger" by moving the XY table, using hand-over-hand assistance. This step is used to demonstrate the difference between direct viewing and CCTV viewing. Once the client finds the tip of his finger, magnification is increased. This exercise can be continued, but as an advanced exercise later until the client can find his finger by feel. Another demonstration that might help a user understand CCTV magnification is to place the cutout of a square window on an enlarged print version of the initial worksheet. The window can be moved along the paper to illustrate the necessary limitations in field of view that occur with magnification.

Before this instruction begins, the therapist should setup the CCTV with the appropriate focus and natural color. The CCTV should now be setup in reading

mode, optimized contrast and color for reading, focused, and set to lowest magnification. If available, XY table friction setting should allow greater vertical than horizontal resistance. If this is done by a therapist, the therapist should describe this setup process to the client.

The starting exercise teaches the client to develop systematic horizontal and vertical scanning. An example of a practice sheet might be rows of repeating, sequential single digit numbers, with five spaces between numbers and double spaces between lines. The numbers are connected by a horizontal line (see CCTV instruction documents in the Appendices). The therapist first shows the client how to position the paper on the XY table, against the lip and centered. The sheet is previewed at the lowest magnification at which the client can see start and stop of lines, and the margin stops (if any) are set. The client is then shown how to increase magnification until the letters or numbers can be easily recognized. The client is then instructed to move the table horizontally, starting at the first line. Sequential numbers and letters are generally easy to recognize and provide immediate feedback if a client loses his or her place. At the end of the line, the client is instructed to retrace back over the line to the beginning and move up to the next line. If available, a margin stop should be set to stop tray movement when the beginning of the line is reached. If the XY table does not have margin stops, the client can position his finger or a heavy object to the left of the tray on the table so that it stops the tray movement when the beginning of a line is centered in the display. The client should be reassured that once CCTV use is mastered, this scan can be performed very quickly.

If the therapist anticipates the client may have difficulty reading sheets with standard 12-point print, the size of the letters and numbers on the paper being viewed can be increased to allow magnification of the CCTV to be reduced. An enlarging copier should not be used, rather the overall size of the layout should remain the same so that the numbers are larger but the same distance apart.

With electronic devices and the resistant client, the therapist should attempt to make the task as easy as possible. To upgrade the activity and teach problem solving, position the paper incorrectly so that the lines are on a diagonal and challenge the client to identify and correct the problem. Move the table so that a few words are skipped or a line is skipped, and have the user find the beginning of the line once again.

Reading and Writing

Reading instruction continues from scanning sequential numbers and letters, to simple sentences, isolated short words, and more complicated sentences, as described in Chapter 9. At first, the exercises should only involve reading successive horizontal lines of task across a full page. Wright and Watson's workbook is an excellent source of graded engaging exercises for reading rehabilitation.[4] Initially, the material should be selected that involves sentences or sequenced words or numbers to provide immediate feedback if the user skips a line or some words. Activities involving random words and numbers can be presented once skipping errors are minimal. As this practice can be somewhat tedious, the exercises should involve games such as counting words that describe people or finding numbers that add up to 10. Practice writing can be incorporated into the reading exercises in a graded manner. First, the client might simply draw a line through selected words or numbers, then draw a line under the word, then a circle around, and finally a square around selected words or numbers.

If the client is having difficulty writing at the magnification level used for reading, then writing practice should occur separately at first. To begin, the client must learn to find the pen under the CCTV camera and become accustomed to a different visual-motor orientation. The client points to a high-contrast target on the XY table at a random location and then moves his hand on the table until the target and tip of the finger are displayed on the screen. This task is first performed at minimum magnification and graded to increased difficulty with higher magnification, and finally the use of a pen is added. Practice with this task should enable the client to adapt visual motor coordination with the CCTV so that positioning objects for a better view feels more natural. With writing, the table might be locked at first or the friction increased if this setting is available. The setup for writing should involve a thick felt-tip pen with thick lined paper, lower magnification and natural color settings. Start with a signature, simple shapes, and then move on to writing. Once the client feels comfortable writing enlarged print at a lower CCTV magnification setting, grade up the difficulty of the task by using the contrast/color settings used for reading, then progressively increase CCTV magnification with paper or forms with smaller, more typical lines.

Completion tasks, in which the user must fill in a missing word guessed from context, provide excellent practice. This teaches writing, as well as close strategies for reading as described in Chapter 9. Once the user is competent reading lines of text, the difficulty of the task might be increased by presenting reading material in columns and then interspersed with figures, tables, and ads, as is typical of a newspaper or many books.

Localization

A more difficult but functionally important task with a CCTV is localization. This involves spotting

strategies where first the material is viewed with lower magnification and the approximate location of the critical information is estimated from the layout of the material as seen with lower magnification. The user centers the suspected location of the critical information on the screen, and increases magnification to read. If in the wrong place, the user uses the material just read to better estimate the location of the critical information. The user decreases magnification somewhat to enlarge the field of view and moves the material and increases the magnification to read when the target is expected.

Functional reading, such as reading medicine labels, finding the total on a bill, finding information in a printed advertisement, reading a recipe or instructions, and finding and identifying faces in a photograph all involve localization strategies. Localization practice proceeds first with having the client locate sequential numbers in the corner of a blank page, then to the middle of a page. Then the client might practice finding and naming the first word in successive paragraphs, locating the byline or headline, and reading a picture caption. This phase of instruction can be completed using bills, medicine labels, instructions, and recipes. Note that the user is frequently changing magnification. Users require convenient access to the magnification control for such advanced skills.

Skimming and Scanning

Skimming and scanning is the most advanced reading task. In some cases, the user cannot use localization strategies because the layout of the page in an unmagnified view does not indicate where critical information is located on a page. The client must now magnify the text until it can be read and perform systematic left-right-vertical scanning to look for some text. This task might be to search text for particular words or numbers. In most cases, a combination of scanning and localization can be used. For example, looking up a word in the dictionary or a name in the phone directory might initially involve localization. The client must check first letters and then decrease magnification, using the less magnified view to skip pages and whole blocks of text until the expected location of the expected starting letter is centered and then magnified. Once the reader is close to the target, scanning methods can be used to find the target.

Grooming/Diabetic Management/Reading Labels

To begin this step in instruction, the client should demonstrate competency with CCTV setup and problem solving, especially with focusing. Tabletop CCTVs can be used to inspect hands and trim nails visually. The client should be competent with visual-motor coordination with a CCTV, such as writing tasks.

To start, a target is applied to a finger or picked up and viewed after focus is adjusted. The therapist instructs the user to inspect his hand and find the target. The goal is for the client to be able to move an object and position it so that it is in focus. Subsequent practice tasks might include fastening buttons, adjusting zippers, simple sewing activities like separating seams, cutting, and painting three-dimensional objects. These activities require that the CCTV be frequently refocused. Subsequent activities can be varied according to the client's interests and needs.

To read a medicine label, syringe, or to blot a bead of blood onto a test strip, the hand or object being viewed should rest in the center of the XY table so the distance from the camera does not change. In most cases, the table should be locked or friction increased for stability. A medicine bottle or syringe might be rotated while resting on a firm surface. To facilitate this activity for someone with impaired motoric control, the therapist might easily fabricate stands and holders from scraps of splinting material or dispense some firm putty to a client to stabilize objects.

Working With Crafts and Three-Dimensional Objects, Grooming, Skin Inspections, and Self-Catheterization

These activities are more easily performed with component CCTV systems (see Figure 14-2). With a detachable or adjustable camera, the objects are often viewed at odd angles so the image on the display appears rotated. If the camera does not have a rotational adjustment, the user should position the camera with direct horizontal or vertical alignment with the object rather than direct the camera at an oblique angle. For example, if setting a camera to magnify a screen at the end of a rectangular table, the user should position the camera directly in front of screen, at the other end of the table, rather than from the side. If a component CCTV is used as a mirror substitute for grooming, the camera might be directed at a mirror so the view is reversed like a real mirror. Otherwise, the user will need to readapt because the view will appear reversed from working in front of a mirror. Some component CCTVs have a setting that will reverse the display on a screen horizontally just like a mirror for just such an application. If the camera can be handheld, component CCTVs can be used for skin inspections. Component systems may also allow the camera to be mounted for self-catheterization. The challenge with all of these tasks is learning to approximate the correct camera positioning by feel or with the use of visible markers or tactile cues.

COMPUTER SYSTEMS

The increasing popularity of the personal computer in the early 1980s was a breakthrough for people who were blind. The first operating systems, eg, MS DOS, displayed text, one line at a time, in a form that could be easily transmitted to text-to-speech conversion hardware. People who had difficulty reading visually, now could read and write as quickly and efficiently as a typically sighted user. The advent of the now-standard graphical user interface (eg, Microsoft Windows, Apple MacIntosh) and dependence on the mouse has subsequently presented the blind user with a major obstacle to full access to the world of computing. Since the advent of the graphic interface, software developers and computer engineers, many of whom were blind, fought back with innovation and advocacy that encouraged manufacturers of operating system software to make their operator interface systems accessible. This was true not only for people with visual impairment, but also for those with a variety of other impairments as well. Currently, operating systems have built-in features that enable relatively easy access by people with mild impairment. Those with more severe impairment can access software, and other manufacturers of hardware and software have developed screen readers and display magnifiers that enable access by people with any level of vision loss. Full access to software and resources now is limited by the design of more specialized software and design of fully accessible Web pages. For example, few available instructional typing programs or computer games are fully accessible by people who are blind.

The personal computer stands as the potentially most powerful assistive device to enable a user with any level of vision loss to easily access print and numerical information and to recover inclusive functional written communication. As discussed in Chapter 9, people who can read by listening as quickly, comfortably, and efficiently as a typically sighted person. Not only can a user with low vision access email and much information on the Web, but with document readers that are now reasonably inexpensive, the computer user can scan and read printed information with magnification and visual enhancement with screen magnifiers or with speech or Braille using a screen reader.

Getting Started

To provide clients with access to these powerful tools, the therapist must learn how to adapt computer systems and operate common assistive equipment, but he or she does not need to become a computer expert. This chapter provides a "getting started guide" down the road of computer assistive systems. The information changes so rapidly, specific instructions and product recommendations would become quickly outdated. We will direct the reader to resources where this information can be found and provide recommendations about what to look for when evaluating equipment and software. This chapter will provide the reader with an overall strategy on how to narrow in on specific equipment, skills, and procedures for using computer-based assistive technology. For the service that cannot afford to stock and maintain the expertise to teach all competing products, selection of one or two preferred systems often is sufficient. Therapists can obtain free demonstration software for evaluation and introductory instruction. Extended instruction on use of the equipment typically is beyond the scope of a low vision service and can be provided by vendors or separate agencies.

Although the vendors of such equipment and instructors have special expertise with computers and the specialized programs and applications, these individuals often do not have special training in low vision rehabilitation and require a collaborating therapist with such training. These instructional and equipment providers require a therapist to setup the equipment and workplace so that the client with low vision can easily read the display. To share the equipment, the collaborating therapist providing vocational rehabilitation might consider working in the same facility with computer instructors and vendors.

Required Equipment and Skills

In typical outpatient, home-based, or workplace-based low vision rehabilitation settings, the therapist needs to be prepared to perform basic evaluation and introductory instruction with affordable equipment and basic skills. The hardware, software, skills, and resources required are listed in Table 14-6. A therapist can avoid the necessity of owning and learning many devices by having just one or two available. Most clients will depend on the therapist for specific product recommendations. Using the guideline in this chapter, the therapist should periodically evaluate the different devices available and select one or two of the best products for demonstration and instruction.

Carrying electronic devices such as computer monitors presents a problem for those doing home-based or workplace-based low vision practice. Those interested in computers usually already own a computer. It is recommended that the therapist have all of the necessary software on his or her own (portable) computer and use that computer for evaluation and demonstration rather than the client's computer. Computer programs for the visually impaired often conflict with other programs and require special hardware. Loading the software on a client's computer often results in many

Table 14-6.

Basic Equipment and Skills for Evaluation and Instruction

Equipment

- A 19-inch monitor.
- A height- and distance-adjustable monitor stand.
- A personal computer with speakers, scanner, regular keyboard, popular operating system, Web browser, word processor, and email program.
- Demonstration screen magnification programs.
- Demonstration screen reader programs.
- Demonstration document reader programs.
- Press-on enlarged keyboard letters (www.maxiaids.com)

Skills

- How to setup operating system with simplified menus and presentation.
- How to set user profiles (names used to log onto an operating system).
- Set accessbility display features of an available operating system, word processor, Web browser, and email system including:
  * Enlarged icons and text
  * Different and enhanced color contrast
  * Change print spacing if possible
  * Turn on/off text-to-speech features if available
  * Enlarge and enhance the mouse pointer
- Use other magnification features under accessibility options.
- Know how to use the demonstration magnification, screen reader, and document reader program.
- Know how to teach a client to use the very basic features of a simplified word processor, email system, Web browser and to change "templates" so these programs automatically start with required user settings.

Resources

- A relationship with local vendors and agencies who provide instruction.
- A commitment to continuing education on technology for the visually impaired.

---

technical problems. The therapist, however, usually can easily connect his or her own computer to the client's monitor and keyboard without such problems. If a client wishes to use a program for instruction and home practice, these programs will need to be loaded on the client's own computer. At this stage, the compatibility of the software with the client's computer will be important to consider in evaluating this device. The therapist is advised to refer the client to a vendor who can address installation and compatibility issues.

Minimally necessary equipment and skills include the following:

1. An approximately 17- to 19-inch monitor on a height and distance adjustable stand (Figure 14-8).

2. A personal computer with headphone jacks, speakers, and a scanner.

3. Summaries in large print and audio format to provide to clients describing modifications to operating systems, common web browsers, word processors, and email programs, as well

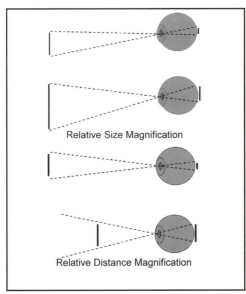

Relative Size Magnification

Relative Distance Magnification

Figure 14-8. Illustration of how relative distance magnification and relative size magnification enlarge the retinal image.

as recommended computer programs. These modifications can be made to a client's computer or a shared computer and saved under a user log-in name to be automatically recalled later when the user signs onto the computer. These instructions should indicate how to:

- Change display font and background colors.
- Enlarge icons and print.
- Enlarge and change the contrast of print.
- Turn on text-to-speech systems.
- Use other magnification features under accessibility options.

4. Demonstration screen magnifiers (eg, MAGic or ZoomText). These programs enlarge and enhance text displays much like a CCTV enlarges printed material. Select a screen magnifier that can be combined with a screen reader or incorporates screen reading features. Selection depends on availability of product sales and support (eg, MAGic or ZoomText).

5. Demonstration screen readers (eg, JAWS, Window-Eyes). These programs read text or numbers displayed on a screen aloud using computer speech or display the text on a Braille display. Many will indicate the position of graphics and even descriptions of graphics in some cases.

6. Demonstration document reader (eg, Kurzweil) software. This includes optical character recognition software and a display enhancement

7. A simplified computer system for word processing and typing instruction. On the demonstration computer, create a user "Mr. Easy" under the operating system, then remove all icons and features from the operating system except those minimally necessary to operate a word processor, the typing teaching program, the operating system email system, and a simplified Web page. If possible, disable all specialized key combinations that can initiate features unexpectedly if a user strikes the wrong keys. The goal here is to create a close equivalent to a typewriter.

8. Necessary computer skills. The therapist needs to develop the skills and a summary of instructions to introduce a client to a word processor, one or two demonstration Web pages, and email with the demonstration screen magnifier and screen readers. Focus on one common email program, such as Microsoft Outlook. Avoid Web-based mail systems, as websites are often incompatible with screen readers. Choose sample Web pages with good compatibility and generally high interest value, such as the website for a news source. Web pages for demonstration and instruction can often be duplicated on the hard drive of the therapist's computer so the therapist can avoid problems with Internet access.

9. A template for a written report. The therapist should have a document template that can be completed to describe all of the steps required to setup a system so that a user can see what is on a screen, including necessary optical devices, magnification, screen enhancements, working distance, and ancillary devices such as an adjustable monitor stand. A sample template is provided in the Appendices. The summaries describing changes to software described above can be added to this document. This report is provided to consumers and all instructors working with consumers who depend on the vision therapist to communicate the optimal visual settings.

10. A relationship with a local vendor or agency that provides instruction on use of computer assistive equipment.

11. A commitment to attending continuing education on assistive technology.

Resources

Access World, one of best sources of objective information about assistive technology by and for consumers of these products, is published by the American

Foundation for the Blind and available online for no cost (http://www.afb.org/aw/main.asp). The publication provides product reviews and unbiased information on what's new in computer technology. The following websites are also good sources of information for updated product information:

> http://www.abledata.com
> http://www.closingthegap.com
> http://www.resna.org/taproject
> http://www.afb.org
> http://www.csun.edu
> http://www.disabilityresources.org/AT-BLIND.html

Maintaining updated versions of the software can be very costly unless one has demonstration versions that are free of cost. Demonstration software usually is fully operational with time limits. There are two basic strategies for limiting time. First, the therapist may limit the time a person can access the software to about 30 minutes each time the computer is turned on. This limitation is usually sufficient for evaluation and initial instruction. The second strategy is for the software to run normally for a fixed number of days, then stop functioning. This, of course, is not satisfactory. Therapists are encouraged to contact vendors and manufactures to provide demonstration versions that can be used by practitioners for evaluation and instruction for more than a limited number of days.

Prerequisite Client Skills and Abilities

Unfortunately, computer assistive devices continue to be difficult to use. Until manufacturers simplify use of this technology, clients must have intact problem solving, semantic and procedural memory, reasoning, and frustration tolerance. For a person who has worked with computers for most of his or her life, many operations that may be somewhat challenging for the therapist, may for this client be as familiar and easy as getting dressed in the morning. These individuals often can use this equipment despite some cognitive limitations.

The major prerequisite skill for computer use is touch typing. A potential user with even moderate vision loss must learn to touch type before he or she can use a computer with efficiency. Close working distances in order to see the screen or the keys generally renders the "hunt and peck" method impossible. Fortunately, programs like Talking Typing Teacher (MarvelSoft Enterprises Inc, Abbotsford, British Columbia) have been developed that teach people who are blind to type on a computer, and the Hadley School for the Blind has a correspondence typing course for people who are blind. Simplified, talking word processors are also available. To locate typing programs for the blind, search the Web using the key terms "typing instruction blind" and "word processor blind." In general, if a person is physically able, typing is preferred to speech recognition software. Detecting and correcting errors that inevitably result from speech recognition is slower than typing it correctly the first time.

The complexity and instability of computers presents a major obstacle to use of computer assistive devices. Enabling someone with cognitive limitations and/or low frustration tolerance to access computer assistive low vision devices is limited by the resourcefulness and skill of the therapist. Simplifying computer access, however, requires special training on operating systems and software modifications, and setup of screen magnification and screen reader programs. Even sophisticated computer users with functional vision should have available optical devices, usually a handheld magnifier sufficient to enable a computer screen to be read if assistive software or the computer fails to work properly or does something unexpected. The available optical device allows the user to see the screen and solve the problem.

Screen Magnification Options

Display Enhancement: Mild/ Moderate Vision Loss

For those with approximately 20/80 to 20/100 acuity or better, who can read 2M print or smaller print fluently at 40 cm (16 in) (required magnification of less than 10 diopters [D] equivalent power [EP]), use of optical devices with a standard operating system is usually sufficient. The user requires an adjustable monitor stand and an ability to touch type. Icons, text, and mouse pointers can be easily enlarged 2X (5 D EP) using standard operating systems (see Figure 14-6). These modifications do not change the essential layout of the operating system and are thus easiest to learn. The setup steps are as follows:

- The mouse setup features allow enlarged mouse pointers to be used. An "inverted" feature should be selected so that the pointer automatically changes color on a background to reverse contrast.

- By finding the "accessibility" options in the setup software (in "Control Panel" in Windows) the operating system can be set to double the size of all text displayed. The accessibility setting also allows various reverse and color contrast settings as well. The setup features for the display also can be adjusted to provide white on black or any required color contrast. Icons can be enlarged using the display control as well.

Table 14-7.
Important Properties of Screen Magnifiers

- Stability (most important): the computer does not stop working properly while program is running.
- Ease of use for simple applications such as email and word processing and the programs used by the client.
- Magnification 2X to 10X.
- Quick and easy magnification adjust.
- Use with screen reader.
- Quick and easy change from contrast best for reading and normal view.
- Script files can be written so setups can be customized for applications.
- Targeting feature: the view can be preset to jump to targets frequently accessed with a keystroke.
- Font modifiability.
- Scroll features.

- Once set in the operating system, the screen enhancements should automatically apply to the menus of common word processors, spreadsheets, database programs, and Web browsers. If one needs to enlarge the text displayed within the particular program (the text the user is typing in a word processor), the "normal template" must be modified so the "view" or "zoom setting" is set to an appropriate magnification. In the view menu, Web browsers can be set to enlarge the print of pages and change contrast of Web pages as well.

- Despite all of these changes, sometimes messages will appear in an unmagnified view. For this reason, the user should always have additional optical magnification devices available that allow seeing normal displays in a pinch.

To magnify the screen, up to 5 D EP or 2X enlargement, sometimes up to 10 D (4X) will be tolerated. The use of a full-field microscope prescribed by an eyecare provider along with an adjustable monitor stand will enable the user to sit up straight and bring the monitor closer to the eyes (see Figure 14-5). Because the hands are now obscured by the monitor, touch typing is required. By combining relative distance magnification and operating system enhancements, one can achieve up to 4X to 6X enlargement (10 to 20 EP magnification). Additional screen reader features are available that allow the user to highlight text and have the computer read the text aloud.

We do not recommend use of large monitors and optical Fresnel magnifiers (magnifiers that adhere to

the screen), or optical magnifiers that are positioned in front of the screen. One can achieve the same magnification more easily and inexpensively with a clearer image of the screen with relative distance magnification. For example, increasing the monitor size from about 19 to 25 inches might nearly double the cost, while achieving an enlargement of only about 1.25%. The same magnification can be achieved by decreasing working distance from 40 cm (16 in) to 32 cm (12 in) at the cost of new reading glasses.

If a client must use a number of different computers, eg, a computer support person, he or she should have optical devices available that are sufficient to access computers on a regular basis. Examples of such devices are full-field microscopes, with hand magnifiers for additional magnification, and a telemicroscope if the client is instructing someone or needs to provide hardware repairs.

Display Enhancement: Moderate to Severe Vision Loss

For those requiring more than 2X to 4X enlargement, separate screen magnifier programs like MAGic (www.freedomscientific.com) or Zoomtexz (www.aisquared.com) should be considered as an option. For larger magnification, or text-to-speech, screen magnifiers and screen readers packaged with operating systems are generally unsatisfactory. The screen magnifier has more additional features than a CCTV (Table 14-7). While a CCTV enlarges a portion of the printed page, screen magnifiers enlarge a portion of the screen (see Figure 14-6). The user must now learn scanning skills, often using the mouse to scan

the entire screen. As with a CCTV, scanning can be a time-consuming and difficult skill to master. Screen magnifier programs, unlike CCTVs, have features that allow one to automatically jump to areas of interest on a screen. For example, with a word processor one might use a mouse to scan and read a document being typed, but as soon as a letter key is pressed, the screen magnifier will jump to the place in the text where the text is being typed. If a message box appears on the screen, the screen magnifier can be set to automatically jump to the text displayed in the box and then back to where the user was previously reading once the box is closed.

With software that a client uses often, such as database programs, screen magnifiers can be preprogrammed using script programs. When the software is started, the script file will change magnification and display characteristics for that particular software. For example, the script program will assign special control keys so that the user can, with a key press, jump to a particular area on the screen for data entry. This is called a targeting feature. This feature allows users to enter data in a program by quickly jumping to the data entry fields most commonly used with the press of a key rather than searching the screen to find it. These are used primarily by clients with vocational goals and require advanced instruction and support beyond the scope of a general low vision service.

Screen magnifier programs have features that can modify text characteristics, such as font type and spacing, to allow the user to more easily read without changing the font of the document being read or written. For example, ZoomText (Ai Squared, Manchester Center, VT) will display the text in a long document in a marquee fashion, scrolling the text from left to right at a preset speed. The reader no longer needs to hunt for the beginning of lines, but can use the steady eye technique to more easily read without moving his or her head or gaze position. This feature can be set up and used for training steady eye technique for people with central field loss (see Chapter 9). Most importantly, several screen magnifiers can be combined with screen readers, allowing users to read and listen to text at the same time. These combined systems are the software of choice for most people with low vision—even moderate vision loss. Table 14-7 lists the important properties of screen magnifiers. The most important property is stability. Stability indicates that the program operates consistently and does not stop working unexpectedly. For someone with normal vision, software malfunctions are frustrating but generally obvious. For someone with low vision, it is often difficult to distinguish a software malfunction from a routine operational problem.

Text-to-Speech/Braille Software

Once used only by people with profound vision loss, the screen reader allows a blind individual to navigate a computer screen. The screen reader reads text and numbers displayed on a screen at the cursor to the reader using computer speech or Braille displays. Screen readers might also read entire documents, lines, sentences, or paragraphs at a time at a preset speed so that a user can read a document of several pages at a time. Braille displays are pads that are about twice the length of a spacebar or more with moveable pins that are usually positioned just under the spacebar. The device in Figure 14-7 can be used as a Braille display. The pins, representing Braille characters, are raised and correspond to the text displayed on a line in the screen. Special translation software converts text to Braille.

Some screen readers work with a mouse, reading whatever text or numbers are displayed where the mouse pointer stops. Indeed, a special mouse will provide the user with tactile feedback as the user scans a page. For example, the mouse might bump when the user leaves a window. In general, someone with low vision will use a computer much more efficiently with only keyboard controls, avoiding the mouse as much as possible. Using the keyboard, the user must, therefore, memorize dozens of key combinations that direct the cursor to scan a page horizontally or vertically, to jump through text a word, sentence, or paragraph at a time, start reading, read faster or slower, or jump to preset locations in a particular application.

Using only the keyboard, a user can control all of the features as well as position the cursor on all major operating systems, word processors, spreadsheets, database programs, and Web browsers. The screen reader still reads what is being displayed at the location of the cursor. Since most people use a mouse, the instructions and help features on these programs sometimes neglect to summarize keyboard controls. One needs to search the website for the software manufacturer, and search for this information. In general, a convention has developed where the control features are listed in text format at the top of the screen, starting with "File/Edit." One can press the ALT key and the underlined or first letter on this menu for keyboard access. For example, holding the ALT key down and pressing F followed by a P will open the File menu to the print screen. The script file feature and targeting feature described above for screen magnifiers actually were first developed for screen readers and are thus available from major commercially available screen readers to allow one to jump the cursor to preset locations with key combinations.

Graphics, graphical icons, and unusual format in Web pages, documents, and software present a con-

Table 14-8.
Important Properties of Screen Readers

- Stability.
- Ease of use for simple, common applications and the applications used by the user.
- Use with magnification software using the same controls as magnification software.
- The screen reader used with magnifier uses the same controls as a screen reader used alone.
- Quick speed adjust, repeat reading a line or sentence with a single keystroke.
- Script files and targeting features.
- Web compatibility.
- Compatibility with software applications required by the client, including DOS.
- Full compatibility with common applications such as Outlook, Microsoft Word, Excel, Internet Explorer, and Access.
- Adobe PDF file compatibility.
- Visual dependence to use is not required to set up or use.

tinual challenge to the operation of screen readers. At the very least, screen readers normally announce to the user that it has encountered a graphic, or a graphic control. All major programming languages, operating systems, and Web designs now have a feature where the programmer or designer can provide text that describes a graphic or a control. Many, unfortunately, have not used these features. One useful service a therapist might provide is to identify software and websites that are fully accessible by a blind user using a screen reader. Software is available that checks sites for accessibility. These programs can be found by searching "accessible web sites blind" on the Internet. Of the many features that are most important for the beginning user (Table 14-8), stability remains the most important. Screen readers tend to have the most problems with stability, especially with the Web.

Print Reading Systems

This author recalls the first document or print reader (the Kurzweil machine), which cost $40,000 and was very slow and developed for people who were blind. Scanners and software are now available for a few hundred dollars and have features that convert printed text into speech and are relatively fast. Although the sophisticated, visually impaired client can use the inexpensive systems, commercial systems were not developed with blind users in mind and thus are often difficult to access with screen readers. Several manufacturers currently sell programs that work on the standard PCs. Document readers are also sold as stand-alone document readers that are specifically designed for users with low or no vision and are easier to use than computer-based systems. Inevitably,

document readers make mistakes and sometimes do not read print in the correct sequence when textbooks or documents have multiple columns. The systems designed for the blind user allow errors to be avoided or more easily corrected. Stand-alone systems are more expensive but easier to use and more stable than systems designed to work with conventional computers. The features that are most important for successful use by the beginner are summarized in Table 14-9.

Recordings for the Blind and Sighted Readers

The National Library for the Blind and Physically Handicapped (NLBPH) is a federally-funded agency that provides recordings or Braille transcriptions of current novels and magazines to users who cannot read because of visual, physical, or cognitive disability. Recordings for the Blind (RFB) is a private agency that provides a similar service for little or no fee. RFB more often provides textbooks and teaching materials.

The technology involved in presenting recordings of books and magazines is rapidly changing. In 2005, recordings were generally available on audiotape cassettes that were specially formatted to work more slowly and store twice as much as conventional cassettes. Special players are required; these are generally available for free from NLBPH. As the audio quality of these players is often poor, earphones are recommended, especially for elderly clients who likely have at least mild hearing loss. The major disadvantage of audiotapes is that the tone of the speaker

Table 14-9.

Important Properties of Document Readers

- Stability.
- Ease of use for the reluctant client.
- Low error frequency even with poor quality print and unpredictable formats (evaluation with a newspaper is recommended).
- Low error frequency if original is not aligned properly.
- Fast scan rates, automatic feed with multiple pages.
- For low vision users, documents can be read aloud while document, charts, and figures are simultaneously viewed with screen magnification.

changes (the "Mickey Mouse effect") if the speaking rate is increased or decreased. It becomes difficult to skim a book. As is often the case with visual reading, users fall asleep when listening. Unlike visual reading, the tape keeps playing. The reader must now try to rewind to where he or she fell asleep. Audiotapes are "tone indexed." Chapters and sections are marked so that during the fast rewind, a tone or tones can be heard marking the beginning of a chapter, for example. The user can rewind until the tone is heard, then stop the recorder near the beginning of the chapter. Note that special switches are now available that shut off the player if the listener falls asleep and releases the switch.

Digital talking books, available from RFB and other private suppliers, uses CDs to store both a recording by a reader (as opposed to computer speech) and a digital transaction of the material. With digital talking books, the user can much more easily scan the recording. The user must acquire special CD players or software that can be installed on any PC to use this technology. Ipods (Apple Computer) and other MP3 players are able to store music, audio books, and radio broadcasts that can be downloaded from the Web to play on demand.

Personal Organizers and Other Devices

Blind users used personal organizers before they became widely used by those with typical vision. These devices essentially are keyboards. Instead of a display, the device uses text-to-speech played through standard earphones. Some models have special keyboards and displays for Braille users as well. Talking cell phones, talking global positioning devices, and echolocation devices that use sound to indicate obstacles are available as well.

EVALUATION

Computer systems should be considered as assistive devices as well as adaptations for those who aspire to use computers as a performance goal. As a general rule, clients for whom a CCTV would be seriously considered for a reading or writing goal might benefit from adapted computer systems as well. For those with reading and writing goals that do not necessarily involve computers, evaluation of clients for use of assistive computer systems is virtually identical to the evaluation performed for the CCTV, except the criteria for frustration tolerance and problem-solving ability is more stringent for computer systems.

Computers should be considered for clients who must engage in writing more than required for activities of daily living (ADL). Word processing is often easier than handwriting for those with moderate vision loss, especially if they already can touch type or have incoordination impairment or arthritis. People with vocational goals involving extensive reading and writing, data processing, searching for information, and virtually anyone working at a desk will benefit from consideration of assistive computer systems. In addition, therapists should perform an evaluation of people with mild vision loss who have included computer use in their performance goals.

Computer systems are similar to CCTV, except:
- Evaluate reading performance with text-to-speech versus reading versus both.
- Evaluation of other physical requirements relevant to ergonomics.
- Evaluation of cognitive capability. The client requires good frustration tolerance, ability to learn and recall multistep operations, and trial and error problem solving. Computer systems are routinely used successfully for many with

developmental disabilities and can be adapted for cognitive impairment.

Instructional Strategies

In general, instruction with computer systems depends on the specific configuration provided and is beyond the scope of this text. Some general strategies for the more reluctant user are as follows:

- Choose systems primarily on the basis of stability. Nothing is more frustrating to a beginning user than when a computer stops working and the user cannot tell if it was a user error or a program error.
- The first skills to learn are how to start and restart a computer. The user should be taught "escape strategies"---how to return to a comfortable, familiar place in the computer such as the start menu if the computer starts doing the unexpected.
- Do not begin with instructions on setup. Often setup can be automated, so that when the client signs onto the computer as a user, the assistive programs start and configure automatically, and the desktop will appear in a familiar format. Once the therapist determines the optimum setup, this information can be stored onto a CD or other storage media and transferred to another computer with the help of a computer-savvy assistant.[5]
- Begin with typing instruction program if necessary, then a simplified word processor and then to email.
- Use optical devices and modifications in operating system software if possible, rather than special screen magnifiers or screen readers.
- Remove all icons from the desktop. Place applications frequently used on the top of the start-up menu. See the help menu for the operating system for instructions on how to do this.
- Have available a simplified computer for demonstration using a different name (Mr. Easy) for evaluation and initial instruction.

ACCESSORIES AND ERGONOMICS

A visually impaired student, worker, or leisure participant using a computer system or CCTV will be moving a lot more than a typically-sighted user and is thus at risk for repetitive strain injury. When recommending electronic systems, the therapist must use a variety of methods to enable good ergonomics (see Table 14-9). The use of a monitor stand is the most

important. The workspace should be set up so that the user can switch quickly among all of the devices that must be used. For example, a user providing customer service by telephone needs to easily access the telephone, so a headset is essential. Someone using an optical device to read documents requires a task light and work space for visual reading. Someone typing from print might require the magnified view of the original positioned to be read with good posture with a reading stand or CCTV. The corner of a corner desk with a swivel chair allows one to avoid lateral back movement. Split-screen CCTVs also have a feature where the user can switch between the CCTV and computer display with a foot switch, allowing one to copy without moving the head (see Figure 14-5).

Another configuration involves having the computer read the typed material aloud while the client is reading visually. This is an excellent strategy for the beginning typist. Glare is often a problem in a large office area. A privacy screen positioned in front of the monitor allows only the person directly in front of the monitor to see what is displayed without decreasing the light from the display. This is the best method to eliminate glare and allows for privacy for someone who is displaying a magnified image on the screen.

SUMMARY AND VIEW OF THE FUTURE

CCTV technology and computer technology continue to converge. Many types of devices (see Table 14-1) will soon be available in one portable system. In 2006, CCTVs with digital cameras store an image that a user can view just like the image on a standard CCTV. Systems such as the Myreader (Eschenbach Optik of America, Ridgefield, CT) provide most of the visual enhancements described above for screen magnifiers, the ability to change fonts, letter spacing, and scroll text for easier visual reading. CCTVs that read text aloud are on the horizon. As computer systems continue to become miniaturized, handheld, and more cosmetically acceptable, head-mounted systems will allow someone to look at a book and immediately have the book displayed in a visual format optimized by his or her therapist and eyecare provider, as well as read aloud.

One area that still requires considerable attention is development of systems that are easier for clients to use. For example, we need an accessible word processor or email system that is as easy to use as a typewriter. Most of the additional features available are simply unimportant to many consumers with low vision. One must not forget that most clients with recent vision loss simply wish to recover the familiar. They

often approach new ground with fear and trepidation. For example, replacing a dial or lever that adjusts magnification with a push button control neglects to consider what is familiar to most older consumers.

Finally, one unfortunate consequence of emerging technology has been an apparent decline in human to human contact that for all of us is most important. For the older, often lonely, client who has recently lost vision, a friend reading the newspaper or helping read mail provides so much more than the achievement of efficient reading performance.

REFERENCES

1. Hensil J, Whittaker SG. Comparing visual reading versus auditory reading by sighted persons and persons with low vision. *J Vis Impair Blind*. 2000;94(12):762-770.
2. De l'Aune W, Watson GR, Stelmack J, Maino J, Long S. A national survey of veterans' use of low vision devices. *Optom Vis Sci*. 1997;74:249-259.
3. Lund R, Watson GR. *The CCTV Book: Habilitation and Rehabilitation With Closed Circuit Television Systems*. Frolond, Norway: Synsforum ANS; 1997.
4. Wright V, Watson GR. *Learn to Use Your Vision for Reading* (LUV Reading Series). Lilburn, GA: Bear Consultants; 1996.
5. Whittaker SG, Young T, Toth-Cohen S. Universal tailored access: automating setup of public and classroom computers. *J Vis Impair Blind*. 2002;96(6):448-451.

Adaptive Diabetes Self-Management Tools and Techniques

Debra A. Sokol-McKay, MS, CVRT, CDE, CLVT, OTR/L

STATISTICS

Diabetes is a national health issue. According to the American Diabetes Association (ADA), diabetes affects 20.8 million people in the United States, or 7% of the population. While an estimated 14.6 million people were diagnosed in 2005, 6.2 million (or nearly one-third) are unaware that they have the disease. One and a half million new cases of diabetes were diagnosed in people aged 20 years or older in 2005. A research analysis completed by members of the Centers for Disease Control and Prevention (CDC) and the Research Triangle Institute projected a 165% increase in the prevalence of diabetes between the years 2000 and 2050, from 11 million cases of diagnosed diabetes in 2000 to 29 million cases in 2050.

Diabetes is a systemic disease for which there is no cure, and its complications affect every major system of the body. Stroke and risk of death from heart disease are two to four times higher in adults with diabetes than without. Diabetes is the leading cause of new blindness in adults 20 to 74 years of age. Forty-four percent of the new cases of kidney failure can be attributed to diabetes. More than 60% of nontraumatic lower limb amputations in the United States occur among persons with diabetes. Mild to severe forms of nervous system damage are evident in 60% to 70% of persons with diabetes.[1]

According to ADA statistics dated 2002, the total direct and indirect costs of diabetes in the United States is $132 billion, with direct medical costs of $92 billion and indirect costs of $40 billion, including disability, work loss, and premature mortality. Per capita medical expenditures totaled $13,243 for people with diabetes and $2,560 for people without diabetes. When adjusting for differences in age, sex, and race/ethnicity between the population with and without diabetes, people with diabetes had medical expenditures that were 2.4 times higher than expenditures that would be incurred by the same group in the absence of diabetes. The projected increase in the number of people with diabetes suggests that the annual cost in 2002 dollars of diabetes could rise to an estimated $156 billion by 2010 and to $192 billion by 2020. The financial costs are rivaled by the overwhelming physical and psychosocial toll that diabetes places on those who have it and their loved ones. Incidence of depression is reported to range from 30% to 70% in persons with diabetes and may be as high as 75% in persons with more than one complication.

Two premier studies, the Diabetes Control and Complications Trial (DCCT) and the United Kingdom

Prospective Diabetes Study (UKPDS) have demonstrated the benefit of tight blood glucose control on the reduction in the development and progression of chronic complications. The results of the DCCT (1983 to 1993) showed a reduction in risk of complications (eye disease: 76%; kidney disease: 50%; nerve disease: 60%; cardiovascular disease: 35%) when persons with type 1 diabetes were treated with an intensive management regime consisting of four injections per day or use of an insulin pump and blood glucose monitoring four or more times per day. The UKPDS (1977 to 1991) showed the importance of intensive blood glucose control to persons with type 2 diabetes. It reported that better blood glucose control through intensive antidiabetic therapy resulted in a 25% reduction in microvascular complications, including retinopathy, and a 35% reduction in early kidney damage. In addition, improved blood pressure control through medication in persons with high blood pressure and diabetes resulted in reductions in: stroke (33%), death from the long-term complications of diabetes (33%), and serious deterioration of vision (33%).

INTRODUCTION TO DIABETES AND ITS IMPACT ON VISION

Diabetes mellitus is a group of metabolic diseases characterized by hyperglycemia or high blood glucose. Diabetes occurs when the body cannot use the glucose in the blood because the pancreas is not able to make or release enough insulin, the insulin that is made is not effective because of resistance of the cells receiving it, or both. The symptoms of acute hyperglycemia include frequent urination, excessive thirst, extreme hunger, blurred vision, fatigue, headache, poor wound healing, and muscle cramps.

The two major types of diabetes are type 1 (formerly juvenile-onset, type I, or insulin dependent) and type 2 diabetes (formerly adult-onset, type II, or noninsulin dependent). The other two forms of diabetes include gestational and secondary. Type 1 diabetes affects 5% to 10% of persons with diabetes and most often develops before age 30.[1] Persons with type 1 diabetes require an external source of insulin to sustain life, due to autoimmune destruction of the insulin producing cells of the pancreas. A genetic predisposition underlies the cause of type 1 diabetes.

Type 2 diabetes affects about 90% to 95% of persons with diabetes. It is usually diagnosed after 30 years of age; however, it is becoming increasingly more prevalent in young children and adolescents. Both insulin deficiency (although variable) and insulin resistance are present in persons with type 2 diabetes. Major risk factors for type 2 diabetes include age (high prevalence in older adults), ethnic background, positive family history of type 2 diabetes, and obesity. Type 2 diabetes may initially be treated with weight loss, diet, and exercise. Oral medications and then ultimately insulin may be needed as the disease progresses.

Diabetes can contribute to a multitude of conditions affecting the eyes, including diabetic retinopathy, macular edema, cataracts, glaucoma, ocular palsies, and fluctuating vision. In addition, the incidence of macular degeneration, although unrelated to diabetes, is also strongly related to increased age and thus another prevalent eye condition in persons with type 2 diabetes. Eye disease is 25 times more common in persons with diabetes than in the general population. The CDC estimates that 3 million people in the United States report both vision loss and diabetes, out of an estimated total of 20.8 million people with diabetes.

Diabetic retinopathy, the most common eye condition, is often detectable within 5 years of diagnosis. Nonproliferative retinopathy is present in 90% of persons with type 1 diabetes after 20 years; 50% will progress to the proliferative stage. After 20 years, 80% of persons with type 2 diabetes treated with insulin will have nonproliferative retinopathy; 40% will progress to the proliferative stage. Twenty percent of persons with type 2 diabetes but not treated with insulin will have nonproliferative retinopathy, with 5% advancing to the proliferative stage. Macular edema affects 10% to 15% of persons in all groups.[7]

Diabetic retinopathy can occur in a mild to very advanced form, from nonproliferative (formerly background or preproliferative) to the proliferative stage. The nonproliferative stage is further broken down into mild, moderate, severe, and very severe. Mild nonproliferative diabetic retinopathy (NPDR) occurs when the microvasculature of the retina becomes weakened and begins to leak fluids. Small deposits are formed on the retina and tiny hemorrhages appear. Often no vision loss is noted at this stage. During moderate to very severe NPDR, further vascular damage occurs, resulting in capillary closure and retinal ischemia; however, persons at this stage may not detect changes in vision.

In the final stage, proliferative diabetic retinopathy (PDR), new blood vessels begin to grow along the retina in response to the hypoxia. However, these vessels are very fragile and will rupture, causing preretinal and vitreous hemorrhages. At this stage, vision impairment may range from mild blurring to severe vision loss. Persons experiencing bleeding may report a veil, cloud, or streaks of red material within their field of vision. In addition, the fibrous scar tissue that develops between the vessels, retina, and vitreous can contract and pull on the retina, causing retinal tears and detachment. A retinal detach-

ment can cause total blindness in the affected eye. If neovascularization occurs in the optic disc, the risk for major vision loss is high.

Macular edema can be present in NPDR or PDR and it may impair central vision. The impact on vision may vary from mild blurring to severe loss. Fluctuating vision may arise from swelling in the lens of the eye as a result of high and low blood glucose levels, or it may be in response to postural changes, environmental conditions such as lighting, eye fatigue, or general fatigue.

A major treatment for severe to very severe NPDR and PDR is panretinal photocoagulation or laser surgery, which is applied in a scatter pattern to the peripheral retina. This treatment does not target the new abnormal blood vessels themselves, but is thought to halt their proliferation by destroying enough tissue that the demand for oxygen is decreased.[9] A vitrectomy may be performed when hemorrhages do not resolve or when retinal detachment has or may occur. During vitrectomy, the vitreous contents are removed and replaced with a clear solution. Clinically significant macular edema is treated with focal photocoagulation to seal leaking blood vessels. The goal of these treatments is to reduce vision loss.

The functional vision in persons with diabetic eye disease is quite variable, ranging from mild blurring, irregular patches of vision loss in the central or peripheral field of vision, to severe vision loss or total blindness. Vision loss may vary between both eyes. It is not uncommon for a person with diabetes and vision loss to have a preferred, better-seeing eye. An eye report may be helpful to provide visual acuity and visual field measurements within a clinical setting; however, it is also important to obtain a sense of what a client can see during functional activities in a natural environment. An individual's subjective acuity or personal experience of his or her vision loss is just as important as objective acuity or results from an eye chart, especially with respect to low vision. The client's performance of activities requiring vision may be better than acuity suggests, or in some cases worse. Two clients with diabetic eye disease and similar vision changes may use their residual vision differently. A client may well have, through experience, discovered areas of usable vision, which may not appear consistent with actual acuity measurements.

CHRONIC COMPLICATIONS OF DIABETES AND GENERAL PRECAUTIONS

Prolonged hyperglycemia is the cause of the many chronic and systemic complications of diabetes. These complications affect both the large and small blood vessels in the body and therefore are divided into two major categories: microvascular and macrovascular. The microvascular conditions include retinopathy, neuropathy, and nephropathy. Twenty percent of persons with type 2 diabetes will have microvascular complications upon diagnosis. Macrovascular complications include: coronary artery disease, cerebral vascular disease, and peripheral vascular disease. These complications contribute significantly to the morbidity and mortality associated with diabetes, particularly in persons with long-standing diabetes.

Retinopathy that has advanced to the proliferative stage carries with it a number of precautions to prevent retinal bleeding. These include avoiding the following behaviors: lifting objects heavier than 5 pounds (or limit as determined by physician), bending so the head is lower than the waist, engaging in activities that raise blood pressure in the eyes, moving suddenly, and straining. A primary care provider and ophthalmologist should be consulted before engaging in strenuous activities.

Diabetic neuropathy, another microvascular complication, can be diffuse, affecting the peripheral and autonomic nervous systems, or it can be focal, affecting a single nerve or group of nerves. It is chronic and progressive in nature. Peripheral neuropathy is the most prevalent form. Symptoms include a "pins and needles" sensation, pain, numbness, the inability to detect temperature or position, and inability to feel feet when walking. Precautionary measures include care in use and disposal of sharp objects, exposure to and handling of hot items, and implementing proper foot care.

Autonomic neuropathy involves nerves that control automatic body functions and affect mostly internal organs. This form of neuropathy tends to occur later in the course of diabetes. Fifty percent of persons with diabetes who have peripheral neuropathy also have autonomic neuropathy. Autonomic neuropathy may affect many systems, including the genitourinary, the gastrointestinal, the cardiovascular, and the sudomotor (responsible for the body's temperature regulation).

Cardiovascular effects of autonomic neuropathy are noteworthy. They include postural hypotension, which can cause lightheadedness, dizziness, and weakness. Precautions include slow positional changes and transitional movements. Cardiac denervation syndrome, a fixed heart rate that does not change in response to stress, exercise, breathing patterns, or sleep, may be present. In later stages of cardiac denervation, a silent or painless myocardial infarction (MI) can occur. Other typical symptoms of a MI, such as nausea, shortness of breath, sweating, and vomiting, may be present. These symptoms require imme-

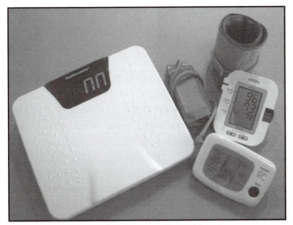

Figure 15-1. Large display or talking blood pressure monitors and weight scales.

diate medical attention. Stress testing should precede any type of exercise program.

Focal neuropathy is generally acute and time-limited, with pain often being the primary symptom. The most common form of focal neuropathy is carpal tunnel syndrome, which is three times more common in persons with diabetes than among the rest of the population.[13]

Nephropathy is the final microvascular complication. End-stage renal disease may result in symptoms of nausea, vomiting, dyspnea, lethargy, hypertension, and fluctuating blood glucose levels. Ninety-five percent of persons with diabetic nephropathy have some retinopathy, with 50% being blind or having lost significant vision. This syndrome is entitled renal-retinal syndrome. Monitoring blood pressure by use of a large display or talking blood pressure cuff may be required.

Macrovascular complications are responsible for 80% of the mortality of adults with diabetes. Macrovascular complications are characterized by both arteriosclerosis and atherosclerosis. Coronary artery disease can lead to congestive heart failure (CHF) or a heart attack. Monitoring CHF-related fluid retention by use of a large display or talking scale becomes critical.

Cerebral vascular disease can lead to a stroke. Symptoms such as dizziness, slurred speech, numbness or weakness in an arm or leg, or sudden loss of sight may occur. Ability to access emergency medical services is important. Peripheral vascular disease can lead to lower leg and foot ulcers and the need for amputation. Symptoms can include pain with standing, walking, or at rest. Guidelines may include remaining seated during tasks, incorporating rest periods into standing/walking activities if pain is relieved by rest, and seeking medical attention if pain interferes with program or is reported at rest.

With respect to the health maintenance devices suggested above, the following guidelines should be considered. Large, LCD (liquid crystal display) devices should be evaluated by the individual with diabetes and vision loss to insure that they can consistently be read; getting close to the display may not be an option. When suggesting any talking device, many voice-related features need to be considered before recommending a specific model. These include voice clarity, volume, speed, pitch, and accent. In many cases where a hearing impairment is present, a male voice may be preferable due to the lower pitch (Figure 15-1).

ACUTE COMPLICATIONS OF DIABETES

Hypoglycemia

The major acute complication of diabetes is hypoglycemia or low blood glucose, which is defined as a blood glucose level of less than 70 mg/dL. Hypoglycemia is not a result of diabetes itself but is a consequence of its treatment. Typical causes relate to the amount and timing of: 1) insulin or certain anti-diabetes medications (but not all), 2) physical activity, and 3) food or carbohydrates eaten. Common symptoms can include: sweating, shakiness, difficulty concentrating, blurred vision, dizziness, weakness, or trouble performing a routine task. Severe hypoglycemia can result in pronounced confusion, seizures, coma, and death.

Hypoglycemia is treated with carbohydrate containing foods or beverages such as juice/soda, honey, or commercially made products such as glucose tablets or gel. If possible, the person should check his or her blood glucose level to determine the amount of carbohydrates required to raise his or her blood glucose to a safe level. Regardless of whether or not the person is able to test, the symptoms should be treated as soon as possible. It is recommended that clients consume 15 grams of carbohydrate (4 ounces juice or regular soda, 1 tablespoon honey, or 3 to 4 glucose tablets) and then retest their blood glucose in 15 minutes to determine if additional treatment is required. This is known as the 15/15 rule. If a meal is not planned within 1 to 2 hours of treating a hypoglycemic reaction, then a snack containing 15 to 30 grams of carbohydrate should be consumed to prevent another episode of hypoglycemia.

Several safety measures and adaptations can be implemented to assist the client with vision impairment to avoid or manage hypoglycemia. Persons with diabetes should always wear diabetes identification

and carry a blood glucose monitor and a readily available carbohydrate source at all times. Physical activity that might lower blood glucose should be scheduled 1 to 3 hours after mealtime. The individual with diabetes should be referred to a physician or diabetes educator if: 1) symptoms of low blood glucose are no longer recognized, 2) a significant episode of low blood glucose occurs, or 3) if blood glucose levels are low for 2 days at the same time of day.

Low vision, talking, or Braille timepieces will enable clients with vision loss to insure timeliness of meals and medications. Large-print or taped blood glucose records will allow the person with diabetes and his or her physician to determine events that may have contributed to low blood glucose. Noncaloric/low sugar products like diet soft drinks can be marked with a rubber band to distinguish them from those that are nondiet. Immediate access to emergency phone numbers is critical and several possible adaptations include: large print, preprogramming telephone, and speed or voice dialing. Low vision and nonvisual methods for blood glucose monitoring, measuring insulin and obtaining desired portions of carbohydrate foods will be addressed later in this chapter.

Very high blood glucose levels can lead to two different acute and life-threatening conditions: diabetic ketoacidosis (DKA) and hyperosmolar hyperglycemic state (HHS). DKA occurs most frequently in persons with type 1 diabetes, while HHS is more common in elderly persons with type 2 diabetes. Both conditions are characterized by pronounced hyperglycemia, dehydration, and altered mental state and if left untreated, may result in coma and death. Both require immediate medical attention.

DEFINITION OF DIABETES SELF-MANAGEMENT AND THE ROLE OF THE LOW VISION THERAPIST

Diabetes self-management consists of a variety of tasks: 1) blood glucose monitoring, 2) medication management (including insulin), 3) meal planning, 4) exercise or physical activity, and 5) foot and skin care. Each of the above tasks is interrelated, and taken together, the client can achieve improved blood glucose control by implementing an integrated diabetes self-management program. By this means, the client can live a healthy lifestyle and avoid, delay, reduce, and/or manage the long-term complications of diabetes. Each of the above task areas poses unique challenges to a person with vision impairment.

The basic role of the low vision therapist is to provide support, reinforcement, and referral. This role requires knowledge of diabetes, its complications, functional implications, and precautions, in addition to knowledge of professionals in the field of diabetes. In an advanced role, the low vision therapist provides: 1) general training in low vision and nonvisual skills and environmental modification related to organization, contrast, lighting, and magnification; and 2) specific training in the tools and techniques of adaptive diabetes self-management. This advanced role requires in-depth, current knowledge of all facets of diabetes and diabetes self-management, as well as practical knowledge of low vision tools and techniques relative to diabetes management.

In 1994, the Visually Impaired Persons Specialty Practice Group (VIP-SPG) of the American Association of Diabetes Educators (AADE) and Division 11 (Rehabilitation Teaching) of the Association for Education and Rehabilitation of the Blind and Visually Impaired (AER) jointly developed Guidelines for the Practice of Adaptive Diabetes Education for Visually Impaired Persons (ADEVIP). Specific guidelines are included in ADEVIP for professional educational background, the respective role of the low vision therapist and the certified diabetes educator, and the expected process and content of adaptive diabetes education. The ADEVIP offered the following guidelines:

- Continuing education in diabetes treatment must be updated every 2 years.
- Contact client's primary healthcare professional to assure that client has had basic diabetes self-care instruction.
- Only teach adaptations and not basic diabetes self-care (should reinforce proper self-care).
- Never give specific advice on medication, nutrition, or exercise.
- No direct care, such as prefilling of syringes.
- After client has learned adaptive techniques, but before relying on it for self-care, refer client back to client's primary healthcare professional for confirmation of skill.

Although the ADEVIP practice guidelines were designed for AER vision rehabilitation professionals, they are equally applicable to low vision therapists in the field of occupational therapy.

MEMBERS OF THE DIABETES SELF-MANAGEMENT TEAM AND THEIR ROLES

It is important to be aware of members of the diabetes management team, each member's role, rea-

sons to refer to these other healthcare providers, and resources for reimbursement for their services. The core diabetes team should consist of the client, a physician, a nurse diabetes educator, a dietician, an ophthalmologist, and a low vision optometrist. Persons with diabetes should be educated as to the availability and roles of these team members.

In general, everyone with type 1 diabetes should be seen by an endocrinologist, which is a physician who specializes in endocrine disorders, including diabetes. Many persons with diabetes, particularly uncomplicated type 2, can have a primary care provider such as an internist or family physician effectively manage their diabetes. An endocrinologist may be recommended for an individual with type 2 diabetes if he or she is following an intensive diabetes self-management program requiring three or more insulin injections a day or is using an insulin pump. Other circumstances that may warrant follow-up by an endocrinologist include: blood glucose levels consistently higher than desired, one or more diabetes complications, other medical conditions that make diabetes management more difficult, or an individual's desire for a change in his or her diabetes care plan. Routine follow-up visits should be scheduled every 3 to 6 months, or more frequently if the client has difficult keeping blood glucose levels under control, is experiencing complications, or becomes ill.[19]

The nurse diabetes educator provides comprehensive training in diabetes as well as basic and more advanced diabetes self-management tasks. Referral for initial or follow-up training by a nurse diabetes educator is recommended when an individual: lacks information or has misperceptions about what diabetes is and its effects on the body, has not received basic diabetes self-management training, or has difficulty with at least one diabetes-related task. A diabetes nurse educator should also be consulted when a client would like to incorporate physical activity into his or her diabetes self-management program or needs a plan for managing stress or illness.

A dietician provides training in healthy meal planning and develops individualized meal plans, taking into account many variables, including caloric requirements, food preferences, and cultural background. Referral to a dietician is recommended when an individual does not know what to eat or how much to eat, feels restricted by his or her meal plan or makes unhealthy food choices, lacks or has an outdated food/meal plan, or has not seen a dietician in several years.

An ophthalmologist is necessary to diagnosis eye disease(s), monitor disease progression, and provide medical treatment inclusive of prescription eyewear, medications, and eye surgery. This team member is especially important when diabetic retinopathy, macular edema, glaucoma, or even macular degeneration are already present, in order to maintain optimum eye health and visual functioning. All persons with diabetes should receive routine dilated eye exams at least every year, or more frequently depending on the presence and degree of eye disease. It is recommended that persons with proliferative retinopathy receive an ophthalmologic exam every 2 to 4 months or more often.[7]

The role of the optometrist is to determine whether a change in the traditional eyeglass prescription might be of benefit and to perform a detailed evaluation of distance and near visual acuity, contrast sensitivity, assessment of central scotomas, and peripheral visual field. Based on the results of this evaluation and the case history, the optometrist begins the process of determining the magnification needs of the patient for various activities of daily living (ADL) and selects and prescribes appropriate low vision optical aids. To be most effective, the optometrist and occupational therapist should work together to determine the appropriate optical devices for a patient. Optometrists will often make suggestions about lighting, contrast, and glare and how these issues affect the patient's ability to effectively use the optical device. The optometrist then refers the patient to the occupational therapist for training in the use of the prescribed device in various ADL.

Other potential members of the diabetes self-management team may include, but are not limited to, a dentist, psychologist, podiatrist, and nephrologist.

Most insurances pay for diabetes self-care training provided by a nurse or a dietician who is a diabetes educator and who is affiliated with a healthcare setting or medical office. Outpatient diabetes self-management education is reimbursable under Medicare and includes up to 10 hours of one-time initial training within a continuous 12-month period, and 2 hours of follow-up training each year thereafter. A physician must order these services. The approved providers include physician-run clinics and hospital-based outpatient programs that include a registered dietician and a certified diabetes educator and are accredited by the Health Care Finance Administration (HCFA), now called the Centers for Medicare and Medicaid Services (CMS). In January 2002, Medicare added a new Part B benefit for Medical Nutrition Therapy (MNT). Eligible persons with diabetes can receive 3 hours of initial MNT and up to 2 hours annually thereafter in addition to the hours for basic diabetic self-management education (DSME).

Medicare Part B reimbursement has been available for blood glucose monitoring equipment since October 1998. Medicare covers 80% of the cost of a blood glucose monitor and ancillary supplies, including test

strips, lancets, and glucose control solution. They will reimburse for replacement of a blood glucose monitor and lancing device every 5 years. Many other insurances will provide coverage for blood glucose monitoring equipment; the level of coverage varies and certain plans may limit an individual's choice to specific models. Rebates are often available for visual display monitors, and monitor manufacturers may be willing to provide a free monitor to acquire a new customer or maintain a current customer. A listing on blood glucose monitor manufacturers is provided at the end of this chapter under Resources. Under Medicare and many third party reimbursers, an individual must be declared legally blind to qualify for a talking blood glucose monitor. Insurance coverage of a monitor and supplies requires a physician's prescription.

According to the CMS, under Medicare Parts A and B: "Syringes and insulin aren't covered (unless used with an insulin pump) unless you join a Medicare Prescription Drug Plan." Many prescription drug plans exist under Medicare Part D, include coverage for insulin, and appear to include coverage for syringes and insulin pens. Such plans vary according to their coverage and cost. Insurance coverage for insulin, syringes, and insulin pens may be available under other third party reimbursement plans. Both insulin and insulin pens require a physician's prescription. Some insulin and insulin pen manufacturers have patient assistance programs that are income-based and will assist individuals with diabetes to obtain insulin in vial or pen format, on an ongoing basis. One manufacturer requires an annual financial assessment and will provide insulin products in 90-day increments, with a form completed every 90 days to confirm insulin dose. Customer representatives from manufacturers of insulin products may provide samples of their products to physicians and diabetes centers to offer to their clients.

In July 2002, Medicare Part B and Medicaid approved coverage for biannual foot exams for persons with peripheral neuropathy and loss of protective sensation.[9] A Medicare recipient under Part B may qualify for therapeutic shoes (depth-inlay shoes, custom-molded shoes, and shoe inserts or shoe modification) with a physician's prescription and if certain conditions are met.

ASSESSMENT

The assessment of a person with diabetes and vision loss has numerous components. It is important to initially assess an individual's prior level of knowledge about diabetes, its treatment, and the daily self-care tasks that are required to manage diabetes. The diabetes equipment and resources with which the person with diabetes is familiar should be determined. It is critical that the individual have a basic foundation of knowledge and skills before adaptive diabetes education can be initiated.

It is important to know the outcome of an eye exam and if the individual will be or has recently undergone eye surgery, as the level of vision currently present may change. The assessment should include information on whether visual decline has been gradual or sudden, its stability, and what the primary and secondary eye conditions are, as these will vary in their functional implications and therefore the intervention techniques and tools chosen will vary also. The low vision therapist should also determine if the individual has been diagnosed as legally blind.

Functional vision must also be assessed to determine if residual vision is sufficient to safely and accurately complete daily diabetes self-management tasks. It is critical to know if vision is reliable or if it fluctuates day to day or throughout the day, as will occur with low or high blood glucose levels, eye fatigue, postural changes, ambient lighting, or general fatigue. It should be determined whether the person has undergone a low vision examination, and if so the results and recommendations. If the client has not undergone a recent low vision examination, a referral should be made to a low vision optometrist. It is important that the therapist prepare the individual with diabetes and vision loss for the low vision exam by explaining what will occur in the exam and how it differs from a conventional eye exam. Encouraging the individual to make a list of activities he or she wishes to accomplish and bringing samples of items or materials that need to be "viewed or read" is critical; these may include a syringe, medication/food labels, a blood glucose monitor instruction manual, or an insulin pump with a digital display.

If the person with diabetes has received or will receive optical devices, it is important to know whether these devices can be incorporated into diabetes self-care. Training in use of optical devices as well as eccentric viewing techniques (use of the preferred retinal locus or PRL) may be required to optimize use of residual vision. The low vision optometrist should be consulted with respect to any specific recommendations regarding optical device use or PRL location and use as it impacts on diabetes self-management tasks. Specific areas to assess in diabetes self-management may include blood glucose monitoring, medication management and/or insulin measurement, nutrition management, foot/skin care, healthcare/sick day management, and physical activity/exercise (Table 15-1).

Physical impairments secondary to or independent of diabetes need to be taken into consideration. These may include weakness, decreased or altered sensation,

Table 15-1.

Sample Assessment Questions

Blood Glucose Monitoring

Do you monitor your blood glucose? If so, how often?
Have you received formal training in using a blood glucose monitor and from who?
What blood glucose monitor do you use?
Can you consistently read the display?
Do you have difficulty or require assistance in any aspect of using your blood glucose monitor? Inserting the strip, locating the blood sample on the finger, placing the blood drop on the test site of the test strip?
Can you and do you record your blood glucose results? Who uses these results and how?
How do you discard lancets?
What pharmacy do you use for your supplies?

Medication Management and/or Insulin Measurement

Are you able to accurately and consistently identify your medications or see the lines on your syringe? If so, describe your method?
Do you use insulin? If so, what type(s) of insulin, their dosage(s), and time(s) of day taken?
What brand/size of syringe do you use?
How do you know when your insulin vial is empty?

Nutrition Management

Have you ever received instruction in how and what to eat with diabetes? How long ago did you receive this instruction and from where?
Do you have special guidelines or a meal plan to follow? If so, describe.
Are you able to read your meal plan, food labels and other nutritional information?
How do you determine portions and measure food quantities?
Do you prepare your own meals? If you have difficulty or receive assistance, identify in what tasks? Setting stove and oven dials, determining when food is done, cutting food?
Have you ever burned yourself? If so, describe how?

Foot and Skin Care

Are you able to bath your feet and don socks and shoes?
Do you inspect your feet? If so, how often and by what method?
Do you have your physician inspect your feet every visit or do you regularly see a podiatrist?
Do you have numbness or tingling in your hands and feet?
Do you cut your nails? If so, how?
What do you do if you have an injury to your foot or a foot infection?

Physical Activity/Exercise

Do you have an exercise program or are you interested in beginning one?
Do you have any difficulty getting around indoors or outside?
Does your vision prevent you from engaging in physical activity? Describe what activities.
Have you ever been instructed in exercise related precautions?
Do you wear a diabetes identification tag?

Healthcare/Sick Day

Can you readily access emergency phone numbers or emergency assistance?
Do you have a sick day plan? If so, are you able to read it?
Do you have a sick day kit that you can readily access?
Does your physician want you to monitor your weight or blood pressure?
Can you take your temperature when you are not feeling well?

and coordination deficits related to the complications of diabetes, such as peripheral neuropathy, carpal tunnel syndrome, and stroke. Additional diagnoses that may require further adaptations include arthritis, tremors, and hearing loss. Often, vision loss necessitates the use of other senses for task completion, including sense of touch and hearing. The ability to localize touch; detect position, movement, pressure and pain; and discriminate temperature are all necessary.

Cognitive functioning needs to be assessed in the areas of concentration, ability to follow multiple-step directions, problem-solving skills, ability to form mental images, capacity to learn new information, and memory. Learning adaptive diabetes self-management often requires that the individual interpret and integrate information, perform mathematical computations, and implement algorithms. Psychosocial functioning is important to assess due to the high rates of depression and anxiety in persons with diabetes. Social, emotional, and physical support systems; insurance coverage and/or financial resources; and level of independence the client desires should all be noted.

AREAS OF INTERVENTION IN ADAPTIVE DIABETES SELF-MANAGEMENT

General Intervention Strategies

Many persons with diabetes and vision impairment will want to utilize their residual vision to complete diabetes self-management tasks. The low vision therapist's role is to insure the client achieves accurate, safe, consistent results when incorporating remaining vision. Methods to maximize use of residual vision include: modification of the task environment through lighting, organization, and contrast; use of optical devices; and labeling and marking techniques. Both general and specific applications of the above principles will be provided. Depending on the extent and type of vision loss, the client may achieve varying degrees of independence in a diabetes self-care task and may need to also supplement performance with nonvisual techniques or devices as well.

Lighting

Lighting is the most essential environmental consideration to enable a person with low vision to use his or her remaining vision (see Chapter 10). If additional lighting is beneficial, then it is important to incorporate a flexible arm task lamp that permits the level of wattage preferred by the client. The task lamp needs to be positioned nearest the better-seeing eye or opposite the person's working hand in order to avoid casting shadows on the immediate work surface. Glare from the work surface, such as the table, or from the equipment, such as the blood glucose monitor display, needs to be minimized by a covering in the former example and repositioning the lamp in the latter.

Organization can include reduction in clutter, advanced preparation, and consistency in placement of task materials. Keep like equipment together. Using a tray with a lip is helpful for organizing task equipment. A tray can help the user maintain orientation to supplies, can assist to define the workspace, and can prevent materials from "getting away" from the user. The latter is especially important where "sharps," such as lancets or syringes, and liquids from measuring beverage portions, can drop or be spilled onto the floor. Advanced preparation is helpful so that a diabetes task can be completed in a sequential, timely fashion with a minimum of stress. Assembling a lancing device before turning on a blood glucose monitor or having beverages labeled to enable the user to discern noncaloric from caloric are both examples where prior preparation is very beneficial.

Enhancing contrast can be achieved by placing light-colored supplies on a dark surface and vice versa. The background should be solid in color to avoid having items "lost" in busy patterns. Placing a syringe against a white background permits the black plunger tip and syringe markings to stand out, while a dark blood glucose monitor and dark test strips will be more visible on a light tray.

Optical Devices

Optical devices can be incorporated into many diabetes self-management tasks, although each type of device has it benefits and limitations and must be tailored to the individual and the task (see Chapter 13). The low vision optometrist and the low vision therapist work together as a team to educate the individual with diabetes and vision loss regarding devices that are available, their features, and their applications. Portable optical devices allow the user to perform a task such as blood glucose monitoring or nutrition label reading away from the home. Spectacle format magnification and stationary closed circuit televisions (CCTVs) allow both hands to be used during a task such as insulin measurement. Magnification, however, will not resolve the decreased contrast present in blood glucose monitor and insulin pump liquid crystal displays. Relative distance magnification can also be used by bringing the eye closer to the task or the task closer to the eye (see Chapter 10).

Figure 15-2. Blood glucose monitoring setup with environmental adaptations and marked large display monitor and lancing device.

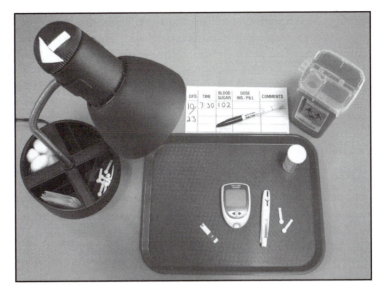

Marking and Labeling Techniques

Marking can also be incorporated to bring attention to features of objects that are less visible to a person with diabetes and vision impairment. Markings can be visual, focusing on high-contrast, bright colors; they can be tactile, emphasizing textural properties such as raised or rough markings; or they can combine elements of both. The features that can be marked include indiscernible features such as a test strip port on a blood glucose monitor or weight markings on a food scale. Due to potential contact with blood, marking materials should be durable, permanent and washable, such as tactile marking liquid or fabric paint, bump or touch dots, or even rubber bands (Figure 15-2).

General Teaching Strategies

Provide choices and alternatives to clients, outline the benefits and limitations of a piece of equipment or a technique, and provide guidance to elicit safe choices. Remember always that retinopathy and other forms of eye disease as well as diabetes are all progressive, and the client needs to be aware of other equipment that may be available to satisfy his or her future needs. Adaptive diabetes self-management techniques and devices are rarely ideal, and it is up to the client to determine what is most suitable and workable for his or her own needs. The following is a list of general teaching strategies that will enhance the learning experience for the person with diabetes and vision loss:

- Allow for visual and tactile exploration of equipment and its setup.

- Be very descriptive and specific in the explanation, relying on low vision, tactile, and auditory cues.
- If beneficial, provide information on what might be seen so that the person with vision loss can sense what a sighted person might experience.

- Establish agreement on spatial positioning and directional concepts, such as front and back, right and left.
- Have client decide where to place or how to position an object, or explain positioning in established frames of reference, such as clock or cardinal positions.
- Always establish a point of reference to guide orientation to other objects around it.
- Establish a common terminology, introducing new terms as desired or needed by the client.
- Allow the client to direct his own learning experience by working through a process as independently as possible, providing feedback as needed. Build on client's knowledge and experience.
- Encourage client to make suggestions regarding problem-solving approaches.
- Let client know what is being done at all times and why, in order to provide a complete and integrated experience.

Process and Outcomes

A high degree of accuracy in performing the tasks of diabetes self-management is necessary. Therefore, the following is strongly recommended:

- Any adaptations or techniques chosen must be effective when the user's vision is at its lowest. Fluctuating vision may occur when the user needs most to test blood glucose levels (when blood glucose is very low or very high).

- Accurate insulin measurement and blood glucose monitoring should be observed on at least three separate occasions, or two times each on each of two separate occasions.

BLOOD GLUCOSE MONITORING

Blood glucose monitoring is a vital tool in diabetes self-management. It determines the effectiveness of medication, diet, and physical activity in normalizing blood glucose levels; it guides adjustment of treatment and it prevents and detects hypoglycemia. The treating physician individually determines the frequency and timing of blood glucose monitoring. Guidelines from the ADA recommend that persons with type 1 diabetes self-monitor blood glucose (SMBG) three or more times daily, while persons with type 2 diabetes treated with insulin should SMBG at least daily, and up to three to four times per day when treated with multiple daily injections.

The ADA also has published target ranges for blood glucose control. The recommended blood glucose range for plasma glucose is 90 to 130 mg/dL prepandial (prior to a meal) and <180 mg/dL postprandial (1 to 2 hours after start of a meal).[27] These goals apply to most persons with diabetes, however, each person needs to have specific goals set by his or her physician that takes into account age, comorbid diseases, or other unusual circumstances or conditions.

A blood glucose monitor is a device that measures glucose in the blood by a chemical change or an electric current that is produced when blood comes in contact with the test site of the test strip. The lancing device used to obtain the blood sample is spring-loaded and resembles a refillable pen. A small, sharp lancet is placed in the device and should be removed after each use. Generally, the blood sample is obtained from the finger, although there are now many monitors on the market that are alternate site approved. Alternate sites may include the forearm, thigh, and palm, but specific guidelines need to be followed when using an alternate site monitor. Several products are also available for semi- or noninvasive blood glucose monitoring, however, none are currently recommended for daily home blood glucose monitoring.

Many steps are involved in the maintenance and use of a blood glucose monitor. Maintenance issues include: keeping track of expiration date of test strips and glucose control solution, coding or calibrating the monitor, setting the time and date, performing glucose control solution check, accessing monitor memory, cleaning the monitor, replacing the battery, and accessing instruction manual or resource person when in need of assistance. Generally, all of these steps are performed on an as-needed basis.

Coding or calibrating a blood glucose monitor is required to match the test strips being used to the monitor, and therefore is done each time a new bottle or box of strips is opened. Some monitors now have automatic calibration, some require the manual insertion of a code key or calibration strip, and others entail reading a number from the test strip container and manually inputting into it the monitor. A second important maintenance task is performing a glucose control solution test. This is performed to insure the monitoring procedure is being done correctly and that the monitor and strips are working properly. Opening a new bottle of strips, obtaining blood glucose results higher or lower than expected, and leaving the test strip bottle open all warrant a glucose control solution check. This test is performed by applying control solution rather than blood to the test strip.

Numerous steps are also required in daily use of a blood glucose monitor. These steps include: assembling and using a lancing device, opening the strip bottle/foil, knowing if there is one or multiple strips in the hand, properly orienting and inserting the test strip, attaining and identifying a sufficient blood sample, determining the location of the blood sample on the finger, achieving proper placement of the blood sample on the test strip, and reading the monitor display. Assembling a lancing device and removing the lancet is a multistep task in and of itself.

There are a variety of tools, adaptations and techniques that can assist a person with mild vision loss to continue to use a LCD monitor. A number of monitors have large displays and bold numbers, but a person with vision loss needs to try out different models to see which is best. Providing or enhancing task lighting and contrast, as well as incorporating different forms of optical and nonoptical magnification, may also prove beneficial. Optical devices can be used for reading expiration dates and code numbers. Propping or stabilizing the magnifier upright can allow hands-free use, which may assist the user in locating and placing a blood sample on the test strip. Many monitors are designed to be brought to the blood sample, so they also can be picked up and brought closer to the eye.

Visual features of test strips (underside of strip white or solid colored, combined light and darker areas on topside with shiny electrodes at one end) may aid in proper orientation of the test strip prior to insertion. High-contrast or tactile markings can be placed on salient features of a monitor or lancing

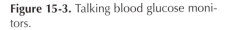
Figure 15-3. Talking blood glucose monitors.

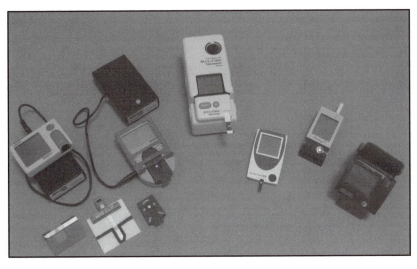

device to highlight the location of buttons, settings, or openings. Producing a larger, more visible blood drop or using a white towel for contrast will help to discern and obtain a sufficient blood sample. For some blood glucose monitors, placement of high-contrast markings on the monitor or creation of a high-contrast test strip guide may assist the user in locating and placing the blood drop on the test site.

Blood glucose monitors with speech capability are available for persons who are unable to use large display monitors; however, legal blindness is required before insurance coverage can be obtained with the exception of one model. Currently there are four options on the US market for blood glucose monitors with speech capability, with a fifth model seeking FDA approval. The Accu-chek Voicemate is a two piece unit, designed to fit together, wherein the standard blood glucose monitor inserts into and is sold with the voice unit. Two older monitors, the One Touch Basic and the One Touch Surestep, can be coupled with a separate voice attachment by a data cable. These two monitors can be purchased separately from their respective voice attachment or as a package. The fourth and fifth monitors, the Prodigy and the SensoCard, are newer, fully integrated talking models, as the speech component is incorporated into the monitor itself. The SensoCard is awaiting FDA approval, which is expected to be received in the near future (Figure 15-3).

The Voicemate can be coded nonvisually by insertion of a code key. It has a bar code reader to identify different types of Lilly insulin. It has a relatively large strip, called the Comfort Curve strip. This strip has a small curved cutout on the right side of the strip, which is where the blood is applied. A moderate amount of blood is needed. The monitor will beep when it detects blood at the test site. A second

drop of blood can be applied within 15 seconds. The Voicemate comes with instructions in large print and on cassette tape.

The One Touch Basic has a relatively large strip, with the test site located on top of the strip. This monitor requires visual calibration and cleaning. The test site on the Basic test strip should not be touched during blood drop application and requires a moderate to large drop of blood. A blood drop guide, called the Suredrop, can be used to facilitate successful blood placement, but it must be purchased separately. "Not enough blood retest" appears on the display and is verbalized when the blood drop is too small or was smeared.

The One Touch Surestep also requires visual calibration and cleaning. It has a relatively large strip, with the test site on the top. It requires a relatively large blood drop. Blood can be dabbed on the test site. This monitor requires blood placement on the strip before insertion into the monitor. A blood drop guide, called the Sureguide, can be purchased separately to aid in blood sample placement on the test strip.

The SensoCard is a slim, compact unit, which can be coded nonvisually by a code strip. It has a relatively small test strip. The blood is applied to the end or tip of the strip, and a very small amount of blood is required. The monitor automatically turns on with strip insertion and beeps when blood is applied. It only requires battery replacement in a single unit. Directions will be made available in large print and audio format. The SensoCard can be switched from English to German within the same unit. The manufacturer is anticipating FDA approval in September, 2006. Cost is moderate.

The Prodigy is a small, compact unit that currently requires visual coding. The manufacturer indicates (as of September 2006) that a "no code" feature will

be included. The strip is small in size. The blood is applied to the end or the tip of the strip and a very small amount of blood is required. The monitor automatically turns on with strip insertion and beeps when blood is applied. The Prodigy only requires battery replacement in a single unit. Directions will be made available in large print and cassette upon request. The Prodigy can be switched from English to Spanish within the same unit. The current Prodigy announces blood glucose readings and room temperature. The manufacturer is currently modifying its monitor to give it greater speech capability. The Prodigy Duo combines a Prodigy meter with a wrist style blood pressure cuff, which announces both blood pressure and heart rate data. The combination unit is compact, lightweight and simple to use. Both units are low cost..

When vision is insufficient, additional nonvisual techniques may be required. Tactile features on monitors, strips, or lancing equipment can aid in locating and identifying key parts, or equipment can be adapted with raised markings. Features such as notches or cutouts and smooth or textured surfaces can aid in properly orienting and inserting the test strip, or locating the test site. The monitor's manual will aid in determining how a strip can be explored. Sighted assistance may be used to determine the number of times a finger needs to be milked before an adequate blood sample is achieved. Feeling for wetness on the finger or making a mental map may help the user to locate the blood drop on the finger after lancing.

Blood glucose monitors and their supplies are provided and billed for by pharmacies (these may include hospital-based, local, mail order, or chain drugstores; regional/national general merchandise stores; and grocery stores). Talking blood glucose monitors are also available through many of the above suppliers. Many pharmacies, however, are unaware of the availability of talking models and require education as to their features and the reimbursement criteria and process. Each therapist needs to develop resources in his or her local area. Many individuals with diabetes have developed a relationship with a particular pharmacy and it is preferable to utilize this pharmacy if possible. It is important to determine if the pharmacy will bill insurance directly or will bill the individual, who then must seek reimbursement from his or her insurance. A mail order medical supplier or a pharmacy that delivers may be an added benefit for the person with diabetes and vision loss.

Many physicians and endocrinologists are also unaware of the availability of talking blood glucose monitors and would benefit from similar education. A prescription must be written by the physician treating the individual's diabetes in order for a blood glucose monitor to be covered by insurance. The prescription should include the following information: the name of the blood glucose monitor, the diagnosis code, the testing frequency, and the quantity of test strips and lancets desired beyond that provided by the starter kit. If a talking model is being sought, a statement of legal blindness should also be included on the prescription. A corroborating eye report from the eyecare physician may be required by the pharmacy, the insurance company, or the medical physician to support the diagnosis of legal blindness.

ORAL MEDICATION MANAGEMENT

Being able to identify, track, and administer medications, both in oral and injectable form, is a critical component of diabetes self-management. Most adults diagnosed with diabetes take oral medication, insulin or both. According to the CDC, between the years 2001 and 2003, 16% of the adults diagnosed with diabetes took insulin only, 12% took both insulin and oral medications, 57% took oral medications only, and 15% did not take either insulin or oral medication.[1] It is important to have some fundamental knowledge about the different kinds of oral medications and insulin, as well as some of their key properties/characteristics.

There are five categories of oral agents used to normalize blood glucose levels. Several classes, including the sulfonylureas and meglitinides, work on the pancreas to increase the release of insulin. These two categories of medications are capable of reducing blood glucose levels below normal and therefore can result in hypoglycemia.

Commonly used medications in this category include: Glucotrol, Amaryl, Prandin, and Starlix. The remaining three categories, because of the site of their action, only reduce high blood glucose, but do not produce hypoglycemia. Two of these categories of medication, the biguanides, which includes Glucophage, and the thiazolidinediones (TZDs), which includes Actos and Avandia, all function as insulin sensitizers, enhancing glucose transport into fat and skeletal tissue. The final category, the alpha-glucosidase inhibitors, such as Precose, work on the small intestine, reducing the rate of starch digestion and glucose absorption.

Clients may initially be treated with a single medication, progressing to combination therapy wherein two or more oral agents, or an oral agent and insulin, may be used. Several of the medications above have now been combined, forming such drugs as Glucovance (Glyburide and Glucophage), Metaglip (Glucophage and Glucotrol) and Avandamet (Avandia and Glucophage) enhancing medication compliance. The dosing frequency, the time(s) of day, and whether

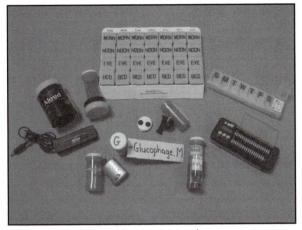

Figure 15-4. Selected low vision medication management systems.

it is taken before or with food varies with each medication.

A wide array of adaptive techniques and equipment are available that incorporate low vision and/or nonvisual features to enable independent identification and tracking of oral medications. Task lighting, a contrasting background, optical magnification, and pill vial magnifiers all can assist a person to use remaining available vision to identify medication. Pill containers can be labeled in large print or a color-coding system can be implemented. When vision is insufficient, wooden or plastic letters can be used as tactile labels or small adhesive-backed dots can be applied to the container representing the number of pills to be taken (Figure 15-4).

Many of the visual and tactile labels convey only a limited amount of information, such as a medication's name or how many pills are to be taken; however, auditory medication labels are capable of recording additional label information. Some of the auditory labels, such as the Tel Rx, consist of a small recording device that attaches to the medication bottle, while other systems, such as the Aloud Audio Labeling System, have a recording/playback mechanism and separate labels.

Several methods are also available to enable a person to track his or her medication usage. One technique is to apply elastic bands to the bottle equal to the number of daily doses, remove one band after taking each dose, and then reapply all bands after taking the last dose. Large-print and Braille pillboxes are also popular alternatives. Such pillboxes are available in different shapes and sizes, ranging from 1x/day to 4x/day. Many pillboxes come in different colors so that one color can be used for the morning, another for the night. Some pillboxes come equipped with timers and auditory alarms, such as the e-pill Multi

Alarm system, to remind the client to take his or her medication.

INSULIN MANAGEMENT

Insulin is the medication most often associated with diabetes. It is currently used in an injectable form. Several inhaled insulins are on the horizon (Exubera recently obtained FDA approval), and oral insulin is being tested outside of the United States. Currently, three companies manufacture injectable insulin in the United States: Lilly (brand names Humulin and Humalog), Novo Nordisk (Novolin, Novolog, and Levemir), and Aventis (Lantus and Apidra). Insulins are classified according to their onset of action, peak effect, and duration of action. The four classifications of insulin include fast-acting or rapid-acting (Humalog, Novolog, Apidra), short-acting (R or regular), intermediate-acting (N or NPH), and long-acting (Lantus and Levemir). Lantus, one of the newer insulins, is a "peakless" insulin. Several premixed insulins are also available (70/30, 50/50, 75/25). Some insulins are clear, colorless solutions, while other insulins are suspensions, which should be evenly cloudy.

Insulin dosing frequency is dependent on the type of diabetes, level of insulin deficiency or resistance, timing and carbohydrate content of meals, physical activity, and waking and sleeping patterns. Common dosing frequencies include a single daily injection administered in the morning or at bedtime or a two-injection regime with insulin administered in the morning before breakfast and before the evening meal or at bedtime. Intensive insulin therapy ranges from three to four times per day, with a four-injection regime requiring one injection in the morning and one at each mealtime. Some persons take a "fixed" dose of insulin that is set by their physician. Others take a "variable" dose, which is a dose that can be altered by the individual, taking into account his or her current blood glucose level and carbohydrate amounts eaten or to be eaten, among other factors.

Many steps are required for safe insulin use. They include: insulin storage, identification (if more than one is taken), insulin/vial preparation, measurement, mixing (if more than one is taken), air bubble management, administration, injection site management, determination of quality and quantity of vial contents, and sharps disposal. Specific information regarding insulin itself can be obtained from the manufacturer's guidelines. Low vision therapists should adhere to standard procedures for preparing, mixing, and drawing up insulin and can begin to familiarize themselves with these basic procedures through educational materials available through syringe manufac-

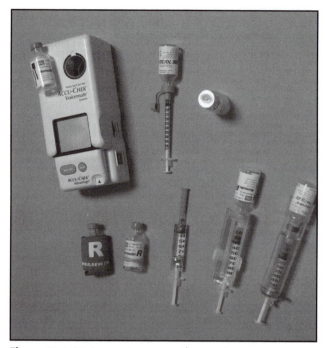

Figure 15-5. Various syringe magnifiers and accessory devices.

turers such as Becton-Dickinson (B-D). Following are some very basic principles:

- Suspension insulins should be rolled between the palms to resuspend the insulin contents in the vial.

- Pressurize insulin vial by filling vial with amount of air corresponding to desired insulin dose, prior to drawing out insulin.

- When preparing a mixed dose, the clear insulin should be drawn into the syringe before the cloudy/suspension insulin.

- Always insure syringe and vial are vertical, with the vial inverted, when drawing out insulin.

- Sharps (needles and lancets) should be disposed of in a hard plastic, opaque container with a screw cap.

Many low vision and nonvisual techniques and devices are now available to assist in insulin management. All insulin bottles are the same size and shape except for those manufactured by Aventis, such as Lantus and Apidra, which are taller and thinner. To distinguish two similar vials, a rubber band can be placed around one of the insulins, or a commercially made color-coded, large-print sleeve, such as the Insuleeve, can be incorporated. One of the talking blood glucose monitors has a bar code reader, however it will only read one of the insulin manufacturer's bar codes (the Lilly brand).

A wide range of visual and nonvisual devices can be used for insulin measurement. The primary method of insulin delivery is the vial and syringe. It is important to be aware of the features of a syringe, which include: syringe/barrel size, needle gauge (width), and needle length. For visual accuracy in dosing, the syringe size is matched to the insulin dose to be injected, as follows:

- 0.25 cc (for doses < 25 units)
- 0.30 cc or 3/10 cc (for doses -< 30 units)
- 0.5 cc or ½ cc (for doses < 50 units)
- 1 cc (for doses 50 to 100 units)

In addition to the environmental modifications and optical devices identified earlier in this chapter, several magnifiers are made specifically to fit on the syringe and they may enable a person with mild vision loss to read the dose markings on the barrel. These include the clip-on syringe magnifier, the B-D Magni-Guide, and the Tru-Hand. The syringe magnifiers currently available provide up to 2X magnification and will fit any syringe. They vary in their features, which may include a holder for the insulin vial, the plunger, or the syringe barrel, all of which will assist the user to align the syringe needle with the rubber stopper on the vial. Two separate devices, the Center-aid and the Insul-cap, will guide the syringe needle into the rubber stopper of the vial; the latter device also holds the syringe firmly to the vial (Figure 15-5).

When choosing a nonvisual insulin measurement device, several factors need to be considered. These include: amount of insulin taken (large or small dose), whether the dose is fixed or variable, single or mixed, the current type of syringe used, and the person's desire to be fully independent. The fixed dose devices require setting by a sighted person, while the variable dose devices do not require any sighted assistance (Figure 15-6).

Three fixed dose devices are currently available: the Safe Shot, the Unit Calibration Aid, and the InjectAssist. These measuring devices hold the syringe and can be preset for either one or two doses. The plunger is pulled back to the preset stop, which measures a specific insulin dose. The Unit Calibration Aid requires a 1 cc syringe. The two devices available for variable insulin doses are the ½ cc Count-a-Dose and the Syringe Support. Both can be used for single or mixed doses. The Count-a-Dose requires a B-D ½ cc syringe with a ½-inch needle. Each unit of insulin is measured by a single click that can be felt and heard. The second device, the Syringe Support, uses a B-D 1 cc syringe. The device is set by a calibrated screw, with a single turn of the screw measuring 2 units of insulin.

Although the procedure for using each insulin measurement device differs, the nonvisual technique

Figure 15-6. Left to right: fixed dose (3) and variable dose (2) insulin measurement devices; insulin pens and dosers.

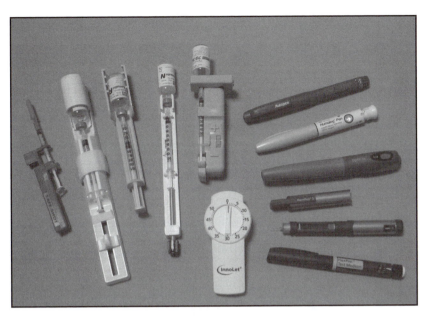

for removing air bubbles in the syringe and knowing when the insulin vial is empty is universal. Removing air bubbles is critical because air bubbles take up space that insulin should be occupying and therefore the insulin dose will be less. Expelling air bubbles is performed by drawing insulin into the syringe, pushing it back into the vial at least three times, then filling the syringe with the desired dose on the fourth time. Tapping the syringe will help release air bubbles.

It is important to avoid using an almost empty insulin vial, as air can be drawn in instead of insulin. Using no more than 950 units out of 1000 unit vial will insure that there is sufficient insulin in the vial at all times. Always determine how many doses an insulin vial contains without using the last 50 units. For example, if a person took 50 units each day from a 1000 unit vial of NPH, one vial would last 19 days (950 ÷ 50 = 19). The person should set aside 19 syringes and start a new vial when these are used. A second technique is to mark off each successive day on a calendar that a dose is taken (in this case 19 days), using different marking symbols for each 19-day period.[29]

Insulin pens and insulin dosers, another method of insulin delivery, can be operated nonvisually, although most are not endorsed by the manufacturer for this use. Pens come in a wide range of insulin formulations. Some pens are reusable and require refilling with insulin cartridges; other pens are prefilled and disposable. Depending on the model, pens can deliver insulin in ½ unit, 1 unit, or 2 unit increments. An audible and tactile click is noted for each increment when dialing a dose. The three insulin manufacturers listed earlier all manufacture at least one insulin pen.

The insulin pump, a continuous method of insulin delivery, can be used with some success by some persons with vision loss. An insulin pump is a miniaturized, computerized device the size of a pager that delivers insulin through flexible plastic tubing to a small needle inserted just under the skin. It is programmed to closely mimic the body's normal release of insulin. The pump releases a steady trickle of insulin 24 hours a day (preprogrammed basal rate/dose) and at the press of a button it can deliver a specific amount of insulin (bolus dose) calculated by the pump user to handle the rise in blood glucose caused by meals. Some models come with tactile buttons and audio features for programming bolus insulin doses. Candidates for the insulin pump must meet specific requirements including, but not limited to, type of diabetes and residual insulin levels, in order to obtain insurance coverage.

Insulin administration itself may focus on methods to achieve increased control during the injection process. By pinching the skin, gently placing the needle on the skin, and then inserting the needle, the person with vision loss can avoid the usual dart-like motion and can control where the needle is inserted.[7] A product called the NeedleAid can also help to stabilize an insulin syringe or pen against the skin and insures injection at proper angle and to proper depth.

Insulin measurement devices that are used in conjunction with syringes are available through the several specialty low vision catalogs listed at the end of this chapter under Resources. Many can also be purchased directly from the manufacturer and some from select pharmacies. These devices are paid for out of pocket. Insulin pens and dosers, as well as pen

needles, are obtained and billed for by a pharmacy and require a physician's prescription. General medical physicians may need to be educated regarding the benefits and feasibility of insulin pens and dosers for persons with vision loss; however, a general prescription is sufficient.

NUTRITION MANAGEMENT

MNT is an important component of successful diabetes self-management, not only to control blood glucose levels, but also blood lipids, blood pressure, and overall health. There is no such thing as a "diabetic diet;" eating with diabetes means eating in a healthy manner. A person with diabetes should have an individualized food/meal plan developed for him or her by a registered dietician, preferably one who is a certified diabetes educator.

Persons with type 2 diabetes, whose diabetes is controlled by diet and exercise, are encouraged to spread food throughout the day, eating three meals or smaller meals with snacks, although generally they can eat according to their own schedule. When persons with type 2 diabetes also take oral medications, meals need to be kept small to moderate in size, with snacks for persons on specific medications that can result in hypoglycemia. Meal times and carbohydrate content of meals needs to be consistent. These approaches are designed to help even out blood glucose levels.

Persons with type 1 or type 2 diabetes who are on a fixed-dose insulin regime need to be consistent in the times meals are eaten and the carbohydrate content of meals in order to maintain a balance between insulin and food. Timing and amount of insulin taken is determined by timing and frequency of meals and their carbohydrate content. Persons on a flexible-dose insulin regimen can determine their insulin dose based on the carbohydrate content of meals that they have eaten or plan to eat. This approach helps to maintain a "flexible" balance between insulin and food. Timing and frequency of meals and carbohydrate content of meals are based on the person's own schedule and food preferences. Insulin is integrated into usual eating habits.

Several common methods for teaching nutrition management and meal planning include the food pyramid, the plate method, the exchange list, and carbohydrate counting. The food pyramid provides basic nutrition information but generally does not address issues specific to persons with diabetes. The plate method provides general guidelines for relative quantities of each food group at each meal, based on a 9-inch plate (eg, dinner plate consists of ¼ plate meat, ¼ plate starch, and ½ plate low carbohydrate/

nonstarchy vegetables; one fruit serving and 1 milk serving complete the meal). The exchange list groups foods into categories based upon amount of carbohydrate, protein, fat, and calorie content. An exchange is a measured amount of food within a group, which may be exchanged or traded for another food within the same category because the food values are the same (eg, can trade 1 slice of bread for ½ cup cooked cereal because each is one starch exchange containing 15 grams of carbohydrate and 80 calories).

The method of meal planning most useful to persons with diabetes—carbohydrate counting—focuses on counting carbohydrate choices or grams. This approach focuses on the total carbohydrates in food being eaten (not just sugar), with a carbohydrate choice consisting of 15 grams. In basic carbohydrate counting, each meal is allowed a certain number of carbohydrates or carbohydrate choices. Reading food labels or using a nutrition guide is essential to determining carbohydrate content of foods. A sample meal would appear as: 2 slices of toast (30 grams carbohydrate) + 4 ounces orange juice (15 grams carbohydrate) + 1 small 4 ounce banana (15 gram carbohydrate) = 60 grams carbohydrate or 4 carbohydrate choices. More advanced methods of carbohydrate counting, which involve matching units of insulin to carbohydrate grams, are also used, but are beyond the scope of this chapter.

Many low vision and nonvisual techniques and adaptations can assist a person with vision loss in nutrition management and meal planning. The following areas should be addressed: making a grocery list and locating needed items in grocery store; identifying and labeling food products; measuring food and portion sizes; safe food preparation and cooking and accessing meal plans, cookbooks, nutritional information, and food labels. Some of the above areas will be discussed below.

Optical devices or sighted assistance can be used to identify food products in the store, but alternate systems need to be implemented once these items are placed in kitchen storage areas. Food products can be identified through organization (locate all cans of fruit together), by other senses (cream soup sounds different when shaken than broth soup), or by labeling (large print, raised letters, rubber bands, audio labels such as the Talking Can lid). A labeling system needs to be designed for a person's specific needs and should be sustainable by the client and/or significant others.

Measuring food amounts and determining portions is a prerequisite to using the above meal planning methods. Using contrasting plates, cups, and bowls that hold particular portion sizes may assist some persons in using their remaining vision to estimate portions. For example, a dark, 1.5 cup cereal

Figure 15-7. Tactile, large display, talking food scales; food measurement tools; food templates/models.

bowl may be used to estimate a single carbohydrate choice of puffed cereal. A food template or model can also be utilized to tactilely estimate a portion of cake or baked potato. More specific measurement of solid foods and beverages can be obtained by using nested, large-print, color-coded, or tactilely marked measuring cups. Portion-controlled serving utensils for hot foods can be purchased from restaurant supply stores. A large display, or talking or tactilely marked scale can be used to measure foods by weight (Figure 15-7).

Meal plans and nutrition information may be enlarged on a copier, but maintaining contrast and clarity is critical. Reformatting material into large print or in audio by means of a cassette tape or digital recorder may be required. A meal plan can be reformatted and customized in print size for each individual. Some general guidelines when reformatting a meal plan into large print include the following: use black print on white or yellow paper that has a dull finish, choose a plain versus fancy font, increase spacing between lines of print, left justify print, use headings that are larger and bolder than regular large print, and avoid columns and charts. It is beneficial to become very familiar with any material to be audio recorded so that recording proceeds at a natural but even pace; scripting may be helpful.

FOOT CARE

Regular and thorough foot care is essential for avoiding or minimizing lower-extremity complications in persons with diabetes. Foot and skin care becomes an extremely important task in light of peripheral neuropathy and vascular complications. In the United States, about 86,000 lower limbs are amputated every year due to diabetes; this is about 50% of

all lower limb amputations. About 60% of people with diabetic retinopathy have had foot problems. Foot care includes basic hygiene, proper foot inspection, appropriate footwear, and special precautions. Many techniques and devices are available to assist the person with vision loss to perform these tasks safely.

Basic hygiene includes: washing the feet daily with mild soap and warm water, drying between the toes, and avoiding foot soaks. Lowering the water temperature on the water heater, using a scald-free adapter, or a low vision or talking bath thermometer may be helpful to insure bathwater temperature is within a safe range (98° to 100° Fahrenheit). Applying alcohol-free moisturizing lotion to the feet (but not between toes) prevents dry, cracked skin. Cutting or using chemical corn or callus removers should be avoided; however, if at low risk/approved by the physician, a pumice stone may be used for smoothing purposes. Sighted assistance for cutting nails should be obtained from a reliable friend or family member. A podiatrist should be seen when thick, hard nails or foot problems are noted. An emery board may be used to file and smooth rough edges of toenails. Toenails can be periodically checked with fingertips to insure they are filed straight across and not too short.

A foot inspection should be done daily at a consistent time and place, such as after bathing or before bed. Visual techniques are to be used only if remaining vision is adequate and reliable. Visual methods may include incorporating appropriate lighting, a handheld magnifier, contrast (dark towel behind foot), and magnifying/lighted mirrors. However, sighted assistance should be obtained weekly or if a new problem is detected. In addition, a physician should perform a foot inspection every visit, and a podiatrist should be seen at least annually.

Nonvisual methods can be utilized when vision is insufficient. A tactile foot inspection requires intact sensation in the hand and fingertips. The fingertips are used to explore the entire foot in a careful, organized fashion. The skin is inspected for cuts, blisters, swelling, new calluses, and other irregularities, with particular attention to any previous or existing foot problems. Changes in foot shape are noted and the back of the hand can be used to feel for excessively cool areas (decreased circulation) or warm areas (possible inflammation), in comparison to other areas of the foot or the opposite foot.

In addition, changes in foot odor should be noted, especially when removing socks and shoes. A bad or unusual foot odor can be sign of a fungal infection; often a suddenly offensive or foul odor will be the first indication of an infection. Socks should be felt for wet or crusty areas that might be indicative of blood or discharge. If discharge has adhered to the sock, a sticking or pulling sensation may be noted during sock removal. Following inspection, if a cut, blister, or

sore has not begun to heal within a day, the physician should be contacted. A foot that is painful or swollen requires immediate medical attention.

Socks and shoes should be worn at all times and socks should be changed daily. Socks should not be lumpy or mended, and they should be made of materials that "breathe" and keep feet dry (such as wool and synthetic blends). Shoes should be of a closed style and should fit well upon purchase. Similarly, they should be made of materials that allow air to circulate, such as canvas or leather. Persons with diabetes should feel inside their shoes before putting them on each time to make sure the lining is smooth and that there are no hidden objects, nail points, or rough areas.

Additional precautions include avoiding artificial heat, such as heating pads and electric blankets; crossing the legs for extended periods; and wearing tight socks and garters, which hinders blood circulation.

PHYSICAL ACTIVITY/EXERCISE AND PRECAUTIONS

The role of exercise and physical activity in maintaining and improving health is well known. Additional benefits to the person with diabetes include: improving blood glucose control, allowing muscles to use insulin more effectively, assisting in controlling blood pressure, decreasing LDL cholesterol while increasing the beneficial HDL cholesterol and reducing stress (stress can increase blood glucose levels). Several risks are also associated with exercise in persons with diabetes; however, these risks can be avoided with proper exercise program design and adherence to precautions. These risks include: hypoglycemia during or after physical activity/exercise (even several hours after), hyperglycemia (usually in type 1), exacerbation of heart disease, and worsening of complications, including retinopathy.

A physician should always be consulted before starting an exercise program, particularly if the individual is over 35 years of age, has not exercised in a long time, or has medical conditions such as heart disease or breathing difficulties. General exercise guidelines include: maintaining hydration; incorporating stretching, warm-up and cool-down; avoiding vigorous exercise in extreme environmental conditions; and beginning an exercise program slowly. Exercise should be stopped if pain, lightheadedness, or shortness of breath occurs.

Additional guidelines should be implemented when an individual has diabetes. Diabetes of greater than 5 years' duration or the presence of complications requires a physician to be consulted. Exercise

precautions such as wearing diabetes identification, exercising with someone who is familiar with diabetes, wearing proper shoes, and inspecting feet after exercise are all important. A range of safety measures should be implemented during exercise to avoid or manage hypoglycemia. The safest time to exercise is 1 to 3 hours after a meal. Body areas that are likely to be involved in the exercise should be avoided as injection sites, when planning to exercise immediately after insulin administration.

Blood glucose levels should be monitored before and after exercise, as well as during if symptoms of low blood glucose are experienced. Persons with diabetes should always carry a fast-acting source of carbohydrates at all times. Exercise should be avoided when blood glucose levels are greater than 250 mg/dL and urine testing reveals ketones are present. Although not a typical occurrence, it would be more likely to occur in a person with type 1 diabetes.

An ophthalmologist should be consulted when a person wants to engage in exercise and has diabetes and vision loss, especially more advanced retinopathy. Proliferative retinopathy requires avoidance of the following activities:[7]

- Activities that raise the blood pressure in the body or head (doing resistance exercises with weight machines, lifting free weights, or using rubber exercise bands).

- Bending the head forward below the level of the heart/waist (toe touches, sit-ups, some yoga exercises).

- Holding breath or straining (as when tightening abdominal muscles and lifting legs).

- Activities that jar or involve bouncing of the head (jogging, contact sports).

- Strenuous, high impact activities (high impact aerobic dance, racquet sports, intense competitive sports).

- Strenuous arm exercises (rowing or arm bike exercise).

- Activities involving severe atmospheric pressure changes (diving, mountain climbing).

Various adaptations are available to enable persons with diabetes and vision loss to participate in physical activity and exercise. A walking program is an easy and readily accessible form of exercise. Walking can be done by means of a treadmill or in familiar areas using points of reference such as walls and furniture. Walking with a friend (using sighted guide technique), a guide dog, or using a mobility cane is also an option. A guide wire, rope, or railing can be used to mark off an area such as a yard or indoor track. Persons

with vision impairment can use a tandem or stationary bike for cycling. Swimming can be a year round activity requiring minimal adaptation. Alternatives include: swimming near a wall of the pool, using lane markers, or participating in water aerobics.

Safety measures should be implemented when participating in aerobic exercise. The floor area should be checked for hazards and obstacles. Positioning near a wall or chair helps to maintain orientation. Exercise can be performed in a seated position. Several exercise videos are now available that are designed specifically for persons with vision loss. Talking pedometers and large-print exercise records can be used to track and record exercise progress.

RESOURCES

Educational Offerings

- American Associate of Disease Educators (AADE) "ABC Course," a 1-day introductory course for beginning diabetes educators. This program is not offered according to a fixed schedule. Interested parties should contact AADE at 1-800-338-3633 or visit www.aadenet. org

- AADE's "Core Concepts: The Art and Science of Diabetes Education," a 3-day intensive course. For dates and locations, contact AADE as above.

Organizations

- American Association of Diabetes Educators (AADE) - Disabilities/Visual Impairment Specialty Practice Group; www.aadenet.org or 1-800-338-3633

- American Diabetes Association (ADA); www. diabetes.org or 1-800-342-2383

- American Dietetic Association; www.eatright. org or 1-800-877-1600

- National Library Service for the Blind and Physically Handicapped (NLS), Library of Congress, www.loc.gov/nls publications in accessible formats.

- National Diabetes Information Clearinghouse of National Institute of Diabetes & Digestive & Kidney Diseases (NIDDK); www.niddk.nih.gov or 1-800-860-8747

- National Federation of the Blind (NFB); www. nfb.org, Materials Center (410) 659-9314

Publications

Professional Publications

- American Association of Diabetes Educators. *Diabetes Education: A Core Curriculum for Health Professionals*. 5th ed. AADE; 2003.

- Chous AP. *Diabetic Eye Disease*. Auburn, WA: Fairwood Press; 2003.

- National Federation of the Blind (NFB). *Diabetes Resources: Equipment, Services, and Information* (2004-2005 Edition). Available in accessible format.

- Sokol-McKay D, Buskirk P, Whittaker P. Adaptive Low-Vision and Blindness Techniques for Blood Glucose Monitoring. *Diabetes Educator*. 2003;29:614-630.

- Williams A. Using participatory action research to make diabetes education accessible for people with visual impairment. (Doctoral dissertation, Saybrook Graduate School, San Francisco, CA.). UMI Proquest Digital Dissertations. Publication #AAT 3174539. 2005.

Consumer Publications

- Diabetes Action Network Articles, NFB. Accessible format.

- Diabetes Burnout – What To Do When You Can't Take It Anymore, American Diabetes Association (ADA). Accessible format.

- Diabetes: The Basics. Diabetes Association of Greater Cleveland. Accessible format. www. dagc.org or (216) 591-0800.

- Diabetes Forecast, a monthly publication available through membership of ADA. Publishes a yearly Resource Guide. Accessible format through NLS.

- The Diabetes Home Video Guide – Skills for Self-Care, Milner-Fenwick, Inc., produced in affiliation with AADE, accessible format, www.milner-fenwick.com or 1-800-432-8433

- Diabetes Self-Management; www. DiabetesSelfManagement.com or 1-800-234-0923

- Exchange Lists for Meal Planning 2003 Edition, American Dietetic Association and American Diabetes Association, available through NFB in accessible format.

- Living with Diabetes and Visual Impairment, Diabetes Association of Greater Cleveland, Accessible format. www.dagc.org or 1-216-591-0800

- Resource Guide to Aids and Appliances, NFB. Accessible format.

- You, Your Eyes and Diabetes, distance education course in accessible format, Hadley School for the Blind, www.hadley-school.org or 1-800-323-4238

- Voice of the Diabetic, NFB. Accessible format.

Products

Adaptive Equipment and Blood Glucose Monitors

- The Eye-Dea Shop: 1-216-791-8118 ext. 278/279 or www.clevelandsightcenter.org

- e-pill, LLC, Medication Reminders: 1-781-239-8255 or www.e-pill.com

- Independent Living Aids, Inc: 1-800-537-2118 or www.independentliving.com

- Insuleeve: 1-201-791-9024 or www.insuleeve.com

- LS&S Group, Inc.: 1-800-468-4789 or www.lss-group.com

- MaxiAids: 1-800-522-6294 or www.Maxi-Aids.com

- Pharma Supply, Inc.: 1-866-373-2824 or www.pharmasupply.com

- Science Products: 1-800-888-7400 or www.scienceproducts.org

Insulin Pens and Other Forms of Insulin Dosers

- Eli Lilly and Company: 1-800-545-5979 or www.lillydiabetes.com

- Novo Nordisk: 1-800-727-6500 or www.novo-nordisk-us.com

- Owen Mumford, Inc: 1-800-421-6936, or www.owenmumford.com

- Sanofi-Aventis: 1-800-981-2491 or www.sanofiaventis.com/us

Blood Glucose Monitors

- Abbott Laboratories, Abbott Diabetes Care: 1-888-522-5226 or www.abbottdiabetescare.com

- Bayer Health Care, LLC., Diabetes Care Division: 1-800-348-8100 or www.ascensia.com

- BBI Healthcare, BBI Holdings Plc: Sensocard. It is expected that this product will be marketed through catalog distribution and WalMart.

- BD: 1-888-232-2737 or www.bddiabetes.com

- Diagnostic Devices Inc: Prodigy and Prodigy Duo. www.prodigymeter.com. Marketed through catalog distribution and PharmaSupply.

- Home Diagnostics, Inc: 1-800-342-7226 or www.homediagnostics.com

- Hypoguard: 1-800-818-8877 or www.hypoguard.com

- LifeScan, Inc.: 1-800-227-8862 or www.lifescan.com

- Roche Diagnostics: 1-800-858-8072 or www.roche.com or www.accu-chek.com

- U.S. Diagnostics, Inc.: 1-866-216-5308 or www.usdiagnostics.net

REFERENCES

1. American Diabetes Association, National Fact Sheet, 2005, p. 3, Available at http://www.diabetes.org/uedocuments/nationaldiabetesFactSheetRev.pdf, accessed November 25, 2005.

2. American Diabetes Association, Projection of Diabetes Burden Through 2050, 2001. Available at http://care.diabetesjournals.org/cgi/content/full/24/11/1936#SEC2. Accessed January 25, 2005.

3. American Diabetes Association, Economic Costs of Diabetes in the U.S. in 2002, 2002, Available at http://care.diabetesjournals.org/cgi/content/full/26/3/917. Viewed November 25, 2005.

4. Andrus M, Leggett-Frazier N, Pfeifer M. Chronic complications of diabetes: an overview. In: Franz M, Ed. *A Core Curriculum for Diabetes Educators*. 5th ed. Diabetes and Complications. Chicago, IL: American Association of Diabetes Educators; 2003:56.

5. National Institute of Diabetes and Digestive and Kidney Diseases, Diabetes Control and Complications Trial, NIH Publication No. 94-3874, September, 1994. 1-2.

6. Diabetes Trials Unit, University of Oxford, UK Prospective Diabetes Study, 2002. Available at http://www.dtu.ox.ac.uk/index.html?maindoc=/ukpds/. Accessed January 28, 2006.

7. Bernbaum M, Stich T. Eye disease and adaptive diabetes education for visually impaired persons. In: Franz M, Ed. *A Core Curriculum for Diabetes Educators*. 5th Ed. Diabetes and Complications. Chicago, IL: American Association of Diabetes Educators; 2003:125.

8. Centers for Disease Control and Prevention. Diabetes surveillance system: visual impairment. Available at: http://www.cdc.gov/diabetes/statistics/visual/fig1.htm. Accessed July 21, 2005

9. Chous AP. *Diabetic Eye Disease*. Auburn, WA: Fairwood Press; 2003:106.

10. Sokol-McKay D, Buskirk K, Whittaker P. Adaptive Low-Vision and Blindness Techniques for Blood Glucose Monitoring. *Diabetes Educator.* 2003;29:614-630.

11. Ratner R. Pathophysiology of the diabetes disease state. In: Franz M, Ed. *A Core Curriculum for Diabetes Educators.* 5th ed. Diabetes and Complications. Chicago, IL: American Association of Diabetes Educators; 2003:10.

12. Koenig P. The eye, retinopathy and other pathologies. In: Cleary M, Ed. *Diabetes and Visual Impairment: An Educator's Resource Guide.* Chicago, IL: The American Association of Diabetes Educators Education and Research Foundation; 1994:34.

13. Funnell M, Feldman E. Diabetic Neuropathy. In: Franz M, Ed. *A Core Curriculum for Diabetes Educators.* 5th Ed. Diabetes and Complications. Chicago, IL: American Association of Diabetes Educators; 2003:200.

14. Coonrod B, Ernst K. Nephropathy. In: Franz M, Ed. *A Core Curriculum for Diabetes Educators.* 5th Ed. Diabetes and Complications. Chicago, IL: American Association of Diabetes Educators; 2003:156.

15. A.D.A.M. Inc., 15/15 Rule. [Medline Plus Website, Medical Encyclopedia, published by the National Institutes of Health] Aug. 1, 2004, Available at: http://www.nlm.nih.gov/medlineplus/ency/imagepages/19815.htm. Accessed January 21, 2006.

16. Mullooly C, Chalmers K. Physical activity/exercise. In: Franz M, Ed. *A Core Curriculum for Diabetes Educators.* 5th Ed. Chicago, IL: American Association of Diabetes Educators; 2003:69.

17. Hinnen D, Guthrie D, Childs D, et al. Pattern management of blood glucose. In: Franz M, Ed. *A Core Curriculum for Diabetes Educators* 5th Ed. Diabetes Management Therapies. Chicago, IL: American Association of Diabetes Educators; 2003:218.

18. ADEVIP Task Force. Guidelines for the practice of adaptive diabetes self-care equipment for visually impaired persons (ADEVIP). *Diabetes Educator.* 1994;20(2):111-118.

19. Williams A. Working with your diabetes team. *Voice of the Diabetic.* 2005;20(3):12-13.

20. American Association of Diabetes Educators and Roche Diagnostics Corporation. Reimbursement Primer. Chicago, IL; 2000:38.

21. American Diabetes Association, Part B Medicare Benefits for Medical Nutrition Therapy. 2002. Available at: http://www.diabetes.org/for-health-professionals-and-scientists/recognition/dsmt-mntfaqs.jsp. Accessed January 21, 2006.

22. American Association of Diabetes Educators. Guide to Medicare Reimbursement Diabetes Education and Supplies. Available at: http://members.aadenet.org/scriptcontent/MNTMedicareGuide.cfm. Accessed January 21, 2006.

23. Centers for Medicare & Medicaid Services, Medicare and You – 2006 Handbook, 2006, Available at: http://www.medicare.gov/Publications/Pubs/pdf/10050.pdf. Accessed January 28, 2006.

24. Lidke R. How to choose footwear. *Diabetes Self-Management.* 2005;July/August: 37.

25. Sokol-McKay D, Buskirk K, Whittaker P. Adaptive low-vision and blindness techniques for blood glucose monitoring. *Diabetes Educator.* 2003;29:614-630.

26. Task Force on ADEVIP. Guidelines for Practice of Adaptive Diabetes Education for Visually Impaired Persons. In: Cleary M, Ed. *Diabetes and Visual Impairment: An Educator's Resource Guide.* Chicago, IL: The American Association of Diabetes Educators Education and Research Foundation; 1994: xxxiii.

27. American Diabetes Association. Clinical Practice Guidelines 2005. *Diabetes Care.* 2005;28(1):S10.

28. White J, Campbell R. Pharmacologic therapies for glucose management. In: Franz M, Ed. *A Core Curriculum for Diabetes Educators.* 5th Ed. Diabetes Management Therapies. Chicago, IL: American Association of Diabetes Educators; 2003:104.

29. Petzinger R. Adaptive medication measurement and administration. In: Cleary M, Ed. *Diabetes and Visual Impairment: An Educator's Resource Guide.* Chicago, IL: The American Association of Diabetes Educators Education and Research Foundation; 1994:129-130.

30. Kitchel JE. Large Print: Guidelines for Optimal Readability and APHontTM a font for low vision. American Printing House for the Blind; 2004. Available at: www.aph.org/edresearch/lpguide.htm. Accessed January 22, 2006.

31. Vinicor F. Macrovascular disease. In: Franz M, Ed. *A Core Curriculum for Diabetes Educators.* 5th Ed. Diabetes and Complications. Chicago, IL: American Association of Diabetes Educators; 2003:101.

32. Williams A. Foot care. *Diabetes Self-Management.* 1999:32-34.

Section IV

Practice Management

Establishing a Low Vision Rehabilitation Specialty Practice

INTRODUCTION

Throughout this text, we have tried to establish the research and clinical basis for providing low vision rehabilitation as part of occupational therapy practice. We have emphasized that the ability to evaluate and treat low vision is necessary to meet the needs of many clients. Occupational therapists working with the adult population will encounter many clients with low vision, even if this is not the primary reason the client has been referred for occupational therapy.

The prevalence and incidence of low vision in the United States are high and experts predict a large increase over the next two decades because the prevalence of low vision increases sharply in persons older than 65 years. In the study by Congdon et al,[1] persons older than 80 years made up only 7.7% of the population but accounted for 69% of the severe visual impairment. It is this group that is the fastest-growing segment of the US population. Based on this information, the American Occupational Therapy Association (AOTA) has called low vision rehabilitation one of the top 10 emerging fields in occupational therapy.

It is our hope that if you have reached this section of the book, you have a strong interest in becoming more involved in this new and exciting practice area of occupational therapy. If so, you are likely to be left with a number of important questions about educational requirements, certification, practice opportunities, billing, and reimbursement.

Some of the important questions that need to be addressed include:

1. What are the educational requirements for an occupational therapist to provide low vision rehabilitation services?
2. Is certification necessary to provide low vision rehabilitation services?
3. How does the occupational therapist interact with other vision rehabilitation professionals?
4. What practice opportunities are available?
5. How do I market my services as a provider of low vision rehabilitation services?
6. Are low vision rehabilitation services provided by occupational therapists covered by Medicare and other insurance?
7. How do I properly bill insurance for low vision rehabilitation services?
8. Are optical aids and other devices covered by insurance?
9. What equipment do I need to get started in the field of low vision rehabilitation?

This chapter is designed to provide answers to these critical questions.

DIDACTIC EDUCATION/CLINICAL TRAINING

Although information about the visual system is certainly part of every occupational therapy curriculum, the information provided is generally basic and introductory. Few programs are designed to prepare the entry-level occupational therapist for the practice of low vision rehabilitation, either from a didactic or clinical training perspective. Mary Warren states that "Although occupational therapists have been involved in the rehabilitation of persons with vision loss since the inception of the profession in 1917, we never played an extensive role in low vision rehabilitation."[2] Occupational therapists have indeed always played a role in low vision rehabilitation because nearly two-thirds of older adults with low vision have at least one other chronic medical condition that may interfere with activities of daily living (ADL) and require occupational therapy.[3] Thus, in the context of providing care for other chronic conditions, occupational therapists must routinely manage issues related to low vision in their elderly clients.

Perhaps the entry-level occupational therapy program curricula need to be reconsidered, given the prevalence of low vision in the adult population. However, at the present time, most occupational therapy graduates, as well as experienced occupational therapists need to gain additional information and clinical experience to feel comfortable practicing low vision rehabilitation at a sophisticated level, much as hand therapists seek specialized training. A useful guide to the core knowledge base required to practice low vision therapy is provided by the Academy for Certification in Vision Rehabilitation Professionals (ACVRP) (www.acvrep.org).

A wide range of educational opportunities are now available for occupational therapists to receive this additional educational experience. These opportunities include graduate degree level programs, multiple-day continuing education workshops (both on-site and online), presentations from companies that sell and produce optical aids, home study courses, and of course, textbooks like this one.

While all registered/licensed occupational therapists are legally qualified and currently able to provide and bill for low vision rehabilitation services without any additional education or certification, most will need additional education and clinical experience to competently function as low vision therapists. The decision about how much additional educational expe-

rience and the nature of the educational experience is a personal one that each occupational therapist must make. Individuals vary in their preferred learning style. For an assertive, self-assured individual with strong independent learning skills, reading a book, taking a home-study course, and gaining some experience with optical aids from a manufacturer's workshop may be sufficient to develop the core knowledge base. Additional clinical practice supervised by an experienced low vision therapist is also recommended and is required for certification. Some may prefer to enroll in a formal graduate program in low vision rehabilitation that includes clinical training. The various opportunities are listed with contact information in Table 16-1. We have tried to make this listing as complete as possible. Of course, organizations come and go and new programs are being developed. Thus, it is important to use this table as a starting point and be aware that new programs and educational opportunities will certainly be available after publication of this book.

CONTINUING EDUCATION COURSES

It is common for occupational therapists to gain knowledge about new areas of practice through postgraduate, continuing education seminars and workshops. One- and two-day workshops are offered periodically for low vision rehabilitation. Some of the companies offering such workshops are listed in Table 16-1. These workshops generally cover information about epidemiology of low vision, diseases causing low vision, basic optics, the occupational therapy evaluation and low vision rehabilitation, billing for services, and hands-on experience with optical aids. After completing one or two of these courses most occupational therapists would feel comfortable providing basic low vision rehabilitation services to clients presenting with low vision as a secondary diagnosis. Some self-assured occupational therapists might feel comfortable enough to initiate a low vision service in a hospital setting, or provide home-based low vision rehabilitation services with clients presenting with a primary diagnosis of low vision.

Companies that produce and sell optical devices sometimes provide inexpensive continuing education for occupational therapists and these seminars offer an excellent opportunity to gain hands-on experience with microscopes, magnifiers, telescopes, closed circuit televisions (CCTVs), and other video display technology. For example, Eschenbach Optik of America (http://eschenbach.com/seminars.php) has been providing this service for many years and this

Table 16-1.

Postgraduate Educational Opportunities for Education in Low Vision Rehabilitation

Name of Organization	Type of Education	Contact Information
Pennsylvania College of Optometry	Graduate level All distance learning Certificate or Masters in Low Vision Rehabilitation Certificate or Masters in Rehab Teaching Certificate or Masters in Orientation and Mobility	www.pco.edu/acad_progs/grad/gs_lvr.htm
University of Alabama, Birmingham	Graduate level education Masters or Certificate in Low Vision Rehabilitation	www.uab.edu/ot/lvrcert/program_description.htm
Vision Education Seminars	2-Day Workshops on Low Vision presented across the United States	www.visionedseminars.com
Lighthouse courses	Workshops on Low Vision presented across the United States	www.lighthouse.org
Eschenbach courses	2-Day Workshops on Low Vision presented across the United States	www.Eschenbach.com
visAbilties	2-Day Workshops on Low Vision presented across the United States	www.visabilities.com
AOTA home study course	Home study course	www.aota.org
AOTA/Jewish Guild for the Blind Online Study Course	Online course	www.aota.org
The Hadley School for the Blind	Online course	www.hadley-school.org/
Lions Vision Research and Rehabilitation Center at the Johns Hopkins Wilmer Eye Institute	Online course	http://lowvisionproject.org/
Ocusource	Online course	www.ocusource.com/

company offers seminars in many cities around the country on an annual basis. The Eschenbach course is entitled "Low Vision Care...What's it All About?" This low vision care presentation for eyecare and rehabilitation professionals is designed as an introduction to low vision care and optical devices.

The primary missing ingredient from short continuing education courses is clinical experience with clients. Gaining meaningful clinical experience is the greatest challenge facing the therapist who would like to be involved in low vision rehabilitation. Opportunities may exist in some communities for an interested occupational therapist to volunteer or find employment in a situation in which low vision rehabilitation is already being provided by another experienced therapist. In any case, finding a setting to acquire supervised clinical instruction is a challenge. Recognizing this challenge, ACVREP will arrange supervision of applicants

for certification from a distance using technological methods.

HOME STUDY AND DISTANCE EDUCATION

In 1995, the AOTA devoted its entire October issue to the topic of low vision and in 1998 developed the AOTA Occupational Therapy Practice Guidelines for Adults with Low Vision. In 2000, Mary Warren edited a home study course entitled Low Vision: Occupational Therapy Intervention with the Older Adult, published by AOTA.[4] These three documents provide a wonderful starting point for independent learning. In 2006, the AOTA published revised practice guidelines for a specialty certification in low vision (www.aota.org).

A recent trend in education is online or distance learning and many opportunities now exist for this type of education in the area of low vision rehabilitation. The Hadley School for the Blind (http://www.hadley-school.org) currently offers a number of online courses for professionals, including coursework in Braille, low vision technology, introduction to low vision, self-esteem and adjusting with blindness, and macular degeneration. These courses are provided without any tuition charge.

The Lions Vision Research and Rehabilitation Center at the Johns Hopkins Wilmer Eye Institute offers some exceptional distance learning opportunities and outstanding up-to-date information about low vision rehabilitation at their website (http://lowvisionproject.org). This site is also the gateway to the Low Vision Rehabilitation Network (LVRN). This is a network of low vision providers and researchers, and membership allows individuals to participate in a number of collaborative projects, including:

- Free online continuing professional education courses.
- Exchange ideas and views with colleagues in online forums.
- Participate in live online low vision case conferences.
- Participate in live online low vision research symposia.
- Participate in an online "What's New in Low Vision" website.
- Help plan the Low Vision Rehabilitation Outcomes Project.

Membership in LVRN is free and open to low vision rehabilitation practitioners, researchers, students, educators, administrators, policy-makers, business people, and anyone else who is interested in advances in the field of low vision rehabilitation.

A course currently offered on this website is entitled "Understanding Visual Impairments and Functional Rehabilitation of Visually Impaired Patients." The course consists of 22 lectures and supplemental material that cover the following topics: anatomy and physiology of vision, diseases of the visual system, optics and optical devices, functional and ADL assessments, visual skills training, rehabilitation services and resources, and vision enhancement and adaptive technology.

An organization called Ocusource (http://www.ocusource.com) uses a different approach to distance learning and provides extensive information and resources about low vision, including continuing education. This organization, founded by Dr. Lou Lipschultz, a low vision practitioner, offers a web-based voice-conferencing system, all in an accessible format. Participants are able to view presentations, and meet live with speakers and vendors.

An online course entitled "Low Vision in Older Adults: Foundations for Rehabilitation" is the result of collaboration between the AOTA and SightCare, a program of The Jewish Guild for the Blind. The course was written by a low vision optometrist, a certified environmental design specialist, and an occupational therapist. It is made up of three lessons:

- Lesson 1: An orientation to vision loss: its causes, effects, and interventions
- Lesson 2: Vision enhancement with magnification: theory and practice.
- Lesson 3: Environmental considerations.

Of course, the professional journals listed in Table 16-1 and textbooks like this one are available to assist occupational therapists in gaining information about low vision rehabilitation as independent learners.

UNIVERSITY-BASED GRADUATE EDUCATION

Some occupational therapists may prefer more formal, university-based graduate education. Two excellent programs designed for occupational therapists are now available to meet this need and are listed in Table 16-1. Both programs offer a certificate or master's degree in low vision rehabilitation.

The Department of Graduate Studies in Vision Impairment of the Pennsylvania Colleges of Optometry (http://pco.edu/acad_progs/grad/grad_prgs.htm) prepares a variety of professionals to work with people who are visually impaired. These programs include the:

- Master of Science and Certificate in Low Vision Rehabilitation

- Master of Education and Certificate in Education of Children and Youth with Visual and Multiple Impairments
- Master of Science and Certificate in Orientation and Mobility
- Master of Science and Certificate in Vision Rehabilitation Therapy (formerly Rehabilitation Teaching)

The program most likely to be of interest to occupational therapists is the Master of Science and Certificate in Low Vision Rehabilitation. All of these programs, with the exception of the full-time Master's degree in Orientation and Mobility, are now available through distance education.

The University of Alabama, Birmingham Department of Occupational Therapy offers a graduate certificate program in low vision rehabilitation (http://main.uab.edu/Shrp/default.aspx?pid=76987). This program is designed for occupational therapists with bachelors, masters, or doctorate degrees. It consists of 17 credit hours of specialized courses in low vision rehabilitation. Students take 11 credits of core courses designed to provide a foundation in providing low vision rehabilitation services, 4 credits of elective courses to address specific aspects of intervention in greater depth, and a 2-credit course in advanced application. All of the courses are offered online through a web-based curriculum. The curriculum is designed with the working occupational therapist in mind. Coursework emphasizes practical application of the information taught. Students can enroll in the certificate program or combine completion of the certificate program with a postprofessional master's degree in occupational therapy. Students completing the certificate program need to complete an additional 10 credits of coursework and 6 credits of research to receive the postprofessional master's degree. Coursework for the postprofessional degree is also online.

Thus, many educational opportunities are available for an occupational therapist who would like to become involved in low vision education. It is simply a matter of deciding on one's learning style and researching some of the available options.

CERTIFICATION

Certification in low vision therapy is not required at this time for occupational therapists. Any registered/licensed occupational therapist is able to provide low vision rehabilitation and bill for these services. In Chapter 1, we discussed the various professionals involved in low vision rehabilitation of adult clients.

These include occupational therapists, low vision therapists, vision rehabilitation therapists (formerly rehabilitation teachers), and orientation and mobility (O&M) specialists. Of these three groups, only occupational therapists are licensed and function as independent service providers in the Medicare system and in some regions for other commercial insurance programs. Vision rehabilitation therapists, low vision therapists, and O&M specialists often work for state agencies, private organizations, and school systems. In 2006, the services of these professionals were not reimbursed by Medicare, Medicaid, or most private insurance.

Although occupational therapists do not require certification to practice low vision rehabilitation, it is a desirable goal for the following reasons:
- Certification demonstrates that the therapist has advanced skills low vision rehabilitation.
- Certification may be required in the future by insurers for reimbursement, even for occupational therapists.

ACADEMY FOR CERTIFICATION OF VISION REHABILITATION AND EDUCATION PROFESSIONALS

Currently there are two active certification programs for low vision therapy. The first is a certification process run by ACVREP, which was established in January 2000. It is an independent and autonomous legal certification body governed by a volunteer Board of Directors. ACVREP's mission is to offer professional certification for vision rehabilitation and education professionals in order to improve service delivery to persons with vision impairments. As of January 2006, there were approximately 2,100 certified O&M specialists, 600 certified vision rehabilitation therapists, and 300 certified low vision therapists. Although ACVREP does not release data on how many occupational therapists are certified, it is likely that many of the 300 who are certified low vision therapists are occupational therapists.

The ACVREP certification program that is appropriate for occupational therapists is called the Certified Low Vision Therapist (CLVT). To be eligible to take the written certification test, candidates must meet the eligibility criteria listed in Table 16-2. Candidates passing a 100-item written examination receive certification that is valid for a 5-year period (Table 16-3). Certified low vision therapists must go through a recertification process every 5 years. To be recertified, an individual must demonstrate that he or she has maintained continuing professional competence

---

Table 16-2.

Criteria for Eligibility for Certification (Academy for Certification of Vision Rehabilitation and Education Professionals)

A. Proof of a minimum of a Bachelor's degree in a related health, education or rehabilitation field.

B. Have completed 350 hours of "discipline specific, supervised practice that includes, but is not limited to, direct service hours, and related phone calls, meetings, observations, report writing, etc." The practice must be supervised by a CLVT and a physician (OD or MD) practicing in low vision. The CLVT practice supervisor may be offsite. The applicant must meet the CLVT clinical competencies.

C. The CLVT practice supervisor must verify that the applicant possesses knowledge of the 13 CLVT core curriculum areas, which are as follows:

1. The human visual system including pathology and disorders, treatment, and implications for daily functioning.

2. Human development and the visual system.

3. Psychosocial aspects of vision impairment.

4. Basic optics of the eye and optical principles of lenses, including magnification, minification, prisms, and correction of refractive errors.

5. Principles of teaching and learning in general and specifically related to low vision.

6. The components of the low vision clinical examination, including procedures, instruments, and equipment.

7. Optical and non-optical devices for enhancing low vision, and their characteristics, uses, advantages, and disadvantages.

8. Techniques and strategies for assessment of environmental factors impacting visual efficiency.

9. Techniques and strategies for enhancing vision through visual environmental adaptations and the use of environmental cues.

10. Techniques and strategies for assessment of visual efficiency when completing everyday tasks of daily living.

11. Instruction in the use of adaptive techniques and strategies for using vision efficiently.

12. Techniques for teaching visual skills, such as fixating, focusing, eccentric viewing, tracing, scanning, tracking, and localizing with and without optical devices.

13. The impact of additional disabilities on low vision, and resources for meeting these needs.

Note: check www.acrep.org for updates.

---

in the field of vision rehabilitation and education, much like the requirements for occupational therapy certification. Acceptable activities include continuing education, professional experience, publications and presentations, and professional service. Full details of all requirements can be obtained from the ACVREP website.

The advantages of ACVREP certification are:

- The guidelines for the examination and study program have been developed by experienced professionals in the field. The applicant must have his or her study program reviewed and a multiple choice

examination must be passed to insure that the occupational therapist has the requisite knowledge base for competent practice.

- The organization will help applicants locate and arrange for clinical supervision. Although some direct supervision is necessary, most of the 360 hours of clinical practice may be supervised by a certified therapist off-site.

- Certification allows the occupational therapist to join rather than compete with the professionals who have been providing low vision and blindness rehabilitation services

Table 16-3.

Low Vision Therapist Test Summary: The 100 Multiple-Choice and True/False Questions

Content Categories	Approximate Percentage of Examination
Functional Implications of Eye Pathologies	16%
Interpretation of Reports of the Clinical Examination	10%
Preclinical Functional Assessment	15%
Optics and the Visual System	11%
Optical Devices	12%
Human Development	8%
Therapeutic Intervention	16%
Psychosocial Aspects	8%
Driving and Low Vision	4%

long before the recent increase in occupational therapy practitioners in the field.

- ACVREP is a member of the National Organizations for Competency Assurance (www.noca.org) according to standards established by the National Commission for Certifying Agencies.

AMERICAN OCCUPATIONAL THERAPY ASSOCIATION CERTIFICATION

In 2006, the AOTA initiated Board Specialty Certification in low vision. The purpose of this new specialty certification is to provide a framework for professional development that is specifically geared to occupational therapy. Through its Specialty Certification programs, AOTA provides formal recognition for those who have engaged in a voluntary process of ongoing, focused, and targeted professional development. The program is voluntary and certification is not required for practice.

The process for Specialty Certification is self-directed. There is no test involved; rather, certification is based on peer review of the candidate's professional development portfolio and a series of narrative reflections covering the following topics:[5]

1. Performs an individualized occupational therapy low vision evaluation to identify factors that may facilitate, compensate for, or inhibit use of vision in occupational performance.

2. Develops and implements an individualized occupational therapy low vision intervention plan in collaboration with the client and rel-

evant others that reflects the client's priorities for occupational performance.

3. Recognizes immediate and long-term implications of psychosocial issues related to vision loss and modifies therapeutic approach and occupational therapy service delivery accordingly.

4. Advances access to occupational therapy services and advocates for policies, programs, and products that promote engagement in occupations by persons with low vision.

OTHER PROFESSIONS AND INTERPROFESSIONAL ISSUES

It is important that occupational therapists have a firm understanding of the history of low vision in the United States (see Chapter 1). Vision rehabilitation therapists and O&M specialists have been in low vision rehabilitation for many more years than occupational therapists. With the inclusion of low vision as a disability under Medicare guidelines in the early 1990s, occupational therapists suddenly became involved in low vision rehabilitation and this created controversy. The primary basis for this controversy is that the impetus for occupational therapy's entrance into the low vision arena was not a change in education and preparation of its practitioners; rather, it was purely based on reimbursement issues. Thus, other vision rehabilitation therapists have raised questions about the qualifications, education, and clinical experience of occupational therapists in the area of low vision. For example, Lambert[6] raised the following concerns about occupational therapists:

1. They may be unfamiliar with the various disciplines in the field, and thereby fail to appropriately refer clients for other needed services.

2. They have inadequate knowledge or specialized training in low vision.

3. Clinics may favor occupational therapy in the delivery of low vision services, even though more disability-specific professionals may be the most appropriate providers.

Similar concerns were raised by Orr and Huebner in 2001,[7] when they expressed their unease about occupational therapists' lack of specialized knowledge base and skills needed to work with the low vision population.

Others have argued that there are a number of important reasons why occupational therapists should play a primary role in low vision rehabilitation:[2,8]

1. Although the elderly comprise the majority of the low vision population, they are the most underserved by existing state, charitable, and private programs. Because of the lack of availability of services treatment through the blindness system, rehabilitation may be delayed and these individuals are likely to become socially isolated, depressed, and dependent. Involvement of occupational therapists through the healthcare system provides significantly greater access to low vision rehabilitation for the elderly.[8]

2. Two-thirds of older persons have at least one other chronic condition, in addition to low vision, that limits their independent functioning. Occupational therapists are already primary providers for older clients with other chronic conditions.[2,8] Occupational therapists are trained in the physical, cognitive, sensory, and psychological aspects of disability and aging, and therefore, may be the natural choice of professionals to work with older persons whose limitations in ADL are a result of a combination of deficits.[2]

3. Occupational therapists are more evenly distributed throughout the United States than O&Ms and vision rehabilitation therapists, who tend to be located in larger metropolitan areas. Low vision services can be more widely disseminated through the healthcare delivery system.[2]

Occupational therapy as a profession, as well as individual therapists, have reacted in a positive way to this debate. In the past 15 years, many occupational therapists have gained the knowledge base and clinical skills necessary to provide excellent care to clients requiring low vision rehabilitation. This has been accomplished though a variety of learning formats, including independent study, continuing education courses, clinical internships, and university-based training. In addition, many occupational therapists have completed the certification process run by the ACVREP.

Occupational therapists active in low vision rehabilitation may work closely with vision rehabilitation therapists and O&M specialists in various clinical settings. As occupational therapists become involved, it is critical to be aware of the history of low vision rehabilitation in the United States, the various professions involved, and some of the sensitivities and important political issues described above.

PRACTICE OPPORTUNITIES

There are many potential practice opportunities available for occupational therapists who wish to become involved in the field of low vision rehabilitation. These opportunities range from employment in hospitals (both inpatient and outpatient), nursing homes, assisted living facilities, offices of ophthalmologists and optometrists, and both independent home healthcare, as well as employment in home health agencies. The underlying essential ingredient to finding these opportunities is to know where to look for patients with low vision. Based on the information about prevalence and incidence of low vision, we know this means looking for patients who are 65 years of age and older. These patients are found in nursing homes, assisted living facilities, and hospital settings. The ophthalmologists most likely to see patients with low vision are the retinal, cataract, and glaucoma specialists. Optometrists with a specialty practice in low vision, of course, are also likely to be good resources for patients with low vision.

HOME HEALTHCARE

A wonderful private practice opportunity for occupational therapists is providing low vision evaluations and rehabilitation in the client's home. To function in this capacity, the occupational therapist must first enroll as a private practitioner in Medicare and obtain a Medicare provider number. Information about becoming a provider and an application are available at: http://new.cms.hhs.gov/center/provider.asp. A list of Medicare carriers can be found at the CMS website: http://cms.hhs.gov/contacts/incardir.asp. Once this provider number is obtained, the therapist is able to perform both evaluation and treatment services and

bill Medicare. The essentials of this billing and necessary documentation process required for Medicare will be reviewed later in this chapter. In this mode of practice the occupational therapist is a private practitioner and must have an office address for billing while providing care in the client's home. The therapist must market him- or herself to other professionals who are likely to encounter elderly clients with low vision. Such professionals include ophthalmologists (primarily retinal, glaucoma, and cataract specialists), low vision optometrists, geriatricians, large eye hospitals, and other rehabilitation therapists such as physical therapists, speech-language pathologists, other occupational therapists, recreational therapists, and social workers.

We have provided a sample brochure and introductory letter in the Appendices. These documents can be used to develop these relationships with other professionals.

NURSING HOMES

Research has shown that a high percentage of nursing home residents are visually impaired. For example, Horowitz[9] conducted a study of a 250 bed, long-term facility and found that 23% of the residents were visually impaired. Vision loss among nursing home residents complicates many of the care-related tasks for providers of nursing home services, and interferes with the clients' ability to engage in ADL.[10]

Thus, there is a significant need for occupational therapists who currently work in nursing homes to become involved in low vision rehabilitation in order to care for a large percentage of their clients.

ACUTE CARE/REHABILITATION HOSPITAL

We know that the two most common causes of low vision are macular degeneration and diabetic retinopathy. Older people with cardiovascular disease and diabetes make up a significant percentage of the patients in acute care and rehabilitation hospitals. These are the same people who are likely to have macular degeneration and low vision. In addition, many patients admitted to rehabilitation hospitals with cerebral vascular accident or traumatic brain injury may experience significant visual field loss, which also falls into the category of low vision impairment. Thus, occupational therapists working in this setting have an opportunity to establish a low vision service within such rehabilitation departments. Development of such a service helps to insure that there are therapists with appropriate clinical ability and that clients receive appropriate and timely treatment. Occupational therapists may practice in outpatient and home health services associated with rehabilitation hospitals, enabling reimbursement from private insurers as well as Medicare and Medicaid.

RETIREMENT/ASSISTED LIVING COMMUNITIES

Opportunities also exist in assisted living communities because of the aging population that live in such facilities. The basic underlying theme when looking for the population that is likely to need low vision care is to find older adults. An occupational therapist can arrange to make educational presentations about low vision and low vision rehabilitation in assisted living communities. Providing such education and helping people better understand what can be accomplished in spite of permanent vision loss can be quite important for people. Many individuals do not even seek care because they have simply been told by previous professionals that there is not much that can be done. The occupational therapist can develop a working relationship with an ophthalmologist and/or a low vision optometrist. People seeking more information or additional care for their visual impairment can be referred to an eyecare professional for an evaluation. If low vision rehabilitation is required, the eyecare professional can then refer the client to the occupational therapist for such care. This care would be provided by the occupational therapist as an independent provider.

COMMUNITY-BASED AGENCIES

Until the late 1990s, most of the low vision rehabilitation in the United States was provided within the service delivery system that has been called the "blindness system" (see Chapter 1). This system is also sometimes referred to as the educational rehabilitation model, or the nonmedical vision rehabilitation system.[11] This system is a comprehensive nationwide

network of services consisting of state, federal, and private agencies serving children and adults with blindness and low vision.[12] Because of limited public funds to support these services, however, only a limited percentage of people requiring low vision rehabilitation are able to receive these services in community-based, state, or federally-funded agencies. This scarcity of resources has led some vision rehabilitation agencies to hire occupational therapists to provide services.[7] The advantage is that occupational therapists can be reimbursed by Medicare, while vision rehabilitation therapists and O&M specialists cannot. Thus, there may be opportunities for occupational therapists in these agencies. Occupational therapists working in these agencies would generally be salaried employees.

LOW VISION OPTOMETRIST

A nonconventional opportunity would be to become affiliated with a low vision optometrist. They design and prescribe low vision devices (eg, optical, nonoptical, electronic) and make recommendations about lighting, contrast, and other environmental factors that influence vision. Although low vision optometrists should ideally work closely with low vision therapists, this may not always be the case. Some low vision optometrists are not fully aware of the capabilities of occupational therapists. Thus, once an occupational therapist identifies a low vision optometrist in the area, one challenge may be to educate this eyecare professional about the role of occupational therapy in low vision rehabilitation.

A second challenge is trying to locate a qualified low vision optometrist. The profession of optometry does not recognize "specialties". Therefore, any optometrist can provide low vision services, regardless of his or her experience in this area. However, the American Academy of Optometry Low Vision Section has a Diplomate program for interested optometrists. To become a Diplomate in Low Vision, an optometrist must pass a written test, an oral examination, and a practical low vision examination. Currently, there are only about 45 practicing Low Vision Diplomats worldwide. A current list of optometrists that have successfully completed this process can be found at the website for the American Academy of Optometry.[13] The American Optometric Association also has a Low Vision Section. Although there is no testing program required to become a member of this section, optometrists that have joined are likely to have a strong interest in the area of low vision. Some low vision optometrists have completed a residency program, while others have chosen to specialize in this area

and have acquired additional knowledge and clinical skills through continuing education and independent learning. Currently, there are about 36,000 optometrists in the United States, and there are about 1,000 members in the low vision section of the American Optometric Association.

There are two potential ways of working with the low vision optometrist. The first method would be as an employee. The low vision optometrist would refer patients to the occupational therapist working in his or her practice. The therapist would evaluate and provide treatment in the doctor's office. The office would bill and be reimbursed for the therapist's services and provide an hourly salary to the occupational therapist. Another scenario would be for the low vision optometrist to refer patients to an occupational therapist functioning as an independent provider. In this case, the therapist would not provide services in the doctor's office. Rather, he or she would need an office and also could provide services in the client's home. In either case, the occupational therapist would require registration as an independent provider. In some states, not all private insurers recognize occupational therapists as independent providers. In these situations, occupational therapists may work for and bill through agencies or outpatient rehabilitation services.

OPHTHALMOLOGIST

Perhaps the most effective way of finding clients who require low vision rehabilitation is to work with an ophthalmologist. Ophthalmologists are physicians who specialize in the diagnosis and treatment of eye disease by completing a residency in ophthalmology. Many ophthalmologists also complete a fellowship program to further specialize in an area of ophthalmology. A number of specialty areas exist, including specialists in cataract, glaucoma, retina, cornea, pediatric ophthalmology, and neuro-ophthalmology. Ophthalmologists most likely to treat clients with low vision are the retinal, glaucoma, and cataract specialists. Since most patients who have low vision have retinal problems or loss of vision due to glaucoma, these are the types of specialists with whom the occupational therapist should develop relationships. Doctors in these offices examine a high percentage of patients with various retinopathies on a daily basis. A very high percentage of their patients require further care. Unfortunately, many ophthalmologists do not refer for low vision rehabilitation.[14] Occupational therapists can identify these ophthalmologists and arrange a visit, at which the therapist can educate the physician about his or her capabilities, and the potential advantages for the patients in the practice. There is

no specific subspecialty of low vision in the profession of ophthalmology. There are currently about 16,000 practicing ophthalmologists in the United States.

The primary areas of interest and responsibility of the ophthalmologist are the diagnosis and treatment of eye disease. Treatment modalities generally involve the use of medication and surgery. Thus, clients often see the ophthalmologist first because of a perceived significant change in vision. The ophthalmologist attempts to restore normal visual function by treating the eye disease. In some cases this fails, or in other cases the vision can never be restored to normal and the client is now faced with permanent low vision. It is at this point that the ophthalmologist should refer the client with low vision to other professionals for further evaluation and rehabilitation.

A similar working relationship described above for the low vision optometrist also applies to working with the ophthalmologist, although few ophthalmologists specialize in low vision rehabilitation. Thus, the occupational therapist would need advanced skills in vision evaluation and optics.

EYE HOSPITAL

Some large metropolitan areas in the United States have free-standing eye hospitals. A high percentage of adult patients seen at these hospitals have low vision. Many of these institutions have a low vision optometrist on staff and some may already have established low vision rehabilitation programs. If not, eye hospitals represent a potential opportunity for occupational therapists. Our recommended approach would be to use some of the evidence for the effectiveness of low vision rehabilitation reviewed in Chapter 9 in a presentation to key personnel at the hospital. The article written by Mary Warren entitled "Providing Low Vision Rehabilitation Services with Occupational Therapy and Ophthalmology: A Programs Description" is an excellent article to include in such a discussion. Occupational therapists working in such a setting would generally be employees.

COLLEGES OF OPTOMETRY – PATIENT CARE CLINICS

There are 17 Colleges of Optometry in the United States and Puerto Rico. All of these colleges have large patient care clinics with a low vision service. These low vision services are used to train optometry students in all aspects of low vision care, including rehabilitation. The low vision departments are staffed by optometrists who have completed residencies in low vision and/or have many years of experience as low vision specialists. They are generally well-versed in the current trends in low vision care and research and should have an understanding of the important role that occupational therapy has begun to play in low vision rehabilitation. Some of these clinics may already employ rehabilitation therapists. Others, however, may not offer full-scope low vision care. Thus, this is a potential opportunity for an occupational therapist. The key contact person would be the Chief of the Low Vision Service at the College of Optometry. The occupational therapist would not have to convince this individual of the importance of low vision rehabilitation. Rather, the presentation would emphasize the unique contributions that occupational therapists could make in the low vision service.

MARKETING AND PUBLIC RELATIONS

Whether an occupational therapist establishes a low vision rehabilitation service in a nursing home, rehabilitation hospital, the office of an eyecare provider, or starts a private practice, there will be a need for marketing and public relations to make the service grow. In the following section, we present a series of internal and external marketing and public relations ideas that could be used in a variety of practice settings.

Internal Marketing

Within each practice setting, there will already be a client base that may be unaware of low vision and low vision rehabilitation. The first and least expensive method of marketing is to make current clients aware of the new low vision service.

Handouts and Brochures in Waiting Area

Most professionals utilize handouts and brochures in their waiting rooms to market various aspects of their practices. It is a matter of selecting appropriate materials to market the low vision rehabilitation aspect of your practice.

1. Handouts: Many materials are available that could be used as handouts in a waiting area. For example Lighthouse International offers a series of brochures for consumers that explain

Table 16-4.

Sample Resources for Consumer Education

Company/Vendor	Topic	Contact Information
Glaucoma Research Foundation	Understanding and Living with Glaucoma Glaucoma: What You Need To Know Cataracts and Glaucoma	http://www.glaucoma.org/learn/literature.php
National Eye Institute	Don't Lose Sight of Diabetic Eye Disease Age Related Eye Disease Study Information Packet Age-Related Macular Degeneration: What You Should Know Don't Lose Sight of Age Related Macular Degeneration Glaucoma: What You Should Know	http://www.nei.nih.gov/lowvision/default.asp
Lighthouse International	Low Vision Defined: A Guide to the Major Causes of Vision Loss and What Can Be Done to Improve Functional Vision Vision Loss Is Not a Normal Part of Aging—Open Your Eyes to the Facts! Newsletters for consumers	http://lighthouse.org/

various aspects of low vision. They also offer a monthly newsletter designed for consumers called "Consumer Times: Living Better with Vision Loss". Table 16-4 lists some other resources for consumer education.

2. Brochures: Think about developing your own brochure that explains low vision and the importance of low vision rehabilitation. An example of such a brochure is included in the Appendices.

Internal Mailings

If your office/hospital is computerized, you have the ability to make a selective mailing to clients by age and by diagnostic condition, such as macular degeneration, diabetic retinopathy, and diabetes. You can periodically send out information about low vision and low vision rehabilitation. Sample handouts are included in the Appendices.

Grand Rounds/Seminar Presentations

In most institutional settings, case conferences, grand rounds, and seminars are periodically scheduled. This is an outstanding opportunity to make the rest of the staff aware of your service, the clients you can help, and the expected outcomes.

External Marketing

In addition to marketing directly to current clients, it is important to make potential clients and other professionals aware of your service. We refer to this as external marketing.

Speaking Engagements

One of the best marketing tools available is to present educational information in a seminar/workshop format. Few people take advantage of this opportunity, however, because of discomfort with public speaking. Suggested audiences include groups of older adults, consumers with low vision, families of consumers with low vision, civic organizations, churches, and synagogues. We suggest that instead of waiting for an invitation from an organization, that the occupational therapist take the initiative and contact potential organizations.

Establish a Working Relationship With Other Professionals

In addition to ophthalmologists and optometrists, there are many other professionals who work with older adult clients with low vision. These include other occupational therapists, physical therapists, speech-language pathologists, recreation therapists, nurses,

social workers, psychologists, family physicians, neurologists, neuro-ophthalmologists, and geriatricians.

One way to cultivate a working relationship with an optometrist or general ophthalmologist with an interest or specialization in low vision is to refer clients. If other physicians or professionals refer to an occupational therapist, the occupational therapist, who must work under the prescription of a physician, may then refer the client to the optometrist or ophthalmologist.

There is no simple way to get the names and addresses of these people. You can sometimes get names and addresses from telephone directories, and from professional organization websites on the Internet. Mailing lists can be purchased from organizations such as the AOTA and similar organizations from other fields. We have included a letter of introduction for professionals in the Appendices that could be used to initiate contact. The goal is to develop true inter-referral relationships with a group of professionals that share an interest in the care of clients with low vision.

BILLING, INSURANCE, AND MEDICARE ISSUES

Reimbursement Sources

The impetus for occupational therapy's involvement in the area of low vision rehabilitation was the 1991 amendment by the Health Care Financing Administration (HCFA) that allowed Medicare coverage for the first time for licensed healthcare providers for low vision rehabilitation. Medicare is currently the main source of reimbursement for low vision rehabilitation for occupational therapists. Other potential reimbursement sources are HMOs, private insurance companies, state agencies for the blind and visually impaired, and private paying clients.

MEDICARE AND LOW VISION REHABILITATION (OUTPATIENT SETTINGS)

The information we provide in this section was current when this book was published. However, it is important to understand that the CMS occasionally makes policy changes and the reader should carefully review the CMS website and seek current information about billing for low vision rehabilitation services (www.cms.gov).

The current CMS policy on low vision rehabilitation in an outpatient setting (Medicare B) states that occupational therapy is a covered service if it meets the following criteria:

1. Services must be prescribed by a physician and furnished under physician-approved plan of care.

2. Services must be performed by an occupational therapist or occupational therapy assistant under supervision of occupational therapist.

3. Services must be reasonable and medically necessary for treatment of an individual's illness (must result in significant improvement in level of function within reasonable period of time). Medically necessary is defined by the diagnostic code and rehabilitation potential.

According to CMS, the purpose of vision rehabilitation therapy is to maximize the use of residual vision and provide patients with many practical adaptations for ADL. In doing so, it builds the confidence that is necessary for ongoing creative problem solving. Rehabilitation appears to be more effective if it is started as soon as functional visual difficulties are identified.

There can be coverage variations among Medicare contractors, called fiscal intermediaries, which are allowed to establish local policies. Thus, it is important to check with your local Medicare fiscal intermediary before initiating any low vision rehabilitation with clients.

According to CMS, coverage of low vision rehabilitation services is considered reasonable and necessary only for patients with a clear medical need. To meet the criteria established by CMS you must demonstrate that:

1. The patient has a moderate to severe visual impairment not correctable by conventional refractive means or certain types of visual field loss.

2. The patient has a clear potential for significant improvement in function following rehabilitation over a reasonable period of time.

Before providing services, the occupational therapist must develop a written evaluation and treatment plan. The treatment plan should include:

1. An initial assessment that documents the level of visual impairment.

2. A plan of care identifying specific goals to be fulfilled during rehabilitation.

3. A definition of specific rehabilitation services to be provided during the course of rehabilitation.

4. A reasonable estimate of when the goals will be reached and the frequency at which the services will be provided.

Periodic follow-up evaluations must be performed by the referring physician during the course of the rehabilitation.

Currently, CMS bases the maximum number of treatment sessions on the severity of the visual impairment, and the level of visual impairment is based on visual acuity with best correction and some forms of field loss. As of March 2006, individuals with central field loss, generalized field constriction, homonymous and heteronymous bilateral field deficits, or acuity loss of worse than 20/60 in the better eye are eligible for services.

Sessions are generally conducted over a 3-month period of time with intervals appropriate to the patient's rehabilitation needs. If additional sessions are necessary, medical record documentation must indicate the need for additional sessions.

Coding Guidelines

Vision rehabilitation therapy should be provided by an occupational therapist or a physician or "incident to a physician's professional services, when performed by non-physician personnel under direct supervision". The incident to a physician rules apply to vision rehabilitation therapists and O&M specialists who are not licensed and are unable to perform these services independently. Occupational therapists can perform these services independently and do not require direct supervision by the physician.

Proper coding requires determination of the primary and secondary diagnoses and the use of ICD-9-CM codes. The 369 codes reflect the level of visual impairment and this must always be the primary diagnosis. The secondary codes are the 362-377 codes and these reflect the actual eye disease causing the visual impairment. The eye disease must always be listed as the secondary diagnosis.

Table 16-5 is a convenient chart that can be used to determine the appropriate code to be used for a client based on the distance visual acuity measurement. In most cases, the visual acuity will be provided by the referring eyecare professional. If for some reason the visual acuity is not provided, the occupational therapist can use the acuity charts suggested in Chapter 8 to determine the visual acuity. An example would be a client for which the ophthalmologist or optometrist refers the patient with the following information. The right eye visual acuity is 20/120 and the left eye visual acuity is "counting fingers". The term "counting fin-

gers" is used by some eye doctors inappropriately. Generally, it means that he or she had a traditional eye chart that has no symbols greater than 20/400. As a result, if the patient is unable to see the 20/400 letter, some doctors will simply stand some distance in front of the patient, ask if the patient can see his or her fingers, and count how many he or she is holding up. This is not proper testing protocol. The doctor should have an appropriate chart, and if not, reducing the distance of the patient from the chart will allow more accurate determination of acuity. Nevertheless, in the real world, it is not uncommon for an occupational therapist to receive a referral with the acuity as "counting fingers". In such a case, the occupational therapist would have to retest visual acuity.

To demonstrate the use of the chart in Table 16-5, let us assume we have a client who has been referred to us for low vision rehabilitation. The referring eye doctor reports that the visual acuity in the right eye is 20/120 and the visual acuity in the left eye is 20/1500. The first step is to determine the level of impairment that each visual acuity represents. Looking at Table 16-5, one can determine that 20/120 falls into the category of "moderate impairment" (refer to left column of table), and 20/1500 falls into the category of "near total impairment" (left column of table). The next step is to locate the category of "moderate impairment" on the left column of the chart and move across that row until it intersects with the column with the heading of "near total impairment". The code found at the intersection of the row and column is the primary diagnosis used for Medicare billing. In this case, the code would be 369.17. A second example is a client with a visual acuity of 20/200 in the right eye and 20/300 in the left eye. Use the approach suggested above. In this case, both acuities fall in the category of "severe impairment". Locate "severe impairment" in the left column and move across this row until it intersects with "severe impairment" on the top column. The diagnostic code is 369.22.

The secondary diagnosis must be determined by the referring eye doctor. Table 16-6 lists some of the more common diagnoses of low vision clients.

The treatment codes for low vision rehabilitation are the traditional PM&R codes used by occupational therapists and are listed in Table 16-7.

REFERRALS FOR LOW VISION REHABILITATION

Medicare requires that an occupational therapist receive a referral from a physician before initiating an evaluation or low vision rehabilitation. Initially, this referral could only be issued by an ophthalmolo-

Table 16-5.

ICD-9CM Codes for Visual Impairment – Primary Diagnosis [15]

	Normal Vision	Near Normal Vision	Moderate Impairment	Severe Impairment	Profound Impairment	Near Total Impairment	Total Impairment
Normal vision 20/20- 20/25			369.76	369.73	369.69	369.66	369.63
Near normal vision 20/30-20/60			369.75	369.72	369.68	369.65	369.62
Moderate impairment 20/80-20/160	369.76	369.75	369.25	369.24	369.18	369.17	369.16
Severe impairment 20/200- 20/400 or VF =<20 degrees	369.73	369.72	369.24	369.22	369.14	369.13	369.12
Profound impairment 20/500- 20/1000 or VF <=10 degrees	369.69	369.68	369.18	369.14	369.08	369.07	369.06
Near total impairment 20/1250-20/2500 or VF<=5 degrees	369.68	369.65	369.17	369.13	369.07	369.04	369.03
Total impairment no light perception (NLP)	369.63	369.62	369.16	369.12	369.06	369.03	369.01
Visual field defects	368.41 Scotoma involving central area		368.45 Visual field defects, generalized contraction or constriction		368.46 Homonymous bilateral field defects		368.47 Heterony-mous bilat-eral field defects

Table 16-6.

Common ICD-9-CM Billing Codes for Secondary Diagnosis

362.01 - Diabetic retinopathy, background
362.02 - Diabetic retinopathy, proliferate
362.35 - Central retinal vein occlusion
362.51 - Macular degeneration, dry
362.52 - Macular degeneration, wet
362.74 - Retinitis Pigmentosa
365.10 - Glaucoma, open angle, unspecified
365.20 - Glaucoma, primary, angle-closure, unspecified
366.10 - Cataract, senile, unspecified
368.46 - Field deficit homonymous, bilateral
377.10 - Optic nerve atrophy
377.41 - Optic neuritis

Table 16-7.

PM&R Codes Used for Low Vision Rehabilitation

Evaluations

97003	Occupational therapy evaluation
97004	Occupational therapy reevaluation

Therapeutic Procedures

97110	Therapeutic procedure, one or more areas, each 15 minutes; therapeutic exercises to develop strength and endurance range of motion, and flexibility.
97112	Neuromuscular reeducation of movement, balance, coordination, kinesthetic sense, posture, and proprioception
97530	Therapeutic activities, direct (one on one) patient contact by the provider (use of dynamic activities to improve functional performance) 1 on 1 treatment each 15 minutes.
97533	Sensory integrative techniques to ehnance sensory processing and promote adaptive responses to environmental demands, direct (1 to 1) patient contact by provider, each 15 minutes.
97535	Self-care/home management training (eg, ADL and compensatory training, meal preparation, safety procedures, and instructions in use of adaptive equipment), direct one-on-one contact by provider, each 15 minutes.
97537	Community/reintegration training (eg, shopping, transportation, money management, avocational activities, and/or work environment/modification analysis, work task analysis), direct one-on-one contact by provider, each 15 minutes

Table 16-8. Recertification – Time Requirements	
Type of Facility/Care	# of Days
Skilled Nursing Facility	After 14 days and then every 30 days
Home Health A	Every 62 days
Home Health B	Every 60 days
Comprehensive Outpatient Rehab Facility	Every 60 days

gist or other medical doctor. However, the Balanced Budget Refinements Act (P.L. 106-113) signed into law November 29, 1999, includes a technical amendment that recognizes optometrists as "physicians" for purposes of certifying a Medicare beneficiary's need for occupational therapy services under Medicare Part B. This new federal law does not, however, supersede state law. Therapists in states with broad or no referral requirements will be able to accept referrals from optometrists in 36 states, the District of Columbia, and Puerto Rico have no referral requirements in either their OT statute or regulations. However, it is possible for the state occupational laws to specifically require an MD or podiatrist as a referral source, for example. In such cases, the state law would have precedence and in such a state an occupational therapist could not accept a referral from an optometrist. Currently, optometrists can provide a referral to an occupational therapist in 37 of the 50 states. To determine the regulation in your state, it is important to check with your state occupational therapy association. You can check your state law on the AOTA website (www.aota.org) by searching for the State OT Law Database.

well-defined goals. The Individual Rehabilitation Plan must be signed by physician and must be reviewed by a physician every 60 days.

Recertification/Reevaluations

Medicare also requires periodic recertification for all clients receiving low vision rehabilitation. To be recertified, the client must be examined by the referring physician and the Individual Rehabilitation Plan must be signed. The required time period varies depending on the environment, as listed in Table 16-8.

Documentation

The documentation requirements for vision rehabilitation therapy are identical to those required for any other condition. Therapists must document that the treatment is reasonable and necessary, provide a plan of care and regular progress notes, must demonstrate progress over time, and at the end of treatment provide a discharge summary.

OTHER MEDICARE REQUIREMENTS

Individual Rehabilitation Plan

Medicare requires an Individual Rehabilitation Plan for each client being treated by the occupational therapist. The Individual Rehabilitation Plan prospectively documents the treatment to meet reasonable,

CURRENT REIMBURSEMENT RATES FOR VISION REHABILITATION SERVICES

Information about Medicare reimbursement rates can easily be accessed for any location in the United States at the CMS website (www.cms.gov/physicians/mpfsapp/step0.asp).

Table 16-9. Suggested Equipment for Low Vision Evaluation			
Equipment	Cost	Source	Phone
Minnesota Low-Vision Reading Test (MN Read Test)	$175	Lighthouse	800-829-0500
Feinbloom Visual Acuity Chart	$50	Lighthouse	800-829-0500
Veterans Affairs Low-Vision Visual Functioning Questionnaire VA LV VFQ-48	Free	www.slackbooks.com/otvisionforms	
Low Vision Rehabilitation Evaluation form	Free	www.slackbooks.com/otvisionforms	
Mars Letter Contrast Sensitivity Test	$350	Lighthouse	800-829-0500
The Pepper Visual Skills for Reading Test (Pepper VSRT)		Lighthouse	800-829-0500
Occupational Therapy Low Vision Aids Starter Kit	$2000	Eschenbach	800-396-3886

MEDICARE AND LOW VISION REHABILITATION (HOSPITAL INPATIENT AND NURSING HOMES)

Prospective Payment System

Rehabilitation services in nursing homes and hospitals are limited by a prospective payment system (PPS). In this system, patients may receive therapies only for needs that have been documented within a few days after the patient is admitted to the nursing home. Under a PPS, hospitals receive a fixed amount for treating patients diagnosed with a given illness, regardless of the length of stay or type of care received. There must be a method to insure that proper testing (visual acuity) is performed in the first few days if occupational therapy for low vision rehabilitation is to be provided.

Supplies and Equipment

Some basic equipment and supplies are necessary to start a low vision rehabilitation service/practice. Suggested equipment necessary for the evaluation is listed in Table 16-9 and therapy equipment is listed in Table 16-10.

SUMMARY

In this chapter, we tried to provide answers about many of the critical questions and issues that occupational therapists encounter when they begin to provide low vision rehabilitation services. We have included information about low vision education, certification, interaction with other vision rehabilitation professionals, practice opportunities, marketing low vision services, reimbursement and coding, Medicare requirements, and recommendations for equipment and supplies.

Table 16-10.

Suggested Therapy Equipment

Equipment	Cost	Source	Phone
LS&S Equipment	$2033.07	LS & S	800-468-4789
LUV Reading Workbook	$25	Lighthouse	800-829-0500

Low Vision Supplies (From LS&S Catalog)

Kitchen	Catalog Number	Price
Long Oven Mitts	OM15	3.50
Low Vision Timer	8402	12.95
Boil Alert	5739	2.95
Liquid Level Indicators	EZ-1	12.95
Measuring Cups	4839	6.95
Measuring Spoons	6138	3.95
Talking Kitchen Scale	851059	114.95
Cutting Boards	826024	7.95
Jar Openers	75358-1002	8.95
Iron Safety Guard	75464-1000	53.95
Bright Dish Brush	3143	3.59
Bright Colored Dish Brush	3137	2.49
Talking Indoor/Outdoor Thermometer	888S	13.95
Total		**$253.03**

Make-up	Catalog Number	Price
Handsome 5X Stand Mirror	MC111	$21.95
7X Gooseneck Stand Mirror	Z6V7	22.95
Z'Zoom 5X Compact	ZZ30	11.95
5X Fluorescent	ZLP05	59.95
Double Sided Lighted Makeup	BE4	25.95
Total		**$142.75**

Personal Care	Catalog Number	Price
5X Magnifying Clippers	MC1	5.25
6X Tweezer Magnifyer	424	2.49
Superb Quality Talking Scale	LHS-3	79.95
Talking Clinical Thermometer	8842	12.95
32" Metal Rehab Reacher	571000	12.95
Jumbo Plastic Pill Box	67199	1.75
Magnifying Pill Cutter	67168	5.95
Total		**$128.54**

Leisure	Catalog Number	Price
Visual Mate	LM747	49.95
Needle Threader	THREADER	2.75
Low Vision Pinochle Cards	CC1A	1.25
Marinoff Large Symbol Playing Cards	GPM	4.45
Jumbo Face Playing Cards pack	1223	2.45
Playing Card Holder	71252-0010	4.95

Continued

Table 16-10, Continued
Suggested Therapy Equipment

New York Times Large Print		9.95
40 Crossword Puzzles	0-812-91044-3	4.95
Giant Print Bible	883C	17.95
Low Vision Bingo Cards	CC1A	1.25
Super Large Laminated Bingo Cards	LBC	1.25
10 Digit Talking Calculator Alarm Clock	99025	14.95
Total		**$116.10**

Reading/Writing	*Catalog Number*	*Price*
Able Table	AT-1	46.95
Easy Reader	ER1	21.95
20/20 Pen	13101	0.94
Flair/Gel Pens	Staples	3.95
Large Print Appointment Book	BP3	14.45
Big Print Address Book	BP!	13.95
Large Print Calendar	LPC	6.49
Bold Line Paper	BLP100	2.95
Superior Letter Writing Guide	LTG	3.95
Original Easy Writer Guide	EWG	19.95
Original Marks Script Guide	MS-1	23.95
Large Print Check Register	BP2	6.49
Signature Guide	STSG	1.85

Reading/Writing	*Catalog Number*	*Price*
Large Envelope Writing Guide	ENG	1.95
Deluxe Check Writing Guide	KJV-1611	4.95
Leather Coin Purse MOW-3	7.95	
Total	**$182.67**	

Talking Watches/Clocks	*Catalog Number*	*Price*
Black Face Silver Band	LHS-127 MENS	
	LHSL LADIES	32.95
White Face Silver Band	LHS-131 MENS	
	LHS-131L LADIES	32.95
Jumbo Low Vision Watch (leather)	LHS-107	22.95
Quartz Low Vision Mens	4211	69.95
Quarts Low Vision (leather)Men/Women	4211 GMENS	
	4211 LADIES	74.95
Talking Atomic Clock	AT1000	49.95
Curved Talking Alarm Clock	6695	9.95
Silver Beauty Talking Metal Watch	SW5	11.75
Casual Talking W	3220163	9.95
Total	**$315.35**	

Continued

Table 16-10, Continued.

Suggested Therapy Equipment

Labels/Identifiers	Catalog Number	Price
Bump On Tactile Markers	BP-BL	2.75
	BP-W	
	BP-CLEAR	
Loc Dots	LD-2	1.09 per pack
Original Touch Dots	TDB	2.09
	TDW	
	TDY	
Wide Label Maker	LM300	119.95
AC Adapter	40077	18.95
Tape Cartridges	53713	
	53721	15.95
Note-It	91420	4.99
Key Pager	822028	12.95
Touch To See Braille/Tactile	TTS	11.95
Sock Sorters	825029	3.45
Total		**$190.28**

Telephone/Computers/TV	Catalog Number	Price
Big Button 900 MHz	614030	39.95
Big Button Plus 905	HI-905	29.95
Big Size Computer Magnifier	CTC-21H	49.95
Big Button Remote	BWO120	17.95
Jumbo Button Phone	HI-JB20	69.95
Total		**$302.70**

Lighting/Lamps	Catalog Number	Price
Economical Illuminated 3D Magnifying Lamp	3700	52.95
Chromalux Full Spectrum Bulbs	A21FR/75	
	A21FR/100	7.45 ea
All Purpose Economy Lamp	2225-Z	54.95
Gooseneck Lamp	2030BLK	14.95
Economical Swing Lamp	2000BLK	14.95
Ott Lite Desk Lamp	OTL-13	54.95
Deluxe Lamp	30302	74.95
Big Eye Lamp	01042.95	
Total		**$401.65**

It is our hope that many readers will use the information in this book to help meet the growing demand for low vision rehabilitation services in the adult client.

REFERENCES

1. Congdon N, O'Colmain B, Klaver CC, et al. Causes and prevalence of visual impairment among adults in the United States. *Arch Ophthalmol.* 2004;122(4):477-485.
2. Warren M. Including occupational therapy in low vision rehabilitation. *Am J Occup Ther.* 1995;49(9):857-860.
3. Elliott DB, et al. Demographic characteristics of the vision-disabled elderly. *Invest Ophthalmol Vis Sci.* 1997;38:2566-2575.
4. Warren M. *Low Vision: Occupational Therapy Intervention with the Older Adult.* Bethesda, MD: American Occupational Therapy Association; 2000.
5. American Occupational Therapy Association website (www.aota.org).
6. Lambert J. Occupational therapists, orientation and mobility specialists and rehabilitation teachers. *J Vis Imp Blind.* 1994;88:297-298.
7. Orr AL, Huebner K. Toward a collaborative working relationship among vision rehabilitation and allied health professionals. *J Vis Imp Blind.* 2001;95(8):468-482.
8. McGinty Bachelder J, Harkins D. Do occupational therapists have a primary role in low vision rehabilitation? *Am J Occup Ther.* 1995;49(9):927-930.
9. Horowitz A. Vision impairment and functional disability among nursing home residents. *The Gerontologist.* 1994;34:316-323.
10. Horowitz A, et al. Visual impairment and rehabilitation needs of nursing home residents. *J Vis Impair Blind.* 1995;88:7-15.
11. Mogk L, Goodrich G. The history and future of low vision services in the United States. *J Vis Impair Blind.* 2004;(Oct):585-600.
12. Ponchillia PE, Ponchillia SV. *Foundations of Rehabilitation Teaching With Persons Who Are Blind or Visually Impaired.* New York: American Foundation for the Blind; 1996:3-21.
13. American Academy of Optometry. Low Vision Section List of Low Vision Diplomates. 2005.
14. Pankow L, Luchins D. Geriatric low vision referrals by ophthalmologists in a senior health center. *J Vis Impair Blind.* 1998;92(11):748-753.
15. Hart AC. *The Professional ICD-9-CM Code Book.* Reston, VA: St. Anthony Publishing; 2000.

RESOURCE

- Academy for Certification of Vision Rehabilitation and Education Professionals (ACVREP) http://www.acvrep.org/

Goal Writing

The *Occupational Therapy Practice Framework* divides the intervention process into three substeps: the intervention plan, intervention implementation, and intervention review.[1] According to the *Framework*, the intervention plan includes objective and measurable goals with a timeframe, an occupational therapy intervention approach, and mechanisms for service delivery.[1] In Chapters 9 through 15, we described an organized approach for this intervention process with specific vision rehabilitation techniques that fall into four of the five categories of intervention approaches suggested in the *Occupational Therapy Practice Framework*, including: establishing or restoring performance skills, maintaining performance skills, modifying context or activity demands, and preventing problems in performance skills. Our goal in this chapter is to help therapists structure the development and writing of intervention goals. To do so, we have identified four components that should be incorporated into each goal. These components include: the areas of occupation and performance skills to be addressed, the type of assistance required, criteria for success, and the method of assessment. When developing intervention goals, it is important to develop goals that are realistic and achievable,[2] have a positive effect on the quality of the patient's life, are measurable and quantifiable, are related to function, and appropriately reflect the patient's needs.

A common problem when trying to establish client-centered goals is that clients with low vision may lose interest in activities because visual difficulties may reduce the ability to concentrate and sustain visual attention.[3] In such cases, the client may actually deny that the vision loss causes any limitation in function.[4] Warren states that this could result in problems with client safety and well-being.[4] Such clients may survive by expending a great deal of effort and by taking greater risks. It is, therefore, vital that therapists make goal development an essential part of the low vision rehabilitation evaluation. We describe our recommended approach for goal development in Chapter 8. This approach includes an assessment of the client's functional ability before the loss of vision as well as a detailed discussion to systematically develop a list of realistic client-based goals for vision rehabilitation.

Clients typically want things to be the way they were before the eye disease caused the vision loss. In most cases, the client will need to realize that some significant changes will be required in lifestyle. It is not unusual to hear some very unrealistic expectations from clients. Remember that the prior experience of this client was that new glasses always

restored clear vision. Patients often expect the same result even when the vision loss is caused by disease. They either fail to understand that the vision loss is permanent, or refuse to accept this prognosis. By the time the client is being examined by the occupational therapist, he or she has had numerous examinations with the ophthalmologist and perhaps a low vision optometrist. The client should certainly be well aware that there are no miracle glasses, devices, or drugs that will restore normal vision. Yet, it is not unusual for the client, when asked what he wants to be able to do, to say "I want to be able to see well again", or "I am hoping you can prescribe glasses that will help me see well again".[5]

The therapist's role is to help clients with low vision fulfill realistic vision-related goals.[5] It is useful to review Table 7-4, which lists a series of questions modified from a "personal eyesight evaluation" developed by Paul Freeman, OD. These questions allow the therapist to help the client systematically develop a list of realistic goals for vision rehabilitation.

Table 17-1 represents an example of the approach we suggest for goal writing. In this table, there are four columns and the therapist can select an item from each of the categories in order to write a goal. For example, from Table 17-1, the therapist might select one item from each column to construct the following goal:

Goal: The client will be able to apply lipstick using a magnifying mirror and spot lighting, with minimal assistance. The client's performance will be assessed by direct observation.

Tables 17-2 through 17-11 provide similar suggestions for some of the more common areas of occupational performance and performance skills, such as managing medication, personal hygiene, clothing management, eating, home management, food preparation, communication, and financial management. These tables are not designed to be comprehensive. Rather, they represent one possible method that the therapist may use to organize the essential skill of goal writing. The therapist can use these tables to mix and match items from each of the four columns to assist in goal writing. We suggest therapists use these tables as a starting point and add to them as they write new goals.

Table 17-1.
Sample—Low Vision Goal Writing

Area of Occupation/ Performance Skill	Type of Assistance	Criterion for Success	Method of Assessment
Will be able to identify medication	**Optical Aids**	Independently	Direct observation
Will be able to use an electric razor	handheld magnifier	With minimal assistance	Stop watch
Will be able to apply lipstick	stand magnifier	Moderate assistance	
Will be able to measure shampoo and conditioner	microscopic spectacles telemicroscope portable video magnifier stand video magnifier telescope magnifying mirror		
Will be able to identify clothing and accessories	**Lighting/Contrast**		
Will be able to locate items on the table or on the plate	gooseneck lamp		
Will be able to set the stove or oven controls	lighted mirror		
Will be able to slice a piece of bread and butter	spot lighting		
Will be able to write a letter, address an envelope, or sign name	contrasting towels		
Will be able to read newspaper print, headlines/articles	contrasting bath mat		
	Nonoptical Devices		
	Rx talking machine		
	identifying buttons		
	identifying labels		
	liquid level indicator		
	"bump" dots		
	hi-marks		

Continued

Table 17-1, Continued.			
Sample—Low Vision Goal Writing			
Area of Occupation/ Performance Skill	Type of Assistance	Criterion for Success	Method of Assessment
	Other Aids		
	auditory sense		
	tactile sense		
	pill organizers		
	transfer equipment		
	grab bars		
	CCTV		
	Computer assisted device		

Table 17-2.			
Low Vision Goal Writing—Medication			
Activity of Daily Living	Type of Assistance	Criterion	Method of Assessment
Will be able to identify medication	Using handheld magnifier, gooseneck lamp, CCTV, Rx talking machine	Independently, or with minimal or moderate assist	Direct observation
Will be able to self-administer medication	Using a predetermined system to insure a specific pill is measured, pill organizers	Independently, with minimal or moderate assist, and without any errors	Direct observation
Will be able to inject medication	Using adaptive techniques and aids	Independently	Direct observation

Table 17-3.

Low Vision Goal Writing—Personal Care/Hygiene

Activity of Daily Living	Type of Assistance	Criterion	Method of Assessment
Will be able to put toothpaste on a toothbrush	Scoop toothpaste from a jar, squeeze toothpaste in the hand or in the mouth	Independently, with minimal or moderate assist	Direct observation
Will be able to take a bath or shower	Transfer equipment, grab bars, contrasting towels, bath mat	Independently, with minimal or moderate assist	Direct observation
Will be able to identify simulated skin lesion	Using mirror, telescope, handheld magnifier, CCTV	Independently (100% accuracy) or with assistance (<100% accuracy)	Direct observation
Will be able to use an electric razor	Magnifying mirror, lighted mirror spot lighting, tactile sense	Independently, set up assistance, minimal, moderate assistance	Direct observation

Table 17-4.

Low Vision Goal Writing—Applying Make-Up/Nail Care

Activity of Daily Living	Type of Assistance	Criterion	Method of Assessment
Will be able to apply lipstick	Using magnifying mirror, lighted mirror spot lighting	Independently, with no more than 1 deviation from the lips	Direct observation
Will be able to care for nails	Using magnifying nail clippers, CCTV, spot lighting	Independently with no errors, with minimal or moderate assist	Direct observation
Will be able to apply skin products	Using magnifying mirror, lighted mirror, spot lighting, adaptive techniques	Independently, with set up assistance, minimal assist	Direct observation

Table 17-5.

Low Vision Goal Writing—Hair Care

Activity of Daily Living	Type of Assistance	Criterion	Method of Assessment
Will be able to part and comb hair	Using magnifying mirror, lighted mirror, spot lighting	Independently, with minimal assist to part hair	Direct observation
Will be able to measure shampoo and conditioner	Using tactile sense	Independently, with minimal or moderate assist	Direct observation
Will be able to maintain a hairpiece	Using tactile sense	Independently	Direct observation

Table 17-6.

Low Vision Goal Writing—Clothing Management

Activity of Daily Living	Type of Assistance	Criterion	Method of Assessment
Will be able to identify clothing and accessories	Using tactile sense and identifying beads, buttons, labels, clothing ID, etc	Independently	Direct observation
Will be able to clean and/or polish shoes	Using tactile sense	Independently, with minimal or moderate assist	Direct observation
Will be able to sort clothing for the laundry	Using tactile sense and adaptive identifiers	Independently, set up assistance	Direct observation

Table 17-7.

Low Vision Goal Writing—Eating

Activity of Daily Living	Type of Assistance	Criterion	Method of Assessment
Will be able to locate items on the table or on the plate	Using the locating technique	Independently or with minimal or moderate cueing	Direct observation
Will be able to use salt, spices, sugar during eating	Using adaptive techniques	Independently, minimal cueing	Direct observation
Will be able to cut, and scoop foods	Using the "clock" model, scoop plates, plate guards	Independently, with set up assistance	Direct observation

Table 17-8.

Low Vision Goal Writing—Home Management

Activity of Daily Living	Type of Assistance	Criterion	Method of Assessment
Will be able to set the stove or oven controls	Using "bump" dots, hi-marks	Independently, with minimal, moderate assist	Direct observation
Will be able to make a bed	Using tactile sense, safety pin technique	Independently, minimal or moderate assist	Direct observation
Will be able to use the television	Using telescope, reducing the distance, voice description, "bump" dots	Independently, minimal, moderate assistance	Direct observation

Table 17-9.

Low Vision Goal Writing—Food Preparation

Activity of Daily Living	Type of Assistance	Criterion	Method of Assessment
Will be able to pour cold liquids into a cup	Using a liquid level indicator, ping pong ball, finger technique	Independently, set up assistance	Direct observation
Will be able to slice a piece of bread and butter it	Using an adapted knife, low vision cutting board, "spreading" technique	Independently, set up assistance	Direct observation
Will be able to measure liquids	Using low vision measuring utensils, adaptive techniques	Independently, set up assistance, minimal, moderate assistance	Direct observation

Table 17-10.

Low Vision Goal Writing—Communication

Activity of Daily Living	Type of Assistance	Criterion	Method of Assessment
Will be able to tell time	Using voice response watch/ clock, bold numbered watches/clocks, Braille numbered watch, tactile sense	Independently	Direct observation
Will be able to dial a telephone	Using "bump" dot marked phone, CCTV, magnifier, voice memory phone, large dial phone	Independently	Direct observation
Will be able to write a letter, address an envelope, or sign name	Using various tachistoscopes, CCTV, magnifier	Independently, set up assistance, minimal or moderate assistance	Direct observation
Will be able to read newspaper print, headlines/articles	Using stand magnifier, telemicroscope, CCTV, spot, lighting, eccentric viewing, computer assistive device	Independently, words per minute word identification accuracy	Direct observation timed reading
Will be able to write and read written correspondence	Using stand magnifier, telemicroscope, CCTV, spot lighting, eccentric viewing, computer assistive device	Independently Word identification accuracy Words per minute	Timed reading and writing, % correct
Will be able to locate and performed simulated purchase of 3 items	Using handheld magnifier, telemicroscope, computer		

Table 17-11.

Low Vision Goal Writing—Mobility

Activity of Daily Living	Type of Assistance	Criterion	Method of Assessment
Will identify target in right field within 2 seconds of presentation.	Compensatory scanning	X/10	Direct observation
Will identify approach of persons/cars on right and left with 100% accuracy.	Auditory cues Compensatory scanning	X/10	Direct observation
Will identify exit signs, restroom and directional signs	Telescope	X/10	Direct observation
Will identify and avoid potential tripping obstacles in unfamiliar setting.	Sighted guide Telescope Compensatory scanning	X/10	Direct observation
Will navigate 4 turn indoor course from verbal directions	Trailing technique, using visual, auditory, and olfactory cues	Independent, modified Independent, minimum, moderate cues	Direct observation

Table 17-12.

Low Vision Goal Writing—Financial Management

Activity of Daily Living	Type of Assistance	Criterion	Method of Assessment
Will be able to identify money	Using adaptive techniques to fold paper money, tactile sense to identify coins	Independently, minimal, moderate assistance	Direct observation
Will be able to maintain a checking account	Using a large-print check register, large-print checks, signature guide, check writing guide, talking calculator	Independently, set up assistance, minimal, moderate assistance	Direct observation
Will be able to pay bills	CCTV, magnifier, signature guide, check writing guides	Independently, set up assistance, minimal, moderate assistance	Direct observation

REFERENCES

1. American Occupational Therapy Association. Occupational Therapy Practice Framework: Domain and Process. *Am J Occup Ther.* 2002;56(6):609-639.
2. Warren M. Providing low vision rehabilitation services with occupational therapy and ophthalmology: a program description. *Am J Occup Ther.* 1995;49(9):877-883.
3. Horowitz BP. Gerontic occupational therapy practice: focus on vision. In: Gentile M, Ed. *Functional Visual Behavior: A Therapist's Guide to Evaluation and Treatment Options.* Bethesda, MD: AOTA; 1997.
4. Warren ML, Lampert J. Assessing daily living needs. In: Fletcher DC, Ed. *Ophthalmology Monographs: Low Vision Rehabilitation: Caring for the Whole Person.* San Francisco: American Academy of Ophthalmology; 1999:89-125.
5. Freeman P, Mendelson R. *Believing is Seeing: Hope for Those Victimized by Macular Degeneration and Other Conditions That Cause Low Vision.* 1st ed. Pittsburgh, PA: Freeman and Mendelson; 1996.

Appendices

- Activities of Daily Living Assessment and Treatment Plan
- Optimizing Lighting for Low Vision
- Sighted Guide Techniques
- Teaching Compensatory Scanning for Field Cuts or Unilateral Visual Inattention
- Low Vision Rehab Brochure
- Occupational Therapists and Low Vision Rehabilitation
- Practice Sentences

ACTIVITIES OF DAILY LIVING ASSESSMENT AND TREATMENT PLAN

Client:_____ DOB: __/__/__ Date: __/__/__
Address _____ City _____ State____ Zip_____
Telephone: _____ Referring Physician: _____
Visual Acuity: Right Eye_____ Visual Acuity: Left Eye_____
Eye Disease Diagnosis: _____

OT Evaluation of Visual Status if Not Available from Physician

VA (Distance) OD: _____ Feinbloom Chart	VA (Distance) OS: _____ Feinbloom Chart	VA (Distance) OU: _____ Feinbloom Chart
VA (Near) OD: _____ Reading Speed ____ MNRead Chart	VA (Near) OS: _____ Reading Speed ____ MNRead Chart	VA (Near) OU: _____ Reading Speed ____ MNRead Chart
MARS Contrast Sensitivity Test (OU)		
Eccentric Viewing Evaluation: Right Eye	Eccentric Viewing Evaluation: Right Eye	
Evaluation of Scotoma (Clockface or Tangent Screen) OD	Evaluation of Scotoma (Clockface or Tangent Screen) OS	

Veterans Affairs Low-Vision Visual Functioning Questionnaire (VA LV VFQ-48): _____

Background Information

How long have you experienced trouble seeing? _____
What is most difficult to see? _____
Have you ever had a low vision evaluation? Y / N
When: _____ Where: _____
Do you use any magnifiers or special glasses? Y / N
   Who gave them to you? _____
Any previous vision rehabilitation services? Y / N Describe. _____
_____
Any previous Home Health Therapy?_____

Other Health Issues

__ Hearing loss __Hearing Aid __Diabetes __Dialysis __Stroke __Hypertension __Angina
__Cardiac problems __Arthritis __Respiratory
Medications: _____
_____

Sensorimotor/Cognitive Function

AROM UE:	AROM LE	Sensation:	Problem Solving:
PROM UE:	PROM LE	Initiation:	Awareness:
Strength UE:	Strength LE	Organization:	Orientation:

Further Cognitive Evaluation Indicated?

Living Situation

Members of household and relationship to you: _____

How do you currently spend your time? _____

How did you spend it before your vision loss? _____

What activities are the most difficult for you since your vision decreased? _____

_____

Do you receive assistance from anyone?

_____

Food Preparation and Shopping

What food preparation do you do now? _____

What foods did you prepare before your vision loss? _____

Do you do your own grocery shopping? Y/N   Small trips   Full list

Describe assistance received with shopping _____

Do you have any difficulty completing the following tasks?

Describe any food preparation difficulties: _____

Cooking and Appliance Use

Appliances used in cooking: Stove   Oven   Microwave   Toaster oven   Broiler

Other: _____

Do you have any problems cooking?   Y/N

     Visual _____

     Physical _____

Table Techniques

Once food is prepared, do you have any difficulty finding food on the plate? _____

Do you have any difficulty when eating out? _____

Would you like to review any of the following table techniques?

Locating technique	Y/N
Identifying the contents of a plate of food	Y/N
Cutting food with a knife and fork	Y/N
Scooping food with a fork	Y/N
Seasoning food	Y/N
Carrying containers of food and liquids	Y/N
Buffer technique	Y/N

Other: _____

Communications

Do you have any problem:

Signing your name?	Y/N	Method: _____
Reading any form of print?	Y/N	Large Standard
Writing letters?	Y/N/NA	

Dialing the operator in an emergency?   Y/N
Dialing the telephone independently?   Y/N   Difficulty?
Are you aware of the directory assistance exemption?   Y/N
How do you manage:
Telephone/address directory: _____
Appointments _____
Paperwork/written records _____
Identifying your money?
      Coins   Y/N   NA   Difficulty:
      Bills   Y/N   NA   Difficulty:
Giving correct change when shopping?   Y/N   N/A
Checking account _____
Do you write out checks independently?   Y/N
     If not, who assists you in maintaining the account and paying bills? _____
Do you need a talking calculator?   Y/N
Are you familiar with the Library of Congress recorded books program?   Y/N
     Receiving   Not receiving   Not interested   Want to apply
If already participating, do you use EZ machine   Standard machine
Any problems with EZ machine? _____

Home Management

Identifying your keys?   Y/N
Inserting the key in the lock and opening the door?   Y/N
Identifying the time?   Y/N   Method: _____

Who does the majority of your house cleaning? Self   Other (specify): _____
Do you find any of the following tasks difficult?
__ Washing dishes __ Cleaning a surface __ Cleaning a refrigerator/stove
__ Cleaning a floor (sweeping/vacuuming) __ Making a bed __ Operating a thermostat
__ Operating a television __ Operating a radio
Other:_____

Clothing Management

Do you have any difficulty identifying clothing? _____
Are there any items/colors that you find particularly difficult to identify?   Y/N
Describe:_____
Do you do your own laundry?   Hand   Machine   Don't do
Operating the washing machine?   Y/N   NA   Dryer? Y/N / NA
Do you have a need to sew?   Y/N
Any Difficulties: _____
_____

Personal Care and Hygiene

__ Do you have any difficulty locating and identifying items in your bathroom?
__ Do you experience problems taking a bath/shower independently and safely?
__ Do you feel you might need a grab bar to get in and out of the tub or a tub seat?

Do you have any difficulty when completing the following tasks?
__ Applying toothpaste, __ Cleaning dentures, __ Filing/cutting nails, __ Using a spray can,
__ Shaving with a manual razor, __ Shaving with an electric razor
    Other: _____

For persons with diabetes:
Do you have a podiatrist or family member: __ Routinely check your feet for cuts and sores
                                                __ Assist with toenail care
__ Do you have difficulty identifying your medications?
Method used: _____
What technique do you use to keep track of 'the medications that you are supposed to take? _____
__ Any difficulty administering your medications? __ Splitting pills? __ Crushing pills?
__ Measuring liquid medication? __ Self injecting?
Does anyone help you with your medications? Y / N Who_____
Recommended adaptations: _____

Hair Care

__Do you have any difficulty with hair care?

Cosmetics

Do you wear makeup? _____

Indoor Travel/O&M Screening

Are you able to find your way around your home without assistance?_____
Are you able to go up and down the stairs independently?_____

DIAGNOSIS

Primary Impairment: Diagnostic Code:
Secondary Impairment: Diagnostic Code:

TREATMENT PLAN

Rehabilitation Potential: _____
Frequency: ___ per month, ___ units each visit, for a total estimate of visits
Duration/Projected Achievement Date: _____
Date Planned Established: _____

Recommended Nonoptical Adaptive Aids
_____
_____
_____
_____

Recommended Optical Aids
_____
_____

Recommended Rehab Techniques:
__ Eccentric Viewing
__ Scanning
__ Locating Techniques
__ Other: _____
_____
_____

Referrals:
___ O and M
___ Low Vision Exam
___ CCTV

TREATMENT GOALS:

Functional Level	Goal

OT Signature: _____ Date: ___/___/___

Physician Signature _____ Date: ___/___/___

OPTIMIZING LIGHTING FOR LOW VISION

Stephen G. Whittaker, PhD, OTR/L, CLVT, Moss Rehabilitation Hospital

Teach a patient how to identify glare sources

- Glare sources are light sources or reflections of light that shine directly into the patient's eyes (Figure 1).
- Teach patient to identify light sources (windows, lights) or reflections.
- A light directly behind or above the client often will reflect off a light colored or shiny surface (tile floors, countertops, TV screen, white pages of a book or newspaper) into the patient's eyes (see Figure 1).
- Too much light (even indirect light) can cause glare dysfunction in some patients.

Teach a patient how to reduce glare

- Position a directional source or the patient so light is from the side (Figure 2).
- Use light shades and eye shades.
- Adjust the brightness of a light level by changing distance of work from the light source.
- Use eye shades or wear a hat with a brim.
- Use sunglasses or tints on regular glasses (yellow tint is usually best).
- Select color schemes that maximize contrast.
- Use flat white or flat black placemats on work surfaces.
- Use light or dark plates.
- Use contrasting grooming items.
- Usually darker work surfaces are best if objects are light enough.
- Use color schemes to categorize places and items.
- Mark the bottom and top steps with contrasting tape. A directional light should shine on the steps.
- Tie a big bright bow or use a contrasting color collar on pets.
- Don't use more than the maximum rated wattage bulb in a light. The newer energy efficient lights are excellent sources if they can be properly shaded. Consider Vision Max by Tensor ($30) or OTT lights ($80). OTT lights can be purchased at sewing stores and Tensor lights at Staples or Office Max.

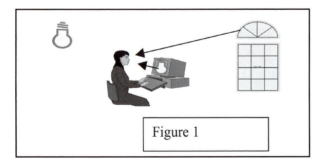

Figure 1

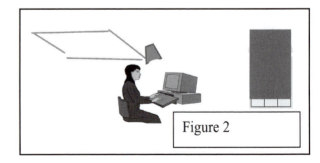

Figure 2

SIGHTED GUIDE TECHNIQUES

Stephen G. Whittaker, PhD, OTR/L, CLVT, Moss Rehabilitation Hospital

Sighted Guide Techniques describe how a person who has low vision can use a person with sight to get around. The person with low vision should be taught to teach others these techniques.

- Please ask before helping. Unexpected help often is disorienting, and sometimes insulting.

- Offer a person your arm; ask which side, then tap the back of your hand to the back of his hand. The person should grasp your arm just above the elbow. *The person you are guiding should grab you—you never grab the person.*

- Walk a pace in front of the person you are guiding at whatever speed is comfortable for him or her. Always pause or slow down when changing directions, stepping up or down, or walking around an obstacle. Look up as well as down—you might miss a tree branch or puddle but walk the person you are guiding into it.

- Describe your surroundings.

- When leading someone through a tight space, put your arm behind your back.

- Be careful of doors. Describe how the door is swinging and let the person you are guiding help open and close the door if he or she is physically able.

- When guiding someone, never walk away without saying you are leaving. Never leave a blind person in free space. Lead the person to a wall, railing, or chair and describe the surroundings before you leave.

- In giving directions to a blind person or a person with low vision, orient the person to sounds, or, if he or she has some vision, lights or windows, patches of color, or high-contrast edges like baseboard. Direct her to walls, or edges that she can follow.

- When leading a blind person to a seat, place your hand on the back of the seat. The person will follow your arm down, grab the back of the chair and, by touch orient himself to the chair.

Source: Lighthouse of Central Florida. www.cite-fl.com/pdf/Sighted_Guide_Technique.doc

Teaching Compensatory Scanning for Field Cuts or Unilateral Visual Inattention

Stephen G. Whittaker, PhD, OTR/L, CLVT, Moss Rehabilitation Hospital

Visual scanning with right/left/up/down eye movements is the best treatment for a unilateral field cut or an overall peripheral field restriction. This compensatory method generalizes to occupational performance because there is no need for special optical devices or artificial supports. Using learning theory or behavioral paradigms, there are two phases to this (or any) instructional technique. During the instructional phase, one uses more artificial situations (cues that provide frequent, salient, and immediate feedback) to establish the compensatory scanning behavior. One then changes to more complicated, natural settings and gradually withdraws the cues. The goal is to establish automatic scanning eye movements all of the time in natural settings, especially during mobility.

Instruction

- *Verbal explanation*: Explain the nature of the field loss, and demonstrate how one can use searching eye movements to find objects in the blind side. Verbally instruct the client for all tasks described below.

- *Search markers*: Place the client's hand or a high contrast (orange) search marker to the far periphery of the blind side. Instruct the client to look until he or she sees the marker. Using Sarah Appel's technique, place a colored filter on the left or right side of both lenses of glasses or cut inexpensive sunglasses so that the client sees a color change when he or she looks in the correct direction. Have the client locate one, and then multiple objects on a clear surface—scanning to the marker. Tell the client ahead of time how many objects he or she is looking for. Try symbol or letter cancellation tasks or word finds. Decrease task demand by adding auditory and tactual stimuli or reducing distraction on the unaffected side. Increase task demand by adding elements to search, decrease object contrast and size, increase background clutter, and decrease the salience of the field marker. Divide attention by playing Connect-4, Dominoes, checkers, or other spatial games.

- *Laser tag*: The client holds one laser pointer; the therapist holds the other. The therapist points the laser spot first in different positions on the unaffected side; the client is to find the spot and "tag it" with his pointer. Now flash the spot back and forth between predictable positions on the right and left side. Finally, randomize the location on the right and left. Decrease task demand by making the movement predictable and on a blank, uncluttered surface. Increase task demand by positioning the pointer to project onto a cluttered surface, at different distances, and finally during mobility or other tasks. Measure and record the number of tags within 2 seconds within about 40 degrees and between 40 and 80 degrees of the midsagittal plane.

- *Obstacles during mobility*: Walk about a foot or two in front of your client on the affected side insuring mobility, then veer into him or her. Bump shoulders if she doesn't see you. Likewise, distract the client when passing an obstacle on the affected side, allowing the client to bump. Let the client bump—taking care to avoid falls, of course. Play two-on-one games like soccer or basketball.

Generalization

- Gradually withdraw the cues until the client habitually scans to the affected side at all times. At first, the client will scan when looking for something. Using laser tag during mobility, one can start presenting the spot intermittently—less frequently and while the client is distracted. The client should get into the habit of scanning to the affected side at all times—especially during mobility—much as someone uses a rearview mirror in a car.

LOW VISION REHAB BROCHURE

Services Provided

- Home Safety Recommendations
- Lighting Recommendations
- Reading Training
- Visual Skills Training
- Cooking Safety Suggestions
- Computer Training
- Financial Management Adaptations
- Adaptive Equipment
- Daily Living Skill Training
- Scotoma Awareness Training
- Preferred Retinal Loci Training
- Handwriting Training
- Optical and other Low Vision Aids/Equipment Training
- Mobility Training
- Support Groups

Vision Function Rehab Associates

> OT Name, OTR/L, CLVT
> Occupational Therapist
> Certified Low Vision Therapist
>
> Specializing In Low Vision Rehabilitation
>
> Address
> City, State Zip
>
> For Information Call:
>
> Phone

What is Low Vision?

Low vision is a visual impairment, not correctable by standard glasses, contact lenses, medicine, or surgery, that interferes with a person's ability to perform everyday activities.

What Causes Low Vision?

Low vision can result from a variety of diseases and injuries that affect the eye. Many people with low vision have age-related macular degeneration, cataract, glaucoma, or diabetic retinopathy. Age-related macular degeneration accounts for almost 45 percent of all cases of low vision.

How Does Low Vision Affect People's Lives?

People with low vision experience physical, economic, and psychological changes that diminish their quality of life. Without assistance and training, patients may have difficulty using low vision devices and completing necessary daily living tasks such as:

- Grooming
- Meal preparation
- Financial management
- Home maintenance
- Shopping
- Reading
- Community and leisure activities

OCCUPATIONAL THERAPISTS AND LOW VISION REHABILITATION

What is Occupational Therapy?

Occupational therapy is a unique healthcare profession that is concerned with the ability of people to independently participate in their meaningful daily activities, or "occupations".

Low Vision Rehabilitation

Occupational therapists help people with low vision impairment who have a loss of ability to perform necessary activities of daily living in the following ways:

- Teach people to use their remaining vision as best as possible to complete activities.
- Help modify activities so that they can be completed even with reduced vision.
- Train people in the use of adaptive equipment to compensate for vision loss.
- Create a safe home environment to prevent falls and injuries.

Therapists also work closely with the doctor. They help determine if any other factors may interfere with the use of equipment, ie, arthritic joints, upper and lower extremity weakness, and lack of endurance.

Questionnaire

Do you have any difficulty with the following activities, even when using glasses or magnification devices?

- Reading labels
- Reading books and newspapers
- Managing finances
- Counting money
- Using home appliances
- Using utensils
- Doing fine handiwork
- Preparing meals
- Dressing
- Performing self-care, grooming
- Managing medications
- Maintaining balance
- Navigating stairs, steps, curbs

OCCUPATIONAL THERAPISTS AND LOW VISION REHABILITATION

What Is Low Vision?

Low vision is a visual impairment, not correctable by standard glasses, contact lenses, medicine, or surgery, that interferes with a person's ability to perform everyday activities.

What Causes Low Vision?

Low vision can result from a variety of diseases and injuries that affect the eye. Many people with low vision have age-related macular degeneration, cataract, glaucoma, or diabetic retinopathy. Age-related macular degeneration accounts for almost 45% of all cases of low vision.

How Does Low Vision Affect People's Lives?

People with low vision experience physical, economic, and psychological changes that diminish their quality of life. Without assistance and training, patients may have difficulty using low vision devices and completing necessary daily living tasks such as:

- Grooming
- Meal preparation
- Financial management
- Home maintenance
- Shopping
- Reading
- Community and leisure activities

What Is Occupational Therapy?

Occupational therapy is a unique health care profession that is concerned with the ability of people to independently participate in their meaningful daily activities, or "occupations".

Low Vision Rehabilitation

Occupational therapists help people with low vision impairment that have a loss of ability to perform necessary activities of daily living in the following ways:

- Teach people to use their remaining vision as best as possible to complete activities
- Help modify activities so that they can be completed even with reduced vision
- Train people in the use of adaptive equipment to compensate for vision loss
- Create a safe home environment to prevent falls and injuries

Occupational therapists work closely with the eye doctor. The eye doctor may prescribe optical aids and the occupational therapist teaches the patient how to use these aids in various activities of daily living. Occupational herapists also help determine if any other factors may interfere with the use of equipment, ie, arthritic joints, upper and lower extremity weakness, and lack of endurance.

12 Pt (~1.6M) Practice Sentences

These are the same lengths as MNRead sentences. Use these to evaluate CCTV's or optical devices. If larger print is read faster (shorter reading time), additional magnification is indicated. If smaller print is read as quickly as larger print, try decreasing magnification. Not graded for reading difficulty.

I glanced up to see her standing in the doorway watching me.

I parked my blue car in the small lot near the motel office.

I need to take another call so why don't you ring him back.

I punched the button for line two and prepared myself fast.

There's nothing wrong with a man's spending his own savings.

She stepped into her office and closed the door behind them.

Then Roger realized that his father had been standing there.

Everyone had moved from the dining room onto the back porch.

He picked up a large fluffy towel and wrapped it around twice.

He was surprised to see John and Eric sitting on the lounge.

Lisa returned to the office carrying two cups of hot coffee.

She was using every ounce of self-control to not break down.

He informed her that he would be working late at the office.

For a few moments he stood at the rail in the cold damp air.

There was a stack of newspapers close by meant for kindling.

I locked up the cabin door and headed back toward the house.

They began to move in opposite directions to their entry.

He stood up and walked to the window and looked down on her.

10 PT (1.3M) PRACTICE SENTENCES

The sidewalks were crowded with pedestrians and automobiles.

She looked down at the yellow legal pads on the round table.

He didn't want to talk about her but he wanted it over with.

My mission, I believe, is to help the men and woman of Asia.

Where did the singer get the lyrics to the song in the play?

The barking and growling dog frightened four little children.

Speeding down the narrow road, the yellow car almost crashed.

The alarm rang when the smoking waste bin burst into flames.

The older man in a gray suit jumped up after he sang a song.

She looked at her watch and leaned forward, fear in her eye.

He parked down the street and listened to the ringing bells.

He found the work enjoyable and was glad he could finish it.

He could see almost all northbound lanes of the expressway.

Right after he opened the beer, his tiny red telephone rang.

He looked up and did a double-take when he saw me advancing.

I stopped in my office and checked an address on the poster.

We feel that the government has no right to interfere with those.

Spring green sparkled on the trees and in the young grasses.

Concealing the truth would destroy everything else he loved.

8 Pt (~1.0M) Practice Sentences

I glanced up to see her standing in the doorway watching me.

I parked my blue car in the small lot near the motel office.

I need to take another call so why don't you ring him back.

I punched the button for line two and prepared myself fast.

There's nothing wrong with a man's spending his own savings.

She stepped into her office and closed the door behind them.

Then Roger realized that his father had been standing there.

Everyone had moved from the dining room onto the back porch.

He picked up a large fluffy towel and wrapped it around twice.

He was surprised to see John and Eric sitting on the lounge.

Lisa returned to the office carrying two cups of hot coffee.

She was using every ounce of self-control to not break down.

He informed her that he would be working late at the office.

For a few moments he stood at the rail in the cold damp air.

There was a stack of newspapers close by meant for kindling.

I locked up the cabin door and headed back toward the house.

They began to move in opposite directions to their entry.

He stood up and walked to the window and looked down on her.

8 PT (~1.0M) PRACTICE SENTENCES

The morning sun was coming through the sparkling window now.

It was the same today as it had been on the first of August.

He listened as if she were the only person in this universe.

I now know it is more important than almost everything else.

Once he started running he found it hard to take a new path.

The strong but short man listened to them as they told Alan.

The horizon was a featureless black line in every direction.

He lets his head roll back on the chair and closes his eyes.

I looked forward to these visits with my old friend Stephen.

I think about all the people I know and about my own family.

Sometimes you cannot believe what you see or what you learn.

You must feel that you can trust other people like yourself.

He studied very hard by the dim light over the kitchen sink.

He can never tell when his influence over children will end.

There was a handsome young man riding on a beautiful donkey.

They have very little understanding about the story we tell.

Index